A Gale Ready Reference Handbook

Fast Answers to Common Questions

ISSN 1526-2731

A Gale Ready Reference Handbook

Fast Answers to Common Questions

Compiled by The Carnegie Library of Pittsburgh and the Saint Louis Public Library

Carolyn A. Fischer, editor

Detroit
San Francisco
London
Boston
Woodbridge, CT

Fast Answers to Common Questions
A Gale Ready Reference Handbook

Carolyn A. Fischer
Editor

Dawn Conzett DesJardins and Kristin Mallegg
Contributing Editors

Amy L. Rance, *Associate Editor*
Kevin B. McCoy, *Intern*
Kathleen Lopez Nolan, *Managing Editor*

Dorothy Maki, *Manufacturing Manager*
Wendy Blurton, *Senior Buyer*

Cindy Baldwin, *Product Design Manager*
Pamela A. E. Galbreath, *Senior Art Director*

27500 Drake Road
Farmington Hills, MI 48331-3535

ISBN 0-7876-3947-8
0-7876-3946-X (complete set)

ISSN 1526-2731

Printed in the United States of America

Contents

Gale Ready Reference Handbooks

A series of books designed to quickly answer questions on a number of subjects, the *Gale Ready Reference Handbooks* are a great addition to any library. The *Gale Ready Reference Handbooks* feature four task-specific references, containing high-quality data, including essays, overviews, and contact information. Also featured are six related titles--sourcebooks which are industry targeted and contain a comprehensive cross-section of data, including information on associations, directories, periodicals, databases and online services, and leading companies and suppliers.

Fast Answers to Common Questions

Presented in a question and answer format, *Fast Answers to Common Questions (FACQ)* contains answers to 4,500 commonly asked ready-reference questions on a variety of subjects. For easier look-up, *FACQ* is arranged by subject and features a keyword index.

Fast Help for Major Medical Conditions

Fast Help for Major Medical Conditions (FHMMC) features essays about 100 common medical diseases and conditions, including an explanation of the disease/condition, symptoms, treatment, prognosis, prevention, and alternative treatments. For each disease, a list of associations, agencies, clinics, and treatment centers is provided.

First Stop for Jobs and Industries

With information on more than 500 jobs and 1,100 industries, *First Stop for Jobs and Industries (FSJI)* is a great source for job seekers, career counselors, investors, and entrepreneurs alike. In *FSJI*, researchers will gain valuable information on job duties, outlook and earnings, and industry trends, statistics, and leaders.

Where to Go / Who to Ask

Where to Go/Who to Ask (WGWA) contains contact information for approximately 4,900 associations, 8,600 publications, 1,600 databases, and 3,200 agencies and research centers and organizations. Arranged in a yellow pages-type format by keyword, *WGWA* will point you in the right direction whatever your need.

Related Titles

Gale's Guide to Genealogical and Historical Research
Contains associations, directories, periodicals, databases and online services, and leading companies relevant to genealogy.

Gale's Guide to Nonprofits
Contains associations, directories, periodicals, databases and online services, and leading companies relevant to the nonprofit industry.

Coming Soon

Gale's Guide to the Arts
Gale's Guide to the Government
Gale's Guide to Industry
Gale's Guide to the Media

Introduction

Fast Answers to Common Questions (FACQ) is exactly what the title implies--a handy book to grab when you are looking for the answer to a commonly asked reference question. This useful product contains answers to more than 4,500 common questions, and a few answers to questions not asked quite as often!

From the recipe for sugar starch to the current location of Orville and Wilbur Wright's famous airplane, this book contains answers to a myriad of questions in a variety of subject areas.

Content and Arrangement

The information in this product is arranged in an easy-to-read question and answer format. There is also a keyword index which lists important words and phrases from each question and answer and the page(s) on which each can be found.

Descriptive Listings

Fast Answers to Common Questions is arranged in thirteen broad subject categories. Each subject category is then divided again into sections pertinent to that subject. The thirteen subject categories include:

- Arts and the Media
- Business and Economics
- Education
- Food and Beverages
- Government, Politics, and Law
- History and Geography
- Language and Literature
- Medicine and Health
- Recreation and Sports
- Religion and the Occult
- Science and Mathematics
- Sociology and Social Issues
- Technology

Master Index

The index contains an alphabetical listing of all key words and phrases mentioned in the text. The numbers following the index citations refer to the page or pages on which the word or phrase can be found.

Method of Compilation

The questions and answers listed in this book were originally derived from the files of commonly-asked reference questions of two prestigious libraries--The Carnegie Library of Pittsburgh and the Saint Louis Public Library.

Acknowledgements

The base data for this product came from the ready reference files of The Carnegie Library of Pittsburgh and the Saint Louis Public Library.

The editor gratefully acknowledges the help of her colleague Carol Schwartz, whose guidance and advice helped enormously. Last but not least, Darren S. Roney must be commended for his support, as well as his proofreading and programming skills. This book is dedicated to him.

Comments and Suggestions

We invite comments and suggestions for improvement. Please contact:

Fast Answers to Common Questions

The Gale Group
27500 Drake Rd.
Farmington Hills, MI 48331-3535

Telephone: (248)699-4253
Toll-free: 800-347-4253
Fax: (248)699-8070

User's Guide

Fast Answers to Common Questions (FACQ) comprises questions with corresponding answers and a keyword index. Each is fully explained below.

Descriptive Listings

Questions and their corresponding answers are listed in thirteen separate chapters. Each chapter is further broken down into sections, as outlined below. Within sections, questions and answers appear in random order. They are not listed alphabetically nor in any other manner.

- Arts and the Media
  - Crafts
  - Media
  - Performance
  - Visual Arts
- Business and Economics
  - Consumer Issues
  - Economics
  - Finance
  - General Business
  - Labor
  - Markets, Sales, and Trade
- Education
  - Colleges and Universities
  - Libraries, Museums, and Research Institutions
  - Pre-College Education
- Food and Beverages
  - Beverages
  - Culinary Arts
  - Diet and Nutrition
  - Food
- Government, Politics, and Law
  - Government
  - Law
  - Politics
- History and Geography
  - General History
  - Geography and Maps
  - Beginning of History to 475
  - 476 to 1500
  - 1500 to 1789
  - 1789 to 1918
  - 1918 to present
- Language and Literature
  - Languages
  - Poetry
  - Prose
  - Quotations
  - Words and Symbols
- Medicine and Health
  - Animal Care and Health
  - Drugs and Medicinal Herbs
  - General Psychology
  - Health Institutions and Practitioners
  - Health Care
- Recreation and Sports
  - Games, Toys, and Hobbies
  - Individual Awards
  - Outdoor Activities
  - Team Sports
- Religion and the Occult
  - Occult
  - Philosophy
  - Religion and Mythology
- Science and Mathematics
  - Biology, Zoology, Botany, Anatomy
  - Chemistry, Physics, Astronomy
  - Geology, Meteorology, Oceanography
  - Mathematics
  - Weights, Measures, and Times
- Sociology and Social Issues
  - Community Services
  - Crime and Criminals
  - Cultures and Customs
  - General Sociology
  - Social Issues
  - Social Statistics
- Technology
  - Agriculture
  - Buildings, Bridges, and Other Structures
  - Communication
  - Energy and Related Industries
  - Manufacturing and Mining
  - Transportation

Index

The index provides alphabetical access by keyword to all entries included in the book. Index references are to page numbers.

Crafts

What is the recipe for the sugar starch used for handmade crochet?

To prepare the starch used to stiffen crochet, mix 1/2 cup granulated sugar with 1/2 cup water in a small pan; heat to boiling, being careful not to burn mixture; immediately remove from heat. Cool to room temperature. Wet crochet in clear water, then immerse in starch. Remove from starch and place on a padded surface covered with clean, white paper. Insert rust-proof pins to hold tightly in shape. Let dry thoroughly before removing pins.

The Great Christmas Crochet Book (New York: Sterling Publishing, 1981), 21.

What were the occupations of Paul Revere?

Paul Revere (1735-1818) was most renowned as a silversmith, but his energy and skill along with the necessity of supporting a growing family led him in many directions. He not only worked in silver but also made surgical instruments, sold spectacles, replaced missing teeth, and engraved copper plates.

New Encyclopaedia Britannica, 15th ed. (Chicago: Encyclopaedia Britannica, 1990), s.v. "Revere, Paul."

How would one make a toga?

Togas were rectangular blankets or cloths made from undyed wool. For a man five feet six inches tall, four yards of fabric, about a yard and three-quarters wide was needed. The lower corners of the rectangle were rounded off. Togas were thrown over the left shoulder from the front, with the front end hanging just below the knee. The rest of the cloth was drawn across the back, passed under the right arm, and up across the breast, then thrown backwards over the left shoulder.

Mary Johnston, *Roman Life* (Glenview, IL: Scott, Foresman, 1957), 191.

How can a quilt be cleaned?

Although many contemporary quilts can be machine-washed and dried, hand-washing is preferred. If the fabric is colorfast, soak the quilt briefly, using mild soap and tepid water, in a bathtub from which all traces of scouring powder and detergent have been removed. Rinse the quilt well and let it drain in the tub until water no longer drips out of it when it is lifted. Dry flat on a rack. Do not hang the quilt on a line. A very old or fragile quilt should not be washed. If necessary, gently hand vacuum it, covering the vacuum nozzle with a piece of fine, soft netting held in place with a rubber band.

Mary K. Levenstein, *Caring for Your Cherished Possessions* (New York: Crown, 1989).

What is the origin and process of the craft batik?

Batik is a very ancient craft dating back at least 2,000 years. It is a method of applying a colored design on textiles by waxing those parts that are not to be dyed. White pure cotton or white pure silk are the best materials to use. Hot wax is applied to the fabric in the areas that are to be kept white and then the dye is added. The lightest color is the first dye. The fabric is then waxed in those areas that are to retain the first color and the process is repeated with a second color. Once all the dyeing is completed, the wax is removed, revealing the design.

Heather Griffin, *Introduction to Batik* (Cincinnati, OH: North Light Books, 1990), 4.

Media

Who wrote a full-page letter to Saddam Hussein in *The New York Times*?

Hotel magnate Leona Helmsley responded with indignation to Iraqi president Saddam Hussein's (1937-) use of the word "guest" in reference to hostages taken in Kuwait. On September 17, 1990, she used a full-page open letter in *The New York Times* as her means of communication. In the letter, she decried the treatment of the hostages, who were beaten and starved. She also told Hussein that it was "time to check out." Helmsley bid him to release the hostages and implied that it was an act of cowardice to wage war behind these "human shields."

New York Times 17 September 1990.

In what year did the television series "The Fugitive" win an Emmy?

The popular television series "The Fugitive" won an Emmy for Outstanding Dramatic Series in 1966.

Thomas O'Neil, *The Emmys: Star Wars, Showdowns, and the Supreme Test of TV's Best* (New York: Penguin Books, 1992), 105.

Which actor played "Little Beaver" in the "Red Rider" series?

Robert Blake (1933-) portrayed the "Little Beaver" character in 27 movies in Republic's "Red Rider" series during the 1940s. As a child actor, Blake also appeared in the *Our Gang* series of movie shorts as "Mickey Gubitosi." He enjoyed a lucrative career as an adult, appearing in several films, most notably, the 1967 murder thriller *In Cold Blood.* Blake was also a successful television actor and appeared in several made-for-television movies and specials. He won an Emmy Award for Outstanding Lead Actor in a Drama Series in 1975, for his portrayal of Detective Tony Baretta, in the popular ABC series, "Baretta" (1975-1978.) In 1985 Blake appeared as Father Noah "Hardstep" Rivers in the NBC movie *Father of Hell Town,* and later in the series "Hell Town."

David Dye, *Child and Youth Actors: Filmographies of Their Entire Careers, 1914-1985* (Jefferson, NC: McFarland & Company, Inc., 1988.

Ray Milland won an Academy Award in 1945 for which film?

Ray Milland (1908-1986) won an Academy Award for Best Actor in 1945 for his performance in *The Lost Weekend.*

Richard Shale, comp., *The Academy Awards Index: The Complete Categorical and Chronological Record* (Westport, CT: Greenwood Press, 1993), 93.

Who did *Life* magazine name as the 100 most important Americans of the twentieth century?

In 1990 *Life* magazine listed the following persons as the most important Americans of the twentieth century: Jane Addams; Muhammad Ali; Elizabeth Arden; Roone Arledge; Louis Armstrong; George Balanchine; John Bardeen; Irving Berlin; Edward L. Bernays; Leonard Bernstein; Marlon Brando; Wernher von Braun; Dale Carnegie; Wallace Carothers; Willis Carrier; Rachel Carson; Bing Crosby; Clarence Darrow; Robert de Graff; Eugene V. Debs; John Dewey; Walt Disney; W.E.B. Du Bois; Allen Dulles; Bob Dylan; Albert Einstein; T.S. Eliot; William Faulkner; Abraham Flexner; Henry Ford; John Ford; Betty Friedan; Milton Friedman; George Gallup; A.P. Giannini; Billy Graham; Martha Graham; D.W. Griffith; Joyce C. Hall; Ernest Hemingway; Oliver Wendell Holmes; J. Edgar Hoover; Robert Hutchins; Helen Keller; Jack Kerouac; Billie Jean King; Martin Luther King, Jr.; Alfred Kinsey; Willem Kolff; Ray Kroc; Edwin Land; William Levitt; John L. Lewis; Charles Lindbergh; Raymond Loewy; Henry Luce; Douglas MacArthur; George C. Marshall; Louis B. Mayer; Claire McCardell; Joseph R. McCarthy; Frank McNamara; Margaret Mead; Karl Menninger; Charles E. Merrill; Ludwig Mies van der Rohe; Robert Moses; William Mulholland; Edward R. Murrow; Ralph Nader; John von Neumann; Reinhold Niebuhr; Eugene O'Neill; J. Robert Oppenheimer; William Paley; Jackson Pollock; Emily Post; Elvis Presley; Jackie Robinson; John D. Rockefeller, Jr.; Richard Rodgers; Will Rogers; Eleanor Roosevelt; Babe Ruth; Jonas Salk; Margaret Sanger; Alfred P. Sloan, Jr.; Benjamin Spock; Alfred Stieglitz; Roy Stryker; Bill W.; Andy Warhol; Earl Warren; James D. Watson; Thomas J. Watson, Jr.; Tennessee Williams; Walter Winchell; Frank Lloyd Wright; Orville Wright; Wilbur Wright; and Malcolm X.

Life Fall 1990.

What single broadcast is attributed to the success of commercial radio?

On November 2, 1920, in a broadcast sponsored by Westinghouse to promote the sale of receivers, ham radio operator Frank Conrad went on the air at station KDKA in Pittsburgh to announce the returns of the Harding-Cox presidential election. His broadcast of the election returns thrilled the public and commercial radio was suddenly an overnight success. His broadcast is considered to be the beginning of American radio programming. By 1923 more than 700 radio stations were in operation, and General Electric was selling 11 million sets a year.

Jane Polley, ed., *Stories Behind Everyday Things* (Pleasantville, NY: The Reader's Digest Association, 1980), 270. Fred J. MacDonald, *Don't Touch That Dial!: Radio Programming in American Life, 1920-1960* (Chicago: Nelson-Hall, 1979), 2-3.

What was the first significant American magazine?

Magazines have been published in the United States since 1741. One of the earliest magazines published in America was Rogers' and Fowle's *American Magazine and Historical Chronicle.* Founded in 1743, it has been dubbed the "first really important American magazine" according to magazine historian Frank Luther Mott. The *American Magazine and Historical Chronicle* folded in 1746.

M. Thomas Inge, ed., *Handbook of American Popular Culture,* (Westport, CT: Greenwood Press, 1981), 3:139.

What was the first daily newspaper published in the United States?

America's first daily newspaper was published by Benjamin Towne shortly after the Revolutionary War. Towne's *Pennsylvania Evening Post* began publication in Philadelphia on May 30, 1783. Following increased competition from another Philadelphia newspaper, the *Pennsylvania Evening Post* folded in October of 1784.

M. Thomas Inge, ed., *Handbook of American Popular Culture,* (Westport, CT: Greenwood Press, 1981), 3:234.

Who played the character Kathy on the television show "Father Knows Best"?

Actress Lauren Chapin played the role of Kathy, the lovable youngest daughter of Jim and Margaret Anderson on "Father Knows Best," a popular television show dating from the 1950s. Kitten, as she was called, attended Springfield Grammar School and played baseball for the Maple Street Tigers. She also had a teddy bear named Bear.

Vincent Terrace, *Television Character and Story Facts: Over 110,000 Details from 1,008 shows, 1945-1992* (Jefferson, NC: McFarland & Company, Inc., 1993)

Which newspaper publisher was responsible for helping to shape the views of the United States population in challenging Spain to war over Cuba?

Among the many influential newspaper barons during the late nineteenth century, American newspaper publisher William Randolph Hearst (1863-1951), with his *New York Journal,* stirred up the American public to go to war with Spain over Cuba in 1898.

M. Thomas Inge, ed., *Handbook of Popular American Culture* (Westport, CT: Greenwood Press, 1981), 3:325.

When was the first Pulitzer Prize for editorial cartooning awarded, and who received it?

In 1922 the first Pulitzer Prize for editorial cartooning was awarded to Rollin Kirby of the *New York World.* Kirby was a transitional figure in the history of cartooning, whose work fell between the earlier multifigure cartoons and the modern single-figure panels. He won the prize again in 1925 and 1929, becoming the most important editorial cartoonist of the decade.

M. Thomas Inge, ed., *Handbook of American Popular Culture* (Westport,CT: Greenwood Press Inc., 1978), 2:111.

When were the first major sporting events broadcast on television?

The first baseball telecast occurred on May 17, 1939. It was a game between Princeton University and Columbia University at Columbia's Baker Field. Only one camera was used, and the announcer was Bill Stern. The first major league baseball game on television occurred on August 26, 1939, between the Brooklyn Dodgers and the Cincinnati Reds at Ebbets Field. Red Barber was the announcer.

The first boxing match telecast was on June 1, 1939, of a heavyweight fight between Lou Nova and Max Baer at Yankee Stadium.

On August 9, 1939, the first tennis match to be telecast took place at the Eastern Grass Court Championships in Rye, NY.

The first football game to be televised was between Fordham University and Waynesburg on September 30, 1939, at Triborough Stadium on Randall's Island, New York. The first professional football game on television occurred on October 22, 1939, between the Brooklyn Dodgers and the Philadelphia Eagles at Ebbets Field.

Washington Post 23 January 1975.

What is the A. Philip Randolph Messenger Award?

The A. Philip Randolph Messenger Award recognizes outstanding journalism in African-American publications. It is named after civil rights leader and activist Asa Philip Randolph (1889-1979), who founded the monthly civil rights activist publication, *The Messenger,* in 1917. In 1994, the *Milwaukee Community Journal* and the *Philadelphia Tribune* were presented with the award.

USA Today 20 June 1994. *Webster's New Biographical Dictionary* (Springfield, MA: Merriam-Webster, 1988), s.v. "Randolph, Asa Philip."

On what radio program did Orson Welles broadcast his famous "War of the Worlds"?

On October 30, 1938 during the radio program the "Mercury Theatre on the Air," host and producer Orson Welles (1915-1985) also presented what has come to be known as his "War of the Worlds" broadcast. As a Halloween stunt Welles interspersed regularly scheduled presentations with gradually alarming but seemingly real documentary reports of first strange lights and finally an invasion of space creatures centered on Grovers Mills, New Jersey. Many listeners, believing what they were hearing was real, became panic-stricken and in many families and communities chaos ensued. Although disclaimers were given throughout the broadcast, nonetheless an outraged public lobbied the federal government to prevent future re-occurrences. The broadcast was based on Howard Koch's adaptation of H.G. Wells' story *War Of The Worlds.* Orson Welles went on to have a distinguished career as a movie producer, actor and director.

Frank Buxton and Bill Owen, *The Big Broadcast, 1920-1950* (New York: Viking Press, 1972), s.v. "the Mercury Theatre on the Air." *The World Book Encyclopedia* (Chicago: World Book, 1993), s.v. "Welles, Orson."

What are the names of the California Raisins?

The California Raisins, Claymation characters featured in a series of popular television commercials advertising raisins, consisted of Tiny Goodbite (the lead singer), Ben Indasun (the one always wearing sunglasses), and Justin X. Grape (the one in the blue sneakers).

USA Today 22 April 1988.

What were the names of the relatives and friends of the Walt Disney cartoon character Donald Duck?

The Walt Disney cartoon character Donald Duck, had three nephews—Huey, Louie, and Dewey. They made their film debut in *Donald's Nephews* (1938), when Donald's sister, Dumbella, sent them for a visit. He was not able to send them home again. Donald's girlfriend Daisy Duck had three nieces—April, May, and June.

Kevin Neary and Dave Smith, *The Ultimate Disney Trivia Book* (New York: Hyperion, 1992), 12. Fred L. Worth, *The Trivia Encyclopedia* (Los Angeles: Brooke House, 1974), 71.

What was printed on the business card of the fictional gun slinging Paladin in the hit TV show "Have Gun, Will Travel"?

In the popular television western "Have Gun, Will Travel" (1957-1962), the black-garbed hired gun, Paladin, played by actor Richard Boone (1917-1981), handed out business cards with the printed notation: "Have Gun. Will Travel. Wire Paladin, San Francisco." The card expresses in modern terms what Paladin's medieval namesake, one of Charlemagne's legendary knights, pledged to do: protect the weak of Charlemagne's realm.

Sylvia Cole, *The Facts On File Dictionary of 20th-Century Allusions* (New York: Facts On File, 1991), 117.

Who is the composer of the music in the popular Gallo Wine commercial of the late 1970s?

The music in the popular Gallo Wine commercial that ran in the late 1970s is entitled "Hymne" and is from Vangelis Papathanassiou's album *Opera Sauvage.* Papathanassiou also composed the score for the hit movie *Chariots of Fire.*

Parade 1987.

What was the name of the real-life sheriff whose heroic story was presented in the motion picture *Walking Tall*?

The real-life modern day Tennessee sheriff in the motion picture *Walking Tall* (1973) was Buford Pusser. The film told the heroic tale of a man fighting corruption and starred Joe Don Baker as Pusser.

Richard B. Armstrong, *The Movie List Book* (Cincinnati, OH: Betterway Books, 1994), 401.

In the 1939 film *The Wizard of Oz,* who played the Cowardly Lion?

American comic actor Bert Lahr (1895-1967) is probably best remembered for his portrayal of the Cowardly Lion in the 1939 film *The Wizard of Oz.*

The Encyclopedia Americana (Danbury, CT: Grolier Inc. 1989), s.v. "Lahr, Bert."

When did the cartoon "Little Orphan Annie" make its debut?

The cartoon character Little Orphan Annie was created by Harold Gray, and the comic strip of the same name first appeared in 1924. New York *Daily News* publisher Joseph Patterson requested a cartoon strip featuring a child, and Gray obliged with a little girl character at a time when some 40 other comic strips were featuring little boys.

David Manning White and Robert H. Abel, eds., *The Funnies: An American Idiom* (New York: Free Press of Glencoe, 1963).

Who were the Marx Brothers?

The Marx Brothers started as a vaudeville comedy troupe of the early twentieth century, and consisted of five brothers-Groucho, Chico, Harpo, Gummo, and Zeppo. Chico (1886-1961), named Leonard in real-life, was known for his unusual Italian accent and his piano playing. Harpo (1888-1964), whose real name was Adolph, played the harp and never spoke in any of the acts. Groucho (1890-1977), whose real name was Julius, was ready with a wisecrack and known for his trademark cigar. Gummo (1893-1977), actually named Milton, left the act before the brothers made their films. Herbert (1901-1979), nicknamed Zeppo, was the romantic relief in the troupe for the first five films—*Coconuts* (1929), *Animal Crackers* (1930), *Monkey Business* (1931), *Horsefeathers* (1932), and *Duck Soup* (1933) but left soon after. The remaining three brothers went on to make their most commercially successful film *A Night At the Opera* (1935).

Leslie Halliwell, *Filmgoer's Companion, 9th ed.* (New York: Charles Scribner's Sons, 1988), s.v. "Marx brothers." Scott Siegel and Barbara Siegel, *The Encyclopedia of Hollywood* (New York: Facts on File, 1990), s.v. "Marx brothers."

Where is Lake Wobegon?

Lake Wobegon is a fictional town created by writer and radio humorist Garrison Keillor, who was born Gary Edward Keillor on August 7, 1942 in Anoka, Minnesota. In 1974 Keillor introduced National Public Radio audiences to the eccentric but nonetheless endearing residents of Lake Wobegon, Minnesota, with his now famous opening line, "It's been a quiet week in Lake Wobegon, my hometown." His now famous radio show, "A Prairie Home Companion" ran until 1987. Keillor has made a number of Lake Wobegon recordings and published various collections of Lake Wobegon stories. He has also written a number of books on other subjects and in 1987 hosted "Garrison Keillor's American Radio Company of the Air."

James G. Lesniak, ed., *Contemporary Authors* (Detroit: Gale Research, 1993) 36:216-17. Diane Roback, "Leaving the Shores of Lake Wobegon," *Publishers Weekly* 21 August 1987.

Who played the Wicked Witch of the West in the motion picture *The Wizard of Oz*?

Although she did not consider it her finest performance, Margaret Hamilton is best known for her role as the Wicked Witch of the West in the 1939 film *The Wizard of Oz.* Hamilton was a teacher in her hometown of Cleveland, Ohio, until she landed a role in *Another Language* (1932), a New York-bound play destined to become a Broadway hit. Hamilton felt that her work in this play was her finest. From there she went on to appear in over 70 films and numerous plays including over a dozen Broadway productions. She declined numerous offers to portray a witch in TV commercials because she did not want to trivialize her portrayal of the Wicked Witch.

Richard Lamparski, *Whatever Became of...? All New Tenth Series* (New York: Crown Publishers, Inc., 1986), 70.

Who were the Hollywood Ten?

The Hollywood Ten were a group of performing-arts industry professionals who were jailed during the height of anti-Communist fervor in the early 1950s. Alvah Bessie, Herbert Biberman, Lester Cole, Edward Dmytryk, Ring Lardner, Jr., John Howard Lawson, Albert Maltz, Samuel Ornitz, Adrian Scott, and Dalton Trumbo were some of the many Hollywood insiders called before the United States Senate in 1947 to testify before the House Committee on Un-American Activities. Invoking the Fifth Amendment the ten refused to testify about alleged Communist-related conspiracies in Hollywood, or about their own political activities. As a result, they were fined and given one-year jail terms; Dmytryk served only two months of his sentence. All lost their jobs at Hollywood studios and were blacklisted in the industry for over a decade.

Fred L. Worth, *The Trivia Encyclopedia* (New York: Bell Publishing Co., 1974), 119.

In the hit television show "The Honeymooners," Ralph Kramden and Ed Norton belonged to what lodge?

In the hit comedy television show "The Honeymooners," the loud-mouthed Gotham City bus driver Ralph Kramden and his sewer-worker friend and neighbor Ed Norton belonged to the Raccoon Lodge. Kramden was portrayed by Jackie Gleason (1886-1987), and Norton by Art Carney. Actress Audrey Meadows was cast in the role of Alice Gibson, who married Kramden and moved to their first and only apartment at 728 Chauncey St. in Bensonhurst, Brooklyn, New York.

Vincent Terrace, *Encyclopedia of Television Series, Pilots and Specials 1937-1973* (New York: Baseline, 1985).

What fictional character has been most often portrayed in films?

British physician and author Sir Arthur Conan Doyle's (1859-1930) world famous fictional detective Sherlock Holmes has been portrayed in films more than any other single character. Since 1900, Holmes has been played by 75 actors in more than 211 films. The literary character created by Bram Stoker (1847-1912), Count Dracula, has been portrayed 160 times in horror films, whereas Frankenstein has only been in 115 movies.

Mark Young, ed., *The Guinness Book of Records 1995* (New York: Facts On File, 1994), 163.

Which famous actress was so obsessed with death that she often slept in a coffin?

The great French actress Sarah Bernhardt (1844-1923) was so obsessed with death that as a teen-ager she asked her mother to buy a coffin in which Bernhardt occasionally slept. Bernhardt was also a frequent visitor to the Paris morgue and was eventually buried in the coffin she used as a bed.

Isaac Asimov, *Isaac Asimov's Book of Facts* (New York: Bell Publishing, 1981), 433.

Does Cuban dictator Fidel Castro have a Hollywood connection?

At one time the future Cuban dictator Fidel Castro (1926-) evidently worked as an extra in a number of Hollywood films, including *Bathing Beauties* starring Esther Williams (1923-). Bandleader Xavier Cugat (1900-1990) called him a "...young, ambitious, attractive boy" but also "a ham."

John May, *Curious Trivia* (New York: Dorset Press, 1984), 46-47.

In the television series "Father Knows Best," what did lead actor Robert Young do for a living?

In the popular 1950s television family sitcom "Father Knows Best" (1954-62), actor Robert Young (as Jim Anderson) was the manager of the fictitious General Insurance Company. Young played the head of the Anderson family, living at 607 South Main Street, in the town of Springfield. His wife Margaret was portrayed by Jane Wyatt, and Elinor Donahue played Betty, also know as "Princess," the eldest child. The middle child, James, Jr., or "Bud," was played by Billy Grey, and Lauren Chapin was cast in the role of Kathy, or "Kitten," the youngest member of the family. The series title aptly summarizes the outcome of each episode in which Jim Anderson has the uncanny ability to solve any family problem that occurs.

Vincent Terrace, *Television Character and Story Facts* (Jefferson, NC: MacFarland & Company, Inc., 1993), 147.

In the television sitcom "M*A*S*H," what is the name of the character who continually tries to win an army discharge by cross-dressing?

In the very popular television series "M*A*S*H" (1972-83), Corporal Klinger, played by Jamie Farr (1934-), continually tried to win a discharge from the army by dressing in women's clothes. Based on Robert Altman's (1925-) hit movie of the same title, field surgeons and medical staff involved in the Korean Conflict used dark humor to keep their sanity amid the pain and death. The cast of characters included: Alan Alda (1936-) as Captain Benjamin Franklin (Hawkeye) Pierce; Loretta Swit (1937-) as Major Margaret (Hot Lips) Houlihan; Mike Farrell (1939-) as Captain B.J. Hunnicutt; Henry Morgan (1915-) as Colonel Sherman Potter; David Ogden Stiers (1942-) as Major Charles Emerson Winchester III; Gary Burghoff (1943-) as Corporal Walter (Radar) O'Reilly; Wayne Rogers (1933-) as Captain John F.X. (Trapper John) McIntyre; Larry Linville (1939-) as Major Frank Burns.

Les Brown's Encyclopedia of Television (Detroit, MI: Visible Ink Press, 1992), s.v. "M*A*S*H." Laurence Urdang and Frederick G. Ruffner, Jr., eds., *Allusions-Cultural, Literary, Biblical, and Historical: A Thematic Dictionary* (Detroit, MI: Gale Research Co., 1986), 483.

The classic phrase "Gort! Klaatu barada nikto" is spoken in what 1950's science fiction film?

The classic phrase "Gort! Klaatu barada nikto" is spoken in the American science fiction film *The Day The Earth Stood Still* (1951).

Directed by Robert Wise, this allegorical story starred Michael Rennie as the alien Klaatu, sent to give the Earth an ultimatum, and Patricia Neal (1926-) and the earthling who helps to prevent the planet's destruction.

Phil Hardy, *The Film Encyclopedia: Science Fiction* (New York: William Morrow and Co., 1984) 127.

Is there a book in Boston bound in human skin?

There is a book in the Boston Athenaeum that is said to be bound in skin of its author. It is the deathbed confession of a highwayman named George Walton in 1837. The Library of Congress also has a book bound in human skin.

Library Notes, *More Books* May 1944.

Which real-life mother and daughter have also played mother-and-daughter roles on film?

American actresses Diane Ladd (1932-) and daughter Laura Dern (1967-) have reprised their real-life roles on film. Ladd started her career on the stage, segued into film, and married her co-star Bruce Dern (1936-) from *The Wild Angels* (1966). She and Dern had a daughter together, and the grown-up Laura followed her parents' footsteps into the entertainment industry. Ladd was cast as the younger Dern's dysfunctional mother in the David Lynch film *Wild at Heart* (1990). The following year, Ladd portrayed a more sympathetic mother character opposite her daughter in *Rambling Rose* (1991), and their performances garnered the duo separate Academy Award nominations. It was the first such mother-daughter nomination in Oscar history.

Robyn Karney, ed., *The Hollywood Who's Who: The Actors and Directors in Today's Hollywood* (New York: Continuum, 1993), s.v. "Ladd, Diane."

What was the television series about reptilian aliens who assumed a human disguise?

The television series about reptilian aliens with sinister plans for conquering Earth was called "V" and ran on NBC from the fall of 1984 until the summer of 1985. The aliens were known as the Visitors and their plans for conquest were eventually thwarted by a group of resistance fighters. It was based on two separate mini-series that had aired on the network in 1983 and 1984.

Alex McNeil, *Total Television: A Comprehensive Guide to Programming from 1948 to the Present, 3d ed.* (New York: Penguin, 1991), s.v. "V."

Where did the phrase "the $64 question" originate?

The phrase "the $64 question" originated on a CBS radio quiz show called "Take It or Leave It" broadcast during the 1940s. The host of the program, Phil Baker, queried contestants chosen from a studio audience. Baker often joked with the participants and liked to remind them that he was posing "the $64 question." Later the "$64 question" became the "$64,000 Question" (1955-58), title of a short-lived prime time television quiz show hosted by Hal March. The show ended after a scandal erupted over the coaching of contestants.

Les Brown's Encyclopedia of Television (Detroit, MI: Visible Ink Press, 1992), s.v. "game shows." *New York Times* 2 December 1963.

In what famous film of the 1970s do two men storm into the office of newswriter Rudyard Kipling and ask him to witness a contract?

In *The Man Who Would Be King*, Michael Caine (1933-) and Sean Connery (1930-) play two con artists who barge into Rudyard Kipling's (1865-1936) newspaper office, portrayed by

Christopher Plummer (1929-), to have him witness their contract. The con-artists turned adventurers promise to forswear women and alcohol in their quest to find the ancient city of Kafiristan, and become the first white men since Alexander the Great to enter it. John Huston (1906-1987) directed the adventure film.

Robert Bookbinder, *The Films of the Seventies* (Secaucus, NJ: Citadel Press, 1982), 134.

In which film does the story begin with someone being swindled out of his bankroll?

The Sting begins as young con man Johnny Hooker, portrayed by Robert Redford (1937-), learns the tricks of the trade from Robert Earl Jones in the role of Luther Coleman, his more experienced mentor. Together they cheat a patsy out of his loot, not knowing that the man is involved with the Chicago mob. Luther soon turns up dead, and Redford's Hooker searches for and finds another legendary con man that his murdered mentor had spoken of—Henry Gondorff. Paul Newman (1925-) was cast as Gondorff, and the exploits of the two in their attempt to exact retribution for the murder carried the rest of *The Sting's* plot to box-office success.

Robert Bookbinder, *The Films of the Seventies* (Secaucus, NJ: Citadel Press, 1982), 76.

Who played the memorable villains in the 1960s television series "Batman"?

The television series "Batman" (1966-68), based on the comic book characters of Bob Kane, featured the following villains: Catwoman—Eartha Kitt (1928-), Julie Newmar (1935-), and Lee Meriwether (1935-); Egghead—Vincent Price (1911-1993); Joker—Cesar Romero (1907-1994); Penguin—Burgess Meredith (1908-1997); Riddler—Frank Gorshin (1934-).

Gabe Essoe, *The Book of TV Lists* (Westport, CT: Arlington House, 1981), 82. *Les Brown's Encyclopedia of Television* (Detroit, MI: Visible Ink Press, 1992), s.v."Batman."

Who is Captain Africa?

Appearing in 1987, Captain Africa is a Nigerian comic book superhero whose mission is to fight "evil and dark forces that threaten Africa and the whole world." When not battling evil, Captain Africa is Rokko Zullu, a successful businessman. The comic book series is drawn by Andy Akman, written by a committee, and published by African Comics Ltd.

Created as a role model for urban Africans, Captain Africa lives in an airbrushed, idyllic Africa, a place with comfortable vills, clean hospitals, and he battles superstition and ignorance.

James Brooke, "Goodbye to Tarzan, Meet Captain Africa," *New York Times* 27 September 1988.

In the movie screen epic *Gone With The Wind*, who played the role of Belle Watling?

In the American Civil War movie epic *Gone With The Wind* (1939), the role of Belle Watling was played by Ona Munson (1906-1955).

William Pratt, *Scarlet Fever: The Ultimate Pictorial Treasury of Gone With The Wind* (New York: Macmillan Publishing, 1977), 226.

Who was the host of the 1950s' television game show "Beat The Clock"?

Bud Collyer was the original host of the television game show "Beat The Clock." He emceed the popular show from 1950 to 1961. His assistant was Roxanne Arlen, who was replaced in 1955 by Beverly Bentley. Jack Narz was the emcee of "The New Beat the Clock" from 1969 to 1972, being replaced by Gene Wood, who hosted the show from 1972-1974. Monty Hall was host from 1979-1980.

Les Brown's Encyclopedia of Television (Detroit, MI: Visible Ink Press, 1992), s.v. "game shows." David Schwartz, *The Encyclopedia of TV Game Shows* (New York: New York Zoetrope, 1987), 34.

What famous American literary magazine, founded in 1925, is also known for its covers?

The *New Yorker* is a weekly literary magazine that is also famous for its cover artwork. Founded by editor Harold Ross in 1925, it has included poetry and short stories as well as articles on literature, art, theater, films, music, and dance. Many famous authors have contributed to its pages.

Jack Salzman, ed., *The Cambridge Handbook of American Literature* (Cambridge: Cambridge University Press, 1986), 177.

Why have print journalists traditionally closed their news copy with the notation "30"?

There are numerous reasons given why print journalists have traditionally closed their news copy with the notation "30." One theory holds that the first news story sent by telegraph to a press association during the American Civil War (1861-65) contained 30 words. Others believe that before the invention of the typewriter, "X" designated the end of a sentence, "XX," the end of a paragraph, and "XXX," which is also the Roman numeral for 30, the end of a story. Less likely stories deal with a reporter named "Thirtee," the number of slugs a typesetting machine could cast, and an early Associated Press rule that allowed a subscriber a maximum of 30 stories per day.

William Metz, *Newswriting: From Lead to "30"* (Englewood Cliff, NJ: Prentice-Hall, Inc., 1977), p. 26.

What former television situation-comedy actress is receiving high marks as a movie director?

Former television situation-comedy actress Penny Marshall, who portrayed Laverne De Fazio on "Laverne and Shirley," has gone on to receive high marks as a movie director. Movies to her credit are *Jumpin' Jack Flash*, *Awakenings*, and *Big*.

Ronald L. Smith, *Who's Who in Comedy: Comedians, Comics, and Clowns From Vaudeville to Today's Stand-Ups* (New York: Facts On File, 1992), 304-05.

What does TARDIS stand for?

TARDIS is an acronym for Time and Relative Dimensions in Space, which is the time-traveling vehicle of the Timelords of Gallifrey from the longest-running British science fiction television series "Dr. Who."

Bill Harry, *Heroes of the Spaceways* (London: Omnibus Press, 1981), s.v. "TARDIS, the."

What was the name of comic-strip caveman Alley Oop's pet dinosaur?

Comic-strip caveman Alley Oop shared many a prehistoric adventure with his pet dinosaur, Dinny. Alley Oop was created by American cartoonist V.T. Hamlin in 1933.

David Pringle, *Imaginary People: A Who's Who of Modern Fictional Characters* (New York: World Almanac, 1987), s.v. "Alley Oop."

What was the name of Superman's dog?

Superman's dog was known as "Krypto the Super Dog." Mort Weisinger, an editor at DC Comics, created the Man of Steel's canine pal.

Ron Goulart, ed., *The Encyclopedia of American Comics* (New York: Facts On File, 1990), s.v. "Superman."

Why did NBC reject in 1965 the first "Star Trek" episode, "The Cage"?

The National Broadcasting Company (NBC) rejected the first "Star Trek" episode, "The Cage," in February of 1965 because it was considered too intellectual. NBC was still interested, however, and commissioned a second pilot for the series, entitled "Where No Man Has Gone Before." Premiering in September 8, 1966, the series focused of the adventures of the crew of the Starship NCC 1701, called the "USS Enterprise." Led by Captain James T. Kirk (portrayed by William Shatner (1931-) when Jeffery Hunter turned down the role), the major crew members were the half-human, half-Vulcan science officer, Spock (played by Leonard Nimoy (1931-), Dr. Leonard "Bones" McCoy (portrayed by DeForest Kelly (1924-1999). Despite a very strong cult following, "Star Trek" only had a three-season run, ending in March of 1969. Yet, years after its initial debut, its reruns would be carried by 140 stations in 48 countries, cartoons and "Star Trek" merchandise-licensing would be extremely successful, and a new generation of Star Trek movies and television series would made, such as "Star Trek: The Next Generation."

Allan Asherman, *The Star Trek Compendium* (New York: Pocket Books, 1993), 17, 173. *Les Brown's Encyclopedia of Television* (Detroit, MT: Visible Ink Press, 1992), s.v. "Star Trek."

Which actor gave actress Jane Wyman Hollywood's then-longest screen kiss?

Actor Regis Toomey gave Jane Wyman a 185-second kiss in *You're in the Army Now,* released in 1941. Toomey's kiss made motion picture history and set a Hollywood record for the longest kiss on film.

Pittsburgh Post-Gazette 14 October 1991.

How long is a script for a television play?

The script length for a television play varies according to time. A 15-minute script would average about 20 pages; a 30-minute script, 40 pages; a 60-minute script, 100 pages, and a 90-minute script, 150 pages.

Edward Barry Roberts, *Television Writing and Selling, 4th ed.* (Boston: The Writer, 1964).

What is the name of France's over-the-air pay television channel?

Canal Plus is the hugely successful French pay television channel that premiered in 1984.

Les Brown's Encyclopedia of Television, 3d ed. (Detroit, MI: Gale Research Inc., 1992), s.v. "Canal Plus."

When and where did the first Dick Tracy comic strip appear?

The first Dick Tracy comic strip appeared in the Detroit *Mirror* on Sunday, October 4, 1931. Artist Chester Gould (1900-1985) created the long-running strip based on the adventures of a strong-jawed police detective.

Bill Crouch Jr., *Dick Tracy: America's Most Famous Detective* (Secaucus, NJ: Citadel Press, 1987), 24.

What is a "spin doctor"?

A "spin doctor" is either a press agent or a public relations representative who puts a flattering slant, or "spin," on a given story about his or her client.

Harold LeMay, Sid Lerner and Marian Taylor *The Facts On File Dictionary of New Words* (New York: Facts On File, 1985), 112.

Who was the voice of the nearsighted cartoon character Mr. Magoo?

Actor Jim Backus (1913-1989) was the voice of the nearsighted cartoon character Mr. Magoo, a comical old man, much of whose humor was derived from mistakes made because of his poor eyesight. The animated character had great success in movie theater cartoons before coming to television in 1962 as Ebeneezer Scrooge in "Mr. Magoo's Christmas Carol." In 1964-65, he had his own television series, "The Famous Adventures of Mr. Magoo."

Tim Brooks and Earle Marsh, *The Complete Directory to Prime Time Network TV Shows, 1946-Present, 5th ed.* (New York: Ballantine Books, 1992), s.v. "Famous Adventures of Mr. Magoo, The."

Which comic book character had a jet birdplane with flapping batwings?

"Airboy" was a comic book character of the 1940s and 1950s who had a jet birdplane with flapping batwings.

Don Thompson and Dick Lupoff, eds., *The Comic-Book Book* (New Rochelle, NY: Arlington House, 1974), 189.

On whose life was the film *Funny Lady* based?

The film *Funny Lady* was based on the life of Fanny Brice and featured Barbra Streisand as actress/singer Brice and James Caan as Billy Rose, a songwriter/businessman.

Pauline Kael, *Reeling* (Boston: Atlantic Monthly Press Book, Little, Brown and Co., 1976), 457.

Which dance director wowed moviegoers with his overhead kaleidoscopic shots of dance routines?

Director/choreographer Busby Berkeley (1895-1976) revolutionized the film musical in the 1930s with his extravagant, kaleidoscopic numbers in which he used the camera to create innovate effects, such as overhead shots of dance routines. Some critics feel the greatest representation of his art was "The Lullaby of Broadway" in the movie *Gold Diggers of 1935* (1935).

Ted Sennett, *Great Movie Directors* (New York: Harry N. Abrams, 1986), 33.

What was the name of Plastic Man's sidekick?

Woozy Winks was the reformed criminal turned sidekick of comic book superhero Plastic Man. Although the red-suited rubber crime fighter was first introduced to readers in the first issue of *Police Comics* in August of 1941, Woozy didn't come along until issue #13.

Ron Goulart, ed., *The Encyclopedia of American Comics* (New York: Facts On File, 1990), s.v. "Plastic Man."

What is the origin of "Shazam," the magic word that transforms Billy Batson into superhero Captain Marvel?

Shazam, the word that transforms young Billy Batson into crime-fighting comic book superhero Captain Marvel, was the name of a wizard who transferred his powers to Batson. Shazam is an acronym for Solomon, Hercules, Atlas, Zeus, Achilles, and Mercury.

Ron Goulart, ed., *The Encyclopedia of American Comics* (New York: Facts On File, 1990), s.v. "Captain Marvel."

What was the first American paperback book?

The first American paperback book was *Maleska: The Indian Wife of the White Hunter* by Ann S. Stephens. The book was published in 1860 by Erastus and Irwin P. Beadle as part of their "Dime Novels" series.

Karen L. Rood, *American Literacy Almanac* (New York: Facts On File, 1988), 32.

At what newspaper did Ernest Hemingway get his first job?

Upon his graduation from high school in June of 1917, Ernest Hemingway (1899-1961) got his first job as a cub reporter for the Kansas City *Star* newspaper. Hemingway went on to become a Nobel prize-winning novelist.

Samuel Shaw, *Ernest Hemingway* (New York: Frederick Ungar, 1973), 18.

Who wrote the short story about two never-married daughters of a Norwegian Lutheran minister that became the best foreign-language film of 1987?

Danish writer Karen Blixen (1885-1962), under the name, Isak Dinesen, wrote a short story about a Norwegian Lutheran minister's two daughters who, in their younger days, capture the interest of many young men. The sisters, however, never marry. This story was the basis for the winner of the 1987 Academy Award for best foreign-language film, *Babette's Feast.* The film focuses on a meal cooked for the sisters and their guests by an enigmatic woman who has become their servant.

Geoffrey Hill, *Illuminating Shadows: The Mythic Power of Film* (Boston: Shambhala, 1992), 137-138.

Who was the founder of *Pravda?*

Leon Trotsky (1879-1940) was the founder of newspaper *Pravda,* which is the Russian word for truth, and which was the official organ of the Communist party in the former Soviet Union. Trotsky was a Russian revolutionary leader who escaped from exile in Siberia to Vienna, where he produced the first *Pravda* in 1908.

Martin Walker, *Powers of the Press: Twelve of the World's Influential Newspapers* (New York: Pilgrim Press, 1983), 139.

How many categories are there for Pulitzer Prizes in Journalism and how much money are the winners awarded?

The Pulitzer Prizes in journalism were established in 1917 to recognize achievement in journalism, letters, music, and drama. Awards are given in the following fourteen categories of journalism: public service journalism; spot news reporting; investigative reporting; explanatory journalism; beat reporting; national reporting; international reporting (two prizes); feature writing; commentary; criticism; editorial writing; editorial cartooning; spot news photography; and feature photography. Awards are also made in letters and drama; fiction; history; biography; poetry; general non-fiction; drama; and music.

The winner in each category is awarded $3,000 from an endowment established by Joseph Pulitzer (1847-1911), the Hungarian-born American journalist who founded the Columbia University School of Journalism. The winner for Public Service in Journalism is awarded a gold medal in addition to the $3,000 monetary prize.

Debra M. Kirby, ed., *Awards, Honors & Prizes,* (Detroit: Gale Research, Inc., 1994), 1:485. Kendall J. Wills, ed., *The Pulitzer Prizes* (New York: Simon & Schuster, 1988), 14.

When did media mogul Rupert Murdoch launch Fox Broadcasting?

The U.S. television network Fox Broadcasting was launched by Australian media mogul Rupert Murdoch (1931-) in June of 1988.

Martin A. Lee and Norman Solomon, *Unreliable Sources* (New York: Carol Publishing Group, 1990), 95.

Who provided the voice of "Francis the Talking Mule" in the movie *Francis* (1950)?

In the 1950 movie hit *Francis,* actor Chill Wills (1903-1978) provided the voice of "Francis the Talking Mule."

Scott Siegel and Barbara Siegel, *The Encyclopedia of Hollywood* (New York: Facts On File, 1990), 15.

How are Nielsen television ratings gathered?

Nielsen Television Research is gathered from home viewers who keep a diary of the shows they watch. The A.C. Nielsen Company, a marketing research firm, randomly selects households and asks family members to keep and submit a viewer diary for one week. Information gathered from a cross-section of American homes is used to produce the Nielsen ratings.

Nielsen Television Research 1990.

What was D.W. Griffith's controversial 1915 film *Birth of a Nation,* based on?

Birth of a Nation, the controversial 1915 film by D.W. Griffith (1875-1948) was based on Thomas Dixon's melodramatic play *The Clansman.* The play and the movie are set in the post-Civil War south and both present the War, its aftermath, and Reconstruction from the southern viewpoint. The villains are the carpetbaggers and recently freed slaves, while the heroes are members of the emerging Ku Klux Klan and sympathetic southerners. The film opened to great technical acclaim because of its sweeping historical panorama, battle scenes, human drama, and the climactic ride of the Klan. *Birth of a Nation* was one of the first movies to unite the terms "film epic." The movie opened to considerably less enthusiasm in northern cities with large

African-American populations; many demonstrations and protests ensued.

Leonard Maltin, ed., *Leonard Maltin's Movie Encyclopedia* (New York: Dutton, 1994), s.v. "Griffith, D.W.." Juliet P. Schoen, *Silents to Sounds: A History of the Movies* (New York: Four Winds Press, 1976), 29.

What movie actor played the 1950s cowboy hero Hopalong Cassidy?

A western series created William Boyd (1898-1972) for the movies during the 1930s and 1940s featured Boyd as the black-garbed cowboy hero Hopalong Cassidy. These movies were shown again on television in 1948. Children enjoyed them so much that Boyd produced 52 half-hour shows for television during 1951-52. Cassidy's sidekick in the television series was Red Connors, played by Edgar Buchanan.

Bernard A. Drew, *Motion Picture Series and Sequels* (New York: Garland Publishing, 1990). *Les Brown's Encyclopedia of Television, 3d ed.* (Detroit, MI: Gale Research Inc., 1992), s.v. "Hopalong Cassidy."

What was the first Technicolor film?

Color films were a reality in England by 1906 when the process called Kinemacolor was developed by George A. Smith. The first full-length color film in Kinemacolor, called *The World, the Flesh, and the Devil,* was produced in 1914, but the expense of this color process made it a commercial failure. The first practical, commercial color process known as three-color Technicolor was used in Walt Disney's 1932 film *Flowers and Trees,* also known as *Silly Symphony.* The first feature film to be produced in Technicolor was *Becky Sharp,* directed by Rouben Mamoulian in 1935.

Dennis Sanders, *The First of Everything* (New York: Delacorte Press, 1981), 253.

What was the first commercial 3-D feature film?

The first commercial 3-D feature film was Arch Obler's *Bwana Devil,* released in the early 1950s with promises of a "lion in your lap." Hollywood viewed 3-D as a way to combat the growing popularity of television, but the demand for stereoscopic films was short lived and by the mid-1950s the craze had passed. The 1980s and 1990s saw a few futile attempts to revive the 3-D fad.

Richard B. Armstrong and Mary Willems Armstrong, *The Movie List Book* (Cincinnati, OH: Betterway Books, 1994), 376.

In what movie did Swedish actress Greta Garbo utter her famous line "I want to be alone"?

Swedish actress Greta Garbo (1905-1990) uttered the line "I want to be alone" in the 1931 movie *Grand Hotel.* The phrase soon became part of the popular idiom with people saying "I vant to be ahlone" in mockery of Garbo's accent.

Stuart Berg Flexner, *Listening To America* (New York: Simon and Schuster, 1982), 407.

In the two movies *The Cat People* of what gender are those who turn into great cats?

The 1942 RKO movie *The Cat People* was based on a Serbian folktale of a woman who, in jealous rages, is able to turn herself into a panther and kill her lovers. The movie starred Simone Simon and Kent Smith and received good reviews considering it was produced as a B film. The 1982 remake by Universal starred Nastassia Kinski and Malcolm McDowell and featured a male character who was able to turn himself into a killer cat. The remake had strong sexual and incestuous overtones and received generally poor reviews, especially when compared to the original.

Jay Robert Nash and Stanley Ralph Ross, *The Motion Picture Guide* (Chicago: Cinebooks, 1985), 2:379-80.

When comic-book hero Batman is not fighting crime, who is he and where does he reside?

Comic-book Batman is the alter-ego of Gotham City socialite and philanthropist Bruce Wayne. He dedicated his life to fighting crime when, as a nine-year-old boy, he witnessed the murder of his parents, Thomas and Martha Wayne, by a thug in Gotham City. Batman began his crime-fighting career in 1939 with the May issue of *Detective Comics.* He was originally drawn by Bob Kane with much of the writing done by Bill Finger. The caped crusader is aided in his quest for a crime-free world by boy wonder Robin, also known as Dick Grayson. Over the decades there have been numerous movies, movie serials, and television shows featuring the two characters and their seemingly eternal nemeses "The Joker," "The Penguin," and "Catwoman."

David Pringle, *Imaginary People* (New York: World Almanac, 1987), s.v. "Batman." Tom Sabulis, "A Trivia Quiz for true Batman fans," *Pittsburgh Press* 22 June 1989.

On what television series did Carol Burnett first appear?

Although viewers associate comedienne Carol Burnett (1936-) with the Gary Moore Show (1958-64), she first appeared on television in the series "Stanley," which ran on the National Broadcasting Company (NBC) network from September of 1956 to March of 1957.

James Robert Parish and Vincent Terrace, *The Complete Actors' Television Credits, 1948-1988, 2d ed.* (Metuchen, NJ: The Scarecrow Press, 1990), 2:52.

Who played the Bickersons?

The Bickersons were a radio comedy skit that featured a quarreling husband and wife; they were first heard on Edgar Bergen's "Chase and Sanborn Hour." The cast included Don Ameche (1908-1993) as the husband, Francis Langford and then Marsha Hunt as the wife, and Danny Thomas (1914-1991) as the husband's brother.

Frank Buxton and Bill Owen, *The Big Broadcast, 1920-1950* (New York: The Viking Press, 1972), 34.

What film classic features a mad scientist in pursuit of a somnambulist who has kidnapped a girl?

The Cabinet of Dr. Caligari (1919), a German silent movie, is a pioneering film made in the most extreme expressionistic style; the plot involves a mad scientist in pursuit of a somnambulist who kidnapped a girl. The film was highly influential and was much imitated in its approach to lighting, composition, design, and acting.

Baird Searles, *Films of Science Fiction and Fantasy* (New York: AFI Press, 1988), 77. David J. Weiner, ed., *The Video Source Book, 11th ed.* (Detroit, MI: Gale Research Inc., 1990), 1:248.

Who designed the dream sequences in Alfred Hitchcock's movie *Spellbound?*

Spellbound, by English film director Alfred Hitchcock (1899-1980), was produced in 1945 and is considered one his finest movies from the 1940s. It is about a young man suffering from amnesia and a female psychologist who falls in love with him. The film stars Gregory Peck and Ingrid Bergman and features dream sequences that were designed by the Spanish surrealist Salvador Dali (1904-1989).

Robert A. Harris and Michael S. Lasky, *The Films of Alfred Hitchcock* (Secaucus, NJ: The Citadel Press, 1976), 122.

Which movie did Alfred Hitchcock direct twice?

The Man Who Knew Too Much was Alfred Hitchcock's (1899-1980) first international success and the first English-speaking film for actor Peter Lorre (1904-1964). Produced in 1934, the film centered on a British family man on vacation in Switzerland who is told about an assassination plot by a dying agent. Hitchcock remade the film in 1956, but this time it is an American family vacationing in Marrakech who becomes involved in international intrigue. The second version, which is over a half hour longer than the original, featured James Stewart (1908-1997) and Doris Day (1924-).

Robert A. Harris and Michael S. Lasky, *The Films of Alfred Hitchcock* (Secaucus, NJ: The Citadel Press, 1976), 48.

What is the name of Gumby's horse?

Gumby was a 1957 children's television program about the misadventures of a boy Gumby, who was an animated green clay figure, and his orange horse friend, Pokey.

Vincent Terrace, *The Complete Encyclopedia of Television Programs, 1947-1979, 2d ed.* (New York: A.S. Barnes, 1979), 1:402.

What was the only X-rated film to win an Oscar?

Directed by John Schlesinger, *Midnight Cowboy* (1969) dealt with the relationship between a naive newcomer to New York city played by John Voight (1938-) and his companion, a street-wise derelict portrayed by Dustin Hoffman (1937-). The film touched on the theme of homosexual prostitution and became the first X-rated movie to win an Academy Award for best picture, although it has subsequently been given an R rating.

David A. Cook, *A History of Narrative Film* (New York: W.W. Norton & Co., 1981), 633.

Who played the character Pp Le Moko in the movie *Algiers*, and what line from the movie became part of the popular idiom?

In 1938 French actor Charles Boyer (1899-1978) portrayed the character Pp Le Moko in the American film version of Roger d' Ashelbe's (Henri La Barthe) novel of the same name. Entitled *Algiers*, the movie contained the line "Come with me to the Casbah," which soon became part of the popular idiom. The 1936 French film version of the novel retained Ashelbe's title and starred Jean Gabin as Pp Le Moko. The 1948 American film version, *Casbah*, featured Tony Martin.

David Pringle, *Imaginary People: A Who's Who of Modern Fictional Characters* (New York: World Almanac, Pharos Books, 1987), s.v. "Pp Le Moko."

What is the memory test that is used for persons applying for jobs as radio announcers?

The phrase used as a memory test for radio announcer applicants is: "one hen; two ducks; three squawking geese; four Limerick oysters; five corpulent corpuscles; six pairs of Don Alverzo's tweezers; seven Macedonians in full battle array; eight brass monkeys from the ancient sacred crypts of Egypt; nine apathetic, sympathetic, athletic, diabetic old men on roller skates with a marked propensity for delinquency and sloth; ten lyrical spherical, diabolical demons of the deep who haul, stall around the corner of the quo of the quay of the quivy all at the same time."

RQ Fall 1992.

Who played the son of Tarzan and Jane in the Tarzan films?

In the 1920 movie *The Son of Tarzan*, Kamuela C. Searle played the natural son of Tarzan. His name in the movie was Korak. Most people remember Boy, who was played by Johnny Sheffield. In *Tarzan Finds a Son!* (1939) Tarzan finds the child as the only survivor of a plane crash in the jungle. Jane and Tarzan "adopt" the child as their own son. Sheffield appeared in eight Tarzan movies with John Weismuller as Tarzan. In *Tarzan's Savage Fury* (1952), Tarzan played by Lex Barker finds an orphan boy, Joey, who is "adopted" by Tarzan and Jane. Tommy Carlton played the part of Joey. In other Tarzan movies there were young boys who were befriended by Tarzan but not considered his son.

David Fury, *Kings of the Jungle: An Illustrated Reference to "Tarzan" on Screen and Television* (Jefferson, NC: McFarland, 1994).

Who did the classic baseball spoof "Who's on First"?

The comedy skit "Who's on First"? was first presented on the radio by slapstick comedians Bud (William) Abbott (1895-1974) and Lou Costello (1908-1959) on *The Abbott and Costello Program* during the 1940s.

Frank Buxton and Bill Owen, *The Big Broadcast 1920-1950, rev. ed.*, (New York: Viking Press, 1972), s.v. "the Abbott and Costello program." John Dunning, *Tune in Yesterday: The Ultimate Encyclopedia of Old-Time Radio 1925-1976* (New Jersey: Prentice-Hall, 1976), s.v. "the Abbott and Costello show."

What were the names of the movies comprising the "Planet of the Apes" series?

Based on a science fiction novel by Pierre Boulle about a post-apocalyptic race of ape-like beings discovered by American astronauts, the films in the "Planet of the Apes" series were *Planet of the Apes, Beneath the Planet of the Apes, Escape From the Planet of the Apes, Conquest of the Planet of the Apes*, and *Battle for the Planet of the Apes*. Roddy McDowall appeared in all but *Beneath the Planet of the Apes*.

Bernard A. Drew, *Motion Picture Series and Sequels: A Reference Guide* (New York: Garland, 1990), 268. John Walker, ed., *Halliwell's Filmgoer's and Video Viewer's Companion, 10th ed.* (New York: HarperCollins, 1993), s.v. "McDowall, Roddy."

When did the first American comic book appear?

A reprint of *Mutt and Jeff* comic strips printed by the *Chicago American* in 1911 is considered the first U.S. comic book, although cheap volumes of the *Yellow Kid* comic strip had appeared as early as 1904. Printed more like a traditional book, readers could get a copy by collecting six coupons from the papers which carried the strip. The initial printing of 10,000 sold out, and 35,000 additional copies had to be printed. Despite its success, the next comic book, which was the size of a newspaper tabloid, was not published until 1929. Issued by Dell under the title *The Funnies* and containing original strips, it ran for only 13 issues.

The first American comic magazine in modern format to be placed for sale independently of a newspaper or coupons/premiums was *Famous Funnies* in May of 1934. Subject-oriented comic books with original stories started with *Detective Comics* in 1937. *Superman* appeared as issue number one of *Action Comics* in 1938.

Robert McHenry, ed., *The New Encyclopaedia Britannica, 15th ed.* (Chicago: Encyclopaedia Britannica, 1993), s.v. "caricature, cartoon, and comic strip." Reinhold Reitberger and Wolfgang Fuchs, *Comics: Anatomy of a Mass Medium* (Boston: Little, Brown, 1971), 17-19. Coulton Waugh, *The Comics, 1947 reprint* (New York: Luna Press, 1974), 333-51.

What are the "Fourth and Fifth Estates"?

The "Fourth Estate" refers to the press as a distinct and influential power in the state. The term is usually credited to Sir Edmund Burke (1729-1797), who claimed that there were three estates in the English Parliament but that in the Reporters' Gallery there was a fourth more important than them all. The other three estates are the nobility, the commoners, and the clergy.

The phrase "Fifth Estate" is an adaptation of Burke's allusion to more modern times when the electronic press is so influential. The term refers to television and radio journalism.

William Morris and Mary Morris, *Morris Dictionary of Word and Phrase Origins, 2d ed.* (New York: Harper & Row, 1988), 229. Laurence Urdang, ed., *Picturesque Expressions: A Thematic Dictionary, 2d ed.* (Detroit, MI: Gale Research, Co., 1985), 457. Jay M. Shafritz, *The HarperCollins Dictionary of American Government and Politics* (New York: HarperCollins, 1992), 241.

When did the Walt Disney cartoon character Donald Duck make his first appearance?

The Walt Disney cartoon character Donald Duck made his first appearance in the animated film *The Wise Little Hen* (1934). The ill-tempered duck was created by Art Babbit, and Dick Huemer, and Clarence Nash gave Donald a voice. Donald's full name is Donald Fauntleroy Duck, as evidenced his military draft notice in *Donald Gets Drafted.*

David Pringle, *Imaginary People* (New York: World Almanac, 1987), s.v. "Donald Duck." Kevin F. Neary and Dave Smith, *The Ultimate Disney Trivia Book* (New York: Hyperion, 1992), 12.

What were the names of the characters that appeared in the Walt Disney version of *Pinocchio*?

Pinocchio, the wooden puppet-turned-boy, had many friends and some not-so-nice acquaintances, human and otherwise in the Walt Disney animated feature film of the same name. The bad guys were J. Worthington Foulfellow, Gideon, Stromboli, and the Coachman. Much more likeable were Geppetto, Jiminy Cricket, Figaro, Lampwick, Monstro, and the Blue Fairy. *Pinocchio,* Walt Disney's second animated feature, was released in 1940.

John Grant, *Encyclopedia of Walt Disney's Animated Characters* (New York: Hyperion, 1993), 158-68.

How many cartoons has Walt Disney's Mickey Mouse appeared in?

Between 1928 and 1990 Walt Disney's Mickey Mouse appeared in 136 cartoons, including two commercials, two remakes of previous cartoons and two cameo appearances. Mickey Mouse, drawn by Ub Iwerks, first appeared in the animated cartoon, *Steamboat Willie* (1928). He was so popular that in 1929, Mickey Mouse Clubs were formed at local movie houses. That was also the year Mickey got a voice, that of his creator, Walt Disney, in the cartoon *The Karnival Kid.* Disney voiced Mickey until 1946, when James Macdonald took over, and in 1983, Wayne Allwine replaced Macdonald.

John Grant, *Encyclopedia of Walt Disney's Animated Characters* (New York: Hyperion, 1993), 31-32. Kevin Neary and Dave Smith, *The Ultimate Disney Trivia Book* (New York: Hyperion, 1992), 4.

Who were the Fantastic Four?

Created in 1961 by Stan Lee and Jack Kirby, the comic heroes called the Fantastic Four battled criminals and evildoers. They included scientist Reed Richards (Mr. Fantastic), who could stretch his body into various contortions; his wife, Sue (The Invisible Girl); Ben Grim (The Thing), who had the power of a thousand horses; and Johnny Storm (The Human Torch).

Ron Goulart, *Ron Goulart's Great History of Comic Books* (Chicago: Contemporary Books, 1986) , 281-82. Jeff Lenburg, *The Encyclopedia of Animated Cartoons* (New York: Facts on File, 1991), 323.

When did "The Lone Ranger" first air?

Created as a radio series by George W. Trendle and Fran Striker, "The Lone Ranger" made its debut on January 30, 1933, and lasted over twenty years. The television series ran from 1948-1961. The Lone Ranger's horse was named Silver and Tonto's horse was Scout. The famous cry of the Lone Ranger was "Hi-Yo, Silver, Away!" The person to play the Lone Ranger on television was Clayton Moore (except for 1952-1954, when he was played by John Hart) and Tonto was played by Jay Silverheels, a Mohawk Indian.

Tim Brooks and Earle Marsh, *The Complete Directory of Prime Time Network TV Shows 1946-Present, 5th ed.* (New York: Ballantine Books, 1992), 522. Vincent Terrace, *The Complete Encyclopedia of Television Programs 1946-1976* (New York: A.S. Barnes and Co., 1976), 2:34-35. Ruthven Tremain, *The Animals' Who's Who* (New York: Charles Scribner's Sons, 1982), 232, 237.

What were the first newspaper and periodical to be published by African-Americans?

The first African-American newspaper edited by African-Americans for African-Americans was *Freedom's Journal,* a four-page weekly published in New York City from March 16, 1827, to March 28, 1829, and edited by John Brown Russwurm (1799-1851) and Samuel E. Cornish. In 1830, Cornish, who had left the paper in 1827, resumed his editorship of the newspaper under the name *Rights of All.*

The first African-American periodical was *The Mirror of Liberty,* a quarterly of 16 pages, edited and published in New York City by David Ruggles. The first issue was dated July 1838.

Joseph Nathan Kane, *Famous First Facts, 4th ed.* (New York: H. W. Wilson, 1981), s.v. "newspaper." Kenneth Estell, ed., *The African-American Almanac, 6th ed.* (Detroit: Gale Research, 1994), 855, 879.

What are vanity presses?

Publishers who offer author subsidy or co-publishing arrangements are also known as vanity presses. They offer services ranging from printing a person's book to distributing and promoting it. Subsidy publishers are paid by the author to produce a book while co-publishers pay part of the production costs.

Mark Garvey, ed., *1994 Writer's Market* (Cincinnati: OH: Writer's Digest Books, 1993), 244.

What is the history behind the *Superman* radio program?

The DC comic book character Superman became the star of a successful radio program that started shortly after the comic book debuted. The *Adventures of Superman* began in 1938 in 15-minute syndicated programs. Sponsored by Mutual, it became a three-times-a-week program on February 12, 1940. When the program was dropped in 1942, the demand of young listeners brought it back on August 31, 1942, and it aired five times a week. It was very popular during World War II, and Superman's enemies were often Nazis or the Japanese. Kellogg's Pep cereal became the sponsor from 1943 through 1946. Mutual sponsored it again until 1949, when *Superman* went to ABC for a half-hour show on Saturdays. Programs increased to two times a week in 1950 until the show ended in 1951.

Clayton (Bud) Collyer was the voice of Superman (alias Clark Kent) until the program moved to ABC, where the voice was that of Michael Fitzmaurice. Joan Alexander was Lois Lane, Julian Noa was Perry White, and Jackie Kelk was Jimmy Olsen. The announcer was Jackson Beck.

To let the audience know that Clark Kent was changing to Superman, the voice was deepened for the super hero and he would say, "This looks like a job for . . . . (voice changes) SUPERMAN!" To let the listeners know Superman was taking flight, he would say, "Up, up, and away!"

Frank Buxton and Bill Owen, *The Big Broadcast 1920-1950* (New York: Viking Press, 1972), 230-31. John Dunning, *Tune in Yesterday: The Ultimate Encyclopedia of Old-Time Radio 1925-1976* (New Jersey: Prentice-Hall, 1976), s.v. "Adventures of Superman, The."

Which television shows have featured Superman?

From 1952 to 1957, George Reeves appeared as Superman in the syndicated television series "The Adventures of Superman," based on the DC comic book character. He had also appeared in the 1951 movie *Superman and the Mole Men.* Phyllis Coates continued her role as Lois Lane from the same movie for 26 episodes and was replaced by Noel Neill for the remaining episodes. Neill had appeared in the original Superman movie with Kirk Alyn in 1948 and in *Atom Man vs. Superman* in 1950.

"Superboy" appeared on television as a syndicated series from 1988 to 1992 starring John Haymes Newton as Superboy in 1988-89 and Gerard Christopher from 1989-92.

In the fall of 1993, the ABC series "Lois & Clark: The New Adventures of Superman" premiered with Dean Cain as Superman and Teri Hatcher as Lois Lane.

There have been numerous cartoon series on television with Superman as the main character or as one of many other "super heroes."

Tim Brooks and Earle Marsh, *The Complete Directory to Prime Time Network TV Shows: 1946-Present, 5th ed.* (New York: Ballantine Books, 1992), s.v. "Adventures of Superman, The, Superboy." Harry Castleman and Walter J. Podrazik, *Harry and Wally's Favorite TV Shows* (New York: Prentice Hall Press, 1989), s.v. "Superboy, Superman, The Adventures of." Rick Marin, "Super Chat," *TV Guide,* November 1993.

Whose footprints were the first to be placed in cement outside Grauman's Chinese Theater in Hollywood?

On May 18, 1927, actress Norma Talmadge (1893-1957) was the first to place her footprints in wet cement outside Grauman's Chinese Theater in Hollywood. According to legend it was an accident, but it gave restauranteur Sid Grauman the idea for a publicity stunt that continues still.

Patrick Robertson, *Guinness Movie Facts & Feats* (New York: Guinness Publishing, 1988), 18. Evelyn Mack Truitt, *Who Was Who On Screen* (New York: R. R. Bowker, 1984), s.v. "Talmadge, Norma."

Who was Miss Jane Pittman?

Miss Jane Pittman was a fictional character created by author Ernest J. Gaines. In the 1970s a novel and television movie came out entitled *The Autobiography of Miss Jane Pittman.* Her life spans the most significant periods of African-American history, from slavery to the civil rights era. The fact that Gaines wrote an introduction, signed the end of the introduction as "the editor," and referred to the book as an autobiography, created the false impression that Pittman was real.

Valerie Melissa Babb, *Ernest Gaines* (Boston: Twayne Publishers, 1991), 76-78. Martin Seymour-Smith, *Dictionary of Fictional Characters, rev. ed.* (Boston: The Writer, 1992), s.v. "Pittman, Jane, Miss."

Which television station provided the first educational programming?

In May of 1953 KUHT Houston became the first educational television station in the United States. It was a forerunner to PBS, the Public Broadcasting System. Created in November 1969, PBS became the central educational and cultural source of programming for public television stations.

Les Brown's Encyclopedia of Television, 3d ed. (Detroit: Gale Research, 1992), s.v. "PBS (Public Broadcasting Service)." Cobbett Steinberg, *TV Facts* (New York: Facts on File, 1985), 400.

What television comedian was known for saying the famous line, "My name . . . Jose Jiminez"?

Comedian Bill Dana (born October 5, 1924), most famous for the line "My name ... Jose Jiminez," got his big break in comedy in the late 1950s during an appearance on "The Steve Allen Show" when he uttered that quip. Dana, born William Szathmary in Quincy, Massachusetts, is a graduate of Boston's Emerson College. He is also an accomplished comedy writer, having worked for such luminaries as Don Adams. Dana built much of his comedic image upon his accent in which he replaces the sound of "hs" with those of "js," though never relying upon ethnic humor for laughs.

Ronald L. Smith, *Who's Who in Comedy: Comedians, Comics, and Clowns From Vaudeville to Today's Stand-Ups* (New York: Facts on File, 1992), s.v. "Bill Dana."

What is the name of the Woody Allen film that parodies a documentary?

Zelig (1983) is the name of the Oscar-winning director Woody Allen's (1935-) film that parodies a documentary. The film traces the life of a chameleon-like non-entity who contrives to have been associated with all the major events of the 20th century. It starred Allen and Mia Farrow (1945-), and employed advanced technological film-making techniques to place the Allen character alongside such historical figures as German leader Adolf Hitler (1889-1945) and American dramatist Eugene O'Neill (1888-1953). Film critic Roger Ebert commented that "The movie is a technical masterpiece, but in artistic and comic terms, only pretty good."

Leslie Halliwell, *Halliwell's Film Guide, 8th ed.* (New York: HarperCollins, 1991), s.v. "Zelig."

What actor is famous for playing the characters: Duke Mantee, Roy "Mad Dog" Earle, Sam Spade, and Rick Blaine?

American actor Humphrey Bogart (1899-1957) is famous for his great characterizations, which earned him three Academy Award nominations, winning once for his 1951 role in *The African Queen* opposite Katharine Hepburn. Bogart was born in 1899, the son of a respected physician and an artist. He served in the Navy during World War I (1914-1918), and was wounded during the shelling of *Leviathan.* He began his acting career in 1922, acting on stage in New York City, making his film debut in 1930 in a short film titled *Broadway's Like That.*

He is most famous for the following roles: Duke Mantee in *The Petrified Forest,* 1936; Frank Taylor in *Black Legion,* 1937; David Graham, *Marked Woman,* 1937; Baby Face Martin, *Dead End,* 1937; James Frazier, *Angels With Dirty Faces,* 1938; Roy "Mad Dog" Earle, *High Sierra,* 1941; Sam Spade, *The Maltese Falcon,* 1941; and Rick Blaine in *Casablanca,* in 1942.

Robert Nowlan and Gwendolyn Wright Nowlan, *Movie Characters of Leading Performers of The Sound Era* (Chicago: American Library Association, 1990), s.v. "Bogart, Humphrey."

What were the names of the Seven Dwarfs?

The Seven Dwarfs, depicted in the animated Walt Disney movie, *Snow White and the Seven Dwarfs* (1937), were named Happy, Sneezy, Bashful, Grumpy, Doc, Dopey, and Sleepy. They befriended Snow White and popularized the now-famous songs "Whistle While You Work" and "Heigh Ho, Heigh Ho."

Sylvia Cole, *The Facts on File Dictionary of 20th-Century Allusions: From Abbott and Costello to Ziegfeld Girls* (New York: Facts on File, 1991), 241.

What was the original title for "The Phil Silvers Show," whose main character was Sergeant Ernest Bilko?

"You'll Never Get Rich" was the original title of the Phil Silvers' show, which featured the main character Sergeant Ernest Bilko. Later dubbed "The Phil Silvers Show," the program ran on CBS from September 20, 1955 through September 18, 1959. Bilko was a con man who tried to make a profit off his Army service. The show also starred Paul Ford, Elisabeth Frazer, and Maurice Gosfield. Producers were Edward J. Montagne and Aaron Ruben.

Vincent Terrace, *Fifty Years of Television: A Guide to Series and Pilots, 1937-1988* (New York: Cornwall Books, 1991), s.v. "The Phil Silvers Show."

What is a gaffer?

In the theater, a gaffer is the foreman of a stage crew; in film or television, the gaffer is the head electrician. The word's etymological roots trace back to the 16th century, when gaffer was used as an altered form of godfather or grandfather. In the 19th century, a foreman or overseer became known as a gaffer.

Richard Weiner, ed., *Webster's New World Dictionary of Media and Communications* (New York: Webster's New World, 1990), s.v. "Gaffer."

What was Mr. Magoo's first name?

Jim Backus (1913-1989) supplied the voice of Quincy Magoo, the lovable, but nearly blind, animated cartoon character in the children's television show "Mr. Magoo," which was first aired in 1960.

George W. Woolery, *Children's Television: The First Thirty-Five Years, 1946-1981* (Metuchen, NJ: Scarecrow Press, 1983), s.v. "Mr. Magoo."

Who was the substitute host on the "Howdy Doody Show" during Bob Smith's illness in 1954?

George "Gabby" Hayes was the substitute host on the "Howdy Doody Show" during Bob "Buffalo Bob" Smith's illness in 1954. The "Howdy Doody Show" ran on NBC for 2,543 episodes, from December 27, 1947 to September 24, 1960. The show depicted the adventures of the orphan Howdy, whose guardian was Buffalo Bob, a ventriloquist, who was the creator and host for this children's series.

Vincent Terrace, *Encyclopedia of Television Series, Pilots, and Specials 1937-1973* (New York: Zoetrope, 1986), s.v. "Howdy Doody."

What was the Pink Panther in the 1964 film of the same name?

Directed by Blake Edwards in 1964, *The Pink Panther* was a comedy about a jewel thief known as the Phantom, who attempts to steal a famous diamond, the Pink Panther. The movie had an all-star cast, but its success was based on the performance of Peter Sellers (1925-1980) as a bumbling policeman Inspector Clouseau, who infuriates his associates by solving crimes correctly and usually capturing the affections of the heroine despite all his ridiculous blunders.. Blake Edwards directed six sequels with Sellers, two of which were made after the actor died by using outtakes from previous films. In 1993 Edwards made another comedy on the same theme, *Son of the Pink Panther* (1993), which starred Roberto Benigni as Clouseau's son. In 1968 Alan Arkin played the title role in *Inspector Clouseau,* a movie Edwards did not direct. The Pink Panther, a animated cat who introduced the credits in each of the movie adventures, went on to become a popular cartoon character.

Richard B. Armstrong and Mary Willems Armstrong, *The Movie List Book* (Cincinnati, OH: Betterway Books, 1994, 288. Michael R. Pitts, *Famous Movie Detectives* (Metuchen, NJ: Scarecrow Press, 1991), 21.

What was the name of the family dog on the television program "Petticoat Junction"?

Boy was the name of the Bradley family dog on the television comedy series "Petticoat Junction" (1963-70). Press releases referred to Boy as the "Shady Rest Dog," named for the family's Shady Rest Hotel in Hooterville, where Kate Bradley and her three daughters, Billy Jo, Bobby Jo, and Betty Jo lived. He was owned by Betty Jo, whom he followed home from school one day.

Vincent Terrace, *Television Character and Story Facts: Over 110,000 Details from 1,008 Shows, 1945-1992* (Jefferson City, NC: McFarland & Co., 1993, 564.

In which Mike Hammer film does author Mickey Spillane play the role of Mike Hammer?

In *The Girl Hunters* (1963), directed by Roy Rowland, author Mickey Spillane (1918-) plays his own central character, the tough-talking detective Mike Hammer.

Max Allan Collins and James L. Traylor, *One Lonely Knight: Mickey Spillane's Mike Hammer* (Bowling Green, OH: Bowling Green State University Popular Press, 1984), 185.

What were the first words Mr. Ed spoke to Wilbur on the syndicated television series "Mr. Ed"?

On the syndicated television series "Mr. Ed" (1960-61), the first words Mr. Ed, the talking horse said to Wilbur, played by Alan Young, were: "It's been a long time since I was a pony."

Vincent Terrace, *The Ultimate TV Trivia Book* (Boston: Faber and Faber, 1991), 148.

Who played Major Seth Adams in the original television version of "Wagon Train"?

Actor Ward Bond (1904-1960) played the character Adams, who led wagon trains westward in the original television version of "Wagon Train" (1957-62). He established the role, but died before the start of the 1961-62 season. John McIntire (1907-1991) was chosen to replace Bond and continued to play the character throughout the rest of the series. The western drama also starred Robert Horton, who was later replaced by actor Robert Fuller.

Les Brown's Encyclopedia of Television, 3d ed. (Detroit, MI: Visible Ink Press, 1992), s.v. "Wagon Train." Richard West, *Television Westerns* (Jefferson, NC: McFarland & Co., 1987), 103.

What were two early radio networks of the National Broadcasting Company?

The National Broadcasting Company (NBC) had two early radio networks known as "Red" and "Blue." The names came from a map which showed red and blue lines connecting each network's respective affiliate stations. The networks were known as NBC-Red and NBC-Blue and in 1931, each had 61 stations.

J. Fred MacDonald, *Don't Touch That Dial!: Radio Programming in American Life, 1920-1960* (Chicago, IL: Nelson-Hall, 1979), 25.

To what tribe did Tonto, Lone Ranger's companion, belong?

In the television legend of "The Lone Ranger," the faithful companion Tonto was a Potawatomi Indian, who is riding through a western valley hunting for game, discovers a lone survivor of an attack on five Texas Rangers by the infamous Butch Cavendish Gang, who have ridden off believing that all the Rangers are dead. Tonto takes the severely wounded John Reid into a cave and nurses him back to health. Tonto and Reid form a close partnership, but Reid must conceal his identity so that Cavendish will believe him dead until he can gain his revenge, and wears a mask from that day forward. In token of their lifelong friendship, Tonto calls him "Kemo Sabe," translated as both "trusted scout" and "faithful friend."

Vincent Terrace, *Television Character and Story Facts: Over 110,000 Details from 1,008 Shows, 1945-1992* (Jefferson, NC: McFarland & Company, 1993), 264.

How many women have been named "Man of the Year" by *Time* magazine?

Individual women who won the "Man of the Year" designation by *Time* magazine were Wallis Warfield Simpson (1936); Madame Chaing Kai-Shek (who shared the honor with her husband, 1937); Queen Elizabeth II (1952); and Corazon Aquino (1986). *Time's* 1985 award went to American women, as a group.

New York Times 20 December 1993.

What was the name of the classic 1926 Fritz Lang film about a city of the far future?

Once described as "the first big budget and fully aware science fiction film," *Metropolis* (1926) was directed by German film maker Fritz Lang (1890-1976). The film took 16 months to shoot at a time when most motion pictures required only a few weeks. It featured a cast of 37,383, a host of special effects, and a sentimental story in which love conquers all. Lang was inspired to create his futuristic city by his first glimpse of the New York City skyline in 1924.

Phil Hardy, *The Film Encyclopedia: Science Fiction* (New York: William Morrow, 1984), s.v. "Metropolis."

Who was the first U.S. president to broadcast over the radio?

Warren G. Harding was the first U.S. president to be heard on the radio. His speech dedicating the Francis Scott Key Memorial was broadcast on June 14, 1922; Baltimore, Maryland, radio station WEAR carried the broadcast. A message from Harding was transmitted on November 5, 1921 from Washington, D.C. This program was sent to 28 countries; it was transmitted in code via RCA's 25,000-volt station at Rocky Point, New York. The results of Harding's presidential election were broadcast on November 2, 1921, by radio station KDKA of Pittsburgh, Pennsylvania, considered to be the first commercial radio broadcast.

Joseph Nathan Kane, *Facts About the Presidents* (New York: H.W. Wilson Co., 1989), 179.

What Pulitzer Prize-winning journalist in a collaborative effort produced a documentary on the daily lives of Southern sharecroppers?

In 1940 American Pulitzer prize-winning journalist James Agee (1909-1955) collaborated with American photographer Walker Evans (1903-1975) to produce *Let Us Now Praise Famous Men*, a documentary on the daily lives of Southern sharecroppers. Agee was also a successful poet, novelist, and screenplay writer. He wrote the screenplay for the Academy award-winning movie *The African Queen* (1951), starring Humphrey Bogart (1988-1957) and Katharine Hepburn (1907-).

Louis Untermeyer, ed., *Modern American Poetry, Modern British Poetry* (New York: Harcourt, Brace & World, 1962), 603.

What was the name of the actor who played Captain Kangaroo on television?

The longest running children's program on television, "Captain Kangaroo" featured actor Robert Keeshan in the title role. It debuted on October 3, 1955, and ran until it was canceled in 1984.

Les Brown's Encyclopedia of Television (Detroit, MI: Visible Ink Press, 1992), s.v. "Captain Kangaroo." Stuart Fischer, *Kids' TV*, (New York: Facts on File, 1983), 79.

What were "penny dreadfuls"?

The publications known as "penny dreadfuls" were weekly periodicals that were devoted to sensational stories and which cost a penny.

Edward Latham, *A Dictionary of Names Nicknames and Surnames of Persons Places and Things* (1904, reprint, Detroit: Gale Research, 1966), 241.

Is there a *Who's Who of American Pets?*

In the tradition of the many "Who's Who" publications, a *Who's Who of American Pets* was established by pet owner John Breen. Unlike directories for pure bred animals, this book is a biographical listing of the most ordinary pets, including animals of all kinds. For five dollars per entry, the book will include biographies of up to one hundred words long. For example, Breen described his dog: "Her favorite activities include playing with her friend Pirate, stealing cheese, and rolling her ball under the sofa." Registered owners then get a five dollar discount on the book, which costs $35 plus shipping.

Pittsburgh Press 31 March 1992.

What is the origin story of Spider-Man?

The comic book character of Spider-Man was introduced during the summer of 1962. Marvel comics presented the new character in "Amazing Fantasy #15" and gave Spider-Man his own title "The Amazing Spider-Man" a year later. The origin story of this superhero tells of young Peter Parker, a scholarly high school student who gained special powers after being bitten by a radioactive spider. He was then able to cling to any surface and had extraordinary strength. After a brief career in show business, Ben's uncle was murdered. The boy used his new powers to catch the killer and turned to a life of crime fighting. Like other superheros, Spider-Man kept his identity secret and, as Peter Parker, worked as a photographer for the *Daily Bugle.*

Ron Goulart, *The Comic Book Reader's Companion* (New York: HarperPerennial, 1993), 153.

What is meant by the terms "Golden Age" and "Silver Age" in the comic book trade?

The "Golden Age" of comic books refers to the highest-priced and most sought-after editions, published during the 1930s and 1940s, especially from 1938 through 1945. The "Silver Age" of comic books refers to the period when superheroes made a comeback in popular comics, from 1956 till 1969.

Ron Goulart, *The Comic Book Reader's Companion* (New York: Harper Perennial, 1993), 77, 148.

What was the title of the American version of the film, *Profume di Donna,* for which Al Pacino won the best actor Oscar?

Al Pacino (1940-) won the best actor Oscar for his role as a blind man in *Scent of a Woman,* which was the title of the American version of the Italian film, *Profume di Donna.*

Peter Cowie, ed., *Variety International Film Guide 1994* (London: Samuel French Trade, 1993), 351-352.

Does the little red-haired girl from Charles Schulz's *Peanuts* comic strip have a real-life counterpart?

Donna Wold, a Minneapolis grandmother, was the real-life counterpart for the little red-haired girl in the popular *Peanuts* comic strip by American cartoonist Charles Schulz (1922-).

Rheta Grimsley Johnson, *Good Grief, The Story of Charles M. Schulz* (New York: Pharos Books, 1989), 84.

Who broadcasted the first regular Sunday evening religious service on the radio?

Two months after KDKA in Pittsburgh became the first licensed radio station in America, on January 2, 1921, the Calvary Episcopal Church started to broadcast its regular Sunday evening service. Religious broadcasting, however, is as old as radio itself. The first amateur transmission of a human voice was made at a Christmas service in 1906.

Charles H. Lippy and Peter W. Williams, *Encyclopedia of the American Religious Experience* (New York: Charles Scribner's Sons, 1988), 1711.

How should one format a television or film script?

Professional script writers follow certain standard format rules when submitting manuscripts. On the title page, the script's title should be in quotation marks and underlined, with a series title indicated where appropriate. The script title is followed by the phrase "Written by" or "Screenplay/Teleplay by" and the author's name. If the work is based on material from another source this is indicated by the phrase "Based on a story/play/article by [source's name]." This information appears under the scriptwriter's name. Title pages must also include the author's name, address, and phone number, as well as an agent's name, address, and phone number.

A line at the head of each scene specifies an exterior or interior location, describes the location, and indicates time of day or night. Descriptions of action are single-spaced and run from margin to margin. Double spacing separates descriptions and dialogue. In order to show who is speaking, character names are centered over the first line of dialogue and capitalized. In descriptions, character names are only capitalized the first time they appear in the script. All dialogue is single-spaced and set in a column three inches wide and centered. Double-space between all lines of dialogue and other transitions. Scenes extending over several pages are marked "CONTINUED" in the upper left corner of each following page. With speeches that run to a second page, the name of the character speaking is repeated, followed by "(Cont.)" centered over the dialogue, at the head of the second page.

Joseph Gillis, *The Screen Writer's Guide: (almost) Everything You Need to Know to Get Your Script Produced, 2nd ed.* New York: New York Zoetrope, 1987), 15-16.

How did Loony Tunes differ from Merrie Melodies?

Warner Brothers Pictures produced both the Loony Tunes cartoons and the Merrie Melodies cartoons in the 1930s and 1940s. At first the Merrie Melodies were supposed to feature one-shot characters and be in color, while the Loony Tunes were supposed to feature on-going characters and be shot in black and white. The boundaries were blurred by 1935, when Merrie Melodies began to use Daffy Duck and a Bugs Bunny prototype. By 1943 Warner Brothers had consolidated its Merrie Melodies and Loony Tunes production staffs under one roof. After that, all characters appeared in both series, and all director units worked on both as well. The separate names were kept as a matter of prestige.

Will Friedwald and Jerry Beck, *The Warner Brothers Cartoons* (Metuchen, NJ: Scarecrow Press, 1981), ix.

What is the epitaph of the cantankerous comedian W.C. Fields?

The cantankerous comedian W.C. (William Claude) Fields (1880-1946) wrote his own epitaph, "On the whole, I'd rather be in Philadelphia." Having grown up wretchedly poor in Philadelphia, the comedian, radio and movie star, raconteur, and alcoholic held no love for the "City of Brotherly Love." Fields died on Christmas Day.

John Bartlett, *Familiar Quotations: A collection of passages, phrases, and proverbs traced to their sources in ancient and modern history, 16th ed.* (Boston: Little, Brown, 1992), 641.

Who was the silent film pioneer in the field of slapstick comedy as exemplified by the "Keystone Kops"?

Mack Sennett (1880-1960) was an early silent film pioneer best known for producing slapstick comedies as exemplified by the "Keystone Kops." The names of the "Keystone Kops" were Roscoe "Fatty" Arbuckle, Charles Avery, Billy Bletcher, Glenn Cavender, Charley Chase, Eddie Cline, Andy Clyde, Pinto Colvig, Chester Conklin, Heinie Conklin, Vernon Dant, George Dillon, Bobby Dunn, James Finlayson, Billy Gilbert, George Gray, Eddie Gribbon, Harry Gribbon, Billy Hauber, Del Henderson, Rea M. Hunt, Bud Jamison, George Jesky, Buster Keaton, Edgar Kennedy, Tom Kennedy, George "Fats" Lebeck, Grover G. Ligen, Horace McCoy, Hank Mann, Rube Miller, Kewpie Moran, Joe J. Murray, Kalla Pasha, Ingram Pickett, Victor Potel, Mack Riley, Wesley Ruggles, Al St. John, Ford Sterling, Slim Summerville, Eddie Sutherland, Al Thompson, Ben Turpin, and Bobby Vernon.

Sylvia Cole, *The facts On File Dictionary of 20th-Century Allusions* (New York: Facts On File, 1991), 239. John Stewart, comp., *Filmarama* (Metuchen, NJ: The Scarecrow Press, Inc., 1975).

Who popularized the cartoon character "Casper the Friendly Ghost"?

Cartoon mogul Alfred Harvey (1910-1994) popularized "Casper the Friendly Ghost." "Casper" and other cartoon characters were part of a comic book empire started in 1939 by brothers Leon and Alfred Harvey. After undergoing a number of name changes Harvey Comics was decided on in 1941. Over the decades Harvey has published over 6400 comic books and over 250 titles covering such fields as humor, crime, western, romance, and super-hero. Some of Harvey's early titles were *Green Hornet* (1940), *Black Cat Comics* (1946), *Terry & the Pirates* (1947), and *Li'l Abner* (1947). In 1952 Harvey acquired the rights to "Casper the Friendly Ghost" from Paramount and St. John Publishing and published the first "Casper" comic book in 1953. The cartoon character has also been marketed in various merchandising campaigns and was featured in an animated television series and a 1995 movie release.

Mike Benton, *The Comic Book in America* (Dallas: Taylor Publishing, 1989), 126-27. Hubert H. Crawford, *Crawford's Encyclopedia of Comic Books* (Middle Village, NY: Jonathan David, 1978), 408. *Variety* 18-24 July 1994.

In the 1946 motion picture *The Postman Always Rings Twice*, which actors portrayed the lead characters Cora Smith Papadakis and Frank Chambers?

Lana Turner portrayed Cora Smith Papadakis and John Garfield played Frank Chambers in the 1946 hit MGM film version of the novel *The Postman Always Rings Twice* by James Cain.

Otto Penzier, el al., eds., and comps., *Detectionary* (Woodstock, NY: Overlook Press, 1977), 171.

Did the "Amos and Andy" television series feature an all-black cast, and who played the title roles in the early radio version?

"Amos and Andy" (1951-53) was the first comedic television series with an all-black cast. The show was based on a radio program of the same name that began in 1928, in which white dialecticians Freeman Gosden and Charles Correll played Amos and Andy, respectively.

Not until 1965, when Bill Cosby co-starred in *I Spy*, would there be a black performer again featured in a regular dramatic or comedy series.

Literary Digest April 1930.

Who was the first Miss America to be dethroned?

Vanessa Williams was the first Miss America to be dethroned. The 1984 winner relinquished her crown to first runner-up Suzette Charles of New Jersey after it was learned that Williams had once posed for nude photographs. The photos subsequently appeared in the September 1984 issue of *Penthouse Magazine*.

USA Today 24 July 1984.

In the television series "Alien Nation," what planet did the aliens come from?

The television series "Alien Nation," which first aired on Fox in 1989, focused on the lives of the Franciscos, a family that landed on earth with thousands of other aliens from the planet Tencton in 1990. Unable to return to their own planet, the aliens are assimilated into Los Angeles society.

Vincent Terrace, *The Ultimate TV Trivia Book* (Boston: Faber and Faber, 1991), 10-11.

What was the original name of Walt Disney's Mickey Mouse?

Walt Disney's famous cartoon character Mickey Mouse was almost called Mortimer Mouse. In 1928 Disney was traveling by train to California from New York where he had just lost the contract rights to one of his early cartoon characters "Oswald the Lucky Rabbit." Trying to think of another cartoon character free of contract infringements, he came up with Mortimer Mouse. His wife Lillian liked the idea of a mouse but not the name Mortimer, which she found to be pompus. She suggested the name Mickey as being more egalitarian. Disney liked the name and the world's most famous mouse was born. He made his first public appearance on November 18, 1928, in *Steamboat Willie*, the first animated cartoon with sound. The debut took place at 2 p.m. at the Colony Theater in New York City. Disney had actually produced two other animated shorts featuring the mouse previous to *Steamboat Willie*, but neither *Plane Crazy* nor *Gallopin' Gaucho* found a distributor. Mortimer Mouse did, however, make an appearance in *Mickey's Rival* (1936) as Mickey's rival for the affections of Minnie Mouse.

Leslie Halliwell, *Halliwell's Filmgoer's Companion* (New York: Charles Scribner's Sons, 1988), 482. *Walt Disney's Mickey Mouse Memorabilia* (New York: Abrams, 1986), 20. John Culhane, "A Mouse for All Seasons," *Saturday Review* 11 November 1978.

When did the soap opera "General Hospital" debut?

The soap opera "General Hospital" was first aired on April 1, 1963, on the ABC network. For more than two decades, the relationship between Dr. Steve Hardy, played by John Beradino, and his nurse, Jesse Brewer, portrayed by Emily McLaughlin, was a pivotal point in this medical drama.

Christopher Schemering, *The Soap Opera Encyclopedia* (New York: Ballantine Books, 1985), 108.

What is the most commercially successful hard-core pornographic film ever released in the United States?

The most commercially successful hard-core pornographic film in the United States is *Deep Throat.* Released in 1972, the film had grossed approximately five million dollars by mid-1973.

M. Thomas Inge, ed., *Handbook of American Popular Culture* (Westport, CT: Greenwood Press, 1981), 3:289-299.

What was the first radio broadcast?

The Christmas story told from the Gospel of St. Luke, music, and a voice wishing everyone a merry Christmas made up the first radio broadcast. The voice belonged to Canadian inventor Reginald Fessenden, and the broadcast originated from his laboratory on the Massachusetts coast on December 24, 1906. It was heard by shipboard operators off the coast of New England.

Jane Polley, ed., *Stories Behind Everyday Things* (Pleasantville, NY: The Reader's Digest Association, 1980), 270.

Who is considered to be the founder of radio broadcasting?

David Sarnoff (1891-1971), a Russian immigrant, was a pioneer in the development of both radio and television broadcasting. He came to the United States in 1900, peddling newspapers to help support his family and later got a job as a messenger boy for a telegraph company. With the money he earned, he purchased his first telegraph instrument and eventually found work as a radio operator for the Marconi Wireless Telegraph Service. Sarnoff worked both on shore and at sea for the next few years after which he became radio operator of the most powerful station in the world, atop Wanamaker's department store in New York. It was there, on April 14, 1912, that Sarnoff picked up the distress signal from the sinking passenger liner *Titanic.* U.S. President Taft ordered all other stations off the air, and Sarnoff became the nation's only link with the scene. He remained at his post for 72 hours, receiving information and passing on the news.

In 1916 Sarnoff submitted a proposal to his boss at the Marconi company for a commercially marketed radio receiver he called a "radio music box." The proposal was ignored initially, and it was only after the company was absorbed by the newly formed Radio Corporation of America (RCA) in 1919 that Sarnoff would try again. In 1921 as general manager of RCA, to demonstrate the marketing potential of radio, Sarnoff broadcast the Dempsey-Carpentier boxing match. It created a sensation, and in three years RCA sold more than $80 million worth of radio receivers. In 1926 under Sarnoff's guidance, RCA formed the National Broadcasting Company (NBC). In 1928 Sarnoff established an experimental NBC television station, and by 1939 he had successfully demonstrated the medium with the first telecast from the New York World's Fair.

Jane Polley, ed., *Stories Behind Everyday Things* (Pleasantville, NY: The Reader's Digest Association, 1980), 271. *The New Encyclopaedia Britannica, Micropaedia, 15th ed.* (Chicago: Encyclopedia Britannica, 1991), 10:456.

What was the first newspaper of continuous publication in the American colonies?

Newspapers have been published in the United States since colonial times. In 1704 Boston postmaster John Campbell began publishing the *Boston News-Letter* on a weekly basis. This was the first newspaper of continuous publication in colonial America. Like many other newspapers of its day, the *Boston News-Letter* had the phrase "Published by Authority" on its nameplate. This phrase meant that the newspaper had the blessing of colonial authorities and allowed the publisher access to lucrative printing contracts.

M. Thomas Inge, ed., *Handbook of American Popular Culture,* (Westport, CT: Greenwood Press, 1981), 3:233.

What was the real name of Batman's arch-enemy the Penguin?

The comic strip character Batman's nemesis the Penguin began life as a chubby boy named Oswald Chesterfield Cobblepot. Oswald's father died of pneumonia after being caught in a rainstorm without his umbrella; after his death, Oswald helped his mother to run the Cobblepot Bird Shop. Due to Mr. Cobblepot's untimely demise, Mrs. Cobblepot became extremely protective of her son, insisting that he carry an umbrella with him whenever he went out. This habit, in combination with Oswald's large nose and his round physique, inspired the other children in his neighborhood to bully and tease him unmercifully. Oswald withdrew more and more into the world of birds and eventually majored in ornithology in college. When his mother died after a long, costly illness, creditors seized the family business. Infuriated and embittered, Oswald turned to a life of crime. But even the local underworld gang ridiculed and rejected him, calling him a "bulgy little penguin." Oswald adopted the name as his alias and set out to take his revenge on the gang and the world at large.

Jeff Rovin, *The Encyclopedia of Super Villains* (New York: Facts on File Publications, 1987), 260.

What was the first broadcast network, and when and how was it formed?

The first broadcast network was the National Broadcasting Company (NBC), which was formed in 1926 by the General Electric Corporation, Westinghouse, and the Radio Corporation of America. After World War I there was a proliferation of independent stations as radio equipment became inexpensive. Large corporations like American Telephone and Telegraph, newspapers, and even amateurs working out of their garages began to broadcast. NBC could supply local stations with a number of quality programs that originated mostly from New York and still leave them considerable time for their own shows. This format proved very popular, and in 1927 a second network, the Columbia Broadcasting System (CBS), was established.

M. Thomas Inge, ed., *Handbook of American Popular Culture* (Westport, CT: Greenwood Press, Inc., 1978), 1:227.

Was the movie *Call Northside 777* based on a true story?

The movie *Call Northside 777* was based upon the murder of Frank Lundy, a Chicago policeman, who was killed in 1932 as he attempted to foil a holdup, and the subsequent implication of Joseph Majczek in the crime. Despite a weak case, Majczek was sentenced to 99 years in prison, but his mother, who scrubbed floors for a living, offered a reward in 1944 for the arrest of the real killer. James McGuire, a reporter for the *Sun*, was moved by her devotion and eventually proved that the evidence against her son was fabricated. Majczek was released, although the perpetrator was never apprehended.

Jay Robert Nash, *Crime Chronology; A Worldwide Record, 1900-1983* (New York: Facts on File Publications, 1984), 89.

What led to the success of Karl Baedeker's travel guidebooks?

Karl Baedeker's claim to fame are the guidebooks that he created from his travels throughout Europe. As a young man in search of his fortune, Baedeker (1801-1859) traveled to the German city of Mainz during the 1820s. Although he saw beautiful sights such as castles and historic towns along the way, Baedeker found that the information contained in the guidebook he was carrying was woefully inadequate. He bought the rights to the guidebook and rewrote it. The wealth of valuable, accurate information quickly made the book popular, thus launching a very lucrative business for Baedeker.

All of the information contained in Baedeker's guidebooks on accommodations, restaurants, historical sites, and other points of interest was based on Baedeker's personal experiences. His standards regarding accommodations were very exacting, and innkeepers often coveted Baedeker's highest rating. Baedeker loved art, and his ratings of art works in countries throughout the world were held in high esteem.

Although Karl Baedeker died in 1859, subsequent generations of the Baedeker family continued to publish guidebooks for an increasing number of countries and added features such as highly detailed maps. During World War II (1939-1945), the Baedeker publishing headquarters in Leipzig, Germany, was severely damaged during Allied bombing campaigns. Much of the valuable information in the Baedeker files was destroyed. However, Karl Baedeker's great-grandson rebuilt the company and resumed publishing the still-prized guidebooks.

Jane Polley, ed., *Stories Behind Everyday Things* (Pleasantville, NY: The Reader's Digest Association, Inc., 1980).

What did the mysterious word "rosebud" symbolize in the film *Citizen Kane*?

"Rosebud" was the last word uttered by the dying tycoon, Charles Foster Kane, in the opening scene of Orson Welles' acclaimed film *Citizen Kane* (1941). At the end of the movie it is revealed that "Rosebud" was the name on the sled that Kane had as a boy and symbolized the unspoiled happiness of youth and its innocence. The film's plot centers around the quest to find the key to the word's significance by reporter Jerry Thompson (played by William Alland), who delves into Kane's past life by interviewing five people who were close to him. Each gives Thompson a different prospective of the successful newspaper publisher Kane's life.

The film, called one of the ten best of all time, was noted for the advanced film techniques used in its production-quick cuts, imaginative dissolves, as well as deep-focus photography. Comparison has been made between Kane and the real-life newspaper mogul William Randolph Hearst (1863-1951), although Welles disputed that Kane was wholly modeled after Hearst.

Sylvia Cole and Abraham H. Lass, *Dictionary of 20th-Century Allusions* (New York: Facts On File, 1991), 230. Jay Robert Nash and Stanley Ralph Ross, *The Motion Picture Guide* (Chicago: Cinebooks, Inc., 1986), 2:431.

What is Wilma Flintstone's maiden name?

The maiden name of cartoon character Wilma Flintstone is Slaghoople. She and Betty Jean McBricker were hotel waitresses who met bellboys Fred Flintstone and Barney Rubble while working at the Honeyrock Hotel.

Vincent Terrace, *The Ultimate TV Trivia Book* (Boston: Faber and Faber, 1991), 83.

What was the name of Charlie Chaplin's famous comic character?

"The Tramp," who first appeared in 1914, was probably silent film comic Charlie Chaplin's (1889-1977) most famous character. Sometimes called "the Little Fellow," he looked undersized and malnourished and walked in a shuffling manner. Complete with a derby hat, a bamboo walking cane, and gloves, the penniless but spirited character wore a too-small coat and too-big pants that emphasized his poverty.

World Book Encyclopedia (Chicago: World Book Inc. 1992), s.v. "Chaplin, Charlie."

What was the name of the "Millionaire" in the early television classic of the same name?

In the television classic "The Millionaire," which ran from 1955 to 1960, the name of the billionaire giving away all that money was John Beresford Tipton. Tipton was never seen, just heard. His voice was that of Paul Frees. Marvin Miller played the character Michael Anthony, the assistant who presented the anonymous surprise million-dollar checks to ordinary people.

Vincent Terrace, *Television Character and Story Facts,* (Jefferson, NC: McFarland & Company, 1993). *Les Brown's Encyclopedia of Television* (Detroit, MI: Visible Ink Press, 1992) s.v. "The Millionaire."

What was a "Living Newspaper"?

A "Living Newspaper" was the theatrical innovation of Elmer Rice, who headed the New York branch of the Federal Theatre Project in the 1930s. His productions dealt with controversial current events such as the Italian invasion of Ethiopia and American societal problems. Many of his productions were viewed as left-wing propaganda and drew opposition, especially among conservatives. Congress abolished the project in 1939 after heated debate.

Gerald Martin Bordman, *The Oxford Companion to American Theatre,* (New York: Oxford University Press, 1984), 249.

What was the name of the night-club singer played by Marlene Dietrich in the film *The Blue Angel*?

In the film *The Blue Angel* (1930) Marlene Dietrich (1901-1992) played a night-club singer with the unlikely name of Lola-Lola.

David Pringle, *Imaginary People: A Who's Who of Modern Fictional Characters* (New York: World Almanac, 1987), 273. Louise Mooney, ed., *Newsmakers 1992* (Detroit: Gale Research Inc., 1992), 567.

What is a "key grip"?

A key grip is the individual who is in charge of the stagehands. Stagehands are called "grips" on movie sets.

Ira Konigsberg, *The Complete Film Dictionary* (New York: NAL Books, 1987), 179.

What is a scopitone?

The scopitone is a video jukebox from France that was popular in American bars and restaurants in the 1960s.

New Yorker July 1964.

What was the name of Eleanor Roosevelt's newspaper column?

Eleanor Roosevelt, wife of American president Franklin Delano Roosevelt, wrote a syndicated newspaper column called *My Day* beginning in 1936. When the column made its debut, it covered women's issues and excluded politics. By 1939, however, the subject matter in the column had changed, and Mrs. Roosevelt subsequently used it as a forum for her political philosophy and her husband's programs.

Anna Roth, ed., *Current Biography: Who's News and Why, 1949* (New York: H.W. Wilson Co., 1949), 530.

Has *Time* magazine ever featured something other than a human as its "Man/Woman of the Year"?

There were two instances when *Time* magazine's "Man/Woman of the Year" issue was not devoted to a representative of the human race. In 1982, the award was given to "The Computer," and in 1988 to an "Endangered Earth."

New York Times 20 December 1993.

What is "The 700 Club"?

"The 700 Club" is a daily 90-minute television program hosted by the Rev. Pat Robertson and Ben Kinchlow. The program, which began in 1963, combines news, interviews, current events, and feature segments. "The 700 Club" is the dominate offering of CBN, Christian Broadcasting Network Corporation, a highly successful cable network which provides family programming from a Christian perspective.

"Change Brings Success For Christian Network," *New York Times* 3 September 1984.

Which Pulitzer Prize-winning playwright has also enjoyed careers in screenwriting, acting, and directing?

Sam Shepard is a Pulitzer Prize-winning playwright who has also made a name for himself as a screenwriter, actor, and director. Shepard's involvement in the entertainment industry began when his first few works for the New York stage were produced before he was twenty-one. Since then he has authored over 40 other dramas and has won several theater-industry awards for such dramas as *True West* and *Fool for Love*. His motion-picture career began with the co-authorship of screenplays for *Me and My Brother* (1967) and *Zabriskie Point* (1970). Shepard has written for other films, such as German filmmaker Wim Wenders's opus *Paris, Texas* (1984), as well as writing and directing the release *Far North* (1988). A Bob Dylan project entitled *Renaldo and Clara* (1978) was Shepard's first appearance before the camera. He was also cast as a cowboy in *Days of Heaven*, and went on to appear in a number of screen roles during the 1980s and '90s. For his portrayal of aviation notable Chuck Yeager in *The Right Stuff* (1983) Shepard received an Academy Award nomination.

Robyn Karney, ed., *The Hollywood Who's Who: The Actors and Directors in Today's Hollywood* (New York: Continuum, 1993), 428-29.

What was Yaddo?

Yaddo was a residence for well-connected artists near Saratoga Springs, New York. It was primarily a haven for aspiring writers who stayed there by invitation. The main building of the compound was a luxuriously appointed Victorian mansion.

John Malcolm Brinnin, *Truman Capote: Dear Heart, Old Buddy*, (New York: Delacorte/Seymour Lawrence, 1986), I.

What was the address of "The Addams Family" home in the 1960s television series?

In the 1960s television situation comedy series "The Addams Family" (1964-66), the morbid clan's home was located in the municipality of Cemetery Ridge on 000 Cemetery Lane. John Astin (1930-) played Gomez Addams, Carolyn Jones (1933-1983) was Morticia, and Jackie Coogan (1914-1984) was Uncle Fester. The characters were based on the macabre cartoons of Charles Addams.

Les Brown's Encyclopedia of Television, 3d ed. (Detroit, MI: Visible Ink Press, 1992), s.v. "The Addams Family." Vincent Terrace, *The Ultimate TV Trivia Book* (New York: Faber, 1991), 4.

What is the pseudonym used by directors when they do not wish to receive film credit for their work?

When "Alan Smithee" is listed as the director of a film, one can assume that the real director does not want his name associated with the project. A dispute with the producing agency-either the studio or the network-over the way the work has been edited is usually the primary reason behind a director's wish to remain anonymous. The pseudonym's use is sanctioned by the Directors Guild of America.

Michael Singer, ed., *Michael Singer's Film Directors: A Complete Guide* (Los Angeles: Lone Eagle, 1993), 280.

Who was the performer who warned others about placing burning embers in the mouth?

American magician Harry Houdini (1874-1926) offered the sage advice not to "bite a piece of red-hot iron unless you have a good set of teeth."

Ricky Jay, *Learned Pigs & Fireproof Women* (New York: Villard Books, 1986), 273.

Who are some short celebrities and how do they measure up?

Some of Hollywood's shortest leading men are as follows:
Tom Cruise—5 ft. 6 3/4 in.
Woody Allen—5 ft. 5 in.
Michael J. Fox—5 ft. 4 in.

Mickey Rooney—5 ft. 3 in.
Dudley Moore—5 ft. 2 1/2 in.
Danny DeVito—5 ft. 0 in.
Herve Villechaize—3 ft. 11 in.

Good Housekeeping May 1987.

Where was King Kong's home before he was brought to New York City?

In the movie *King Kong*, the giant gorilla named King Kong lived in a cave atop Skull Mountain on Skull Island in the middle of the Indian Ocean. It was from this island that he was brought to New York City.

Jay Robert Nash and Stanley Ralph Ross, *The Motion Picture Guide* (Chicago: Cinebooks, 1986), s.v. "King Kong."

What was Walt Disney's first successful cartoon creation?

Walt Disney's first successful cartoon creation was the floppy-eared Oswald the Rabbit. Oswald was abandoned by Disney when his New York distributor, Charles Mintz, attempted to swindle him. This misfortune pushed Disney to design a new character, which became the legendary Mickey Mouse.

Craig Yoe and Janet Morra-Yoe, eds., *The Art of Mickey Mouse* (New York: Hyperion, 1991).

What is a bouquiniste?

A bouquiniste is someone who purchases and sells used books.

Stephen Glazier, *Random House Word Menu* (New York: Random House, 1992), 545.

What was the title of Stanley Kubrick's first film?

American film director Stanley Kubrick's (1928-1999) first film was *Day of the Flight*, a 1950 documentary. Among his most noted films are *2001: A Space Odyssey*, *Dr. Strangelove*, and *A Clockwork Orange*.

Ann Lloyd and Graham Fuller, eds., *The Illustrated Who's Who of the Cinema* (New York: Macmillan, 1983), s.v. "Kubrick, Stanley."

What is yellow journalism and what American publisher is identified with it?

In 1898 the term "yellow journalism" was used for the first time. "Yellow" had already appeared in 1846 in reference to sensational newspapers and books which sometimes came in yellow covers. "Yellow journalism" came into use in response to the sensational newspaper stories that appeared in Joseph Pulitzer's (1847-1911) *New York World* and William Randolph Hearst's (1863-1951) *New York Journal* about atrocities Spain was inflicting on Cuba. Hearst defended his use of sensationalism when he said that, "the public is even more fond of entertainment than it is of information."

Robert Hendrickson, *The Henry Holt Encyclopedia of Word and Phrase Origins* (New York: Henry Holt, 1987), s.v. "Yellow journalism." Michael Schudson, *Discovering the News: A Social History of American Newspapers* (New York: Basic Books, 1978). *Webster's Ninth New Collegiate Dictonary* (Merriam-Webster, 1988). *Who Was Who in America: A Companion Biographical Reference Work to Who's Who in America* (Chicago: Marquis—Who's Who, 1960), s.v. "Hearst, William Randolph."

In the movie *The Wizard of Oz*, who played the Munchkin advising Dorothy to follow the yellow brick road?

Nita Krebs, who had been the oldest surviving Munchkin from the movie *The Wizard of Oz*, died January 18, 1991, at the age of 85. In the movie, Krebs played a member of the Lullabye League and was the woman who darted out as Dorothy was preparing to leave and said, "Follow the yellow brick road." Born in Czechoslovakia, Krebs stood 3 feet, 8 inches tall.

Stephen Cox, *The Munchkins Remember: The Wizard of Oz and Beyond* (New York: E.P. Dutton, 1989), 42. *St. Louis Post-Dispatch* 20 January 1991.

Who portrayed Tarzan and Jane in the Tarzan films?

The first Tarzan story by Edgar Rice Burroughs (1875-1950) was in print in 1913; five years later the first movie was made with the role of Tarzan being played by Elmo Lincoln in the 1918 silent film *Tarzan of the Apes*. Lincoln also appeared in two others. The most well-known Tarzan is Johnny Weismuller, who was in twelve of the films. Other actors who have portrayed the King of the Jungle on the big screen were: Gene Pollar, P. Dempsey Tabler, Jim Pierce, Frank Merrill, Buster Crabbe, Herman Brix (also known as Bruce Bennett), Glenn Morris, Lex Barker, Gordon Scott, Denny Miller, Jock Mahoney, Mike Henry, Ron Ely, Miles O'Keeffe, and Christopher Lambert. The television Tarzans were Gordon Scott, Ron Ely, Joe Lara, and Wolf Larson.

The first screen Jane was Enid Markey in the 1918 silent film *Tarzan of the Apes*. The most well-known Jane is Maureen O'Sullivan, who appeared in *Tarzan, the Ape Man* in 1932 and five other films. Other actresses who portrayed Jane on the big screen were Karla Schramm, Louise Lorraine, Dorothy Dunbar, Natalie Kingston, Brenda Joyce, Vanessa Brown, Virginia Huston, Dorothy Hart, Joyce MacKenzie, Eve Brent, Joanna Barnes, Bo Derek, Andie MacDowell. Television Janes were Eve Brent, Kim Crosby, and Lydie Denier.

Richard B. Armstrong and Mary Willems Armstrong, *The Movie List Book: A Reference Guide to Film Themes, Settings, and Series* (Jefferson, NC: McFarland, 1990), s.v. "Tarzan." Bernard A. Drew, *Motion Picture Series and Sequels: A Reference Guide* (New York: Garland, 1990), s.v. "Tarzan of the Apes." David Fury, *Kings of the Jungle: An Illustrated Reference to "Tarzan" on Screen and Television* (Jefferson, NC: McFarland, 1994).

Who was known as "The Voice of Experience"?

"The Voice of Experience" was Dr. Marion Sayle Taylor (1889-1942), a teacher and lecturer, who began dispensing advice on domestic affairs over the radio in 1933.

Frank Buxton and Bill Owen, *The Big Broadcast, 1920-1950, rev. ed.* (New York: Viking Press, 1972), s.v. "the voice of experience." *Current Biography: Who's News and Why 1942* (New York: H.W. Wilson, 1942), s.v. "Taylor, M(arion) Sayle."

What was the first newspaper published in America?

The first newspaper published in the American colonies was *Publick Occurrences Both Forreign and Domestick*. After the publication of only one issue in Boston in September of 1690, it was suppressed by the colonial governor of Massachusetts. In 1704 the *Boston News-letter* began publication as a weekly and was issued by the postmaster.

The New Encyclopaedia Britannica: Micropaedia (Chicago: Encyclopaedia Britannica, 1993), s.v. "newspaper."

When were the Olympic Games first televised?

The first Olympic Games were telecast in 1936 in Berlin. Twenty-five large television screens were set up in theaters throughout the city, allowing citizens to view the event for free.

David Wallechinsky, *The Complete Book of the Olympics* (New York: Penguin Books, 1988), xxii.

What was the first radio broadcasting station?

The identity of the "first" radio broadcasting station is open to debate, credit for being the first station has customarily gone to Westinghouse station KDKA in Pittsburgh for its broadcast of the Harding-Cox presidential election returns on November 2, 1920. Although it did not receive its regular license until November 7, 1921, it produced programming under a different authorization. Moreover, while there were other earlier radio transmissions, KDKA was one of the first stations to use electron tube technology to generate the transmitted signal and hence to have what could be described as broadcast quality. It was the first to have a well-defined commercial purpose-it was not a hobby or a publicity stunt. It was the first broadcast station to be licensed on a frequency outside the amateur bands. Records of the U.S. Department of Commerce, which then supervised radio, indicate that the first station to receive a regular broadcasting license was WBZ of Springfield, Massachusetts, on September 15, 1921.

Andrew F. Inglis, *Behind the Tube: A History of Broadcasting Technology and Business* (London: Focal Press, 1990), 61. *Broadcasting & Cable Yearbook 1994* (New Providence, NJ: R. R. Bowker, 1994), xiii. Joseph Nathan Kane, *Famous First Facts* (New York: H. W. Wilson, 1981), 528. Dennis Sanders, *The First of Everything* (New York: Delacorte Press, 1981), 292.

When was the first scientific journal published?

A proposal to publish a French weekly scientific journal was submitted in 1664 by Sir Denis de Sallo, Counselor of the Court of Parliament under Louis XIV (1638-1715). In August 1664, a privilege was signed establishing *Le Journal des Scavans* (Journal of Learned Men), and the privilege was registered in December 1664. The first weekly issue of the *Journal des Scavans* was published on January 4, 1665.

Krishna Subramanyam, *Scientific and Technical Information Resources* (New York: Dekker, 1981), 31.

Was Lassie a male or female?

Although all of the dogs who have played Lassie were males, the character of the movie and television series was always depicted as being female.

Tim Brooks and Earle Marsh, *The Complete Directory of Prime Time Network TV Shows 1946-Present, 5th ed.* (New York: Ballantine Books, 1992), 493-94.

When was *Life* magazine first published?

Founded by Henry Robinson Luce (1898-1967), *Life* magazine was published weekly from 1936 until 1972. Luce had envisioned a market for a "ten-cent photo magazine" as he observed the growing popularity of movies and tabloids. The invention of a superfast camera lens by Paul Wolff for Leica of Germany made candid photography and thus his magazine possible.

Providing a pictorial account of World War II, *Life's* readership rose to 5.2 million copies per week. During the postwar years 36 percent of American families read *Life.*

Despite its unique niche in the marketplace with its much heralded photojournalism, fiscal problems plagued *Life* during the 1960s and in 1972 publication was suspended. Only two special issues per year were published from 1973 to 1977. *Life* resumed publication as a monthly magazine in 1978 and continues to be published monthly in the tradition it established in photojournalism.

Alan Nourie and Barbara Nourie, eds., *American Mass-Market Magazines* (New York: Greenwood Press, 1990), s.v. "Life."

How can an international telephone call be made without using operator assistance?

For international telephone calls most countries have a "dialing out code" and a "dialing in code." The caller first uses the "dialing out code" of the country from which the call is made. In some countries it is necessary to wait for a dial tone or an announcement before proceeding further. Then one must dial the "dialing in code" of the country being called, followed by the area or city code and the telephone number. The "dialing out code" for the United States is 011, and the "dialing in code" is 1.

David Crystal, ed., *The Cambridge Encyclopedia* (Cambridge: Cambridge University Press, 1990), RR88.

What is the real name of actor Mr. T?

Born Lawrence Tero on May 21, 1952, actor Mr. T. was raised in the Chicago tenements. In high school he was a star football player and a three-time city wrestling champion. After graduation he served as a celebrity bodyguard to Muhammad Ali, Michael Jackson, and others. His role as Clubber Lang in the film *Rocky III* was the big break that eventually led to *The A-Team* and other television shows.

Tim Brooks, *The Complete Dictionary to Prime Time TV Stars 1946-Present* (New York: Ballantine Books, 1987), s.v. "T, Mr."

Where was the first U.S. motion picture theater?

During the early 1900s motion pictures were traveling expositions shown as part of a vaudeville program or in a storefront theater. Due to a shortage of films and the competition from vaudeville, the specialized storefront theaters operated for short periods only.

A U.S. storefront picture show for which detailed records exist was the Searchlight Theater run by Mrs. S.C. Sloan. Located in Tacoma, Washington, the theater opened in November of 1900 and closed June 1, 1902.

One of the best-known movie theaters was Thomas L. Tally's Electric Theater in Los Angeles. The theater, which opened on April 16, 1902, was open daily from 7:30 p.m. to 10:30 p.m. and featured the same attraction for a month or more. For ten cents, customers saw such features as *Capture of the Biddle Brothers, New York City in a Blizzard,* and *The Great Bull Fight.* Tally closed his theater after six months.

Charles Musser, *The Emergence of Cinema: The American Screen to 1907* (New York: Charles Scribner's Sons, 1990), 297-99.

Who has played Superman and Lois Lane in the movies?

The character of Superman from the DC comics has appeared in movies since 1948. Actors who have played the "Man of Steel" include:

Superman (1948) (15-episode serial) with Kirk Alyn as Super-

man and Noel Neill as Lois Lane
Atom Man vs. Superman (1950) with Kirk Alyn as Superman and Noel Neill as Lois Lane
Superman and the Mole Men (1951) with George Reeves as Superman and Phyllis Coates as Lois Lane
Superman (1978) with Christopher Reeve as Superman and Margot Kidder as Lois Lane
Superman II (1980) with Christopher Reeve as Superman and Margot Kidder as Lois Lane
Superman III (1983) with Christopher Reeve as Superman
Superman IV: The Quest for Peace (1987) with Christopher Reeve as Superman.

There was also the movie *Supergirl* (1984) starring Helen Slater, based on the comic book character.

Bernard A. Drew, *Motion Picture Series and Sequels: A Reference Guide* (New York: Garland Publishing, 1990), s.v. "Superman." Leonard Maltin, ed., *Leonard Maltin's Movie and Video Guide 1994 Edition* (New York: Signet, 1993), s.v. "Superman," "Superman II," "Superman III," "Superman IV: The Quest for Peace," "Superman and the Mole Men." Roy Pickard, *Who Played Who in the Movies* (New York: Schocken Books, 1981), s.v. "Superman."

How was Superman described in the opening to the 1950s television series "The Adventure of Superman"?

The Superman television series opened each show with the following: "Faster than a speeding bullet! More powerful than a locomotive! Able to leap tall buildings in a single bound. ...Superman ... strange visitor from another planet who came to Earth with powers and abilities far beyond those of mortal men! Superman, who can change the course of mighty rivers, bend steel in his bare hands, and who, disguised as Clark Kent, mild-mannered reporter for a great metropolitan newspaper, fights a never-ending battle for truth, justice, and the American way!"

Tim Brooks and Earle Marsh, *The Complete Directory to Prime Time Network TV Shows: 1946-Present, 5th ed.* (New York: Ballantine Books, 1992), 18.

Who played "The Shadow" on the CBS radio program?

The character called The Shadow first appeared on a CBS radio program titled *Detective Story* in August of 1930. The Shadow was based on a series of 282 books by Walter Gibson, using the pseudonym of Maxwell Grant. James LaCurto played the character who simply narrated a story. LaCurto was succeeded by Frank Readick, George Earle, and Robert Hardy Andrews. It was in 1937 that The Shadow went from narrator to the principal character. Orson Welles played the role of "The Shadow whose identity was Lamont Cranston, a man of wealth, a student of science and a master of other people's minds...." In the fall of 1938 when *The War of the Worlds* made Welles an overnight celebrity, he was replaced by Bill Johnstone, who held the role until 1943. Johnstone was succeeded by John Archer (1943), Steve Courtleigh (1945), and in 1949 Bret Morrison played the last Shadow until 1954.

John Dunning, *Tune in Yesterday: The Ultimate Encyclopedia of Old-Time Radio 1925-1976* (Englewood Cliffs, NJ: Prentice-Hall, 1976), s.v. "the shadow." Michael R. Pitts, *Famous Movie Detectives II* (Metuchen, NJ: Scarecrow Press, 1991), 130.

What was the name of Dudley Do-Right's horse?

Various sources cannot agree on the name of cartoon character Dudley Do-Right's horse. Some call the horse "Steed" and others give the name "Horse." Despite the short run from April 27, 1969, to September 6, 1970, many remember this animated cartoon on ABC. Other characters were Inspector Ray K. Fenwick, Dudley's boss in the Canadian Mounties; Snidely Whiplash, the most diabolical of fiends who Dudley must capture; and Nell Fenwick, the inspector's daughter who loved Dudley's horse rather than Dudley.

Alex McNeil, *Total Television, 3rd ed.* (New York: Penguin Books, 1991), s.v. "The Dudley Do-Right Show." Vincent Terrace, *Television Character and Story Facts* (Jefferson, NC: McFarland, 1993), s.v. "Dudley Do-Right of the Mounties." Terri A. Wear, *The Horse's Name Was...* (Metuchen, NJ: Scarecrow Press, 1993), s.v. "Steed."

Who created the concept of "The Tonight Show"?

NBC executive Sylvester L. "Pat" Weaver is considered the father of "The Tonight Show." He created "Broadway Open House" as a late night, live variety show that premiered May 22, 1950, on NBC. The original host was to be comedian Don "Creesh" Hornsby, but he contracted infantile paralysis and died the weekend before the show was to start. Jerry Lester was called in after a series of guest appearances by leading comics. Lester's announcer was Wayne Howell and the bandleader was Milton DeLugg. Morey Amsterdam, who later went on to "The Dick Van Dyke Show," and Jack E. Leonard, also worked as hosts. "Broadway Open House" only lasted one year and three months, going off the air on August 23, 1951. "The Tonight Show" would premiere in 1954.

Jeff Greenfield, *Television: The First Fifty Years* (New York: Harry N. Abrams, 1977), 75. Robert Metz, *The Tonight Show* (New York: Playboy Press, 1980), 26, 33-34, 40-52. James Van Hise, *40 Years at Night: The Story of The Tonight Show* (Nevada: Pioneer Books), 14.

Who was the first African-American "Playmate of the Month" and "Playmate of the Year?"

Jennifer Jackson appeared as the first African-American "Playmate of the Month" in the March 1965 issue of *Playboy.* Renee Tenison of Melba, Idaho, became the first African-American "Playmate of the Year" in 1990.

Editorial Research Library (Chicago: Playboy Enterprises). *Jet* 7 May 1990. *Playboy* March 1965.

What was Harry's last name in the film *Dirty Harry*?

Clint Eastwood (1930-) starred in the Warner Brothers film *Dirty Harry* (1971), in which he played the tough police officer, Harry Callahan, who was most famous for uttering the line: "Go ahead, make my day," in this film directed by Don Siegel. Eastwood's tough guy has since returned to film in the movies *Magnum Force, The Enforcer, Sudden Impact,* and *The Dead Pool.*

Bernard Drew, *Motion Picture Series and Sequels: A Reference Guide* (New York: Garland Publishing, 1990), s.v. "Dirty Harry."

In the early 1950's TV series, who played the wife of Mr. Peepers?

Pat Benoit played school nurse Nancy Remington, who marries Robinson Peepers, played by Wally Cox, in the television comedy series, "Mr. Peepers" (1952-1955). Also starring the comedy were Tony Randall as English teacher Harvey Weskitt, and Marion Lorne as the Peepers' landlady.

Les Brown, *Les Brown's Encyclopedia of Television, 3rd ed.* (Detroit, MI: Gale Research, 1992), s.v. "Mr. Peepers."

Who was the actor who played Santa Claus in the 1947 film *Miracle on 34th Street*?

Welsh actor Edmund Gwenn (1875-1959) played a benevolent old man who may or may not have been Santa Claus in George Seaton's 1947 film, *Miracle on 34th Street*.

Leslie Halliwell, *Halliwell's Filmgoer's Companion, 9th ed.* (New York: Charles Scribner's Sons, 1988), s.v. "Miracle on 34th Street."

With what actress was William Randolph Hearst so enamored that he invested in a motion picture studio to showcase her talents?

Marion Davies (1897-1961) is the actress in whom William Randolph Hearst (1897-1961) was enamored, investing in a motion picture studio to showcase her talents. Davies was considered a talented actress with a particular gift for light comedy. A silent film actress, Davies' transition to talkies was difficult. Her popularity declined in the 1930s, after which she retired from films. She is, perhaps, best remembered for her role opposite Bing Crosby in *Going Hollywood*. Other films include *Runaway Romany, Cecilia of the Pink Roses, Getting Mary Married, April Folly, The Bride's Play, Peg o' My Heart*, and *Cain and Mabel*.

Larry Langman, *Encyclopedia of American Film Comedy* (New York: Garland Publishing, 1987),s.v. "Davies, Marion." Jay Robert Nash and Stanley Ross, *The Motion Picture Guide* (Chicago, IL: Cinebooks, 1985), s.v. "Citizen Kane."

Who was the first African-American actress to win an Academy Award since Hattie McDaniels in *Gone With The Wind* in 1939?

In 1990, Whoopi Goldberg (1950-) became the first African-American actress to win an Academy Award since Hattie McDaniels had done so for her performance in *Gone With The Wind* in 1939. Goldberg won the Best Supporting Actress Award for her performance as a psychic in *Ghost*, starring with Demi Moore and Patrick Swayze. Goldberg beat Annette Bening, nominated for *The Grifters*; Lorraine Bracco, *GoodFellas*; Diane Ladd, *Wild at Heart*; and Mary McDonnell, *Dances With Wolves*.

John Harkness, *The Academy Awards Handbook* (New York: Windsor Publishing, 1994), 282-284.

What famous film actress disliked and avoided publicity and retired from the screen in 1941 at the height of her fame?

Greta Garbo (born Louisa Gustafsson, 1905-1991) was the Swedish film actress who so disliked and avoided publicity that she retired from the screen in 1941 at the height of her fame. She is famous for uttering the line, which may or may not have been correctly reported to be: "I want to be alone." She replied that she said "I want to be left alone." Garbo starred in such film classics as *Anna Christie, Queen Christina, Anna Karenina, Camille, Grand Hotel*, and *Ninotchka*.

Barry Jones, *The St. Martin's Press Dictionary of Biography* (New York: St. Martin's Press, 1986), s.v. "Garbo, Greta."

When and why was the television program "60 Minutes" moved to its now-familiar Sunday 7:00 p.m. time slot?

The television program "60 Minutes" debuted on CBS on September 24, 1968, alternating with "CBS Reports." Not overwhelmingly popular at first, it was moved around in the weekly schedule and, as late as 1975, the program still suffered from low ratings when a network vice president suggested moving it to the 7:00 p.m. Sunday slot, a time that had been specifically set aside by the Federal Communications Commission (FCC) as part of the prime-time access rule for either public affairs or children's programming. Because the other major networks, American Broadcasting System (ABC) and the National Broadcasting System (NBC) would routinely show something for children, "60 Minutes" had little opposition in that slot on the largest viewing night of the week. By 1980 it was the most watched program in the United States.

Robert Slater, *This . . . Is CBS: A Chronicle of 60 Years* (New York: Prentice Hall, 1988), 247.

Who was the first continuing character in an American comic strip?

The "Kid" in *The Yellow Kid*, the creation of Richard Felton Outcault, which first appeared in February, 1895, was the first continuing comic character created in an American newspaper. Named for the yellow shirt he wore, the Kid's gaping grin, preposterous ears, impudence, and catch phrase, "keep de change," made him a success. The sensation of the Kid and other comic strips as aids to increase newspaper circulation gave rise to the term "yellow journalism," named after the Kid's brightly colored shirt.

David Kunzle, *The History of the Comic Strip* (Berkeley, CA: University of California Press, 1990), 1. John Matuszak, "'Yellow Kid' was a Comic Trailblazer," *Sarasota Herald-Tribune* 23 May 1995.

When did "The McLaughlin Group" program first appear on television?

"The McLaughlin Group" political roundtable television program debuted in 1982, beginning on a local commercial station in Washington, D.C., but soon being carried by NBC affiliates in four major cities and over 275 public television stations around the country. In format, "The McLaughlin Group" was similar to its competitor, "Agronsky and Company," having one moderator and four respected Washington commentators discuss current political issues for thirty minutes.

Alan Hirsch, *Talking Heads: Political Talk Shows and Their Star Pundits* (New York: St. Martin's Press, 1991), 31.

During the opening theme of the "Brady Bunch" television series, the Bradys are seen in a series of squares arranged like a tic-tac-toe board: in what sequence are they arranged?

In the opening theme of the comedy show of the "Brady Bunch" television series, the Bradys are seen in a series of squares arranged like a tic-tac-toe board. In the top sequence, from left to right are Marcia, Carol, and Greg. Left to right in the middle sequence are Jan, Alice, and Peter. Cindy, Mike, and Bobby are in the bottom sequence, left to right. The "Brady Bunch" (1969-74), Robert Reed and Florence Henderson played the widow Carol, and widower Mike whose families were merged with their marriage. Ann B. Davis played the Bradys' house keeper.

Lester L. Brown, *Les Brown's Encyclopedia of Television, 3d ed.* (Detroit: Visible Ink, 1992), s.v. "Brady Bunch, The." Vincent Terrace, *The Ultimate TV Trivia Book* (Boston: Faber and Faber, 1991), 37.

What is the Patsy Award?

The Patsy Award is a trophy presented annually by the American Humane Association for outstanding film appearances by animals. The Humane Association receives nominations from producers and directors, its own field officers, and animal trainers. A Patsy Committee narrows these to a field of nominees for selection by a blue-ribbon panel of prominent people. Beginning in 1978, awards were made by animal categories rather than media categories.

Claire Walter, *Winners: The Blue Ribbon Encyclopedia of Awards, rev. ed.* (New York: Facts on File, 1982), 298.

What song by folk singer Pete Seeger was deleted from the final tape of a 1967 episode of "The Smothers Brothers Show"?

"Waist Deep in the Big Muddy" was the song by American folk singer Pete Seeger (1919-) that was deleted from the final tape of a 1967 episode of "The Smothers Brothers Show." Seeger had written the song to convey his opposition to U.S. President Lyndon Johnson (1908-1978) policies on the Vietnam Conflict. Using a parable to make a point, his song tells of a reckless military commander who orders his platoon to forge a turbulent river while on a routine training march, nearly drowning the entire platoon before he is swept away himself. At the taping session, Seeger sang the song, but a Columbia Broadcasting System (CBS) network programmer ordered the song deleted from the final tape to avoid political embarrassment, but it set off a storm of controversy.

Robert Slater, *This . . . Is CBS: A Chronicle of 60 Years* (Englewood Cliffs, NJ: Prentice Hall, 1988), 241.

Who was *Time* magazine's first "Man of the Year"?

Time magazine's first "Man of the Year" recipient was aviator Charles A. Lindbergh (1902-1974), who won the honor in 1927.

New York Times 20 December 1993.

What were the names of the characters on the popular television show "Bonanza"?

"Bonanza" (1959-1973), a Western soap opera television series which ran on NBC, told of the Cartwright family at the ranch The Ponderosa near Virginia City, Nevada, during the mid 1800s. It featured the following characters: the patriarch Ben (played by Lorne Greene), Adam (played by Pernell Roberts for six seasons), Hoss (played by Dan Blocker), and "Little" Joe (played by Michael Landon).

Les Brown's Encyclopedia of Television, 3rd ed. (Detroit, MI: Gale Research, 1992), s.v. "Bonanza." Vincent Terrace, *Fifty Years of Television: A Guide to Series and Pilots, 1937-1988* (New York: Cornwall Books, 1991), s.v. "Bonanza."

Where did the famous quote "Me Tarzan, you Jane" originate?

The famous quote "Me Tarzan, you Jane" has come to symbolize the great gulf between Tarzan, a character raised in the jungle by apes, and Jane, a civilized and cultured modern woman. In fact, the phrase in its best-known form was never uttered in any of the numerous Tarzan films produced in Hollywood. It may have originated based on dialogue in an early Tarzan adventure in which the ape man learns his name and Jane's by pointing his finger back and forth and saying, ever more rapidly, "Jane— Tarzan. Jane— Tarzan. Jane—Tarzan. Jane—Tarzan. Jane— Tarzan." According to the book *Saturday Afternoon at the Bijou*, this is the closest any Tarzan character ever came to saying the immortal line, "Me Tarzan, you Jane."

David Zinman, *Saturday Afternoon at the Bijou* (New Jersey: Castle Books, 1973), 32.

In the book trade, what is a remainder?

Books that publishers have decided not to stock any longer are called "remainders." The remainder of the stock is sold to wholesalers, who offer the books at extremely discounted prices. Bookstores will reserve special shelves for remainders and designate them as such.

Allen Ahearn, *Book Collecting: A Comprehensive Guide* (New York: G. P. Putnam's Sons, 1989), s.v. "Remainders."

Actor Ed Byrnes became well known portraying "Kookie" on the hit television series "77 Sunset Strip." What was Kookie's full name in the show?

Actor Ed Byrnes (1933-) is best known for his role as "Kookie" in the hit television series "77 Sunset Strip." In the show the full name of his character was Gerald L. Lloyd Kookson III. The private detective drama was first telecast during the 1958 season and starred Efrem Zimbalist Jr. (1923-) and Roger Smith (1932-) as posh private eyes operating on Sunset Strip. Next to their No. 77 Sunset Strip office was Dino's, an upscale restaurant where Kookie was employed parking cars. Kookie had dreams of being a private detective and, while the character originally provided comic-relief, he began to figure more prominently in the show as it progressed through the season. This was especially true as Kookie developed a large following; his habit of constantly combing his ducktail haircut led to the hit novelty song "Kookie, Kookie, Lend Me Your Comb." Byrnes' demands for a larger salary and a major role in the series led to his walking off the set and being replaced by heart-throb Troy Donahue (1936-) who portrayed a long-haired bookworm. A few months later, with salary issues resolved, Kookie (Byrnes) returned as a full partner in the detective firm until the show ended in September of 1964.

Tim Brooks and Earle Marsh, *The Complete Directory to Prime Time Network TV Shows, 1946-Present* (New York: Ballantine Books, 1992), s.v. "Sunset Strip." Vincent Terrace, *Encyclopedia of Television Series, Pilots, and Specials, 1937-1973* (New York: Baseline, 1986),391. Ed Weiner, *The TV Guide TV Book* (New York: HarperPerennial, 1992), 197.

What is the origin of the term "muckraker"?

"Muckraker" is a term used to describe one who, perhaps overzealously, seeks out and exposes real or alleged corruption, scandal, or misconduct in government, business, or public life. It was coined by U.S. President Theodore Roosevelt (1858-1919) in the early 1900s; he used it as a derisive label for a group of American writers and journalists-including Upton Sinclair (1878-1968), Ida Tarbell (1857-1944), and Lincoln Steffens (1866-1936)-whose writings revealed corruption and exploitation in the business and politics of that era.

Kathleen Morner and Ralph Rausch, *NTC's Dictionary of Literary Terms* (Lincolnwood, IL: National Textbook Co., 1991), 140.

In the hit television series "All In The Family" what was the home address of Archie Bunker?

In the hit television series "All In The Family," Archie Bunker, his wife Edith, his daughter Gloria, and his son-in-law "the Meathead," all lived at 704 Houser Street in the borough of

Queens, New York. The show ran with a varying cast from January 12, 1971 to September 21, 1983 and starred Carroll O'Connor (1928-) as Archie Bunker, Jean Stapleton (1923-) as his "Dingbat" wife, Sally Struthers (1948-)as his blond and not-so-bright daughter, and Rob Reiner (1947-) as her husband. "All In The Family" was one of the first television series to bring the social upheaval of 1970s America to the television screen. Rob Reiner, as son-in-law Mike Stivac, portrayed a long-haired, non-working, college student majoring in sociology who thought his liberal idealism could solve the world's problems, if only the world and Archie would listen to him. Stivac was the perfect foil for Archie's blue-collar outlook on life which could only be described as non-progressive. Edith was the family mediator while Gloria was always walking a tightrope between her father and her husband. The show often dealt with serious themes such as rape, breast cancer, terrorism, the Vietnam War and racial prejudice but managed, without preaching to the audience, to portray them as part of the "human comedy." In 1979 the show's title was changed to "Archie Bunker's Place."

Tim Brooks and Earle Marsh, *The Complete Directory to Prime Time Network TV Shows, 1946-Present* (New York: Ballantine Books, 1992), s.v. "All in the Family." Alex McNeil, *Total Television: A Comprehensive Guide to Programming from 1948 to the Present* (New York: Penguin Books, 1991), 25-6.

Who were the "Happiness Boys"?

The "Happiness Boys" were Ernie Hare and Billy Jones, who in 1921 formed the first radio comedy team under that name. They were also the first team to have a commercial sponsor, the first to have a theme song ("How do you do, everybody, how do you do") and the first to incorporate the sponsor's name into the name of the show (Happiness Candy-Happiness Boys).

Newsweek 20 March 1939.

What is the name of the *New Yorker's* logo character with the monocle and top hat?

The *New Yorker's* logo character with the monocle and top hat is Mr. Eustace Tilley. This depiction of a Regency dandy represents the reader-a suave twentieth-century figure. It was drawn for the first cover of the magazine by Rea Irvin.

Brendan Gill, *Here at the New Yorker* (New York: Random House, 1975), 87-89.

Who were the "Quiz Kids"?

The "Quiz Kids" were a collection of extremely bright, precocious kids, aged six to 16, who answered tough questions as part of a radio show. The show, which ran every Sunday evening for 13 years beginning in 1940, had a vast audience and even crossed over to television in the early 1950s. Many parents admonished their children for not studying as hard as the "Quiz Kids." In the early 1980s former "Quiz Kid" Ruth Duskin Feldman wrote *What Ever Happened to the Quiz Kids?*

Fred Ferretti, "Quiz Kids: Where Are they Now?," *Pittsburgh Post-Gazette* 28 December 1982. *New York Times* 26 December 1982.

In book binding what is a fly-leaf and why is it so named?

In book binding a fly-leaf-or end-leaf-is a blank leaf at the beginning and end of a book. There often are two leaves at the beginning and end of the book; one is pasted down while the other is left "flying," hence a fly-leaf.

Ainsworth Rand Spofford, *A Book for All Readers* (New York: G.P. Putnam's Sons, 1900), 67.

What real life character did Mickey Rooney portray in a 1981 Emmy-winning performance?

In 1981 Mickey Rooney (1920-) won an Emmy for his portrayal of real life Bill Sackter. In 1920 Sackter was institutionalized in Minnesota as being "mentally deficient," but, with the aid of friends and a social worker, managed to overcome his deficiencies and lead a productive life.

Alvin H. Marill, *Movies Made For Television* (New York: Baseline Books, 1987), 43. *New York Times* 22 December 1981.

How old is the paperback book in America?

The paperback book celebrated its 50th anniversary in America in 1989. Some of the first titles published by Pocket Books included: James Hilton's *Lost Horizons*; *Five Great Tragedies*, William Shakespeare; *Wuthering Heights*, Emily Bronte; Thorton Wilder's *Bridge of San Luis Rey*.

USA Today 13 June 1989.

Who was John Wendell Smith?

John Wendell Smith (1914?-1972) was one of the first African-American member of the Baseball Writers Association of America. Hailing from Detroit, Smith graduated from West Virginia State College. He wrote for the *Pittsburgh Courier*, the largest African-American weekly newspaper published in the 1930s, and the *Chicago American*. A contemporary of Jackie Robinson, Smith was once hired to be Robinson's roommate when the Brooklyn Dodgers were on the road. Smith went on to write the first biography of Robinson. He is also credited with helping to integrate spring baseball training facilities in Florida.

Tom Weir, "Commentary," *USA Today* 7 February 1994.

What novel was inspired by a coffee commercial?

Love Over Gold, a novel by English mystery writer Susan Moody under the pseudonym Susannah James, was inspired by the Gold Blend coffee commercial. The commercial was "serialized" on British television and featured a growing romance between a coffee-loving couple. The advertisement was popular in the United States; the coffee is known here as Taster's Choice.

Writer June 1993.

How did Stanley Kubrick's movie, *A Clockwork Orange* get its name?

Stanley Kubrick's controversial movie, *A Clockwork Orange* (1971), takes its name from a 1962 novel by the same name written by English journalist and author Anthony Burgess (1917-1993). Burgess pointed out that there is no such thing as a clockwork orange and that the phrase refers to an old Cockney expression,"Queer as a clockwork orange." It meant that the person referred to was "queer to the limit of queerness." Burgess, who stated that he also enjoyed "raping and ripping by (the) proxy" of his characters said that he meant the title to "stand for the application of a mechanistic morality to a living organism oozing with juice and sweetness." The term did not refer primarily to homosexuals.

Kubrick (1928-1999) has long generated rancor and accolades amongst film-goers and critics for his films. His *Dr. Strangelove, or: How I Learned To Stop Worrying and Love the Bomb* (1964) epitomizes black humor with its blending of comedy and horror in presenting a world plunging into an inevitable nuclear holocaust. His hit *2001: A Space Odyssey* (1968) is a quest beginning at the dawn of time and ending in the future of outer space as space and time travelers pursue the alien "presence" responsible for mankind's ability to think and create. *A Clockwork Orange* however was his most devisive. The movie featured Malcolm McDowell as Alex, a street thug of a futuristic but bleak and dreary London who wreaks havoc on his fellow citizens along with the "droogs," a pack of similarly vicious thugs. Kubrick's pessimistic and depraved view of humanity won him applause from some critics while others viewed the movie as "...intellectual waste put to film instead of being flushed."

Anthony Burgess, *A Clockwork Orange, rev. ed.* (New York: Ballantine Books, 1988), x-xi. Leonard Maltin, ed., *Leonard Maltin's Movie Encyclopedia* (New York, Dutton Books, 1994), 485-86. Jay Robert Nash and Stanley Ralph Ross *The Motion Picture Guide* (Chicago: Cinebooks, 1985), 2:444.

What one-time sailor and ballet dancer turned movie director became well known for his controversial films about devils, women in love, and boyfriends?

Ken Russell, former ballet dancer and sailor turned movie director, made a number of controversial films in the 1960s and 1970s, including *The Devils, Women In Love,* and *The Boy Friend.*

Time 20 December 1971.

Who is the villain responsible for Superman's death?

The villain responsible for Superman's death is Doomsday, an maniacal escapee from a cosmic insane asylum.

People Weekly 21 September 1992.

What was the name of comic book superhero Tom Terrific's dog?

The name of comic book superhero Tom Terrific's dog was Mighty Manfred the Wonder Dog. Both appeared in the *Tom Terrific* series of comic books, which were popular in the late 1950s.

Denis Gifford, *The International Book of Comics* (New York: Crescent Books, 1984), 233.

What was the prequel to the movie *The Carpetbaggers* which was based on Harold Robbin's novel of the same name?

Nevada Smith was the prequel to the movie *The Carpetbaggers,* which was based on a novel of the same name by Harold Robbins (1916-1997). Robbin's novel was published in 1961 and came to the screen in 1964 starring George Peppard (1928-1994) as Jonas Cord Jr. and Alan Ladd (1913-1964) as Nevada Smith. *The Motion Picture Guide* called the movie "first-rate third-rate trash" because of a convoluted, trashy plot dealing not with Reconstruction as the title might imply but rather the dirty, greedy side of Hollywood filmdom. *Nevada Smith* was produced in 1966 and starred Steve McQueen (1930-1980) in the role previously played by Alan Ladd. McQueen as "Nevada" tracks down his parent's killers and then sets out to become a cowboy hero of the silver screen. Surprisingly, *Nevada Smith* was better received than *The Carpetbaggers.*

Bernard A. Drew, *Motion Picture Series and Sequels, New York* (New York: Garland Publishing, 1990), 67. Jay Robert Nash and Stanley Ralph Ross, *The Motion Picture Guide* (Chicago: Cinebooks, 1985), 1:363, 2:2121.

In motion picture terminology, what is a MacGuffin?

In motion picture terminology, a MacGuffin is an inanimate object-often with a suspenseful nature-which is central to the scene being shot. The term originated with director Alfred Hitchcock (1899-1980) and has two variant synonyms: McGouffin or Maguffin.

Richard Weiner, *Webster's New World Dictionary of Media and Communications* (New York: Webster's New World, 1990), 276.

What was the name of Federico Fellini's prize-winning film about a young woman who is bought from her poor mother by a circus strongman?

La Strada, Federico Fellini's prize-winning film, told the unlikely story of a circus strongman who buys a young woman from her poor mother. Fellini (1920-1993) has won accolades, prizes, and awards throughout his cinematic career from both filmgoers and film critics. One critic maintains that Fellini's craft is so distinctive that the word "Felliniesque" has entered the popular idiom of the movie world. Released in 1954 but not shown in the U.S. until 1956, *La Strada* starred Anthony Quinn (1916-)as Zampano the brutish strongman who buys Gelsomina, played by Giulietta Masina (1921-) in order to give his one man traveling circus a boost and to provide him with a sexual partner, cook, performer, etc. *La Strada* won Fellini his first Oscar for Best Foreign Film. He went on to win Oscars for *Nights of Cabiria* (1957), *8 1/2* (1963), *Amacord* (1974), and a special Academy Award in 1993 honoring his long and fruitful career.

Leonard Maltin, ed., *Leonard Maltin's Movie Encyclopedia* (New York: Dutton Books, 1994), 275-76. Jay Robert Nash and Stanley Ralph Ross, *The Motion Picture Guide* (Chicago: Cinebooks, 1986), 5:1569-70.

Who was the director of a 1972 landmark erotic film and what was its title?

In 1972 Bernardo Bertolucci directed *Last Tango in Paris* which has since come to be regarded as a landmark erotic film.

Pauline Kael, *Reeling* (Boston: Atlantic Monthly Press Book/Little, Brown and Co., 1976), 27.

Which Peckinpah film of the late 1960s told the bloody and violent story of a group of misfits in a changing West?

In 1969 Sam Peckinpah (1925-1984) directed *The Wild Bunch,* a violent movie chronicling the last tumultuous days of a group of misfit outlaws in a changing West that no longer valued friendship, honor, or courage.

Ted Sennett, *Great Movie Directors* (New York: Harry N. Abrams, 1986), 190.

What is the meaning of the French phrase *Faire les quatre cent coups*?

The French phrase *Faire les quatre cent coups* means "To sow one's wild oats," or "to run wild" as a child. Truffaut's film *The 400 Blows* takes its title and cue from this expression.

Suzanne Brock, *Idiom's Delight: Fascinating Phrases and Linguistic Eccentricites* (New York: Times Books, 1988), 87.

What is the slogan of the *New York Times*?

The slogan appearing on the masthead of the *New York Times* is "All the News That's Fit To Print."

Joseph C. Goulden, *Fit To Print: A.M. Rosenthal and His Times* (Secaucus, NJ: Lyle Stuart, 1988), 15.

Which actress is generally regarded as playing the first great African-American screen heroine, and what was the film?

Actress Cicely Tyson (1942-) is regarded by many film critics as playing the first great African-American screen heroine in the film *Sounder*, based on a novel by William H. Armstrong the won the Newbery Medal Award in 1970. In the film, Tyson portrayed Rebecca, the strong, dignified, loving wife of a sharecropper in the South during the Great Depression.

Pauline Kael, *Reeling* (Boston: Atlantic Monthly Press Book, Little, Brown and Co., 1976), 5. Jessie Carney Smith, ed., *Notable Black American Women* (Detroit, MI: Gale Research Inc., 1992), s.v. "Cicely Tyson."

When was the Book-of-the-Month Club established and what was its first selection?

Believing that he could sell books by mail, Harry Scherman established The Book-of-the-Month Club in 1926 in order to reach a market that the bookstores were missing. His success was dependent on two innovations. First he developed a negative option distribution system by which the member had to reject the month's selection by postcard in order to avoid receiving it. Second he established a committee of literary experts that would select books for the club and so lend their authority to them. By the end of the first year the club had 45,000 subscribers, although its first selection, *Lolly Willowes* by Sylvia Townsend Warner (1893-1978), was returned in droves.

Karen L. Rood, ed., *American Literary Almanac* (New York: Facts On File, 1988), 35-36.

In what sci-fi movie thriller of the early 1950s did the invading Martians succumb to earthly disease?

In an adaptation of the English author H.G. Wells' (1866-1946) novel, the 1953 sci-fi movie thriller *War of the Worlds* featured invading Martians, who were technologically advanced but lacked natural immunity to bacteria and eventually succumbed to Earthly disease.

Baird Searles, *Films of Science Fiction and Fantasy* (New York: AFI Press, 1988), 120.

How many movies featured the duo of Spencer Tracy and Katharine Hepburn?

Over a span of 25 years, nine Hollywood films combined the talents and sexual spark of Spencer Tracy (1900-1967) and Katharine Hepburn (1907-), who were first paired together in *Women of the Year* (1942). Another 1940s screen duo that had sexual chemistry was Humphrey Bogart and Lauren Bacall, first appearing together in *To Have and Have Not* (1944). During the 1930s the onscreen pairings of Clark Gable with Jean Harlow, Alan Ladd with Veronica Lake, Gable with Joan Crawford, and Errol Flynn with Olivia De Haviland all had a similar chemistry. Finally, much earlier, during the silent film era, Greta Garbo and John Gilbert started it all with their sizzling onscreen chemistry.

Scott Siegel and Barbara Siegel, *The Encyclopedia of Hollywood* (New York: Facts On File, 1990), 369-70.

In the hit 1953 movie *Gentleman Prefer Blondes*, who played the blonde?

In the 1953 movie hit *Gentleman Prefer Blondes*, the blonde was played by Marilyn Monroe (1926-1962). The movie is a modernization of the 1949 Broadway musical of the same name.

Derek Elley, ed., *Variety Movie Guide* (New York: Prentice Hall General Reference, 1992), 224.

What was the name of the first host of TV's "Death Valley Days," and who was the actor who played him?

For 12 years the "Old Ranger" as played by Stanley Andrews was the first host of TV's "Death Valley Days" (1952-1972). A long-running western anthology series that had its start in radio in 1930, other hosts that followed Andrews included Ronald Reagan, Robert Taylor, and Merle Haggard.

Ed Weiner, *The TV Guide TV Book* (New York: HarperPerennial, 1992), 189, 197.

In the popular "Dr. Kildare" movies, why was the focus shifted from the character Dr. Kildare to Dr. Gillespie in 1942?

In 1942 the popular "Dr. Kildare" movie series shifted its focus away from the Dr. Kildare character played by Lew Ayres (1908-1996) because of bad publicity generated by Ayres. The actor claimed that he was a conscientious objector and thus exempt from the World War II draft. The wheelchair-bound Dr. Gillespie, played by Lionel Barrymore (1878-1954), became the focal character in the 1942 movie *Calling Dr. Gillespie*. Ayres eventually enlisted and saw combat during the war.

Richard B. Armstrong and Mary Willems Armstrong, *The Movie List Book* (Cincinnati, OH: Betterway Books, 1994), 219.

Which film introduced moviegoers to the characters Ma and Pa Kettle?

Universal Studios introduced moviegoers to Ma and Pa Kettle in the comedy *The Egg and I* (1947). Based on the book of the same name written by Betty McDonald, the movie starred Marjorie Main and Percy Kilbride as the zany "Kettles."

Richard B. Armstrong and Mary Willems Armstrong, *The Movie List Book* (Cincinnati: Betterway Books, 1994), 218.

In the 1968 film *The Lion In Winter* who played King Henry II?

In the 1968 film *The Lion In Winter* the role of King Henry II was played by English actor Peter O'Toole (1932-). Set in England in 1183, the film tells the story of familial intrigues and in-fighting aimed at unseating Henry II from his throne. The movie was based on the play of the same name by James Goldman; it also starred Katharine Hepburn (1907-), who won her third Oscar for her portrayal of Queen Eleanor of Aquitaine, and Anthony Hopkins (1937-) who played Prince Richard the Lion-Hearted. O'Toole also played Henry II in the movie *Becket*.

Jay Robert Nash and Stanley Ralph Ross, *The Motion Picture Guide* (Chicago: Cinebooks, 1986), 5:1684.

What was the inspiration behind Harvey Pekar's comic book series *American Splendor*?

The inspiration behind Harvey Pekar's "new wave" comic book series *American Splendor* was *All-American" Comics* and *Splendor in the Grass*. Pekar's 1976 *American Splendor* series was hailed by comic book critic Donald Phelps as "one of the most encouraging and deeply engaging phenomena to appear in American comic-books." Born in Cleveland, Ohio, Pekar dropped out of college after three semesters and worked at various menial jobs before he began contributing articles on jazz, popular culture, and political and social issues to various periodicals. In the 1970s Pekar began writing and illustrating underground comic books including *Bizarre Sex, Flaming Baloney,* and *Comix Book. American Slendor* was self-printed and self-distributed.

Ron Goulart, *The Encyclopedia of American Comics* (New York: Facts On File, 1990), s.v. "Pekar, Harvey." Stanley Wiater and Stephen R. Bissette, *Comic Book Rebels* (New York: Donald I. Fine, 1993), 131.

Who created the cartoon characters "the Smurfs"?

The cartoon characters collectively known as the Smurfs are the creation of Belgian comic-strip artist Pierre Culliford, also known as Peyo. In Europe the Smurfs were originally known as *Les Schtroumpfs* and were first featured in Culliford's 1957 comic strip *Johan et Pirlouit.* By 1960 the pixie-like Smurfs were starring in their own comic-strip, and soon appearing in other mediums such as books, television series, and mass merchandising.

David Pringle, *Imaginary People,* (New York: World Almanac, 1987), s.v. "Smurfs, The."

In which cartoon did Walt Disney's Minnie Mouse first appear?

Walt Disney's Minnie Mouse made her first appearance in the cartoon *Steamboat Willie* in 1928. By 1988 she had appeared in 70 cartoons including the full-length feature *Who Framed Roger Rabbit* (1988).

John Grant, *Encyclopedia of Walt Disney's Animated Characters* (New York: Hyperion, 1993), 35.

What was the first U.S. soap opera to feature supernatural characters?

The first soap opera to feature supernatural characters (vampires, witches, werewolves, and black magic) was "Dark Shadows" (1966-1971), in which the Collins house is inhabited by the present people and their nineteenth century ancestors.

Vincent Terrace, *The Complete Encyclopedia of Television Programs, 1947-1979, 2nd and rev. ed.* (South Brunswick: A.S. Barnes and Company, 1979), 224.

How did cable TV originate?

Cable TV originated as a means of providing television signals to remote areas or areas with natural impediments such as mountains. Television signals, however, were not transmitted directly by cable but rather relayed to a powerful local antenna and then transmitted to the receiver via a coaxial cable. The first such community antenna went into service in Astoria, Oregon, in 1949 and relayed TV signals from Seattle. The first actual cable TV company was established in Lansford, Pennsylvania, in 1950.

Philip Mattera, *Inside U.S. Business: A Concise Encyclopedia of Leading Industries, 1994 ed.* (New York: IRWIN, 1994), 29-31.

Who created the cartoon "The Addams Family"?

The ghoulish, macabre but nonetheless endearing Addams Family was the creation Charles Addams (1912-1988), a cartoonist for the *New Yorker* magazine. Addams Family cartoons began running in the magazine in the early 1930s and translated well into other mediums over the years including a television series "The Addams Family" (1964-66), two full-length motion pictures with live actors, and a cartoon series for television. Many of the cartoons were published collectively in book form including: *Drawn and Quartered* (1942), *Monster Rally* (1950), and *Creature Comforts* (1982).

Charles Moritz, ed., *Current Biography Yearbook, 1988* (New York: H.W. Wilson, 1988), s.v. "Addams, Charles." David Pringle, *Imaginary People* (New York: World Almanac, 1987), s.v. "Addams Family, The."

Who was Betty Boop?

Betty Boop was the cute, sexy, wide-eyed, and sometimes quite shocking cartoon star of short animated feature films produced by Max Fleischer in the 1920s and the 1930s. Betty Boop's skimpy skirts and various stages of undress served to raise the eyebrows if not the ire of the Hays Office, which served as censor of the American cinema industry. Ms. Boop was the first cartoon character to receive such attention.

David Pringle, *Imaginary People,* (New York: World Almanac, 1985), 54.

In which state did the cartoon character Deputy Dawg uphold law and order?

During the 1960s and the 1970s, the state of Mississippi was protected (at least, in the cartoon universe) by Deputy Dawg, a pot-bellied, dim-witted cartoon dog who appeared on Saturday morning television.

George W. Woolery, *Children's Television: The First Thirty-Five Years, 1946-1981* (Metuchen, NJ: Scarecrow Press, 1983), 79.

What are the names of three films with only one letter as their title?

Three films that have only one letter as their titles include: *M* (1951), *Q* (1982), and *Z* (1969).

Leonard Maltin, ed., *Leonard Maltin's Movie and Video Guide 1994 Edition* (New York: Signet, 1993), 771, 1023, and 1457.

Who played Mork's son on the television show "Mork & Mindy"?

On the television comedy series "Mork & Mindy" (1978-82), Mork's son was played by Jonathan Winters. Winters was introduced in 1981 as the full-grown hatchling Mearth to counteract sagging ratings after the show, moved to a different timeslot, was pitted against another successful sitcom "Archie's Bunker's Place." Even with the addition of Winters as the son of Mork (played by Robin Williams,) a quirky alien from the planet Ork, and his earthling wife Mindy (played by Pam Dawber,) ratings did not improve and the show was canceled in 1982.

Ed Weiner, *The TV Guide TV Book: 40 Years of the All-Time Greatest: Television Facts, Fads, Hits, and History* (New York: HarperPerennial, 1992), 193.

Is there a technical manual for the "Star Trek" space ships?

Franz Joseph researched and compiled a *Star Trek Star Fleet Technical Manual,* which contains blueprints and dimensions of starships. The manual was published by Ballantine Books in 1975, and is subtitled *Official Version for Cadets from United Nations, Earth, Sol System.*

Franz Joseph, comp., *Star Trek Star Fleet Technical Manual* (New York: Ballantine Books, 1975).

Who starred as the phantom in the 1925 film version of *Phantom of the Opera*?

American actor Lon Chaney (1883-1930) starred as the mysterious phantom in the 1925 film version of *Phantom of the Opera.*

Michael F. Blake, *Lon Chaney: The Man Behind the Thousand Faces* (Vestal, NY: The Vestal Press, 1990), 132.

In "The Man from U.N.C.L.E." television series, what did the acronym U.N.C.L.E. stand for?

In "The Man from U.N.C.L.E." television series (1964-1968), the acronym U.N.C.L.E. stood for United Network Command for Law Enforcement. The series starred Robert Vaughn (1932-) as Napoleon Solo, David McCallum (1933-) as Ilya Kuryakin, and Leo G. Carroll (1892-1987) as Alexander Waverly, head of U.N.C.L.E. The agency battled against opponents of democracy, most notably the malevolent organization T.H.R.U.S.H., a group bent on world domination.

Jeff Rovin, *The Great Television Series* (Cranbury, NJ: A. S. Barnes and Co., Inc., 1977), 90.

What was the title of the television adaption of John Ehrlichman's "The Company"?

The television adaption of John Ehrlichman's (1925-1999) "The Company" was entitled "Washington: Behind Closed Doors" and was generally considered to be a fictitious account of the actual Watergate scandal which led to U.S. President Richard Nixon's (1913-1994) resignation and imprisonment of Ehrlichman for his involvement in the Watergate break-in.

Newsweek 5 September 1977.

What are the names of the four famous Gabor women?

The four famous Gabor women are mother Jolie and daughters Magda, Eva, and Zsa Zsa.

Peter Harry Brown, *Such Devoted Sisters: Those Fabulous Gabors* (New York: St. Martins Press, 1985).

Who were the regular cast members of the "Batman" television series?

Regular cast members of the ABC television series "Batman" (1966-68) were the following:
Adam West—Batman/Bruce Wayne
Burt Ward—Robin/Dick Grayson
Neil Hamilton—Police Commissioner Gordon
Stafford Repp—Chief O'Hara
Alan Napier—Alfred
Madge Blake—Aunt Harriet Cooper
Yvonne Craig—Batgirl/Barbara Gordon

Gary Gerani and Paul H. Schulman, *Fantastic Television* (New York: Harmony Books, 1977), 96.

What were the opening words for "The Twilight Zone" television program?

Each episode of "The Twilight Zone" (1959-64), a science fiction television series, was hosted by its creator Rod Serling who recited the following explanation:

"There is a sixth dimension beyond that which is known to man. It is a dimension as vast as space and as timeless as infinity. It is the middle ground between light and shadow-between science and superstition; between the pit of man's fears and the sunlight of his knowledge. It is the dimension of the imagination. It is an area that we call the Twilight Zone."

Gary Gerani and Paul H. Schulman, *Fantastic Television* (New York: Harmony Books, 1977), 35.

How did the Emmy Award get its name?

The National Academy of Television Arts and Sciences created the Emmy Award in 1949, as a means of recognizing outstanding achievement in the television industry. The awards, first given in 1949, were originally to be called Ikes, after the television iconoscope tube. Ike was also the nickname of World War II (1939-45) General (and future U.S. president) Dwight D. Eisenhower, however, and this association was considered a problem. The name of the award was changed to the word "immy"-a slang reference to the basic component-the image orthicon tube. Harry Lubcke, then president of the Society of Television Engineers, suggested "Emmy," a feminization of "Immy," as an acceptable alternative to "Ike," and the name stuck.

Les Brown, *Encyclopedia of Television, 3d ed.* (Detroit: Gale Research, 1992), s.v. "Emmy Awards." Thomas O'Neil, *The Emmys: Star Wars, Showdowns, and the Supreme Test of TV's Best* (New York: Penguin Books, Wexford Press, 1992), 8.

Which Academy Awards were last given in 1927-28 and 1929-30?

Awards for writing were among the original categories when the Academy Awards were established in 1927-28, but the nature of the awards has changed considerably since then. Originally there was an award for supplying the written material to silent movies to make them more intelligible. The task was called title writing, but the award for it was only offered once, in 1927-28, because the rise of the talkies soon rendered the job of title writer obsolete. A single award for achievement in writing was given until 1929-30, but after that presentation the category was split into two and sometimes three divisions. At present there are two awards, one for a screenplay written directly for the screen, and another for a screenplay based on material adapted from another medium.

Richard Shale, comp., ed., *Academy Awards* (New York: Frederick Ungar Publishing, 1978), 82-83.

On what television program did Mary Tyler Moore first appear?

The actress Mary Tyler Moore (1936-), who is probably best known for her roles as Rob Petrie's wife, Laura, in the domestic comedy, the *Dick Van Dyke Show* (1961-66) and as a Minneapolis television newsroom career woman on the "Mary Tyler Moore Show" (1970-77), made her first television appearance in 1955 as the dancing elf in the Hot Point commercials on "The Adventures of Ozzie and Harriet."

Les Brown's Encyclopedia of Television (Detroit, MI: Visible Ink Press, 1992), s.v. "Dick Van Dyke Show," "The Mary Tyler Moore Show." James Robert Parish and Vincent Terrace, *The Complete Actors' Television Credits, 1948-1988, 2d ed.* (Metuchen, NJ: The Scarecrow Press, 1990), 2:260.

What is the most valuable comic book?

The most valuable comic book is *Detective Comics, Number 27,* which was worth $92 thousand in 1994 for a copy in excellent condition. It dates from May of 1939 and marks the first appearance of Batman.

Robert M. Overstreet, *The Overstreet Comic Book Price Guide, 24th ed.* (New York: Avon Books, 1994), A-40, A-98.

Who played the title role in the 1951 version of *The Thing?*

The 1951 movie thriller *The Thing (From Another World)* was about an eight-foot, anthropomorphic alien who drank human blood. The title role was played by James Arness, who later became famous as the sheriff in the television series "Gunsmoke." The story revolves around the struggle between this creature and members of scientific station in the Arctic who discover him in a flying saucer buried in the ice. Although its moral that scientific curiosity is not as important as survival is simplistic, it was an effective science fiction, and horror film.

Frank N. Magill, ed., *Magill's Survey of Cinema* (Englewood Cliffs, NJ: Salem Press, 1980), 1712.

Who was the NBC TV newscaster dubbed the "Golden Girl" by *Newsweek*, and who died in a car crash in 1983?

Jessica Savitch, who was called the "Golden Girl" of TV news by *Newsweek*, died in an automobile accident in 1983 at the age of 36. Her life, which involved two failed marriages, three abortions, and cocaine addiction, has been used as a cautionary tale about the difficulties of working in the high-pressure world of television news.

Ron Powers, *The Beast, the Eunuch, and the Glass-Eyed Child: Television in the '80s* (San Diego: Harcourt Brace Jovanovich, 1990, 62-65.

In which of his movies did Alfred Hitchcock make his first cameo appearance?

English film director Alfred Hitchcock (1899-1980), who became famous as a master of suspense and for his skill in film technique, was known for making brief appearances in his movies. Although he could be seen in two scenes in *The Lodger* (1926), he was almost unrecognizable. The first movie in which he created a genuine cameo character was in the first successful British talking picture, *Blackmail* (1929).

Michael Haley, *The Alfred Hitchcock Album* (Englewood Cliffs, NJ: Prentice-Hall, 1981), 27.

What was *The Hitch-Hiker's Guide to the Galaxy*?

The Hitch-Hiker's Guide to the Galaxy was originally a British radio serial about an earth man and an extraterrestrial who travel through space and time following a guidebook for the galaxy. It was a successful blend of science fiction and comedy that was created by Douglas Adams, the story editor of "Doctor Who," a popular British science-fiction television series. Begun in 1977, "The Hitch-Hiker's Guide" soon developed a cult following and was adapted for the stage and for television. It also spawned a record album and three books.

Gene Wright, *Who's Who & What's What in Science Fiction Film, Television, Radio & Theater* (New York: Bonanza Books, 1985), 187.

On what American actor had the Germans placed a $5,000 bounty during World War II?

German Field Marshall Hermann Gring (1896-1946), whom Adolf Hitler (1889-1945) had designated as his successor, offered a $5,000 reward to any flier who could bring down the plane containing the American movie star Clark Gable (1901-1960), who was serving in the Air Force. Gable refused to carry an escape kit and stated that he would never bailout of his aircraft, because he did not want to be used by the Nazis for propaganda purposes.

Lyn Tornabene, *Long Live the King: A Biography of Clark Gable* (New York: G.P. Putnam's Sons, 1976), 311.

What was the name of the television series where the main character is the computer-generated alter-ego of newscaster Edison Carter?

The television series "Max Headroom" was seen on the ABC network from March to October of 1987. It featured the title character, a computer-generated alter-ego of the character Edison Carter, Carter's co-worker Theora Jones, and his friends and enemies in the television industry. The series presented a futuristic world where television cannot be shut off. The viewing audience is known as the Blank Generation and the television industry is totally driven by ratings.

Vincent Terrace, *The Ultimate TV Trivia Book* (Boston, MA: Faber and Faber, 1991), s.v. "Max Headroom."

Who played the gangster Johnny Rocco in the 1948 film *Key Largo*?

In the movie *Key Largo* (1948), Edward G. Robinson played the crude and egotistical Johnny Rocco, a gangster who was eager to recapture his former power after having been run out of the country.

Susan Lieberman and Frances Cable, eds., *Memorable Film Characters* (Westport, CT: Greenwood Press, 1984), 173.

Who was the child actress who played the "little sweetheart" in the "Our Gang" series?

The child actress who played Darla, the sweetheart of all the boys in the "Our Gang" film shorts, was Darla Hood. Born in Leedy, Oklahoma, she was only four years old when her mother took her to New York City, with the hope that she would make it into show business. A screen test resulted in a 9 year contract with the Hal Roach Studios in Hollywood. Darla Hood appeared in over 150 "Our Gang" pictures.

Richard Lamparski, *Whatever Became of...?* (New York: Crown Publishers, 1968).

What was the Professor's name on the television program "Gilligan's Island"?

The full name of the "Gilligan's Island" character that is commonly known as the Professor is Dr. Roy Hinkley. Many other facts about the Professor were revealed throughout the course of the television series: he had six college degrees, and had expertise in areas including medicine, astronomy, psychology, law, and chess. The reason Dr. Hinkley took the tour on the Minnow was to write a book "Fun with Ferns."

Russell Johnson and Steve Cox, *Here on Gilligan's Isle* (New York: HarperPerennial, 1993), 88.

What was the first superhero team to appear in comics?

The first superhero team to be featured in a comic book was the Justice Society of America. The group appeared in late 1940 in the DC publication "All Star Comics #3." A joint creation of editor Sheldon Mayer and writer Gardner Fox, the superhero team continued in the comics until early 1951, ending with issue #57. The original members of the Justice Society of America were the Flash, the Green Lantern, Hawkman, the Spectre, and Dr. Fate. Each had been presented individually in other DC titles; now these characters gathered together to fight crime, to thwart anti-American spies, and to combat super-villains such as the Brain Wave, the Psycho-Pirate and Solomon Grundy. Eventually new superheros, including Wonder Woman, were introduced to the Justice Society.

Ron Goulart, *The Comic Book Reader's Companion* (New York: HarperPerennial, 1993), 97.

What is a Dalek?

A Dalek is an evil, robot-like character created for the British television series, "Doctor Who." The pot-shaped, metal-shelled enemies of the space hero, Doctor Who, are programmed to enslave or destroy all other life forms in the galaxy. The doctor and his cohorts spend much of their time thwarting the Dalek's plans. The Daleks were introduced to the TV series in 1964 and also starred in two films, *Dr. Who and the Daleks,* released in 1965, and *Daleks—Invasion Earth 2150 A.D.*, in 1966.

Gene Wright, *Who's Who & What's What in Science Fiction* (New York: Bonanza Books, 1985), 105.

Why was "The Untouchables" television series boycotted by the Federation of Italian-American Democratic Organizations?

The Federation of Italian-American Democratic Organizations boycotted the ABC television series, "The Untouchables" (1959-63), for unfairly depicting Italian-Americans as gangsters. The boycott forced a pullout of the show's chief sponsor, Liggett & Myers (L&M) products, and led to an agreement by Desi Arnaz, whose studio produced the show, to highlight the role of Italian-Americans as law abiding, law enforcing citizens. The series squared off government agents led by Elliot Ness (played by Robert Stack) against the Prohibition era gangsters.

Jay S. Harris, comp. and ed., *TV Guide, The First 25 Years* (New York: Simon and Schuster, 1978), 52-53.

Which French actress starred opposite Gene Kelly in *An American In Paris*?

Leslie Caron (1931-) was the French actress who starred opposite Gene Kelly (1912-1996) in the film, *An American in Paris* (1951).

Earl Blackwell's Entertainment Celebrity Register (Detroit, MI: Visible Ink Press, 1991), 83.

What was the name of the dog in "The Little Rascals: Our Gang"?

Pete, or Petie, was the name of the pup who starred in "The Little Rascals: Our Gang." During the series' long, on-screen history, many different dogs played Pete. He was notable for a large halo painted around one eye, and his alternately docile, then vicious behavior. Pete was a Staffordshire terrier, or pit bull.

Leonard Maltin and Richard W. Bann, *The Little Rascals: The Life and Times of Our Gang* (New York: Crown, 1992), 281.

What is the difference between microfiche and ultramicrofiche?

Ultramicrofiche is similar to microfiche but can include up to 3,000 images in the space that microfiche can store only 100 images.

Publishers Weekly 6 January 1969.

When was the first televised presidential inauguration?

The inauguration of U.S. president Harry S. Truman (1884-1972) was the first such event to be televised. When Truman took the oath of office on January 20, 1949, an estimated ten million people were watching the ceremony on television. One hundred million were thought to have listened to the event on radio.

Joseph Nathan Kane, *Facts About the Presidents* (New York: H. W. Wilson, 1989), 213.

Who was the first U.S. president to have his inaugural speech broadcast by radio?

Calvin Coolidge (1872-1933) was the first U.S. president to have his inaugural speech broadcast by radio. On March 4, 1925, twenty five radio stations carried his forty one minute inaugural speech. His audience is thought to have numbered 22 million. This was Coolidge's second inaugural and it was in sharp contrast to the first. Coolidge originally became president upon the death of president Warren G. Harding (1865-1923), after which he took the oath of office by the light of a kerosene lamp in his parents' sitting room. At the second inaugural, Coolidge also became the first president to be sworn in by a former U.S. president, U.S. Supreme Court chief Justice William Howard Taft (1857-1930).

Joseph Nathan Kane, *Facts About the Presidents* (New York: H. W. Wilson, 1989), 185.

Who was the first U.S. president to appear on television?

On April 30, 1939, Franklin Delano Roosevelt (1882-1945) became the first U.S. president to appear on television. His speech at the New York World's Fair opening ceremonies was telecast by the National Broadcasting Company (NBC). The speech was given from the exposition's Federal Building overlooking the Court of Peace.

Joseph Nathan Kane, *Facts About the Presidents* (New York: H. W. Wilson, 1989), 204.

What is the New Clio Award?

The Clio Awards were established in 1959 by Wallace Ross as the American TV Commercials Festival to recognize creative excellence in advertising worldwide. Entries are submitted annually from television, print, radio, poster, and outdoor advertising. United States entries and international entries are judged separately. There are approximately 150 categories judged on criteria which include concept, execution, music, illustration, and direction. A statuette is presented to the winners in each category.

In 1991, the awards were restructured and renamed the New Clio Awards.

Debra M. Kirby, ed., *Awards, Honors, and Prizes, 11th ed.,* (Detroit: Gale Research, Inc., 1994), s.v. "New Clio Awards." Clarence L. Barnhart and Robert K. Barnhart, eds., *The World Book Dictionary* (Chicago: World Book, Inc., 1990), s.v. "Clio."

Who played the title role in *The Bride of Frankenstein*?

The actress who starred as the female creation in the 1935 film *The Bride of Frankenstein* was English actress-comedienne Elsa Lanchester (1902-1986).

Jack Sullivan, ed., *Horror and the Supernatural* (New York: Viking, 1986), 53.

What is a *Kammerspielfilm*?

Kammerspielfilm is German for "chamber-talk film." The term describes a type of German silent film made during the 1920s which developed from Max Reinhardt's (1873-1943) *Kammerspiel* theater, and was also a reaction to then current expressionist films. *Kammerspielfilm* was naturalistic, psychological, and bleak, with few titles, and great emphasis on characters' facial expressions.

Ira Konigsberg, *The Complete Film Dictionary* (New York: New American Library Books, 1987), s.v. "Kammerspielfilm."

How many Japanese-produced Godzilla-style movies are there?

The science-fiction dinosaur monster Godzilla (or its clones) has appeared in 17 Japanese-produced motion pictures. They are:
Godzilla, King of the Monsters (1954)
Gigantis, the Fire Monster (1955)
King Kong vs. Godzilla (1962)
Godzilla vs. the Thing (1964)
Ghidrah, the Three-Headed Monster (1965)
Monster Zero (1965)
Go Sea Monster (1966) [a.k.a. *Godzilla vs. the Sea Monster*]
Son of Godzilla (1968)
Destroy All Monsters (1968)
Godzilla's Revenge (1969)
Godzilla vs. the Smog Monster (1971)
Godzilla vs. Gigan (1972)
Godzilla vs. Megalon (1973)
Godzilla vs. the Cosmic Monster (1974)
Godzilla vs. Megagodzilla (1975)
Monsters from the Unknown Planet (1975)
Godzilla 1985 (1985).

Bernard A. Drew, *Motion Picture Series and Sequels: A Reference Guide* (New York: Garland Publishing, 1990), 140.

Performance

The musical *Cats* is an interpretation of which poet's collection of poems about his favorite pets?

The musical *Cats* is Andrew Lloyd Webber's interpretation of a 1939 collection of poems by T.S. Eliot (1888-1965) about his favorite pets. Originally written in letters to his godchildren, the cunning lyrics of the poems that eventually became *Old Possum's Book of Practical Cats* appeal to adults as well. Webber's production, which takes its dialogue almost exclusively from Eliot's work, cleverly blends catlike and human movements and emotions. The score, with its impressive array of musical styles including jazz, rock, folk, big band, and western, appeals to a broad audience.

Janet Karsten Larson, "Eliot's Cats Come Out Tonight," *The Christian Century* 5 May 1982.

Who is the only actor to have killed someone in a theater?

A member of a famous stage family, John Wilkes Booth (1838-1835), is the only actor to have killed someone in a theater. He assassinated U.S. President Abraham Lincoln (1809-1865) in Ford's Theater on April 14, 1865.

Michael Billington, *The Guinness Book of Theatre Facts & Feats* (London: Guinness Superlatives Limited, 1982), 68.

Was there actually a Frankie and Johnny, as immortalized in various folk songs?

Devotees of folk music have often wondered whether Frankie and Johnny, the couple immortalized in several folk ballads, are based on the lives of a real couple. However, according to folklorists, the Frankie and Johnny ballads are not based on a real couple but memorialize the eternal man-woman-adultery dilemma.

Frank W. Hoffmann and William G. Bailey, *Arts & Entertainment Fads* (New York: The Haworth Press, 1990), 201.

Who created Rudolph the Red-Nosed Reindeer?

Rudolph the Red-Nosed Reindeer was created in 1939 by copywriter Robert May, who wrote a story about Rudolph that was printed as a giveaway booklet for Montgomery Ward. Over 2,400,000 copies were distributed free in 1939 and over 3,600,000 in a 1946 reprint. May obtained the copyright to the story in 1947, adapted the story into verse, and issued a hardcover edition. The recorded song, first released in 1949, has sold over 50 million copies. The most famous recordings are by Gene Autry (1949) and Johnny Marks. An animated version of the story was created for television in 1964 with the folksinger Burl Ives as the narrator.

May died at the age of 71 on August 11, 1976, in Evanston, Illinois. He had a statue of the reindeer on the lawn of his home near Skokie, Illinois.

Peter Gammond, *The Oxford Companion to Popular Music* (New York: Oxford University Press, 1991), 27, 371. James Cross Giblin, *The Truth about Santa Claus* (New York: Thomas Y. Crowell, 1985), 71-73. *Newsweek* 23 August 1976, p.59. Vincent Terrace, *Encyclopedia of Television: Series, Pilots and Specials, 1974-1984* (New York: New York Zoetrope, 1985), 356-57.

What is the African-American National Anthem?

James Weldon Johnson (1871-1938) and his brother J. Rosamond Johnson (1873-1954) wrote the words and music to "Lift Every Voice and Sing" for schoolchildren to sing at an Abraham Lincoln birthday celebration in 1900. Later as executive secretary to the National Association for the Advancement of Colored People (NAACP), James Weldon Johnson encouraged this inspiring song to be used as an Afro-American national anthem.

Lift every voice and sing
Till earth and heaven ring,
Ring with the harmonies of Liberty;
Let our rejoicing rise
High as the listening skies,
Let it resound loud as the rolling sea.
Sing a song full of the faith that the dark past has taught us,
Sing a song full of the hope that the present has brought us,
Facing the rising sun of our new day begun
Let us march on till victory is won.

Stony the road we trod,
Bitter the chastening rod,
Felt in the days when hope unborn had died;
Yet with a steady beat,
Have not our weary feet
Come to the place for which our fathers sighed?
We have come over a way that with tears has been watered,
We have come, treading our path through the blood of the slaughtered,
Out from the gloomy past,

Till now we stand at last
Where the white gleam of our bright star is cast.

God of our weary years,
God of our silent tears,
Thou who hast brought us thus far on the way;
Thou who hast by Thy might
Led us into the light,
Keep us forever in the path, we pray.
Lest our feet stray from the places, our God, where we met Thee,
Lest, our hearts drunk with the wine of the world, we forget Thee;
Shadowed beneath Thy hand.
May we forever stand.
True to our God,
True to our native land.

Arna Bontemps, comp., *Golden Slippers: An Anthology of Negro Poetry for Young Readers* (New York: Harper & Row, 1941), 69-70. James Weldon Johnson, *Lift Every Voice and Sing* (New York: Walker and Co., 1993).

Where did karaoke originate?

Originating in Japan, karaoke, the recent entertainment fad in American bars and nightclubs, is the latest variation of the sing-along. Customers sing into a microphone to recorded background music (instrumental and back-up voices). Special effects, such as reverb, enhance the crooner's voice quality. The word "karaoke" is derived from the Japanese words "kara" (meaning empty) and "okesutora" (meaning orchestra).

Merriam-Webster's Collegiate Dictionary, 10th ed. (Springfield, MA: Merriam-Webster, 1993), s.v. "karaoke." Edward C. Baig, "So you think you can sing," *U.S. News & World Report* 4 March 1991.

Which Edward Albee play won him his first Pulitzer Prize and who starred in it?

A Delicate Balance (1967) garnered the American playwright Edward Albee (1928-) his first Pulitzer Prize; the critics' accolades went to Hume Cronyn, Jessica Tandy, and Rosemary Murphy, who had leading roles in the play.

Philip C. Kolin and J. Madison Davis, *Critical Essays on Edward Albee* (Boston: G.K. Hall, 1986), 23.

Did Senator Everett Dirksen of Illinois ever have a hit record?

In 1966 Senator Everett Dirksen (1896-1969) of Illinois recorded "Gallant Men." It made *Billboard's* Top 100 Records List, reaching position 29 for six weeks.

Amy Wallace, *The Book of Lists # 3* (New York: William Morrow, 1983), 185.

What is the progression of characters in the children's song or game, "The Farmer in the Dell"?

The progression of characters in the children's song or game, "The Farmer in the Dell," is:

The farmer takes a wife
The wife takes the child
The child takes the nurse
The nurse takes the dog
The dog takes the cat
The cat takes the rat
The rat takes the cheese
The cheese stands alone.

William L. Simon, ed., *The Reader's Digest Children's Songbook* (Pleasantville, NY: Reader's Digest Association, 1985).

Listening to which music can make you smarter?

Researchers at the Center for the Neurobiology of Learning and Memory at the University of California, Irvine, have recently determined that listening to Mozart actually makes the listener smarter. I.Q. scores of college students rose nine points after exposure to ten minutes of Mozart, and Mozart's music proved to assist in the solution of spatial puzzles involving folded cutout shapes.

Alex Ross, "Listening to Prozac...Er, Mozart," *New York Times* 28 August 1994.

Has a dispute arisen regarding the origin of the "Star Spangled Banner"?

A 1972 publication by the director of the Maryland Historical Society questioned whether Americans have learned an idealized story of the origins of "The Star Spangled Banner." In fact, P. William Filby, an Englishman, ruffled a few feathers with his monograph on the U.S. national anthem. Filby felt it was his duty to point out that during the bombardment of Baltimore's Fort McHenry, on the night of September 13, 1814, it poured rain. This was the battle which inspired Francis Scott Key (1779-1843) to write the song's lyrics, which assert that the flag "was so gallantly streaming." This would have been impossible, according to Filby, with a soggy 42-by-30-foot flag. Other eye-opening details include the national anthem's melody is an English drinking song; and Key is not likely to have written the lyrics on an envelope, as is commonly believed, because envelopes were not in general use for another thirty years.

New York Times 4 July 1972.

Who were the Ritz Brothers and what kind of act did they perform?

The Ritz Brothers were a comic dance team that performed on vaudeville stages beginning in the late 1920s. Al, Harry, and Jimmy Joachim started as a precision dance group; they took the name "Ritz" when an employer told Al that his name was too long. They also changed their act and focused on its comic effect, for which they became famous. Their trademark song was "The Man in the Middle Is the Funny One." Brother Harry was best known as the group's funny man, and for his line "Don't holler—please don't holler," which he delivered at the top of his lungs.

Bill Smith, *The Vaudevillians* (New York: Macmillan Publishing Co., 1976), 179.

What playwright wrote *Torch Story Trilogy*, a play about the life and loves of a drag queen?

Harvey Fierstein (1954-) is the award-winning playwright who wrote the 1981 *Torch Story Trilogy*, a play that catalogues the life and loves of a drag queen. Fierstein was born in Brooklyn, New York, and educated at the Pratt Institute, from which he received a Bachelor of Fine Arts degree in 1973. He was a drag performer and actor himself, and appeared in more than 60 plays and in several films. He is the recipient of several awards and grants including: Rockefeller, Ford, and Creative Artists

Public Services grants; an Obie Award in 1982; a Tony Award in 1983 (for both writing and acting); an Oppenheimer Award in 1983; and a Drama Desk Award in 1983.

D.L. Kirkpatrick, ed., *Contemporary Dramatists, 4th ed.* (Chicago, IL: St. James Press, 1988), s.v. "Fierstein, Harvey Forbes."

What are the theme songs of the Walt Disney cartoon characters Mickey Mouse and Goofy?

The theme song of Walt Disney's famous cartoon mouse Mickey is "Minnie's Yoo Hoo" which was written by Carl Stalling and first heard in *Mickey's Follies* in 1929. Mickey's sidekick Goofy also has his own theme song "The World Owes Me A Living" from the 1934 Silly Symphony *The Grasshopper and the Ant.*

Kevin F. Neary and Dave Smith, *The Ultimate Disney Trivia Book* (New York: Hyperion, 1992), 20-21.

Who was the "little sparrow" of Paris?

Singer Edith Piaf (1915-1963) was born Edith Giovanna Gassion. She was literally born on the streets of Paris and raised in a brothel. Around 1930, when she was working as a Paris street singer, she was discovered by cabaret owner Louis Leple, who changed her name to Piaf, a slang word for sparrow. She gained an international reputation for her songs about tragic love affairs, like "La Vie en Rose," and became known as the "little sparrow." When Piaf died, 40,000 fans covered her bier with mounds of flowers.

Simone Berteaut, *Piaf* (New York: Harper & Row, Publishers, 1969).

What was the initial purpose of a stage bow?

Stage bows were originally a way for actors to thank the audience. It also allowed the audience to indicate how much they enjoyed individual performances, modulating their response as each actor bowed in turn.

David Louis, *Fascinating Facts* (New York: Ridge Press/Crown Publishers, 1977), 166.

What does the title of Ingmar Bergman's film, *The Seventh Seal*, refer to?

The title of Ingmar Bergman's film *The Seventh Seal* refers to seven seals on a scroll in the Bible's Book of Revelation. As each seal is broken curses are unleashed upon the earth, visiting tragedy and death upon its inhabitants. In Bergman's film the figure of Death appears seven times before taking its victims captive.

Geoffrey Hill, *Illuminating Shadows: The Mythic Power of Film* (Boston: Shambhala, 1992), 61.

What is the name of the opera that features a beautiful, life-like, mechanical doll?

Les Contes d'Hoffmann (The Tales of Hoffman), was the only grand opera composed by Jacques Offenbach (1819-1880), a well-known French musician and composer of operettas. Not produced until after his death in 1880, the opera relates the fictional experience of a historical character, the German writer Ernst Theodor Hoffmann (1776-1822). In the second of these tales, which is set in Venice, Hoffmann become infatuated with a life-like mechanical doll Olympia, whom Hoffmann thinks is a real person. In fact, she is the creation of an evil scientist, Dr. Miracle, and Hoffmann becomes aware of the deception when Olympia breaks down at the end of her aria. The opera has been made into a movie twice: once in 1951 when the famous ballerina Moira Shearer played Olympia, and in 1981 when a Royal Opera performance featured John Gielgud (1904-) and Placido Domingo (1941-).

Baird Searles, *Films of Science Fiction and Fantasy* (New York: AFI Press, 1988), 89. Julia C. Furtaw, ed., *The Video Source Book, 15th ed.* (Detroit, MI: Gale Research Inc., 1994), 2:2556.

Which Shakespearean play was the basis for the Broadway musical *The Boys From Syracuse*?

The 1938 Broadway musical *The Boys From Syracuse* was an adaptation of English dramatist William Shakespeare's (1564-1616) *The Comedy of Errors.* The Pulitzer Prize-winning show was by Richard Rodgers and Larry Hart (1895-1943).

Isaac Asimov, *Isaac Asimov's Book of Facts* (New York: Bell Publishing Company, 1981), 440.

Who were the Ringling brothers?

The Ringling brothers, whose name was to dominate the world of the American circus, were christened Rngeling, but they anglicized it when they entered show business. Their father, a German saddle maker who came to the United States in the middle of the nineteenth century, had five sons who would organize their first circus in Wisconsin in 1884: Albert (1852-1916), Otto (1858-1911), Alfred (1861-1919), Charles (1863-1926), and John (1866-1936).

Peter Verney, *Here Comes the Circus* (New York: Paddington Press, 1978), 63.

Who was Toby the sapient pig?

Toby the sapient pig was a sideshow animal who performed in England in the early nineteenth century. The pig participated in a magic show and was said to have the ability to read minds. In fact, his owner Nicholas Hoare maintained that the pig had composed an autobiography, which Hoare published in 1817. Animals who purportedly had human intelligence were a popular diversion in the eighteenth and nineteenth centuries. In 1786 another literary pig claimed to have written *Hamlet* in a previous life in memoirs that he "dictated" to a retired member of the Royal Navy.

Ricky Jay, *Learned Pigs & Fireproof Women* (New York: Villard Books, 1987), 19-23.

What is a passion play?

A passion play is a religious drama that represents the trials, crucifixion, and resurrection of Jesus Christ. Performances can be traced back to thirteenth-century Europe. The most famous example today is the Oberammergauer Passionsspiel, performed in Bavaria at ten-year intervals.

Chris Baldick, *The Concise Oxford Dictionary of Literary Terms* (Oxford: Oxford University Press, 1990), S.V. "passion play."

Where is "The Great White Way"?

"The Great White Way" is the term used to describe the New York City theater district along Broadway as it passes through Times Square. At the turn of the century, famous theaters filled the area from 14th Street to 42nd, and it was known then as the "Gay White Way." Today's commercial theater district stretches from 42nd Street to 53rd, between Sixth and Eighth Avenues.

Jack Burton, The*Blue Book of Tin Pan Alley, expanded new ed.* (Watkins Glen, NY: Century House, 1962), 227. *The 1995 Grolier Multimedia Encyclopedia* (Danbury, CT: Grolier Electronic Publishing, 1995), s.v. "Broadway."

What is labanotation ?

Invented by Rudolph von Laban around 1927, labanotation is a system for recording movement, especially movement connected to dance. In order to notate a movement in the system, one must observe or know four basic things: the part of the body that is moving; the direction of the movement; the level of the movement; the duration/rhythm of the movement.

The Dance Notation Bureau, which promotes the study of labanotation, was founded in New York City in 1940.

Mary Ann Kinkead, *Elementary Labanotation,* (Palo Alto, CA: Mayfield Publishing Company, 1982), 274.

How did the Academy Award trophies acquire the nickname "Oscar"?

Nicknaming the Academy Award trophies "Oscar" is generally attributed to Margaret Herrick, who was the librarian and subsequent executive director of the Academy of Motion Picture Arts and Sciences. In 1931, when first viewing sketches of the trophy at the Academy offices, she reportedly exclaimed, "Why, he looks like my Uncle Oscar!" Hollywood columnist Sidney Skolsky first used the term "Oscar" in his column dated March 18, 1934. To him, the gold statuette was too dignified and snobby, and he wanted to humanize it, so he borrowed the name from a vaudeville routine that included the line "Will you have a cigar, Oscar"?

Anthony Holden, *Behind the Oscar: The Secret History of the Academy Awards* (New York: Simon and Shuster, 1993), 84. *Parade* 23 February 1986.

During what event did Francis Scott Key write the poem that became "The Star Spangled Banner"?

Francis Scott Key (1779-1843) is best remembered for writing the words of "The Star Spangled Banner" during the War of 1812. Well known by his contemporaries in Washington, D.C., as a lawyer and composer of amateur verse, Key was aboard a prisoner-exchange boat trying to win the release of his friend, William Beanes, whom the British had taken with them during their retreat from Washington, D.C., during the War of 1812. According to the widely-accepted account of the events, on that September night in 1814 the boat was temporarily in the custody of a British warship while the British fleet bombarded Fort McHenry in Baltimore Harbor. From his vantage point in the midst of the enemy, Key anxiously watched the bombardment all night and was so overcome with joy to see the colonists' flag still flying in the morning that he wrote the poem that would become the lyrics for the National Anthem. The words were set to the tune of an English drinking song, "To Anacreon in Heaven," and in 1931 the U.S. Congress designated it the national anthem.

World Book Encyclopedia (Chicago: World Book, 1987), s.v. "Key, Francis Scott."

What famous humorist was killed along with well known aviator Wiley Post in a 1935 airplane crash in Alaska?

American humorist Will Rogers (1849-1935) was killed with well-known American aviator Wiley Post (1900-1935) in a plane crash near Point Barrow, Alaska, on August 15, 1935. Roger was known and revered for his many sayings, such as "I never met a man I didn't like," and "Everything is funny as long as it is happening to somebody else."

The Encyclopedia Americana, intl. ed. (Danbury, CT: Grolier Incorporated, 1990), s.v. "Rogers, Will."

What is Disneyland's "Secret Club"?

Club 33 is Disneyland's secret club, and few people, including Disney employees, are aware of it's existence. Club 33 is the only Disneyland facility to serve alcoholic beverages, and access is strictly limited to members and their guests. Membership is limited to approximately 1,000, and a $10,000 membership fee is said to be a prerequisite for joining. An ornate but discreet plaque with the number "33" on it marks the entrance to the club at 33 Rue Royale in New Orleans Square near the Blue Bayou restaurant.

William Poundstone, *Bigger Secrets* (Boston: Houghton Mifflin Company, 1986), 221.

What Olympic gymnast starred in the Broadway play "Peter Pan"?

Cathy Rigby (1952-), American Olympic gymnast, starred as the character Peter Pan in the Broadway production "Peter Pan" during 1990-1991. Rigby went to her first Olympics when she was fifteen-years old. In the 1972 Munich Olympics, she placed tenth in the gymnastics category.

John Willis, *Theatre World: 1990-1991 Season* (New York: Applause Theatre Book Publishers, 1992), 21. The World Almanac, eds., *The God Housekeeping Woman's Almanac* (New York: Newspaper Enterprise Association, 1977), 424.

How did trumpeter Ish Kabibble get his name?

Serving as a trumpeter in the Kay Kyser Band during the big band era, Merwyn Bogue would often be yelled at by dancing couples to play the song entitled "Ish Kabibble." The name Ish Kabibble stuck with him ever since.

Merwyn Bogue, Ish Kabibble: *The Autobiography of Merwyn Bogue* (Baton Rouge: Louisiana State University Press, 1989), 7-8.

What is the Hollywood Walk of Fame?

Founded in 1958, the Hollywood Walk of Fame is a strip of sidewalk on Hollywood Boulevard that honors stars who have contributed greatly to the entertainment industry. In order to be added to the Walk of Fame, one must be in the industry at least five years, be involved in the community, and must attend the unveiling. Stars can be nominated by a fan club, studio, or friends; nominations are reviewed by a committee.

A few celebrities have been honored with more than one star. Bette Davis and Lucille Ball both have two; Bud Abbott and Lou Costello have three; Tony Martin has been given four; Gene Autry has the most stars at five. Several non-humans also have stars on the Walk of Fame: Lassie, Rin Tin Tin, Mickey Mouse, Bugs Bunny, and Snow White.

"The Astral Facts on the Walk of Fame," *USA Today* 23 January 1987. "Someday My Star Will Come," *USA Today* 1 April 1987. *Parade Magazine* October 1987.

To what does the term "dog show" refer?

The theatrical term "dog show" refers to a play that first opens outside the New York City theater circuit. This expression for a provincial debut is roughly derived from the sentiment to "try it on the dog."

Jonathon Green, *Newspeak: A Dictionary of Jargon* (London: Routledge & Kegan Paul, 1985), s.v. "dog show."

Who was the "doctor" who ultimately provided the basis for a character created by Charlie Chaplin?

"Walford Bodie, M.D." was the stage name of Samuel Murphy Brodie, a British music hall performer of the early twentieth century. He falsely promoted himself as a physician for an act that included magic, ventriloquism, and hypnotism, as well as a stage full of electrical gadgetry. Billing himself as a doctor earned Bodie scorn, and in 1909 Glasgow medical students disrupted one of his performances by throwing fruit, fish, and eggs at Bodie and then storming the stage. A seventeen-year-old Charlie Chaplin (1889-1977) once satirized the infamous Bodie onstage in 1906 to great success, and later incorporated some of the mannerisms into his "Little Tramp" character.

Ricky Jay, *Learned Pigs & Fireproof Women* (New York: Villard Books, 1986), 127, 137.

Who was "Bricktop"?

"Bricktop" was a red-headed cabaret star of the 1920s who entertained cafe society on two continents. Born Ada Beatrice Queen Victoria Louise Virginia Smith on August 14, 1894, in Alderson, West Virginia, she often described herself as a "100 per cent Negro American with an Irish temper."

Raised in Chicago, she was in the chorus of a black theater at age 15. In the 1920s she was singing in Harlem before moving to Paris where she opened her own cabaret. She entertained in Paris, Mexico City, and Rome. A friend to everyone in the cabaret scene from Cole Porter to the Duke of Windsor, "Bricktop" was the mentor to Mabel Mercer, Josephine Baker, and even influenced Duke Ellington. "Bricktop" died in 1984 at the age of 89 in New York City.

Albin Krebs, "Bricktop, Cabaret Queen In Paris, Dead," *New York Times*, 8 February 1984. *Variety Obituaries, 1905-1986* (New York: Garland Publishing Inc., 1988).

What are "tropes"?

Tropes are Latin responses set to music and originated in the tenth century as a liturgical elaboration. They are a brief dialogue in song and are given before the "Resurrexi" of the Easter Mass. Tropes have their beginnings in chants sung by monks during the Easter Mass and may be regarded as being among the first medieval dramas.

Representative Medieval and Tudor Plays (New York: Sheed & Ward, 1942), 3.

What is the history behind the song "The Twelve Days of Christmas"?

The song "The Twelve Days of Christmas" celebrates the twelve days linking the birth of Jesus Christ on Christmas (December 25) and the Feast of Epiphany (January 6) when the Magi or Three Wisemen presented gifts to the newborn baby. Dating back to at least the thirteenth century, the song is essentially a "forfeit game" song. As each day was cumulatively sung out by a leader, each player repeated the ever-growing verses. When a player failed to mimic the leader's lengthening verses, the player had to pay some sort of forfeit or penalty.

Duncan Emrich, *American Folk Poetry* (Boston: Little, Brown and Co., 1974), 404.

Who invented the saxophone?

Intending to improve upon the bass clarinet, Adolphe Sax (1814-1894), a Belgian, patented the saxophone in 1846. Made of metal, with a single-reed mouthpiece and a conical bore, the instrument has subsequently added to the richness of military fanfares, classical pieces, and of course, jazz.

Valerie-Anne Giscard d'Estaing, *The Second World Almanac Book of Inventions* (New York: World Almanac, 1986), 86. Nicolas Slonimsky, *Baker's Biographical Dictionary of Musicians 7th ed.* (New York: Schirmer Books, 1984), s.v. "Sax, (Antoine-Joseph-) Adolphe."

When was the Marines Hymn written?

The Marines Hymn, which became especially popular during World War II, was written shortly after the Marines captured Mexico City in 1847 during the Mexican War. It is thought a Marine officer involved in this campaign wrote the words. The "shores of Tripoli" refers to the war against the Barbary pirates in 1805. The term "The halls of Montezuma" refers to the National Palace in Mexico City, which was captured during the Mexican War. After this, the inscription on the Marine Corps Colors, which had been "To the Shores of Tripoli," was amended to read "From the Shores of Tripoli to the Halls of the Montezumas." The melody is adapted from a modified version of "Gendarmes' Duet" from Jacques Offenbach's opera-bouffe *Genevieve de Brabant.*

David Ewen, ed., *American Popular Songs: From the Revolutionary War to the Present* (New York: Random House, 1966), 249. James Morehead and Albert Morehead, *Best Loved Songs and Hymns* (Cleveland, OH: World Publishing, 1965), 16-17. Philip N. Pierce and Frank O. Hough, *The Compact History of the United States Marine Corps* (New York: Hawthorne Books, 1960), 98-99.

Who wrote the U.S. Navy song "Anchor's Aweigh"?

The words to "Anchor's Aweigh" were written by U.S. Navy midshipman Alfred H. Miles, and its music by Lieutenant Charles A. Zimmerman. Miles was a member of the 1907 class of the U.S. Naval Academy at Annapolis and later leader of its chapel choir; Zimmerman was bandmaster at the academy.

The song was first introduced during the 1906 Army-Navy football game. With some additional verses by midshipman Royal Lovell, it was published in 1926 by the academy's Trident Literary Society under the title "Anchor's Aweigh." Although the general public regards this song as the navy's theme song, the official navy song is "The Navy Hymn" written by William Whiting and John Bacchus Dykes.

David Ewen, ed., *American Popular Songs: From the Revolutionary War to the Present* (New York: Random House, 1966), s.v. "Anchors Aweigh." James

Morehead and Albert Morehead, eds., *Best Loved Songs and Hymns* (Cleveland, OH: World Publishing, 1965), 12-15.

Does the U.S. Coast Guard have an official song?

The official song of the U.S. Coast Guard is "Semper Paratus," (Always Prepared) which was composed by Captain Francis S. Van Boskerck in 1928.

C.A. Browne, *The Story of Our National Ballads* (New York: Thomas Y. Crowell, 1960), 283. Walter Ehret, Lawrence Barr, and Elizabeth Blair, *Time for Music* (New Jersey: Prentice-Hall, 1959), 92-93.

Who wrote the words to "The Battle Hymn of the Republic"?

Julia Ward Howe (1819-1910) wrote the words to "The Battle Hymn of the Republic" after hearing Union soldiers singing "John Brown's Body" near the Potomac River in Virginia in 1861. She felt that the lyrics of the stirring tune were somewhat out of place, and one of her companions, the Reverend James Freeman Clarke, challenged her to compose more appropriate words worthy of the music and the soldiers. Howe was a writer, abolitionist, advocate of women's rights, and was active in many other causes during her life.

James Morehead and Albert Morehead, eds., *Best Loved Songs and Hymns* (Cleveland, OH: World Publishing, 1965), 8-9. C. A. Browne, *The Story of Our National Ballads* (New York: Thomas Y. Crowell, 1960), 180-91.

Who wrote "Taps"?

The present version of "Taps," which is played by a military bugler at the end of the day and at a soldier's funeral, is attributed to General Daniel Butterfield during the American Civil War. The bugle was used to signal many things, including wake up, start a march, stop a march, and so on. Butterfield was said to have been dissatisfied with the music used for night call and in 1862 worked out a new version with his bugler, Oliver Willcox Norton, and named it "Taps." Upon hearing the music, other units asked for a copy and adopted it; thus its popularity spread.

Fairfax Downey, *Fife, Drum & Bugle* (Fort Collins, CO: The Old Army Press, 1971), 109-11. Oliver Willcox Norton, *Army Letters 1861-1865* (Chicago: O.L. Deming, 1903), 323-29. George W. Stimpson, *Nuggets of Knowledge* (New York: A. L. Burt, 1934), 41-42.

Why was Elvis Presley successful?

The precise reasons for the success of Tupelo, Mississippi, native Elvis Aaron Presley (1935-1977) are of course conjectural, but his singing style, which blended black rhythm and blues with white rockabilly, was clearly original and is probably the major reason for his immense popularity. Elvis also had a unique stage presence. He was six feet tall and weighed 170 pounds. With blue eyes and dishwater blond hair dyed jet black, he made an imposing figure in his stylized costumes, glittering with sequins, as he strummed his guitar and gyrated his hips. He became a national phenomenon with his first hit recording, "Heartbreak Hotel," in 1956 and his subsequent appearance on "The Ed Sullivan Show." Before he died at age 44, Elvis sold over 600,000,000 records and starred in 33 motion pictures.

Fred L. Worth and Steve D. Tamerius, *Elvis: His Life from A to Z* (Chicago: Contemporary Books, 1988), 157.

Who were the "Florodora girls"?

On November 12, 1900, the Broadway show *Florodora* opened and ran for 505 performances, one of the longest runs of its era. Part of the show's popularity was due to a sextette of women the "Florodora girls," who, along with six men, sang "Tell Me Pretty Maiden." According to legend, the six original "Florodora girls"-Daisy Greene, Marjorie Relyea, Vaughn Texsmith, Margaret Walker, Agnes Wayburn, and Marie L. Wilson-all married millionaires.

Gerald Bordman, *The Oxford Companion to American Theatre* (New York: Oxford University Press, 1984), s.v. "Florodora."

Who wrote the "U.S. Air Force Song"?

"The Army Air Corps Song," which is now known as "The U.S. Air Force Song," was written by Robert M. Crawford in 1939. While a member of the music faculty at Princeton University, he wrote the words and music to the song for a competition conducted by *Liberty* magazine and won the first prize of $1,000. The song became popular as the Army Air Corps hymn during World War II (1939-45).

David Ewen, ed., *American Popular Songs* (New York: Random House, 1966), s.v. "Army Air Corps Song, the." C. A. Browne, *The Story of Our National Ballads* (New York: Thomas Y. Crowell, 1960), 274-84. Charles D. Bright, ed., *Historical Dictionary of the U.S. Air Force* (New York: Greenwood Press, 1992), s.v. "U.S. Air Force Song, the."

What is black comedy?

Black comedy is that which finds its source of humor in tragedy. According to Eric Bentley, "the extreme virulence of modern tragi-comedy—like that of a Goya in painting—is not easy to account for. Yet most observers would concede that, in modern times, a peculiar vehemence of attack is called for both by the conditions which provoke it and the torpor of the public [to which it] is addressed. 'Black' tragi-comedy not only gives a somber account of the world, it also gives the public a shaking. Modern art is upsetting—and for a reason: for the double reason I have just given."

Eric Bentley, *The Life of the Drama* (New York: Atheneum, 1965), 344.

How did the English rock group, the Beatles, get its name?

Before settling upon the name of the Beatles, the renowned rock group, which started in 1960, was known in its earlier days as the Moon Dogs, the Quarry Men, the Moonshiners, and the Silver Beatles. The name the Beatles was a pun on the name of an insect-the beetle-and a pulsating rhythm or beat. In 1961 the group's new manager, Brian Epstein, changed their image. He successfully booked them into the London Palladium in 1963, which brought the group national attention. The following year, their American television appearance gave the group's members-John Lennon, Paul McCartney, George Harrison, and Ringo Starr-international exposure. In 1970 the group disbanded.

Collier's Encyclopedia (New York: Macmillan Educational, 1991), s.v. "Beatles."

In what year did James Coco win a Tony Award for his work in the play *The Last of the Red Hot Lovers?*

Actor James Coco won a Tony Award in 1970 for his performance in the *The Last of the Red Hot Lovers.*

Isabelle Stevenson, ed., *The Tony Award* (New York: Crown, 1989), 107.

What was the name of ventriloquist Paul Winchell's dummy?

Paul Winchell was born in New York City in 1923 and at the age of thirteen he was appearing on vaudeville. Winchell became a successful ventriloquist and his famous dummy, "Jerry Mahoney," was originally whittled as part of a class project at New York's High School of Industrial Arts. In 1958 Winchell added another dummy, "Knucklehead Smith," to his act.

While performing at various children's camps and hospitals Winchell became interested in medicine and eventually earned a degree in medical engineering. In 1963 he designed and patented a device relating to mechanical hearts. He also designed a blood plasma defroster and a suit for surgery patients.

Celebrity Register (New York: Harper & Row, 1963), s.v. "Winchell, Paul." Stuart Fischer, *Kids' TV: The First 25 Years* (New York: Facts on File, 1983), 11.

What is Crosby's Law?

Theater critic John Crosby was quoted in *Playbill* in the *New York Herald Tribune* in 1967 as stating, "You can tell how bad a musical is by how many times the chorus yells, 'hooray.'"

Harold Faber, *The Book of Laws* (New York: Times Books, 1979), 46.

What were some of sharpshooter Anne Oakley's nicknames?

Sharpshooter Annie Oakley (1860-1926) had two nicknames, "Little Missy" and "Little Sure Shot." She started being called "Little Missy" after William "Buffalo Bill" Cody introduced her act to his Wild West Show audiences with the opening line, "Boys, this little missy here is Miss Annie Oakley." Chief of the Sioux Indians, Sitting Bull, dubbed Oakley "Little Sure Shot" in 1881 after watching an exhibition of her shooting skills in St. Paul, Minnesota.

Born Phoebe Anne Oakley Mozee in Drake County, Ohio; Oakley learned to shoot as a means of helping the family following her father's death. She eventually won a shooting match against vaudeville star Frank Butler; Oakley married Butler a few years later and with her new husband-manager she joined Buffalo Bill Cody's traveling Wild West Show in 1885. For 17 years Oakley entertained audiences with her remarkable shooting act. From 30 paces she could slice a playing card with the thin edge facing her, break 4,772 out of 5,000 thrown glass balls in a single day, shoot the ashes off a lighted cigarette held in the mouth of her assistant. Crown Prince Wilhelm of Germany saw Annie Oakley perform this last feat in Buffalo Bill's Wild West Show in 1890 or 1891. When the prince asked Oakley to repeat the trick while he held the cigarette, she compromised and offered to shoot at a cigarette held in his hand. It is a matter of speculation whether Wilhelm, the future Emperor of Germany, was trying to prove that the shot was faked or if he wanted to demonstrate his bravery. Her life straddled the transition of the American west from a wild frontier to settlement, finally, and statehood, and she was mourned nationwide when she died. In 1950 Irving Berlin's smash musical *Annie Get Your Gun*, introduced a new generation of Americans to "The Peerless Lady Wing-Shot."

Shirl Kasper, *Annie Oakley* (Norman: University of Oklahoma Press, 1992), 114. *McGraw-Hill Encyclopedia of World Biography* (New York, McGraw-Hill, 1973), s.v. "Oakley." George Earl Shankle, *American Nicknames: Their Origin and Significance, 2nd ed.* (New York: H.W. Wilson Company, 1955), s.v. "Oakley, Annie."

What was the worst American theater disaster in history?

On December 30, 1903, just five weeks after it opened, the Iroquois Theater in Chicago, Illinois, caught fire. "Standing Room Only" signs were posted as the light operetta, "Mr. Bluebeard," played to an over-capacity holiday crowd of 2,000. The theater had been billed as "absolutely fireproof." However, the seats were wooden and stuffed with hemp and the fire equipment was still waiting to be installed.

During a moonlit scene a powerful spotlight caught the draperies on fire. An asbestos curtain was dropped and the operetta's featured comedian, Eddie Foy, came onstage and made a valiant attempt to calm the audience. When the flames escaped from under the curtain, the audience panicked. Of the 2,000 theatergoers, 602 people died.

After the incident regulations were put into effect which required theaters to display lit exit signs, install sprinkler systems, and use fire-resistive scenery.

Marshall Everett, *The Great Chicago Theater Disaster* (Chicago: Publishers Union of American, 1904), 33. *Great Fires of America* (Waukesha, WI: Country Beautiful, 1973) 134-41.

When was the "Star Spangled Banner" written?

Francis Scott Key (1779-1843) wrote the words to the "Star Spangled Banner" while a prisoner on the British warship *Supreme* during the British attack on Fort McHenry, Baltimore, Maryland, on September 13, 1814. Set to the English tune of "Anacreon in Heaven," it was originally known as "The Defense of Fort McHenry" and printed on a handbill on September 15, 1814. It was designated as the U.S. national anthem by an act of Congress and signed into law by U.S. President Herbert Hoover (1874-1964) on March 3, 1931.

Dick Jacobs and Harriet Jacobs, *Who Wrote That Song?* (Cincinnati, OH: Writer's Digest Books, 1994), s.v. "Star Spangled Banner." Joseph Nathan Kane, *Famous First Facts, 4th ed.* (New York: H. W. Wilson, 1981), s.v. "National Anthem."

What are the Tony Awards?

The Tony Awards officially called the Antoinette Perry Awards were established in 1947 by the American Theatre Wing to honor its founder, actress Antoinette Perry (1888-1946). Currently administered by the League of American Theatres and Producers, the annual awards recognize outstanding theatrical achievement presented in an eligible Broadway house with 499 or more seats during the Tony season (May to May). The actual award is a silver medallion embossed with masks of comedy and tragedy mounted on a black lucite base. The award categories include Best play, Best book of a musical, Best original score of a musical, Best revival, Best actor/actress, Best featured actor/actress, Best actor/actress in a musical, Best play direction, Best musical direction, Best scenic design, Best costume design, Best lighting design, and Best choreography.

Gerald Bordman, *The Oxford Companion to American Theatre* (New York: Oxford University Press, 1984), 673. Gita Siegman, ed., *Awards, Honors & Prizes, 10th ed.* (Detroit, MI: Gale Research, 1992), 287, 711.

What was the title of the play on which the movie *Casablanca* was based?

The movie *Casablanca*, which starred Humphrey Bogart (1899-1957) and Ingrid Bergman (1915-1982), and which won Academy Awards in 1943 for Best Picture, Best Director, and Best

Screenplay, was based on *Everybody Comes to Rick's*, a three-act play by Murray Burnett and Joan Alison.

Charles Francisco, *You Must Remember This. . . The Filming of Casablanca* (Englewood Cliffs, NJ: Prentice-Hall, 1980), 28.

What was the Feejee Mermaid?

The Feejee Mermaid was an 1842 creation of master showman and hoaxman Phineas Taylor Barnum (1810-1891) in a scheme to attract people to his American Museum in New York. Barnum started the hoax by mailing letters to the media from various locations around the world claiming a mermaid had been discovered in the Feejee Islands and preserved in China. After arousing public interest, Barnum then announced he had the preserved mermaid on display. People were willing to pay 25 cents to see this oddity and, from a financial and publicity standpoint, the Feejee Mermaid was a great success although Barnum in his later years admitted the mermaid was really the torso and head of a monkey grafted to the lower half of a fish.

Amy Wallace, et al., *The Book of Lists #3* (New York: William Morrow, 1983), 485.

How old was Wolfgang Amadeus Mozart when he composed his first piece of music?

Wolfgang Amadeus Mozart (1756-1791) composed a concerto for the clavier when he was only four years old. Born in Salzburg, Austria, Mozart is one of the world's greatest composers, not only for of his music but also his mastery of all the musical forms of his day-including symphony, concerto, chamber music and opera.

Dennis Fradin, *Remarkable Children* (Boston: Little, Brown and Company, 1987), 4. *McGraw-Hill Encyclopedia of World Biography* (New York: McGraw-Hill, 1973), s.v. "Mozart."

How much did it cost to attend the Woodstock concerts in 1969 and 1994?

The 1994 attempt to recreate Woodstock on its twenty-fifth anniversary changed the rock concert in at least one way: it raised the cost of attending considerably. Tickets in 1969 were six dollars; adjusted for inflation, that was equivalent to $23.96 in 1994. The second concert cost $67.50 per day.

"Price of music goes up," *USA Today* 12 August 1994.

Who was America's most famous striptease artist, known as the "Queen of Burlesque"?

Rose Louise Hovick (1914-1970) better known as "Gypsy Rose Lee," was America's most famous striptease artist. Contemporaries called her the "Queen of Burlesque." Lee made an art out of the striptease and rose from the Burlesque circuit to appear in movies, on the stage, and on television. She also associated with New York intellectuals, such as H. L. Mencken and Damon Runyon. Mencken even coined a word in her honor, dubbing striptease artists "ecdysiasts."

Sylvia Cole and Abraham H. Lass, *The Facts on File Dictionary of 20th-Century Allusions: From Abbott and Costello to Ziegfeld Girls* (New York: Facts on File, 1991), s.v. "Gypsy Rose Lee."

What was the name of the three instrumentalists dressed in ape suits who were featured on Ernie Kovacs' television shows?

The Nairobi Trio was the name of a group of three instrumentalists dressed in ape suits who were featured on innovative comedian Ernie Kovacs' television show.

Alex McNeil, *Total Television, 3d ed.* (New York: Penguin Books, 1991), s.v. "Ernie Kovacs."

What year did *A Chorus Line* win a Tony award for best musical?

A Chorus Line won a Tony award for best musical in 1976. Written by James Kirkwood and Nicholas Dante, it features music by Marvin Hamlisch and lyrics by Edward Kleban. The story of *A Chorus Line* revolves around an audition for the chorus of Broadway show, revealing the backgrounds of the individual characters in speech and song. The musical first opened at the Public Theater in New York on April 15, 1975 and proceeded to become the longest running musical in Broadway history. It opened on Broadway at the Shubert Theater on July 25, 1975, and ran for 15 years; when the play ended its run in 1990, there had been 6,137 performances.

Kurt Gnzl, *The Encyclopedia of the Musical Theatre* (New York: Schirmer Books, 1994), s.v. "Chorus line." Mike Kaplan, ed., *Variety Presents the Complete Book of Major U.S. Show Business Awards,* (New York: Garland Publishing, 1985), 294.

What was the military significance of the Spanish tune called the "Deguello"?

The "Deguello" is a Spanish tune that was used to signal that no quarter or mercy would be given to opposing troops.

John Pimlott, *The Military Quiz Book* (Harrisburg, PA: Greenhill Books and Stackpole Books, 1993), 39-40.

What is the derivation of the term "belly dancing"?

The term "belly dancing" is the Western name for a Middle Eastern style of dance. In 1893 a group of dancers visited the United States to perform the *danse du ventre* at the Chicago Columbian Exposition. The star of the show was called Little Egypt, and her dance style originated in the Middle East. When Americans learned the literal translation for her *danse du ventre* was "belly dance," the sensual style and suggestive term were linked.

Dahlena Meilach and Dona Z. Meilach, *The Art of Belly Dancing* (New York: Bantam Books, 1975), 5.

What are the "Chester Plays" and the "Chester Cycle"?

The "Chester Plays" are a "Corpus Christi" cycle of 25 biblical plays by a 14th century anonymous author. The 11,000 extant lines of script make up five manuscripts and were probably written about 1325-1375 A.D. The plays were produced on successive days at the back of pageant wagons that made stops throughout a city. The 25 plays deal with various themes from the scriptures including:
Fall of Lucifer
Creation and fall of man
Moses and the Ten Commandments
Flight into Egypt
Last Supper and the betrayal of Christ

Coming of the Antichrist
Last Judgment.

John Gassner and Edward Quinn, *The Reader's Encyclopedia of World Drama* (New York: Thomas Y. Crowell Co., 1969), 122-23.

What is moshing?

Moshing is a variation on slam-dancing; in addition to dancers aggressively crashing into each other, it involves high stepping and jumping around.

"Among the New Words," *American Speech: A Quarterly of Linguistic Usage* Winter 1993.

Who were the first male and female winners of the annual Hasty Pudding Awards?

The Hasty Pudding Institute of 1770 annually bestows its Woman of the Year and Man of the Year award, usually to entertainment personalities. The first woman to win the award was Gertrude Lawrence (1898-1952), an English actress, in 1951; the first man, Bob Hope (1903-), won in 1967. Award celebrations include a banquet, parade, gifts and a plaque. Harvard University students comprise the institutes membership.

Claire Walter, *Winners: The Blue Ribbon Encyclopedia of Awards* (New York: Facts On File, 1982), 215-16.

What is the source of Brecht's *Three Penny Opera?*

The text of *Der Dreigroschenoper (The Three Penny Opera)* was written by Bertold Brecht (1898-1956), a German poet and playwright, in 1928; its music was composed by Kurt Weill (1900-1950). Although the work with its cynical, anti-bourgeois theme reflected the contemporary, avante-garde mind-set, it was based on a much older work, *The Beggar's Opera* (1728) by John Gay, an English playwright and poet who lived between 1685 and 1732.

Peter Thomson and Glendyr Sacks, eds., *The Cambridge Companion to Brecht* (New York: Cambridge University Press, 1994), 62-63.

What operetta is based on George Bernard Shaw's *Arms and the Man*?

Premiering in 1909, the operetta *The Chocolate Soldier* by Oscar Straus (1870-1954) is based on the play *Arms and the Man* by George Bernard Shaw (1856-1950). Produced in 1894, *Arms and the Man* lampoons romantic views of war and soldiering. The comedy, set in Bulgaria in 1885, is a romantic farce featuring would-be heroes, lackluster soldiers and a beautiful heroine born to wealth and refinement. Strauss' operetta takes its name from the character Captain Bumerli, a Swiss mercenary who carries chocolates instead of rifle shells in his cartridge box.

Joseph T. Shipley, *The Crown Guide to the World's Greatest Plays* (New York: Crown Publishers, 1984), 675-77. *McGraw-Hill Encyclopedia of World Biography* (New York: McGraw-Hill, 1973), 10:24-25.

By what unofficial title was George Jessel known?

George Jessel (1898-1981), an American entertainer who entered vaudeville as a child, wrote, produced, and starred in motion pictures. He is probably best known for his appearances at benefit performances, where he sparkled as the master of ceremonies or as an after-dinner speaker, becoming known as the "toastmaster general." His autobiography *Hello Momma*, was published in 1946.

Frank Buxton and Bill Owen, *The Big Broadcast, 1920-1950* (New York: The Viking Press, 1972), 124.

For which city did P.T. Barnum serve as mayor?

P. T. Barnum (1810-1891), an American showman who is probably best known as a circus owner, established "The Greatest Show on Earth" in 1871 and collaborated with James Bailey to form the Barnum and Bailey Circus in 1881. From 1846 he was a resident of Bridgeport, Connecticut, where he built a Moorish-style home he called Iranistan, and where he was very active in city life, showing a great deal of civic spirit and generosity. He also represented that district four times in the state legislature and served as mayor for one term.

A.H. Saxon, ed., *Selected Letters of P.T. Barnum* (New York: Columbia University Press, 1983), xvi.

In 1947 who won the Tony Award for best dramatic actor?

In 1947 the Tony Award for best dramatic actor was awarded to both Jose Ferrer for *Cyrano de Bergerac* and Fredric March for *Years Ago.*

Mike Kaplan, ed., *Variety Presents: The Complete Book of Major U.S. Show Business Awards* (New York: Garland Publishing, 1985), 271.

Who are Punch and Judy?

Punch and Judy are the stars of an English puppet show, *Punch and Judy,* that originated during the seventeenth century. Presented on the miniature stage of a collapsible, portable theater/booth, the show's plot varies, but always features Punch, a humped-back, hooked-nose comic-villain, his wife, Judy, and faithful terrier, Toby. The characters were featured in numerous slap-stick plots and were favorites throughout England.

Phyllis Harnoll, ed., *The Oxford Companion to the Theatre* (Oxford: Oxford University Press, 1983), s.v. "Punch and Judy."

What are Miss Piggy's measurements?

The popular Muppet character Miss Piggy (who is madly in love with Kermit the Frog), created by Jim Henson (1936-1990), has a well-rounded figure. Her real-life costume designer, Calista Hendrickson, has acknowledged that Miss Piggy measures 3 feet tall, 27-20-32 with a broad beam and short legs.

Grace Proven, "A Star is Born—in Hog Couture," *Pittsburgh Post-Gazette* 14 December 1982).

What was Theodore Dreiser's brother's name and profession?

Songwriter Paul Dresser (1857-1911) was the brother of American author Theodore Dreiser (1871-1945). Dresser composed popular music in the heart of New York's Tin Pan Alley during 1890s.

Jack Burton, *The Blue Book of Tin Pan Alley, expanded new ed.* (Watkin's Glen, NY: Century House, 1962), 175.

Who were the stars of the 1930 hit movie classic *Min and Bill*?

The classic 1930 movie hit *Min and Bill* starred Marie Dressler (1869-1934) as Min Divot and Wallace Beery (1886-1949) as Bill. Dressler and Beery both portrayed gruff but lovable characters in this MGM drama spiced with romantic comedy. Dressler won an Oscar for her portrayal of the owner of a rough-and-tumble hotel on California's waterfront who befriends a waif abandoned by her mother. Beery is a fisherman and the object of Dressler's affection. Dressler and Beery were so popular with movie-goers as Min and Bill that a sequel *Tugboat Annie* was released three years later.

Jay Robert Nash and Stanley Ralph Ross, *The Motion Picture Guide* (Chicago: Cinebooks, Inc., 1986), 5:1959.

What was the figure on the price tag hanging from country comedian Minnie Pearl's straw hat?

Country comedienne Minnie Pearl's (1912-1996) trademark was a price tag hanging from her straw hat. The price on the tag is $1.98. Pearl, who first won the hearts of "country and western" audiences in the South and then in the rest of the country was born Sarah Ophelia Colley on October 25, 1912 in Centerville, Tennessee. Although she wanted to be a dramatic actress for as long as she could remember, she later decided to pursue a comedic career and based her now-famous character, Minnie Pearl on a real life woman she stayed with in northern Alabama. As she was quoted in Current Biography Yearbook, Cannon chose the name "Minnie Pearl" because "Everybody in the country knows Minnies and Pearls..... They are the most wonderful names, soft and euphonious to say." "Minnie Pearl" is from the fictional town of Grinder's Switch which was the name of a railroad station where her real-life father loaded his lumber onto freight cars. Minnie's organdy dress, straw hat, and black Mary Jane shoes are what a country girl would dress in when going to a Sunday meeting or wear to town on a Saturday to do a little "trading and flirting." Cannon eventually became established with the Grand Old Opry show in Nashville which was her springboard to national popularity.

Judith Graham, ed., *Current Biography Yearbook, 1992* (New York: H.W. Wilson, 1992), s.v. "Pearl, Minnie." Melvin Shestack, *The Country Music Encyclopedia* (New York: Thomas Y. Crowell, 1974, s.v. "Pearl, Minnie."

Which hymn was played by the band aboard the *Titanic* as the ship sank?

In 1912, the great ocean liner *Titanic* sank in the frigid waters of the North Atlantic Ocean. Over 1,500 people drowned. During the evacuation of the *Titanic*, a band aboard the ship played music in an attempt to calm the passengers. Survivors who were able to board lifeboats and row away from the ship reported that the band was playing the hymn "Nearer, My God to Thee" when the *Titanic* sank.

Thomas H. Russell, ed., *Sinking of the Titanic: World's Greatest Sea Disaster* (Chicago: Homewood Press, 1912), 94.

Which London theater was most intimately associated with William Shakespeare?

The Globe Theatre, which was built in 1599, was intimately associated with the great English playwright William Shakespeare (1564-1616). The Globe burned to the ground in 1613, was re-built in 1614, but ultimately was demolished in 1644.

Phyllis Hartnoll, ed., *The Concise Oxford Companion to the Theatre* (Oxford: Oxford University Press, 1992), 188.

How tall was Tom Thumb?

Tom Thumb, the midget made famous by American showman P.T. Barnum (1810-1891), was 25 inches tall. Born Charles Sherwood Stratton, Tom Thumb was first exhibited in 1843 at the age of five. He eventually grew to a height of 40 inches before his death in 1883.

Gerald Martin Bordman, *The Oxford Companion to American Theatre,* (New York: Oxford University Press, 1984), 668.

What is the height and weight of the "Oscar" statuettes presented annually by the Academy of Motion Picture Arts and Sciences?

The Academy Award of Merit known as "Oscar," which is awarded annually for achievement in the motion picture industry, was conceived by Cedric Gibbons, a member of the Academy of Motion Picture Arts and Sciences in 1926. As he reflected on the need to build a strong corporate image for the motion picture industry, he drew a sketch of a naked knight with a crusader's sword impaled in a reel of film. The slots of the reel represented the five original branches of the academy: producers, writers, directors, actors, and technicians. Frederic Hope, Gibbon's assistant, was charged with finalizing the design. George Stanley, an out-of-work artist, was commissioned to model the statuette in clay, cast it in bronze, and produce twelve copies of the statuette. He did this under the supervision of Guido Nelli of the California Bronze Foundry. The final statuettes weighed eight pounds and were thirteen inches high. The formula for the composition of the metal statuettes remains a secret, although in 1971 its interior composition was listed as 92.5 percent tin and 7.5 percent copper. A 24-karat gold-plated finish is applied to the final product. The first statuettes were presented on May 16, 1929.

Awards are granted in the following categories: acting in a leading role by an actress and an actor; acting in a supporting role by an actor and an actress; art direction; cinematography; costume design; directing; documentary for both feature and short subject; filmediting; foreign language film; makeup; music for best original score, original song score, and best original song; best picture; both animated and live action short films; sound; sound effects editing; visual effects; writing for the best screenplay written for the screen; and best screenplay based on material previously produced or published.

Anthony Holden, *Behind the Oscar: The Secret History of the Academy Awards,* (New York: Simon & Schuster, 1993), 83-84. John May, *Curious Trivia* (Dorset Press, 1980), 188. Debra Kirby, ed., *Awards, Honors, and Prizes* (Detroit: Gale Research, Inc., 1994), s.v. "Academy Awards of Merit (Oscar)."

Who were Frick and Frack?

Frick and Frack were ice-skating performers in the mid-twentieth century. They were known as "the Clown Kings of the Ice" while working for the Ice Follies. Mr. Frick was born Werner Groebli in Basel, Switzerland, on April 21, 1915. Mr. Frack was born Hansreudi Mauch on May 4, 1919 also in Basel.

The boys who would later be known as Frick and Frack started clowning around at the local ice rink, where the owner took an interest in their antics and suggested they perform professionally at an ice carnival at St. Moritz. Their parents would not allow them to use their given names because the Swiss took ice skating extremely seriously, and their parents might have been embarrassed by the comedy act, so the boys called themselves "Zig and Zag."

Soon they were playing in England and Hollywood. By this time they had changed their billing to "Frick and Frack;" "Frick" being the name of a Swiss border town and "Frack" being the German word for frock They appeared in two movies: *Silver Skates* (1942) and *Lady, Let's Dance* (1943).

They performed with the Ice Follies from May 13, 1939, to August 24, 1954, when Frack had to retire due to a bone disease. Frick continued with the Ice Follies until a sudden accident on December 1, 1979, ruined his knee.

Hansreudi "Frack" Mauch died in June of 1979. Werner "Frick" Groebli retired with his wife after his accident that same year.

Richard Lampaski, *Whatever Became Of?* (New York: Crown Publishers, Inc., 1989), 58-59.

Who first played Little Orphan Annie in the hit musical *Annie*?

The 1977 hit musical Annie opened on August 10 at the Alvin Theatre in New York, with Andrea McArdle playing the lead role of Little Orphan Annie. The production, which went on to win the Tony Award for Best Musical, was produced by Thomas Meehan, with music by Charles Strouse and lyrics by Martin Charnin. The musical was based on the comic strip "Little Orphan Annie" which was the creation of Harold Gray (1894-1968). The strip first appeared on August 5, 1924, with a theme based loosely on the format of many successful Mary Pickford movies. A vulnerable waif, but with a lot of pluck and ambition, finds herself through circuitous circumstances in a palatial home, headed by an overbearing patriarchal figure with a strong will but possessing a heart of gold. To further pull at the heart strings, add a lovable pooch! The musical, like the comic strip, was an overnight success. In 1982 Columbia pictures brought *Annie* to the screen starring Carol Burnett, Albert Finney, and Aileen Quinn.

Kurt Gnzl and Andrew Lamb, *Gnzl's Book of the Musical Theatre* (New York: Schirmer Books, 1989), 851. Ron Goulart, ed., *The Encyclopedia of American Comics* (New York: Facts On File, 1990), s.v. "Little Orphan Annie."

How did Bill "Bojangles" Robinson get his nickname?

Tap dancer Bill "Bojangles" Robinson, a popular stage and screen star of the early twentieth century, earned his nickname after winning a sum of money in a poker game one night in Harlem. As he and his friends exited the basement apartment where the game had been held, the young Robinson started to dance out of joy over his good fortune. At that point, his losing friend Des Williams dismissed Robinson as a "bojangles," an appellation thought to mean "happy-go-lucky." Robinson later became a household name known for his ebullient personality.

Richard Strouse, "At 70, Still Head Hoofer," *New York Times Magazine* 23 May 1948.

What was the "Breastplate of St. Patrick"?

The "Breastplate of St. Patrick" was a hymn written by Patrick to protect himself and his fellow clerics against ambush by his enemies. It is also known as "Deer's Cry."

Alice-Boyd Proudfoot, ed., comp., *Patrick: Sixteen Centuries with Ireland's Patron Saint* (New York: Macmillian, 1983), 49.

Who was Seor Wences?

Seor Wences, one of the best known ventriloquists in comedy was, in reality, Wenceslao Moreno. Born in Penaranda, Spain, in 1912, Moreno's most famous and bizarre creation was "Johnny," a face with a high-pitched voice painted on the side of his fist with a wig over the knuckles. A standard opening between the two was an endearing "Be nice." "Nice." "Are you nice"? "Yes." "Nice." Wences also had a disembodied head known as "Pedro" kept in a box who was known for saying "S'all right"? Senor Weces was very popular in the 1940s through the 1970s, and he made a brief comeback in the 1980s.

Ronald L. Smith, *Who's Who in Comedy: Comedians, Comics and Clowns From Vaudeville to Today's Stand-Ups* (New York: Facts On File, 1992), 487.

How did the phrase "Tin Pan Alley" originate?

Theatrical man Robert H. Duiree claimed to have originated the phrase "Tin Pan Alley" in reference to New York City's songwriting district-West 28th Street. Shortly before his death in 1935, Duiree recalled to Epes W. Sargent, the drama critic for the *New York Morning Telegraph*, "Listen to those pianos banging, this is a regular tin pan alley." Sargent used the phrase in his next day's column and it has been an American idiom ever since.

"Originator of term 'Tin Pan Alley' Dies," *New York Times* 6 October 1935.

What is the Susie-Q?

Susie-Q is a dance of African-American roots. The origin of its name is unknown. In the Susie-Q, dancers interlace the fingers of both hands, raise them to chest height, and with elbows extended outward, move them from left to right across the body while doing crossover footwork. The dance is also spelled Suzie-Q, Suzi-Q, Suzy-Q, Susy-Q, and without the hyphen.

The Oxford English Dictionary, 2d ed. (Oxford: Clarendon Press, 1989), s.v. "Susie-Q." Charles Panati, *Panati's Parade of Fads, Follies, and Manias* (New York: HarperCollins, 1991), 168. *Webster's Third New International Dictionary of the English Language Unabridged* (Springfield, MA: Merriam-Webster, 1986), s.v. "susy-q."

Who wrote the song titled "Wabash Cannon Ball"?

The folk song "Wabash Cannon Ball" is a folk song believed to have originated by and for train-hopping hoboes in the 1880s. While the song is about a train which traveled between the Atlantic and Pacific oceans, there was a "Wabash Cannon Ball" which operated between St. Louis, Missouri, and Detroit, Michigan. The song, recorded by Roy Acuff, gained popularity and sold over a million copies. The song was featured in *Rolling Home to Texas*, a 1941 film.

Donald J. Heimburger, *Wabash* (Illinois: Heimburger House Publishing, 1984), 9. Theodore Raph, *The Songs We Sang: A Treasury of American Popular Music* (Cranbury, NJ: A. S. Barnes, 1964), 367-69.

Who wrote the official U.S. Army song?

In 1908 General Edmund L. Gruber wrote "The Caissons Go Rolling Along" (sometimes called the Caisson song) when he was a first lieutenant for the U.S. Field Artillery in the Philippines. In 1918 during World War I (1914-18) John Philip Sousa (1854-1932) expanded the song into a band arrangement entitled "Field Artillery March." Sousa introduced this rendition to the public during a Liberty Loan concert at the Hippodrome in New York City. Because he helped popularize the song, Sousa has, at times, been erroneously credited as the song's composer. When Dr. H.W. Arberg was asked to select an official song for the U.S. army, he adapted Sousa's and Gruber's works into "The Army Goes Rolling Along."

David Ewen, ed., *American Popular Songs: From the Revolutionary War to the Present* (New York: Random House, 1966), s.v. "Caissons Go Rolling

Along, The (or, The Caisson Song)." James Morehead and Albert Morehead, eds., *Best Loved Songs and Hymns* (Cleveland, OH: World Publishing, 1965), 10-11.

What was the first full-length talking picture made with an all-African-American cast?

The first full-length, all-African-American Hollywood film with sound was *Hearts in Dixie.* Released in 1929, it was followed later in the year by *Hallelujah.* Oscar Micheaux (1884-1951) in 1918 made the first full-length, all-African-American film called *Birthright.* Three years earlier, the Lincoln Motion Picture Company, an African-American production company, which made black films for black audiences produced the *Realization of a Negro's Ambition.*

Joan Potter and Constance Taylor, *African-American Firsts* (New York: Pinto Press, 1994), 56-59. *The Ebony Handbook* (Chicago: Johnson Publishing Co., 1974), 450.

Who wrote the patriotic song "America the Beautiful"?

"America the Beautiful" was written by Katherine Lee Bates in 1893. A professor of English at Wellesley College in Massachusetts, she traveled to Pikes Peak, Colorado, in a mule-drawn wagon on an outing sponsored by Colorado College where she was lecturing. She had traveled west by train and upon seeing the breathtaking view from Pikes Peak, wrote the words to the poem that evening. Two years after her trip, the poem was published in the magazine *The Congregationalist.* Many musical settings were composed for her verses, but the most popular one was the music of the hymn "Materna," written by Samuel A. Ward in 1882.

James Morehead and Albert Morehead, eds., *Best Loved Songs and Hymns* (Cleveland, OH: World Publishing, 1965), 6-7. *The Denver Post* 4 July 1993. Theodore Raph, *The Songs We Sang* (Cranbury, NJ: A. S. Barnes, 1964), 350.

Which bands performed at Woodstock?

On August 15-17, 1969, a crowd of 300,000 to 500,000 people attended the Woodstock Music Festival near Bethel, New York. The performers were Joan Baez, Blood, Sweat and Tears, The Jeff Beck Group, The Paul Butterfield Blues Band, The Band, Creedence Clearwater Revival, Canned Heat, Country Joe McDonald and the Fish, Crosby, Stills and Nash, Joe Cocker, Arlo Guthrie, Grateful Dead, Tim Hardin, Jimi Hendrix, Richie Havens, Keef Hartley, The Incredible String Band, Janis Joplin, The Jefferson Airplane, The Joshua Light Show, Melanie, Mountain, Quill, John Sebastian, Ravi Shankar, Sly and the Family Stone, Bert Sommer, Santana, Sweetwater, Ten Years After, Johnny Winter, and The Who.

On August 12-14, 1994, a Woodstock 25th Anniversary Concert was held in Saugerties, New York, with approximately 300,000 to 350,000 attending. There were 50 performing acts including original performers Joe Cocker, Santana, Country Joe MacDonald, and Crosby, Stills and Nash. New performers included Bob Dylan, Aerosmith, Metallica, Nine Inch Nails, Arrested Development, Traffic, the Allman Brothers Band, Peter Gabriel, The Band, the Spin Doctors, Porno for Pyros, Cypress Hill, James, Salt-N-Pepa, Green Day, and Sheryl Crow. Some people boycotted the anniversary concert, calling it too expensive and commercial. Approximately 20,000 to 45,000 people showed up at the original site to hear free performances by local bands and by Woodstock veterans such as Arlo Guthrie and Melanie.

*Facts on File: World News Digest with Index,*18 August 1994. Robert McHenry, ed., *The New Encyclopaedia Britannica, 15th ed.* (Chicago: Encyclopaedia Britannica, 1993), s.v. "Woodstock." Robert Stephen Spitz, *Barefoot in Babylon: The Creation of the Woodstock Music Festival, 1969* (New York: Viking Press, 1979), xvii-xviii.

Who were the members of Frank Sinatra's "Rat Pack"?

Also referred to as "The Clan," singer Frank Sinatra's "Rat Pack" included actor/singer Dean Martin, actor Tony Curtis, actor Peter Lawford, actor/singer Sammy Davis, Jr., comedian Joey Bishop, and actor Henry Silva. Pairings of some of the members of the pack occurred in the movies *Ocean's Eleven* (1960), *Sergeants Three* (1962), *Johnny Cool* (1963), *Robin and the Seven Hoods* (1964), *Salt and Pepper* (1968), and *One More Time* (1970).

Beverly Baer and Neil E. Walker, eds., *Almanac of Famous People, 5th ed.* (Detroit: Gale Research, 1994), s.v. "Bishop, Joey," "Curtis, Tony," "Lawford, Peter," "Martin, Dean," "Sinatra, Frank." Peter Chapman, *The Players: Actors in Movies on Television and Videocassette* (New York: Windsor Press, 1994), 419. Patricia Seaton Lawford, *The Peter Lawford Story: Life with the Kennedys, Monroe, and The Rat Pack* (New York: Carroll & Graf, 1988), 111-17. Charles Moritz, ed., *Current Biography Yearbook 1978* (New York: H. W. Wilson, 1978), s.v. "Davis, Sammy, Jr."

Who wrote the national ballad "America"?

Boston minister Samuel Francis Smith (1808-1895) wrote the words to the song "America" while studying at the Andover Theological Seminary in 1832. Smith wrote over 600 poems in his 93 years including the hymn "The Morning Light is Breaking." He saw the music in a German book which inspired the words, not realizing he was setting his song to the British royal anthem "God Save the Queen." "America" was first performed at a church service on July 4, 1832, and printed in a collection of songs with the name "America, National Hymn" four years later. It became very popular with the Union Army during the American Civil War (1861-65). It originally had four verses but Smith continued to write additional stanzas for special occasions.

James Morehead and Albert Morehead, eds., *Best Loved Songs and Hymns* (Cleveland, OH: World Publishing, 1965), 2-3. C. A. Browne, *The Story of Our National Ballads* (New York: Thomas Y. Crowell, 1960), 78-92.

Visual Arts

What is the Amber Chamber?

The Amber Chamber is a legendary masterpiece conceived by King Frederick I of Prussia as a magnificent gift to the Russian royal family to seal the alliance of the two powers. Master craftsmen took years to create the full-sized room designed in the Baroque and Rococo styles and consisting of 22 wall panels, intricate bas-reliefs, busts, figures, monograms, coats-of-arms, candelabra, mirrors, and inlaid decorations depicting Tuscan landscapes and scenes from ancient mythology-all fashioned entirely of amber.

The Amber Chamber was installed at the Catherine Palace outside St. Petersburg in 1755. It remained there until 1941 when Nazi troops captured the palace, dismantled the chamber, and removed it. The search continues for this priceless art treasure, with most efforts concentrated at Karl-Marx-Platz, Germany.

New York Times 24 November 1991. *New York Times International* 27 May 1992.

What is Carhenge?

Located in Alliance, Nebraska, Carhenge is a rough recreation of the famous stone monument Stonehenge, located in England. The difference lies in the material used to create the sculpture. While Stonehenge is composed of large stone pillars, Carhenge is made up entirely of junked automobiles. It was built by Jim Reinders and his family during the summers of 1987 and 1988.

Motor Trend March 1990.

What does the placement of horses' hooves signify on statues of soldiers on horseback?

A custom observed by sculptors around the time of the American Civil War was to use the placement of the horse's hooves in their statues to indicate the status of the rider. If the horse has all four hooves firmly planted on the ground, the rider survived unharmed. If the rider was wounded, there is one hoof off the ground. If the horse has two hooves, raised the rider was killed in battle.

James W. Wensyel, "Tales of a Gettysburg Guide," *American Heritage* April 1994.

What is the riddle of the Portland Vase?

Among the treasures of the British Museum in London, England, there is a cobalt blue urn called the Portland Vase. Named after an early owner, the Dowager Duchess of Portland, it is considered to be one of the finest examples of ancient glass. Crafted between 27 B.C. and 34 A.D. by an unknown artist who was probably from Alexandria, the urn is decorated with a frieze that seems to tell a story, the meaning of which is obscure and has long been a topic of scholarly debate. In 1992 Randall L. Skalsky, an American graduate student from the University of Massachusetts, claimed to have solved the riddle of the Portland Vase. He postulated that the frieze contains two different marriage scenes taken from mythology, that of Peleus and Thetis and of Paris and Helen. Not all scholars have accepted his theory as plausible.

Saturday Evening Post September/October 1992.

Who was the model for Leonardo da Vinci's *Mona Lisa*?

For approximately two years, Leonardo da Vinci had been making sketches of Lisa di Anton of Naples, Italy, who was married to Francesco del Giocando, a local politician and businessman. She became the model for da Vinci's painting, *Mona Lisa* in 1507. However, she accompanied her husband that spring on a long business trip to Calabria, leaving before the portrait was finished.

James Trager, *The People's Chronology: A Year-by-Year Record of Human Events from Prehistory to the Present, rev. ed.* (New York: Henry Holt and Co., 1992), 165.

Which president is most responsible for improving the aesthetics of U.S. coins?

U.S. President Theodore Roosevelt (1858-1919) is greatly responsible for improving the aesthetics of U.S. coins. At Roosevelt's urging, Augustus Saint-Gaudens, a highly regarded U.S. sculptor, submitted designs for the cent, $10 eagle and $20 double eagle coins. Roosevelt personally approved Saint-Gaudens' designs for the "eagles." Although there was some animosity towards Saint-Gaudens on the part of many U.S. Mint staff members, his double eagle design (1907) is considered by many collectors to be the aesthetic high point of U.S. coinage.

Beth Deisher, ed., *Coin World Almanac: A Handbook for Coin Collectors, 5th ed.,* (Sidney, OH: Amos Press Inc., 1987), 288.

Who introduced lithographic theater posters in the United States?

Michael B. Leavitt, an owner of numerous touring burlesque companies, claims to have introduced colorful lithographic theater posters in the United States. Leavitt brought samples back from a tour of Europe in 1872 and, by the end of the decade, he was spending $8,000 to $20,000 each theater season on posters, which replaced block printing in advertisements.

Robert C. Allen, *Horrible Prettiness: Burlesque and American Culture* (Chapel Hill, NC: University of North Carolina Press, 1991), 204.

What is the Iron Pillar of Delhi?

The Iron Pillar of Delhi is an ancient monument made of solid iron. The pillar is buried so deep that its length can only be estimated; it is perhaps as long as 60 feet, with 22 feet visible above ground. Located in Delhi, India, the monument is also known as "the arm of fame" of Raja Dhv. According to a nineteenth-century translation by James Prinsep, the Sanskrit inscription describes the Raja's immortal fame and how he "obtained with his own arm an undivided sovereignty on the earth for a long period." The inscription has been dated to as early as 319 A.D.

Various Indian legends give different accounts of how the monument came to be erected. In one version B lan Deo, who founded the Tomara dynasty, drove the pillar into the ground until it rested on the head of Vasuki, King of the Serpents and supporter of the earth. This was done at the recommendation of a Brahman counselor; the now immovable pillar would guarantee the Raja's everlasting power. But the Raja, doubting this, had the pillar unearthed, only to discover that it was indeed stained with the serpent's blood. He found it was impossible to replace the pillar. It was now loose, or "dh la" in the Indian language. That is supposedly how the city became known as Dhili, and finally as Delhi.

Alexander Cunningham, *Archaeological Survey of India* (Simla, India: Government Central Press, 1871), 169-75.

Why did posters originate?

Poster refers to a bill or placard that is put in a public place usually for some commercial purpose, and that has a decorative effect. Posters as we know them did not come into prominence until the nineteenth century; the word poster dates only from 1838, but the first one ever discovered was made around 3000 B.C. and comes from Thebes in ancient Egypt. It offered a reward for an escaped slave. Poster-like placards seem to have been common in the ancient world. There were engraved announcements for theatrical events in ancient Athens, and political and commercial advertisements were found during the excavations of the Roman cities of Pompeii and Herculaneum.

Synergy May/June 1970.

What is remarkable about the Altamira Cave in Spain and who discovered its wonders?

The Altamira Cave in Spain, about 19 miles southwest of Santander, is remarkable for the awe-inspiring brightly painted, realistic Palaeolithic art on its walls and ceilings. The renditions of life-size stags and bisons were done sometime during the Upper Palaeolithic Period which began around 38,000 B.C. The Altimira Cave consists of multiple chambers each with its own set of paintings and each done at different times from the late Solutrean to the late Magdalenian (17,000 B.C. -10,000 B.C.). The ceilings were discovered in 1879 by Don Marcelino de Sautuola, a Spanish nobleman who became interested in archaeology after visiting the Paris International Exhibition in 1878, and his eight-year-old daughter Maria. While in the cave, Maria looked up at the ceiling and suddenly exclaimed "Toros, Toros" which means "Bulls, Bulls." Don Marcelino presented his findings to the Archaeological Congress in 1879 and published his findings in 1880 only to find both efforts greeted with skepticism. In 1905 the archaeological community recognized his find as authentic.

Edward Bacon, ed., *The Great Archaeologists* (Indianapolis: Bobbs-Merrill, 1976), 137. Dennis Brindell Fradin, *Remarkable Children: Twenty Who Made History* (Boston: Little, Brown, 1987), 67. Jacquetta Hawkes, ed., *Atlas of Ancient Archaeology* (New York: McGraw-Hill, 1974), 88.

What is the history of London's Drury Lane Theatre?

Drury Lane in London is England's most famous theater. Although occupying the present site since 1662, the building has been replaced four times. The first theater was built by Killigrew (1612-1683) and chartered by Charles II (1630-1685). Seating 700, it opened in 1663 with Francis Beaumont (1584-1616) and John Fletcher's (1579-1625) *The Humorous Lieutenant.* Then known as the Theatre Royal it was closed during parts of 1665 and 1666 because of the plague and burned down in 1672. The theater was re-built and opened in 1674 under the name Theatre Royal in Drury Lane, seated 2,000 and may have been designed by Sir Christopher Wren (1632-1723). In 1791 the theater was again re-built and opened in 1794 with seating for 3,611. This theater burned to the ground in 1809, was re-built and opened in 1812 with a production of *Hamlet.* Although there were now four tiers of seating, capacity was reduced to 2,283.

Phyllis Hartnoll and Peter Found, eds., *The Concise Oxford Companion to the Theatre* (Oxford: Oxford University Press, 1992), s.v. "Drury Lane."

Which ear did Vincent Van Gogh cut off and what happened to it?

Artist Vincent Van Gogh (1853-1890) cut off part of his left ear in December of 1888, while living in Arles, France. He wrapped the ear in newspaper and went to a brothel. He handed the package to a prostitute he knew by the name of Rachel saying, "Guard this object carefully." He was then taken home by an acquaintance.

Upon unwrapping the paper, Rachel began to faint. The police, alerted to the commotion and informed of the incident, went to Van Gogh's house. By the time he was taken to the hospital it was too late to save the ear. It was put into alcohol to preserve it in case it was needed as evidence, and several months later the ear was thrown out.

David Sweetman, *Van Gogh: His Life and His Art,* (New York: Crown Publishers, Inc., 1990), 292-93.

What is the correct pronunciation of the surname of the French artist douard Vuillard ?

The correct pronunciation of the surname of the French artist douard Vuillard (1868-1940) is: vwee-yar. A painter, printmaker and decorator, Vuillard was a member of the Nabis group and collaborated with his friend Pierre Bonnard to develop a style known as the Intimist Manner, which featured small domestic scenes rendered in subtle colors. He also created mural decorations for the Thtre des Champs-lyses in Paris and the League of Nations in Geneva, Switzerland.

Wilfred J. McConkey, *Klee as in Clay: A Pronunciation Guide* (Lanham, MD: University Press of America, 1985), 52.

When were Courrges' shiny white fashion boots introduced?

French fashion designer Andr Courrges introduced his tall, shiny white fashion boots in his spring collection of 1964, creating a trend which survived more than a decade.

Christina Probert, *Shoes in Vogue Since 1910* (New York: Abbeville Press, 1981), 62-63.

How does an armoire differ from a built-in cupboard?

An armoire is a free-standing cupboard, distinguishing it from most cupboards, which are built-in.

A.J. Bliss, *A Dictionary of Foreign Words and Phrases in Current English* (London: Routledge & Kegan Paul, 1983), s.v. "armoire."

What is pointillism or divisionism?

Pointillism is the neo-impressionistic artistic technique of placing adjacent to one another two dots of differing primary colors, such as blue and yellow. When viewed, the two dots appear as a third color, in this example, green. Divisionism is another term for this technique. French painters Georges Scurat (1859-1891) and Paul Signac (1863-1895) were the founders of pointillism.

Mario Pei, ed., *Language of the Specialists: A Communications Guide to Twenty Different Fields* (New York: Funk & Wagnalls, 1966), s.v. "pointillism or divisionism."

Which former American film actress appeared on a postage stamp in 1981?

The former American film actress Grace Kelly, who became the Princess of Monaco, was pictured on a stamp along with her husband Prince Rainier in 1981. Monaco honored the couple's twenty-fifth wedding anniversary with a commemorative stamp that featured their portrait and two crowns.

Samuel A. Tower, "For U.N. Energy Parley," *The New York Times* 17 May 1881.

How tall is the figure on the Statue of Liberty, and how much does it weigh?

The Statue of Liberty, conceived and designed by the French sculptor Frderic-Auguste Bartholdi (1834-1904), was given to the United States to commemorate its first centennial. Called (in his patent, U.S. Design Patent no. 11,023, issued February 18, 1879) "Liberty Enlightening the World," it is 152 feet (46.3 meters) high, weighs 225 tons (204 metric tons), and stands on a pedestal and base that are 151 feet (46 meters) tall. Its flowing robes are made from more than 300 sheets of hand-hammered copper over a steel frame. Constructed and finished in France in 1884, the statue's exterior and interior were taken apart piece-by-piece, packed into 200 mammoth wooden crates, and shipped to the United States in May 1885. The statue was placed by Bartholdi on Bedloe's Island, at the mouth of New York City Harbor. On October 28, 1886, ten years after the centennial had passed, the inauguration celebration was held.

It was not until 1903 that the bronze inscription "Give me your tired, your poor,/Your huddled masses yearning to breathe free ..." was added. The verse was taken from the third stanza of *The New Colossus*, composed by New York City poet Emma Lazarus in 1883. The statue, the tallest in the United States, and the tallest metal statue in the world, was recently refurbished for its own centennial, at a cost of $698 million, reopening on July 4, 1986. One visible difference is the flame of her torch is now 24-karat gold-leaf, just as in the original design. In 1916 the flame was redone into a lantern of amber glass. Concealed within the rim of her crown is the observation deck that can be reached by climbing 171 steps or by taking the newly installed hydraulic elevator.

Mark C. Young, ed., *Guinness Book of Records 1995* (New York: Facts on File, 1994), 333-34. *How in the World* (Pleasantville, NY: Reader's Digest Association, 1990), 359-61. Charles Panati, *Panati's Extraordinary Origins of Everyday Things* (New York: Perennial Library, 1987), 291-93.

What is the oldest indoor theater in the world?

The oldest indoor theater is the Teatro Olimpico in Vicenza, Italy. It was begun three months before the death of its designer, Andrea di Pietro (1502-1580), better known as Palladio, in 1580.

Mark C. Young, ed., *The Guinness Book of Records 1995* (New York: Facts On File, 1994), 156.

Who designed the Vietnam War Memorial?

The Vietnam War Memorial was built in Washington, D.C., in 1982. The design by Maya Ying Lin, a 21-year-old architecture student at Yale University was selected from the 1,421 entries in a national competition. The memorial is a granite wall, 494 feet long, containing the names of over 58,000 men and women who died or were declared missing in action while serving in the armed forces. The wall is 10 feet high at its center and bends at a 125-degree angle. The names are listed chronologically by their dates of casualty on the two black granite walls. The first name is from July of 1959 and the last from May of 1975. Names denoted with a plus mark indicate missing in action, while a diamond symbol indicates the death was confirmed. The symbol is changed from a plus to a diamond if remains returned by the Vietnam government are identified. Guidebooks are available at the Memorial to help visitors locate a particular name. A book entitled *Vietnam Veterans Memorial Directory of Names* includes an alphabetical listing of the names. The memorial was built with private donations from the American people and over 30 million people have visited it since its dedication on November 13, 1982.

Jan C. Scruggs and Joel L. Swerdlow, *To Heal A Nation: The Vietnam Veterans Memorial* (New York: Harper & Row 1984), 78-80, 159. *USA Today* 6 November 1992. *Vietnam Veterans Memorial Directory of Names* (Washington, DC: Vietnam Veterans Memorial Fund, 1991). *The World Book Encyclopedia* (Chicago: World Book, 1994), s.v. "Vietnam Veterans Memorial."

What is the French name given to the representation of the stable at Bethlehem?

In France, the representation of the stable at Bethlehem is called a *crche.* It includes figures of Mary, Joseph, the infant Jesus, the shepherds, the Wise Men, and the Star of the East. Many churches put this nativity scene on display during the Christmas season as a reminder of the birth of Jesus Christ-the first Christmas. Many *crches* in churches are valued as beautiful antique works of art.

Elizabeth Hough Sechrist, *Christmas Everywhere: A Book of Christmas Customs of Many Lands, new rev. and enlarged ed.* (Philadelphia: Macrae Smith, 1962), 110.

Where is the Buffalo Soldier Monument and how did it get its name?

The Buffalo Soldier Monument is a 12-foot bronze statue located in Fort Leavenworth, Kansas, that was built in tribute to the all-black regiments serving in the United States Army from the Civil War to the Korean War, when the armed forces were finally integrated. The monument was named for the all-black Ninth and Tenth Cavalries, who protected wagon trains and helped settle the Wild West. They were dubbed "Buffalo Soldiers" by the Indians because of their curly hair, large coats, and fighting tactics.

New York Times 26 July 1992. *USA Today* 24 July 1992.

What are the Seven Ancient Wonders of the World?

The Seven Wonders of the Ancient World are:
the Pyramids of Giza—three pyramids constructed during the fourth dynasty on the west bank of the Nile in Egypt, are the oldest and only one of the wonders substantially in existence today
the Hanging Gardens of Babylon—a series of landscaped roof gardens constructed within the walls of the royal palace at Babylon between the eighth and sixth centuries B.C.
the Statue of Zeus at Olympia—a 40-foot statue of the Greek god sitting on a throne was done by sculptor Phidias of Athens around 430 B.C.
the Temple of Diana at Ephesus—famous for its size and for the artworks it contained, built by Croesus, king of Lydia, around 550 B.C.
the Mausoleum of Halicarnassus—constructed between 353 and 351 B.C. for the Anatolian king Mausolus, by his widow Artemisia
the Colossus at Rhodes—a giant bronze statue of the sun god Helios that stood by the harbor in the city of Rhodes, constructed between 292 and 280 B.C.
the Pharos of Alexandria—a lighthouse built for Ptolemy II of Epypt in about 280 B.C. which stood in the harbor of Alexandria on the island of Pharos.

Philip W. Goetz, ed., *The New Encyclopaedia Brittanica, Micropaedia, 15th ed.* (Chicago: Univ. of Chicago, 1989), s.v. "Seven Wonders of the World."

What is the most beautiful United States coin ever issued?

Many coin collectors consider a 20-dollar gold piece designed by American sculptor Augustus Saint-Gaudens (1848-1907) as the most beautiful United States coin. Originally minted in 1907, the Saint-Gaudens gold piece (1907-1933) has a representation of Liberty on one side and a depiction of the American bald eagle on the other.

R.S. Yeoman, *1994 Handbook of United States Coins* (Racine, WI: Western Publishing Company, Inc., 1993), 147.

Where is the house built of newspapers located?

The Paper House, a house built of 215 thicknesses of newspaper, is located in Rockport, Massachusetts. Almost all of the furnishings are made of newspaper, including a piano, a grandfather clock, and a desk created from newspapers describing American aviator Charles Lindbergh's (1902-1974) historic solo flight across the Atlantic Ocean to France in 1927.

AAA TourBook: Connecticut, Massachusetts, Rhode Island (Heathrow, FL: American Automobile Association, 1994), 118.

What is a Mutoscope?

A Mutoscope is a hand-crank device for showing a one-minute flip-card movie, commonly known as a peep-show. Peep-shows were a popular form of entertainment in the first and second decades of the twentieth century.

New York Times 2 August 1967.

What is Monticello?

Monticello is the stately Virginia mansion built by Thomas Jefferson (1743-1826), when he was still an up-and-coming 26-year-old lawyer in the British colony. The future third President of the United States designed it himself in homage to the celebrated landmarks built by sixteenth-century Italian architect Andrea Palladio. Although possessing an elevation of only 600 feet, Jefferson's home affords a 20-mile view of the nearby Blue Ridge Mountains. Hence, Jefferson called it "Monticello"—the Italian word for "little mountain."

James Trager, *The People's Chronology: A Year-by-Year Record of Human Events from Prehistory to the Present, rev. ed.* (New York: Henry Holt and Co., 1992), 314.

How have U. S. coinage portraits of Liberty changed over the years?

The allegorical female figure, Liberty, has graced U.S. coins, both in bust and full-length portraits, for over 115 years. Liberty has always reflected a man's perception of the "ideal woman" since U.S. coins have always been engraved by men. Early renditions of Liberty were "Rubenesque" by modern standards but later coins have reflected a slimmer woman.

Coin World, *Coin World Almanac* (Sidney, OH: Amos Press Inc., 1987), 286.

Why does the Statue of Liberty wear a crown with rays?

There is no explanation for why the Statue of Liberty, sculpted by Frederic Bartholdi, is adorned with a crown with rays. The sunburst was the heraldic emblem of the Bartholdi family. Similar crowns had been used in symbolic representations of France, Liberty, and the French Republic in 1848. Bartholdi may have used symbols of antiquity to convey the grandeur of his work, but he was also attracted to Freemasonry. In a Masonic ritual, the sun is an important symbol in which the Great Architect of the Universe has given the sun to the world to enlighten it, and Liberty to sustain it. More than likely, Bartholdi fused these two images together by crowning Lady Liberty with the sun's rays.

Bernard A. Weisberger, *Statue of Liberty: the First Hundred Years* (New York: American Heritage, 1985), 47.

When Walt Disney created Tinker Bell for the animated film *Peter Pan*, what actress served as a model for the cartoon character's figure?

The gorgeous figure on Walt Disney's cartoon character Tinker Bell, seen in the *Peter Pan*, was modeled after actress Margaret Kerry.

John Grant, *Encyclopedia of Walt Disney's Animated Characters* (New York: Harper & Row, 1987), 228.

What is the story behind the famous "Hollywood" sign?

The famous "Hollywood" sign was erected atop Mount Wilson in 1923 as a publicity gimmick by a land-developer. In 1932 actress Peg Entwistle, disillusioned at not being able to find work, committed suicide by jumping to her death off the 45-foot letter "H." The sign was originally "HOLLYWOODLAND" but by 1978 it had fallen into disrepair and the "LAND" was removed. The Hollywood Sign Trust was formed in that year and is now responsible for maintenance and repair of the landmark.

Parade 3 May 1992.

How can Walt Disney's capricious chipmunks "Chip an' Dale" be identified?

Walt Disney's capricious cartoon chipmunks "Chip an' Dale" can be identified by the color of their noses. Chip has a black nose while Dale's is red. Their personalities also differ; Chip is more level-headed, while Dale is more whimsical.

John Grant, *Encyclopedia of Walt Disney's Animated Characters* (New York: Hyperion, 1993), 96.

What is the history behind the carved Indian figures that used to stand outside of cigar stores?

Cigar store carved Indians were not the only figures gracing the sidewalks of tobacco shops, and not all figures were stereotypes or caricatures. The Museum of Tobacco Art and History in Nashville, Tennessee, has in its collection a figure of the Shawnee leader Tecumseh, as well as figures of sultans, Punch (of Punch and Judy), fire chiefs, police officers, baseball players, and highlanders. The latter advertised snuff and were popular in Scotland. Ship's carvers who had carved masts crafted these figures, especially as ships began using iron and steel for parts. Cigar store figures were popular from about 1870 to 1920, when master carvers operated large shops with apprentices. With the advent of the automobile, sidewalk space became more valuable and displays started disappearing. Figures created from zinc were taken away for their scrap metal value during World War I. Cigar store figures are collectors' items today, with prices ranging from $3,000 to $35,000.

Antique Trader's Collector July 1994.

What is the derivation of the Louis heel?

Louis heels are named for Louis XIV (1638-1715), King of France from 1643 to 1715. The curvy heel was about two inches high, and waisted all around to create a splayed-out effect at its base.

Christina Probert, *Shoes in Vogue since 1910* (New York: Abbeville Press, 1981), 8.

What was the controversy over an award presented to author Alice Walker?

When author Alice Walker was named "state treasure" in California, her award was a foot-tall sculpture of a woman's torso designed by Robert Graham. Since Walker's latest work was a film and book about female mutilation entitled *Warrior Marks*, she was horrified by the nude sculpture which was missing arms, legs, and head. "Though these mutilated figures are...considered 'art' by some," Walker was quoted as saying in *USA Today*, "the message they deliver is of domination, violence and destruction."

USA Today 18 April 1994.

What is the origin of the word *credenza*?

Americans adapted the Italian word *credenza* to describe a sideboard, which is a piece of dining room furniture used to hold linens and tableware. Originally a *credenza* was the table at which food was tasted before being served to a king.

Suzanne Brock, *Idiom's Delight: Fascinating Phrases and Linguistic Eccentricities* (New York: Times Books, 1988), 93.

Which cartoon characters did Andy Warhol commit to canvas?

American pop artist Andy Warhol (1928-1987) painted five cartoon characters: Dick Tracy, Nancy, Batman, Popeye, and Mickey Mouse.

Craig Yoe and Janet Morra-Yoe, eds., *The Art of Mickey Mouse* (New York: Hyperion, 1991).

What is a thaumatrope?

The thaumatrope (or wonder turner) consists of a piece of cardboard with a picture drawn or pasted on each side, the two pictures being upside-down from one another. Two pieces of string are attached to the cardboard and when they are spun it produces the visual effect of merging the two pictures into one. Invented by J. A. Paris in 1826, it is believed to be the first cinematographic device.

Eugene F. Provenzo, *47 Easy-To-Do-Classic Science Experiments* (New York: Dover, 1989), 28.

Who designed the Indian Head or Buffalo nickel?

The two themes of the Indian Head, Bison, or Buffalo nickel makes this coin the most American, most dramatic, most artistic, and most original of all United States coins. For the Indian head on the obverse side, American sculptor and designer James Fraser (1876-1953) created a composite portrait from three Indians: Two Moons, Iron Trail, and Chief John Tree. For the American bison on the reverse side of the coin, Fraser took his sketching equipment to the Bronx Zoo. The coin was produced from 1913 until 1938.

Coin World Almanac, 5th ed. (New York: Amos Press, 1987), 288. Marc Hudgeons, *The Official 1994 Blackbook Price Guide of United States Coins* (New York: Random House, 1993), 171.

What are the dimensions of the statue of Jesus Christ which overlooks Rio de Janeiro?

The statue Christ the Redeemer overlooks Rio de Janeiro, Brazil, from Corcovado Mountain. The total height of the monument is 38 meters, with the statue itself being 30 meters tall. The head is 3.75 meters high, the hands 3.20 meters long, and the outstretched arms 28 meters. The total weight is 1,145 tons. Designed by the French sculptor Landowski, the statue and took five years (1926-31) to erect.

Jean Cau and Jacques Bost, *Brazil, 5th ed.* (Geneva: Nagel, 1979), 129.

What is the most famous monument in Copenhagen?

One of the most popular monuments in Copenhagen is the sculpture of the Little Mermaid (*Den Lille Havfrue*) in Copenhagen Harbor. Created by Edvard Eriksen in 1913, the figure was inspired by a story by Danish author Hans Christian Andersen (1805-1875). Eriksen used a ballerina from the Royal Ballet as a model. The statue was beheaded in 1964, but another head was created from the original cast. The first mermaid statue crafted by Eriksen-the same as the one in the harbor but much smaller-was deemed too diminutive by brewery magnate Carl Jacobsen, who had commissioned the work. The original statue can now be found on the Carlsberg Brewery grounds.

Frommer's Budget Travel Guide: Copenhagen '92-'93 on $50 a Day (New York: Prentice Hall, 1992), 97.

Consumer Issues

What is "kiting"?

"Kiting" is taking unlawful advantage of the "float," which is the time interval between the writing of a check and its collection at a bank. Checks are sometimes written with the knowledge that there are insufficient funds to cover them, but with the hope or belief that funds will be deposited before the check reaches the bank account on which it is written.

Henry Campbell Black, *Black's Law Dictionary: Definitions of the Terms and Phrases of American and English Jurisprudence, Ancient and Modern, 6th ed.* (St. Paul, MN: West Publishing Company, 1990), s.v. "kiting."

What is a reverse mortgage?

A reverse mortgage is a loan that allows a consumer to take the equity in their home and turn it into regular monthly payments while still owning their property. A reverse mortgage was designed for elderly homeowners who in their twilight years need money for monthly living expenses. Each monthly payment is deducted with interest from the accumulated equity in the property. The loan is paid off when the owner dies or the house is sold.

There are two types of reverse mortgages: "short-term" reverse mortgages and "long-term" reverse mortgages. "Short-term" mortgages are set from 3 to 10 years. After this time the customer must repay the loan in full, refinance, or sell the house. In "long-term" reverse mortgages the payments are set until the owner dies or sells the house.

The amount of the loan depends on the value of the house, the age of the owner, and the current interest rates.

Since the early 1980s about 150,000 reverse mortgage loans have been made in the United States. Federally insured reverse mortgages are available in 41 states.

Dun & Bradstreet Guide to $Your Investment$: 1994 (Harper Perennial, 1994).

What is sweat equity?

Sweat equity is a way to keep costs down in building or remodeling a house by the consumer contributing his own labor or "sweat" to the project. Opting to use one's own time and labor rather than a professionals should be done with great caution since there may be little or no return on the investment. Many schools have popped up around the country to take advantage of this trend by teaching consumers the how-to's of construction.

Margaret DiCanio, *The Encyclopedia of Marriage, Divorce, and the Family* (New York: Facts on File, 1989), s.v. "sweat equity."

What criteria should be used in choosing a Health Maintenance Organization (HMO)?

When choosing a health maintenance organization (HMO), it is wise to find out the following information from which you can make your own assessment. Ask how the HMO pays its doctors to see if compensation is commensurate with the amount of care provided. Research records of complaints against providers, including patient satisfaction. Ask if statistics are available on provider turnover within the HMO. Check for provider accreditation, looking in particular for ratings compiled by the National Committee for Quality Assurance.

M. Jenks Brian L.P. Zevnik, *Employee Benefits Plain and Simple: The Complete Step-By-Step Guide to Your Benefits Plan* (New York: Collier Books, 1993), 46.

How can one call to find out if any technical defects have been discovered in a particular car model?

To find out about any potential technical defects in a specific car model, call the National Highway Traffic Safety Administration at (202) 366-2768.

Clarence Ditlow, "Automobiles -Technical Defects," *Consumer Reports* February 1994.

What are travel clubs and are they cost effective?

There are three major types of travel clubs: full service travel clubs, limited service travel clubs, and clubs and associations with a non-travel focus that also arrange cut-rate travel services. Discounted services offered by travel clubs may include hotel discounts, airfare discounts, car-rental discounts, cruise discounts, last-minute cruises and tours, and commission rebates. Travel clubs may be cost effective depending on the individual's needs; however, a travel club's prices may be beat by finding a discount agency for cruises, a discount agency for air tickets, a rebating agency for the times list price is paid, and a half-price hotel program.

Ed Perkins and Janet A. Smith, *Consumer Reports 1993 Travel Buying Guide* (Yonkers, NY: Consumer Reports Books, 1993), 38-44.

How much humidity should be maintained in the house during the winter?

When the outside temperature is at freezing (32 degrees Fahrenheit or 0 degrees Celcius) or above, an indoor air humidity of 35 percent to 40 percent is satisfactory. When the outside temperature decreases to 15 degrees Fahrenheit (9 degrees Celcius), a 30 percent indoor air moisture content is desirable. At 0 degrees Fahrenheit (-18 degrees Celcius), the humidity should be dropped to about 20 percent.

Roger C. Whitman, *More First Aid for the Ailing House* (New York: McGraw-Hill, 1977), 191.

In the early 1990s why was Procter & Gamble the object of a sales boycott?

In the early 1990s Procter & Gamble was accused of using satanic symbols and supporting the so-called "Church of Satan." The totally unfounded rumors and subsequent sales boycott had much to do with the "man-in-the-moon and stars" logo which had represented the corporation since 1851. Because of bad publicity, Procter & Gamble was forced to modernize its logo.

Laura Blumenfeld, "Ugly rumor puts Procter & Gamble in a devil of a bind," *Pittsburgh Press* 20 July 1991.

Is it possible for a homeowner to cancel or rescind a second mortgage or home equity loan?

A homeowner can cancel or rescind a second mortgage or home equity loan within three business days of closing if:
The homeowner refinances with a new lender; or
The homeowner takes out a larger loan to pay off the old loan from the same lender.

The rescission right does not apply to homeowners who apply to a state agency for refinancing unless that state agency is the original lender, nor does it apply to those who seek a loan from the current lender to pay off the original loan. There is no right of rescission to those seeking a loan to buy or build a home. These regulations also apply to home equity loans, and in rescinding such agreements the homeowner will be due refunds on so-called "non-refundable" fees and third-party fees for title searches, appraisals, and credit checks. The three-day rescission period begins upon receipt of the Truth In Lending disclosure. These regulations are covered by the U.S. Federal Truth In Lending Act.

"Law allows cancellation of refinance loan," *Pittsburgh Press* 8 March 1992.

How long should canceled checks, financial documents, and other related information be retained?

According to *Consumer Reports* the retention of canceled checks, financial documents, and other related information should adhere to the following schedule:

Document	Location	Time
Canceled checks, bank statements, etc.	Current file	One year
Itemized deductions	Dead storage	Five years
Credit-card numbers	Current file	Current
Contracts	Safe-deposit box	Current
Household inventory	Safe-deposit box	Up-to-date
Insurance policies	Current file	Indefinitely
Loan information	Current file	Until closed
Medical records	Current file	Up-to-date
Mortgage records ownership	Safe-deposit box	Life of ownership
Net worth statements	Current file	Indefinitely
Personal records	Safe-deposit box	Indefinitely
Real estate deeds	Safe-deposit box	Life of ownership
Receipts	Current file	Life of ownership
Stock and bond certificates	Safe-deposit box	Until sold

"Keeping records," *Consumer Reports* September 1986.

What are the benefits of travel insurance?

The high cost of travel has increased the popularity of travel insurance, policies that cover trip interruption or cancellation. Most of these policies prevent financial loss in the event of illness, injury, or death. Consumer advocates warn that these policies must be chosen carefully to assure the desired amount of coverage. Things to watch include: clauses that exclude preexisting medical conditions, cutoff dates before departure, and coverage that is worth more than the amount that could be lost in deposits and prepayments. It is also best to buy travel insurance directly from an insurance company. Insurance purchased from tour operators and travel agencies is worthless if the firms go out of business before the trip takes place.

Pittsburgh Press 13 January 1991.

What are one's rights under the Fair Credit Reporting Act?

Under the U.S. Fair Credit Reporting Act one has the following rights:
To learn the name and address of the credit reporting agency used in connection with your application for credit or a job.
To discover the nature and substance of all non-medical information in your credit report.
To know the sources of information used to compile your credit report, excluding investigative sources.
To know the names of all people who have received a credit report on you in the previous six months or 12 months depending on certain circumstances.
To have all incomplete and inaccurate information investigated and expunged.
To have the credit reporting agency notify all relevant parties of mistakes in your credit report made by the agency.
To have your side of the story appear in your credit report if differences cannot be resolved with the credit reporting agency.
To have no information older than seven years sent out, or ten years in the case of bankruptcies, except when applying for certain types of insurance policies and, jobs with salaries above certain limits.

Jonathan D. Pond, *The New Century Family Money Book* (New York: Dell Publishing, 1993), 407-08.

What is the difference between a Certified Financial Planner (CFP) and a Chartered Financial Consultant (ChFC)?

The difference between a Certified Financial Planner (CFP) and a Chartered Financial Consultant (ChFC) is a matter of degrees.

A CFP has completed a study program and passed a subsequent examination given by the College for Financial Planning in Denver, Colorado. A ChFC has passed two examinations after completing a ten section course of study administered by the American Society of Chartered Life Underwriters and Chartered Financial Consultants of Bryn Mawr, Pennsylvania.

Jonathan D. Pond, *The New Century Family Money Book* (New York: Dell Publishing, 1993), 282-83.

What are some "rules" for buying a car, particularly a used car?

When buying a car, particularly a used car, the following "rules" will help to get a good bargain:
Wear old clothes.
Don't show too much emotion or interest.
Don't be afraid to ask why the car is being sold.
Let the seller believe you have more cars to look at.
Don't be swayed when the seller tells you others are ready to buy the car.
Bring a friend to act as devil's advocate.
Don't make the first offer to buy, let the seller make the first offer to sell.
Take enough cash to at least hold the car if you decide to buy, and don't be shy about casually showing the cash to the seller.
If a bargaining stalemate is reached have your friend play good guy with the seller.
Make a fair offer and stick to it, and remember there are a lot of other cars out there.

Don Biggs, *How to Avoid Lawyers: A Step-by-Step Guide to Being Your Own Lawyer in Almost Every Situation* (New York: Garland Publishing, 1985), 445.

What are some rights of credit card holders?

Credit card holders have numerous rights including the following:
The annual fee need not be paid if the card is canceled by written notification within 40 days of receiving the bill for the annual fee.
If a card is stolen and the issuers are notified immediately, the card holder is only liable for $50 of unauthorized charges.
The lender must be notified about billing errors within 60 days. Card companies must respond to the complaint with in 30 days and resolve the problem within 90 days. The card cannot be canceled while the investigation is ongoing, and if the lender fails to respond they cannot hold the card holder for the charge.
If charged merchandise is defective and valued at $50 or more and the dispute cannot be resolved with the merchant, refusal to pay is legal. Oftentimes, however, the purchase must have been made in-state or within a 100 mile radius of the card holder's address.

Kenneth M. Morris and Alan M. Siegel, *The Wall Street Journal Guide to Understanding Personal Finance* (New York: Lightbulb Press, 1992), 44-45.

What are some ways to avoid personal bankruptcy?

Before filing for personal bankruptcy, a debtor in trouble can contact the local Consumer Credit Counseling Service. This umbrella nonprofit organization will provide names of reputable credit counseling centers. For a nominal charge, a credit counselor will offer advice and act as a go-between with creditors. In lieu of using a formal counseling service, a debtor can also speak directly with creditors to arrange alternative payment plans.

Edward A. Haman, *How to File Your Own Bankruptcy* (Clearwater, FL: Sphinx Publishing, 1992) 28-31.

What criteria do mortgage lenders use to determine whether or not the applicant can afford a particular house?

Mortgage lenders use a number of general guidelines in determining whether or not the applicant can afford a particular house. These guidelines include the following:

Mortgage lenders generally feel that home buyers can afford a house worth two and one-half times their annual income, providing they have ten percent of the purchase price as a down payment. Mortgage lenders also feel that homeowners can afford to spend 28 percent of their total income on mortgage payments, property taxes, and homeowners' insurance. However, mortgage payments and other debt payments—such as credit cards and automobile loans—must not total more than 36 percent of total income. This is known as the 28/36 qualifying ratio. Simply multiply monthly income by .28 to determine the maximum acceptable mortgage payment or multiply monthly income by .36 to determine the acceptable maximum monthly payments for all debts.

Kenneth M. Morris and Alan M. Siegel, *The Wall Street Journal Guide To Understanding Personal Finance* (Lightbulb Press, 1992), 54.

What are some guidelines regarding auction participation?

There are several common sense rules that should be utilized by prospective buyers at an auction. The first is to avoid "auction fever"—becoming swept away by the frenzy of the moment and involved in a bidding war on an item. This may lead to a disastrous financial situation. It is also a good idea to thoroughly investigate any item that you might wish to purchase before the bidding opens. Get an official appraisal on it or find the market value of a comparable piece. Fix a spending limit. Become familiar with the conditions of the sale, especially regarding the method of payment required as some auctions are cash and carry only, and the merchandise pick-up procedure. First time auction attendees should first avoid bidding but should simply observe. It's also wise to remember that an auction is essentially a sale and the auctioneer a professional sales person—working on commission—and often quite proficient at high-pressure sales techniques.

George C. Chelekis, *The Official Government Auction Guide* (New York: Crown Publishers, 1992), 48-49.

What are the basic types of auctions?

There are four basic types of auctions: public, sealed bid, spot bid, and negotiated sale. A public auction is conducted by vocal bids from the audience until the highest price for an item is called out. If no one shouts a higher bid, the item goes to the last bidder. In a sealed bid auction, a bid is mailed and opened in secret. The highest offer receives the item, and the bidder is usually informed of the purchase by mail. A spot bid auction combines the first two: -the bidder brings a secret bid to the auction site, and the auctioneer opens up the bids. The purchaser is the one with the highest sealed bid. A negotiated sale takes place through the mail or over telephone wires. The offers are accepted by phone or mail by the seller, either a government agency or an auctioneer. Again, the highest offer wins—and pays for—the merchandise.

George C. Chelekis, *The Official Government Auction Guide* (New York: Crown Publishers, 1992), 24-25.

Economics

What was the significance of the Schuman Plan?

The European Economic Community (Common Market) had its origin in the Schuman Plan. On May 9, 1950, Robert Schuman (1886-1963), the French foreign minister, made a proposal for the integration of the Western European coal and steel industry. Principally the French hoped to create an economic bond with Germany that would ensure a regular supply of coal from the Ruhr valley and diminish the threat of German militarism. On April 18, 1951, France, Germany, Italy, and the Benelux countries formed the European Coal and Steel Community, and in 1957 these same countries created the Common Market.

George C. Kohn, *Dictionary of Historic Documents* (New York: Facts on File, 1991), s.v. "Schuman Plan."

What economic indicators do financial experts look at when evaluating the direction of the economy?

When evaluating the direction of the economy, financial experts look at various economic indicators for danger signals including auto sales, consumer credit, housing starts, GNP, industrial production, capacity utilization, labor productivity, producer prices, consumer prices, consumer sentiment, and the Dow Jones P/E ratio.

Michael B. Lehman, *The Dow Jones-Irwin Guide to Using the Wall Street Journal, 3d ed.* (Homewood, IL: Dow Jones-Irwin, 1990), 158-59.

What is dialectical materialism?

Dialectical materialism is an economic theory created by Karl Marx (1818-1883) and Friedrich Engels (1820-1895). According to this theory, labor is a valuable commodity while capital is "stored" labor alienated from the proletariat. Workers are constantly in danger of losing their employment because as they produce more and more capital, they are replaced in factories by automation. This leads to a tremendous increase in unemployed labor. Eventually, the pool of desperate and impoverished unemployed workers will rise up in revolution and seize the productive capacity of the state. The state itself, Marx theorized, would collapse because its only purpose is to foster competing economic interests. Marx's theory of dialectical materialism has been widely criticized by economists as flawed and implausible.

Chris Cook, *Dictionary of Historical Terms: A guide to names and events of over 1,000 years of world history* (New York: Peter Bedrick Books, 1983), "dialectical materialism."

What is Gresham's Law?

Gresham's Law states, "Bad money drives out good." Postulated by English financier Sir Thomas Gresham (1519-1579) to Queen Elizabeth I (1596-1662), his law was formulated in relation to the debasement of English coin. His law asserts that when coins made of a valuable metal are followed by the same coins made of a lesser metal, the former will be hoarded and will disappear from use.

William A. Sabin and Nancy Warren, eds., *The McGraw-Hill Dictionary of Modern Economics: A Handbook of Terms and Organizations, 3d ed.* (New York: McGraw-Hill Book Company, 1983), s.v. "Gresham's law."

What is Adam Smith's "invisible hand" theory?

Scottish economist Adam Smith's (1723-1790) "invisible hand" theory purports that when individuals pursue their own self-interests, this will simultaneously promote the interests of their society, as if guided by an "invisible hand." A competitive marketplace would, therefore, hold greed and excess in check. Smith's theory first appeared in his *Wealth of Nations* (1776).

The Encyclopedic Dictionary of Economics, 3d ed. (Guilford, CT: Dushkin Publishing Group, 1986), s.v. "invisible hand."

What is mercantilism?

Mercantilism, a popular economic theory among trading nations during the seventeenth and early eighteenth centuries, held that a nation's wealth and power would increase by exporting goods for gold. Mercantilism, however, often led to high tariffs, trading wars, and restrictions on the sale of precious metals. Director of the East India Company and defender of the theory of balance of trade Thomas Mun (1571-1641) put forth the precepts of mercantilism in *England's Treasure by Foreign Trade* (1621) which later Scottish economist Adam Smith (1723-1790) criticized the theory in *The Wealth of Nations* (1776).

William A. Sabin and Nancy Warren, eds., *The McGraw-Hill Dictionary of Modern Economics: A Handbook of Terms and Organizations, 3d ed.* (New York: McGraw-Hill Book Company, 1983), s.v. "mercantilism."

Who are "The Group of Thirty"?

The Group of Thirty is a group of economics experts who meet continually to discuss the world's economic and monetary systems. It was established in December of 1978. Among the founders were two officials-turned-private bankers, a former British treasury official, a vice-chairman of the board of trustees of the Rockefeller Foundation, a Federal Reserve governor, a former president of Germany's central bank, the prime minister of the Philippines, a deputy governor of the Bank of Hungary, and the president of the French bank Crdit National.

The Rockefeller Foundation launched the group with a grant of about $1.5 million, to be spread over three years. Its office is in New York, and meetings are organized every two to three months, with several study groups going on at any given time. Each meeting lasts two and a half days and starts with a roundtable discussion on world economic developments, with particular emphasis on inflation and unemployment. Subsequent discussions focus on special issues, usually backed up by background papers or study group reports. A strong focus of the group is on ways to strengthen international cooperation among major countries in economic policymaking.

Marjorie Deane, "The Group of Thirty," *RF Illustrated* June 1982.

In business what is meant by outsourcing?

The business practice known as outsourcing involves contracting other businesses for services that are normally provided in-house. Generally, big businesses contract smaller, specialized companies to provide them with services such as housekeeping, architectural design, grounds maintenance, food service, and security, to name a few.

"Out is in," *Entrepreneur* May 1994.

What is the meaning of supply-side economics?

The name "supply-side" was invented in 1976 by economist Herbert Stein, who was actually a critic of this theory which is based on the idea that the economy should not be influenced by government manipulation of demand for goods and services. Instead, government should influence the supply by encouraging producers to increase output, thereby increasing employment and controlling inflation. To accomplish this, economists advocate tax cuts and deregulation, both of which were practiced by the administration of U.S. president Ronald Reagan (1911-).

Christine Ammer and Dean Ammer, *Dictionary of Business and Economics, rev. ed.* (New York: Free Press, 1984), s.v. "supply-side economics, Reaganomics."

What is "Bolton's Law"?

"Bolton's Law" states that under current practices expenditures and revenues rise to meet each other, regardless of which one may be in excess.

Time 6 April 1974.

What is meant by the term cheese-pare?

The term cheese-pare refers to an attempt to save money through economizing in a manner similar to paring cheese.

Oxford English Dictionary Additions Series (Oxford: Clarendon Press, 1993), s.v. "cheese-paring."

What is the meaning of the terms macroeconomics and microeconomics?

The terms macroeconomics and microeconomics refer to specific methodologies of analyzing an economy. Macroeconomics looks at the large picture—the total output of an economy, its gross income and expenditures, employment data, and cost factors. These segments of information are collected for study and the economy's overall health is assessed with these figures in mind. In contrast, microeconomics analyzes one small segment of an economy— one business enterprise, or one family—to determine its overall fiscal health and future.

The Encyclopedic Dictionary of Economics, 3d ed. (Guilford, CT: Dushkin Publishing, 1986), s.v. "macroeconomics" and "microeconomics."

In Marxist thought, what is the proletariat?

In Marxist thought, the proletariat is the class of wage earners denied control of the implements and means of production. The proletariat, together with the capitalist class who do control the implements and means of production, compose a bourgeois society.

Great Soviet Encyclopedia (New York: Macmillan, 1978), s.v. "proletariat."

What is the relationship between war and inflation?

The United States has frequently seen dramatic price increases during times of war. The additional military spending often causes production surges and a shortage of products for the average consumer. Prices rise as demand outstrips supply. Dramatic inflation was experienced during the American Revolutionary War (1775-1783), when prices rose 201 percent. The American Civil War (1861-1865) caused prices in Union states to jump 117 percent; Confederate states, however, suffered far worse, their prices were multiplied 9,210 percent. World War I (1914-1918)inflated prices 126 percent and World War II (1939-1945) created an increase of 108 percent. During the Vietnam Conflict (1957-1975), American prices rose 69 percent.

Sylvia Nasar, "An Exception to Rule of War: Inflation Threat Is Receding," *New York Times* 10 March 1991.

Finance

What is meant by net asset value when referring to a mutual fund?

In discussing mutual funds, the net asset value is the dollar value of one share of the stock of a mutual fund. A mutual fund is a professionally managed investment opportunity in which a large group of people pool their money to invest in the stock market. A prospective joiner of the fund will want to know its net asset value. This can be obtained by tallying up the fund's total holdings, subtracting any debt, and dividing that figure by the number of shares.

Kenneth M. Morris and Alan M. Siegel, *The Wall Street Journal Guide to Understanding Personal Finance* (New York: Lightbulb Press, 1992), 142.

How long does it take the average taxpayer to prepare his or her federal income tax return?

The U.S. Internal Revenue Service estimates it takes the average taxpayer ten hours and 27 minutes to prepare his or her federal income tax return. Three hours and 23 minutes are spent filling out the 1040 form, one hour and 26 minutes are devoted to filling out schedules A and B, and five hours and 38 minutes are usually spent gathering tax forms and records together and familiarizing oneself with the materials and tax regulations.

Kenneth M. Morris and Alan M. Siegel, *The Wall Street Journal Guide to Understanding Personal Finance* (Lightbulb Press, 1992), 155.

When was the private ownership of gold outlawed in the United States?

Private ownership of gold coin, currency, and bullion was illegal from 1933 to 1974. When the law took effect during the Depression, citizens and companies were forced to turn over their personal gold reserves to the U.S. Treasury, but received compensation. According to U.S. President Franklin D. Roosevelt's (1882-1945) Executive Order No. 6260, the order was necessary "to provide relief in the existing national emergency in banking and for other purposes."

Beth Deisher, ed., *Coin World Almanac, 5th ed.* (New York: World Almanac, 1987), 79-80.

What is an ESOP?

An employee stock ownership plan is known as an ESOP and is considered an excellent financial strategy for all parties concerned. An ESOP falls under the company's benefit plan and typically gives workers shares of its nonvoting common stock. The company receives a tax credit for the donation of stock. It is assumed that stock-holding employees will be better motivated to see the company perform well in its field and thus increase the value of their stock. The ESOP plan is allowed to borrow from banks in order to purchase additional shares, and the financial institution that advances the money does not pay income tax on the interest the loan has generated. In the 1980s many companies began ESOPs as a way to fend off hostile takeovers when "corporate raiders" obtained large blocks of shares of a company in an attempt to take it over. Granting stock to employees meant that management was placing it the hands of those least desirous to let go of it— and least desirous of seeing a change in the status quo of their working environment—no matter what price the raiders were offering for the shares.

Paul A. Argenti, *The Portable MBA Desk Reference: An Essential Business Companion* (New York: John Wiley & Sons, 1994), s.v. "employee stock ownership plan." Michael Blumstein, "The New Role for ESOP's," *New York Times* 2 January 1984.

What face designs were used on the first paper money?

In 1862 the United States government issued its first legal tender paper money in the form of demand notes made payable by the United States Treasury Department. The new notes were soon nicknamed "greenbacks," a term that remains in use today. The five-dollar note featured a portrait of the first U.S. Secretary of the Treasury Alexander Hamilton (1755-1804) at right and a statue of Columbia at left. Lincoln (1809-1868) was portrayed on the right on the ten-dollar note, with a stylized woman representing Art on the left. The 20-dollar note featured Liberty.

Beth Deisher, ed., *Coin World Almanac: A Handbook for Coin Collectors, 5th ed.* (Sidney, OH: Amos Press, 1987), 244-45, 262-64.

What is meant by the term "Black Monday"?

The term "Black Monday" refers to a stock market crash that occurred on October 19, 1987. During the course of the day, Wall Street's barometers of economic health fell to record lows. This occurrence mirrored the stock market crash of 1929, called "Black Friday," that preceded the Great Depression. The Dow Jones Industrial Average—a fluctuating number based on the stock performances of the thirty leading companies on the New York Stock Exchange—fell 508 points on that day in 1987. The 22.6 percent drop in the value of these stocks was the most precipitous since before World War I, and some analysts held modern technology partly to blame. The speed with which shares could be bought and sold electronically helped create a panic-selling situation among Wall Street traders. World financial markets also plummeted over the next few days, while domestic politicians and fiscal policy experts assured American citizens and business leaders that the economy was in good health.

Facts on File 23 October 1987. Allan H. Pessin and Joseph A. Ross, *The Complete Words of Wall Street: The Professional's Guide to Investment Literacy* (Homewood, IL: Business One Irwin, 1991), 66.

How does the over-the-counter (OTC) market differ from the regular stock market?

The over-the-counter market differs from the regular stock market in that its trading does not take place in a fixed location. Instead, it is a network of brokers and dealers who buy and sell shares from one another via the telephone or other means of electronic communication. The transactions of New York Stock Exchange (NYSE) and the American Stock Exchange (AMEX), on the other hand, occur on the exchanges' trading floors on Wall Street in New York City. The types of stocks traded also differ between the regular stock and OTC markets. The nation's largest companies are generally traded on the NYSE, while the stocks of smaller firms are bought and sold on the AMEX as well as on regional stock exchanges. Stocks from new or small niche companies are bought and sold on the OTC market. Some, but not all, of the transaction data in a day's OTC trading is tracked by the National Association of Security Dealers Automatic Quote System (NASDAQ) index.

Sumner N. Levine and Caroline Levine, eds., *The Irwin Business and Investment Almanac 1994* (Burr Ridge, IL: Irwin Professional Publishing, 1994), 432.

What is a junk bond?

The term junk bond refers to a bond with low credit rating, generally BB or below. They are considered speculative, or risky, investments.

Allan H. Pessin and Joseph A. Ross, *The Complete Words of Wall Street: The Professional's Guide to Investment Literacy* (Homewood, IL: Business One Irwin, 1991), 368.

What is a zero coupon security?

The term "zero coupon" refers to a debt security issued by a corporation or government at a price well below its face value. At maturity, it can be redeemed for its face value, and the difference in the amounts is considered interest income. Zero coupon bonds are sometimes redeemable prior to maturity and generally do not mature until at least a year after issuance.

Allan H. Pessin and Joseph A. Ross, *The Complete Words of Wall Street: The Professional's Guide to Investment Literacy* (Homewood, IL: Business One Irwin, 1991), s.v. "zero coupon."

What effect do presidential elections have on the stock market in the United States?

In general, presidential elections usually coincide with an increase in the value of stocks. Since 1900, the Dow Jones Industrial Average—a performance barometer of the 30 leading stocks on the New York Stock Exchange—has risen an average of ten points during the last few months of nearly every election year. Several theories have been offered to explain this, one being that during their campaigns, incumbent politicians up for reelection often insure that the economy appears to be thriving.

New York Times 10 July 1992.

What is seigniorage?

Seigniorage is the difference between the cost of coin production and the monetary value of a coin.

Beth Deisher, ed., *Coin World Almanac: A Handbook for Coin Collectors, 5th ed.* (Sidney, OH: Amos Press, 1987), 197.

When did the Dow Jones closing average first go over 1000?

In November 14, 1972, the Dow Jones average closed over 1000 for the first time. The closing average was 1003.16.

Fred L. Worth, *The Trivia Encyclopedia* (New York: Bell Publishing Company, 1974), 189.

What do the terms "bull" and "bear" mean when applied to the stock market?

The term "bear market" refers to a declining stock market. According to one theory, it was so named because bears fight by striking downward with their paws. "Bull market" indicates a rising stock market, because bulls toss their horns upward when attacking.

Jane Polley, ed., *Stories Behind Everyday Things* (Pleasantville, NY: The Reader's Digest Association, 1980), 332.

Who was America's first millionaire?

Elias Hasket Derby, a merchant of Salem, Massachusetts, became America's first millionaire. Nicknamed "King," Derby made his money from the profitable sea trade of his time.

Isaac Asimov, *Isaac Asimov's Book of Facts* (New York: Bell Publishing, 1981), 62.

When were the first one-, two-, and five-dollar bills issued?

The currently used small-sized paper money notes were first issued in mid-1929, although some carry the series year designation 1928. The one-dollar bill, featuring a portrait of the first U.S. President George Washington (1732-1799), bears the Series 1928 imprint. The two-dollar note, featuring U.S. President Thomas Jefferson (1743-1826) on the front and his home, Monticello, on the back, was first printed in the Series 1928 and was discontinued in 1966. The five-dollar note, featuring U.S. President Abraham Lincoln (1809-1865) on the front and the Lincoln Memorial on the back, was also issued with the Series 1928 imprint.

Beth Deisher, ed., *Coin World Almanac: A Handbook for Coin Collectors, 5th ed.* (Sidney, OH: Amos Press, 1987), 255-56.

When were United States postage stamps used as currency?

Shortages of silver coinage during the American Civil War led the U.S. Congress to propose the use of postage stamps as currency. An Act of July 17, 1862, monetized the postage and other stamps of the United States. By August 21, 1862, the first notes of a postage currency issue were released by the Treasury Department. These notes bore the imprints of the contemporary five-and ten-cent postage stamps. U.S. presidents, Thomas Jefferson (1743-1826) appeared on the five-and 25-cent issues and George Washington (1732-1799) on the ten-and 50-cent notes. Counterfeiting became a prevalent problem with this currency. The small notes continued to circulate until an Act of January 14, 1875, provided for their retirement.

Beth Deisher, ed., *Coin World Almanac: A Handbook for Coin Collectors* (Sidney, OH: Amos Press, 1987), 254.

What is "arbitrage"?

"Arbitrage" is the process of simultaneously buying a security, currency, or commodity on one market and selling it in another in order to profit from a price discrepancy. The cumulative effect of this eventually evens out the price of security, currency, or commodity in both markets.

Parul A. Argenti, ed., *The Portable MBA Desk Reference: An Essential Business Companion* (New York: John Wiley & Sons, 1994), s.v. "arbitrage."

What would a nickel buy in the first automat vending machine in 1902?

A nickel could buy virtually everything at an automat in 1902 when the first one opened, including the following items: a cup of coffee, a slice of apple pie, a bowl of tapioca pudding, a bowl of macaroni and cheese, a ham sandwich, and a bowl of baked beans.

Bethany Kandel, "Glass door closes on the automat era," *USA Today* 9 November 1990.

What is the oldest form of money?

The cowrie shell, a small, delicately shaded mollusk native to the shores of the Indian and Pacific Oceans, is probably the oldest form of money. Cowries were evidently used as early as 20,000 B.C., having been discovered in Cro-Magnon graves dating from that time. They were also discovered in the Neolithic ruins of Nineveh. Marco Polo (1254-1324) described their use by Chinese merchants. As late as the nineteenth century cowrie shells were used as currency in Africa, and as late as the onset of World War II (1939-45) they were an accepted medium of exchange in parts of Southeast Asia.

Jane Polley, ed., *Stories Behind Everyday Things,* (Pleasantville, NY: The Reader's Digest Association, 1980), 223.

Where did the term "underwriter" from the insurance industry originate?

Edward Lloyd (d. 1713), whose name was eventually adopted by the most well-known group of insurance underwriters in the world, Lloyd's of London, owned a coffeehouse in London in the 1680s and 1690s that became a gathering place for sailors and ships' captains. As time passed Lloyd established a network of correspondents all over the continent. Money was put up by many of his patrons to insure safe passage of ships to various ports of call. Lloyd's insurers oftentimes wrote their names on brokers' slips below the amounts they were willing to cover in the event of loss. From this practice the term "underwriter" probably evolved.

Jane Polley, ed., *Stories Behind Everyday Things,* (Pleasantville, NY: The Reader's Digest Association, 1980), 193.

In financial parlance what are "liquid assets"?

In financial parlance the phrase "liquid assets" refers to either currency or other holdings that are quickly convertible to currency such as bank demand deposits or U.S. government savings bonds.

William A. Sabin and Nancy Warren, eds., *The McGraw-Hill Dictionary of Modern Economics: A Handbook of Terms and Organizations, 3d ed.* (New York: McGraw-Hill Book Company, 1983), s.v. "liquid asset."

What is a negative income tax?

A negative income tax (NIT) guarantees a minimum income for families with no other source of income, or a supplemental income for families whose income falls below the minimum preset level.

The Encyclopedic Dictionary of Economics, 3d ed. (Guilford, CT: Dushkin Publishing Group, 1986), s.v. "negative income tax (NIT)."

Who was the first American billionaire?

The first American billionaire was oil tycoon John D. Rockefeller (1839-1937). According to *Forbes Magazine,* in March 2, 1918, Rockefeller was far ahead of the other nine wealthiest men in the United States. The rest were only millionaires . Below are the wealthiest men in 1918:

Name	Estimated fortune (millions)	Yearly income (millions)	Chief source
John D. Rockefeller	$1,200	$60.00	oil
H. C Frick	$225	$11.25	coke, steel
Andrew Carnegie	$200	$10.00	steel
George F. Baker	$150	$7.50	banking
William Rockefeller	$150	$7.50	oil, railroads
Edward S. Harkness	$125	$6.25	oil
J. Ogden Armour	$125	$6.25	packing
Henry Ford	$100	$5.00	automobiles
W. K. Vanderbilt	$100	$5.00	railroads
Ed H. R. Green	$100	$5.00	banking

"Our 30 Richest Americans," *Forbes,* Fall 1983. Dennis Sanders, *First of Everything* (New York: Delacorte Press, 1981), 164.

When was the copper dollar coin first proposed by the United States Treasury?

The copper dollar coin was first proposed by the United States Treasury in 1978. Treasury officials argued that it would be relatively cheap to produce and last at least fifteen years, compared with the 18-month lifespan of an average dollar bill. The new coin would join the Eisenhower silver dollar, which had yet to enter general circulation. The new copper dollar— actually a copper-nickel blend—was introduced in July of 1979. It bore the likeness of Susan B. Anthony, a nineteenth-century American suffragette who campaigned to win women and African-Americans the right to vote.

Pittsburgh Post-Gazette 22 February 1978. *Pittsburgh Press* 1 October 1978, 1 July 1979.

What was the first country to use the word "dollar" on a coin?

The word "dollar" was first used on a coin by the West African nation of Sierra Leone. In 1791, it began issuing coins with the words "One Dollar." The United States Treasury had been minting coins in dollar denominations since 1794, but did not use the word until after 1836.

"First 'dollar'," *Pittsburgh Press* 3 February 1987.

What is a tontine?

A financial term named for a seventeenth-century Italian, Tonti, the tontine is a financial arrangement between several parties in which the parties agree that if one of the partners dies or defaults, his or her advantages are distributed to the other participants. When only one person remains, all the benefits of the other participants go to this person. If the agreed-upon period of the tontine expires and several members remain, all of the available benefits are distributed equally among the participants. The tontine is often used in some types of life insurance policies.

Henry Campbell Black et al., *Black's Law Dictionary* (St. Paul, MN: West Publishing Co., 1990), s.v. "tontine."

How is the grade of a coin determined?

The grade of a coin describes its level of preservation. Determinants used in grading coins are contact marks (surface marks caused by collision between the coin and other objects), luster (reflection of light off the surface of the coin), wear (especially at the coin's high points), strike (evenness of metal-flow into the crevices of the die), and toning and color (changes caused by oxidation, reaction to pollutants, etc.).

Beth Deisher, ed., *Coin World Almanac: A Handbook for Coin Collectors, 5th ed.* (Sidney, OH: Amos Press and New York: World Alamanac, 1987), 505-8.

What are blue chip stocks?

Blue chip stocks come from large companies with long-term track records of high performance. The term is derived from poker chips, of which blue are the most valuable.

Michael Johnson, *Business Buzzwords: The Tough New Jargon of Modern Business* (London: Basil Blackwell, 1990), s.v. "blue chip."

What is "Ginnie Mae"?

"Ginnie Mae" is affectionate stock market slang for the Government National Mortgage Association (GNMA). GNMA is a government-owned corporation that purchases, packages, and resells mortgages and often uses them as collateral for securities issues.

Michael B. Lehmann, *The Dow Jones-Irwin Guide to Using the Wall Street Journal, 3d ed.* (Homewood, IL: Dow Jones-Irwin, 1990), 238-39.

What were the beginnings of the Rothschild banking dynasty?

The Rothschild banking dynasty was begun by Mayer Amschel Rothschild (1744-1812) with his founding of a Frankfurt banking house. By the 1820s under the leadership of Mayer, and eventually his five sons: Amschel Mayer (1773-1855), Salomon Mayer (1774-1855), Nathan Mayer (1777-1836), Karl Mayer (1788-1855), and Jakob or James Mayer (1792-1868), the bank had branches in London, Paris, Vienna, and Naples.

The New Encyclopaedia Britannica, 15th ed. (Chicago: Encyclopaedia Britannica, 1989), s.v. "Rothschild family."

What August 1914 event caused a virtual collapse of financial and security markets in the United States and Europe?

The August 1914 outbreak of World War I (1914-18) in Europe caused a virtual collapse of financial and security markets in the United States and Europe. According to financial reporters, all of the world's leading stock exchanges were closed, the foreign exchange market was demoralized, there was a tremendous outflow of gold from New York, and there was a rise in the price of grain, cotton, and other commodities. The issuance of weekly bank statements by the New York Clearing-House Association was suspended on August 8 not to be resumed until December.

Commercial and Financial Chronicle 1 August 1914, 5 December 1914.

What was the original name of the Bank of America?

The original name of San Francisco's Bank of America, one of the largest in the world, was surprisingly the Bank of Italy. It was founded in 1904 by A.P. Giannini who felt that existing banks ignored the large Italian colony in the North Beach section of San Francisco. In 1930 the name of the institution was changed to the Bank of America.

Marquis James and Bessie Rowland James, *Biography of a Bank: The Story of the Bank of America* (New York: Harper & Brothers, 1954), 1-3.

Whose signatures appear on U.S. paper money?

The various handwritten and signature facsimiles that appear on U.S. paper money lends an aura of authority to the note. Postage currency, second issue of fractional currency, and 3-cent third issue fractional currency do not bear signatures. National bank notes bear the signatures of the Register, Treasurer, bank president, and bank cashier. Federal Reserve Bank notes also bear the signatures of two Federal Reserve officers. By the time of the Lincoln presidency (1861-65) signing currency had become an arduous task and legislation was passed allowing Treasury personnel to sign first demand notes with their name and "For The" before the respective titles. Beginning in 1863 paper money plates were engraved with the signatures of Treasury officials. Beginning in 1862 the signature of the Register of the Treasury appeared on paper money to be replaced in 1925 with the signatures of the Secretary of the Treasury and the Treasurer of the United States.

Beth Deisher, ed., *Coin World Almanac, 5th ed.* (New York: Amos Press, 1987), 277-78.

What value was placed on treasure found on a sunken Spanish galleon in 1986?

In 1986 divers in the Bahamas found the remains of the Spanish galleon Nuestra Senora de la Maravilla, which sank in 1656. Over the centuries many adventurers had tried but failed to find the wreck. The galleon's treasure of gold, silver, emeralds, and other artifacts was valued at $1.6 billion. One of the first jewels recovered was a 49.5 carat emerald worth $1 million. Spanish records indicate that the ship carried 30 to 40 tons of silver and a solid gold three-foot statue of the Madonna and Child. The wreck was discovered in only thirty feet of water about 50 miles north of Grand Bahama Island by a team of divers and archaeologists that had been assembled by Memphis businessman Herbert Humphreys, Jr. Under Bahamian law the government gets 25 percent of the total worth of a treasure trove and first choice of what to keep. The remainder of the treasure is then returned to the finder.

In January of 1656 the Maravilla left Vera Cruz with its precious cargo and 650 mostly wealthy passengers. After stopping in Havana, the Maravilla collided with another ship in heavy fog and sank. Spanish salvage efforts failed but not before ripping open the hull and scattering the treasure around the wreck.

Pittsburgh Press 26 November 1986.

What are the Seven Laws of Money?

In his book *The Seven Laws of Money,* author Michael Phillips states what he considers are the properties of money. His seven laws are the following:

Money will come when you are doing the right thing.
Money has its own rules, records, budgets, savings, borrowings.
Money is a dream: a fantasy as alluring as the Pied Piper.
Money is a nightmare: in jail, robbery, fears of poverty.
You can never really give money away.
You can never really receive money as a gift.
There are worlds without money.

Harold Faber, *The Book of Laws* (New York: Times Books, 1979), 59

To what does the term "Private Gold" refer?

There have been instances in the history of the United States where Private coins were circulated due to a shortage of regular currency. These coins are referred to as "Private Gold" because they were not minted at the United States Mint. Private gold comes in various shapes and denominations. In the past, private gold had been circulated in isolated areas of the country by bankers, assayers, and private citizens.

R.S. Yeoman, *1994 Handbook of United States Coins, 51st ed.* (Racine, WI: Western Publishing Company, 1993), 169.

What are some of the pitfalls of an annuity?

The tax-deferred advantages of an annuity can sometimes be offset by sales charges, surrender fees, management costs, and other expenses. Some of these disadvantages can be avoided by choosing a no-or low-load annuity; shop around.

Nancy Dunnan, *Dun & Bradstreet Guide to Your Investments: 1994* (New York: HarperPerennial, 1994), 317.

How can a person calculate currency exchange?

If a person plans on traveling overseas for business or pleasure, it is essential to learn how to calculate currency exchange, which is a fairly straightforward process. Suppose a person wants to exchange 50 British pounds for the equivalent in United States dollars and one British pound is equal to 1.50 U.S. dollars. Multiply 50 British pounds and $1.50. The answer would be 50 British pounds is equal to 75 U.S. dollars.

In order to exchange U.S. dollars for foreign currency, division is used. Suppose a person wants to exchange 20 U.S. dollars for the equivalent number of Columbian pesos. A table of exchange rates indicates that one dollar is equal to .001583 Columbian pesos. Divide 20 U.S. dollars by .001583 Columbian pesos. The answer would be 20 U.S. dollars is equal to 12,634 Columbian pesos.

Susan H. Munger, *The International Business Communications Desk Reference* (New York: American Management Association, 1993), 136.

Where can a person buy foreign currency?

Persons who plan on traveling abroad may wish to buy foreign currency before their departure. One of the best places to obtain foreign currency is an exchange or money broker. Money brokers are companies that specialize in the buying and selling of currencies. Most money brokers are located in major metropolitan areas and international airports. A visit to a large money broker is recommended, especially if someone is attempting to obtain currency from a country that is rarely visited by Americans.

Foreign currency can sometimes be purchased through a travel agency. Large travel agencies in major metropolitan areas are usually the best bet for obtaining foreign currency.

Hotels that cater to a large number of foreign visitors may also convert American dollars to foreign currency. However, hotels may convert only a limited number of currencies and charge more for their services than a money broker.

It should be noted that some countries do not allow their currency to be sold outside their borders. In these cases, a traveler must wait until the destination is reached before converting currency.

Susan H. Munger, *The International Business Communications Desk Reference* (New York: American Management Association, 1993), 137-38.

What is an S corporation?

An S corporation is a type of corporation that is not subject to personal holding company or accumulated earnings penalty taxes, but allows for limited liability and transferability of interests. S corporations do not pay federal taxes, but pass all of their income to shareholders or owners. The S corporation is considered a favorable option for new business entrepreneurs.

Gustav Berle, *The Small Business Information Handbook* (New York: John Wiley and Sons, 1990), s.v. "S corporation."

Where did the dollar sign, $, come from?

Explanations for the origin of the dollar sign vary. The predominant theory traces the symbol's origins to Greek mythology and later Spanish conquest. In ancient times, the Greeks believed the Straits of Gibraltar were the end of the world. According to Greek mythology, the two land masses flanking the straits—the rock of Gibraltar and the Jebel Muza—had been placed there by Hercules during his twelve labors and thus came to be known as the Pillars of Hercules. In 1492 when the Christian Spanish monarchs finally succeeded in expelling the Muslim Moors from Spain and King Ferdinand was able to place Gibraltar under Spanish rule, he commemorated the event by incorporating two pillars draped by a ribbon inscribed with the words "Non plus ultra"—"there is nothing more beyond" or "the unsurpassable"—into his royal arms. In that same year Christopher Columbus discovered the Americas, prompting the Spanish kings to change the inscription to "Plus ultra"—"there is something beyond" or "onward." To the Spaniards, the Pillars of Hercules became symbolic of the New World and the wealth in gold and silver that they discovered there.

The symbolic Pillars of Hercules was minted on the coins the Spaniards produced, along with their coat of arms. It became so common and popular in colonial America that it was copied by other European states, who incorporated the pillars into their own currency. When the United States established its own currency after 1776, they used a simplified version of the sign on the Spanish coin, which is the dollar sign as we know it today—an S-like shape intersected by two vertical lines.

Sven Tito Achen, *Symbols Around Us* (New York: Van Nostrand Reinhold, 1978), 216-18.

What was the subject of the first special issue stamp printed in the United States?

The printing of special issue stamps by the United States government began in 1893 with the release of a stamp commemorating Christopher Columbus's discovery of America. Generally, up until 1890 most governments issued portrait stamps, with George Washington appearing on the common United States stamp. Many governments saw an interest in collecting stamps as an opportunity to turn a hobby into a big government business. It was felt that colorful and pictorial stamps might attract the interest of stamp collectors.

M. Thomas Inge, ed., *Handbook of American Popular Culture* (Westport, CT: Greenwood Press, 1981), 3:462.

How does a pawnshop work?

A pawnshop is a place where loans are issued on personal property brought into the store as collateral. When the loan and the interest fee is paid off, the property is returned to the owner.

Although it is up to the individual pawnbroker what items the pawnshop will accept, generally brokers prefer articles such as jewelry, musical instruments, cameras, computers, typewriters, and silverware. The article should have a good resale value.

If the loan is not paid in the time agreed upon, the broker usually notifies the client that the payment is past due. If the loan remains unpaid, the pawnbroker usually puts the article up for sale. So, the broker sells articles as well as makes loans and stores items.

There are several laws controlling the activities of pawnbrokers and pawnshops. In most cities the interest rates charged on the borrowed money is regulated by state or local laws. Likewise, many states require that pawnbrokers give the local police a list of items brought in as collateral for loans. The list describes the articles and provides serial numbers so the police can check if the merchandise was stolen. If the items were stolen property, the articles have to be returned to the rightful owner.

The Book of Inside Information (New York: Boardroom Classics, 1991), 19.

How has the mutual fund industry grown in the United States in recent years?

The U.S. mutual fund industry underwent great growth in the years between 1986 and 1993. In 1986 the total assets of all mutual funds were $716.2 billion. There has been a steady rise in mutual fund assets since 1990, when the funds recorded values at $1 trillion. By mid-1993 mutual assets registered values of $1.8 trillion.

The rise in financial values was reflected in the growth in the number of funds and the increase in shareholder accounts. In 1986, for example, the number of reporting mutual funds was 1,843 with a total of 46.1 million shareholder accounts recorded. In 1990, the number of reporting mutual funds rose to 3,105, with a total of 62.6 million shareholder accounts reported. By 1993, there were 4,224 reporting mutual funds, with over 77.2 million shareholder accounts. This dynamic and unprecedented growth can be attributed to several factors, including lower interest rates and the ensuing infusion of cash into mutual funds, plus record performance for the securities markets in the United States and abroad. Looking for a greater return on their investment dollar, large numbers of customers turned from the low interest rates paid on more traditional savings accounts to the higher profits reaped from mutual funds.

U.S. Industrial Outlook 1994 (Washington, DC: U.S. Department of Commerce, 1994), 46-5.

What is red-lining?

Red-lining means to circle or mark in red ink but it also refers to the crossing off of areas that are considered off limits or unacceptable. Today the term "red-lining" applies to the refusal of certain lending institutions to lend money on property in areas considered undesirable. It has racial connotations in that redlined neighborhoods often have a large minority population.

The Oxford English Dictionary, 2nd ed. (Oxford: Clarendon Press, 1989), s.v. "red-line."

How many old pesos equal a new peso?

On January 1, 1993, the Mexican peso lost three zeros as new peso coins and bills went into circulation. The new peso equals 1,000 former pesos, in a move aimed at simplifying calculations without devaluing the national currency.

"'New Peso' for Mexico on Jan. 1," *New York Times* 20 December 1992.

What is Black Tuesday?

Black Tuesday, the most devastating day in the history of the New York Stock Exchange, occurred on October 29, 1929. Over 16,410,030 shares were sold at rapidly declining prices--more than three times the number usually sold on a big day. The panic to sell stock had begun on the prior Thursday, known as Black Thursday, when 12,894,650 shares changed hands. This period, known as the Great Stock Market Crash, contributed to the beginning of the Great Depression.

John Kenneth Galbraith, *The Great Crash, 1929* (New York: Avon Books, 1980), vii, 87-89, 99-101, 149.

Who was the first African-American millionaire?

The first African-American millionaire was William A. Liedesdorff (1810-1848). He opened San Francisco's first hotel, launched its first steamboat, and organized it first official horse race.

Joan Potter, *African-American Firsts* (Elizabethtown, NY: Pinto Press, 1994), 3. Jessie Carney Smith, *Black Firsts: 2,000 Years of Extraordinary Achievements* (Detroit, Gale Research, 1994), 59.

What was the New York Curb Exchange?

The New York Curb Exchange is the former name of the American Stock Exchange, the largest stock exchange in the United States. It was called "curb" because it began as an outdoor, sidewalk ("curbstone") operation, moving indoors in 1921. In 1953 the name changed to the American Stock Exchange.

Christine Ammer and Dean S. Ammer, *Dictionary of Business and Economics, rev. ed.* (New York: The Free Press, 1984), s.v. "American Stock Exchange."

Who invented the traveler's check?

At the direction of J.C. Fargo, president of the American Express Company, the first traveler's check system was originated in 1891 by American Express agent Marcellus Fleming Berry. In the first year, checks amounting to only $9,120 were sold; by 1900 six million dollars were sold; and sales to date are in terms of billions.

Alden Hatch, *American Express, A Century of Service* (New York: Doubleday, 1950), 92-97. *The World Book Encyclopedia* (Chicago: World Book, 1994), s.v. "traveler's check."

Why is Wall Street in New York City so named?

Wall Street is both an actual street located in downtown Manhattan in New York City and a term symbolizing American finance. The street's name derives from its location near a wall that was built during Dutch ownership of the land. The principal financial institutions of the city have been located on this street since the early nineteenth century.

Robert Hendrickson, *The Henry Holt Encyclopedia of Word and Phrase Origins* (New York: Henry Holt, 1987), s.v. "wall street."

What flaw created the U.S. three-legged buffalo five-cent coins?

Minted in Denver, Colorado, in 1937, the three-legged buffalo nickels were the result of the die being polished too much, which erased the detail of one leg. Dies are polished to extend their lives and to remove marks, scratches, dirt, and grease from their surfaces. This 1937-D Indian Head is considered a collector's item.

Coin World Almanac, 5th ed. (New York: Amos Press, 1987), 353. *1994 Handbook of United States Coins With Premium List, 51st ed.* (Wisconsin: Western Publishing, 1993), 68.

How long is a check valid?

Adopted by many U.S. states, the Uniform Commercial Code declares that "A bank is under no obligation to a customer having a checking account to pay a check, other than a certified check, that is presented more than six months after its date."

Vernon's Annotated Missouri Statutes (Minnesota: West Publishing, 1994), 443.

General Business

What is a "banana republic"?

The term "banana republic" is used to describe a country, usually a Central American country, that is run by a corrupt dictatorship with close ties to foreign business interests.

At the beginning of the twentieth century, banana companies such as United Fruit of America and Cuyaxel Fruit Company virtually controlled many Central American countries. The banana companies controlled all port and transportation facilities, meddled in the country's internal political affairs by promoting their own candidates, and used the country's police force to suppress revolts by peasants and plantation workers. The first country to be known as a "banana republic" was Honduras whose government was controlled by U.S. fruit companies.

Kofi Buenor Hadjor, *Dictionary of Third World Terms* (London: I.B. Tauris & Co., 1992), s.v. "banana republic." *The World Book Encyclopedia* (Chicago: World Book, 1987), 9:281.

In business parlance, what is the meaning of the phrase quality circles?

In business parlance, the phrase quality circles refers to small groups or teams of employees who meet on a regular basis to discuss ongoing production issues and procedures. Quality circles operate with the approval of management and have come to be regarded as playing an important role in organizational methodology. The results of quality circles, however, have met with mixed reviews.

Jack P. Friedman, *Dictionary of Business Terms* (Hauppauge, NY: Barron's, 1994), 494.

What is the world's oldest industry?

Flint knapping, which involves the production of hand axes and chopping tools, originated in Ethiopia over 2.5 million years ago and is probably the world's oldest industry. Agriculture, which some consider to be the world's oldest occupation, did not begin until around 11,000 B.C.

Mark Young, ed., *The Guinness Book of Records 1995* (New York: Facts on File, 1994), 168.

What U.S. industrialist commissioned a coin bearing his likeness?

In 1917, U.S. automobile industrialist Henry Ford (1863-1947) commissioned a penny-like coin which bore his likeness rather than Abraham Lincoln's. The coin was engraved with the phrase "Help the Other Fellow" under Ford's portrait and was meant to be a goodwill gesture rather than a unit of exchange.

Irving Wallace, David Wallechinsky, and Amy Wallace, *Significa* (New York: E.P. Dutton, Inc., 1983), 304.

What are W. Edwards Deming "14 points toward quality"?

William Edwards Deming (1900-93) was a statistician with the U.S. Department of Agriculture, Bureau of Standards, and the Bureau of the Census between 1927 and 1946. Following World War II (1939-45) he founded a consulting firm and took a teaching position at New York University's Graduate School of Business Administration. After many of his theories of management, production, and quality control were rejected by U.S. companies he was invited to Japan by that country's war-shattered but soon-to-burgeon industries. He had much to do with the emergence of Japan as a major economic and manufacturing power but his work and theories did not become appreciated in the United States until the 1980s. Deming is famous in manufacturing circles for his "14 points toward quality," which follows:

Create constancy of purpose for improvement of product and service.
Management must be responsible for change.
Do not depend on mass inspection, build quality into the product.
Do not award contracts on basis of price alone.
Improve constantly, and thus constantly decrease costs.
Institute training on the job.
Supervisors should aim to help people and gadgets do a better job.
Drive out fear, so that everyone may work effectively.
Break down barriers between departments to make teams.
Eliminate slogans and targets for the workforce.
Eliminate numerical quotas for the workforce (and management).
Remove barriers that rob people of pride of workmanship.
Encourage education and self-improvement for everyone.
Take action to accomplish the transformation.

Judith Graham, *Current Biography Yearbook 1994* (New York: H. W. Wilson, 1994), s.v. "Deming, William Edwards." Department of Labor, *Learning a Living: A Blueprint for High Performance* (Washington, DC: Government Printing Office, 1992), 18.

What is the difference between a general and a limited partnership?

General partnerships give each partner an equal stake in the furtherance of the business through their time, money and effort. Each partner has equal liability and authority to act within the scope of their agreement. Limited partnerships have active and inactive partners. The inactive or limited partner does not have any managerial assignments, nor does his or her liability extend beyond their monetary contribution.

Christopher Neubert and Jack Withiam, Jr., *How to Handle Your Own Contracts* (New York: Sterling Publishing, 1991), 126-27.

What is an appropriate gift in Germany?

In Germany a gift of knives should be reciprocated by a coin so that the friendship won't be cut. The preference is for high quality items as gifts even if they are very small.

"Beware When Bearing Gifts In Foreign Lands," *Business Week* 6 December 1976.

What are appropriate gifts in business relationships in Brazil?

The customs of Brazil make giving anything purple inappropriate except at funerals. Purple is the color of death. To make a good impression liquor is a good option. The preference is for Scotch.

"Beware When Bearing Gifts In Foreign Lands," *Business Week* 6 December 1976.

What gifts are appropriate in India?

In India gifts of white are inappropriate because it is the color of mourning. Certain products can cost twice their amount due to tariffs so it is a sound idea to check with government officials about such matters. Liquor is a good gift option.

"Beware When Bearing Gifts In Foreign Lands," *Business Week* 6 December 1976.

What are appropriate business gifts in Great Britain?

The English find gifts of apparel and soap as too personal. Flowers and potted plants are popular but avoid white lilies because they are used in funerals. If you give liquor avoid bourbon. Scotch is a more acceptable gift.

"Beware When Bearing Gifts In Foreign Lands," *Business Week* 6 December 1976.

What is an appropriate business gift in France?

If you wish to thoroughly offend someone in France give them yellow flowers. Yellow flowers represent infidelity. If you give another color of flower give an odd number but not thirteen. Any French luxury item will go over well.

"Beware When Bearing Gifts In Foreign Lands," *Business Week* 6 December 1976.

What is an appropriate gift for a business relationship in Greece?

In Greece gifts of wearing apparel to men are not greatly appreciated. The men prefer to choose their own gifts. Flowers should be reserved for girlfriends. General gifts for the home are appreciated.

"Beware When Bearing Gifts In Foreign Lands," *Business Week* 6 December 1976.

What are appropriate gifts in Hong Kong?

Giving gifts in Hong Kong can be touchy due to the anticorruption mood in the city. Red flowers are popular but white should be reserved for funerals. Blooming exotic plants are popular also.

"Beware When Bearing Gifts In Foreign Lands," *Business Week* 6 December 1976.

What is an appropriate business gift in Canada?

Canadians enjoy French and California wines. They also appreciate native crafts, especially carvings from Eskimo and Indian tribes. Giving to government employees is frowned upon.

"Beware When Bearing Gifts In Foreign Lands," *Business Week* 6 December 1976.

What are appropriate gifts in Israel?

In Israel gifts to government officials should be only of a token nature. Anything with religious overtones should be avoided.

"Beware When Bearing Gifts In Foreign Lands," *Business Week* 6 December 1976.

Who was the first female business executive?

The first female business executive in the United States was probably Margaret Getchell La Forge. R. H. Macy, the future retail magnate, hired her in 1860 or 1861 as a cashier for his fancy New York City dry-goods store, R. H. Macy & Co. She became the superintendent of the store, and Macy credited her for much of the legendary store's success.

Jane Polley, ed., *Stories Behind Everyday Things* (Pleasantville, NY: The Reader's Digest Association, 1980), 106.

What are quality circles?

Quality circles are an organizational management technique in which a small number of employee volunteers, usually six to twelve people from the same work area, meet regularly to discuss positive ways to solve problems. Persons who participate in quality circles usually receive training in decision-making and conflict resolution. Quality circles are considered better alternatives to suggestion boxes as a vehicle for airing grievances because they solicit direct employee participation.

Robert L. Barker, *The Social Work Dictionary,* (Silver Spring, MD: National Association of Social Workers, 1987), s.v. "quality circles."

What is the origin of coins as they are known today?

Since the advent of organized societies, there has been a need to have objects, tokens, or goods to represent fixed values. In simple agrarian societies, agricultural products, tools, and cattle were bartered as a means of exchange. However, as societies became increasingly advanced, a less cumbersome means of exchange was needed. One of the precursors to currency as it is known today was pieces of metal valued by weight, which were usually guaranteed by a private banker or the state.

The first society to use coins as they are known today was that of the Lydians of the eighth century B.C. In the early seventh century B.C., coins first appeared in China and Greece.

Arnold Whittick, *Symbols, Signs and their Meaning* (Newton, MA: Charles T. Branford Company, 1960), 83.

What is a pac-man defense?

In the parlance of corporate takeovers a pac-man defense occurs when the original target company turns the tables and attempts to gain control of the attacking company. The phrase is derived from the popular video game Pac-Man.

Harold LeMay, *The Facts On File Dictionary of New Words* (New York: Facts On File, 1988) 87.

What are appropriate gifts in Italy?

When giving gifts in Italy one should not give handkerchiefs, silk, or linen. Red roses connote tenderness. Gifts should be festive and bright or very refined.

"Beware When Bearing Gifts In Foreign Lands," *Business Week* 6 December 1976.

What are appropriate gifts in Japan?

In Japan anything with the English word four in it or giving four of something is a bad idea. Four sounds like the Kanji word for death. White flowers should be avoided. Potted plants are not to be sent to those who are ill. Liquor is a good gift. A small gift is expected when visiting.

"Beware When Bearing Gifts In Foreign Lands," *Business Week* 6 December 1976.

What is an appropriate gift in Mexico?

In Mexico yellow is the color of death. Red and white flowers are said to have magical properties. Red casts spells while white dispels spells. Most other items are appropriate for giving.

"Beware When Bearing Gifts In Foreign Lands," *Business Week* 6 December 1976.

What is an appropriate gift in Saudi Arabia?

When giving gifts in Saudi Arabia one should never include wives. Alcohol is verboten since this is a devout Islamic nation. Flowers are not given. Hunting and equestrian related goods are appropriate gifts. Hunting falcons are highly prized and will make a grand impression.

"Beware When Bearing Gifts In Foreign Lands," *Business Week* 6 December 1976.

What are appropriate gifts to be given in Spain?

In Spain gifts of flowers are welcomed. Chrysanthemums are associated with funerals. Electronic items are prized due to their cost.

"Beware When Bearing Gifts In Foreign Lands," *Business Week* 6 December 1976.

What is an appropriate gift to give in Sweden?

In Sweden gifts of flowers are appropriate as long as they are kept simple and do not include white lilies. Lilies are funeral flowers. Items used in sailing are popular.

"Beware When Bearing Gifts In Foreign Lands," *Business Week* 6 December 1976.

What are appropriate gifts in Taiwan?

In Taiwan fruits are better gifts than flowers. If you opt to go with flowers avoid yellow and white since they are used in funerals. Clocks are not good gifts since the word sounds like "terminate." Money is fine when given in a red envelope. Don't give a man a green hat, it means he has an unfaithful wife.

"Beware When Bearing Gifts In Foreign Lands," *Business Week* 6 December 1976.

What is an appropriate gift in Venezuela?

In Venezuela gift giving should not include handkerchiefs since they are unlucky. Any kind of flower is appropriate.

"Beware When Bearing Gifts In Foreign Lands," *Business Week* 6 December 1976.

Who made the decision to break up AT&T?

The U.S. Justice Department initiated the breakup of AT&T on January 8, 1982. Under the direction of William French Smith, the department coordinated a deal to end what had been seen as long term violation of antitrust laws. The final divestiture agreement between the company and the Justice Department was approved by U.S. District Judge Harold Greene on August 5, 1983.

Walter Scott, "Telephone Co. Break-up," *Parade* 4 March 1984.

Who started the first American automobile company?

Charles Duryea (1861-1938), a cycle manufacturer from Peoria, Illinois, and his brother, Frank (1869-1967), founded America's first auto manufacturing firm and became the first to build cars for sale in the United States. The Duryea Motor Wagon company, set up in Springfield, Massachusetts, in 1895, built gasoline-powered, horseless carriages similar to those built by Benz in Germany.

However, the Duryea brothers did not build the first automobile factory in the United States. Ransom Eli Olds (1864-1950) built it in 1899 in Detroit, Michigan, to manufacture his Oldsmobile. Over ten vehicles a week were produced there by April 1901 for a total of 433 cars produced in 1901. In 1902 Olds introduced the assembly-line method of production and made over 2,500 vehicles in 1902; and 5,508 in 1904. In 1906 there were 125 companies making automobiles in the United States. In 1908 the American engineer Henry Ford (1863-1947) improved the automobile assembly line techniques by adding the conveyor belt system that brought the parts to the workers on the production line, this made automotive manufacture quick and cheap cutting production time to ninety-three minutes; his company sold 10,660 vehicles that year.

Tom Burnam, *The Dictionary of Misinformation* (New York: Harper & Row, 1975), 12. Harry Harris, *Good Old-Fashioned Yankee Ingenuity* (Chelsea, MI: Scarborough House, 1990, 36-37, 183. Patrick Robertson, *The Book of Firsts* (New York: Clarkson N. Potter, 1974), 104. David Burgess Wise, *The Motor Car* (New York: Putnam, 1979), 74.

When were frozen foods first available commercially?

Clarence Birdseye (1887-1956) discovered that quick freezing of food enabled the food to retain its texture, flavor, and nutrients. The faster the freezing process takes place the less danger of ice crystals rupturing the cell walls of the food item and releasing its natural juices. Birdseyes patented this quick-freezing technique of pressing the food item between two metal plates that have a below zero degrees Fahrenheit (-18 degrees Centigrade) temperature to permit rapid heat exchange. In 1929 he sold his company to Postum Cereal Co., which founded General Foods. At the time of the sale it was agreed that Birdseye's name (as two words) would become the brand name for the frozen food items-peas, spinach, raspberries, cherries, fish, and meat-that were marketed in September in 1930.

Edward DeBono, *Eureka!* (New York: Holt, Rinehart and Winston, 1974), 116. Harry Harris, *Good Old-Fashioned Yankee Ingenuity* (Chelsea, MI: Scarborough House, 1990), 133-34. Patrick Robertson, *The Book of Firsts* (New York: Clarkson N. Potter, 1974), 75-76.

Was April 15 always the filing date for income tax returns?

Nineteen fifty-five was the first year individual income tax returns had to be filed by April 15. Prior to that year the filing date was March 15.

U.S. Treasury Department, Bureau of Internal Revenue, *Income Tax Primer* (Washington, DC: Government Printing Office, 1921), 4. U.S. Treasury Department, Internal Revenue Service, *Internal Revenue Bulletin: Cumulative Bulletin 1954-2* (Washington, DC: Government Printing Office, 1955), 36. U.S. Treasury Department, Bureau of Internal Revenue, *Regulations III: Income Tax* (Washington, DC: Government Printing Office, 1943), 296.

When was the first life insurance company in America established?

The first life insurance company in America was founded on January 11, 1759. It was called the Corporation for Relief of Poor and Distressed Widows and Children of Presbyterian Ministers.

Laurence J. Peter, *Peter's Almanac* (New York: William Morrow, 1982).

What should be included in a letter of recommendation?

A letter of recommendation should include the applicant's name, the relationship the writer has or had with the applicant, including relevant details, and the general abilities of the applicant. Before writing the letter, which should be sincere and friendly in tone, the writer should become familiar with the position being sought. The letter should be concise but complete.

Meg Whitcomb, *"Dear Meg" tells you...How to Write the Most Important Letters of Your Life* (New York: Warner Books, 1986), 124-25.

How should one respond to a letter of complaint?

One should always respond promptly to a letter of complaint and adopt a friendly and concerned tone. One should keep in mind that the complainant is a customer whose business is worth having, and the response must protect that relationship. The letter might begin with a note of gratitude for bringing up the problem. Always agree with the complainant on some point and state what action has been taken. Try to be positive, even if nothing can be done, perhaps by offering another recourse that the customer might follow. End the letter with a goodwill statement.

Harold E. Meyer, *Lifetime Encyclopedia of Letters, rev. ed.* (Englewood Cliffs, NJ: Prentice Hall, 1992), 214-15.

What was America's first multinational corporation?

America's first multinational corporation was the Singer Company, known worldwide for its sewing machines. The company was founded by Isaac Merritt Singer, who was born in Pittstown, New York, in 1811. At the age of 12, Singer ran away from home and joined a troupe of traveling actors. By 1850 Singer had tired of acting and went to Boston with a device he had patented which carved wood block type for the printing trade.

It was there that Singer became interested in sewing machines, which had first been patented in England in 1790 and later improved by Elias Howe. These early machines however were unreliable, and in 1851 Singer received a patent on what he thought was a better design. Singer's design was an immediate success, but he had to fend off a patent infringement suit by Elias Howe. Singer won in court; in exchange for legal services, he made his lawyer Edward Clark a full partner in the company. Clark eventually brought Singer's competitor into their firm, thus forming the Singer Machine Combination. With Clark handling finances, Singer was free to pursue the manufacturing side of the business. Clark soon offered their sewing machines to customers on the installment plan. Sewing machines were quite expensive and, until Clark's marketing innovation, could only be afforded by commercial enterprises.

In 1867, in an attempt to open up the European market, Singer began manufacturing his machines in Glasgow, Scotland, and in 1873 a plant was opened in Montreal. This made the Singer Company America's first multinational corporation and by the 1970s Singer had facilities in over 200 countries.

Tom Mahoney and Leonard Sloane, *The Great Merchants, updated ed.* (New York: Harper & Row, 1974), 71-72. Lisa Mirabile, ed., *International Directory of Company Histories, Vol. II* (Chicago: St. James Press, 1990), 9-11.

What four Asian nations are called the Four Tigers?

South Korea, Hong Kong, Taiwan, and Singapore are called the Four Tigers, a reference to the business success of the four countries. Along with Japan, the Four Tigers are known for alternative economic strategies that rival U.S. policies of free markets and free trade.

David Murray, "Fiction Comes to the Killing Fields," *New York Times Book Review* 18 February 1990.

What two brothers lost a fortune trying to corner the silver market in 1980?

Brothers Herbert and Bunker Hunt tried to corner the silver market in 1979 and 1980. They used a letter of credit to purchase large quantities of silver and then withdrew it from the market. Therefore, for every one thousand dollars down payment they made on silver futures contracts, the brothers had actually only paid ten dollars. They also brought in four Saudi Arabian partners to help them corner the market. When silver prices went up they made a large profit, on paper.

As others started losing money in the silver market, those in control of the exchanges became concerned. In March of 1980, the Chicago and New York exchanges changed the rules on how silver futures were sold. Margin requirements were lifted from two thousand dollars per contract to forty thousand dollars. The number of contracts that an individual could own was also reduced. This forced the Hunt brothers to sell their silver in a falling market and to find cash to cover their obligations to banks and brokerage houses. This resulted in a controversial bailout by the Federal Reserve, which loaned the Hunts $1 billion in order to insure the stability of the silver market.

William J. Quirk, "The Hunt Silver Caper," *New Republic* 24 May 1980.

Why did the Bayer chemical company lose the right to sell aspirin in the United States under the Bayer name and trademark in 1918?

More than 75 years after losing the U.S. rights to sell aspirin, Bayer, a German chemical company, regained the ability to sell the pain killer in Canada and the United States. The company had been stripped of its name and product, which were claimed as confiscated enemy property in 1918 by the U.S. Alien Property Custodian. Bayer developed the popular pain killer only to have it auctioned off as a franchise to the Sterling Drug Company for $5.3 million. In 1994 it was sold to SmithKline Beecham, who negotiated a $1 billion agreement with Bayer for the rights to use the Bayer name and trademark.

Milt Freudenheim, "Trademark Reclaimed," *New York Times* 18 September 1994.

Who were the creators of the first McDonald's restaurant, which was discovered and franchised by Ray Kroc?

The first McDonald's restaurant was created by brothers Maurice and Richard McDonald in San Bernardino, California. The drive-in restaurant was opened in 1948; it featured a streamlined operation that impressed Ray Kroc, a salesman who sold them Multimixer machines. The McDonald's restaurant was exceptionally clean, the quality of the food was consistent, and the meals were served quickly. Kroc convinced the brothers to become partners in a franchise agreement. Using their restaurant as a guide, he formulated guidelines for the chain restaurants and sold the franchise licenses.

Stan Luxenberg, *Roadside Empires: How the Chains Franchised America* (New York: Viking Penguin, 1985), 72.

As used in the business world, what is a "bottleneck"?

As used in the business world, a "bottleneck" occurs when an industry has to slow production because the supply of necessary parts or materials cannot keep up with demand. The term alludes graphically to the bottle's structure.

E. D. Hirsch Jr., Joseph F. Kett, and James Trefil, *The Dictionary of Cultural Literacy* (Boston: Houghton Mifflin, 1988), s.v. "bottleneck."

In the nineteenth century where was America's whaling industry centered?

In the nineteenth century America's whaling industry was centered in Nantucket, Massachusetts, which has become, since then, a resort area.

E. D. Hirsch Jr., *The Dictionary of Cultural Literacy* (Boston: Houghton Mifflin, 1988), s.v. "Nantucket."

How did the Sears, Roebuck company begin?

The Sears, Roebuck & Co. story is the epitome of an American success story. It began when the young Richard W. Sears (1863-1914), a railway worker, bought a shipment of watches that had been refused by the potential purchaser. Sears decided to sell the watches, but by a way that was novel at the time—through the mail. He did remarkably well, mostly because he required very little markup to sell through the mail. His business grew and before long Alvah C. Roebuck, a watch repairer, had joined him. In 1893, they took the name Sears, Roebuck & Co., and their sales totaled $388,000. They began selling clothing in 1895 when Julius Rosenwald, a clothing manufacturer, joined the company.

Godfrey M. Lebhar, *Chain Stores in America, 1859-1962, 3d ed.* (New York: Chain Store Publishing 1963), 47-49.

How did the A&P grocery store begin?

George F. Gilman (d. 1901) and George Huntington Hartford (1833-1917) began what was to become the A&P grocery store chain in a small store in New York in 1859. The store sold tea that they had imported directly from the Orient at a very low price. Their success kept increasing and before long they had opened 25 stores under the name of the Great American Tea Company. They added groceries to their list of items to sell and changed the name to the Great Atlantic & Pacific Tea Company in 1869.

Godfrey M. Lebhar, *Chain Stores in America, 1859-1962, 3rd ed.* (New York: Chain Store Publishing, 1963), 25-26, 31.

How did the concept of self-service begin in the food retailing industry?

Clarence Saunders, founder of the Piggly Wiggly grocery store chain in 1916, was the person who invented the idea of self-service. Customers had to pass through a turnstile to enter the store, and were then ushered through the aisles in a prescribed way. Other in the food retailing industry bought Piggly Wiggly franchises and operated them in different areas to see how the idea would catch on before the major chain stores were converted to self-service.

Godfrey M. Lebhar, *Chain Stores in America, 1859-1962, 3rd ed.* (New York: Chain Store Publishing, 1963), 34.

What is a Gantt chart, and what is it best used for?

Henry Gantt developed the Gantt chart that is used primarily for planning projects and scheduling work. It is a bar chart that plots actual output versus planned output over a period of time.

Hano Johannsen and G. Terry Page, *International Dictionary of Management: A Practical Guide* (Boston: Houghton Mifflin, 1975), 153.

What is the Good Housekeeping Seal?

The Good Housekeeping Seal indicates that a product is covered by a limited warranty, promising "replacement or refund if defective" within four years of purchase. *Good Housekeeping* magazine offers the seal to its advertisers; some 500 products currently wear this mark. The magazine created the seal in 1909 as a way of encouraging manufacturers to guarantee the quality of their products. A University of Baltimore study has shown that there is a general misconception regarding the seal. A majority of people surveyed thought it indicated that the product had been tested for safety, that the magazine was endorsing the product as being superior to others, and that was a promise to meet all advertising claims.

Kathleen Day, "Sealed with misconceptions," *USA Today* 27 January 1983.

What does the term "agribusiness" mean?

"Agribusiness" is a broad term encompassing the production, processing, and marketing of all farm and related commodities and services. Included in the term are the obvious food products and non-food items such as farm machinery and fertilizer, as well as services such as meatpacking and grocery sales.

McGraw-Hill Dictionary of Modern Economics: A Handbook of Terms and Organizations, 3d ed. (New York: McGraw-Hill Book Company, 1983), s.v. "agribusiness."

When did the practice of "buying on time" originate?

The practice of "buying on time," or taking possession and using a product while it is still being paid for, originated with the American inventor Isaac Singer (1811-1875) in 1856. Singer wanted a way to boost sales of his $125 sewing machines at a time when the average annual family income was only $500. Singer made it possible for such a family to buy one of his machines for $5 down and $5 a month.

Kenneth M. Morris and Alan M. Seigel, *The Wall Street Journal Guide to Personal Finance* (New York: Light Bulb Press, 1992), 31.

What are some do's and dont's for writing an effective resume?

There are several rules for writing an effective resume.
It should be clearly organized and attractively presented.
Avoid abbreviations, except for the middle initial of a name, as well as the pronoun "I."
Do not lie.
Keep the tense of the verbs the same, the sentences brief and factual.
Action verbs are crucial to presenting one's skills impressively, as is concise language.
Present the most important skills first.
The name and address of the resume writer should be centered at the top of the document. Categories such as "Education" and "Employment" should be set off to the left, and the items falling under these headings to the right.
Certain devices, such as capital letters, underlines, and bullets to draw the eye, are acceptable.
The resume should be free from typographical errors and other mistakes.

Ronald L. Krannich and Caryl Rae Krannich, *The Complete Guide to Public Employment, 2d ed.* (Woodbridge, VA: Impact Publications, 1990), 157-58.

What was the cost of a telephone call made on the first coin-operated telephone?

In 1889 in Hartford, Connecticut, the cost of making a telephone call on the first coin-operated telephone was five cents.

Dennis Sanders, *The First of Everything* (New York: Delacorte Press, 1981), 60.

What is the origin of mission furniture?

Mission furniture originated as a marketing ploy by furniture manufacturers and dealers in the early 1900s when some rather rough and crude furniture pieces were being shown as a novelty at an exhibition. A Chicago dealer, knowing there was a great deal of interest in old Spanish missions in California, dubbed the pieces "mission furniture" and the name and the furniture quickly caught on, especially after Maltese crosses were incorporated into the design.

William Walsh, *A Handy Book of Curious Information* (Philadelphia: J.B. Lippincott, 1913), 550-51.

What are the responsibilities of the presiding officer of a meeting?

The presiding officer of a meeting has several duties. The first of these takes place before the meeting is actually held and centers around the planning of the meeting. This includes choosing the site (finding accommodations where the attendees are comfortable and conducive to the business at hand) and notifying all members of the time and place of the meeting. It is expected that the meeting will be at an hour convenient to a majority of them. The presiding officer is also responsible for the efficient and proper conduct of the meeting according to standard rules of procedure, and should insure that a general consensus is satisfied during the proceedings that the will of the majority is determined without infringing on the minority's rights.

James E. Davis, *Rules of Order* (Chicago: Chicago Review Press, 1992), 89-91.

What is the usual order of a standard business meeting?

According to *Robert's Rules of Order*, a business meeting should be organized into six sections:
Reading and approval of minutes
Reports of officers, boards and standing committees
Reports of special (select or ad hoc) committees
Special orders
Unfinished business and general orders
New business

Henry M. Robert, *The Scott, Foresman Robert's Rules of Order, 9th ed., ed. Sarah Corbin Robert, et al.* (Glenview, IL: ScottForesman, 1990), 347.

Labor

When were the first pensions in the United States established?

In 1875 one of the first formal pension plans in the United States was launched by the American Express Company. On August 14, 1935, the U.S. Congress enacted the Social Security Act, legislation to establish a permanent national old-age insurance program that would provide elderly Americans with a financial cushion against poverty and illness through employer and employee contributions.

Jane Polley, ed., *Stories Behind Everyday Things,* (Pleasantville, NY: The Reader's Digest Association, 1980), 247.

What is the "Peter Principle"?

The "Peter Principle" contends that an employee is often promoted beyond his or her abilities. The promotion is based upon work well performed at a level compatible with ability, where the employee should have remained. The term was coined by the late Professor Laurence Peter, a Canadian-born U.S. academic.

Michael Johnson, *Business Buzzwords: The Tough New Jargon of Modern Business* (Basil Blackwell, 1990), s.v. "Peter Principle."

Have there been any studies done on age discrimination in employment?

The American Association of Retired Persons (AARP) conducted a study of older Americans and concluded that older people are discriminated against in job offers. The discrimination is less prevalent among successful companies than among less successful ones, the study showed. In the research, AARP mailed virtually identical resumes of two people to 775 large companies. The results indicated that companies discriminated 26.5 percent of the time against a 57-year-old fictional applicant whose resume was virtually identical to a 32-year-old applicant's. In cases of both male and female pairs applying for jobs as writer-editor, executive secretary, and management information specialist, there were less favorable responses to the older applicant, the association reported. Discrimination against older people in the job market is a violation of federal law.

"Job Applicants Face Age Bias, Study Finds," *New York Times* 23 February 1994.

What does the term gandy dancer mean?

A gandy dancer is a track laborer. The name derived from the special tools used for track work made by the Gandy Manufacturing Company of Chicago, Illinois. These tools were used during the nineteenth century almost universally by section gangs.

James H. Beck, *Rail Talk* (Gretna, NE: James Publications, 1978).

Who were the Luddites?

The Luddites were a group of British workers who, as a social protest, went around smashing newly introduced industrial machinery in the years 1811-1816. Luddites claimed that the machines were the cause of their distress. They named themselves after Ned Ludd, a boy who broke a machine during a temper tantrum years earlier.

J.L. Hanson, *A Dictionary of Economics and Commerce* (London: MacDonald & Evans, 1965), s.v. "Luddites."

What is the history of the Red Caps organization?

The United Transport Service Employees of America is a labor union that was originally organized as the International Brotherhood of Red Caps in 1937. The name was changed in 1940 and the group became affiliated with the Congress of Industrial Organizations in 1942. The organization represented all service employees in the transportation industry.

Florence Peterson, *Handbook of Labor Unions* (Washington, DC: American Council on Public Affairs, 1944), 389.

What was controversial about the 1950 "fee for red cap porters"?

The 1950 "fee for red cap porters" was controversial because it gave porters a raise they did not want. Prior to December of 1950 red cap porters working at various railroad stations received 15 cents for every bag they carried and whatever tips their patrons gave them. The Interstate Commerce Commission (I.C.C.) in mandating the increase was following a trend started in 1940 of setting and periodically raising the fee porters charge for each bag carried under terms of the 1940 Federal Wage and Hour Law. Under the new increase the porters received 25 cents for every bag carried. The porters and their union feared that any gain made from the fee increase would be more than offset by a decline in tips. Although the union did not attempt to block the raise in court, they did support spending nearly $18,000 to oppose the increase. The increase was supported by railroad management and what the union called the "pro-railroad attitude of the I.C.C."

New York Times 1 December 1950.

In the business world, what is a "headhunter"?

In the business world, an executive search consultant is often referred to as a "headhunter."

Michael Johnson, *Business Buzzwords: The Tough New Jargon of Modern Business* (Basil Blackwell, 1990), s.v. "headhunter."

In the business world, what is a "golden parachute"?

In the business world, a "golden parachute" is a termination clause in an executive's contract that guarantees he or she will be well rewarded upon leaving the company regardless of job performance or circumstances surrounding termination. The practice of granting a "golden parachute" has come under much criticism recently.

Michael Johnson, *Business Buzzwords: The Tough New Jargon of Modern Business* (Basil Blackwell, 1990), s.v. "golden parachute."

When was the 40 hour work week instituted?

The forty hour work week was legislated into existence with passage of the Public Contract Act of 1936. This legislation mandated that workers on all government contracts over $10,000 be paid time and one half for every hour worked over 40 hours in a week, and overtime pay at the same rate for more than 8 hours worked in one day.

Joseph Nathan Kane, *Famous First Facts: A Record of First Happenings, Discoveries, and Inventions in American History, 4th rev. ed.* (New York: H.W. Wilson Company, 1981), 339.

How long should a cover letter accompanying a resume be and what information should it contain?

A cover letter accompanying a resume should be just long enough to persuade the reader a further look at the resume. The cover letter should indicate which job is being applied for and one or two points concerning your qualifications for that position.

Harold E. Meyer, *Lifetime Encyclopedia of Letters, rev. ed.* (Englewood Cliffs, NJ: Prentice Hall, 1992), 229-30.

What is the significance of a "Green Card"?

The "Green Card," or Alien Identification Document, enables a foreign citizen to work in the United States and grants its bearer permanent legal residence in the United States.

"How to Apply For a Green Card," *New York Times* 4 February 1993.

Markets, Sales, and Trade

Who portrayed Aunt Jemima in the Quaker Oats advertising campaign?

The role of Aunt Jemima in the 1950s advertising campaign for the Quaker Oats pancake mix was played by Ethel Ernestine Harper. In addition to the Quaker Oats campaign, Harper also performed in the theatrical production of "The Hot Mikado" and "The Negro Follies." Along with two other women, Harper performed in a singing group known as the Three Ginger Snaps. The Ginger Snaps toured Europe and became well known in many countries, especially Italy. Harper died in 1979.

"Ethel Harper, Actress Was Aunt Jemima In Ads for Pancakes," *New York Times* 3 April 1979.

Were women the "goods" sold at the earliest public auctions?

One of the first public auctions recorded occurred in Babylon more than 2,500 years ago. Each year all the women eligible for marriage were gathered together and sold by auction to the men that had congregated to bid for them.

Jane Polley, ed., *Stories Behind Everyday Things* (Pleasantville, NY: The Reader's Digest Association, 1980), 24.

What was the first product sold from a vending machine?

The coin-operated vending machine dates back to the first century A.D. At certain Greek temples worshippers could drop money in a mechanical device and receive a dollop of purifying water.

Jane Polley, ed., *Stories Behind Everyday Things* (Pleasantville, NY: The Reader's Digest Association, 1980), 77.

When did discount stores become popular?

One of the first discounters was Anderson Little, a manufacturer of men's clothing who had a large order canceled in 1936. In order to sell the surplus merchandise, he opened his factory in Massachusetts to the public. New England was the main site of these mill outlets which were opened in abandoned factories and warehouses. After World War II (1939-1945) discount houses or "mass merchandisers" became a major player in the retail business as more people became willing to sacrifice personal service and atmosphere for a lower price.

Jane Polley, ed., *Stories Behind Everyday Things* (Pleasantville, NY: The Reader's Digest Association, 1980), 115-16.

Who was the real Chef Boy-ar-dee?

Hector Boiardi was the founder of Chef Boy-ar-dee Foods, one of America's first packaged Italian food businesses. The company he started in 1928 was first called Chef Boiardi. But customers and salesmen had difficulty pronouncing his name, so the brand name was changed to the phonetic spelling, "Boy-ar-dee."

He served as president of the company until 1946, when he sold it to American Home Foods Company. Boiardi served as a consultant to American Home Foods until 1978. He died in 1985 at the age of 87.

"Hector Boiardi Is Dead. Began Chef Boy-ar-dee," *New York Times* 23 June 1985.

What was the full name of the famous fried chicken purveyor, Colonel Sanders?

The full name of the famous fried chicken purveyor was Colonel Harland Sanders. "Colonel" was an honorary title granted to Sanders by Governor Ruby Laffoon of Kentucky in 1935. Sanders developed his famous fried chicken recipe in 1939 when he was running a restaurant in Corbin, Kentucky.

Chuck Bartelt and Barbara Bergeron, eds., *Variety Obituaries, 1905-1986, Vol. 9* (New York: Garland Publishing, 1988).

What is the trademark character of the Maytag Corporation?

The trademark character of the Maytag Corporation is the repairman "Ol' Lonely," since he never gets a call to repair a Maytag product.

Joseph Mendenhall, *Character Trademarks* (San Francisco: Chronicle Books, 1990), 104.

When was the first radio commercial broadcast?

The first radio commercial was broadcast on August 28, 1922, by station WEAF. The commercial was for Hawthorne Court, a complex of tenant-owned apartments in the Jackson Heights section of New York City. The commercial, which was long and drawn out by present standards, earned the radio station $100.

J. Fred MacDonald, *Don't Touch That Dial!: Radio Programming in American Life, 1920-1960* (Chicago: Nelson-Hall, 1979), 18.

When did infomercials begin?

The phenomenon of infomercials began in 1984. That year the Federal Communications Commission (F.C.C.) eliminated a 1973 guideline banning program-length commercials. Deregulation of the television industry also increased the demand for new programming and revenue. The new "infomercials" follow the traditional television talk show format but use it to sell a product or service. Usually 30 minutes long, the programs combine a sales pitch, product information, and a toll-free telephone number for placing orders.

Forbes 15 October 1990.

When was cigarette advertising banned from television and radio?

January 1, 1971, was the last day cigarettes could be advertised on television and radio. The ban came in the wake of the U.S. Surgeon General's 1964 report linking cigarette smoking to lung cancer, heart disease and various other respiratory ailments.

Stuart Berg Flexner, *Listening To America: An Illustrated History of Words and Phrases from Our Lively and Splendid Past* (New York: Simon and Schuster, 1982), 153.

Which cigarette brands were the first, historically, to attract a nationwide market?

Following World War I (1914-18), cigarette smoking was becoming increasingly popular in the United States, and the major manufacturers began competing to establish national brands. The top three brands were Camels, brought out by R.J. Reynolds in 1913, American Tobacco's Lucky Strikes in 1916, and Liggett & Myers's Chesterfields which soon followed.

Philip Mattera, *Inside U.S. Business: A Concise Encyclopedia of Leading Industries, 1994 ed.* (New York: Irwin, 1994), 154.

What company is the world's oldest retailer?

The world's oldest retailer is the Hudson's Bay Company which received its charter to exploit Canada's burgeoning fur trade in 1670. In its earliest years the company functioned as much like a government than as a commercial enterprise with a string of forts, its own printed money, a flag, and coat of arms. Today Hudson's Bay Company has 250 modern retail stores across Canada. The company has, however, held on to many of its traditions over the centuries, such as paying the reigning English monarch an annual rent of two beaver pelts and two elk heads and, until recently, referring to its shareholders as proprietors and paying them in pounds sterling rather than the Canadian dollar. In 1970 during the company's tercentenary, its headquarters were moved from London, England, to Winnipeg.

Tom Mahoney and Leonard Sloane, *The Great Merchants: America's Foremost Retail Institutions and the People Who Made Them Great* (New York: Harper & Row, 1974), 20.

What is bait-and-switch?

One of the purposes of advertising is to develop and utilize various techniques designed to lure customers into business establishments. However, some unscrupulous business owners may use techniques that are unethical. Among these unethical techniques is the bait-and-switch.

The bait-and-switch involves offering customers an enticing bargain in order to bring them into a store. However, once the customer asks to purchase the item at the alluring bargain price, the salesperson claims that the item is sold out. The salesperson offers a similar product and insists that it is a better buy than the bargain item when, in fact, the offered item is more expensive and may not be of superior quality.

Ralph De Sola, *Crime Dictionary, rev. ed.* (New York: Facts on File Publications, 1988), s.v. "bait-and-switch."

Who was the Gerber Baby?

Numerous rumors exist regarding the identity of the baby whose face appears on the labels of Gerber Foods baby products; one even names the American film actor Humphrey Bogart (1899-1957) as the infant (actually, his baby portrait did appear on another brand of baby food at one time). The famous Gerber Baby is actually Ann Turner Cook, whose father was a comic strip illustrator for the *Saturday Evening Post*, The Gerber Baby illustrator, Dorothy Hope Smith, used a photo of then-six-month-old Ann for the portrait.

"Follow-up on Baby," *Woman's Day* 26 June 1979.

What does the term loadline mean in shipping?

A loadline or load waterline is an immersion mark on the hull of a merchant ship. This indicates her safe load limit. The lines vary in height for different seasons of the year and areas of the world. Also called the Plimsoll Line or Plimsoll Mark, it was accepted as law by the British Parliament in the Merchant Shipping Act of 1875, primarily at the instigation of Samuel Plimsoll (1824-1898). This law prevented unscrupulous owners from sending out unseaworthy and overloaded, but heavily insured, vessels (so-called "coffin ships"), which risked the crew's lives.

Encyclopedia Americana (Danbury, CT: Grolier, 1990), 17:632. George H. Peters, *The Plimsoll Line* (London: Barry Rose, 1975), 129, 184.

When did the first used-car dealership open?

The first used-car dealership in Britain, the Motor Car Company of London, England, opened in September 1897 with 17 second-hand vehicles.

Patrick Robertson, *The Book of Firsts* (New York: Clarkson N. Potter, 1974), 162.

When did gasoline stations open?

The first service station (or garage) was opened in Bordeaux, France, in December 1895 by A. Borol. It provided overnight parking, repair service, and refills of oil and "motor spirit." In April 1897 a parking and refueling establishment, Brighton Cycle and Motor Co., opened in Brighton, England.

The pump which would be used to eventually dispense gasoline was devised by Sylanus Bowser of Fort Wayne, Indiana, but in September 1885, it dispensed kerosene. Twenty years later Bowser manufactured the first self-regulating gasoline pump. In 1912, a Standard Oil of Louisiana superstation opened in Memphis, Tennessee, featuring 13 pumps, a ladies' rest room, and a maid who served ice water to waiting customers. On December 1, 1913, in Pittsburgh, Pennsylvania, the Gulf Refining Company opened the first drive-in station as a 24 hour-a-day operation. Only 30 gallons (114 liters) of gasoline were sold the first day.

Harry Harris, *Good Old-Fashioned Yankee Ingenuity* (Chelsea, MI: Scarborough House, 1990), 136-37. Joseph N. Kane, *Famous First Facts: A Record of First Happenings, Discoveries, and Inventions in American History, 4th ed.* (New York: Wilson, 1981), 598.

What was the name of the dog portrayed in the "His Master's Voice" trademark, associated with RCA Victor?

Little Nipper was the name of the black and white fox terrier listening to "His Master's Voice" in the RCA trademark. The work was originally painted by Francis Barraud, an Englishman, for exhibition at the Royal Academy. When he was denied space at the exhibition, Barraud repainted part of the picture, painting over the cylinder machine portrayed in the original and painting in the gramophone, and sold it to the Gramophone Company, Ltd. in the early 1890s. In 1901, the Victor Talking Machine Company, which later merged with Radio Corporation of America (RCA), acquired the American rights to "His Master's Voice" and adopted the picture as its trademark. RCA did not use Nipper in its advertisements until 1929. In 1968 RCA announced a new logo, retaining Nipper for some products in a modified form. In 1990, Nipper made a comeback accompanied by a puppy originally called Little Nipper. In 1991, a promotional contest was held to name the Nipper's miniature sidekick, and Chipper was the winning entry out of 81,000. Nipper now represents RCA's traditional products, whereas Chipper is used for newer electronic products and developing technology.

New York Times 19 January 1968. Oliver Read *From Tin Foil to Stereo* (Indianapolis: Howard W. Sams, 1976), 134. Ruthven Tremain, *The Animals' Who's Who* (New York: Charles Scribner, 1982), s.v. "Nipper."

Why are clocks in catalogs and stores set to 8:20?

Clocks shown in catalogs and stores are often set to 8:20 because this position makes for a pleasingly symmetrical arrangement of the hands, as does 10:10, which shows up almost as often.

Cecil Adams, *More of the Straight Dope* (New York: Ballatine Books, 1988), 330-31.

What was the phrase "Call for Philip Morrraaiiss!" all about?

"Call for Philip Morrraaiiss!" was famous in radio advertising from 1933 into the 1950s. It was an advertisement for Philip Morris cigarettes featuring a bellhop paging Philip Morris in a hotel lobby. The voice and the spokesperson for this ad was Johnny Roventini, who was originally a $15-a-week bellhop at the Hotel New Yorker. Roventini was a four-foot midget who could sing a perfect B-flat note. After the ad aired, his salary went to $20,000 a year. Connected with "The Philip Morris Playhouse," Roventini also did the ad for other shows sponsored by Philip Morris and appeared on billboards and in magazines.

John Dunning, *Tune in Yesterday: The Ultimate Encyclopedia of Old-Time Radio, 1925-1976* (New Jersey: Prentice-Hall, 1976), s.v. "Philip Morris Playhouse, The."

What was the world's first billion dollar corporation?

The first billion dollar corporation was created by J. Pierpont Morgan when he formed the United States Steel Corporation. The American financier accomplished this business feat in 1901.

E.D. Hirsch, Joseph F. Kett, and James Trefil, *The Dictionary of Cultural Literacy* (Boston: Houghton Mifflin, 1988), 427.

Who was Howard Johnson and how did his orange-roofed restaurant chain originate?

Howard Johnson, a former cigar wholesaler, was one of the first to create a successful chain of franchised restaurants. The original Howard Johnson's restaurant was opened in 1935, on Cape Cod in Orleans, Massachusetts. Johnson had been selling ice cream, made with his mother's recipe, at a soda fountain but lacked the capital to open a proper restaurant. The franchise approach solved this problem: Johnson sold the rights to run his restaurant to an agent or franchisee. The other elements, beyond ice cream, that made his restaurants a success were a colonial style decor, the quick preparation of decent food, and the trademark orange roof. The color was selected for its ability to reflect light and the resulting high visibility.

Harvey Levenstein, *Paradox of Plenty, A Social History of Eating in Modern America* (New York: Oxford University Press, 1993), 47.

Why are three balls usually found on signs for pawnshops?

The three golden balls which most pawnshops display on their signs originate with the family crest of the Italian money lenders, the Medici family.

Henry Dreyfuss, *Symbol Sourcebook* (New York: Van Nostrand Reinhold, 1972), 65-66.

When did Sears, Roebuck and Company sell homes by mail order?

Sears sold 100,000 mail-order homes mostly in the East and Midwest from 1908 to 1940 through the Sears and Roebuck catalog. All construction materials and detailed plans for electric wiring were included. The price for the precut homes ranged from $595 to $5,000. Carlinville, Illinois, has an entire nine-block neighborhood of 152 houses, known as Standard Addition area, ordered from the Sears catalog.

Nell DuVall, *Domestic Technology* (Boston: G. K. Hall, 1988), 251. "For Sears Houses, a Catalogue Like No Other," *New York Times* 7 February 1993.

In the name of the well-known department store chain, J.C. Penney, what do the initials "J.C." stand for?

In the department store chain J.C. Penney, the initials "J.C." indicate the first and middle name of the store's founder—James Cash Penney. In 1902 Penney managed a store in Kemmerer, Wyoming, in which he had a one-third interest. Penney soon bought out his partners and was on his way to becoming a department store magnate. By 1929 he was selling $209,000,000 worth of goods a year.

The National Cyclopaedia of American Biography (New York: James T. White, 1930), s.v. "Penney, James Cash."

What are some unusual indicators of stock market performance?

Some unusual indicators of stock market performance includes the length of women's hemlines, whether an AFL or NFL team wins the Super Bowl, which presidential term is current, and the "Fibonacci number sequence."

Smart Money: The Wall Street Journal magazine of Personal Business June, 1994.

What is a "poison pill"?

The purposeful acquisition of debts and liabilities by a company to make it less attractive as a takeover target is often referred to as a "poison pill." The "poison pill" strategy is often viewed with skepticism.

Michael Johnson, *Business Buzzwords: The Tough New Jargon of Modern Business* (Basil Blackwell, 1990), 112.

Who were some traveling salesmen who went on to become entrepreneurs or illustrious personalities?

With the advent of the railroad the traveling salesman become a popular fixture of the American landscape. Many, however, tiring of seedy hotel rooms and cramped railroad cars, went on to become entrepreneurs, inventors, or illustrious personalities. Retail barons Marshall Field (1834-1906) and Aaron Montgomery Ward (1844-1913) once sold their wares out of a suitcase, as did George W. Cole of "3-in-1 Oil" fame and King C. Gillette, inventor of the safety razor blade. Huey P. Long (1893-1035), the "Kingfish" of Louisiana politics, was once a traveling salesman for Cottolene, a cotton seed oil shortening.

Gerald Carson, *The Old Country Store* (New York: Oxford University Press, 1954), 170.

Who was responsible for popularizing the cash register?

While John Henry Patterson (1844-1922) did not invent the cash register, he can be recognized as chief proponent for popularizing it. Patterson was born on a farm near Dayton, Ohio, and after his schooling, service in the American Civil War, and a stint as a canal toll-gate keeper, he went into the coal business with his brothers. The business, which included three coal mines, a store, and a chain of coal yards, was barely breaking even. Much to his disbelief, Patterson soon discovered why. Many of his clerks, in an effort to build personal customers, were surreptitiously discounting prices by nearly 50 percent. After firing the guilty employees, Patterson turned to the newly invented cash register to keep track of business.

Patterson was so impressed with the machine and its potential profits that in 1884 he bought the National Manufacturing Company from James Ritty, the machine's inventor and manufacturer. Later that year he gave the company the name it is known by today, the National Cash Register Company. The cash register as improved by Patterson became an instant success—by 1906 he was marketing over 400 models and sizes—and as they became more sophisticated, cash registers radically altered retailer's bookkeeping systems. The register made a record of sales and transactions between clerks and customers. This kept clerks honest, yet saved time and labor.

Gerald Carson, *The Old Country Store* (New York: Oxford University Press, 1954), 107. Samuel Crowther, *John H. Patterson: Pioneer in Industrial Welfare* (Garden City, NY: Doubleday-Page, 1923), 58. Dumas Malone, ed., *Dictionary of American Biography* (New York: Charles Scribner's Sons, 1934), s.v. "Patterson, John Henry."

What was the first chain store business in the United States?

The first chain store business in the United States was the Great American Tea Company, which was established in 1859. In 1925 the company was incorporated in Maryland as the Great Atlantic & Pacific Tea Co. By 1994 the company owned 1,173 grocery stores operating under a variety of trade names including A&P and Farmer Jack. Other chain stores established during the nineteenth century include Montgomery Ward (1872), Woolworth Company (1879), Kroger Company (1882), and Sears, Roebuck and Company (1886).

Moody's Industrial Manual, Vol. 1 (New York: Moody's Investors Services, 1994), 3233. *The World Book Encyclopedia* (Chicago: World Book, 1990), s.v. "chain store."

What was the first department store in the United States?

Naming the first department store in the United States is difficult because of the category. The U.S. Bureau of the Census defines a department store as a large store organized by departments, which sells a variety of merchandise, is under one management, and has annual sales in excess of $100,000. Using this definition it is impossible to say which store first met all of these criteria. Such well-known stores as Macy's, Wanamaker's, and A.T. Stewart's could be called the first department stores, as could be the lesser-known Zion's Co-Operative Mercantile Institution founded by Brigham Young in Salt Lake City in 1868.

Tom Mahoney and Leonard Sloane, *The Great Merchants: America's Foremost Retail Institutions and the People Who Made Them Great, Updated ed.* (New York: Harper & Row, Publishers, 1974), 9-10.

Who was "Little Debbie," the model which appeared since 1960 in the snack cake advertisements?

"Little Debbie," the smiling girl model wearing a sunbonnet in the snack cake advertisements, was Debbie McKee, the granddaughter of O.D. McKee, founder of McKee Foods. The company used "Little Debbie" in its advertisements since 1960 for cupcakes, fruit cookies, and oatmeal cream pies.

Mary B.W. Tabor, "Defeat for Dubious Debbie In Battle Over Trademark," *New York Times* 5 April 1994.

Who was the real Betty Crocker?

Betty Crocker is a fictitious character created by admen in the 1920s for the Washburn Crosby Co., the predecessor of General Mills. She originated out of the company's desire to feminize response letters going out to answer questions from customers. The surname Crocker was chosen to honor a retired director, William G. Crocker. Pictures of Betty Crocker are composites that are revised from time to time to reflect changes in style.

The woman who helped create General Mills' well-known Betty Crocker trademark was Marjorie Child Husted, who died in 1986 at the age of 94. She developed the concept and likeness of the domestic-engineer-extraordinaire in the 1920s while working at a Minnesota company called Washburn-Crosby. In 1928 her employer became part of General Mills, and Husted—a home economist by training—eventually became head of its Betty Crocker Homemaking Service. This department answered volumes of mail about the domestic arts, especially cooking and baking, and even fielded marriage proposals for the winsome but elusive Betty.

Husted was also involved with the popular Betty Crocker cookbooks and served as the voice of the character on a radio program that began in 1927. In a 1948 survey, the trademark homemaker was familiar to 91 percent of American homemakers. Husted's success earned her a number of honors, including the first-ever Woman of the Year award from the Women's National Press Club in 1948 and the Advertising Federation of America's Advertising Woman of the Year in 1949. Until her retirement Husted held the title of Consultant in Advertising, Public Relations and Home Services at General Mills.

Changing Times March 1972. *New York Times* 28 December 1986.

What was the original brand name for Kleenex?

Kleenex was first marketed under the brand name Celluwipes. The product was introduced in 1924 by the Kimberly-Clark Company as a throwaway handkerchief. The name was later changed to Kleenex 'Kerchiefs, which evolved into the shortened form of Kleenex.

Dennis Sanders, *The First of Everything: A Compendium of Important, Eventful, and Just-Plain-Fun Facts About All Kinds of Firsts* (New York: Delacorte, 1981), 12.

What was the first trading stamp company?

The first trading stamp company was formed by Thomas Sperry and Shelly Hutchinson in 1896, and called the Sperry & Hutchinson Company. A stamp was issued for each dollar purchased, and consumers soon were thrilled with the idea of filling up stamp books to redeem prizes. In 1914 six percent of purchases were sold with trading stamps.

Dennis Sanders, *The First of Everything: A Compendium of Important, Eventful, and Just-Plain-Fun Facts About All Kinds of Firsts* (New York: Delacorte, 1981), 8.

Whose advertising slogan was "never underestimate the power of a woman"?

Ladies' Home Journal used the advertising slogan "never underestimate the power of a woman."

William H. Laughlin, *Laughlin's Fact Finder: People, Places, Things, Events* (West Nyack, NY: Parker Publishing, 1969), 578.

Which colors were discontinued by the makers of Crayola crayons in 1990?

The makers of Crayola crayons, Binney & Smith Inc., discontinued eight colors of crayon in 1990: maize, raw umber, violet blue, orange yellow, blue gray, green blue, orange red, and lemon yellow. To replace them, the Eaton, Pennsylvania-based company substituted neon shades, and the many devotees of the brand were outraged. "Raw umber and maize represent a bygone time in America. You can't draw a picture of Nebraska or Kansas or South Dakota without using these colors," Kenneth E. Lang, head of Rumps--the Raw Umber and Maize Preservation Society—told the *New York Times*. In response, Binney & Smith reintroduced the discontinued colors as "classics" in 1991 and sold them separately in a commemorative tin.

New York Times 3 October 1991.

What was the first product to extend a refund offer?

The first product to extend a refund offer was Grape Nuts and Flakes, a cereal manufactured by the C. W. Post Company. In an 1895 promotion, a penny was offered to consumers who tried the product.

Lynn Langway and Janet Huck, "Promotion: Coupon Clippers of '77," *Newsweek* 20 June 1977.

What is the *"hui"* method of financing?

The *"hui"* method of financing is an Asian business practice in which both business owners and would-be entrepreneurs become members of an investment club and contribute as much money as they can. When a member is ready, he or she approaches the *hui* at one of its meetings to request a loan to establish a new business or expand an existing one, indicating the amount of interest that can be paid. Bids are opened and announced, with the highest bidder receiving the loan. This venture capital system has gone on for generations and has allowed thousands of Asian small businesses to get their start in the United States.

Gustav Berle, *The Small Business Information Handbook* (New York: John Wiley & Sons, 1990), 12.

What is a foreign trade zone or FTZ?

A foreign trade zone (FTZ) is a zone where exported foreign merchandise can be kept duty-free for an unlimited time until it is shipped out to an American destination. The FTZ charges a fee, but customs duties are not paid until the merchandise actually leaves the FTZ. Foreign trade zones are attractive options for small importers or budding entrepreneurs.

Gustav Berle, *The Small Business Information Handbook* (New York: John Wiley & Sons, 1990), 85.

Colleges and Universities

What is the rank order of titles held by college or university instructors?

From highest to lowest, in terms of pay and prestige, the order of titles held by college or university instructors is professor, associate professor, assistant professor, instructor, fellow, and assistant (teaching assistant or graduate assistant). Professors are addressed as Professor or Dr. (surname) both orally and in writing; associate and assistant professors as Mr., Ms., Mrs., Miss, or Dr. (surname) orally and as Professor (surname) in writing; instructors as Mr., Ms., Miss, Mrs., or Dr. (surname) both orally and in writing.

Tom Burnam, *The Dictionary of Misinformation* (New York: Thomas Y. Crowell, 1975), s.v. "professor, as title." Anna L. Eckersley-Johnson, ed., *Webster's Secretarial Handbook* (Springfield, MA: Merriam-Webster, 1983), 189-90.

What is the oldest historically black college in the United States?

Lincoln University in Pennsylvania and Wilberforce University in Ohio are the oldest historically black colleges established in the United States. Both remained in their original locations, developed fully into degree-granting institutions and awarded baccalaureate degrees. Lincoln, originally called Ashmun Institute, was incorporated in 1854 and opened its doors in 1856; Wilberforce was incorporated in 1856 and awarded its first baccalaureate degree in 1857. In 1862 the latter came under black control, making it the oldest college operated by African Americans. Ashmun became Lincoln in 1866 in honor of the slain president.

Jessie Carney Smith, ed., *Black Firsts: 2,000 Years of Extraordinary Achievement* (Detroit: Gale Research, 1994), 98-99. Alton Hornsby, Jr., *Chronology of African-American History: Significant Events and People from 1619 to the Present* (Detroit: Gale Research, 1991), 27. Joan Potter, *African-American Firsts: Famous, little-known and unsung triumphs of blacks in America* (New York: Pinto Press, 1994), 21.

What is the difference between the degrees doctor of dental surgery (DDS) and doctor of medical dentistry (DMD)?

The title depends entirely on the school's preference in terminology. The degrees are equivalent.

Reader's Digest Consumer Adviser (Pleasantville, NY: Reader's Digest Association, 1989), 302.

What is the "Rule for Academic Deans"?

The so-called "Rule for Academic Deans" advises first to hide and second, if discovered, to lie! The rule originated with Father Damian Fandal of the University of Dallas.

Time 26 February 1979.

What was the first Greek letter sorority for African Americans?

Alpha Kappa Alpha, the first Greek letter sorority for African Americans, was founded in 1908 at Howard University in Washington, D.C. and was incorporated in 1913.

John Robson, ed., *Baird's Manual of American College Fraternities, 18th ed.* (Menasha, WS: George Banta Company, 1968), 466.

How did the term "Ivy League" schools originate?

The original Ivy League colleges were Army, Brown, Columbia, Cornell, Dartmouth, Harvard, Navy, Pennsylvania, Princeton, and Yale. The two military academies are not members of the present Ivy group. Organized for athletic contests, chiefly football, the League was not officially formed until 1954 but the term was used much earlier. One theory attributes the phrase to a sportswriter of the *New York Herald Tribune* in the 1930s. A second theory attributes the phrase's origin to the Four League of the 1800s. This was an interscholastic league for athletic competition comprising Harvard, Yale, Columbia, and Princeton. The Roman numeral IV was used instead of "four" and was pronounced vocally as "ivy."

Ralph Hickok, *The Encyclopedia of North American Sports History* (New York: Facts on File, 1992), s.v. "ivy league." William Morris and Mary Morris, *Morris Dictionary of Word and Phrase Origins, 2nd ed.*, (New York: Harper & Row, 1988), s.v. "ivy league."

What is the only collegiate circus in the United States?

Florida State University's "Flying High Circus" is the only collegiate circus in the nation. It was founded in 1948. Students work as their own riggers, put up the Big Top, spread sawdust, and string lights. Performers can receive one academic credit, but no academic scholarships or tuition waivers are available. Circus performances take place in Tallahassee each spring, in early April.

Office of the Registrar, *General Bulletin, 1992/1993* (Tallahassee: Florida State University, 1992), 66-67. James T. Black, "A Capital Salute to Spring," *Southern Living* April 1993.

In academic dress, what is correct attire?

The pattern and fabric of academic gowns varies with the degree. Although some universities allow those who have received doctor's degrees to wear gowns in colors distinctive to the university, most graduates wear black. A bachelor's gown has pointed sleeves and is worn closed. A master's gown has oblong sleeves that are open at the wrist. The base of the sleeve hangs in the usual manner, but the rear section is square cut, and an arc has been cut out of the front. The sleeves of a doctor's gown are bell shaped. Designed to be worn either open or closed, the gowns can vary in weight depending on the climate, for they can be made from a variety of materials, including broadcloth, silk, rayon, or cotton poplin.

Although neither the bachelor's nor the master's gown is trimmed, the front of the doctor's gown is faced with black velvet. It also may have three bands of velvet across the sleeves that are black or in a color appropriate to the degree awarded.

Hoods for all degrees are black and made of the same material as the gown. They vary in length according to the degree. The bachelor's hood must be three feet long and the master's, three and a half. The doctor's is four feet and has side panels. Hoods are lined with the official color or colors of the institution conferring the degree. The pattern of the colors is determined by the institution. Often there is a chevron in the field color. The edges of the hoods are bound in velvet or velveteen in a color appropriate to the subject area. The bachelor's is two inches wide; the master's, three inches; and the doctor's, five inches.

Academic caps are black, and for the bachelor's and master's degree, they are made of the same material as the gown. The doctor's cap is made of velvet. They have flat square top, called a mortarboard, from the middle of which a tassel is fastened. The doctor's tassel may be gold, and the others are either black or the color of the discipline.

American Universities and Colleges, 14th ed. (New York: Walter de Gruyter, 1992), 1880.

What was the first American coeducational college?

On December 3, 1833, the first American coeducational college Oberlin Collegiate Institute in Oberlin, Ohio, opened with 44 students (29 men and 15 women). In 1835 it was the first school to admit students without respect to color. In 1837 it awarded its first degrees to 34 students, four of which were women. On March 21, 1850, the college's name was changed to Oberlin College.

Gorton Carruth, *The Encyclopedia of American Facts and Dates, 9th ed.* (New York: HarperCollins, 1993), 191. Joseph Nathan Kane, *Famous First Facts, 4th ed.* (New York: H. W. Wilson, 1981), s.v. "coeducational college."

Which institution did Benedict Arnold plot to betray to the British during the American revolution?

During the American Revolution American army officer Benedict Arnold (1741-1801) plotted to betray West Point to the British. Arnold's plan was discovered but he escaped, he subsequently became a general in the British army. After the British defeat in America, Arnold went to England where he died June 14, 1801.

Dictionary of American History, rev. ed. (New York: Charles Scribner's Sons, 1976), s.v. "Arnold's treason."

What does the script monogram "SP" that appears on Phi Beta Kappa keys represent?

The meaning of the script monogram "SP" that appears on Phi Beta Kappa keys has been open to question. At various times members have felt the letters represent *Signum Principum*, which can be translated "the mark of those who are the best," or *Societas Philosophorum*, which means society of philosophers or lovers of wisdom. In 1907, however, Dr. Edward A. Birge, a Phi Beta Kappa Senator, concluded after careful investigation that the letters stand for *Societas Philosophiae*, which means the society of philosophy or the society of the love of wisdom.

Phi Beta Kappa News & Notes 1929.

Who was the first Native-American to receive an International Rhodes Scholarship Award?

The first Native-American to win a International Rhodes Scholarship Award to study at Oxford University in England was John Joseph Mathews, a member of the Osage tribe. Mathews went on the be a successful writer, who includes among his many publications *The Osages*, *Wahkontah*, and *Talking to the Moon*. In 1934, Mathews wrote a semibiographical novel called *Sundown*, which was one of the earliest novels written by a Native American about Native Americans.

Henry C. Dennis, *The American Indian 1492-1970: A Chronological Fact Book* (Ferry, NY: Oceana Publications, 1971), 103. Sharon Malinowski, ed., *Notable Native Americans* (Detroit: Gale Research, 1995), s.v. "John Joseph Mathews."

What was the only college in New England to remain open during the American Revolutionary War?

Dartmouth College in Hanover, New Hampshire, was the only New England college to remain open throughout the American Revolution. The charter for the college was approved by King George III in 1769 and classes, such as they were, began in 1770. The school is named after the 2nd earl of Dartmouth who was the president of the school's trustees.

David Louis, *Fascinating Facts* (New York: Ridge Press/Crown Publishers, 1977), 37.

What prominent Americans have been Rhodes Scholars?

The Rhodes Trust provides the funds for the famed Rhodes Scholarship, which allows graduate students from the British Commonwealth, South Africa, the United States, and Europe, to study at Oxford University for at least two years. Established in 1902 in the will of British colonial administrator Cecil Rhodes (1853-1902) for the purpose of promoting unity between English-speaking peoples. Of the 3,000 Americans who have been Rhodes scholars at England's Oxford University since 1904, a good number have achieved prominence in their professions. U.S. president Bill Clinton (1946-) was a Rhodes scholar, as were several of his advisors. The list of politicians with this distinction includes these senators: Indiana Republican Richard Lugar, Oklahoma Democrat David Boren, Maryland Democrat Paul Sarbanes, and South Dakota Republican Larry Pressler. Senator J. William Fulbright, who created his own famous scholarship, was a Rhodes scholar.

Rhodes scholars in other fields include: former pro football quarterback Pat Haden, Metro Goldwyn Mayer co-chairman Dennis Stanfill, singer and actor Kris Kristofferson, Harvard University president Neil Leon Rudenstine, Walt Disney Company president Frank Wells, and Librarian of Congress James

H. Billington. A number of famous writers have been Rhodes scholars, such as Caroline Alexander, Cleanth Brooks, Reynolds Price, Robert Penn Warren and Naomi Wolf.

The following athletes from the United States Olympic teams have been awarded Rhodes Scholarships over the years: Norman Taber (1912-track and field); Eddie Eagan (1920, 1924-boxing, 1932-bobsled); John Carleton (1924-nordic ski); Bill Stevenson (1924-track and field); Alan Valentine (1924-rugby); Bill Bradley (1964-basketball); and Tom McMillen (1972-basketball).

Philip W. Goetz, ed., *The New Encyclopaedia Britannica, Micropaedia, 15th ed.* (Chicago: Encyclopaedia Britannica, 1989), s.v. "Rhodes scholarship." "Alumni who made their mark back home," *USA Today* 3 December 1992.

Is there a sorority for lesbians?

Lambda Delta Lambda is the sorority formed by lesbians and first given official recognition by the University of California at Los Angeles. Any women are welcome to join the sorority, whether homosexual or heterosexual, per university rules. The group was formed for social and philanthropic purposes.

"Lesbian-formed sorority recognized," *The Pittsburgh Press* 24 February 1988.

Walt Disney's Donald Duck is the mascot for what university?

Walt Disney's Donald Duck is the mascot for the University of Oregon. Disney gave Oregon exclusive rights to have the famous cartoon character as a mascot, and no other school may use him.

Kevin Neary and Dave Smith, *The Ultimate Disney Trivia Book* (New York: Hyperion, 1992), 12.

What was the first medical college in the United States?

The College of Philadelphia Department of Medicine, now the University of Pennsylvania School of Medicine, was established on May 3, 1765, by Dr. John Morgan and Dr. William Shippen, Jr. The first commencement was held on June 21, 1768, when the first medical diplomas were presented to the ten members of the graduating class.

Joseph N. Kane, *Famous First Facts, 4th ed.* (New York: Wilson, 1981), 383.

What is the world's oldest existing university?

The University of Karueein is the oldest existing university in the world. It was established in Fez, Morocco, in A.D. 859. In the United States the oldest college is Harvard University, founded in 1636. Originally called Newtowne College, its named changed in 1638 to honor its benefactor, John Harvard.

Mark C. Young, ed., *The Guinness Book of Records 1995* (New York: Facts on File, 1994), 191.

What is the name given to the lowest student (in terms of grades) in the United States Naval Academy's graduating class?

The United States Naval Academy graduate with the lowest grades in any given year is called the "anchorman."

Fred L. Worth, *The Trivia Encyclopedia* (New York: Bell Publishing, 1974), 10.

Where do officers in the U.S. Armed Forces receive their training?

Officers in the U.S. Armed Forces receive their training in a variety of programs and institutions including Federal service academies (Military, Naval, Air Force, and Coast Guard); the Reserve Officers Training Corps (ROTC); Officer Candidate School (OCS); the National Guard (State Officer Candidate School programs); the Uniformed Services University of Health Sciences; and other programs.

Department of Labor, Bureau of Labor Statistics, *Occupational Outlook Handbook: 1994-95 Edition* (Washington: Government Printing Office, 1994), 455.

Who was the first woman in the world to receive a university degree?

The first woman in the world to receive a university degree was Elena Cornaro Piscopia (1646-1684) who was awarded a degree from the University of Padua.

Pittsburgh Post Gazette 10 July 1936.

What is meant by the phrase "academic freedom"?

The phrase "academic freedom" has three related meanings. In the most general sense it refers to intellectual freedom in any educational setting. More specifically it means the right of teachers to pursue all aspects their vocation without the threat of political or institutional censorship, and the freedom to express oneself in the context of an academic setting.

Jay M. Shafritz, Richard P. Koeppe, and Elizabeth W. Soper, *The Facts On File Dictionary of Education* (New York: Facts on File, 1988), s.v. "academic freedom."

Did any First Lady before Hillary Clinton have an advanced degree?

The first "first lady" with a college degree was Lucy Ware Webb Hayes. She became first lady in 1887 and had received her degree from Cincinnati Wesleyan College. More than a hundred years later, with a Yale law degree, Hillary Clinton became the first first lady to have a postgraduate education. Seven other "first ladies" held college degrees: Frances Folsom Cleveland, Grace Anna Coolidge, Lou Henry Hoover, Jacqueline Lee Bouvier Kennedy, Lady Bird Johnson, Pat Ryan Nixon, and Nancy Reagan.

USA Weekend, Tribune Review 27 December 27, 1992.

What was the Institute of 1770?

The Institute of 1770 was the oldest social club at Harvard University, in Cambridge, Massachusetts. It was known variously as the Speaking Club, the Patriotic Association, and the Social Fraternity of 1770. Secret until it ventured into the public in 1825 as "The American Institute of 1770," the club merged with the Hasty Pudding Club in 1924.

Stewart Mitchell, *Official Guide to Harvard University* (Cambridge: Harvard University, 1929), 154-57. Charles A. Wagner, *Harvard: Four Centuries and Freedoms* (New York: E. P. Dutton, 1950), 82.

Who were the first African-American graduates of the Air Force Academy?

Charles Vernon Bush, Issac Sanders Payne IV, and Roger Bernard Sims were the first African Americans to graduate from the United States Air Force Academy at Colorado Springs. They graduated on June 5, 1963, with each receiving a Bachelor of Science degree.

Joseph Nathan Kane, *Famous First Facts, 4th ed.* (New York: H. W. Wilson, 1981), 9.

Libraries, Museums, and Research Institutions

Where is the National Baseball Hall of Fame and Museum located?

The National Baseball Hall of Fame and Museum is located in Cooperstown, New York, where Abner Doubleday is credited with inventing the game in 1839. It opened in 1939 in honor of baseball's first one hundred years. This large brick building houses such treasures as Lou Gehrig's New York license plate, Dwight Gooden's hat, the bat Babe Ruth used in 1927 when he hit his record-breaking 60th home run, a collection of all the World Series rings, and, of course, tobacco and gum cards, some dating back to 1887.

Joyce Jurnovoy and David Jenness, *America on Display* (New York: Facts On File Publications, 1987), 37.

Who founded the American Philosophical Society?

The American Philosophical Society is an organization composed of scholars, statesmen, and scientists who gather together to exchange information and promote scientific research. It was founded in 1743 by U.S. statesman Benjamin Franklin (1706-90).

Howard L. Hurwitz, *An Encyclopedic Dictionary of American History* (New York: Washington Square Press, 1968), s.v. "American Philosophical Society."

Is there a Coca-Cola museum?

The World of Coca-Cola is a four-story building, located near company headquarters in downtown Atlanta, Georgia. It was built at a cost of $10 million and contains Coke memorabilia like a 90-year-old serving tray worth $20,000, a working soda fountain, and video displays that include a collection of past Coke advertisements. There is an admission charge.

James Cox, "Coca-Cola to enshrine soft drink," *USA Today* 23 November 1988.

What is the name of the national library of France?

The Bibliothque Nationale is the national library of France and the oldest European national library, with a continuous history dating from the reign of Louis XI (1461-83).

Academic American Encyclopedia (Danbury, CT: Grolier, 1990), s.v. "Bibliothque Nationale."

What are the names of the two lions on the front steps of the New York Public Library?

The two lions on the front steps of the New York Public Library are affectionately known to New Yorkers as "Lady Astor" and "Lord Lenox." The amiable lions were fashioned by Edward C. Potter.

Marshall B. Davidson, *Treasures of the New York Public Library* (New York: Harry N. Abrams, 1988), 18.

What is the Center for Reformation Research?

The Center for Reformation Research, formerly the Foundation for Reformation Research, is a library holding the largest single collection of sixteenth-century documentation of the Reformation on microfilm in the United States. It is located in St. Louis at the Concordia Lutheran Seminary. The center was established in 1957 to assist scholars in reexamining the issues that led to the division between the Protestant and Catholic Churches, providing a Protestant counterpart of the Pius XII Memorial Library's Vatican collection at St. Louis University.

"Library Holds Reformation Answers: World's Scholars Visit 16th Century In St. Louis," *Pittsburgh Press* 20 July 1966.

Where are the British Crown Jewels kept for protection?

The Tower of London is home to the British Crown Jewels. They are located in the Tower's Waterloo Barracks. This collection is made up of gem covered pieces of gold and silver, including: the ampulla and spoon used to anoint English kings and queens, the Imperial Mantle, as well as various royal orbs, scepters, rings, and crowns.

Louise Nicholson, *Fodor's London Companion* (New York: Fodor's Travel Publications, 1987), 103.

When was the first library established in the United States?

Although Boston established a public library in the seventeenth century, most of the first libraries on the North American continent belonged to colleges or were in the hands of private individuals. The library of Harvard College in Cambridge, Massachusetts, was probably the oldest, since the school had a library almost before it was founded. In 1638, John Harvard donated 380 books and a small cash endowment to the college. The first private libraries were owned by early colonial leaders like William Bradford (1590-1657) and John Winthrop ((1588-1649) of Massachusetts. Cotton Mather (1663-1728) was the first man to amass a library of any size, building it to 4,000 volumes.

Captain Robert Keayne of Boston endowed the first public library in America, when he willed his collection of books to the city for public use 1656. The building for the library was completed in 1658, but by all accounts it was small and probably lacked patrons. If the public library is defined as being a book collection that is publicly supported, publicly controlled, and for general public use, there were few such libraries in the United States before 1850. The town usually considered as the pioneer in providing permanent library service was Peterborough, New Hampshire. In 1833, its citizens took part of the State Literary Fund that was usually applied to schools and used it for the purchase of books for a free public library.

Aline C. Wisdom, *Introduction to Library Services for Library Media Technical Assistants* (New York: McGraw-Hill, 1974), 24, 37-8, 41.

Where is the Ambrosian Library and why is it famous?

The Ambrosian Library (Biblioteca Ambrosiana) is in Milan, Italy, and is named after St. Ambrose (339-397), a former bishop of that city and its patron saint. The library was started by Federigo Borromeo, a cardinal of the Roman Catholic Church and also a Milanese bishop, whose episcopate spanned the years 1595 to 1631. Known for his charity and his heroism during the plague of 1630, the bishop was also an avid bibliophile who wanted to establish a center of culture that would restore scholarly prestige to Italy and make Milan a center of learning in a world torn by religious controversy. So in 1609 he founded a library that was to become one of the most important repositories of manuscripts in Europe. Among its many treasures it includes fragments from a fourth or fifth-century copy of the Iliad, an album of drawings by Leonardo da Vinci, the love letters of Lucretia Borgia, and three orations of Cicero that were unknown until they were discovered in the library in the early nineteenth century. The building was bombed by the Allies during World War II (1939-45), and although the manuscripts had been removed for safety reasons, 50,000 books and the beautiful reading room that Bishop Federigo had built was destroyed. After the war the building was carefully restored.

Anthony Hobson, *Great Libraries* (New York: G.P. Putnam's Sons, 1970), 186-95.

Where was the great library of ancient Egypt located? How large was the collection?

Located in Alexandria, Egypt, the Alexandrian Library was the greatest library of ancient Egypt. It was established by Alexander the Great in the 330s B.C. Under Alexander's successors, Ptolemy I and Ptolemy II, this Greek institution became the greatest repository of papyrus scrolls in ancient history. Although no trace of the library remains, at one time its collection totaled more than 400,000 scrolls. The library's administrators borrowed scrolls from other libraries, including libraries in other countries, and had them copied for the Alexandrian collection. The library owned a copy of every scroll known to the library's administration. The library, which was headed by a number of noted scholars, eventually became known not only for its collection, but also for the scholarly work it supported.

World Book Encyclopedia (Chicago: World Book, 1987), s.v. "libraries of papyrus."

What is the size of the collection at the Smithsonian Institution?

The Smithsonian Institution in Washington D.C. houses approximately 140 million objects. The Smithsonian's collection are the Institution's main focus. The Smithsonian Bill of Incorporation was passed by the U.S. Congress in 1846.

Smithsonian Year, 1992 (Washington, DC: Smithsonian Institution Press, 1993), 4.

Where is the Money Museum?

The Money Museum is affiliated with, and located in, the Federal Reserve Bank of Richmond, Virginia. It contains nearly 600 specimens of coins from around the world, as well as exhibits detailing the history of American currency.

James F. Tucker, *Your Money: A Review of Money in Use in the United States, 3d ed.* (n.p.: Federal Reserve Bank of Richmond, 1991), 19.

Which libraries have large collections of pornography?

Some of the world's libraries with large collections of pornography include the Vatican Library in Rome, the Kinsey Institute in Indiana, the U. S. Library of Congress, the British Museum in London, and the Bibliothque Nationale in Paris.

David Loth, *The Erotic in Literature: A historical survey of pornography as delightful as it is indiscreet* (New York: Julian Messner, 1961), 183-84.

What are some of the problems that beset rare book collections in libraries?

Rare book collections present a unique array of problems for librarians. The first of these is whether or not a work is "rare" and needs to be placed in a special collection. Next, once an edition has entered the rare book collection there is the question of if, and how, it should be marked. Some libraries stamp or pencil catalog and accession numbers, others consider such actions as defacements. The strict control of materials and supervision of those using the collection is also an important concern to rare book librarians to prevent deterioration, defacement, or theft.

Lawrence Clark Powell, "Problem of Rare Books In The College and University Library," *Library Journal* 1 April 1939.

Where is the Big Foot Museum located?

The Big Foot Museum, which includes newspaper clippings, photos, charts, and drawings of the legendary but elusive hairy ape-man of the American Northwest, is located in The Dalles, in north-central Oregon, at the foot of Mt. Hood's north slope. The museum's founder, Irish explorer Peter Byrne, in 1974 offered a $1,000 reward to anyone providing information that would lead directly to a find by the center's investigative team. To date, no one has claimed the reward. Just across the Columbia River in Skamania County, Washington, the county board of commissioners passed a law in 1969 that provided for a five-year jail sentence for any person or persons who "willfully and wantonly" kills a Big Foot.

Jack Pement, "Scientific Team Launches Search For Northwest's Fabled 'Big Foot,'" *Pittsburgh Press* 15 June 1974.

Pre-College Education

What is the "whole language" approach to reading?

The whole language approach operates from the basic premise that reading and writing are meaningful activities that cannot be taught separately from their natural social contexts and purposeful uses. Whole language advocates eschew the teaching of reading through drills on language parts, such as letters, syllables, words, and grammar rules.

Gary A. Woodill, Judith Bernhard, and Lawrence Prochner, eds., *International Handbook of Early Childhood Education* (New York: Garland Publishing, 1992), 516.

What issues were raised by California's Proposition 174, which would have initiated a school voucher plan?

California's Proposition 174 would have given parents vouchers worth about $2,600 per child, which could be used as tuition payments to send their offspring to the school of their choice. The measure aroused strong feelings on both sides. Since the vouchers could be used at religious schools, some maintained that the proposition violated the constitutional provision for the separation of church and state. They argued further that under a voucher system the budgets of public schools would shrink and the quality of their education decrease. On the other hand, parents of children in private schools asserted that they were unfairly subsidizing public education by relieving the state of the cost of their children's tuition. They also claimed that the public educational system would benefit as well by introducing choice and competition.

USA Today 9 September 1993.

Who founded the kindergarten movement?

Educational reformer Friedrich Froebel (1782-1852) was the founder of the kindergarten movement. Froebel opened an infant school in Germany in the late 1830s. Originally it was called the Child Nurture and Activity Institute, but he later renamed it the Kindergarten. The school put into practice his belief that infant education needed to be improved. Although banned by the Prussian government from 1851 until 1860 as subversive, Froebel's educational concept of kindergarten won worldwide support. He also published the widely popular *Mother-Play and Nursery Songs* and other educational materials for children.

Philip W. Goetz, ed., *The New Encyclopaedia Britannica, 15th ed., "Micropaedia"* (Chicago: Encyclopaedia Britannica, 1989), s.v. "Froebel, Friedrich."

What is "hothousing"?

The term "hothousing" became well known in the mid-1980s in reference to a style of education that involves formal instruction for infants and toddlers. The term reflects the controlled environment created by this practice and the negative side effects that can accompany it. Educational experts speak of a child being "hothoused" when he or she is not given the opportunity to experience unstructured play, and to follow their own natural learning impulses. Such children often believe that their personal value is based on their achievements, causing a higher level of anxiety.

Glenn Collins, "Experts Say Don't Rush Child's Natural Pace of Early Learning," *Pittsburgh Post-Gazette* 28 November 1985.

Why is Shakespeare's *Julius Caesar* still a standard in high school curriculums?

The great English dramatist Shakespeare's historical work, *Julius Caesar* was once popular in high school Latin classes as an adjunct to Caesar's *Commentaries.* Once rooted in the school curriculum, it has stayed there even though Latin is no longer taught.

Another reason for its popularity may be because it lacks sexual puns or allusions which usually cause embarrassed titters and giggles among high school students.

Norrie Epstein, *The Friendly Shakespeare* (New York: Viking, 1993), 13.

What is the Montessori Method of education?

The Montessori Method of education for children was developed by Maria Montessori (1870-1952), an Italian physician, nineteenth-century champion of women's rights, and innovative educator, who focused on the cognitive development of the child. In 1894 Montessori became the first woman to receive a medical degree in Italy and her first professional position was as an assistant doctor in the University of Rome's psychiatric clinic. In 1898 she became the director of the State Orthophonic School in Rome where she worked with "deficient" children. In 1906, after having various academic positions at the University of Rome, she was put in charge of a state-supported school in a Rome slum. It was there that she began developing what was later called the Montessori Method of education.

This method, which eventually found its way into various private schools, stressed independent thinking and initiative sense perception, creativity, and responsible self-discipline on the part of the student. The teacher was regarded not as an instructor but rather as an "adviser and guide" who sets up the learning atmosphere through a selection of materials, exercises, and experiences that is individualized for each student's need. Montessori felt that children went through "sensitive periods" which were characterized by "spontaneous interest" and a "greater ability" to learn. She did not believe in formal classes, classroom settings, or curriculums. Her educational methods reached cyclical periods of popularity in Europe and the United States.

McGraw-Hill Dictionary of World Biography (New York: McGraw-Hill, 1973), s.v. "Montessori." Irene Franck and David Brownstone, *The Parent's Desk Reference* (New York: Prentice Hall, 1991), 328.

When did organized child care services begin in the United States?

The earliest child care in the United States was derived from the extended family. Aunts, uncles, and older siblings would care for children who were too young to work. In the early nineteenth century the European concept of the infant school was brought to America. The idea originated in Great Britain with a businessman's desire to free more laborers from child care responsibilities, but the group of Christian women who founded the first day care center in America in 1828 also viewed it as a training ground for religion and morality. In spite of their concern for character building, the infant schools fell into disfavor because many leading authorities believed early learning would lead to disease of the mind and body. The decline of infant schools was a disaster for poor women, who had to work and thus were often forced to abandon their children at foundling homes or even to sell them.

Yet, the catalyst for child care services had nothing to do with a sense of social outrage. World War II (1939-45) brought large numbers of women back into the work force in order to replace men who were needed for military service. Since the Works Progress Administration (WPA) had funded child care centers during the Great Depression to provide jobs for unemployed adults, legislation was enacted to continue and expand WPA centers. Their funding was provided by the Federal Works Agency (FWA) under the Latham Act. After the war, most of these centers were closed; California was the only state to continue funding Latham Act centers.

Edward F. Zigler and Mary E. Lang *Child Care Choices: Balancing the Needs of Children, Families, and Society* (New York: The Free Press, 1991), 28-37.

What is the worst school disaster in U.S. history?

The worst school disaster in U.S. history occurred on March 18, 1937, in New London, Texas, when a natural gas explosion ripped through the Consolidated School tragically killing 412 children.

Woody Gelman and Barbara Jackson, *Disaster Illustrated: Two Hundred Years of American Misfortune* (New York: Harmony Books, 1976), 100.

When did kindergarten begin in the United States?

The kindergarten was introduced in the United States during the 1800s by German immigrants who had fled Germany to escape the aftermath of the Revolution of 1848. The first kindergarten was started in Watertown, Wisconsin, by Margarethe Schurz in 1855. The kindergarten movement was largely a province of the German-American community and by 1870, of the 11 kindergartens in the United States, only one of them was English-speaking. The movement continued to expand through the turn of the century, and by 1914 every major urban center in the United States had a public kindergarten.

Gary A. Woodill, Judith Bernhard, and Lawrence Prochner, eds., *International Handbook of Early Childhood Education* (New York: Garland Publishing, 1992), 504-5.

Beverages

Who invented instant coffee?

Powdered coffee has been known since the eighteenth century and in 1838 the United States Congress used instant coffee in the form of a liquid extract as a substitute for rum in the rations of American soldiers and sailors. This extract was not practical to produce and it was not accepted by the public.

During the American Civil War (1862-65) a cake form of powdered coffee was a convenient but less-palatable alternative for union troops. In 1901 Japanese chemist Sartori Kato created the first powdered instant coffee that was sold to a receptive public at the 1901 Pan-American Exhibition in Buffalo, New York. In 1906 American chemist G. Washington created a more-refined, better-tasting powder. The Nestle Company in Switzerland in 1938 marketed the first commercially available instant coffee and again in the 1960s introduced freeze-dried instant coffee.

Barbara Berliner, *The Book of Answers* (New York: Prentice-Hall, 1990), 108. John F. Mariani, *The Dictionary of American Food and Drink* (New York: Ticknor & Fields, 1983), 119. Bridget Travers, ed., *World of Invention* (Detroit: Gale Research, 1994), s.v. "instant coffee."

Who invented iced tea?

Iced tea was first created in 1904 at the St. Louis World's Fair. At the time Chinese tea was the most popular in the United States, but a group of tea producers from India wanted to introduce Americans to their product. As people were not interested in drinking hot tea during the fair's warm summer days, the Indians poured their tea over ice. The new drink was quite popular with fair attendees.

Madeline Matson, *Food in Missouri: A Cultural Stew* (Missouri: University of Missouri Press, 1994), 121.

Who invented soda pop?

Joseph Priestley (1733-1804), the British clergyman and chemist who discovered oxygen, created the first carbonated water in 1767, from injecting carbon dioxide gas into water—but it was not very tasty. In 1807 Dr. Philip Syng Physick asked a Philadelphia druggist, Townsend Speakman, to prepare carbonated water for some of his patients. In order to make it more palatable, Speakman mixed fruit flavors with Priestley's invention, and marketed it as Nephite Julep.

Merriam-Webster's Collegiate Dictionary, 10th ed., (Springfield, MA: Merriam-Webster, 1993), s.v. "tonic." George Stimpson, *A Book About a Thousand Things* (New York: Harper & Brothers, 1946), 173-4. David Wallechinsky and Irving Wallace, *The People's Almanac* (New York: Doubleday, 1975), 914.

What is the origin of the trade name *Pepsi Cola*?

The trade name *Pepsi Cola* originated because of its similarity to *Coca Cola* and its supposed aid in relieving dyspepsia or indigestion. Invented by a pharmacist Caleb D. Bradham of New Bern, North Carolina, the soda first was called "Brad's Drink" by the locals, until Bradham chose the name Pepsi Cola in 1898.

Leslie Alan Dunkling, *The Guinness Book of Names,* (Enfield, Middlesex: Guinness Books, 1986), 158. Bridget Travers, ed., *World of Invention* (Detroit: Gale Research, 1994), s.v. "soda pop."

At what temperature is milk pasteurized?

Most milk sold for direct human consumption is pasteurized—heated hot enough and long enough to destroy all disease-causing organisms, especially the heat resistant *Mycobacterium tuberculosis.* Pasteurization, a process invented by the French chemist, Louis Pasteur (1822-1895), also retards spoilage by killing most of the bacteria that affect the milk's freshness and by inactivating the inherent milk enzymes (especially the fat-splitters) that make milk unpalatable. One standard method among the different combinations of temperature and time is to heat milk in a batch process to 144 degrees Fahrenheit (62 degrees Centigrade) for 30 minutes (at that temperature). In the continuous process, the milk is heated to at least 160 degrees Fahrenheit (71.7 degrees Centigrade) for at least 15 seconds. The first method stays well below the temperature at which a "cooked" flavor develops, whereas the temperature of the second method of continuous process approaches this temperature limit.

Encyclopedia of Chemical Technology, 3d ed. (New York: Wiley, 1978), 15:530. Harold McGee, *On Food and Cooking* (New York: Collier Books, 1988), 13.

How is coffee decaffeinated?

There are two methods generally used: solvent method or water process. In the first, coffee beans are placed in a rotating drum and softened by steam for 30 minutes. Then the beans are soaked in a chemical solvent such as methylene chloride for approximately ten hours. When the chemical has absorbed the caffeine out of the beans, both caffeine and chemical are drained away. The beans are steamed for another 8 to 12 hours to allow any remaining solvent to evaporate. A minute amount of the chemical-approximately 0.1 parts per million-remains in the beans. The concern over this solvent residue's effect on human health has prompted producers to turn more and more to water process methods.

In the second method-the water process-green coffee beans are soaked in hot water until the caffeine is drawn out from the beans. The drained water containing the caffeine is treated with a chemical, such as methylene chloride, to absorb the caffeine. Then the mixture is heated until both the chemical and caffeine evaporate. The remaining water is returned to the beans, wherein, according to coffee experts, the beans regain most of their flavor. In this method, the solvent does not come in contact with the bean. The Swiss Water Process extracts the caffeine through carbon filtering rather than using a chemical solvent. But the drawback is that decaffeinated coffee made by this method does not taste as well.

Some producers have used ethyl acetate in place of methylene chloride, but it is not as effective as the latter in decaffeination. Its use is sometimes labeled "the natural process" because ethyl acetate has been found to occur naturally in minute quantities in ripening fruit, such as apples and bananas. Another solvent, liquid carbon dioxide, has also been used as an effective decaffeination agent which dissipates afterward, leaving no residue. Decaffeination processes still can leave one to five milligrams of caffeine compared to 100 milligrams present in a regular cup of coffee.

Corby Kummer, "The Flavor Factor," *American Health* September 1995. *Prevention's Giant Book of Health Facts* (Emmaus, PA: Rodale Press, 1991), 111. Neil Schlager, ed., *How Products Are Made* (Detroit: Gale Research, 1994), s.v. "coffee."

How is egg cream made?

Egg cream is a New York City soda fountain drink, popular since the 1930s. It does not contain any eggs. It is a mixture of milk and chocolate syrup into which seltzer water is spritzed, causing the mixture to foam. Egg cream is so named for its frothy head that resembles beaten egg whites.

Sharon Taylor Herbst, *Food Lover's Companion* (Hauppauge, NY: Barron, 1990), 153.

Is mead an alcoholic drink?

Mead is an alcoholic drink made by fermenting a solution of water and honey with malt and yeast. Sometimes mead is flavored with wild flowers or spices. One of the oldest liquors, the name is derived from the Sanskrit *madhu*, meaning honey. In medieval Europe, spiced mead was also called *metheglin*, deriving from the Welsh word *meddyglyn*.

Oscar Mendelsohn, *The Dictionary of Drink and Drinking* (London: Macmillan, 1965), 215-16. *Woman's Day Encyclopedia of Cookery* (New York: Fawcett, 1966-67), 12:1116.

What are the different sizes of wine bottles?

The standard wine bottle is 757 milliliters, which is almost equivalent to an "American fifth" (4/5 of a quart or 1 pint 9.6 fluid ounces or 25.6 fluid ounces). Other bottle sizes used to contain wine are:

Split—1/4 of a standard wine bottle or 6.4 ounces
Half-bottle—1/2 of a standard wine bottle or 12.8 fluid ounces or 4/5 pint
Magnum—1.5 liters equivalent to 2 standard bottles (usually champagne)
Jeroboam—4 bottles in one or 1.6 magnums, or 6.4 pints (usually champagne and brandy)
Gallon—5 bottles in one
Rehoboam—6 bottles in one or 3 magnums (usually champagne)
Methuselah—8 bottles in one or 4 magnums (usually champagne)
Salmanazar—12 bottles in one or 6 magnums (usually champagne)
Balthazar—16 bottles in one or 8 magnums (usually champagne)
Nebuchadnezzar—20 bottles in one or 10 magnums (usually champagne)

Sharon Tyler Herbst, *Food Lover's Companion* (Hauppauge, NY: Barron, 1990), 502. Jeff Rovin, *Laws of Order* (New York: Ballantine, 1992), 50. *World Almanac and Book of Facts* (New York: World Almanac, 1991), 305.

What is the difference between a vintner, a viticulturist, and an enologist?

A vintner is a winemaker; a viticulturist is a grape grower. An enologist is one who directs and coordinates all activities concerned with production of wine; a wine taster is an enologist.

Department of Labor, *Dictionary of Occupational Titles, 4th ed.* (Washington, DC: Government Printing Office), 124. Philips Seldon, *The Vintage Magazine Consumer Guide to Wine* (New York: Doubleday, 1983), 3, 18. Richard P. Vine, *Commercial Winemaking, Processing and Controls* (Westport, CT: AVI, 1981), 460.

What does the term "proof" on a liquor bottle mean?

In the United States, the term proof is a measurement of strength of (ethyl) alcohol contained in a volume of liquor at 68 degrees Fahrenheit (20 degrees Celsius). One degree of proof equals 0.5 of one percent of alcohol. For example, a bottle labeled "80 proof" contains 40 percent alcohol.

Mr. Boston Official Bartender's Guide, 63rd ed. (New York: Warner Books, 1988), 212.

How is casein used?

Casein is the main protein in milk and is not found in any food other than milk. It gives milk its white color and coagulates in milk as little white flecks when milk becomes slightly sour. Prior to the discovery of plastics, casein was used extensively in various manufacturing processes such as button-making. It is now dried and used as powdered creamer for tea and coffee and is also used in the manufacture of paint and glue.

Patricia Cleveland-Peck, *Making Cheeses, Butters, Cream and Yoguart at Home* (Wellingborough, England: Thorsons Publishing, 1980), 12-13.

What is the formula for Coca-Cola?

Only one or two senior corporate officers know the exact proportions of the ingredients for Coca-Cola. The cola has never been patented, so its composition remains a secret. Fourteen of its ingredients-including caramel, sugar, coca leaves (with cocaine content removed), cola nut extract, citric acid and sodium nitrate, caffeine, phosphoric acid, lemon, orange, lime, cassia (a type of cinnamon), nutmeg oils, etc., vanilla, and glycerine-are generally well known. The name of the fifteenth ingredient, known only as "7X," is one of the best-guarded secrets in the industry. The ingredients are mixed with carbonated water.

How in the World (Pleasantville, NY: Reader's Digest Association, 1990), 389. Adrian Room, *Dictionary of Trade Name Origins* (London: Routledge & Kegan Paul, 1982), 56.

Has cocaine ever been an ingredient in Coca-Cola?

Yes, cocaine had been an ingredient at one time. Like so many other early soda drinks, cola originated as one of the tonics and elixirs mixed by neighborhood druggists for their customers' maladies. A pharmacist in Atlanta, Georgia, Dr. John Styth Pemberton, in 1885, mixed a number of ingredients including purified cocaine to create Coca-Cola. The name was derived from two of the constituents of the drink; extract from *coca* leaves (cocaine) and extract from the *cola* or kola nut. Around 1899 Asa Candler, an Atlanta pharmacist who bought Pemberton's business, was convinced by Benjamin F. Thomas and Joseph Whitehead of Chattanooga, Tennessee, to join them in bottling the drink. The cocaine was removed from the soft drink shortly before the passage in 1907 of the Pure Food and Drug Act.

Tom Burnam, *The Dictionary of Misinformation* (New York: Perennial Library, 1986) 48. John C. Flynn, *Cocaine* (New York: Carol Publishing Group, 1991), 27. Adrian Room, *Dictionary of Trade Name Origins* (London: Routledge & Kegan Paul, 1982), 56.

What is the beverage known as Moxie?

Moxie is the tradename for a fairly tart or bitter soft drink which in the 1880s had been one of the most popular sodas in the United States. It began as a concentrated tonic bottled by the Moxie Nerve Food Company of Lowell, Massachusetts, in 1885; soon afterward carbonation was added. The word itself has come to mean "courage," "nerve," or "shrewdness."

John F. Mariani, *The Dictionary of American Food and Drink* (New York: Ticknor & Fields, 1983), 260. Bridget Travers, ed., *World of Invention* (Detroit: Gale Research, 1994), 562-63.

What are the ingredients in beer?

Beer is made from water, malt, sugar, hops, yeast (dried beer yeast, not baker's or wine yeast), a little salt, and a little citric acid. Malt gives beer its characteristic body and flavor. Hops, the ripe and carefully dried fruit of the herb *Humulus lupulus*, give beer flavor and bitterness; hops are the single most expensive ingredient in beer.

Bob Abel, *The Book of Beer* (Chicago: Regnery, 1976), 64.

Why do bubbles rise in a glass of beer?

Beer bubbles, made of carbon dioxide, have a lower density than the surrounding beer liquid. The density difference causes these bubbles to rise in the liquid. The bubbles grow as they accumulate carbon dioxide during their ascension upward through the beer.

Physics Today October 1991.

How many calories are there in light beer?

In order for a company to call a beer "light," it must have 1/3 fewer calories than the same company's regular beer. Regular beers average about 150 calories; light beers average about 100 calories. Light beers usually contain a lower percentage of alcohol than their regular counterparts do.

Mary Blocksma, *Reading the Numbers* (New York: Penguin, 1989), 112.

What is the derivation of the drink wassail?

This warmed drink, once popular in England on special occasions such as Christmas and Twelfth Night, is made from ale or wine flavored with spices (such as cinnamon, nutmeg, and cloves) and usually contains roasted apples. Originally it was used as a toast to someone's health or for good luck. The word itself is derived from the Old Norse word *vesheill*, which means "be in good health." Often at Christmastime in Old England, groups of carolers would go *a-wassailing*, traveling from house to house caroling their hosts in return for a cup of this delicious drink.

Woman's Day Encyclopedia of Cookery (New York: Fawcett, 1966-67), 12:1918.

How many gallons are in a barrel of beer?

There are 31 gallons of beer in a U.S. barrel.

O.T. Zimmerman, *Conversion Factors and Tables* p. 13.

What are the leading tea-producing countries?

The leading tea producing countries include India, China, Sri Lanka, Kenya, Indonesia, Soviet Union, Turkey, Japan, and Iran. India and China outproduce the others by significant amounts.

The World Book Encyclopedia (Chicago: World Book, 1993), 19:63.

What are the leading coffee producing countries?

The leading coffee producing country is Brazil which produces nearly triple the amount the next leading country, Columbia, does. Indonesia, Mexico, the Ivory Coast, India, Ethiopia, Guatemala, Uganda and El Salvador also lead in the production of coffee.

The World Book Encyclopedia (Chicago: World Book, 1993), 4:754.

Did the ancient Egyptians brew beer?

In 1994 Cambridge archaeologist Barry Kemp claimed to have uncovered a large combination brewery and bakery, possibly from the reign of ancient Egypt's Queen Nefertiti. A 4,000-year-old beer recipe names some of the ingredients as olives and dates.

Steve Marshall, "Tut's Tipple Soon on Tap," *USA Today* 23 March 1994.

Who were the two engaging old timers who appeared as Bartles & Jaymes in the Bartles & Jaymes California Wine Cooler commercials of the mid-1980s?

The two engaging old timers who appeared as Bartles & Jaymes in the Bartles & Jaymes California Wine Cooler commercials are David Rufkahr as Bartles and Dick Maugg as Jaymes. Neither are professional actors.

Parade 9 November 1986.

What kind of drinks have been dubbed New Age beverages?

Clear, fruit-flavored drinks and clear colas have been called New Age beverages.

John Algeo and Adele Algeo, "Among the New Words," *American Speech: A Quarterly of Linguistic Usage* Spring 1994.

What does an order of macchiato at a coffee bar mean?

To order a macchiato at a coffee bar means to order a petit cup of espresso with a touch of milk (for a bit of foam). Espresso is a dark roasted coffee produced from a rapid "shot" of very hot water through the coffee grounds and served in petit cups, sometimes with a twist of lemon. The name comes from the Italian world macchiare which means to mark or stain.

Myles H. Bador, *4001 Food Facts and Chef's Secrets, rev. ed.* (San Diego, CA: Mylin Publishing, 1993), 150-51. *New York Times Magazine* 31 July 1994.

What do the letters *A.O.C.* stand for on a wine label, and how is it pronounced?

The highest quality French wines have the letters *A.O.C.* on their labels. The letters stand for the French phrase *"appellation d'origine contrle,"* which is a pledge that the wine was grown in the location stated on the label and in the correct manner. It is pronounced *ap-el-ah-syom-do-ri-zheen-kon-trohl-ay.*

B.A. Phythian, *A Concise Dictionary of Foreign Expressions* (New York: Barnes & Noble Books, 1982), s.v. "appellation d'origine contrle."

What were the popular beverages in the American colonies?

In the American colonies chocolate was the most popular nonalcoholic drink. In New England rum was the favorite alcoholic beverage, while the middle colonies preferred beer.

Isaac Asimov, *Isaac Asimov's Book of Facts* (New York: Grosset & Dunlap, 1979), 90.

It is usually suggested that red table wine be served at "room temperature," but just what is room temperature?

Red table wines are commonly served at room temperature, which is considered to be 65 to 68 degrees Fahrenheit. Therefore, in warm weather red wine should actually be cooled slightly.

The New York Public Library Desk Reference (New York: Webster's New World, 1989), 529.

Why are so many wines sold in tinted bottles?

Many wines are bottled in tinted glass in order to protect it from harmful ultraviolet light. Extended exposure to light can turn wine brown and give it a flat taste; this effect is called oxidation or maderization. For this reason it is recommended that wine also be stored in a dark place. The specific color of glass is often an indication of where the wine was produced. Rhine wine is bottled in brown glass, White Bordeaux in clear glass, and Moselles and Red Bordeaux in green glass.

Alexis Lichine, *Alexis Lichine's New Encyclopedia of Wines & Spirits* (New York: Alfred A. Knopf, 1987), 25. Hugh Johnson, *Hugh Johnson's Modern Encyclopedia of Wine* (New York: Simon & Schuster, 1983), 508.

How did the decaffeinated coffee, *Sanka,* get its name?

The process of decaffeinating coffee was perfected by Ludwig Roselius who began selling it in Europe circa 1900 under the name *Sanka.* The word loosely translates as "sans caffeine" in French. The product was marketed in the United States around 1911. By 1928 General Foods had obtained the distribution rights and in 1932 the company purchased the patent and rights to the name.

Stuart Elliott, "Advertising," *New York Times* 13 September 1994.

How does a whole pear get into a bottle of pear brandy?

Pear growers, such as those in France, tie a bottle on a pear branch over a blossom or a tiny developing fruit, which proceeds to grow and ripen inside the bottle. Bottle and pear are sent to brandy makers where distilled brandy is added. The contents are sealed and then shipped to distributors. Connoisseurs of brandy find this a conversation piece more than anything else, since the pear does not guarantee high quality.

Caroline Sutton and Duncan M. Anderson, *How Do They Do That?* (New York: Quill, 1982), 27.

What are the primary ingredients in the beverage bishop?

Bishop, which is another name for mulled wine, can be served either hot or cold. In Great Britain it is normally made with mulled wine, oranges, sugar, and spices and is served hot. In America it is served cold and is usually made of fruit juice, sugar, burgundy, rum, and soda water.

Ruth Martin, *International Dictionary of Food and Cooking* (London: Constable, 1973), s.v. "bishop."

What is the "water of life"?

The term "water of life" refers to distilled alcoholic beverages. At one time "water of life" was the term given to a magical elixir that would provide perpetual youth or immortality to those who drank it. The early Romans used the term to refer to a drink that would elicit temporary feelings of euphoric immortality.

Robert O' Brien et al., *The Encyclopedia of Drug Abuse, 2d ed.* (New York: Facts on File, 1992), s.v. "water of life."

How was coffee discovered?

It is said that coffee was discovered by an Arab goatherd Kaidi in east Africa in the year 850 who observed that the animals became energetic after eating the berries of certain wild bushes. He ate one of these and experienced a similar exhilaration and passed his discovery on to others. True or not, it is known that by 1000 A.D., Ethiopian Arabs were collecting the fruit of the coffee trees, which grew wild, and preparing a beverage from its beans. Eventually by the fifteenth century it became popular in Arabia and Turkey, and the berries were roasted and brewed into a hot drink. The Arab fondness for coffee spread along the trade routes to Venice by 1600.

Europeans were drinking coffee and it was even considered to be a cure for such ailments as gout, scurvy, headaches, constipation, and colds. The first coffeehouse opened in London in 1652 and soon after cafes flourished in Europe. The popularity of coffee in the United States arose from a particular blend produced by Joel Cheele in Nashville, Tennessee. Served at the Maxwell House hotel, U.S. president Theodore Roosevelt (1858-1919) called this blend "good to the last drop." This became the motto of the brand Maxwell House.

Coffee generally is a blend of several varieties of coffee berries or beans produced mainly in Brazil, Columbia, Costa Rica,

Mexico, Cuba, and Java. The best beans are considered to be those from Jamaica and Hawaii, known as Kona.

John F. Mariani, *The Dictionary of American Food and Drink* (New York: Ticknor & Fields, 1983), 119. Neil Schlager, ed., *How Products Are Made* (Detroit: Gale Research, 1994), s.v. "coffee." Bridget Travers, ed., *World of Invention* (Detroit: Gale Research, 1994), s.v. "instant coffee."

What is the origin of the soft drink's name, "Dr. Pepper"?

The soft drink "Dr. Pepper" was named in 1885 after Dr. Charles Pepper of Virginia. A druggist who worked with Dr. Pepper and later went into the soft drink business in Texas named the syrup "Dr. Pepper" in an effort to win the doctor's approval to marry his daughter.

Amal Naj, *Peppers: A Story of Hot Pursuits* (New York: Alfred A. Knopf, 1992), 33.

Where did Irish Coffee originate?

A plaque outside the Buena Vista bar in San Francisco proclaims that:

> "America's First Irish coffee was made here in 1952. It was inspirationally invented at Shannon Airport [Ireland] by Joe Sheridan. It was fortuitously introduced by [newspaper writer] Stan Delaplane. It was nurtured to a national institution by [the bar's owner] Jack Koeppler."

John F. Mariani, *The Dictionary of American Food and Drink* (New York: Ticknor & Fields, 1983), 210.

Culinary Arts

What can be substituted for cream fraiche in a recipe?

One cup of sour cream, combined with a dash of baking soda, will serve as a substitute for creame fraiche in a recipe.

Debbie Khoee, *1000 Cooking Substitutions* (Bethany, OK: Global Trade Co., 1989), 33.

What are the ingredients in the seasoning five-spice powder?

Frequently used in preparing Chinese dishes, five-spice powder consists of equal parts of cinnamon, cloves, fennel seed, star anise, and szechuan peppercorns. The seasoning can be found prepackaged in oriental markets and many grocery stores.

Sharon Tyler Herbst, *Food Lover's Companion: Comprehensive Definitions of over 3,000 Food, Wine and Culinary Terms* (Hauppauge, NY: Barron's Educational Series, 1990), s.v. "five spice powder."

Is it possible to substitute something else for an egg in a recipe?

Two tablespoons of mayonnaise can be substituted for one egg in a recipe or two tablespoons of vegetable oil and one tablespoon of water.

Debbie Khoee, *1000 Cooking Substitutions* (Bethany, NY: Global Trade Co., 1989), 44.

What does "a la carte" mean?

"A la carte" is according to the bill of fare; each item on the menu is separately priced.

C. O. Sylvester Mawson, *Dictionary of Foreign Terms: Found in English and American Writings of Yesterday and Today* (New York: Thomas Y. Crowell, 1934), 17.

How many items constitute a "baker's dozen"?

A "baker's dozen" is an amount of something totaling thirteen. The term may have originated in the custom of bakers adding the extra amount to twelve to keep a lawful weight. A heavy penalty was levied against bakers who short weighted their customers.

Alfred H. Holt, *Phrase and Word Origins: A Study of Familiar Expressions* (New York: Dover Publications, 1961), 12.

What is a salamandre used for in cooking?

A salmandre is an iron implement which is heated red hot and then held close to a piece of food such as fish or sausage in order to brown it. Salamandres were especially popular during the era of wood-or charcoal-burning stoves. A modern salamandre is an electric or gas grill that produces especially intense heat.

Len Deighton, *ABC of French Food* (New York: Bantam Books, 1990), s.v. "salamandre."

What is the origin of the table napkin?

Towel-size table napkins were commonly used by the ancient Greeks, Romans, and Egyptians. Large napkins were needed as most meals were eaten with one's fingers. Roman dinner guests often carried leftovers home in their napkins. Napkins later called "serviettes," also served to dry the hands after cleansing them in finger bowls during the many-coursed meals. With the introduction of the fork, napkins became a more manageable size. The word derives from the French word *naperon* which means "little tablecloth." The British tying these "towels" around their waists corrupted the word into *napron*, which soon became pronounced *apron*.

Charles Panati, *Extraordinary Origins of Everyday Things* (New York: Harper & Row, 1987), 81-82.

How long will food keep in the refrigerator or freezer after the power goes off?

Assuming the refrigerator door remains closed, food in the refrigerator will stay chilled for six hours after the power goes off. Adding bags of regular ice on the upper shelves will help keep the temperature down. After power has been restored, check the temperature in various parts of the refrigerator to make certain that milk products, meat, fish, poultry, mayonnaise, and cooked food have been kept colder than 45 degrees Fahrenheit (seven degrees Centigrade). Likewise, if the food in the freezer is allowed to thaw and warm up to above 45 degrees Fahrenheit (seven degrees Centigrade), harmful bacteria will thrive and food will spoil. A fully-loaded freezer will stay cold for up to two days, a half-loaded one will do so for one day, but only if the freezer is not opened. Dry ice can be added to extend this time period. A ten-cubic-foot freezer, fully loaded, will need 25 pounds (11.34 kilograms) of dry ice to keep food cold for up to three days. Always wear gloves when handling dry ice; cover the food first with cardboard and place the dry ice on the cardboard. Once the ice is in place, only open the freezer to add more ice.

Janet Bailey, *Keeping Food Fresh, rev. ed.* (New York: Harper & Row, 1989), 376-78. *Rodale's Complete Home Products Manual* (Emmaus, PA: Rodale Press, 1989), 125, 253.

Why is fresh pineapple not used in jello?

A pineapple *(Ananas comosus)* contains a protease, an enzyme that breaks down proteins. This must be destroyed by boiling if the fruit is to be used in a gelatin preparation-gelatin is a protein derived from meat. The protease will simply digest the gelatin away, leaving a soupy, unappealing dish.

Harold McGee, *On Food and Cooking* (New York: Collier Books, 1988), 188.

What is the origin of the chef's hat?

The tall white hat is a copy of the "toque" hat worn by Orthodox priests. To escape persecution, some famous cooks sought refuge in monasteries. The cooks sought a distinction from other monks, which was found in the innovation of a white hat instead of the conventional black. This was authorized and is now the white hat worn by chefs the world over.

Andr L. Simon and Robin Howe, *Dictionary of Gastronomy, 2d ed.* (Woodstock, NY: Overlook Press, 1978), 114.

When were table forks first used?

Table forks were not used until the late Middle Ages, while spoons and knives have been in use since prehistoric times. The first known use of a table fork was in eleventh-century Italy when the wife of the Doge of Venice ate with a small gold fork. Forks were not generally used outside of Italy until the seventeenth century, and then the practice was slowly adopted elsewhere. English writer and traveller Thomas Coryate (1577?-1617) introduced the fork to his countrymen in 1608, following his return from Italy. Common use of the fork was not evidenced until the eighteenth century. Before then, most Europeans used their fingers to convey food to their mouths.

George Stimpson, *Information Roundup* (New York: Harper & Brothers Publishers, 1948), 205-16.

When did spoons originate?

Spoons have been found in Asia, dating back to the Paleolithic Age 20,000 years ago. Spoons were first made of thin, and slightly concave, chips of wood. The Anglo-Saxon word *spon* means "chip." It is surmised that spoons were originally meant to eat food such as gruel or porridge, which are too thick to sip from a bowl but too thin to eat with one's fingers.

Charles Panati, *Extraordinary Origins of Everyday Things* (New York: Perennial Library, 1987),79-80.

What is a porringer?

A porringer is a shallow circular bowl with a single flat handle, often made of silver, and used in the American colonies. It was probably used for children's food of a soft nature—porridge, broths, or perhaps sugar.

Francis Hill Bigelow, *Historic Silver of the Colonies and Its Makers* (New York: Macmillan Company, 1917), 297-99.

What is a bundt?

A bundt is a fluted pan of Swedish or Danish origin and is used for making cakes commonly called bundt cakes.

New York Times 9 July 1979.

In 1976 what cooking implement was heralded as the greatest culinary event in twenty years?

In 1976 the *New York Times* heralded the introduction of the Cuisinart, a French-made food processor, as the "food news event of the ... last couple of decades!"

New York Times 7 January 1976.

To what level should wine and water glasses be filled?

Wine glasses should be filled half-way, while water glasses should be filled approximately two-thirds.

Letitia Baldrige, *Letitia Baldrige's Complete Guide to the New Manners for the '90s* (New York: Rawson Associates, 1990), 424.

What contribution to the food industry has put Avery Island, Louisiana, on the map?

Avery Island, Louisiana, was made famous by Tabasco brand pepper sauce, a condiment made of hot peppers, salt, and vinegar. Made by the McIlhenny Company on Avery Island since 1868, Tabasco sauce is a key ingredient in Bloody Marys, gumbo, and jambalaya; it is also popular with eggs, steaks, salads, and soups. The pepper sauce is made only on the island, a small, subtropical spot in the bayous about 120 miles west of New Orleans. Avery Island now features a visitor's center where guests can learn about the process of making Tabasco, and where they can purchase miscellaneous Tabasco-related items.

Patricia Mandell, "Louisiana Hot," *Americana* February 1991.

What makes a good cold cellar?

A cold cellar, or root cellar for storing fruits and vegetables, should have high humidity, low temperature, and some ventilation. The humidity should be around 90 percent, the temperature between 32 degrees Farenheit (0 degrees Celsius) and 40 degrees Farenheit (4.4 degrees Celsius), with enough air circulation to remove the ethylene gas that fruits give off. Most modern houses have dry warm basements that are not useful for fruit and vegetable storing.

Janet Bailey, *Keeping Food Fresh, rev. ed.* (New York: Harper & Row, 1989), 331. Robert Rodale, *The Best Gardening Ideas I Know* (Emmaus, PA: Rodale Press, 1978), 76-79.

Diet and Nutrition

Are oranges the best source of Vitamin C?

Contrary to popular opinion, the best sources of Vitamin C are green peppers, parsley, broccoli, brussels sprouts, turnip greens, and guava. Tomatoes, strawberries, and citrus fruits are good but not the best sources. Green, leafy vegetables and even potatoes are relatively good sources.

Ann M. Holmes, *Nutrition & Vitamins* (New York: Facts on File, 1983), 100.

What are RDAs (Recommended Dietary Allowances)?

RDAs (Recommended Dietary Allowances) are estimates for meeting the nutritional needs of a group of people. They are not averages but are calculated for individuals with the highest requirements. These levels are intended to apply to persons whose physical activity is considered light and who live in temperate climates. They provide a safety margin for each nutrient above the minimum level that will maintain health. The United States RDAs are formulated by the U.S. Food and Drug Administration. These values are generally the highest values for each nutrient given in the RDA tables produced by the Food and Nutrition Board of the National Research Council. The Food and Drug Administration RDAs were established primarily in connection with legal labeling requirements of foods and vitamin preparations.

Benjamin T. Burton and Willis R. Foster, *Human Nutrition, 4th ed.* (New York: McGraw-Hill, 1988), 176-77. Levon J. Dunne, *Nutrition Almanac, 3rd ed.* (New York: McGraw-Hill, 1990), 10, 118.

How do essential amino acids differ from non-essential ones?

There are twenty different amino acids that make up all the proteins in humans. These are needed to replenish tissue, red blood cells, and enzymes, etc. Of these, twelve can be made by the body. They are known as non-essential amino acids because they do not need to be obtained from the diet. The other eight (some authorities say nine), the essential amino acids, cannot be made by the body and must be obtained from the diet. Proteins in meat have all the essential amino acids; vegetables with the exception of soybeans are "incomplete proteins" in that they do not have all the essential amino acids. By combining certain foods, collectively, all essential amino acids can be ingested. For example, whole grain cereal combined with legumes and eaten together as "complimentary foods" form a complete source.

American Medical Association Encyclopedia of Medicine (New York: Random House, 1989), 94. Howard Hillman, *Kitchen Science, rev. ed.* (Boston: Houghton Mifflin, 1989), 256-57.

Why are there daily recommended allowance of cholesterol and salt in the diet?

The American Heart Association recommends a restriction of dietary cholesterol to three hundred milligrams per day and of sodium to three grams per day. Too much salt (in particular the sodium content of salt) in the diet causes extra water to be drawn into the blood vessels, increasing the pressure on the artery walls and causing high blood pressure. Generally 1 and 1/2 teaspoons of sodium a day is sufficient to get the three grams or three thousand milligrams needed. However, the average American ingests two to four times that much. Cholesterol, an essential element for bodily functions, can be supplied by eating high dietary cholesterol foods of animal origin (egg yolks; meat, poultry, and fish, and milk and milk products), or foods having high saturated fat content (butter, cheese, whole milk, ice cream, cream, meat, poultry, and shellfish (in particular fatty meats), and a few vegetable fats (coconut oil, cocoa butter (found in chocolate), palm and palm kernel oil). Of all the things in one's diet, saturated fats seem to raise blood cholesterol levels the most. Too high of a blood cholesterol could lead to coronary heart diseases and atherosclerosis, so researchers stress avoiding or limiting foods that contain high dietary cholesterol (organ meats, egg yolks, fat portions of meat, milk products) or high saturated fats (butter, ice cream, cream portions of milk products, fatty meats), and baked or fried products and snack foods containing coconut, palm, or palm kernel oil.

Eating to Lower Your High Blood Cholesterol (Washington, DC: U.S. Department of Health and Human Services, 1989), 4-8. Nigel H. Hopkins, John W. Mayne, and John R. Hudson, *The Numbers You Need* (Detroit: Gale Research, 1992), 84. James B. Wyngaarden and Lloyd H. Smith, *Cecil Textbook of Medicine, 18th ed.* (Philadelphia: Saunders, 1988), 1208.

How many glasses of water should humans drink every day?

In the course of a day, the body uses between 1 and 1/2 and three quarts (1.4 to 2.8 liters) of water just in breathing, sweating, and releasing waste fluids. Less than a quart is supplied by food. The rest is from about six glasses of liquid a day. The experts recommend six to eight glasses as a safe amount. However active persons may need 15 glasses, while small and inactive persons only need two glasses.

Vegetarian Times April 1992.

What is pica?

Pica refers to the craving for unnatural or non-nutritious substances. It is named after the magpie (*Pica pica*) which has a reputation for sticking its beak into all kinds of things to satisfy its hunger or curiosity. It can happen in both sexes, all races, and in all parts of the world, but is especially noted in pregnant women.

FDA Consumer December 1985/January 1986.

What is Chinese restaurant syndrome?

Monosodium glutamate (MSG), a commonly used flavor-enhancer, is thought to produce flushing, headache, and numbness about the mouth in susceptible individuals. Because many Chinese restaurants use MSG in food preparation, these symptoms may appear after a susceptible person eats Chinese food.

Mayo Clinic Family Health Book (New York: Morrow, 1990), 470.

What is good and bad cholesterol?

Chemically a lipid, cholesterol is an important constituent of body cells. This fatty substance, produced mostly in the liver, is involved in bile salt and hormone formation, and in the transport of fats in the bloodstream to the tissues throughout the body. Both cholesterol and fats are transported around as lipoproteins—units having a core of cholesterol and fats in varying proportions with an outer wrapping of carrier protein (phospholoids and apoproteins). An overabundance of cholesterol in the bloodstream can be an inherited trait, can be caused by dietary intake, or can be the result of a metabolic disease, such as diabetes mellitus. Fats (from meat, oil, and dairy products) strongly affect the cholesterol level. High cholesterol levels in the blood may lead to a narrowing of the inner lining of the coronary arteries from the build-up of a fatty tissue called atheroma. This increases the risk of coronary heart disease or stroke. However, if most cholesterol in the blood is in the form of high density lipoproteins (HDL), then it seems to protect against arterial disease. HDL picks up cholesterol in the arteries and brings it back to the liver for excretion or reprocessing. HDL is referred to as good cholesterol. Conversely, if most cholesterol is in the form of low density lipoproteins (LDL), or very low density lipoproteins (VLDL), then arteries can become clogged. Bad cholesterol is the term used to refer to LDL and VLDL.

The American Medical Association Encyclopedia of Medicine (New York: Random House, 1989), 275. Isaac Asimov, *The Human Body, rev. ed.* (New York: Mentor Book, 1992), 179-83. Richard B. Brennan, *Dictionary of Scientific Literacy* (New York: John Wiley & Sons, 1992), 137.

Which cooking oil contains the lowest level of saturated fat?

Canola oil is the cooking oil containing the lowest level of saturated fat (6 percent as opposed to 14 percent in olive oil and 51 percent in palm oil). Made from a variety of rape plant, canola oil received FDA approval in 1985. It has a long shelf life, remains odorless at high temperatures, averages only 120 calories per tablespoon, and contains high levels of fatty acids necessary for good nutrition.

Time 12 November 1990. *World Book Encyclopedia,* (Chicago: World Book, Inc., 1994), s.v. "canola oil."

Is there a difference in nutritional value between brown-shelled eggs and white-shelled eggs?

There is no difference either in nutritional value or in flavor between brown-shelled and white-shelled eggs. Shell color is no indication of quality. The color of the eggshell is determined by the breed of hen. Most chicken eggs are white or brown. Brown eggs come in a variety of shades from light brown to dark brown. The Single Comb White Leghorn is the dominant breed in the United States because it lays white eggs. In New England, where brown eggs bring a premium price, Rhode Island Reds, New Hampshires, and Plymouth Rocks are popular.

Egg Science and Technology, 3d ed. (Westport, CT: AVI, 1986), 13, 66. Harold Hillman, *Kitchen Science, rev. ed.* (Boston: Houghton Mifflin, 1989), 125.

Food

How can the freshness of an egg be tested?

Changes that take place in an egg as time goes by can be observed without opening it up. One way is to place the egg in water. If it rests flat on its side on the bottom, it is fresh. If it tends to stand up at the broad end, it is stale. If it floats under water, it is several weeks old. If it floats on top, it is several months old and may be bad. Inspectors judge an egg's freshness by "candling" it-holding it up to an intense light to see what is inside. When the yolk is obscured by cloudy white, or when the pocket of air is small (dime-sized), the egg is fresh. Grades are assigned based on freshness determined by candling: Grade AA eggs are freshest, Grade A are slightly older, and Grade B are older and can be slightly misshapen. Any dating on the egg carton is based on the day the eggs were packed (not laid). A three-figure code for the packing date represents the day of the year-numbered consecutively from 001.

Janet Bailey, *Keeping Food Fresh, rev. ed.* (New York: Harper & Row, 1989), 165-67. Tom Stobart, *The Cook's Encyclopedia* (New York: Harper & Row, 1981), 178.

How do the holes form in Swiss cheese?

Swiss cheese, also called Emmentaler cheese, is a cow's milk cheese that originated in the Emme River Valley in Switzerland. Its curd, formed from rennet, is shaped into large wheels about 36 inches (90 centimeters) in diameter with a thickness of 6 inches (15 centimeters). The wheels are salted in strong brine and wrapped to prevent drying. Complete ripening, taking three to six months, occurs in humidity-and temperature-controlled rooms, where the microbial enzymes present in the "green" cheese slowly change the cheese's composition, its texture, and its flavor. Different bacteria used especially in the ripening process give different cheeses their characteristic flavors. In Swiss cheese, the enzymes are *Streptococcus thermophilus, Lactobacillus bulgaricus,* and *Propionibacterium shermanii.* The latter bacterium lives on lactic acid excreted by the first two bacteria, giving off large amounts of propionic acid and carbon dioxide gas. The gas collects in large pockets to form the "eyes" or holes in the cheese.

Harold McGee, *On Food and Cooking* (New York: Collier Books, 1988), 48-49. Philip W. Goetz, ed., *New Encyclopaedia Brittanica, 15th ed.* (Chicago: Encyclopaedia Britannica, 1990), 4:477.

How much sweeter than sugar is aspartame?

Aspartame, or Nutrasweet, is 180 times sweeter than sugar. Created in 1965 by the pharmaceutical firm G.D. Searle and Company, it was hailed as a low-calorie alternative to the controversial saccharin.

Ingo W.D. Hackh, *Grant & Hackh's Chemical Dictionary, 5th ed.* (New York: Mcgraw-Hill, 1987), 55. Harry Harris, *Good Old-Fashioned Yankee Ingenuity* (Chelsea, MI: Scarborough House, 1990), 33.

From what is the fat substitute Simplesse made?

Simplesse is a blend of proteins from egg whites and milk with processed sugar. Approved by the U.S. Food and Drug Administration as the first low-calorie fat substitute in 1990, it was developed by the Nutrasweet Company.

New York Times 23 February 1990. *Yearbook of Science and the Future 1991* (Chicago: Encyclopaedia Britannica, 1990), 356.

How is guar gum used?

Guar gum is a food additive that is used as an emulsifier, firming agent, stabilizer, or thickener. It is added to such foods as baked goods, beverages, breakfast cereals, dairy products, jellies, sauces, and processed vegetables.

Richard J. Lewis, *Food Additives Handbook* (New York: Van Nostrand Reinhold, 1989), 237.

Why is saffron so costly to buy?

Saffron is the world's most expensive spice-ounce for ounce, it is more precious than gold. One pound (.4536 kilogram) of saffron threads costs well over $2,000. Saffron threads are the roasted stigmas (female organs) of a small purple crocus *(Crocus sativus).* Packed by hand it takes at least 4,000 stigmas to make one ounce (28.3 grams) of this spice. Aromatic when dried, with a pungent smell, it adds flavor and coloring in cooking, and is also used as a dye and a medicine. Originating in the Near East, and known to the Assyrians as early as 4000 B.C., the term originates from the Arabic word *za'faran* (meaning yellow). The main producers of saffron today are Spain and Kashmir.

Smithsonian August 1988. *Woman's Day Encyclopedia of Cooking* (New York: Fawcett, 1966-67), 10:15-77.

When was the GRAS list established?

The Generally Recognized As Safe (GRAS) list was established by the U.S. Congress in 1958 to designate food additives safe for human consumption. The original list consisted of substances that had been added to food over a long time, which were recognized as safe by qualified scientists. Such items as salt, pepper, yeast, common spices, and flavorings are on the GRAS list. These items are exempt from pre-market clearance. The list has been reviewed and revised by the U.S. Food and Drug Administration, using a panel of expert pharmacologists and toxicologists.

Richard J. Lewis, *Food Additives Handbook* (New York: Van Nostrand Reinhold, 1989), 5-6. *McGraw-Hill Encyclopedia of Science and Technology, 7th ed.* (New York: McGraw-Hill, 1992), 7:281-82. Ruth Winter, *A Consumer's Dictionary of Food Additives, 3d ed.* (New York: Crown, 1981), 16-17.

When was the first moisture-proof cracker marketed?

The first moisture proof cracker was marketed by the National Biscuit Company in 1898. Sold under the brand name Uneeda Biscuit, it was the first cracker to be marketed nationally under a brand name and sold for five cents per package.

Gerald Carson, *The Old Country Store* (New York: Oxford University Press, 1954), 274.

In early America to what did the terms "dry goods," "produce," and "groceries" refer?

During the late 1700s and early 1800s in America, "dry goods" referred to merchandise and foodstuffs that was not poured or weighed; "produce" was foodstuffs that stored well, such as flour, smoked and pickled meat, and dried fruits and vegetables, and could be shipped. "Groceries" were expensive foodstuffs, like raisins, citron, and spices, usually from exotic places. Wine was often included as a "grocery." "Grocery store" was an early term for a saloon.

Gerald Carson, *The Old Country Store* (New York: Oxford University Press, 1954), 13-14.

Who was John Cadbury?

John Cadbury (1801-1889) was the founder of the world famous Cadbury cocoa and chocolate firm. Born in Birmingham, England, Cadbury was apprenticed to a retail tea firm at the age of 15 and later worked at a bonded tea house in London. In 1824 he established his own business as a tea and coffee processor and dealer. By 1830 instant cocoa drinks had become popular and in 1831 Cadbury converted a former malthouse into a cocoa processing facility. By 1841 he was marketing a line of 16 chocolate and 11 cocoa products. In 1846 when his brother entered the business the firm's name was changed to Cadbury Brothers and in 1853 it gained its most famous customer to that time, Great Britain's Queen Victoria (1819-1901). Cadbury was also a social reformer, temperance advocate, and a strident opponent of the use of young boys as chimney sweeps.

C.S. Nicholls, *The Dictionary of National Biography* (Oxford: Oxford University Press, 1993), s.v. "Cadbury, John."

What do the "M"s in "M&M"s stand for, and why are there no seams on these candy pieces?

The name for the candy-coated chocolate pieces "M&M" comes from the names Mars and Murrie, who were the heads of M&M Candies during the early 1940s. There are no seams on M&M's because they are coated by a process called "panning," whereby individual pieces of chocolate are placed in a revolving pan, rotated, and sprayed with colored sugar, which hardens as cool air is blown into the pan to create a coating. After evaporation, an even layer of dry shell is formed. No seams show because the coating is uniform and no cutting or binding was necessary to form a shell.

David Feldman, *Why Do Clocks Run Clockwise? and Other Imponderables; Mysteries of Everyday Life Explained* (New York: Harper & Row, 1988), 227-29.

What is a Moon Pie?

A Moon Pie is a marshmallow cookie sandwich that is smothered with icing. This confection has been satisfying the sweet tooth of southern Americans since its introduction in 1917. In that year the Chattanooga Bakery sent an employee into the countryside to survey the snack preferences of potential customers. *Bon Appetit* noted that the employee reported, "They said they wanted something big and round with marshmallow and chocolate, and it needed to be as big as the moon." What they got then, and what they now get 50 million of every year, is the five and a half inch Moon Pie! Moon Pies have become a cultural icon in the South being celebrated in song ("Oh Champagne and caviar is an RC Cola and a Moon Piieee") and the object of Moon-Pie-eating contests. The Moon Pie is occasionally available in such radical flavors as lemon, but the old standbys of chocolate, vanilla, and banana continue to pay the bills. The Moon Pie is sold in 43 states and, while lacking a low fat/no fat label, sales are still rising.

Madelyn Rosenberg, "Dreaming of Moon Pies," *Bon Appetit* 24 June 1995.

How does butter differ from margarine and oleo?

Butter is made from dairy cream, and U.S. law requires it to be at least 80 percent butterfat, with 18 percent water and 2 percent milk solids (casein, milk sugar, lactose, etc.). The first palatable margarine was invented by French chemist Hippolyte Mege-Mouries in 1869. It is a non-dairy product containing at least 80 percent fat. Generally, the fat content is derived from plant oils, such as corn, soybean, safflower, or cottonseed. The name "oleomargarine" was required by law until 1952. Since that time, the terms "margarine" and "oleomargarine" have been used interchangeably.

Janet Bailey, *Keeping Food Fresh, rev. ed.* (New York: Harper & Row, 1989), 142. Harold McGee, *On Food and Cooking* (New York: Collier Books, 1988), 19-23.

What is a poor boy sandwich?

The poor boy sandwich is a small loaf of bread, sliced lengthwise, that contains cheese and meat. Its history reaches back to Europe, where the baguettes and the habit of slicing them lengthwise originated. Later, in New Orleans, nuns from France added meat and cheese to the bread. Beggars who came to their convents beseeching a *pourboire*—the French term for "handout"—were given the sandwich. The mispronunciation of the word over the years led to the moniker "poor boy."

Webb Garrison, *How It Started* (Nashville: Abingdon Press, 1972), 41.

Why are there more brown M&M's than any other color?

M&M/Mars conducts continual market research to determine the desired mix and ratio of colors in a package. Consumers have shown a consistent preference for brown M&M's, so this color predominates. Red M&M's were victims of the Red Dye No. 2 scare of the mid-seventies, and were dropped in 1976; although the company didn't actually use Red Dye No. 2 to color the red M&M's, the company was concerned that the public might be frightened. Once it was determined that consumers would welcome red M&M's again, Mars, Inc. complied.

An earlier survey had found that the most popular M&M colors were brown, 33 percent preference; yellow and red, each with 20 percent; 15 percent liked orange; 10 percent liked green; and only 5 percent liked tan. The company used these preferences to determine the mix of colors for the candy pieces. When the company took another survey to replace the color tan, ten million people responded with their selections. Blue received 54 percent of a consumer vote, beating out pink and purple. So now the candy pieces contain blue-coated ones.

David Feldman, *Why Do Clocks Run Clockwise? and Other Imponderables; Mysteries of Everyday Life Explained* (New York: Harper & Row, 1988), 227-29. "What Would Fay Wray Say"? *New York Times* 30 March 1995. "M&M's Candies Singing the Blues," *USA Today* 5 September 1995.

What kind of food was served at the first Thanksgiving?

Although no menu exists from the first Thanksgiving, the following foods were generally available for a bountiful table fare: oysters, fish, duck, goose, venison, partridge, turkey, barley loaf, cakes of Indian meal, beans, peas, parsnips, carrots, turnips, onions, melons, cucumbers, radishes, beets, cabbage, squash, pumpkin, strawberries, gooseberries, plums, and wild grapes.

W. DeLoss Love Jr., *The Fast and Thanksgiving Days of New England* (Boston: Houghton, Mifflin and Co., 1895),73-75.

What is the origin of Key Lime pie?

Key Lime pie originated in Florida in the mid-1850s because the available condensed milk tasted too sweet and tinny. In an effort to make the milk more palatable housewives mixed in lime juice, and eventually the mixture was tried as pie filling. The limes used in this dessert are not the usual dark green Persian limes, but small yellowish lime that grows in the Florida Keys. The type of lime, also grown in Mexico and parts of the Southwest, has a mild, delicate flavor that is quite different from the more commonly-known limes.

Martha Stewart, *Martha Stewart's Pies Tarts* (New York: Clarkson N. Potter, 1985), 102. Webb Garrison, *How It Started* (Nashville: Abingdon Press, 1972), 37-38.

What dessert is named after a French lawyer who wrote a book about food?

Savarin, a sweet, rich yeast cake that is usually soaked with rum, is named after Anthelme Brillat-Savarin (1755-1826), a French lawyer, who is probably best known for his book of gastronomy *The Physiology of Taste* (1825). A politician, he was a member of the National Assembly before the Terror forced him to leave France in 1892. He returned to Paris in 1896 and became a judge during the Consulate.

The Washington Post Book World, *Book Bag Treasury of Literary Quizzes* (New York: Charles Scribner's Sons, 1984), 127-28.

What was the purpose of a trencher at a medieval dinner table?

At a medieval dinner table before the introduction of plates, meat was often served on large slices of stale bread. The bread, known as trenchers, soaked up the juices from the meat and was eaten with the meal.

Isaac Asimov, *Isaac Asimov's Book of Facts* (New York: Grosset & Dunlap, 1979), 92.

When did ready-to-eat cereals become available?

Ready-to-eat cereals came on the market packed in boxes ready for consumers in the late 1890s and early 1900s. Processing innovations in this burgeoning market included flaking, rolling, baking, grinding, and extruding the various cereal grains. Some early innovators in the field were Henry D. Perky who created Shredded Wheat, C.W. Post who originated Grape Nuts and Postum, and the famous Kellogg brothers John and W.K. (1860-1951) of Battle Creek, Michigan. These and other cereal entrepreneurs attempted to imbue their breakfast goods with "product personality" by the use of such appealing brand names as Granola, Malta-Vita, Egg-O-See, Elijah's Manna, and Post Toasties.

Gerald Carson, *The Old Country Store* (New York: Oxford University Press, 1954), 273-74.

Are there any fruits native to North America?

Only three fruits are native to North American soil: the cranberry, the blueberry, and the Concord grape.

John Larrabee, "Cranberries break out of Thanksgiving," *USA Today* 28 October 1991.

When was the American consumer first enticed by the TV dinner?

TV dinners first appeared on U.S. supermarket shelves to entice hungry, media-addled consumers in 1954. They were the idea of researchers at the C.A. Swanson and Sons Company.

Dennis Sanders, *The First of Everything: A Compendium of Important, Eventful, and Just-Plain-Fun-Facts About All Kinds of Firsts* (New York: Delacorte Press, 1981), 9.

What was the first paper wrapped-candy to be sold?

The first paper-wrapped candy to be sold was a chewy, cylindrical piece of chocolate named after Clara "Tootsie" Hirschfield, daughter of the candy's maker, Leo Hirschfield. First sold in 1896, the candy later became known as the Tootsie Roll.

Dennis Sanders, *The First of Everything: A Compendium of Important Eventful, and Just-Plain-Fun Facts About All Kinds of Firsts* (New York: Delacorte Press, 1981), 20.

What are the ingredients in the English desert known as *fool*?

Similar to *trifle*, the traditional English dessert *fool*, is composed of two parts whipped cream mixed into one part sweetened fruit pureed (especially gooseberries). Served in sherbet glasses, it makes a delicious summer dessert. Its obscure name might derive from the French word *fol* (meaning "mod"). This mixed fruit and cream concoction might have been considered analogous to the condition of craziness.

Evelyn Grant, ed., *Women's Day Encyclopedia of Cookery* (New York: Fawcett Publications, 1966), 5:714.

How many pounds of potatoes does it take to make one pound of potato chips?

It takes four pounds of potatoes to make one pound of potato chips.

USA Today 31 January 1994.

What was a "sugar loaf"?

A "sugar loaf" was produced by the 15th century process of compressing sugar into a compact cone shaped mass.

Francis Hill Bigelow, *Historic Silver of the Colonies and Its Makers* (New York: Macmillan Company, 1917), 398-99.

How did the dessert cake baba get its name?

The dessert cake baba is named after Ali Baba, the hero of the classic tale *The Thousand and One Nights*. It was named by King Stanislas Leszcsynski of Poland who was a dedicated reader of the stories.

Jenifer Harvey Lang, ed., *Larousse Gastronomique* (New York: Crown Publishers, Inc., 1988), s.v. "baba."

Was cheese ever used as a weapon of war?

Cheese was once used as a weapon—and a deadly weapon at that—of war. During a mid-19th century naval battle between Brazil and Uruguay, hard balls of stale Dutch cheese were used by the latter in lieu of cannonballs, which were in short supply during the conflict. Reportedly, two Brazilian sailors were struck and killed by the cheese.

William Walsh, *A Handy Book of Curious Information* (Philadelphia: J.B. Lippincott, 1913), 202-3.

What is tiramisu?

Tiramisu is an Italian dessert made from an espresso-soaked sponge cake with a filling made from double-cream cheese, eggs, and sugar. It is usually topped off with shaved chocolate or cocoa. The name literally means "pull me up" or "pick me up" in Italian, referring to the high caffeine content of the dessert.

Harold LeMay, Sid Lerner, and Marian Taylor*Dictionary of New Words* (New York: Facts On File, 1988), s.v. "tiramisu."

What is Saint John's-bread?

Saint John's-bread is the gum from the pod from the carob tree. It is used to feed cattle and is also eaten raw by people. The name is derived from the biblical allusion to John the Baptist, who survived in the wilderness by eating honey and "locusts." The "locusts" probably were the fruit or beans of this carob or "locust" tree. It is used as a substitute for chocolate by those who are allergic to chocolate. The carob tree is an evergreen that can grow as large as 50 feet high and has blossoms of red flowers. It is found in the Mediterranean and in the Southwest United States.

Philip Grove, ed., *Webster's Third International Dictionary* (Springfield, MA: Merriam-Webster, 1986), s.v. "saint-john's-bread." *The World Book of Encyclopedia, vol. 3,* (Chicago: World Book, Inc., 1993) s.v. "carob."

What is the origin of fruitcake?

Fruitcake, a perennial Christmas treat, originated in ancient Egypt. Similar cakes were made in Spain and Italy. Centuries later, British sailors returning from foreign ports brought back the ingredients for the delicious fruit-filled cakes so that they could be baked at home.

Norah Smaridge, *The Story of Cake* (Nashville: Abingdon, 1978), 19-21.

Why does a Hostess cupcake have seven loops of white icing?

The Hostess cupcake has seven loops of white icing instead of a straight line of white frosting because a straight line doesn't look fancy enough.

Time 22 May 1989.

What is the origin of pasta?

Pasta (the word translates as "dough paste") was introduced to Europe by the Polo brothers, Niccolo and Maffeo, and Niccolo's famous son Marco. Returning from China at the end of the thirteenth century, they brought with them recipes for Chinese noodles. The Chinese had been preparing pasta from rice and bean flour since before 1000 B.C. By the mid-1300s pasta was firmly established in Italy, especially spaghetti-like noodles and turnip-shaped ravioli. Period books mention various sauces and cheese toppings for pasta dishes.

Charles Panati, *Extraordinary Origins of Everyday Things* (New York: Perennial Library, 1987) 405-406.

What is the origin of the hors d'oeuvre tray?

The hors d'oeuvre tray, containing several varieties of bite-sized edibles, was introduced in Athens, Greece. Other Greeks reputedly took this tradition of small portions as proof of the miserly nature of the Athenians.

Reay Tannahill, *Food in History, rev. ed.* (New York: Crown Publishers, 1988), 69.

What is the name of the summer fruit which, although much enjoyed by Singaporeans, is banned in their subways?

Residents of Singapore are very fond of the durian, a large, round, spiky fruit with sweet, custardy yellow flesh. The smell of the durian, however, is so offensive that eating the fruit is forbidden in the subway system of the island city-state. The fruit's scent has been described as being akin to rotting fish, overripe cheese, a city dump, and carrion. Despite its foul odor, the fruit also has the reputation of being an aphrodisiac.

Philip Shenon, "Love It or Hate It, It's the Forbidding Fruit," *New York Times* 18 July 1994.

What is lutefisk?

Lutefisk is a Scandanavian dish made from dried cod. In order to soften the dried fish it often has to be soaked in a lye solution of birch ashes for up to two weeks. Lutefisk means "lye fish" and takes its name from this process. Ling, a relative of the cod, is often prepared in the same manner in Sweden as a Christmas dish. This Swedish dish dates back hundreds of years to when Sweden was a predominantly Catholic country. It was served as part of a fast, rather than part of a feast. On Christmas Day lutefisk is served with a white sauce, melted butter, green peas, boiled potatoes and a rice-porridge desert. In spite of the popularity of lutefisk many regard it as having more sustenance than flavor.

Dale Brown, *The Cooking of Scandinavia* (New York: Time-Life Books, 1968), 75, 188. Willy Kirkeby, *Gyldenals Ordboeker Norsk-Engelsk* (Oslo: Gyldendal Norsk Forlag, 1974), s.v. "lutefisk."

Is the tomato a fruit or a vegetable?

Botanists class the tomato (*Lycopericon esculentum*) technically as a berry, which in a strictly scientific sense, is a simple fruit. In botany, a fruit is the ovary of a plant—the section of the plant that surrounds the seeds. All other edible plant parts are considered vegetables. By this definition, tomatoes, pumpkins, eggplants, peppers, peapods, cucumbers, and corn kernels are fruits. But horticulturists and the U.S. Department of Agriculture in its bulletins and reports class the tomato as a vegetable. On May 10, 1893, the U.S. Supreme Court ruled that the tomato is a vegetable and that it was subject to import duties under the U. S. Tariff Act of 1883, which levied duties on imported vegetables but not on fruits. Common usage dictates that a plant is a vegetable if it is usually eaten as part of a meal's main course. A fruit is eaten as a dessert or a between meal snack.

Howard Hillman, *Kitchen Science, rev. ed.* (Boston: Houghton Mifflin, 1989), 130. Harold McGee, *On Food and Cooking* (New York: Collier Books, 1988), 124-26. George Stimpson, *Information Roundup* (New York: Harper, 1948), 210.

Why were tomatoes called "love apples"?

Tomatoes (*Lycopersicon esculentum*), of the nightshade family, were cultivated in Peru and introduced into Europe by Spanish explorers. Tomatoes were brought via Morocco into Italy where they were called *pomi de Mori* (apples of the Moors). The French called the tomato *pommes d'amore* (apples of love). This may be because tomatoes were thought by some to have aphrodisiac powers, or it may simply be a corruption of the Italian term.

Sharon Tyler Herbst, *Food Lover's Companion* (Hauppauge, NY: Barron, 1990), 473. Andre L. Simon and Robin Howe, *Dictionary of Gastronomy , 2d ed.* (Woodstock, NY: Overlook Press, 1978), unpaged alphabetical entry.

What is an ugli?

An ugli (*Citrus reticulata*) is a tropical fruit originating in Jamaica. Possibly a hybrid between a grapefruit and a tangerine, this unattractive fruit with a loose, wrinkled, yellowish-red skin with a greenish tinge, ranges in size between that of a navel orange and a giant grapefruit. Its acid-sweet flavor suggests grapefruit with hints of orange.

Donald Wyman, *Wyman's Gardening Encyclopedia, 2d ed.* (New York: Macmillan, 1986), 1135. Andre L. Simon and Robin Howe, *Dictionary of Gastronomy, 2d ed.* (Woodstock, NY: Overlook Press, 1978), s.v. "ugli."

What is Indian corn?

Indian corn is flint corn, a hard starch corn that predominated in the northern United States and Canada centuries before the Europeans arrived. Early native growers produced red, blue, black, yellow, white, and multicolored corns. Later growers continued to cultivate and selectively breed this corn, producing ears of every conceivable hue. It is usually this colored flint corn, also called Indian corn, that is used in autumn decorations.

Rebecca Rupp, *Blue Corn and Square Tomatoes* (Pownal, VT: Garden Way, 1987), 194.

Will an orange ripen after it is picked?

An orange *(citrus sinesis)*, unlike many fruits, does not continue to ripen after being picked; it is either tree-ripened, or not ripened at all. But some green color on its skin does not mean that it is unripe. The skin of a Florida orange is commonly dyed "orange" to have a pleasing consumer appeal. The orange, a berry in the botanical classification of fruits, originated in southern China about 2200 B.C., and the Romans introduced it into Europe in the first century A.D. Spanish explorer Christopher Columbus (1451-1506) brought it to Hispaniola in 1493, and in 1539, Spanish explorer Hernando De Soto (1500?-1542) planted seedlings in St. Augustine, Florida. Its cultivation slowly moved westward to California, where it did not thrive. In 1873 two Washington navel orange trees from Brazil were planted in California; these orange trees are the ancestors of all California navel oranges.

Jane E. Brody, *Jane Brody's Goodf Food Book* (New York: W.W. Norton, 1985), 158. Charles Panati, *Panati's Browser's Book of Beginnings* (Boston: Houghton Mifflin, 1984), 103-4. Waverly L. Root, *Food* (New York: Simon and Schuster, 1980), 306.

What is a beefalo?

Beefalo is a cross between the American bison (commonly called a buffalo) and cattle. The dark red meat beefalo is very lean and has a somewhat stronger flavor than beef. It may be cooked in any manner suitable for beef.

Sharon Tyler Herbst, *Food Lover's Companion* (Hauppauge, NY: Barron, 1990), 32.

What is muktuk?

Muktuk is the skin of the narwhal, an unusual whale of the Arctic. It is eaten as food by the native peoples.

World Book Encyclopedia (Chicago: World Book, 1990), 4:21-22.

Who invented the ice cream cone?

Many versions exist of the ice cream cone's origin, although most attribute it to a vendor (Ernest Hamwi, David Avayou, Abe Doumar) or visitor (Charles E. Menches and his lady friend) at the World's Fair in St. Louis in 1904. These versions indicate someone folded a waffle or wafer into a cone to hold some ice cream. By the end of the fair, "cornucopias," later shortened to "cone," were being sold. However, upon Italo Marchiony's death in 1954, it came to the public's attention that this Italian immigrant had applied for a patent for a cone mold he had been using since 1896. The patent was issued on December 13, 1904, before the fair opened. Others claim cones originated in France before the turn of the century.

Paul Dickson, *The Great American Ice Cream Book* (New York: Atheneum, 1972), 66-73. Joseph Nathan Kane, *Famous First Facts: A Record of First Happenings, Discoveries, and Inventions in American History, 4th ed.* (New York: H. W. Wilson, 1981), s.v. "ice cream cone." Joe Pollack, "Norfolk Drive-In Has Cone-Nection to 1904 World's Fair," *St. Louis Post-Dispatch* 4 July 1993.

Where did the hamburger originate?

The hamburger, originating in Hamburg, Germany, arrived in the United States with German immigrants in the 1880s. It is not known exactly when the hamburger was put into a bun, but by the time of the St. Louis World's Fair in 1904, it was already served as a sandwich. Originally called the Hamburg steak, it became the hamburger steak, then the hamburger.

William Morris and Mary Morris, *Morris Dictionary of Word and Phrase Origins, 2nd ed.* (New York: Harper & Row, 1987), s.v. "hamburger." Charles Panati, *Extraordinary Origins of Everyday Things* (New York: Harper & Row, 1987), 399-400.

Who created the first chocolate bar?

Until the nineteenth century chocolate was not a candy, only a beverage. In 1819 Francois-Louis Cailler made chocolate in a bar form in Vevey, Switzerland. In 1828 C.J. van Houten in the Netherlands isolated the cocoa bean's creamy butter. This extraction remained a curiosity until, in 1847, the English firm of Fry and Sons mixed the cocoa butter with chocolate liqueurs to make a sweet-tasting dark eating chocolate. In 1849 Daniel Peter in Switzerland added dry milk to produce milk chocolate.

Valerie-Anne Giscard d'Estaing, *The World Almanac Book of Inventions* (New York: World Almanac, 1985), 75. Charles Panati, *Panati's Browser's Book of Beginnings* (Boston: Houghton Mifflin, 1984), 122.

Where did spaghetti originate?

Historians argue over the origin of pasta. It is probably indigenous to Italy, having been developed by the Etruscans from a Greek recipe, a dough cake cut into strips and called "laganon," from which the word "lasagna" is ultimately derived. "Tri," one of the earliest words for pasta, suggests an Arabic origin. The word is from the Arabic "itriyah," which means "string" or literally "little threads." Spaghetti's thinner form, vermicelli ("little worms") was known in Italy in the fifteenth century. There are now over 600 different shapes for pasta.

Adrian Bailey, *Cooks' Ingredients* (New York: William Morrow, 1980), 259-61. Jane Horn, ed., *Cooking A to Z* (San Ramon, CA: Ortho Books, 1988), 409.

What is the origin of chop suey?

The mixture of chopped simmered vegetables and strips of meat known as chop suey is not a Chinese food dish, but rather, American. As the story goes, when Viceroy Li Hung-chang, the first Chinese statesman to visit the United States, arrived in New York in August of 1896, he was asked by the media what kind of food he ate. "Chop suey" was supposed to be their transcription of the Mandarin words "tsa tsui," which means "a little of this and that." However, "chop suey" is seen in print as early as 1888. The dish may have originated with Chinese cooks for railroad workers in the 1850s. By the late nineteenth century, "chop suey parlors" were appearing in major cities.

Jenifer Harvey Lang, *Larousse Gastronomique: The New American Edition of the World's Greatest Culinary Encyclopedia* (New York: Crown Publishers, 1990), s.v. "chop suey." John Mariani, *The Dictionary of American Food and Drink, rev. ed.* (New York: Hearst Books, 1994), s.v. "chop suey."

Who invented potato chips?

Potato chips were created in 1853 by American Indian George Crum, who worked as a chef at a resort in Saratoga Springs, New York. The French-fried potatoes at the Moon Lake Lodge's restaurant were not acceptable to a customer who kept sending them back to be cut thinner. Exasperated, Crum made the fries so thin and crisp that a fork could not be used. The customer and others loved the potatoes, which became known as Saratoga Chips. They were eventually packaged and sold in other places in New England. Herman Lay in the 1920s began selling the chips in the South. Lay's potato chips became the first successfully marketed national brand. In 1961 Herman Lay merged his company with Frito, famous for Fritos Corn Chips, to form the company Frito-Lay.

Charles Panati, *Extraordinary Origins of Everyday Things* (New York: Harper & Row, 1987), 388-89.

Who invented the Reuben sandwich?

The Reuben sandwich, or more popularly referred to simply as the "Reuben," is made with corned beef, Swiss cheese, and sauerkraut on rye bread which is then fried like a grilled-cheese sandwich. Most attribute the creation of the sandwich to Arnold Reuben (1883-1970), owner of Reuben's Restaurant in New York City in 1914. Another theory is that Reuben Kolakofsky, a grocer, invented the sandwich in 1922 during a poker game with friends at the Blackstone Hotel in Omaha, Nebraska. A waitress at the hotel, Fern Snider, later submitted the recipe and won first prize at the National Sandwich Contest in 1956.

Robert K. Barnhart and Sol Steinmetz, *The Barnhart Dictionary of New English* (New York: H. W. Wilson, 1990), s.v. "Reuben sandwich." John Mariani, *The Dictionary of American Food and Drink, rev. ed.* (New York: Hearst Books, 1994), s.v. "Reuben sandwich."

When were Animal Crackers introduced?

Animal cookies or crackers originated in England in the 1890s and were introduced in America by the National Biscuit Company (Nabisco) in time for the Christmas of 1902. Eighteen different animal-shaped cookies came in a small rectangular box printed to resemble a circus wagon, and it was labeled "Barnum's Animals," named after the popular P.T. Barnum's (1810-1891) Greatest Show on Earth. The box had a string handle, originally intended for hanging the boxes on Christmas trees. The eighteen creatures cast in cookie dough were: bison, camel, cougar, elephant, giraffe, gorilla, hippopotamus, hyena, kangaroo, lion, monkey, rhinoceros, seal, sheep, tiger, zebra, sitting bear, and walking bear.

Over the years thirty-seven different animals have been featured. Among the animals that no longer appear in Animal Crackers are the alligator, polar bear, reindeer, musk ox, moose, antelope, and the jaguar. Only 18 different animal shapes are featured in the boxes of Animal Crackers produced in the 1990s, with the bear appearing twice—sitting and standing. In 1986, consumers bought 50 million Barnum's boxes, or one billion cookies—enough to cross the United States 11 times.

Charles Panati, *Extraordinary Origins of Everyday Things* (New York: Harper & Row, 1987), 412.

What is canola oil?

Canola oil is the market name for the bland-tasting rapeseed oil used in cooking and salad dressings. It has become popular in the United States because it is about six percent lower in saturated fat than any other oil and contains more cholesterol-balancing monosaturated fat than any oil except olive oil. In addition, it contains omega-3 fatty acids-the polyunsaturated fat reputed to not only lower both cholesterol and triglyceride values, but to enhance brain growth and development as well.

Sharon Tyler Herbst, *Food Lover's Companion* (Hauppauge, NY: Barron, 1990), 65.

How did Toll House cookies originate?

Long before chocolate was sold in small chips, homemakers cut up bars of chocolate when making chocolate chip cookies. Ruth Wakefield (1905-1977), who ran the Toll House Inn in Whitman, Massachusetts, made these cookies popular. She sold the rights to the name "Toll House cookies" to the Nestle Company. In 1939, the company began packaging chocolate chips.

James Beard, *James Beard's American Cookery* (Boston: Little, Brown, 1972), 713. Charles Panati, *Panati's Extraordinary Origins of Everyday Things* (New York: Perennial Library, 1987), 414-15.

How are truffles found?

Truffles, found near the roots of oak, elm, aspen, and willow trees, are located by specially trained dogs or pigs that scent out and dig up these underground fungi. Dogs are preferred for this activity, because unwatched pigs tend to eat their finds.

Prized by gourmets for centuries, truffles are used to flavor cooked foods. The French black truffles (Perigord variety) or the Italian white truffles (Piedmont variety) are considered the finest, but English black truffles are also hunted. Another main variety of truffle, which grows below the soil in North Africa and the Middle East, is a whitish pear-shaped mushroom, called *terfez* or lion's truffle, desert truffle, sand truffle, or Arab truffle.

Andre L. Simon and Robin Howe, *Dictionary of Gastronomy, 2d. ed.* (Woodstock, NY: Overlook Press, 1978), s.v. "truffle."

What is the name of the dog on the Cracker Jack box?

In 1918, Sailor Jack and his dog, Bingo, first appeared on the red-white-and-blue Cracker Jack box. The caramelized popcorn with peanuts inside the box was first made in 1893 by the Rueckheim brothers for the World Columbian Exposition held in Chicago, Illinois. In 1896, they named their product "Cracker Jack" after a slang expression—that's crackerjack—an expression of approval. It sold in bulk until 1899, when a wax-sealed, moisture-proof box was developed for it. During World War I (1914-18), Sailor Jack and Bingo were first put on the patriotically-colored box. They were modeled after F.W. Rueckheim's grandson Robert and his dog. The tiny prizes inside each box are older, and probably date from 1913. Before this time, the box carried a discount coupon toward subsequent purchase.

Martin Elkort, *The Secret Life of Food* (Los Angeles: Jeremy P. Tarcher, 1991), 99. Alex Jaramillo, *Cracker Jack Prizes* (New York: Abbeville Press, 1989), 7-8, 10-12. Charles Panati, *Panati's Extraordinary Origins of Everyday Things* (New York: Perennial Library, 1987), 395.

Who inspired the name for the Baby Ruth Candy Bar?

The Baby Ruth candy bar was named after Baby Ruth Cleveland, daughter of U.S. President Grover Cleveland (1837-1908). The origin of the candy bar's name is sometimes erroneously attributed to baseball's Babe Ruth.

Dennis Sanders, *The First of Everything: A Compendium of Important, Eventful, and Just-Plain-Fun Facts About All Kinds of Firsts* (New York: Delacorte Press, 1981), 21.

What is the origin of the word "sandwich"?

The sandwich is named for the 4th Earl of Sandwich, John Montagu (1785-1792). Known for long gambling bouts, the Earl placed a slice of beef between two pieces of bread so he could eat while continuing his card game on August 6, 1762. The Sandwich Islands (Hawaii) in the Pacific Ocean discovered by Captain James Cook (1728-1779) in 1778 were also named after him, in recognition of the earl's interest in naval affairs and his promotion of exploration in his office of First Lord of the Admiralty.

The New Encyclopaedia Brittanica, 15th ed., "Micropaedia" (Chicago: Encyclopaedia Britannica, 1993), s.v. "Sandwich, John Montagu." David Wallechinsky and Irving Wallace, *The People's Almanac* (New York: Doubleday & Co., 1975), 766-67.

How long can chocolate be stored?

Mass-market produced chocolate can last from nine to 15 months in bars and 15 months in morsels, if stored at a constant room temperature. Mechanically-made commercial chocolates produced by smaller manufacturers have shelf lives of three to four months, if the temperature is held at 68 degrees Fahrenheit to 70 degrees Fahrenheit (20 to 21 degrees Centigrade) and the humidity at 50 to 60 percent. Smaller manufacturers that produce "homemade" chocolates estimate the shelf lives of their products at a maximum of four to six weeks. Baking chocolate, dry cocoa, or hot chocolate mix will last one year at room temperature if kept in a tightly closed container so as not to absorb moisture and odor. Unopened liquid chocolate can be stored up to 18 months, after opening, it should be stored in the refrigerator and can be kept for one year.

Jane Bailey, *Keeping Food Fresh, rev. ed.* (New York: Harper & Row, 1989), 317-19. Frank Kendig and Richard Hutton, *Life-Spans* (New York: Holt, Rinehart & Winston, 1979), 157-58.

What are the different kinds of sugar?

Sugar from sugar beets or sugar cane are sucrose sugar. Sucrose is 66 percent as sweet as fructose (sugar from fruits); but sucrose is twice as sweet as dextrose, which is a glucose sugar known as corn or grape sugar. Sucrose is three times as sweet as maltose (malt sugar) and about six times sweeter than lactose (milk sugar).

Granulated or white sugar is highly refined cane or beet sugar. Superfine sugar, known in Britain as castor sugar, is more finely granulated. Confectioners' or powdered sugar is granulated sugar that has been crushed into a fine powder. A small amount of cornstarch is added. Confectioners' sugar is known as icing sugar in Britain.

Decorating or coarse sugar (also called sugar crystals) has granules about four times larger than those of regular granulated sugar. Brown sugar is white sugar combined with molasses (a by-product of the cane sugar refining process).

Sharon Tyler Herbst, *Food Lover's Companion* (Hauppauge, NY: Barron, 1990), 452-53. Howard Hillman, *Kitchen Science, rev. ed.* (Boston: Houghton Mifflin, 1989), 182-83.

Where did pizza originate?

Pizza is thought to have evolved from early Egyptian flat bread. In ancient Pompeii, coarse bread dough was brushed with olive oil and baked. Naples, Italy, is considered the place of origin of pizza as it is known today, although its date of origin is unknown. Pizza was brought to the United States by immigrants and made popular by soldiers returning from Italy after World War II (1939-45).

Webb Garrison, *How It Started* (Nashville: Abingdon Press, 1972), 40-41. Sharon Tyler Herbst, *Food Lover's Companion* (Hauppauge, NY: Barron, 1990), 354.

What is manna that is mentioned in the Book of Exodus in the Bible?

Some sources say that manna is a sweet, granular substance secreted by two varieties of scale insects that live on tamarisk shrubs. Today in the Sinai region, this substance is collected in June; it is used to make candy.

Bruce Felton and Mark Fowler, *Felton & Fowler's Best, Worst, and Most Unusual* (New York: Crowell, 1975), 228-29.

Who invented peanut butter?

The inventor of peanut butter could have been a St. Louis physician who in 1890 ground up peanuts to serve as a nutritious and easily digested food for his elderly patients. But antecedents of this peanut puree can be found earlier in South American, Asian, and African cooking in the United States. A note in an 1883 Savannah newspaper suggests that peanut butter was already a Georgian favorite. However, the peanut butter boom in the United States did begin around the time of the St. Louis "discovery." By 1900 grocers were selling it by the pound in big tubs, stirring the oil that rose to the top. In the 1920s hydrogenated fats, to prevent oil separation, and sweeteners were added. To meet the U.S. Food and Drug Administration Standards, peanut butter must contain 90 percent peanuts and have no artificial flavoring or sweetener, no preservative, color additive, or added vitamins.

Irena Chalmers, *Great American Food Almanac* (New York: Harper & Row, 1986), 154. Webb Garrison, *How It Started* (Nashville: Abingdon Press, 1972), 27-28. Harry Harris, *Good Old-Fashioned Yankee Ingenuity* (Chelsea, MI: Scarborough House, 1990), 219-20.

From what is tofu derived?

Also known as soybean curd and bean curd, this custard-like white block is made from curdled soy milk. The process starts with soaked soybeans that are pureed, cooked, and filtered through cloth. The resulting milk is curdled with a coagulant, such as magnesium chloride. The formed curds are pressed into soft cakes, allowing the whey to drain off.

Tofu is perishable and should be refrigerated for no longer than a week. When storing, it should be covered with water that is changed daily. Tofu may be frozen up to three months, although freezing will cause it to have a chewier texture. High in protein, low in salt and calories, with no cholesterol, tofu is very bland and readily picks up the flavor of whatever it is cooked with.

Jane E. Brody, *Jane Brody's Good Food Book* (New York: W.W. Norton, 1985), 99-100.

What are rose hips?

Though too tart to eat raw, the ripe reddish-orange fruit or seed capsule of the rose—located between the stem and petals—is often used to make jellies and jams, syrup, tea, and wine. An excellent source of Vitamin C, rose hips can be ground into powder and compressed into tablets and sold in health food stores.

Another part of the rose is edible as well—rose petals. Rose petals may be included in a fruit or vegetable salad, soup, or puree. To prepare them for a sandwich, butter them and refrigerate. Then add enough fresh petals to cover. Ground or powdered, they can be incorporated into all cooked foods, baked or broiled meat, casseroles, baked goods, jellies and preserves, or omelets. Finely ground or dried petals may be added to cottage cheese, sour cream, or other spreads.

Rosewater is an essence distilled from rose petals and has a delicious scent and flavor of the flower. Used for extensive cosmetic uses, for finger washing, and for rinsing fine linens, it is also used in the kitchen, where it makes an admirable flavoring-used in place of various extracts or in combination with them, especially in Indian, Iranian, and Turkish cooking as well as in Victorian and medieval cookery. The production of true rosewater is a long and complicated process.

Ben C. Harris, *Make Use of Garden Plants* (New York: Barre, 1978), 167. Julia Jones and Barbara Deer, *Royal Pleasures and Pastimes* (Devon, England: David and Charles, 1990), 14. *Woman's Day Encyclopedia of Cookery* (New York: Fawcett, 1966-67), 10:1560.

What is a prawn?

This term can have several definitions:

A species that is part of the lobster family. These prawns have bodies shaped like tiny Maine lobsters, including minuscule claws. The meat has a sweet delicate flavor. They are six to eight inches (15 to 20 centimeters) long and have pale-red bodies deepening to dark-red tails. The crustaceans included are the Dublin bay prawn, Danish lobster, Italian scampi, langostino (Spanish), langoustine (French), Caribbean lobsterette, and Florida lobsterette.

"Freshwater" prawns (macrobrachium) which migrate from saltwater to freshwater to spawn. They look like a cross between a shrimp and a lobster. Their bodies have narrower abdomens and longer legs than shrimps.

The term "prawn" is also loosely used to describe any large shrimp, especially those that number 15 or fewer to one pound (0.4536 kilograms).

Sharon Tyler Herbst, *Food Lover's Companion* (Hauppauge, NY: Barron, 1990), 367-68.

What are sea legs or sea claws?

Sea legs are a mixture known as "surimi," processed in Japan. It consists mainly of pollack, a cousin of cod fish, which is mixed with the meat of the sea crab and given body by the addition of starches and stiffeners, usually egg whites. Dyed a pretty pink, this agglomeration is formed into the shape of a crab leg, and frozen. It is far cheaper than real crabmeat and frequently passes for the real thing.

Irena Chalmers, *Great American Food Almanac* (New York: Harper & Row, 1986), 180.

Is the puffer fish, eaten as a delicacy in Japan, toxic?

The tiger puffer *(Fugu rubripes rubripes)*, also known as *fugu* or *tora fugu*, contains a powerful natural poison. It takes a special skill to prepare a dish that is definitely safe to eat. When imported into the United States, it is subject to rigid laboratory testing, and must be FDA-approved and guaranteed by the Japanese government to be toxin-free.

Albert J. McClane, *McClane's Fish Buyer's Guide* (New York: Henry Holt, 1990), 76. *Science 82* May 1982.

Which fish have the most nutrients and are the least susceptible to contamination?

The purer and most nutritious fish are cod, halibut, red snapper, haddock, salmon, sea bass, and sea trout. They all swim at the middle to upper level of the sea. The more fatty the fish, the more flavorful the fish is and the more vitamins and nutrients it has. Fat content of a fish generally decreases in relation to the depth of the fish's environment. Lobster, shrimp, mussels, and clams are scavengers that live off debris at the bottom of the ocean and are more likely to be contaminated. For instance, bottom-dwelling shellfish ingest toxic mercury wastes that settle on the ocean floor. Fish that eat these toxic shellfish likewise have higher concentrations of toxins and the fish such as tuna, sharks, and swordfish, that ingest the toxic fish, in turn increase their mercury contamination. Because these bigger fish live longer than smaller fish, they can eat more toxic fish and have high mercury levels within their tissues. Tuna fish and swordfish are the most frequently contaminated with mercury poisoning.

James D'Adamo, *One Man's Food—Is Someone Else's Poison* (New York: R. Marek, 1980), 41-42. Howard Hillman, *Kitchen Science, rev. ed.* (Boston: Houghton Mifflin, 1989), 76-77, 85-86.

Are oysters good to eat only in months ending with an "R"?

Now oysters can be eaten any month of the year. The belief that oysters should not be eaten in May, June, July, and August stems from pre-refrigeration days when with the warm weather came more danger of contaminated oysters with harmful toxins. However, since oysters tend to be more watery and less meaty during the summer months when they spawn, the dictum still carries some meaning in terms of good taste.

Charles J. Cazeau, *Science Trivia* (New York: Berkley Books, 1986), 126-27. Howard Hillman, *Kitchen Science, rev. ed.* (Boston: Houghton Mifflin, 1989), 96.

Why are pistachio nuts dyed red?

In Turkey and Iran, where pistachio trees grow, the nuts are roasted in the sun in a salt brine, which turns the shells a pinkish color. American importers and California producers attempted to imitate this color and in the process came out with the now familiar shocking red. The California Pistachio Commission states that these nuts are still dyed red because many people find this form familiar and they are easier to spot in a bowl of mixed nuts.

Sharon Tyler Herbst, *Food Lover's Companion* (Hauppauge, NY: Barron, 1990), 353. Helen McCully, *Nobody Ever Tells You These Things About Food and Drink* (Fort Worth: Holt, Rinehart & Winston, 1967), 202.

Where did bagels originate, and why are genuine bagels boiled before baking?

There are as many stories for the origin of the bagel as there are ethnic and immigrant groups in America. Most groups can claim a roll or roll-like bread with a hole as its distinguishing feature. In general though, the bagel is acknowledged as a Jewish contribution to America, and today it is a universal American food. Boiling (*kettling* in Yiddish) is traditional and apparently serves to "lock" in flavor prior to baking and to give bagels their sheen.

The bagel's origin has been traced back to Austria in 1683. As a token of thanks for defeating the Turks, a Jewish baker made a hard-roll in the shape of a stirrup as a way of recognizing the king's bravery and love of riding. The word "stirrup" in Austrian-German is *beugel*. Eventually this word evolved from German to Yiddish into English as *bagel*.

Marilyn Bagel and Tom Bagel, *The Bagels' Bagel Book* (Herndon, VA: Acropolis Books, 1985), 4-5, 11.

What were medieval banquets like and what foods were served?

A medieval banquet could consist of ten courses. The menu may have included roast capons and partridges, civet of hare, meat and fish aspics, lark pasties and rissoles of beef marrow, black puddings and sausages, lamphreys and savory rice, entremet of swan, peacock, bitterns, and heron, pasties of venison and small birds, fresh-water and salt-water fish, white leeks with plovers, duck with roast chitterlings, stuffed pigs, eels reversed, frizzled beans, a whole calf with trout, roasted kid, peacocks with cabbage, French beans, pickled ox-tongue, junkets and cheese, fruit wafers, cherries, pears, comfits, medlars, peeled nuts, and spiced wine.

Oftentimes medieval banquets accommodated hundreds of people. Care was taken in decorating the halls with tapestries and other ornamentation. There were high and low tables reflecting the status of the guests. The service of the meal could be quite elaborate and at times was served from horseback by noble servitors. The banquets were always accompanied by entertainment and frequently concluded with a spectacular pageant.

Barbara W. Tuchman, *A Distant Mirror* (New York: Alfred A. Knopf, 1978), 242-243, 310-311.

What is Devon cream?

Devon cream, also known as clotted cream, is a specialty of Devonshire, England. Rich, unpasteurized milk is gently heated until a semisolid layer of cream forms on the surface of the liquid. After being allowed to cool, the thickened Devon cream is removed and can be spread on bread, fruits, or other desserts.

Sharon Tyler Herbst, *Barron's Cooking Guide, Food Lover's Companion: Comprehensive Definitions of over 3000 Food, Wine and Culinary Terms* (New York: Barron's Educational Series, 1990), s.v. "clotted cream."

What is the only food that does not spoil?

The only food that does not spoil is honey. Upon discovery centuries later, honey from tombs of Egyptian pharaohs has been found to still be edible.

David Louis, *Fascinating Facts* (New York: Ridge Press, 1977), 62.

What is the origin of the crepe suzette?

The crepe suzette was created accidentally by chef Henri Charpentier (1841-1910) while serving at a function for the then Prince of Wales, who later became Edward VII. Charpentier inadvertently set the brandy sauce on fire. The result was apparently quite delicious and pleasing to the prince, who was delighted when Charpentier named the dish for one of his female guests.

New York Times 12 December 1961.

How did the pretzel get its name and crisscross-shape?

Legend has it that a medieval northern Italian monk was the first to twist pretzels. The shape was chosen because it resembled the folded arms of someone praying. The pretzels were presented by him to children for memorizing prayers. The term "pretzel" may have come from the Latin word "pretium" for "reward," as in a little gift to a child, or the Italian word "bracciatelli" for "small arms." By the time pretzels had spread to Germany in the thirteenth century, they were called "bretzitella" and then "brezel"-the immediate predecessor of their name today.

John Mariani, *The Dictionary of American Food and Drink* (New York: Hearst Books, 1994), s.v. "pretzel." Charles Panati, *Extraordinary Origins of Everyday Things* (New York: Harper & Row, 1987), 389.

When did tomatoes become popular as a food?

Early explorers of the New World carried tomato seeds back to Europe, where the tomato was used only as an ornamental plant. Identified by botanists as a member of the nightshade family, it was assumed the fruit was toxic, when actually the leaves and stems are dangerous. During the middle of the nineteenth century, attitudes began to change and cooked tomatoes were eaten. It was not until the twentieth century that eating raw tomatoes became a widespread practice.

Jane Horn, ed., *Cooking A to Z* (San Ramon, CA: Ortho Books, 1988), 580.

Where did fortune cookies originate?

Fortune cookies originated in the United States rather than China. The cookies were probably first made and served in California around World War I (1914-1918). Fortune cookie factories were in existence by the 1930s. The cookies had to be folded by hand, so that a "fortune" could be inserted. The fortune was usually a proverb written on a small slip of paper. In the late 1960s a machine was invented that would do the folding. By 1992, an American company in New York was planning to open a fortune cookie factory in China.

John Mariani, *The Dictionary of American Food and Drink* (New York: Hearst Books, 1994), s.v. "fortune cookie."

What is MSG?

MSG is the abbreviation for monosodium glutamate, a white crystalline powder derived from glutamic acid, a common amino acid. It occurs naturally in seaweed, soybeans, and beets or can be produced by fermenting glucose or by processing wheat, corn, soybean, or sugar beet proteins. In 1909 Kikunae Ikeda isolated it as a flavoring agent. It is added to foods, especially high-protein or processed foods, to improve or enhance flavors. In the 1950s, a bacterium was isolated that synthesizes and excretes glutamic acid when fed the nitrogen in ammonium ions (NH4+). Today most MSG is made using this fermentation technique, with world production at 250 thousand tons (226,800 kilograms). There is evidence that high doses of MSG might cause physical problems but it continues to be on the list of food additives generally regarded as safe by the U.S. Food and Drug Administration (FDA).

Nicholas Freydberg, *The Food Additives Book* (New York: Bantam, 1982), 555-56. Harold McGee, *On Food and Cooking* (New York: Collier Books, 1988), 570.

What is the difference between an herb and a spice?

Spices are pungent or aromatic seasonings obtained from the bark, buds, fruit, roots, seeds or stems of various plants and trees; whereas, herbs usually come from the leafy part of a plant.

Sharon Tyler Herbst, *Food Lover's Companion* (Hauppauge, NY: Barron, 1990), 440.

Why does the smoking of meat act as a preservative?

Smoked meat (or any food) is preserved because the traces of formaldehyde present in the wood smoke arrest bacterial development.

Frank Kendig and Richard Hutton, *Life-Spans* (New York: Holt, Rinehart and Winston, 1979), 112.

Which hypobaric system is used for food storage?

Hypobari-controlled atmosphere systems are a precisely controlled combination of low pressure, low temperature, high humidity, and ventilation that extends up to six times the length of time a perishable commodity remains fresh. Atmospheres are tailored to each perishable item. For example, iceberg lettuce uses oxygen, carbon dioxide, and nitrogen. Seafood, avocados, cherries, limes, mushrooms, tomatoes, chicken, pork, and lamb may be kept under hypobaric conditions.

Van Nostrand Reinhold Encyclopedia of Chemistry, 4th ed. (New York: Van Nostrand Reinhold, 1984), 482.

How is acidulated water used?

Acidulated water is cold water to which vinegar, lemon juice, or lime juice has been added to prevent cut fruit or vegetables from discoloring. The proportions are one tablespoon (14.8 milliliters) of juice in one quart (946 milliliters) of water.

Helen McCully, *Nobody Ever Tells You These Things About Food and Drink* (Fort Worth: Holt, Rinehart & Winston, 1967), 21.

How is food freeze-dried?

The freeze-drying food preservation process, first used in the 1950s, can be used on 600 different foods. It is a two-step process of rapid freezing and subsequent dehydration (removal of moisture from a substance). To preserve its nutrients, flavor, etc., food is fast-frozen by placing the item between two hollow plates that contain a refrigerant liquid in a tightly-sealed chamber. While the food is being frozen, a high-powered pump creates a vacuum in the chamber. Then the refrigerant liquid in the hollow plates is replaced with warm gas, which converts the ice in the food *directly* into vapor. This dehydration process takes 20 hours. The dehydrated food can be reconstituted by the addition of boiling water. The food must be packaged to seal out oxygen and moisture, which would cause the food to decay.

How in the World (Pleasantville, NY: Reader's Digest Association, 1990), 379.

Which foods cannot be frozen?

Bananas, cream fillings and puddings, custards, gelatin dishes, hard-cooked eggs, cooked potatoes, raw vegetables, such as celery and radishes, and soft cheeses.

Helen McCully, *Nobody Ever Tells You These Things About Food and Drink* (Fort Worth: Holt, Rinehart & Winston, 1967), 11.

Can food be left in the can once it has been opened?

Yes, but it must be securely covered and refrigerated. Modern cans are lined with a thin layer of pure tin that in no way affects food.

Helen McCully, *Nobody Ever Tells You These Things About Food and Drink* (Fort Worth: Holt, Rinehart & Winston, 1967), 9.

Is it possible to freeze eggs?

Yes, but never freeze eggs in their shells; the contents will expand, causing the shells to break. Liquid egg white can be frozen as is. When thawed, it will act just as if it had been taken right from the shell. Whole eggs and, to a greater extent, egg yolks, become more viscous after they have been frozen. To prevent this, mix the eggs or yolks thoroughly with sugar or salt before freezing. Add either one half teaspoon of salt or two to three tablespoons of sugar per cup of eggs. The method chosen depends on the intended use of the eggs. One cup of eggs is equal to five large eggs.

Janet Bailey, *Keeping Food Fresh, rev. ed.* (New York: Harper & Row, 1989), 169-70.

Government

What were the names of the women's reserve units in the U.S. armed services during World War II?

Women were recruited into reserve units of the U.S. armed forces to free men for war duty. Many of the jobs were administrative with the exception of the women pilots.

Women's Auxiliary Ferrying Squadron (WAFS)-The first women to fly aircraft on military missions as part of a United States military organization. Absorbed into the WASP. Part of the Air Transport Command of the United States Army Air Corps.

Women's Airforce Service Pilots (WASP)

Women's Army Auxiliary Corps (WAAC)-Later changed to Women's Army Corps (WAC).

Women's Army Corps (WAC)

(SPARS)-Women in the Coast Guard. The name comes from first letters of Coast Guard motto, *Semper Paratus*, and its English translation, "Always Ready."

Women Accepted for Voluntary Emergency Service (WAVES)-Women's Reserve of the United States Naval Reserve.

Women Marines.

The Encyclopedia Americana, intl. ed. (Danbury, CT: Grolier, 1994), s.v. "Women in the Armed Forces." Adela Riek Scharr, *The WAFS, vol. 1 of Sisters in the Sky* (Gerald, MO: Patrice Press, 1986), 1-14. *World Book Encyclopedia* (Chicago: World Book, 1994), s.v. "Coast Guard, United States."

How many U.S. female military personnel served during the Vietnam conflict?

Between 7,500 and 11,000 U.S. female military personnel were stationed in Vietnam during U.S. participation in the war. Eight nurses lost their lives in the conflict.

Ann Butler, "Vietnam vets, D.C. project," *The Pittsburgh Press* 27 May 1990.

To what address are requests for a congratulatory letter from the president of the United States sent?

In order to arrange for a congratulatory letter from the president of the United States to honor someone on the occasion of their eightieth or older birthday, or to honor a couple celebrating their fiftieth-or beyond-wedding anniversary write to the following address:

The White House
Greetings Office
Room 39
1600 Pennsylvania Ave., N.W.
Washington, DC 20500

The office should be contacted six weeks in advance. The phone number, the name and address of the honoree, and the occasion being celebrated should be included.

Parade Magazine 20 March 1994.

How does one apply for a Social Security card?

In order to apply for a new, replacement, or corrected Social Security card, one must provide evidence of your age, identity, and U.S. citizenship. The preferred document for proof of age and U.S. citizenship is a public birth certificate, or foreign birth certificate, that shows the date and place of birth recorded before age five. Other documents that are acceptable include church records, certificates of naturalization, hospital records of birth, U.S. consular reports of birth, and U.S. passports. Identity must be verified by providing a document showing name, signature, photograph, or other identifying information. Acceptable documents include a driver's license, state identity cards, U.S. passport or citizen ID cards, school records, marriage licenses, divorce decrees, military or draft records, and voters' registration cards.

Persons who are not citizens of the United States and were born outside the United States must provide evidence of their lawful alien status before they are eligible for a Social Security card. Any document issued by the U.S. Immigration and Naturalization Service (INS) will suffice.

All persons requesting a Social Security card must fill out application Form SS-5; the card should be received within two weeks of application.

Ken Skala, *American Guidance for Those Over 60, 2d ed.* (Falls Church, VA: American Guidance, 1990), 51-52.

What percentage of U.S. federal outlays is applied toward the public debt?

The percentage of U.S. federal outlays applied toward the public debt, that is, the amount owed by state, local, and national government, has been steadily increasing since 1960 when 10.0 percent was applied according to the Bureau of Public Debt, Department of the Treasury. In 1970, 9.9 percent of outlays was applied toward the public debt; in 1980, 12.7 percent; in 1990,

21.1 percent; in 1991, 21.5 percent; in 1992, 21.1 percent; and in 1993, 20.8 percent.

Robert Famighetti, ed., *The World Almanac and Book of Facts 1995* (Mahwah, NJ: World Almanac, 1994), 101, 133.

When were the first official U.S. postage stamps printed and when did the federal government gain a monopoly on their production?

The first postage stamps were introduced in Great Britain in 1840 by Sir Rowland Hill, but not until July 1, 1847, were the first U.S. postage stamps issued. Previously some local postmasters had issued their own stamps. In two denominations, the stamps were printed without perforations on thin bluish paper, one hundred to a sheet. The brown five-cent stamp bore a portrait of U.S. statesman, Benjamin Franklin, and the black ten-cent stamp depicted U.S. president George Washington. The U.S. government did not gain a monopoly on the production of postage stamps until 1863.

M. Thomas Inge, *Handbook of American Popular Culture* (Westport, CT: Greenwood Press, 1981) 3:461. Carl H. Scheele, *Neither Snow Nor Rain...: The Story of the United States Mails* (Washington, DC: Smithsonian Institution Press, 1970), 32.

Have officials in American cities ever solicited financial aid from a foreign government?

On occasion, officials of American cities have solicited foreign aid from a foreign government. In 1977 the West Virginia city of Vulcan asked for financial aid from the Soviet Peace Committee after the state and federal governments denied funding for a new bridge. Although Vulcan officials claimed the request was made in jest, the Soviet Peace Committee offered to send financial aid for construction of the bridge. In 1980 New York City officials hosted a delegation from the Soviet Peace Committee and requested five billion dollars in foreign aid to help rebuild the South Bronx.

New York Times 17 December 1977. *New York Times* 21 June 1980.

What does the acronym SSI stand for?

Supplemental Security Income, or SSI, is a federal public assistance program established in 1972 and administered by the Social Security Administration. It provides a minimum cash income for underprivileged people, or people who are old, disabled, or blind. Eligibility is determined by a means test and is not related to a person's employment record. Funding for the program is provided by the federal treasury.

Source: Robert L. Barker, *The Social Work Dictionary,* (Silver Spring, MD: National Association of Social Workers, 1987), s.v. "Supplemental Security Income (SSI)."

What is the full name and title of Prince Charles of Great Britain?

Prince Charles (1948-) has four given names, Charles Philip Arthur George, and an assumed name, Windsor, which is the surname of his mother, Queen Elizabeth II (1926-). He does not share the surname of his father, Philip Mountbatten, because his mother is the ruling Queen of England.

The full royal title of Prince Charles is His Royal Highness Charles, Prince of Wales, Duke of Cornwall, Earl of Chester and, in the Scottish peerage, Duke of Rothesay, Earl of Carrick, and Baron Renfrew, Lord of the Isles and Prince and Great Steward of Scotland.

Pittsburgh Post Gazette 4 March 1988.

Who was Meir Kahane, and why was he deprived of his U.S. citizenship?

Rabbi Meir Kahane was a U.S. citizen who emigrated to Israel in 1971 and was elected to the Israeli parliament in 1984. Upon his election, he stated that he had kept his U.S. citizenship only as a travel convenience. Because, with few exceptions, it is illegal for a U.S. citizen to serve in a high ranking government position as a citizen of a foreign power, Kahane was stripped of his American citizenship in 1985.

Martin Tolchin, "U.S. Declares Kahane Is No Longer a Citizen," *New York Times* 5 October 1985.

What is the old-boy network called in China?

The old-boy network in China is known as guanxi, which is a Chinese word meaning connections. Being properly connected with the guanxi is vital to success in any enterprise in China.

Harold LeMay, Sid Lerner, and Marian Taylor, *Dictionary of New Words* (New York: Facts On File, 1988), s.v. "guanxi."

What is the Greek parliament called?

Greece is a republic with a president as head of state, a prime minister as head of government, and a 300-seat parliament known as the Vouli. Members of the Vouli are elected every four years.

Stephen Brough, ed., *The Economist Business Traveller's Guides: Europe's Business Cities* (New York: Prentice Hall, 1989), 181.

What is the Iron Cross?

The Iron Cross was a German military honor first established in 1813 by Frederick William III (1770-1840). The German leader Adolf Hitler (1889-1945) revived its use during World War II (1939-45). Hitler allowed variations of the medal, to which adornments such as golden oak leaves, diamonds, and swords could be added. The medal was given not only for military heroism, but was used as a diplomatic ploy.

James L. Collins, ed., *The Marshall Cavendish Illustrated Encyclopedia of World War II* (New York: Marshall Cavendish, 1972), 3380.

What are the benefits provided or mandated by the U.S. government for employees?

Besides providing for and mandating Workers' Compensation benefits, the United States government provides or mandates the following eight benefits: unemployment benefits, Social Security Disability payments, Social Security retirement benefits, Social Security survivors' benefits, Social Security Supplemental Security Income (SSI), Medicare and Medicaid, state disability payments, and death benefits from Workers' Compensation programs.

James M. Jenks and Brian L.P. Zevnik, *Employee Benefits Plain and Simple: The Complete Step-By-Step Guide to Your Benefits Plan* (New York: Collier Books, 1993), 178-79.

What was the Gulf of Tonkin Resolution?

On August 7, 1964, the U.S. Congress passed the Gulf of Tonkin Resolution, a measure that gave U.S. president Lyndon B. Johnson (1908-1973) power to respond to attacks on U.S.

forces. It became the basis for further involvement by the United States in the Vietnam Conflict. In addition, this resolution allowed the president to provide military aid to any member or protocol nation of the Southeast Asia Collective Defense Treaty. The measure passed by a 416-0 vote in the House and a 88-2 vote in the Senate. It was intended to expire when the president felt the security of the area was restored.

The resolution was a response to alleged attacks earlier in August by North Vietnamese torpedo boats on the U.S. destroyers *Maddox* and *C. Turner Joy*, which were in the Gulf of Tonkin for electronic surveillance of North Vietnam. President Johnson used the resolution as a vehicle to conduct the Vietnam War, and later President Richard Nixon (1913-1994) used the measure as authority to invade Laos and Cambodia. Congress repealed the Tonkin Gulf Resolution in 1970.

James S. Olson, ed., *Dictionary of the Vietnam War* (New York: Greenwood Press, 1988), s.v. "Gulf of Tonkin Resolution."

What were the minimum age and physical requirements for being drafted into the armed services during World War II?

When registration for the United States' first peacetime draft began on October 16, 1940, the minimum physical and age requirements were a minimum weight of 105 pounds and a minimum height of five feet; correctable eyesight problems; and at least sixteen of thirty-two natural teeth. Hernias, venereal disease, and flat feet disqualified men from joining the armed services. Congress later lowered the upper age limit to twenty-seven. The age limit changed again when the United States entered World War II (1939-45) and the U.S. Congress amended the draft law to give the president power to defer certain age groups. In 1943 as World War II raged on, some men who had been ineligible were declared eligible. In some cases, less stringent physical standards were applied. In other cases, men who had been rejected because of quotas imposed on the number of limited-service men, illiterates, or those with venereal disease, could now be drafted.

Norman Polmar and Thomas B. Allen, *World War II: America at War, 1941-1945* (New York: Random House, 1991), 724-25.

When were Native Americans granted United States citizenship?

On June 2, 1924, the United States Congress granted American citizenship to all "non-citizen" American Indians born in the United States.

Henry C. Dennis, ed., *The American Indian, 1492-1970: A Chronology and Fact Book* (Dobbs Ferry, NY: Oceana Publications, 1971), 52.

What duty restrictions are placed on American citizens traveling abroad?

Duty restrictions placed on Americans traveling abroad follow laws governed by the U.S. Customs Service. An American resident who has traveled to another country for a period of at least 48 hours is allowed to bring back into the United States $400 worth of goods without being subject to customs taxes. The goods must accompany the traveler, be for personal or household use, and be declared to customs agents upon re-entry into the United States. Travelers to the United States territories of American Samoa, Guam, or the United States Virgin Islands are allowed to bring back $1,200 worth of duty-free articles with certain restrictions.

In a little-known exemption to the above duty-free regulations, American travelers to certain countries in Latin America, Africa, or Asia are allowed more leeway in bringing back merchandise. The Generalized System of Preferences (GSP) Program was enacted to provide indirect economic support to underdeveloped nations. Items manufactured from endangered species and plants are not covered under this law.

Robert Famighetti, ed., *The World Almanac and Book of Facts 1995* (Mahwah, NJ: World Almanac, 1994), 721-22. *U.S. and Worldwide Travel and Accommodations Guide, 13th ed.* (Fullerton, CA: Campus Travel Service, 1993), 88.

How many U.S. military personnel were granted conscientious-objector status in the major wars of the twentieth century?

The total number of U.S. military personnel granted conscientious-objector status in the major wars of the twentieth century is 200,000. In the two years of U.S. involvement in World War I from 1917 to 1918, 2,000 were granted such status; between 1940 and 1946, during World War II, the figure was 15,000; for the five-year Korean Conflict that began in 1950, 12,000; and during the Vietnam War, a record number of 171,000 were granted conscientious-objector status between 1963 and 1973.

USA Today 24 October 1990.

Who was the first legislator to be expelled from the United States Senate?

In 1797, William Blount (1749-1800) became the first legislator to be expelled from the United States Senate. The North Carolina politician was a delegate to the 1787 Constitutional Convention and a signer of the Constitution. He moved from North Carolina westward over the Allegheny Mountains around 1790; and in that same year, he was appointed by the future U.S. president George Washington (1732-99), then territorial governor of the region, which later became Tennessee. Over the next few years, Blount became illicitly involved in profitable real estate deals that were technically illegal because of his gubernatorial post. After Tennessee became a state in 1796-in part due to his political involvement-Blount became a United States senator.

While Blount's real estate deals were no longer unlawful because of his new legislative office, they nevertheless soured and he looked for ways to avoid financial ruin. Playing upon the animosities and allegiances between settlers, Native Americans, and the British and Spanish in the South, Blount became an agent of the English crown. He devised a 1797 military campaign to eject the Spanish out of Florida and Louisiana, but the plan was foiled by sheer bad luck: a letter from Blount to his Native American allies about the plot was accidentally delivered to U.S. president John Adams (1735-1826), who brought it to the attention of the U.S. Congress. The United States Senate voted 25 to 1 to expel Blount on July 8, 1797, and to start putting in motion the impeachment process. Thus Blount also became the first United States official to be threatened with impeachment, although the action was dropped a few years later. In 1798 he was elected to Tennessee's state senate and even became speaker of its house. The stress of his financial and political troubles took its toll on Blount, however, and he died in 1800.

George C. Kohn, *Encyclopedia of American Scandal* (New York: Facts on File, 1989), s.v. "William Blount: impeachment through conspiracy."

What are the occupational categories for military personnel?

Occupational categories for military personnel can be broken down into two areas: officers and enlisted. According to 1992 Department of Defense statistics, among all five branches of the Armed Forces-Army, Navy, Air Force, Marines, and Coast Guard-1,621 officers served in top management positions; 110,270 as tactical operations officers; 12,872 as intelligence officers; 35,530 as engineering and maintenance officers; 12,346 as scientists and professionals; 44,695 as medical officers; 19,474 as administrators; 23,568 as supply, procurement, and allied officers; and an additional 12,279 officers serve in nonoccupational positions.

In the Armed Forces' enlisted personnel, electrical and mechanical equipment repairers made up the largest occupational category at 301,523; infantry, gun crews, and seamanship specialists numbered 246,702; functional support and administration, 234,740; electronic equipment repairers, 151,724; communications and intelligence specialists, 145,513; service and supply handlers, 128,609; health care specialists, 93,938; craftsworkers, 62,664; other technical and allied specialists, 35,036; and finally, 117,810 enlisted personnel held nonoccupational positions.

Department of Labor, Bureau of Labor Statistics, *Occupational Outlook Handbook, 1994-95 edition* (Washington, DC: 1994), 453.

Which countries are members of the League of Arab States?

The League of Arab States or Arab League has twenty-two members. The members are Algeria, Bahrain, Comoros, Djibouti, Egypt, Iraq, Jordan, Kuwait, Lebanon, Libya, Mauritania, Morocco, Oman, Palestine, Qatar, Saudi Arabia, Somalia, Sudan, Syria, Tunisia, United Arab Emirates, and Yemen. The Arab League strives towards better cooperation between Arab states and presenting a more united front on the world political scene.

The Europa World Year Book 1994 (London: Europa Publications, 1994), 1:172.

Can an individual hold more than one citizenship?

Depending on the countries involved, an individual can hold more than one citizenship. Persons who marry a foreign national may be granted citizenship of the country of their spouse. The legalities involved with dual citizenship are extremely complex and fraught with questions over taxes, military service, politics, and other matters.

D. O'Nes, *The Guide to Legally Obtaining a Foreign Passport: The Easy Way to Get Additional Citizenships* (New York: Shapolsky Publishers, 1990), 185-87.

Are mail order passports available?

Four countries will give passports to individuals through the mails: Bolivia, Jamaica, Dominican Republic, and Portugal. A substantial investment in the local economy of the country issuing the passport is involved.

In Bolivia the government will give one a passport for an investment of $25,000. This should be viewed as an investment in a passport not as a profitable business venture.

The Jamaican government provides an opportunity to get a mail order passport through the Jamaican National Investment Program or JAMPRO. The initial investment is $120,000, which gets the investor a travel permit and document of permanent residence in Jamaica.

The Dominican Republic has a residency requirement that the authorities may choose to ignore if one is on good terms with the authorities. It takes only two to twelve months to get the passport. There is no set amount of investment..

In Portugal one must fill out an application at the nearest embassy, and a permanent residency paper is issued within two weeks. For about $2,000, not including the cost to the actual investment, one may obtain a passport.

D. O'Nes, *The Guide to Legally Obtaining a Foreign Passport: The Easy Way to Get Additional Citizenships* (New York: Shapolsky Publishers, 1990), 129-34.

Does the United States government accept unsolicited proposals?

It is possible for a small business or individual to enter into the lucrative world of government contracts. Usually a government agency will invite solicited bids for products or services they need to purchase. In other cases, because of the newness of the product or service, there is no solicitation, and a small business owner might wish to submit a proposal. The proposal should detail the name and nature of the enterprise, the person to contact, whether any of the information enclosed is proprietary data, which other government agencies are also receiving the same proposal, the date, and a signature. The technical area of the proposal should include a 200-word summary detailing how the governmental agency would benefit from the product or service. Its developers or researchers should be identified by name, and the proposal should also include what kind of nonfinancial support is needed from the government to fully implement the product or service. In another section of the proposal, a price estimate should be given, the duration of the proposal's validity, what type of contract the small business owner would prefer, a general time frame, a brief history of the company or personal resume, and any signed affidavits or security clearances.

Charles R. Bevers, Linda Gail Christie, and Lynn Rollins Price, *The Entrepreneur's Guide to Doing Business with the Federal Government: A Handbook for Small and Growing Businesses* (New York: Prentice Hall, 1989), 250-52.

Who are "minority" presidents?

"Minority" presidents are those serving in the nation's executive office who did not win a majority of the popular vote in the general U.S. election. Either the electoral college or the U.S. House of Representatives cast the deciding votes that made them president. Of the fifteen who have been minority presidents, John Quincy Adams (1767-1848), Rutherford B. Hayes (1822-1893), and Benjamin Harrison (1833-1901) actually received less votes than their opponents in the popular election.

Congressional Quarterly's Guide to U.S. Elections, 2d ed. (Washington, DC: Congressional Quarterly, 1985), 321.

How do you do business with the federal government?

The following steps are recommended when attempting to do business with the federal government:

Analyze the market. Make certain that the product or service will be of use to the government.

Decide what to put in a bid. Have a sound business plan done to analyze the profitability of the bid.

Get on the government's "bidders' lists" of contractors.

Marketing products or services to the government is not automatic; Develop a marketing plan that will establish the business' reputation and convince the government of the merits of the proposal.
Go after the contract.
Complete the contract.
Prepare for future contracts.

Charles R. Bevers, Linda Gail Christie, and Lynn Rollins Price *The Entrepreneur's Guide to Doing Business with the Federal Government: A Handbook for Small and Growing Businesses* (New York: Prentice Hall, 1989), 19-21.

What is a quorum?

According to *Robert's Rules of Order*, a quorum is the minimum number of members of a group who must be present to officially conduct business. This rule is set up to keep a small number from making decisions that may not be representative of the whole. In the U.S. Congress, a quorum is considered to be a majority of the members. Organizations may specify what constitutes a quorum; often this is a majority of the members, or the number of members who may be counted on to show up at any given normal meeting during normal circumstances.

Sarah Corbin Robert et al., *The Scott, Foresman Robert's Rules of Order, 9th ed.* (n.p.: ScottForesman, 1990), 19-20.

When did the deadline to file personal income tax change from March 15 to April 15?

Until the year 1954, U.S. residents had to file their income tax by March 15. The deadline was changed to April 15 in 1955.

Harry Hansen, ed., *The World Almanac and Book of Facts for 1955* (New York: New York World-Telegram and Sun, 1955), 645.

Which country spends the most money on its military?

The United States ranks behind Israel in military spending when it is figured as a percentage of gross domestic product. A United Nations report in 1994 showed Israel spent 8.6 percent of its gross national product on the military, followed by the United States at 5.1 percent. The United Kingdom spent 4.2 percent, Canada spent 2 percent, and Japan spent 1 percent.

USA Today 2 August 1994.

What is the central banking system in the United States?

Established in 1913, the Federal Reserve Board, appointed by the president, is the central banking system in the United States. The system is made up of 12 regional Federal Reserve Banks, with each regional bank serving over 6000 member commercial banks. These member banks own the Federal Reserve Bank's capital and receive fixed dividends. The U.S. Internal Revenue Service (IRS) collects surpluses earned by the Federal Banking System. Federal Reserve Banks are located in Boston, New York, Philadelphia, Cleveland, Richmond, Atlanta, Chicago, St. Louis, Minneapolis, Kansas City, Dallas, and San Francisco.

Hano Johannsen and G. Terry Page, *International Dictionary of Management, 3d ed.,* (New York: Nichols Publishing, 1986), s.v. "Federal Reserve System."

When was the Medal of Freedom established and why was it renamed the Presidential Medal of Freedom?

On July 6, 1945, U.S. president Harry Truman established the Medal of Freedom. It was later amended by Executive Order on April 5, 1952. The medal was awarded to any civilian who performed a meritorious act or service after December 6, 1941, that aided the United States or its allies. The award was reestablished as the Presidential Medal of Freedom by U.S. president Kennedy (1917-1963) on February 22, 1963. Then the medal's scope was broadened to include nominees who should be honored for meritorious contributions to national security, world peace, cultural, or other significant public or private endeavors. The medal is awarded at the discretion of the sitting president of the United States.

David Borthick and Jack Britton, *Medals, Military and Civilian of the United States* (Tulsa, OK: MCN Press, 1984), 169-70.

In the British government, what are MI-5 and MI-6?

MI-5, also known as the Security Service, is Great Britain's intelligence agency charged with internal security and counterintelligence activities for the United Kingdom. It is authorized to investigate any person or movement that might threaten the nation's security, but it has no powers of arrest. MI-6, also known as the Secret Intelligence Service, is the British government agency responsible for collecting, analyzing, and using foreign intelligence. It was founded in its present form in 1912 and was particularly active and effective during the Second World War 1939-1945), at which time its agents trained American officers who would later work for the U.S. Central Intelligence Agency (CIA). The names MI-5 and MI-6 derive from the Second World War, when Security Service was "section five" of "military intelligence" and Secret Intelligence was "section six" of "military intelligence."

Philip W. Goetz, *The New Encyclopaedia Britannica, 15th ed., "Micropaedia"* (Chicago: Encyclopaedia Britannica, 1989), s.v. "MI-5," "MI-6."

What is the Israeli parliament called?

The Israeli parliament is called the Knesset. There are 120 members, and who are elected in national general elections. Israeli citizens over 18 years have the right to vote. Those over 21 years have the right to serve in the Knesset.

The Europa World Year Book 1994 (London: Europa Publications, 1994), 1:1552.

What is a "Most Favoured Nation"?

"Most Favoured Nation" status is a much sought after international trading convention which gives a country the best trading and tariff arrangements. It is usually reciprocal between countries but only in the sense that the recipient will respond with the best trade terms it grants to other countries.

Rupert Pennant-Rea and Bill Emmott, *The Pocket Economist* (Oxford: Basil Blackwell, 1987) s.v. "most favoured nation."

When was personal income first taxed in the United States?

The personal income of Americans was first taxed in 1914 at a rate of one per cent on taxable income over $3000 or $4000 for married couples. The law went into effect in October of 1913.

Gerald Carson, *The Golden Egg* (Boston: Houghton Mifflin, 1977), 1.

How did Anthony Sampson, a British journalist, describe members of the British Civil Service?

British journalist Anthony Sampson's description of Britain's civil servants is "Members rise from CMG (known sometimes in Whitehall as 'Call Me God') to the KCMG ('Kindly Call Me

God') to—for a select few governors and super-ambassadors—the GCMG ('God Calls Me God')."

Angela Partington, ed., *The Oxford Dictionary of Quotations, 4th ed.* (Oxford: Oxford University Press, 1992), s.v. "Anthony Sampson."

What British prime minister negotiated the Munich Pact of 1938?

The Munich Pact of 1938 was negotiated by Adolf Hitler (1889-1945) and British prime minister Neville Chamberlain (1869-1940). By its terms Hitler received the right to annex those parts of Czechoslovakia that had a heavy German population, but in fact it allowed Hitler to destroy and absorb the whole country. According to Chamberlain it was a document that was to bring "peace in our time," but the start of World War II (1939-45) was only a year away. It is often taken as an example of the failure of appeasement and need to oppose forcefully tyrants. Chamberlain was a skilled administrator, but he was not skilled at foreign policy and badly misread the European situation throughout the 1930s.

Marcel Baudot, et al., eds., *The Historical Encyclopedia of World War II* (New York: Facts on File, 1980), s.v. "Chamberlain, (Arthur) Neville."

Who was the first official American "woman in combat"?

The first official American "woman in combat" was U.S. Army Captain Linda Bray who participated in the 1989 invasion of Panama. Bray was in charge of a military police platoon that went into battle against a Panama Defense Forces stronghold. However, her Army career later came under a cloud however when her military police company was investigated by the Army Criminal Investigation Division. Disillusionment and resentment from her superiors forced Bray to eventually accept a medical discharge from the Army.

New York Times 4 January 1990. *New York Times* 7 January 1990. "America's First Woman in Combat," *Pittsburgh Press* 30 June 1991.

How many rooms are there in the White House?

The White House, located at 1600 Pennsylvania Ave., Washington, DC, is a 132 room mansion designed by James Hoban. Its design is based on a Georgian country home in Ireland, Leinster Hall. First occupied in 1800, the White House was not fully completed until 1829. Many presidents have directed structural changes and restoration projects, including the addition of terraces, the installation of running water and elevators, and the addition of a second-story porch to the south portico.

Fodor's 92, Washington, D.C. (New York: Fodor's Travel Publications, 1991), 63.

What was the first U.S. state to require the licensing of motor vehicles?

In 1901 New York became the first state to require the licensing of motor vehicles.

David Louis, *Fascinating Facts* (New York: Ridge Press/Crown Publishers, 1977), 87.

What is INTERPOL?

INTERPOL, an acronym for the International Criminal Police Organization, coordinates international law enforcement efforts through cooperation between member national police agencies. Founded in 1923 INTERPOL, by the early 1980s, had 126 members each with its own national central bureau. The international headquarters, known as the General Secretariat, is located in France, while the central bureau for the United States is in Washington, DC. INTERPOL conducts criminal investigations especially those relating to counterfeiting, fraud, drug and weapons trafficking, theft, murder, and rape and it tracks fugitives, suspects, potential witnesses, and missing persons. Funding for INTERPOL comes from member nations with the United States contributing approximately five percent of the organization's total budget.

The Guide to American Law: Everyone's Legal Encyclopedia (St. Paul, MN: West Publishing, 1984), s.v. "Interpol."

What is fascism?

Fascism originally referred to the form of government that Benito Mussolini (1883-1945) introduced in Italy beginning in 1919. The term, however, has become part of the popular idiom and is often used to refer to any authoritative and repressive right-wing government, regardless of internal structure. Generally speaking, however, a fascist government is characterized by one party control or dictatorship while allowing tightly controlled but private ownership of the means of production.

Walter J. Raymond, *International Dictionary of Politics* (Lawrenceville, VA: Brunswick Publishing, 1980), s.v. "fascism."

Why was the South African gold coin known as the Krugerrand banned in the United States?

The Krugerrand is a one-ounce South African gold coin that was banned in the United States in 1985 because of the anti-apartheid movement. Apartheid laws were put in place by South Africa's minority Caucasian government and placed severe limitations on the rights and freedoms of the non-Caucasian majority population. As part of worldwide economic sanctions against South Africa U.S. president Ronald Reagan (1911-) banned importation of the coin in accordance with Executive Order 12535 on October 1, 1985. The Krugerrand was the world's best-selling gold bullion coin and featured a graceful springbok on one side and the bust of Paul Kruger, former president of the Republic of South Africa, on the other side. The Krugerrand was minted in one-quarter, one-half, and one ounce, weights but the latter was most common in the United States.

Coin World Almanac (New York: Amos Press, 1987), 54-55. M. A. Olsen, *The Gold Book* (Westminster, CO: Westminster Publishing, 1992), 65.

What is "trench warfare"?

"Trench warfare" is a term used to describe the style of warfare that typified much of World War I (1914-1918). The fighting was conducted from long, barbed wire fortified trenches that had been dug across much of the landscape, particularly in France. Rather than being haphazardly dug, the trenches were carefully planned and could be quite sophisticated. Oftentimes there were communications, secondary-defense, and support trenches leading to the rear. Some trenches even had their own railway systems. The narrow strip of land that lay between the trenches of opposing sides was called "no man's land." Front line trench duty could be exceedingly dangerous with periods of terrifying enemy action and then periods of silence. To keep troop morale up with the psychology seesaw of terror and boredom, troops were usually rotated between front line trenches, reserve or support trenches, and rear guard trenches for training and if possible, rest and recuperation. Much of the activity in the trenches was conducted under the cover of night including supply replenishment, repair of barbed wire and bulwarks, and nocturnal raids and larger offensives. Closely associated with trench warfare were withering artillery barrages, intersecting fields of machine gun fire, gas warfare, and "over the top" assaults. Toward the end of the war, massive losses inherent in trench warfare led to a rethinking of strategy and the concept of a more fluid "zonal defense" began to emerge.

Philip J. Haythornthwaite, *The World War One Source Book* (London: Arms and Armour, 1992), 76-81.

What was the "bamboo curtain"?

The "bamboo curtain" referred to the Communist governments of the People's Republic of China and other regimes in Asia, which exercised complete control over the movement of people, goods, and ideas, making intelligence gathering and political interaction by Western agencies and governments difficult. "Bamboo curtain" is undoubtedly derived from British statesman's Winston Churchill (1874-1965) "iron curtain,"-a term he used to describe similar despotic conditions in eastern Europe. Although popular in the 1950s, 1960s, and 1970s, by the 1990s "bamboo curtain" as a term had fallen into disuse.

Walter J. Raymond, *International Dictionary of Politics, 6th ed.* (Lawrenceville, VA: Brunswick Publishing Company, 1980), 42.

How do Jeffersonian democracy and Jacksonian democracy differ?

The difference between Jeffersonian democracy and Jacksonian democracy was a matter of degree. Named after U.S. president Thomas Jefferson (1743-1826), Jeffersonian democracy emphasized able leadership via the electoral process. Jacksonian democracy was more radical and was founded in the belief that the "common citizen was the best judge of measures." While President of the United States, Andrew Jackson (1767-1845) strengthened the presidency by vetoing more bills than all his predecessors combined-asserting that by the electoral process the President better represents the will of the people.

E.D. Hirsch Jr., et al., *The Dictionary of Cultural Literacy* (Boston: Houghton Mifflin, 1988), s.v. "Jeffersonian democracy."

How was it determined that the first Tuesday after the first Monday in November would be federal election day?

The current federal election day, the first Tuesday after the first Monday in November, was established in 1845 as the day on which all states must appoint presidential electors. The day became the election day for members and delegates to the U.S. House of Representatives in 1872, and with the ratification of the 17th Amendment in 1915 it also became the election day for senators.

The selection of the particular month and day resulted from several practical considerations. The first was to prevent election abuses in the selection of Presidential electors that could arise if states held elections on different days. Also November was a convenient time of the year for the country's farmers, who had finished harvesting, and it still allowed for easy travel in advance of winter weather. The selection of Tuesday gave voters a travel day to reach the polls, since many Americans observed Sunday as a day of rest.

Our American Government (Washington, DC: U.S. Government Printing Office, 1993), 61.

Who lives at the addresses of 10, 11, and 12 Downing Street in London, England?

The London addresses of 10, 11, and 12 Downing Street are the official residences and offices of Britain's top government officers. Number 10 Downing Street is the official residence of England's prime minister; Number 11 is the residence of the chancellor of the exchequer; and Number 12 is the office of the government whips, members of Parliament who act as liaisons for their political parties.

Whitaker's Almanack (London: J. Whitaker & Sons, 1994), 598.

Which U.S. presidents were sworn in on a Sunday?

Two U.S. presidents have been sworn in on a Sunday, breaking the tradition of delaying the ceremonies when inauguration day falls on a Sunday. During the period when inaugurations were held on March 4, four presidents postponed taking the oath of office until the following day: James Monroe (1758-1831) in 1821, Zachary Taylor (1784-1850) in 1849, Rutherford B. Hayes (1822-1893) in 1877, and Woodrow Wilson (1856-1924) in 1917. Since the inauguration date was moved to January 20, inauguration day has fallen on a Sunday twice. In each of these instances the president was officially sworn in on Sunday, followed by public ceremonies the next day. Dwight D. Eisenhower (1890-1969) was sworn in on Sunday, January 20, 1957, in a private ceremony and Ronald Reagan (1911-)took his oath of office on Sunday, January 20, 1985, in a semi-private ceremony. The next inauguration days to fall on Sunday will be in the years 2013 and 2041.

Joseph Nathan Kane, *Facts About the Presidents, 5th ed.* (New York: H.W. Wilson, 1989), 375.

What was the British name for the Persian Gulf War?

Americans know the Persian Gulf War by the name "Operation Desert Storm," its U.S. military code name. The English, however, had their own name for the war. They called it "Operation Granby." The code name Granby, selected at random by computer, refers to an 18th century British hero. The Marquess of Granby was a cavalry commander who is famed for his courage.

USA Today 20 February 1991.

Who received the first Social Security card and number?

Social Security Card Number 1 was assigned on December 1, 1936 to John David Sweeney, Jr., a 23-year-old shipping clerk from New York. His name was chosen by lot when Joseph L. Fay, chief of the Federal Social Security Bureau in Baltimore, found Sweeney's name on top of the stack of applications he started processing.

"Republican Gets No. 1 Security Card," *New York Times* 2 December 1936.

What is the origin of the name for the state of Virginia?

Virginia was named by the English navigator Sir Walter Raleigh (1552?-1618) for Queen of England Elizabeth I (1533-1603) who was known as the virgin queen. Virginia was the tenth of the 13 original colonies to become a state in 1788.

Lillian Eichler, *The Customs of Mankind* (Garden City, NY: Garden City Publishing, 1924), 679-81. William H. Harris and Judith S. Levey, *The New Columbia Encyclopedia* (New York: Columbia University Press, 1975). *Pittsburgh Press* 24 February 1974.

What is the origin of the name for the state of West Virginia?

Originally West Virginia was part of the state of Virginia. Sir Walter Raleigh (1552?-1618) named Virginia in honor of Queen of England Elizabeth I (1533-1603) who was known as the virgin queen. When the western counties of Virginia rejected secession prior to the outbreak of the American Civil War (1861-1865), they chose to retain Virginia but in order to distinguish themselves from their rebellious neighbor adopted West Virginia as their official name. West Virginia was the 35th state admitted to the Union in 1863.

Lillian Eichler, *The Customs of Mankind* (Garden City, NY: Garden City Publishing, 1924), 679-81. William H. Harris and Judith S. Levey, *The New Columbia Encyclopedia* (New York: Columbia University Press, 1975). *Pittsburgh Press* 24 February 1974.

What is the origin of the name for the state of Wyoming?

Wyoming probably derives its name from a Delaware Indian or Leni-Lenape word, "maugh-wau-wama," meaning "extensive plains" or "mountains with valleys alternating." It is named for the Wyoming Valley of northeastern Pennsylvania, the site of the Indian massacre of 1778. Wyoming was the 44th state admitted to the Union in 1890.

Lillian Eichler, *The Customs of Mankind* (Garden City, NY: Garden City Publishing, 1924), 679-81. William H. Harris and Judith S. Levey, *The New Columbia Encyclopedia* (New York: Columbia University Press, 1975). *Pittsburgh Press* 24 February 1974.

What is the origin of the name for the state of New Jersey?

New Jersey was named by George Carteret (1610-80) after the Isle of Jersey in the English Channel where he was born. Carteret settled the area after it had been granted to him by the Duke of York, later James II (1633-1701). New Jersey was the third of the original thirteen colonies to join the Union in 1787.

Lillian Eichler, *The Customs of Mankind* (Garden City, NY: Garden City Publishing, 1924), 679-81. William H. Harris and Judith S. Levey, *The New Columbia Encyclopedia* (New York: Columbia University Press, 1975). *Pittsburgh Press* 24 February 1974.

What is the origin of the name for the state of Connecticut?

The name for the state of Connecticut, one of the Thirteen Colonies, appears to be derived from the Native North American word "Quonoktacut" or "Quonecktacut," which has been interpreted by some to mean "river whose water is driven in waves by tides or winds," "long river," and "long river place."

Lillian Eichler, *The Customs of Mankind* (Garden City, NY: Garden City Publishing, 1924), 679-81. William H. Harris and Judith S. Levey, eds., *The New Columbia Encyclopedia* (New York: Columbia University Press, 1975). *Pittsburgh Press* 24 February 1974.

What is the origin of the name for the state of Florida?

In 1513 Spanish explorer Juan Ponce de Len, set out on a quest to find the fabled Fountain of Youth, said to be located somewhere in the Bimini isles. When he landed near the site of St. Augustine, he claimed the area—what he thought was an island—for Spain and named it "Florida," probably because it was during the Easter season, the Spanish *Pascua Florida*, (Feast of Flowers), that he made the discovery. Florida was admitted as the 27th state of the Union in 1845.

Lillian Eichler, *The Customs of Mankind* (Garden City, NY: Garden City Publishing, 1924), 679-81. William H. Harris and Judith S. Levey, eds., *The New Columbia Encyclopedia* (New York: Columbia University Press, 1975). *Pittsburgh Press* 24 February 1974.

What is the origin of the name for the state of Hawaii?

The name Hawaii comes from the English spelling of "Owhyhee," possibly derived from a native word meaning "homeland." The islands were discovered by English explorer James Cook in 1778. He named them the Sandwich Islands after the English Earl of Sandwich. The island chain, located in the central Pacific Ocean, became the 50th state of the Union when it was admitted in 1959.

Lillian Eichler, *The Customs of Mankind* (Garden City, NY: Garden City Publishing, 1924), 679-81. William H. Harris and Judith S. Levey, eds., *The New Columbia Encyclopedia* (New York: Columbia University Press, 1975). *Pittsburgh Press* 24 February 1974.

What is the origin of the name for the state of Illinois?

The name Illinois is derived from an Illini Indian word meaning "men" or "warriors." This Native North American word was supplemented by the French adjective ending "ois," probably by the early French explorers when they came to this region. Illinois was admitted as the 21st state of the Union in 1818.

Lillian Eichler, *The Customs of Mankind* (Garden City, NY: Garden City Publishing, 1924), 679-81. William H. Harris and Judith S. Levey, eds., *The New Columbia Encyclopedia* (New York: Columbia University Press, 1975). *Pittsburgh Press* 24 February 1974.

What is the history of the presidential veto and how often are presidential vetoes overridden?

Early U.S. presidents did not find much occasion to use their veto power over bills in Congress. U.S. President George Washington (1732-1799) used his veto only twice and was never overridden. Ulysses S. Grant (1822-1885) was the first president to near the 100 mark with his use of the veto; he denied 93 bills and was only overturned four times. Over the course of two non-successive terms, Grover Cleveland (1837-1908) utilized the presidential veto a record 414 times. He was only surpassed by Franklin D. Roosevelt (1882-1945), who exercised his veto power 635 times. The least successful use of the veto was shown by Franklin Pierce (1804-1869) who was overridden 56 percent of the time.

The New York Times 29 September 1991.

What illnesses have been suffered by different U.S. presidents while they were in office?

Many U.S. presidents have suffered from illness while in office, though not all were made known to the public. Some of these illnesses have been directly attributed to the stresses of being president. For example, Thomas Jefferson (1743-1826) had epileptic fits and had a paranoid fear of audiences. Abraham Lincoln (1809-1865) is known to have suffered from periods of depression. Woodrow Wilson (1856-1924) had hypertension and experienced many strokes, impairing his mental powers while in office. Pneumonia temporarily disabled Warren G. Harding, (1865-1923) who later died in office of a stroke. Franklin D. Roosevelt (1882-1945) suffered from the effects of polio, as well as heart disease and hypertension; he died early in his fourth term of office of a cerebral hemorrhage. Several ailments struck Dwight D. Eisenhower (1890-1969), who had a heart attack, Chron disease, and a stroke. John F. Kennedy (1917-1963) had chronic back problems and Addison's disease, although he denied it during the 1960 campaign. Gall bladder surgery and removal of a polyp were needed by Lyndon B. Johnson (1908-1973), during his presidency. During his second term, Richard M. Nixon (1913-1994) had phlebitis in his left leg. One of many presidents who showed rapid signs of aging, Jimmy Carter (1924-) was once near collapse while running in a race. Ronald Reagan (1911-) survived being shot by a gunman while in office; he also had a malignant tumor removed and prostate surgery. While in office, George Bush (1924-)was diagnosed with a thyroid disorder known as Grave's disease.

John B. Moses and Wilbur Cross, *Presidential Courage* (New York: Norton, 1980), 233. *New York Times* 6 May 1991. *USA Today* 9 June 1993.

What is the WARN Act?

WARN is an acronym for the Worker Adjustment and Retraining Notification Act which was enacted August 4, 1988, and went into effect February 4, 1989. The act requires employers with 100 or more employees to give sixty days' notice of covered plant closings or covered mass layoffs. Not included in the minimum figure of 100 employees are those employees who have worked less than six months in the previous 12, or those who average less than 20 hours of work per week. Companies covered by the act include private for-profit, private nonprofit, and public and quasi-public institutions "which operate in a commercial context and are separately organized from the regular government." Federal, state, and local governmental units are exempted from the act.

Department of Labor, Employment and Training Administration, *A Guide to Advance Notice of Closings and Layoffs* (Washington, DC: Government Printing Office, 1989), 1-8.

What are some statistics on U.S. military personnel that are listed killed in action (KIA) and missing in action (MIA)s in the Vietnam conflict?

Of approximately 2.6 million Americans who served in the Vietnam conflict, 47,357 are listed as killed in action and 10,796 as noncombat deaths. As of 1992, the Pentagon listed 2,266 U.S. military personnel who took part in the war as still unaccounted.

USA Today 23 September 1992.

What is the origin of the name for the state of Minnesota?

The state name Minnesota is derived from a Sioux Indian word meaning "cloudy water" or "sky-tinted water," and was taken from the river of the same name. In 1858 Minnesota was admitted as the 32d state of the Union.

Lillian Eichler, *The Customs of Mankind* (Garden City, NY: Garden City Publishing, 1924), 679-81. William H. Harris and Judith S. Levey, eds., *The New Columbia Encyclopedia* (New York: Columbia University Press, 1975). *Pittsburgh Press* 24 February 1974.

What is the origin of the name for the state of Missouri?

The state of Missouri was named for the large river that flows through the region. It was derived from a Native North American tribal name meaning "muddy water." Missouri was admitted as the 24th state of the Union in 1821.

Lillian Eichler, *The Customs of Mankind* (Garden City, NY: Garden City Publishing, 1924), 679-81. William H. Harris and Judith S. Levey, eds., *The New Columbia Encyclopedia* (New York: Columbia University Press, 1975). *Pittsburgh Press* 24 February 1974.

How have U.S. presidents been rated for their success on the job?

Americans are becoming more critical of the country's presidents, according to a USA Today/CNN/Gallup poll. U.S. president Ronald Reagan (1911-), George Bush (1924-), and Bill Clinton (1946-)have all struggled for higher marks on their presidential "report cards." In the first quarter of his term, Clinton received a C+ for his overall grade, reflecting the fact that he only received 43 percent of the popular vote. Bush ended his term with a solid B, having lost points gained in the Persian Gulf War to economic problems. After two terms, Reagan finished the presidency with a C+ despite his overwhelming victory in the 1984 election. The study calculated the following grades for each president since Dwight D. Eisenhower (1890-1969): Jimmy Carter (1924-), C-; Gerald Ford (1913-), C-; Richard Nixon (1913-1994), C-; Lyndon B. Johnson (1908-1973), C+; John F. Kennedy (1917-1963), A-; Eisenhower, B. When Harvard professor Arthur Schlesinger, Sr. asked 75 presidential experts to rate the greatest U.S. Presidents in 1962, the top vote getter was Abraham Lincoln (1809-1865), followed by George Washington (1732-1799), Franklin D. Roosevelt (1882-1945), Woodrow Wilson (1856-1924), and Thomas Jefferson (1743-1826).

Samuel Rosenman and Dorothy Rosenman, *Presidential Style* (New York: Harper and Row, 1976), 551. *USA Today* 28 April 1993.

How successful have recent U.S. presidents been in getting bills passed by Congress?

The success rate of bills that were proposed or supported by the president has greatly varied over the course of the last several presidents. The U.S. Congress did not create many obstacles for U.S. president Dwight D. Eisenhower (1890-1969), who had 72 percent of his bills succeed in Congress. John F. Kennedy (1917-1963) received the greatest amount of support from the legislature, which approved 85 percent of his bills. His successor, Lyndon B. Johnson (1908-1973) and Gerald Ford (1913-) were less fortunate; they were victorious 64 and 58 percent of the time. Jimmy Carter (1924-) succeeded with 77 percent of his bills. Ronald Reagan (1911-) had a 62 percent success rate with Congress. George Bush (1924-) was one of the least successful presidents in getting bills passed; only 52 percent of his bills were victorious.

USA Today 15 June 1993.

When was the first congressional investigation?

The first congressional investigation occurred in 1792. There have been 33 major congressional investigations since that time.

U.S. News & World Report 25 July 1994.

What is the name of the mutual assistance pact between Australia, New Zealand, and the United States?

In 1951 the United States, Australia, and New Zealand signed the ANZUS Pact, a treaty which pledged each country to come to the aid of the other country(ies) in the event of an attack from Asia.

Howard L. Hurwitz, *An Encyclopedic Dictionary of American History* (New York: Washington Square Press, 1968), s.v. "ANZUS Pact."

When was the bald eagle adopted as the national bird of the United States?

On June 20, 1782, the citizens of the newly independent United States of America adopted the bald or "American" eagle as their national emblem. At first the heraldic artists depicted a bird that could have been a member of any of the larger species, but by 1902, the bird portrayed on the seal of the United States of America had assumed its proper white plumage on head and tail. The choice of the bald eagle was not unanimous; The American statesman, scientist, and philosopher, Benjamin Franklin (1706-1790) preferred the wild turkey bird. Oftentimes a tongue-in-cheek humorist, Franklin thought the turkey a wily but brave, intelligent, and prudent bird. He viewed the eagle on the other hand as having "a bad moral character" and "not getting his living honestly: but would prefer to steal fish from hardworking fish-hawks." He also found the eagle a coward who readily flees from the irritating attacks of the much smaller kingbird.

American Heritage December 1959, October 1960. Ernest Ingersold, *Birds in Legend, Fable and Folklore* (New York: Longmans, Green and Co., 1923), 37. *Marshall Cavendish International Wildlife Encyclopedia* Marshall Cavendish, 1989. *McGraw-Hill Encyclopedia of World Biography* (New York: McGraw Hill, 1973), s.v. "B. Franklin."

Where was the first automobile license plate issued?

Leon Serpollet of Paris, France, obtained the first automobile license plate in 1889. They were first required in the United States by New York State in 1901. Registration was required within 30 days. Owners had to provide their names and addresses as well as a description of their vehicles. The fee was one dollar. The plates bore the owner's initials and were required to be over 3 inches high. Permanent plates made of aluminum were first issued in Connecticut in 1937.

Automotive Industries 4 October 1930. Joseph N. Kane, *Famous First Facts, 4th ed.* (New York: Wilson, 1981), 56.

Is there a national flower of the United States?

The national flower of the United States is the rose, adopted on October 7, 1986.

Encyclopedia Americana (Danbury, CT: Grolier, 1990), s.v. "flowers." *World Book Encyclopedia* (Chicago: World Book), s.v. "flowers."

How many votes does it take to close debate on an issue in the U.S. Senate?

Cloture, or closure, in the U.S. Senate is a parliamentary procedure used to close debate and bring a motion or a bill to a vote. It is used especially against the filibuster-a delaying tactics designed to prevent action on a measure-and prior to 1975 required the vote of two-thirds of the senators present. That rule was amended in 1975 to require a three-fifths' vote of the entire Senate membership. On current proposed changes to Senate rules, however, a vote of two-thirds of the members present and voting would be required.

Our American Government: A Primer on the Operation of the Three Branches of Government: 150 Questions & Answers (Washington, DC: WANT Publishing, 1985), 15-16. *World Book Encyclopedia* (Chicago: World Book, 1994), s.v. "cloture."

Who was the first woman elected to the U.S. Senate?

Hattie Ophelia Wyatt Caraway (1878-1950) of Jonesboro, Arkansas, became the first woman elected to the U.S. Senate in 1932. She was appointed on November 13, 1931, by the Arkansas governor to fill the vacancy left by the death of her husband Senator Thaddeus Caraway. She served in the U.S. Senate until January 3, 1945.

Joseph Nathan Kane, *Famous First Facts, 4th ed.*, (New York: H.W. Wilson, 1981), 572.

Who owns the Liberty Bell?

The Liberty Bell is located in the Liberty Bell Pavilion by Independence Hall (Independence National Historical Park) in Philadelphia, Pennsylvania. The city owns the bell but it is under the custody of the U.S. National Park Service.

The bell was first cast in London by Thomas Lester's foundry in 1752 for the state house of the British province of Pennsylvania. It bore the inscription "Proclaim Liberty throughout all the land unto all the inhabitants thereof." (Leviticus: 25:10) The bell was cracked when tested in Philadelphia, then recast locally by Charles Stow and John Pass.

It was rung on July 8, 1776, to proclaim the adoption of the Declaration of Independence and on each anniversary of this occasion until 1835. The bell suffered another major crack on July 8, 1835, when it was used to toll the death of Chief Justice of the United States John Marshall (1755-1835). It was muffled and tolled at the death of U.S. President William Henry Harrison (1773-1841) in 1841 and was last rung during the commemoration for U.S. President George Washington's (1732-1799) birthday in 1846.

Charles Michael Boland, *Ring in the Jubilee* (Riverside, CT: Chatham Press, 1973), 7, 34, 40-41, 44, 48, 93-94, 98. *The Encyclopedia Americana, intern. ed.* (Danbury, CT: Grolier, 1994), s.v. "Liberty Bell."

Who can declare a national emergency?

A national emergency is defined as a state of national crisis; a situation demanding immediate and extraordinary national or federal action. The National Emergency Act of 1976 terminated various emergency powers of the U.S. President and established clear guidelines for such a declaration which would have to be decided jointly by the President and Congress.

This act culminated the work of the Special Senate Committee on the Termination of the National Emergency Act. Established on January 6, 1973, the committee found that the United States had been living in a state of declared national emergency since March of 1933. Then the U.S. Congress ratified the declaration of an emergency by President Franklin D. Roosevelt's (1882-1945). The emergency was invoked to bring stability to the country during the chaotic economic upheaval called the Great Depression. President Harry Truman (1884-1972) had declared a state of national emergency in December of 1950, in response to China's invasion of Korea. President Richard Nixon (1913-1994) had declared a state of emergency twice; first on March 23, 1970, for federal troops to handle mail in New York during a postal strike, and on August 15, 1971, to cope with an international monetary crisis that developed when Nixon imposed a surcharge on dutiable imports. The committee found 470 laws which gave emergency powers to the president. PL95-223 established a new set of economic controls the President could implement and provided some Congressional review of future presidential declarations of emergency.

Henry Campbell Black, *Black's Law Dictionary, 6th ed.* (Minnesota: West Publishing, 1990), s.v. "national emergency." *Congress and the Nation* (Washington, DC: Congressional Quarterly, 1977), 4:801-2. *Congress and the Nation* (Washington, DC: Congressional Quarterly, 1981), 5:139. Jay

M. Shafritz, *The HarperCollins Dictionary of American Government and Politics* (New York: HarperCollins, 1992), s.v. "national emergency act of 1976."

How many Hispanics have served in the U.S. Congress, and who was the first?

From 1877 to 1993, there were 31 Hispanics who had served in the U.S. Congress. The first Hispanic representative was Romualdo Pacheco, a Republican from California, in 1877. The first Hispanic senator was Dennis Chavez, a Democrat from New Mexico who held the position from 1935 to 1962.

This figure does not include the territorial delegates from Puerto Rico, Guam, or the Virgin Islands, nor the 14 resident commissioners of Puerto Rico.

Congress A to Z: A Ready Reference Encyclopedia, 2d ed. (Washington, DC: Congressional Quarterly, 1993), 461.

How much does it cost to print United States paper money?

United States paper currency cost 2.6 cents per bill to produce in 1990.

Marc Hudgeons, *Official 1995 Blackbook Price Guide of United States Paper Money, 27th ed.* (New York: House of Collectibles, 1994), 30.

What does "PT" in "PT boat" signify?

The "PT" in "PT boat" stands for "Patrol Torpedo." These boats were used by the U.S. Navy during World War II (1939-45) in the South Pacific against the Japanese. Powered by diesel or gasoline engines, PT boats could reach speeds of 40 knots and carried a significant gun armament in addition to torpedoes.

The New Encyclopaedia Britannica, 15th ed. (Chicago: Encyclopaedia Britannica, 1993), s.v. "war, technology of."

When was the first minimum wage rate established and how much was it?

The U.S. Fair Labor Standards Act of 1938 set the first minimum wage as 25 cents an hour. The rate applies only to specific nonsupervisory employment categories. Over the past 40 years, the minimum wage has increased not quite sixfold.

Bureau of the Census, *Statistical Abstract of the United States: 1993, 113th ed.* (Washington, DC: Government Printing Office, 1993). *New York Times* 7 May 1976. *New York Times* 21 November 1977. *The World Almanac and Book of Facts, 1995* (Mahwah, NJ: World Almanac, 1994), 151. *The World Book Encyclopedia,* (Chicago: World Book, 1994), s.v. "Fair Labor Standards Act."

If only 41 individuals have served as President of the United States, then why is Bill Clinton the 42nd president?

If the number of people who have held the office of President of the United States is counted, the total will be 41. However, Grover Cleveland is usually counted twice. He served two terms but the terms were not concurrent. He was the 22nd and 24th president. Bill Clinton is the 42nd.

Dmitri A. Borgmann, *Language on Vacation: An Olio of Orthographical Oddities* (New York: Charles Scribner's Sons, 1965), 263.

When was the Purple Heart established?

Originally called the Badge of Military Merit, U.S. President George Washington (1732-1799) established the Purple Heart in 1782. It was a heart made of purple cloth and was awarded to Revolutionary War (1775-1783) soldiers for unusual bravery. The Purple Heart of today, which has a profile of Washington on it, was established in 1932 for the Army and 1942 for the Navy. It is awarded for having been wounded or killed in the line of duty.

Tom Burnam, *The Dictionary of Misinformation* (New York: Thomas Y. Crowell, 1975), s.v. "Purple Heart." *The World Book Encyclopedia* (Chicago: World Book, 1994), s.v. "medals, decorations, and orders."

What is Red Skelton's version of "The Pledge of Allegiance"?

Red Skelton on Flag Day, June 14, 1972, addressed the U.S. House of Representatives saying:

If I may I would like to recite the Pledge of Allegiance and give you a definition for each word.
I-me, an individual, a committee of one.
Pledge-dedicate all of my worldly goods to give without self-pity.
Allegiance-my love and my devotion.
To the Flag-our standard, Old Glory, a symbol of freedom. Wherever she waves, there is respect because your loyalty has given her a dignity that shouts freedom is everybody's job.
Of the United-that means that we have all come together.
States-individual communities that have united into 48 great states, 48 individual communities with pride and dignity and purpose, all divided with imaginary boundaries, yet united to a common purpose, and that's love for country.
Of America.
And to the Republic-a state in which sovereign power is invested in representatives chosen by the people to govern. And government is the people and it's from the people to the leaders, not from the leaders to the people.
For which it stands.
One nation-meaning, so blessed by God.
Indivisible-incapable of being divided.
With liberty-which is freedom and the right of power to live one's own life without threats or fear or some sort of retaliation.
And justice-the principle or quality of dealing fairly with others.
For all-which means 'it's as much your country as it is mine.'

Suzy Platt, ed., *Respectfully Quoted: A Dictionary of Quotations Requested from the Congressional Research Service* (Washington, DC: Library of Congress, 1989), 257.

What is the difference between the Freedom of Information Act and the Privacy Act?

Both the Freedom of Information Act and the Privacy Act provide public access to U.S. federal government records. The Freedom of Information Act applies to federal executive agency administrative files, while the Privacy Act applies to personal records maintained by those same agencies. Anyone can request records covered by the Freedom of Information Act, while the Privacy Act allows individual citizens to request information about only themselves.

Judith Schiek Robinson, *Tapping the Government Grapevine: The User-Friendly Guide to U.S. Government Information Sources, 2d ed.* (Phoenix, AZ: Oryx Press, 1993), 1015.

Who was the first African-American representative in the U.S. Congress?

The first African American to serve in the U.S. House of Representatives was Joseph Hayne Rainey (1831-1887) of South Carolina. He was elected to fill a vacancy in the House in 1870 and was regularly elected until 1878, when he lost his bid for re-election.

Joan Potter and Constance Claytor, *African-American Firsts* (Elizabethtown, NY: Pinto Press, 1994), 104-5. Jessie Carney Smith, ed. *Black Firsts: 2,000 Years of Extraordinary Achievement* (Detroit: Gale Research, Inc., 1994), 173.

Who wrote the "Pledge of Allegiance"?

Although authorship of the pledge has been attributed to both Francis Bellamy, an associate editor of the Boston magazine *Youth's Companion*, and to James Upham, one of the owners of the magazine, the United States Flag Association in 1939 assigned the authorship of the pledge to Bellamy, who had served on a State Superintendents of Education program committee for the national Columbus anniversary celebration.

U.S. president Benjamin Harrison (1833-1901) had proclaimed October 21, 1892, a holiday, designating the day as the 400th anniversary of the European discovery of America by the explorer Christopher Columbus (1451-1506). During a time of a great influx of immigrants to America, Harrison used this occasion to impress upon America's youth the patriotic duties of U.S. citizenship. The committee was charged to design exercises that would be enacted in American schools on that day. Bellamy penned the *Pledge of Allegiance*, also known as *Flag Pledge*, or *Salute to the Flag*, in August 1892. His original version appeared in the September 8, 1892, issue of *Youth's Companion* and read:

I pledge allegiance to my flag, and to the Republic for which it stands one nation indivisible, with liberty and justice for all.

The ambiguous phrase "my flag" was changed to "the flag of the United States of America" by the committee. The pledge was to be recited before the flag in an approved ceremony in which students would salute the flag during the pledge's recitation.

In 1942 during World War II (1939-1945) the pledge was made part of the U.S. Congress' code for the use of the flag. The original wording has been changed over the years. On June 14, 1954, the U.S. Congress added the words "under God." The pledge currently reads:

I pledge allegiance to the flag of the United States of America and to the republic for which it stands, one nation under God, indivisible, with liberty and justice for all.

Chronicle of America (Liberty, MO: International Publishing, 1993), 497. Robert Famighetti, ed., *The World Almanac and Book of Facts 1995* (Mahwah, NJ: World Almanac, 1994), 468. Ernie Gross, *This Day in American History* (New York: Neal-Schuman Publishers, 1990), 285. George W. Stimpson, *Nuggets of Knowledge* (New York: A. L. Burt, 1934), 339-40.

How much does the federal government spend each year on AIDS?

U.S. government spending on Acquired Immune Deficiency Syndrome (AIDS) research, prevention, and services has been rising steadily since 1990. Expenditures in 1990 for AIDS were $1.35 billion; in 1991, $1.73 billion; in 1992 $1.82 billion; in 1993, $1.90 billion; and in 1994 $2.42 billion.

USA Today, 2 December 1993.

Was there ever a state in the United States that was later dissolved?

The self-proclaimed state of Franklin existed from 1784 to 1788 in the western portion of North Carolina. The state, named for U.S. statesman, Benjamin Franklin (1706-1790), was established in 1784 by western settlers attempting to establish self-government in the midst of land disputes between the federal government and the state of North Carolina. Franklin elected a governor, negotiated for the purchase of additional land, and petitioned the U.S. Congress for recognition as a state but petition denial, factionalism, infighting, and confusion subsequently led to its demise. When its governor's term expired in 1788, so too did the state of Franklin. The area would later be incorporated into the state of Tennessee.

The Encyclopedia Americana, intern. ed. (Danbury, CT: Grolier, 1990), s.v. "Franklin, state of."

What is AFDC?

AFDC is an acronym for the public assistance program known as Aid to Families with Dependent Children. The purpose of AFDC is to provide financial aid to families with children who have lost parental support due to infirmity, death, or abandonment. Eligibility for AFDC benefits is determined on the individualized basis of need compared to assets. Originally created in 1935 as part of the Social Security Act, AFDC is administered at both the state and local levels, usually through county departments of public welfare.

Robert L. Barker, *The Social Work Dictionary* (Silver Spring, MD: National Association of Social Workers, 1987), s.v. "Aid to Families with Dependent Children."

What are the steps taken when a U.S. citizen dies in a foreign country?

In the event of a U.S. citizen dying in a foreign country, the U.S. consulate should be contacted. If the deceased was carrying disposition instructions with his or her passport, the consul will carry out those wishes as closely as local law will allow. If there were no instructions, the consul will arrange for disposition according to the survivors' wishes, including a report of death (similar to a death certificate), and will act as the "provisional conservator" of any property involved.

Transporting of the body home requires that the body be embalmed and packed in a hermetically-sealed coffin with an additional outside shipping case. As this can be quite expensive, cremation is an alternative. However, one may find that embalming and cremation facilities are not readily available in many countries.

The remaining alternative is to have the body buried in the country of death. However, this may require that the survivors follow local laws and customs of that country.

Patricia Anderson, *Affairs in Order: A Complete Resource Guide to Death and Dying* (New York: Macmillan Publishing, 1991), 216.

What is Amnesty International?

Amnesty International is an organization that was established to promote the release of political prisoners who have neither committed nor advocated acts of violence. It was founded in Britain in 1961 by Peter Benenson, a lawyer, and has grown to include over 50,000 members in 57 countries. Privately sponsored, it has no political or religious affiliation. Having done much to publicize cases of murder, torture, and unjust imprisonment, it also aims to improve the standards for the treatment of prisoners and to help the families of those imprisoned. In 1972 Amnesty International was awarded the Nobel Peace Prize.

Chris Cook, *Dictionary of Historical Terms: A Guide to Names and Events of over 1,000 Years of World History* (New York: Peter Bedrick Books, 1983), s.v. "Amnesty International."

What is the significance of the Philippine Constitution of 1987?

The Philippine Constitution of 1987 was an attempt by Corazon Aquino and other reformers to return the Philippines to a democracy after the overthrow of the Marcos dictatorship in 1986. It allowed for a bicameral legislature, a presidency with clear limits on its power, and a judiciary free of political influence.

George C. Kohn, *Dictionary of Historic Documents* (New York: Facts on File, 1991), s.v. "Philippine Constitution of 1987."

What was the GI Bill of Rights (Servicemen's Readjustment Act)?

On June 22, 1944, the U.S. government enacted the GI Bill of Rights (Servicemen's Readjustment Act), which gave economic and educational assistance to veterans of World War II (1939-45). It allowed subsidies for vocational training or a college education for up to four years, and about 12 million veterans took advantage of the educational benefits. In addition, it provided grants for veteran's hospitals, vocational rehabilitation, job placement and restoration of peacetime jobs, substantial unemployment benefits, and low-interest mortgages.

It was extended to Korean Conflict veterans in 1952 and, in 1966, a new GI Bill was passed for Vietnam Conflict veterans. Vietnam Conflict veterans received similar benefits as well as medical assistance and a preference when applying for federal jobs.

Family Encyclopedia of American History (Pleasantville, NY: Reader's Digest Association, 1975), s.v. "GI Bill of Rights." George G. Kohn, *Dictionary of Historic Documents* (New York: Facts on File, 1991), s.v. "GI Bill of Rights (Servicemen's Readjustment Act)."

What are the *Federalist Papers*?

One of the hallmarks of United States constitutional history are the *Federalist Papers*. Originally published as a series of 85 newspaper articles, the *Federalist Papers* sought to explain some of the concepts in the new American Constitution. They were reprinted and distributed throughout the states as debate raged over the ratification of the American Constitution. The authors of the *Federalist Papers* included some of the principal architects of the U.S. Constitution such as James Madison (1751-1836), Alexander Hamilton (1755-1804), and John Jay (1745-1829).

Michael Nelson, ed., *The Presidency A to Z* (Washington, DC: Congressional Quarterly, 1992) s.v. "Federalist Papers."

What symbols appear on the great seal of the United States?

Many countries in the world have an official seal. The great seal of the United States was first adopted in 1782 and formally accepted in 1789. On the front side of the seal appears an American eagle, a traditional symbol of power and victory. The eagle's breast is covered by a shield or escutcheon with thirteen red and white stripes, symbolizing America's original colonies. In the eagle's mouth is a ribbon containing the words "E Pluribus Unum," meaning "one out of many" to symbolize the unity of the country. The eagle's right talon contains an olive branch with thirteen leaves which signifies peace, while the left talon has thirteen arrows symbolizing a strong defense. Above the eagle's head is a ring of light breaking through a cloud. Inside the ring are thirteen stars, one for each new state, on a blue background, symbolizing a sovereign country taking its place in the community of nations. The blue field represents the U.S. Congress.

The opposite side of the seal contains a central pyramid, which expresses the building of a strong nation. At the base of the pyramid is the date "1776" in Roman numerals, the year in which the United States was founded. the pyramid has 13 courses of stone representing the 13 original states in the Union and is watched over by the Eye of Providence enclosed in its traditional triangle. The eye enclosed in a triangle with rays of light is positioned above the pyramid. The light rays represent the light of the universe. Above the triangle are the words "Annuit Coeptis" which means "God has favored our undertakings." Below the pyramid the phrase "Novis Ordo Sectorum" meaning "a new order of the ages" is inscribed on a ribbon.

This ornamental stamp is used to seal documents 2,000 to 3,000 times a year, and is kept in the custody of the Secretary of State. Documents include treaties, appointments by the president other than those issued under another seal, and ceremonial communications The seal is also seen on public buildings, uniforms, coins, money, and many other things representing the U.S. government.

Department of State, *The Great Seal of the United States* (Washington, DC: Government Printing Office, 1986), 6, 12-15. Arnold Whittick, *Symbols, Signs and their Meaning* (Newton, MA: Charles T. Branford Company, 1960), 48. *World Book Encyclopedia* (Chicago: World Book, 1994), s.v. "Great Seal of the United States.."

What are Clinton's "Laws of Politics"?

The "Laws of Politics" of President William Clinton refers to his light-hearted attempt to distill his political experience into the following six maxims:

Always be introduced by someone you have appointed to high office.

When you are starting to have a good time, you should be somewhere else.

There is no such thing as enough money.

If someone tells you it's not a money problem, it is someone else's problem.

When someone tells you it is not personal, they are fixing to stick it to you.

Nearly everyone will lie to you given the right circumstances.

New York Times 17 September 1992.

Which of the last four presidents made the most initial appointments of women and minorities to their cabinet?

U.S. president Bill Clinton (1946-) made significantly more initial appointments of women and minorities to his cabinet than any of the last four presidents.

USA Today 22 December 1992.

Which states limit the terms of their state legislators?

Arizona, Arkansas, California, Colorado, Florida, Michigan, Missouri, Montana, Nebraska, Ohio, Oklahoma, Oregon,

South Dakota, Washington, and Wyoming all have term limits imposed on their state legislators.

Election Results Directory: A Complete Listing of State and Federal Legislative and Executive Branch Officials (n.p.: National Conference of State Legislatures, 1993), xi.

What are the general military enlistment requirements?

It is essential that persons who are considering a military career know the general military enlistment requirements. Enlisted members must enter a legal agreement called an enlistment contract, which usually involves a commitment to eight years of service. Depending on the terms of the contract, two to six years are spent on active duty, the balance in the reserves. Enlistees must be between the ages of 17 and 35, must be a U.S. citizen or immigrant alien holding permanent resident status, must not have a felony record, and must possess a birth certificate. Applicants who are seventeen years old at the time of enlistment must have the consent of a parent or legal guardian. Applicants must pass both a physical examination and a written examination, the Armed Services Vocational Aptitude Battery, and must meet minimum physical standards such as height, weight, vision, and overall health. All applicants should have at least a high school diploma or equivalent.

Department of Labor, *Occupational Outlook Handbook, 1994-95, ed.* (Washington DC: Government Printing Office, 1994), 454.

Which states in the United States are called "Commonwealths"?

In the United States, Kentucky, Massachusetts, Pennsylvania, and Virginia carry the official designation "Commonwealth." The word represents the antithesis of despotic and an autocratic government. The word embodies the principle of popular sovereignty.

The Encyclopedia Americana, intern. ed. (Danbury, CT: Grolier, 1990), s.v. "commonwealth."

What is the smallest independent state in the world?

From a practical standpoint the world's smallest independent state is Vatican City. The Vatican is the seat of the Roman Catholic Church and its 108 acres are completely within the city of Rome. From a technical standpoint however the smallest independent state is The Sovereign Military Order of Malta (SMOM). The SMOM, which originated with the eleventh century crusades is also located in Rome and comprises about three acres or roughly one-half of a football field. In 1961 the Civil Courts of Rome declared the order an "international sovereign society," free to issue passports and conduct diplomatic business.

Wayne C. Thompson, *Western Europe 1994, 13th ed.* (Harper's Ferry, WV: Stryker-Post Publications, 1994), 414, 422. *World Book Encyclopedia* (Chicago: World Book, 1987), s.v. "Vatican City."

How was the U.S. Treasury's gold reserve saved in 1895?

The U.S. Treasury's gold reserve was saved in 1895 when the financial houses of American bankers J. P. Morgan (1837-1913) and August Belmont (1816-90) loaned the federal government $65 million in gold. The debt was to be paid off in government bonds. The financial panic of 1893 was fomented by an inflexible banking system, low immediate profit on capital investments made during the 1880s, the failure of the British banking house Baring Brothers and Company, the slowing down of foreign investment capital, and a New York stock market crash. Substantial exports of gold coupled with rumors that the United States was about to go off the gold standard resulted in large scale gold hoarding. By April of 1893 the gold reserves of the United States had fallen below the accepted minimum of $100 million and by 1895 that figure stood at $41,393 million. This made it necessary for the U.S. Treasury to borrow the gold.

Dictionary of American History (New York: Charles Scribner's Sons, 1976), s.v. "panic of 1893." James Trager, *The People's Chronology* (New York: Henry Holt, 1992), 610.

Who was the first living U.S. President to appear on paper money?

The first living U.S. President to appear on paper money was Abraham Lincoln (1809-1865). Lincoln's portrait appeared on an 1861 ten dollar demand note.

Alex Trebek and Merv Griffin, *The Jeopardy Challenge: The Toughest Games from America's Greatest Quiz Show!* (New York: Harper Perennial, 1992), 15, 17.

In what order were the states admitted to the Union?

The states joined the union in the following order: Delaware, Pennsylvania, New Jersey, Georgia, Connecticut, Massachusetts, Maryland, South Carolina, New Hampshire, Virginia, New York, North Carolina, Rhode Island, Vermont, Kentucky, Tennessee, Ohio, Louisiana, Indiana Mississippi, Illinois, Alabama, Maine, Missouri, Arkansas, Michigan, Florida, Texas, Iowa, Wisconsin, California, Minnesota, Oregon, Kansas, West Virginia, Nevada, Nebraska, Colorado, North Dakota, South Dakota, Montana Washington, Idaho, Wyoming Utah Oklahoma New Mexico, Arizona, Alaska, and Hawaii.

Robert Farmighetti, ed., *World Almanac and Book of Facts 1995* (New York: World Almanac, 1995), 426. Milo M. Quaife, *The History of the United States Flag* (New York: Harper & Brothers, 1961), 426.

What were President Franklin D. Roosevelt's "Four Freedoms"?

President Franklin D. Roosevelt's "Four Freedoms" were the freedom of speech and expression, freedom of worship, freedom from fear, and freedom from want. Roosevelt's concept of the "Four Freedoms" was presented in a speech before Congress in 1941.

John Wagman, *On This Day In America* (New York: Gallery Books, 1990).

Do U.S. Senators ever leave the Senate to run for a seat in the House of Representatives?

Between 1962 and 1987 not one U.S. Senator relinquished their position to run for a seat in the House of Representatives. In the same period, however, 117 House members ran for Senate seats.

American Leaders, 1789-1987: A Biographical Summary (Washington, DC: Congressional Quarterly, 1987), 57.

What is the origin of the term "G.I." Joe?

By 1935 G.I. was a stamped or stenciled acronym appearing on every "Government Issue" item. About the same time, "Joe" was in popular usage in such expressions as "Joe College," "Joe Blow," and "just an ordinary Joe." A Joe wearing government issue quite naturally became "G.I. Joe," which during World War II (1939-45) was a slang expression for an ordinary U.S. soldier. In Lieutenant Dave Gerger's comic strip for *Yank*, the army weekly, on June 17, 1942, the term was first used in print. Recruits finding themselves caught up in the impersonal process soon began referring to themselves as Government Issue.

Charles Panati, *Parade of Fads, Follies, and Manias* (New York: HarperCollins, 1991), 202. Louis L. Snyder, *Louis L. Snyder's Historical Guide to World War II* (Westport, CT: Greenwood Press, 1982) s.v. "GI."

Who was the first African-American woman elected to the U.S. Congress?

The first African-American woman to serve in the U.S. Congress was Shirley Chisolm (1924-). She was elected to the U.S. House of Representatives in 1968. In 1972 Chisolm became the first African-American woman to seek nomination as the Democratic party's presidential candidate.

Jessie Carney Smith, ed., *Black Firsts* (Detroit: Gale Research, 1994), 180.

What was the name of the book published by Saddam Hussein in 1977?

Saddam Hussein's book *Our Struggle* attracted little attention at the time of its publication in 1977. The Arab leader published the book in Arabic, as well as in German-under the title *Unser Kampf*, startlingly similar to Hitler's *Mein Kampf*. Interest in the book started when excerpts surfaced in February of 1991 in the German newspaper *Hamburger Rundschau*. A collection of speeches and interviews, the publication outlines Hussein's goals to unite Arabs against western nations and to prepare for war against the West.

"Saddam's book also a 'kampf,'" *Pittsburgh Post-Gazette* 23 February 1991.

What two leaders joined President Carter in 1974 to sign an historic peace treaty?

To end a war that had lasted nearly 31 years, on March 26, 1979, U.S. president Jimmy Carter (1924-), President Anwar Sadat of Egypt (1918-81), and Premier Menahem Begin of Israel signed a peace treaty in Washington, DC. Carter succeeded in facilitating peace in two countries that had never before had a peace treaty.

Facts on File 30 March 1979.

What was the Friendship Force?

President Jimmy Carter's Friendship Force, founded by the Reverend David Wayne Smith, was an international exchange program. Delegates from a foreign city exchanged places with delegates from a United States city.

Pittsburgh Post-Gazette 14 January 1978.

What is eminent domain?

Eminent domain is a legal term describing the right of a national, state, or municipal government or an individual assigned such powers to confiscate private property for public use following due process and just compensation.

The Guide To American Law: Everyone's Legal Encyclopedia (St. Paul, MN: West Publishing, 1983), s.v. "eminent domain."

What is a kangaroo court?

A kangaroo court is a colloquial expression for a court without any legal power. The phrase also refers to a court in which because of bias an individual's right to due process is completely ignored.

The Guide to American Law: Everyone's Legal Encyclopedia (St. Paul, MN: West Publishing, 1984), s.v. "kangaroo court."

How many African-American soldiers have been awarded a U.S. Medal of Honor?

In 1993, the U.S. Army decided to reexamine its record for awarding the Medal of Honor to African-American soldiers. At that time, 79 African-American soldiers had received the country's highest award for heroism, which has been given out since 1862. Most of those 79 awards were given out in the nineteenth century. In fact, of the more than 400 Medal of Honor decorations made in World War II (1939-45), none of the awards went to African-American soldiers, despite the fact that 1.2 million African Americans were in the U.S. Armed Forces. Most of these troops were segregated into units that did service tasks rather than fight in combat.

Mark W. Wright, "Army asks why no WWII black won Medal of Honor," *Pittsburgh Post-Gazette* 5 April 1993.

What were the Northwest Ordinances?

The Northwest Ordinances were three acts passed by the U.S. Congress that provided a framework for the settlement and governing of the "Old Northwest," that vast wilderness west of Pennsylvania and north of the Ohio River. Much of this land had been controlled by the various states but under the Articles of Confederation it was ceded to the Union. The Ordinance of 1784 was drafted by Thomas Jefferson (1743-1826) and divided the region into sixteen districts and set down guidelines for the admittance of future states from this region.

The Ordinance of 1785 regulated the surveying, sale, and final disposition of land. It mandated surveying the territory into townships six miles on a side and comprised of 36 sections, each a square mile. Section 16 of each new township was to be used to support education. Boundaries would be based on meridians of longitude and parallels of latitude. Some land was set aside to be used as bounty payments to veterans while other lands would be sold in exchange for special or continental certificates.

The Ordinance of 1787 established the governmental framework through the creation of the Northwest Territory. As population increased, responsibility for the seating of governors, legislators, and others would gradually shift from the Congress to the electorate. An important part of the 1787 ordinance was the outlawing of slavery in the Northwest Territory.

Dictionary of American History, rev. ed. (New York: Charles Scribner's Sons, 1976), s.v. "Northwest Territory." *Family Encyclopedia of American History* (Pleasantville, NY: Reader's Digest Association, 1975), s.v. "Northwest Ordinance."

What is the name given to the first ten amendments of the U.S. Constitution?

The first ten amendments to the U.S. Constitution are collectively known as the Bill of Rights. The concept of a list enumerating the rights of citizens arose with the English Bill of Rights of 1689 which was a result of the Glorious Revolution of 1688. Originally the drafters of the U.S. Constitution did not plan on a formal bill of rights. Specific rights, such as a writ of habeas corpus, were folded into the body of the constitution but less specific rights such as freedom of speech were notoriously absent. In 1789, however, James Madison (1751-1836), a leading Federalist, drafted the Bill of Rights which by mid-December of 1791 had been ratified by the various state legislatures.

The Bill of Rights protects three general areas of human endeavor: rights of conscience, which include such rights as freedom of speech freedom of religion; rights of the accused which include such rights as freedom from self-incrimination; and the rights of property that include such rights as just compensation for public confiscation..

The Guide to American Law: Everyone's Legal Encyclopedia (New York: West Publishing, 1983), 2:95-99.

What does the design on the Treasury seal represent?

The seal of the Department of the Treasury, which can be traced back to the Continental Congress of 1778 is overprinted on the face of each U.S. note. Supposedly Governeur Morris, and others designed the first seal and after that Francis Hopkinson may have had a hand in the design which was adopted officially by the Continental Congress in 1789. In 1861 Spencer Clark modified Hopkinson's design; then in 1968 the seal again underwent revision. The new seal has the English inscription "The Department of the Treasury" which replaced the inscription "Thesaur. Amer. Septent. Sigil.," (i.e. the Latin abbreviation for "The Seal of the Treasury of North America"). The seal also bears the date 1789 to symbolize the year the U.S. government and the U.S. Treasury Department were created. The balance scales on the seal represent justice, the key signifies authority, and the chevron with 13 stars the original states. On United States notes the seal is overprinted in red, on Federal Reserve notes it is in green.

Beth Deisher, ed., *Coin World Almanac, 5th ed.* (New York: Amos Press, 1987), 151. Gene Hessler, *Comprehensive Catalog of U.S. Paper Money, 5th ed.* (Port Clinton, OH: BNR Press, 1977), 28-29.

What were the 3 R's of President Franklin Roosevelt's "New Deal"?

The 3 R's are the elements of the "New Deal" legislation, proposed or approved by U.S. president Franklin Roosevelt (1882-1945), between 1933 and 1939 intended to deal with the economic and social ravages of the Great Depression. The legislation fell into three broad categories-relief, recovery, and reform. Relief was aimed at alleviating the social strife caused by the depression, recovery referred to the state of the national economy, and reform was aimed at those practices that were not good for the general welfare. Roosevelt first used the term "New Deal" when addressing the Democratic convention in Chicago on July 2, 1932.

Dictionary of American History, rev. ed. (New York: Charles Scribner's Sons, 1976), s.v. "New Deal."

What was the Assay Commission?

The Assay Commission was established by the Act of April 2, 1792, Section 18 and was mandated to test the weight and fineness of samples of coins produced by the various mints. Coins were randomly selected quarterly each year and shipped to the Philadelphia Mint where they were stored waiting inspection the following February. If the coinage did not pass weight and quality standards those responsible mint officers would be released. If the coins passed the various tests those not assayed would be returned unmarked for circulation. The purpose of the Assay Commission was to provide an impartial check on the quality of the nation's coinage beyond those checks performed by U.S. Mint employees. The commission had three ex-officio members: a judge of the United States District Court for the Eastern District of Pennsylvania; the Comptroller of the Currency; and the Assayer of the United States Assay Office at New York. A representative of the National Bureau of Standards was also on the commission. In 1837 members of the public were authorized to serve on the commission and between 1874 and the Jimmy Carter administration members of the public were in fact continually nominated. U.S. president Jimmy Carter (b. 1924) did not nominate any public members to the commission. No meetings of the statutory members of the Assay Commission were held during the Reagan administration and the closing of the New York Assay Office eliminated the statutory members' positions.

Coin World Almanac, 5th ed. (New York: World Almanac, 1987), 199-200.

When did the United States begin striking coins?

United States coinage began at the Philadelphia Mint in 1793. The first coins produced were copper cents and half cents. By 1794 the mint was striking silver half dimes, half dollars, and dollars. In 1795 the gold eagle and half eagle were being produced and in 1796 the silver dime and quarter dollar was minted. Since the opening of the mint, 21 denominations of circulating and commemorative coins have been issued. Gold denominations have included $50, $25, $20, $10, $5, $3, $2.50, and one dollar coins. Silver denominations include the one dollar, 50-cent, quarter dollar, 20-cent, dime, half-dime and 3-cent coins. Five-cent, three-cent, and one-cent coins have been produced in copper-nickel alloy. There have also been bronze two-cent coins and one-cent coins in copper, bronze, steel, and zinc as well as a copper half-cent. As mandated by the Mint Act of 1965, silver coins were changed to copper-nickel alloy.

Coin World Almanac, 5th ed. (New York: Amos Press, 1987), 284.

What was the subject of Lord Byron's first speech in the House of Lords?

The English poet Lord Byron's (1788-1824) first speech in Great Britain's House of Lords on February 27, 1812, was on the Frame-Work Bill, dealing with government handling of worker riots and the violence during the period of the Industrial Revolution in Great Britain.

Michael Foot, *The Politics of Paradise: A Vindication of Byron* (New York: Harper & Row, 1988), 398.

What was the Mandelbaum Gate?

The Mandelbaum Gate, the symbol of divided Jerusalem, was demolished on August 22, 1967. From 1958 through that date, it had been the only authorized crossing point between the Israeli and Jordanian sectors of Jerusalem, although for a few days at Christmas and Easter each year the barrier had been lifted to permit Christian pilgrims to visit shrines in the city. By demolishing the gate, Israeli municipal authorities hoped to eliminate all physical barriers that had previously divided Jerusalem, making it a single city once again. It was hoped at the time that repair of all damage done during several wars would facilitate an era of peace and free access to all parts of the city.

Terence Smith, "Mandelbaum Gate, Symbol of Divided Jerusalem, Coming Down," *New York Times* 23 August 1967.

How can one contact a missing person?

The Social Security Administration will forward an unsealed letter to persons whose names are listed in their files, for certain humanitarian reasons. The communication will be forwarded to their last-known employer or directly to the person if he or she is drawing Social Security benefits. To qualify for this service, one must submit a request in writing, and supply the missing person's name and Social Security number, if known. If the number is unknown, include date and place of birth, names of parents and last-known employers, plus dates of employment. The Social Security Administration also must know the reason for wanting to contact the missing person, last time he or she was seen, and other attempts at contact already exhausted. The letter to be forwarded must be enclosed in an unsealed, stamped envelope to a local Social Security Administration office.

The Internal Revenue Service will also forward letters to persons in their files for humane reasons. They will not release the missing person's address or any tax information, and the decision to reply is up to the missing person. A local telephone company may also offer some help. Information operators can search an entire area code for a missing person, provide an address, or verify that the person has telephone service even if the number is unlisted. Computers have made it easier to find missing persons, too, especially through Internet web pages and online services.

Ted L. Gunderson, *How to Locate Anyone Anywhere* (New York: Plume, 1988), 50. Richard S. Johnson, *How to Locate Anyone Who Is or Has Been in the Military* (Ft. Sam Houston, TX: Military Information Enterprises, 1991), 113-15.

What is the origin of the name for the state of Ohio?

Ohio derives its name from an Iroquois Indian word meaning "beautiful river." The Indians had called the river that flows there by this name. Ohio became the 17th state when it was admitted to the Union in 1803.

Lillian Eichler, *The Customs of Mankind* (Garden City, NY: Garden City Publishing, 1924), 679-81. William H. Harris and Judith S. Levey, *The New Columbia Encyclopedia* (New York: Columbia University Press, 1975). *Pittsburgh Press* 24 February 1974.

What is the origin of the name for the state of Nebraska?

The name Nebraska has two possible sources of origin. One says that the name is derived from a Sioux Indian meaning "shallow water" or "broad water," possibly describing the Niobrara River from which the state reportedly gets its name. Another source cites an Otos Indian word meaning "flat river," in reference to the Platte River which flows through the state. Nebraska was admitted as the 37th state of the Union in 1867.

Lillian Eichler, *The Customs of Mankind* (Garden City, NY: Garden City Publishing, 1924), 679-81. William H. Harris and Judith S. Levey, eds., *The New Columbia Encyclopedia* (New York: Columbia University Press, 1975). *Pittsburgh Press* 24 February 1974.

What is the origin of the name for the state of Oregon?

The name of the state of Oregon could have been derived from *origanum*, the name of a species of wild sage indigenous to its coast lands. Some say the name came from the Spanish word "Oregones" meaning "bigeared men," in reference to the Indian tribes which inhabited the area. Joaquin Miller, a poet of the Sierras, suggested that the name originated with the Spanish "aura aqua" which means "gently falling waters." Oregon became the 33rd state when it was admitted to the Union in 1859.

Lillian Eichler, *The Customs of Mankind* (Garden City, NY: Garden City Publishing, 1924), 679-81. William H. Harris and Judith S. Levey, *The New Columbia Encyclopedia* (New York: Columbia University Press, 1975). *Pittsburgh Press* 24 February 1974.

What is the origin of the name for the state of Rhode Island?

Rhode Island was originally called "Roode Eylandt," most likely from the redness of the clay characteristic of the land of that area, by the Dutch Navigator Adrian Block (fl. 1610-1624). Later the name was anglicized to Rhode Island. Little credence is given to a theory that Rhode Island is named after the Island of Rhodes in the Mediterranean. Rhode Island was the last of the thirteen original colonies to join the Union in 1790.

Lillian Eichler, *The Customs of Mankind* (Garden City, NY: Garden City Publishing, 1924), 679-81. William H. Harris and Judith S. Levey, *The New Columbia Encyclopedia* (New York: Columbia University Press, 1975). *Pittsburgh Press* 24 February 1974.

What is the origin of the name for the state of South Dakota?

South Dakota like its sister state North Dakota derives its name from a North American Indian name meaning "allies." The name denoted the confederated Sioux tribes that inhabited the area. There are several versions of the name depending on the dialect -Lakota, Nakota, or Dakota. South Dakota was admitted as the 40th state of the Union in 1889.

Lillian Eichler, *The Customs of Mankind* (Garden City, NY: Garden City Publishing, 1924), 679-81. William H. Harris and Judith S. Levey, *The New Columbia Encyclopedia* (New York: Columbia University Press, 1975). *Pittsburgh Press* 24 February 1974.

What is the origin of the name for the state of Texas?

Texas derives its name from the North American Indian term *tejas* meaning "friends" or "allies." The spelling was changed to Texas when the area was organized as the Republic of Texas in 1836. Texas became the 28th state when it entered the Union in 1845.

Lillian Eichler, *The Customs of Mankind* (Garden City, NY: Garden City Publishing, 1924), 679-81. William H. Harris and Judith S. Levey, *The New Columbia Encyclopedia* (New York: Columbia University Press, 1975). *Pittsburgh Press* 24 February 1974.

What is the origin of the name for the state of Vermont?

Vermont was named for its mountains by the French explorer Samuel de Champlain (1567?-1635). The name is derived from the French *vert mont* (Green Mountains). Vermont became the 14th state when it was admitted to the Union in 1791.

Lillian Eichler, *The Customs of Mankind* (Garden City, NY: Garden City Publishing, 1924), 679-81. William H. Harris and Judith S. Levey, *The New Columbia Encyclopedia* (New York: Columbia University Press, 1975). *Pittsburgh Press* 24 February 1974.

What led to the establishment of the U.S. Mint in San Francisco?

The discovery of gold at Sutter's Mill in California in 1848 led to an unprecedented boom and more gold than the Philadelphia mint could process. Because of a lack of U.S. coinage in California many different coins were in circulation, everything from Dutch guilders to Indian rupees. In an effort to create a standardized medium of exchange in the West, and to relieve pressure on the Philadelphia facility, the San Francisco Mint was authorized by the U.S. Congress in 1852 and began limited operations in 1854.

Coin World Almanac, 5th ed. (New York: World Almanac, 1987) 164.

In the U.S. system of government what are "checks and balances"?

In the U.S. system of government, "checks and balances" refers to the concept that the respective powers of the three branches of government-executive, judicial, and legislative-hold the powers of the others in check in a complementary fashion to prevent one branch from dominating another. This constitutional mandate requires the branches to interact, since generally the legislative branch makes the laws while the executive branch enforces them, and the judicial branch interprets them. For instance, the U.S. Congress can pass legislation by a simple majority, which can be vetoed by the president, but in turn the veto can be overridden by a two-thirds congressional vote. The U.S. Supreme Court in turn, whose members are appointed for life by the president, but with the advice and consent of the Senate, can declare legislation and executive actions unconstitutional.

Kenneth C. Davis, *Don't Know Much About History* (New York: Crown Publishers, Inc., 1990), 88. *Dictionary of American History, rev. ed.* (New York: Charles Scribner's Sons, 1976), s.v. "checks and balances."

Are there any disadvantages to government employment?

There are several disadvantages to being employed by government. The first of these drawbacks is the salary cap. Since compensation for many government positions is regulated by legislative bodies and must follow budgetary constraints, the pay is often lower than comparable positions in the private sector. Secondly, opportunities for advancement are often constricted within a particular agency or department. Thirdly, red tape and other bureaucratic minutiae often hamper day-to-day job performance. Finally, political considerations-due to interference from other agencies, the needs of special-interest groups, or a particular individual's desire to be re-elected-also affect all levels of decision making and policy implementation in government jobs.

Ronald L. Krannich and Caryl Rae Krannich, *The Complete Guide to Public Employment, 2nd ed.*, (Woodbridge, VA: Impact Publications, 1990), 224.

What are the highest and lowest ZIP codes?

The lowest five-digit ZIP postal code of the United States is 00401 for the Reader's Digest Association in Pleasantville, NY. The town of Ketchikan, AK, holds the highest ZIP code of 99950.

U.S. News and World Report 5 July 1993.

How many ZIP code areas are added each year in the United States

The United States Postal Service adds about 200 ZIP code areas each year. In 1993, the total number of areas was 43,412.

U. S. News and World Report 5 July 1993.

Which former child film star was the first woman to serve as the U.S. chief of protocol?

Former child film star Shirley Temple Black served as chief of protocol under U.S. president Ford making her the first woman to hold that post. Black was also the U.S. ambassador to Ghana under U.S. presidents Nixon and Ford.

Shirley Jane Temple was born on April 23, 1928, in Santa Monica, California; almost before she could walk she began taking dancing lessons. A talent scout spotted her, arranged a screen test, and she soon began appearing in low-budget one-reel comedy films. Her first full length feature came quickly however, with the release of *Stand Up and Cheer* in 1934. On her way to becoming an overnight sensation Black also appeared in *Little Miss Marker, Now And Forever, Baby Take A Bow*, and *Bright Eyes*, all released in 1934. That year ended with her being awarded a special Oscar by the Academy of Motion Picture Arts and Sciences. Her popularity seemed endless and through the 1930s she made numerous hit movies including *The Little Colonel, Curly Top, Wee Willie Winkie*, and *Rebecca of Sunnybrook Farm*. As she grew older her films began earning less revenue and her popularity slipped but never faded. In 1945 she married to Army Air Force Sergeant John Agar Jr. but the couple separated and were divorced two years later following the birth of their daughter Linda Susan. In 1950 she married Charles A. Black, a wealthy San Francisco socialite and business executive.

Charles Moritz, ed., *Current Biography Yearbook, 1970*, (New York: H.W. Wilson, 1971), s.v. "Black, Shirley Temple."

What was the Civil Liberties Act?

The Civil Liberties Act of 1988 awarded financial compensation to Japanese-Americans interned during World War II. After the American naval base in Pearl Harbor, Hawaii was bombed by Japanese aircraft in late 1941, the United States declared war on the Asian power. As a result, domestic tensions developed and U.S. government officials feared that Japanese-American residents, some of them naturalized citizens or born on American shores, would collaborate with Japan if Japan launched an invasion along the Pacific coast. Under Executive Order No. 9066 Japanese-American property was appropriated and over 100,000 Americans of Japanese ancestry were forcibly interned until 1944. The 1988 Act provided the 60,000 survivors a sum of $20,000 each as restitution.

Ted Yanak and Pam Cornelison, *The Great American History Fact-Finder* (Boston: Houghton Mifflin, 1993) s.v. "Japanese-American Internment."

How long has the Grimaldi family ruled Monaco?

The Grimaldi family's governance over the tiny Mediterranean coastal principality of Monaco dates back to 1297.

Arthur S. Banks, ed., *Political Handbook of the World: 1993* (Binghamton, NY: CSA Publications, 1993), 549.

What is the origin of the name for the state of New York?

New York was originally called the New Netherlands. In 1664 the English took control of the area and renamed it New York after the Duke of York, later James II (1633-1701). New York was the 11th of the original 13 colonies to be admitted to the Union in 1788.

Lillian Eichler, *The Customs of Mankind* (Garden City, NY: Garden City Publishing, 1924), 679-81. William H. Harris and Judith S. Levey, *The New Columbia Encyclopedia* (New York: Columbia University Press, 1975). *Pittsburgh Press* 24 February 1974.

What is the origin of the name for the state of North Dakota?

North Dakota derives its name from a North American Indian name meaning "allies." The name was used to denote the confederated Sioux tribes that inhabited the area. There are several versions of the name depending on the dialect-Lakota, Nakota, or Dakota. North Dakota was admitted as the 39th state of the Union in 1889.

Lillian Eichler, *The Customs of Mankind* (Garden City, NY: Garden City Publishing, 1924), 679-81. William H. Harris and Judith S. Levey, *The New Columbia Encyclopedia* (New York: Columbia University Press, 1975). *Pittsburgh Press* 24 February 1974.

What is the origin of the name for the state of Arizona?

The name for the state of Arizona has several possible sources of origin. Some authorities have said that the name was derived from the Aztec word "arizuma" meaning "silver bearing," possibly for the silver deposits found there. Others cite the *Papagos* Indian tribe of the Southwest, said to have named it for the area in which they lived, called "Arizonac" meaning "site of small springs" (for the lack of water) in the region. Another version attributes the meaning to a word for "arid zone" or "desert." Arizona was admitted as the 48th state of the Union in 1912.

Lillian Eichler, *The Customs of Mankind* (Garden City, NY: Garden City Publishing, 1924), 679-81. William H. Harris and Judith S. Levey, eds., *The New Columbia Encyclopedia* (New York: Columbia University Press, 1975). *Pittsburgh Press* 24 February 1974.

What is the origin of the name for the state of California?

The origin of the name California can be traced to Spanish conquistador Hernando Cortez, who first applied the name to the lower region of the area he discovered during a maritime expedition in 1536. He likened that region to the imaginary island of California, found in the pages of an old Spanish romance written by Garcia Ordoez de Montalvo in 1510. Montalvo described the isle as an earthy paradise, abundant with gold and other precious gems and this was undoubtedly the image Cortez perceived as he arrived upon California's golden shores. In 1850 California was admitted as the 31st state of the Union.

Lillian Eichler, *The Customs of Mankind* (Garden City, NY: Garden City Publishing, 1924), 679-81. William H. Harris and Judith S. Levey, eds., *The New Columbia Encyclopedia* (New York: Columbia University Press, 1975). *Pittsburgh Press* 24 February 1974.

What is the origin of the name for the state of Iowa?

The state of Iowa is reputedly named for the Ioway or "Ah-hee-oo-ba" Indian tribe, which translates as "sleepy ones" or "drowsy ones." The Native North American tribe lived in a valley along the state's principal river, which is also named after the group. Iowa, the 29th state of the Union, was admitted in 1846.

Lillian Eichler, *The Customs of Mankind* (Garden City, NY: Garden City Publishing, 1924), 679-81. William H. Harris and Judith S. Levey, eds., *The New Columbia Encyclopedia* (New York: Columbia University Press, 1975). *Pittsburgh Press* 24 February 1974.

What is the origin of the name for the state of Kentucky?

The origin of the name for the state of Kentucky is somewhat controversial. Some claim that the name comes from the Wyandot Indian word "Ken-tah-ten," meaning "land of tomorrow." Others claim the name is derived from a Shawnee Indian word meaning "at the head of a river," relating to their use of the Kentucky River to travel throughout the region. American pioneer George Rogers Clark claimed the name stemmed from the Native North American word "Kentake," which means "meadowland." Kentucky is the 15th state of the Union, admitted in 1792.

Lillian Eichler, *The Customs of Mankind* (Garden City, NY: Garden City Publishing, 1924), 679-81. William H. Harris and Judith S. Levey, eds., *The New Columbia Encyclopedia* (New York: Columbia University Press, 1975). *Pittsburgh Press* 24 February 1974.

What is the origin of the name for the state of Maine?

The name for the state of Maine has two possible origins. One version attributes the origin to early explorers who named the region to honor Queen Henrietta Maria, wife of Charles I of England, who had a private estate in the French province of Maine. The territory that would become Maine was granted to Sir Fernando Gorges and Captain John Mason by the Council for New England in 1620. In 1629 Gorges and Mason divided their grant and the area taken by Gorges would later be confirmed by Charles I, who in 1639 issued a royal charter to Gorges for "the Province and County of Mayne." The other version says that the region was named so by the fishermen of the islands dotting the coast who referred to the area as "main" or "mainland." Maine, largest of the New England states, is the 23d state of the Union, admitted in 1820.

Lillian Eichler, *The Customs of Mankind* (Garden City, NY: Garden City Publishing, 1924), 679-81. William H. Harris and Judith S. Levey, eds., *The New Columbia Encyclopedia* (New York: Columbia University Press, 1975). *Pittsburgh Press* 24 February 1974.

What is the origin of the name for the state of Massachusetts?

The name Massachusetts is derived from the Algonquin Indian word "Massadch-es-et," meaning "great hill-small place." Massachusetts, one of the original Thirteen Colonies, was the first of the states to have a Native North American name.

Lillian Eichler, *The Customs of Mankind* (Garden City, NY: Garden City Publishing, 1924), 679-81. William H. Harris and Judith S. Levey, eds., *The New Columbia Encyclopedia* (New York: Columbia University Press, 1975). *Pittsburgh Press* 24 February 1974.

What percentage of total income does Social Security provide for eligible older Americans?

In 1990, 13 percent of all beneficiaries received 100 percent of their income from Social Security, while 11 percent of beneficiaries received 90-99 percent; 35 percent of beneficiaries received 50 to 89 percent and 41 percent of beneficiaries received less than 50 percent of their total income from Social Security.

Income of the Aged Chartbook 1990 (Washington, D.C.: Department of Health and Human Services, Social Security Administration, Office of Research and Statistics, 1992), 9.

When did Lithuania declare its independence?

On March 11, 1990, Lithuania proclaimed itself a sovereign state, independent of the Soviet Union. The Lithuanian parliament voted 124-0 to restore its sovereign powers, 50 years after it was annexed by the Soviets. The legislators also elected Vytautas Landsbergis, leader of the independence movement, to be the country's new president.

Bill Keller, "No Soviet Reaction," *New York Times* 12 March 1990.

Who was the first official chaplain to serve the U.S. Congress?

Appointed by the first U.S. Congress in 1789, the Reverend Samuel Provoost, (1742?-1815) a Protestant Episcopal clergyman became the first chaplain of the U.S. Senate. Provoost, previously was the rector of Trinity Church and had been chaplain of the Continental Congress in 1785. The U.S. House of Representatives chose the Reverend William Linn, a Presbyterian minister. Formerly, Linn had served as a chaplain in the Continental Army.

The duties of the chaplains include opening the daily session with a prayer and serving as spiritual counselor to members, their families, and their staffs.

Congress A to Z: A Ready Reference Encyclopedia, 2d ed. (Washington, DC: Congressional Quarterly, 1993), s.v. "chaplain." George W. Stimpson, *Uncommon Knowledge* (Indiana: Bobbs-Merrill, 1936), 161-62.

What are the seating arrangements in both the U.S. Senate and the U.S. House of Representatives?

In both chambers of the U.S. Congress, as they face the front of the chamber, Democrats sit to the left of the center aisle and Republicans sit to the right. Each Senator has an assigned place, while in the House of Representatives, the members occupy any vacant chair on their side of the aisle.

George B. Galloway, *History of the House of Representatives, 2d ed.* (New York: Thomas Y. Crowell, 1976), 51. U.S. Congress, *1993-1994 Official Congressional Directory* (Washington, DC: Government Printing Office, 1993), 662, 664.

How did the thirteen colonies officially become the United States of America?

The thirteen original colonies entered the Union on the date each ratified the Constitution. These dates are as follows:
Delaware—December 7, 1787
Pennsylvania—December 12, 1787
New Jersey—December 18, 1787
Georgia—January 2, 1788
Connecticut—January 9, 1788
Massachusetts—February 6, 1788
Maryland—April 28, 1788
South Carolina—May 23, 1788
New Hampshire—June 21, 1788
Virginia—June 25, 1788
New York—July 26, 1788
North Carolina—November 21, 1789
Rhode Island—May 29, 1790

The World Almanac and Book of Facts, 1995 (Chicago: World Almanac, 1994), 426, 460.

What is the origin of Uncle Sam?

Widely-known and well-respected, Samuel Wilson (1766-1854) of Troy, New York, was commonly known as "Uncle Sam." As a meat packer he supplied the U.S. Army with provisions during the War of 1812. The barrels in which the supplies were shipped were stamped with the initials "U.S.," which at the time were not commonly accepted as an abbreviation for United States. Soon all government property was referred to as being Uncle Sam's and the words eventually came to be a nickname for the federal government.

As early as 1814 allusions linking Uncle Sam as the nickname for the federal government appeared in print in broadsides. In 1851, an unknown parade marcher billed himself as "Uncle Sam." He dressed in a patriotic costume of red-and-white striped pants, a high hat , and had a goatee. The nation's cartoonists were delighted to finally have a colorful visual symbol to match the already accepted nickname for the U.S. and made his appearance recognizable to all. In 1950, the U.S. State Department commissioned artist Herbert Noxon to paint an official portrait of "Uncle Sam" which depicts him as a tall man, friendly and smiling with a hand outstretched in greeting. In 1961, the U.S. Congress passed a resolution saluting Samuel Wilson as the person who inspired America's national symbol.

Fred Blumenthal, "The Story of Uncle Sam," *Parade* 4 July 1976. *Dictionary of American History, rev. ed.* (New York: Charles Scribner's Sons, 1976), s.v. "Uncle Sam." Alton Ketchum, *Uncle Sam: The Man and the Legend* (New York: Hill and Wang, 1959), 34-44. *World Book Encyclopedia* (Chicago: World Book, 1993), s.v. "Uncle Sam."

What were the NKVD and the KGB?

The NKVD, or the Narodnyi Kommissariat Vnutrennikh Del (People's Commissariat for Internal Affairs), was founded in 1934 and succeeded by the MGB, or the Ministerstvo Gosurdastvennoi Bezopastnosti (Ministry of State Security), in 1946, and the KGB, or the Komitet Gossudarrstvennoi Bezopastnosti (Committee of State Security), in 1954. All were essentially Soviet Union secret police agencies which concentrated on maintaining Communist control. Earlier organizations were the Cheka (1917) and the OGPU, or the Obiedinennoye Gosudarstvennoye Politicheskoye Upravlenie (United State Political Administration) (1922). In 1991 after the fall of Communism, the KGB was formally disbanded and its functions divided among smaller agencies.

Academic American Encyclopedia (Danbury, CT: Grolier, 1988), s.v. "KGB." Ralph De Sola, *Abbreviations Dictionary, 7th ed.* (New York: Elsevier Science, 1986), s.v. "KGB," "MGB," "NKGB," "NKVD," "OGPU." *The World Book Encyclopedia* (Chicago: World Book, 1994), s.v. "KGB."

What percentage of the U.S. armed forces served abroad during the major wars in which the United States has been involved?

During the Spanish-American War 29 percent of the total armed forces served abroad. During World War I it was 53 percent and 73 percent during World War II. Fifty-six percent served overseas during the Korean War. The percentage which served in the Vietnam War is unavailable.

Department of Commerce, *Statistical Abstract of the United States 1993* (Washington, DC: Government Printing Office, 1993), 359.

What is a township?

In a government survey, a township is a square tract of land with six miles on each side. Each square mile area within the township is called a "section." There are 36 sections in each township . Each section has 640 acres. Sections may be further divided into halves, quarters, and so on. Survey or congressional townships were created by the United States Public Land Survey (USPLS) from the Land Ordinance of 1785 in order to transfer land in an orderly way to settlers. Townships are now considered subdivisions of counties and have varying degrees of importance as a unit of government within the twenty states which still list townships.

Edith R. Horner, ed., *Almanac of the 50 States* (Palo Alto, CA: Information Publications, 1993), 54, 110, 118, 134, 158, 174, 182, 190, 206, 222, 238, 246, 262, 278, 286, 310, 318, 334, 366, 398, 414. Phillip C. Muehrcke,

Map Use: Reading, Analysis, and Interpretation, 2d ed. (Madison, WI: JP Publications, 1986), 194-96. Jay M. Shafritz, *The HarperCollins Dictionary of American Government and Politics* (New York: HarperCollins, 1992), s.v. "township."

To whom was the first social security check issued in the United States?

The first person to receive a social security check in the United States from the retirement benefits program established by the Social Security Act of 1935, was Ida Fuller of Brattleboro, Vermont. The check was for the amount of $22.54 in January of 1940. Three thousand seven hundred other women and men received checks that month. She had her footprints preserved in concrete at the U.S. Social Security Administration headquarters in Washington, DC. Born September 6, 1874, she died at the age of 100 in January of 1975.

Phyllis J. Read and Bernard L. Witlieb, *The Book of Women's Firsts* (New York: Random House, 1992), 169. *Time* 24 May 1982.

What were the "Pentagon Papers?"

The "Pentagon Papers," as it is popularly known, was a 47-volume study of American involvement in Vietnam from 1945-1968. It included internal working papers from the presidential administrations with analytical commentary by 36 military and civilian analysts. U.S. Secretary of Defense Robert S. McNamara had commissioned the Rand Corporation to do the study. Employees Daniel Ellsberg and Anthony J. Russo illegally copied the classified study and gave it to newspapers. After the material began appearing in print, the Justice Department under President Richard Nixon (1913-1994) attempted to stop publication, but the U.S. Supreme Court in *New York Times v. United States* (1971) allowed the publication under freedom of the press. Ellsberg and Russo were indicted for espionage, theft, and conspiracy, but actions by the Nixon administration to ensure that Ellsberg would be discredited, by authorizing a break-in of Ellsberg's psychiatrist's office, resulted in dismissal of charges on the grounds of gross government misconduct.

Concise Dictionary of American History (New York: Charles Scribner's Sons, 1983), s.v. "Pentagon Papers." Jay M. Shafritz, *The HarperCollins Dictionary of American Government and Politics* (New York: HarperCollins, 1992), s.v. "Pentagon Papers."

Who were the first African-American generals in the U.S. armed forces?

Benjamin Oliver Davis, Sr. (1877-1970), was promoted to brigadier general under U.S. president Franklin Roosevelt (1882-1945) in 1940, the first African American to attain that rank. He served in the U.S. Army.

Benjamin Oliver Davis, Jr., the son of Benjamin Oliver Davis, Sr., was promoted to the rank of brigadier general in the U.S. Air Force in 1954, the first African American to become an Air Force general. He led the 99th Pursuit Squadron, better known as the Tuskegee Airmen, in World War II (1939-1945). He was further promoted to lieutenant general in 1965, the first African American to reach that rank. He was also the first African American to command an airbase.

Frank E. Petersen, Jr., commanded what was recognized as the best fighter squadron in the U.S. Marine Corps in Vietnam. He was promoted to the rank of brigadier general in 1979. He was the first African American to become an aviator in the Marine Corps and the first to become a brigadier general in the Marines.

The first African-American admiral in the U.S. Navy was Samuel Gravely, appointed in 1971 to the rank of rear admiral. In 1962 he had become the first African American to command a warship since the American Civil War.

Daniel H. "Chappie" James, Jr. (1920-1978), became the first African-American four-star general in 1976. He served in the U.S. Air Force.

The first African American to serve as Chairman of the Joint Chiefs of Staff was General Colin L. Powell (1937-). He had served as national security adviser to U.S. president Ronald Reagan (1911-) in 1987 and was appointed to head the Chiefs of Staff in 1989 by president George Bush (1924-). He also was the youngest man to hold that office.

Walter L. Hawkins, *African American Biographies* (Jefferson, NC: McFarland, 1992), s.v. "Davis, Benjamin Oliver, Jr.," "Gravely, Samuel Lee," "Petersen, Frank E., Jr.," "Powell, Colin L.." W. Augustus Low, ed., *Encyclopedia of Black America* (New York: McGraw-Hill, 1981), s.v. "Davis, Benjamin Oliver, Jr.," "Davis, Benjamin Oliver, Sr.." Jessie Carney Smith, ed., *Black Firsts: 2,000 Years of Extraordinary Achievement* (Detroit: Gale Research, 1994), 239, 245.

Is it considered permissible to display the American flag at night?

It is not against the law to fly the flag at night. It is the universal custom, however, to display it only from sunrise to sunset. It should only be flown for 24 hours for patriotic reasons, never for convenience. Ships at sea display the flag 24 hours, as do some sights that have been authorized by law or proclamation. These include:

Fort McHenry National Monument, Baltimore, Maryland
Flag House Square, Baltimore, Maryland
United States Marine Corps (Iwo Jima) Memorial, Arlington, Virginia
Battle Green, Lexington, Massachusetts
The White House, Washington, D.C.
Washington Monument, Washington, D.C.
United States Customs Ports of Entry
Valley Forge State Park, Valley Forge, Pennsylvania

Mary Jane McCaffree and Pauline Innis, *Protocol: The Complete Handbook of Diplomatic, Official and Social Usage* (Washington, DC: Devon Publishing, 1989), 355-57.

Was Benjamin Franklin Postmaster General?

In 1753 the British appointed William Hall and the future American statesman, Benjamin Franklin (1706-1790), deputy postmaster generals for the colonies. At the time of their appointment mail service was bad and the post office was consistently losing money. So Franklin traveled throughout the colonies in order to improve schedules and map better routes. He extended postal service to Canada and Florida and convinced the British to keep transatlantic service open when hostility with France threatened to end it. In conjunction with Hall he allowed newspapers to be sent through the mail and permitted them to be mailed free of charge if they were traveling between printers. At least initially Franklin's innovations seemed to be in part responsible for an increase in the volume of mail, but as American opposition to British rule grew, the postal service worsened. In 1774 the British dismissed Franklin from office, because they considered him a troublemaker.

Cheryl Weant McAfee, *The United States Postal Service* (New York: Chelsea House Publishers, 1987), 21.

During the 1933 Bank Holiday how long were bank operations suspended?

By presidential proclamation, U.S. president Franklin D. Roosevelt (1882-1945) suspended all bank operations and gold transactions on March 6, 1933. What became known as the "1933 Bank Holiday" lasted for four days. This action was taken due to the increasing number of bank failures during the Great Depression. When President Roosevelt was inaugurated on March 4, 1933, most of the banks in the country had already been closed by state action. The Emergency Banking Act was passed by the U.S. Congress on March 9, 1933, ratifying the presidential closures and providing for the opening of sound banks.

Howard L. Hurwitz, *An Encyclopedic Dictionary of American History* (New York: Washington Square Press, 1968), s.v. "Bank Holiday (1933)."

What medical expenses are deductible for federal income tax purposes?

Only unreimbursed medical expenses that exceed 7.5 percent of adjusted gross income may be claimed as deductions on one's federal income tax. Deductible medical expenses include:

Professional services
Dental services
Medical equipment and supplies
Medical treatments
Prescription medicines and drugs
Laboratory examinations and tests
Hospital services
Premiums for medical care policies

Miscellaneous expenses include:

Alcoholic inpatient care
Asylum
Birth control pills or other birth control items prescribed by a doctor
Braille books (cost over regular editions)
Childbirth classes for an expectant mother
Clarinet lessons advised by a dentist for treatment of tooth defects
Convalescent home care for medical treatment only
Drug treatment center—inpatient care costs
Fees paid to a health institute where the exercises, rubdowns, etc. are prescribed by a physician as medically necessary
Kidney donor's or possible kidney donor's expenses
Lead-based paint removal to prevent a child who has had lead poisoning from eating the paint
Legal fees for guardianship of a mentally ill spouse where Commitment was medically necessary
Life time care i.e. advance payments made either monthly or as a lump sum under an agreement with a retirement home
A nurse's board and wages, including Social Security taxes paid on wages
Remedial reading for a child suffering from dyslexia
Sanitariums and similar institutions
school—payments to a special school for a mentally or physically impaired person if the main reason for using the school is its resources for relieving the disability
A seeing-eye dog and its maintenance
Special school costs for physically and mentally handicapped children
Telephone-teletype costs and television adapter for closed Caption service for deaf persons
Wages of a guide for a blind person.

A tax attorney should be consulted for specific deductions.

J.K. Lasser Institute, *J.K. Lasser's Your Income Tax 1994* (New York: Prentice Hall, 1993), 196.

Which agencies protect the savings of Americans in banks, savings and loan associations, and credit unions?

Most banks, savings and loan associations, and credit unions insure the deposits of Americans. A government agency, the Federal Deposit Insurance Corporation (FDIC), insures most of the commercial banks in the United States. The FDIC insures bank deposits up to $100,000. Formerly the Federal Savings and Loan Insurance Corporation (FSLIC), the FDIC insures qualifying financial institutions through two separate funds: the Bank Insurance Fund and the Savings Association Insurance Fund.

Although some savings and loan associations are insured by private companies or individual states, the Savings Association Insurance Fund (SAIF) protects deposits up to $100,000 in most savings and loan associations.

Many Americans choose to deposit their savings in credit unions. The vast majority of credit unions are insured through the National Credit Union Administration (NCUA). The NCUA insures deposits up to $100,000.

Janet Bodnar, "New name, same rules: How to make the most of deposit insurance," *Changing Times*, October 1989. Nancy Dunnan, *Dun and Bradstreet Guide to Your Investments: 1994* (New York: Harper Perennial, 1994), 39-40.

What is the "notch controversy"?

The "notch controversy" refers to a situation where, as a result of a transitional benefit formula, retired workers born between 1917 and 1921 may reduced Social Security benefits. When a flaw in the Social Security benefit formula that would bankrupt the system was discovered, the U.S. Congress amended the Social Security Act and phased in a new formula in 1977. To ease the transition from the old formula to the new one special calculations were included for people born between 1917 and 1921. As a result of this formula, however, the Social Security benefits of workers born in this period are often significantly lower than the benefits payable to workers with identical earnings retiring at the same time who, because they were born before 1917, have their benefits computed under the pre-1977 formula.

Workers born between 1917 and 1921 are often referred to as "notch babies," a phrase coined in a 1983 "Dear Abby" column when letter detailing their plight was published.

Ken Skala, *American Guidance for Those Over 60, 2d ed.*, (Falls Church, VA: American Guidance, 1990), 72-73.

How solvent is the Social Security system?

For years, rumors have persisted that the U.S. Social Security system will eventually run out of funds. Workers who pay into the system often worry that they will not receive their hard-earned benefits when they reach retirement age. Although the future solvency of Social Security is arguable it is projected by some that the Social Security fund will swell to a $5 trillion surplus by the time the "Baby Boomers" begin retiring around 2010. At that time however more funds will begin going out in benefits that will be taken in from taxes. It is further projected that if benefits are not reduced or if taxes are not raised by 2030 that all income revenue of the federal government will be needed to meet entitlement obligations. Solutions would include scaling back benefits, downward changes in the cost-of-living allowance, reduced payments for wealthy retirees, and an increase in payroll taxes.

Ken Skala, *American Guidance for Those Over 60, 2d ed.* (Falls Church, VA: American Guidance, 1990), 46-47. Marysue Wechsler, "Can You Depend on Social Security"? *USA Today* March 1995.

What was the "Shamrock Summit"?

The "Shamrock Summit" is the nickname given to the 1985 economic summit between U.S. president Ronald Reagan (1911-) and Canadian Prime Minister Brian Mulroney. At this summit, both leaders agreed to negotiate a free trade accord. The summit was nicknamed the "Shamrock Summit" because both Reagan and Mulroney are of Irish descent.

The Arthur Andersen North American Business Sourcebook (Chicago: Triumph Books, 1994), 12.

How many persons have been named honorary U.S. citizens by the federal government?

On April 9, 1963, U.S. president John F. Kennedy (1917-1963) declared that Sir Winston Churchill (1874-1965) would be named the United States' first honorary citizen. The proclamation had been approved by the U.S. House of Representatives vote of 377-21 on March 12, 1963. Since then three other persons have been named as honorary U.S. citizens by the federal government. They are the English religious reformer, colonist, and founder of Pennsylvania William Penn (1644-1718),and his wife Hannah Callowhill Penn; and the Swedish diplomat Raoul Wallenberg (1912-1947, who saved thousands of Hungarian Jews during World War II (1939-1945).

Facts on File, 4-10 April 1963. *Pittsburgh Press,* 20 October 1984.

Where did Prince Charles and Princess Diana reside after their wedding?

After their wedding on July 29, 1981, and an extensive honeymoon, Charles (1948-), Prince of Wales and heir to the throne and Princess Diana took up principal residence at Highgrove, a nine-bedroom Georgian house on 348 acres in Gloucestershire, about 90 miles west of London, England.

While in London, the English royal couple resided at Kensington Palace, built in the seventeenth century by the English architect and astronomy professor, Sir Christopher Wren (1632-1723). The palace also served as home to Princess Margaret, sister of Queen Elizabeth II (1926-).

New York Times 25 June 1981.

When was paper money first issued in the United States?

The first issue of paper money by the United States government was made in 1861. But states had been printing their own paper money even before the American Revolutionary War, and the Continental Congress also issued paper currency. Most of these Colonial notes are worth from $3.00 to $10.00 today, but a few are quite rare and very expensive.

R.S. Yeoman, *1994 Handbook of United States Coins, 51st ed.* (Racine, WI: Western Publishing, 1993), 12.

What is Jacquin's Postulate?

Jacquin's Postulate is from an anonymous source and states:

> No man's life, liberty, or property are safe while the legislature is in session.

Time 26 February 1979.

What were the founding countries of NATO?

On August 24, 1949, the North Atlantic Treaty Organization (NATO) was formed. NATO is a military organization that was created to deter any possible attack by the Soviet Union against the countries of Western Europe. The founding countries of NATO were Belgium, Canada, Denmark, France, Iceland, Italy, Luxembourg, the Netherlands, Norway, Portugal, the United Kingdom, and the United States. Members of NATO considered an attack on one or more of the members as an attack against all and pledged to defend each other. In 1966, France withdrew from NATO and the headquarters of the organization was moved from Paris to Brussels, Belgium. The Federal Republic of Germany (West Germany), Turkey, and Greece were admitted to NATO at a later date. Following the Turkish invasion of Cyprus in 1974, Greece withdrew from NATO.

Walter J. Raymond, *International Dictionary of Politics* (Lawrenceville, VA: Brunswick Publishing Co., 1980), s.v."North Atlantic Treaty Organization."

What percentage of Americans participate in the Social Security system?

Since 1935, many American workers have received Social Security benefits upon retirement, provided they have met eligibility requirements. However, not all Americans are covered by the Social Security system. Approximately three percent of the American workforce are in jobs that are not covered by the Social Security system. Consequently, these workers do not pay Social Security taxes and do not receive any benefits upon retirement. Roughly 13 percent of American workers are in jobs that offer employees the option of paying or not paying Social Security taxes. Approximately 72 percent of workers who are given this option decide to pay the taxes and receive benefits upon retirement. 84 percent of all Americans work in jobs where Social Security taxes are deducted automatically from each paycheck. All of these workers will receive Social Security benefits upon retirement.

A. Haeworth Robertson, *Social Security: What Every Taxpayer Should Know* (Washington, DC: Retirement Policy Institute, 1992), 181.

Which U.S. President adopted as his motto "the buck stops here"?

U.S. president Harry S. Truman (1884-1972) adopted as his motto the phrase "the buck stops here" and had a sign made with those words on it for his desk. The phrase implied that final decisions and final responsibilities went along with the office of the presidency. Although most often associated with Truman, who held office from 1945 to 1953 many subsequent presidents and journalists made use of Truman's motto, which comes from the phrase "passing the buck" or not taking responsibility or fault by passing it on to others. This phrase originated as a poker expression during the late nineteenth century. In 1872 Mark Twain wrote that poker players would pass a "buck" or marker to signify which player would have the next deal. Since a silver dollar was occasionally used as the marker, a dollar came to be referred to as a "buck."

Barbara Berliner, ed., *The Book of Answers: The New York Public Library's Telephone Reference Service's Most Unusual and Entertaining Questions* (New York: Simon & Schuster, 1992), 61. William Safire, *Safire's Political Dictionary* (New York: Random House, 1978), s.v. "buck stops here, the."

What is the American's Creed?

The American's Creed is a 100-word statement written by William Tyler Page in 1918 in response to a national contest soliciting the best summary of American political faith. Tyler, who was then clerk of the U.S. House of Representatives, was awarded $1,000 for the following composition. His statement appears in the paragraph below.

I believe in the United States of American as a Government of the people, by the people, for the people; whose just powers are derived from the consent of the governed; a democracy in a republic; a sovereign Nation of many sovereign States; a perfect union, one and inseparable; established upon those principles of freedom, equality, justice and humanity for which American patriots sacrificed their lives and fortunes. I therefore believe it is my duty to my country to love it; to support its Constitution; to obey its laws; to respect its flag, and to defend it against all enemies.

Tyler's creed used passages and phrases from the Declaration of Independence, the Preamble to the Constitution, and Lincoln's Gettysburg address. The U.S. House of Representatives accepted the statement on April 3, 1918.

Encyclopedia Americana (Danbury, CT: Grolier, 1989), s.v. "American's Creed." William Rea Furlong and Byron McCandless, *So Proudly We Hail: The History of the United States Flag* (Washington, DC: Smithsonian Institution Press, 1981), 229.

When was an income tax first enacted in the United States?

The first income tax in the United States occurred during the American Civil War in 1862. It remained in effect until 1872. An income tax was reintroduced in 1894 but the U.S. Supreme Court quickly pronounced it unconstitutional because it was a direct tax that was not equitably divided among the states according to each state's population. In 1913 the Sixteenth Amendment imposed a permanent income tax.

John Eatwell, Murray Milgate, and Peter Newman, eds., *The New Palgrave: A Dictionary of Economics* (London: Macmillan Press, 1987), 4:404.

Who killed Alexander Hamilton in a duel?

Aaron Burr (1756-1836) shot Alexander Hamilton (1755?-1804) in a duel on July 11, 1804, in Weehawken, New Jersey, and Hamilton died the following day. Hamilton and Burr had been on opposite ends of the political spectrum for years. Hamilton had actively worked to undermine Burr's election to the presidency in 1800 and his election to the New York governorship in 1804; Burr lost both times. Following his second defeat Burr challenged Hamilton to a duel with pistols.

World Book Encyclopedia (Chicago: World Book, 1987), s.v. "Hamilton, Alexander."

What military specialties are open to women?

Women are eligible to enter almost 90 percent of all military specialties. Traditionally, women in the military have served in medical and administrative support positions, but women also work as mechanics, missile maintenance technicians, heavy equipment operators, airplane pilots, and intelligence officers. Most of the positions that exclude women involve a high probability of direct exposure to combat. The Coast Guard has no occupational limitations for women.

Department of Labor, Bureau of Labor Statistics, *Occupational Outlook Handbook, 1994-95 edition,* (Washington, DC: Government Printing Office, 1994), 454.

How can E-mail be sent to the president and vice-president of the United States?

E-mail refers to electronic messages transmitted from one computer modem to another, and such messages can be sent to the president and vice-president of the United States on the Internet at the following addresses:
president@whitehouse.gov
vice.president@whitehouse.gov

To receive a response, White House personnel ask that senders include their regular street address.

John R. Levine and Carol Baroudi, *The Internet for Dummies* (San Mateo, CA: IDG Books, 1993), 88.

What were the laws regarding military conscription in 1940?

The laws regarding military conscription in 1940 stated that "each male citizen and declarant alien between the ages of 21 and 36 is liable for training and service in the land and naval forces of the United States," according to the Selective Training and Service Act of 1940. Deferments could be granted on the basis of the subject's occupation, number of dependents, or by being declared physically, mentally, or morally unfit for military service. Some non-citizens, clergy, divinity students, those already having conscientious-objector status, and civilians with prior military service could also receive a lower classification in their eligibility status. Such deferments were under the jurisdiction of local Selective Service boards.

Conscription Law and Regulation (New York: Commerce Clearing House, 1940), 77-78.

How many people serve in the United States military?

According to 1992 Department of Defense statistics, 1.8 million persons were listed on active duty in the five branches of the U.S. military. The Army had the largest number of personnel at 606,000; 466,000 were serving in the Air Force; the Navy counted 537,000; the Marine Corps, 184,000; and the Coast Guard numbered 38,000. Roughly 11 percent of the 1.8 million were female. Of all military personnel on active duty, 393,000 were posted overseas, with European and Western Pacific region bases hosting the majority.

Department of Labor, Bureau of Labor Statistics, *Occupational Outlook Handbook, 1994-95 ed.* (Washington, DC: Government Printing Office, 1994), 453-54.

When was the last time the federal budget of the United States was without a deficit?

The last time the United States federal budget did not show a deficit-a year when expenditures did not exceed receipts-was

1969. A surplus of $3.2 billion was posted that year. Since then, the deficit has grown to astronomical sums, with estimates for 1995 predicting a $165.1 billion shortage for that year alone.

Economic Report of the President (Washington, DC: Government Printing Office, 1994), 359.

What is UNESCO?

Established in 1946, the United Nations Educational, Scientific, and Cultural Organization (UNESCO) is an organization devoted to advancing the objectives of international peace and the common welfare through the educational, scientific, and cultural relations of the peoples of the world. UNESCO has a special interest in literacy, especially among women and people with disabilities in underdeveloped countries.

The Europa World Year Book 1994 (London: Europa Publications, 1994), 1:84.

Who was Gary Davis?

Gary Davis was a U.S. Air Force fighter pilot who renounced his citizenship and claimed to be a citizen of the world. After reflecting on his views about life while a prisoner of war in World War II (1939-45) he concluded that national identities were the root of all the troubles in the world and created the universal passport. The first of the universal passports was issued in 1945. Many individuals in circumstances which preclude the use of national passports use the universal passport. It has been recognized by the governments of Ecuador, Togo, Zambia, Burkina Faso, Mauritania, and Yemen. Some other countries have allowed its use on a case by case basis.

The document is printed in the six official languages of the United Nations: English, Russian, French, Spanish, Chinese, and Arabic. A seventh language, Esperanto, an artificial language based on word roots common to many European languages that promotes universalism, is also used. The universal passport provides for all of the documentation a national passport would except it lists sectors rather than countries for places of birth; Davis has divided the globe into sectors without regard to national boundaries. This is advantageous for those who do not want their country of origin known.

Davis is associated with the World Service Authority District III in Washington D.C.

D. O'Nes, *The Guide to Legally Obtaining a Foreign Passport: The Easy Way to Get Additional Citizenships* (New York: Shapolsky Publishers, 1990), 169-73.

What are the requirements for applying for naturalization as a United States citizen?

A person can apply for formal U.S. citizenship if he or she is at least 18 years of age, has been a lawful, permanent resident for at least five years, or, in the case of those currently married to a U.S. citizen, has been a lawful, permanent resident for at least three years while married and cohabiting with the spouse, or if he or she has served in the U.S. armed forces for a specified period with a good record.

Gladys Alesi, *How to Prepare for the U.S. Citizenship Test* (Hauppauge, NY: Barron's, 1992), 29-30.

What is the history of parliamentary procedure?

Parliamentary procedure has its roots in the assemblies of Greek and Roman officials of the ancient classical period. Later, in medieval England, barons were often summoned by the king for feudal assemblies to discuss matters of government. These assemblies evolved into formal bodies known as parliament; and by the sixteenth century one of the official chambers of England's parliament, the House of Commons, made its journal the official precedent for its meetings. John Hatsell published *Precedence of Proceedings in the House of Commons* (1781), which became the established source on parliamentary law. The American system was naturally patterned from the British; Thomas Jefferson adapted Hatsell's work for American assemblies, such as the Senate. However, in smaller organizations and groups rules and procedures often varied greatly, following local custom. Henry Martyn Robert, an army engineer, published *Robert's Rules of Order* (1876), which has become the accepted source for the conduct of meetings of all sizes and purposes. He based his rules on procedures used to conduct Congressional sessions and offered detailed technical protocol.

James E. Davis, *Rules of Order* (Chicago: Chicago Review Press, 1992), 1-3.

Who was the first African-American woman ever to be elected to the U.S. Senate?

In 1992 Carol Moseley Braun, a Democrat from Illinois, became the first African-American woman to be elected to the U.S. Senate. In fact, Braun was only the second African-American to be elected to the Senate in the years after Reconstruction.

In the years prior to her election, Braun had broken through other racial barriers. She became the first woman and the first African-American to hold executive office in Cook County, Illinois, government. Braun had also been an assistant U.S. attorney as well as a state representative in the Illinois House.

Jeffrey B. Trammell and Gary P. Osifchin, *The New Members of Congress Almanac, 103rd Congress* (Washington, DC: Almanac of the Unelected, Inc., 1992), 8.

Which nations signed the Nuclear Test Ban Treaty of 1963?

On August 5, 1963, in Moscow, the Nuclear Test Ban Treaty was signed by the United States, the United Kingdom, and the U.S.S.R. The treaty went into effect on October 10, 1963.

Department of State, *United States Treaties and Other International Agreements* (Washington, DC: Government Printing Office), 1313.

Is there a room in the White House called the Fish Room?

Lesser known than the Lincoln bedroom and the Oval Office, the White House also includes a conference room known as the Fish Room. It is so named because of the mounted fish displayed on its walls and because it once contained an aquarium. The Fish Room is located in the West Wing Office Building at the White House.

Ralph A. Dungan, Special Assistant to the President, *letter to R.E. Fitzmier* 16 November 1964.

What is a totalitarian state?

A totalitarian state is characterized by a number of features, all of which serve to place the interests of the controlling power first and the interests of the individual second. All branches of government are under the control of one centralized authority, generally a representative of the only acknowledged political party. Laws demand the greatest efficiency and prohibit waste. The value of individual citizens and their rights are prescribed and limited by the governing authority. Totalitarianism is characteristic of Communism, Fascism, Nazism, and Caesarism.

Walter J. Raymond, *International Dictionary of Politics, 6th ed., rev.* (Lawrenceville, VA: Brunswick Publishing Co., 1980), s.v. "totalitarian state."

What was the first public building to be built by the U.S. government?

A national mint was the first building to be built by the U.S. government. The passage of an act by the U.S. Congress on April 2, 1792, established the United States Mint. A site was selected in Philadelphia. The building that was built would serve as the U.S. Mint for the next 40 years.

Coin World Almanac, 5th ed. (New York: World Almanac, 1987), 160.

What is a kibbutz?

A kibbutz is an Israeli collective settlement, usually agricultural and often also industrial, in which the wealth is held in common. The organization provides clothing, food, shelter, and medical services for its members, who vote on policies and elect their administrative leaders. Adults have private quarters, but children are often raised in groups. Labor is divided equally, with each member performing tasks that are assigned. The first kibbutz was founded at Deganya in Palestine in 1909. In 1989 Israel contained an estimated 200 kibbutzim with a total population of more than 100,000.

The New Encyclopaedia Britannica, 15th ed. (Chicago: Encyclopaedia Britannica, 1989), s.v. "kibbutz."

Who is the chief law enforcement officer of the U.S. government?

The U.S. Attorney General, who heads the U.S. Department of Justice, is the chief law enforcement officer of the U.S. federal government. The Attorney General represents the United States in legal matters and gives advice and opinions to the president and other members of government as requested. The affairs and activities of the Department of Justice are directed by the Attorney General, who often also serves as the department's spokesperson.

Office of the Federal Register, *United States Government Manual 1993/1994* (Lanham, MD: Bernan Press, 1993), 366.

Which countries make up the European Union?

The European Union (EU), effected on November 1, 1993, consists of the following countries: Belgium, Denmark, France, Germany, Greece, Ireland, Italy, Luxembourg, Netherlands, Portugal, Spain, and the United Kingdom. On March 29, 1994 the EU admitted four new members: Austria, Sweden, Norway and Finland. Previously the EU was the called European Economic Community.

The Europa World Year Book 1994 (London: Europa Publications, 1994), 137. *Facts On File* 21 April 1994.

What is "affirmative action"?

"Affirmative action" is a controversial program designed to increase the participation of women and minorities in the work force in proportion to their numbers. Legislation mandating affirmative action programs is contained in Title VII of the U.S. Civil Rights Act. At the federal contract level the program is enforced by the Office of Federal Contract-Compliance Programs (OFCCP). Many have charged that affirmative action promotes reverse discrimination.

Encyclopedic Dictionary of Economics, 3d ed. (Guilford, CT: Dushkin Publishing Group, 1986), s.v. "affirmative action."

When did the Great Seal of the United States first appear on paper money?

The Great Seal of the United States debuted on the 1935 one dollar silver certificates, the first time it had been used on paper money. The two-sided seal contains an eagle with the Latin motto *E Pluribus Unum*, meaning "from many one" while the reverse side features a pyramid with an eye at the top of it, and the phrases *Annuit Coeptis* meaning "God has favored our undertakings" and *Novus Ordo Seclorum*, meaning "a new order of the ages." The motto "In God We Trust" was added to the back of the one dollar silver certificates in 1957.

Gene Hessler, *Comprehensive Catalog of U.S. Paper Money, 5th ed.* (Port Clinton, OH: BNR Press, 1977), 28-29.

How did the British civil service develop?

In the early nineteenth century government administration was organized into ministries, and its officials were from the nobility and upper gentry who were appointed to ; these positions by patronage. It was seen as a public service that could be conducted in an amateurish fashion rather than as a serious profession. In 1870 a competitive examination and promotions by merit were introduced into government service, but these reforms made little difference, since only the well-to-do could afford the education needed to pass the examination, and there were few positions anyway. It was not until World War I (1914-18), when there was a tremendous growth in government, that the government or civil service expanded into a modern bureaucracy run by professional managers.

David Grote, *British English for American Readers* (Westport, CT: Greenwood Press, 1992), 115-16.

What "rights" were listed in the French "Declaration of the Rights of Man and of the Citizen"?

The French "Declaration of the Rights of Man and of the Citizen" listed man's inherent rights as "liberty, property, security, and resistance to oppression." The Declaration did not create these rights, which as stated are inherent, but rather acknowledged and described them.

Samuel F. Scott and Barry Rothaus, eds., *Historical Dictionary of the French Revolution, 1789-1799* (Westport, CT: Greenwood Press, 1985), s.v. "Declaration of the Rights of Man and of the Citizen."

Who were the five men awarded two U.S. Medals of Honor?

Five men were awarded two Medals of Honor by the United States: Frank D. Baldwin, Captain, Company D, nineteenth Michigan Infantry; Thomas Custer, Second Lieutenant, Company B, sixth Michigan Cavalry; Henry Hogan, First Sergeant, Company G, fifth U.S. Infantry; Patrick Leonard, Sergeant, Company C, second U.S. Cavalry, in 1870, and Corporal, Company A, twenty-third U.S. Infantry, in 1876; and William Wilson, Sergeant, Company I, fourth U.S. Cavalry. The award, established in 1862 by an Act of the U.S. Congress, can no longer be awarded more than once to one person. Army regulations concerning the medal were changed accordingly in 1918.

The Medal of Honor of the United States Army (Washington, DC: Government Printing Office, 1948), 22.

What is a poll tax and which amendment to the U.S. Constitution prohibits poll taxes for federal elections?

A poll tax is a financial sum required of each voter. The 24th Amendment to the U.S. Constitution prohibits such a tax on federal elections; poll taxes have also been declared unconstitutional in state elections.

The Guide to American Law (New York: West Publishing, 1984), s.v. "poll tax."

What federal agency assigns code names to various presidents, politicians, and visiting celebrities and what are some examples?

The White House Communications Agency assigns a list of suggested code names for the president, various politicians, visiting celebrities and other notables. The U.S. Secret Service chooses names from the list and assigns the names to those people under their watch. Since the introduction of "encrypted" radios has made these deceptions unnecessary, the Secret Service has the option of using the person's title during communications.

Vanity Fair September 1993.

What is the British Commonwealth?

The British Commonwealth also known as the Commonwealth of Nations, is a grouping of current sovereign countries that once were former members of the British Empire. The phrase was first used in 1884 by the Earl of Rosebery who said in a speech that "the British empire is a commonwealth of nations." This was said, of course, long before these colonies had achieved independence. Every two years the current heads of state of these former colonies meet at the Commonwealth Conference in accordance with the 1931 Statute of Westminster. India broke ranks with other former colonies when it decided to become a republic and no longer recognize the British monarch as a head of state. As a result members now recognize the reigning British monarch as head of the Commonwealth. As of 1992 there were 50 members in the Commonwealth. Ireland withdrew in 1949 and South Africa withdrew in 1961. Pakistan withdrew in 1972 but rejoined in 1989.

Bamber Gascoigne, *Encyclopedia of Britain* (New York: Macmillan, 1993), s.v. "Commonwealth."

Which American zoo once had the dubious distinction of exhibiting a human being?

For a while in the early 1900s, the Bronx Zoo in New York City had a caged exhibit featuring Ota Benga, a 23-year-old Congolese Pygmy. Ota Benga was brought to the United States by African explorer Samuel Verner to participate in the 1904 St. Louis Exposition. Tribal wars prevented Ota Benga from being returned to his homeland and the four foot, eleven inch tall African became an adoptee of the Bronx Zoo. Over the vigorous protests of New York's African-American community, Ota Benga was placed in a cage with a parrot and an orangutan. The zoo maintained that the exhibition was educational, Ota Benga was free to come and go as he pleased, and was an employee of the zoo. The protesters won, but Ota Benga continued to attract the curious as he strolled through the grounds in a white suit and canvas shoes helping zookeepers with tasks. The gawkers often became unruly and Ota Benga eventually left the zoo and committed suicide near Lynchburg, Virginia, in 1916.

Irving Wallace et al., *Significa* (New York: E. P. Dutton, 1983), 26-27.

Which branch of the U.S. government has the constitutional authority to declare war?

In the United States only the federal government, not any state or territorial government, can declare war. Within the federal government the constitution only empowers the U.S. Congress with the authority to declare war.. A president cannot declare war, but that office does have the authority in the absence of congressional action to repel an invasion and carry hostile action to the invader's homeland. Through much of American history, various presidents have found ways to circumvent the constitutional legal restraints.

The Guide to American Law: Everyone's Legal Encyclopedia (New York: West Publishing Company, 1983), s.v. "war and national defense."

In the American governmental structure, what is the Joint Chiefs of Staff?

In the American governmental structure, the Joint Chiefs of Staff serves as an advisory body to the U.S. president, the National Security Council, and the Department of Defense on military and defense matters. The body is also responsible for overseeing and implementing strategic plans and goals of the country as they relate to military and defense matters. The Joint Chiefs of Staff consists of the Chairman of the Joint Chiefs of Staff; the Vice Chairman; the Chief of Staff, U.S. Army; the Chief of Naval Operations, US. Navy; the Chief of Staff, U. S. Air Force; and the Commandant of the Marine Corps.

Office of the Federal Register, National Archives and Records Administration, *The United States Government Manual 1993/1994,* (Lanham, MD: Bernan Press, 1993), 183-84.

What were the Alien and Sedition Acts?

Various controversial legislative acts passed in the United States in 1798 came to be known as the Alien and Sedition Acts. These acts were passed by the anti-Republican Federalists and were meant to stymie opposition to the John Adams's (1735-1826) administration and stem the perceived or real threat of French Jacobians in the United States. The Act of June 18, 1798, (1 Stat. 566) put restrictions on aliens entering the country, sometimes demanding a surety or bond to insure "peace and good behavior" and stiffened requirements for citizenship. The Act of June 25, 1798, (1 Stat. 570) gave the U.S. president extraordinary authority to deport aliens and required a ship's master to provide the government with detailed information on any alien brought into the country. The third Act of July 6, 1798, (1 Stat. 577) gave the government the power to detain and hold in custody any 14 years or older foreign male citizen of a country involved in hostile or threatened action against the United States. The last of the four measures-the Act of July 14, 1798 (1 Stat. 596)-was the most stringent. It mandated severe penalties against any person who opposed any measure by the U.S. government. The act's most controversial section in effect created a law of seditious libel threatening anyone who published "...false, scandalous and malicious writing...against the Government of the United States."

Public support of the "Alien and Sedition Acts" rose and fell in accordance with U.S. relations with France. Once the threat of a French invasion vanished, so did support for the political philosophy that fomented the acts. Although there were a large number of prosecutions under the various acts, some in retrospect seemed to be so ludicrous that the acts authority were further eroded. Further legislative attempts throughout U.S. history to control dissent have subsequently been largely unsuccessful.

The Guide to American Law: Everyone's Legal Encyclopedia (St. Paul, MN: West Publishing, 1983), 1:173-76.

What were Mao Tse-tung's directives to his guerrilla army?

The directives issued by the Chinese Communist leader Mao Tse-tung (1893-1976), still in effect, which made the Chinese guerrilla army so well-liked and respected by the Chinese people, were: "Do not take a single needle or piece of thread from the masses. . .pay fairly for what you buy. . .do not take liberties with women."

Parade Magazine 26 March 1972.

What were the provisions and consequences of the Molotov-Ribbentrop Pact?

A secret 1939 pact between the Soviet Union and Nazi Germany was known as the Molotov-Ribbentrop pact, named after the signatories to the agreement, the Soviet Union's Foreign Minister Vyacheslav M. Molotov (1890-1986) and Germany's Joachim von Ribbentrop (1896-1946), respectively, for their nations. Described at the time as a "friendship" treaty, the pact carved Eastern Europe into Soviet and German spheres of influence and paved the way for the German invasion of Poland in September of 1939. The pact also laid the ground for Stalin's annexation of the Baltic countries of Lithuania, Latvia, and Estonia.

"Archives Yield Soviet-German Pact," *New York Times* 30 October 1992.

Who was the first U.S. vice president to live in a home officially designated as the vice president's home?

In 1975, the U.S. vice president and his family finally received an officially designated home of their own. It is Admiral's House, a three-storied gabled and turreted white brick Victorian mansion of 33 rooms on Embassy Row, 2.5 miles northwest of the White House. Gerald and Betty Ford were supposed to move into the house themselves during Ford's vice presidency, but encountered substantial delays while the roof was replaced and a new heating-cooling system was installed. The first residents of the official vice president's Home were Nelson and Happy Rockefeller, who moved in on September, 1975, by which time the Fords had moved on to occupy the White House.

"A Place to Call Home," *Time* 15 September 1975.

What was a U.S. House of Representatives Committee probing when Dick Clark testified on April 29, 1960?

Dick Clark (1929-) testified in a 1960 House Committee investigation into payola, the practice of record companies who give money to disk jockeys in return for playing their songs. The top disk jockey in the country, and the host of the television program *American Bandstand*, (1952-1990) Clark was among some 30 disk jockeys who were questioned. The investigators were skeptical of the legitimacy of Clark's stock purchases that made $409,020 in gains from an initial $53,773 in investments. The committee also showed that when Clark had a financial interest in a record he played it twice as often as others. Clark countered that he simply had shown good business sense and that he was only guilty of making "a good deal of money in a short time." He said that he did not favor the records intentionally, and that he had dropped such involvement when the conflict of interest issue was shown to him. When Clark asserted that he had never "agreed" to take payola, the committee objected to the statement, and argued that payola was never based on an overt agreement.

Anthony Lewis, "Dick Clark Denies Receiving Payola. Panel Skeptical," *New York Times* 30 April 1960.

What is contained in the text of United Nations Resolution 242 regarding political developments in the Middle East?

United Nations Resolution 242, issued by the U.N. Security Council on November 22, 1967, has often been referred to during continued political turmoil in the Middle East. The resolution spoke of the "grave situation" created by the Arab-Israeli War of 1967 and it asserted that Israel should withdraw from the occupied territories that were taken by force. It stressed the need to guarantee "the territorial inviolability and political independence of every state in the area." The resolution also requested that a U.N. representative be appointed to work on behalf of peace efforts in the Middle East.

George C. Kohn, *Dictionary of Historic Documents* (New York: Facts on File, 1991), 342.

When were the first U.S. government war bonds issued?

While bonds were sold to finance the repayment of Revolutionary War debts, the first "war bonds" to be sold in preparation for war, were created in 1812. The U.S. government wanted to purchase ordnance and equipment and to build up the Army for what is now known as the War of 1812. The war bonds were authorized on March 14, 1812, for the amount of $11 million. Sales eventually totaled $8,134,700.

Joseph Nathan Kane, *Famous First Facts* (New York: H.W. Wilson, 1981), 696.

What international crisis prompted the installation of the "hot line" between Washington and Moscow?

The Cuban Missile Crisis, which occurred in late 1962, was the impetus behind installing a "hot line" that connected the United States and Soviet governments. The new direct link was an effort to improve communications as the two governments negotiated nuclear arms control policies.

Raymond L. Garthoff, *Reflections on the Cuban Missile Crisis* (Washington, DC: The Brookings Institution, 1989), 134.

How long would it take after retirement to recover all of the Social Security taxes the average wage earner paid in?

It would take seven years for an individual retiring at age 65 to recover all of the Social Security taxes paid, plus interest, if one's year of retirement was 1992. By comparison, it only took one year and eleven months for an individual to recover all Social Security taxes paid if retirement occurred in 1972. It has been projected that by the year 2012, it will take eleven years and nine months to recover taxes paid into Social Security for individuals retiring that year. For the person retiring in 2032, it will only take eleven years to recover taxes paid.

USA Today 23 August 1993.

What is the origin of the name for the state of Nevada?

Nevada derives its name from the Spanish word meaning "snowy," "snowy land," or "snow-clad." Among the mountain ranges in this state are the rugged Sierra Nevada mountains where the name was probably originally used. Nevada was admitted as the 36th state of the Union in 1864.

Lillian Eichler, *The Customs of Mankind* (Garden City, NY: Garden City Publishing, 1924), 679-81. William H. Harris and Judith S. Levey, *The New Columbia Encyclopedia* (New York: Columbia University Press, 1975). *Pittsburgh Press* 24 February 1974.

What is the origin of the name for the state of Washington?

The state of Washington is named in honor of George Washington (1732-1799) known as the "Father of Our Country." In 1932 a bill was introduced in the 32d Congress creating the Territory of Columbia. Because of the existence of the District of Columbia, the name was changed to Washington. Washington became the 42d state when it was admitted to the Union in 1889.

Lillian Eichler, *The Customs of Mankind* (Garden City, NY: Garden City Publishing, 1924), 679-81. William H. Harris and Judith S. Levey, *The New Columbia Encyclopedia* (New York: Columbia University Press, 1975). *Pittsburgh Press* 24 February 1974.

What is the origin of the name for the state of Wisconsin?

Wisconsin is named after its principal river, the Wisconsin River. The name is derived from a North American Indian name for which the meaning is uncertain. Several versions are "wild rushing channel," "meeting of the rivers," or a reference to "holes in the banks of a stream in which birds nest." Early chroniclers spelled Wisconsin "Ouisconsin" and "Misconsing." Wisconsin was admitted to the Union as the 30th state in 1848.

Lillian Eichler, *The Customs of Mankind* (Garden City, NY: Garden City Publishing, 1924), 679-81. William H. Harris and Judith S. Levey, *The New Columbia Encyclopedia* (New York: Columbia University Press, 1975). *Pittsburgh Press* 24 February 1974.

What is the origin of the name for the state of New Hampshire?

New Hampshire was named by James Mason in 1629 after the county Hampshire in England. Admitted to the Union in 1788, New Hampshire was the ninth of the 13 original colonies to become a state.

Lillian Eichler, *The Customs of Mankind* (Garden City, NY: Garden City Publishing, 1924), 679-81. William H. Harris and Judith S. Levey, *The New Columbia Encyclopedia* (New York: Columbia University Press, 1975). *Pittsburgh Press* 24 February 1974.

What is the origin of the name for the state of Colorado?

The state of Colorado gets its name from the Spanish word "colorado," meaning "red" or "ruddy," describing the color of the river bearing the same name. The name was chosen by William Gilpin, the first territorial governor of the region during the early 1860s. Colorado is the 38th state of the Union, being admitted in 1876.

Lillian Eichler, *The Customs of Mankind* (Garden City, NY: Garden City Publishing, 1924), 679-81. William H. Harris and Judith S. Levey, eds., *The New Columbia Encyclopedia* (New York: Columbia University Press, 1975). *Pittsburgh Press* 24 February 1974.

What is the origin of the name for the state of Delaware?

The state of Delaware was named for Thomas West, 12th Baron De La Warre, the first governor of Colonial Virginia. In 1610 Lord De La Warre sailed with British captain Sir Samuel Argall for the colony of Virginia; Argall would name one of the capes they sailed through for De La Warre. The river formerly known as the South River would also bear the name "Delaware."

Lillian Eichler, *The Customs of Mankind* (Garden City, NY: Garden City Publishing, 1924), 679-81. William H. Harris and Judith S. Levey, eds., *The New Columbia Encyclopedia* (New York: Columbia University Press, 1975). *Pittsburgh Press* 24 February 1974.

What is the origin of the name for the state of Georgia?

The state of Georgia was named by and for King George II of England. In 1732 English philanthropist James Oglethorpe received a charter from the king to settle the colony of Georgia. England and Spain had been engaged in ongoing territorial disputes and England wanted to settle Georgia as a buffer colony to protect South Carolina from Spanish invasion from the South. Georgia was the last of the Thirteen Colonies, being founded by Oglethorpe in 1733.

Lillian Eichler, *The Customs of Mankind* (Garden City, NY: Garden City Publishing, 1924), 679-81. William H. Harris and Judith S. Levey, eds., *The New Columbia Encyclopedia* (New York: Columbia University Press, 1975). *Pittsburgh Press* 24 February 1974.

What is the origin of the name for the state of Idaho?

The origin of the name for the state of Idaho is uncertain. One claim attributes the name to a Shoshone Indian translation of "Edah Hoe," meaning "light on the mountains." Others claim that the name translates from a Native North American word of unknown meaning. Because Native North American translations generally referred to the natural features of the surrounding country, some have said that the name stems from a word meaning "gem of the mountains," describing the beauty of the mountainous terrain. Idaho, one of the Rocky Mountain states, is the 43d state of the Union, admitted in 1890.

Lillian Eichler, *The Customs of Mankind* (Garden City, NY: Garden City Publishing, 1924), 679-81. William H. Harris and Judith S. Levey, eds., *The New Columbia Encyclopedia* (New York: Columbia University Press, 1975). *Pittsburgh Press* 24 February 1974.

What is U.S. law regarding the succession of the president?

The U.S. Constitution did not originally call for the vice president to succeed the president if he should die, resign, or be unable to discharge his duties. That arrangement was not made law until the 25th amendment was ratified in 1967. This was however done in practice since 1841, when vice president John Tyler (1790-1862) assumed the presidency upon the death of U.S. president William Henry Harrison (1773-1841). Formerly, the vice president was expected to act as president only until a new president was elected. If the president and the vice president are unable to serve, the line of succession is as follows:

Speaker of the House
President pro tempore of the Senate
Secretary of State
Secretary of the Treasury
Secretary of Defense
Attorney General
Secretary of the Interior
Secretary of Agriculture
Secretary of Commerce
Secretary of Labor
Secretary of Health and Human Services
Secretary of Housing and Urban Development

Secretary of Transportation
Secretary of Energy
Secretary of Veteran Affairs.

"Nomination and Election Presidential Succession" (Washington, DC: Government Printing Office), 1992, 377-84.

Why must one member of the President's cabinet not attend the President's annual State of the Union message?

When the President of the United States gives his annual State of the Union message, one of the Cabinet members does not attend the speech. The reason for this practice is to ensure that a successor is safe from any accident that could harm the president and the 16 other officials in the line of succession. This tradition probably dates to the administration of U.S. president Woodrow Wilson (1856-1924), who began the practice in 1913.

Parade 18 March 1991.

What is the origin of the name for the state of Michigan?

The name for the state of Michigan is said to have been derived from the Algonquin Indian word "Mishigamaw" which means "big lake" or "great water," undoubtedly for the lakes that surround the region. It is also said to come from the Native North American words "michi" and "gama," meaning "great" and "water." In 1837 Michigan was admitted as the 26th state of the Union.

Lillian Eichler, *The Customs of Mankind* (Garden City, NY: Garden City Publishing, 1924), 679-81. William H. Harris and Judith S. Levey, eds., *The New Columbia Encyclopedia* (New York: Columbia University Press, 1975). *Pittsburgh Press* 24 February 1974.

What is the origin of the name for the state of Mississippi?

The state of Mississippi derives its name from the mighty river bearing the same name. It comes from a Native North American word meaning "great waters" or "gathering in of all the waters." It was also referred to by Native North Americans as the "father of waters," indicating an awareness among the inhabitants on the region of the immensity of the waterway. The name was first written as "Michi Sepe" by French explorer Henri de Tonti, who sailed the river with Rne Robert Cavelier de La Salle in 1681. Mississippi was admitted to the Union as the 20th state in 1817.

Lillian Eichler, *The Customs of Mankind* (Garden City, NY: Garden City Publishing, 1924), 679-81. William H. Harris and Judith S. Levey, eds., *The New Columbia Encyclopedia* (New York: Columbia University Press, 1975). *Pittsburgh Press* 24 February 1974.

What is the origin of the name for the state of Montana?

The origin of the name for the state of Montana is as controversial as most other states. It is unclear whether the name is of Spanish or Latin origin but it is derived from a word that means "mountainous," most likely to describe the terrain of the region. Montana is the 41st state of the Union, admitted in 1889.

Lillian Eichler, *The Customs of Mankind* (Garden City, NY: Garden City Publishing, 1924), 679-81. William H. Harris and Judith S. Levey, eds., *The New Columbia Encyclopedia* (New York: Columbia University Press, 1975). *Pittsburgh Press* 24 February 1974.

What is the history of U.S. presidential pardons?

The president of the United States has the power under Article 2 of the U.S. constitution to "grant reprieves and pardons for offences against the United States." It is a power that is frequently used, usually with little public notice. Instances that have been historically significant have usually involved large groups of offenders or famous people. In 1800, U.S. president Thomas Jefferson (1743-1826) pardoned everyone who had been convicted by the Alien and Sedition Acts, which were later found unconstitutional. Confederate soldiers received amnesty from both Presidents Abraham Lincoln (1809-1865) and Andrew Johnson (1908-1875). And Jimmy Carter (1924-) gave amnesty to all draft evaders from the Vietnam conflict.

Famous individual pardons include Dr. Samuel Mudd, who was pardoned by Andrew Johnson. Mudd had been convicted of assisting Lincoln's assassin, John Wilkes Booth, by setting his broken leg. Socialist Eugene V. Debs was pardoned by Warren G. Harding (1865-1923), while serving time for sedition in 1921. Former Teamsters' union president Jimmy Hoffa was pardoned by Richard Nixon (1913-1994) in 1971. Three years later, Nixon was himself pardoned by Gerald Ford (1913-), in the wake of his resignation and the Watergate scandal. Nixon's name again came up at the 1989 pardons of George Steinbrenner and Armand Hammer, who had each made illegal contributions to Nixon's reelection campaign. Ronald Reagan (1911-) and George Bush (1924-) granted these pardons.

"Presidential Pardons, Historically," *New York Times* 25 December 1992.

How did the South Tyrol Package regulate relations between the different linguistic groups?

In 1992 Italy and Austria officially ended their dispute over South Tyrol, land that was given to Italy as a reward for uniting with the Allies in World War I. This was in part the result of the South Tyrol "Package," an agreement made between the two countries in 1961. The package listed 137 measures to give the German-speaking majority of South Tyrol autonomy. It also regulated relations between the three linguistic groups in the area, German, Italian, and Ladin. Accordingly, the civil service requires bilingual ability in German and Italian and court cases must be conducted in the language of the person involved.

Austria Today March 1992.

What was the purpose of the Marshall Plan?

The Marshall Plan was a U.S. program for assisting European countries that were suffering economically after World War II (1939-45); it was named after the U.S. Secretary of State, George C. Marshall (1880-1959). The three-year plan was developed immediately after the war, when Great Britain showed that it could not maintain the convertibility of the pound sterling. The plan is credited with speeding up the economic and political recovery of Western Europe.

J.L. Hanson, *A Dictionary of Economics and Commerce* (London: MacDonald & Evans, 1965), s.v. "Marshall Plan."

What benefits does the federal government provide to ex-presidents?

A 1958 congressional report stated that "We expect a former President to engage in no business or occupation which would demean the office he has held or capitalize upon it in any improper way.... We believe that a former President should take very seriously his obligation to maintain the dignity of that office...for the remainder of his life." To this end, Congress passed the Former Presidents Act which awarded ex-presidents a $25,000 annual salary, $50,000 for clerical support, and free postage. Other benefits included free office space on federal property, and an annual pension of $10,000 for widows of former presidents. The 1963 Presidential Transition Act provided $300,000 tax-free dollars to help the out-going president with his return to private life. This allowance was later increased to $1 million. In 1970 Congress decided that an ex-President's salary should be equal to that of a cabinet official. The $50,000 for staff support had risen to $150,000 tax-free dollars by 1993. Upon his retirement, George Bush began to receive not only the ex-president's annual pension ($143,800), but also federal pension monies for his service as vice-president, United Nations ambassador, director of the Central Intelligence Agency, member of Congress, and a naval officer.

In 1968 Congress decreed that former chief executives and their wives or widows should receive Secret Service protection for life, unless a widow remarries. Minor children are guarded until they reach sixteen years of age.

"Into the Sunset," *The Economist* 16 January 1993. Bernard A. Weisberger, "Expensive Ex-Presidents," *American Heritage* May/June 1989.

What is the difference between Great Britain, England, the United Kingdom, and the British Isles?

The terms Great Britain, England, United Kingdom, and British Isles are all related. Great Britain is the geographical name given to the British Isles, which comprised of England, Scotland, and Wales. In 1801 the Act of Union formed the United Kingdom of Great Britain and Ireland. In 1921 when Ireland separated and became the Republic of Ireland, the union became known as the United Kingdom of Great Britain and Northern Ireland, or the United Kingdom. The Channel Islands and the Isle of Man are not part of the United Kingdom but are direct dependencies of the Crown. Like England, Wales and Scotland are administrative units or entities of the United Kingdom of Great Britain and Northern Ireland.

Brian Hunter, ed., *The Statesman's Year-Book* (New York: St. Martin's Press, 1994), 1318.

What is the ground area of the Pentagon Building in Washington, DC.?

The Pentagon, the headquarters of the U.S. Department of Defense, is the world's largest office building in terms of ground space. Its construction was completed on January 15, 1943-in just over 17 months. With a gross floor area of over 6.5 million square feet, this five-story, five-sided building has three times the floor space of the Empire State Building and is 1-times larger than the Sears Tower in Chicago. The World Trade Center complex in New York City, completed in 1973, is larger with over 9 million square feet (836 thousand square meters), but it basically is two structures (towers). Each of the five sides is 921 feet (281 meters) long with a perimeter of 4,610 feet (1,405 meters). The Secretary of Defense, the Secretaries of the three military departments, and the military heads of the Army, Navy, and Air Force are all located in the Pentagon. The National Military Command Center, which is the nation's military communications hub, is located in the area of the Joint Chiefs of Staff. It is commonly called the "war room."

The largest commercial building in the world under one roof is the flower auction building of the cooperative VBA in Aalsmeer, Netherlands. In 1986, the floor plan was extended to 91.05 acres (36.85 hectares). It measures 2,546 by 2,070 feet (776 by 639 meters). The largest building in the United States, and the largest assembly plant in the world, is the Boeing 747 assembly plant in Everett, Washington, with a capacity of 200 million cubic feet (5.5 million cubic meters) and covering 47 acres (19 hectares).

Mark C. Young, *The Guinness Book of Records 1995* (New York: Facts on File, 1994), 98. *New Encyclopaedia Brittanica, 15th ed.* (Chicago: Encyclopaedia Britannica, 1990), 9:267. *The Pentagon: A National Institution* (Berlin, MD: D'OR Press, 1986), 9, 13, 17.

What environmental landmarks soon followed the celebration of the first Earth Day?

Important official actions by the U.S. government that began in 1970 or shortly thereafter were: the birth of the EPA (Environmental Protection Agency), the enactment of the National Environmental Policy Act, the creation of the President's Council on Environmental Quality, and the passage of the new Clean Air Act establishing national air quality standards for the first time.

EPA Journal January/February 1990.

When was the Outer Space Treaty signed?

The United Nations Outer Space Treaty was signed on January 23, 1967. The treaty provides a framework for the exploration and sharing of outer space. It governs the outer space activities of nations that wish to exploit and make use of space, the moon, and other celestial bodies. It is based on a humanist and pacifist philosophy and on the principle of the nonappropriation of space and the freedom that all nations have to explore and use space. A very large number of countries have signed this agreement, including those from the western alliance, the former Eastern bloc, and non-aligned countries.

Space law, or those rules governing the space activities of various countries, international organizations, and private industries, has been evolving since 1957 when the General Assembly of the United Nations created the Committee on the Peaceful Uses of Outer Space (COPUOS). One of its subcommittees was instrumental in drawing up the 1967 Outer Space Treaty.

The Cambridge Encyclopedia of Space (New York: Cambridge University Press, 1990), 360-61. Frank N. Magill, *Magill's Survey of Science: Space Exploration Series* (Engelwood Cliffs, NJ: Salem Press, 1989), 3:1111.

What were the first official coins of the United States?

The first coins struck by the United States were half dimes or half dismes as they were called (five-cent pieces). U.S. president George Washington (1732-1797) was said to have contributed silverware from which these first coins were made. They were stamped with a plump Liberty on the obverse and a scrawny eagle in flight on the reverse.

David C. Harper, ed., *1994 North American Coins & Prices: A Guide to U.S., Canadian, and Mexican Coins, 3d ed.* (Iola, WI: Krause Publications, 1993), 5. Marc Hudgeons, *The Official 1994 Blackbook Price Guide of United States Coins* (New York: House of Collectibles, 1993), 39. R.S. Yeoman, *1994 Handbook of United States Coins, 51st ed.* (Racine, WI: Western Publishing, 1993), 5.

What is the oldest legislative body or oldest government?

Because of its continuous existence since 930, the Althing, Iceland's parliament, is probably the oldest legislative body.

Robert McHenry, ed., *The New Encyclopaedia Britannica, 15th ed.,* (Chicago: Encyclopaedia Britannica, 1993), s.v. "Iceland." Johannes Nordal and Valdimar Kristinsson, eds., *Iceland 874-1974* (Iceland: Central Bank of Iceland, 1975), 130.

When was the Medal of Honor established, and who were the first recipients?

The highest military award for bravery above and beyond the call of duty that can be bestowed upon any individual in the United States, the Medal of Honor, was created by the U.S. Congress in 1861. A bill passed by both Houses of Congress and approved by U.S. president Abraham Lincoln (1809-1865) on December 21, 1861, established a Medal of Honor for enlisted men of the Navy and Marine Corps. A joint resolution with President Lincoln's approval on July 12, 1862, extended the medal to enlisted men of the Army and to military officers and made the law retroactive to the beginning of the American Civil War (1861-1865).

The first Medals of Honor were awarded to 19 Union Army volunteers of the raiding party sent by General George Mitchell in April of 1862 to sabotage the vital Confederate rail link between Atlanta and Chattanooga. The medals were presented to six of the party on March 25, 1863, after the men were released from a Confederate prison. The remaining 13 were subsequently awarded, some posthumously.

General Arthur MacArthur, American Civil War hero, and General Douglas MacArthur (1880-1964) of World War II (1939-1945), are the only father and son who have both received the Medals of Honor. The first woman to be awarded the medal was Dr. Mary Walker in 1861.

Today this award is often called the Congressional Medal of Honor. It is usually presented by the president and awarded in the name of the U.S. Congress.

U.S. Senate, Committee on Veterans' Affairs, *Medal of Honor Recipients 1863-1978* (Washington, DC: Government Printing Office, 1979), 1-17. *The World Book Encyclopedia* (Chicago: World Book, 1994), s.v. "medals, decorations, and orders."

Who was called the "Father of the American Constitution"?

James Madison (1751-1836), the fourth president of the United States, is considered to be the "Father of the American Constitution" because he was the dominant figure at the convention that was called in 1787 to draft that document. A believer in a strong central government, Madison wrote a letter to Washington in which he outlined a series of proposals that became the basis of the Virginia Plan, which was introduced at the convention by Edmund Randolph. It advocated a national government that could exercise its will directly over each citizen rather than depend upon the individual states to assert authority for it. Fifteen resolutions from the Virginia Plan were adopted by the convention to serve as the basis for further discussion. Madison was able to manage these debates with great skill and prevented the convention from becoming deadlocked by making a number of compromises with those who wanted a greater it on states' rights. He also kept a fastidious record of the deliberations, providing us with the fullest account of the proceedings.

Dictionary of American History, rev. ed. (New York: Charles Scribner's Sons, 1971), s.v. "Constitution of the United States." *Webster's Guide to American History: A Chronological, Geographical, and Biographical Survey and Compendium* (Springfield MA: G. & C. Merriam Company, Publishers, 1971), s.v. "Madison, James."

When did the White House get its name?

The White House was not officially called the White House until 1901, when the title was authorized by U.S. President Theodore Roosevelt (1858-1919). The first official name was the President's House and then the Executive Mansion. The White House had been the popular name since the early 1800s, and it was firmly in place by 1820. Its white-washed walls were the source of the nickname.

William Seale, *The President's House: A History* (Washington, DC: White House Historical Association, 1986), 1:163. *The World Book Encyclopedia* (Chicago: World Book, 1994), s.v. "white house."

Where is the Klondike?

The Klondike is an approximately 800-square-mile area which lies on both sides of the Klondike River in the Yukon Territory of Canada. Rich gold-bearing gravel was discovered along the small creeks of the area in August of 1896. When the news reached the United States in January of 1897, there followed a rush of 30,000 people from 1897 through 1899. By 1929 the area had produced gold valued at $175,000,000.

Webster's New Geographical Dictionary (Springfield, MA: Merriam-Webster, 1988), s.v. "Klondike."

Why do soldiers wear "dog tags"?

The two metal identification tags worn by U.S. soldiers are called "dog tags" because they resemble dog license tags. Identification tags were worn voluntarily since the American Civil War (1861-65) but were required by 1906. The term "dog tags" did not become popular until World War I (1914-18). Serial numbers were added in 1918 to differentiate between soldiers with similar or identical names. In July of 1969 social security numbers replaced serial numbers. In the event of death, one tag is buried with the soldier and the other is kept as a record. The current number is known as the Social Security account number.

John R. Elting, Dan Cragg, and Ernest L. Deal, *A Dictionary of Soldier Talk* (New York: Charles Scribner's Sons, 1984), s.v. "serial number." Robert Hendrickson, *The Henry Holt Encyclopedia of Word and Phrase Origins* (New York: Henry Holt, 1987), s.v. "dog tags."

Who was U.S. president for a day?

Zachary Taylor (1784-1850) refused to take the oath of office of president on Sunday and was not inaugurated until Monday, March 5, 1849. U.S. president Polk's (1795-1849) term constitutionally ended at noon on Sunday, March 4, and his Vice President had resigned as president of the Senate on Friday, March 2. U.S. Senator David Rice Atchison of Missouri was elected as president of the Senate pro tempore on March 2. According to the Succession Act of 1792, the president of the Senate is designated next in the line of succession as president. Without a president or vice president, many considered Atchison as President of the United States for one day until Taylor was sworn in on March 5. Some maintain that Atchison was neither president of the Senate on March 4 nor President, because the U. S. Senate had adjourned March 3.

Joseph Nathan Kane, *Facts About the Presidents, 6th ed.* (New York: H.W. Wilson, 1993), 77. *St. Louis Post-Dispatch* 27 January 1991.

Who was the "father of the Seabees"?

E. Jack Spaulding, known as the "father of the Seabees," is credited with helping to organize the construction battalions of Pacific war fame that built and repaired overseas bases to support Navy and Marine Corps forces. Spaulding enlisted the cooperation of the press, radio, the construction industry, and union labor to build Seabee battalions out of the country's most skilled workmen. The name is taken from the initials of the official name, Construction Battalion. The Seabees were authorized on January 5, 1942. They were made a permanent part of the U.S. Navy in 1947.

William Bradford Huie, *Can Do! The Story of the Seabees* (New York: E.P. Dutton, 1944), 67. "Death of E. Jack Spaulding, Called Father of Seabees," *St. Louis Post-Dispatch* 3 April 1953. *World Book Encyclopedia* (Chicago: World Book, Inc., 1994), s.v. "Seabees."

What is the origin of the term "dollar"?

The term "dollar" is derived from "thaler" (short for "Joachimsthaler"), a large silver coin made of silver from the Joachimsthal mine in Bohemia, Germany. First produced in 1518, the coin was widely circulated in both Europe and the New World. Finding the word "thaler" difficult to pronounce, the English gradually changed it to "dollar."

J. P. Jones, *The Money Story* (New York: Drake Publishers, 1973), 42. David Wallechinsky and Irving Wallace, *The People's Almanac* (Garden City, NY: Doubleday & Co., 1975), 340. *World Book Encyclopedia* (Chicago: World Book, 1994), s.v. "dollar."

Are American recipients of the Nobel and Pulitzer Prizes required to pay U.S. taxes on the amounts they receive?

The Nobel, Pulitzer, or other prizes awarded in recognition of past accomplishments in religious, charitable, scientific, artistic, educational, literary, or civic fields are not taxable as long as all of the following are satisfied: the person was selected without any action on his or her part to enter the contest or proceeding; the person selected is not required to perform substantial future services as a condition to receiving the prize or award; and the person selected transfers the prize or award directly to a governmental unit or tax-exempt charity.

Department of the Treasury, Internal Revenue Service, *Your Federal Income Tax* (Washington, DC: Government Printing Office, 1993), 109-10.

Which vice-presidents of the United States subsequently became presidents?

The following vice-presidents became president of the United States upon the death or resignation of the president:
John Tyler (1790-1862) when William H. Harrison (1773-1841) died in 1841.
Millard Fillmore (1800-1874) when Zachary Taylor (1784-1850) died in 1850.
Andrew Johnson (1808-1875) when Abraham Lincoln (1809-1865) was assassinated in 1865.
Chester A. Arthur (1829-1886) when James Garfield was assassinated in 1881.
Theodore Roosevelt (1858-1919) when William McKinley (1843-1901) was assassinated in 1901.
Calvin Coolidge (1872-1933) when Warren Harding (1865-1923) died in 1923.
Harry Truman (1884-1972) when Franklin D. Roosevelt (1882-1945) died in 1945.
Lyndon Johnson (1908-1973) when John F. Kennedy (1917-1963) died in 1963.
Gerald Ford (1913-) when Richard Nixon (1913-1994) resigned in 1974.

The following vice-presidents were elected to the presidency:
John Adams (1735-1826)
Thomas Jefferson (1743-1826)
Martin Van Buren
George Bush (1924-)

Richard M. Nixon was elected president, but not immediately following his vice-presidency; it was eight years later.

American Leaders 1789-1991 (Washington, DC: Congressional Quarterly, 1991), 23. Joseph Nathan Kane, *Facts About the Presidents, 6th ed.* (New York: H.W. Wilson, 1993), 420.

What was the Athenian oath?

Having attained adult status at the age of eighteen, Athenian males in ancient Greece began a two-year period of compulsory military training before being granted citizenship. At the end of their first year, they took an oath of loyalty to the state. The text of the oath is as follows:

> I will not disgrace my sacred arms
> Nor desert my comrad, wherever
> I am stationed.
> I will fight for things sacred
> And things profane.
> And both alone and with all to help me,
> I will transmit my fatherland not diminished
> But greater and better than before.
> I will obey the ruling magistrates
> Who rule reasonably
> And I will observe the established laws
> And whatever laws in the future
> May be reasonably established.
> If any person seek to overturn the laws,
> Both alone and with all to help me,
> I will oppose him.
> I will honor the religion of my fathers.
> I call to witness the Gods ...
> The borders of my fatherland,
> The wheat, the barley, the vines,
> And the trees of the olive and the fig.

Suzy Platt, ed., *Respectfully Quoted: A Dictionary of Quotations Requested from the Congressional Research Service* (Washington, DC: Library of Congress, 1989), 22.

Who was Richard Nixon's running mate in the U.S. presidential campaign of 1960?

Henry Cabot Lodge (1902-1985) of Massachusetts was the Republican vice-presidential candidate in 1960, running with Richard Nixon (1913-1994). At the time of his nomination, Lodge was the permanent United States representative to the United Nations. He had been appointed in 1953 after he had lost his bid for a third term in the United States Senate to then Representative John F. Kennedy (1917-1963). He later served as ambassador to South Vietnam from 1963-67 and was chief negotiator at the talks in Paris on peace in Vietnam (1969).

Facts On File 28 July 1960. Robert McHenry ed., *The New Encyclopaedia Britannica, 15th ed.* (Chicago: Encyclopaedia Britannica, 1993), s.v. "Lodge, Henry Cabot."

How do the Social Security tax laws apply to household or domestic employees?

Household employees including cooks, gardeners, cleaning persons, companions, and caretakers must have their wages reported and pay Social Security taxes on them if they earn more than $1000.00 per calendar year. Reimbursement for transportation costs and room and board are reportable as cash wages. Consult a tax advisor for full information.

Ken Skala, *American Guidance for Those Over 60* (Falls Church, VA: American Guidance, 1989), 113-114.

When and why have foreign forces been sent to Africa?

Over the past 30 years, subsequent to colonial rule, foreign forces have been sent into African nations on many occasions. In 1993, after rebels in Rwanda launched an offensive against the government, France sent troops to protect foreigners. The United Nations sent an intervention force to Somalia in 1992 to protect international relief efforts necessitated by civil war. After Zairian soldiers mutinied in 1991, Belgium, the United States, and France sent troops and planes to evacuate foreigners. In 1991 French troops were sent to Benin to protect French nationals during instability in neighboring Togo. Also in 1991, France sent troops to Djibouti to repel rebels. Rioting in Zaire prompted France and Belgium to send troops there in 1991. After rebels overthrew the pro-American government in Chad in 1990, American troops helped 600 Libyan prisoners of war return home. French Legionnaires and Belgian paratroopers were sent to Rwanda in 1990 to evacuate Europeans and Americans when they were threatened by battles between the government and rebels. American Marines rescued 2,400 foreigners from Monravia, Liberia in 1990 during a rebellion. Armed rebellion in Somalia in 1990 necessitated the evacuation of diplomats and expatriates by United States Marines, Italian troops, and a French frigate. Israeli troops, with secret American support, evacuated 8,000 Ethiopian Jews from Ethiopia in 1984. Israel sent commandos to Uganda in 1976 to rescue hostages aboard a French airliner that had been hijacked by Palestinians. In 1960 Belgian troops intervened in the Republic of Congo, later Zaire, to protect Belgian nationals during an armed forces mutiny. United Nations forces intervened in Katanga in 1960 to suppress its secession from Zaire.

New York Times, 11 April 1994.

How much is the federal debt?

The federal debt has been increasing steadily since 1929 when it was $16.9 billion. In 1940 it was $50.7 billion; in 1950, $256.9 billion; in 1960, $290.5 billion; in 1970, $380.9 billion; in 1980, $908.5 billion; in 1990, $3,206.2 billion; in 1993, $4,351.2 billion. The estimated federal debt for 1995 is $4,960.1 billion.

Economic Report of the President (Washington, DC: Government Printing Office, 1994), 359.

Which country was the first to adopt a national flag that included stars?

The United States was the first country in the world to incorporate stars into its national flag. In 1776 when the thirteen British colonies declared their independence from the mother country, the founding fathers had to choose a flag to fly over their new country. The initial flag was a variation of the British Union Jack in which the solid red field was changed into a series of horizontal red and white stripes. The British union emblem would remain for a time but, when the Puritans of New England expressed misgivings about the cross it incorporated for religious reasons, in 1777 it was resolved to change the design, which became a blue field with 13 white five-pointed stars to represent each state in the union.

Sven Tito Achen, *Symbols Around Us* (New York: Van Nostrand Reinhold, 1978), 26.

What is an entitlement?

An entitlement is a right granted to an individual that he may exercise freely. An example of an entitlement in the United States would be the right to free education. The level of education provided has changed throughout the years, as well as which persons in the country are entitled to receive it.

Most entitlements in the United States deal with the social welfare system and with programs such as Social Security and Medicare. In many instances, a "mean test" is necessary in deciding who should receive certain entitlements.

George L. Maddox, ed., *The Encyclopedia of Aging* (New York: Springer Publishing Co., 1987), s.v. "entitlement."

What was the U-2 incident?

The U-2 incident refers to the downing of a United States spy plane, a Lockhheed U-2, over Sverdlovsk in the former Soviet Union on May 1, 1960. The captured pilot Francis Gary Powers (1929-1977) was given a trial and sentenced to prison. Later, in February of 1962, he was exchanged for a Russian spy. The event damaged relations between the two countries. The Soviet Union broke off a summit conference in Paris in 1960 after the United States refused to apologize for the incident. Since there was also a great deal of criticism of the affair in America, further U-2 spy flights were canceled.

Chris Cook, *Dictionary of Historical Terms: A Guide to Names and Events of over 1,000 Years of World History* (New York: Peter Bedrick Books, 1983), s.v. "U-2 incident."

What was "apartheid"?

"Apartheid" was the name given to a social policy followed by various South African governments through the early 1990s that called for strict segregation between whites and blacks and highly restrictive laws governing black life. When the Nationalist Party came to power in 1948 in the Republic of South Africa, oppressive measures against the non-white population steadily increased. "Apartheid" is an Afrikaans word that means "separateness."

Chris Cook, *Dictionary of Historical Terms* (New York: Peter Bedrick Books, 1983), s.v. "apartheid." Graham Evans and Jeffrey Newnham, *The Dictionary of World Politics: A Reference Guide to Concepts, Ideas and Institutions* (New York: Simon & Schuster, 1990), s.v. "apartheid."

What was Rousseau's *Social Contract (Du Contrat Social)*?

The *Social Contract (Du Contrat Social)* was a book written by the philosopher Jean Jacques Rousseau (1712-1778) and published in 1762. In it he argued that in a properly ordered society there is a contract by which each citizen, all of whom have equal rights and obligations, agree to surrender their rights to the general will, which is represented by a responsible monarch. Although Rousseau emphasized that government must rely on the consent of the governed, the concept of general will has been used to justify modern totalitarian regimes.

George C. Kohn, *Dictionary of Historic Documents* (New York: Facts on File, 1991) s.v. "Social Contract."

What do the initials "FS" found on certain nickels stand for?

Beginning in 1966, U.S. nickels included the letters "FS" under the bust of Jefferson. They are the initials of Felix Schlag, who beat out some 390 other artists with his design for the five-cent coin. The Jefferson type coin was first minted in 1938; it represented a new trend toward the use of portrait and pictorial devices on U.S. coins. Other changes to the coin have been a new metal composition that eliminated the use of nickel, the mark "P" to indicate the new alloy, and moving the mint mark to the obverse side of the coin.

R.S. Yeoman, *1994 Handbook of United States Coins* (Racine, WI: Western Publishing Company, Inc., 1993), 68.

Which countries have the highest tobacco taxes?

Throughout the world, efforts are being made to discourage people from smoking. One way to do this is to increase the tax on a pack of cigarettes. While proposals to raise the cigarette tax in the United States have been met with a storm of protest, several other countries have raised their cigarette taxes dramatically. Among the countries with the world's highest cigarette taxes are Denmark, with a tax of $3.68 per pack; Canada, with $3.00 per pack; Britain, $2.55 per pack; and Germany, $2.11 per pack. Several studies have shown that a $2.00 per pack tax increase on cigarettes in the United States could reduce consumption by 23 percent within a few years and prevent two million premature deaths.

Business Week 22 March 1993.

Which U.S. presidents were judged "great" by historians?

In 1948 and 1962, noted historian Arthur Schlesinger polled a number of distinguished historians and asked them to evaluate each U.S. president's regarding performance in office. Presidents were rated on a scale of great, near great, average, below average, and failure. The result of the first survey indicated that Abraham Lincoln (1809-1865); George Washington (1732-1799); Franklin D. Roosevelt (1882-1945); Woodrow Wilson (1856-1924); Thomas Jefferson (1743-1826); and Andrew Jackson (1767-1845) were considered great presidents. In the second survey, Jackson slipped to near great, and Harry S. Truman (1884-1972), who had been in office during the first poll, was placed in the same category.

Michael Nelson, ed., *The Presidency A to Z* (Washington, DC: Congressional Quarterly, 1992), 210-11.

What is the honeymoon period of a presidency?

The honeymoon of a presidency refers to a period of good feeling between the public and the president, usually the first few weeks or months of his administration, during which there is a widely shared belief that the new regime can bring peace and prosperity to the nation. It is often the period of the administration's greatest strength and the best time for it to implement its legislative program. Since the public's expectations are commonly set too high, a president's popularity will begin to decline when it becomes apparent that he cannot fulfill everyone's hopes.

Michael Nelson, ed., *The Presidency form A to Z* (Washington, DC: Congressional Quarterly, 1992), s.v. "honeymoon period."

What percentage does the United States contribute to the budget of the United Nations?

The United States contributes 25 percent of the United Nations' annual budget.

The Europa World Year Book 1994 (London: Europa Publications, 1994), 1:3-4.

What was the Golden Fleece Award?

Senator William Proxmire was a powerful Democratic senator from Wisconsin who served in the U.S. Senate from 1957 to 1988. Considered a "tax and spend" liberal early in his career, Proxmire became a staunch critic of wasteful government expenditures. In 1975, Proxmire created the Golden Fleece Award. This monthly "award" was given to government agencies whom Proxmire accused of spending money frivolously.

The Encyclopedia Americana, intern. ed. (Danbury, Ct.: Grolier, 1990), s.v. "Proxmire, William."

What was the closest governor's race in modern American politics?

In 1990, Nebraska was the site of the closest governor's race in modern U.S. history. Ben Nelson defeated Bill Hoppner 44,721 to 44,679 in the Democratic primary for governor of Nebraska. Nelson won the election by a razor-thin margin of 0.047 percent.

"Winner in Nebraska at Last. The Margin 0.047 Percent," *New York Times* 4 July 1990.

Where were some former branch mints located in the United States?

Former U.S. branch mints were located in: Charlotte, North Carolina (1835-1935); Dahlonega, Georgia (1838-1878); Carson City, Nevada (1863-1933); and New Orleans (1838-1909). The dates given are not necessarily inclusive of minting operations. There were many interruptions of service at each mint due to falling demand for coinage, expansion of other facilities, the American Civil War, and so on. A number of mints were closed, only to be reopened for ancillary government activities.

Beth Deisher, ed., *Coin World Almanac: A Handbook for Coin Collectors, 5th ed.* (Sidney, OH: Amos Press, Inc., 1987), 168-73.

Who were the four fleet admirals of the U.S. Navy in World War II?

In the U.S. Navy and most other navies throughout the world, admiral is the highest rank an individual can achieve. During World War II (1939-45), the U.S. Navy instituted the new rank of fleet admiral. Fleet admirals wore an insignia with five stars. Four men were awarded this rank during World War II: Ernest J. King, Chester W. Nimitz, William F. Halsey, and William D. Leahy.

World Book Encyclopedia (Chicago: World Book, 1987), s.v. "admiral."

Is the U.S. Central Intelligence Agency (CIA) authorized to conduct espionage operations in the United States?

Prior to 1981 the U.S. Central Intelligence Agency (CIA) was not allowed to conduct espionage operations within the United States. President Ronald Reagan (1911-) changed that when he issued Executive Order 12333 which allows internal CIA activities under certain prescribed circumstances. By this order the CIA was empowered to collect foreign intelligence or counterintelligence within the United States, in coordination with the Federal Bureau of Investigation (FBI), when such information is not otherwise obtainable. Collection, production, and dissemination of intelligence on foreign aspects of drug trafficking was also included. The CIA can also conduct special activities approved by the President or perform services within the United States of common concern to the intelligence community as directed by the National Security Council (NSC).

President, Executive Order, "United States Intelligence Activities, Executive Order 12333," *The Weekly Compilation of Presidential Documents* 4 December 1981.

Can a living person be pictured on U.S. currency?

The portrait of a living person may not appear on U.S. currency. Only a deceased individual can be portrayed, and his or her name shall be inscribed beneath the portrait.

United States Code: 1988 Edition (Washington, DC: Government Printing Office, 1989), 545.

What U.S. currency was known as a "jackass note"?

Eagles engraved on U.S. legal tender notes of 1869, 1875, 1878, and 1880, during the Republican administration of U.S. president Ulysses S. Grant (1822-1885), when turned upside down, resembled the head of a donkey. These became known as "jackass notes" and were a source of embarrassment to Grant. It is thought that the engraving was done by a disgruntled engraver, possibly a Democrat, at the U.S. Mint.

Irving Wallace and David Wallechinsky, *Significa* (New York: E.P. Dutton, 1983), 309.

Where is England's Royal Military Academy located?

England's Royal Military Academy is located near the town of Sandhurst, which lies about 30 miles west-southwest of London. In 1799 the Royal Military Academy was founded at Woolwich, London, and in 1802 the Royal Military College was established at Great Marlow before moving to Sandhurst in 1812. In 1939 the functions of both institutions were combined at Sandhurst.

Philip W. Goetz, ed., *New Encyclopaedia Britannica, 15th ed., "Micropaedia"* (Chicago: Encyclopaedia Britannica, Inc., 1989), s.v. "Sandhurst."

How many women followed their husbands into Congress and how many women preceded their husbands to Congress?

By the beginning of 1987, 37 percent of women elected to Congress had husbands who previously served in that same institution. Of that group 44 were married to former congressional members, while 41 filled unexpired terms of their late husbands either through election or appointment. Only one woman, U.S. Representative Emily Taft Douglas, Democrat from Illinois, preceded her husband Senator Paul H. Douglas in Congress.

American Leaders, 1789-1987 (Washington, DC: Congressional Quarterly, 1987), 50.

How long should federal tax related records and receipts be kept?

If you use an itemized federal income tax return, any records relating to income or deductions must be kept until the statute of limitations for that return expires, usually three years from the filing date. Any receipts for items that may affect capital gain or loss, such as improvements on a home or piece of property, should be kept as long as the home or property is owned. Consult a tax advisor for full information.

Jonathan D. Pond, *The New Century Family Money Book* (New York: Dell Publishing, 1993), 22.

What was the first cabinet position in the United States government?

The first cabinet position in the United States government was U.S. Secretary of State, created on July 27, 1789. Although the future president Thomas Jefferson (1743-1826) officially was the first secretary, John Jay (1745-1829) held a similar position under the Articles of Confederation and acted in this position until Jefferson could assume the responsibilities on March 22, 1790. The starting salary was $3,500.

Dennis Sanders, *The First of Everything* (New York: Delacorte Press, 1981), 144.

Where can mutilated paper money be exchanged?

The U.S. Department of the Treasury will exchange lawfully held mutilated paper currency if more than one half of the bill remains. If less than half of the note exists the possessor must have evidence that the other portions have been destroyed. Totally destroyed paper currency is unredeemable. Inquiries regarding mutilated currency should be addressed:

Department of the Treasury
Bureau of Engraving and Printing
OCS/BEPA, Room 344
P.O. Box 37048
Washington, DC 20013.

Coin World Almanac: A Handbook for Coin Collectors (Sidney, OH: Amos Press, 1987), 223.

How does the original cost of the statue Freedom, that sits on the top of the U.S. Capitol, compare to the cost of refurbishing it in 1993?

The beautiful statue Freedom, which graces the top of the U.S. Capitol building, cost a mere $23,797 in 1863. Cleaning and refurbishing the statue cost $780,000 in 1993.

USA Today 22 October 1993.

What is the Court of St. James?

The official name of the royal court in Great Britain is the Court of St. James, and it is to this court that newly arrived ambassadors are accredited when they arrive in Great Britain. The name derives from St. James's palace, which was the royal residence in the eighteenth century when the phrase was established.

Bamber Gascoigne, *Encyclopedia of Britain* (New York: Macmillan Publishing, 1993) s.v. "Court of St. James."

Why is the U.S. Department of State often referred to as "Foggy Bottom"?

The U.S. Department of State is often referred to as "Foggy Bottom" because its offices are built over a swampy area of the same name, which was known for its heavy mists and vapors.

E.D. Hirsch, Jr., *The Dictionary of Cultural Literacy* (Boston: Houghton Mifflin 1988), s.v. "Foggy Bottom."

What is the meaning of the phrase "divine right of kings"?

The phrase "divine right of kings" referred to the supposed right of a monarch to rule or govern his kingdom by virtue of his birth. Because the monarch's ancestors were appointed by God to serve, this right is passed from generation to generation.

The Guide to American Law: Everyone's Legal Encyclopedia (St. Paul, MN: West Publishing, 1983), s.v. "divine right of kings."

What were the principal ships used by Great Britain during World War I?

During World War I (1914-1918), Great Britain had some 65 battleships, giving them the strongest naval forces in the world. The country's principal ships included many pre-dreadnought battleships. These were superseded by the development of the dreadnought, a battleship that was armed with large caliber guns that were mounted in turrets, allowing all guns to be pointed in the same direction at one time. The first such ship was the *Dreadnought*, built in 1906. The British Navy also deployed faster and less heavily armored battlecruisers, light battlecruisers and cruisers.

Philip J. Haythornthwaite, *The World War One Source Book* (London: Arms and Armour Press, 1992), 227.

What government agencies were the forerunners of the Central Intelligence Agency?

Prior to the outbreak of World War II (1939-45), the United States did not have a centralized intelligence-gathering agency. With war clouds on the horizon, Colonel William J. ("Wild Bill") Donovan (1883-1959) persuaded U.S. president Franklin Roosevelt (1882-1945) of the need for such an agency. In July of 1941 Roosevelt created the Office of Coordinator of Information (COI) with Donovan as its head.

The COI did not have an aggressive mandate; its role was to passively gather and analyze information vital to the security of the United States. Following the bombing of Pearl Harbor in 1941 however, the COI was replaced with the Office of Strategic Services (OSS), again with Donovan at its helm.

The OSS was under military jurisdiction and its tactics for gathering information and shaping events became much more forceful including sabotage, propaganda, and support of guerrilla warfare in hostile territory. In 1945 the OSS was disbanded and U.S. president Harry Truman (1884-1972) signed into law the legislation creating the civilian-controlled Central Intelligence Agency (CIA).

Family Encyclopedia of American History (Pleasantville, NY: Reader's Digest Association, 1975), s.v. "Office of Strategic Services."

What is meant by a "fifth column"?

In warfare parlance the term "fifth column" refers to the use of irregular forces-partisans, guerillas, paramilitary groups-to overthrow a government, often acting surreptitiously but in concert with regular forces. The term originated during the Spanish Civil War of the mid-1930s when Francisco Franco (1892-1975) attacked Madrid with four columns of troops. Franco claimed his victory was due in part to a "fifth column" of insurgents operating within the city.

Walter J. Raymond, *International Dictionary of Politics, 6th ed.* (Lawrenceville, VA: Brunswick Publishing, 1978), s.v. "fifth column."

Where and when was the first U.S. Mint established?

In 1782 Secretary of Finance Robert Morris (1734-1806) put a plan before the Continental Congress urging the creation of a U.S. mint. In 1786 the Board of Treasury at the request of Congress began studying the proposal and in 1792 a mint was authorized. It opened in Philadelphia, which was then the nation's capitol, in 1793, although other federal facilities moved to Washington, DC, when it became the nation's capitol. In 1794 the mint was producing silver coinage and began striking gold coins in 1795. As the country and its economy grew, so did output of the mint. In 1794-1795 it produced $500,000 worth of coins; by 1807 it reached the million dollar mark, and in the year 1851 it produced $63.5 million in coinage. Although the government opened numerous branch mints and assay offices, the Philadelphia mint continued in operation.

Coin World Almanac, 5th ed. (New York: Amos Press, 1987), 159. *Dictionary of American History* (New York: Charles Scribner's Sons, 1976), s.v. "mint, federal."

What is an alderman?

An alderman is an elected official of a city council, or local legislative body, or the public officer of a town. Like other elected officials, an alderman represents those who elected this official to office.

The Guide to American Law: Everyone's Legal Encyclopedia (St. Paul, MN: West Publishing, 1983), s.v. "alderman."

How did the United States of America come to be named?

The name "United States of America" first officially appeared in the Declaration of Independence. There were many antecedents including the "United Colonies of New England," "United Colonies," "United Colonies of America," and the "United Colonies of North America." For instance the British rules for troops published in 1775 made reference to the "...Twelve United Colonies of North America." As the idea of independence burgeoned the word "states" gradually began to replace the word "colony." The Virginia resolution of 1776 stated "...these United Colonies are, and of the right ought to be, free and independent States." In the Declaration of Independence "United Colonies" gave way to "United States" which was subsequently used in the Articles of Confederation (1777) and the Constitution (1787). Political theorist, pamphleteer, and American Revolutionary War propagandist Thomas Paine (1737-1809) is often attributed with coining the name.

Isaac Asimov, *Isaac Asimov's Book of Facts* (New York: Grosset & Dunlap, 1979), 447. *Dictionary of American History, rev. ed.* (New York: Charles Scribner's Sons, 1976), s.v. "United States of America."

What are "Barr notes"?

"Barr notes" are notes signed by Joseph W. Barr who was the U. S. Secretary of the Treasury for only one month, from December 21, 1968, to January 20, 1969. Barr had a long history of public service including U.S. representative from Indiana, assistant to the Secretary of the Treasury, and various positions with the International Monetary Fund, International Bank for Reconstruction and Development, and the Asian Development Bank. In the private sector Barr served with the American Society Corporation and the Franklin National Bank of New York. It was felt by many paper money collectors that because Barr served as Secretary of the Treasury for such a short time those notes bearing his signature would become collector's items. However, the notes continued to be issued until June of 1969 even though David Kennedy had already succeeded him. The notes have no particular collector's value.

Coin World Almanac, 5th ed. (New York: World Almanac, 1987), 259.

In U.S. politics, what is a "pocket veto"?

As mandated by the U.S. Constitution if the White House receives a bill from Congress and the president decides to either sign it or veto it this must be done within ten days of receipt of the bill, excluding Sundays. If Congress adjourns within those ten days, however, the bill cannot be returned and thus does not become law. Situations often arise when the president objects to a bill but for reasons of political expediency does not wish to go on record as exercising the presidential veto. In such a case, if timing permits such action, the president can "sit" on the bill until Congress adjourns, thus killing it by default. This veto by default or inaction is known as the pocket veto.

Jay M. Shafritz, *The Facts On File Dictionary of Public Administration* (New York: Facts On File, 1985), s.v. "veto."

What is "Maggie's drawers"?

"Maggie's drawers" is a military term for a red flag that is waved by firing range personnel when a rifleman misses the target completely.

New York Times 5 January 1962.

How many times in U.S. history have there been no living former presidents?

The United States has been without a living former president five times during its history. George Washington died in 1799, more than a year before U.S. president John Adams (1735-1826) completed his term. Andrew Johnson died in 1877, eight months before U.S. president Ulysses S. Grant's (1822-1885) second term ended. Grover Cleveland died in 1908, nine months before U.S. president Theodore Roosevelt (1858-1919) left office. Calvin Coolidge died in 1933, two months before Herbert Hoover (1874-1964) left office. Lyndon B. Johnson died in 1973, before U.S. president Richard Nixon (1913-1994) resigned in 1974.

New York Times 23 January 1973.

What is the origin of the "twenty-one gun salute"?

The twenty-one gun salute, the most famous military salute, originates from the early days of the British Navy. The firing of guns represented a form of honor in which the saluter, upon firing his weapon, disarmed himself in respect to the individual being saluted. The greater the number of guns fired, the greater the degree of respect to the individual. A twenty-one gun salute—the number of guns found on one side of the larger "ships of the line"—became the highest mark of respect accorded to an individual and was usually reserved for heads of state. Because of an old seagoing superstition against even numbers, only odd numbers were used for salutes. Seven may have been selected because of its symbolic and mystic significance in sacred literature and three because it represents omnipotence and the Deity. Thus, seven times three was the ultimate honor that could be conferred upon an important individual.

The international salute was officially recognized by the United States on August 16, 1875. Previously it was set at 21 guns in the regulations of the U.S. Army revised in 1841. The president, as commander-in-chief of the armed forces, is accorded a salute of twenty-one guns. It is fired to honor the arrival or departure of a sovereign, a member of a reigning royal family or chief of state of a foreign country and when a U.S. Navy ship enters a port of a foreign nation recognized by the U.S. Government on ceremonial occasions. Each Memorial Day all military installations that can fire a twenty-one-gun salute do so, and it is fired at one-minute intervals on the day of an interment for a president, ex-president, or president-elect.

Mary Jane McCaffree and Pauline Innis, *Protocol: The Complete Handbook of Diplomatic, Official and Social Usage* (Washington, DC: Devon Publishing, 1981), 337-41. William Morris and Mary Morris, *Dictionary of Word and Phrase Origins* (New York: Harper and Row, 1967), s.v. "twenty-one gun salute." George W. Stimpson, *Nuggets of Knowledge* (New York: A.L. Burt, 1934), 21-22.

What is the origin of the name for the state of Alabama?

The state of Alabama derives its name from a Native North American tribe of the Creek Confederacy called the *Alabamas* or *Alibamons*, who had given the name to a river that flowed through the territory. Alabama was admitted as the 22d state of the Union in 1819.

Lillian Eichler, *The Customs of Mankind* (Garden City, NY: Garden City Publishing, 1924), 679-81. William H. Harris and Judith S. Levey, eds., *The New Columbia Encyclopedia* (New York: Columbia University Press, 1975). *Pittsburgh Press* 24 February 1974.

What is the origin of the name for the state of Oklahoma?

Oklahoma derives its name from a Choctaw Indian word meaning "red people." Oklahoma was admitted as the 46th state to the Union in 1907.

Lillian Eichler, *The Customs of Mankind* (Garden City, NY: Garden City Publishing, 1924), 679-81. William H. Harris and Judith S. Levey, *The New Columbia Encyclopedia* (New York: Columbia University Press, 1975). *Pittsburgh Press* 24 February 1974.

What is the origin of the name for the state of Pennsylvania?

Pennsylvania was named after its founder William Penn (1644-1718). In 1681 king of England Charles I (1600-1649) made Penn the sole proprietor of the settlement to be known as Pennsylvania as partial repayment of a debt owed Penn's father the English admiral Sir William Penn (1621-1670). Penn had proposed naming the tract of land "Sylvania" derived from the Latin word *sylva* (wood); but the king prefixed it with the surname "Penn" in honor of Penn's father. Pennsylvania was the second of the original thirteen colonies to enter the Union in 1787.

Lillian Eichler, *The Customs of Mankind* (Garden City, NY: Garden City Publishing, 1924), 679-81. William H. Harris and Judith S. Levey, *The New Columbia Encyclopedia* (New York: Columbia University Press, 1975). *Pittsburgh Press* 24 February 1974.

What is the origin of the name for the state of South Carolina?

Like its sister state North Carolina, the area now known as the state of South Carolina was referred to as Carolina by some English newspapers in the early 1600s which was probably a reference to the English king Charles I (1600-1685). When Charles II (1630-1685) actually made a land grant of the area around 1663 it was officially called Carolina in his honor. South Carolina was the twelfth of the original 13 colonies to become a state of the Union in 1889.

Lillian Eichler, *The Customs of Mankind* (Garden City, NY: Garden City Publishing, 1924), 679-81. William H. Harris and Judith S. Levey, *The New Columbia Encyclopedia* (New York: Columbia University Press, 1975). *Pittsburgh Press* 24 February 1974.

What is the origin of the name for the state of Tennessee?

Tennessee derives its name from the name given to the state's principal river the Tennessee River. The river had been named after the site of a Cherokee Indian village that was called Tanasse (also spelled Tennese). This could mean "bend in the river," however, this has never been substantiated. Tennessee was admitted as the 16th state to the Union in 1796.

Lillian Eichler, *The Customs of Mankind* (Garden City, NY: Garden City Publishing, 1924), 679-81. William H. Harris and Judith S. Levey, *The New Columbia Encyclopedia* (New York: Columbia University Press, 1975). *Pittsburgh Press* 24 February 1974.

What is the origin of the name for the state of Utah?

Utah was named for the Ute Indians, the tribe that inhabited the region when the area was settled. The origin of the word is unknown. Utah was admitted as the 45th state of the Union in 1896.

Lillian Eichler, *The Customs of Mankind* (Garden City, NY: Garden City Publishing, 1924), 679-81. William H. Harris and Judith S. Levey, *The New Columbia Encyclopedia* (New York: Columbia University Press, 1975). *Pittsburgh Press* 24 February 1974.

Which states make up the United Arab Emirates?

The United Arab Emirates, formerly known as the Trucial States, is made up of seven member states: Abu Zabi, Ajman, Dubayy, Al Fujayrah, Ra's al Khaymah, Shariqah, and Umm al Qaywayn.

David Munro, *Chambers World Gazetteer: An A-Z of Geographical Information* (Edinburgh: W & R Chambers; Cambridge: University of Cambridge, 1988), s.v. "United Arab Emirates."

What is the "Granite Lady" and who is responsible for saving her?

"Granite Lady" is the affectionate nickname bestowed on the 1874 San Francisco Mint. Closed by the Mint in 1937 the building housed various government offices while continuing to deteriorate until 1968 when it was closed by the federal government. In 1972 then president Richard Nixon (1913-1994) ordered it restored and transferred back to the Mint for continued government use. In 1973 the Old San Francisco Mint was re-opened as a public museum.

Coin World Almanac, 5th ed. (New York: World Almanac, 1987), 166.

What is the salary of the Prime Minister of Great Britain?

The Prime Minister of Great Britain received a salary of 53,007 British pounds in 1993.

Whitaker's Almanack (London: J. Whitaker & Sons, 1994), 282.

What was California's Proposition 13?

California's Proposition 13 was a radical referendum item, formally known as the Jarvis-Gann initiative, that voters in the state approved in 1978. Its origins were a grass-roots response to what voters perceived as the state's unsound fiscal policies. Proposition 13 cut property taxes by over 50 percent and required a two-thirds popular majority vote before the implementation of any further local non-property taxes.

Encyclopedia Americana, intern. ed. (Danbury, CT: Grolier, 1990), s.v. "California."

What percentage of the world's mail circulates through the U.S. Postal Service?

Over forty percent of all mail in the world passes through the U.S. Postal Service.

U.S. News and World Report 5 July 1993.

What are the advantages of government employment?

There are numerous advantages to holding a job with the government. The first of these is the pay-in certain non-technical, unskilled positions, salaries are often quite good, as are fringe benefits such as health insurance and pensions. Overtime or an unfailing seven-day-a-week dedication to hold one's job is rare. Since the government is not a profit-driven enterprise, working conditions are generally more relaxed than in private business. Studies show that among government employees job satisfaction is high, especially among those who work directly with the public. Most positions are relatively secure. Additionally, advancement within the hierarchy of government employment is equitable, with promotions often based on merit or equal-employment considerations. Lastly, a position with the government is an excellent stepping-stone for similar work within the private sector.

Ronald L. Krannich and Caryl Rae Krannich, *The Complete Guide to Public Employment, 2d ed.* (Woodbridge, VA: Impact Publications, 1990), 222-24.

Who became known as "Nixon's Rabbi"?

Rabbi Baruch Korff of Taunton, Massachusetts, became known as "Nixon's Rabbi" after founding the *Citizen's Committee for Fairness to the Presidency* in reaction to the perceived unfair media treatment U.S. president Richard M. Nixon (1913-1994) was getting during the Watergate scandal.

Newsweek 1 October 1973.

What are the different methods of voting in a meeting?

There are several appropriate methods for taking a vote at meetings. One method, acclamation, requires that members respond "aye" or "no." A show of hands is another method. A variation on this is to ask adherents of one side to stand, and a count is taken; the process is repeated for the opposing side. Members may also vote by secret ballot. In a fifth method, the secret roll-call ballot, the voters must sign their names to the ballot slip.

In a simple roll call vote, the names of the eligible voting members are called out loud, and they respond "aye" or "no."

Marjorie Mitchell Cann, *Cann's Keys to Better Meetings: Parliamentary Procedure Simplified* (Mobile, AL: HB Publications, 1990), 15-16.

What is the origin of the name for the state of New Mexico?

The origin of the name New Mexico can be traced to the Mexicans of the 16th century when they referred to the territory north and west of the Rio Grande as Nuevo Mexico. The word may have been derived from the name *Mexitli*, the Aztec war god. Some say that it means "habitation of the god of war." New Mexico became the 47th state of the Union when it was admitted in 1912.

Lillian Eichler, *The Customs of Mankind* (Garden City, NY: Garden City Publishing, 1924), 679-81. William H. Harris and Judith S. Levey, *The New Columbia Encyclopedia* (New York: Columbia University Press, 1975). *Pittsburgh Press* 24 February 1974.

What is the origin of the name for the state of North Carolina?

As early as the 1600s the area now known as the state of North Carolina was referred to by some English newspapers as Carolina-probably for Charles I of England (1600-1649). Around 1663, when a land grant was made by Charles II (1630-1685), the area was officially called Carolina in honor of this king of England. North Carolina was the 12th of the original thirteen colonies to be admitted to the Union in 1789.

Lillian Eichler, *The Customs of Mankind* (Garden City, NY: Garden City Publishing, 1924), 679-81. William H. Harris and Judith S. Levey, *The New Columbia Encyclopedia* (New York: Columbia University Press, 1975). *Pittsburgh Press,* 24 February 1974.

What is the origin of the name for the state of Alaska?

Alaska derives its name from the Eskimo word "alashak," meaning "peninsula" and "great lands." Admitted to the Union as the 49th state in 1959, it is also the largest state, nearly one fifth the size of the rest of the United States.

Lillian Eichler, *The Customs of Mankind* (Garden City, NY: Garden City Publishing, 1924), 679-81. William H. Harris and Judith S. Levey, eds., *The New Columbia Encyclopedia* (New York: Columbia University Press, 1975). *Pittsburgh Press* 24 February 1974.

What is the origin of the name for the state of Arkansas?

The origin of the name Arkansas is somewhat uncertain. Most state names find their origins in the loose translations of Native North American words and some of the various spellings for this state name include names like "Alkansia," "Alkansas," and "Akamsea." Some authorities have said the name is of Algonquin origin and its meaning is unknown. Still others say that Arkansas is the French interpretation of the word "Kansas," a Sioux Indian name that translates as "south wind people." Arkansas is the 25th state of the Union, admitted in 1836.

Lillian Eichler, *The Customs of Mankind* (Garden City, NY: Garden City Publishing, 1924), 679-81. William H. Harris and Judith S. Levey, eds., *The New Columbia Encyclopedia* (New York: Columbia University Press, 1975). *Pittsburgh Press* 24 February 1974.

What is the origin of the name for the state of Indiana?

The origin of the name for the state of Indiana is somewhat uncertain. Some claim that it was named for the Native North American tribes who had settled in the Western Pennsylvania region of the country. Others say that territory was named so because the land, bordering the Ohio River, was purchased from the "Indians"—hence the name, "Indiana."

Lillian Eichler, *The Customs of Mankind* (Garden City, NY: Garden City Publishing, 1924), 679-81. William H. Harris and Judith S. Levey, eds., *The New Columbia Encyclopedia* (New York: Columbia University Press, 1975). *Pittsburgh Press* 24 February 1974.

What is the origin of the name for the state of Kansas?

The state of Kansas was named for one of the tribes of the Sioux Indian family that lived in the region along a river and gave it their tribal name "Kanza" or "Kansas," which means "south wind people" or "wind people." Kansas was admitted as the 34th state of the Union in 1861.

Lillian Eichler, *The Customs of Mankind* (Garden City, NY: Garden City Publishing, 1924), 679-81. William H. Harris and Judith S. Levey, eds., *The New Columbia Encyclopedia* (New York: Columbia University Press, 1975). *Pittsburgh Press* 24 February 1974.

What is the origin of the name for the state of Louisiana?

The name Louisiana was first used by the French explorer Ren Robert Cavelier de La Salle. In 1862 on an expedition down the Mississippi, La Salle, upon reaching the Gulf of Mexico, claimed all the lands drained by the river and its tributaries for France and named the region Louisiana in honor of King Louis XIV. Louisiana is the 18th state of the Union, admitted in 1812.

Lillian Eichler, *The Customs of Mankind* (Garden City, NY: Garden City Publishing, 1924), 679-81. William H. Harris and Judith S. Levey, eds., *The New Columbia Encyclopedia* (New York: Columbia University Press, 1975). *Pittsburgh Press* 24 February 1974.

What is the origin of the name for the state of Maryland?

The state of Maryland, one of the original Thirteen Colonies, was named so in honor of Queen Henrietta Maria, wife of Charles I, of England. The king granted by charter the territory that would become Maryland to George Calvert, 1st Baron Baltimore, in 1632.

Lillian Eichler, *The Customs of Mankind* (Garden City, NY: Garden City Publishing, 1924), 679-81. William H. Harris and Judith S. Levey, eds., *The New Columbia Encyclopedia* (New York: Columbia University Press, 1975). *Pittsburgh Press* 24 February 1974.

What are the options in federally subsidized rental housing for the poor elderly?

Among federally subsidized rental options available to poor elderly persons are:

Low-rent public housing for low-income elderly persons

Section 8 certificates and vouchers (federal subsidies provided to income-eligible households for use on the private market to help defray their housing costs)

Section 202 Housing for the Elderly, for elderly renters and handicapped persons

Elderly Americans: Health, Housing, and Nutrition Gaps Between the Poor and Nonpoor (Washington, DC: U.S. General Accounting Office, 1992), 30-32.

How many workers currently pay into Social Security for each person receiving benefits?

Statistics reveal that the number of workers paying into Social Security for each person getting benefits continues to dwindle. In 1970, there were approximately 3.7 payers for each recipient. By 1980, that number was down to 3.2, recovering slightly by

1990 to 3.4. The U.S. Social Security Administration projects, however, that in the year 2000, there will once again be 3.2 payers per recipient, and the ratio will be 2.9 in 2010, 2.4 in 2020, 2.0 in 2030, and 2.0 in 2040.

"Entitlements for the Retired Take Ever More Money," *New York Times* 30 August 1992.

Who was the first woman ambassador for the United States?

The first woman ambassador for the United States was Ruth Bryan Owen (later Rohde)(1885-1954). In April of 1933 U.S. President Franklin D. Roosevelt (1882-1945) appointed her as Envoy Extraordinary and Minister Plenipotentiary to Denmark.

Current Biography: Who's News and Why 1994 (New York: H. W. Wilson, 1994), s.v. "Owen, Ruth Bryan."

When was the law establishing Social Security signed?

The United States initiated the first national pension system when the Social Security Act was signed on August 14, 1935. At first it covered only retired private sector employees, but was changed in 1939 to cover survivors of deceased workers and to cover certain dependents of a retired worker. In the 1950s, coverage was extended to include most self-employed persons, most state and local employees, household and farm employees, and members of the armed forces and clergy. Upon retirement, most Americans receive Social Security benefits. The purpose of Social Security is to provide a portion of a person's earnings that are lost due to disability, old age, or death. In 1954, disability insurance was added to protect workers against loss of income due to total disability. The Social Security program was expanded once again in 1965 with the enactment of Medicare, which assured hospital and medical insurance protection to persons 65 years of age and over.

Jay M. Shafritz, *The HarperCollins Dictionary of American Government and Politics* (New York: HarperCollins, 1992), s.v. "social security." *Shepard's Acts and Cases by Popular Name, Federal and State, 4th ed.* (Colorado: Shepards/McGraw-Hill, 1992), s.v. "social security act."

How many African Americans have served in the U.S. Congress?

From 1870 to 1993, 86 African Americans had served in Congress; 4 in the U.S. Senate and 82 in the U.S. House of Representatives. Thirty-eight of the 86 were in office in January of 1993.

Congress A to Z: A Ready Reference Encyclopedia, 2d ed. (Washington, DC: Congressional Quarterly, 1993), 459-60.

Which session of the U.S. Congress holds the record for the most recorded votes?

The second session of the 95th Congress, which met in 1978, holds the record for the most recorded votes in a session with 1,350 total votes, one more than the previous record set in 1976.

95th Congress, 2nd Session, 1978, *Congressional Quarterly Almanac* (Washington, DC: Congressional Quarterly, 1979), 9. 103rd Congress, 1st Session, 1993, *Congressional Quarterly Almanac* (Washington, DC: Congressional Quarterly, 1994), 8. *How Congress Works, 2d ed.* (Washington, DC: Congressional Quarterly, 1991), 148.

Servicemen from which wars are buried at the Tomb of the Unknown Soldier?

On March 4, 1921, the U.S. Congress approved both the construction of the Tomb of the Unknown Soldier in Arlington National Cemetery and the return of an unknown American serviceman killed in France during World War I (1914-1918). At the ceremony consecrating the memorial site and burial of the U.S. World War I serviceman on November 11 of that year, President Warren G. Harding (1865-1923) presented the Medal of Honor and delivered a eulogy. The tomb was completed in 1932 and dedicated on Veteran's Day of that year.

On June 24, 1946, Congress approved the designation of an Unknown Soldier for World War II (1939-1945) and set May 30, 1951, as the date for burial. When the Korean War (1950-1953) broke out in November of 1950, U.S. president Harry S. Truman (1884-1972) postponed the interment, which finally took place on May 30, 1958, when servicemen from both World War II and the Korean War were buried. President Dwight D. Eisenhower (1890-1969) awarded each the Medal of Honor.

On June 18, 1973, Congress directed the remains of an Unknown American representing the servicemen and women who died during the Vietnam Conflict (1961-1975) be interred in the Memorial. The burial took place on Memorial Day of 1984 (May 28), with U.S. president Ronald Reagan (1911-) awarding the Medal of Honor.

The tomb carries the inscription: "Here rests in honored glory an American soldier known but to God." The reason behind the great amount of time between the end of the wars and the ceremonies is the arduous process of identifying as many of the remains as possible. Identification of the remains of soldiers from Vietnam continues although the ceremony has already been held.

Encyclopedia Americana, intern. ed. (Danbury, CT: Grolier, 1992), s.v. "Unknown Soldier, tomb of the." William M. Hammond, *The Unknown Serviceman of the Vietnam Era* (Washington, D.C.: Government Printing Office, 1985), iii, 3-4.

What were the capitals of the original thirteen colonies?

The capitals of the original thirteen colonies were as follows:

Connecticut—Hartford and New Haven
Delaware—Dover
Georgia—Savannah
Maryland—Annapolis
Massachusetts—Boston
New Hampshire—Exeter
New Jersey—Burlington
New York—Kingston
Pennsylvania—Philadelphia
Rhode Island—Newport and Providence
North Carolina—New Bern
South Carolina—Charles Town
Virginia—Williamsburg

The New Encyclopaedia Britannica (Chicago: Encyclopaedia Britannica, 1993), s.v. "Kingston." *Encyclopedia Americana, intern. ed.* (Danbury, CT: Grolier, 1994), s.v. "Charleston." *Webster's New Geographical Dictionary* (Springfield, MA: Merriam-Webster, 1988), s.v. "Annapolis," "Boston," "Burlington," "Dover," "Exeter," "Hartford," "New Bern," "New Haven," "New Port," "Philadelphia," "Savannah," "Williamsburg."

Which U.S. cities are considered independent, that is, not part of a county?

The independent cities within the United States that are not part of a county are Baltimore, Maryland; St. Louis, Missouri; Carson City, Nevada; and the following cities in Virginia: Alexandria, Bedford, Bristol, Buena Vista, Charlottesville, Chesapeake, Clifton Forge, Colonial Heights, Covington, Danville, Emporia, Fairfax, Falls Church, Franklin, Fredericksburg, Galax, Hampton, Harrisonburg, Hopewell, Lexington, Lynchburg, Manassas, Manassas Park, Martinsville, Newport News, Norfolk, Norton, Petersburg, Poquoson, Portsmouth, Radford, Richmond, Roanoke, Salem, South Boston, Staunton, Suffolk, Virginia Beach, Waynesboro, Williamsburg, and Winchester.

Randata City Index: The Reliable Source to U.S. Places of Over 100 People (Chicago: Rand McNally, 1988), 121, 149, 162, 269-70.

How are social security numbers determined?

Before 1973, the first three digits of a U.S. social security number simply established that the social security card had been issued by one of the Social Security offices in a particular state. Now an area code is also factored into the first set of three numbers indicating the state or territory the applicant is residing currently. For example, social security cards issued in Michigan can begin with the numbers 362 through 386. The second group of two numbers relates to the year the card was issued, but these numbers are not necessarily the same digits as those used in that year (for example, 95 may not indicate 1995). These middle numbers begin with 01 and proceed in a set pattern from there, so if a particular three-digit number is being used for the first time, the two-digit number would be 01. The third part of a social security number consists of four random digits.

Mary Blocksma, *Reading the Numbers* (New York: Viking Penguin, 1989), 162-64.

Which states do not have income or sales taxes?

Seven states do not have an income tax. They are Alaska, Florida, Nevada, South Dakota, Texas, Washington, and Wyoming. There are five states that do not have a state sales tax. They are Alaska, Delaware, Montana, New Hampshire, and Oregon.

Information Please Almanac Atlas and Yearbook 1995, 48th. ed. (Boston: Houghton Mifflin, 1994), 79. *The World Almanac and Book of Facts 1995* (Mahwah, NJ: Funk & Wagnalls, 1994), 148.

What is the history of the U.S. silver dollar?

U.S. silver dollars were first produced in 1794. They were designed by Robert Scot and had a composition of .8924 silver and .1076 copper. There were slight modifications in design from 1794 to 1803, and then the production of silver dollars was suspended. Although a design was ready for 1804 dollars, they were not produced until the 1830s and again in 1859 for proof sets but carried the 1804 date. Only 15 of these dollars still exist. A 1836 dollar designed by Christian Gobrecht was tested on the public, but full-scale production of silver dollars was not resumed until 1840. In 1866 the words "In God We Trust" were added. Production ceased once again in 1873. Pressure to create a heavier and larger silver dollar to be used in American commerce with Japan in order to compete with European crowns of this size resulted in the design of the "Trade Dollar." It was the heaviest U.S. silver dollar made and was composed of nine parts silver to one part copper. Trade dollars were produced until 1885 and had limited use in the United States. They were designed by William Barber and carried the words "Trade Dollar" on the coin. Demands by the U.S. public for the regular silver dollar caused resumption of production in 1878. The Liberty Head or Morgan dollars, named after designer George T. Morgan, were nine parts silver to one part copper. They were produced from 1878 to 1904, when a shortage of silver halted production until 1921, when over 80 million Morgan coins were made in that one year. A silver dollar commemorating world peace was designed by Anthony DeFrancisci, carried the word "Peace," and was produced from 1921 to 1935. This was the last true silver dollar (90 percent silver and 10 percent copper), as the following issues had a different metallic composition.

Marc Hudgeons, *Official 1995 Blackbook Price Guide of United States Coins, 33rd ed.* (New York: House of Collectibles, 1994), 226-35.

Who was the first black cabinet member in the United States?

Robert Clifton Weaver was the first African-American to serve as a cabinet member. He was appointed as Secretary of Housing and Urban Development (HUD) by U.S. President Lyndon Johnson in 1966. Before this Weaver had served in the U.S. Department of Interior under U.S. President Franklin Roosevelt and was the first African-American to head a major government agency when named administrator of the Housing and Home Finance Agency in 1961.

Jessie Carney Smith, ed., *Black Firsts: 2,000 Years of Extraordinary Achievement* (Detroit: Gale Research, 1994), 158. Joan Potter, *African-American Firsts* (Elizabethtown, NY: Pinto Press, 1994), 116. Shirelle Phelps, ed., *Who's Who Among Black Americans 1994/95, 8th ed.* (Detroit: Gale Research, 1994), s.v. "Weaver, Robert C."

What are the highest ranks in the U.S. military?

"General" is a senior officer rank that is used in most countries for the highest land officers. In the United States there are five grades. Brigadier general, the lowest level, is denoted by one star and commands a brigade. A major general has two stars and usually commands a division or a corps. A lieutenant general is denoted by three stars and usually commands a corps or an army. A general is denoted by four stars and usually commands an army or an army group. In many European countries, the rank of field marshall was created as an officer senior to the four star general. General of the Army is the equivalent in the United States, and during World War II (1939-1945), five star general rank was created so that the United States officers would be on equal footing. The only persons to hold this rank have been Dwight D. Eisenhower, Douglas MacArthur, and George C. Marshall, on whom the titles were conferred in 1944, and Omar Bradley, in 1950. The title General of the Armies had been posthumously created for George Washington and John J. Pershing for his command of United States troops in World War I (1914-1918).

The titles of General of the Air Force and Fleet Admiral are equivalent to the five star general. William Leahy, Ernest King, Chester Nimitz in 1944 and William "Bull" Halsey in 1945 won their fifth stars. In 1944, Henry "Hap" Arnold who led the Army Air Forces was the first and only air force officer to win five stars.

John R. Elting, Dan Cragg, and Ernest L. Deal, *A Dictionary of Soldier Talk* (New York: Charles Scribner's Sons, 1984), s.v. "General of the Army." *The Encyclopedia Americana, intern. ed.* (Danbury, CT: Grolier, 1994), s.v. "general." Robert McHenry, *The New Encyclopaedia Britannica, 15th ed.* (Chicago: Encyclopaedia Britannica, 1993), s.v. "general."

Can someone continue to work past age 65 and still collect Social Security?

Social Security benefits are intended to replace part of the income that U.S. workers and their families were receiving before the worker's retirement, disability, or death. Because Social Security covers only part of the earnings, persons often work after retirement. There are set limits as to how much someone can earn and also receive benefits unless they are 70 years old or older. The limit is determined by whether the beneficiary is under age 65 or 65 through 69. The limit varies from year to year in accordance with increases in the level of nationwide earnings. For example, in 1985 someone under the age of 65 receiving benefits was limited to $5,400 in earnings while someone from age 65 through 69 was limited to $7,320. In 1994 the limits were $8,040 for those under age 65 and $11,160 for those 65 through 69. If someone earns over these limits, then benefits are reduced. For someone from age 65 through 69, $1 would be deducted from the benefits for every $3 earned above the limit. For someone under age 65, the deduction would be $1 in benefits for every $2 in earnings above the limit.

U.S. Department of Health and Human Services, Social Security Administration, *How Work Affects Your Social Security Benefits: A Factsheet from Social Security* (Washington, D.C.: Government Printing Office, 1994). U.S. Department of Health and Human Services, Social Security Administration, *Social Security Handbook 1993, 11th ed.* (Washington, D.C.: Government Printing Office, 1993), 291.

What were some of the important events in the Persian Gulf War of 1990-91?

On August 2, 1990, Iraq invaded Kuwait, and the United Nations Security Council demanded it withdraw all troops, imposing sanctions and an embargo four days later. The first United States troops (40,000) arrived on August 6; it was the first wave of an American force that would eventually reach 430,000. On November 29, 1990, the United Nations Security Council authorized all necessary means to liberate Kuwait, and on January 16, 1991, coalition forces began an air campaign (Operation Desert Storm) against Iraqi targets. In all there would be over 106,000 missions over Iraq and Kuwait, which effectively broke Iraq's ability to make war. On February 24, 1991, coalition forces, which then numbered over 680,000, began an mechanized infantry attack (Operation Desert Sabre) on the estimated 545,000 Iraqi troops in Kuwait and southern Iraq. Coalition forces met little opposition from retreating Iraqi troops, and liberated Kuwait City on February 27. The next day Iraq agreed to conditions of the United Nations for a temporary cease-fire, and formal hostilities were suspended. A permanent cease-fire was made effective on April 11, 1991, after Iraq agreed to the terms of a United Nations resolution for a permanent peace.

Dilip Hiro, *Desert Shield to Desert Storm* (New York: Routledge, 1992), 500-520.

When did airmail service begin in the United States?

In 1911 Postmaster General Frank H. Hitchcock hired Earl Ovington to carry the mail by air from Garden City, New York to Mineola, New York during the International Aviation Tournament. In this demonstration Ovington did not land but simply dropped the mail to the ground for the postmaster. The first regular United States mail flight began the next year, on April 10, 1912, when pilot George Mestach transported the mail from New Orleans to Baton Rouge, Louisiana. In 1918 the Post Office Department received $100,000.00 in congressional funding to join with the War Department and use Army Signal Corp pilots to fly the mail. The new service began on May 15, and was a success, improving delivery time from Washington to New York by two to three hours. On October 12, 1918, the Post Office created its own service, purchasing six especially designed mail planes and hiring pilots. Transcontinental service started the next year; the journey from New York to San Francisco was divided into four legs with stops in Cleveland, Chicago, and Omaha. The first transcontinental flights took place on February 22-23, 1921, during which the planes touched down only for refueling. The trip involved four planes, two of which left from each coast. The journey took just over 33 hours, much faster than the 72 hour train service. Although there was a steady improvement in airfields and equipment, in 1925 Congress passed legislation that encouraged commercial airlines to carry the mail, and the response was so great that by 1927 there was no need for a separate postal air force. But the limited space on planes and the few number of flights initially made airmail service more expensive than regular first-class service. By the mid-1950s, however, commercial aviation had expanded so that regular first-class mail began to travel by air whenever space was available. By 1977 airmail became so common that the post office eliminated the additional charge for the service.

Cheryl Weant McAfee, *The United States Postal Service* (New York: Chelsea House Publishers, 1987), 45-49.

Who was the first African-American to appear on a postage stamp?

In 1940 Booker T. Washington (1856-1915) became the first African American to be commemorated on a postage stamp. The ten-cent stamp was first placed on sale at Tuskegee Institute, a vocational school for blacks that Washington founded.

Joan Potter, *African-American Firsts* (Elizabethtown, NY: Pinto Press, 1994), 27.

Why was the Magna Carta important?

The Magna Carta (Magna Charta) or Great Charter was a list of personal and political freedoms demanded from the crown by English barons in the thirteenth century. The document was unwillingly granted by King John (1167-1216) on June 15, 1215, at Runnymede, a meadow in Surrey County, England. The articles included a "free" English church, limitation on taxes, freedom of trade and travel, and the king's assurance of what today is called "due process of law." The English Magna Carta has become the model for many statements of basic rights throughout the world and is the foundation of modern constitutional government.

George C. Kohn, *Dictionary of Historic Documents* (New York: Facts on File, 1991), 202.

Is it required to pay income tax on employer-paid life insurance premiums?

Group-term life insurance premiums paid by an employer are not taxable for coverage up to $50,000. Premiums for coverage exceeding $50,000 are taxable at rates determined by the U.S. Internal Revenue Service. Consult a tax advisor for full information.

J.K. Lasser Institute, *J. K. Lasser's Your Income Tax 1994* (New York: Prentice Hall General Reference, 1993), 31.

What is the Stewart B. McKinney Homeless Assistance Act?

The Stewart B. McKinney Homeless Assistance Act is designed to champion educational opportunities for homeless children. Signed into U.S. law on July 22, 1987, the Act entitles homeless children to free public school education and prohibits communities from using residency requirements to deny homeless children access to public education.

The act provides limited funding for special educational programs to address the concerns of homeless children. The Act is the first of its kind to establish national guidelines for the education of homeless children.

Mary Ellen Hombs, *American Homelessness: A Reference Handbook* (Santa Barbara: ABC-CLIO, 1990), 47.

What were the first coins struck in England's New World colonies?

Because England was ambivalent about providing gold or silver coins to the colonists, there were no single coins in use by the colonists. At first they used any European coins in circulation. The first coins to be struck for the English colonies in America were issued about 1616 on the Sommer Islands in Bermuda and were commonly known by the colonists as "Hogge Money" or "Hoggies." They were lightly silvered copper coins in denominations of a shilling, sixpence, threepence, and twopence. The coins received their nickname because a hog appeared on the obverse side of each coin.

The first coins minted on the North American mainland by Englishmen were those of John Hull in the Massachusetts Bay Colony by authorization from the General Court of the colony. In 1652 shillings (such as the famous N.E. pine tree) were struck at the Boston mint. In addition a wide variety of coins in North American colonies circulated and were often commissioned by individuals, such as Lord Baltimore's series of silver pieces struck in London around 1658. Mark Newby introduced the St. Patrick's halfpence into the province of New Jersey in 1682, while the Rosa Americana and Hibernia coppers struck in London by William Woods circulated in the colonies in the early 1720s. In the late 1690s New England Elephant tokens became a popular medium of exchange.

R.S. Yeoman, *A Guide Book of United States Coins, 47th rev. ed.* (Racine, WI: Western Publishing, 1993), 7-8. R.S. Yeoman, *1994 Handbook of United States Coins, 51st ed.* (Racine, WI: Western Publishing, 1993), 13.

Law

What was importance of the *Brown v. Board of Education* case?

In 1954, the U.S. Supreme Court ruled in *Brown v. Board of Education* that U.S. public schools could not deny admission to students on the basis of race. The Court's decision in *Brown v. Board of Education* struck down as unconstitutional the 1896 case of *Plessy vs. Ferguson,* which allowed the creation of "separate but equal" schools.

Jay M. Shafritz, Richard P. Koeppe, and Elizabeth W. Soper, *The Facts on File Dictionary of Education,* (New York: Facts on File, 1988), 71.

Has there been an increase in the number of lawsuits filed in recent years?

Although it seems that the number of frivolous lawsuits is increasing daily, statistics show that this is not the case. The number of tort cases, those general lawsuits that exclude contract disputes, actually dropped in 1992. According to Marc Galanter, a professor at the University of Wisconsin Law School, "One of the things that has happened in recent years is that lawsuits have become a lot more expensive, so that's probably screened out a lot of these (frivolous) cases."

Pittsburgh Post-Gazette 11 June 1994.

What is the difference between Chapter 7, Chapter 11, and Chapter 13 bankruptcies?

A Chapter 7 bankruptcy is a liquidation proceeding in which the nonexempt assets owned by the debtor at the time the bankruptcy petition is filed are collected and sold. The proceeds are distributed to the creditors and the debtor is usually discharged from liability for prebankruptcy debts excluding debts such as tax obligations or alimony and child support obligations.

Chapter 11 and Chapter 13 bankruptcies are rehabilitation proceedings in which a debtor is permitted to keep assets while making payments to creditors following a plan approved by the bankruptcy court.

The Guide to American Law, (St. Paul, MN: West Publishing Co., 1983), 2:30.

How much alcohol must be in the blood before a person is considered to be driving under the influence of alcohol (DUI)?

Most states use a 0.10-percent blood alcohol baseline to determine whether a person is driving under the influence of alcohol (DUI). But in six states—California, Maine, Oregon, Utah, Vermont, and Virginia—the percentage is 0.08.

David Savageau and Richard Boyer, *Places Rated Almanac: Your Guide to Finding the Best Places to Live In North America* (New York: Prentice Hall Travel, 1993), 228.

What is the Code of Hammurabi?

King Hammurabi of Babylonia developed and promulgated a collection of laws circa 1700 B.C. that became known as the Code of Hammurabi. The 3,600 lines of Akkadian cuneiform were carved on a diorite stele or slab below the carved portrait of Hammurabi with the introduction: "Before this portrait let every man who has a legal dispute come forward, read the text, and heed its precious words." The laws were based on Hammurabi's decisions in regard to civil, commercial, criminal, familial, and other matters. For the most part they were humanitarian. The stele was stolen from Babylon's temple of Marduk by a conquering Elamite king about 1000 B.C. After being discovered in 1901 by Frenchmen at Susa, a ruined city in Western Iran, the stele was deposited in the Louvre Museum in Paris, France.

George C. Kohn, *Dictionary of Historic Documents* (New York: Facts on File, 1991) s.v. "Hammurabi, Code of."

What was the Treaty of Guadalupe-Hidalgo?

The Treaty of Guadalupe-Hidalgo was signed on February 2, 1848, at Guadalupe-Hidalgo, Mexico. It ended boundary and annexation disputes that had plagued relations between the United States and Mexico, resulting in the 1846-1848 war. Terms of the treaty required Mexico to relinquish California,

Nevada, Arizona, New Mexico, and Utah. Mexico was also required by the treaty to recognize Texas as U.S. territory as far south as the Rio Grande. U.S. troops were withdrawn from Mexican soil, and the United States paid an indemnity of $15 million for Mexico's ceded territory. Mexico lost approximately one half of her territory by terms of the treaty. The United States agreed to assume claims made by U.S. citizens against Mexico totaling $3.25 million. The territory acquired by the United States from this treaty came to be known as the "Mexican Cession."

George C. Kohn, *Dictionary of Historic Documents* (New York: Facts on File, 1991), s.v. "Gradalupe-Hidalgo, Treaty of."

If a person dies without a will, who gains custody of that person's children?

If a person dies without a will, the surviving biological parent has priority rights regarding guardianship. If both parents die at the same time or the surviving biological parent does not want to retain guardianship rights, the court chooses a suitable guardian for the surviving children. If a suitable guardian is not available, the children may be cared for by a government agency.

Patricia Anderson, *Affairs in Order: A Complete Resource Guide to Death and Dying* (New York: Macmillan, 1991), 6.

What points do people often forget when writing their will?

Writing a will can often be a complicated process. Sometimes, people forget to consider certain points, such as: allocation of death taxes among beneficiaries; consideration of all insurance arrangements; provision to establish legally who died first should both spouses die at the same time; confirmation that the will takes full advantage of the marital deduction, which allows a tax exemption of up to the full amount of the gross estate; safe guards to ensure minimum double taxation of the estate upon the death of each spouse; and determination of whether the executor of the estate will have the power to run or dispose of any business assets.

The Book of Inside Information (New York: Boardroom Classics, 1991), 147.

What is probate?

The word "probate" comes from a Latin root meaning "to prove" and refers to the process of proving or accepting as approved, the will of a dead person. The probate process offers a forum that allows the federal government an opportunity to collect its taxes and to ensure that a deceased person's estate is properly administered.

Patricia Anderson, *Affairs in Order: A Complete Resource Guide to Death and Dying* (New York: Macmillan Publishing Co., 1991), 14.

What did the Adamson Act involve?

In 1916, the U.S. Congress passed a law that imposed an eight-hour work day for railroad employees. This was done to divert a possible major railroad strike. A commission was also set up to look at railroad employment problems. U.S. president Woodrow Wilson urged Congress to pass the bill after talks had failed with railroad management representatives, who did not want to reduce the working hours.

Howard L. Hurwitz, *An Encyclopedic Dictionary of American History* (New York: Washington Square Press, 1968). s.v "Adamson Act."

What do the English call a lawyer who has the right to argue cases in higher courts?

The term "barrister" refers to lawyers in Great Britain who have the right to argue cases in higher courts of law. A barrister who represents the king is called a "king's counsel." Other terms for lawyer include attorney, solicitor, or counselor.

World Book Encyclopedia (Chicago: World Book, 1987), s.v. "lawyer."

What are the copyright laws regarding titles of books?

Titles of books are not covered by copyright laws. Only the actual text is protected under the U.S. Copyright Act of 1978, for the span of the author's life plus fifty years.

Parade 15 January 1989.

What is a bright-line rule?

A bright-line rule is a simple, straightforward ruling from a court of law that simply ignores any ambiguities of the case.

Bryan A. Garner, *A Dictionary of Modern Legal Usage* (New York: Oxford University Press, New York, 1987), s.v. "bright-line rule."

What is a contingent fee?

A contingent fee is an agreement between an attorney and his client where the attorney will only receive compensation if the settlement is worthy of division.

Edward J. Bander, *Dictionary of Selected Legal Terms and Maxims* (Dobbs Ferry, NY: Oceana Publications, 1979), s.v. "contingent fee."

Is a cross or an "X" ever a substitute for a signature on a legal document?

If a person is unable to write, a cross or an "X" may be substituted for a signature on a legal document, although it should be properly attested.

William Edward Baldwin, ed., *Bouvier's Law Dictionary: Baldwin's Students Edition* (Cleveland: Banks-Baldwin Law Publishing Company, 1934), 757.

When is it worthwhile to take a dispute to small claims court?

It is often worthwhile to file a claim in small claims court for the following types of disputes:

Problems with poorly done repairs such as auto, appliance, or home repairs
Damage to property such as a dented fender by a parking lot attendant
Rent, lease, and security deposit disputes
Loss of wages because of failure to conclude a service call or delivery
Damage due to negligence of the defendant
Failure to collect a debt of limited size

To take a dispute to small claims court it must be able to be settled by a monetary award and the amount of the award must not exceed the legal limit of the small claims court. Before taking a dispute to small claims court you should first determine who to sue, where to sue, what to sue for, how much to sue for, and when to sue.

Don Biggs, *How To Avoid Lawyers* (New York: Garland Publishing, 1985), 138.

What does the phrase "fair use" mean as it relates to copyright?

The phrase "fair use" refers to the limited use of copyrighted material without the permission of the owner of the copyright. Fair use of copyrighted material is only legal under specifically defined circumstances, and experts warn that there is a fine line between fair use and copyright infringement. If the user does not fully understand the fair use doctrine or has any questions, he or she is strongly advised to contact either the owner of the copyright or a copyright attorney.

Robert B. Chickering and Susan Hartman, *How to Register a Copyright and Protect Your Creative Work* (New York: Charles Scribner's Sons, 1980), 174.

What are the grounds for an annulment of a marriage?

The grounds for annulment of marriage vary from state to state. An annulment differs from a divorce in that a divorce deals with problems occurring after the union has begun; an annulment invalidates the marriage altogether because it was entered into improperly. The most common reasons for annulments are that one of the parties was either underage, still married to someone else, coerced by the other into the marriage, or was incapable of making a sound judgment due to drug or alcohol abuse. An inability to consummate the union is also a valid reason for dissolution in most states.

Richard A. Leiter, ed., *National Survey of State Laws* (Detroit: Gale Research, 1993), 219.

What are the penalties for drunk-driving in each state?

Penalties for operating a vehicle while under the influence of alcohol vary from state to state, but most call for suspension of the driver's license upon conviction for the first offense. The length of the initial suspension, however, varies greatly among states. The legal level of intoxication-measured by the blood alcohol content-may also be determined by the individual state, but most have set it at 0 .10 percent. Upon the third drunk-driving offense, a court may revoke the license; in Michigan this can be done upon conviction for a second offense. Almost all states now order such offenders to attend some sort of alcohol-rehabilitation program.

Richard A. Leiter, *National Survey of State Laws* (Detroit: Gale Research, 1993). 81.

What court case declared unconstitutional the states requiring students to salute the flag?

In the 1943 court case, *West Virginia State Board of Education v. Barnette* the U.S. Supreme Court of the United States declared that the states could not require students to salute the flag because it was an abridgement of their first amendment rights.

William Rae Furlong, *So Proudly We Hail: The History of the United States Flag* (Washington, DC: Smithsonian Institution Press, 1981), 216.

What should the constitution and bylaws of a new organization contain?

The constitution and bylaws of a new organization should follow a standard blueprint that delineates several items. The constitution should spell out its name, purpose, membership requirements, its high-level offices and method of election to them, provisions for an executive committee, required number of meetings each year, and the manner by which the constitution is to be amended. The by-laws of a new organization should further delineate its members' rights and responsibilities as well as those of the officers and executive committee. It should make provisions for a standing committee, address frequency of regular meetings, define the quorum needed for a meeting and the method of notification for regular and special meetings, spell out all election matters (time of year, method of nomination, and type of installation), indicate the cycle of the organization's fiscal year, standing rules and special rules, the member or officer who will be in charge of parliamentary procedure, and the method by which the by-laws can be amended.

Marjorie Mitchell Cann, *Cann's Keys to Better Meetings: Parliamentary Procedure Simplified* (Mobile, AL: HB Publications, 1990), 12.

Can an idea be copyrighted?

Copyright protection only extends to the expression of an idea, and not the idea itself. A copyright protects against plagiarism, paraphrasing, and abridgment; it does not protect the actual idea, methods, or facts in the work.

Robert A. Gorman, *Copyright Law* (Washington, DC: Federal Judicial Center, 1991), 15-17.

What was the significance of the 1978 U.S. Supreme Court decision in *Regents of University of California* v. *Bakke*?

In the 1978 U.S. Supreme Court decision *Regents of University of California* v. *Bakke*, the Court ruled that Allan P. Bakke's constitutional rights were violated by his not being admitted to medical school on the basis of his Caucasian race. The Court also ruled that race may be used under certain circumstances as an entrance criteria to educational institutions seeking ethnic balance and diversity. Bakke applied to the University of California Medical School in 1973 and 1974. He was denied admission while minority applicants with lower qualifications were enrolled. Bakke sued claiming his rights under the Equal Protection Clause of the Fourteenth Amendment were violated. The case wound its way through various courts finally reaching the Supreme Court after a lower court agreed with Bakke. The Supreme Court upheld the lower court saying Bakke should have been admitted but the Court's decision still allowed for racial preferences as opposed to the suddenly suspect racial quotas in pursuit of a more integrated society.

The Guide to American Law: Everyone's Legal Encyclopedia (New York: West Publishing, 1983), 2:17-21.

Who was the second woman to join the U.S. Supreme Court?

Ruth Bader Ginsburg became the second woman to sit on the bench of the high court, as well as the 107th Supreme Court Justice on August 3, 1993. The first woman justice was Sandra Day O'Connor. Ginsburg was confirmed by a Senate vote of 96-3, replacing Justice Byron R. White, upon his retirement. Appointed by U.S. president Bill Clinton, she was the first Democratic nominee to be confirmed since Thurgood Marshall was nominated by U.S. president Lyndon B. Johnson. The U.S. Senate vote reflected her appeal as a jurist with moderate views. She received criticism from only one member of the Senate, North Carolina senator Jesse Helms who condemned her support of abortion rights and homosexuality.

Facts on File 1993.

How are U.S. Federal Court juries selected?

Title 28 of the United States Code, specifying judiciary and judicial procedure, includes instruction on the "selection and summoning of jury panels." Section 1866 outlines the procedures for the following seven points:

Maintenance of a jury wheel and the random selection of persons for assignment to juries

How to summon persons drawn for a jury

Circumstances under which a juror may be excused or disqualified, including instruction on reinserting their name into the jury wheel

Maintaining records regarding the reasons why a juror is excluded from service

The time limit which a juror may be required to serve

The course of action to be taken if there is shortage of available jurors

The penalty for not responding to the court's summons

Office of the Law Revision Counsel of the House of Representatives, *United States Code, 1988 ed.* (Washington, DC: Government Printing Office, 1989), 12:372.

Why is a jury composed of 12 jurors?

In fourteenth century England impaneling people to weigh evidence was coming into practice. By the seventeenth century jurors were called upon to be judges of fact. However, the reason for limiting the jury to 12 remains a mystery. After all Socrates (ca. 700-399 B.C.), the great ancient Greek philosopher, had 501 Athenian freemen judging him guilty for corrupting the city state's youth and for denying honor to the city-state's gods in 399 B.C. Speculation by one author suggests the Anglo-Saxon dislike of the decimal system led to the number of jurors being set at 12.

Jane Polley, ed., *Stories Behind Everyday Things* (Pleasantville, NY: Reader's Digest Association, 1980), s.v. "jury."

How can one contact the local bankruptcy court?

In the United States, bankruptcy courts are under federal jurisdiction rather than city, county, or state law. When looking for addresses and phone numbers of federal courts in a phone book, consult the "blue pages" under "Government Offices-United States."

Henry Campbell Black, *Black's Law Dictionary, 6th ed.* (St. Paul, MN: West Publishing, 1990), s.v. "bankrupt," " bankruptcy courts."

What are "sunshine laws" in the United States?

"Sunshine laws" require that the meetings of governmental agencies and departments and the records of those meetings be open to the public. The term comes from the idea that agencies are required to do their work in public, and as a result, the process is sometimes called "government in the sunshine."

Black's Law Dictionary: Definitions of the Terms and Phrases of American and English Jurisprudence, Ancient and Modern, 6th ed. (St. Paul, MN: Minnesota: West Publishing Co., 1990), s.v. "sunshine law." *The Guide to American Law: Everyone's Legal Encyclopedia,* (St. Paul, MN: West Publishing Co., 1984), s.v. "sunshine laws."

What are the longest recorded filibusters in the U.S. Senate?

The U.S. Senate has long been famous for using prolonged debate and delaying tactics to block action supported by the majority of its members. The longest continuous such debate, or filibuster, lasted 74 days and took place when the Senate was debating the civil rights bill of 1964. Senator Strom Thurmond of South Carolina holds the record for the longest individual filibuster in the history of the Senate. While debating passage of an earlier civil rights bill in 1957, Thurmond spoke for 24 hours and 18 minutes.

Congress A to Z, 2d ed. (Washington, D.C.: Congressional Quarterly, 1993), s.v. "filibuster."

In jurisprudence, what is known as the "Great Writ"?

In jurisprudence, a writ of habeas corpus is also known as the "Great Writ." A writ of habeas corpus demands a judicial decision on the cause and legality of someone being held in custody by civil authorities. Habeas corpus translates as "you have the body."

Steven H. Gifis, *Law Dictionary, 2d ed.* (New York: Barron's Educational Series, Inc., 1984), s.v. "habeas corpus."

What is the loud intonation made by the marshall of the U.S. Supreme Court to open its session?

Just before the opening session of the Supreme Court the marshall of the Court, acting as a court cryer, makes the following intonation:

The Honorable, the Chief Justice and the Associate Justices of the Supreme Court of the United States. Oyez! Oyez! Oyez! All persons having business before the Honorable, the Supreme Court of the United States, are admonished to draw near and give their attention, for the Court is now sitting. God save the United States and this Honorable Court.

Robert J. Wagman, *The Supreme Court: A Citizen's Guide* (New York: Pharos Books, 1993), 18.

What disastrous fire spurred safety legislation to improve working and safety conditions in factories?

The tragic Triangle Waist Company fire, which killed 145 young women workers in New York City on March 25, 1911, spurred legislation to improve working and safety conditions in factories. The Greenwich Village shirt factory and "sweatshop," had been infamous for its oppressive working conditions and total disregard for worker safety but this tragedy occurred before it became apparent that legislation needed to be enacted.

Woody Gelman and Barbara Jackson, *Disaster Illustrated* (New York: Harmony Books, 1976), 54.

What is the Freedom of Information Act and how can it be utilized?

The Federal government, and state and local governments, generates a great deal of information concerning their operations and activities in the form of documents. The Freedom of Information Act (FOIA) asserts that citizens have the right to access any document, file or record of any government agency, although there are exceptions written into the FOIA. In general requests must be sent to the governmental agency generating the document and requests must "reasonably describe" the desired material. Most federal government agencies have an FOIA request response department. These are the people to contact for more specific information. Information may be legally be withheld if that information compromises national defense, foreign policy, or law enforcement activities; concerns internal personnel rules and practices; is specifically exempted from the FOIA by statute; concerns commercial trade secrets; invades the privacy of another person; is privileged information concerning banks, financial institutions or certain geological surveys.

Stephen G. Christianson, *100 Ways to Avoid Common Legal Pitfalls Without a Lawyer* (New York: Citadel Press, 1992), 81.

What is the copyright law governing performance of another's work?

The copyright law governing performance of another's work states that a protected work—one that has been officially copyrighted—may not be performed before a public audience without consent of its creator. A person who wishes to perform the work of another in public must first contact the holder of its copyright; to not gain permission is termed copyright infringement. In some cases a performing-arts industry group such as the American Society of Composers, Authors, and Publishers (ASCAP) may be the holder of the copyright.

Robert B. Chickering and Susan Hartman, *How to Register a Copyright and Protect Your Creative Work* (New York: Charles Scribner's Sons, 1980), 151-52.

Are there any unusual laws regarding whales?

There are three unusual state laws regarding whales. In California it is a misdemeanor to shoot at any animal from a moving vehicle or airplane, with the exception of whales. Even more oddly, the state of Ohio bans whale fishing in any of its territorial waters on Sundays. A similar but even more stringent law is also on the books in Oklahoma that prohibits whale fishing on any day of the week in its jurisdiction.

Robert Wayne Pelton, *Loony Laws* (New York: Walker & Co., 1990), 65.

What type of assets are generally considered exempt in bankruptcy cases?

Certain assets are considered exempt from seizure or forfeiture when a person files for bankruptcy. The list of specific items is determined by state law, but it almost always allows cars, clothing and other personal items, furniture, work-related tools or equipment, home equity, life insurance, public employee pensions, and any accumulated savings of government-provided benefits such as Social Security or unemployment compensation. Most of these assets do have limits, however; for instance, a person filing for bankruptcy would not be able to keep two automobiles.

Edward A. Haman, *How to File Your Own Bankruptcy (or How to Avoid It)* (Clearwater, FL: Sphinx Publishing, 1992), 220.

What is the difference between a "tort" and a "crime"?

The terms "tort" and "crime" are used to differentiate two separate types of activity or wrongdoing punishable in a court of law. A tort is an offense committed against an individual. Unintentional property damage would be an example of a tort-the property owner would be able to initiate a lawsuit for damages against the wrongdoer in a court of civil law. A crime, on the other hand, is a violation of an existing statute, or an offense against the general public or governmental entity. Prosecution for a crime is done within the criminal court system.

You and the Law (New York: Reader's Digest Association, 1984), 850.

What was the Volstead Act?

The Volstead Act of 1919, ratified on January 16, 1919, was passed as a means to enforce the Eighteenth Amendment to the U.S. Constitution. This amendment prohibited the "manufacture, sale, or transportation of intoxicating liquors, for beverage purposes. "Intoxicating beverage" was defined as any beverage containing more than one half of one percent of alcohol. The years following the passage of the Volstead Act became known as the Prohibition Era.

Otto Johnson, ed., *1995 Information Please Almanac* (Boston: Houghton Mifflin, 1994), 623. Thomas H. Johnson, *The Oxford Companion to American History* (New York: Oxford University Press, 1966), s.v. "Volstead Act."

What is common law and how does it differ from statutory law?

Common law is a body of principles and rules which derive their authority from usages and customs of tradition, and not from enactments by legislatures. Much of American common law is derived from the ancient unwritten law of England and has been instituted through judicial decisions. Statutory law is created by legislation.

Henry Campbell Black, *Black's Law Dictionary, 6th ed.* (St. Paul, MN: West Publishing, 1990), s.v. "common law," "statutory law."

What is the significance of the 1803 U.S. Supreme Court case, *Marbury v. Madison*?

The 1803 U.S. Supreme Court case, *Marbury v. Madison* is significant because it firmly established the federal judiciary as the final and supreme interpreter of the Constitution of the United States and able to invalidate those acts of the U.S. Congress that the Court found to be unconstitutional.

The Guide to American Law (St. Paul, MN: West Publishing, 1984), 7:267.

What is limited immunity?

Limited immunity is a method attorneys use to solve the problem of witnesses giving information that is self-incriminating. It is used to keep witnesses from being prosecuted at a later date as a result of their testimony.

Glen Elsasser, "Limited Immunity: Its Format and What It Can Accomplish," *Pittsburgh Press* 17 December 1986.

What is the power of attorney?

Power of attorney is the legal process by which a mentally competent adult transfers the power to perform some legal function or task to another mentally competent adult. The transfer is made by means of a written document, which can specify the duration and when and under what circumstances the transfer takes effect. Power of attorney is often useful to older adults who can have the comfort of knowing that some one is designated to look after their affairs when they are no longer capable.

Legal Counsel for the Elderly, *Legal Hotline for Older Americans* (Pittsburgh: n.d.).

What is "sedition"?

"Sedition" is a hostile or harmful activity aimed at undermining state authority. Although often a crime, sedition is not as serious of transgression as treason.

Walter J. Raymond, *International Dictionary of Politics* (Lawrenceville, VA: Brunswick Publishing, 1980), s.v. "sedition."

Is there a Juror Bill of Rights?

The American Board of Trial Advocates has put together an 11-point Juror Bill of Rights in hopes of assuring a juror's rights:
To privacy, to be free from harassment, and to choose whether or not to discuss the verdict.
To be treated with courtesy and respect as is fitting for an officer of the court and to have service to physical comfort and convenience in the jury room.
To have the trial process explained.
To have safe passage to and from the courthouse.
To be properly compensated for jury service.
To have input in court scheduling and have court schedules made available whenever possible.
To be randomly selected for jury service and not be excluded on the because of race, sex, religion, physical disability, or country of origin.
To have the law explained in plain language.
To have judges and lawyers be sensitive to and supportive of the jurors' needs that are a result of jury service.
To have the ability to communicate effectively concerns, complaints and recommendations to courthouse authorities.
To be free from exposure to billboards erected in proximity to the courthouse placed by special interest groups or actual parties to a lawsuit who are attempting to influence their verdict.

USA Today 21 December 1992.

What was the Miranda decision?

In *Miranda* v. *Arizona*, 1966, the U.S. Supreme Court ruled that before police authorities could question a custodial suspect in a crime he or she must be given certain warnings. The phrase "Miranda warnings" has since entered the popular idiom. The suspect must be told that he or she:
Has the right to remain silent.
Anything said can be held against them in a court of law.
The suspect has the right to have an attorney present during the interrogation.
If the suspect cannot afford a lawyer a public defender will be made available.

If a suspect is not given these warnings, anything said by the suspect during the interrogation cannot be admitted to court as evidence. The Court's ruling was based on the Fifth Amendment to the U.S. Constitution which protects citizens against self-incrimination. It is important to note that *Miranda* only applies to persons in police custody. If the suspect is not under arrest then the suspect is not in custody; and casual questioning or voluntary divulgence of information is not covered by the Miranda decision. Problems with the Miranda decision center around the definition of "interrogation" and the "voluntary" waiving of the right to have an attorney present.

The Guide to American Law: Everyone's Legal Encyclopedia (New York: West Publishing Company, 1984), 7:349-51.

What types of patents are available?

There are three types:
Utility patents, granted for new, useful, and nonobvious process, machine, manufactured article, composition, or an improvement in any of the above. There are three types: chemical, mechanical, and electrical.
Design patents, granted for new, original, and ornamental designs for an article of manufacture.
Plant patents, provided to anyone who has invented or discovered and asexually reproduced any distinct and new variety of plant.

Department of Commerce, Patent and Trademark Office, *General Information Concerning Patents* (Washington, DC: Department of Commerce, 1992), 3, 29.

Must all U.S. patent applications be accompanied by a drawing?

It is required by law in most cases that a drawing of the invention accompany the patent application. Composition of matter or some processes *may* be exempt, although in these cases the commissioner of Patents and Trademarks may require a drawing for a process when it is useful. The required drawing must show every feature of the invention specified in the claims, and be in a format specified by the Patent and Trademark Office. Drawings must be in black and white unless waived by the Deputy Assistant Commissioner for Patents. Color drawings are permitted for plant patents where color is a distinctive characteristic.

U.S. Department of Commerce, Patent and Trademark Office, *General Information Concerning Patents* (Washington, DC: Department of Commerce, 1992), 16, 30.

How do copyrights differ from patents and trademarks?

Copyrights are very different from patents and trademarks. A patent primarily prevents inventions, discoveries, etc., of useful processes, machines, etc., from being manufactured, used, or marketed without the permission of the patent holder. It is a grant of property rights to the inventor and heirs by the government. A trademark is a word, name, or symbol to indicate the origin or source of goods and to distinguish the products and services of one company from those of another. Copyrights protect the form of expression rather than the subject matter of the writings or artistic works. They protect the original work of authors and other creative people against copying and unauthorized public performance and recording.

Department of Commerce, Patent and Trademark Office, *General Information Concerning Patents* (Washington, DC: Department of Commerce, 1992), 2.

When and why did cigarette packages begin carrying the label warning that smoking could be a health hazard?

The Federal Cigarette Labeling and Advertising Act (PL 89-92) required that as of January 1, 1966, all cigarette packages and cartons sold in the United States, whether domestic or imports, bear the following statement: "Caution: Cigarette Smoking May Be Hazardous to Your Health." The bill was Congress's response to the conclusion of the January 11, 1964, Surgeon General's report that cigarette smoking was "a health hazard of sufficient importance in the United States to warrant appropriate remedial action." Legislation in 1970 (PL 91-222) banned all cigarette commercials on radio and television, or on any other medium of electronic communications subject to the jurisdiction of the U.S. Federal Communications Commission, effective January 2, 1971.

Congress and the Nation (Washington, DC: Congressional Quarterly Service, 1969), 2:675. *Congress and the Nation,* (Washington, DC: Congressional Quarterly Service, 1973), 3:671.

What is an "act of God" and in what profession is the term frequently used?

An "act of God" is an act brought about solely by natural forces that was unable to be foreseen, prevented, escaped, or controlled by humankind. Accidents resulting from storms, tornadoes, earthquakes, lightning, and dangers at sea are all examples of an act of God. Lawyers use the term to describe disasters such as these for which there is no legal means of redressing the losses sustained. Sir Alan Patrick Herbert (1890-1971) is credited with saying that "an Act of God was defined as something which no reasonable man could have expected."

John Bartlett, *Familiar Quotations: A Collection of Passages, Phrases, and Proverbs Traced to Their Sources in Ancient and Modern Literature, 16th ed., ed. Justin Kaplan* (Boston: Little Brown and Company, 1992), 678. Henry Campbell Black, *Black's Law Dictionary: Definitions of the Terms and Phrases of American and English Jurisprudence, Ancient and Modern, 6th ed.* (St. Paul, MN: West Publishing, 1990), s.v. "Act of God.." Ivor H. Evans, *Brewer's Dictionary of Phrase and Fable, 14th ed.* (New York: Harper & Row Publishers, 1989), s.v. "Act of God."

What is a "living will"?

A "living will" is a legal document in which a person requests the right to die with dignity and without artificial prolongation of their lives by modern medical technology. A person who obtains a living will can designate someone to serve as "durable power of attorney." The person serving as durable power of attorney can make medical decisions in the event that the subject of the living will becomes incapacitated. Forty-six states and the District of Columbia have some provision for living wills; but each of these jurisdictions have varying requirements on the content of the declaration. The states of Massachusetts, Michigan, New York, and Pennsylvania gave no statutory provisions.

Richard Leiter, ed., *National Survey of State Laws* (Detroit: Gale Research, 1993), 338-54. Ken Skala, *American Guidance for Those Over 60, 2d ed.* (Falls Church, VA: American Guidance, 1990), 321-22.

What is reverse discrimination?

Reverse discrimination is generally perceived as the practice of discrimination against white males while concurrently giving preferential treatment to women and minorities. Traditionally, employment advancements were determined by such criteria as seniority or test scores. Sometimes affirmative action policies are in direct conflict with traditional employment policies. There is no legal basis for the practice of reverse discrimination. Section 703(j) of Title VII of the U.S. Civil Rights Act of 1964 holds that nothing in the title shall be interpreted to permit any employer to "grant preferential treatment to any individual or group on the basis of race, color, religion, sex, or national origin."

Jay M. Shafritz, Richard P. Koeppe, and Elizabeth W. Soper, *The Facts on File Dictionary of Education,* (New York: Facts on File, 1988), 401.

What are the abortion laws around the world?

Countries in which abortion is legal in most circumstances and available on demand at least through the first trimester include Canada, the United States, Great Britain, Czechoslovakia, Denmark, Finland, France, Greece, Italy, Netherlands, Norway, Romania, Russia, Sweden, China, and Japan.

In some countries abortion is legal with restrictions. Approval is based on whether or not the mother's life is in danger or the fetus deformed. Consideration is given in cases of rape or incest. These countries include Israel, Germany, Spain, Switzerland, South Africa, Zimbabwe, Australia, India, and South Korea.

Countries in which abortion is illegal in most cases include Brazil, Chile, Mexico, Peru, Egypt, Lebanon, Saudi Arabia, Ireland, Poland, Indonesia, and the Philippines.

Pittsburgh Post-Gazette 29 May 1993.

What were the laws of Draco?

The first written law code of the city-state of Athens is alleged to have been compiled from customary law by the magistrate (archon) Draco in 621 B.C. Until that time the laws were unwritten and known only to nobles. Although Draco's code enlarged the franchise and provided a more equitable system of justice for the poorer classes, criminal offenses were harshly punished. Therefore, the adjective *draconian* has developed an unpleasant connotation. It is defined by *Webster's Collegiate Dictionary*, tenth edition, as meaning "cruel" or "severe."

George C. Kohn, *Dictionary of Historic Documents* (New York: Facts on File, 1991), s.v. "Draco, laws of (Draconian Code)."

What was the *Dred Scott v. Sandford* lawsuit?

The *Dred Scott v. Sandford* lawsuit was decided by the U.S. Supreme Court on March 6, 1857. After being taken in 1834 from Missouri, a slave state, to Illinois, a free state, then to Wisconsin Territory, where slavery was prohibited by the Missouri Compromise, and later returned to Missouri, Dred Scott sued his owner, John F. A. Sanford, whose name was officially misspelled in the court records as "Sandford," for freedom. Scott maintained that he had become free by virtue of his residency in a free state and a free territory. The U.S. Supreme Court ruled that residency in a free state did not confer freedom on a slave; and furthermore it ruled that blacks were not citizens, they could not sue in federal courts, and that the U.S. Congress had no power to prohibit slavery in the territories, rendering the Missouri Compromise unconstitutional.

George C. Kohn, *Dictionary of Historic Documents* (New York: Facts on File, 1991), s.v. "Dred Scott v. Sanford."

Which states have parental consent laws concerning abortion?

Several states have laws which require a minor or an unemancipated minor to receive parental consent before an abortion can be performed. These states are as follows:

Alaska
Arizona
Arkansas
California
Colorado
Delaware
Florida
Illinois
Indiana
Kentucky
Louisiana
Maine
Maryland
Massachusetts
Michigan
Missouri

Montana
Nevada
New Mexico
North Dakota
Ohio
Pennsylvania
Rhode Island
South Carolina
South Dakota
Tennessee
Wyoming

Richard Leiter, ed., *National Survey of State Laws* (Detroit, MI: Gale Research, 1993), 189-207.

What is primogeniture?

Primogeniture is the position of being the firstborn of a number of children who have the same parents. It can also refer to the eldest son's exclusive right to inherit from his parent and especially to his right to succeed to his parent's estate. Younger sons are excluded from this right to inherit the estate.

Henry Campbell Black, *Black's Law Dictionary, 6th ed.* (St. Paul, MN: West Publishing, 1990), s.v. "primogeniture."

Which provision of the Revenue Act of 1919 was invalidated by the U.S. Supreme Court in 1922?

In 1922, the U.S. Supreme Court's decision in *Bailey v. Drexel Furniture Co.* repealed the child labor tax provision of the Revenue Act of 1919. The Revenue Act stipulated that mines, factories, and other businesses that employed children under the age of 14 should be subject to a ten percent federal excise tax upon all profits. The Court ruled this provision Revenue Act of 1919 was unconstitutional because it allowed the federal government to interfere in a matter that was completely the province of the state government and beyond the taxing power of Congress.

Howard L. Hurwitz, *An Encyclopedic Dictionary of American History* (New York: Washington Square Press, 1968), s.v. "Bailey v. Drexel Furniture Co."

What was the subject of the Desmond decision by the New York State Court of Appeals in 1955?

The mid-1950s to the mid-1960s was a period of experimentation for film makers in the United States. During this period, film makers increasingly introduced more nudity and violence into their films. In 1955 the New York State Court of Appeals ruled in the Desmond decision that the nudity in the film *Garden of Eden* was not indecent. This ruling was pivotal because it allowed nudity to appear increasingly in American films.

M. Thomas Inge, ed., *Handbook of American Popular Culture* (Westport, CT: Greenwood Press, 1981), 3:297.

What law was ruled invalid by the U.S. Supreme Court in the *Adkins v. Children's Hospital* case?

In 1923, the U.S. Supreme Court ruled invalid the minimum wage law for women in the District of Columbia that was passed by the U.S. Congress in 1918. The majority decision stated that there was no relationship between a woman's wages and her morals, welfare, or health. The Court felt that the law could put at risk the liberty of contract between employers and their women workers.

The decision was overruled in 1937 during the *West Coast Hotel Co. v. Paris* case.

Howard L. Hurwitz, *An Encyclopedic Dictionary of American History* (New York: Washington Square Press, 1968), s.v. "Adkins v. Children's Hospital."

What are the dram shop laws?

Dram shop laws are a means of controlling drunk driving and other forms of illegal behavior done under the influence of alcohol. This legislation permits the last person to serve an alcoholic beverage to those who are intoxicated, as well as the establishment in which they are served, to be held legally responsible for the drunk's actions immediately afterward. For example, victims of drunk drivers may sue bar owners or party hosts in addition to the actual culprit.

David Savageau and Richard Boyer, *Places Rated Almanac: Your Guide to Finding the Best Places to Live In North America* (New York: Prentice Hall Travel, 1993), 227.

Where is an International Drivers Permit necessary, and how can it be obtained?

Many countries in the Caribbean, Central or South America, some areas of Mexico, and nations in the Pacific region of Asia require an International or Inter-American Drivers Permit. Travelers are advised to determine prior to departure if the permit is required or recommended in the country to which they are going. Either permit can be obtained from any local Automobile Association office. A permit fee and recent photographs are required. The permit is valid for one year and is restricted to persons at least 18 years of age who hold a valid drivers license.

OAG Business Travel Planner, North American ed. Spring 1994.

Which countries require motorists to drive on the left side of the road?

Several countries require motorists to drive on the left side of the road. Great Britain is the best-known example, but there are 53 others: Anguilla, Antigua, Australia, the Bahamas, Bangladesh, Barbados, Bermuda, Bhutan, Botswana, Brunei, Cayman Islands, Channel Islands, Cyprus, Dominica, Fiji, Finland, Grenada, Guyana, Honduras, Hong Kong, India, Indonesia, Ireland, Jamaica, Japan, Kenya, Lesotho, Macao, Malawi, Malta, Mauritius, Montserrat, Mozambique, Namibia, Nepal, New Zealand, Papua, the Seychelles, Singapore, South Africa, Sri Lanka, St. Christopher, St. Lucia, St. Vincent, Suriname, Swaziland, Tanzania, Thailand, Trinidad and Tobago, Uganda, West Malaysia, Zambia, and Zimbabwe.

Parade 9 May 1993.

What is a nolo contendere plea?

The nolo contendere plea means neither guilty or innocent but that the defendent will not defend himself or herself. However, it does have basically the same effect as a guilty plea.

Edward J. Bander, *Dictionary of Selected Legal Terms and Maxims* (Dobbs Ferry, NY: Oceana Publications, 1979), s.v. "nolo contendre."

What is "double jeopardy"?

"Double jeopardy" is being prosecuted a second time for the same offense following an acquittal or conviction at an initial trial. It also refers to multiple punishments for the same offense.

U.S. citizens are protected against "double jeopardy" by the Fifth and Fourteenth Amendments to the Constitution.

Henry Campbell Black, *Black's Law Dictionary: Definitions of the Terms and Phrases of American and English Jurisprudence, Ancient and Modern, 6th ed.* (St. Paul, MN: West Publishing Co., 1990), s.v. "double jeopardy."

What was the first year that the Supreme Court was composed entirely of law school graduates?

Until 1957 the U.S. Supreme Court had never been composed entirely of law school graduates. The last justice never to have attended law school was James F. Byrnes (1879-1972), who served from 1941 to 1942. Byrnes had little formal education and dropped out of school at age fourteen. He studied law by reading and clerked until he passed the bar at age twenty-four.

American Leaders, 1789-1987 (Washington, DC: Congressional Quarterly, 1987), 27.

How long does a copyright endure?

The duration of a copyright is largely dependent on the circumstances of authorship and the date when the work was created. Copyright protection for a created work—which normally lasts the duration of its author's life plus fifty years—is not renewable. This statute applies to works originating after January 1, 1978. For works created before then, the renewal terms of the Copyright Act of 1909 still apply, and under certain circumstances the descendants or executors of the creator may apply for renewal.

Basic term—For works created after January 1, 1978, the copyright endures for fifty years after the death of the author.

Joint works—The copyright is in effect for fifty years following the death of the last surviving author.

Anonymous and pseudonymous works—The copyright term will last for 75 years after publication or 100 years from the year of creation, whichever expires first. However, if authorship becomes known the copyright term is the life of the author plus fifty years as in Basic term.

Works created by hire—The copyright will extend for 75 years from publication or 100 years from creation, whichever is shorter.

Presumption of author's death—If there is no knowledge of when an author died the copyright will endure for 75 years after publication or 100 years after creation, whichever expires first.

Donald M. Dible, ed., *What Everybody Should Know About Patents, Trademarks and Copyrights* (Fairfield, CA: Entrepreneur Press, 1978), 118.

What are the various exceptions to the exclusive rights of copyright owners?

There are various exceptions to the exclusive rights of copyright owners including: library copying, first-sale doctrine, educational and other performances and displays, cable transmissions and other re-transmissions, musical compulsory licenses for recordings and jukeboxes, fair use, parody, and library and educational usage. It must be stressed that these exceptions are not absolute but only allowable under specific circumstances.

Robert Gorman, *Copyright Law* (Washington, DC: Federal Judicial Center, 1991), 88.

Are there any states that allow prayer in public schools?

Thirty states have laws that permit a moment of reflection or meditation for students in public schools. However, the wording of these statutes is purposely vague in order to circumvent a 1962 U.S. Supreme Court ruling banning prayer in public schools. The controversial decision was based on the theory that enforced prayer violated constitutional precepts of separation of church and state. In some cases, the states' laws were already on the books and have not been repealed, while in other states the ordinances allowing prayer or meditation were enacted after 1962.

Richard A. Leiter, ed., *National Survey of State Laws* (Detroit: Gale Research, 1993), 159-61.

What is the difference between criminal and civil law?

The field of law can be divided into two categories: criminal and civil. Criminal law concerns the breaching of specific federal, state, or local statutes designed to protect the rights of an individual. Murder, robbery, and fraud are typical misdeeds that fall under this category. A government prosecuting agency brings the charges forth against the wrongdoer. In contrast, civil law deals with violations against one party by another, and the charges are introduced by the complaining party. A divorce, for instance, is a civil lawsuit to settle a dispute between two aggrieved parties. Another example of civil law is an individual's lawsuit against a corporate entity for damages inflicted by a product that has malfunctioned. Some court cases fall under both criminal and civil categories-a car thief may be prosecuted by the state for the criminal act of stealing the automobile, but the car's owner may also bring a civil suit against the perpetrator for damage incurred when the car was in his or her illegal possession.

Don Biggs, *How to Avoid Lawyers: A Step-by-Step Guide to Being Your Own Lawyer in Almost Every Situation* (New York: Garland Publishing, 1985), 8.

How does a civil lawsuit progress through the court system?

A civil lawsuit is a lengthy and complicated process that seems best avoided by all parties except attorneys in need of work. To begin a civil suit, the wronged party—called the plaintiff—must file a legal document detailing the person to be sued, the reason for the suit and the amount of compensation requested. The defendant—the party being sued—must then submit a response that either denies wrongdoing, admits guilt, or counters the claim with a civil suit of their own. The monetary compensation determines which judicial body will rule on the case. If the monetary award is low, the case goes to the small-claims court where the judge renders the decision. These cases are usually heard within a reasonable amount of time. In other suits having higher monetary compensation, however, a period of pre-trial discovery begins and a judge assigned. Attorneys for the adversarial parties can subpoena evidence from one another, talk to witnesses on both sides under oath, and submit and argue pre-trial motions before the assigned judge. Both sides must notify the judge when they are finally ready to go to trial.

If one side requests a jury trial, the legal issues become even more complicated. Attorneys for both plaintiff and defendant begin a battle to dismiss from the jury pool the highest number of citizens they believe favor the other side. This is perfectly within the law and goes by the legal term "challenging." When, and if the trial ever gets under way, each side presents its arguments to either the judge and/or jury. The burden of proof is on the plaintiff to prove the defendant's wrongdoing.

Next, the defense is allowed to ask the judge for a directed verdict if the plaintiff has not presented enough evidence to continue the trial. If this is denied, the defense then proceeds to explain its side of the issue before the court. A period of rebuttal follows, when the lawyers for both sides are allowed to present more information or new evidence. Then comes the decision. If it is to be a trial by jury, the judge, with the help of both attorneys, issues a set of instructions to the jury concerning the statute that has supposedly been violated. If it is not a jury trial, the judge sometimes asks that the lawyers on each side present to him a written summation of their court representation.

Sometimes a jury can only decide for or against the plaintiff and the judge sets the award, but in some states they may also determine the amount. The judge has final determination over the monetary compensation, if any, that is to be awarded the plaintiff. Either side can make post-trial motions when they do not agree with the outcome or the amount.

An appeals process to a higher court can be initiated by the "loser" if this judicial body accepts why there is disagreement with the verdict. Then the opposition is allowed to advance their reasons why they think the decision was fair. These written documents are called memoranda of appeal.

If the case advances formally to the appeals court docket, the judges on the higher court sometimes decide the case on the basis of the memoranda. Other times the lawyers need to argue their cases in front of the bench. The appeals court either confirms the lower court's decision, reverses it, orders a new trial held, or assigns it to another judge for review. If one side does not agree with the decision of the appeals court, the case may next move to the next higher court level until it reaches the state's supreme court for review and finally, the U.S. Supreme Court.

The World Almanac of U.S. Politics (New York: World Almanac, 1989). 91.

What is negligence?

Negligence is failing to exhibit the kind of care that an ordinary person would take under similar circumstances. The court makes the determination as to the degree of care a prudent person would take in the same situation. Negligence cases are extremely common.

Don Biggs, *How to Avoid Lawyers: A Step-by-Step Guide to Being Your Own Lawyer in Almost Every Situation* (New York: Garland Publishing, 1985), 15-17.

What distinction does Anne Clarke have in U.S. history?

Anne Clarke is remembered for having been the first woman in U.S. history to be granted a divorce. According to records of the Colony of the Massachusetts Bay, the Quarter Court at Boston granted her divorce on January 5 in 1643 or 1644. It was determined that her husband, Denis Clarke, had deserted her and become an adulterer, fathering two children by another woman.

Joseph Nathan Kane, *Famous First Facts: A Record of First Happenings, Discoveries, and Inventions in American History, 4th ed.* (New York: H.W. Wilson, 1981), s.v. "divorce."

According to a 1971 *Life* magazine article, who are the twelve greatest U.S. Supreme Court justices?

In 1971 a panel of 65 scholars, selected by Professors Roy Mersky of the University of Texas and Albert Blaustein of Rutgers, was asked to judge the quality of the contributions of 96 U.S. Supreme Court Justices. Associate Justice Harry Blackman and Chief Justice Warren Burger were not considered because they had only recently been appointed. At the top of the list are those justices that the experts deemed "The Twelve Great Justices of All Time," as they were called in a *Life* magazine article. These were Joseph Story, Roger B. Taney, John M. Harlan I, Oliver Wendell Holmes, Charles Evans Hughes, John Marshall, Louis D. Brandeis, Harlan F. Stone, Benjamin N. Cardozo, Hugo L. Black, Felix Frankfurter, and Earl Warren. Most of the judges chosen held legal opinions which expanded the influence of the U.S. Supreme Court. However, at least one, Felix Frankfurter, an appointee of U.S. president Richard Nixon, held a "strict constructionist" view.

"The Twelve Great Justices of All Time," *Life* 15 October 1971.

Which works can a person copyright?

A copyright protects original works of authorship that are fixed in a tangible form of expression Copyrightable works include the following categories:
Literary works
Musical works, including any accompanying words
Dramatic works, including any accompanying music
Pantomimes and choreographic works
Pictorial, graphic, and sculptural works
Motion pictures and other audiovisual works
Sound recordings
Architectural works

Library of Congress, *Copyright Basics* (Washington, DC: Government Printing Office, 1993), 1-12. Library of Congress, *Duration of Copyright* (Washington, DC: Government Printing Office, 1993), 1-4. *Library of Congress Extension of Copyright Terms* (Washington, DC: Government Printing Office, 1994), 1-4.

How many laws passed by Congress have been vetoed by U.S. presidents, and which president holds the record number of vetoes?

From George Washington (1732-1799) through George Bush's (1924-) term as president, there have been 2,431 presidential vetoes of laws passed by Congress. Of this total, 95 were overridden by Congress to become law. Eight presidents never used the veto. They were John Adams (1735-1826), Thomas Jefferson (1743-1826), John Q. Adams (1782-1862), Martin Van Buren (1782-1862), William Henry Harrison (1773-1841), Zachary Taylor (1784-1850), Millard Fillmore (1800-1874), and James Garfield (1882-1945). The three U.S. presidents who used their veto power the most were Franklin D. Roosevelt (1837-1945) with 635 vetoes in 12 years, Grover Cleveland (1837-1908) with 584 vetoes in 8 years, and Harry Truman (1884-1972) with 250 vetoes in 8 years.

Joseph Nathan Kane, *Facts About the Presidents, 6th ed.,* (New York: H.W. Wilson, 1993), 394-95.

Do 18-year-old men still register for the draft?

The United States drafted men during the Civil War from 1861 to 1865, World War I from 1917 to 1918, World War II from 1940 to 1946, and from 1948 to 1972 which included the Korean War and most of the Vietnam War. A stand-by draft continued until 1975, although the armed forces were accepting only volunteers. In 1980, Congress instituted registration of 19- and 20-year-old men. The law also stipulated that beginning in 1981 all men reaching the age of 18 were required to register with the Selective Service System. The idea was that the government would know how many "battle age" men would be available in the event of a national emergency. In 1994, President Bill Clinton decided to keep this policy in place.

Associated Press News Service 24 May 1994. *World Book Encyclopedia* (Chicago: World Book, 1994), s.v. "draft, military."

What is bankruptcy?

Bankruptcy is a legal status whereby a court declares an individual or corporation to be insolvent. To be bankrupt is not necessarily to be penniless. A state of bankruptcy can be declared when liabilities are greater than assets. There may be enough assets to partially pay off debts. These assets are usually administered by a court appointee. Debtors and creditors alike may petition a court to begin bankruptcy proceedings.

Susan Lee, *ABZ's of Economics* (New York: Poseidon Press, 1987), s.v. "bankruptcy."

Is there a city that fines owners of dripping automobiles?

In Green Bay, Wisconsin, the owner of a dripping automobile can be fined one dollar for every drop dripped!

Robert Wayne Pelton, *Loony Laws* (New York: Walker and Company, 1990), 84.

What documentation is needed to legally change one's name?

Although the statutes covering the changing of one's name varies from state to state a checklist of required items of the applicant would probably include:
Proof of citizenship
Current residence and legal name
Place and date of birth
Proposed new name
Previous criminal record if any
Form of notice of publication if required
Names and addresses of living relatives, especially parents
List of financial obligations
Formal request to change name
Notification of legal entanglements -lawsuits etc.
Name and address of spouse
Parental consent in case of a minor
Reason for name change
Name, age and address of any children
Names and addresses of creditors
Information on bankruptcy or insolvency proceedings if any
Notarization of the application
Applicant's signature.

Stephen G. Christianson, *100 Ways to Avoid Legal Pitfalls Without a Lawyer* (New York: Citadel Press, 1992), 160.

What are the essential elements of a valid contract?

The essential elements of a valid contract are as follows: offer, acceptance, consideration, legal capacity of the parties, legal subject matter, and a writing if required by law.

Christopher Neubert and Jack Withiam Jr., *How to Handle Your Own Contracts,* (New York: Sterling Publishing Co., 1991), 9.

Are there any laws specifying how long a kiss may last?

There are laws on the books in two jurisdictions that regulate how long a kiss may last. Tulsa, Oklahoma, prohibits kisses lasting longer than three minutes, regardless of marital status. Pauses must be taken at three-minute intervals. Kisses delivered anywhere in Iowa may not last any longer than five minutes.

Robert Wayne Pelton, *Loony Laws: That You Never Knew You Were Breaking* (New York: Walker, 1990), 101.

Does the state of Connecticut have any unusual laws regarding the barber industry?

The state of Connecticut has some unusual regulations pertaining to the barber industry. One states that a haircut must be round and "to fit a cap." Another ordinance prohibits men from shaving on Sunday, whether receiving a shave in a barber shop or doing it themselves at home. Finally, Connecticut barbers, as well as private citizens, are prohibited from discarding used razor blades.

Robert Wayne Pelton, *Loony Laws* (New York: Walker & Co., 1990), 54.

Which amendment to the U.S. Constitution abolished slavery?

The 13th Amendment to the U.S. Constitution abolished slavery. It was introduced in January of 1865 and ratified in December of that year. The amendment is separate, but related to, the Emancipation Proclamation of 1863, which freed all slaves in the Confederacy. U.S. president Abraham Lincoln (1809-1865) signed the Proclamation into law during the American Civil War against the rebelling southern states that were fighting to secede from the Union over this very issue. The 13th Amendment at the end of the Civil War finalized the abolition of slavery within U.S. borders.

World Book Encyclopedia (Chicago: World Book, 1987) s.v. "Constitution of the United States."

What is the chain of command in the system of U.S. federal and state courts?

The chain of command in the federal and state court system is rather complex, but begins at the bottom with local tribunals—traffic, municipal, small claims, and other such courts. Above them are trial courts, sometimes referred to as county, superior, or district courts. Trial courts also supersede special tribunals, such as juvenile and probate. Next in the chain of judicial command are the intermediate appellate courts, although not all states have these. This body reviews appeals of decisions made by the trial courts. All states do have a state supreme court, however. Above that sits the Supreme Court of the United States, the final arbiter. In addition to hearing disputes not resolved within the previously mentioned chain of local and state courts, the U.S. Supreme Court has jurisdiction over the federal tribunals. These include two U.S. courts of appeal, and below that the U.S. claims, district, and tax courts. An international trade tribunal sits under the court of appeals for the federal circuit, and decisions made by the two bankruptcy courts can be appealed in the U.S. district courts.

You and the Law (Pleasantville, NY: Reader's Digest Association, 1984), 30-31.

In the U.S. Supreme Court decision in the case *Cohens* v. *Virginia*, of what crime were the Cohens found guilty?

In the 1821 U.S. Supreme Court case of Cohens v. Virginia, the court upheld the conviction of the Cohens for violating a state law prohibiting the sale of lottery tickets. The case is perhaps better known because of the State of Virginia's claims that the case did not fall under the U.S. Supreme Court jurisdiction and the subsequent affirmation that reviewing state decisions was within the high court's rights.

Howard L. Hurwitz, *An Encyclopedic Dictionary of American History* (Washington Square Press, 1968), s.v. "Cohens v. Virginia."

What does the expression to "take the Fifth" mean?

The popular expression "taking the Fifth" refers to a person's assertion of his or her Fifth Amendment to the U.S. Constitution right, which protects against self-incrimination. "Pleading the Fifth" is an alternative expression for protection against self-incrimination.

Steven H. Gifis, *Law Dictionary, 2d ed.* (New York: Barron's Educational Series, 1984), s.v. "taking the fifth."

What Supreme Court decisions opened the door for the so called "Jim Crow" laws?

The so-called "Jim Crow" laws came into use after five U.S. Supreme Court decisions in 1883. The high court ruled that it was not unconstitutional for a proprietor to deny equal accommodations at inns, theaters, or public conveyances. The effect of the "Jim Crow" laws was to segregate African Americans from whites in public places.

Howard L. Hurwitz, *An Encyclopedic Dictionary of American History* (New York: Washington Square Press, 1968), s.v. "civil rights cases of 1883."

What does it mean to copyright a book, and when was the first book copyrighted in the United States?

A copyright grants the exclusive legal right to reproduce, publish, or sell a literary or musical production. The practice became regularized in England in 1557 when Queen Mary granted to the Stationer's Company the right to print matter for sale in the kingdom. All books had to be entered in their register for a small fee, and the publisher then gained the exclusive right to "copy" it. It was a way of controlling content as well as protecting the holder of the copyright from unscrupulous printers who might pirate the work. The first book registered for copyright in the United States was *The Philadelphia Spelling Book*, which was registered by its author John Barry June 9, 1790.

Stephen Gilbar, *The Book Book* (New York: St. Martin's Press, 1981), 4. Philip W. Goetz, *The New Encyclopaedia Britannica, 15th ed.* (Chicago: Encyclopaedia Britannica, 1991), s.v. "publishing."

In medieval England what was the "Star Chamber"?

In medieval England the "Star Chamber" was a court of law that began in the fourteenth century. It was made up of the privy council and was quite apart from the common law courts of the day. During the reign of Charles I (1600-1649) the "Star Chamber" developed a reputation for despotism and began to impose arbitrary punishments against citizens which led to the courts abolishment in 1641 by the "Long Parliament." The origins of its name are murky although the Star Chamber did meet in a room with a star decorated ceiling in Westminster Palace.

Bamber Gascoigne, *Encyclopedia of Britain* (New York: Macmillan Publishing Company, 1993), s.v. "Star Chamber."

What was the impact of *Plessy* v. *Ferguson* and under what circumstances was it later overturned?

Plessy v. *Ferguson* was an 1896 U.S. Supreme Court decision that upheld an 1890 Louisiana statute calling for "separate but equal" accommodations in railroad cars for Caucasian and African-American passengers. Homer Plessy was a seven-eighths Caucasian and one-eighth African who purchased a first-class ticket but was refused a seat in the Caucasian-only car. When he objected he was arrested, imprisoned and eventually prosecuted for violating the law. Plessy argued that the Louisiana statute was unconstitutional under the Thirteenth Amendment which abolished slavery and the Fourteenth Amendment which prohibited restrictive state legislation. The U.S. Supreme Court disagreed stating that the concept of "separate but equal" accommodations was a reasonable exercise of state power in order to promote the public good and if there was to be social intercourse between the two races it must be by mutual consent. U.S. Justice John Marshall Harlan (1833-1911) was the lone dissenter.

In 1954 the Supreme Court overruled *Plessy* v. *Ferguson* in the landmark case *Brown* v. *Board of Education of Topeka*, 1954. The court ruled that so-called "separate but equal " accommodations were inherently unequal.

The Guide to American Law: Everyone's Legal Encyclopedia (St. Paul, MN: West Publishing, 1983), s.v. "Plessy v. Ferguson."

Can race or gender be a criteria in jury selection?

In 1986 the U.S. Supreme Court ruled in *Batson* v. *Kentucky*, that excluding African-Americans and other minorities from juries on the basis of their race violated the fourteenth Amendment's guarantee of "equal protection of the laws." Prior to the 1986 decision, it was not unusual for prosecutors to use their peremptory challenges to exclude minorities from juries when the defendant was a member of the same minority group. Lawyers are limited to a specific number of peremptory challenges (usually around 11) in which a juror can be dismissed without cause. A peremptory challenge itself can now be challenged if the defendant feels it was made on the basis of race. This ruling and a subsequent 1992 ruling severely limits the use of peremptory challenges. The 1992 decision prohibits the defendant's use of peremptory challenges based on race. In 1994 the U.S. Supreme Court made a similar ruling as to excluding jurors on the basis of gender.

"Court rules gender alone can't disqualify jurors," *Detroit News* 20 April 1994. "A bar to peremptory jury challenges," *Time* 29 June 1992.

As it relates to the free speech clause of the First Amendment of the U.S. Constitution, what is the "clear and present danger test"?

As it relates to the free speech clause of the First Amendment of the U.S. Constitution, the "clear and present danger test" is used to determine the constitutionality of statutes and other government actions that impede free speech. The test attempts to demarcate the line between innocent speech and illegal speech that presents a clear and present danger. It was first used by Justice Oliver Wendell Holmes (1841-1935) in *Schenck* v. *United States* (1919). During World War I (1914-18) Schenck claimed the free speech clause of the First Amendment shielded him from prosecution for encouragement of insubordination among the soldiers of the U.S. army and for the obstruction of military enlistment. Holmes rejected this defense claiming:

"The question in every case is whether the words are used in such circumstances and are of such a nature as to create a clear and present danger that they will bring about the substantive evils that Congress has a right to prevent. It is a question of proximity and degree."

Other U.S. Supreme Court cases involving the "clear and present danger test" include *Abrams* v. *United States* (1919), *Thornhill* v. *Alabama* (1940), *Bridges* v. *California* (1941), and *Dennis* v. *United States* (1951). The test has often been criticized by civil libertarians for being vague and imposing undue restraint on free speech.

The Guide to American Law (New York: West Publishing, 1983), 2:378-79.

How long does a patent or a trademark protect the holder?

The term of a utility or a plant patent is 17 years from the date of issue, subject to the payment of maintenance fees. The term of a design patent is 14 years from the date of issue and is not subject to the payment of maintenance fees. The term of a trademark is potentially infinite.

Richard C. Levy, *Inventing and Patenting Sourcebook* (Detroit: Gale Research, 1990), 55.

What cannot be patented?

Many things are not open to patent protection:

The laws of nature, physical phenomena, and abstract ideas.

A new mineral or a new plant found in the wild.

Inventions useful solely in the utilization of special nuclear material or atomic energy for weapons.

A machine that is not *useful* (i.e. does not have a useful purpose or does not operate to perform the intended purpose).

Methods of doing business.

Printed matter.

In the case of mixtures of ingredients, such as medicines, a patent cannot be granted unless the effect of mixture is more than the effect of its components.

Human beings cannot be patented.

Mere substitution of one material for another or changes in size to a previously known useful invention without "novelty."

Richard C. Levy, *The Inventor's Desktop Companion* (Detroit: Visible Ink Press, 1991), 10.

Where did the term "lynch-law" originate?

There exists a number of explanations for the origin of the term "lynch-law," which is the execution of punishment to an offender by a self-constituted court, which has no legality whatsoever. The most popular one traces the term "lynch-law" to Colonel Charles Lynch (1736-1796), a justice of the peace in Bedford County, Virginia, at the time of the American Revolution. He and other justices of the court decided to punish Tories and others without taking the felony cases to Williamsburg as the law indicated. The "guilty" would be sentenced to receive thirty-nine lashes on their backs, and hung by their thumbs until they shouted "Liberty Forever."

James Elbert Cutler, *Lynch-Law: An Investigation into the History of Lynching in the United States* (New York: Longmans, Green and Co., 1905), 1, 13-40. *The Oxford English Dictionary, 2d ed.* (Oxford: Clarendon Press, 1989), s.v. "lynch law."

Politics

What were Sun Yat-sen's "Three People's Principles"?

The three principles of Chinese revolutionary leader Sun Yat-sen (1866-1925) are nationalism, democracy, and socialism. Sun first formulated the "Three People's Principles" in 1905 and continually modified them until 1924. Both the Chinese Nationalist Party and the Communist Party followed these principles to overthrow the imperialist powers of China during the early part of the twentieth century, and today both parties claim them as their own.

George C. Kohn, *Dictionary of Historic Documents* (New York: Facts on File, 1991), s.v. "Sun Yat-sen's Three People's Principles."

How many of the thirteen states participated in the first U.S. presidential election?

Of the 13 original states, only ten of them participated in the first U.S. presidential election. Both North Carolina and Rhode Island had not ratified the Constitution in time for the election. New York was experiencing too much debate between Federalists and Anti-Federalists, and so no electors were chosen by the deadline.

Eileen Shields-West, *The World Almanac of Presidential Campaigns* (New York: World Almanac, 1992).

When did political conventions begin?

The use of national political party conventions to nominate presidential candidates began in the 1820s and was fully in place by 1840. Prior to this new era, candidates had been selected by a Congressional caucus, but the phenomenal growth in the number of voters in the country demanded a more fair and less autocratic system. Citizens who joined a political party then had a voice say in the nomination of the candidate. The nominating convention method also led to the reappearance of the two-party system.

Congressional Quarterly's Guide to U.S. Elections, 2d ed. (Washington, DC: Congressional Quarterly, 1985), 11-12.

What state has had two female senators serving simultaneously?

In the 1992 elections, California voters elected two female U.S. Senators to represent their state. This was the first time a state had two female Senators serving simultaneously. Democrats Barbara Boxer and Diane Feinstein were also the first female Senators elected by the state of California.

Jeffrey B. Trammell and Gary P. Osifchin, *The New Members of Congress Almanac: 103rd Congress* (Washington, DC: The Almanac of the Unelected, 1992), 4.

In British political history who were the Tories?

In British political history the Tories were members of the conservative Tory party. The term was first used in 1679 among supporters of James (1623-1701), then the Duke of York and comes from a Gaelic word meaning "pursued" or "pursued man." The Tories evolved into a major British political party in opposition to the Whigs but by the mid-1800s the word "Tory" began giving way to the term "Conservative."

World Book Encyclopedia (Chicago: World Book, 1987), s.v. "Tory Party."

In politics, what is "jingoism"?

Jingoism is a political term referring to hawkish foreign policies. It may be of Basque origin, "Jainko" is the name of a Basque god, stemming from the English king Edward I's (1239-1307) use of Basque mercenaries in the thirteenth century. A popular English music hall song of 1878 brought the word into common usage; written by G.W. Hunt, it ran, "We don't want to fight, yet by Jingo! if we do / We've got the ships, we've got the men, and got the money too." U.S. president John F. Kennedy (1917-63) used the term when he described an unhealthy, isolationist form of U.S. policy as "belligerent jingoism."

Graham Evans and Jeffrey Newnham, *The Dictionary of World Politics: A Reference Guide to Concepts, Ideas, and Institutions* (New York: Simon & Schuster, 1990), s.v. "jingoism."

What is the importance of the electoral college?

In the American political system, U.S. presidents are elected through the electoral college system. According to this system, a citizen who votes for a particular presidential candidate is actually voting for a slate of electors pledged to that candidate. The number of electors a state receives depends on the number of senators and congress persons in that state. The winning electors in each state meet in their state capital on the first Monday after the second Wednesday in December to cast their votes for president and vice president. A statement regarding the results is sent to Washington, D.C., where Congress counts the votes. In order for a person to be elected president, he or she must capture at least 270 out of a possible 538 votes.

If no suitable candidate for president receives a majority of electoral votes, the responsibility for choosing the president is given to the House of Representatives. Each state has one vote in the House, and a majority of states is needed for a candidate to win election. In the history of the United States, the House of Representatives has elected a president only three times.

The electoral college system offers the possibility that a candidate may be elected president even if he or she loses the popular vote. In fact, three presidents have been elected after losing the popular vote: John Quincy Adams (1767-1848) in 1824, Rutherford B. Hayes (1822-1893) in 1876, and Benjamin Harrison (1833-1901) in 1888.

Since the founding of the United States, the electoral college system has been widely criticized as an unsatisfactory means of electing a president. Many proposals for revamping the system, including electing the president by direct vote only or granting bonus electors for the winner of the popular vote in each state, have been presented at various times in American history. However, the electoral college remains firmly in place.

Michael Nelson, *The Presidency A to Z* (Washington, DC: Congressional Quarterly, 1992), s.v. "electoral college."

What is the meaning of "dark horse" in U.S. politics?

A "dark horse" as referred to in U.S. politics is a relatively unknown person who is nominated for an important office by a major party. Dark horse candidates have been selected to run for the U.S. presidency on occasions when party conventions have become locked between two or more strong candidates. A dark horse is generally unobjectionable with respect to issues, unidentified with party factions, and untarnished with respect to his public and private persona.

The first dark horse was James Polk (1795-1849), who became a nominee at the Democratic Convention in Baltimore in 1844. Polk won the nomination when the convention became deadlocked following successive balloting for Martin Van Buren (1782-1862) and Lewis Cass (1782-1866). Other dark-horse candidates were Franklin Pierce (1804-1869), Rutherford B. Hayes (1822-1893), Warren G. Harding (1865-1923), and Wendell Willkie (1892-1944).

The term "dark horse" was used in *The Young Duke* (1831), a novel by Benjamin Disraeli (1804-1881). He wrote: "A dark horse which had never been thought of, and which the careless St. James had never even observed in the list, rushed past the grandstand in sweeping triumph."

Hans Sperber and Travis Trittschuh found its first printed reference in a quoted statement by Hamilton Fish (1808-1893) speaking for Abraham Lincoln (1809-1865) in 1860: "We want a log-splitter, not a hair-splitter; a flat-boatman, not a flat-statesman; log cabin, coonskin, hard cider, old Abe and dark horse-hurrah!"

Dictionary of American History, rev. ed. (New York: Charles Scribner's Sons, 1976), s.v. "dark horse." William Safire, *Safire's Political Dictionary* (New York: Random House, 1978), s.v. "dark horse."

Why was the U.S. Presidential election of 1876 controversial?

The 1876 U.S. Presidential election was between the Democratic nominee Samuel J. Tilden (1814-86) and the Republican runner, Rutherford B. Hayes (1822-93). Because of much dispute over the counting of ballots, the U.S. Congress established a 15-man, bipartisan electoral commission. In 1877 the commission, voting 8-7 along strict party lines, awarded Hayes the disputed ballots. Tilden won 4,284,757 popular votes to Hayes' 4,033,950 but ultimately lost the election by one electoral vote, 185 to 184.

William A. DeGregorio, *The Complete Book of U.S. Presidents, 2d ed.* (New York: Dembner Books, 1989), 285-86.

How did the Progressive Party come to be known as the Bull Moose Party?

President Teddy Roosevelt (1858-1919) was the source of yet another American colloquialism when he inadvertently coined the term "Bull Moose" Party. The Republican politician had served as the nation's chief executive from 1901 to 1909, but announced himself dissatisfied with the policies of his Republican successor, William Howard Taft (1857-1930). In 1912 Roosevelt gained the nomination of the Progressive Party in another bid for the presidency. When the press inquired as to his health, the candidate replied that he felt "fit as a bull moose." The term soon became the unofficial moniker of the party, and Roosevelt lost the election despite his hearty constitution.

Howard L. Hurwitz, *An Encyclopedic Dictionary of American History* (New York: Washington Square Press, 1968), s.v. "Bull Moose party."

What is the "revolution of rising expectations"?

The "revolution of rising expectations" was a loosely defined political movement in the late 1950s and early 1960s that swept through many "Third World" countries. Because of the economic disparity between the developed and the undeveloped countries, "Third World" leaders promised their countrymen economic modernization as a way of closing the gap between them and the developed countries.

Eugene Staley, *The Future of Underdeveloped Countries* (New York: Harper & Brothers, 1961), 15-18.

At a political convention, what is a "favorite son"?

When, in a national election or at a national party convention, a state's votes are primarily cast for a candidate from within that same state, the candidate is referred to as a "favorite son." In the event that the candidate is not elected, these votes can give the candidate bargaining power and the ability to trade them in for political favors.

Walter J. Raymond, *International Dictionary of Politics* (New York: Brunswick Publishing, 1978), s.v. "favorite son."

Which New Hampshire hamlet rises early to vote first in presidential elections?

The New Hampshire northern town of Dixville Notch is famous for being the first voting place to call in its votes in presidential elections. The tiny town is considered by some to be a means of predicting an election's outcome, despite the fact that it only represents some 20 votes.

Dana Facaros and Michael Pauls, *New England: A Handbook for the Independent Traveler* (Chicago: Regnery Gateway, 1982), 194.

What is the Eastern Establishment?

Eastern Establishment refers to those from the eastern part of the United States who because of family wealth, family connections, and Ivy League educations and networking exert a political influence in this country disproportionate to their numbers. People from the Eastern Establishment, in spite of their vested interests in the status quo, are generally viewed as being more liberal than conservative.

Walter J. Raymond, *International Dictionary of Politics* (Lawrenceville, VA: Brunswick Publishing, 1980), s.v. "Eastern Establishment."

What is a "lame duck" official?

The term "lame duck" refers to any official, although most often a president, whose leaving of office is imminent because of a pending resignation or retirement, loss of reelection or reappointment, or term limit restrictions. The "lame duck" official loses that portion of political power that is dependent upon continuity of office or position.

Walter J. Raymond, *International Dictionary of Politics, 6th ed.* (Lawrenceville, VA: Brunswick Publishing, 1980), s.v. "lame duck."

What is the history of the Moral Majority?

The Moral Majority, which made history by helping to marshal the religious right into a political force, came into being in 1979, when the Reverend Jerry Falwell gathered religious leaders from around the country in his office conference room in Lynchburg, Virginia, to discuss how to engage conservatives in politics. The political action group got its name from that meeting, at which Paul Weyrich (president of the Free Congress Foundation in Washington, D.C.) said, "I believe there is a moral majority in this country," and somebody responded, "That's the name!"

Over a ten-year span, the lobbying group took much of the credit for helping elect three Republican administrations and for rallying conservatives behind issues ranging from abortion to pornography. Falwell resigned as president of the Moral Majority in 1987, and announced in 1989, that the organization was to dissolve at the end of that fiscal year.

The group's work has since been taken over by lobbying groups of religious conservatives, such as the American Coalition for Traditional Values, Concerned Women for America, the Rutherford Institute, the Freedom Council, and the American Family Association.

Pittsburgh Press 12 June 1989.

Who stood before a column of tanks in Tiananmen Square in 1989?

The man who captured the spirit of the 1989 pro-democracy movement in China by stopping a column of tanks on June 5 of that year was Wang Weilin, a 19-year-old student. After stopping the column, he climbed onto the turret of the lead tank and pleaded with the soldiers to turn back and stop killing people. Ultimately, bystanders led him away and he disappeared into the crowd. While a 1990 news report from China reported that Wang had vanished and was feared to have been executed by the Communist government, there is, to date, no hard evidence concerning his fate.

Pittsburgh Post-Gazette 2 June 1990.

What is the correct way to compose a petition?

A well written petition is clear, well-organized, persuasive and dignified. Two approaches are traditionally used in arranging the document: the first begins with a list of reasons for forming the petition, the second starts by announcing who is organizing the request for signatures. In determining the legal impact of a petition it may be necessary to study relevant laws or regulations. Some kinds of petitions require the signatures of registered voters, residents, or other specific kinds of individuals; others may require special language or a certain number of signatures. Signers should always be reminded to write their full, legal name.

Sarah Augusta Taintor and Kate M. Monro, *The Secretary's Handbook, 9th ed.* (Toronto, ON: Collier-Macmillan, 1969), 412.

What was the full name of Adolf Hitler's Nazi party?

The full name of Adolf Hitler's (1889-1945) political party was the Nationalsozialistische Deutsche Arbeiterpartei (National Socialist German Workers Party). The party ideology, as set forth in Hitler's *Mein Kampf* (My struggle), had several elements: a belief in an Aryan German race superior to all others, extreme nationalism which called for the unification of all German-speaking peoples, belief in corporative state socialism, a private army, a youth cult, massive use of propaganda, and submission of all decisions to a supreme leader.

Academic American Encyclopedia (Danbury, CT: Grolier, 1988), s.v. "nazism."

How did U.S. President Harry Truman get the nickname "Give 'em Hell, Harry"?

While running for re-election to the presidency in 1948, Harry Truman (1884-1972) told his running mate, Alben Barkley (1877-1956), "I'm going to fight hard. I'm going to give them hell." Crowds picked up the quote and yelled, "Give 'em hell, Harry!" during the campaign. The phrase became one of his nicknames.

William A. DeGregorio, *The Complete Book of U.S. President, 2d ed.* (New York: Dembner Books, 1989), s.v. "Truman, Harry S.." David McCullough, *Truman* (New York: Simon & Schuster, 1992), 663. William Safire, *Safire's New Political Dictionary* (New York: Random House, 1993), s.v. "give 'em hell, Harry."

Who created the Democratic and Republican political party symbols-the donkey and the elephant?

Caricaturist Thomas Nast (1840-1902) is credited as being the creator of the symbols for the two major U.S. political parties. The Democratic donkey first appeared in a political cartoon in *Harper's Weekly* on January 15, 1870, in which Nast spoofed the party by illustrating the old folktale about the jackass kicking a dead lion. The Democrats had attacked the policies of President Lincoln's Secretary of War at a time when he could not respond. The secretary, E. Stanton (1814-1868) represented as the dead lion had recently died. Some believe that Nast had just reused rather than invented the donkey symbol. The first appearance of the Democratic party symbol was in 1848, in the Whig party newspaper in Chicago, called the *Field Piece.*

There is no dispute about Nast's depiction of the Republican Party, also known as the "Grand Old Party" (GOP). The Republican elephant appeared in one of Nast's political cartoons in *Harper's Weekly* on November 7, 1874, satirizing the GOP as the biggest vote getter in the political jungle.

Albert Bigelow Paine, *Thomas Nast: His Period and His Pictures* (New York: Macmillan, 1904), 146-47, 300-01. Jay M. Shafritz, *The HarperCollins Dictionary of American Government and Politics* (New York: HarperCollins, 1992), s.v. "donkey," "elephant." "Words and Wisdom," *Pittsburgh Post-Gazette* 26 June 1984.

What is the origin of the term "Viet Cong"?

The Viet Nam Cong San, which means Vietnamese Communists in English, was the guerrilla force that, with the support of the North Vietnamese Army, fought against South Vietnam and the United States between the late 1950s and 1975. In 1957 Ngo Dinh Diem, president of South Vietnam, applied the term "Viet Cong" to the rebels who opposed his rule.

Robert McHenry, ed., *The New Encyclopaedia Britannica, 15th ed., "Micropaedia"* (Chicago: Encyclopaedia Britannica, 1993), s.v. "Viet Cong." *The World Book Encyclopedia* (Chicago: World Book, 1994), s.v. "Vietnam War."

What is a "plebiscite?"

A plebiscite is a vote by the people of an entire country or district. It differs from other kinds of elections, in that it does not ask voters to choose between various candidates or proposals. A plebiscite requires that the voters confirm or reject one ruler, form of government, or course of action. The purpose is to bypass political parties and representatives. Plebiscites are often associated with totalitarian regimes and with the French Revolution because Napoleon (1769-1821) was made emperor in a plebiscite.

Philip W. Goetz, ed., *Encyclopaedia Britannica, 15th ed., "Micropaedia"* (Chicago: Encyclopaedia Britannica, 1989), s.v. "plebiscite."

What is the Bubba factor?

The Bubba factor is a reference to the impact of conservative southern votes on an election. Bubba, a common man's nickname, has come to mean a white, southern male who is seen, by non-Southerners as unsophisticated and boorish.

American Speech: A Quarterly of Linguistic Usage Spring 1993.

What does the term "Byzantine" mean in reference to politics?

"Byzantine" is defined as a devious, scheming, and double-crossing manner of behavior in power politics. The term was not used in this way until the twentieth century when the former U.S. president Theodore Roosevelt (1858-1919) criticized the U.S. president Woodrow Wilson (1856-1919). The word is actually derived from the manner of politics and foreign affairs of the East Roman Empire (327-1453), whose capital of Constantinople was built on the site of the earlier Greek city of Byzantium. Although the achievement of the Byzantine Empire was impressive, it had a reputation for a labyrinthine foreign policy and domestic politics marked by intrigue and palace revolution.

William L. Safire, *Safire's Political Dictionary* (New York: Random House, 1978), s.v. "Byzantine."

In British politics what was a "rotten borough"?

In British politics a "borough" was originally any fortified town. It eventually came to designate an area that could send a representative to Parliament. An area came to be known as a "rotten borough" when it declined to where its votes could be easily bought because of few electors.

Bamber Gascoigne, *Encyclopedia of Britain* (New York: Macmillan Publishing, 1993), s.v. "borough."

In political terminology what is a "nonperson"?

In political terminology a "nonperson" is a former political figure, alive or dead, that has fallen out of favor with the political regime in power. Because the nonperson's political views are contrary to those of the current regime a pretense is made that for all practical purposes the nonperson never officially existed. This practice is most often prevalent among totalitarian governments such as the Communist regimes of the former Soviet Union which struck Nikita Khrushchev (1894-1971) and Leon Trotsky (1879-1940) from its official histories.

E.D. Hirsch, Jr., *The Dictionary of Cultural Literacy* (Boston: Houghton Mifflin Company, 1988), s.v. "nonperson."

What does the political expression "at large" mean?

The political expression "at large" refers to an elected official who represents the entire electorate of a specific geographic area. A senator is elected by and represents all of a state's citizens "at large" as contrasted to a congressional representative who is elected by and represents only those citizens that reside in the respective congressional district.

Walter J. Raymond, *International Dictionary of Politics, 6th ed.* (Lawrenceville, VA: Brunswick Publishing Company, 1980), s.v. "at large."

In political parlance, what is a fellow traveler?

In political parlance, a fellow traveler originally described people who traveled to Russia to view first-hand the wonders of the socialist state following the Bolshevik Revolution of 1917. Coined by Bolshevik leader Leon Trotsky (1879-1940), the term then referred to people believing in the Communist ideology but not having any formal Communist party affiliation. Its usage gradually became more widespread and described various intellectuals who promoted communism such as journalist John Reed, singer Paul Robeson, and political activist Angela Davis. During the McCarthy era in the United States, it was also used to describe Americans sympathetic to the Communist cause but who did not overtly act on their beliefs.

Walter J. Raymond, *International Dictionary of Politics, 6th ed.* (Lawrenceville, VA: Brunswick Publishing, 1980), s.v. "fellow traveler."

What was the first town in the United States to have a member of the Libertarian Party in high office?

Big Water, Utah, became the first town in the United States to have a member of the Libertarian Party in high office when Alex Joseph became its mayor. Besides being a Libertarian, Joseph was a polygamist with 10 wives and 20 children. The population of Big Water at that time was 350.

The Libertarian Party was founded in 1971 and ran candidates in the 1972 presidential election and the 1974 federal election. The party stands for "...individual freedom, voluntarism, a free-market economy, civil liberties, and an anti-interventionist foreign policy."

Alan J. Day, ed., *Political Parties of the World, 3d ed.* (Chicago: St. James Press, 1988), s.v. "Libertarian Party." *USA Today* 1 May 1986.

What are some world events in which one vote made a difference?

The following events were decided by one vote:
In 1645 Oliver Cromwell (1599-1658) gained control of England by one vote.
In 1649 Charles I of England (1600-1649) was executed because of one vote.
In 1845 the entrance of Texas into the Union was decided by one vote.
In 1868 U.S. president Andrew Johnson (1808-1875) avoided impeachment by one vote.
In 1923 one vote gave Adolf Hitler (1889-1945) control of the Nazi party.
In 1960 one vote change in each Illinois precinct would have caused the defeat of U.S. president John F. Kennedy (1917-1963).

Library Journal 1 June 1989.

When did the earliest political parties emerge in the United States?

One of the first modern political parties formed in the United States was the Federalist party which evolved from a group of statesmen active in the constitutional movement of 1787. Federalist party ideology, known as Hamiltonianism, centered around Alexander Hamilton (1755-1804), his financial policies, and a strong central government complimented by a strong national judiciary. The Federalists were elitist believing that the country would be best governed by "the wise and good and rich." This led to a strong centralized government which the Federalists believed could best govern the development, especially the industrial development, of the emerging nation. Hamiltonians also felt that their preferred form of government could best keep in check the excesses of the citizenry. Opposing the Federalists were Thomas Jefferson (1743-1826) and the Republican party which advocated that the federal government take a smaller role in the country's affairs, complemented by strong state and local governments which would be more responsive to the citizenry. Their political philosophy came to be known as Jeffersonianism. The Federalists all but disappeared from the national scene in the years following Jefferson's election to the Presidency.

Mark Mayo Boatner, *Encyclopedia of the American Revolution* (New York: David McKay, 1974), s.v. "Federalist party." E.D. Hirsch Jr., et al., *The Dictionary of Cultural Literacy* (Boston: Houghton Mifflin, 1988), s.v. "Jeffersonianism versus Hamiltonianism." Eileen Shields-West, *The World Almanac of Presidential Campaigns* (New York: World Almanac, 1992), 10.

What 1990 pact failed to cement a unified Canada?

Canada hoped to create a constitutional confederation with the Meech Lake accord in 1990, but failed to get unanimous support from the country's 10 provinces. The accord was comprised of a series of constitutional amendments aimed at cementing Quebec as a part of Canada, after years of separatist agitation. Manitoba and New Brunswick, however, would not endorse the accord based on the fact that it recognized Quebec as a "distinct society." Newfoundland also joined these provinces in opposing the accord after the Newfoundland House of Assembly rescinded a vote of approval. These provinces were concerned that the pact would give Quebec superior powers and that it would enable the province to pass laws that would be in conflict with national legislation. The Meech Lake accord was also criticized for its failure to address the issues of Senate reform and the rights of Canada's native peoples. In Quebec, separatists celebrated the failure to make the province part of a constitutional confederation.

Facts on File 29 June 1990.

Who started Earth Day?

The first Earth Day was April 22, 1970. It was coordinated by Denis Hayes at the request of U.S. Senator from Wisconsin, Gaylord Nelson, who is sometimes referred to as the father of Earth Day. His main objective was to organize a nationwide public demonstration so large it would get the attention of politicians and force the environmental issue into the political dialog of the nation.

EPA Journal January/February 1990. *Smithsonian* April 1990.

When were bilingual ballots first required?

A 1975 amendment was made to the 1965 Voting Rights Act which added provisions to protect minority language rights. Based on that amendment the U.S.Justice Department, on September 25, 1975, ordered 276 counties in six states to hold bilingual elections and obtain federal clearance of changes in voting or election procedures. The states affected were Arizona, California, Colorado, Florida, New York, and Texas.

Pittsburgh Press 26 September 1975.

What was the purpose of the U.S. attorney general's list of subversive organizations?

On March 22, 1947, U.S. president Harry Truman issued an executive order authorizing the Federal Bureau of Investigation (FBI) and the Civil Service Commission to conduct background checks on prospective government employees. The purpose of this background check was to determine if applicants were avowed Communists or harbored Communist sympathies. As a result of this executive order, U.S. attorney general Tom Clark compiled a list of 90 organizations that were believed to be disloyal to the United States.

Howard L. Hurwitz, *An Encyclopedic Dictionary of American History* (New York: Washington Square Press, 1968), s.v. "attorney general's list of subversive organizations."

What is the John Birch Society and how did it get started?

The John Birch Society was established by Robert Welch, a candy tycoon, to counter what he perceived to be a threat against the United States by Communists and Communist sympathizers. He decided that only his personal leadership could deter the Red menace. In December of 1958 he invited 11 friends from all parts of the nation to Indianapolis to found the society. It was to be a highly structured, monolithic organization with Welch at its head. He conceived it to be an educational, not a political, movement, but one that had revolutionary implications, because it was to change the pattern of American thinking by awakening the nation to the dangers of communism. The society had a religious dimension as well and welcomed members of all religions. In fact, it was named after a fundamentalist Baptist preacher, John Birch, who was killed by the Chinese Communists after World War II (1939-1945) ended. Because of the unreasonable nature of many of Welch's statements, the society has been denounced by responsible commentators on both the left and the right.

John George and Wilcox Laird, *Nazis, Communists, Klansmen, and Others on the Fringe* (Buffalo, NY: Prometheus Books, 1992), 214-16.

Who is generally considered to be the first politician to become president of the United States?

Martin Van Buren (1782-1862) is generally considered the first politician to become president of the United States. His political work began with the associations he formed with New York's Regency-a group that ran the Democratic-Republican party of that state. He proceeded to organize the national Democratic party and succeeded in establishing a coalition that elected Andrew Jackson (1767-1845) president in 1828. Van Buren was the Democratic presidential candidate in 1836 and won that election.

Microsoft Encarta '95 (Redmond, WA: Microsoft Publishing Group, 1992-1994), s.v. "Martin Van Buren." Eileen Shields-West, *The World Almanac of Presidential Campaigns* (New York: World Almanac, 1992), 56.

How much do political candidates spend on their campaigns?

Despite the debate among politicians concerning ways to limit the high cost of political campaigns, the cost of political campaigns continues to escalate. In 1992, for example, candidates for Congress spent a combined $504 million on their campaigns.

USA Today 31 December 1992.

Who campaigned for the U.S. Senate in 1992 with the motto "Just a Mom in Tennis Shoes"?

With her unique slogan of "Just a Mom in Tennis Shoes," Patty Murray, a Washington state Democrat, launched a successful campaign for the U.S. Senate in 1992. Early in the race, Murray was being characterized by her opponent as a left-wing liberal democrat who was unsure of her stance on issues. Murray countered with a successful grass roots campaign that allied her with traditional working class ideals.

Her slogan originally was derived from a warning by a state legislator who in 1979 told her that her drive to save a parent education program was ill-advised. "You're just a mom in tennis shoes; you can't make a difference," was his comment. Murray ignored his advice and went on to save the program.

Murray began her political career in 1981 as a lobbyist for the Organization for Parent Education in Washington, continued as a lobbyist for environmental issues until 1988, when she was elected a state senator in Washington.

Jeffrey B. Trammell and Gary P. Osifchin, *The New Members of Congress Almanac, 103rd Congress* (Washington, DC: The Almanac of the Unelected, 1992), 13.

What was meant by the "white man's burden"?

The expression "the white man's burden" refers to a political concept from the turn of the century, that the white man through superior technical development and colonization would "save" the other races, even if it was necessary to use force. This school of thought saw the colonization of other nations as a means for fulfilling their responsibility for spreading modern technology and Christianity.

Walter J. Raymond, *International Dictionary of Politics* (Lawrenceville, VA: Brunswick Publishing, 1980), s.v. "white man's burden."

What is the political meaning of the term "hundred days"?

"Hundred days" has several political meanings. Historically the term was first used to describe the time period in 1815 when King Louis XVIII of France (1755-1824) was forced to leave Paris after Napoleon's (1769-1821) escape from Elba. In the United States, "hundred days" more commonly refers to a controversial time in 1933 when U.S. president Franklin Delano Roosevelt (1882-1945) convened a special session of Congress to focus on the problems of the Depression. In addition, the first "hundred days" of a U.S. president's term in office is a period designated by journalists and critics for analysis and review.

William Safire, *Quoth the Maven* (New York: Random House, 1993), 190-91.

In politics, what is "brinkmanship"?

The political strategy known as brinkmanship is used during times of international crisis, particularly when there is threat of war, to make one's adversary back down. It has been likened to a high stakes game of "Chicken;" while war is clearly undesirable on both sides, one state manipulates "the shared risks of violence" to pressure the other into conciliatory action.

Graham Evans and Jeffrey Newnham Evans, *Dictionary of World Politics: A Reference Guide to Concepts, Ideas, and Institutions* (New York: Simon & Schuster, 1990), s.v. "brinkmanship."

In South Africa what is the AWB?

In South Africa, AWB stands for the Afrikaanse Weetstandsbeweging, or Afrikaner Resistance Movement, an extreme right-wing paramilitary group organized in 1973. In a 1994 interview with *Esquire*, Eugene Terre Blanche, the leader of the AWB, vowed to continue to oppose Nelson Mandela, the democratically elected president of South Africa and the head of the African National Congress. The AWB supports the idea of an Afrikaner homeland within South Africa.

Tim Guyse Williams, ed., *BBC World Service Glossary of Current Affairs* (Chicago: St. James Press, 1991), s.v. "AWB." Daniel Voll, "Into the Heart of Whiteness," *Esquire* August 1994.

What was awkward about the Adams/Jefferson election of 1796?

The presidential election of 1796 found the Federalists, a political group that favored a strong central government, opposing the Republicans, also called the Democratic-Republicans, who favored states rights over central government rights. The Federalists supported the candidacy of John Adams (1735-1826) and Thomas Pinckney (1750-1828) while the Democratic-Republicans supported Thomas Jefferson (1743-1826) and Aaron Burr (1756-1836). For this election each of the sixteen states chose electors to represent their state in the presidential election. When electors cast their votes, no distinction was made between voting for president or vice-president. The result was a situation the designers of the Constitution had not foreseen. When all the votes were counted John Adams had received seventy-one votes and Thomas Jefferson had received sixty-eight. Therefore, even though they were political opponents who had each sought the presidency, Adams became president and Jefferson became vice-president. Later legislation was enacted to prevent a reoccurrence of this situation.

Joseph Nathan Kane, *Facts About the Presidents: A Compilation of Biographical and Historical Information, 5th ed.* (New York: H.W. Wilson Co., 1989), 15.

What is the Concord Coalition?

Many Americans are concerned about the large national debt carried by the federal government. In 1992 Senator Warren Rudman, a Republican from New Hampshire, and Senator Paul Tsongas, a Democrat, formed the Concord Coalition, a nonpartisan grass-roots movement designed to pressure the President and the federal government to reduce the federal budget deficit.

"Debt-Busting Duo," *People* 2 November 1992.

What is a "pork barrel" project?

"Pork barrel" is a synonym for a tax-funded project that earns a politician proverbial brownie points with his or her constituency. The term is usually used for attention-getting construction projects-like highways-that an elected official has helped push through the legislative process.

The World Almanac of U.S. Politics (New York: World Almanac, 1989), s.v. "pork barrel."

How has political party affiliation changed in the United States in recent years?

Political party affiliation in the United States showed significant changes in 1992. The number of Americans who identified themselves as Democrats dropped, while the proportion of Independents increased. In the four previous presidential elections 52 to 48 percent of voters identified themselves as Democrats; in 1992 only 38 percent declared themselves Democrats. There was also a smaller drop in the number of Republicans, which shifted from 41 percent to 35 percent. The number of Independents jumped from 11 percent in 1988 to 27 percent in 1992.

"Who are the Democrats"? *USA Today* 25 January 1993.

What was the first political speech to be broadcast nationwide on radio?

The first political speech to be broadcast nationwide was delivered by Wisconsin Senator Robert M. LaFollette (1855-1925) on Labor Day, 1924. The Progressive presidential candidate was seeking an advantage over the Republican candidate Calvin Coolidge (1872-1933) and the Democratic candidate John W. Davis (1873-1955). The broadcast, however, was generally thought to be a failure, as LaFollette was unaccustomed to such a presentation. His speaking style had been developed for public meetings; LaFollette liked to walk as he spoke, using facial expressions and gestures to punctuate his oration. Nevertheless, radio proceeded to become an important political tool in the next election; the Democratic party increased radio spending from $40,000 in 1924 to $600,000 in 1928.

Congressional Quarterly's Guide to U.S. Elections, 3d ed. (Washington, DC: Congressional Quarterly, 1994), 88. Kenneth Campbell MacKay, *The Progressive Movement of 1924* (New York: Octagon Books, 1966), 213.

What controversial and often eccentric politician held the office of British prime minister four times during the reign of Queen Victoria?

During the reign of the English queen, Victoria (1819-1901), William Gladstone (1809-1898) held the office of prime minister four times. A major shaper of the Liberal Party, Gladstone held his country's top office from 1868-74, 1880-85, 1886, and 1892-94. Gladstone entered Parliament as a Tory in 1832 but became disillusioned with many of his party's positions such as the controversial Corn Laws and joined others in a gradual move toward liberalism. Gladstone favored fiscal responsibility, more individual freedom and rights, a less martial foreign policy, and home rule for Britain's colonies.

Queen Victoria, who characterized Gladstone as "an old, wild, and incomprehensible man" much preferred his Tory political rival Benjamin Disraeli. Gladstone's personal habits often contrasted with those of other British politicians. Gladstone felled trees for relaxation, used public transportation rather than private cabs, and wandered the streets of London's slums at night offering advice and moral comfort to prostitutes.

Bamber Gascoigne, *Encyclopedia of Britain* (New York: Macmillan Publishing Company, 1993), s.v. "William Gladstone."

What controversial clause was dropped from an early version of the Declaration of Independence?

In an early version of the Declaration of Independence, the future U.S. president Thomas Jefferson (1743-1826) had inserted a clause abolishing slavery. Because of pressure from South Carolina and Georgia, Jefferson later struck the clause.

Dictionary of American History, (New York: Charles Scribner's Sons, 1976), 2:305. David Louis, *Fascinating Facts* (New York: Ridge Press/Crown Publishers, 1977), 176.

In the politics of the former Soviet Union, what is the difference between a bolshevik and a menshevik?

In Russian "bolshevik" means "majority" or "a member of a majority." The word is commonly used in reference to Vladimir Lenin's Communist followers which through the revolution of 1917 overthrew and assassinated the Russian czar and gained control of the country. Lenin's party was officially known as the Russian Social-Democratic Labor Party. In the Russian language "menshevik" means "minority" or the "member of a minority." It was used in reference to Lenin's political rivals in the Russian Social-Democratic Workers Party.

Walter J. Raymond, *International Dictionary of Politics* (Lawrenceville, VA: Brunswick Publishing, 1980), s.v. "Bolshevik," "Menshevik."

What were the ten commitments proposed by Common Cause in 1972?

John Gardner, chairman of the citizens' lobby called Common Cause, requested that candidates for high public office should answer the following ten questions:

Will you support in every possible way the openness of your party's nominating process, from precinct caucus to (and through) the national convention?

Will you disclose the names of your chief financial backers, the total amount donated to you or to committees operating in your behalf from all sources?

Will you pledge not to engage in appeals to hatred, fear and prejudice?

Will you announce early enough the list of your vice-presidential preferences, and will you ask the convention to make the final decision from that list?

Will you fight for legislative controls on lobbying to let the public know precisely who is spending how much for what purpose?

Will you work to eliminate the secrecy that corrupts so much of the public process? Will you fight for "freedom of information" and "open meetings statutes covering both the executive branch and the legislature?

Will you fight to eliminate conflicts of interest in which a public official has a stake in the very matters he is legislating; and will you disclose your own sources of income?

Will you do everything possible to eliminate the antiquated and tyrannical seniority system in Congress?

Will you support a constitutional amendment for direct election of the president?

Will you use television spot announcements to clarify your position on certain issues, using preferably no spots under five minutes in length?

Parade Magazine 23 April 1972.

Who were the "three tailors of Tooley Street"?

The "three tailors of Tooley Street" refers to three tradesmen who lived near London Bridge during a time of nineteenth century political turmoil. By some accounts they were actually all tailors; others insist they were simply fictional characters. Robert Hogg, in *Notes and Queries*, identified them as tailors John Grose and Thomas Satterley, and grocer George Sandham, all of different streets. The activists gained some notoriety when they issued a proclamation commenting on a topical religious/political dispute that began with the words, "We, the people of England."

William S. Walsh, *A Handy Book of Curious Information* (Philadelpia: J.B. Lippincott Company, 1913), 851.

What is the origin of the modern usage of the political designations "left," "center," and "right"?

The use of the words "left," "center," and "right" to describe liberal, moderate, and conservative political viewpoints dates back to the French Revolution. In 1789, the first gathering of the French National Assembly brought together representatives of the common people, the clergy, and the nobility. At the event, the nobles were seated to the right of the president, a place of honor; the revolutionaries were placed on the left. The terms "right" and "left" came to be associated with the corresponding political views of each group. The first such use of these words was in Thomas Carlyle's *The French Revolution* in 1837. "Center" eventually came to represent a moderate political viewpoint.

Craig M. Carver, *A History of English in its Own Words* (New York: HarperCollins Publishers, 1991), s.v. "left, center, right."

Where were women first allowed to vote?

The Isle of Man, an island dependency of Great Britain, was first to extend suffrage to women in 1880. In 1893 the country of New Zealand gave women the right to vote. Although the United States nationally did not grant women the vote until 1920, the state of Wyoming gave women voting rights in 1869; with Colorado following in 1894; Utah, 1895; and Idaho, 1896. At first the right to vote was limited to women property owners.

Susan B. Anthony and Ida Husted Harper, eds., *History of Woman Suffrage* (Indiana: Hollenbeck Press, 1902), 4:1025. Russell Ash, *the Top 10 of Everything* (London: Dorling Kindersley, 1994), 58.

Who were the first African-American U.S. presidential and vice-presidential candidates?

The first African-American U.S. vice-presidential candidate was Frederick Douglass (1817-1895). He represented the People's Party (Equal Rights Party) in 1872. He was also the first African American to be nominated as a presidential candidate. This took place at the Republican convention in 1888, where he received one vote. The first African-American presidential candidate was Clennon King of Georgia, who was the representative of the Independent Afro-American Party in 1960.

Jessie Carney Smith, ed., *Black Firsts: 2,000 Years of Extraordinary Achievement* (Detroit: Gale Research, 1994), 170-71.

How many U.S. presidents have been elected even though they received fewer popular votes than their opponents?

Only three candidates have been elected president of the United States with fewer popular votes than their opponents: John Q. Adams in 1824, Rutherford B. Hayes in 1876, and Benjamin Harrison in 1888. Sixteen presidents have been elected without receiving a majority of the votes cast: John Q. Adams, 1824; James Polk, 1844; Zachary Taylor, 1848; James Buchanan, 1856; Abraham Lincoln, 1860; Rutherford B. Hayes, 1876; James Garfield, 1880; Grover Cleveland, 1884; Benjamin Harrison, 1888; Grover Cleveland, 1892; Woodrow Wilson, 1912; Woodrow Wilson, 1916; Harry S. Truman, 1948; John F. Kennedy, 1960; Richard Nixon, 1968; and Bill Clinton, 1992.

Joseph Nathan Kane, *Facts About the Presidents, 6th ed.* (New York: H. W. Wilson, 1993), 375-6.

Has a U.S. presidential election ever been postponed because of war?

War has never postponed a U.S. presidential election. In fact, no president has lost a bid for reelection during wartime.

Lu Ann Paletta and Fred L. Worth, *The World Almanac of Presidential Facts, rev. ed.* (New York: World Almanac, 1992), 210-211.

What is the Freedom Socialist Party?

The Freedom Socialist Party was formed in 1967 when the Seattle chapter separated from the Socialist Workers Party. Women's equality issues were at the heart of the split. In the following years, the issue of women's rights became even more emphasized because two of its key members, Clara and Richard Fraser, went through a divorce. Under Washington law, she was definitely at a disadvantage, but Clara fought back to gain better custody rights. In so doing, the Freedom Socialist Party became more feminist in its ideology.

Freedom Socialist Spring 1979.

What does "realpolitik" mean?

"Realpolitik" is diplomacy or power politics based on practical factors such as strength rather than on theoretical or ethical grounds. It need not imply ruthlessness or selfishness. "Realpolitik" is a German word that literally means the politics of reality and was coined in 1853 by Ludwig von Rochau, who was criticizing the unrealistic policies of German liberals. The term has been especially applied to the policies of the German chancellor Otto von Bismarck (1815-1898), who was responsible for the unification and growth of Germany during the nineteenth century.

William L. Safire, *Safire's Political Dictionary* (New York: Random House, 1978), s.v. "realpolitik."

Who were the Jacobins?

The Jacobins were members of the most influential political clubs of the French Revolution. Started in Versailles in 1789, the club was housed at Paris in the dwelling of a religious order, the convent of the Dominicans of the rue Saint-Jacques, who were known as Jacobins. The name was soon transferred to the political club, which was more properly called the Society of the Friends of the Constitution. It began as a society for constitutional monarchists, and became very popular, forming chapters all over the country, and becoming something like a political party. Later under the leadership of Robespierre (1758-1794) it became radical and was associated with the assassination of the king and the Reign of Terror. In the reaction against the Terror the club was suppressed on November 12, 1794. The word "jacobin" has come to mean a member of an extremist or radical political group.

Samuel F. Scott and Barry Rothaus, eds., *Historical Dictionary of the French Revolution, 1789-1799* (Westport, CT: Greenwood Press, 1985) s.v. "Jacobins."

In political jargon what is "log rolling"?

In political jargon "log rolling" is the granting of mutual favors among legislators. When favors are granted it is expected that they will be reciprocated.

Walter J. Raymond, *International Dictionary of Politics* (Lawrenceville, VA: Brunswick Publishing Company, 1980), s.v. "log rolling."

What was William Jennings Bryan's "Cross of Gold" speech?

William Jennings Bryan (1860-1925), an American lawyer, editor, and politician was known as the "Great Commoner" and was a fierce advocate of agrarian democracy. In 1896 while he was a presidential candidate seeking nomination at the Democratic Party convention, Bryan made his famous "Cross of Gold" speech. Opposed to the gold standard, he advocated the free coinage of silver in order to help debt-ridden farmers and aroused the convention and gained the democratic nomination with his stirring words, "You shall not press down upon the brow of labor this crown of thorns. You shall not crucify mankind upon a cross of gold." Bryan ran unsuccessfully for president on the Democratic ticket three times. His last public appearance before his death was at the infamous Tennessee Scopes trial where he assisted in the prosecution of a high school instructor named Scopes who was charged with teaching Darwin's theory of evolution.

E.D. Hirsch Jr., et al., *The Dictionary of Cultural Literacy* (Boston: Houghton Mifflin, 1988, s.v. "Cross of Gold speech." *McGraw-Hill Encyclopedia of World Biography*, (New York: Mcgraw-Hill,1973), s.v. "Bryan."

What American policy was reflected by Jefferson's phrase "entangling alliances with none"?

In 1801 during Thomas Jefferson's (1743-1826) first inaugural address he used the phrase "...entangling alliances with none." In his address Jefferson was advocating U.S. isolationism. As an American political concept isolationism refers to American nonintervention or involvement in European wars and alliances. Isolationism has always been an influence in American foreign policy.U.S. president George Washington (1732-1799) warned America to avoid permanent alliances, during the War of 1812 Americans did not fight on European soil, and the Monroe Doctrine of 1823 cautioned America not to "...interfere in the internal concerns" of European countries. Throughout American history advocates of isolationism have believed in foreign trade, American expansionism, and a strong military presence in the western hemisphere. Their strong distrust of inter-European politics and alliances, especially among England and France, however, strongly influenced their thinking and gave rise to isolationism. American isolationism reached its apex in the early twentieth century with opposition to involvement in World War I (1914-1919) and the subsequent League of Nations.

Dictionary of American History, rev. ed. (New York: Charles Scribner's Sons, 1976), s.v. "isolationism."

What role did Constance Gore-Booth play in Irish politics?

Constance Gore-Booth (1868-1927) was the daughter of Sir Henry Gore-Booth, an Irish landlord and Arctic explorer, and his wife Georgina Mary, herself the daughter of Colonel Charles Hill of Tickhill Castle. After studying art in Paris and London and marrying Count Casimir de Markievicz of Poland in 1900, she became an impassioned supporter of the Irish nationalist movement. In 1908 she became involved with Sinn Fin, the Irish nationalist society that fought for and eventually helped achieve Irish independence from Great Britain. In 1909 Gore-Booth founded Na Fianna, an organization that taught martial skills to Irish boys. In 1916 she was implicated in the Easter Rising, tried and sentenced to death. Her sentence was commuted to a life sentence of penal servitude but in 1917 she was released under the terms of a general amnesty. In 1918 Gore-Booth became the first woman elected to the British Parliament but following Sinn Fin tradition, she declined to be seated. The rest of her life was a repetitive series of pamphleteering, arrests, and jail sentences for radical political activity, elections to Parliament, and refusal to take her seat.

C. S. Nicholls, ed., *The Dictionary of National Biography: Missing Persons* (Oxford: Oxford University Press, 1993), s.v. "Gore-Booth, Constance." A.C. Ward, *Longman Companion to Twentieth Century Literature* (London: Longman, 1970), s.v. "Markievicz, Countess."

What was the Know-Nothing Party?

The Know-Nothing Party was formed in New York in 1849 as a semisecret patriotic society that was officially known as the Order of the Star Spangled Banner. Also known as the American Party, it had secretive initiation rites and a stoic close-mouthed membership who, when asked about the group, would unerringly reply "I know nothing about it." Hence the name Know-Nothing Party originated. The success of the party was also due to its pledge to support only native-born Americans for elected office, its firm stand against the perceived encroachment of Catholicism and the Papacy in American life and government, and its desire to ban immigration for a period of 21 years. The party was particularly influential in the 1854 and 1855 elections, especially in the border states and New England. Passage of a pro-slavery resolution, however, at its 1855 convention hopelessly split the party along regional lines and its 1856 presidential candidate Millard Fillmore was only able to carry Maryland.

Thereafter the Know-Nothings quickly passed from the political scene.

Dictionary of American History, rev. ed. (New York: Charles Scribner's Sons, 1976), s.v. "American Party."

When was the Federalist party dismantled?

The last Federalist presidential candidate Rufus King ran for office in 1816; he lost that election to James Monroe (1758-1831). The party was effectively dismantled as a national party by the next election in 1820.

Eileen Shields-West, *The World Almanac of Presidential Campaigns* (New York: World Almanac, 1992), 32.

Which American women have been U.S. presidential candidates?

As of the year 1989, fourteen women have been national party candidates for the office of U.S. president. Victoria Woodhull ran in 1872 and 1892 as the nominee of the People's Party, also known as the Equal Rights Party. In 1884 and 1888, Belva Ann Lockwood was the candidate for the Equal Rights Party. Each of these suffragists faced difficulties on election day; Woodhull was jailed the first time and, in 1888 and 1892, the ballots that were cast for these candidates were not counted. The next three women to be presidential candidates did not run on feminist platforms: Anna Millburn, the National Greenback Party, 1940; Ellen Jensen, the Washington Peace Party, 1952; and Yette Bronstein, the Best Party, 1964. Other female candidates were: Ventura Chavez, the People's Constitutional Party, 1968; Charlene Mitchell, the Communist Party, 1968; Linda Jenness, the Socialist Workers Party, 1972; Margaret Wright, the People's Party, 1976; Deirdre Griswold, the Workers World Party, 1980; Ellen McCormack, the Right to Life Party, 1980; Margaret Smith, the Peace and Freedom Party, 1980; and Sonia Johnson, the Citizens Party, 1984. Lenora B. Fulani, the presidential nominee for the New Alliance Party in 1988, was the first female presidential candidate to appear on the ballot in all 50 states.

Joseph Nathan Kane, *Facts About the Presidents, 5th ed.* (New York: H.W. Wilson, 1989), 354. *Ms.* February 1980.

What was the Kuomintang and who was its founder?

Kuomintang was the name of the Chinese Nationalist Party when it was founded in 1911 by leader Sun Yat-sen and his lieutenant Sung Ch'iao-jen. The political party took 269 out of 596 seats in the lower house of the Chinese parliament, and 123 out of 274 seats in the upper house, giving them a majority in the election year of 1912. The group was nevertheless outlawed in 1913, causing Sun to flee to Japan where he formed the Chinese Revolutionary Party. When Chinese leader Yuan Shih-k'ai died, Sun returned to China as leader of the renamed Chinese Nationalist Party and formed a government in Canton in 1921. After Sun's death the party was led by Chiang K'ai-shek (1887-1975), who governed during the reunification of most of China, as well as during the Japanese invasion of the country and the Japanese defeat at the end of World War II (1939-45). Civil war, however, eventually pushed the Chinese Nationalist Party out of mainland China to Taiwan, when the Chinese Communists were victorious in 1948.

Michael Dillon, *Dictionary of Chinese History* (London: Frank Cass, 1979), s.v. "Kuomintang."

Where did Tipper Gore get the nickname "Tipper"?

Tipper Gore, wife of U.S. Vice President Al Gore, was born Mary Elizabeth Aitcheson. Her nickname, "Tipper," comes from a favorite childhood lullaby, "Tippy Tippy Tin."

Jennet Conant, "Family First," *Redbook* March 1994.

General History

Where is Blair House and what is its historical significance?

Blair House is located in Washington, DC, across the street from the White House. Constructed in 1824, Blair House was purchased by Francis Preston Blair in 1836. Blair became a close friend of U.S. president Andrew Jackson (1767-1845) and often hosted frank political discussions in his kitchen with Jackson and his cabinet, which earned Jackson's cabinet the nickname "Kitchen Cabinet."

Prior to the outbreak of the American Civil War, representatives from both the Union and the Confederacy met at Blair House to discuss issues of concern. In Blair House's Lincoln Room, General Robert E. Lee (1807-70) refused President Abraham Lincoln's (1809-65) request to command the Union armies.

"At the Nation's Guest House, An Elegant New Beginning," *New York Times* 13 June 1988.

Who were the Bourbons?

Bourbon is the family name of what was once one of the most powerful ruling houses of Europe, which held the thrones of France and Spain as well as kingdoms and dukedoms in Italy. The duchy of Bourbon was established in France in the tenth century, and the family that controlled it married into the French royal house, the Capetians, in the thirteenth century. It was not until the late sixteenth century, however, when Henry of Navarre became Henry IV (1553-1610), that the Bourbons assumed the crown. The greatest of their kings, Louis XIV (1638-1715), was able to extend the family's influence to Spain by having his grandson Philip V (1683-1746) named monarch of that country in 1701. A branch of the Spanish family ruled in Naples and Sicily from 1738 to 1860. The Bourbon's power was largely broken by various democratic revolutions in the late eighteenth and nineteenth centuries, but even today the king of Spain, Juan Carlos, is from that family.

Chris Cook, *Dictionary of Historical Terms: A Guide to Names and Events of over 1,000 Years of World History* (New York: Peter Bedrick Books, 1983), s.v. "Bourbons."

When were medals first awarded for military service?

Many countries today award medals to their soldiers for exemplary service or valor in battle. However, the awarding of medals did not become common until the nineteenth century. The soldiers of British ruler Oliver Cromwell (1599-1658) were among the first to receive medals for military service. Following their victory at the Battle of Dunbar in 1650, Cromwell's soldiers and officers received a medal designed by Thomas Simon bearing a likeness of Cromwell on the front and a representation of the English Parliament in session on the back.

Arnold Whittick, *Symbols, Signs and Their Meaning* (Massachusetts: Charles T. Branford Company, 1960), 94.

Have U.S. presidents always worked long hours at their jobs?

Before 1930 most U.S. presidents were not expected to work long, hard hours at their job. It was believed that states, local governments, and Congress should do most of the labor. Benjamin Harrison (1833-1901) was typical in working only two or three hours a day. Since the 1930s, however, as the nation has confronted problems that seem to demand a stronger central government and an active president, most leaders have started the day early and worked late. However, three immensely popular presidents, Dwight Eisenhower (1890-1969), John F. Kennedy (1917-1963), and Ronald Reagan (1911-), have bucked that trend and had more relaxed work schedules.

Michael Nelson, ed., *The Presidency A to Z: A Ready Reference Encyclopedia* (Washington, DC: Congressional Quarterly, 1992), s.v. "daily and family life."

What is the official name of Prince William?

Prince William, the son of Prince Charles (1948-) and Princess Diana (1961-1997), was born on June 21, 1982. His official name is William Arthur Philip Louis. William is a name that has been used in Diana's Spencer family for many generations. Arthur was selected because it is part of Prince Charles' full name, Charles Philip Arthur George. Philip was chosen because it is the name of Prince Philip (1921-), Charles' father and the husband of Queen Elizabeth II (1926-). Louis was selected because it was the name of Prince Charles' great-uncle Earl Louis Mountbatten (1900-79) of Burma. Mountbatten, who was loved and respected by Prince Charles, was killed in an Irish Republican Army terrorist bombing in 1979.

"William is new prince's name," *Pittsburgh Post-Gazette* 29 June 1982.

How long have the Tutsi and Hutu tribes been enemies?

Since the sixteenth century, intense ethnic hatred has existed between the central African Tutsi and Hutu tribes. The roots of the conflict are long and deep. In the sixteenth and seventeenth centuries, the Tutsis migrated to central Africa from the area of present-day Ethiopia and Somalia. The Tutsis are very tall in stature and established themselves as masters over the smaller Hutus who lived in the area. Hutus were considered inferior and denied many basic human rights. Since the seventeenth century, periodic conflicts have occurred between the Tutsis and Hutus. The results of these conflicts are the horrific massacres of thousands of Tutsi and Hutu civilians, usually innocent women and children.

Two of the most recent outbreaks of hostilities between the Tutsis and Hutus have occurred in the central African nations of Burundi and Rwanda. In August of 1988, Hutus living in Burundi attacked Tutsi villages with rocks and knives. In return, Burundi's Tutsi-dominated army retaliated against Hutu villages. The conflict lasted roughly one week and resulted in the deaths of 5,000 Tutsis and Hutus. On April 6, 1994, Rwanda's Hutu president was killed in a plane crash. Many Hutus within the country claimed that members of Rwanda's minority Tutsi population sabotaged the plane. Soon, Rwanda's Hutu-dominated army and its supporters launched a wave of massacres of Tutsi civilians and government officials. Many Tutsis fled to refugee camps in neighboring Zaire or Tanzania. In July of 1994 a rebel army of Tutsis who had been fighting a long civil war against Rwanda's government defeated the Hutus and set up an interim government. Fearing retaliation, many Hutus who had participated in the massacre of Tutsis fled the country.

Lee Davis, *Man-Made Catastrophes: From the Burning of Rome to the Lockerbie Crash* (New York: Facts on File, 1993), 61-62.

What is the origin of the term "doughboy," used to describe American soldiers?

Until World War II (1939-45) American soldiers were called "doughboys," a term that can be traced back at least as far as 1854 when it was used along the Texas border. American infantrymen of that time wore white belts which were cleaned periodically with "dough" made of pipe clay. Although "doughboy" was originally a derogatory term by the time it was replaced by "GI" it was being used with pride.

Dictionary of American Hstory, rev. ed. (New York: Charles Scribner's Sons, 1976), s.v. "doughboy."

What role has hostage taking played in U.S. history?

In the *New York Times* political scientist Graham E. Fuller has described the taking of hostages as "a basic characteristic of war," and as such, it is something the U.S. government has dealt with since the country's birth. Beginning in 1785, more than 100 Americans were held prisoner for 12 years in North African dungeons; the U.S. Congress voted to pay a ransom of nearly one million dollars. Ransoms were also paid to Barbary Coast pirates during the presidency of John Adams (1735-1826). In 1904, U.S. president Theodore Roosevelt (1858-1919) negotiated the release of an American hostage, after sending warships to Tangiers. In 1981, a group of Americans was held hostage in Iran. After the release of eight billion dollars in frozen Iranian assets, they were given their freedom. While the negotiations were handled by U.S. president Jimmy Carter (1924-), the release occurred less than an hour after U.S. president Ronald Reagan took office. The Iran-contra, a secret attempt to free American hostages in Lebanon, affair also took place during Reagan's presidency. And while recent U.S. policy statements have claimed that there will be no deals struck with terrorists, each new hostage situation has been treated individually, with no regular pattern of response.

Richard D. Lyons, "Since Ancient Times, Hostages Have Been Used, and Misused, in Wars," *The New York Times* 22 August 1990.

What is populism?

Populism is a reoccurring movement in American history that portrays the government as the defender of the common man against the tyranny of the wealthy classes.

Jay M. Shafritz, *The Facts On File Dictionary of Public Administration* (New York: Facts on File, 1985), s.v. "populism."

During World Wars I and II, what was a Service Flag?

Displayed throughout World Wars I and II, a display Service Flag was a banner hung in the front window that displayed a star for each member of the family, usually sons, performing military service. The idea of a Service Flag originated with Captain R. L. Quiesser of Cleveland, Ohio, just prior to the outbreak of World War I (1914-18). Quiesser was injured while serving with "Black Jack" Pershing's expedition into Mexico in pursuit of Pancho Villa. Although his injury ended his military career, Quiesser wanted people to know that his two sons in the Ohio National Guard, would soon be headed overseas because of inevitable American involvement in the European war. In April of 1917 he devised a red-bordered flag with two blue stars, representing his two sons on a white background.

The idea of such a flag became so popular that the Ohio State Legislature made the Service Flag the official symbol to represent men in service. Service Flags spread nationwide and during World War II (1939-45) the U.S. War Department issued design and display regulations for this flag.

"Service Flag's Origin," *Pittsburgh Sun-Telegraph* 11 April 1945.

What are some of the coincidences between the lives and deaths of the two U.S. presidents Abraham Lincoln and John F. Kennedy?

According to a report published in *The Pittsburgh Press Roto* in 1977, there are at least 20 coincidences between the lives and deaths of Presidents Lincoln and Kennedy. Some of these are as follows:

Both Lincoln and Kennedy were over six feet tall.

Both were active in civil rights legislation favoring African Americans.

Both presidents were assassinated by southerners.

Both assassins were themselves shot before they came to trial.

The names Lincoln and Kennedy comprise seven letters each.

The names of their assassins, John Wilkes Booth and Lee Harvey Oswald, comprise 15 letters each.

Both presidents were shot in the head, from behind, on a Friday, with their wives present.

Lincoln was elected to Congress in 1847; Kennedy in 1947.

Lincoln was elected to the presidency in 1860; Kennedy in 1960.

Both were succeeded by vice presidents who were southerners named Johnson.

Andrew Johnson was born in 1808; Lyndon Johnson in 1908.

Lincoln's secretary was named Kennedy; Kennedy's secretary was named Lincoln.

Allen Spraggett, "The Presidential Death Cycle," *The Pittsburgh Press Roto* 17 April 1977.

What was "Operation Just Cause"?

The U.S. invasion of Panama in December of 1989 was known as "Operation Just Cause." After a six-day period that saw the appointment of General Manuel Noriega as the head of the Panamanian government and the country's declaration of war against the United States, U.S. President George Bush (1913-) ordered troops to invade Panama. The effort was intended to overthrow Noriega's government and to capture Noriega, who managed to escape U.S. forces. In conjunction with the attack, a Panamanian government headed by Guillermo Endara was officially recognized. The biggest U.S. military action since the Vietnam War, Operation Just Cause involved 24,000 American troops. The invasion was well received in the United States, but was criticized internationally.

"U.S. Forces Invade Panama, Seize Wide Control. Noriega Eludes Capture," *Facts on File* 22 December 1989.

What was acclaimed as "the world's most ambitious underwater archaeological operation"?

The raising of the *Mary Rose,* a sixteenth-century British warship, has been dubbed "the world's most ambitious underwater archaeological operation." On October 11, 1982, the ship was recovered from its resting place in the waters a mile off Portsmouth, England. Covered and protected by mud, most of its oak frame remained intact. A special steel cage was used to lift the remains of the ship to the surface, the first step in a long restoration project. Over 17 thousand artifacts are estimated to be preserved in the wreck, making it a "Tudor time capsule."

The *Mary Rose* was a famous warship, part of the navy of King Henry VIII (1491-1547); it sank in 1545 while preparing to do battle with the French. It is believed that the cannons on board were not properly secured, breaking through the ship's side as it heaved in the wind. Recovery of the ship cost seven million dollars and involved 17 years of research and planning.

"Sea Gives Up the Mary Rose, Warship That Was Henry VIII's Pride," *New York Times* 12 October 1982.

What are the major periods identified in the history of India?

Historians have divided the history of India into 13 major periods, based on political activity and cultural development. Beginning as early as 5000 B.C., the Dravidian Period is known only through it artifacts, including coins, writing instruments, architecture, and pottery. The Vedic Period began in 3000 B.C.: the Aryans invaded Northwest India, and created the first Aryan literature, the Vedas. The Epic Period, which started in 1500 B.C., saw even greater Aryan influence in India. The year 1000 B.C. marked the start of the Magadha Period, which provided the first true record of India's political history. Buddha was born in 557 B.C., and little more than 50 years later the first Buddhist Period began. The first Buddhist missionary work and commerce in other countries began during this age.

The later Buddhist Period included the years A.D. 1 to A.D. 300; Buddha's image was now an object of worship and commerce had begun with Rome and Alexandria. A period of Orthodox Hinduism began in 300 B.C. This period also included the first Hun War in A.D. 455 and the dominance of Sanskrit literature. In the year 600, a period typified by the rise of small kingdoms began. The period of Hindu Reformation started in 1200; India was using brass and copper currency and Indian writers used many different languages. The Mogul Period began in 1500, and was marked by the introduction of smoking and the appearance of the first Jesuit missionaries. The Period of Unsettlement, which started in 1700, saw a greatly increased European presence in India; the French were defeated by the British at Wandiwash. In the Victorian Age, 1850-1900, a war of independence failed and Britain claimed sovereignty over India. During the twentieth Century, India has seen the rise of Nationalism. Civil disobedience campaigns organized by Mohandras Gandhi in the 1930s solidified the Indian independence movement. The Union of India was established in 1947, when the British transferred power to an Indian government.

Stephen G. Krishnaya, comp., "Comparative Chart of Indian History," *The Scholastic* 8 January 1927. Harry Judge, ed., *World History From Earliest Times to 1800, vol. 3 of Oxford Illustrated Encyclopedia* (Oxford: Oxford University Press, 1988), s.v. "India." Robert Blake, ed., *World History From 1800 to Present Day vol. 4 of Oxford Illustrated Encyclopedia* (Oxford: Oxford University Press, 1988), s.v. "India."

What is the "Stone of Scone"?

The "Stone of Scone" is an important artifact of Scottish royal history. It is a rectangular slab of reddish-grey sandstone purported to be the stone Jacob used for a pillow *(Genesis 28).* Originally used as a coronation throne in Ireland, it was brought to Scotland by Kenneth I (d. 858) and was used in Scottish coronations until 1296. In that year it was removed by Edward I (1239-1307) to Westminster Abbey and was made the centerpiece of the Coronation Chair. In 1950 it was stolen by four Glasgow University students but was returned in 1952.

Bamber Gascoigne, *Encyclopedia of Britain* (New York: Macmillan Publishing, 1993), s.v. "Scone."

What are history's nine turning points?

According to *U.S. News & World Report,* the nine turning points in history are as follows:

The writings of the Apostle Paul that greatly influenced acceptance of Christianity.

The bubonic or Black plague which killed roughly one-third of Europe's population and subsequently fomented a social revolution which ended serfdom and issued in the Renaissance.

The voyages of Christopher Columbus which sparked European colonization of the New World.

The policies of French emperor Napoleon Bonaparte which helped create a middle class and subsequent democracy.

The Japanese rejection of Western technology, especially firearms.

The publication of Mark Twain's *Huckleberry Finn,* "which told thing as they were."

The charisma of Madame Chiang Kai-shek in the 1940s which blinded U.S. foreign policy, skewed U.S. views toward nationalist movements, and led to U.S. involvement in Korea and Vietnam.

The birth control pill and the resultant sexual revolution of the 1960s and 1970s.

Japan's post World War II economic revolution.

Del Jones, "Work finds place in world history," *USA Today* 21 December 1993.

What is a concentration camp?

A concentration camp is a place of confinement for those whom the state considers dangerous because of their political views or ethnic background. Usually persons are sent to concentration camps without trial or legal indictment. Prisoners are confined because of who they are, not what they have done, although often the state fears that they may engage in subversive activity.

The term "concentration camp" was coined by the British during the Boer War (1899-1902) in South Africa, but many other countries have used them. For example, the United States set up internment camps during World War II for more than 100,000 Japanese-Americans. By 1922 the Soviet Union had established 23 forced labor camps for those convicted of political and criminal offenses. They were expanded during World War II to include prisoners of war and citizens from Eastern Poland and the Baltic states, which had been absorbed by the Soviet Union.

Perhaps the most notorious camps were those of Nazi Germany. In 1933 the German chancellor Adolf Hitler (1889-1945) first established a concentration camp at Dachau, a small town outside of Munich, to incarcerate political prisoners. Soon minority groups, especially Jews, were also imprisoned. Since prisoners were expected to earn their food by their labor, those who were too sick to work or weakened by overwork often died of starvation. In 1940 new camps were built, usually in Poland, to serve as extermination centers for all those whom Hitler considered subhuman, subversive, or socially undesirable. At some camps humans were used for medical experimentation. About four millon people died in these facilities, about three quarters of whom were Jewish.

Konnilyn G. Feig, *Hitler's Death Camps; The Sanity of Madness* (New York: Holmes & Meier Publishers, 1981), xiii-xvi. *Encyclopedia Americana, intern. ed.* (Danbury, CT: Grolier, 1994), s.v. "concentration camp." Philip W. Goetz, ed., *The New Encyclopaedia Britannica, 15th ed., "Micropaedia"* (Chicago: Encyclopaedia Britannica, 1989), s.v. "concentration camp."

Who owns the Hope Diamond?

In 1958 the 44-carat Hope Diamond, legendary as a jinx for its possessors, was donated to the Smithsonian Institution by gem dealer Harry Winston. Winston acquired it in 1949 when he paid $1,500,000 for the jewel collection of Evalyn Walsh McLean. Among the diamond's previous owners were Marie Antoinette and London banker Henry Thomas Hope, who gave the diamond his name.

Current Biography Yearbook 1965 (New York: H. W. Wilson, 1966), s.v. "Winston, Harry." J. G. Lockhart, *Curses, Lucks and Talismans* (Detroit: Singing Tree Press, 1971), 68-71.

Are there any surviving American veterans of the Spanish-American War?

Nathan E. Cook, the last American veteran of the Spanish-American War, which began on February 15, 1898, and lasted for 112 days, died at the age of 106 on September 10, 1992.

St. Louis Post-Dispatch 31 May 1993.

What is the only state in the United States over which no foreign flag has ever flown?

Idaho is the only state that has never had a foreign flag fly over it.

Fred L. Worth, *The Trivia Encyclopedia,* (New York: Bell Publishing, 1974), s.v. "Idaho."

When did the French Indochina Wars occur?

During the late nineteenth and early twentieth centuries, French Indochina was the site of four wars. The French under Napoleon III wanted a greater share of the overseas markets in Indochina and to stop the persecution of French missionaries by the Vietnamese. The first French Indochina War, waged from 1858 to 1863, was a major success for the French, who secured from Vietnamese King Tu Duc a pledge for religious freedom for French missionaries, greater access to trade routes, and control of the provinces of Saigon, My Tho, and Bien Hoa.

The second French Indochina War 1873 to 1874, erupted when French explorer Francis Garnier (1839-73) was sent to the Vietnamese capital, Hanoi, to settle a dispute between the local Hanoi officials and an imprisoned French trader-smuggler. When the Vietnamese refused to agree to Garnier's request, he sent a French force to seize Hanoi. The force captured Hanoi and several other key Vietnamese cities. The Vietnamese and their Chinese allies formed a military force to oppose Garnier. Calling themselves the "Black Flag Pirates," this force put up strong resistance and eventually killed Garnier in late 1873. The French quickly lost interest in the war and eventually withdrew from Hanoi and the other cities they had captured. In return, the Vietnamese agreed to respect the religious freedom of French missionaries.

The third French Indochina War commenced in 1882 after the French accused the Vietnamese and their Chinese allies of persecuting French missionaries and opposing French expansion into Laos and Cambodia. The war lasted only one year and, as a result, the French gained control of Laos and strengthened their control over Vietnam.

Following the end of World War II (1939-45), the French were again embroiled in problems in French Indochina. In 1946, the Vietminh, a Communist group led by Ho Chi Minh (1890-1969), declared an independent Democratic Republic of Vietnam in the north. The Vietminh attacked the French throughout the north and in 1951, allied themselves with Communist groups in Laos and Cambodia. The war went quite badly for the French. The turning point of the war occurred in 1954 when a large Vietminh force under the command of General Vo Nguyen Giap besieged a French garrison at Dien Bien Phu. After 56 days, the French surrendered on May 7, 1954. All French forces were withdrawn shortly after. A peace agreement was signed dividing Vietnam at the seventeenth parallel. The Vietminh were given control of territory north of the parallel, while the non-Communist Vietnamese gained control of all territory south of the seventeenth parallel.

George C. Kohn, *Dictionary of Wars* (New York: Facts on File Publications, 1986), s.v. "French Indochina War of 1858-63," "French Indochina War of 1873-74," "French Indochina War of 1882-83," "French Indochina War of 1946-54."

What is the formal name of England's Prince Henry?

On September 15, 1984, Prince Henry was born to Prince Charles and Princess Diana. His official name is Henry Charles Albert David. Henry was chosen because it is a reminder of great English monarchs of the past, such as Henry V, Henry VIII, and Henry II. Charles was selected because it is a name strongly connected with Princess Diana's Spencer family heritage. Albert was the name of Prince Charles' grandfather, George VI, and Queen

Victoria's husband. David was the name of the Queen Mother's brother, David Bowes Lyon.

"The Newest Prince: Plain Harry at Home," *New York Times* 17 September 1984.

What are grace-and-favor apartments?

The British royal family owns many prestigious residences, such as Buckingham Palace, Hampton Court Palace, and Kensington Palace. All of these royal properties contain apartments that are rented free of charge to many of the queen's relatives, ambassadors and civil servants or their widows, retired or active members of the royal household staff, and senior military officers. Although tenants do not pay rent, they are expected to pay for heating and electricity. These royal apartments are often referred to as grace-and-favor apartments because the occupants are favored by the grace of the king or queen.

"Home a castle: They live free in palaces of royalty," *Pittsburgh Press* 18 April 1986.

Who were some of history's most prolific readers?

The following list of history's "most prolific readers" has been taken from remarks by the American critic and writer, Van Wyck Brooks (1886-1963), who, when seeing these numbers in print, contested their validity using his own experiences as a measure. His profession required Brooks to read on the average six to eight hours a day for the past twenty years. At this rate, he calculated, he read less than 6,000 books-less than one per day.

Adolf Hitler, who reportedly read over 7,000 military history titles.

Lawrence of Arabia, who was said to have read 40,000 books from the Oxford library.

Thomas Wolfe, who supposedly read 20,000 books during his life.

Time 13 January 1958.

Which United States president made the shortest inauguration speech?

The shortest inaugural speech by a United States president, only 135 words, was delivered by George Washington (1732-99) during his inauguration for a second term on March 4, 1793, in Philadelphia. By comparison, the longest inaugural speech was delivered by William Henry Harrison (1773-1841) in 1841. Lasting two hours his speech contained 8,445 words and was delivered during a snowfall. Harrison contracted pneumonia and died exactly one month later, becoming the first United States president to die in office.

Joseph Nathan Kane, *Facts About the Presidents, 5th ed.,* (New York: H. W. Wilson, 1989), 337.

In what ways are presidents Martin Van Buren and George Bush alike?

United States presidents Martin Van Buren (1837-41) and George Bush (1989-93) share a number of similarities. Both served in a variety of political positions before becoming president. Both served as vice president for two terms under popular presidents, with Van Buren serving under Andrew Jackson (1829-37) and Bush under Ronald Reagan (1981-89), before becoming president.

Like Bush, Van Buren served as vice president during a time of tremendous change in America, with the economy and social institutions undergoing profound transformations.

On the morning after his victory in the presidential election of 1988, George Bush gave thanks to Martin Van Buren, formerly the last sitting vice president elected to the presidency—152 years previous. Unfortunately for Bush, four years later another similarity with Van Buren arose—he was defeated for reelection and became a one-term president.

Arthur Levine, "President-Elect Martin Van Bush?," *New York Times* 28 December 1988.

Who was the last emperor of China?

Throughout history, China has had many dynasties and emperors. The last Chinese emperor was Henry Pu Yi (or P'uei) (1906-1967), who was the tenth emperor of the Ch'ing dynasty. Pu Yi was crowned emperor at the age of three. He abdicated power in 1912, was imprisoned following the Communist revolution in 1949, and was released from prison in 1959.

Following his release from prison, Pu Yi married Li Shuxian, a nurse. Although he underwent hormone treatments due to a problem with impotence, Pu Yi never fathered any offspring. When Pu Yi died in 1967 at the age of 61, the last Chinese dynasty came to an end. The life of Pu Yi was the subject of the highly acclaimed 1987 film *The Last Emperor.*

Parade 20 November 1988.

When did the British royal family officially change its name to Mountbatten-Windsor?

In 1960, Queen Elizabeth II (1926-) announced that the British royal family would officially change its name to Mountbatten-Windsor. The Queen announced the change so that her husband's family name, Mountbatten, would be added to her own family name of Windsor. The name change did not apply to the Queen or her children. However, all of her descendants, other than those entitled to the title of royal highness, prince, or princess, will take the Mountbatten-Windsor name. The Queen made her decision to change the family name to Mountbatten-Windsor to honor her husband, Prince Philip (1921-).

Drew Middleton, "Elizabeth Alters Royal Line's Name," *New York Times* 9 February 1960. "New Rule for Royal Name," *Pittsburgh Post-Gazette* 9 February 1960.

What is a cousin chart?

In genealogy, a cousin chart is a grid with branches where researchers can put the names of their family members and work back several generations. The chart can help an individual determine the difference between a first cousin (the child of one's aunt or uncle), a first cousin once removed (a first cousin's child), and a second cousin (the grandchild of one's great-aunt or great-uncle). By putting together a cousin chart, many people have found that they are related to famous persons.

"Cousins: from kissing to fourth 4 times removed," *Good Housekeeping* November 1981.

What well-known people became famous posthumously?

Many artists, scientists, and writers acquired fame posthumously. For example, composer Johann Sebastian Bach (1685-1750) was indeed known in musical circles during his life but primarily for his skill as an organist. Public interest in Bach's music didn't develop until 1829, some eighty years after his death; it has truly flourished in the 20th century.

French impressionist painter Paul Gauguin (1848-1903) was destitute at the end of his life, after leaving his home and family to paint in the South Pacific. Ridiculed for his unorthodox technique and subjects at the turn of the century, his works are now some of the highest valued paintings in the world.

Gregor Johann Mendel (1822-1884) was a monk and natural science teacher who quietly pursued advanced research in botany. His testing of pea plants was the basis for what are now known as "Mendel's Laws," which provided the first scientific explanation of how hereditary traits are transmitted. When three botanists presented the same findings 35 years later, they were shocked to find that Mendel had preceded them.

Physicist Robert Hutchings Goddard (1882-1945) wrote a paper in 1919 describing rockets that could fly to the moon. Ignored and ridiculed during his life for this idea, the United States government eventually spent a million dollars to avoid infringing on his 214 patents.

A pencil-maker, surveyor, and tutor, Henry David Thoreau (1817-1862) wrote what was to become an inspiration for twentieth century anarchist political thought. *Civil Disobedience* greatly influenced social leaders Mahatma Gandhi and Martin Luther King, Jr. His work, *Walden* was first published in 1854 and has never been our of print since.

The works of novelist Franz Kafka (1883-1924) may have never reached the public eye if his request to burn all of his writings had been fulfilled. Kafka died in 1924, considering himself a failure. His books began to be published the following year and are now considered modern classics.

Posthumous fame also came to composer Franz Schubert, poet Emily Dickinson, painter Vincent Van Gogh, railroad engineer Casey Jones, composer Scott Joplin, and diarist Anne Frank, among others.

David Wallechinsky and Irving Wallace, *The People's Almanac #3* (New York: William Morrow, 1981), 616-24.

What historian is associated with the "great man" theory?

The nineteenth-century Scottish historian Thomas Carlyle (1795-1881) is most often associated with the "great man" theory of history. Carlyle believed that all history is biography and that heroes shape history via their intellect and divine inspiration. Carlyle's theory is largely discounted today.

E.D. Hirsch, Jr., Joseph F. Kett, and James Trefil, *The Dictionary of Cultural Literacy* (Boston: Houghton Mifflin Company, 1988), s.v. "great man theory."

Who were some illustrious customers of Brooks Brothers, the famous men's clothing store?

Brooks Brothers, founded in 1818, is America's oldest and undoubtedly America's most famous men's apparel store. Over the decades it has had many illustrious customers including Abraham Lincoln, Franklin D. Roosevelt, John Foster Dulles, Charles Lindbergh, Gene Tunney, and Marlene Dietrich. Presidents Ulysses S. Grant, Theodore Roosevelt, and Woodrow Wilson wore Brooks Brothers's clothing when they took the oath of office. Franklin Roosevelt wore a Brooks Brothers Navy cape at Yalta, and Lincoln was wearing its Prince Albert coat, waistcoat, and trousers when he was assassinated. During the American Civil War, Brooks Brothers made uniforms for many Union generals, such as Grant, Sheridan, Sherman, and Hooker. Diplomats including Dean Acheson have long patronized the store and Charles Lindbergh was even loaned a Brooks Brothers suit by Ambassador Myron T. Herrick after his famous trans-Atlantic flight.

Tom Mahoney and Leonard Sloane, *The Great Merchants* (New York: Harper & Row, 1974), 39-40.

What is the inscription above the grave of the Unknown Soldier of Great Britain?

The inscription "A British Warrior, Who Fell in the Great War, 1914-1918, for King and Country" lies at the foot of a grave in London's Westminster Abbey. It honors this unknown soldier and all British soldiers who were killed in World War I. The grave was left open for one week and was attended by a continuous crowd of people, who filed past the memorial. When it came time to close the grave, it was filled with soil from French and Flemish battlefields.

Current History January 1921.

In which presidential inaugurations did Reverend Billy Graham participate in the swearing-in ceremonies?

The American evangelist the Reverend Billy Graham (1918-) has participated in seven inaugural ceremonies for both U.S. Democratic and Republican presidents. He has led prayer for the following presidents: Bill Clinton, George Bush, Ronald Reagan, Richard Nixon, Lyndon Johnson, and Dwight Eisenhower.

USA Today 21 January 1993.

What is the largest U.S. flag?

The largest U.S. flag on record is so big it almost covers two acres. Conceived by Len Silverfine of Bakersfield, Vermont, the flag is 411 feet by 210 feet. It requires a 25 foot crane and 100 volunteers to unfurl it. Silverfine's mission to make the largest flag began in 1976, when he made an enormous nylon flag that was to be hung from the Verrazano Narrows Bridge in New York City. That flag was a failure, being unable to bear the winds of New York Harbor. In 1980, the new polyester flag was displayed on Flag Day in Washington D.C. and it was later unfurled in honor of the return of U.S. hostages from Iran. The flag's size has created some problems for the Government Services Administration, its current owner. After sitting in a government warehouse for eight years the flag was to be displayed on Flag Day in 1991. A massive cleaning effort was required. Hundreds of workers in Humboldt, Tennessee sponge mopped the flag but were unable to dry it in 38 degree weather. The flag was then moved to a Marine parade ground in Quantico, Virginia where it could be spread out to dry. The laundering problems are typical of the relationship between Silverfine and the GSA; the flagmaker has frequently pressed officials to make more use of his flag.

Maria Puente, "Red Tape, Mildew Can't Keep Largest Flag from Flying," *USA Today* 14 June 1991.

What is the meaning and origin of Saddam Hussein's name?

Iraqi president Saddam Hussein (1937-) is known in his own country simply as "Saddam." His first name means "one who confronts," and is used exclusively in Iraqi news reports. His last name, Hussein, was the first name of his father; he also once had the regional surname Al-Takriti, indicating that he was from the town of Takrit. But Saddam has since abolished all use of such surnames, presumably to conceal the number of relatives included in his government.

"Name muddle: Say Saddam? Use Hussein"? *Pittsburgh Post-Gazette* 6 August 1990.

Do the "ramparts" mentioned by Francis Scott Key in "The Star-Spangled Banner" still stand?

Baltimore's Fort McHenry was the site of the battle that inspired Francis Scott Key (1779-1843) to write the words to "The Star-Spangled Banner." On September 13 and 14, 1814, the fort received a 25-hour bombardment by the British fleet, as Key watched from a distance. By the 1980s, Fort McHenry, a tourist site operated by the U.S. Park Service, was in disrepair. A multimillion dollar fundraising effort has been spearheaded by the "Patriots of Fort McHenry" to finance the fort's restoration. The outer battery, seawall, drainage system, a American Civil War powder magazine, buildings, and walls were all in need of repair.

"$6 Million Sought to Restore Fort McHenry," *New York Times* 12 October 1984.

Is there a list of the 100 most influential people in the history of the world?

In 1978 astronomer Michael Hart published *The 100*, a book that lists, in his opinion the 100 most influential people in world history. Actually 101 names appear as Hart listed the Wright brothers as a single entry. Individuals were included based on "the total influence that each of them had on human history and on the everyday lives of other human beings." The top ten most influential people on his list are: Muhammad, Isaac Newton, Jesus Christ, Buddha, Confucius, Saint Paul, Tsai Lun, Johann Gutenberg, Christopher Columbus, and Albert Einstein.

Kenneth L. Woodward, "All-Stars of History," *Newsweek* 31 July 1978.

What is "Little America"?

Polar explorer Richard Evelyn Byrd (1888-1957) of Virginia called his base of operations in the Antarctic "Little America." From this location he explored the region during the years 1928-30, including his flight over the South Pole, and 1933-35. His explorations were the basis for U.S. territorial claims in the Artic.

Howard L. Hurwitz, *An Encyclopedic Dictionary of American History* (New York: Washington Square Press, 1968), s.v. "Byrd, Richard Evelyn."

Does more than one cast of the Liberty Bell exist?

Fifty-three replicas of the Liberty Bell were cast at a foundry in Annecy, France. The replicas are the same in size, tone, and inscription, but the crack is only etched in outline on the surface. All fifty states, District of Columbia, and Puerto Rico have one. One was given to U.S. President Harry S. Truman, (1884-1972) which is now located at the Truman Library in Independence, Missouri.

Charles Michael Boland, *Ring in the Jubilee: The Epic of America's Liberty Bell* (Riverside, CT: The Chatham Press, 1973), 118.

Which U.S. presidents have been left-handed?

James Garfield (1821-81), Harry S. Truman (1884-1972), Gerald Ford (1913-), George Bush (1924-) and Bill Clinton (1946-) are the left-handed U.S. presidents. During the 1992 campaign, the three main candidates for the presidency were left-handed: Bush, Clinton, and Ross Perot.

William A. DeGregorio, *The Complete Book of U.S. Presidents, 2d ed.* (New York: Dembner Books, 1989), 293, 603, 663. *Parade Magazine* 13 September 1992. David Wallechinsky and Irving Wallace, *The People's Almanac* (New York: Doubleday, 1975), 1226-27.

When did the United States officially enter the First and Second World Wars?

At 1:18 p.m. on April 6, 1917, the United States officially announced that it was declaring war against Germany, thus entering World War I (1914-18). On April 2, U.S. president Woodrow Wilson (1856-1924) had asked Congress to recognize a state of war, which the Senate did two days later, with the House following suit on April 6.

At 12:30 p.m. on December 8, 1941, U.S. president Franklin D. Roosevelt (1882-1945) appeared before a joint session of Congress to ask that it declare a state of war between the United States and Japan. In less than an hour both houses of Congress approved the declaration and at 4:10 p.m. Roosevelt signed it, bringing the United States into World War II (1939-45). Three days later Japan's Axis partners, Germany and Italy, declared war on the United States, and Congress replied in kind.

Ronald H. Bailey, *The Home Front: U.S.A.* (Chicago: Time-Life Books, 1978), 23. *Chronicle of America* (Liberty, MO: JL International, 1993), 599.

Was Princess Diana related to any U.S. presidents?

Genealogists have discovered that through her father, the eighth Earl Spencer, Great Britain's Princess Diana was related to seven U.S. presidents, including John Adams and Franklin D. Roosevelt.

James Lemoyne and Lea Donosky, "England's Second Family," *Newsweek* 9 March 1981.

Who was Dennis Hart Mahan?

Dennis Hart Mahan was one of the United States' most noted military theorists. He graduated at the top of his class at West Point in 1824 and became an assistant professor there. In 1830, after two years of teaching, he became Professor of Engineering at West Point. The military academy at this time lacked any credible engineering texts, so Mahan wrote his own. Because his books were so well-written, they became principal engineering texts in colleges throughout the country.

Mahan was also a noted military theorist who extensively studied the military tactics of the French emperor and military genius Napoleon Bonaparte (1769-1821). Mahan's analyses of many military operations were so well-received that they became the basis for the first course on military tactics at West Point. One of Mahan's most famous books, *Advanced Guard, Outpost and Detachment Service of Troops, with the Essential Principles of Strategy and Grand Tactics*, was studied extensively by both Union and Confederate military leaders during the American Civil War.

R. Ernest Dupuy and Trevor N. Dupuy, *The Encyclopedia of Military History: From 3500 B.C. to the Present, 2d ed.* (New York: Harper & Row, 1986), 742.

What was the process used to name Princess Beatrice, the daughter of the Duke and Duchess of York?

The naming of a new member of the British royal family is a lengthy, complicated process. Royal protocol dictates that over 200 people in the royal family must be contacted to receive their imput on a name for a new heir. The Duke and Duchess of York eventually decided on the name Beatrice because of their close relationship with Spain's King Juan Carlos and his wife Sophie. Beatrice was the name of Juan Carlos' great-grandmother. Britain's Beatrice was born on August 8, 1988.

Barbara Reynolds and Princess Simmons, "Naming a princess is tedious work, 200 relatives must say OK," *USA Today* 23 August 1988.

Who was Ariel Durant?

Ariel Durant, a well-known popularizer of history, was born Ida Kaufman in Prosurov, Russia, in 1898 and came to New York with her parents in 1900. At the age of 15 she married her teacher, Will Durant, and soon legally changed her name to Ariel. In 1926 Will Durant published *The Story of Philosophy*, which sold over two million copies. Ariel collaborated with her husband on the highly acclaimed 11 volume series *The Story of Civilization*. The first volume was written in 1935, and the final volume was completed in 1975. Although Ariel contributed to all of the volumes in this series, she was not listed as a co-author until the publication of the seventh volume in 1961.

The writings of Ariel and Will Durant earned the accolades of many critics. In 1968, the Durants won the Pulitzer Prize for general nonfiction for their work *Rousseau and Revolution*. They also received the Presidential Medal of Freedom in 1977. Ariel Durant died on October 25, 1981, at the age of 83. Her husband died just seven days later, on November 7.

New York Times 28 October 1981.

Geography and Maps

What is the former name of Zimbabwe?

The nation of Zimbabwe, located in southern Africa, was formerly known as Rhodesia. In 1980, during a change of government rule from the white minority to the black majority, the name of the country changed to Zimbabwe.

World Book Encyclopedia (Chicago: World Book, 1987), s.v. "Zimbabwe."

Who discovered Greenland?

The island of Greenland was discovered accidentally by the Norseman Gunbjorn in A.D. 900. While sailing from Norway toward Iceland, Gunbjorn was blown off course and landed at an ice-covered island that is known today as Greenland.

James Trager, *The People's Chronology: A Year-by-Year Record of Human Events from Prehistory to the Present, rev. ed.* (New York: Henry Holt, 1992), 73.

What country was known as Persia until 1935?

In 1935 the former country of Persia became known as Iran. The official name of the country is the Islamic Republic of Iran.

David Munro, ed., *Chambers World Gazetteer* (Edinburgh: W & R Chambers; Cambridge: Cambridge University Press, 1988), s.v. "Iran."

What are the world's largest countries in size?

In terms of sheer geographic area, the list of the five largest countries in the world is led by the Russia. It stretches 6.6 million square miles. Next is Canada, with 3.9 million square miles; the People's Republic of China, with 3.7 million square miles; and the United States, at 3.6 million square miles. Brazil is the planet's fifth-largest country at 3.3 million square miles.

Information Please Almanac Atlas & Yearbook 1995, 47th ed. (Boston: Houghton Mifflin, 1995), 128.

What is the Northwest Passage?

The Northwest Passage is the fabled route from Europe to Asia via North America's northernmost waters near the Arctic Circle. European navigators sought to reach important Asian trading centers the quickest way possible and made several attempts during the sixteenth century. English explorers such as Martin Frobisher (1535-94), Humphrey Gilbert (1539-83), and Henry Hudson (d. 1611) were frustrated in their attempts to reach Asia via this route; they were not aware that the waters of the elusive passage were frozen much of the year.

Kenneth C. Davis, *Don't Know Much About History* (New York: Crown Publishers, 1990), 12-13.

What are the geographic extremes of the United States?

The geographic extremes of the United States include Ka Lae (South Cape), Hawaii; as the southernmost point (Key West, Florida, if only the 48 contiguous states are counted); Point Barrow, Alaska as the northernmost point (Warroad, Minnesota, if only the lower 48 contiguous states are counted); a point near Eastport and Lubec, Maine, as the easternmost point; and Attu Island, Alaska, as the westernmost point (Cape Alava, Washington, if only the lower 48 contiguous states are counted).

William H. Laughlin, *Laughlin's Fact Finder* (West Nyack, NY: Parker Publishing, 1969), 271.

Which American city's name means "red stick"?

The name of Louisiana's capital of Baton Rouge translates from the French into "red stick." Its roots date back to the Choctaw Native Americans who originally settled the area. They referred to the area as *istrouma*, a word believed to mean "red pole." It is assumed that this refers to a boundary pole between the Choctaw lands and a neighboring region belonging to another Native American group.

Kelsie B. Harder, ed., *Illustrated Dictionary of Place Names: United States and Canada* (New York: Facts on File, 1985), s.v. "Baton Rouge."

What was the former name of the country of Suriname?

The present day country of Suriname was formerly known as Dutch Guiana, having been a Dutch colony. Before it achieved independence in 1975 Suriname was an autonomous region of the Netherlands. The country, which has an area of 63,036 square miles, is located on the north-central coast of South America. In its early days African slaves, European colonists, and contract laborers from Asia came or were brought to the equatorial Dutch colony resulting in a very diverse ethnic mix. Its 1991 population of 404,310 was 35 percent Creole, 33 percent Indian, 16 percent Javanese, 10 percent Black, and 3 percent Amerindian. Nearly half of the population lives in Paramaribo, the country's capital. Mainstays of the economy are Bauxite mining and agriculture, especially rice, citrus fruits, plantains and bananas.

Arthur S. Banks, ed., *Political Handbook of the World* (Binghamton, NY: CSA Publications, 1993), s.v. "Suriname." Brian Hunter, ed., *The Statesman's Year-Book* (New York: St. Martin's Press, 1994), s.v. "Suriname."

What was the only country that bordered the Soviet Union but not in the Eastern Bloc?

Finland was the only European country that bordered the Soviet Union, but was not in the Eastern Bloc.

E.D. Hirsch, Joseph F. Kett, and James Trefil, *The Dictionary of Cultural Literacy* (Boston: Houghton Mifflin Company, 1988), s.v. "Finland."

What two rivers formed the boundary of ancient Mesopotamia?

Mesopotamia is a Greek word that means "land between the rivers." The two rivers that formed the traditional boundaries of ancient Mesopotamia were the Tigris and the Euphrates. Much of the land that was part of Mesopotamia is now part of Iraq.

Philip W. Goetz, ed., *The New Encyclopedia Britannica, 15th ed., "Micropaedia"* (Chicago: Encyclopaedia Britannica, 1989), s.v. "Mesopotamia."

What is a savanna?

A savanna is a tropical grassland which occurs in both hemispheres between equatorial forests and deserts. Savanna climates are marked by distinct wet and dry seasons while the ground cover is largely grass with scattered trees.

W. G. Moore, *A Dictionary of Geography, rev. ed.* (New York: Frederick A. Praeger, 1967), s.v. "savanna."

What is the oldest public park in the United States?

Boston Common is considered to be the oldest public park in the United States. The Common was established in 1634 with the purchase of 45 acres of land, for which the Reverend William Blaxton received thirty pounds. The land was used as a grazing area for two centuries, and it served as the militia's training area until the American Civil War. There have never been any permanent buildings on Boston Common.

Fodor's Boston, 1986 (New York: Fodor's Travel Guides, 1986), 32. Lawrence W. Kennedy, *Planning the City Upon a Hill: Boston Since 1630* (Boston: University of Massachusetts Press, 1992), 19.

In which European city was Archduke Francis Ferdinand assassinated and was much later the site of Olympic games?

Francis Ferdinand (1863-1914), archduke of Austria-Este, was assassinated with his wife in the streets of Sarajevo, Bosnia, on June 28, 1914, by Bosnian Serb Gavrilo Princip. This event is generally regarded as being the flashpoint of World War I (1914-18). In 1984 the winter Olympic games were held in Sarajevo, by then a Yugoslavian city.

Holger H. Herwig and Neil M. Heyman, *Biographical Dictionary of World War I* (Westport, CT: Greenwood Press, 1982), s.v. "Francis Ferdinand." Philip W. Goetz, ed., *The New Encyclopedia Britannica, 15th ed., "Micropaedia"* (Chicago: Encyclopaedia Britannica, 1989), s.v. "Sarajevo."

Where is the Petrified Forest?

The 93,533 acre Petrified Forest National Park is located 19 miles east of Holbrook, Arizona, in the east-central portion of the state. It features the rainbow colored, fossilized logs of the Petrified Forest as well as the Painted Desert, a spectacularly colored area of sand and stone, and Anasazi Indian village ruins and petroglyphs. The Petrified Forest is further divided into five areas known as Blue Mesa, Jasper Forest, Crystal Forest, Rainbow Forest, and Black Forest.

AAA Tourbook: Arizona, New Mexico (Heathrow, FL: American Automobile Association, 1994), 53.

Where is the southernmost city in the world?

Punta Arenas (formerly Magallanes), Chile, is farther south than any other settlement of sufficient size and having enough commercial importance to deserve being called a city. It lies on the extreme southern end of Patagonia on the Strait of Magellan at 53 degrees 10 minutes south latitude. The world's southernmost village is Puerto Williams (population about 350), Tierra del Fuego, Chile, being 680 miles (1,094 kilometers) north of Antarctica.

George Stimpson, *Information Roundup* (New York: Harper, 1948), 285. *Webster's New Geographical Dictionary* (Springfield, MA: Merriam-Webster, 1988), s.v. "Punta Arenas"; Robert Famighetti, ed., *The World Almanac and Book of Facts 1995* (Mahwah, NJ: World Almanac, 1994), 166.

Where are the northernmost and southernmost points of land?

The most northern point of land is Cape Morris K. Jesup on the northeastern extremity of Greenland. It is at 83 degrees, 39 minutes north latitude and is 440 miles (708 kilometers) from the North Pole. However, the *Guinness Book of Records 1995* reports that, an islet of 100 feet across, called Odaaq, is more northerly at 83 degrees, 40 minutes north latitude and 438.9 miles (706 kilometers) from the North Pole. The southernmost point of land is the South Pole, since the South Pole, unlike the North Pole, is on land.

Mark C. Young, ed., *Guinness Book of Records 1995* (New York: Facts on File, 1994), 25. George Stimpson, *Information Roundup* (New York: Harper. 1948), 416.

What are relief maps, and when were they first used?

A relief map is a three-dimensional map in which the topographical features project above and below a level surface. The Chinese were the first to use relief maps where the contours of the terrain were represented in models. Relief maps in China go back at least to the third century B.C. Some early maps were modeled in rice or carved in wood. It is likely that the idea of making relief maps was transmitted from the Chinese to the Arabs and then to Europe. The earliest known relief map in Europe was a map showing part of Austria, made in 1510 by Paul Dox.

Robert K. G. Temple, *The Genius of China* (New York: Simon and Schuster, 1986), 179-81.

Who was the first person to map the Gulf Stream?

In his travels to and from France as a diplomat, Benjamin Franklin (1706-1790) noticed a difference in speed in the two directions of travel between France and America. He was the first to study ships' reports seriously to determine the cause of the speed variation. As a result, he found that there was a current of warm water coming from the Gulf of Mexico that crossed the North Atlantic Ocean in the direction of Europe. In 1770, Franklin mapped it.

Isaac Asimov, *Asimov's Chronology of Science and Discovery* (New York: Harper and Row, 1989), 215-216.

What is the slogan of Los Angeles County, California?

In 1995 Los Angeles County, California adopted "Together, we're the best. Los Angeles." The slogan was chosen to improve the city's tarnished image. It will be used in billboards, celebrity television and radio commercials, and a jingle.

Annie Shooman, "Los Angeles' new slogan lacks punch-for a reason," *Detroit News* 7 June 1995.

Where is Adam's Peak?

Adam's Peak is the name of one of Sri Lanka's highest mountains. The cone-shaped peak is 7,360 feet high and is located in the island's southern region. It's name is derived from a formation on the summit that looks like a giant footprint, which is attributed to Adam. That is according to Mohammedan lore; Hindu legend gives this role to the god Siva; and Buddhists believe that the footprint belongs to Gautama Buddha.

Dorothy Rose Blumberg, *Whose What? Aaron's Beard to Zorn's Lemma* (New York: Holt, Rinehart and Winston, 1969), s.v. "Adam's Peak."

Where is the Valley of the Fallen, also known as Valle de los Cados?

The memorial to the Spainish Civil War dead, the Valle de los Cados or Valley of the Fallen, is located northwest of Madrid, near the Escorial, the sixteenth-century palace. Set in a state park, it is a crypt cut in living rock that is topped by a 429-foot concrete and stone cross. The site also includes a Benedictine monastery and the grave of former Spanish state head General Francisco Franco (1892-1975).

Fodor's Spain, 1987 (New York: Fodor's Travel Guides, 1987), 138.

Who named America?

Martin Waldseemller (1454-1512), a German geographer, used the name "America" in his *Cosmographiae introductio* (1507). He derived the term from the name of the Italian navigator Amerigo Vespucci who had sighted the South America mainland in 1797. Waldseemller was apparently unaware that Christopher Columbus (1451-1506) had voyaged to the new world five years earlier than Vespucci. Because the book became very popular, the term became universally accepted.

Clarence L. Barnhart, ed., *The New Century Cyclopedia of Names* (New York: Appleton-Century-Crofts, 1954), s.v. "America." Philip W. Goetz, ed., *The New Encyclopaedia Britannica, 15th ed., "Micropaedia"* (Chicago: Encyclopaedia Britannica, 1991), s.v. "Americas."

What is the largest county in the United States?

Excluding Alaska, the largest U.S. county in area is San Bernardino, California, at 20,064 square miles. According to the 1990 U.S. census it has a population of 1,418,380, growing 58 percent in number from the 1980 census. However, the largest county in terms of population is Los Angeles, California, with a population of 8,863,052 (1990 census; increase of 18.5 percent over 1980 census).

Robert Famighetti, ed., *The World Almanac and Book of Facts 1995* (Mahwah, NJ: World Almanac, 1994), 378, 424, 497.

How did Piccadilly in London, England, get its name?

Piccadilly, the famous thoroughfare of London, England, is said to have received its name from the word "pickadel," a collar worn by men of fashion in the seventeenth century. Robert Baker, a retired tailor, built a house at the corner of Windmill Street, which became known as Piccadilly Hall. Baker never referred to his home by that name but others did. It is surmised that neighbors nicknamed it after an article of apparel formerly sold by Baker.

Arthur Irwin Dasent, *Piccadilly in Three Centuries* (London: Macmillan, 1920), 8-17.

How is Iceland's capital, Reykjavk, heated?

Reykjavk, the capital of Iceland, was once a tiny fishing village and is now an attractive modern city that serves as the country's cultural, economic, and industrial center. Most of Reykjavk's buildings are made from concrete and are heated by underground hot springs.

Philip W. Goetz, ed., *The New Encyclopaedia Britannica, 15th ed., "Micropaedia"* (Chicago: Encyclopedia Britannica, 1989), s.v. "Reykjavk."

Why is Ireland called the "Emerald Isle"?

The "Emerald Isle" is a poetic name for Ireland, popular in part because of the country's deep green fields and trees. Irish poet William Dronnan claimed to have coined the name because it first appeared in print in his 1795 poem entitled "Erin." The stanza in question reads as follows:

> "Arm of Erin! prove strong; but be gentle as brave,
> And, uplifted to strike, still be ready to save;
> Nor one feeling of vengeance presume to defile
> The cause, or the men, of the Emerald Isle."

The World Book Encyclopedia (Chicago: World Book, 1987), s.v. "emerald isle."

What are the most common county names in the United States?

The most common names for counties in the United States are Washington, Jefferson, Franklin, Jackson, and Lincoln.

USA Today 20 July 1989.

Which three state capitals lie on the Missouri River?

The Missouri River is the second-longest river in the United States, measuring 2,315 miles. Three state capitals are located on the Missouri River: Jefferson City, Missouri; Bismarck, North Dakota; and Pierre, South Dakota.

The Encyclopedia Americana, intern. ed. (Danbury, CT: Grolier, 1990), s.v. "Missouri River."

What is the most frequently crossed international border?

In 1993, the busiest international frontier is the 1,933-mile Mexico-United States border. In fiscal year 1993 (ending in September of 1993) there were 452,657,133 crossing.

Mark Young, ed., *The Guinness Book of Records, 1995* (New York: Facts on File, 1994), 175.

What is the name of the group of islands at the extreme southern tip of South America?

The Tierra del Fuego archipelago is at the extreme southern tip of South America, south of the Strait of Magellan. The archipelago covers 26,872 square miles, and the largest island in the group is also named Tierra del Fuego, which means "Land of Fire."

Webster's New Geographical Dictionary (Springfield, MA: G & C Merriam, 1972), s.v. "Tierra del Fuego." *World Book Encyclopedia* (Chicago: World Book, 1987), s.v. "Tierra del Fuego."

What is the oldest surviving map ?

The oldest known map is a Babylonian clay tablet dating from about 2500 B.C. The map resides in the Semitic Museum of Harvard.

Isaac Asimov, *Isaac Asimov's Book of Facts* (East Brunswick, NJ: Bell Publishing Company, 1981).

Geographically, how is Paris divided?

Paris is geographically divided by the Seine River, which courses through the middle of the city. Traditionally the Left Bank has been associated with the city's intellectual life, while the Right Bank has had a more commercial orientation. However, as Paris has developed, these distinctions have become blurred.

Stephen Brough, ed., *The Economist Business Traveller's Guides. Europe's Business Cities* (New York: Prentice Hall, 1989), 57.

Is there a town known as the "Dachshund Capital of the World"?

The German village Gergweis is known as the "Dachshund Capital of the World." This Lower Bavarian village, located 90 miles northeast of Munich, has a population of over 1,000 dachshunds, outnumbering its human population by nearly two-to-one.

Marcy Rosenberg, "A Very Shaggy Dog Story," *New York Times* 5 January 1975.

What are the five largest islands in the world?

The five largest islands in the world in square miles are Greenland, 839,999; New Guinea, 316,615; Borneo, 286,914; Madagascar, 226,657; and Baffin, 183,810.

Information Please Almanac Atlas & Yearbook, 1995, 48th ed. (Boston: Houghton Mifflin, 1994), 489.

Who were the first men to reach the top of Mt. Everest?

On May 29, 1953, Sir Edmund Hillary and Da Tenzig became the first men to reach the peak of Mt. Everest, the world's highest mountain.

John Hunt, *The Conquest of Everest* (New York: E. P. Dutton, 1954), 237.

What are the "Seven Seas"?

The "Seven Seas" is an ancient term that is generally used to refer to the Arctic, Antarctic, North and South Atlantic, North and South Pacific, and Indian Oceans. The term is more romantic than literal and carries no official geographic authority.

World Book Encyclopedia (Chicago: World Book, 1987), s.v. "seven seas."

What are the Maritime and Prairie Provinces of Canada?

The Maritime Provinces of Canada are Nova Scotia, New Brunswick, and Prince Edward Island and the Prairie Provinces are Manitoba, Saskatchewan, and Alberta.

Encyclopedia Canadiana (Toronto: Grolier of Canada, 1972), s.v. "maritime provinces," "prarie provinces."

How did Cape Canaveral in Florida get its name?

The origin of the word "Canaveral," as in Cape Canaveral, Florida, is a Spanish word meaning "thicket of canes." The Cape was named by Pedro de Menendez, the first Spanish governor of Florida who found sugarcane growing there.

"Space-Age Sight-Seeing," *New York Times* 7 December 1958.

Where is No Man's Land?

Three areas in the United States are referred to as No Man's Land. One is a small island near Martha's Vineyard, Massachusetts. Another is the panhandle of Oklahoma, so called because Congress failed to assign it to any state or territory after the Compromise of 1850. The third is a local name given to a strip of land on the boundary of Pennsylvania and Delaware, which by official survey belongs to Pennsylvania, but by habit and custom of the people, to Delaware.

Mitford M. Matthews, ed., *A Dictionary of Americanisms: On Historical Principles* (Chicago: University of Chicago Press, 1951) s.v. "No Man's Land."

What is the origin of India's coat of arms?

India's coat of arms is an adaptation of a monument in Bhopal, known as the Asoka Pillar. Named for a famous emperor, it features a pedestal mounted by three lions. The base shows figures of native animals and a symbolic "Wheel of Destiny."

New York Times 23 April 1950.

How did the atlas get its name?

A picture of the Greek mythological figure Atlas, noted for his great strength, bearing the world on his back was the frontispiece for a book of maps by Gerhard Mercator, a French geographer of the late sixteenth century. Shortly thereafter a collection of maps came to be called an atlas.

Robert Hendrickson, *The Literary Life and Other Curiosities* (New York: Viking Press, 1981), 245. *Webster's Ninth New Collegiate Dictionary* (Springfield, MA: Merriam-Webster, 1988), s.v. "atlas."

What is a tundra?

A tundra is a treeless plain of North America and northern Eurasia, much of which lies above the Arctic Circle. The tundra climate has mean monthly temperatures below the freezing point for much of the year with long, severe winters and short, hot summers. A characteristic of much of the tundra is the permanently frozen ground which lies a few inches below the surface. Trees, other than stunted willows and birches are not part of the landscape but the tundra does support mosses, lichens and a few flowering plants. There is no landscape comparable to the tundra in the southern hemisphere.

Wilfred G. Moore, *A Dictionary Of Geography* (New York: Frederick A. Praeger, 1967), s.v. "tundra."

What is the length of a degree of longitude?

The length of a degree of longitude shortens as one moves through the north or south latitudes towards the poles. At the equator a degree of longitude is approximately 69 miles, very close to the length of a degree of latitude. At 30 degrees north or south latitude, a degree of longitude is about 60 miles; at 60 degrees north or south latitude, it measures 34.6 miles; and 12 miles, at 80 degrees of latitude. At the poles a degree of longitude has no measurement.

W. G. Moore, *A Dictionary of Geography* (New York: Frederick A. Praeger, 1967), s.v. "longitude."

What are Landsat maps?

They are images of the earth taken at an altitude of 567 miles (912.3 kilometers) by an orbiting Landsat satellite, or ERTS (Earth Resources Technology Satellite). The Landsats were originally launched in the 1970s. Rather than cameras, the Landsats use multispectral scanners, which detect visible green and blue wavelengths, and four infrared and near-infrared wavelengths. These scanners can detect differences between soil, rock, water, and vegetation; types of vegetation; states of vegetation (e.g., healthy/unhealthy or underwatered/well-watered); and mineral content. The differences are especially accurate when multiple wavelengths are compared using multispectral scanners. Even visible light images have proved useful-some of the earliest Landsat images showed that some small Pacific islands were up to 10 miles (16 kilometers) away from their charted positions.

The results are displayed in "false-color" maps, where the scanner data is represented in shades of easily distinguishable colors-usually, infrared is shown as red, red as green, and green as blue. The maps are used by farmers, oil companies, geologists, foresters, foreign governments, and others interested in land management. Each image covers an area approximately 115 miles (185 kilometers) square. Maps are offered for sale by the United States Geological Survey.

Other systems that produce similar images include the French SPOT satellites, the Russian Salyut and Mir manned space stations, and NASA's Airborne Imaging Spectrometer, which senses 128 infrared bands. NASA's Jet Propulsion Laboratories are developing instruments which will sense 224 bands in infrared, which will be able to detect specific minerals absorbed by plants.

How In the World? (Pleasantville, NY: Reader's Digest Association, 1990), 174-75. *The Map Catalog* (New York: Vintage, 1986), 123, 125. Caroline Sutton and Duncan M. Anderson, *How Do They Do That?* (New York: Quill, 1982), 174.

Where is the world's deepest lake?

Lake Baikal, located in southeast Siberia, is 5,314 feet (1,620 meters) deep at its maximum depth, making it the deepest lake in the world. The lake is 385 miles in length and varies between 20 and 46 miles in width. Lake Tanganyika in Africa is the second deepest lake with a depth of 4,708 feet (1,435 meters).

Otto Johnson, ed., *1995 Information Please Almanac* (Boston: Houghton Mifflin Company, 1994), 486. Rupert O. Matthews, *The Atlas of Natural Wonders* (New York: Facts on File, 1988), 96. Mark C. Young, ed., *The Guinness Book of Records 1995* (New York: Facts on File, 1994), 65.

How large is Dinosaur National Monument?

Dinosaur National Monument consists of 211,272 acres (85,499 hectares) on the border of northeast Utah and northwest Colorado. It contains the largest known concentration of fossilized bones. Most of the monument is a scenic wilderness area of canyons formed by the Green River and its tributary the Yampa.

World Book Encyclopedia (Chicago: World Book, 1993), 14:51. John W. Wright, ed., *The Universal Almanac 1994* (Kansas City, MO: Andrews and McMeel, 1993), 39-40.

Is Chicago the windiest city?

Although Chicago has been called the "windy city," it ranked 21st in the list of 68 windy cities with an average wind speed of 10.3 miles (16.6 kilometers) per hour in 1990. Cheyenne, Wyoming, with an average wind speed of 12.9 miles (20.8 kilometers) per hour, ranks number one, closely followed by Great Falls, Montana, with an average wind speed of 12.8 miles (20.6 kilometers) per hour. The highest surface wind ever recorded was on Mount Washington, New Hampshire at an elevation of 6288 feet (1.9 kilometers). On April 12, 1934 its wind was 231 miles (371.7 kilometers) per hour and its average wind speed was 35 miles (56.3 kilometers) per hour. According to the *Weather Alamanac*, Cheyenne has dropped from first place to fifth.

As for Chicago, its nickname has nothing to do with the forces of nature but rather comes from its history. Chicago received its nickname "the windy city" when it was one of four cities competing to be the site of the world's Columbian Exposition of 1893. Bidding was started in 1889 when the U.S. Congress authorized the exposition and set hearings for the site. During the intense competition, Charles A. Dana, in his *New York Sun*, wrote of Chicago, "Don't pay any attention to the nonsensical claims of that windy city. Its people couldn't build a world's fair even if they won it."

Herman Kogan and Lloyd Wendt, *Chicago: A Pictorial History* (New York: E.P. Dutton, 1958), 162. Les Krantz, *The Best and Worst of Everything* (New York: Prentice Hall, 1991), 102-3. Jack Williams, *The Weather Alamanac 1995* (New York: Vantage Books, 1994), 125. Jack Williams, *The Weather Book* (New York: Vintage Books, 1992), 43.

What are the U.S. sunbelt states?

The U.S. sunbelt states include the southern states of Alabama, Arkansas, Delaware, Florida, Georgia, Kentucky, Louisiana, Maryland, Mississippi, North Carolina, South Carolina, Tennessee, Virginia, and West Virginia; and the southwestern states of Arizona, New Mexico, Oklahoma, and Texas; and Hawaii.

Library of Congress Subject Headings (Washington, DC: Library of Congress, 1993), s.v. "Sunbelt States." *World Book Encyclopedia* (Chicago: World Book, 1994), 20:103

Which countries had been satellites of the Soviet Union?

The satellites of the Soviet Union were Bulgaria, Czechoslovakia, Hungary, Poland, Romania, and East Germany. The communist regimes in Albania and Yugoslavia were also influenced by the Soviet Union.

The World Book Encyclopedia (Chicago: World Book, 1994), s.v. "Russia."

Where is the geographic center of the United States?

If one includes Alaska and Hawaii, the geographic center of the United States is in Butte County, west of Castle Rock, South Dakota, approximately latitude of 44 degrees, 58 minutes north and longitude 103 degrees, 46 minutes west.

If referring only to the contiguous (48 states) United States, the geographic center is near Lebanon, Smith County, Kansas, latitude 39 degrees, 50 minutes north and longitude 98 degrees, 35 minutes west.

Robert Famighetti, ed., *The World Almanac and Book of Facts 1995* (Mahwah, NJ: Funk & Wagnalls, 1994), 427.

What is the Indian name for Lake Superior?

Lake Superior, the largest and deepest of the Great Lakes, is known by the Chippewa Indians as "Gitche Gumee." The most popular references to this name are in Henry Wadsworth Longfellow's (1807-1882) poem "The Song of Hiawatha" and in popular song-writer Gordon Lightfoot's ballad "The Wreck of the Edmund Fitzgerald."

Henry Wadsworth Longfellow, *The Poems of Longfellow* (New York: Random House, 1944), 135. Grace Lee Nute, *Lake Superior* (Indianapolis: Bobbs-Merrill, 1944), 331.

What is the "matabeleland" in Zimbabwe?

In Zimbabwe, the "matabeleland" is the name of the region around Bulowayo in which Ndebele-speakers live.

Tim Guyse Williams, ed.*BBC World Service Glossary of Current Affairs,* (Chicago: St. James Press, 1991), 729.

How many miles of international boundaries does the United States have?

According to the U.S. Geological Survey of the Department of the Interior, the United States has 7,458 miles of international boundaries. The northern boundary between Canada and the United States, excluding Alaska, but including the boundaries of the Great Lakes, is 3,987 miles, which makes it the longest continuous frontier in the world. The border between Alaska and Canada is 1,538 miles. The border between Mexico and the United States measures 1,933 miles from the Pacific Ocean to the Gulf of Mexico.

Robert Famighetti, ed., *The World Almanac and Book of Facts 1995* (Mahwah, NJ: World Almanac, 1994), 50.

Why is New York City called the Big Apple?

The term the Big Apple in reference to New York City had its origins with jazz musicians and their booking agents back in the 1920s and 1930s. Club dates in small towns were referred to as "little apples," while gigs in jazz clubs in large cities came to be known as a "big apples." Since the premiere jazz clubs were located in Harlem, "the Big Apple" became synonymous with New York City. Previously the phrase was used in New Orleans, Louisiana by jazz musicians about 1910. It was a loose translation of *manzana principal,* where the Spanish word manzana meant city block or apple. The term was little-known outside of jazz circles until 1971, when Charles Gillett, president of the New York Convention and Visitors Bureau, adopted the term for a large-scale advertising campaign to boost the city's image and tourism business.

Pittsburgh Post-Gazette 14 March 1978. *Pittsburgh Press* 4 October 1981.

What are the nicknames of various cities throughout the United States?

By state, the nicknames of some cities in the United States are as follows:

Alabama-Huntsville, The Rocket City, U.S.A.; Alaska-Point Barrow, The Top of the World; Arizona-Tombstone, The Town Too Tough to Die; Arkansas-Hot Springs, Valley of the Vapors; California-Castroville, The Artichoke Center of the World; Colorado-Leadville, The Cloud City; Connecticut-New Canaan, The Next Station to Heaven; Delaware-Wilmington, The Chemical Capital of the World; District of Columbia-Washington, D.C., The Capital City; Florida-St. Augustine, The Nation's Oldest City; Georgia-Claxton, The Fruit Cake Capital of the World; Hawaii-Waikiki, The Birthplace of Surfing; Idaho-Boise, The City of Trees; Illinois-Kewanee, The Hog Capital of the World; Indiana-Jasper, The Nation's Wood Capital; Iowa-Le Claire, The Birthplace of Buffalo Bill Cody; Kansas-Dodge City, The Cowboy Capital of the World; Kentucky-Lexington, The Horse Capital of the World; Louisiana-Gonzales, Jambalaya Capital of the World; Maine-Eastport, The Easternmost City in the U.S.; Maryland-Annapolis, Crabtown; Massachusetts-Boston, Beantown; Michigan-Detroit, Motor City; Minnesota-International Falls, Icebox of the Nation; Mississippi-Jackson, Chimneyville,; Missouri-St. Louis, The Gateway to the West; Montana-Anaconda, Where Main Street Meets the Rockies; Nebraska-Lincoln, The Star City; Nevada-Virginia City, The World's Liveliest Ghost Town; New Hampshire-North Walpole, Steamtown, U.S.A.; New Jersey-Metuchen, The Brainy Borough; New Mexico-Los Alamos, The Atomic City; New York-New York City, The Big Apple; North Carolina-High Point, Furniture Capital of the World; North Dakota-Fargo, Agricultural Capital of the World; Ohio-Toledo, The Home of the Mud Hens; Oklahoma-Ponca City, The Home of the Pioneer Woman; Oregon-Tillamook, Land of Cheese, Trees and Ocean Breeze; Pennsylvania-Bethlehem, The Christmas City; Rhode Island-Newport, The Yachting Capital of the World; South Carolina-Sumter, The Gamecock City; South Dakota-Lead, City with the Heart of Gold; Tennessee-Gleason, The Tater Town; Texas-Crystal City, The World's Spinach Capital; Utah-St. George, Utah's Dixie; Vermont-Rutland, The Marble City; Virginia-Winchester, The Top of Virginia; Washington-Enumclaw, The Home of the Evil Spirits; West Virginia-Bluefield, Nature's Air-Conditioned City; Wisconsin-Rhinelander, The Home of the Hodag (a legendary hairy beast with a dozen gleaming white horns); Wyoming-Dubois, The Rock Capital of the Nation.

USA Today 26 September 1989.

What is the center of population in the United States?

The center of population is defined as that point at which an imaginary flat, weightless, and rigid map of the United States would balance if weights of identical value were placed on it so that each weight represented the location of one person on the date of the census. On August 2, 1790, it was 23 miles east of Baltimore, MD; June 1, 1850, it was 23 miles southeast of Parkersburg, West Virginia; June 1, 1900, it was six miles southeast of Columbus, Indiana; April 1, 1950, it was eight miles north-northwest of Olney, Richland County, Illinois; April 1, 1960, it was in Clinton County 61/2 miles northwest of Centralia, Illinois; April 1, 1970, it was 5.3 miles east-southeast of the Mascoutah City Hall in St. Clair County, Illinois; April 1, 1980, it was 1/4 mile west of De Soto in Jefferson County , Missouri; and April 1, 1990, it was 9.7 miles southeast of Steelville in Crawford County, Missouri.

Bureau of the Census, *Statistical Abstract of the United States 1993, 113th ed.* (Washington, DC: Government Printing Office, 1993), 26.

Where was Camelot located?

The existence of King Arthur and his legendary castle Camelot is a subject often debated by archeologists. However, in 1966, the noted British archeologist Sir Mortimer Wheeler announced that he and a team of archeologists had discovered the fabled Camelot. According to Wheeler, the remains of Camelot are located at South Cadbury near the southwestern England town of Yeovil. Artifacts found at the site, such as eastern Mediterranean pottery, metalwork, iron knives, and a bronze pin were dated to the sixth century—the time when King Arthur is believed to have lived.

"Camelot Site Is Reported Found," *New York Press* 30 July 1966.

Which American city is built entirely on Indian land?

Salamanca, New York, is the only incorporated city in the United States built entirely on Indian land. The Seneca Nation holds the lease, for which each homeowner must make a payment. The situation arose after the Revolutionary War when the Senecas, one of six Iroquois tribes, were forced to settle on two reservations in the southwestern corner of the state. In the nineteenth century railroad workers flocked into the area, and leasing land from the Indians, they founded Salamanca.

Rae Tyson, "Tribe wants to raise rent for town on Indian land," *USA Today* 24 July 1990.

What is the largest island in the Mediterranean Sea?

The largest island in the Mediterranean Sea is Sicily located at the "toe" of Italy. The island, which is separated from Italy by the narrow Strait de Messina, has an area of 9,814 square miles and a population of about 5.1 million, 700,000 of whom live in Palermo, the island's largest city and capital. Sicily was originally inhabited by the Sicans but was colonized by the Greeks in the eighth century B.C., and conquered by Rome in the third century B.C., the Muslims in the ninth century A.D., and the Normans beginning in 1060. Sicily was part of various European dynasties through the following centuries and became a part of the Italian kingdom in 1860. Presently it is an autonomous region of Italy. Because of its history, climate, and Mediterranean setting, Sicily is a popular tourist area but agriculture (wine, olive oil, olives, wheat, and fruit), fishing, oil and natural gas reserves, and limited engineering, shipbuilding, and petrochemical facilities also contribute to the island's economy.

Other large islands in the Mediterranean are Cyprus, 3,570 square miles; Crete, 3,410 square miles; and Corsica, 3,350 square miles.

Baedeker's Sicily (New York: Prentice Hall, 1993), 9-23. David Munro, ed., *Chambers World Gazetteer* (Edinburgh: W & R Chambers; Cambridge: Cmabridge University Press, 1988), s.v. "Sicilia." *Webster's New Geographical Dictionary* (Springfield, MA: Merriam-Webster, 1988), s.v. "Sicily."

What are the Tropics of Cancer and Capricorn?

The Tropics of Cancer and Capricorn are imaginary latitudinal lines that run parallel to the Earth's equator. The Tropic of Cancer lies 23.5 degrees north of the Equator, and the moment the midsummer sun crosses it marks the day of the year when the sun hangs directly over the northern hemisphere. The Tropic of Capricorn is the equivalent line in the southern hemisphere, located 23.5 degrees south of the Equator.

John Kingston, *Longman Illustrated Dictionary of Geography: the Study of the Earth, its Landforms and Peoples* (New York: Longman, 1988), 239.

Which African country was set up in the nineteenth century as a haven for freed American slaves?

The West African republic of Liberia was created in the nineteenth century as a home for former American slaves. An American charity founded the country in 1822 to provide a fresh start for those who wished to return to Africa. During this period, most of the land in Africa was under European control, and Liberia became the first independent black nation in tropical Africa in the modern era. Its Declaration of Independence dates to 1847. The United States provided financial assistance for the defense of the fledgling country against European and African foes.

World Book Encyclopedia (Chicago: World Book, 1987), s.v. "Liberia."

Why is Oklahoma called the Sooner State?

The "Sooner" nickname for the state of Oklahoma is a result of its rather unruly history. For most of the nineteenth century its boundaries had marked official Indian Territory, but U.S. authorities opened the area up to white settlement during the country's westward migration. There was a rush to settle the land when it was first declared legal to homestead there in April of 1889. Federal troops guarded the borders until a specified hour when the lands could be officially taken. Many eager future Oklahomans transgressed both the rules and the cordons, and those who did so were termed "Sooners."

George Earlie Shankle, ed., *State Names, Flags, Seals, Songs, Birds, Flowers, And Other Symbols: A Study based on historical documents giving the origin and significance of the state names, nicknames, mottoes, seals, flags, flowers, birds, songs, and descriptive comments on the capitol buildings and on some of the leading state histories, with facsimiles of the state flags and seals, rev. ed.* (Westport, CT: Greenwood Press, 1973), 140-141.

What are steppes?

Steppes are areas of unobstructed grassland almost completely devoid of shrubs or trees in the interior of eastern Europe and Asia.

Hot summers, cold winters and relatively low annual rainfall characterizes the climate of these areas. High evaporation rates and low rainfall create inadequate soil moisture, so that there is a lack of tree and shrubs generally in these areas.

John Small and Michael Witherick, *A Modern Dictionary of Geography* (London: Edward Arnold, 1986), s.v. "steppe."

What is a megalopolis?

A megalopolis is an area where originally separate cities or suburbs have grown together by increasing population density, creating a larger urban structure. The Greek word was applied by Gottman in 1964 to describe the urban and suburban area from Boston to Washington D.C. Since then it has been used to describe the Axial Belt in Great Britain, the Pacific coastlands of S. Honshu, Japan, the Rhne valley between Lyons and Marseilles, France, and the area encompassing Los Angeles and San Diego, California.

John Small and Michael Witherick, *A Modern Dictionary of Geography* (London: Edward Arnold, 1986), s.v. "megalopolis."

What is the largest inland body of water in the world?

The largest inland body of water in the world is the Caspian Sea, whose name derives from the Caspii tribe that once lived along its southern shore. Covering 143,000 square miles (371,000 square kilometers), the Caspian lies between Iran and various republics of the former Soviet Union. Its salinity level is kept relatively low because of the fresh water flowing into it largely from the Volga, Kuria, Embra, and Terek rivers. It has no outlet or tides.

The largest fresh water lake in the world is Lake Superior, which covers 31,800 square miles (82,362 square kilometers).

Encyclopedia Americana (Danbury, CT: Grolier, 1990), s.v. "Superior, Lake." David Munro, ed., *Chambers World Gazetteer* (Edinburgh: W & R Chambers; Cambridge: Cambridge University Press, 1988), s.v. "Caspian Sea."

How did San Salvador, a city in the Central American country of El Salvador, get its name?

There are two versions on the naming of San Salvador (Holy Savior), a city in the Central American country of El Salvador (The Savior). The first claims that the city is named directly after Jesus Christ, who according to practice of Spanish Catholics is often referred to as El Salvador del Mundo,—The Savior of the World—or Santsimo Salvador—The Most Holy Savior. The name may have been chosen for the city because there was a decisive battle against the Cuzcatl n Indians on August 6, the feast of the Transfiguration when, according to the Bible, Jesus Christ appeared in all his glory to several of his disciples.. Others suggest that the city was named by Diego de Holgun, who had ties to a city named San Salvador de Bayamo in Spain.

Lilly de Jongh Osborne, *Four Keys to El Salvador* (New York: Funk & Wagnalls, 1956), 25.

What are the most common street names in the United States?

Common street names in the United States are named after trees, presidents, and numbers. A list of the most common names taken from the U.S. Post Office *ZIP Code Directory* 24 are Park, Washington, Maple, Oak, Lincoln, Walnut, Elm, Jefferson, Highland, Madison, Pine, Cedar, Sunset, Jackson, Franklin, Willow, Third, Wilson, Second, Laurel, Fifth, Chestnut, Fourth, Adams, Virginia, Linden, Woodland, Cherry, Rose, and First.

Irving Wallace, *The Book of Lists #2* (New York: William Morrow, 1980), 42-43.

What are the shortest and longest geographical names?

Villages in France and Wales are known for having the shortest and the longest geographical names. The village of Oo, France is located in the Pyrenees between Lourdes and the state of Andorra. The name Oo is pronounced like the letter "o." The Welsh village of Llanfairpwllgwyngyllgogerychwyrndrobwyllllantysiliogogogoch is in north Wales. This fifty-eight-letter and practically unpronounceable name means "St. Mary's Church in the hollow of the white hazel near the rapid whirlpool of Llantysilio of the red cave." Local residents simply call the village Llanfair. The local railroad station features the full name, however, on a sign that is nearly nineteen feet long.

New York Times 18 May 1975.

What area of the United States is known as the Rustbelt?

The Rustbelt designates an area across the northeastern and midwestern United States. It includes many urban areas which have seen the decline of industries such as steel and textiles.

E.D. Hirsch, Joseph F. Kett, and James Trefil, *The Dictionary of Cultural Literacy* (Boston: Houghton Mifflin, 1988), s.v. "rustbelt."

What and where is the continental divide of North America?

The continental divide is a continuous line that runs north and south the length of North America. About 50 miles west of Denver, U.S. Highway Route 40 crosses Berthoud Pass at an altitude of 11,314 feet (3,450 meters) above sea level. At the crest of this pass is the continental divide. West of this divide, all water flows eventually to the Pacific Ocean. East of this line, the waters will flow toward the Atlantic Ocean.

Frank Press, *Earth, 2d ed.* (San Francisco: W.H. Freeman, 1978), 180.

Who was the first person on Antarctica?

Historians are unsure who first set foot on Antarctica, the fifth largest continent covering 10 percent of the earth's surface with its area of 5.4 million square miles (14 million square kilometers). In 1773-1775 British Captain James Cook (1728-1779) circumnavigated the continent. American explorer Nathaniel Palmer (1799-1877) discovered Palmer Peninsula in 1820, without realizing that this was a continent. In this the same year Fabian Gottlieb von Bellingshausen (1779-1852) sighted the Antarctic continent. American sealer John Davis went ashore at Hughes Bay on February 7, 1821. In 1823, sealer James Weddell (1787-1834) travelled the farthest south (74 degrees south) that anyone had until that time and entered what is now called the Weddell Sea. In 1840, American Charles Wilkes (1798-1877), who followed the coast for 1,500 miles, announced the existence of Antarctica as a continent. In 1841, Sir James Clark Ross (1800-1862) discovered Victoria Land, Ross Island, Mount Erebus, and the Ross Ice Shelf. In 1895, the whaler Henryk Bull landed on the Antarctic continent. Norwegian explorer Roald Amundsen (1872-1928) was the first leader to reach the South Pole on December 14, 1911. Thirty-four days later, Amundsen's rival Robert Falcon Scott (1868-1912) stood at the South Pole, the second leader to do so, but he and his companions died upon their return trip.

Robert Famighetti, ed., *The World Almanac and Book of Facts 1995* (New York: World Almanac, 1994), 544-45. Otto Johnson, ed., *1995 Information Please Almanac* (Boston: Houghton Mifflin, 1994), 474. John May, *The Greenpeace Book of Antarctica* (New York: Doubleday, 1989), 16, 110-13. John Stewart, *Antarctica: An Encyclopedia* (Jefferson, NC: McFarland, 1990), s.v. "Amundsen, Roald," "Scott, Robert Falcon." *World Book Encyclopedia* (Chicago: World Book, 1990), 530, 536.

What is the prime meridian?

The north-south lines on a map run from the North Pole to the South Pole and are called "meridians," a word that meant "noon," for when it is noon on one place on the line, it is noon at any other point as well. The lines are used to measure longitudes, or how far east or west a particular place might be, and they are 69 miles (111 kilometers) apart at the equator. The east-west lines are called parallels, and unlike meridians, are all parallel to each other. They measure latitude, or how far north or south a particular place might be. There are 180 lines circling the earth, one for each degree of latitude. The degrees of both latitude and longitude are divided into 60 minutes, further divided into 60 seconds each.

The prime meridian is the meridian of 0 degrees longitude, used as the origin for measurement of longitude. The meridian of Greenwich, England, is used almost universally for this purpose.

Mary Blocksma, *Reading the Numbers* (New York: Penguin, 1989), 107. *The McGraw-Hill Dictionary of Scientific and Technical Terms, 4th ed.* (New York: McGraw-Hill, 1989), 1492.

What is the Piri Re'is map?

In 1929, a map was found in Constantinople that caused great excitement. Painted on parchment and dated in the Moslem year 919 (1513 according to the Christian calendar), it was signed by an admiral of the Turkish navy known as Piri Re'is. This map might be one of the earliest maps of America. It shows South America and Africa in their correct relative longitudes. The mapmaker also indicated that he had used a map drawn by Columbus for the western part. It was an exciting statement because for several centuries geographers had been trying to find a "lost map of Columbus" supposedly drawn by him in the West Indies.

Charles H. Hapgood, *Maps of the Ancient Sea Kings* (Radnor, PA: Chilton, 1966), 1.

In terms of geographical area, what is the largest city in South America?

Sao Paulo covers a greater area than any other South American city. The Brazilian city covers 451 square miles.

Robert Famighetti, ed., *The World Almanac and Book of Facts, 1994, 126th ed.* (Mahwah, NJ: World Almanac, 1994), 829.

What is the history of Greenbelt, Maryland?

President Franklin D. Roosevelt's (1882-1945) Resettlement Administration sought to ease the plight of low-income residents of Washington, DC, by creating Greenbelt, Maryland. The community was constructed beginning in 1936 to provide 1,000 affordable, high-quality homes surrounded by an 11,000-acre greenbelt. The plan also included a 22-acre artificial lake and a layout that minimized the amount of land used for streets. The project followed the example of British social reformer Ebenezer Howard who originated the greenbelt or garden city concept in 1898.

Two other such towns were built in America: Boulder, Colorado, and Radburn, New Jersey, although Radburn was only partially completed. The American green belt movement was hindered by the expense of creating belts of open space and by the circular design of such communities. Most American cities are shaped by rivers, coasts, and highways, giving them a linear shape.

Duncan Aikman, "Tugwelltown," *Current History* August 1936. Ruth A. Eblen and William R. Eblen, eds., *The Encyclopedia of the Environment* (Boston: Houghton Mifflin, 1994), s.v. "Green Belts."

What two countries occupy the Island of Hispaniola in the West Indies?

Previously in the hands of Spain and France, two-thirds of the island of Hispaniola in the West Indies is occupied by the Dominican Republic. The remaining third is occupied by Haiti. In 1870 President Grant's proposal that the United States annex the embattled island was rejected by the Senate.

Howard L. Hurwitz, *An Encyclopedic Dictionary of American History* (New York: Washington Square Press, 1968), s.v. "Dominican Republic."

How long is the Grand Canyon?

The Grand Canyon, cut out by the Colorado River over a period of 15 million years in the northwest corner of Arizona, is the largest land gorge in the world. It is 4 to 13 miles (6.4 to 21 kilometers) wide at its brim, 4,000 to 5,500 feet (1,219 to 1,676 meters) deep, and 217 miles (349 kilometers) long, extending from the mouth of the Little Colorado River to Grand Wash Cliffs (and 277 miles, 600 feet or 445.88 kilometers if Marble Canyon is included).

However, it is not the deepest canyon in the United States; that distinction belongs to Kings Canyon, which runs through the Sierra and Sequoia National Forests near East Fresno, California, with its deepest point being 8,200 feet (2,500 meters). Hell's Canyon of the Snake River between Idaho and Oregon is the deepest U.S. canyon in low-relief territory. Also called the Grand Canyon of the Snake, it plunges 7,900 feet (2,408 meters) down from Devil Mountain to the Snake River.

Robert Famighetti, ed., *The World Almanac and Book of Facts 1995* (Mahwah, NJ: World Almanac, 1994), 512. *Webster's New Geographical Dictionary* (Springfield, MA: Merriam-Webster, 1988), s.v. "Grand Canyon." Mark C. Young, ed., *Guinness Book of Records 1995* (New York: Facts on File, 1994), 66

Where is the largest port in the world?

The largest ocean port is the Port of New York and New Jersey, with a navigable waterfront of 755 miles.

The largest freshwater port in the world is located on the Delaware River about 88 miles from the Atlantic Ocean. Known as the "Ports of Philadelphia," the area includes Philadelphia and Chester, Pennsylvania; Camden and Gloucester, New Jersey; and Wilmington, Delaware.

Encyclopedia Americana, intern. ed., (Danbury, CT: Grolier, 1994), s.v. "Philadelphia." Mark C. Young, ed., *The Guinness Book of Records 1995* (New York: Facts On File, 1994), 113.

Why is Missouri called the Cave State?

Missouri is known as the Cave State because it has over 4,000 caves. New ones are listed each year as they are discovered.

Benjamin F. Shearer and Barbara S. Shearer *State Names, Seals, Flags, and Symbols, rev. ed.* (Westport, CT: Greenwood Press, 1994), 10. H. Dwight Weaver, *Missouri the Cave State* (Jefferson City, MO: Discovery Enterprises, 1980), 15.

How long is the Mississippi River?

At 2,348 miles the Mississippi River is the second longest river in the United States. Only the Missouri River is longer with 2,466 miles. Along its length the Mississippi passes through or forms the boundary of the states of Minnesota, Wisconsin, Iowa, Illinois, Missouri, Kentucky, Tennessee, Arkansas, Mississippi, and Louisiana. Its depth ranges from 9 to 100 feet and its widest point is approximately 3-miles just north of Clinton, Iowa, in a backwater formed by Lock and Dam No. 13.

Webster's New Geographical Dictionary, (Springfield, MA: Merriam-Webster, 1988), s.v. "Mississippi." *The World Book Encyclopedia* (Chicago: World Book, 1994), s.v. Mississippi River."

What is the oldest continuously inhabited city?

Damascus, the capital city of Syria, is believed by many scholars to be the world's oldest continuously inhabited city. Lying 50 miles east of the Mediterranean Sea, Damascus' roots can be traced as far back as the 3rd millennium *B.C.* Historical records also reveal that it was called Damascus at least as early as the 15th century *B.C.* and that it served as the capital of the Islamic empire from *A.D.* 661-750.

Philip W. Goetz, ed., *The New Encyclopedia Britannica, 15th ed., "Microp-dia"* (Chicago: Encyclopedia Britannica, 1989), s.v. "Damascus."

Why is La Paz, Bolivia, nearly a fireproof city?

The fire engines in the city of La Paz, Bolivia, are virtually unused. Because La Paz is approximately 12,000 feet above sea level there is barely enough oxygen to sustain a fire.

Isaac Asimov, *Isaac Asimov's Book of Facts* (New York: Bell Publishing, 1981), 75.

What are the 50 largest counties in the United States?

The list of the nation's largest counties is led by Los Angeles County, California, according to 1990 population data. The other counties in the top-ten list are, in descending order, those of Cook (Illinois), Harris (Texas), San Diego (California), Orange (California), Kings (New York), Maricopa (Arizona), Wayne (Michigan), Queens (New York), and Dade (Florida). The eleventh-largest county in the U.S. is Dallas County, Texas. Following it are the counties of Philadelphia (Pennsylvania), King (Washington), Santa Clara (California), New York (New York), San Bernadino (California), Cuyahoga (Ohio), Middlesex (Massachusetts), Allegheny (Pennsylvania), Suffolk (New York), Nassau (New York), Alameda (California), Broward (Florida), and Bronx (New York). The No. 25 spot is held by Bexar County, Texas. The next largest twenty-five counties, in successive order, are those of Riverside (California), Tarrant (Texas), Oakland (Michigan), Sacramento (California), Hennepin (Missouri), St. Louis (Missouri), Erie (New York), Franklin (Ohio), Milwaukee (Wisconsin), Westchester (New York), Hamilton (Ohio), Palm Beach (Florida), Hartford (Connecticut), Pinellas (Florida), Honolulu (Hawaii), Hillsborough (Florida), Fairfield (Connecticut), Shelby (Tennessee), Bergen (New Jersey), Fairfax (Virginia), New Haven (Connecticut), Contra Costa (Ccalifornia), Marion, (Indiana), DuPage (Illinois), and lastly, New Jersey's Essex County.

Governing July 1993.

Which countries are referred to as the Baltic States?

The Baltic States refer to the nations adjacent the Baltic Sea at the far northeastern end of Europe. They are Latvia, Estonia, and Lithuania. Despite the fact that throughout history they were invaded and governed by a succession of their neighbors-Poland, Russia, Sweden, Germany, and Denmark-the three main Baltic States managed to retain their own languages and cultural identities. They belonged to the Russian Empire at the onset of World War I (1914-18), but won independence after the 1917 Bolshevik Revolution. Unfortunately, their strategic location made both the Soviet Union and Nazi Germany covetous, and the area was again occupied by its Russian neighbors in 1940. After World War II (1939-45), Latvia, Estonia, and Lithuania remained part of the Soviet Union until the collapse of communism in the early 1990s. All three were independent republics again by 1992.

Alan J. Day, ed., *Annual Register: A Record of World Events: 1992* (White Plains, NY: Longman, 1993). *The World Book Encyclopedia* (Chicago: World Book, 1987), s.v. "Baltic states."

What is the most populous urban area in the world?

The most populous urban area in the world is the Tokyo, Japan. In 1990 this area had a population of 25,000,000, with the projected population in the year 2,000 to be 28,000,000.

Mark Young, ed., *The Guinness Book of Records, 1995* (New York: Facts on File, 1994), 178.

Which South American countries are landlocked?

Two South American countries Paraguay and Bolivia, are landlocked.

Michael Milone and Robert Dahl, *The Do-It-Yourself Book of Blank Maps* (Honesdale, PA: Willow Spring Press, 1991), 23.

Where exactly did Columbus land in the New World?

According to a National Geographic Society team of navigators, mathematicians, archaeologists, and computer experts, Spanish explorer Christopher Columbus' (1451-1506) landed at Samana Cay, an isolated Bahamian island. According to the team, Columbus reached the island on October 12, 1492.

Kim Painter and Mark Lewyn, "Columbus landed somewhere else," *USA Today* 9 October 1986.

Before the break-up of the Soviet Union, what was the composition of the All-Union Supreme Soviet?

Before the break up of the Soviet Union, the All-Union Supreme Soviet was comprised of 15 Republics: Russia (RSFSR), Ukraine, Kazakhstan, Uzbekistan, Byelorussia, Azerbaijan, Georgia, Moldavia, Tadzhikistan, Kirgizia, Lithuania, Armenia, Turkmenistan, Latvia, and Estonia.

Ian Derbyshire, *Politics in the Soviet Union: from Brezhnev to Gorbachev* (Edinburgh: W & R Chambers, 1987), 133.

What is the largest lake in Africa?

Lake Victoria is the largest body of freshwater in the continent of Africa. Most of the lake is in Tanzania and Uganda but it also straddles the border with Kenya. Lake Victoria has a surface area of 69,485 square kilometers (26,828 square miles) making it the second largest body of freshwater in the world after Lake Superior. Lake Victoria is also known as Victoria Nyanza and serves as the chief reservoir of the Nile River.

Philip W. Goetz, ed., *The New Encyclopaedia Britannica, 15th ed., "Micropaedia"* (Chicago: Encyclopaedia Britannica, 1989), s.v. Lake Victoria."

Which two African countries united to form the present country of Tanzania?

In 1964 the African countries of Zanzibar and Tanganyika signed an Act of Union to form the United Republic of Tanzania.

David Munro, ed., *Chambers World Gazetteer: An A-Z of Geographical Information* (Edinburgh: W & R Chambers; Cambridge: Cambridge University Press, 1988), s.v. "Tanzania."

Who made the first assault on the summit of Mt. Everest?

The first assault on the summit of Mt. Everest was made by George Finch and George Mallory in 1922.

John Hunt, *The Conquest of Everest* (New York: E. P. Dutton, 1954), 225.

On what natural phenomena is Mexico City built?

Mexico City is situated in a depression known as the Valley of Mexico and lies between mountains on the country's Central Plateau. The depression lacks drainage and is subsequently a dry but spongy lake bed locally called Lake Texcoco. The city also lies along a major east-west geologic fault which makes the area prone to frequent tremors and occasional earthquakes.

Encyclopedia Americana, intern. ed. (Danbury, CT: Grolier, 1990), s.v. "Mexico City."

Where is "Land's End"?

"Land's End" is a name for the southwestern tip of Britain. It is the western most land in England.

Laurence Urdang and Frederick G. Ruffner, Jr., eds., *Allusions—Cultural, Literary, Biblical and Historical: A Thematic Dictionary, 2nd ed.* (Detroit: Gale Research Company, 1986), 421.

What do you call a resident of Accident, Maryland?

A resident of Accident, Maryland, is usually referred to as an Accidental.

Paul Dickson, *What Do You Call A Person From...?* (New York: Facts on File, 1990), s.v. "Accident, Maryland, USA."

What is Indonesia's coat of arms?

The Indonesian coat of arms shows an eagle with a shield over its body, holding a banner in its claws. The shield bears a star in the center, symbolizing Divine Omnipotence. It is surrounded by a bull's head to symbolize "Democracy;" a banyan tree, representing "National Consciousness;" a chain symbolizing "Humanity;" and rice and cotton stalks, which stand for "Social Justice." The banner carries the words "Bhinneka Tunggal Ika" meaning "Many Remain One."

New York Times 23 April 1950.

What is the "Inland Empire"?

The "Inland Empire" is a region covering parts of eastern Washington, northern Idaho, and western Montana. It is famous for its productivity in the forest, mining, and agricultural industries. The area grows Idaho white pine, ponderosa pine, sugar pine, and other trees, accounting for one quarter of the nation's soft timber. Mining in the Coeur d'Alene and Metaline districts produces lead, silver, and zinc. Farms in the "Inland Empire" are best known for their hops, apples, pears, and wheat.

Encyclopedia Americana, intern. ed. (Danbury, CT: Grolier, 1994), s.v. "Spokane."

What is the only place in the world where one can see the sun rise on the Pacific Ocean and set on the Atlantic?

Because of a bend in the isthmus, Panama is the only place on earth where it is possible to see the sun rise on the Pacific Ocean and set on the Atlantic.

David Carroll, *Fascinating Facts* (New York: Ridge Press and Crown Publishers, 1977), 70.

What country is Black Africa's oldest state?

Ethiopia, located in northeastern Africa and bordering on the Red Sea is Black Africa's oldest state with its formal history going back over 2,000 years. Human-like fossils have been found in Ethiopia dating back 3.5 million years, an agricultural culture began there around 5000 B.C., and the ancient Greeks knew and wrote about Ethiopia. Originally the country was known as the Aksumite or Axumite Empire and Menelik I, who was the son of King Solomon and the Queen of Sheba, was an early emperor. Ethiopia became a Christian nation in the fourth century and, over the centuries, was one of the few countries in that part of the world able to resist the spread of Islam.

Ethiopia was also one of the few African nations able to resist European colonization although it was under Italian rule for six years from 1935 to 1941. Ethiopia's most famous ruler was Haile Selassie, known as Ras Tafari Makonnen (1892-1975), who is best remembered for his impassioned plea before the League of Nations in the face of the Italian invasion. Selassie returned to power in 1941 but was overthrown in a leftist coup in 1974 and died shortly thereafter. Once known as Abyssinia, the country today has an area of 435,186 square miles. Its 1994 estimated population was 58,359,664 of which nearly 2 million live in the capital Addis Ababa.

E.D. Hirsch, Jr., Joseph F. Kett, and James Trefil, *The Dictionary of Cultural Literacy* (Boston: Houghton Mifflin, 1988), s.v. "Ethiopia." *Worldmark Encyclopedia of the Nations: Africa* (Detroit, Gale Research, 1995), s.v. "Ethiopia."

What are antipodes?

Antipodes are any two points on the globe that can be connected by a straight line passing through the center of the earth. The north and south poles are antipodes while London, England, and Antipodes Island, southeast of New Zealand, are approximate antipodes.

W.G. Moore, *A Dictionary Of Geography,* (New York: Frederick A. Praeger, 1967), s.v. "antipodes."

What is the highest and lowest elevation in the United States?

Named in honor of U.S. president William McKinley (1843-1901), Mt. McKinley, Alaska, at 20,320 feet (6,194 meters), is the highest point in the United States and North America. Located in central Alaska, it belongs to the Alaska Range. Its South peak measures 20,320 feet high and the North Peak is 19,470 feet high. It boasts one of the world's largest unbroken precipices and is the main scenic attraction at Denali National Park. Denali means the "high one" or the "great one" and is a native American name sometimes used for Mt. McKinley. Mt. Whitney, California, at 14,494 feet (4,421 meters), is the highest point in the continental United States. Death Valley, California, at 282 feet (86 meters) below sea level, is the lowest point in the United States and in the western hemisphere.

Robert Famighetti, ed., *The World Almanac and Book of Facts 1995* (Mahwah, NJ: World Almanac, 1994) 547, 556. Otto Johnson, ed., *1995 Information Please Almanac* (Boston: Houghton Mifflin Company, 1994), 491. *The World Book Encyclopedia* (Chicago: World Book, 1987), s.v. "Mount McKinley.."

Which U.S. city has the greatest number of trees?

According to a survey of 20 cities, Houston, Texas, has the most trees with 956,700.

American Forests March/April 1992.

What are the Seven Natural Wonders of the World?

The Seven Natural Wonders of the World are:
Mount Everest on the Nepal-Tibet border

Victoria Falls on the Rhodesia-Zambia border
Grand Canyon of the Colorado River
Great Barrier Reef of Australia, the world's largest coral formation
Caves in France and Spain with their prehistoric paintings
Parcutin, a young volcano in Mexico
The harbor at Rio de Janeiro.

Other natural wonders often listed include the giant sequoia trees of California, Rainbow Natural Bridge of Utah, Yellowstone Falls in Yellowstone National Park, Crater Lake and Wizard Island in Oregon, and the Carlsbad Caverns of New Mexico.

World Book Encyclopedia (Chicago: World Book, 1971), s.v. "Seven Wonders of the World."

What is the highest navigable lake?

Lake Titicaca, located partially in Peru and partially in Bolivia, is the highest navigable lake with a maximum depth of 1,214 feet. It is 12,506 feet above sea level. While there are higher lakes in the Himalayas, they are glacial and of a temporary nature only.

Mark C. Young, ed., *The Guinness Book of Records 1995* (New York: Facts on File, 1994), 65.

Why does the Zuider Zee no longer appear on maps of the Netherlands?

Now called Ijsselmeer, the Zuider Zee (meaning South Sea) was a landlocked inlet of the North Sea penetrating the Netherlands. A dike completed in 1932 was built across the Zuider Zee, separating it into the outer Waddenzee (open to the North Sea) and the inner IJsselmeer (Lake IJssel). Much of the IJsselmeer has been reclaimed as agricultural land.

Philip W. Goetz, ed., *The New Encyclopaedia Britannica, 15th ed.* (Chicago: Encyclopaedia Britannica, 1993), s.v. "IJsselmeer," "Netherlands," "Zuiderzee." *Webster's New Geographical Dictionary* (Springfield, MA: Merriam-Webster, 1988), s.v. "Zuider Zee."

Which city and town names in the United States are suggestive of Christmas?

The following city and town names in the United States have Christmas connotations; zip codes appear in parentheses:

Bethlehem, Connecticut (06751); Bethlehem, Georgia (30620); Bethlehem, Indiana (47104); Bethlehem, Kentucky (40007); Bethlehem, Maryland (21609); Bethlehem, New Hampshire (03574); Bethlehem, Pennsylvania (18016); Bethlehem, South Dakota (57708); Christmas, Florida (32709); Christmas Cove, Maine (04542); Christmas Valley, Oregon (97638); North Pole, Fairbanks, Alaska (99705); North Pole, Colorado (80901); North Pole, New York (12946); Noel, Missouri (64854); Noel, Virginia (23047); Santa Claus, California (93013); Santa Claus, Indiana (47579); Santa, Idaho (83866.

"Post Office lists Christmas cities in U.S.," *Monroeville Times-Express* 1972.

What is the proper term to use when referring to someone from the Ivory Coast?

A resident of the Republic of the Ivory Coast (formerly French West Africa) is referred to by most sources as an "Ivorian." A few sources may refer to such a person as an "Ivory Coaster."

Paul Dickson, *What Do You Call a Person From...?: A Dictionary of Resident Names* (New York: Facts on File, 1990), 73.

Where can beaches of various colored sands be found?

On any given beach, one of five different colors of sand can commonly be found. The locations of the beaches containing sand of each color are as follows:

Black—the Big Island, Santorini, St. Vincent, Stromboli; red—Seward Peninsula, Alaska; green—Hanauma Bay, Oahu; Papakolea Beach, the Big Island; pink—Bermuda, Bonaire, Rangiroa, Bahamas' Harbour Island; and white—Anguilla; Cephalonia, Greece; Kauai; Maui; Mustique.

"Sand: A User's Guide," *Cond Nast Traveler* July 1994.

Which city was founded by an agent of England's East India Trading Company?

Calcutta, India, was founded in 1690 by Job Charnock (d. 1693), an agent of the East India Company. Located on the Hooghly River, Calcutta is the capital of the West Bengal province of India, formerly the capital of the Bengal Presidency and the Indian Empire. Calcutta was originally founded as a factory settlement in 1690, and was expanded eight years later through the acquisition of the villages of Sutanati, Kalikata, and Govindapur. Its name is derived from the anglicization of Kalikata.

George Thomas Kurian, *Historical and Cultural Dictionary of India* (Metuchen, NJ: The Scarecrow Press, 1976), s.v. "Calcutta."

Beginning of History to 475

What was the Peloponnesian War?

The Peloponnesian War (431-404 B.C.) was fought between the two dominant city-states of ancient Greece, Athens and Sparta. The two cities had different economic and colonial interests as well as different political systems. Sparta was controlled by a militaristic aristocracy, and Athens, although it had a large slave population was a democracy in which all free adult males could vote. The war ended with a Spartan victory, which many scholars consider a disaster for the intellectual life of Greece, since Athens has been its cultural center. A disgraced Athenian general Thucydides (d. ca.401 B.C.) wrote an account of the struggle ending with 411 B.C. in his *The History of the Peloponnesian War*, the finest work of history produced in the ancient world.

D. Brendan Nagle, *The Ancient World: A Social and Cultural History* (Englewood Cliffs NJ: Prentice-Hall, 1979). 122-26, 149-51.

Who was the first ruler of Rome?

Although ancient Rome produced many great historians, none whose works survive in more than fragments wrote before the second century B.C. Since Rome traces its history back to 753 B.C., there are only legends about the origins of the city and its first rulers. According to the mythological accounts that passed for history in ancient Rome, the first ruler of the city was Romulus, the son of the god Mars. Romulus was a twin of Remus, and the two boys were raised by a she-wolf. Later, Romulus murdered his brother in the heat of an argument and went on to establish the ancient capital. Rome's alleged first king died after ruling for almost a quarter-century.

J. W. Fuchs, *Classics Illustrated Dictionary* (New York: Oxford University Press, 1974), s.v. "Romulus."

Was Attila the Hun a dwarf?

Attila the Hun (ca. 370/400-453) was short as were most Huns but whether or not he was a dwarf is open to debate. No portrait is available. The Huns of the mid-400s who terrorized Western Christendom astride their Mongol ponies have been variously described as "ugly," "ferocious," and "awe-inspiring." Attila led the Huns through those parts of Europe that now comprise parts of Austria, Hungary, Croatia, and northern Italy. Attila has been described as being of about the same height as an average Hun, which is short by Western standards, with a broad chest, snub nose, small eyes, and a beard sprinkled with grey.

Anne Commire, ed., *Europe, vol. 2 of Historic World Leaders* (Detroit: Gale Research, 1994), 59-60.

Who founded Alexandria?

When Alexander the Great (356-323 B.C.) of Macedon conquered Egypt in 332 he founded the city of Alexandria on the west side of the Nile delta. Meant to be the capital of Egypt the new city also flourished as a center for trade and a crossroads of Jewish, Greek, and Arab learning and culture. Alexandria served as a distribution point for commodities from India and the east and was especially known for its renowned Ptolemaic library (which was burned when Caesar captured the city in 48 B.C.) and its distinguished schools of theology, philosophy, and astronomy.

Over the centuries, Alexandria was captured by the Romans (48 B.C.), Arabs (640 A.D.), Turks (1517), and the French during Napoleon's Egyptian campaign (1798-1801). The harbor at Alexandria was allowed to deteriorate and with the rising influence of Cairo the importance of Alexandria gradually diminished. By the mid-twentieth century it was a city of approximately two million inhabitants.

John Lemprire, *Lemprire's Classical Dictionary of Proper Names mentioned in Ancient Authors Writ Large, 3d ed.* (London: Routledge & Kegan Paul, 1984), s.v. "Alexandria." James Trager, *The People's Chronology: A Year-by-Year Record of Human Events From Prehistory to the Present, rev. ed.* (New York: Henry Holt, 1992), 22. *Webster's New Geographical Dictionary* (Springfield, MA: G. & C. Merriam, 1972), s.v. "Alexandria."

When did the Xia (Hsia) dynasty rule in China?

Throughout its history, China has been ruled by many dynasties. The Xia (Hsia) dynasty began its rule in China in 2205 B.C. and remained in power for approximately 700 years.

James Trager, *The People's Chronology* (New York: Henry Holt, 1992), 5.

Who was the Carthaginian explorer who led an expedition down the coast of Africa nearly 2,000 years before the Europeans?

Nearly 2,000 years before the Europeans explored Africa, Hanno of Carthage traveled all the way to Mount Kakulima in Sierra Leone, and possibly as far as Mount Cameroun in West Africa, around 500 B.C.

Daniel B. Baker, ed., *Explorers and Discoveries of the World* (Detroit: Gale Research, 1993), s.v. "Hanno."

Who was Alexander the Great's famous teacher?

The ancient Greek philosopher Aristotle (384-322 B.C.) began tutoring Alexander the Great (356-323 B.C.) when the legendary conqueror of the ancient world was 13. The tutelage instilled in the future military leader a love of Greek civilization and culture. These attitudes would have a lasting impact on countries that Alexander would later conquer, like Persia and Egypt. Aristotle is considered to be one of the greatest thinkers of the world, shaping Western rationalism and scientific spirit.

World Book Encyclopedia (Chicago: World Book, 1987), s.v. "Alexander the Great."

What were the Macedonian Wars?

The ancient Roman republic fought four wars with the kingdom of Macedonia between 211 and 146 B.C. Macedonia, which was governed during this period by King Philip V (238-179 B.C.) and his son Perseus(212-165 B.C.), had been the dominant power in Greece since the time of Alexander the Great (356-323 B.C.) and his father Philip. Rome, which had long been under the influence of Greek culture, often posed as the defender of the lost liberties of the Greek city-states against Macedonian oppression. The power of Macedonia was permanently broken during these conflicts, and after Rome's victory in the Second Macedonian War in 196 B.C., the Roman commander, Titius Flaminius, declared the autonomy of Macedonia's former subjects. But the freedom Rome gave was that of client states to pursue a foreign policy harmonious with Rome's interests. The Fourth Macedonian War was an attempt on the part of Greece to break free from Rome's sovereignty. The rebellion was brutally suppressed; the city of Corinth was sacked and her inhabitants enslaved. These wars mark the spread of Rome's power and influence to the eastern Mediterranean area and were important landmarks in the creation of the Roman empire.

J.W. Fuchs, *Classics Ilustrated Dictionary, trans. Livia Visser-Fuchs* (New York: Oxford University Press, 1974), s.v. "Macedonian Wars." William G. Sinnigen and Arthur E.R. Boak, *A History of Rome to A.D. 565, 6th ed.* (New York: Macmillan Publishing, 1977), 111 31.

What is the oldest inhabited site in North America?

An Alaskan hilltop is thought to be the oldest inhabited site in North America. Located 225 miles south of Barrow, Alaska, the location showed evidence of an ancient camp. The United States Bureau of Land Management reported that an archaeological dig turned up spear points and wood charcoal that was dated to be between 9,700 and 11,700 years old.

USA Today 26 March 1993.

How did the Roman emperor Diocletian attempt to bring food prices down?

Throughout the third century, the Roman Empire debased its currency in order to meet its expenses. In the course of a hundred years, the most common silver coin, the denarius, had became a copper coin coated with a silver wash. This policy led to inflation, which the Roman Emperor Diocletian (245?-313? A.D.), who ruled between 285 and 305, tried to stem by his Edict of Maximum Prices (in 301 A.D.). It was a long list of goods and services and the maximum price that could be charged for them. Although this decree condemned to death those who overcharged, the measure was unsuccessful because did not take into account the law of supply and demand, wholesale and retail prices, and the quality of workmanship. Romans did not receive any relief from the monetary crisis until the fourth century when coins with a stable content of gold and silver were issued.

Frank Frost Abbott, *The Common People of Ancient Rome: Studies of Roman Life and Literature* (New York: Biblo and Tannen, 1965), 150-60.

Was a horse ever decreed to be a Consul First Class of ancient Rome?

Nicknamed Caligula or "Little Boots" in his youth, Gaius Caesar (A.D. 12-41), the despotic third emperor of Rome, so loved his horse Incitatus that he bestowed upon it the rank of Consul First Class. Thereafter, the horse resided in an ivory manger and drank wine from a gold goblet.

David Louis, *Fascinating Facts* (New York: Ridge Press/Crown Publishers, 1977), 35.

In what impregnable wilderness fortress did more than 900 Jewish rebels commit mass suicide rather than be killed by the Romans?

More than 900 Jewish rebels committed mass suicide in the Masada (Israel), an impregnable wilderness fortress, rather than be killed by the Romans.

Allen C. Myers, *The Eerdmans Bible Dictionary* (Grand Rapids, MI: William B. Eerdmans, 1987), s.v. "Masada."

What was the largest sea battle in the ancient world?

One of the most important battles in naval history was fought at Actium in 31 B.C. between the forces of Octavian and Mark Antony and Cleopatra. Since both sides had a fleet of about 500 ships and an army of 90,000 men, it may have been the largest naval battle fought in the ancient world, but according to some historians the battle itself was a minor engagement that was magnified later by Octavian's propaganda machine. The conflict ended abruptly when Cleopatra fled with her treasure ship, and resistance collapsed as Antony followed her. Actium marked the end of the civil wars that had plagued the late Roman republic, and Octavian used this conquest to portray himself as the savior of Roman liberty and the values of the West. But it really established him as the single most powerful man in the Roman Empire. Under the title Augustus, which was voted him by the Senate, he established a system of government worked successfully for about 200 years, and he can be looked upon as the first Roman emperor.

William G. Sinnigen and Arthur E.R. Boak, *A History of Rome to A.D. 565, 6th ed.* (New York: Macmillan, 1977), 237-38.

How did lead contribute to the fall of the Roman Empire?

Some believe Romans from the period around 150 B.C. may have been victims of lead poisoning. Symptoms of lead poisoning include sterility, general weakness, apathy, mental retardation, and early death. The lead could have been ingested in water taken from lead-lined water pipes or from food cooked in their lead-lined cooking pots or wine cooked in lead-lined goblets. Unaware of its dangers, some ancient Romans unwittingly used lead as a sweetening agent or medicinal treatment for diarrhea. Lead poisoning could have caused infertility in women, leading to a subsequent long-term decline in the birth rate of the Roman upper classes. The effect of this inadvertent toxic food additive on Roman history, however, is only speculative.

Isaac Asimov, *Isaac Asimov's Book of Facts* (New York: Grosset & Dunlap, 1979), 92. George Cazeau, *Science Trivia* (New York: Berkley Books, 1986), 122. Martin Elkort, *The Secret Life of Food* (Los Angeles: Jeremy Tarcher, 1991), 115.

What was Egypt's 1st Dynasty?

One of antiquity's oldest dynasties is Egypt's 1st Dynasty, also known as the Thinite dynasty. Founded in 3400 B.C. it united the northern and southern Egyptian kingdoms under one king, Menes. Menes founded the city of Memphis as the kingdom's capital.

James Trager, *The People's Chronology*, (New York: Henry Holt, 1992), 4.

What caused the Wars of the Diadochi?

The Wars of the Diadochi were a forty-two year power struggle occurring after the death of Alexander the Great (356-323 B.C.). Alexander had subdued Greece, destroyed the Persian empire, which comprised most of the Middle East, and led an army to India. But he died prematurely at age 32 without designating an heir. According to a legend, when he was asked on his death bed to whom he left his kingdom, he replied, "to the strongest." Alexander was survived by a feeble-minded half-brother and a young son, but since neither could rule without regents, and both were eventually murdered, a power struggle developed between his generals and lieutenants. Known as the wars of the Diadochi (successors), these conflicts fragmented Alexander's empire into three major kingdoms, which were ruled by descendants of Alexander's officers. The Antigonids controlled Macedonia and a large part of Greece. The Seleucids ruled Syria, Mesopotamia, much of Iran, and some of Asia Minor. The Ptolemies governed Egypt, Cyprus, Palestine, and Phoenicia. There were other minor states as well, and the politics of this period, which is filled with intrigue and war, is extremely complex.

D. Brendan Nagle, *The Ancient World: A Social and Cultural History* (Englewood Cliffs, NJ: Prentice-Hall, 1979), 192-94. James Trager, *The People's Chronology: A Year-by-Year Record of Human Events from Prehistory to the Present* (New York: Henry Holt and Company, 1992), 23.

What is the Rosetta stone?

The Rosetta stone is a irregular piece of black basalt, measuring roughly four feet by two feet, that was discovered near Rosetta (Rashid), Egypt, in 1799. It contains an inscription that commemorates the accession to the throne of Pharaoh Ptolemy V Epiphanes (205-180 B.C.). Containing three versions of the same text, it was written in Greek, Egyptian hieroglyphics, and demotic, a cursive form of hieroglyphics. Thus it was a key for scholars, especially Jean-Franois Champollion (1790-1832), to decipher hieroglyphics, which until that time had been unintelligible. The Rosetta stone provided the basis for all future translations from hieroglyphics.

Philip W. Goetz, ed., *The New Encyclopaedia Britannica, 15th ed., "MIcropaedia"* (Chicago: Encyclopaedia Britannica, 1989), s.v. "rosetta stone."

Who was the first female pharaoh?

In 1502 B.C. Hatshepsut became Egypt's first female pharaoh. Her father, Thutmose I, designated her as his successor. Her garb as pharoah remained traditional. She had herself depicted as a male in a costume with a beard and without breasts.

Isaac Asimov, *Isaac Asimov's Book of Facts* (New York: Bell Publishing, 1981), 13.

Who led the Israelite migration out of Egypt?

In 1275 B.C., the prophet Moses, along with his brother Aaron, began a 40-year migration of Israelites to escape Egyptian oppression. The tribe's destination was the Dead Sea in Canaan.

Along the way, they traveled through the Sinai Peninsula, Kadesh, Aelana, and Petra.

James Trager, *The People's Chronology: A Year-by-Year Record of Human Events from Prehistory to the Present, rev. ed.* (New York: Henry Holt, 1992), 8.

What was noteworthy about the circumstances surrounding the death of Julius Caesar?

Gaius Julius Caesar (100-44 B.C.) was an aristocrat who became identified with the popular party during the civil strife that beset Rome during the last years of the Roman republic. Because of his success as a military commander, he was able to defy the Senate and march on Rome, where he established himself as dictator (49 B.C.). Although Caesar refused an offer to be made king, a group of aristocrats feared that one day he would be crowned, thus bringing the republic to an end. Led by Brutus and Cassius, they murdered him on the ides of March (March 15, 44). Proclaiming themselves defenders of republican freedom, the assassins were disappointed by the hostility that their action provoked among the common people, who looked upon Caesar as their protector. On the day of his funeral, one of Caesar's supporters, Mark Antony, delivered the funeral oration, during which he read Caesar's will. According to its terms, Caesar's gardens on the right bank of the Tiber were to become a public park, and each Roman was given a bequest of 300 sesterces (about two and a half months' wages). Although he left three quarters of his estate to his adopted son Gaius Octavius, Brutus, one of the assassins, was given a generous legacy. Mark Antony's speech so inflamed the crowd that the city of Rome was no longer safe for the would-be liberators, and the civil war resumed. It was not ended until 31 B.C., when Gaius Octavius, Caesar's heir, emerged victorious, and later, as Augustus Caesar, he became the first Roman emperor.

Manuel Komroff, *Julius Caesar* (New York: Julian Messner, 1955), 174. William Sinnigen and Arthur E.R. Boak, *A History of Rome to A.D. 565, 6th ed.* (New York: Macmillan Publishing, 1977), 209-30.

What are the origins of capital punishment?

While the death penalty most likely occurred long before any written records, the earliest known prescribed capital punishment can be traced back to Babylon about 3,700 years ago. Most ancient societies used it sparingly, but under Greece's Draconian legal code of the seventh century B.C., every crime was punishable by death.

Unique uses of capital punishment include the fifth century B.C. Roman Law of the Twelve Tablets, which used death as a penalty for publishing "insulting songs" and for disturbing the peace at night.

Since ancient times, and well into the twentieth century, public executions were quite common. Citizens were encouraged to attend, with the hope that public display would help deter further crimes. It also served as an honor to the condemned, as they could publicly cry out their innocence for the last time or announce their defiance to the authorities executing them.

Michael Kronenwetter, *Capital Punishment: A Reference Handbook* (Santa Barbara, CA: ABC-CLIO, 1993), 10.

What is considered the earliest European civilization?

The Minoan culture that thrived on the Mediterranean island of Crete, located about 60 miles off the coast of Greece, is considered the earliest important European civilization. This culture flourished between 2500 B.C. and 1400 B.C. Named after mythical king Minos of Crete, the Minoans, who had migrated from Turkey a few millennia earlier, produced groundbreaking achievements in the fine and applied arts, constructed great edifices, made pottery and jewelry, invented a system of writing, and were also excellent engineers. Natural disasters such as fire and earthquakes may have ended Crete's Minoan period. The island was later invaded by the Romans in 68 B.C. and became part of Greece in A.D. 395.

World Book Encyclopedia (Chicago: World Book, 1987), s.v. "Crete."

Who were the Sumerians?

The Sumerians created the oldest known civilization. They settled in the southern part of Mesopotamia, flourishing between 3100 B.C. and 2000 B.C. They were organized into independent city-states and developed complex forms of social organization that enabled them to tame the floods of the Tigris and Euphrates rivers and use the water to irrigate crops. The abundant food produced in this manner gave the Sumerians the leisure to create a vital, inventive culture. They developed the art of writing because their large social groupings forced them to use something other than memory to keep their affairs in order. Soon they began to write literature, and produced *Gilgamesh*, a mythological tale about the human race's yearning for eternal life, and the oldest epic poem in history. In addition to literature the Sumerians contributed to architecture by constructing the first large-scale buildings. These structures were temple complexes, topped by lofty pyramidal towers called ziggurats, that were centers of the social, political, and religious life of the cities. The Sumerians also invented wheeled transportation as well as many of the arts and sciences, including mathematics and astronomy.

Isaac Asimov, ed., *Isaac Asimov's Book of Facts* (New York: Bell Publishing Company, 1981), 31-32. D. Brendan Nagle, *The Ancient World: A Social and Cultural History* (Englewood Cliffs, NJ: Prentice-Hall, 1979), 6, 24-30.

How did Pontius Pilate die?

Pontius Pilate, the Roman governor of Judea who prosecuted Jesus Christ, died by his own hand. Pilate committed suicide during the reign of the Roman emperor Gaius (37-41 A.D.), probably after his trial and subsequent condemnation for the slaughter of the Samaritans.

Geoffrey W. Bromiley, *The International Standard Bible Encyclopedia* (Grand Rapids, MI: William B. Eerdmans Publishing Company, 1979), s.v. "Pilate, Pontius."

What was Julius Caesar's life like?

The most famous Roman Emperor, Julius Caesar (100-44 B.C.), was known for his ability to call audiences to action with his speeches. He was very popular with his people and with the military. His conquests were many—he overtook Gaul and visited Britain.

Caesar was also known for his womanizing. He had many mistresses, including Cleopatra. His birth was apparently by the operation we now call a Caesarian section. His health was marred by deafness in one ear and dizzy spells that may have been due to Mnire's disease. It is believed that he combed his hair forward and wore a laurel wreath around his head to conceal his baldness.

Many pieces of art were inspired by Caesar, as were the words "Kaiser" and "Czar." Julius Caesar continues to be a popular subject for biographers.

Betty Radice, *Who's Who In The Ancient World* (New York: Stein and Day, 1971), s.v. "Julius Caesar, Gaius."

Who was Boudicca?

Often known by the Latinized form of her name, Boudicca, was the first heroine of British history. She was a queen of the Iceni tribe (around the Norfolk area of England) that under her leadership rebelled against Roman invaders in A.D. 60. She was eventually defeated and reportedly committed suicide after playing havoc with Roman settlements as far south as London.

Bamber Gascoigne, *Encyclopedia of Britain* (New York: Macmillan Publishing, 1993), s.v. "Boudicca."

What was the full name of Hannibal?

Legendary Carthaginian general Hannibal (247-183 B.C.), son of Hamilcar Barca, was perhaps Rome's most famous enemy and a brilliant military strategist. Carthage was a city-state in North Africa and Rome's most important rival in the western Mediterranean. Hannibal launched the Second Punic War (218-202 B.C.) by attacking Saguntum, a city allied to Rome in Spain. From there he marched across Gaul, crossed the Alps, and defeated the Romans in three pitched battles, the most famous of which was fought at Cannae in 216. He never, however, had the manpower to attack the city of Rome, nor could he win over enough of Rome's allies in Italy. Recalled to North Africa, he was defeated by the Roman general Scipio Africanus at Zama in 202. Hannibal eventually fled to Asia Minor, where in 183 he committed suicide in order to avoid being handed over to the Romans.

Barry O. Jones and M.V. Dixon, *The St. Martin's Press Dictionary of Biography* (New York: St. Martin's Press, 1986), s.v. "Hannibal." William G. Sinnigen and Arthur E.R. Boak, *A History of Rome to A.D. 565* (New York: Macmillan, 1967).

What was Julius Caesar referring to when he said "Veni, vidi, vici"?

When the Roman general and statesman Julius Caesar (100-44 B.C.) wrote to Amantius he proclaimed "Veni, vidi, vici." Translated, it reads "I came, I saw, I conquered." He was referring to his victory over Pharnaces at Zela, in 47 B.C.

Burton Stevenson, ed., *The Macmillan Book of Proverbs, Maxims, and Famous Phrases* (New York: Macmillan, 1976), 401.

Who was Marcus Aurelius?

The adopted son of Antoninus Pius, Marcus Aurelius (121-180), who ruled the Roman Empire between A.D. 161 and 180, is known as the last of the "five good emperors." A Stoic philosopher, he wrote *Meditations*, a reflection on life and duty. Although attracted to the contemplative life, he had to spend much of his reign fighting to defend the integrity of Rome's borders and died on the Danube frontier in 180. His death marked the end of a 200-year period of prosperity called the Pax Romana (Roman Peace). His son Commodus (177-193) was more interested in developing his gladiatorial skills than ruling an empire, and Edward Gibbon (1737-94) began his famous *The History of the Decline and Fall of the Roman Empire* with his accession.

William G. Sinnigen and Arthur E.R. Boak, *A History of Rome to A.D. 565, 6th ed.* (New York: Macmillan, 1977), 318-21.

Did the Roman emperor Nero really play his fiddle while Rome burned?

The Roman emperor Nero (A.D. 37-68) did not play his fiddle while Rome burned but he did sing his own poem "The Sack of Troy" while enjoying the "spectacle of the flames."

Nero was born Lucius Domitius Ahenobarbus and following his father's death his mother Agrippina the Younger married the emperor Claudius who adopted Lucius and re-named him Nero Claudius. Claudius died in 54 (strongly believed to be poisoned by Agrippina) and Nero, at the age of 17, became Rome's new master. A patron of the arts, Nero was tutored by Seneca, a philosopher. Nero's early reign was marked by peace and harmony but amid growing political intrigue his relationship with the Roman senate, the army and his mother slowly deteriorated. In 59, Agrippina was murdered (her son was suspect) and Nero's life "began a decline into hedonism." His vices are well documented, including jealousy, vanity, and paranoia. Many people were killed in order for him to remain in power. In 64, Rome caught fire, burned for ten days and when the conflagration subsided, three-quarters of the city was destroyed. Although doing much to alleviate the suffering and havoc caused by the fire Nero was accused by his enemies of starting the blaze. He in turn blamed it on the Christians and issued in the systematic persecution and in some instances execution of members of the burgeoning religious sect. Because of his political, economic, and personal indiscretions, the Roman senate condemned him to death by flogging in 68. When Nero learned of this he died by his own hand, plunging a dagger into his throat. His dying words reportedly were "Qualis artifex pereo" or "What a showman the world is losing in me."

Nero left many architectural marvels, including his Golden House with a statue dedicated to himself in the courtyard. He was immortalized in a biography written by Suetonius.

Michael Grant, *The Roman Emperors* (New York, Charles Scribner's Sons, 1985), 38-9. *McGraw-Hill Encyclopedia of World Biography* (New York: McGraw-Hill, 1973), s.v. "Nero." Betty Radice, *Who's Who in Ancient World* (New York: Stein and Day, 1971), s.v. "Nero."

Where is the oldest known human settlement?

The oldest known human settlement is Doln Vestonice in the Czech Republic. It has been dated to about 27,000 B.C.

Mark C. Young, ed., *The Guinness Book of Records 1995* (New York: Facts on File, 1994), 178.

Who was the first Christian emperor of Rome?

The first Christian emperor of Rome was Constantine the Great (A.D. 280-337), who claimed to have had a vision of Jesus Christ before his triumph at the Battle of the Milvian Bridge in 312. In 313 he and his co-emperor Licinius issued the Edict of Milan, which declared the state neutral in matters of religion and granted toleration to Christians. This ended the persecutions that began in the reign of Diocletian (245 or 248-313 or 316). Although Constantine built the first basilica to St. Peter on Vatican hill and was very generous to the church, he was not baptized until shortly before his death. This practice of late baptism was common during this time period; it insured that the deceased would reach the afterlife in a state of innocence.

A. M. H. Jones, *Constantine and the Conversion of Europe* (London: English Universities Press, 1949).

Who was Augustus Caesar?

Augustus Caesar, who ruled from 27 B.C. to A.D. 14, is considered to be the first Roman emperor. With his victory over Marc Antony (83? B.C.-30 B.C.) and Cleopatra (69 B.C.-30 B.C.) at the battle of Actium in 29 B.C., he ended the civil wars that had plagued Rome for a 100 years. He created a system of government that successfully blended the institutions of the republic with the efficiency of an autocracy. His reign initiated the Pax Romana (Roman Peace), an era of prosperity that lasted until A.D. 180. Born Gaius Octavius, Augustus had been adopted by Julius Caesar (100 B.C.-44 B.C.), so he assumed his name. In 27 B.C. when the Roman Senate conferred upon him the title "Augustus," (meaning "Reverend.") He included it as part of his legal name.

William G. Sinnigen and Arthur E.R. Boak, *A History of Rome to A.D. 565, 6th ed.* (New York: Macmillan Publishing, 1977), 253-84. James Trager, *The People's Chronology: A Year-by-Year Record of Human Events from Prehistory to the Present, rev. ed.* (New York: Henry Holt, 1992), 34.

Whose house did Alexander the Great spare when he razed the city of Thebes?

Although Pindar, ancient Greece's best lyric poet, had been dead for approximately a century, he was still held in high esteem when the Macedonian conquerer Alexander the Great (356 B.C.-323 B.C.) razed Thebes. Alexander the Great ordered that the townhouse of Pindar's family in Thebes remain untouched during the Macedonian destruction of that city in 335 B.C. Pindar was best known as a writer of epinicia, choral odes written to celebrate triumphs in the Olympic, Pythian, Nemean, and Isthmian games.

Philip Goetz, ed., *The New Encyclopaedia Britannica, 15th ed., "Micropaedia"* (Chicago: Encyclopaedia Britannica, 1989), s.v. "Pindar."

What are the seven hills of Rome?

The seven hills of Rome are those that are included within the Servian wall, a defensive fortification that was built around the city in 390 B.C. They include the most ancient residential areas in Rome and are filled with reminders of the city's impressive history. They are the Palatine, the Capitoline, the Quirinal, the Aventine, the Caelian, the Esquiline, and the Viminal.

According to legend, Romulus founded the city on the Palatine, and during the Imperial period, the emperor's residence was built there, and its ruin still dominate it. The word "palace" is derived from the name of this hill. On the Capitoline was the temple to Jupiter, Juno, and Minerva, the center of the Roman state religion. The hill was a symbol of Rome's greatness, and triumphal processions of Roman generals ended at the temple on the Capitoline. Among the many treasures on the hill today are the Piazza del Campidoglio, a public square designed by Michelangelo, and two museums that contain many important pieces of classical sculpture. The Quirinal, the highest of seven hills, was originally a shrine to the Quirinus, the name given to the deified Romulus. It is now the site of the Quirinale palace, formerly a papal summer home, which has become the official residence of Italy's head of state.

The Aventine is said to be named for Aventinus, a king from an ancient city near Rome, Alba Longa. The beautiful early Christian church of Santa Sabina, a park that affords an excellent view of St Peter's dome, and the ruins of what was probably a medieval palace now grace its summit. According to Roman legend, the Caelian was settled by Tullus Hostilius (672-640 B.C.), the third king of Rome, who established refugees from Alba Longa, a city he destroyed, on it. The hill is usually associated with one of the most important popes of the Middle Ages Gregory I (590-603), who had lived there and built a monastery. At its apex stands an impressive church dedicated to St. Gregory and St. Andrew, which is reached by a long and wide marble staircase.

The Esquiline has two peaks, both of which are crowned by important churches. On the north peak is St. Mary Major, one of four pontifical basilicas in Rome, and noted for its early Christian mosaics. On the south peak is St Peter in Chains, home to Michelangelo's statue of Moses. At the foot of the Viminal, the last of the seven hills, was built mammoth baths of the Emperor Diocletian (A.D. 245-316), part of which was turned into St. Mary of the Angels, a cavernous Renaissance church designed by Michelangelo.

Catherine Avery, ed., *The New Century Classical Handbook* (New York: Appleton-Century-Crofts, 1962), s.v. "Aventine," "Caelian," "Capitoline," "Esquiline," "Palatine," "Quirinal," "Seven Hills of Rome," "Viminal." Donald R. Dudley, *The Romans: 850 B.C.-A.D. 337* (New York: Alfred A. Knopf, 1970), 8.

476 to 1500

What happened to the Children's Crusade?

The Children's Crusade of 1212 was a spontaneous movement that arose among children to free shrines in Palestine that were sacred to Christians from Muslim control. It came after the failure of the Third Crusade (1187-1192) to recapture Jerusalem, which fell to Islam in 1187, and Fourth Crusade (1202-1204), which never went beyond Constantinople. The Children's Crusade was led by a young man from Cologne named Nicholas and Stephen, a French shepherd boy, who claimed to have seen Christ, and who brought hordes of children and shepherds to Paris. The young crusaders were accompanied by many adults, some of whom were diverted by the clergy to fight in the Albigensian Crusade. The largest group under Nicholas went up the Rhine and crossed the Alps into Lombardy, eventually making their way to Genoa where they dispersed. Some of them seem to have gone to Rome, where Pope Innocent III dispensed them from their vows, which in any case were not valid because of their age. The French contingent may have made its way to Marseille, where, as the story goes, they were tricked by two merchants into embarking on ships for North Africa and sold into slavery.

Jonathan Riley-Smith, *The Crusades: A Short History* (New Haven, CT: Yale University Press, 1987), 141.

When did Marco Polo travel to China?

Venetian explorer and merchant Marco Polo (1254-1324) left for China in 1271 with his father Niccol and his uncle Maffeo. They arrived at the court of Kublai Khan (1215-1294) in Shang-Tu in 1275. Polo entered the khan's diplomatic service and was sent to various parts of the Mongol empire. Remaining in China for 17 years, he left in 1292 and returned to his native Venice in 1295 by way of India and Persia. Later he was captured during a war between Venice and Genoa, and while languishing in a Genovese prison, he dictated an account of his travels in the East to a fellow prisoner Rustigielo (or Rusticiano or Rustichello) of Pisa. *The Travels of Marco Polo* stimulated western interest in this unknown area for purposes of trade as well as travel and sheer curiosity.

Michael Dillon, *Dictionary of Chinese History* (London: Frank Cass, 1979), s.v. "Khubilai Khan." Marco Polo, *The Travels of Marco Polo, trans. Ronald Latham* (New York: Penguin Books, 1958).

Why was the Battle of Hastings important?

The battle of Hastings was fought by the armies of William, Duke of Normandy, and Harold, son of Godwin, earl of Wessex, and leader of the Anglo-Saxon aristocracy, on October 14, 1066. Since Harold's army was defeated and he was killed, William was able to declare himself king of England, which he ruled as William I (1066-87). Because England had been conquered by a Norman-French nobleman, who replaced the local aristocracy with his own knights, the implications of this victory were very great. Until that time the orientation of the country had been toward Scandinavia, but it was then shifted towards France. French became the language of the court, and artistic styles and political institutions were imported from Normandy. For example, feudalism was introduced, and the monarch became more centralized and powerful.

John Dahmus, *A History of Medieval Civilization* (New York: Odyssey Press, 1964).

Why was Joan of Arc burned at the stake?

Sometimes called the Maid of Orleans (La Pucelli) Joan of Arc was a popular French heroine and symbol of French National unity. She was born on January 6, 1412, in northeastern France to a peasant farmer and his deeply religious wife who instilled in Joan a strong belief in Christianity. Around the age of 13 or 14, claimed to hear the voices of saints such as Saint Margaret, Saint Catherine, and Saint Michael instructing her to defeat the English, who were besieging the city of Orleans and to take the dauphin to Reims to be crowned king.

In February of 1429 during the Hundred Year's War, Joan with a small band of soldiers traveled to Orleans, joined with the French army resisting the English siege and led a series of successful assaults against the English army in early May of 1429. These assaults had such a devastating effect on the morale of the English army,that they abandoned their seige of Orleans on May 8, 1429. Joan was hailed as a national hero by the French people.

In April of 1430, Joan with a small group of soldiers went to Compigne to help the French army resist a siege by the Burgundians. During the siege, Joan was captured on May 23, 1430, by Burgundian soldiers. The English, who held Joan responsible for their defeat at Orleans, got the Burgundians to turn her over to them. The English put Joan on trial in January of 1431 charged her with being a witch and a heretic: burned her at the stake on May 30, 1431. Joan was beatified in 1909 and canonized a saint by the Roman Catholic Church in 1920.

The Encyclopedia Americana, intern. ed. (Danbury, CT: Grolier, 1990), s.v. "Joan of Arc."

How did the Crusades start?

The Crusades were Christian military campaigns undertaken in the eleventh, twelfth, and thirteenth centuries to free the land of Palestine, where Jesus Christ lived and died, from the Muslim Turks. The first call for a Crusade was made by Pope Urban II (1042-1099) at the Council of Clermont in 1095. The response to Urban's speech was overwhelming, and the cry "Deus volt," which means in "God wills it," ran through the assembled host. Both nobility and commoners responded in great numbers, pledging to give their lives to free the Holy Land from Muslim control. To go on a Crusade was the considered almost the equivalent of a religious vocation. The lands of men who took the cross were to be free from attack, and they were allowed to wear the distinctive garb of a crusader—a white tunic with a large red cross on the chest.

The military expedition known as the First Crusade, which began in 1096, was the only really successful campaign. It conquered the city of Jerusalem, and established four crusaders states—the kingdom of Jerusalem, the County of Edessa, the Principality of Antioch, and the County of Tripoli. In all, there were between seven and nine crusades, depending on what historian one reads, but none of the campaigns after the first achieved its goal. The later crusades were often called in response to some disaster that had befallen the crusaders. For example, the Second Crusade was organized because the County of Edessa was captured, but it accomplished nothing in its failed siege of Damascus except to help unite the Muslims against the West. The crusader states gradually shrank in size until the westerners were finally pushed off the continent in 1291, when the city of Acre fell.

George C. Kohn, *Dictionary of Wars* (New York: Facts on File, 1986), s.v. "crusade, first."

Why did Britain pass the Iron Act?

In 1750, Britain passed the Iron Act, which prohibited Britain's American colonists from manufacturing iron products but permitted them to exchange iron for manufactured goods. The purpose of the Iron Act was to insure that the American colonies would serve as a ready market for goods produced in Britain and not be able to profit from the wealth of its natural resources. Despite the Iron Act, iron mills continued to prosper throughout the colonies.

James Trager, *The People's Chronology: A Year-by-Year Record of Human Events from Prehistory to the Present* (New York: Henry Holt, 1992), 300.

Was the legendary King Arthur real or imagined?

Although he is not mentioned by historians who were contemporary with him, King Arthur was most probably a real person, a Celtic military leader who defended Britain against Saxon invaders during the fifth century. The Welsh historian Nennius, who wrote about 800, credited him with twelve victories over the Saxons. But if there is a kernel of historical fact in the myths and legends that grew up about the name of Arthur in the later Middle Ages, it is difficult to discern. He most certainly was not a king, and many of the stories told about him owe more to the literary conventions of the eleventh or twelfth centuries than to anything he might have actually done.

Grant Uden, *A Dictionary of Chivalry* (New York: Thomas Y. Crowell Company, 1969), s.v. "Arthur, King."

Who was Charlemagne?

Charlemagne (742-814) was the greatest king of the Franks. They were originally a Germanic tribe that had settled within the confines of the decaying Roman empire during the fifth century. By the time Charlemagne came to the throne in 768, the Franks were the most important political force in western Europe, controlling much of what is now France, the Low Countries, and parts of western Germany. Charlemagne continued the expansion, sending armies into northern Spain, Italy, and deeper into Germany. So impressive were his conquests that in 800 he was crowned by Pope Leo III as emperor of the Romans. In organization and spirit Charlemagne's Roman Empire was a far cry from that of the caesars, but he did reintroduce an imperial ideal that remained part of the European political world for a thousand years. His reign is considered a high point of the early Middle Ages, for in addition to his military successes, he was an effective ruler and also initiated a series of important cultural reforms that sparked a revival we now call the Carolingian renaissance.

Charlemagne is not a name that the emperor would have recognized. It is a French version of the Latin *Carolus Magnus*, which means Charles the Great.

R.H.C. Davis, *A History of Medieval Europe from Constantine to St. Louis, 2d ed.* (London: Longman, 1988), 128-42.

Who established a sea route between Portugal and India by sailing around Africa to India?

Vasco da Gama (1460-1524), a Portuguese explorer, sailed from Lisbon in 1497 with four ships to see if he could discover a sea route to India. He rounded the Cape of Good Hope, at the southern tip of Africa, on November 22 of the same year. In 1498 he arrived at Calicut where the Arab spice dealers feared his competition and, therefore, treated him poorly. Nevertheless, he had accomplished his purpose. Europe would no longer be forced to rely on Venetian merchants, the middlemen of the spice trade.

James Trager, *The People's Chronology: A Year-by-Year Record of Human Events from Prehistory to the Present, rev. ed.*, (New York: Henry Holt and Co., 1992), 161.

Who financed Christopher Columbus' voyage in 1492?

When Christopher Columbus, his captains, and their crews set sail aboard the *Santa Maria*, the *Pinta*, and the *Nia*, on August 3, 1492, his expedition was financed by Spain's Queen Isabella, who had borrowed the funds from Luis de Santangel using her jewelry as collateral.

James Trager, *The People's Chronology: A Year-by-Year Record of Human Events from Prehistory to the Present, rev. ed.* (New York: Henry Holt and Co., 1992), 158.

Which queen of England never once set foot in her country?

Berengeria (1165-1230) never resided or even visited England. A princess from Navarre, a kingdom partly in Spain and in France, Berengeria married Richard the Lion-Hearted (1157-1199) in 1191, who ruled England from 1189 to 1199.

Isaac Asimov, ed., *Isaac Asimov's Book of Facts* (New York: Bell Publishing, 1981), ll.

Who founded the city of Moscow?

Although archaeological evidence shows that settlements have existed at the current site of Moscow, Russia, since the Stone Age, modern history dates the founding of Moscow as April 4, 1147. This is the date of the first written reference to "Moscow." The document in question is a monastic chronicle noting that Yury Vladimirovich Dolgoruky, prince of Suzdal, hosted a "great banquet" for a visiting prince "in Moscow." In 1156 Prince Dolgoruky fortified the city with an earthen rampart topped by wooden walls that he called the "Kremlin."

Philip W. Goetz, ed., *The New Encyclopaedia Britannica, 15th ed., "Macropaedia"* (Chicago: Encyclopaedia Britannica, 1989), s.v. "Moscow."

Which pope granted Portugal the right to a slave trade?

In 1442 Pope Martin V (1368-1431) granted Portugal the exclusive right to the possession and dominion of all countries they could discover from Cape Bojador to India. His purpose was to encourage the Portuguese to convert the Africans to Christianity, educate them, then return the natives to their homes and develop a trade with them.

James Bandinel, *Some Account of The Trade in Slaves From Africa* (1842; reprint, London: Frank Cass, 1968), 12-15.

Who was crowned the first Holy Roman Emperor?

The title Holy Roman Emperor was first used by Frederick I (1152-90), who was known as Barbarossa (Redbeard). Like all medieval emperors, he saw himself as continuing the line of emperors that began with the ancient Romans in the first century. In fact the medieval empire in the west is usually considered to have begun with the coronation of Charlemagne by Pope Leo III on Christmas Day in A.D. 800. After the decline of the Carolingians, the title was revived again by Otto I in 962, and it was in this smaller, more Germanic empire that Frederick was elected to the throne. Throughout the medieval period, however, there was an emperor in Constantinople (modern Istanbul) who also claimed that his authority descended from the ancient caesars. He ruled what is now known as the Byzantine or Eastern Roman Empire.

R. H. C. Davis, *A History of Medieval Europe from Constantine to St. Louis* (London: Longman, 1988), 302-24.

Who was Kublai Khan?

Kublai Khan (1215-1294) was the founder of the Yuan dynasty in China, establishing his capital at Khanbalik, modern Beijing. A grandson of the Mongol leader Genghis Khan, he was a successful soldier as well as an intelligent ruler, whose reign is a high point in the history of China. He conquered Burma and Korea, but failed to take Japan. The writings of the Venetian traveller Marco Polo (1254-1324), who had entered the khan's diplomatic service during his stay in China (1275-92), contains much important historical information about the khan's reign.

James Trager, *The People's Chronology, rev. ed.* (New York: Henry Holt and Company, 1992), 113.

What was the Ottoman Empire?

The Ottoman Empire was a multinational state that was centered in Anatolia, and whose capital after 1453 was Istanbul, the ancient city of Constantinople. At its height the empire included in Europe, the Balkan peninsula, Romania, and parts of Hungary and Russia; in Asia, Iraq, Syria, Palestine, Lebanon, and

Jordan; and in Africa, North Africa, as far as Algeria, and Egypt. The empire lasted over 600 years, from 1290 until 1922 when the modern Turkish republic was established. It was dominated by the Turks, a non-Arab, Islamic people who speak a Turko-Mongolic language, and who originally came from central Asia. The term Ottoman refers to the ruling family, the descendants of Osman I (1258-1326), who established a principality at the expense of the Byzantine Empire in Anatolia in the early fourteenth century, and who is considered the founder of the empire.

Lord Kinross, *The Ottoman Centuries: The Rise and Fall of the Turkish Empire* (Morrow Quill, 1977). James Trager, *The People's Chronology: A Year-by-Year Record of Human Events from Prehistory to the Present, rev. ed.* (New York: Henry Holt, 1992), 117.

What was the battle of Bannockburn?

On June 24, 1314, 30,000 Scotsmen under the leadership of Robert Bruce VIII (1274-1329) became Robert I of Scotland, routed a large English force commanded by Edward II (1284-1327) at Bannockburn. Thus the Scots were able to take the Stirling, the last Scottish castle in English hands, and assure their independence from England.

James Trager, *The People's Chronology: A Year-by-Year Record of Human Events from Prehistory to the Present, rev. ed.* (New York: Henry Holt, 1992), 123.

Why did Lady Godiva ride naked through the streets of Coventry?

Many people are familiar with the story of how Lady Godiva rode naked through the streets of Coventry. However, few people know the reasons for this ride.

In approximately 1040, Lady Godiva's husband, Leofric, imposed heavy taxes on the citizens of Coventry. Realizing that these taxes placed quite a hardship on the common people, Lady Godiva asked Leofric to remove them. Leofric replied that he would revoke all of these taxes, provided that Lady Godiva ride naked through the streets of Coventry. In response to Leofric's challenge, Lady Godiva did indeed ride naked through the streets, her long hair the only covering on her body. She requested that the citizens remain indoors with their windows shut while she did this. According to legend, a tailor was blinded after he tried to sneak a peek at Lady Godiva. Following the ride, Leofric kept his promise and removed all of the taxes.

James Trager, *The People's Chronology: A Year-by-Year Record of Human Events from Prehistory to the Present, rev. ed.* (New York: Henry Holt, 1992), 82.

What were the original names of Christopher Columbus' three ships?

In 1492 the explorer Christopher Columbus (1451-1506) set sail from Spain to explore the New World and took three ships with him. At that time Spanish ships had an official name as well as a nickname. The official name of Columbus' first ship was the *Santa Mara,* which was nicknamed *La Gallega* or "The Galician." The official name of his second ship was the *Santa Clara,* but it was more widely known by its nickname *Nia.* The third ship was known by its nickname *Pinta,* but its official name is unknown.

Samuel Eliot Morison, *Christopher Columbus, Mariner* (Boston: Little, Brown, 1955), 34.

Who was Genghis Khan?

Genghis Khan was a great Mongol ruler and is considered one of history's great military strategists. His date of birth is estimated in the year 1167. After his father was murdered when he was 9 years old, he developed a reputation as a ruthless outlaw. Although he was illiterate, Khan's charisma and excellent organizational skills united the many disparate Mongol tribes into one large, highly disciplined military force.

From 1192 to 1202, Genghis Khan's army engaged in a brutal war with the Mongol's dreaded enemy, the Tatars which ended with Khan's army defeating the Tatars and establishing supremacy throughout central Asia and northern China. Khan developed an impressive armored lance and sword cavalry that struck fear in the hearts of his enemies. He developed an effective military communications network by establishing surveillance outposts along all important caravan routes. His reputation for brutality and ruthlessness often caused commanders of opposing armies to surrender even before Khan's army attacked. By the time of his death in 1227, Genghis Khan's armies had invaded and conquered the Hsia Empire, China's Chin Empire, Russia, India, Persia, and parts of Europe.

George C. Kohn, *Dictionary of Wars* (New York: Facts on File Publications, 1986), s.v. "Genghis Khan, Conquests of."

What were the ten commandments of knighthood?

The ten commandments of knighthood are as follows:

Unswerving belief in the Church, and obedience to her teachings

Willingness to defend the Church

Respect and pity for all weakness, and steadfastness in defending them

Love of country

Refusal to retreat before the enemy

Unceasing and merciless war against the infidel

Strict obedience to the feudal overlord, so long as those duties did not conflict with duty to God

Loyalty to truth and to the pledged word

Generosity in giving

Championship of the right and the good, in every place and at all times, against the forces of evil

Grant Uden, *A Dictionary of Chivalry* (New York: Thomas Y. Crowell, 1969), s.v. "code of chivalry."

How did the slave trade start?

The forcible transporting of Africans into North and South American colonies for free labor actually began when ten Africans were brought into Portugal around 1450. Spanish entrepreneurs soon followed suit in order to provide workers for their holdings in the New World. The Netherlands also copied the idea, and it was a Dutch ship engaged in the slave trade that brought the first West Africans into the English colony at Jamestown, Virginia, in the early years of the seventeenth century. The French and English also participated in the "traffick in men," as it was called then.

Kenneth C. Davis, *Don't Know Much About History: Everything You Need to Know About American History But Never Learned* (New York: Crown Publishers, 1990), 18.

Who was "El Cid"?

One of Spain's most famous military leaders was Rodrigo Diaz de Bivar (ca.1040-1099), better known as "El Cid" or El Cid Campeador. He is best probably best known for his seige and conquest of Valencia, a kingdom inhabited by Spanish Muslims known as Moors. In late 1092, El Cid and his soldiers surrounded Valencia and demanded the surrender of its inhabitants. The Valencians held out stubbornly for over twenty months, but a lack of food supplies forced them to surrender to El Cid on June 17, 1094. El Cid proved to be a capable leader and allowed Valencians freedom of worship and property ownership. Valencia was attacked in October 1094 by the Almoravids, a Muslim tribe. However, El Cid and his soldiers were able to repel the attack. El Cid died in 1099. Three years later, Valencia was captured by the Almoravids.

George C. Kohn, *Dictionary of Wars* (New York: Facts on File Publications, 1986), s.v. "Cid's conquest of Valencia, the."

What treaty divided the globe between Portugal and Spain in 1494?

The 1494 treaty that divided the globe between Portugal and Spain was called the Treaty of Tordesillas. It established a boundary that was similar to the line of demarcation drawn the previous year by Pope Alexander VI. The papal bull specified that the Portuguese would have control over any lands they discovered east of the line and the Spanish would control lands that lay to the west.

James Trager, *The People's Chronology: A Year-by-Year Record of Human Events from Prehistory to the Present, rev. ed.* (New York: Henry Holt and Co., 1992) 159.

What was the Native American population in the Western Hemisphere in 1492?

When Christopher Columbus and his three ships reached the Western Hemisphere in 1492, the New World was populated by about 50 million indigenous peoples.

Isaac Asimov, ed., *Isaac Asimov's Book of Facts* (New York: Bell Publishing, 1981), 30.

What was Spain's financial outlay for Christopher Columbus's voyage to the New World?

In 1902 John Boyd Thacher, a biographer of Christopher Columbus, estimated that 1,167,542 maravedis was the cost of the explorer's voyage for the Spanish Empire. The maravedi was a copper coin used in fifteenth-century Spain, and the equivalent for the 1492 expenditure in 1991 dollars was $151,780. Maintenance amounted to the largest expense for the journey, at $41,558 1991 dollars; officers' salaries, $34,840; sailors' pay, $32,760; the rental cost for one of the ships, $22,464; and furnishings, arms, and trading supplies, $20,158. Spain's financial sponsorship of the voyage was not a troublesome expenditure for its abundant treasury at the time, and historians estimate that the Empire received a 200 million percent return on its investment.

Zvi Dor-Ner, *Columbus and the Age of Discovery* (New York: Morrow, 1991), 119.

What two rival lines of England's royal family were involved in the "Wars of the Roses"?

The "Wars of the Roses" (1455-87) was a dynastic war between two lines of England's royal family. They were the Lancastrians who descended from John of Gaunt (1340-1399), Duke of Lancaster and the Yorkists whos ancestor was Edmund of Langley (1342-1402), Duke of York. Both were sons of King Edward III (1312-1377).

Bamber Gascoigne, *Encyclopedia of Britain* (New York: Macmillan Publishing, 1993), s.v. "Wars of the Roses."

Was there a person named Dracula from Transylvania?

The infamous personage known as Dracula was the son of Vlad II of Romania. As a reward for successfully battling the Turks, Vlad II was admitted to a select group of knights called Order of the Dragon by King Sigismund of Hungary. Since the Latin word for "dragon" is draco, Vlad became known as Vlad Dracul. Dracul's other meaning is "devil," and Vlad was said to be in league with the devil due to his cruelties. However, it was Dracul's son, also named Vlad, who became known as Dracula. He was born about 1430 or 1431 in the Transylvanian town of Schassburg. In his fights with the Turks, he subjected his captives to slow deaths by impalement on wooden stakes; because of this, he was called Vlad the Impaler. Dracula committed hundreds of atrocities, including the torture and killing of his own countrymen. Irish author Bram Stoker (1847-1912) used this historical Dracula for his fictional vampire in his horror novel *Dracula* (1897).

Donald F. Glut, *The Dracula Book* (Metuchen, NJ: Scarecrow Press, 1975), 1-5. *World Book Encyclopedia* (Chicago: World Book, 1994), s.v. "Dracula."

1500 to 1789

What city Is now located on the site of seventeenth-century New Amsterdam?

Dutch settlers once occupied an area on the island of Manhattan with boundaries that are currently marked by Whitehall and Pearl Streets, and by Broad and Beaver Streets. Obliterated by what is now New York City, the settlers called their new home New Amsterdam. Founded in 1625, with the building of a fort, the town changed its name to New York when it became a British possession in 1664. Recaptured by the Dutch in 1673, it was briefly known as New Orange. The British recaptured the land the next year, and the city has been known as New York ever since.

Dictionary of American History, rev. ed. (New York: Charles Scribner's Sons, 1976), s.v. "New Amsterdam."

In colonial America what was the connection between the Townshend Acts of 1767, the Tea Act of 1773 and the Boston Tea Party of the same year?

England's Townshend Acts of 1767, named after Charles Townshend, Chancellor of the Exchequer imposed colonial import duties on glass, paint, paper, oil, lead, and tea to raise revenue to pay for England's North American expenditures, especially defense expenditures. American colonists predictably objected vigorously to the new taxes. On May 10, 1773 the Tea Act was passed by the English Parliament which made it very profitable for the East India Company of England to export tea to the North American colonies while providing a ready market for its seven years supply of tea which was straining the company's storage facilities in England. The Tea Act also allowed the East India Company to sell the tea cheaply and directly with only a three pence Townshend tax to colonial retailers thus eliminating colonial middlemen. The colonists viewed it as an attempt to make Parliamentary taxation palatable. The tea ships in New York and Philadelphia ports had to return to England with the cargo. But in Boston, radical colonists took a different tack that would further worsen the bad relations between the mother country and some of her American colonies. On December 16, 1773 in protest to the Tea Act a group of 60 colonists including Paul Revere and Lendall Pitts disguised themselves as Mohawk Indians, boarded three East India Company ships docked in Boston Harbor and threw 342 chests of tea overboard. Samuel Adams and John Hancock were behind the scenes organizers of the "Party." Angered at the loss of 10,000 pounds and the destruction of property, England sought to punish the Massachusetts colony with the Coercive Acts. This action united the other colonies with Massachusetts, leading them closer to war.

John Mack Faragher, ed., *The Encyclopedia of Colonial and Revolutionary America* (New York: Facts on File, 1990), s.v. "Boston Tea Party," "Townshend Acts." James Trager, *The People's Chronology* (New York: Henry Holt, 1992), 317.

Who assumed command of the Magellan expedition when the explorer was killed in the Philippines?

Ferdinand Magellan (1480?-1521) was a famous Portuguese navigator who received Spanish financial support for his westward voyage around the world. During the journey, Magellan and his party stopped in the Philippines to rest and stock up on provisions. While on the Philippine island of Mactan, Magellan's party was attacked by 1,000 natives. Magellan and eight of his men were killed on April 27, 1521.

Following the death of Magellan, Juan Sebastian de Elcano (ca.1476-1526) had the command of one of Magellan's ships, the *Victoria* to continue the westward voyage around the world. Elcano and his crew sailed from the Philippine island of Cebu through other Philippine islands. They reached the island of Tidore, a part of the Moluccas Islands, on November 8, 1521. After a brief stay, Elcano and his crew left Tidore on December 21, 1521.

Elcano headed first for the island of Timor. He crossed the Indian Ocean as far to the south as possible from the African coast. He did not touch land until he reached Santiago Island in the Cape Verde Islands on July 13, 1522. To deceive the Portuguese who owned the islands, Elcano pretended he was returning from a voyage to the Americas. He needed their help in resupplying his ships, which had traveled for 150 days straight, more than Magellan had taken in going from America to Guam.

Elcano and the *Victoria* arrived at Sanlucar on September 6, 1522, then went on to Seville a few days later. Only 18 men from Magellan's original crew had survived the entire three-year voyage. King Charles V received Elcano with great honor, and a globe was erected in his home village of Guetaria.

Daniel B. Baker, ed., *Explorers & Discoverers* (Detroit: Gale Research, 1993), s.v. "Ferdinand Magellan"

Was 16th century philosopher, Giordano Bruno, really the spy for Elizabeth I of England, Henry Fagot?

Attempting to explain events of 400 years ago, John Bossy, professor at England's York University, suggests that the famed philosopher and priest, Giordano Bruno (1548-1600), also acted as a spy for Queen Elizabeth I (1533-1603) of England. Bossy's sleuthing has uncovered information that points to the possibility that Bruno, while living at the home of the French ambassador to England, helped identify English Catholics plotting to overthrow the Queen.

Bossy theorizes that letters signed by Henry Fagot to the Queen were written by Giordano Bruno. Besides being in the right place at the right time, Bruno was in discord with the papacy and was probably in need of money. One Fagot letter hints that the writer is a priest. None of the details are conclusive evidence of Henry Fagot actually being Bruno.

New York Times 1 September 1991.

After the Boston Massacre of 1770 who defended the British soldiers charged with murder?

After the March 5, 1770 Boston Massacre, in which British soldiers fired on and killed five colonialists, Captain Thomas Preston and seven grenadiers were charged with murder. Preston was defended by the future U.S. president John Adams (1722-1803) and Robert Auchmuty, with the aissistance of Josiah Quincy, Jr. (1744-75). The seven soldiers, who were tried separately, were also defended by Adams and Quincy but with the help of Sampson Salter Blowers. All were acquitted. It has never been fully explained why Adams and Quincy, both colonial radicals, chose to defend the British soldiers.

Dictionary of American History, rev. ed. (New York: Charles Scribner's Sons, 1976), s.v. "Boston Massacre."

What novel but ill-fated solution did Patrick Henry offer to resolve growing hostility between Native Americans and white colonialists?

In 1784, in an effort to resolve growing hostility between Native Americans and white colonialists, American Revolution leader and orator, Patrick Henry (1736-99) proposed a government payment for inter-marriage. Henry's bill, which was introduced in the Virginia legislature would have called for the payment of ten pounds for any free Virginian, male or female, who married a Native American and five pounds following the birth of each child. Included in the bill were tax breaks and educational incentives. The bill passed its first and second readings but failed to pass a third and final reading.

Irving Wallace, *Significa* (New York: E. P. Dutton, 1983), 61.

What insects provided illumination for early cultures?

Early accounts reported that large beetles (although smaller than a sparrow) provided sufficient light for American natives to weave, paint and write by. It was also noted that Spanish invaders attached a beetle to each foot so as to avoid snakes when walking about at night!

F.W. Robins, *The Story of the Lamp (and the Candle)* (1939; reprint, Bath: Kingsmead Reprints, 1970), 125.

Where is Shangri-La?

Shangri-La is a Tibetan lamasery founded by Father Perrault, who was born in Luxembourg in 1681. Perrault, who founded Shangri-La in 1734, reportedly died at the age of 250 years. He is also known for translating Montaigne's *Essay on Vanity* into Tibetan. Shangri-La ("La" is Tibetan for "mountain-pass") is presently under Chinese administration.

The Dictionary of Imaginary Places, exp. ed. (San Diego, CA: Harvest/HBJ, 1987), s.v. "Shangri-La."

How many wives did Henry VIII have?

King Henry VIII of England (1491-1547) had six wives. He first married his brother Arthur's widow Catherine of Aragon (1485-1536). Older than Henry, she was the daughter of Ferdinand and Isabella of Spain and bore Henry one child, Mary, who ruled England from 1553 to 1558. Henry's separation from Catherine in 1533 caused the Church of England to break with the Roman Catholic Church. In that year he married an English noblewoman Anne Boleyn (1507-1536), who was already pregnant with the future Queen Elizabeth I (1533-1603). In 1536 he had Anne beheaded for adultery and married Jane Seymour (1509-1537), who had been a lady-in-waiting to Catherine and Anne. She died 12 days after giving birth to Henry's long-desired son, who eventually became Edward VI. His fourth wife was a German noblewoman Anne of Cleves (1515-1557), with whom he was incompatible; they were divorced after a few months of marriage in 1540. In the same year he married a pretty young English girl Catherine Howard (1520-1542), whom he had beheaded for adultery two years later. In 1543 he married Catherine Parr (1512-1548), who was a good mother to his three children, and who survived him to marry again. On his death bed Henry expressed a desire to be buried next to Jane Seymour.

Charles Panati, *Panati's Extraordinary Endings of Practically Everything and Everybody* (New York: Harper & Row, 1989), 47.

Who was Rob Roy, and what was his real name?

Rob Roy, which means Red Robert, was the nickname of Robert MacGregor (1671-1734). He was a nephew of the chief of Clan MacGregor and involved in the struggles for power and land that took place in Scotland during this period. He eventually became an outlaw, who engaged in cattle stealing and blackmail, age-old Highland practices. He was a Jacobite, a supporter of the Old Pretender, the son of the deposed Stuart monarch James II, but he plundered both sides during that attempt at Stuart restoration known as the Fifteen. His life was glamorized in the Sir Walter Scot novel *Rob Roy* (1818), and he is mentioned in the poems of William Wordsworth.

Robert McHenry, ed., *The New Encyclopaedia Britannica, 15th ed., "Micropaedia"* (Chicago: Encyclopaedia Britannica, 1993), s.v. "Rob Roy."

Which British literary figure wrote books about his dog Tulip?

Joseph Randolph Ackerley (1896-1976) was literary editor of *The Listener* from 1935 to 1959 and attracted many distinguished contributors, such as American writer Christopher Isherwood (1904-1986). Ackerley's writings include *My Dog Tulip* (1956) and a novel *We Think the World of You* (1960), both of which describe his intense relationship his pet, an Alsatian dog named Tulip.

J.R. Ackerley, *My Dog Tulip* (New York: Poseidon Press, 1965), 9. Margaret Drabble, ed., *The Oxford Companion to Literature, 5th ed.* (Oxford: Oxford University Press, 1985).

How long was Karen Ann Quinlan in a coma?

Karen Ann Quinlan, a comatose young woman from New Jersey who became a focal point in the "right to die" debate, existed in a comatose state from April 14, 1975, until her death over ten years later on June 11, 1985. The coma was evidently caused by Quinlan ingesting tranquilizers and alcohol at a party. Her parents petitioned the court to remove her from a respirator and, although they eventually received permission, Quinlan continued in a comatose state until her death.

"Karen Ann Quinlan, 31, Dies 9 Years After Coma Decision," *New York Times* 12 June 1985.

Who was once described as being "first in war, first in peace, and first in the hearts of his countrymen"?

The first president of the United States George Washington (1732-1799) was described by politician Henry (Light-Horse Harry) Lee (1756-1818) as being "first in war, first in peace, and first in the hearts of his countrymen."

Family Encyclopedia of American History (Pleasantville, NY: Reader's Digest Association, 1975), s.v. "Washington, George."

What were the Black Flags?

The Black Flags comprised a private Chinese army that fled to the northern part of Vietnam following the ill-fated Tai-Ping Revolt of 1865. In Vietnam they served as slave traders, pirates, opium traders, and mercenaries. They also fought against French colonialism especially in 1873 and 1882.

Danny J. Whitfield, *Historical and Cultural Dictionary of Vietnam* (Metuchen, NJ: Scarecrow Press, 1976), s.v. "Black Flags."

What saint of the Catholic Church and English statesman was beheaded by King Henry VIII?

Thomas More (1478-1535) an English statesman and later saint of then Roman Catholic Church, was charged with treason and beheaded by King Henry VIII (1491-1547) of England. More fell out of favor with the king because although he accepted the king's marriage to Anne Boleyn, he refused to deny the supremacy of the pope. When the Act of Supremacy was passed in 1534 that recognized Henry VIII as head of the church, More did not swear an oath of allegience, and was charged with treason. More was canonized by the Roman Catholic Church in 1935.

Bamber Gascoigne, *Encyclopedia of Britain* (New York: Macmillan Publishing, 1993, s.v. "Thomas More."

In English history who were the Roundheads and the Cavaliers?

In English history the Cavaliers were supporters of the monarchy during the English Civil War, while the Roundheads opposed the royal cause. Cavalier was an abusive term circa 1640 and was applied to the swashbuckling followers of Charles I (1600-1649). Roundhead also came from the 1640s and was a pejorative term describing the short hairstyles of the Puritans.

Bamber Gascoigne, *Encyclopedia of Britain* (New York: Macmillan Publishing, 1993), s.v. "Cavaliers," "Roundheads."

What artifacts of a 1597 war did Japan recently return to Korea?

In 1992 Japan returned 20,000 noses cut off of Korean soldiers and civilians along with the heads of numerous Korean generals to their homeland. The grizzly artifacts of a 1597 Japanese invasion of Korea were kept at the *senbitsuka*, a tomb near the Japanese city of Bizen. The war trophys will most likely be interred in South Korea's Cholla province where much of the damage and mutilation took place.

USA Today 23 September 1992.

How many fingers did Anne Boleyn have?

It is a matter of speculation as to whether Anne Boleyn (1507?-1536), the second wife of England's King Henry VIII (1491-1547), had the vestiges a sixth finger on one of her hands. Some historians believe that reports of an additional finger and a hideous mole or tumor on her neck were the fictional work of Nicholas Sander. The scholar published a work 50 years after her death which introduced a witch-like description of Boleyn. Contemporary accounts of her appearance, even some that are less than complimentary, do not mention these disfigurements. This supports the theory that these physical marks were created to support the image of Boleyn as an evil, adulterous woman.

Carolly Erickson, *Mistress Anne* (New York: Summit Books, 1984), 12. Retha M. Warnicke, *The Rise and Fall of Anne Boleyn: Family Politics at the Court of Henry VIII* (Cambridge: Cambridge University Press, 1989), 3, 58-59, 65.

What kind of cargo was carried on the *Mayflower* prior to its voyage to America?

The ship the *Mayflower*, famous for its cargo of pilgrims to America, was used on its previous voyage to carry more than 59 tons of French wines to England.

Henry Justin Smith, *The Mast of the Mayflower* (Chicago: Willett, Clark & Company, 1936), 48.

In British history what was the Restoration?

In British history the Restoration marked the event of the return of the monarch Charles II (1630-85) to Britain and his throne in 1660 as well as the time period or the reign of Charles II and James II (1633-1701), which lasted until the Revolution of 1688. The Restoration period was marked by "frivolity, glamour, and licentiousness" that was in sharp contrast to the previous historical period-the dour and drab Commonwealth ear.

Bamber Gascoigne, *Encyclopedia of Britain* (New York: Macmillan Publishing, 1993), s.v. "Restoration."

Who were the two Catholic signers of the U.S. Constitution?

Thomas FitzSimons (1741-1811) and Daniel Carroll (1730-1796) were the two Catholic signers of the U.S. Constitution. FitzSimons, of Philadelphia, was a merchant and public servant who served on the Pennsylvania Navy Board, organized an active-duty Revolutionary War militia, and was a delegate to the Constitutional Convention. Later, FitzSimons was elected to the U.S. Congress. Carroll, a wealthy man, was a successful merchant, tobacco farmer, and plantation owner in Maryland and a delegate to the Constitutional Convention. In addition, he served in the Maryland Senate and Council, the Continental Congress, and eventually the U.S. House of Representatives.

The Catholic University of America, *New Catholic Encyclopedia* (New York: McGraw-Hill, 1967), s.v. "Carroll, Daniel," "FitzSimons, Thomas."

Who claimed the Louisiana territory for France and took possession of the Mississippi Valley?

Rene Robert Cavelier, Sieur de La Salle (1643-1687), claimed the Louisiana territory for France and took possession of the Mississippi Valley. La Salle was a French explorer who originally settled near Montreal and later received grants of lands and trading privileges in the west. He descended the Mississippi River, arriving at the Gulf of Mexico on April 9, 1682. He claimed the whole valley for the French king, Louis XIV (1638-1715), naming the region Louisiana after him.

Bernard Grun, *The Timetables of History, 3d rev. ed.* (New York: Simon & Schuster, 1991),

What role did islands play in the life of Napoleon Bonaparte?

French emperor Napoleon Bonaparte (1769-1821) is regarded by many scholars as being one of the world's most brilliant military strategists. His leadership abilities and the respect and admiration shown to him by his armies were unparalleled as he established French military power and influence throughout Europe and into Russia. Islands have always figured prominently in Napoleon's life. He was born on the island of Corsica in 1769, exiled to the island of Elba in 1814, and died on the island of St. Helena in 1821.

Trevor N. Dupuy, Curt Johnson, and David L. Bongard, *The Harper Encyclopedia of Military Biography* (New York: HarperCollins, 1992), s.v. "Napoleon I."

Who were the "Green Mountain Boys"?

During the American Revolution War, the American colonists received a great deal of outside help in their bid for independence. One source of assistance was from soldiers from Vermont called the Green Mountain Boys. The Green Mountain Boys distinguished themselves in the capture of Fort Ticonderoga and the Battle of Bennington. Through the influence of the Green Mountain Boys, Vermont declared itself an independent republic in 1777, and in 1791, Vermont was incorporated into the United States as the fourteenth state.

The World Book Encyclopedia (Chicago: World Book, 1987), s.v. "Green Mountain Boys."

Who was the first child born of English parents in America?

The first English child to be born on American soil was Virginia Dare on August 18, 1587, to Ananius Dare and Eleanor White Dare on Roanoke Island, North Carolina. The first child born of English parents in New England was Peregrine White, born of Susanna and William White on November 20, 1620. Peregrine was born aboard the *Mayflower* off the New England coast.

Joseph Nathan Kane, *Famous First Facts* (New York: H.W. Wilson, 1981), 117.

In American history what was the "shot heard round the world"?

In American history the "shot heard round the world" is an allegorical reference to the Battle of Concord (Massachusetts), where on April 18, 1775, British troops were fired upon by a small contingent of colonial "Minutemen." One of the earliest engagements of the American Revolution, the Battle of Concord has tremendous symbolic importance for democracy and thus was the "shot heard round the world."

Kenneth C. Davis, *Don't Know Much About History* (New York: Crown Publishers, 1990), 51.

Who made the second circumnavigation of the world following Magellan?

Sir Francis Drake (ca. 1543-1596) made the second circumnavigation of the globe following Ferdinand Magellan (1480?-1521). Born near Tavistock, Devonshire, he went to sea as a young boy, where he became known as a navigator, slaver, pirate, privateer, trader, and admiral. Between 1569 and 1572 Drake amassed a fortune from raiding gold-laden Spanish ships plying the Caribbean area. In 1577 he left England on his around-the-world adventure aboard his ship the *Golden Hind.* Sailing down the South American coast, through the Straits of Magellan, and up the North American coast, he repaired his ship in what is now Drake's Estero, California in 1579 and sailed along the Oregon coast and perhaps as far north as Vancouver Island.

He went on to the Phillipines and the Spice Islands, across the Indian Ocean, and around the Cape of Good Hope of Africa. He returned to London in 1580 where Elizabeth I (1533-1603) granted him knighthood in 1581. Drake died of dysentery off the Panama coast on January 28, 1596.

Helen Delpar, ed., *The Discoverers: An Encyclopedia of Explorers and Exploration* (New York: McGraw-Hill, 1980), s.v. "Drake, Francis."

Was Peter Minuit swindled by the Canarsie Indians when he bought Manhattan Island, and how much would the money be worth today?

In 1626 Peter Minuit, on behalf of the Dutch West India company, purchased Manhattan Island from the Canarsie Indians for about $24 worth of trinkets. Minuit was swindled because the Canarsie Indians did not own the island. A small tribe known as the Manhattan Indians were the true owners, and when Minuit discovered his error, he made payment to them.

If the payment to the Indians were invested in an account that drew 8 percent interest, that $24 would have been worth over 52 trillion dollars in 1993 or $52,776,548,133,120.00 to be exact.

Dictionary of American History, (New York: Charles Scribner's Sons, 1976), s.v. "Manhattan." Michael D. Shook and Robert L. Shook, *It's About Time!* (New York: Plume Books, 1992), 157-58.

Who was Thomas Muntzer?

Thomas Muntzer (1489-1525) was a German religious mystic and political revolutionary who was killed along with five thousand of his followers in 1525 for leading a religious crusade against the established order. In Bad Frankenhausen, Germany, now sits the largest painting in the world, nearly 50 feet high and more than 350 feet long, a vast panorama honoring him and some of his contemporaries, such as Martin Luther, Nicholas Copernicus, Albrecht Durer, Desiderius Erasmus, Johann Gutenberg, and Christopher Columbus. Among German Communists (particularly in the former East Germany), Muntzer has been viewed as a pioneer Socialist hero for his vision of the ideal theocracy, featuring decrees on behalf of the poor, distributing free seeds and livestock, and confiscating a monastery to house the homeless.

Stephen Kinzer, "A Hero and a Picture from History's Attic," *New York Times* 1 May 1991.

What is the "Plymouth Rock" and what is its association with the Pilgrims?

"Plymouth Rock" is a large granite boulder in the present day town of Plymouth, Massachusetts. American folklore has long held that when the Pilgrims landed on December 26, 1620, the first ashore set foot upon the rock. There is little hard evidence supporting this however. While the Pilgrims did land in the area the story is based on the recollections of a Deacon Ephraim Spooner who claimed he was told of the landing by an aged ninety-five-year-old Thomas Faunce whose father John Faunce reached America in 1623 and passed the tale down to his son. Nevertheless such respected historians as Justin Winsor have stood by the veracity of the story.

Presently "Plymouth Rock" is on display but has been moved from its original spot to a safer and protected location. At some point the year "1620" was carved on the face of the rock.

Howard L. Hurwitz, *An Encyclopedic Dictionary of American History* (New York: Washington Square Press, 1968), s.v. "Plymouth Rock."

What was George Washington's career path in the U.S. military?

George Washington (1732-99) served in the Virginia militia (1752-58), rising to the rank of colonel. He was general and commander in chief of the Continental Army (1775-83). After his presidency (1789-97), he was commissioned as lieutenant general and commander in chief of American forces on July 4, 1798, the only former president to hold such a post. At that time, it was feared that war would break out between the United States and France due to the XYZ Affair. Washington held the highest military rank in the United States at the time of his death. Throughout the years, however, additional ranks were created in the army, and he was outranked by subsequent generals. In 1976 Congress posthumously granted Washington the country's highest military title, General of the Armies of the United States. He is now listed as the senior general officer on the army rolls.

Wiliam A. DeGregorio, *The Complete Book of U.S. Presidents, 2d ed.* (New York: Dembner Books, 1989), s.v. "Washington, George." *St. Louis Post-Dispatch, 28 September 1953. World Book Encyclopedia* (Chicago: World Book, 1993), s.v. "Washington, George."

Why was George Washington's birthday changed from February 11 to February 22?

The first U.S. President George Washington (1732-99) was actually born on February 11, 1731, according to the Julian calendar; but in 1750 the British Parliament discarded the Julian calendar and adopted the Gregorian calendar for Great Britain and the colonies. Doing so required adjustments to the years 1751, 1752, and 1753, so that in 1753 and thereafter Washington celebrated his birth on the 22nd.

Joseph Nathan Kane, *Facts About the Presidents, 6th ed.* (New York: H. W. Wilson, 1993), 6.

How many people sailed on the *Mayflower?*

About one hundred and two passengers plus the crew left the English town of Plymouth on September 16, 1620 on the *Mayflower* and landed near Provincetown on November 21. Sources vary as to how many people were aboard. There were estimated 44 men, 19 women, 29 boys and 10 girls. During the voyage a child named Oceanus Hopkins was born, and a servant named William Butten and one of the crew members died. Another child, Peregrine Whire, was born after the ship reached America. The exact number of seamen is unknown, but there were probably about thirty officers and crew.

Azel Ames, *The Mayflower and Her Log* (Boston: Houghton Mifflin, 1901), 143, 193. *Chronicle of America* (Liberty, MO: JL International Publishing, 1993), 53. Vernon Heaton, *The Mayflower* (Mayflower Books, 1980), 80-82, 86.

When was Henry VIII recognized as Supreme Head of the Church in England?

In 1534 the English Parliament passed the Act of Supremacy, which made Henry VIII (1491-1547) the head of the Church in England. His assumption of ecclesiastical authority was related to his desire to rid himself of his wife Catherine of Aragon (1485-1536) and marry Anne Boleyn (1507?-1536), a young English noblewoman. Catherine of Aragon had produced only a daughter, Mary, (1516-1558) and was now past child-bearing age. With the existence of an illegitimate heir, Henry Fitzroy, Duke of Richmond, Henry desired to marry Anne Boleyn and have a legitimate male heir.

Henry attempted to convince Pope Clement VII (1478-1534) that since Catherine had been married previously to Henry's older brother, Arthur (1486-1502), the marriage was invalid because Henry and Catherine had broken Biblical laws against incest. The Pope, who was captured by Catherine's nephew, Charles V (1500-1558), the Holy Roman Emperor, refused to grant an annulment. Henry chipped away at the papacy's influence within England by passing a series oflaws of which the Act of Supremacy was the most blatant. By 1533 he had married Anne Boleyn; his marriage to Catherine of Aragon had been annulled; and he had effectively severed relations with Rome and the Catholic Church. Ironically, Anne Boleyn presented him with a daughter, Elizabeth I (1533-1603). Though another daughter displeased Henry, Elizabeth I came to be one of the most influential monarchs in world history making England a world power.

Bernard Grun, *The Timetables of History, 3d rev. ed.* (New York: Simon & Schuster, 1991), 236. Lacey Baldwin Smith, *This Realm of England 1399 to 1688, 6th ed.* (Lexington, MA: D.C. Heath and Company, 1992), 118-30.

What was the native language of King George I of England?

When at the age of 54 in 1714, George (1660-1727), the Elector of Hanover, became George I, King of Great Britain and Ireland, his native language was German. This noted military strategist inherited the British throne to start the House of Hanover because his mother, Sophie, was the granddaughter of James I (1566-1625), King of England and Scotland. Although historians consider George I a capable monarch, most of his British subjects viewed him as nothing more than a foreign interloper. His refusal to learn English and his insistence that his German mistresses accompany him to England increased the hostility of the British people toward him.

Bamber Gascoine, *Encyclopedia of Britain* (London: Macmillan Press, 1993), s.v. "George I."

Which historical American person had the unlikely first name of "Cotton"?

Cotton Mather (1663-1728) was an American clergyman, historian, scientist of sorts, and man of letters. He was the grandson of Richard Mather, the first minister of Dorchester, and John Cotton, an important first-generation American theologian. His father, Increase Mather, was a minister and president of Harvard College from 1685 to 1701. Cotton Mather's historical reputation has been tarnished by his association with the infamous Salem witchcraft trials. While he thought the punishment of execution was excessive, he nevertheless approved of prosecution for alleged witchcraft, and his writings on the subject helped fuel the witchcraft craze of 1692.

McGraw-Hill Encyclopedia of World Biography (New York: McGraw-Hill, 1973), s.v. "Mather." Ralph P. and Louise Boas, *Cotton Mather: Keeper of the Puritan Conscience* (Hamden, CT: Archon Books, 1964), 6-7.

Who was the first signer of the Declaration of Independence?

In 1776 John Hancock (1737-1793) became the first signer of the Declaration of Independence. His impressive signature, made with a flourish, is still well known. It is from this event that the writing of a signature is sometimes referred to as writing "one's John Hancock."

When his father died, John Hancock was adopted by his uncle, Thomas Hancock, a wealthy Boston merchant whose lucrative business Hancock inherited upon his uncle's death in 1764. In 1768 one of his ships, the *Liberty*, was seized by British customs officials who alleged that Hancock had broken some regulations. The Boston citizenry became enraged and rioted when British troops tried to restore order. It was at this point that John Hancock became known as a revolutionary.

World Book Encyclopedia (Chicago: World Book, 1987), s.v. "Hancock, John."

What early American settlement became known as the Lost Colony?

The Lost Colony refers to an early American settlement on Roanoke Island located off the coast of what is now North Carolina. No one has been able to discover the fate of its settlers. On April 9, 1585, 108 men set sail for North America by order of Sir Walter Raleigh (1554-1618). Their destination was a large territory, then called Virginia, that encompassed what is now the area from Pennsylvania to South Carolina. It is most likely that Raleigh's intent was to found a strategic position from which England could raid Spain's American territories. These colonists endured severe hardships and within a year many returned to England. Within a few days of their departure more settlers and urgently needed provisions arrived. Although most of the colonists from the second group returned to England, fifteen hearty souls remained behind. In 1587 another group of Raleigh's settlers set sail. Originally bound for the banks of the Chesapeake Bay, they were put ashore on Roanoke Island because the ship's crew refused to go any further. None of the fifteen colonists who had remained on the island were found alive.

John White (d. 1593?), one of the newly arrived settlers, and grandfather of the first English baby born in North America, Virginia Dare, went back to England for more supplies. The Spanish war delayed his return to the settlement until 1590. Upon his arrival not one of the colonists was there. Two trees, one with the letters *CRO* carved into it and the other with *Croatoan* carved into it, were the only clues left by the colonists.

Although the National Park Service discovered in 1948 the outlines of a fort the colonists built, the fate of the settlers remains unknown. Perhaps they were captured by Spaniards or left the island following the guidance of helpful Indians to search for food. It is also possible that they were captured by hostile Indians.

World Book Encyclopedia (Chicago: World Book, 1987), s.v. "lost colony."

Who discovered the Philippine Islands?

The Philippine Islands were discovered by the Portuguese explorer, Ferdinand Magellan (1480?-1521) in his attempt to circumnavigate the world. On March 15, 1521, he attempted to overcome Lapu Lapu, a native chief. The following month he and 48 of his men, in full armor, waded ashore onto Mactan, an island in the south central Philippines, where Magellan was killed by Mactan warriors. The survivors of this battle set sail on the two ships that were left of Magellan's original five; two had been lost at sea. The ships sailed towards Moluccas, also known as the Spice Islands.

James Trager, *The People's Chronology: A Year-by-Year Record of Human Events from Prehistory to the Present, rev. ed.* (New York: Henry Holt, 1992), 172. Richard E. Bohlander, ed., *World Explorers and Discoverers* (New York: Macmillan, 1992), s.v. "Magellan, Ferdinand."

Who was Pocahontas?

Pocahontas (1595?-1617) was the teenaged daughter of a Powhatan chief in colonial Virginia who became caught in the conflict between settlers of the area and its Native American population. She had saved the English colonists by supplying them with food after their stores and homes had burnt down during the long winter of 1608. Had she not done so, the English may never have colonized the area and the Native American cultures in the area might have survived. Kidnapped by colonists in 1613, she adopted European customs, converted to Christianity, and took the name Rebecca during her captivity. In April of 1614 she married a colony widower named John Rolfe; she and her father never saw one another again. With their marriage began the Peace of Pocahontas-a friendship between the English and the Native Americans. They had a son, Thomas, in 1615. In 1616 the Rolfes sailed to England and she died there on March 21, 1617, probably from pneumonia or tuberculosis.

Sharon Malinowski, ed., *Notable Native Americans* (Detroit: Gale Research, 1995), 334-37.

Who was the first person killed in the Boston Massacre?

Crispus Attucks (1723-70), a 27-year-old African-American man who sympathized with the colonies during the American Revolution, was the first person killed in the Boston Massacre. Attucks, a former slave born in 1723 in Framingham, Massachusetts, joined a group of several dozen disgruntled colonists in provoking the British troops, possibly assaulting them with stones and snowballs. These actions were in defiance of the policies of Great Britain toward the colonies. Attucks was reported to have said, "They dare not fire." The troops did fire and Attucks, who was highly visible because of his six-foot, two-inch tall frame and his mulatto skin color, was the first to be hit by gunfire. Eleven Americans were injured, and five, including Attucks, were killed that day.

Michael W. Williams, ed., *The African American Encyclopedia* (North Bellmore, NY: Marshall Cavendish, 1993), s.v. "Attucks, Crispus."

What was the first permanent settlement in North America?

The first permanent settlement in North America was St. Augustine, Florida, which was founded by the Spaniards in 1565.

It was not until the seventeenth century that additional settlements were made. The English settled Jamestown (Virginia) in 1607; the French, Quebec (Canada) in 1608; the Spanish, Santa Fe (New Mexico), 1610; and the Dutch, New Amsterdam (New York) in 1626.

Arlene Hirschfelder and Martha Kreipe de Montao, *The Native American Almanac: A Portrait of Native America Today* (New York: Prentice Hall General Reference, 1993), 1.

Who succeeded Queen Elizabeth I of England after her death?

Queen Elizabeth I of England died childless in 1603 and was succeeded by her cousin James VI of Scotland, who then became James I of England and Ireland (1603-25). With Elizabeth's death the Tudor dynasty came to an end, and with James, the son of Mary Queen of Scots, began the reign of the Stuarts, which lasted until the death of Queen Anne in 1714.

Bernard Grun, *The Timetables of History, 3d rev. ed.* (New York: Simon & Schuster, 1991), 268.

What were the Articles of Confederation?

In 1781, the 13 original American colonies agreed to form a government of states. They called this agreement the Articles of Confederation. The Articles guaranteed each state one vote in Congress regardless of its size and guaranteed each state's soverignty and independence. The Articles also insured that Congress could not regulate trade, levy taxes, or meddle in the affairs of individual states. The Articles of Confederation served as the law of the United States until 1789, when the current Constitution of the United States was adopted.

World Book Encyclopedia (Chicago: World Book, 1987), s.v. "Articles of Confederation."

What is first European settlement in the United States?

The oldest European settlement still extant in the United States is St. Augustine, Florida, which was founded by the Spanish admiral Don Pedro Menendez de Aviles on September 8, 1565. The city was burned by Sir Frances Drake in 1586. It is currently a resort town, located 35 miles Southeast of Jacksonville.

It was not until the seventeenth century that additional settlements were made. The English settled Jamestown (Virginia) in 1607; the French, Quebec (Canada) in 1608; the Spanish, Santa Fe (New Mexico), 1610; and the Dutch, New Amsterdam (New York) in 1626.

Arlene Hirschfelder and Martha Kreipe de Montao, *The Native American Almanac: A Portrait of Native America Today* (New York: Prentice Hall General Reference, 1993), 1. *The United States Dictionary of Places* (New York: Somerset Publishers, 1988), 95.

Of the Englishmen who came to America between 1607 and 1776 what percentage had a less than reputable past?

Of the Englishmen who came to America between 1607 and 1776 nearly 40 percent were convicted drunks, debtors, or runaway slaves.

Stephanie Bernardo, *The Ethnic Almanac* (Garden City, NY: Dolphin Books, 1981), 40.

Which cities have served as the United States capital?

Eight other cities besides Washington have served as capital of the United States. During the nation's early years, the capital—where Congressional delegates were meeting—was forced to relocate often because of wartime considerations. The initial assemblies twice met in Philadelphia between 1774 and 1776, but fled to Baltimore when British soldiers invaded the Pennsylvanian city. Lancaster, Pennsylvania hosted the government on September 27, 1777, before it moved on to the neighboring community of York for several months. Between 1778 and 1783 Congress met again in Philadelphia, but removed to Princeton, New Jersey in June of 1783. From November of 1783 until June of 1784 the honor went to Annapolis, Maryland, and in November of 1784 was bestowed on Trenton, New Jersey. New York City was next in line in 1785, and it was there that George Washington was inaugurated as the nation's first president. In 1790 the capital again moved to Philadelphia in a political deal between the fledgling states. However, pressure from the South helped transfer the seat of government to a more centrally located position, and the parcel of land situated between Virginia and Maryland officially became the U.S. capital in 1800.

Thomas H. Johnson and Harvey Wish, *The Oxford Companion to American History* (New York: Oxford University Press, 1966), s.v. "capital of the U.S."

Who were the Minutemen?

Although the term Minutemen was used as early as 1765, it generally refers to a particular type of militia that was organized in Massachusetts prior to the American Revolution. In 1774 many militia organizations in Massachusetts were reorganized in an effort to rid themselves of Tories and Tory sympathizers. Seven new groups were formed and they were organized so one-third of the men could be ready to assemble on a minute's notice, hence the name Minutemen. These groups became known as minutemen companies and were separate from the various militia organizations. Minutemen did fight on Lexington Green and the Concord Bridge alongside members of the various militias.

Mark Mayo Boatner, *Encyclopedia of the American Revolution, rev. ed.* (New York: David McKay, 1974), s.v. "Minutemen."

Did George Washington as a young boy really chop down his father's cherry tree?

It has long been part of American folklore that a young George Washington (1732-1799) when caught red-handed next to a fallen cherry tree with a hatchet in hand replied to his father's accusatory questions with "I can't tell a lie, you know I can't tell a lie. I did cut it down with my hatchet." George was subsequently praised for being honest and his indiscretion with the hatchet was quickly forgotten by his father. This tale is often recited to young people as an example of virtue and honesty, but did it really happen?

The story first appeared in the fifth edition of *A History of the Life and Death, Virtues and Exploits of General George Washington* (1800) by Mason Locke Weems, a prolific writer of moral tracts, and is corroborated by a picture of an earthenware mug (ca. 1770-1790) that is decorated with the events and characters of the tale. Other presidential historians claim that Weems fabricated the entire story, because Washington's father died when George was only 11, and he was subsequently raised by his half-brother Lawrence, 14 years his senior.

William Degregorio, *The Complete Book of U.S. Presidents, 4th ed.*, (New York: Barricade Books, 1993), 3. *New York Times* 4 October 1964.

Who was known as the "Attila of Christendom"?

Count Ernst von Mansfeld (d.1626), a Calvinist general in the Thirty-Years War (1618-48), was known as the "Attila of Christendom." The Thirty-Years War was a bloody conflict that was fought largely in Germany, and although it had many causes, the antipathy between Catholics and Protestants was a major factor in starting the war and making it as vicious as it was. In many ways Mansfeld's conduct reflects a pattern of behavior that was all too common int his period. Although he was the illegitimate son of a famous general who had fought for Spain, he changed his religion and claimed to be a champion of Protestantism. By all accounts Mansfeld was a courageous soldier and a vigorous and flexible commander. Yet, too often he made no provision to feed his men and allowed them to support themselves by pillage and rapine, so that even Protestant areas feared the approach of his army.

Samuel Rawson Gardiner, *The Thirty Years' War, 1618-1648* (Cambridge: Cambridge University Press, 1970), 32-95. John Pimlott, *The Military Quiz Book* (Harrisburg, PA: Stackpole Books, 1993), 51-52.

When was the United States Army established?

In 1792, the United States Congress officially authorized the "Legion of the United States," which was the first United States Army. The force was placed under the command of General Anthony Wayne (1745-96) of Revolutionary War fame. The ideas of U.S. president George Washington (1782-99), Secretary of War Henry Knox (1750-1806), and Friedrich Wilhem von Steuben (1730-94), led to the adoption of a legionary organization. This meant that in place of having separate infantry, artillery, and cavalry branches, all three elements were integrated into four sublegions. The legion won its first battle at Fallen Timbers on August 20, 1794, which broke the power of the Indians in the eastern region of the Northwest. In 1796 legionary organization was abandoned for more conventional forces.

R. Ernest Dupuy and Trevor N. Dupuy, *Military Heritage of America* (New York: McGraw-Hill, 1956), 123. Paul David Nelson, *Anthony Wayne: Soldier of the Early Republic* (Bloomington: Indiana University Press, 1985), 224-7. Wiley Sword, *President Washington's Indian War: The Struggle for the Old Northwest, 1790-1795* (Norman: University of Oklahoma Press, 1985), 232-37. Russell F. Weigley, *History of the United States Army* (New York: Macmillan, 1967), 92-99.

How many sets of dentures did George Washington own, and what were they composed of?

The first U.S. President George Washington (1732-99) had six sets of false teeth; none of which were made of wood. The lightest was made of sea horse ivory and weighed less than an ounce. The heaviest set, made of lead, weighed a pound and a half. Other sets were created from the teeth of humans, cows and other animals.

William A. DeGregorio, *The Complete Book of U.S. Presidents, 2d ed.* (New York: Debmner Books, 1989), 1. *Saturday Review* 18 February 1961.

How much did George Washington earn as head of the Continental Army?

George Washington (1732-1799) was paid a salary of $500 per month for his job as Commander in Chief of the Continental Army during the American Revolutionary War. He refused the salary, choosing instead to be reimbursed only for expenses incurred. He also kept the books on this expense account.

Marvin Kitman, *George Washington's Expense Account* (New York: Simon and Schuster, 1970), 1, 30.

What is the "Black Hole of Calcutta"?

On June 20, 1756, after the capture of the East India Company's Fort William by Indian forces, 146 British prisoners, including one woman, were confined in a poorly ventilated room measuring 18 feet by 14 feet. The next morning only 22 men and the woman remained alive. The term "Black Hole" or "Black Hole of Calcutta" has since come to represent punishment cells in barracks and very dark stuffy places.

Ivor H. Evans, *Brewer's Dictionary of Phrase and Fable, 14th ed.* (New York: Harper & Row, 1989), s.v. "Black Hole of Calcutta."

How did the Mason-Dixon Line get its name?

The Mason-Dixon Line marks the northern boundary of Maryland, Delaware, and West Virginia and the southern border of Pennsylvania. Before the Civil War, the Mason-Dixon Line marked the boundary between slave and free states. The Mason-Dixon Line is named for Charles Mason and Jeremiah Dixon, two English surveyors who surveyed the boundary line in 1763 to end a dispute between Pennsylvania and Maryland.

Dictionary of American History, rev. ed. (New York: Charles Scribner's Sons, 1976), s.v. "Mason-Dixon Line."

What was the importance of the reign of Henry IV of France?

The reign of Henry IV (1553-1610) marked the end of the wars of religion that had plagued France since the middle of the sixteenth century. The struggle, marred by atrocities committed by both sides, determined that the French would remain Roman Catholic rather than convert to Calvinism like the majority of Dutch, Swiss, and Scots had done at about the same time.

Henry, who was king of Navarre from 1572 to 1589, became the heir presumptive to the French throne with the death of Franois, Duke of Alenon in 1584. But since Henry was a Protestant, the Catholic majority refused to accept him as their king in spite of his assumption of the royal title after the death of Henry III in 1589. So in 1593 he became a Catholic and received the widespread support he needed to be sovereign to his people. Yet he did not forget his former co-religionists, for in 1598 Henry issued the Edict of Nantes, which gave French Calvinists the right to civic liberty and to worship freely in certain specific areas. It was a remarkably tolerant document for its time.

The Catholic University of America, *The New Catholic Encyclopedia* (New York: McGraw-Hill, 1967), s.v. "Henry IV, King of France." Bernard Grun, *The Timetables of History, 3d rev. ed.* (New York: Simon & Schuster, 1991), 262.

What two colonial leaders were not included in the British offer of pardons in 1775?

It is not known whether revolutionary politician Samuel Adams (1722-1803), one of the driving forces behind the Boston Tea Party in 1773, was responsible for the loss of British lives at Lexington. Nor is it known whether the British attack at Lexington and Concord in April 1775 was motivated by an effort to capture Adams and revolutionary politician John Hancock (1737-1793), both signers of the Declaration of Independence. What is known is that both Adams and Hancock were present at Lexington and Concord and that both were not included in the British offer of pardons in 1775.

Mark Mayo Boatner, *Encyclopedia of the American Revolution,* (New York: David McKay Co., 1974), s.v. "Adams, Samuel."

What were the Intolerable Acts?

In 1774 when the British Parliament enacted the Intolerable Acts, also known as the Coercive Acts, its purpose was to chastise the residents of Massachusetts for the Boston Tea Party of December, 1773, and to tighten Britain's control of the colony.

The Boston Port Bill, the first act, closed Boston's port with the stipulation that the bill would not be repealed until the residents of Boston demonstrated appropriate respect for British authorities. Under the second act any British soldier or officer accused of murder could return to England for trial. The charter of Massachusetts was altered by the third act which called for a Crown-appointed council and banned all town meetings unless the governor approved. Meetings for electing officers could be held without the governor's permission, however. The fourth act was a mandate for the colonists to provide food and shelter for British soldiers. The fifth act, known as the Quebec Act, expanded the boundaries of the province of Quebec south to the Ohio River. It also granted the province's Roman Catholics freedom of worship. American colonists mistakenly thought that this act, too, was designed to punish them.

Ironically, although the British government had intended these acts to strengthen their control of one colony, they helped to forge a strong bond of unity among all thirteen colonies, a bond that almost drove the colonies to war at that time.

World Book Encyclopedia (Chicago: World Book, 1987), s.v. "Intolerable Acts."

What North American Indian tribes formed the Iroquois?

In 1570 the Mohawk, Onondaga, Oneida, Seneca, and Cayuga tribes joined together and became known as the Iroquois. They were governed by a common council comprised of chiefs from each tribe. This association came about largely due to the efforts of two Indian braves, Hiawatha, a Mohawk, and Dekanawida, originally a Huron brave.

James Trager, *The People's Chronology: A Year-by-Year Record of Human Events from Prehistory to the Present, rev. ed.* (New York: Henry Holt, 1992), 183.

Who was Juan Ponce de Len?

A Spaniard who sailed with Christopher Columbus on his second voyage in 1493, Juan Ponce de Len began (1460?-1521) an exploration of the island of Puerto Rico in 1508. In 1509 he wrested control of the island from the native inhabitants and made himself governor. On Easter Sunday, 1513, he discovered Florida near what would later be called St. Augustine. Ponce de Len called the new land La Tierra Florida (Land of Flowers) in honor of the Easter season. In his second expedition to Florida in 1521, he established a settlement near Sanibel Island. Hostile Indians attached them and Ponce de Len was critically wounded. He later died when the expedition arrived in Havana, Cuba.

James Trager, *The People's Chronology: A Year-by-Year Record of Human Events from Prehistory to the Present, rev. ed.* (New York: Henry Holt, 1992), 166, 168. Richard E. Bohlander, ed., *World Explorers and Discoverers* (New York: Macmillan, 1992), s.v. "Ponce de Len, Juan."

Who founded Rangoon?

The Burmese capital of Rangoon was founded by King Aloung P'Houra in 1755. At the time, the monarch was battling French military personnel; the English East India Company offered P'Houra and the Burmese assistance in this conflict.

James Trager, *The People's Chronology: A Year-by Year Record of Human Events from Prehistory to the Present, rev. ed.* (New York: Henry Holt and Company, 1992), 303.

In colonial America what was the connection between the Townshend Acts of 1767, the Tea Act of 1773, and the Boston Tea Party of the same year?

England's Townshend Acts of 1767, named after Charles Townshend, Chancellor of the Exchequer imposed colonial import duties on glass, paint, paper, oil, lead, and tea to raise revenue to pay for England's North American expenditures, especially defense expenditures. American colonists predictably objected vigorously to the new taxes. On May 10, 1773, the Tea Act was passed by the English Parliament which made it very profitable for the East India Company of England to export tea to the North American colonies while providing a ready market for its seven years supply of tea which was straining the company's storage facilities in England. The Tea Act also allowed the East India Company to sell the tea cheaply and directly with only a three pence Townshend tax to colonial retailers thus eliminating colonial middlemen. The colonists viewed it as an attempt to make Parliamentary taxation palatable. The tea ships in New York and Philadelphia ports had to return to England with the cargo. But in Boston, radical colonists took a different tack that would further worsen the bad relations between the mother country and some of her American colonies. On December 16, 1773, in protest to the Tea Act a group of 60 colonists including Paul Revere and Lendall Pitts disguised themselves as Mohawk Indians, boarded three East India Company ships docked in Boston Harbor and threw 342 chests of tea overboard. Samuel Adams and John Hancock were behind the scenes organizers of the "Party." Angered at the loss of 10,000 pounds and the destruction of property, England sought to punish the Massachusetts colony with the Coercive Acts. This action united the other colonies with Massachusetts, leading them closer to war.

John Mack Faragher, ed., *The Encyclopedia of Colonial and Revolutionary America* (New York: Facts on File, 1990), s.v. "Boston Tea Party," "Townshend Acts." James Trager, *The People's Chronology* (New York: Henry Holt, 1992), 317.

1789 to 1918

Did any African Americans accompany Brigham Young west to Salt Lake City?

When American religious leader Brigham Young (1801-1877) guided the Mormons west to Salt Lake City, Utah, in 1847, three African Americans accompanied him—Oscar Crosby, Hark Lay, and Green Flakc.

Parade 1974.

Who assassinated President William McKinley?

Anarchist and unemployed worker Leon Czolgosz fired a .32-caliber pistol into the abdomen of U.S. President William McKinley (1843-1901) on September 6, 1901, at the Pan-American Exposition in Buffalo, New York. McKinley died eight days later, and Czolgosz was executed by electrocution on October 29.

Jay Robert Nash, *Crime Chronology: A Worldwide Record, 1900-1983* (New York: Facts on File, 1984), 4.

How did the Boxer Rebellion get its name?

Boxer was a popular name given to a member of the Society of Harmonious and Righteous Fists, which was a secret organization that opposed European domination of China at the end of the nineteenth century.

The society's members were well-versed in the Chinese martial art kung fu. Since there was no English equivalent for this method of fighting, the word "boxing" was used to describe it. The Boxers, whose symbol was a clenched fist, had the tacit approval of the Chinese government, attacked Christians and workers on the European-controlled railway system. On June 19, 1900, they began a siege of the European legations in Beijing, which lasted until the beleaguered Westerners were finally relieved by a six-nation expeditionary force in August. There were other Boxer uprisings in Manchuria and Shensi province, but in the end the Europeans prevailed. According to the Beijing (Peking) Protocol of 1901, China had to pay an annual indemnity to European powers in recompense for the uprising. The rebellion, however, spurred Chinese nationalism and led to the eventual end of European colonies in that country.

Chris Cook, *Dictionary of Historical Terms: A Guide to Names and Events of Over 1,000 Years of World History* (New York: Peter Bedrick Books, 1983), s.v. "Boxers." David Louis, *Fascinating Facts* (New York: Ridge Press, 1977), 30.

What was the Treaty of Nanking?

On August 29, 1842, Great Britain and China brought the Opium War (1839-42) to an end by signing the Treaty of Nanking. China was forced to pay an indemnity of 21 million pounds, to surrender Hong Kong, and to open five ports to British traders. It was the first time Chinese markets were open to British commercial interests.

George C. Kohn, *Dictionary of Historic Documents* (New York: Facts on File, 1991), s.v. "Nanking, Treaty of."

What was the U.S. Emancipation Proclamation?

The U.S. president Abraham Lincoln (1809-65) issued the Emancipation Proclamation on January 1, 1863. The edict abolished slavery in the secessionist Southern states and allowed former slaves to enlist in the armed services. Three million slaves were freed by the edict, although there was no immediate effect in the Confederate-controlled Southern states. Lincoln's edict enhanced the Union cause in Europe, but infuriated the Southern confederacy. There was a mixed response to it in the North.

George C. Kohn, *Dictionary of Historic Documents* (New York: Facts on File, 1991), s.v. "Emancipation Proclamation, U.S."

What was the Alaska Purchase Treaty?

The Alaska Purchase Treaty was the agreement by which Russian owned Alaska was sold to the United States for the sum of $7.2 million. The date of the treaty was March 30, 1867. The treaty was negotiated by Baron Edoard de Stoeckl, Russian minister to the United States and U.S. Secretary of State William Seward. The treaty was at first met with derision in the United

States and Alaska was referred to as "Seward's Folly" and "Seward's Icebox."

George C. Kohn, *Dictionary of Historic Documents* (New York: Facts On File, 1991), s.v. "Alaska Purchase Treaty."

What is the Treaty of Brest-Litovsk?

The March 3, 1918 signing of the Brest-Litovsk Treaty ended the World War I fighting between Russia and the Central Powers of Germany, Austria-Hungary and Turkey. Brest is a city in what was Belorussia (Byelarus), a former republic of the Soviet Union. The treaty was excessively punitive towards Russia and was subsequently annuled after Germany's surrender to the Allied forces later that year.

George C. Kohn, *Dictionary of Historic Documents* (New York: Facts On File, 1991), s.v. "Brest-Litovsk, treaty of." United States. Central Intelligence Agency, *The Republics of the Former Soviet Union: An Overview* (Washington, DC: Government Printing Office, 1992).

What was the Bering Sea Dispute?

During the 1880s, fashions for women using sealskin was quite popular, and Canadians began killing seals indiscriminately near the Pribilof Islands, a U.S. territory off the coast of Alaska. In 1889, Congress authorized the President to seize vessels encroaching upon U.S. rights in waters of the Bering Sea. Despite international protests, the U.S. defended its actions, not on the basis of territory, but on the basis of random killing being harmful to public morals.

Despite talks of war, an agreement was settled in Paris in 1893. The U.S. would pay nearly a half million dollars in damages to Canadian schooners, and limits would be set for seal hunting.

Howard L. Hurwitz, *An Encyclopedic Dictionary of American History* (New York: Washington Square Press, 1968), s.v. "Bering Sea dispute."

What was the Battle of Austerlitz?

The Battle of Austerlitz was a major battle that pitted Napoleon's French forces against the combined armies of Austria and Russia. The 1805 battle resulted in an important victory for Napoleon.

Bernard Grun, *The Timetables of History: Of People and Events, 3d ed.* (New York: Simon & Schuster, 1991), 376.

Who was the "Great Compromiser"?

Henry Clay of Kentucky (1777-1852) was known as the "Great Compromiser" for his efforts to make concessions to both southern and northern states in their disputes over slavery. He was a major figure in the political life of the United States in the first half of the nineteenth century, serving in the Senate and the House of Representatives, where he chosen as Speaker on the day he first took office in 1811. Except for two brief periods, he held that position until 1825 when he left the House to become a cabinet member. In 1824, when none of the four candidates received a majority of votes in the electoral college, and the choice of president was given to the House of Representatives, Clay, who dominated that body, was responsible for the election of John Quincy Adams (1767-1848). As a reward Adams appointed Clay his Secretary of State. In 1830 he was elected to the Senate, then reelected in 1836, and again in 1848. He ran for president three times, defeated in 1832 by incumbent Andrew Jackson and narrowly losing in 1844 to James Polk (1795-1849). Clay tried again in 1848 but lost the Whig nomination to Zachary Taylor (1784-1850). He died in 1852, still holding elected office as a senator from Kentucky.

Michael Nelson, ed., *The Presidency A to Z: A Ready Reference Encyclopedia* (Washington, DC: Congressional Quarterly, 1992), s.v. "Clay, Henry."

What were the Boer Wars?

The Boer Wars were fought between the Boers (Dutch) and the British concerning the sovereignty of Transvaal in the area of South Africa. The First Boer War (1880-81) was fought to gain independence for Transvaal, and the Second Boer War (1899-1902) was fought to remove the British from the Republic. The South African Republic was granted its independence during the first war, but British sovereignty was recognized at the conclusion of the second.

George C. Kohn, *Dictionary of Wars* (New York: Facts On File Publications, 1986), s.v. "Boer War, First."

What was the Tet Offensive of the Vietnam Conflict?

The Tet Offensive was a military tactical assault initiated on January 30, 1968, by the Vietcong and North Vietnamese against U.S. and South Vietnam forces during the Vietnam Conflict. A massive attack was launched against the U.S. Marine base at Khe Sanh. Hitting 36 of 44 provincial capitals and five of six major cities, the Vietcong carried out an attack on the U.S. embassy in Saigon, Tan Son Nhut Air Base, the presidential palace, and South Vietnamese general staff headquarters. The goal of the raids was to deceive U.S. intelligence. While the North Vietnamese and National Liberation Front asked for a cease fire during the Tet lunar holiday, 100,000 soldiers and many supplies were moved undetected into the cities.

The Tet Offensive was successful for the Vietcong and North Vietnamese because it illustrated their determination, as well as shocked U.S. public opinion about the war. The offensive was unsuccessful because the South Vietnamese army held their positions and U.S. troops regained control. The Vietcong and North Vietnamese tallied nearly 40,000 battlefield deaths; 1,100 for the United States; 2,300 for the South Vietnamese.

James S. Olson, ed., *Dictionary of the Vietnam War* (New York: Greenwood Press, 1988), s.v. "Tet Offensive."

On what island in the South Pacific Ocean did the mutineers from the HMS *Bounty* settle?

Mutineers from the HMS *Bounty* settled in 1790 on Pitcairn Island in the South Pacific Ocean. Once probably inhabited by Polynesians, the island was discovered in 1767 by Philip Carteret (d. 1796). It was chosen by Fletcher Christian (fl. 1789) and eight other mutineers as their refuge. After removing valuable items, the mutineers burned the ship to avoid detection. Every January 23, the anniversary of the ship's burning, a model of the HMS *Bounty* is launched and burned at Bounty Bay in memoriam.

David Stanley, *South Pacific Handbook* (Chico, CA: Moon, 1989), 224.

What were some of the many descriptive titles bestowed on Susan B. Anthony?

Biographers and journalists dubbed women's rights crusader Susan B. Anthony (1820-1906) with many epithets and laudatory titles. They include Saintly Susan, the Emancipator of Women, the Visionary, the Moses of the Women's Rights

Movement, the Liberator of Women, the Adventurous Miss Anthony, the Great Woman Statesman, the Protagonist, the Woman Who Changed the Mind of a Nation, the Apostle of Freedom, the Trail Blazer, the First Militant, America's Most Honored Woman, Magnificent Maiden Mother of Equal Rights, the Napoleon of Woman Suffrage, the Spirit that Launched the Federal Amendment, Peaceful Warrior, Heroine of Democracy, and the Venerated Herald of Woman Suffrage.

Files of the Anthony Memorial Library.

What Native American served as vice-president of the United States?

The son of a woman descended from Kansa (Kaw) and Osage Indian chiefs and a man whose forbearers were among New England's early settlers, Senator Charles Curtis (1860-1936), of Kansas was the first person of American Indian descent to serve as vice-president of the United States. Born January 25, 1860, Curtis was raised on an Indian reservation in Topeka, Kansas after his mother died when he was three years old.

He began his professional career as a lawyer in 1881 and his political career when he was elected county prosecuting attorney in 1884 and 1886. Later, he was elected to the U.S. House of Representatives and the Senate. When elected by the Kansas legislature to finish an uncompleted term in the U.S. Senate in 1907, Curtis became the first person of Indian descent to serve as a U.S. senator. In 1928 he was Herbert Hoover's (1874-1964) running mate on the Republican ticket. Hoover and Curtis won the election.

Dictionary of Indians of North America (St. Clair Shores, MI: Scholarly Press, 1978), s.v. "Curtis, Charles."

How tall was Napoleon Bonaparte?

Regarded as one of the world's greatest military leaders, the French emperor Napoleon Bonaparte (1769-1821) was approximately five feet six and one-half inches tall, which was small for an average Frenchman. Many of Napoleon's commanding officers were somewhat taller than Napoleon. This disparity in height earned Napoleon the nickname "Little Corporal."

Manuel Komroff, *Napoleon* (New York: Julian Messner, 1955), 73.

What was the first nation to receive foreign aid from the United States?

The first nation to receive foreign aid from the United States was Venezuela. In 1812 the United States sent $50,000 to that South American country as relief aid for earthquake victims.

Joseph Nathan Kane, *Famous First Facts, 4th ed.* (New York: H. W. Wilson, 1981), 258.

What unique leadership duty was Robert Gould Shaw given during the Civil War?

During the American Civil War (1861-65), Union Colonel Robert Gould Shaw was placed in command of the 54th Massachusetts, the first regiment of African-American troops from a free state. Shaw enlisted in the Union Army as a private in 1861, and before receiving his colonel's commission, was promoted to captain in 1862. He was killed at Fort Wagner, South Carolina, on July 18, 1863. The citizens of Massachusetts honored Shaw's service to his country with a statue in Boston Common by Augustus Saint-Gould. His story was told in the film, *Glory.*

Clarence L. Barnhart, ed., *The New Century Cyclopedia of Names* (New York: Appleton-Century-Crofts, 1954), s.v. "Shaw, Robert Gould."

What was the infamous "San Patricio Battalion" of the Mexican War?

The "San Patricio Battalion" of the Mexican War (1846-48) was infamous because it was made up largely of U.S. Army deserters. While some historians claim that members of the Catholic clergy in Monterey, California, urged American regulars to desert to the Mexican cause, other historians believe the San Patricio Battalion was composed mostly of deserters who were not native-born Americans and who found themselves unable to deal with strict army discipline. The battalion then fought against the United States beginning at a battle in Buena Vista, California.

The San Patricio Battalion can trace its origins to the desertion of Sergeant John Riley of Company K, U.S. 5th Infantry who swam across the Rio Grande River and deserted Zachary Taylor's army. In the following months hundreds of soldiers followed Riley and deserted to the Mexican side. Although the reasons varied with each deserter, some common causes were army discipline, Mexican promises of land and money, and Mexican propaganda which developed a split between native-born and foreign-born soldiers. Although most of the deserters were not Irish, their hastily formed battalion flag included a shamrock and the figure of St. Patrick. Many of the deserters were captured and subsequently sentenced to death by hanging. Sergeant John Riley and ten others were spared execution on the grounds that they deserted before war was officially declared. These lucky ones were sentenced to 50 lashes, their cheeks branded with the letter "D," and they had to dig the graves of those executed for desertion.

Jack K. Bauer, *The Mexican War, 1846-1848* (Lincoln: University of Nebraska Press, 1974), 304-5. Lloyd Lewis, *Captain Sam Grant* (Boston: Little, Brown, 1991), 186, 242-48. David Nevin, *The Mexican War* (Alexandria, VA: Time-Life Books, 1978), 209.

Which country was the first to utilize chemical weaponry in war?

Germany was the first country to use chemical warfare against an enemy in battle. Although the idea had been around for centuries-ancient and medieval conflicts often included the throwing of fire-starting substances-the European power was the first to do so in the modern era. Advances in chemistry during the nineteenth century helped German military scientists develop aerosol shells filled with irritating gaseous substances in time for World War I (1914-18). During the fighting at Ypres, Belgium, on April 22, 1915, German forces fired shells filled with noxious chlorine gas at Allied positions. In July of 1917, the Ypres battlefield saw the first use of mustard gas. This chemical caused a significant number of deaths. When combatants inhaled it, they usually died from pulmonary edema. If they survived, they were blinded for life.

Dennis Sanders, *The First of Everything* (New York: Delacorte, 1981), 66.

Which U.S. president was ticketed for speeding?

U.S. president Ulysses S. Grant (1822-85), who held the nation's highest elected office from 1869 to 1877, was stopped by a police officer on M Street one night in Washington, D.C.

A horse and buggy driven by Grant had been careering through the capital at a high rate of speed. When the police officer realized who the culprit was, he began to apologize, but Grant insisted on being ticketed. The president walked back to the White House after the carriage was impounded. Prior to his election, Grant had twice been charged and fined for speeding.

Irving Wallace, David Wallechinsky, and Amy Wallace, *Significa* (New York: E. P. Dutton, 1983), 119.

Who was the soldier who fled the Alamo?

Louis "Moses" Rose is thought to have been the Alamo's only deserter during the 1836 battle between Texas settlers and the Mexican military. The fort in San Antonio, Texas, was the site of a famous two-week conflict in February and March of that year when was occupied by Texans as part of their attempt to secede from Mexico. The disastrous siege became a symbol for the American settlers battle for independence, and it had long been rumored that one lone soldier had abandoned the cause. According to William Zuber, Rose had surfaced in East Texas shortly after the battle and recounted the story to his father, Abraham Zuber. Supposedly, Rose had scaled the Alamo walls, gotten through the Mexican phalanx, and taken off into the night. Although there were no eyewitnesses, historians have corroborated the story.

Susan Prendergast Schoelwer and Tom W. Glser, *Alamo Images: Changing Perspectives of a Texas Experience* (Dallas: Southern Methodist University Press, 1985), 115.

Which American president ordered the words "In God We Trust" removed from coins?

In 1907, U.S. president Theodore Roosevelt ordered the minting of new coins without the "In God We Trust" motto. The president argued that the ubiquitous nature of currency, as well as its ultimate purpose as an element of barter, cheapened the gravity of the words. At the time, there was no law stating that the motto, which had been in use on U.S. currency since 1864, was compulsory. Roosevelt commissioned renowned sculptor Augustus Saint-Gaudens (1848-1907) to design $10 and $20 gold coins in 1907, and when the final prototype was revealed to the public, an uproar ensued. Religious leaders argued that the omission of "In God We Trust" was tantamount to blasphemy. A legislator from Pennsylvania proposed a congressional bill to put the motto back on Roosevelt's new coins, and it passed through both houses in 1908. It was not until 1955 that the motto became specifically required by law on all currency issued by the U.S. Treasury.

Irving Wallace, David Wallechinsky, and Amy Wallace, *Significa* (New York: E.P. Dutton, 1983), 303-304.

What was the strategic importance of Vicksburg, Mississippi, during the American Civil War?

During the American Civil War Vicksburg, Mississippi, was of great strategic importance because it linked Arkansas, Louisiana, and Texas with the rest of the South. Because the city was situated on a high bluff, Union boats trying to move upstream could not elevate their guns high enough to fire on the town's fortifications. In an ill-fated effort to avoid unimpeded Confederate cannon fire Union, forces even tried to divert the, Mississippi River away from the town by building a canal.

Irving Wallace, David Wallechinsky, and Amy Wallace, *Significa* (New York: E.P. Dutton, 1983), 146.

What is the meaning of the archaic word "beal"?

The archaic word "beal" as used in Pennsylvania in the early twentieth century meant to fester or suppurate. During the same period the word was used in Scotland but had become obsolete in England.

Sylva Clapin, *A New Dictionary of Americanisms* (New York: Louis Weiss, 1902), s.v. "Beal."

How much did World War I cost in dollars for the Allied and Axis governments?

World War I (1914-18), cost roughly $186 billion. Of that amount, the Allies-Great Britain, France, Russia, the United States, and several other countries-paid $125.7 billion. The opposing side-the German, Austro-Hungarian, Turkish, and Bulgarian alliance known as the Central Powers—spent over $60.6 billion. In addition, Great Britain loaned $8.7 billion and the United States $9.5 billion to their allies. These figures reflect only the direct military cost of the war and do not take into account the $1.8 billion that neutrals spent defending their borders nor the costs that accrued from destruction, lost revenues, and other war-related expenditures.

Peter Young, ed., *The Marshall Cavendish Illustrated Encyclopedia of World War I* (New York: Marshall Cavendish, 1984), 3546.

Why were shoes rationed during World War II?

Wartime needs limited consumer access to shoes was restricted in the United States beginning February 7, 1943. A shortage of leather was a primary cause, since available material had to be diverted to produce shoes for troops. At the time, statistics showed that the average civilian male went through two pairs per year, but in some combat situations a soldier could wear out a pair in two weeks. Ample supply was needed to be kept on hand by the military for this reason, and necessitated the restricted access to shoes by the civilian population. A ration stamp was needed to purchase a pair.

Office of Price Administration, *Fifth Quarterly Report: For the Period Ended April 30, 1943* (Washington, DC: United States Government Printing Office, 1943), 29-30.

What was Greyfriars Bobby?

Greyfriars Bobby was a Skye terrierdog became who legendary in Edinburgh, Scotland. He is famous for his story of unshakeable devotion and the city's homage to that love. Greyfriars Bobby belonged to policeman, Jock Gray. The pair was inseparable. When Gray died in 1858, the dog would still appear daily for lunch at the eating house frequented by his master. At all other times, he was to be found at his master's grave, where he stayed until his own death.

This touching scenario did not go unnoticed. When a dog licensing law was passed in Edinburgh, the Lord Provost William Chambers paid the fee for Greyfriars Bobby. Greyfriars Bobby maintained his graveside vigil for fourteen years, until his dealth in 1872.

Irving Wallace, David Wallechinsky, and Amy Wallace, *Significa* (New York: E.P. Dutton, 1983), 89-90.

For what purpose did the British once use Australia?

Following the loss of their American colonies, the British turned to Australia for use as a replacement penal colony. By 1830, however, with the introduction of sheep and the opening of lands in New South Wales, the British began allowing freed convicts, discharged prison guards, and free migrants to settle in Australia.

Academic American Encyclopedia (Danbury CT: Grolier, 1988), s.v. Australia, history of.."

How might one identify a reprint of the January 4, 1800, issue of the *Ulster County Gazette* in which the death of George Washington was announced?

No original copy of the January 4, 1800, *Ulster County Gazette* containing the announcement of U.S. President George Washington's (1732-99) death has been identified. Although a number of neat reproductions are available, historians insist an original could be identified only by the coarseness of the yellowish-brown paper and uneven quality of the ink which was standard for the times. Reprints, therefore, would appear much more perfect than an original.

R. W. G. Vail, *The Ulster County Gazette and its Illegitimate Offspring* (New York: The New York Public Library, 1930), 7-8.

What were the conditions of Benjamin Franklin's bequest to the cities of Boston and Philadelphia, and how much money did they receive?

The careful plans of American statesman Benjamin Franklin (1706-90) resulted in a bequest worth $6.5 million in 1990. A man of tremendous foresight, Franklin created a trust for the city of Boston and one for the city of Philadelphia, with the money to be used as loans for young apprentices. He stipulated that one portion of the money could not be used until 100 years had passed, the rest could not be used for 200 years.

Franklin died on April 17, 1790, causing the final installation to become available in 1990. Despite having plenty of time to plan for its use, the recipients had difficulties deciding how the funds should be used. With careful investment the Boston trust was worth $4.5 million in 1990. The Philadelphia trust was considerably smaller at $2 million. It is difficult to calculate exactly how much the money has appreciated; Franklin bequeathed a total of 2,000 pounds sterling, money he earned as Governor of Pennsylvania. The amount is roughly equivalent, in terms of buying power, to $1 million today.

Fox Butterfield, "From Ben Franklin, a Gift That's Worth Two Fights," *New York Times* 21 April 1990.

What queen of France was called "Madame Deficit"?

Once popular with the French court and the common people, Queen Marie Antoinette (1755-1793) came to be known as "Madame Deficit" when she was blamed for a French financial crisis in the mid-1780s. Known for her frivolous tastes prior to the birth of her children, the queen, in fact, became quite restrained in the last years of her life.

Chronicle of the French Revolution, 1788 1799 (London: Chronicle Publications, 1989), 16.

What U.S. president was the recipient of a gift of a 1,400-pound cheese?

In 1837 at the end of his second term as U.S. president, Andrew Jackson (1767-1845) was given a 1,400-pound cheese by the dairymen of New York. It measured four feet in diameter and two feet thick. The gift was made at a public reception, and everyone was invited to eat the cheese, which was consumed within two hours.

Isaac Asimov, *Isaac Asimov's Book of Facts* (New York: Grosset & Dunlap, 1979), 690.

Who is the Napoleon of the Indian race?

Chief Joseph (ca. 1840-1904), a Nez Perce Indian, has often been called the Napoleon of the Indian race because of his able but futile leadership during the Nez Perce War of 1877.

One of four children born to Old Joseph, a chief of the Wallamwatkin band and his wife Khapkhaponimi, Joseph also went by the name Young Joseph, Ehpraim, Chief Joseph, and Hin-mah-too-yah-lat-kekt which means "thunder coming from water over land." Because of numerous treaty violations by Caucasian settlers, Old Joseph refused to sign a new treaty in 1861 which would substantially reduce Nez Perce reservation lands. Old Joseph shortly thereafter died and Young Joseph, along with his brother Ollikut, became chiefs of the so-called Non-treaty Nez Perces. By 1877 skirmishes between the Nontreaty Nez Perces and Caucasian settlers backed by U.S. troops had turned into open conflict. After the Battle of Big Hole on August 9 the Indians lost 60 to 90 warriors and found themselves being pushed eastward into the Absaroka Mountains. During the Battle of Bear Paw on September 30, four Nez Perce chiefs were killed and Joseph realized surrender was imminent. The remaining Nez Perce were eventually sent to the Colville Reservation at Nespelem, Washington. Joseph went on to encourage education and abstinence amongst his band and met U.S. presidents William McKinley (1843-1901) and Theodore Roosevelt (1858-1919). Chief Joseph died at the reservation in 1904.

Henry Frederic Reddall, ed., *Fact, Fancy, and Fable* (1889; reprint, Detroit: Gale Research, 1968), s.v. "Napoleon of the Indian Race." Carl Waldman, *Who Was Who In Native American History* (New York: Facts on File, 1990), s.v. "Joseph."

Who was James J. Andrews and what was his role in the American Civil War's *Great Locomotive Chase*?

James J. Andrews (1829-1862) was a civilian spy for the Union Army during the American Civil War. Under the direction of Brigadier General Don Carlos Buell, Andrews led a small unit of men into Georgia intent on destroying bridges of the Western & Atlantic Railroad. The plan was called off, however, when an accomplice who worked for the railroad failed to make contact. In April of 1862 Brigadier General Ormsby M. Mitchel talked Andrews into making a similar mission in order to sabotage Confederate railroad bridges between Atlanta and Chattanooga. Andrews and 24 Union volunteers broke into small groups and made their way to Marietta, Georgia. Although their plans for destroying bridges, cutting telegraph lines, and road beds were hampered by heavy rains and unexpected Confederate soldiers, Andrews and his group hijacked a locomotive called *The General*, its tender, and three boxcars in Big Shanty, Georgia. They were relentlessly pursued on foot and then by handcar and locomotive by Conductor William A. Fuller and Anthony Murphy, a shop foreman. To Andrew's dismay, the wooden bridges were too wet from the rains to set on fire and, after running out of fuel, *The General* was abandoned 18 miles south of Chattanooga. Andrews and his men were captured within a week and eight were executed including Andrews. Eight of the other raiders managed to escape while the remainder were held prisoner and later exchanged. Andrews's raid came to be known variously as the *Great Locomotive Chase* and the *Great Railroad Raid.*

Patricia L. Faust, ed., *Historical Times Illustrated Encyclopedia of the Civil War* (New York: Harper & Row, 1986), s.v. "Andrews, James J."

Who led the Texans in their struggle for independence from Mexico?

Samuel Houston (1793-1863) was the Texan leader who led the struggle for independence from Mexico. Houston was born in Virginia and had a tempestuous and varied life living with the Cherokee Indians (who called him the Raven), fighting with Andrew Jackson (1767-1845) in the Creek Wars, and serving both as a Tennessee congressman and governor and a Texas senator and governor. His fame, however, comes from his leadership during Texas's fight for independence from Mexico. In 1835 Houston commanded a small and largely unorganized Texas revolutionary army. In 1836 in a surprise attack at the San Jacinto River, Houston fought, beat, and captured General Antonio Lopez De Santa Anna and most of his forces. This battle effectively assured independence and Houston was subsequently elected the first president of the Texas Republic. After Texas joined the Union in 1845, Houston served two terms as an U.S. senator. In antebellum Texas, his pro-Union stance was at odds with many citizens but nonetheless he was elected governor in 1859, but in 1861, however, he was forced out of office. The city of Houston, Texas, is named after him.

Family Encyclopedia of American History (Pleasantville, NY: Reader's Digest Association, 1975), s.v. "Houston, Samuel."

What were President Woodrow Wilson's "Fourteen Points"?

U.S. president Woodrow Wilson's (1856-1924) "Fourteen Points" itemized the U.S. peace terms for the ending of to World War I (1914-18). His "Fourteen Points," given in an address to the U.S. Congress on January 8, 1918, were as follows:

open covenants of peace openly arrived at freedom of the seas
removal of economic barriers and equality of trade conditions
reduction of armaments to the lowest point consistent with public safety
impartial adjustment of colonial claims
evacuation of Russian territory and Russian self-determination
evacuation and restoration of Belgium
evacuation of France and restoration of Alsace-Lorraine to France
readjustment of the Italian frontiers
autonomous development for the peoples of Austria-Hungary
readjustment in the Balkans
autonomous development for the non-Turkish nationalities of the Ottoman Empire and the opening of the Dardanelles
restoration of an independent Poland with access to the sea
establishment of a general association of nations

After much reluctance by the Allied Powers, Wilson's "Fourteen Points" became the basis for the peace treaty.

Dictionary of American History, rev. ed. (New York: Charles Scribner's Sons, 1976), s.v. "fourteen points."

What nineteenth century U.S. president was accused of dodging the draft during the American Civil War?

President-to-be Grover Cleveland (1837-1908) was a lawyer in Buffalo, New York, during the American Civil War (1861-63). In 1863, to avoid military service, Cleveland took the legal but controversial step of paying another person a bounty to serve in the army in his place. Cleveland justified his action by claiming he needed to support his mother, sisters, and two brothers while his other two brothers were in the military. During the presidential campaign 21 years later, he was accused of being a draft dodger, but criticism was soon muted, when it was learned that his Republican opponent for the presidency—John Blaine (1830-1893)—had done the same.

Amy Wallace, David Wallechinsky, and Irving Wallace, *The Book of Lists #3* (New York: William Morrow and Company, 1983), 103.

How many conspirators were implicated in the plot to assassinate U.S. president Abraham Lincoln and what were the results of their trials?

U.S. president Abraham Lincoln (1809-1865) was shot in the head on April 14, 1865 at 10:15 P.M. while watching a performance or "Our American Cousin," a comedy by Tom Taylor, at Ford's Theatre in Washington, DC. Lincoln died the next morning at 7:22 A.M.

Nine persons were implicated in the plot that took Lincoln's life. John Wilkes Booth shot Lincoln and escaped only to be surrounded in a tobacco shed by federal troops on April 26. Booth died of a gunshot wound, possibly inflicted by his own hand while the shed was afire. Seven others were tried by a military commission that met between May 9 and June 30. Four of these, Mary Surrat, George Atzerodt, Lewis Payne, and David E. Herold, were sentenced to death and hanged on July 7, 1865. Dr. Samuel Arnold Mudd and Michael O'Laughlin were sentenced to life imprisonment, and Edward Spangler was given a six-year prison term. The son of Mary Surrat, John H. Surrat, who escaped the country, was tried in 1867 but released after the jury failed to reach a verdict.

Dictionary of American History, rev. ed. (New York: Charles Scribner's Sons, 1976), s.v. "Lincoln, assassination of."

What is important about the Bixby Letter written by Abraham Lincoln?

On November 21, 1864, President Abraham Lincoln (1809-1865) wrote a letter of condolence to Mrs. Lydia Bixby, a Boston widow who reportedly lost five sons in the American Civil War (1861-65). The letter is considered as one of Lincoln's finest even though confusion and mystery surround it. It was later learned that of the five sons, only two died in combat. One was honorably discharged, another deserted, and one either deserted or died as a prisoner of war. The original letter has never been found, and the text is known only through newspaper accounts. Nevertheless, facsimiles exist in what appears to be Lincoln's handwriting.

Mark E. Neely, *The Abraham Lincoln Encyclopedia* (New York: McGraw-Hill, 1982), s.v. "Bixby Letter."

When did World War I end?

The fighting in World War I (1914-18) ended on November 11, 1918, which is known as Armistice Day. The Treaty of Versailles was signed on June 28, 1919, to end the war the Germany. The U.S. Senate, however, did not ratify the treaty. Instead, Congress passed a resolution that U.S. president Harding (1865-1923) signed on July 12, 1921, stating the war with Germany was over.

Chronicle of the 20th Century (Liberty, MO: JL International, 1992), 241, 251, 257, 281-82. *World Book Encyclopedia* (Chicago: World Book, 1994), s.v. "Versailles, Treaty of"

What other jobs did Abraham Lincoln hold other than politician and president?

In 1831 Abraham Lincoln (1809-1865) worked as a clerk in a general store located in New Salem, Illinois. He was paid $15 a month plus lodging. In April of 1832, he enlisted to serve in the Black Hawk War (1832) and served approximately eighty days. Lincoln saw no action and was to joke later that the only blood he lost was to mosquitoes. He received $125 for his service. Lincoln was briefly a partner in a general store that failed before being appointed Postmaster of New Salem, Illinois, in 1833. He held that position until 1836, supplementing his monthly salary of $55 with odd jobs like rail-splitting and surveying. While serving as postmaster, Lincoln began his political career when he was elected to the Illinois legislature in 1834. After being admitted to the Illinois bar in 1836, Lincoln moved to Springfield and practiced law while continuing to pursue politics.

William A. DeGregorio, *The Complete Book of U.S. Presidents, 2d ed.* (New York: Dembner Books, 1989), 230-31.

What was the role of the Australian Light Horse in World War I?

The Australian Light Horse was among the most famous of the country's fighting forces in World War I. This segment of the Australian cavalry benefited from the skills acquired by boundary riders and bushmen in their civilian lives. The Light Horse also featured sturdy horses from New South Wales that were compared to the famed, tough Cossack ponies. Regiments from the Light Horse served in the Dardanelles, on the Western Front, and in Sinai. They were reorganized as the Desert Mounted Corps in 1917. "Light Horse Harry" Chauvel was one of the cavalry's greatest leaders; he was famous for leading the largest body of cavalry to be deployed in modern wartime.

Philip J. Haythornthwaite, *The World War One Source Book* (London: Arms and Armour Press, 1993), s.v. "Australia."

What contribution did Francis Lieber, a German born philosopher, make to the American Civil War effort?

Francis Lieber (1800-72) a German born philosopher and political theorist, wrote at the behest of U.S. president Abraham Lincoln (1809-65) the *Instructions for the Government of the Armies of the United States in the Field.* Issued as General Order 100 in 1863, Lieber's tract codified the required behavior of U.S. troops in regards to the destroying or looting of an enemy nation's "cultural treasures." It protected the "classical works of art, libraries, scientific collections or precious instruments, such as astronomical telescopes." Lieber's code was so well thought of that it was the basis for a similar set of rules issued by the Conference of Brussels in 1874 and subsequently adopted by the Russian and German governments.

Born in Berlin, Germany and educated at various German universities. Lieber fought with other German liberals in a Greek uprising against Turkish rule and later was imprisoned in Germany for his political views and activities. After emigrating to the United States, he edited and published the *Encyclopedia Americana* (1829-1833). He taught at South Carolina College (now the University of South Carolina) and accepted the chair in the history and political science department at Columbia College (now Columbia University). In 1853 he wrote his highly regarded *On Civil Liberty and Self-Government.*

Karl E. Meyer, "Limits of World Law," *Archaeology* July/August 1995. *Webster's Guide to American History* (Springfield, MA: G & C Merriam, 1971), s.v. "Lieber, Francis."

Who was the "Red Baron"?

Manfred Baron von Richthofen (1892-1918), a German fighter pilot during World War I (1914-18), was nicknamed "Red Baron" by the Allies because his Fokker triplane was painted blood red. Although he became the top ace of the war by shooting down 80 Allied planes, only 60 of his kills were confirmed by both sides. The other 20 are disputed and could have been joint kills by Richthofen and his squadron, the Flying Circus. He died on April 21, 1918, when he was attacked both by Canadian ace Roy Brown and by Australian machine gunners on the ground. Both parties have claimed responsibility for his death. The top French ace was Ren Paul Fonck (1894-1953) with 75 kills, and the top British ace was Edward "Mick" Mannock (1887-1918) with 73 kills.

Russel Ask, *The Top Ten of Everything* (London: Dorling Kindersky, 1994), 84. Holger H. Herwig and Neil M. Heyman, *Biographical Dictionary of World War I* (Westport, CT: Greenwood Press, 1994), s.v. "Richthofen, Manfred von."

When was the first United States patent received?

The first U.S. patent was issued on July 31, 1790, to Samuel Hopkins for "making pot and pearl ashes"-a cleaning formula called potash (a key ingredient for soap-making then). However the first patent granted in the American colonies was by Massachusetts in 1641 to Samuel Winslow for an unique process of manufacturing salt.

The first really significant patent issued by the U.S. Patent Office was one for a cotton gin given to Eli Whitney (1765-1825) on March 14, 1794. Its importance lies in the fact that with the mechanical separation of cotton seeds from the lint, cotton became a staple crop of the South. This crop was a major factor in retaining the then-declining institution of slavery.

Between Hopkins's first patent in 1790, and Whitney's in 1794, the U.S. Patent Office issued 70 patents to inventors, some of whom have famous names (Oliver Evans, James Rumsey, John Fitch, and John Stevens) for their work with steam propulsion.

Until July 13, 1836 the 9,957 patents granted were filed alphabetically. Then a new numerical classification system was adopted, and J. Ruggles was granted the first patent in this system for notched train wheels that would giver better uphill traction. During the American Civil War (1861-68) the Confederate states had a patent office, which mostly was destroyed during the battle of Richmond, Virginia, in April of 1865. The first Confederate patent was granted to James Houten for a breech-loading gun on April 1, 1861 and the last one, number 266, was to W. Smith for a percussion cap rammer on December 17, 1864.

Encyclopedia Americana (Danbury, CT: Grolier, 1990), 8:81. *Inventive Genius* (New York: Time-Life Books, 1991), 15. *Patents, vol. 4 of The New American State Papers, Science and Technology* (Wilmington, DE: Scholarly

Resources, 1973), 25-26. Timothy Lee Wherry, *Patent Searching for Librarians and Inventors* (Chicago: American Library Association, 1995), 2.

Was Abraham Lincoln's body snatched after burial?

In 1865 Abraham Lincoln's body was placed in a temporary vault at Oak Ridge Cemetery in Springfield, Illinois, until a permanent tomb could be constructed. However, during the thirty-six years following the death of Lincoln (1809-1865), his body was frequently moved, hidden beneath a floor, and almost kidnapped. His coffin was often cut open to ascertain that Lincoln's-and not somebody else's-remains were inside. Finally, in 1901, following the instructions of Robert Lincoln, his body was placed where only a bomb could reach. In Oak Ridge Cemetery, Lincoln's coffin was put to rest in an iron cage within a concrete block eight feet long and eight feet deep.

Philip B. Kunhardt, Jr., Philip B. Kunhardt III, and Peter W. Kunhardt, *Lincoln: An Illustrated Biography* (New York: Alfred A. Knopf, 1992), 398-99. Mark E. Neely, Jr., *The Abraham Lincoln Encyclopedia* (New York: McGraw-Hill, 1982), s.v. "Tomb, The Lincoln."

Who was the first U.S. native to be elected president?

The first person elected to the presidency who was born a U.S. citizen was U.S. president Martin Van Buren (1782-1862). He was born December 5, 1782, in Kinderhook, New York. All of his predecessors were born prior to American Independence and were British subjects.

The first person elected to the presidency who was born west of the Mississippi River was U.S. president Herbert Hoover (1874-1964). He was born August 10, 1874, in West Branch, Iowa.

Joseph Nathan Kane, *Facts About the Presidents, 6th ed.* (New York: H. W. Wilson, 1993), 303. William A. DeGregorio, *The Complete Book of U.S. Presidents, 2d ed.* (New York: Dembner Books, 1989), 125.

How many general officers were killed in action during the American Civil War?

Of 583 Union flag officers, 47 were killed in battle during the American Civil War. Of 425 Confederate officers, 77 were killed in battle.

Robert Leckie, *None Died in Vain: The Saga of the American Civil War* (New York: HarperCollins, 1990), 657.

Who was the first African-American soldier to be awarded the French *Croix de Guerre* for bravery in battle?

The first African-American soldier to receive the French *Croix de Guerre* for bravery in battle was Army Private Henry Johnson (1897-1929) on May 24, 1918. With the 369th Infantry, 93d Division, in World War I (1914-18), Johnson was injured in an attack by German soldiers but successfully routed his assailants and saved a wounded comrade.

Kenneth Estell, ed., *The African-American Almanac, 6th ed.* (Detroit: Gale Research, 1994), 1311-2. Jessie Carney Smith, ed., *Black Firsts: 2,000 Years of Extraordinary Achievement* (Detroit: Gale Research, 1994), 245. Joseph Nathan Kane, *Famous First Facts* (New York: H. W. Wilson, 1981), s.v. "Croix de Guerre awarded to a black."

Where was the treaty ending the Russo-Japanese War signed?

In August of 1905, U.S. president Theodore Roosevelt (1887-1944) brokered a peace conference at Portsmouth, New Hampshire, between Russia and Japan in an attempt to end the Russo-Japanese War. As a result of the conference, a peace treaty known as the Treaty of Portsmouth was signed. The treaty stipulated that Russia would recognize Japanese control of Korea, cede half of Sakhalin Island below the fifteenth parallel to Japan, and give up its lease on the Liaotung Peninsula. Both countries agreed to cede control of Manchuria to China. As a result of his efforts to end the Russo-Japanese War, Theodore Roosevelt was awarded the Nobel Peace Prize in 1906.

Nicholas V. Riasanovsky, *A History of Russia, 3d ed.* (New York: Oxford University Press, 1977), 447.

Who was Leon Trotsky?

Born Lev Bronstein, the Russian revolutionist Leon Trotsky (1879-1940) became an organizer of Russia's Red Army after the Communists came to power in Russia in 1917. Second in command under Lenin (1870-1924), it was widely believed he would succeed Lenin as leader of the Soviet government. He was, however, no tactical match for Josef Stalin (1879-1953) and was expelled from the Communist party in 1927. Exiled to Soviet Central Asia, he left the Soviet Union. Denied admission to many countries, Mexico finally granted him asylum. Continuing to wage an ideological battle with Stalin, he was silenced when he was murdered by a Soviet agent.

Robert H. Ferrell and John S. Bowman, eds., *The Twentieth Century: An Almanac* (New York: World Almanac Publications, 1984), 155.

Who were Tomas and Jan Masaryk?

Tomas Masaryk (1850-1937) and his son, Jan Masaryk (1896-1948), were Czechoslovakian patriots. Tomas served under the Austro-Hungarian Emperor Franz Joseph (1830-1916). He was elected to the Austro-Hungarian Parliament in 1891, where he worked for the recognition of the rights of the Slavic peoples of the empire. In 1914 Tomas fled to the United States where he lobbied for international support for a separate Czechoslovakia. He was elected Czechoslovakia's first president, after the country was created at the Paris Peace Conference in 1919. His son, Jan, served in the Czech foreign service and later became its foreign minister when the government was in exile during World War II (1039-45). Jan was found dead in 1948 and it was never concluded whether he killed himself or was killed because he denounced the communist seizure of Czechoslovakia.

Robert H. Ferrell and John S. Bowman, eds., *The Twentieth Century: An Almanac* (New York: World Almanac Publications), 128.

Who fired the first shot from Fort Sumter at the beginning of the American Civil War?

In response to a Confederate bombardment, Abner Doubleday (1819-1893) fired the first shot from Fort Sumter in the harbor of Charleston, South Carolina, in the incident that began the American Civil War. Doubleday enjoyed a long military career, including service at the battle of Gettysburg. He was also credited with originating the game of baseball.

Allen Johnson and Dumas Malone, eds., *Dictionary of American Biography* (New York: Charles Scribner's Sons, 1958), s.v. "Doubleday, Abner."

For whom did Mata Hari spy and how was she caught?

Mata Hari was a spy for Germany during World War I (1914-18). Born Margaretha Geertruida Zelle in 1876 to a middle-class Dutch family, she was the ex-wife of an army officer when she assumed the identity of a dancing girl from exotic

India. Her erotic dancing techniques made her popular on the vaudeville stage and at private performances where she gained the confidence of many government leaders.

The French secret service collected evidence against her for several years. Because she had so many friends in the French and Dutch governments absolute proof was necessary to arrest her. Mata Hari was finally was arrested on February 13, 1917, at a hotel in Paris. Allied intelligence agents had intercepted a telegram on its way from German Army headquarters to Mata Hari at the German embassy in Madrid. It directed her to return to Paris to receive 15,000 pesetas. She was carrying the telegram at the time of her arrest. Another piece of evidence against her was her acceptance of 30,000 German marks from the German secret service.

It is possible that she was responsible for the loss of at least 50,000 Allied soldiers. Mata Hari was executed by a firing squad on October 15, 1917, at Vincennes, France.

The Encyclopedia Americana (Danbury, CT: Grolier, 1990), s.v. "Mata Hari."

Who was the first Chief Engraver of the United States Mint?

There is some debate over who is considered to be the first Chief Engraver of the United States Mint. The first person Joseph Wright, appointed by U.S. President George Washington (1732-1799), died before being sworn in. While awaiting a replacement, Henry Voight acted as the Chief Engraver. The first individual to be both appointed and officially confirmed was Robert Scot, about whom very little is known. Scot served from November 23, 1793, until either November 1, 1823, or January of 1824. The later date is in dispute because Scot was believed to have died sometime in November of 1823.

Beth Deisher, ed., *Coin World Almanac: A Handbook for Coin Collectors, 5th ed.* (New York: World Almanac, 1987), 184-85.

How many acres of public land could an individual receive under the Homestead Act of 1862?

According to the Homestead Act of 1862, any individual who was the head of a household and older than 21 could claim up to 160 acres of public land if he or she occupied it with the intention of improving the land. If the settler did not wish to reside on the land, he or she could pay $1.25 per acre instead.

The World Book Encyclopedia (Chicago: World Book, 1987), s.v. "Homestead Act."

What was the Satsuma Rebellion?

The Satsuma Rebellion occurred in Japan between July and September of 1877. The rebellion resulted when 40,000 samurai, members of an elite warrior class, objected to a decision by the Japanese government to create a conscripted national army. This decision infuriated the samurai, and they decided to march on Tokyo in an attempt to overthrow the government. However, the samurai were defeated by national army troops near the city of Kumamoto.

R. Ernest Dupuy and Trevor N. Dupuy, *The Encyclopedia of Military History: from 3500 B.C. to the Present, 2d ed.* (New York: Harper & Row, 1986), 867.

What was the Monroe Doctrine?

In an 1823 speech before the U.S. Congress, president James Monroe (1758-1831) declared that the United States would not tolerate European adventures or interventions in the Americas. This speech, written in collaboration with the Secretary of State (and later U.S. president) John Quincy Adams (1767-1848), became known as the Monroe Doctrine. The doctrine has been variously interpreted as an isolationist move, as a recognition of the decline of European influence in the New World and the rise of U.S. nationalism, or as an excuse for U.S. intervention in Latin-American affairs.

Kenneth C. Davis, *Don't Know Much About History* (New York: Crown Publishers, 1990), 113.

In 1860 what American city was referred to as the "largest Irish city in the world"?

In 1860 New York was referred to as the "largest Irish city in the world" because of its 203,760 Irish-born citizens out of a total population of 805,651.

Stephanie Bernardo, *The Ethnic Almanac,* (Garden City, NY: Dolphin Books, 1981), 19-20.

What was the main port of entry for European immigrants prior to Ellis Island?

The main port of entry into the United States for European immigrants, prior to Ellis Island's tenure, was Castle Garden in New York. It served as the East Coast's main administrative center for immigrants from 1855 to 1892.

Stephanie Bernardo, *The Ethnic Almanac* (Garden City, NY: Dolphin Books, 1981), 19-20,

Who was the American Civil War commander who asked his enemy whether he should surrender?

In 1862, Union Army colonel John T. Wilder crossed over enemy lines to consult with Confederate Army leaders near Munfordville, Kentucky. Wilder-an engineer with little military experience-and his forces were severely outnumbered by those of General Braxton Bragg (1817-76); although Wilder's Union brigade was the first in history to be fully outfitted with repeating rifles. In a quandary, Wilder carried a white flag across the line, entered the Confederate camp, and first consulted with Major General Simon Bolivar Buckner, who sent the Union commander to Bragg. The Confederate general answered Wilder's query by having him count the Confederate cannons trained on the Union soldiers. When Wilder reached the forty-sixth cannon he said, "I believe I'll surrender."

Irving Wallace, David Wallechinsky, and Amy Wallace, *Significa* (New York: E. P. Dutton, 1983), 149.

Which American president kept a cow at the White House?

Pauline Wayne was the name of the bovine that often grazed on the White House lawn after U.S. president William Howard Taft (1857-1930) took office in 1909. The Taft family was apparently too attached to their milk cow to stash her at an area farm during the four-year Republican adminstration.

Sid Frank and Arden Davis Melick, *The Presidents: Tidbits & Trivia* (Maplewood, NJ: Hammond, 1980), 38.

Where were the Barbary Pirates based?

The Barbary pirates took to the sea from Algiers, Morocco, Tripoli, and Tunis. A plague to American ships, they were the target of a law requested by U.S. President Thomas Jefferson (1743-1826) authorizing the U.S. Navy to engage the pirates in battle "for the protection of commerce and seamen." This was not a declaration of war. The Barbary pirates were defeated in 1805 and a peace treaty was signed in Tripoli on June 4, 1805.

Walter J. Raymond, *Dictionary of Politics, 6th ed.* (Lawrenceville VA: Brunswick Publishing Co., 1978), s.v. "Barbary pirates."

Who is credited with introducing the spoils system?

De Witt Clinton (1769-1828), who served as Mayor of New York City and as governor of New York State, is identified with the spoils system. The descriptive phrase was coined early in his political career, when he replaced Federalists in appointed state positions with members of his own Republican party. This took place in 1801 when he served on the New York governor's Council of Appointment.

Howard L. Hurwitz, *An Encyclopedic Dictionary of American History* (New York: Washington Square Press, 1968), s.v. "Clinton, De Witt."

What was allowed by the Burlingame Treaty of 1868?

The Burlingame Treaty of 1868 opened the way for unlimited Chinese immigration to the United States. The treaty was a response to the need for cheap labor in the West, in mines and on the railroads. The treaty was named after Anson Burlingame (1820-1870) who had made the arrangement with the Chinese government after serving as U.S. Minister there.

Howard L. Hurwitz, *An Encyclopedic Dictionary of American History* (New York: Washington Square Press, 1968), s.v. "Burlingame Treaty."

What was the name of the fugitive who was turned over to the United States by the Vatican?

John H. Surratt Jr., a conspirator in the plot to kill President Lincoln, fled the country after the assassination, changed his name to John Watson, and joined the Papal army. He was recognized by an informer in that country, and extradited to the U.S. after an order by the Pope. When Surratt came back to the U.S., he was tried for the crime, but he was released because of a hung jury. His mother was hanged for being a conspirator. She had run the boarding house where John Wilkes Booth stayed.

Pittsburgh Press 31 December 1989.

Who was abb Sieys?

Emmanuel Joseph Sieys (1748-1836) was a priest and a French revolutionary leader who is best known for the publication of a political pamphlet in 1789 *Qu'est-ce que c'est le tiers tat? (What is the Third Estate?)*, the most famous pamphlet of the French Revolution, and one of the most influential political tracts in European history. It was written to influence the debate over the organization and procedures of the French national assembly, the Estates General. In 1789 this body had been called into session for the first time since 1614 to handle the economic and social crisis in which France found itself. According to medieval social theory the nation was divided into three classes or estates. The first two were the clergy and the nobility, and the third comprised everybody else and accounted for about 90 percent of the population. Of middle class origin, abb Sieys identified with the third estate and asserted that sovereign power should rest with the people as a whole. His argument took the question-answer form of a catechism, and although its ideas were not original, its timeliness and clarity with which it was written greatly enhanced its effectiveness. In fact the representatives did act on the tactics recommended by Sieys when the Third Estate declared itself alone to be the national assembly on June 17, 1789.

Samuel F. Scott and Barry Rothaus, eds., *Historical Dictionary of the French Revolution, 1789-1799* (Westport, CT: Greenwood Press, 1985), s.v. "Qu'est-ce que c'est Le Tiers Etat."

How many nations were involved in World War I?

There were 57 nations involved in World War I (1914-18): Aden, Afghanistan, Africa, Albania, Arabia, Australia, Austria-Hungary, Belgium, Brazil, Bulgaria, Canada, Ceylon, China, Costa Rica, Cuba, Czechoslovakia, Egypt, Eritrea, Estonia, Finland, France, Germany, Great Britain, Greece, Guatemala, Haiti, Honduras, India, Italy, Japan, Latvia, Liberia, Lithuania, Luxemburg, Mexico, Montenegro, Newfoundland, New Zealand, Nicaragua, North Africa, Panama, Persia, Philippines, Poland, Portugal, Roumania, Russia, Serbia, Siam, Singapore, Somaliland, South Africa, Sudan, Turkey, Transcaucasia, United States of America, and the West Indies.

Philip J. Haythornthwaite, *The World War One Sourcebook* (London: Arms and Armour Press, 1992).

What were the names of the German "dreadnought" battleships that served in World War I?

The German "dreadnought" battleships that served in World War I (1914-18) were the following:
Westfalen, Nassau, Posen, Rheinland (built in 1909-10)
Helogoland, Oldenburg, Ostfriesland, Thringen (built in 1911-12)
Kaiser, Friedrich der Grosse, Kaiserin, Knig Albert, Prinz Regent Luitpold (built in 1912-13)
Knig, Grosser Kurfrst, Kronprinz, Wilhelm, Markgraf (built in 1914)
Baden, Bayern (built in 1916)

Philip J. Haythornthwaite, *The World War One Sourcebook* (London: Arms and Armour Press, 1992), 205.

What American Civil War battles are referred to as Bull Run and Manassas?

The series of battles that took place along Bull Run, Virginia, are known by two different names: a Confederate name and a Union name. The first fight, which took place on July 18, 1861, was called "The affair at Blackburn's Ford" by Union troops; the Confederate soldiers recalled it as the "First Battle of Bull Run." A bigger clash on July 21, 1861 was considered by the Federals to be the "first" battle of Bull Run, while Southerners dubbed it "First Manassas." The third military engagement in the vicinity took place on August 29 and 30, 1862. It was called "Manassas" by the Union, who also called it the "Second Battle of Bull Run." The Confederates called this battle "Second Manassas."

Mark Mayo Boatner, *The Civil War Dictionary* (New York: David McKay, 1959), 507.

Which U.S. president issued an executive order to ban the sale of alcohol on military bases?

On February 22, 1881, U.S. president Rutherford B. Hayes (1822-93) issued an executive order that prohibited the sale of intoxicating liquors at military installations.

Tim Taylor, *The Book of Presidents* (New York: Arno Press, 1972), 230.

Which battle involved over 100,000 Americans on the field for the first time?

The American Civil War's battle of Shiloh, in April of 1862, was the first event to involve over 100,000 Americans in a battle.

John Pimlott, *The Military Quiz Book* (Harrisburg, PA: Greenhill Books and Stackpole Books, 1993), 69-70.

What was the name of the Mexican colony where defeated Confederate soldiers migrated at the end of the American Civil War?

When the American Civil War ended in 1865, some members of the defeated Confederacy established a Mexican colony rather than live in the unified United States. This was done with the encouragement of Mexican Emperor Maximilian (1832-1867), inspiring the Confederates to name the colony "Carlotta," in honor of the Empress Carlotta (1840-1927). The colony soon failed, however, as did Maximilian; the emperor was executed just two years later.

Howard L. Hurwitz, *An Encyclopedic Dictionary of American History* (New York: Washington Square Press, 1968), s.v. "Carlotta."

Where did the President live after the White House burned in 1814?

U.S. President James Madison (1751-1836) and his wife Dolley (1768-1849) lived in the Octagon House in Washington for more than a year while the White House was being rebuilt. During the War of 1812 it had been burned by the British in August of 1814. The Octagon House belonged to Colonel John Taylor. The building was not octagon-shaped, but had two rectangular wings connected by a circular tower.

William A. DeGregorio, *The Complete Book of the U.S. Presidents, 2d ed.* (New York: Dembner Books, 1989), 58. Joseph Nathan Kane, *Facts About the Presidents, 6th ed.* (New York: H. W. Wilson, 1993), 33.

When did the first U.S. presidential inauguration take place?

Robert Livingston, Chancellor of New York State, administered the first presidential oath of office to George Washington (1732-1799) in New York City, on April 30, 1789. New York City at this time was the temporary capital of the nation. The first inaugural ball was held in this city on May 7, 1789, but Martha Washington did not attend because she was still at Mount Vernon.

Joseph Nathan Kane, *Facts About the Presidents, 6th ed.* (New York: H. W. Wilson, 1993), 8. *Mount Vernon: A Handbook* (Mount Vernon, VA: The Mount Vernon Ladies Association of the Union, 1985), 14. *World Book Encyclopedia* (Chicago: World Book, 1993), s.v. "New York City."

What was the "message to Garcia"?

The "message to Garcia" was supposedly a secret letter sent by President William McKinley (1843-1901) at the outbreak of the Spanish-American War (1898) to Calixto Garcia (1839-98), a Cuban revolutionary and ally of the United States. The letter was entrusted to Lt. Andrew S. Rowan, who carried it in an oilskin pouch strapped over his heart as he wandered the Cuban jungle in search of Garcia's mountain stronghold, the exact location of which he did not know. After three weeks he emerged from the wilderness, having accomplished his mission. The story is apocryphal, for there never was a "message to Garcia" from President McKinley, and Rowan's journey to Cuba was much less dramatic. An American writer, Elbert Green Hubbard (1856-1915), exaggerated the incident in order to write a "preachment" about the importance of industry, promptness, initiative, and devotion to duty. It first appeared as an untitled article in his magazine *The Philistine* in 1899, and it was soon was reprinted throughout the world in newspapers, magazines, and in pamphlet form with the title "A Message to Garcia." Its circulation was estimated at anywhere from ten to forty million readers.

Elbert Hubbard, *A Message to Garcia* (New York: Franklin Watts, 1914), v-xiii.

Which First Lady of the United States was oldest when her husband took office?

Anna Harrison, wife of U.S. President William Henry Harrison, was the oldest First Lady. She was 65 years and 222 days old when her husband took office in 1841.

Joseph Nathan Kane, *Facts About the Presidents, 6th ed.* (New York: H. W. Wilson, 1993), 320.

What is the name of the Virginia woman who claimed to be the Grand Duchess Anastasia?

A Charlottesville, Virginia woman, named Anna Anderson Manahan sought to prove that she was Grand Duchess Anastasia, the youngest daughter of Russia's Czar Nicholas II. She attempted to prove her identity legally, claiming to be the heir to an $85 million dowry deposited in the Bank of England. Her evidence included a family photograph and a document revealing testimony that the princess escaped in 1918 from her Bolshevik captors. Russian history specialists did not credit her and found it strange that she did not speak Russian. A German court ruled that her identity as the Duchess could not be proved, ending her legal case in 1976. Anna Manahan died on February 12, 1984.

National Observer 6 November 1976. "Anna Manahan Dies. 'Anastasia' Claimant," *New York Times* 14 February 1984.

Who were defenders of the Alamo?

The men who defended the Alamo were: Juan Abamillo, R. Allen, Miles DeForest Andross, Micajah Autry, Juan A. Badillo, Peter James Bailey, Issac G. Baker, William Charles M. Baker, John J. Ballentine, Richard W. Ballentine, John J. Baugh, Joseph Bayliss, John Blair, Samuel B. Bair, William Blazeby, James Butler Bonham, Daniel Bourne, James Bowie, Jesse B. Bowman, George Brown, James Brown, Robert Brown, James Buchanan, Samuel E. Burns. George D. Butler, Robert Campbell, John Cane, William R. Carey, Charles Henry Clark, M.B. Clark, Daniel William Cloud, Robert E. Cochran, George Washington Cottle, Henry Courtman, Lemuel Crawford, David Crockett, Robert Crossman, David P. Cummings, Robert Cunningham, Jacob C. Darst, Freeman H.K. Day, Jerry C. Day, Squire Daymon, William Dearduff, Stephen Denison, Charles Despallier, Almeron Dickinson, John H. Dillard, James R. Dimpkins, Lewis Duel, Andrew Duvalt, Carlos Espalier, Gregorio Esparza, Robert Evans, Samuel B. Evans, James L. Ewing, William Fishbaugh, John Flanders, Dolphin Ward Floyd, John Hubbard Forsyth, Antonio Fuentes, Galba Fuqua, William H. Furtleroy, William Garnett, James W. Garrand, James Girard Garrett, John E. Garvin, John E. Gaston, James George, John Camp Goodrich, Albert Calvin Grimes, James C. Gwynne, James Hannum, John Harris, Andrew Jackson Harrison, William B. Harrison, Joseph M. Hawkins, John M. Hays, Charles M. Heiskell, Thomas Hendricks, Patrick Henry Herndon, William D. Hersee, Tapley Holland, Samuel Holloway, William D. Howell, William Daniel Jackson, Thomas Jackson, Green B. Jameson, Gordon C. Jennings, Lewis Johnson, William Johnson, John Jones, Johnnie Kellog, James Kenny, Andrew Kent, Joseph Kerr, George C. Kimball, William P. King, William Irving Lewis, William J. Lightfoot, Jonathon L. Lindley, William Linn, George Washington Main, William T. Malone, William Marshall, Albert Martin, Edward McCafferty, Jesse McCoy, William McDowell, James McGee, John McGregor, Robert McKinney, Eliel Melton, Thomas R. Miller, William Mills, Isaac Millsaps, Edward F. Mitchusson, Edwin T. Mitchell, Napoleon B. Mitchell, Robert B. Moore, Willis Moore, Robert Musselman, Andres Nava, George Neggan, Andrew M. Nelson, Edward Nelson, George Nelson, James Northcross, James Nowlin, Goerge Pagan, Christopher Parker, William Parks, Richardson Perry, Amos Polard, John Purdy Reynolds, Thomas H. Roberts, James Robertson, Isaac Robinson, James M. Rose, Jackson J. Rusk, Joseph Rutherford, Isaac Ryan, Mial Scurlock, Marcus L. Sewell, Manson Shied, Cleland Kinloch Simmons, Andrew H. Smith, Charles S. Smith Joshua G. Smith, William H. Smith, Richard Starr, James E. Stewart, Richard L. Stockton, A. Spain Summerlin, William E. Summers, William D. Sutherland, Edward Taylor, George Taylor, James Taylor, William Taylor, B. Archer M. Thomas, Henry Thomas, Jesse G. Thompson, John W. Thomson, John M. Thurston, Burke Trammel, William Barrett Travis, George W. Tumlinson, Asa Walker, Jacob Walker, Jacob Walker, William B. Ward, Henry Warnell, Joseph G. Washington, Thomas Waters, William Wells, Isaac White, Robert White, Hiram J. Williamson, David L. Wilson, John Wilson, Antony Wolfe, Claiborne Wright, Charles Zanco.

Walter Lord, *A Time to Stand,* (n.p.: n.p., 1961), 214-19.

What was the "Brownsville affray"?

On August 13, 1906, 16 to 20 armed men rode through the streets of Brownsville, Texas, on horseback, shooting into the homes of white residents. One person was killed and several others were injured. The shooting occurred after a fight between a white merchant and an African-American soldier from the First Battalion, resulting in the town being placed off-limits to the battalion, which was quartered in nearby Fort Brown. When the incident drew national attention, an investigation was ordered by President Theodore Roosevelt.

During the investigation, which has come to be known as the "Brownsville affray," the African-American soldiers were accused by the townspeople of being the night riders, but a series of military inquiries and a county grand jury failed to establish the identities of the men involved. When no soldier would speak against his comrades, all of the members of Companies B, C, and D of the First Battalion—167 men—were told that if the persons involved in the shooting did not step forward and identify themselves, the entire group would be dishonorably discharged.

In November of 1906 U.S. President Roosevelt (1858-1919) ordered the 167 soldiers discharged without honor from the Army and barred from reenlistment for what he called their "conspiracy of silence" in refusing to testify against their fellow soldiers. In 1972 the Army announced, after 66 years, that it had cleared the records of the 167 soldiers who were dishonorably discharged. U.S. Secretary of the Army Robert F. Froehlke ordered the discharges changed to honorable and called the action a "gross injustice."

"Army Clears 167 Black Soldiers Disciplined in a Shooting in 1906," *New York Times* 29 September 1972.

How did Rasputin die?

The monk Grigori Rasputin (1872-1916) was killed by a group of Russian noblemen who were apprehensive about his powerful influence over the Russian royal family, which allowed him to interfere in both religious and secular politics. Rasputin was able to control Czar Nicholas II (1868-1918) and especially the Czarina through his ability to stop the bleeding of their hemophiliac son. Invited to the palace of Prince Felix Yusupov, he was given poisoned cakes and wine. When the cyanide failed to work, he was stabbed, then shot, and eventually bound in chains and thrown into a hole cut into the frozen Neva River. Still alive, he had strength enough to break through the ice, but he died of drowning near the river bank.

Jay Robert Nash, *Crime Chronology: A Worldwide Record, 1900-1983* (New York: Facts on File, 1984), 41.

Who were the abolitionists?

Abolitionist was the name given to those who wanted to abolish slavery in the United States in the late eighteenth and nineteenth centuries. An Abolitionist Congress was held as early as 1774, and in 1776 there was an attempt to pass anti-slavery legislation. The movement was given a cohesion it previously lacked when William Lloyd Garrison (1805-1879) founded the American Anti-Slavery Society in 1833, and within seven years it had over 200,000 members nationwide. A splinter group, the American and Foreign Anti-Slavery Society, founded the Liberal Party in 1840 to push the abolitionist cause in national politics, but it was most effective at the state and local levels. Abolitionists were able to keep their program before the American people, and eventually it was adopted by the Republican Party. After the American Civil War (1861-65) and the emancipation of the slaves, the American Anti-Slavery Society dissolved itself in 1870.

Chris Cook, *Dictionary of Historical Terms: A Guide to Names and Events of Over 1,000 Years of World History* (New York: Peter Bedrick Books, 1983), s.v. "abolitionists."

What was the de Lme letter?

The de Lme letter was a private letter written to a Cuban friend by Enrique de Lme, Spanish minister to the United States. It was stolen from a Havana, Cuba, post office and published in the *New York Journal* on February 9, 1898. Since the letter was highly critical of U.S. President William McKinley (1843-1901), it increased the hostility in the United States towards Spanish policies in Cuba and hastened the outbreak of the Spanish American War in April of 1898.

George C. Kohn, *Dictionary of Historic Documents* (New York: Facts on File, 1991), s.v. "De Lme letter."

What was the Council of Five Hundred?

Following the overthrow of the monarchy during the French Revolution, a new government known as the French Directoire was formed. This government, which lasted from November of 1795 to November of 1799, provided for the creation of a legislature with two bodies. One of those bodies was the Council of

Five Hundred, which consisted of 500 delegates, aged 30 or older, who were responsible for proposing legislation. The passage or veto of the proposed legislation, however, was the responsibility of the other legislative body, known as the Council of Ancients.

Philip W. Goetz, ed., *The New Encyclopaedia Britannica, 15th ed., "Micropaedia"* (Chicago: Encyclopaedia Britannica, 1989), s.v. "Dirichlet, Peter Gustav Lejeune."

What is the Balfour Declaration?

The Balfour Declaration was a statement in a letter written on November 2, 1917 in which British Foreign Secretary Arthur J. Balfour endorsed the establishment of a Jewish state in Palestine. The letter was written to British Zionist leader Lionel Walter Rothschild. By his statement Balfour hoped to garner Jewish support for Britain's war effort, protect British interests in the Suez Canal region and thwart Germany's pro-Arab stance in the middle east. Although many British high officials opposed the intent of the Balfour Declaration it found favor amongst the Allied forces and the League of Nations.

George C. Kohn, *Dictionary of Historic Documents* (New York: Facts on File, 1991), s.v. "Balfour Declaration."

What disability did Alexander Graham Bell's wife have?

Mabel G. Hubbard, the wife of Alexander Graham Bell, had been deaf since childhood.

Howard L. Hurwitz, *An Encyclopedic Dictionary of American History* (New York: Washington Square Press, 1968), s.v. "Bell, Alexander Graham."

Who decided that the name of the city of Pittsburgh would be spelled with an "h"?

At the beginning of the twentieth century, the question of whether or not to spell Pittsburgh with an "h" at the end was a subject of intense debate. Members of the United States Geographic Board had decided to officially drop the "h" because they considered it unnecessary. This decision sparked such a huge negative reaction from the public that, on July 20, 1911, the United States Geographic Board sent a letter to Pennsylvania Senator George T. Oliver announcing that they had reversed their decision. With this final, official word, there was no doubt about it—Pittsburgh would be spelled with an "h" at the end.

Robert Simpson, "Pittsburgh Is Spelled With 'H'," *Pittsburgh Post-Gazette* 22 July 1911.

Who was Simon Bolvar?

Simon Bolvar (1783-1830) was a soldier, statesman, and revolutionary leader. He is known in Latin America as the Liberator, the father of its independence movement, since he is responsible for freeing a number of South American countries from Spanish colonial rule. Bolvar served as president of both Peru and Columbia. Bolivia, a country that he organized, is named after him.

Bernard Grun, *The Timetables of History: of People and Events, 3d rev. ed.* (New York: Simon & Schuster, 1991). Gerhard Masur, *Simon Bolvar* (Albuquerque: University of New Mexico Press, 1969).

What led to the Great Chicago Fire of 1871?

A combination of factors led to the Great Chicago Fire of October 8, 1871. At that time, Chicago consisted of 36 square miles of wooden structures—shacks, tenements, buildings, fences, even sidewalks. A long drought beginning in early July and stretching to early October had made the wood tinder dry. Although accounts differ on the actual cause of ignition, there is a consensus that at 8:45 P.M. on the night of Sunday, October 8, Mrs. Katie O'Leary's barn at 137 DeKoven Street on Chicago's West Side went up in flames, and the wind blew sparks from the barn to neighboring buildings, which ignited. This continuing chain reaction caused flames quickly to engulf the dry wooden structures of Chicago, and coupled with a southwest wind, the flames increased in magnitude until they created a draft strong enough to knock people down. The fire raged for over 24 hours, ravaging five square miles of the city from the river to the lake, and from Taylor Street to Lincoln Park. The rain that started Monday night finally extinguished the fire. Miraculously only 250 to 300 persons died, but 17,500 buildings were destroyed; 90,000 people were left without homes; and there was $196 million in property damage.

Lee Davis, *Man-Made Catastrophes: From the Burning of Rome to the Lockerbie Crash* (New York: Facts On File, 1993), 181-86.

Who was King Kamehameha I?

Kamehameha I (ca. 1758-1819) was the first king of the Hawaiian Islands and through conquest united the islands under his rule.

Born to a family that ruled the island of Hawaii under his uncle Kalaniopuu, Kamehameha fought and won a civil war following his uncle's death in 1782. By 1790 Kamehameha was in control of much of the island and soon allied himself with two English sailors who taught him the art of modern warfare and the employment of muskets and cannons. Under their tutelage Kamehameha soon conquered the islands Maui, Molokai, and Lanai. In 1795 he invaded Oahu and drove his opponents to their deaths over the cliffs of Nuuanu. By 1810 he was in control of all of the Hawaiian islands. Kamehameha became known for instituting a centralized government and opening the islands to western trade while maintaining the cultural heritage of his people.

Encyclopedia of World Biography (New York: McGraw-Hill, 1973), s.v. "Kamehameha I." George C. Kohn, *Dictionary of Wars* (New York: Facts on File, 1986), s.v. "Hawaiian War of 1782-1810."

What was the Armenian massacre?

In 1895 the Muslim Turkish government under Sultan Abdal-Hamid II began a campaign of genocide at Sassoun against the Christian Armenians who inhabited the country which would last for 27 years. Armenia had been a long disputed territory which was eventually incorporated into northeast Turkey. Armenians practiced Christianity, since Saint Gregory the Illuminator brought the religion to Armenia during the third century.

From 1895 to 1922, the Turks waged a "holy war" against these "infidels" during which two million Armenians were massacred; others fled across borders or to emigrate. Despite the French occupation of Turkey in 1920, the carnage continued. In 1922 the Treaty of Sevres was signed which restored Armenia as a sovereign state. However at that time most Armenians had no confidence that the massacres would be repeated and emigrated whenever it was possible.

Lee Davis, *Man-Made Catastrophes: From the Burning of Rome to the Lockerbie Crash* (New York: Facts on File, 1993), 59-61.

What is the origin of the phrase "a government of the people, by the people, for the people"?

The oft-quoted phrase "a government of the people, by the people, for the people" originated in the concluding line of U.S. president Abraham Lincoln's (1809-65) Gettysburg Address given at the dedication on November 19, 1863 of a cemetery at the battlefield at Gettysburg, Pennsylvania, where one of bloodiest battles of the American Civil War (1861-68) had taken place. Lincoln urged his audience to dedicate themselves to "the great task remaining before us-that from these honored dead we take increased devotion to that cause for which they here gave the last full measure of devotion-that we here highly resolve that the dead shall not have died in vain-that the nation shall, under God, have a new birth of freedom-and that governments of the people, by the people, and for the people, shall not perish from the earth."

World Book Encyclopedia (Chicago: World Book, 1993), s.v. "Constitution of the United States."

Who was known as "Lemonade Lucy"?

President Rutherford B. Hayes (1822-93) had never allowed alcoholic beverages to be served in his home. He maintained this stance once elected to the presidency. U.S. Secretary of State William Evarts (1818-1901), however, convinced him to have wine served at state dinners. At the first of these dinners two of the guests, who may or may not have been the sons of the Russian Czar in whose honor the dinner was given, behaved so deplorably under the influence of the wine that Hayes never allowed alcoholic beverages to be served at the White House again during his administration. Although his wife, Lucy, a practicing Methodist, had not made the decision, she was quite pleased with it. Secretary Evarts quipped that "water flowed like champagne" at her events. Thus she became known as "Lemonade Lucy."

Margaret B. Bassett, *Profiles and Portraits of American Presidents and Their Wives* (Freeport, ME: Bond Wheelwright, 1969), 183.

What Indian woman served as guide for the Lewis and Clark expedition?

Sacajawea was a Shoshoni Indian woman who accompanied Meriwether Lewis and William Clark as an interpreter and guide on their exploration west from what is now North Dakota to the Pacific Ocean. She was probably born about 1787 in eastern Idaho or western Montana. As a teenager Sacajawea was taken prisoner by the Hidatsa Indians and brought east. She was living in a Mandan (a tribe with close ties to the Hidatsa) village when she was purchased by Toussaint Charbonneau, a French-Canadian fur trader, who made her one of his wives. In 1805 Charbonneau and Sacajawea, carrying her two month old son on her back, left with the explorers.

There is some debate as to whose skills as a guide were needed, Sacajawea's or Charbonneau's. Some historians believe that Charbonneau's experience as a mountain man was needed and that Sacajawea merely accompanied her husband. Others hypothesize that Lewis and Clark let Charbonneau believe that his skills were prized, when it was actually the young Indian woman who knew the language and territory of the Shoshoni, through which they would pass, whose presence was vital. In either case she proved an indispensable member of the expedition. She gathered food, retrieved precious provisions when a boat was almost overturned, and, during their time with the Shoshoni, made sure that the expedition would have enough horses for the trek over the Rocky Mountains. Upon returning from the expedition, Sacajawea rejoined the Indians in the Mandan villages where she remained to care for her baby and her husband.

There is some confusion as to how long Sacajawea lived. In 1812 a fur trader recorded in his journal the death of Charbonneau's Shoshoni wife but the reference may have been to a different Shoshoni wife. Other evidence suggests that she died on an Indian reservation on April 9, 1884, nearly one hundred years old.

Her name is variously spelled as Sakakawea and Sah-cah-gar-we-ah, all of which translate as birdwoman or owl woman.

Dictionary of Indians of North America (St. Clair Shores, MI: Scholarly Press, 1978), s.v. "Sacajawea." Carl Waldman, *Who Was Who in Native American History: Indians and Non-Indians From Early Contacts through 1900* (New York: Facts on File, 1990), s.v. "Sacajawea."

Who were the "Five Civilized Tribes"?

The "Five Civilized Tribes" is the name given to five Native American tribes by American settlers during the early 1800s. The settlers considered members of these five tribes "civilized" because they adopted a number of European customs, attended Christian churches, and sent their children to schools run by Christian missionaries. The Five Civilized Tribes were the Chocotaw, Creek, Seminole, Cherokee, and Chickasaw tribes.

The World Book Encyclopedia (Chicago: World Book, 1987), s.v. "Five Civilized Tribes."

Which two Confederate state capitals were not captured by Union forces during the Civil War?

Tallahassee, Florida, and Austin, Texas, were the two Confederate state capitals that escaped Union capture during the American Civil War.

Alex Trebek and Merv Griffin, *The Jeopardy! Challenge: The Toughest Games from America's Greatest Quiz Show!* (New York: Harper Perennial, 1992), 43, 45.

What two founding fathers died on the 50th anniversary of the signing of the Declaration of Independence?

John Adams (1735-1826), second president of the United States, and Thomas Jefferson (1743-1826), third president of the United States, both died on July 4, 1826, the 50th anniversary of the signing of the Declaration of Independence.

John Wagman, *On This Day In America: An Illustrated Almanac of History, Sports, Science, and Culture* (New York: Gallery Books, 1990), s.v. "July 4."

Who was the first woman to serve as a marine?

The first woman to serve as a marine was Lucy Brewer, who, disguised as a man and using the names George Baker and Louisa Baker, served aboard the *Constitution* during the War of 1812.

Joseph Nathan Kane, *Famous First Facts* (New York: H. W. Wilson, 1981), 363.

What was the first city to undergo aerial bombardment?

Paris, France, was the first locale to suffer from aerial bombardment, during World War I (1914-18) when German planes attacked the city on August 30, 1914.

Dennis Sanders, *The First of Everything: A Compendium of Important, Eventful, and Just-Plain-Fun Facts About All Kinds of Firsts* (New York: Delacorte, 1981), 94.

When was the Liberty Bell put up for sale?

The Liberty Bell was up for sale in 1828, although it was more of a business deal than an outright sale. The hefty relic had been rung for various occasions at the Pennsylvania State House in Philadelphia since 1753. It pealed at the first public reading of the Declaration of Independence, but had not been used since about 1800. When the seat of government moved from Philadelphia to Washington, DC, the Liberty Bell was stored and forgotten. In the process of renovating the State House in 1828, Philadelphia leaders commissioned a replacement for it from a bellmaker named John Wilbank. Wilbank would be given the old one—which he could use as scrap metal—and in return would reduce the bill for the new one by $400. After an attempt to remove it from storage, however, Wilbank decided that the cost of transporting it would be too high in exchange for the $400 credit. The city initiated a lawsuit against Wilbank to take the bell, but it was settled when he agreed to bestow it on the city as a charitable donation.

Irving Wallace, David Wallechinsky, and Amy Wallace, *Significa* (New York: E.P Dutton, 1983), 77-78.

What physical malady chronically plagued the famed naval commander Horatio Nelson?

Horatio Nelson (1758-1805), the famed British naval commander, was plagued by a host of ailments that included seasickness. He also suffered from bouts with malaria, rheumatic fever, and depression.

Ernle Bradford, *Nelson: The Essential Hero* (New York: Harcourt Brace, Jovanovich, 1977), 54.

Did Betsy Ross design and make the first American flag?

The story that Betsy Ross (1752-1836) co-designed and made the first American flag may have been the invention of William J. Canby, her grandson. In an 1870 address to the Historical Society of Pennsylvania, Canby recounted the legend of Betsy Ross as told to him by various relatives. The tale received further impetus from the publication of *The Evolution of the American Flag*, written jointly by Canby's brother and nephew. Although Betsy Ross did sew flags for Pennsylvania state ships, there is no contemporary evidence to indicate she was the flagmaker of the Stars and Stripes, and one of the signers of the Declaration of Independence, Francis Hopkinson (1737-1791), did claim to have designed the flag but made no mention of her. Also the historical papers of George Washington, who supposedly commissioned her to design the flag, has no reference to her work. In fact nothing is told of Betsy Ross' role until 1870 when her grandson presented his paper.

William Rea Furlong, Byron McCandless, and Harold D. Langley, *So Proudly We Hail: The History of the United States Flag* (Washington, DC: Smithsonian Institution Press, 1981), 115-19.

What important American Civil War sea battle was fought in the English Channel?

On June 19, 1864 the chain-plated Union ship *Keersarge* engaged and sank the Confederate raider *Alabama* in the English Channel. The *Alabama*, even though staffed by a mostly British crew, was responsible for the loss or capture of 68 Yankee merchant vessels. In 1872 an international commission rules that Great Britain must pay the United States government an award of $15 million ruled as compensation for losses suffered in this incident.

Irving Wallace, David Wallechinsky, and Amy Wallace, *Significa,* (New York: E.P. Dutton, 1983), 147.

Who commanded British forces during World War I?

A number of military personnel commanded British troops during World War I (1914-18). The Empire's Expeditionary Force were led first by Sir John French (1852-1925), with Sir Douglas Haig (1861-1928) taking over in 1915. In Gallipoli, British forces were under the command of Sir Iain Hamilton (1853-1947) until 1915, then Sir Charles Monro; troops fighting in Italy were led by Sir Herbert Plumer (1857-1932), but later the Earl of Cavan, Frederic Lambart (1865-1946), in the last few months of the conflict. Sir John Jellicoe (1859-1935) headed the British Navy until 1916, when Sir David Beatty (1871-1936) took over the post. Britain's fledgling air combat troops were commanded by Sir David Henderson, H. Trenchard (1873-1952), and finally, J. M. Salmond.

Peter Young, ed., *The Marshall Cavendish Illustrated Encyclopedia of World War I* (New York: Marshall Cavendish, 1984), 3557.

Who was the only American Civil War soldier executed for war crimes?

Confederate captain Henry Wirz (1822-65) was the only man executed after the American Civil War's end for crimes committed during the conflict. Swiss by birth, Wirz emigrated to the United States when he was in his twenties and for a time practiced medicine in Louisiana. At the onset of the American Civil War (1861-65) he enlisted in the Confederate Army and became captain. In 1864 he was named commander of a Georgia military prison officially called Camp Sumter, but known informally as Andersonville. The facility expanded to hold over 33,000 inmates within a few months. Conditions were appalling and many of the prisoners-mostly Union Army enlistees, were weakened by exposure to the elements and a poor diet died from disease that ran rampant through the camp. Advancing Union troops put an end to the situation, as Wirz and Confederate officials transferred some of Andersonville's more hearty residents to Charleston. Officials later found some 13,000 graves at the site, but this was believed to be only a partial count of those who died there. Wirz was charged with war crimes in a court martial and executed in November of 1865.

John S. Bowman, ed., *The Civil War Almanac* (New York: Gallery Books, 1983), 392.

In the post-American Civil War South who were the "carpetbaggers" and "scalawags"?

In the post-American Civil War South "carpetbaggers" were Northerners who hurried south to assume and exploit local political offices strictly for their own financial gain. The term comes from their use of the cloth satchel made of two squares of carpet sewn together called "carpetbags" to carry belongings.

"Scalawags" were Southerners who collaborated with "carpetbaggers."

Mark Mayo Boatner, *The Civil War Dictionary* (New York: David McKay, 1959), s.v. "carpetbaggers," "scalawags." Stuart Berg Flexner, *I Hear America Talking* (New York: Van Nostrand Reinhold, 1976), 293.

What was the first treaty entered into by the United States?

The first treaty entered into by the United States was the Jay Treaty of 1794-95. Its purpose, as negotiated by U.S. Supreme Court's first chief justice John Jay (1745-1829), was to resolve violations to the Treaty of Paris, which had concluded the American Revolution.

Ted Yanak and Pam Cornelison, *The Great American History Fact-Finder* (Boston: Houghton Mifflin, 1993), s.v. "Jay treaty."

What is Calamity Jane's real name?

Martha Cannary (1852-1903), who later became the legendary Calamity Jane of the American west, was born in Princeton, Missouri, but by the time she was 12 or 13 her family had migrated west to Virginia City, Montana. Little is known about Martha until the 1870s when she appeared at Rawlins, Wyoming, dressed as a man and hiring out as a "...mule skinner, bullwhacker, and railroad worker." In 1875 she joined an army troop in pursuit of some Sioux Indians but while bathing nude with her fellow troopers her gender became quite evident and she was forced to leave the expedition. Over the decades her reputation as a hard drinking, hard fighting woman persisted until her death in Deadwood, South Dakota, where she was buried next to Wild Bill Hickok who was reputed to have been one of her lovers.

Stories abound as to the origin of her nickname. She once claimed that during an Indian fight she reached down from horseback to swoop up a wounded army officer who later said to her "I name you Calamity Jane, the heroine of the pains." A less romantic view purports that a common slang term for females of that era was "a Jane" and because of her demeanor a "calamity" was a likely occurrence. The two terms soon came together.

Doris Faber, *Calamity Jane: Her Life and Her Legend* (Boston: Houghton Mifflin, 1992), 16-17. Tony Hillerman, ed., *The Best of the West: An Anthology of Classic Writing from the American West* (New York: HarperCollins, 1991), 219. *McGraw-Hill Encyclopedia of World Biography* (New York: McGraw-Hill, 1973), s.v. "Calamity Jane."

Who were the heroes and villains among African Americans in the Wild West?

The American frontier was filled with a variety of African-American heroes and villains, including: Nate Love, a former slave turned super-cowboy; Cherokee Bill, a guide with the Indians who became an outlaw and was hanged at a very young age; Mary Fields, who, with the alias of Stagecoach Mary, was a tall woman known as a brave mail carrier who loved shootouts; Ben Hodges, an infamous card player who was often equated with Wyatt Earp; and Bill Pickett, an amazing cowboy who claimed to have been the pioneer of bulldogging, a sport which featured wrestling a full-grown steer by the horns.

"Who's who among rogues and heroes," *USA Today* 12 May 1993.

What French pirate helped U.S. General Andrew Jackson at the Battle of New Orleans?

During the War of 1812, French pirate Jean Lafitte (1780-1826) assisted U.S. forces in the defense of New Orleans. Lafitte offered the support of his band of pirates to General Andrew Jackson (1767-1845) when his own stronghold was attacked by the United States Originally, Lafitte was approached by the British, who asked him to take part in their attack on New Orleans. The pirate passed on these plans to the Americans, hoping to gain their goodwill; however,he did not receive apardon until he provided artillery support against the British attack in January of 1815.

Family Encyclopedia of American History (Pleasantville, NY: The Reader's Digest Association, 1975), s.v. "Lafitte, Jean."

Who saved Abraham Lincoln's son Robert from a probable death?

Robert Lincoln, son of U.S. president Abraham Lincoln (1809-65), was saved from what could have been a fatal accident by Edwin Booth (1833-93), the brother of his father's future assassin, John Wilkes Booth (1838-65). The incident took place during 1863 or 1864 as Robert traveled home from college and before the president's death in 1865. By Robert's own account, he was standing on a train platform in a crowd of people who were pressing forward trying to purchase sleeping-car reservations. He was pushed up against the train and off the platform, over a small open space when the train began to move. Robert could easily have been killed and certainly badly hurt if a hand had not reached out to catch him. Edwin Booth grabbed the young man's collar and pulled him to safety. Robert recognized the well-known actor and thanked Edwin Booth.

Ruther Painter Randall, *Lincoln's Sons* (Boston: Little, Brown, 1955), 152.

What was Coxey's Army?

Coxey's Army was part of a larger and loosely organized Populist movement of the unemployed following the financial panic of 1893 in the United States. In the depression following the panic, Jacob Sechler Coxey (1854-1951), a self-made businessman from Massillon, Ohio, started a movement to pressure the U.S. federal government to fund massive road and public improvement programs, thus providing work for unemployed laborers. With Carl Browne, a religious eccentric, Coxey organized a march on Washington, D.C. Because of Browne's influence, the march was also called the Commonweal of Christ. The anticipated 100,000 marchers did not materialize, but 500 supporters did demonstrate at the Capitol on May Day (May 1). Coxey was arrested, sent to jail, and fined for various infractions including carrying banners and walking on the grass of the Capitol grounds. Many similar groups began forming around the country, especially on the West Coast. They attempted to join Coxey in Washington, D.C., and when the railroads rebuffed their demands for free passage many trains were simply hijacked by the protesters. Few of these Coxeyites, Commonwealers, or Industrials made it east of the Mississippi River however, although 1,200 did make it to Washington, DC. These Populist movements had little impact on U.S. economic policy, but they were the precursors to future labor strife in America.

Dictionary of American History, rev. ed. (New York: Charles Scribner's Sons, 1976), s.v. "Coxey's Army."

What fate befell Confederate General Thomas "Stonewall" Jackson during the American Civil War?

American Civil War General Thomas Jonathan "Stonewall" Jackson (1824-63) was one of the Confederacy's most brilliant military officers. Jackson was born in Virginia and graduated from the West Point Military Academy in 1846. At the outbreak of the American Civil War (1861-68) he was made a colonel in the Confederate infantry and within a few weeks he was promoted to general. During the First Battle of Bull Run he acquired his nickname when Brigadier General Bernard E. Bee observed of him in battle "There is Jackson standing like a stone wall." On May 2, 1863, during the Battle of Chancellorsville Jackson was on a scouting mission and returning at dusk he was fired upon and wounded by North Carolina troops mistaking Jackson's party for attacking Union soldiers. Jackson died eight days later, his already deteriorating condition made worse by pneumonia.

Patricia L. Faust, ed., *Historical Times Illustrated Encyclopedia of the Civil War* (New York: Harper & Row, 1986), s.v. "Jackson, Thomas Jonathan 'Stonewall'." Irving Wallace, *The Book of Lists #2* (New York: William Morrow, 1980), 69-70.

What role did camels play in the American West?

Following the Mexican War the United States saw its territory increase by nearly 530,000 square miles of rugged, roadless, dry terrain. In 1855 the U.S. Congress appropriated $30,000 for the purchase of Egyptian and Asian camels for service use in this area. A total of 76 camels were introduced to Texas in 1856 and 28 to California a year later. The camels were originally bought to carry mail, but the government quickly learned they were not going to work out. By 1864 most had been sold to private freight carriers and mining operators with a few going to zoos. Previously during 1860-62, a San Francisco merchant bought 45 camels from Siberia to be used on eastern freight routes, but like their later counterparts they did not fare well and were eventually sold to a British Columbian mining concern. A few camels managed to escape into the wilds and survived for a while but did not establish a breeding population.

Dictionary of American History, rev. ed. (New York: Charles Scribner's Sons, 1976), s.v. "Camels in the West."

What was the Graybeard Regiment of the American Civil War?

Graybeard Regiment of the American Civil War was the nickname given to the 37th Iowa Volunteer Infantry because its recruits were required to be 45 years old and older. In 1862 the U.S. War Department authorized the formation of the unit whose sole purpose was to perform guard and garrison duty thus relieving younger and more able-bodied men for combat duty. Camp Strong, near Muscatine, Iowa, was the assembly site for the original 914 volunteers, including eighty-year-old Private Curtis King. Despite their age, the volunteers trained and lived under the same rigorous conditions as younger soldiers. They performed guard duty at Alton Prison in Illinois, Rock Island Prison in the Mississippi River, Camp Morton in Ohio, and on the Memphis & Charleston Railroad. By the end of the war, three Graybeards had been killed in action, 145 had succumbed to disease, and 364 received discharges for physical disabilities. The regiment was discharged May 24, 1865.

Patricia L. Faust, ed., *Historical Times Illustrated Encyclopedia of the Civil War* (New York: Harper & Row, 1986), s.v. "Graybeard Regiment." Irving Wallace, *Significa* (New York: E. P. Dutton, 1983), 143-44.

Who was the only U.S. vice-president to take the oath of office on foreign soil?

When Franklin Pierce (1804-1869) was elected the U.S. president in 1852, William Rufus De Vane King was elected vice-president. At the time, however, King was in Havana, Cuba, where U.S. Consul William L. Sharkey administered the oath by a special act of Congress. Unfortunately, the new vice-president died a month later before performing any of his new duties. No U.S. president has ever taken the oath of office on foreign soil.

Isaac Asimov, *Isaac Asimov's Book of Facts* (New York: Grosset & Dunlap, 1979), 341-42.

What was meant by the expression "Lafayette, we are here"?

During World War I (1914-18) when an U.S. army officer spoke the words "Lafayette, we are here" at the tomb of Marquis de Lafayette (1757-1834), he was returning a favor more than a century old. Just as Lafayette and France had aided the American colonies in their war with England, so then was America aiding France in its war with Germany.

In 1777 Marquis de Lafayette, a French general, statesman, and soon-to-be hero of the American Revolution, volunteered his services to the fledgling colonial army even though it was against the wishes of his government. Although American authorities looked askance at Lafayette's offer, he was soon given an honorary commission of major general and assigned as General George Washington's aide-de-camp. Lafayette soon distinguished himself both in battle and as a devoted believer in the American cause. For a while Lafayette commanded a division of American troops but soon returned to France to garner further support for the Revolution. In 1780 he returned to America to command a contingent of French auxiliary forces. In 1781 he was instrumental in the defeat of Cornwallis at Yorktown, the battle which ended the war and ushered in the American nation.

E. D. Hirsch, Jr., *The Dictionary of Cultural Literacy* (Boston: Houghton Mifflin, 1988), s.v. "Marquis de Lafayette." *McGraw-Hill Encyclopedia of World Biography* (New York: McGraw-Hill, 1973), s.v. "Marquis De Lafayette."

What was the name of the girl who urged Abraham Lincoln to grow a beard?

On October 15, 1860, 11-year-old Grace Bedell (1848-1936) wrote to Abraham Lincoln (1809-1865) that because his face was so thin, he would look a great deal better if he let his whiskers grow. In his October 19 reply, Lincoln suggested that he doubted the wisdom of doing so. "As to the whiskers," he wrote, "having never worn any, do you not think people would call it a piece of affect[at]ion"? However, Grace's opinion, combined with those of New York Republicans who felt the same, perhaps resulted in Lincoln's decision the next month to let his beard grow.

Philip B. Kunhardt, Jr., Philip B. Kunhardt III, and Peter W. Kunhardt, *Lincoln: An Illustrated Biography* (New York: Alfred A. Knopf, 1992), 13. Mark E. Neely, Jr., *The Abraham Lincoln Encyclopedia* (New York: McGraw-Hill, 1982), s.v. "Bedell, Grace."

What other government officials were meant to die in the plot that took the life of Abraham Lincoln?

The assassination of U.S. president Abraham Lincoln (1809-1865) took place on April 14, 1865, with Lincoln dying the next day, but if the conspirators had their way, the president would not have been their only victim. Both Vice-President Andrew Johnson (1808-1875) and Secretary of State William Seward (1801-1872) were to die simultaneously with Lincoln. George A. Atzerodt was to murder the vice-president but failed to carry it out. Lewis Payne actually stabbed Seward, but the secretary of state survived the attack.

William DeGregorio, *The Complete Book of U.S. Presidents, 2d ed.,* (New York: Dembner Books, 1989), 242.

What city was called the "Cradle of the Confederacy"?

The capitol of Alabama, Montgomery, is known as the "Cradle of the Confederacy" because it was there that Jefferson Davis (1808-1889) was sworn in as President of the Confederate States on February 4, 1861, a position he held until 1865, the year the American Civil War ceased.

Howard L. Hurwitz, *An Encyclopedic Dictionary of American History* (New York: Washington Square Press, 1968), s.v. "Alabama."

What was the first submarine to sink a warship?

The Confederate submarine Hunley was the first to sink a warship. This happened during the American Civil War (1861-65) on the night of February 17, 1864 near the Charleston, South Carolina harbor. The Hunley with nine crew members aboard rammed a mine into the hull of a Union blockade vessel the U.S.S. Housatonic. The Hunley backed off approximately 120 feet and detonanted the mine by means of a pull rope.

The Housatonic sank in five minutes with the loss of five crewmen. The Confederate submarine never made it back to port however, presumably damaged by the detonation it sank with the loss of its entire crew. The submarine long been considered a jinx ship by Confederate sailors having previously sunk three times and each time losing its entire crew including Horace Hunley, the submarine's designer. As a result it was nicknamed the "Peripatetic Coffin." In 1995 the remains of the Hunley were believed to have been found off the South Carolina coast.

Detroit Free Press 12 May 1995.

Which patent was issued to a United States president?

On May 22, 1849, 12 years before he became the 16th U.S. president, Abraham Lincoln (1809-65), was granted U.S. patent number 6,469 for a device to help steamboats pass over shoals and sand bars. The device, never tested or manufactured, had a set of adjustable buoyancy chambers (made from metal and waterproof cloth) attached to the ship's sides below the waterline. Bellows could fill the chambers with air to float the vessel over the shoals and sandbars. It was the only patent ever held by a U.S. president. Lincoln's interest in invention is recognized by the Inventors Hall of Fame, which includes his likeness along with that of Thomas Edison on its medallion presented to inductees. Although Thomas Jefferson (1743-1826), the third U.S. president, is recognized as having invented the swivel chair, pedometer, shooting stick, a hemp-treating machine, and an improvement in the moldboard of a plow.

Inventors Hall of Fame (Akron, OH: Inventors Hall of Fame, 1993), i. *Inventive Genius* (New York: Time-Life Books, 1991), 23. Robert O. Richardson, *The Weird and Wondrous World of Patents* (New York: Sterling, 1990), 38. U.S. Department of Commerce, Patent and Trademark Office, Patent Depository Library Program, *Patent and Trademark Office Collection of Historical and Interesting U.S. Patents in Celebration of Our Nation's Bicentennial: Microfilm Index* (Washington, DC: Government Printing Office, 1987), 6.

Was Napoleon poisoned?

The most common opinion today is that Napoleon Bonaparte (1769-1821), Emperor of France from 1804-1815, died of a cancerous, perforated stomach. A significant minority of doctors and historians have made other claims ranging from various diseases to malign neglect to outright homicide. A Swedish toxicologist, Sten Forshufvud, advanced the theory that Napoleon died of arsenic poisoning, administered by an agent of the French royalists who was planted in Napoleon's household during his final exile on the island of St. Helena.

Arno Karlen, *Napoleon's Glands* (Boston: Little, Brown, 1984), 15. Ben Weider and David Hapgood, *The Murder of Napoleon* (New York: Congdon & Latts, 1982).

Is there any truth to the Abraham Lincoln interviews recorded in "Diary of a Public Man"?

For almost 70 years, many historians used the "Diary of a Public Man" (published in the *North American Review* in 1879) as a source of information on U.S. President Abraham Lincoln (1809-65). The "diary" included accounts that Lincoln called Senator Charles Sumner (1811-74) of Massachusetts "my idea of a bishop," that Lincoln wore black gloves in bad taste at a New York City opera performance, and that archrival Stephen Douglas (1813-61) held Lincoln's hat during his first inaugural address. After 30 years of investigation, Frank Maloy Anderson determined that the first account was certainly fictitious and the other two doubtful.

Mark E. Neely, Jr., *The Abraham Lincoln Encyclopedia* (New York: McGraw-Hill, 1982), s.v. "Diary of a Public Man."

Did anyone survive "Custer's Last Stand"?

The U.S. Seventh Cavalry was divided into three battalions which split up to approach the Indian camp with 225 men-five companies of the Seventh Cavalry-first encountered the Cheyenne and Sioux warriors on June 25, 1876, at the Little Big Horn River, in Montana. Crazy Horse and Sitting Bull defeated Custer's force and then engaged in a standoff with the other two battalions that had come to Custer's aid. The Indians dispersed when reinforcements appeared.

The only survivor of Custer's force at the Battle of the Little Big Horn was a horse by the name of Comanche. He received this name after a Comanche arrow wounded him in his first military action. The horse belonged to Captain Myles Keogh. At the Little Big Horn he was wounded in the neck, lung, and groin, but he was nursed back to health. Once recovered from his wounds, Comanche participated in parades and ceremonies at various posts for the remaining years of his life. No one was allowed to ride him. He died on November 7, 1891, at Fort

Riley, Kansas, at the age of 31. His body was stuffed and put on display at the University of Kansas in Lawrence.

Chronicle of America (Liberty, MO: JL International, 1993), 492. Ruthven Tremain, *The Animals' Who's Who* (New York: Charles Scribner's Sons, 1982), 57. Terri A. Wear, *The Horse's Name Was ....* (Metuchen, NJ: Scarecrow Press, 1993), s.v. "Comanche."

How many battles were there in the American Civil War?

In the American Civil War there were approximately 10,000 recorded military actions, including 76 full-scale battles, 310 engagements, 6,337 skirmishes, and numerous forays, sieges, raids, and expeditions.

Robert Leckie, *None Died in Vain: The Saga of the American Civil War* (New York: HarperCollins, 1990), 657.

How much did the United States pay Russia for Alaska?

On March 29, 1867, U.S. Secretary of State William Henry Seward and Russian minister Baron Eduard Stoeckl completed the transaction granting control of Alaska to the United States. The total cost of the Alaska purchase was $7.2 million.

The purchase of Alaska prompted harsh criticism from many members of the U.S. House of Representatives who believed that Alaska was nothing more than a worthless chunk of ice. Alaska quickly became known as "Seward's Folly."

Dictionary of American History, rev. ed. (New York: Charles Scribner's Sons, 1976), s.v. "Alaska."

What were the "Shoe-black Brigades"?

For many runaway boys in late nineteenth century England, working as a shoeshine boy was one way to earn an income. However, because many of the boys worked long hours in places such as taverns and music halls, they often came into contact with unsavory people. An organization known as the Reformatory and Refuge Union was concerned with the welfare of the shoeshine boys and, in an attempt to save them from the streets, founded the "Shoe-black Brigades."

The Shoe-black Brigades were designed to provide a wholesome environment for shoeshine boys. The boys were dressed in clean clothing and given the opportunity to save some of their earnings. Two-thirds of the boys' earnings were given to the Union, which banked half for the boy and half for the Union's work, while the boys could keep the rest. Reformatory and Refuge Union members provided activities such as reading, playing instruments, and playing cricket. On Sundays, the boys attended worship services together, sang hymns, and read religious tracts. Boys who gained experience in the brigades were also given the opportunity to assume more responsibility, obtain an apprenticeship, or learn a trade. Many boys who belonged to these brigades eventually began their own businesses and became prosperous, responsible citizens.

Jane Polley, ed., *Stories Behind Everyday Things* (Pleasantville, NY: Reader's Digest Association, 1980), 306.

Who was Kemal Ataturk?

Born Mustafa Kemal in 1881 in Turkey, Kemal (1881-1938) adopted the name Ataturk which means "Father of the Turks." Kemal was a fierce military leader, which his triumphs include leading the Young Turks revolt in 1908, that overthrew the sultan, being victorious over the Allied Forces at Gallipoli during World War I; and suppressing Greek invasion of Turkey in 1920. Kemal became president of Turkey in 1923, and transformed the country into a secular state.

Robert H. Ferrell and John S. Bowman, eds., *The Twentieth Century: An Almanac* (New York: World Almanac Publications, 1984), 146.

When was the Sino-Japanese War?

There have been two Sino-Japanese Wars, one waged from 1894-95 and another occurring during 1937-45. The first began in 1894 when the Chinese and Japanese entered southern Korea to restore internal order and gain control. Neither left after the Korean revolt, and in August of the year China and Japan declared war against each other. Japan won the war when China sued for peace in March of 1895. China was forced to cede Formosa and the Pescadores Islands to Japan, recognize the independence of Korea, open ports to Japan, and pay a large war debt.

The second Sino-Japanese War began in 1937 over control of the northeast Chinese province of Manchuria. Japan quickly gained the upper hand by bombing northern Chinese cities. Both the Americans and Russians intervened on behalf of China, affecting greatly the war's outcome. The Japanese surrendered in 1945.

George C. Kohn, *Dictionary of Wars* (New York: Facts on File, 1986), s.v. "Sino-Japanese war of 1894-95."

What was the Trail of Tears?

The Trail of Tears was the route the Chickasaw, Seminole, Cherokee, Creek, and Choctaw were forced to trod to the Oklahoma area when they were evicted from their homelands in the southeastern United States between 1830 and 1842. They had become known as the Five Civilized Tribes because they had lived closely with the white population for over a century and had adopted many of the white people's practices. The journey was arduous and many Indians died along the Trail of Tears.

World Book Encyclopedia (Chicago: World Book, 1987), s.v. "Oklahoma."

Who was President Zachary Taylor's famous son-in-law?

Jefferson Davis (1808-1889), the first and only president of the Confederate States of America, was U.S. president Zachary Taylor's son-in-law. Davis married Taylor's daughter Sarah in 1835; she died of a fever three months later. Zachary Taylor (1784-1850) was president of the United States from 1849 to 1850.

The World Book Encyclopedia (Chicago: World Book, 1987), s.v. "Davis, Jefferson."

What did the nineteenth-century American Zionist Mordecai Manuel Noah try to establish in New York?

Mordecai Manuel Noah (1785-1851), an American Zionist of the nineteenth century, bought a tract of land on Grand Island in the Niagara River near Buffalo, which he wished to turn into a Jewish colony. He named it Ararat and hoped to rule over it. When the colony idea failed, he became a staunch supporter of a Jewish homeland being created in Palestine.

Encyclopaedia Judaica (New York: Macmillan, 1971), s.v. "Noah, Mordecai Manuel."

Who was Cetshwayo and what was role in the Zulu War of 1879?

Cetshwayo (Cetewayo, Ketshwayo) (c. 1832-84) was the last independent king of the Zulu nation in South Africa and a strong and respected military leader of his people. Cetshwayo was the eldest son of the Zulu king Mpande and became the Zulu king following a civil war with his half-brother in 1856 and his father's death in 1872. In 1878 Britain wanted to create a Zululand protectorate in South Africa and issued an ultimatum to that effect. Cetshwayo ignored the ultimatum but soon found himself facing 5,000 British and 8,200 native troops. The Zulu nation was united against the British and Cetshwayo mustered an army of 40,000 warriors. Although they were fierce and disciplined fighters most of the Zulus faced British muskets with only stabbing and throwing spears. After various engagements the war ended on the July 4, 1879 in the Battle of Ulundi, in which 10,000 Zulus were defeated by a smaller but better armed British force of 5,200 men. Cetshwayo was captured and imprisoned in Cape Town. In 1882 he was released from prison and traveled to England where he was surprisingly regarded as a heroic figure. The British government reinstated him as the king of Zululand, but, lacking an effective military force, he was driven out of his capital during a civil war.

R. Ernest Dupuy and Trevor N. Dupuy, *The Encyclopedia of Military History: from 3500 B.C. to the Present, 2d ed.* (New York: Harper & Row, 1986), 850-51. Mark R. Lipschutz and R. Kent Rasmussen, *Dictionary of African Historical Biography* (Berkeley: University of California Press, 1986), s.v. "Cetshwayo."

In the antebellum South what was the first state to secede from the Union?

In the antebellum South the first state to secede from the Union was South Carolina on December 20, 1860; followed by Mississippi, January 9, 1861; Florida, January 10, 1861; Alabama, January 11, 1861; Georgia, January 19, 1861; Louisiana, January 26, 1861; Texas, March 2, 1961; Virginia, April 17, 1861; Arkansas, May 8, 1861; North Carolina, May 20, 1861; and Tennessee, June 8, 1861. The slave states of Delaware, Kentucky, Maryland, and Missouri remained in the Union.

Information Please Almanac Atlas & Yearbook 1994, 47th ed. (Boston: Houghton Mifflin, 1994), 628.

Who faced each other at the legendary "Gunfight at O.K. Corral"?

The legendary "Gunfight at O.K. Corral" pitted the Earp brothers, Wyatt, Virgil, and Morgan, and John H. "Doc" Holliday against the Clanton-McLowery Gang of rustlers and outlaws. The gang consisted of Ike and Billy Clanton, Frank and Tom McLowery, and Billy Claiborne. After the dust settled and the shooting ended, Morgan and Virgil Earp and "Doc" Holliday were wounded. Tom and Frank McLowery and Billy Clanton were dead; Billy Claiborne, although wounded, fled with Ike Clanton. Morgan Earp later died at the hands of Clanton gunmen. The gunfight erupted on October 26, 1881 in Tombstone, Arizona.

Jay Robert Nash, *Encyclopedia of Western Lawmen & Outlaws* (New York: Paragon House, 1992), s.v. "O.K. Corral."

What was the peak decade of Italian immigration to the United States?

In the decade 1901-1910, 2,045,877 Italians emigrated to the United States, more than in any other decade. Between 1821 and 1975, 5,269,992 Italian immigrants came to the United States.

Stephanie Bernardo, *The Ethnic Almanac* (Garden City, NY: Dolphin Books, 1981), 29.

Who was the first chief justice on the U.S. Supreme Court?

The first chief justice to sit on the U.S. Supreme Court was American jurist and statesman John Jay (1745-1829), who served from 1789 to 1795.

Linda S. Hubbard, ed., *Notable Americans: What They Did, from 1620 to the Present, 4th ed.* (Detroit: Gale Research, 1988), 283.

What relative of Napoleon was a member of an American cabinet administration?

After serving one year as U.S. Secretary of the Navy, Charles Bonaparte (1851-1921), a descendant of the French emperor Napoleon Bonaparte (2769-1821), was named U.S. Attorney General by U.S. President Theodore Roosevelt (1858-1919). In 1906 for one historians credit his esteemed ancestor with helping to create the concept of a modern police state in his desire to suppress internal enemies; and the twentieth-century Bonaparte carried on this legacy when he founded the U.S. Federal Bureau of Investigation during his three-year tenure in the Roosevelt Administration.

Charles Mosley, comp., *American Presidential Families* (New York: Macmillan, 1993), 22-23.

What travel agency was hired to take an army to war?

In 1884 the British War Office hired top travel agency Thomas Cook and Son to arrange travel for British troops to the Sudan. General Charles Gordon (1833-1885), stationed in Sudan, had just been attacked by members of a religious leader Mahdi. The travel agency was hired because of its experience booking travel to the Sudan.

Thomas Cook and Son was paid $15 million to get the 18,000 troops and 130,000 tons of supplies to the garrison at Khartoum. A makeshift militia was made from 27 steamboats, 28 ocean liners, 650 sailboats, and 800 whaleboats. Rough waters and a huge waterfall slowed the troops down, and when they arrived in Khartoum, General Gordon and his army were dead.

Irving Wallace, David Wallechinsky, and Amy Wallace, *Significa* (New York:Dutton, 1983), 132-33.

What was the Compromise of 1850?

The Compromise of 1850, also known as the Omnibus Bill (was federal legislation), enacted to balance the interests of slave and free states. Friction between states where slavery was legal and states where slavery was prohibited was increasing. The bill attempted to answer the concerns of both sides, but only did so temporarily.

The bill gave slave owners a better means of recovering slaves with the Fugitive Slave Act of 1850. Abolitionists were appeased by the outlawing of slavery in the District of Columbia and by the admission of California to the Union as a free state. The territories of New Mexico and Utah would be allowed to decide for themselves whether they became free or slave states.

The Guide to American Law: Everyone's Legal Encyclopedia (St. Paul, MN: West, 1983), s.v. "Compromise of 1850.

What did Butler's General Order No. 28 decree?

During the Civil War and the occupation of New Orleans by Union troops, General Benjamin F. Butler (1818-1893) issued Order No. 28 regarding southern women who were disrespectful to the occupying soldiers. The scornful women were to be "treated as women of the town," meaning they were to be treated as prostitutes.

Howard L. Hurwitz, *An Encyclopedic Dictionary of American History* (New York: Washington Square Press, 1968), s.v. "Butler's General Order No. 28."

Was Barbara Frietchie a real person?

John Greenleaf Whittier (1807-92), who penned the famous American Civil War (1861-65) poem, "Barbara Frietchie," claimed that she was a real person and she had waved an American flag while General Stonewall Jackson's troops went through her town of Frederick, Maryland. For years, it was thought that the woman was a literary creation, but in a letter from the author to a Leverett Belknap of Hartford, Connecticut, Whittier emphasized that Frietchie had existed, and that he had met her relations. He added that she was over 90 years old when the Confederate army entered Frederick.

"Barbara Frietchie 'Real,'" *New York Times* 8 January 1923.

Why was Louis XVI executed?

Louis XVI (1754-93) of France was executed during the Terror of the French Revolution, because he was caught up in a period of great historical change that he only dimly perceived. The late eighteenth century has been called the age of democratic revolution and to maintain a monarchy in such an environment would take more skill than he had. He was a weak or average man who was called to the throne when circumstances required a person of outstanding ability. Had he placed himself at the head of the middle class in the early stages of the revolt, he might have been able to lead the nation through a moderate reform that was badly needed. As it was, his indecisiveness cost him allies both among conservatives and revolutionaries, and by preventing France from having any clear direction, Louis aided the more radical elements. He appeared as the man whom no one could trust. Perhaps his attempt to flee the country in July of 1791 was his biggest error. He and his family were captured at Varennes and brought back to Paris as virtual prisoners. Later both he and his wife were convicted of treason and beheaded.

Samuel F. Scott and Barry Rothaus, eds., *Historical Dictionary of the French Revolution, 1789-1799* (Westport, CT: Greenwood Press, 1985), s.v. "Louis XVI."

Who were the *Triumvirate* members that led the attack on the French monarchy in 1789 only to become the monarchy's staunchest defenders in 1791?

A. Barnave (1761-93), A. Duport (1759-98), and A. de Lameth comprised the revolutionary *Triumvirate* that led the attack on the French monarchy in 1789. The *Triumvirs* however had become the monarchy's staunchest defenders by 1791. The conversion was reportedly fueled by Barnave's becoming smitten by the beautiful French queen Marie Antoinette (1755-93).

Samuel F. Scott and Barry Rothaus, *Historical Dictionary of the French Revolution, 1789-1799* (Westport, CT: Greenwood Press, 1985), s.v. "Triumvirate."

Was President Zachary Taylor poisoned?

Amid charges through the years that U.S. president Zachary Taylor (1784-1850) was poisoned by his political opponents, Kentucky medical examiner Dr. George Nichols reported in 1991 that these allegations were untrue. Investigating at the behest of Helene Rufty, a Winston-Salem great-great-great-great granddaughter of "Ol Rough and Ready," Nichols told reporters the exact cause of death cannot be determined but Taylor definitely did not die of poisoning.

"Zachary Taylor's cause of death laid to rest," *Pittsburgh Press* 27 June 1991.

Which U.S. president was embarrassed by a woman's petticoat?

The story of U.S. president William Henry Harrison (1773-1841) and a petticoat continues to puzzle historians. Different accounts assert and deny that the future U.S. president was given a petticoat by disgusted citizens of Chillicothe, Ohio, in criticism of an act of cowardice. The act in question was his 1813 order, as army General to evacuate Fort Stevenson despite threats of a British attack during the War of 1812. The young officer in charge, Major George Croghan, refused and eventually defeated the attacking British troops and their Indian allies. When Whig Party candidate Harrison was on the presidential campaign trail 23 years later, the petticoat reference resurfaced in the town of Bedford, Ohio. Harrison's visit in the county generated a political frenzy between his followers and supporters of his Democratic Party opponent Martin Van Buren (1782-1862). Insults from Harrison supporters prompted members of the opposing party to mimic the candidate's red and white flag by flying a red petticoat from a pole. In response, the Harrison party stormed up with ax in hand, ready to cut down the offending petticoat. Fortunately calmer heads managed to keep the incident from going any further.

Ned Frear, "The Political Incident," *Bedford Gazette* 13 October 1976.

Did the incompetence of the Chicago fire department contribute to the extent of the damage during the great fire of 1871?

Although there were some mistakes, the Chicago fire department performed quite admirably during the great fire of 1871. It was led by Canadian-born Robert A. Williams. The husky six-footer joined the department as a volunteer in 1848, and by the time he was 45 he had risen through the ranks to become Chicago's Chief Fire Marshal. He was a competent leader, but his department was inadequately equipped to fight a fire of that magnitude. Before the conflagration, he had repeatedly asked the city council for more men and equipment but was turned down. The council even refused a fire boat for the Chicago river—a horrendous oversight, since the river flowed directly through the city and was spanned by wooden bridges.

A fire brigade arrived at the scene shortly after the fire started, but one company was not enough to contain it. Because of faulty wiring in an alarm box, reinforcements did not arrive until the fire was out of control. When a fire watcher in the courthouse tower spotted the blaze, he inadvertently gave the wrong location. He soon recognized his mistake, but since the fire operator refused to send out a second message, every other fire company in the city went to the wrong place. This was the most serious blemish on a department that generally worked with great courage and dedication.

Robert Cromie, *The Great Chicago Fire* (New York: McGraw-Hill, 1958), 17. *Dictionary of American History* (New York: Charles Scribner's Sons, 1976), s.v. "Chicago fire."

Who designed the Confederate flag?

The Confederate flag known as "Stars and Bars," a bold "x" of stars and bars on a solid background, was designed by the Confederate General Pierre Gustave Toutant Beauregard. While it was never the official flag of the Confederate government, it was used by its soldiers beginning in 1861. The flag has since become a controversial symbol, used by a political party and by several southern states. The States' Rights Democratic Party took the flag as its official symbol in 1948. The state of South Carolina was criticized for flying the original flag over its state house, while Mississippi and Georgia used the design as part of their official state flags. For some Americans, the flag cannot be disassociated with slavery; they consider it a symbol of racism.

U.S. News & World Report 15 August 1994.

What was Robert E. Lee's horse's name?

Confederate General Robert E. Lee (1807-70) actually had two horses for the duration of the war. The most famous of these was Traveller, purchased in 1861, who stayed with the General for the entire Civil War. Traveller was sixteen hands high (a commonly used equine measurement), a dark iron-gray in color, and was five years old. After the surrender of the Confederate Army at Appomattox in 1865, Lee slowly rode past his troops on Traveller. Those soldiers too emotionally distraught to verbally console the General simply patted the horse as it strode by. It is reported that Traveller was acting happy and excited that day, swaying his head and tail constantly, enjoying all of the attention he was receiving.

After the war, Lee became president of Washington College (later known as Washington and Lee University). Lee rode on Traveller to the college in Lexington, Virginia, and students and visitors would often see him riding Traveller on the campus or witness the horse grazing on the front lawn of the college president's residence. During the post-war years, Traveller's coat grew to a milky-white color, and he became edgy around people due to souvenir hunters plucking hairs from his mane. Lee died in 1870, and Traveller died soon after from lockjaw caused by stepping on a nail which could not be removed. Traveller's remains were buried near the tomb of Robert E. Lee on the college campus.

The second, lesser known horse of Robert E. Lee was a dark-haired mare named Lucy Long. However, it is Traveller that is the more famous of the two, often appearing with Lee in many period paintings and photographs. In 1988, Richard Adams wrote *Traveller: A Novel*, a fictional account of Robert E. Lee's days as a Civil War general through the eyes of his horse.

A.L. Long, *Memoirs of Robert E. Lee* (New York: J. M. Stoddart, 1886), 131-33. Ruthven Tremain, *The Animals' Who's Who* (New York: Charles Scribner's Sons, 1982), s.v. "Traveller."

What is inscribed on George Washington's coffin?

On the first U.S. president's coffin are two inscriptions. At the head of the mahogany coffin is the inscription *Surge Ad Judicium* (Fly to Justice). *Gloria Deo* (Glory Be to God) was inscribed in the middle of the coffin of George Washington (1732-1799). There is also a silver plate with the inscription "General/George Washington/departed this life on the 14th of December/1799, aged 68."

Robert B. Dickerson, Jr., *Final Placement: A Guide to the Deaths, Funerals, and Burials of Notable Americans* (Algonac, MI: Reference Publications, 1982), s.v. "Washington, George."

What was the origin of the Ku Klux Klan?

In 1865 or 1866 six young Confederate veterans of the American Civil War (1861-65) with little to do in Pulaski, Tennessee, decided to establish a secret club to relieve their boredom. They altered the Greek word "kuklos" (circle) and added "klan" to form the name, the ghostly sound of which inspired the white gowns and tall conical hats associated with the group. The club at first engaged only in horseplay and practical jokes, with secret initiations of new members a focal point of its activities. As the Klan expanded in number of members and spread to nearby counties and states, it soon developed into a means of controlling the newly freed slaves.

David M. Chalmers, *Hooded Americanism* (New York: Doubleday, 1965), 8-9. Wyn Craig Wade, *The Fiery Cross: The Ku Klux Klan in America* (New York: Simon & Schuster, 1987), 32-37.

Who were the longest-living Confederate and Union soldiers from the American Civil War?

On August 2, 1956, Albert Woolson, last survivor of the American Civil War's Union Army, died at the age of 109. He had been a drummer and bugler boy.

The last surviving Confederate veteran, Walter Williams, died at the age of 117 on December 19, 1959. Shortly before his death doubts were cast on his claim that he served in the war as a foragemaster. The next-to-last survivor was John B. Salling, who died at the age of 112 on March 16, 1959. Salling enlisted at 15 years of age and spent the war as a member of Company D, 25th Virginia Regiment, mining saltpeter for making ammunition.

Facts On File 1-7 August 1956. *Facts On File* 12-18 March 1959. *Facts On File* 17-23 December 1959.

1918 to present

Who coined the expression "Cold War"?

For most of the latter half of the twentieth century, the United States and the Soviet Union were adversaries. Although the differences between the two countries never erupted into an actual war, there was a constant feeling of tension and a buildup of conventional and nuclear weapons. The conflict between the Soviet Union and the United States was often referred to as the "Cold War."

Bernard Baruch, an American millionaire and advisor to U.S. presidents, used the expression "cold war." He introduced the term in a speech to the South Carolina legislature on April 16, 1947, when he said "Let us not be deceived-we are today in the midst of a cold war." However, in 1961, Baruch credited

Herbert Bayard Swope, a noted American journalist, as the originator of the phrase.

New York Times 1 June 1961. Alan Palmer and Veronica Palmer, *Quotations in History* (Sussex, UK: Harvester Press, 1976), s.v. "Baruch, Bernard."

What was designated by the World War II code names Rankin A, Rankin B, and Rankin C?

The code names Rankin A, Rankin B, and Rankin C were used during World War II (1939-45) by the Allied Forces. Rankin A was a contingency plan to be used in the event that Germany's military or economic situation deteriorated before the Allied Operation Overlord could be enacted. It called for an attack on the Cotentin peninsula or the Normandy coast, as well as landings in Pas-de-Calais or the south of France.

In the event that the Germans should evacuate their forces from occupied Europe, the Allies devised the plan known as Rankin B. This scenario called for the invasion of France at the Cotentin peninsula and landings in the south of France.

Rankin C was a plan to be used in the event of German surrender. It specified that U.S. troops should move into France, Belgium, and southern Germany, while British troops moved into northern Germany and the rest of Europe.

Christopher Chant, *The Encyclopedia of Codenames or World War II* (London: Routledge & Kegan Paul, 1986), s.v. "Rankin A," "Rankin B," "Rankin C."

How many people were killed when the atomic bombs were dropped on the Japanese cities of Hiroshima and Nagasaki?

There is a great deal of debate regarding the number of persons killed in the atomic bombings of Hiroshima and Nagasaki in August of 1945 by the United States. According to the Japanese Welfare Ministry, 260,000 persons died in Hiroshima. This figure differs sharply from the casualty figures issued by U.S. General MacArthur's headquarters, which estimated the death toll in Hiroshima at 78,150. The Atomic Bomb Casualty Commission placed the death toll in Hiroshima at 79,000.

There is more agreement regarding the death toll in the Nagasaki bombing. The Japanese Welfare Ministry stated that 73,884 persons died in Nagasaki. The official American figure also is 73,884 dead. However, the Atomic Bomb Casualty Commission listed the number of those killed in Nagasaki at only 15,220.

"U.S., Japan Differ on Atom Deaths," *New York Times* 3 May 1961.

On what date did the United States recognize Bosnia's independence?

Bosnia declared its independence from Yugoslavia on February 29, 1992, and the United States formally recognized Bosnia on April 7, 1992.

"As War Intensified, So Did Pressure on Serbs," *USA Today* 6 May 1993.

How far did the bullet that killed President John F. Kennedy travel?

Many questions remain regarding the assassination of U.S. President John F. Kennedy (1917-1963). Among the questions raised concerns the distance the bullet that killed President Kennedy travelled. Experts theorize that the bullet fired from the window of the Texas Book Depository building to the Kennedy motorcade travelled between 176.9 feet and 190.8 feet.

The President's Commission on the Assassination of President John F. Kennedy, *Report of the President's Commission on the Assassination of President John F. Kennedy* (Washington, DC: Government Printing Office, 1964), 102-3, 105.

Was there an attempt on Franklin D. Roosevelt's life?

On February 15, 1933, Joseph Zangara (1902-33) attempted to murder President Franklin Delano Roosevelt (1882-1945) on the streets of Miami. The unemployed New Jersey mill hand was influenced by radical political ideas and frustrated by the limited work opportunities in a country that was gripped by a depression. Zangara decided to kill the president when he read that Roosevelt and the mayor of Chicago, Anton J. Cermak (1873-1933), would be visiting Miami, a city in which he himself had just recently arrived in a futile attempt to find a job. Pushing people out of the way as the president's open car was slowed by the press of a crowd, Zangara began to fire wildly when he was about eight feet from the vehicle. Although he missed Roosevelt, he wounded two bystanders and killed Cermak. The assassin was quickly put on trial and executed about five weeks after he committed the crime.

Jay Robert Nash, *Bloodletters and Badmen: A Narrative Encyclopedia of American Criminals from the Pilgrims to the Present* (New York: M. Evans, 1973), s.v. "Zangara, Joseph."

By what name is the Belgian Congo now known?

The name of the Belgian Congo was changed to Zaire in 1971.

World Book Encyclopedia (Chicago: World Book, 1987), s.v. "Zaire."

Why did Spiro Agnew resign as vice president?

Spiro Agnew, vice president under U.S. President Richard M. Nixon (1913-1994), resigned his post on October 10, 1973, in a plea bargain after pleading "no contest" to charges of income tax evasion. At the time, he was under investigation for receiving bribes from contractors during his tenure as governor of Maryland. Along with the resignation, he agreed to pay a $10,000 fine and $150,000 in back taxes. The Justice Department agreed not to prosecute Agnew for taking bribes.

Two days after Agnew's resignation, President Nixon nominated Gerald R. Ford (1913-) for the office of vice president.

Michael Nelson, ed., *The Presidency A to Z: A Ready Reference Encyclopedia* (Washington, DC: Congressional Quarterly, 1992), s.v. "Agnew, Spiro T."

What American city has the nickname "Porkopolis"?

During the 1800s, Cincinnati, Ohio, was a major center for the slaughter of pigs, with over a quarter of a million hogs killed in the city's slaughterhouses. This earned Cincinnati the nickname "Porkopolis." While many Cincinnati residents are proud of their city's heritage as "Porkopolis," others are not as enamored of the image. During Cincinnati's 200th anniversary celebration in 1988, a sculpture featuring four winged swine was unveiled, arousing some controversy.

New York Times 11 July 1988.

How many people were killed under Stalin's rule in the U.S.S.R.?

In bloody purges during the Russian dictator, Joseph Stalin's (1879-1953) rule, approximately 15 to 16 million Soviets died.

Records of the dead are not accurate because birth and death registrations were disrupted during that time.

The death toll includes figures from the 1932 famine, the land collectivization and the massacre of kulaks during 1929-1937 and the reign of terror that started in 1934 to eliminate all party opposition to Stalin's policies

Warren Shaw and David Pryce, *The World Almanac of the Soviet Union: From 1905 to the Present* (New York: World Almanac, 1990), 107.

How did the murder of Sergei Kirov precipitate the Great Purge?

The murder of Sergei Kirov, an influential member of the Politburo of the Soviet Union, served as a catalyst for the Soviet dictator Joseph Stalin (1879-1953) to begin the "Great Purge." Kirov's murder was blamed on a young party member, but historians theorize that Stalin himself was responsible for the assassination. He did it to provide a reason to eliminate all of his political opposition. Stalin investigated Kirov's murder, and then issued a decree stating that those accused of "acts of terror" were to be arrested, judged, and killed with all due speed. Almost instantly thousands were arrested and killed in the major cities, most with only the most summary trial. Stalin's purge soon spread to the military, the provinces, and the police and did not end until 1938.

Warren Shaw and David Pryce, *The World Almanac of the Soviet Union: From 1905 to the Present* (New York: World Almanac, 1990), 102-6.

Why did Stalin eliminate the kulaks?

In 1927 when only two percent of the Soviet land was collectivized, Stalin (1879-1953) decided drastic measures were needed to carry out this basic communist principle. Stalin decided to eliminate the kulaks—peasants who were wealthy enough to hire permanent workers; they also own industrial businesses, hire out their machinery, and be involved in usury. Stalin charged kulaks as being anti-communist, and began to arrest or deport them, and seize their lands. During this period about four and one-half million people were affected. Stalin then targeted the whole peasant class during 1930-32 with the result that ten million were exiled to Siberia and the disruption to agriculture led to the great famine of 1932. The collectivization of land continued aggressively until 1937 when 93 percent of the land was state-owned. During that time period 1930-37, it is estimated that 11 million peasants were killed and 3.5 million later died in Siberian camps. The greatest number of deaths—five million—occurred in the wheat-growing area of the Ukraine.

Warren Shaw and David Pryce, *The World Almanac of the Soviet Union: From 1905 to the Present* (New York: World Almanac, 1990), 8, 107.

When did the first official contact occur between the Japanese and Americans at Pearl Harbor?

At 3:42 a.m. on December 7, 1941, Ensign R.C. McCloy of the mine sweeper *Condor* was the first American to spot a Japanese submarine before the attack on the American naval base at Pearl Harbor, Hawaii. McCloy saw a white wave near his ship and reported it, however, the submarine avoided detection after that sighting.

Timothy B. Benford, *The World War II Quiz & Fact Book* (New York: Harper & Row, 1982), 183.

Where did President Clinton get his name?

U.S. President Clinton (1946-) was born William Jefferson Blythe. His natural father was a young salesman who died in an automobile accident before the future president was born. When young Bill Blythe was 15, he legally changed his name out of respect for his mother and stepfather, Roger Clinton.

Lance Morrow, "The Strange Burden of a Name," *Time* 8 March 1993.

Who was Thomas Eagleton?

Democrat Thomas Eagleton (1929-) was a senator from Missouri for three terms (1968-87), but he is probably best known for the short period when he was George McGovern's (1922-) running mate in the 1972 presidential elections. Although this Harvard Law School graduate was highly qualified, he neglected to tell McGovern that he had been hospitalized three times in the 1960s for psychiatric treatment of fatigue and depression. When this information became widely known, McGovern, after vacillating for a while, asked him to resign and chose R. Sargent Shriver, Jr., as his new vice-presidential nominee.

Michael Nelson, ed., *The Presidency A to Z* (Washington, DC: Congressional Quarterly, 1992), s.v. "Eagleton, Thomas F."

What was D-Prime?

D-Prime was a civil defense evacuation plan from the 1970s that would enable urban residents to evacuate the cities and find shelter in the countryside in case of an imminent nuclear attack. Its supporters argued that the proposal could save as many as 60 million lives, but its opponents countered that it would be very expensive and produce little positive effect.

Susan Fraker and David C. Martin, "Operation Get-Out-Town," *Newsweek* 27 November 1978.

What were the names of Lyndon B. Johnson's beagles?

U.S. president Lyndon B. Johnson's (1908-73) beagles were called Him and Her.

Margaret Truman, *White House Pets* (New York: David McKay, 1969), 174.

What was the Afghan War of 1979?

The Soviet Union invaded the Republic of Afghanistan in December of 1979. Afghanistan rebelled against the attempt to westernize of the region, a stronghold of Muslim faith. The Afghan troops employed fierce guerrilla tactics to repress the Soviets, but were foiled by their own inter-tribal factionalism.

George C. Kohn, *Dictionary of Wars* (New York: Facts on File, 1986), s.v. "Afghan Civil War of 1979-."

What is the U.S. historical date which will live in infamy?

The U.S. historical date which will live in infamy is December 7, 1941, the day of the Japanese attack on the U.S. naval base at Pearl Harbor, Hawaii. The following day, U.S. President Franklin D. Roosevelt (1882-1945) in a speech to Congress asked for a declaration of war against Japan. Roosevelt said, "Yesterday, December 7, 1941—a date which will live in infamy—the United States of American was suddenly and deliberately attacked by naval and air forces of the Empire of Japan.

Hostilities exits . . . . " Roosevelt's speech, six minutes in its entirety, was written without the help of speechwriters.

Elizabeth Frost, ed., *The Bully Pulpit, Quotations from America's Presidents* (New York: New England Publishing Associates, 1988), 259. *Safire's Political Dictionary* (New York: Random House, 1978), 157.

Who was the president of South Korea during the Korean War?

Syngman Rhee (1875-1965) was the controversial president of South Korea during the Korean Conflict. Born in the village of Pyong-san he was educated in Seoul and, while employed as an English instructor, became enamored with the philosophy of the Western Enlightenment and participated in various democratic reform movements. Rhee traveled to the United States in 1905 and eventually received a doctorate in political science from Princeton University in 1910. He became active in international political circles and was highly regarded by conservative politicians and military officers in the United States. Following World War II (1939-45) Rhee returned to Korea and in 1948 was elected chairman of the Korean National Assembly, which soon elected him President of the Korean Republic. In 1950, however, when North Korea invaded South Korea Rhee's government turned autocratic and Korea's capital Pusan was placed under marshal law. In 1952 Rhee was elected president of Korea by popular vote, but following the truce of 1953 his regime continued down its anti-democratic path. In 1960 the Korean military remained neutral during a massive student uprising and Rhee was forced to resign and flee to Hawaii where he lived in exile until his death in 1965.

McGraw-Hill Encyclopedia of World Biography (New York: McGraw-Hill, 1973), s.v. "Rhee." Harry G. Summers, Jr., *Korean War Almanac* (New York: Facts on File, 1990), s.v. "Rhee, Syngman."

What form of government does Saudi Arabia have?

Saudi Arabia is a monarchy and has no formal governing constitution. The current Kingdom of Saudi Arabia was established in 1932 by King Abdul Aziz al-Saud. Saudi Arabia originated in the mid-eighteenth century out of an alliance between Muhammad al-Saud, ruler of the city-state Diriyah and Muhammad ibn Abdul Wahhab, a strict Sunni Islamic scholar. In 1932 al-Saud declared the unity of the Kingdom of Saudi Arabia following centuries of regional expansion and shifting political alliances. The country today is ruled by members of the Saud family and there are no political parties, trade unions, political debate or organized political opposition. Saudi Arabia does have a "constitution" which is based on the Koran and the precepts of the Prophet Muhammad. The country has an area of 2,150,000 square kilometers and 95 percent of its estimated 9 million inhabitants are Sunni Muslims.

Michael Adams, ed., *The Middle East* (New York: Facts on File, 1988), 110-11. Trevor Mostyn, *The Cambridge Encyclopedia of the Middle East and North Africa* (New York: Cambridge University Press, 1988), s.v. "Saudi Arabia.

What were Argentina's "dirty war" activities?

Following a coup on March 24, 1976 by Argentine armed forces, the government of President Isabel Martinez de Pern was overthrown and an inhumane campaign of "dirty war" activities persisted for the next seven years. While President Pern was held in protective custody, a three-man military junta headed by General Jorge Rafael Videla used ruthless tactics against liberals, leftists, and political terrorists. Dirty war activities included arbitrary arrests, unfair prosecution, kidnapping, torture, and imprisonment without due process or trial. It has been estimated that 6,000 to 15,000 Argentines disappeared from 1976 to 1981.

In response to worldwide shock to the violations of human rights and to the United States' refusal to continue to send military aid, several well-known prisoners were released and permitted to leave the country. Slowly, the dirty war activities decreased. On December 10, 1983, Raul Alfonsin was elected president. He promised to prosecute the former military junta.

George C. Kohn, *Dictionary of Wars* (New York: Facts on File, 1986), s.v. "Argentine 'Dirty War.'"

What is the name of the vessel that rammed and sank PT-109, commanded by Lieutenant John F. Kennedy?

On August 2, 1943, the Japanese destroyer *Amigiri* rammed and sank PT-109, the ship that was commanded by Lieutenant John F. Kennedy.

Fred L. Worth, *The Trivia Encyclopedia* (n.p.: Bell Publishing, 1974).

In the U.S. Constitution, which four things is a president prohibited from accepting without Congressional approval?

According to the U.S. Constitution, there are four things a president cannot accept without Congressional approval. The chief executive, or any other holder of high office, may not "accept of any present, emolument, office, or title, of any kind whatsoever, from any king, prince, or foreign state" without permission from Congress.

World Book Encyclopedia (Chicago: World Book, Inc., 1987), s.v. "Constitution of the United States."

What type of weapon did Lee Harvey Oswald use to kill John F. Kennedy?

Lee Harvey Oswald (1939-63) killed U.S. president John F. Kennedy (1917-63) with a Mannlicher-Carcano 6.5 millimeter Italian rifle he obtained through a mail order supplier advertising in *American Rifleman* magazine. He paid a total of $21.45 for the gun and shipping costs. The scope on the rifle increased the price from $12.78.

The President's Commission on the Assassination of President John F. Kennedy, *Report of the President's Commission on the Assassination of President John F. Kennedy* (Washington, DC: Government Printing Office, 1964), 118-9.

Are any First Lady's homes designated as National Historical Sites?

On October 11, 1984, the centennial of the birth of Eleanor Roosevelt (1884-1962), the occasion was celebrated with the dedication of her home, Val-Kill, in Hyde Park, New York, as a National Historic Site, the only one in the United States to honor a First Lady. Speakers at the dedication pointed out that the former first lady merited the honor not merely as an activist First Lady and the wife of U.S. president Franklin D. Roosevelt (1882-1945), but also as a historic figure in her own right. Val-Kill is a complex of five one-and two-story stucco buildings on 179 acres, surrounded by suburban-style homes.

Harold Faber, "Mrs. Roosevelt's Home Becomes a Historic Site," *New York Times* 12 October 1984.

Who was Felix Houphouet-Boigny?

Ivory Coast president Felix Houphouet-Boigny (1905-1993) was the third longest serving national leader at the time of his death in 1993. The only leaders who had held power longer were Kim Il Sung of North Korea and Fidel Castro of Cuba. Houphouet-Boigny had been in command of the African country for 33 years when he died. He had his life support system shut off after suffering from prostate cancer.

Houphouet-Boigny was a rural doctor and planter before becoming involved in politics. He helped found the African Agricultural Syndicate, which organized native planters in what was then a French colony; the group soon became a political party under his direction. This led to a position in the French National Assembly, and in 1956 Houphouet-Boigny became the first African in the cabinet of French premier Guy Mallet. When the Ivory Coast became independent in 1960, Houphouet-Boigny was named president and continued to rule even after the country changed to a multiparty system in 1990.

Facts on File 16 December 1993.

Who was the first presidential spouse to hold the Bible for her husband as he took the oath of office?

"Lady Bird" (Claudia) Johnson (1912-) was the first presidential spouse to hold the Bible for her husband, president Lyndon B. Johnson (1908-1973) as he took the oath of office. It has become a regular practice since that day in 1965; in prior ceremonies a U.S. Supreme Court clerk held the Bible.

USA Today 21 January 1993.

Which U.S. president was pictured on a coin while still in office?

The American Independence Sesquicentennial half dollar features the overlapping busts of U.S. presidents George Washington (1732-99) and Calvin Coolidge (1872-1933). The coin was issued in 1926, while Coolidge was still in office.

David T. Alexander, ed., *Coin World Comprehensive Catalog & Encyclopedia of United States Coins* (New York: World Almanac, 1990), 267.

Which British author created the character Allan Quartermain?

Allan Quartermain was the main character in many of the adventure novels of British author H. Rider Haggard (1856-1925). Haggard was a prolific writer, whose novels number more than fifty, including *Allen Quartermain*, published in London in 1887.

Leslie Henderson, ed., *Twentieth-Century Romance and Historical Writers* (Chicago: St. James Press, 1990), 296.

What is unique about Heather Whitestone, Miss America of 1994-1995?

Heather Whitestone stands out among other winners of the Miss America contest as the first deaf Miss America. Crowned in the 1994-1995 pageant, Whitestone has been deaf since the age of one and one-half, when she lost her hearing after a diphtheria-pertussis-tetanus shot. She is a symbol of pride for many hearing-impaired people and has shown exceptional grace and skill in her appearances. When, at her first press conference, photographers' flashes interferred with her ability to read a reporter's lips, she simply asked the photographers to pause for a moment. Whitestone speaks as well as signs, having five percent hearing in one ear.

Anita Manning and Tracey Wong Briggs, "Miss America, proud sign for the deaf world," *USA Today* 19 September 1994.

Who was the highest scoring ace of the Vietnam War, with six "kills"?

Air Force weapons systems officer Captain Charles DeBellevue was the highest scoring ace of the Vietnam Conflict. He achieved this status on September 9, 1972, when he destroyed his fifth and sixth MIGs. The fifth "kill" or shootdown gave DeBellevue "ace" status, the sixth gave him the highest number of kills.

Carl Berger, ed., *The United States Air Force in Southeast Asia, 1961-1973: An Illustrated Account, rev. ed.* (Washington, DC: Office of Air Force History, United States Air Force, 1984), 95.

Who were the "Flying Tigers"?

They were members of the American Volunteer Group who were recruited early in 1941 by Major General Claire Lee Chennault (1890-1958) to serve in China as mercenaries. Some 90 veteran United States pilots and 150 support personnel served from December 1941 until June 1942 during World War II. The airplanes they flew were P-40 Warhawks, which had the mouths of tiger sharks painted on the planes' noses. It was from these painted-on images that the group got its nickname "Flying Tigers."

Encyclopedia of Twentieth Century Warfare (New York: Orion, 1989), 159-160.

Was Adolf Hitler's body ever found?

According to most historians the body of German leader Adolf Hitler (1889-1945) was doused with fuel and burned by his SS troops on April 30, 1945, shortly after Hitler committed suicide by a gunshot to the head. The showing of a Russian film in 1992, however, raised the spector that Soviet troops had found the body intact during the fighting in Berlin, Germany. According to Russian historian Lev Bezymensky on May 4, 1945, Soviet troops in an area near Hitler's bunker found the body of a man greatly resembling Hitler and dead of a gunshot wound to the head. The corpse was later identified as someone other than Hitler but not before Soviet authorities had it filmed. The film later was used in a documentary in Moscow alleging to show Hitler's body. A second documentary later corrected the erroneous identification. The first documentary was again shown in 1992-without correction-again raising speculation as to Hitler's remains. Bezymensky asserted that historians and archivists have been aware since 1945 that Hitler's burned remains and those of his wife Eva Braun were found in the Chancellery garden on May 4th (but Eva was found later in the day) and that they were positively identified through dental records. The bodies were eventually buried near Magdeburg. Fragments of Hitler's jaw and skull, however, were reportedly removed to an archive near Moscow.

"Archive corpse picture not of Hitler, historian says," *Detroit Free Press* 18 September 1992.

What well-known American was once sued by Adolf Hitler?

Alan Cranston, who went on to represent California in the U.S. Senate, was once sued by Nazi leader Adolf Hitler (1889-1945) for publishing an unauthorized translation of Hitler's *Mein Kampf.*

Parade 14 July 1985.

What is the *Universal Declaration of Human Rights*?

The *Universal Declaration of Human Rights (UDHR)* was formulated by the United Nations and is based on that organization's mandate to protect and promote human rights. The *UDHR* went into effect in 1948 and is based in part on the 1929 New York Institute of International Law's *Declaration of Human Rights and Duties.* An early draft of the *UDHR* was also submitted to the United Nations Human Rights Commission by the 1945 Inter-American Conference, but while the final version of the *UDHR* enumerates rights, it pays scant attention to "human duties." The *UDHR* is a United Nations General Assembly resolution, not a binding treaty. It has, however, been influential in the formulation of subsequent international law. Since the adoption of the *UDHR* in 1948, the United Nations has also formulated the 1959 *Declaration of the Rights of the Child* and the 1963 *Declaration on Elimination of All Forms of Racial Discrimination.* The *UDHR* enumerates the political, social, and economic rights and freedoms of every person.

Edmund Jan Osmanczyk, *The Encyclopedia of the United Nations and International Agreements* (Philadelphia: Taylor and Francis, 1985), 352.

What American war hero said "Uncommon valor was a common virtue"?

American war hero Admiral Chester W. Nimitz (1885-1966) described the American actions in the 1945 conquest of Iwo Jima as "Uncommon valor was a common virtue." Nimitz was the Commander of the U.S. Pacific fleet during World War II (1939-45), directing the naval campaign against the Japanese. By 1945 the Pacific fleet was in effective control of the waters around Japan, and Nimitz recommended the invasion of Japan's southernmost island Kyyushu. However, the dropping of the two atomic bombs on Hiroshima and Nagasaki abruptly ended the war. Nimitz, acting as the official representative of the U.S. government, accepted and signed the Japanese surrender document aboard the U.S. battleship *Missouri.* General Douglas MacArthur (1880-1964) did the same but as Supreme Commander of the Allied forces.

Timothy Benford, *The World War II Quiz & Fact Book* (New York: Harper & Row, 1982), 60. Anne Commire, ed., *North and South America, vol. 5 of Historic World Leaders* (Detroit: Gale Research, 1994), s.v. "Nimitz, Chester W."

Did President John F. Kennedy have any Protestant relatives by marriage?

U.S. president John F. Kennedy (1917-1963) had Protestant relatives by marriage including his mother-in-law, Janet (Lee) Bouvier and her second husband, Hugh D. Auchinloss.

"GOP Affair At JFK's Home," *Pittsburgh Press* 9 September 1962.

Who is Edvard Shevardnadze?

Soviet diplomat Edvard Amvrosievich Shevardnadze is a former Communist Party politician who was involved in some of the Eastern Bloc's most important events during the late twentieth century. A Georgian by birth, the career politician's name was proposed by political ally and new premier Mikhail Gorbachev (1931-) to become the next foreign minister of the Soviet Union in 1985. During Shevardnadze's tenure he was instrumental in negotiating an end to the Soviet conflict with Afghanistan and in winning the confidence of Western nations. His work in international relations helped smooth the transition from the Soviet Union's traditionally adversarial relationship with the West to one of cooperation and mutual beneficence. More conservative Soviets vilified Shevardnadze for these radical policies, and the foreign minister resigned from his post in late 1990. Over the next few years he continued his role in politics from the sidelines and criticized the leadership of Gorbachev successor Boris Yeltsin (1931-).

Andrew Wilson and Nina Bachkatov, *Russia and the Commonwealth: A to Z* (New York: HarperPerennial, 1992), s.v. "Shevardnadze, Edvard Amvrosievich."

Who is Mikhail Gorbachev?

At the height of the Cold War in the mid-1980s, a new leader came to power in the Soviet Union in the person of Mikhail Gorbachev (1931-), a man who would help to radically transform not only his country but the map of the world as well. Gorbachev rose through the ranks of the local Communist Party in the Stavropol area after receiving his law degree from Moscow State University. In 1971 he was elected to the Central Committee of the Soviet Union, and seven years later took charge of its agricultural department. This was followed by appointments to the Supreme Soviet in 1979 and the Russian Parliament the following year. Deaths in the 1980s of aging Politburo members foretold change and necessitated alliances among the ruling body, and Gorbachev's position within its ranks helped bring about his appointment as General Secretary of the Soviet Union in early 1985. Within a few years of taking office, he introduced a series of political, economic, and social reforms that became known around the world by the terms *glasnost* and *perestroika.* In 1988 he became chair of the Presidium of the Supreme Soviet, and in 1990 the country's first executive president, a newly-created office with augmented powers. More conservative elements within the Communist hierarchy of the country attempted to undermine Gorbachev's liberal policies, and these internecine struggles-compounded by resulting economic hardships due to his fiscal reforms-eventually proved Gorbachev's undoing. The attempted coup against him in August of 1991, adamant desires for independence from the Ukraine and other republics, and finally the popularity of Boris Yeltsin (1931-), all helped force Gorbachev's resignation in the last days of 1991.

Andrew Wilson and Nina Bachkatov, *Russian and the Commonwealth: A to Z* (New York: HarperPerennial, 1992), s.v. "Gorbachev, Mikhail Sergeyerich."

How tall was Adolf Hitler?

During German leader Adolf Hitler's (1889-1945) reign, the diminutive Fuehrer was often made fun of because of his stature. He stood five feet five and a half inches, and was often socially awkward with strangers.

William D. Bayles, *Caesars in Goose Step* (Port Washington, NY: Kennikat Press, 1940), 44.

What were the names of the American and British beaches at the battle of Normandy on D-Day?

The Allied landing in Europe during World War II (1939-45) began on D-Day June 6, 1944, with the invasion targeted at Normandy, France. The Americans landed on two beaches at

Normandy, France on D-Day: Utah and Omaha. The British had three beaches: Gold, Juno, and Sword.

Timothy B. Benford, *The World War II Quiz & Fact Book* (New York: Harper & Row, 1982), 76.

What was the full name of Franklin Roosevelt's dog, Fala?

U.S. President Franklin D. Roosevelt (1882-1945) had a faithful traveling companion in the Scottish terrier Fala, whose full name was Murray the Outlaw of Fala Hill. The dog regularly spent the cocktail hour with Roosevelt and traveled with him, confounding the efforts of the Secret Service to keep the president's whereabouts unknown.

John Gunther, *Roosevelt in Retrospect: A Profile in History* (New York: Harper & Brothers, Publishers, 1950), 92. Niall Kelly, *Presidential Pets* (New York: Abbeville Press Publishers, 1992), 69-70.

What was Franklin D. Roosevelt's "court-packing Plan"?

In response to a series of U.S. Supreme Court decisions that weakened his New Deal legislation, U.S. president Franklin Roosevelt (1882-1945) devised a "court-packing Plan" to turn the court's balance in favor of these economic measures. The plan gave the president power to appoint an additional Federal judge "in the event that a sitting judge who had served for at least ten years at that level neither retired nor resigned within six months of his seventieth birthday." This would allow him to 'pack' the court because six of the nine justices were over seventy.

The "court-packing Plan" was unveiled in February of 1937, and received much opposition from both liberal and conservative members of Congress. Although Roosevelt promoted it as a means to manage the increasing number of cases in the Federal courts, opponents quickly labeled the bill as Roosevelt's response to an uncooperative Supreme Court. The bill was never passed. Meanwhile, the U.S. Supreme Court made decisions in a series of cases upholding New Deal legislation including provisions of the Social Security Act and the National Labor Relations Act.

The Guide to American Law: Everyone's Legal Encyclopedia (St. Paul, MN: West Publishing, 1983), 344-349.

What Russian city was under siege by the Germans for 900 days during World War II?

Leningrad, the old capital of Russia and the second largest city in the Soviet Union after Moscow, was besieged by the Germans for 900 days during World War II (1939-45). The German army surrounded the city in August of 1941 and was completely entrenched until January of 1943. During that time, hundreds of thousands of Russian citizens starved to death inside the city, while Soviet naval units sought to bring in supplies across Lake Ladoga. The siege was not completely lifted until January of 1944, after which Stalin declared Leningrad a "Hero City."

Norman Polmar and Thomas B. Allen, *World War II: America at War, 1941-1945* (New York: Random House, 1991), s.v. "Leningrad."

Where did Howard Hughes die?

The reclusive American billionaire, industrialist and aviator Howard Hughes (1905-76) died April 5, 1976, aboard his private jet that was carrying him from Acapulco to Houston for medical treatment. The immediate cause of death was not apparent. Hughes was 70 years old when he died and was reputed to be worth more than $1.5 billion.

"Howard Hughes Dies at 70 On Flight to Texas Hospital," *New York Times* 5 April 1976.

On what page of the Bible did Franklin Delano Roosevelt place his hand while taking his presidential oath?

While taking the oath as thirty-second U.S. President, Franklin Delano Roosevelt (1882-1945) placed his hand on the page containing the passages of charity (or love) in I Corinthians, chapter 13, in the *Bible*.

Holy Bible: The New King James Version (Nashville: Thomas Nelson Publishers, 1982), 1122-23. *New York Times* 5 March 1933.

Why was the abbey on Mount Cassino bombed by Allied Forces?

The abbey on Mount Cassino in central Italy was filled with ancient treasures. It was also in line with the German Gustav Line in World War II. Thinking it was occupied by the Germans as a key position in their line, the Allies ordered it bombed in February, 1944. Unfortunately, after the beautiful abbey was leveled, it was found out that the Germans had never been there.

Norman Polmar and Thomas B. Allen, *World War II: America at War, 1941-1945* (New York: Random House, 1991), 192.

Who was the last survivor of the 19 German officials convicted at the Trials of Nuremberg?

Rudolf Hess, born in 1894 and once second in the line of succession to Nazi leader Adolf Hitler (1889-1945), was the last surviving member of the group convicted by the International Military Tribunal at Nuremberg. He died in August of 1987, at the age of 93. Tried and convicted in 1946 along with 19 other German officials, Hess received a life sentence for "planning, preparing, initiating or waging aggressive war," but was acquitted of other crimes against humanity and thereby escaped execution. He spent the last twenty years of his life as the only prisoner in West Berlin's Spandau Prison. His prison term was marked by a suicide attempt in 1977, and by a heart ailment.

"Rudolf Hess dies at 93: Last of Hitler Inner Circle," *New York Times* 18 August 1987.

Who were James E. Hair and the Golden Thirteen?

James E. Hair was one of 13 black men known as the Golden Thirteen-the first black sailors to become officers in the U.S. Navy. The grandson of a slave, Hair went on to become the first black officer on the U.S.S. *Mason*, a landing ship manned by an all black crew. After World War II (1939-45), he returned to civilian life, earned a master's degree in social work, and worked in foster care and adoption. Many years later, the Navy asked Hair and others from the group to make public appearances with Navy recruiters. Hair died in 1992 at the age of 76.

The Golden Thirteen were commissioned in 1944, despite handicaps placed on them in officers' training school. The Navy was reluctant to create black officers and only allowed Black candidates under pressure from U.S. president Franklin D. Roosevelt (1882-1945). The candidates were then segregated at the Great Lakes Training Station and given half of the usual time allowed to complete their studies. Working together, the group studied through the nights, testing each other on the material. When the Black candidates scored exceptionally well on their exams, the Navy required that they be retested to prove the authenticity of the results.

Bruce Lambert, "James E. Hair, 76, Naval Officer Whose Unit Broke Color Bar, Dies," *New York Times* 11 January 1992.

What was the "40 Committee"?

Once a U.S. secret organization, the "40 Committee" was a subcommittee of the National Security Council that directed the U.S Central Intelligence Agency in covert foreign operations. The group was responsible for U.S. intervention in Chile during the early 1970s. The existence of such a committee, operating under different names, was started during U.S. president Dwight D. Eisenhower's (1890-1969) administration. It was reorganized by U.S. president John F. Kennedy (1917-63) administration, when it was known as the "303 Committee." Membership generally included the national security advisor, the deputy secretary of defense, the undersecretary of state for political affairs, and the director of the C.I.A. During the presidency of Richard Nixon (1913-1994) the committee ceased to meet regularly, when Henry Kissinger began the practice of individual meetings. The "40 Committee" is said to have been so secret that both U.S. presidents Lyndon B. Johnson (1908-1973) and Gerald Ford (1913-) were unaware of its existence when each served as Vice President.

Thomas B. Ross, "Super-Secret 40 Committee Steers CIA," *Pittsburgh Press* 15 September 1974.

Of what religious and political organization was Marcus Garvey the founder?

Marcus Garvey (1887-1940) was a Jamaican black nationalist leader, who tried to achieve dignity and civil rights for people of African descent by emphasizing pride in race and self-sufficiency in economics. In 1914 he founded the Universal Negro Improvement Association (UNIA), originally called Universal Negro Improvement and Conservation Association and African Communities League, which became the largest African-American social movement in the first half of the twentieth century. UNIA's motto was "One God! One Aim! One Destiny!" All subsequent black nationalist movements have been strongly influenced by his beliefs and practices. By 1935 the movement's popularity diminished.

Charles H. Lippy and Peter W. Williams, eds., *Encyclopedia of the American Religious Experience* (New York: Charles Scribner's Sons, 1988), 2:757-58.

Who was Ho Chi Minh?

Ho Chi Minh (1890-1969) was a Vietnamese patriot and a successful revolutionary who ended his life as president of Communist North Vietnam. During World War II (1939-45) he led the resistance against the Japanese as head of the Viet Minh. When the war was over, he established the republic of Vietnam and conducted a war of independence against France, whose colony was Vietnam. After forcing the French to recognize his control over the northern part of the country, he began a war to incorporate the south, which had been established as an independent republic. This endeavor soon brought him into conflict with the United States, and although his side was eventually successful, he died before the reunification was completed.

Marcel Baudot et al., *The Historical Encyclopedia of World War II* (New York: Facts on File, 1980), s.v. "Ho Chi Minh."

When Rudolf Abel spied on the United States in the early 1950s what was his alias and where did he live?

In the early 1950s, while Soviet spy Rudolf Abel (1902-1971) was living in a shabby studio in Brooklyn Heights, New York, he used the alias "Emil R. Goldfus." Abel was arrested and convicted of espionage in 1957, and in 1962 he was exchanged for Gary Powers, the American pilot of the U-2 spy plane that was shot down over the Soviet Union.

James B. Donovan, *Strangers On A Bridge* (New York: Atheneum, 1964), 24.

Who was Kim Philby?

Kim Philby was a master Soviet spy and double agent who betrayed M.I. 6, the British intelligence agency. Along with Guy Burgess and Donald Maclean, Philby compromised British and American intelligence especially during the Cold War after Philby had risen to a high rank within M.I. 6. In 1951 Philby warned Burgess and Maclean of their imminent exposure and they fled to Moscow. Philby remained a "mole" until 1963 when he also fled eastward just ahead of his captors. H.A.R. (Kim) Philby, the so-called "third man" died in Moscow in 1988 at the age of 76.

Steven Erlanger, "Kim Philby, Who Betrayed Britain As Spy and '3d Man,' Dies at 76," *New York Times* 12 May 1988.

Who was the commander of the *U.S.S. Pueblo*, the American navel ship seized by North Korea in 1968?

When seized by North Korea in 1968, Lloyd M. Bucher was naval commander of the *U.S.S. Pueblo*. The ship and its 82 crewmen were captured in international waters on January 23 and held for 11 months. In 1990, the crew was awarded prisoner of war medals, a reversal of an earlier Pentagon decision that they had been detained and not held prisoner.

"Crew of Ship Seized off Korea In '68 Is Awarded War Medals," *New York Times* 7 May 1990.

What is the origin of Japan's plans for attacking Pearl Harbor?

According to William Honan's 1990 book "The Man Who Knew Too Much: How Hector C. Bywater Invented the Great Pacific War," Japan got the idea to the bomb U.S. naval base at Pearl Harbor from a 1925 novel. The novel charged by Honan with predicting the course of the Pacific war was aptly entitled "The Great Pacific War." Bywater's novel was translated into Japanese and became required reading for Japanese naval officers.

"Book spawned Pearl Harbor attack plan," *Pittsburgh Press* 25 September 1990.

What type of car was President Kennedy riding in on the day he was assassinated?

On the day of his assassination, U.S. president John F. Kennedy (1917-63) was riding in a 1961 Lincoln convertible limousine with two collapsible jump seats between the front and rear seats. Kennedy's limousine had a clear plastic bubble-top that was neither bulletproof nor bullet resistant, and this cover was removed because the weather in Dallas, Texas, on November 22, 1963, was clear and sunny.

President's Commission of the Assassination of President John F. Kennedy, *Report of the President's Commission on the Assassination of President John F. Kennedy* (Washington, DC: Government Printing Office, 1964), 43.

What triggered the Watts riots?

The riot in Watts, a predominantly black, 20-square mile area of Los Angeles, started from a seemingly routine incident. On the evening of August 11, 1965, Watts resident Marquette Frye and his brother Ronald were pulled over by a white California Highway Patrolman on the grounds that they were driving erratically. Frye's mother arrived on the scene and began to yell at her son. Marquette Frye, in turn, began to accuse the police of harassing him. A large crowd gathered quickly and began throwing rocks at the officer. The police radioed for help, and the crowd began to stone other officers arriving at the scene. By ten o'clock that evening, the riot was in full swing and police had cordoned off a 16-block area of Watts in an attempt to stop the rioting. The situation continued to deteriorate, and National Guard troops were brought in. The riot raged on for five days and was finally brought under control on August 16, 1965.

As a result of the Watts riot, 34 people were killed and 874 people injured. Property damage to homes and businesses in Watts and the surrounding area was estimated at over 200 million dollars. The cause of the riot was attributed to hot summer weather, poverty, and increased racial tension between Watts residents and the predominantly white Los Angeles police force.

Lee Davis, *Man-Made Catastrophes: From the Burning of Rome to the Lockerbie Crash* (New York: Facts on File, 1993), 80-81.

Who was Hermann Gring?

Hermann Gring was one of the top leaders in the Nazi party and a close lieutenant of the German leader Adolf Hitler (1889-1945). He was born in Rosenheim, Germany, on January 12, 1893, the son of a Reich commissioner in German Southwest Africa. As a result of his father's influential position, Gring lived a life of privilege and wealth. Gring enlisted in the German army in 1912, but soon left the army to join Germany's new air force.

In 1922, Gring met Adolf Hitler and became a trusted colleague of Hitler using his talents and energy to assist Hitler's rise to power. In 1928, Gring was chosen as a representative for the Nazi party in the Reichstag, Germany's parliament. In 1932, Gring was named president of the Reichstag, and in 1934, supreme commander of the Luftwaffe, Germany's air force.

When World War II began in 1939, Gring's Luftwaffe performed extremely well and contributed greatly to Germany's early victories. In gratitude Hitler named Gring a Reichsmarschall, Germany's highest military rank, in 1940. However, as the war began to go poorly for Germany, Gring's Luftwaffe suffered tremendous losses and Hitler and other top lieutenants began to blame him for Germany's impending defeat. In the final days of the war, Hitler expelled Gring from the Nazi party and ordered his arrest. However, Gring surrendered to Allied forces before this could happen.

During the Nuremburg Trials in 1946, Gring and other top Nazi officials were convicted of war crimes and sentenced to death by hanging. However, on October 15, 1946, Gring committed suicide in prison by swallowing poison.

Christian Zentner and Friedemann Bedurftig, eds., *The Encyclopedia of the Third Reich, trans. Amy Hackett* (New York: Macmillan, 1991), s.v. "Gring, Hermann."

What was China's Gang of Four?

The Gang of Four, which supported a policy of strict Marxism and continuous revolution, consisted of Jiang Qing, Wang Hongwen, Yao Wenyuan, and Zhang Chungqiao. Jiang Qing, the wife of Mao Zedong (1893-1976), China's top political leader, was the leader of a radical political faction, members of which supported Mao during the Cultural Revolution in China from 1966 to 1969. Losing their struggle for power after the deaths of Mao and Chou En-lai (1898-1976), their moderate opponents charged them with treason in 1980. All four were convicted, with Jiang and Zhang receiving death sentences, which were later suspended; Wang, life imprisonment; and Yao, a 20-year sentence. Their failure signified the movement of China toward the West and away from the values of the Cultural Revolution.

Chris Cook, *Dictionary of Historical Terms: A Guide to Names and Events of over 1,000 Years of World History* (New York: Peter Bedrick Books, 1983), s.v. "gang of four." *The World Book Encyclopedia* (Chicago: World Book, 1986), s.v. "Jiang Qing."

What was the Chinese "Cultural Revolution"?

Since 1949, China has been ruled by a Communist government. In 1966 China's leader, Mao Tse-tung (1893-1976), decided to encourage China's young people to maintain the values of radical egalitarianism and to root out elitism, revisionism, and bourgeois mentality in Chinese society, especially in Chinese cultural institutions. Mao called this endeavor the Great Proletarian Cultural Revolution. Young people throughout China were encouraged to gather in China's capital, Beijing, to attend political rallies. Hundreds of thousands of young, militant men and women heeded Mao's call and assembled in Beijing. They marched in massive parades in Beijing's Tiananmen Square to declare their devotion to Mao, carried posters and placards denouncing his enemies, and pledged allegiance to China's Communist government.

The fervor of these young militants, known as Red Guards, soon turned violent. They destroyed historical art and relics, burned books, and accused intellectuals of treason against Mao. Many intellectuals and other innocent people were arrested, held without trial, and forced to confess to alleged crimes. As many as 400,00 people were murdered. Throughout China, factions of Red Guards began to fight each other. Economic activity throughout the country was disrupted and schools were closed. Eventually, Mao authorized the creation of Revolutionary Committees in an attempt to restore order. The Committees consisted of peasant workers, representatives from the army, and more rational Red Guards. Eventually, the violence and chaos was brought under control. Schools were reopened in 1969 and universities resumed classes one year later. The movement along with the Red Guards came to an end when Mao died in 1976.

George C. Kohn, *Dictionary of Wars* (New York: Facts on File, 1986), 107-8. Hugh O'Neill, *Companion to Chinese History* (New York: Facts on File, 1987), 253.

Who was Ivan D. Chernyakhovski?

Ivan D. Chernyakhovski (1906-1945) was one of the Soviet Union's most distinguished generals during World War II (1939-45). As commander of the Third Byelorussian Army, Chernyakhovski rallied his troops to retake the strategic Soviet cities of Vilna, Grodno, Minsk, and Kiev from German defenders. In 1945, he was killed in combat during the later stages of the war. He was awarded the Soviet Union's highest military honor, Hero of the Soviet Union, and a town was named in his honor.

Martin H. Greenberg, *The Jewish Lists: Physicists and Generals, Actors and Writers, and Hundreds of Other Lists of Accomplished Jews* (New York: Schocken Books, 1979), 33.

Who imitated his father by becoming lord mayor of Dublin?

In July of 1988, Ben Briscoe was elected lord mayor of Dublin, Ireland. His father, Robert Briscoe, had been elected lord mayor of Dublin in 1956. It was the first time in Dublin's history that a father and son both held the position of lord mayor.

"Son takes the office Dad won in 1956," *Pittsburgh Press* 5 July 1988.

Which Russian spy was exchanged in 1962 for American pilot Francis Gary Powers?

In May of 1960, American pilot Francis Gary Powers' U-2 airplane was shot down over the Soviet Union during a spy mission. Powers was imprisoned in the Soviet Union until 1962, when he was handed over to U.S. authorities in exchange for Colonel Rudolf Abel (1902-1971). Abel was a convicted Soviet spy who was serving a 30-year prison term for espionage.

"Soviet Rebuffed on Berlin In Effort to Curb Flights," *New York Times* 10 February 1962. "Kennedy Invoked Old Pardon Right," *New York Times* 11 February 1962.

Who was the first woman Speaker of the House in a state legislature?

The first woman Speaker of the House in a state legislature was Minnie Davenport Craig of North Dakota. She achieved the position in 1933.

John Wagman, *On This Day In America* (New York: Gallery Books, 1990), s.v. "January 3."

Where was the labor and political leader Eugene Debs residing when he polled nearly a million votes in the 1920 presidential elections?

Labor and political leader Eugene Debs (1855-1926) was occupying a jail cell in 1920 when he polled nearly a million votes as the Socialist candidate for U.S. President. Debs was convicted of violating the Sedition Act in 1918, and was sentenced to ten years in jail. He later was pardoned by U.S. President Warren Harding (1865-1923) in 1921.

Ted Yanak and Pam Cornelison, *The Great American History Fact-Finder* (Boston: Houghton Mifflin, 1993), s.v. "Debs, Eugene."

What battleships were in Pearl Harbor on December 7, 1941, during the surprise Japanese attack?

During the surprise December 7, 1941 Japanese attack on Pearl Harbor the battleships docked there were the *Arizona, Utah, California, West Virginia, Oklahoma, Pennsylvania, Tennessee, Maryland,* and *Nevada.* Although all battleships but the *Tennessee* were damaged-the *Tennessee* was hit by two bombs that failed to explode-all but the *Arizona, Utah* and *Oklahoma* were salvaged and returned to duty. This attack began the U.S. involvement into World War II (1939-45), when on the following day the United States declared war on Japan.

Norman Polmar and Thomas B. Allen, *World War II: America at War, 1941-1945* (New York: Random House, 1991), 632.

What happened to the U.S. Cruiser *Indianapolis* during World War II?

The U.S. Cruiser *Indianapolis* was the last major U.S. warship sunk during World War II (1939-45). The *Indianapolis* was torpedoed by a Japanese submarine while en route to Okinawa, after having delivered atomic bomb parts to a U.S. facility at Tinian. The cruiser sank within two minutes of being hit and only 318 of her 1,199 crew members were saved. Many of the crew survived the sinking only to die of shark attacks before they could be rescued.

Norman Polmar and Thomas B. Allen, *World War II: America at War 1941-1945* (New York: Random House, 1991), s.v. "Indianapolis (CA35)."

What was the Maginot Line?

The Maginot Line was a string of fixed French fortifications, mostly underground, along the French-German frontier between Switzerland and Belgium. Built in the decades prior to World War II (1939-45), the Maginot Line was named after Andr Maginot, the French Minister of War from 1929 to 1931 and was meant to protect France from German invasion. In June of 1940, however, the Germans invaded through the city of Sedan on the French-Belgium border. The Maginot Line was not only a victim of geography, but also the unremitting belief in France that the Line by itself would deter German aggression.

Louis L. Snyder, *Louis L. Snyder's Historical Guide to World War II* (Westport CT: Greenwood Press, 1982), s.v. "Maginot Line."

What Warren Commission member was charged with leaking information to the Federal Bureau of Investigation about the inquest into the assassination of U.S. president John F. Kennedy?

Researcher Mark Lane charged Gerald R. Ford (1913-), a member of the Warren Commission appointed by the U.S. president Lyndon B. Johnson (1908-1973) to investigate the 1963 Kennedy assassination, with leaking information to the U.S. Federal Bureau of Investigation. Lane asserted that Ford—who succeeded to the Presidency himself in 1974—covertly supplied confidential information to the agency during the Commission's inquiries.

James P. Duffy and Vincent L. Ricci, *The Assassination of John F. Kennedy: A Complete Book of Facts* (New York: Thunder's Mouth Press, 1992), s.v. "Ford, Gerald."

What incident put Alamogordo, New Mexico, in the history books?

Alamogordo, New Mexico, has the claim in the history books as being the site of the first atomic explosion. American scientific and military personnel detonated the newly developed device on July 16, 1945. The success of the test made possible the bombing of Hiroshima and Nagasaki, Japan, a few weeks later in the final days of World War II (1939-45).

World Book Encyclopedia (Chicago: World Book, 1987), s.v. "Atomic Bomb."

Was the U.S. mainland ever attacked by the Japanese during World War II?

During World War II (1939-45) the mainland was attacked four times by the Japanese in three different operations. On November 3, 1944, as part of operation "Flying Elephant," the Japanese launched a large number of bomb-bearing balloons toward America's Pacific Northwest. It is believed that nearly

1,000 of the bombs reached the mainland. One of the bombs killed six members of a family on a picnic near Bly, Oregon, in early May of 1945. The picnickers evidently found the unexploded bomb in the woods.

On September 9 and 29, 1942, a warplane piloted by Nobuo Fujita was launched from the Japanese submarine *I-25* making two incendiary raids on an Oregon forest. The plane was an E14Y1, a two-seat, single engine float plane with folding wings designed to be carried, launched and subsequently recovered by a submarine. The E14Y1 was able to carry two 110 pound bombs. Fujita was the only Axis pilot to bomb the United States mainland during World War II.

The coast of Oregon was also targeted when a Japanese submarine fired on Fort Stevens, an old military post near Warrenton. Although the for's old guns were inadequate in responding to the attack, the submarine soon left the area. These operations had no discernible effect on the American war effort.

Thomas Parrish, *The Simon and Schuster Encyclopedia of World War II* (New York: Simon and Schuster, 1978), s.v. "Balloon bomb," "E14Y1," "Flying Elephant," "Fujita Nobuo." Simon Welfare and John Fairley, *The Cabinet of Curiosities* (New York: St. Martin's Press, 1991), 26-27.

When did the former first lady Nancy Reagan marry Ronald Reagan?

Former First Lady Nancy Reagan was born Anna Frances Robbins on July 6, 1923. Nancy was a nickname. Her parents separated at the time of her birth and her mother, Edith Robbins, left Nancy in the care of her aunt so that she could earn a living as an actress. In 1929 Robbins remarried and several years later Nancy was legally adopted by her stepfather, Dr. Loyal Davis. As Nancy Davis, she was introduced to an affluent life-style in Chicago, where she attended Girls' Latin School. As a college student at Smith College, Davis studied acting and graduated with a B.A. degree in 1943. After several years of stage work with touring companies and on Broadway, she signed a contract with MGM Studios. When Davis had been living in Hollywood for about a year, she was shocked to find that her name was on a list identifying Communist sympathizers. Inquiries proved that there was another Nancy Davis with whom she had been confused. In the process of uncovering the mistake, however, she met Ronald Reagan (1911-), then the president of the Screen Actors Guild.

Davis married Ronald Reagan on March 4, 1952. Subsequently, she appeared in a few movies and television programs, but eventually she left acting to be a homemaker and mother. She gave birth to two children, Patricia Ann in 1954 and Ronald Prescott in 1958. Ronald Reagan became politically active in the Republican Party in 1960 and in 1966 was elected Governor of California. Nancy Reagan showed a special interest in the plight of Vietnam Conflict veterans and she supported the Foster Grandparent Program.

Her husband was elected U.S. President in 1980; as First Lady, she continued to promote the Foster Grandparent Program as well as to draw attention to the problem of juvenile drug abuse.

Charles Moritz, ed., *Current Biography Yearbook, 1982* (New York: H.W. Wilson, 1982), s.v. "Nancy Reagan."

Which American General replied to a German surrender demand with a single word, "Nuts"?

General Anthony Clement McAuliffe (1898-1975) is remembered for his reply of "Nuts" to a German surrender demand during World War II (1939-45). Promoted to Brigadier General in 1942, McAuliffe was given command of the 101st Airborne Division's artillery operations, where he gave evidence of his rugged determination. In April, 1944, while preparing for the Allied invasion of Europe, McAuliffe broke his back during a parachute exercise, but by June he had recovered and jumped with his troops over Normandy as part of *Operation Overlord*.

As the allies advanced across France and into Holland and Belgium, the Germans launched a massive counter-offensive, which began the decisive *Battle of the Bulge*. Although McAuliffe rushed with reinforcements to Bastogne, Belgium, this strategic village in the Ardennes forest was soon surrounded by Germans. When two German officers came to McAuliffe's headquarters to demand Bastogne's immediate surrender, he simply replied "Nuts." His effrontery stiffened the resolve of his troops, who were able to hold the town. The successful defense of Bastogne helped break the German counter-offensive, and allowed the allies to carry the war into Germany and Austria. McAuliffe, who became known as the "hero of Bastogne," was promoted to Major General and awarded the Distinguished Service Cross.

Louis L. Snyder, *Louis L. Snyder's Historical Guide to World War II* (Westport, CT: Greenwood Press, 1982), s.v. "McAuliffe, Anthony Clement."

What was Heinrich Himmler's occupation before becoming commander of Adolf Hitler's Gestapo?

Heinrich Himmler (1900-1945) was a chicken farmer near Munich before heading German Nazi leader Adolf Hitler's (1889-1945) Gestapo and Schultzstaffel (S.S.). Himmler was born and raised in the Munich area and studied agriculture at Munich Technical College. In October of 1939 Himmler became the Reich Commissar for the Consolidation of German Nationhood. His foremost task in this position was to eliminate "racial degenerates" through mass extermination. In 1945 after the collapse of the Third Reich of Germany, Himmler fled from Berlin to Bremen, where he was arrested by the British forces. He committed suicide by ingesting potassium cyanide on May 23, 1945.

Louis L. Snyder, *Encyclopedia of the Third Reich* (New York: McGraw-Hill, 1976), s.v. "Himmler, Heinrich." Christian Zentner and Friedemann Bedrftig, eds., *The Encyclopedia of the Third Reich* (New York: Macmillan Publishing, 1991), s.v. "SS."

What was Karl K. Probst oontribution to the winning of World War II?

Karl K. Probst designed the Jeep, one of the most revered American weapons of World War II (1939-45). Probst was a consulting engineer for the Bantam Car Company of Butler, Pennsylvania, when he designed the vehicle. In 1944 there was a dispute between the Ford Motor Company and Willys-Overland as to who actually designed the Jeep, but the Federal Trade Commission ruled in favor of Probst. The Jeep became a favorite of military personnel because of its reliability. In a 1941 demonstration meant to impress Congress, a Jeep was even driven up the steps of the Capitol building in Washington DC.

Probst died in Dayton, Ohio, in 1963 of an apparent overdose of sleeping pills with his plans for the Jeep at his bedside.

Peter Guttmacher, *Jeep* (New York: Crestwood House, 1994), 28. *New York Times* 28 August 1963.

Which of former President Ronald Reagan's children are adopted?

Former United States president Ronald Reagan (1911-) has four children. Maureen and Michael are from his marriage to Jane Wyman. Patricia Ann (Patti) and Ronald Prescott are from his marriage to Nancy Reagan. Michael was adopted in 1945 at the age of four days.

Lloyd Shearer, "Report on the Reagan Four," *Parade* 21 September 1986.

Who coined the phrase "iron curtain"?

The expression "iron curtain" was popularized by the British statesman Winston Churchill (1874-1965) when he declared in an address at Westminster College in Fulton, Missouri on March 5, 1946:

> From Stettin in the Baltic to Trieste in the Adriatic an iron curtain has descended across the continent.

Churchill was referring to the invisible but nonetheless formidable ideological wall separating the Soviet Union and its Eastern European satellites from the democratic nations of the west. Churchill may have been the first to use the term in this geopolitical context but he was not the first to use it as a metaphor. In 1914 Queen Elisabeth (1876-1965) of Belgium in describing German-Belgium relations torn asunder by the war said "...there is now a bloody iron curtain which has descended...." In 1915 George Washington Crile (1864-1943) described France as having "...an iron curtain at its frontier," and during World War II (1939-45) Nazi minister of propaganda Joseph Goebbels (1897-1945) also pre-dated Churchill by using the term in reference to the Soviet Union.

On May 6, 1992, former Soviet president Mikhail S. Gorbachev (1931-) spoke at Westminster College in Fulton, Missouri, where forty-six years earlier Churchill had spoken. During his tenure as the Soviet president, Gorbachev had been greatly credited for improving relations with Western countries, thereby ending the Cold War and removing the "iron curtain."

The original use of the expression was literal and can be traced to the late eighteenth century when actual iron curtains were used to protect theater audiences in case of fire.

John Bartlett, *Familiar Quotations* (New York: Little, Brown and Company, 1992), 622. *Facts On File* 22 October 1992. Walter J. Raymond, *International Dictionary of Politics, 6th ed.* (Lawrenceville, VA: Brunswick Publishing, 1980), s.v. "iron curtain." J. A. Simpson and E. S. C. Weiner, *The Oxford English Dictionary, 2d ed.* (Oxford: Clarendon Press, 1989), s.v. "iron curtain." *World Book Encyclopedia* (Chicago: World Book, 1994), s.v. "Mikhail Sergeyevich Gorbachev."

What is the chronology of Nelson Mandela's career?

In 1940 Nelson Mandela (1918-), South Africa's first African president, was expelled from university after leading a strike with Oliver Tambo, a future African National Congress president. In 1942 he received his bachelor's degree and enrolled in law school. In 1944 he formed the African National Congress (ANC) Youth League with Tambo and Walter Sisulu, and was elected president of that organization in 1950. In 1952 he led a Defiance Campaign, encouraging people to break South Africa's racial separation orders, and in the following year with Tambo, he formed the country's first African law firm. In 1956 he was charged with treason, along with 155 other South Africans of all races who had supported the Freedom Charter calling for a nonracial democracy and a Socialist-based economy. All were acquitted after a four-year trial. In 1960 Mandela's ANC was banned, and in 1962 he was arrested for treason. Two years later, he was convicted of treason and sentenced to life imprisonment. In 1973, and again in 1985, he was offered conditional release from prison, but refused both times until apartheid laws were lifted. In 1990 he was released from prison by President F.W. de Klerk, who also legalized the ANC. In 1991 the government, the ANC, and other groups began formal negotiations on a new national constitution, which opened the way to the 1993 all-race election. During that year, Mandela shared the Nobel Peace Prize with de Klerk. On May 10, 1994, Mandela was sworn in as president.

"From oath of defiance to oath of residency," *USA Today* 10 May 1994.

Who were the first women to become Texas Rangers?

In August of 1993 Cheryl Campbell Steadman, 32, of Houston, and Marrie Reynolds Garcia, 38, of San Antonio, became Texas Rangers, thought to be the first women in the Rangers's 170-year history.

"Newly promoted Texas Rangers," *USA Today* 4 August 1993.

When did the Soviet Union dissolve, and what happened to the republics it comprised?

The Soviet Union was officially disbanded on December 25, 1991, and replaced by the Commonwealth of Independent States (CIS). Twelve of the 15 former Soviet constituent republics joined the Commonwealth; the former Soviet Baltic republics of Estonia, Lativia, and Lithuania were not party to the agreements. The 12 former Soviet republics now part of the Commonwealth are as follow:

Armenia
Azerbaijan
Belarus (or Byelaru, formerly Byelorussia)
Georgia
Kazakhstan (formerly Kazakh Soviet Socialist Republic)
Kyrgyzstan (formerly Kirghizia)
Moldova (formerly Moldavia)
Russia or Russian Federation
Tajikistan (formerly Tadzhikistan)
Turkmenistan (formerly Turkmenia)
Ukraine (formerly *the* Ukraine)
Uzbekistan

David Crystal, ed., *The Cambridge Factfinder* (New York: Cambridge University Press, 1994), 229.

Who was on the Senate Select Committee investigating the Watergate scandal?

The Senate Select Committee on Presidential Campaign Activities was authorized by U.S. Senate Resolutions 60 and 278. The hearings began on May 17, 1973, and the following were the members:

Sam J. Ervin, Jr., Democrat-North Carolina (chairman)
Howard H. Baker, Jr., Republican-Tennessee (vice-chairman)
Herman E. Talmadge, Democrat-Georgia
Daniel K. Inouye, Democrat-Hawaii
Joseph M. Montoya, Democrat-New Mexico

Edward J. Gurney, Republican-Florida
Lowell P. Weicker, Jr., Republican-Connecticut

Edward W. Knappman, *Watergate and the White House, June 1972-July 1973* (New York: Facts on File, 1973), 51. *Watergate: Chronology of a Crisis* (Washington, DC: Congressional Quarterly, 1975), 6-7. Gerald Gold, ed., *The Watergate Hearings: Break-in and Cover-up* (New York: Viking Press, 1973), 130-38.

Who was Axis Sally?

Axis Sally was Mildred Elizabeth Gillars (1900-1988), an American and onetime aspiring actress who was teaching English in Berlin at the outbreak of World War II (1939-1945). She began broadcasting on the German radio, using music and talk to attempt to undermine the morale of the American troops by raising doubts about the war and by suggesting that the women left behind were turning to the men back home. Her radio program was more popular with the soldiers than was the official Army radio, and it was her playing of the song "Lili Marlene" that led to its great popularity. At her trial in 1949, Gillars said that she had broadcast Nazi propaganda for the love of Max Otto Koischwitz, a staff member of the Foreign Ministry. She was convicted of treason and paroled in 1961.

"Axis Sally' Given 10-to 30-Year Term," *St. Louis Globe-Democrat* 26 March 1949. Thomas Parrish, ed., *The Simon and Schuster Encyclopedia of World War II* (New York: Simon and Schuster, 1978), s.v. "Gillars, Mildred Elizabeth."

Which countries signed the Warsaw Pact?

The Warsaw Pact, a military alliance, was signed in Warsaw, Poland, on May 14, 1955, by the Soviet Union, Albania, Bulgaria, Czechoslovakia, East Germany, Hungary, Poland, and Rumania. In 1968 Albania denounced the pact, having played no part in it since 1960. East Germany's membership ended in 1990, and in that same year Hungary announced its intention to withdraw. With the breakup of the Soviet Union, the pact was formally dissolved by the remaining six-member nations in 1991.

The Military Balance: 1969-1970 (London: International Institute for Strategic Studies, 1969), 11-14. *World Book Encyclopedia* (Chicago: World Book, 1994), s.v. "Warsaw Pact."

Who was Tokyo Rose?

During World War II (1939-45) Tokyo Rose was actually the name applied collectively to 13 female radio announcers, all native speakers of American English who worked for a Japanese station which broadcasted a propaganda program entitled "Zero Hour," beamed at U.S. troops. The most famous Tokyo Rose was Iva Toguri D'Aquino, a Japanese-American stranded in Japan when the United States entered the war in 1941. When she returned to the United States in 1947, she was tried and convicted of treason for giving the enemy aid and comfort during the time of war. She served six and one-half years (1949-56) of a ten-year sentence, her time having been reduced due to good behavior. In January of 1977 U.S. President Gerald Ford (1913-) pardoned her after becoming convinced that she had been wrongly accused. Not only had she refused to become a Japanese citizen, she had been recruited to assist two prisoners of war writing the English-language broadcast material while secretly attempting to subvert the entire operation.

Philip W. Goetz, ed., *The New Encyclopaedia Britannica, 15th ed., "Micropaedia"* (Chicago: Encyclopaedia Britannica, 1993), s.v. "D'Aquino, Iva Toguri."

Did General George Patton really slap hospitalized American soldiers?

U.S. General George Patton (1885-1945) caused a scandal during World War II (1939-45) when he twice slapped American soldiers hospitalized for battle fatigue in Sicily. On August 3, 1943, he slapped Private Charles Kuhl and on August 10, 1943, he slapped another soldier. In addition to striking the men, he called them cowards. Upon hearing of these incidents, U.S. General Dwight Eisenhower (1890-1969) reprimanded Patton and instructed him to apologize to the individuals involved and, if necessary, to all those units under his command. Patton complied. Although Eisenhower attempted to keep the news from the media, U.S. newscaster Drew Pearson reported the incidents on his Sunday evening radio program on November 21, 1943. Many other reporters knew of the events but agreed to suppress the information in the national interest.

Ladislas Farago, *Patton: Ordeal and Triumph* (New York: Astor-Honor, 1964), 325-31, 350-53.

Who was the tallest U.S. President?

The tallest U.S. President was Abraham Lincoln (1809-65) at 6 feet 4 inches. The shortest was James Madison (1741-1836) at 5 feet 4 inches. The current President, William (Bill) Clinton, is 6 feet 2 inches tall.

Joseph Nathan Kane, *Facts About the Presidents, 6th ed.* (New York: H. W. Wilson, 1993), 344-45.

How many submarines were sunk in World War II?

There were over 1,200 submarines lost by the major belligerents in World War II (1939-45). Of the Axis powers, the Germans lost 785, the Japanese lost 130, and the Italians lost 84. The Allies suffered 53 losses by the United States of which 49 were in the Pacific; 77 losses by the British, of which 41 were in the Mediterranean; and approximately 100 losses by the Soviet Union.

John Ellis, *World War II: A Statistical Survey* (New York: Facts on File, 1993), 261.

Who was the first African-American woman general in the United States military?

The first African-American woman general in the United States armed forces was Hazel Johnson, who was in the Army. In 1979 she was promoted to the rank of brigadier general and served as chief of the army nurse corps from 1979 to 1983, when she retired.

The first African-American woman general in the United States Air Force was Marcelite J. Harris, promoted to brigadier general in 1990. She was also the first to become an aircraft maintenance officer and one of the first two female commanding air officers.

Jessie Carney Smith, ed., *Black Firsts: 2,000 Years of Extraordinary Achievement* (Detroit: Gale Research, 1994), 239. Joan Potter, *African-American Firsts* (Elizabethtown, NY: Pinto Press, 1994), 177-8.

What are the birthdates of Bill, Hillary, and Chelsea Clinton?

U.S. president William (Bill) Jefferson Blythe IV was born on August 19, 1946, in Hope, Arkansas. His father was killed in an automobile accident before he was born. In 1950 he was legally adopted by his stepfather, Roger Clinton, who gave him his name. Hillary Rodham Clinton was born on October 26, 1947, in Park Ridge, Illinois. Bill and Hillary were married October 11, 1975, in Fayetteville, Arkansas. Their daughter, Chelsea, was born February 27, 1980.

Joseph Nathan Kane, *Facts About the Presidents, 6th ed.* (New York: H. W. Wilson, 1993), 292-93.

What was the Vichy Government in France?

The Vichy Government was a ruling regime that Germany authorized for unoccupied France during World War II (1939-45). The government was established on July 2, 1940, with its capital at Vichy, a town previously known for its mineral water. The government's formation was done by secret pact with Germany, signed by Marshal Henri Philippe Ptain (1856-1951), who thereafter annulled the French Constitution. Despite opposition within France, the Vichy Government won diplomatic recognition from many countries, including the United States.

The Vichy Government was notorious for furthering Nazi interests, including ordering compulsory labor on German projects, enacting laws that stripped French Jews of their rights, and aiding the Germans in their hunt for non-French Jews hiding in France. An extensive French underground force sought to undermine this government during the war.

Clashes between the United States and the Vichy government began when American forces took part in the Allied North African Invasion in 1942. By the time U.S. forces joined in the Normandy Invasion in 1944, the Vichy regime was being ignored by both Germany and the Allies alike. Resistance leaders from the French underground began to effectively replace Vichy officials, and at the end of World War II, those who participated in the Vichy Government were executed, imprisoned, or degraded by the French.

Norman Polmar, *World War II: America at War, 1941-1945* (New York: Random House, 1991), s.v. "Vichy France."

When was the sunken warship the *Bismarck* found? Were there any survivors?

The wreckage of the German battleship the *Bismarck* was discovered at the bottom of the Atlantic Ocean 600 miles west of Brest, France, in June of 1989. Found upright and in good condition, the *Bismarck* had been one of Hitler's premier warships; but it was sunk by the British following a week-long battle in May of 1941. Only 100 members of the 2,300-man crew survived.

"Nazi Warship Bismarck Is Found," *New York Times* 14 June 1989.

Why did President Eisenhower once refuse the use of an umbrella?

In July of 1955 U.S. President Eisenhower (1890-1969) was returning to Washington after attending a conference in Geneva. Upon his arrival it was raining, and when an airport official stood ready with an umbrella, he was pushed aside by a presidental aide, and Eisenhower was soaked before he reached shelter. He wanted to avoid any pictures associated with an umbrella because of what it symbolized.

Before the onset of World War II (1939-1945) another politician, noted British statesman Neville Chamberlain (1869-1940), had set forth a foreign policy calling for avoidance of war by appeasement. One of the things the world would remember most about him throughout his travels was his umbrella. His subsequent meetings with German dictator Adolph Hitler (1889-1945) would ultimately result in failed policies, and as the umbrella had come to be identified with Chamberlain, it became the symbol of appeasement, impotence, or cowardice. The visual significance of this symbol was so important that some 17 years later President Eisenhower would prefer to be drenched rather than be photographed with an umbrella.

Sven Tito Achen, *Symbols Around Us* (New York: Van Nostrand Reinhold, 1978), 7. Philip W. Goetz, ed., *The New Encyclopaedia Brittanica, 15th ed., "Micropaedia"* (Chicago: Encyclopaedia Britannica, 1991), s.v. "Chamberlain, (Arthur) Neville."

What are the circumstances surrounding the incident involving President Jimmy Carter and a rabbit?

During a vacation to his home in Plains, Georgia, during Easter of 1979, U.S. President Jimmy Carter (1924-), while in a canoe on a fishing excursion, was approached by a rabbit swimming in the water. President Carter fought the rabbit off with his canoe paddle.

While some accounts reported that the rabbit attacked the president, most zoologists rejected the idea, claiming that the animal was probably looking for a dry place to land.

"Carter Describes Foe: 'Quiet Georgia Rabbit'," *New York Times* 31 August 1979.

What was the Gulf of Tonkin Resolution?

Becoming the basis for escalation of the war in Southeast Asia, the Gulf of Tonkin Resolution was passed by both houses of the U.S. Congress on August 7, 1964. It provided congressional approval to President Lyndon B. Johnson (1908-73) to take all "necessary measures to repel any armed attack" against U.S. forces and for "all necessary steps" to be taken to assist any Southeast Asian ally seeking to defend its freedom. Two days before the resolution was passed, August 5, 1964, Johnson announced that he had ordered air strikes against North Vietnam in retaliation for alleged North Vietnamese bombings of U.S. destroyers stationed in the Gulf of Tonkin. After a 1968 investigation ordered by the U.S. Senate raised doubts as to the certainty of the Gulf of Tonkin attacks, the resolution was eventually repealed in May of 1970.

George C. Kohn, *Dictionary of Historic Documents* (New York: Facts on File, 1991), s.v. "Gulf of Tonkin Resolution."

What is the Bretton Woods Agreement?

The Bretton Woods Agreement of July 22, 1944 recommended the establishment of the International Monetary Fund (IMF) and the International Bank for Reconstruction and Development (IBRD). Meeting at Bretton Woods, New Hampshire representatives of 44 nations voted for the agreement as a means of re-building those national economies ravaged by World War II.

George C.Kohn, *Dictionary of Historic Documents* (New York: Facts on File, 1994), s.v. "Bretton Woods Agreement."

How did the presidential retreat "Camp David" get its name?

For many American presidents, Camp David has been a welcome place of relaxation and rest. The camp was organized in 1942 during the administration of U.S. President Franklin D. Roosevelt (1882-1945). Roosevelt dubbed the retreat, which is located in Catoctin Mountain State Park near Thurmont, Maryland, "Shangri-La" after the imaginary Tibetan mountain kingdom in James Hilton's novel *Lost Horizon.*

The retreat was well-loved by President Dwight D. Eisenhower (1890-1969), who during his administration, significantly expanded and upgraded the retreat. In 1953, Eisenhower named the retreat "Camp David" after his grandson.

Since the camp was founded, many improvements have been made to the 143-acre compound. As of 1986, Camp David had a two-lane bowling alley, freshwater trout stream, eight-horse stable and riding trails, skeet shooting, badminton, archery ranges, movie auditorium, two free form pools, two clay tennis courts, and a one-hole golf course. It is protected by two layers of ten-foot barbed wire fences, high voltage wires, motion sensors, and several Marine marksmen.

USA Today 11 April 1986.

Which U.S. presidents gave away their salaries?

Two U.S. presidents, Herbert Hoover (1824-1964) and John F. Kennedy (1917-63), never used their salaries earned from being president for their own personal use. Having decided that he did not want citizens to think he ran for office just to make money, Hoover had his entire paycheck deposited in a separate account that was used to supplement salaries of the employees he felt were underpaid. The remainder was distributed to worthy charities. Money from speaking engagements and writing projects was put to similar use. Kennedy donated his salary to charity during the time when he was a U.S. congressman, senator, and president.

Eugene Lyons, *Our Unknown Ex-President: A Portrait of Herbert Hoover* (New York: Doubleday, 1948), 148. "Hoover Never Used Salary As His Own," *New York Times* 2 February 1938. Lu Ann Paletta and Fred L. Worth, *The World Almanac of Presidential Facts* (New York: World Almanac, 1988), 216. *Reader's Digest* November 1947.

What was the New Economic Policy (NEP) introduced by Lenin?

After the Russian revolution of 1917, the strict communist economic policies Russian leader Lenin (1870-1924) imposed on the country were not working. Lenin had to introduce the New Economic Policy (NEP) to quell the protests of the peasants. Private property could once again be willed to relatives, monetary reforms were put in place, and trade and manufacturing were encouraged. Taxes could be paid in the form of goods. These policies reduced collectively-owned land to only two percent of the total. The policies were very popular, but when Stalin (1879-1953) came to power he eliminated the NEP.

Warren Shaw and David Pryce, *World Almanac of the Soviet Union: From 1905 to the Present* (New York: World Almanac, 1990), 83.

What was Adolf Hitler's life like?

Although Adolf Hitler (1889-1945) was born in Branau-am-Inn, Austria, he grew up identifying closely with Germany. He was very attached to his mother, and feared his father. His mother died when he was a young adult, and he spent the next few years wandering around Vienna and Munich, attempting a career at art or architecture.

He joined the Bavarian infantry during World War I (1914-18) and was awarded the Iron Cross, First Class. After the war, inspired by the workers, rebellions taking place in Berlin and Munich, he joined the German Workers' Party, which soon was transformed into the National Socialist German Workers' Party, better known as the Nazi party. Hitler was a charismatic speaker and he was soon elected head of the Nazis.

Wanting to kick out communists and labor leaders from Germany, he planned to have a "revolt" take place during a patriotic demonstration at a beer hall; but failed to arouse them. He managed to get 3,000 sympathizers to march on Munich the next day. Policemen fired into the demonstration, killing sixteen party members. Hitler was put on trial for treason, but his trial became more of a publicity event for him than a punishment for his crime. Because of it, he became a household name and his party rose to national prominence. Given a light sentence at a rather comfortable prison, he used his time to write his autobiography, *Mein Kampf* (My Struggle), in which the German populace learned more about his political ideas, including an agenda of anti-Semitism, nationalistic pride, and genetic purity.

He continued as head of the Nazi party, but soon he took over the German government with the help of his many supporters, and he became chancellor in 1933. He purged his detractors, including leaders of the SA, Nazi thugs who "policed" the streets, during the Night of the Long Knives. He withdrew Germany from the League of Nations and began to build up all areas of the military, in defiance of the Versailles Treaty. A mandatory draft was also reinstated. In 1936, Hitler took his troops into the Rhineland and formed Hitler youth associations and concentration camps where his enemies were imprisoned and slaughtered. He invaded Austria and Czechoslovakia, starting World War II (1939-45). After the Allies landed in France, Hitler was confronted with a two front war, and Germany faced reality of defeat.

An unprincipled tyrant, even his loyal fans began to tire of his tactics that were only plunging Germany deeper into defeat, but he managed to survive several attacks on his life. He was plagued with hypochondria and felt he had to win the war before he died of ill health. As the war went on, he became increasingly agitated and isolated. In 1945 he went into his bunker in Berlin, and made plans to burn all of Germany before the Allied forces could invade. On April 28 he and longtime companion Eva Braun were married. Hitler also dictated a long and rambling will. On April 30 he shot himself in the temple and Braun committed suicide by ingesting poison capsules. Their bodies were hauled outside, doused with gasoline, and set on fire.

Norman Polmar, *World War II: America at War, 1941-1945* (New York: Random House, 1991), 386-89.

How many Americans died during the "Bataan Death March"?

The infamous Bataan Death March, which took place after the U.S.-Filipino surrender of Bataan to Japan during World War II (1939-45), involved 76,000 prisoners of war, of which 12,000 were American. An estimated 5,200 Americans died in the march and many more died in the prison camp. In one of the most brutal prisoner of war incidents in history, prisoners were stripped and searched on April 10, 1942, and sometimes killed simply for having Japanese money. Deprived of food and water, the prisoners were treated cruelly and shot for displaying signs of weakness.

Norman Polmar and Thomas B. Allen, *World War II: America at War, 1941-1945* (New York: Random House, 1991), s.v. "Bataan death march."

What honorary degree did former first lady Barbara Bush receive?

On September 6, 1989, Barbara Bush (1925-), wife of the U.S. President George Bush (1924-), received an honorary doctorate of humane letters from Smith College. Mrs. Bush had attended Smith 45 years earlier, but she left before completing her degree to marry the future president.

"It's Dr. Bush now," *Pittsburgh Press* 7 September 1989.

When is Chelsea Clinton's birthday? What are her favorite hobbies?

Chelsea Clinton, daughter of U.S. President Bill Clinton (1946-) and First Lady Hillary Rodham Clinton, was born on February 27, 1980, in Little Rock, Arkansas. Among her favorite activities are softball, volleyball, soccer, classical ballet, pinochle, cards, ping pong, movies, and shopping.

"The facts on Chelsea Clinton," *USA Today* 25 January 1993.

What was the Iran-Contra affair?

The Iran-Contra affair began in 1986 when the administration of U.S. President Ronald Reagan (1911-) secretly decided to sell military equipment to Iran, although there was an embargo against such transactions. Funds from these sales were used to support the anti-Communist contra rebels in Nicaragua in spite of Congressional restrictions against helping them. When these facts became known, an outcry arose for a special prosecutor and investigation by Congress. There was the possibility that President Reagan might be forced to resign in disgrace. The Congressional hearings, however, were dominated by the testimony of National Security Council staff member Lt. Col. Oliver North, who was able to portray himself as apersecuted war hero and thus change the whole tenor of the investigation by placing the Congressional committee on the defensive. In the end, North's superior, Admiral John Poindexter, the National Security Adviser, took responsibility for the affair, exculpating the president.

Michael Nelson, ed., *The Presidency A to Z: A Ready Reference Encyclopedia* (Washington, DC: Congressional Quarterly, 1992), s.v. "Iran-Contra Affair."

Did Winston Churchill deliver all his own radio speeches during the war?

British statesman Sir Winston Churchill (1874-1965) may not have delivered all his own radio speeches during World War II (1939-45). Actor Norman Shelley claimed that he imitated the voice of the British prime minister in a rebroadcast of his June 1940 speech to Parliament because Churchill was too busy to record it.

Pittsburgh Press 5 October 1979.

What is the Teapot Dome?

Teapot Dome, a location in Wyoming, became the name attached to an notorious political scandal during U.S. President Warren G. Harding's (1865-1923) administration. In 1923 a Senate probe revealed that Albert Fall, Secretary of the Interior under Harding, had transferred government oil reserves in Teapot Dome, Wyoming and Elk Hills, California to his department. Fall then privately leased the reserves to the private oil producers of Harry Sinclair and E.L. Doheny without competitive bidding. Fall resigned following the investigation and joined the oil firm of Harry Sinclair. Later Fall was convicted of accepting a bribe of $400,000.

The World Book Encyclopedia (Chicago: World Book, 1987), s.v. "Teapot Dome."

What was the Iraqi Republican Guard?

The Iraqi Republican Guard was formed as a small politically oriented paramilitary force, originally intended to guard Iraqi President Saddam Hussein (1937-). During the Iran-Iraq War, which began in January of 1991, it grew into a major combat force comprised of 25 brigades and equipped with heavy military artillery.

Frank Chadwick, *Desert Shield Fact Book, 2d ed.* (Bloomington, IL: Game Designer's Workshop, 1991), 51.

What was Dean Acheson's role during the Korean War?

Dean Acheson (1893-1971) served as U.S. secretary of state during the Korean War. He succeeded George C. Marshall (1880-1959) in January of 1949. At first, American's political goal in the war was the restoration of prewar political boundaries. After the Inchon invasion, the goal became the liberation of North Korea, but after the Chinese intervention in November of 1950 the original goal to restore the status quo was restated. While in office, Acheson received much criticism and was accused of having permitted the Communist victory on mainland China in 1949 and of precipitating the North Korean invasion in June of 1950.

One biographer wrote: "Acheson held Moscow accountable for the Korean War." Acheson left office in January of 1953; he was replaced as secretary of state by John Foster Dulles (1888-1959)

Harry G. Summers, Jr., ed., *Korean War Almanac* (New York: Facts on File, 1990), 38-39.

What role did U.S. African-American servicemen play during the Korean war?

U.S. African-American servicemen played a significant role during the Korean war. The largest black Army unit was the 25th Infantry Division's 24th Infantry Regiment, which included the 129th Field Artillery Battalion and the 77th Engineer Company. The 24th Infantry Regiment and its attached units struck the first successful counterattack of the war at Yechon on July 20, 1950.

Other African-American units assigned to Korea were the Second Infantry Division's 503rd Artillery Battalion and the Third Battalion Ninth Infantry; the Third Infantry Division's Third Battalion, 15th Infantry Regiment, 64th Tank Battalion; the separate corps-level 58th Armored Field Artillery; and the 999th Field Artillery Battalion.

In early 1951 African-American soldiers began to be placed into previously white unites, breaking the racially-segregated structure of the units. Because of the urgent need to provide qualified replacements in white units, Commander in Chief Far

East Command General Matthew B. Ridgway integrated all combat units in Korea. The 24th Infantry Regiment was disbanded on October 1, 1951, and the personnel were assigned throughout the Eighth U.S. Army. By July of 1953, more than 90 percent of African-American servicemen in the Army were in integrated units. The U.S. Air Force, Marines, and later the Navy, also joined in assigning African-American servicemen to integrated units. Two African-American U.S. Army service men-Sergeant Cornelius H. Charlton and Private First Class William Thompson-were Medal of Honor recipients for their heroic actions in Korea.

Harry G. Summers, Jr., *Korean War Almanac* (New York: Facts on File, 1990), 63.

When was the country of Jordan created?

The country of Jordan originated in the post-World War I era as Transjordan, a mandatory state administered by the British. The word "Transjordan" referred to that area east of the Jordan River and, prior to the end of the war, this area was part of the Ottoman vilayet of Damascus. The Sykes-Picot agreement in May of 1916 allocated the area to the future British sphere of influence, but Transjordan itself was not part of the 1917 Balfour Agreement which created a national Jewish home in Palestine. In 1920 the Palestine mandate went into effect, officially creating Transjordan and in 1921 Abd Allah was recognized as its ruler. In 1923 Britain recognized Transjordan as an independent state but it remained under British tutelage and was dependent on a British subsidy. In March of 1946, under the Treaty of London, Transjordan was recognized as a truly independent state and two months later Abd Allah was declared King; the country's name was then changed to Jordan.

Jordan remains a monarchy and the King is the head of state. The country has an area of 97,740 square kilometers; including 5,880 square kilometers of the occupied West Bank; and a population of 3.15 million including both East and West banks. Eighty percent of the population are Sunni Muslims and there is a six percent Christian minority.

Michael Adams, ed., *The Middle East* (New York: Facts on File, 1988), 55-6. Trevor Mostyn, ed., *The Cambridge Encyclopedia of the Middle East and North Africa* (New York: Cambridge University Press, 1988), s.v. "Jordan."

Who was Gamal Abdel Nasser?

Gamal Abdel Nasser (1918-1970) was president of Egypt from 1954 until his death in 1970. At the age of 34, he organized the Free Officers, a revolutionary military group that forced King Farouk from the throne in 1952. General Muhammad Naguib became president of the newly proclaimed republic in 1953, but in 1954, Nasser ousted Naguib and assumed the office. A new constitution was written in 1956.

Nasser endorsed an Agrarian Reform Act in 1953, which limited land holdings to 280 acres. Individuals were required to divest acreage in excess of this amount. Existing political parties were abolished and replaced by the Liberation Rally, and later the National Union. By presidential decree industries were nationalized. Nasser's economic system became known as "Arab Socialism." Education was free and university graduates were promised government jobs.

In 1956, after the United States and Great Britain withdrew their support for building Aswan High Dam, Nasser nationalized the Suez Canal Company. His action provoked an Israeli invasion of the Sinai Peninsula and an Anglo-French invasion of the Canal Zone. Pressure from the United Nations forced the invaders to withdraw. Nasser inspired pan-Arab sentiment. A charismatic leader, he is credited with lifting Egypt to the center of international affairs. Muhammad Anwar al-Sadat (1918-1981) succeeded Nasser as president. Nasser died of a heart attack on September 28, 1970.

Source: Michael Adams, ed., *The Middle East* (New York: Facts on File, 1987), 273-82.

Who was the first prime minister of Israel?

The first prime minister of Israel was David Ben-Gurion (1886-1973), who served in that office from 1948 to 1953 and again from 1955 to 1963 when he retired. He also acted as minister of defense during those terms as well. Born David Green, Ben-Gurion moved to Palestine in 1906, where he became an active member of the international Zionist movement, which agitated for the formation of a Jewish state in Palestine. He also served as head of the Executive of the Jewish Agency for Palestine, in which he supervised all Jewish-related matters, from agriculture to espionage, in Palestine until the area was divided into Israel and Jordan in 1948.

World Book Encyclopedia (Chicago: World Book, 1987), s.v. "Ben-Gurion, David."

Was there ever a woman Chief Engraver of the United States Mint?

The first woman to hold the position of Chief Sculptor-Engraver of the United States Mint was Elizabeth Jones, who was appointed by U.S. President Ronald Reagan (1911-) in 1981. She has designed coins to commemorate the 250th birthday of U.S. President George Washington (1732-1799), the Statue of Liberty celebration, and the Los Angeles Olympics.

Beth Deisher, ed., *Coin World Almanac: A Handbook for Coin Collectors, 5th ed.* (New York: World Almanac, 1987), 187-88.

How much money did Jack Ruby's brother receive for the sale of the gun that killed Lee Harvey Oswald?

Earl Ruby, a semiretired dry cleaner from Boca Raton, Florida, sold the snub-nosed .38-caliber colt revolver his late brother Jack Ruby (1911-67) had used to kill Lee Harvey Oswald (1939-63) for $200,000 at an auction at the Omni Park Central Hotel in New York City in December of 1991. Oswald was arrested for the assassination of President John F. Kennedy (1917-63). Ruby said he was selling the gun because he needed the money to pay off legal bills and back taxes. The buyer chose to remain anonymous.

Steven Lee Myers, "Jack Ruby's Brother Sells the Gun for $200,000," *New York Times* 27 December 1991.

What New Orleans District Attorney did an independent investigation of the assassination of President John F. Kennedy?

James Garrison, district attorney for New Orleans, Louisiana, conducted his own investigation into U.S. president John F. Kennedy's (1917-1963) assassination. Garrison claimed that Lee Harvey Oswald (1939-1963) had not killed the president, but rather that he was part of a larger conspiracy engineered by ex-CIA members, who were opponents to Cuban dictator Fidel Castro ((b. 1926). In a press conference on February 18, 1967,

Garrison also claimed that the CIA knew of their plot and knew who actually shot Kennedy.

Facts on File Yearbook, 1967, (New York: Facts on File, 1968).

Who was the man who acted as Joseph Stalin's double?

A man known only as "Rashid" served as the double of the Soviet political leader Joseph Stalin (1879-1953). Rashid would sit at meetings and banquets, passing for the Soviet dictator. Newspaper reports revealed details about the little known double when he died in 1991, at the age of 93. The man was younger than Stalin by twenty years, but closely resembled him; he was given two years of acting lessons in order to "play" the powerful leader. Yet another double is thought to have existed, a man who stood in for Stalin when he was dying.

"Stalin's Double Reported Dead," *New York Times* 16 June 1991.

Which president was listed in the *Webster Encyclopedia Dictionary* as being president before he was elected?

The 1980 edition of the *Webster Encyclopedia Dictionary* listed Ronald Reagan as the fortieth president of the United States, even though the book was issued before he won the election. The citation was the result of a change in press date. Editors had placed Reagan's name in a draft as dummy copy. When the book went to press early, in August, no one remembered to remove his name; the book then reached bookstore shelves before the November election. Buyers snapped up the 50,000 copies of the dictionary, in the hope that it would become a collector's item.

Pittsburgh Post Gazette 1 November 1980.

Who was the first among presidents and vice presidents to appear in a product advertisement?

Former U.S. vice president Dan Quayle (1947-) appeared in an advertisement for Lay's potato chips which was first televised during halftime of the Super Bowl game in January 1994. He was the first former vice president to appear in a product advertisement. No former president has ever appeared in an ad for a product.

USA Today 28-30 January 1994.

Which military general was known as "Dugout Doug"?

General Douglas A. MacArthur (1880-1964) earned the nickname "Dugout Doug," as commander of the U.S. Army troops in the Pacific during World War II (1939-45). MacArthur was given the name by unhappy subordinates who served under him as commanders. The men saw the general as a coward who stole the glory from their individual achievements by placing them under a news blackout.

Norman Polmar and Thomas B. Allen, *World War II: America at War, 1941-1945* (New York: Random House, 1991), s.v. "MacArthur, Gen. of the Army Douglas A."

What World War II event is reflected in the book *The Man Who Never Was?*

In 1954, Ewen Montague was finally able to tell the story of one of World War II's most amazing intelligence stunts in *The Man Who Never Was.* The author, who served as a commander in the British Naval Intelligence Division, was responsible for creating a fictional British officer whose body was to be found by the Germans. Planted on the corpse were letters that appeared to reveal the plans for an Allied assault. In order to convince the Germans that the man and the letters he carried were authentic, Montague created an elaborate background for the fictional Captain William Martin. He carried love letters and the picture of his fiance, as well as the communication he was supposedly delivering to General Sir Harold Alexander in North Africa. The body was released by a submarine and washed up on the coast of Spain. The information it carried was received by the Nazis, who were convinced of its legitimacy. They reacted just as the British Intelligence hoped, by moving Rommel from France to Greece, where the attack was expected, and leaving Sicily lightly guarded.

The New York Times Book Review 31 January 1954.

Who were the Gestapo of the Third Reich in Germany?

Nazi Germany's secret state police was called the Geheime Staatspolizel, commonly known as the Gestapo or the SS. Its aim was to protect Adolf Hitler (1889-1945) and his Third Reich by eliminating those who appeared to pose any possible threat to his power. This dreaded police force grew out of Hitler's own bodyguard, the Stabswache, which had begun to protect him in the early days of the Nazi movement. In 1929 the guard was enlarged and put under the command of Heinrich Himmler. The Gestapo became an autonomous organization that set its own rules, granting itself license to use such extreme force in its quest to annihilate enemies of the state that the word Gestapo became synonymous with the phrase, reign of terror. The Gestapo's victims included Jews, Bolsheviks, Marxists, and, during the Second World War (1939-45), citizens of occupied countries who dared to resist them. The International Military Tribunal at Nuremberg, which was convened after the war to judge the Nazis, cataloged their offenses: "The persecution and extermination of the Jews, brutalities and killings in concetration camps, excesses in the administration of occupied territories, the administration of the slave labour programme and the mistreatment and murder of prisoners-of-war."

Louis L. Snyder, *Encyclopedia of the Third Reich* (New York: McGraw-Hill, 1976), s.v. "Gestapo."

Who was Senpo Sugihara and what was his role in saving European Jews?

In 1940 Senpo Sugihara was in charge of a small Japanese consulate in Kovno, Lithuania. The consulate was besieged daily by Jews seeking visas allowing them to travel eastward into Siberia and Japan, thus escaping the advancing Nazi German armies. Sugihara was ordered by his superiors in Tokyo to deny the visas and close the consulate. Before closing the consulate, however, Sugihara issued visas to over 5,000 Jews, mostly from Poland, allowing them to escape the Nazi onslaught. Sugihara spent the rest of the war in consulates in Germany and Bulgaria. After the war his employment was terminated by the Japanese diplomatic service, but eventually his role in saving thousands of Jews from the Holocaust came to the attention of Israeli officials. He was invited to Jerusalem where his son was awarded a scholarship to the Hebrew University. Japanese television produced a movie on his humanitarian feat and the Holocaust Memorial in Jerusalem recognized him as a "Righteous Gentile." Sugihara died in July of 1986.

Lloyd Shearer, "A Little-Known Story," *Parade* 8 February 1987.

What happened to the house that Adolf Hitler was born in?

Adolf Hitler (1889-1945) was born in a house in Branau-am-Inn, Austria, on April 20, 1889. Over the decades the house has served as a public building, a town library, and a technical school. In 1976 plans were being made to convert the house into a school for retarded children. A few months after Hitler's birth his family moved to the town of Leonding which is near Lintz. That house eventually became a funeral parlor.

"Hitler's Birthplace Will Be School for the Retarded," *New York Times* 19 April 1976.

Who was Fabian von Schlabrendorff and what was his part in an attempt to assassinate Adolf Hitler?

Fabian von Schlabrendorff (1907-1980) was a leading German jurist and a conservative opponent of Adolf Hitler (1889-1945) and other National Socialists. Through his writings Schlabrendorff attempted to thwart Hitler's rise to power and in England he tried to gain support for German opposition. Nonetheless, Schlabrendorff was loyal to Germany and served as an ordnance officer during the World War II (1939-45). He was involved in a failed attempt to assassinate Hitler in 1943. A British-made plastic bomb, made to look like two bottles of brandy, was put aboard Hitler's plane but failed to go off. After another failed attempt on Hitler's life in 1944 in which Schlabrendorff was also involved, he was arrested and tortured but escaped a death sentence when his trial was interrupted by an allied bombing raid. He spent the remainder of the war in a concentration camp and again became a leading jurist but in the new Germany. From 1967 to 1975 he served as a judge in the Federal Constitutional Court.

Louis L. Snyder, *Encyclopedia of the Third Reich* (New York: Macmillan, 1991), s.v. "Schlabrendorff, Fabian von." "Fabian von Schlabrendorff, Made Attempt on Hitler's Life in 1943," *New York Times* 5 September 1980.

Which two Japanese cities were the targets of atomic bombs in 1945?

On July 16, 1945, near Los Alamos, New Mexico, the United States secretly exploded the world's first atomic bomb. After agonized deliberation, President Harry S. Truman (1884-1972) decided to use this weapon against Japan in the hope that it would shorten World War II, save the lives of thousands of Americans that would be lost in an invasion of the Japanese home islands, and relieve the suffering of those in Japanese-occupied territories. General Carl Spaatz, head of the U.S. Strategic Air Forces in the Pacific, was to choose the first target from four preselected military and industrial Japanese cities, and on August 6, 1945, the *Enola Gay*, a B-29 bomber piloted by Colonel Paul W. Tibbets, dropped an atom bomb on Hiroshima, Spaatz's first choice. Suspended from a parachute the bomb exploded several hundred feet above ground level immediately destroying 60 per cent of the city and killing 150,000 people. Since the Japanese government refused to accept Truman's demand for an unconditional surrender, on August 9, the B-29 *Bock's Car*, under the command of Major Charles W. Sweeny, dropped an atomic bomb on Nagasaki. The city was destroyed with the loss of 35,000 lives. On August 10 Emperor Hirohito (1901-1989) ordered his government to accept Truman's terms of surrender, but the military high command did not cede to the surrender until August 14. The first atomic bomb, known as *Little Boy*, was made from fissionable U-235. The second bomb, known as *Fat Man*, was more powerful and made from the plutonium isotope Pu-239.

Marcel Baudot et al., *The Historical Encyclopedia of World War II* (New York: Facts On File, 1980), s.v. "atomic bomb."

Which member of Congress voted against U.S. entry into both World Wars?

Jeanette Rankin, a Republican politician from Montana, was the first woman elected to the U.S. Congress and a committed pacifist. Elected in 1916 to an at-large Congressional seat from her state, Rankin voted against U.S. entry into World War I (1914-18). Later, in 1941, she was the sole dissenting vote in the U.S. House of Representatives when the declaration of war on Japan was put forth. Rankin died in 1973 at the age of 92.

Encyclopedia Americana (Danbury, CT: Grolier, 1990), s.v. "Rankin, Jeanette."

When was the Russian city of Leningrad restored to its previous name of St. Petersburg?

The Russian city of St. Petersburg, made capital of the Russian Empire by the Russian czar Peter the Great (1672-1725), was officially changed from Leningrad back to its former and original appellation in September of 1991. It was not the first time the name of the Gulf of Finland port was changed because of political sentiments. In 1914 it was re-christened Petrograd, then renamed in honor of Communist leader Vladimir Lenin (1870-1924) after his death in 1924.

Andrew Wilson and Nina Bachkatov, *Russia and the Commonwealth: A to Z* (New York: HarperPerennial, 1992), s.v. "Leningrad/St. Petersbury."

Who were the leaders of the 1991 attempted coup in the Soviet Union?

The short-lived 1991 takeover of the Soviet Union was led by a faction in the Communist Party that was dissatisfied with the liberal policies of Mikhail Gorbachev (1931-). On August 19 of that year, a group of high-ranking Communists, including vice-president Gennadi Yanayev, Minister of the Interior Boris Pugo (1937-1991), O. D. Baklanov, deputy chair of the country's Defense Council, and V. A. Starodubtsev, head of the Peasants' Union, issued a statement declaring Gorbachev incapacitated and the reins of government in the hands of an emergency committee. The coup-plotters had visited Gorbachev at his vacation home in the Crimea and demanded that he relinquish power; the Soviet leader had refused and troops under the control of the rebels then occupied several important locations in the capital. Large crowds soon gathered in opposition, and bad planning, overwhelming public opinion, and the divided loyalties of the troops helped put an end to the coup by the close of its third day. The events of August were largely responsible for political demise of Gorbachev, the rise to power of Boris Yeltsin (1931-), and the dissolution of the Soviet Union itself into the Commonwealth of Independent States.

Andrew Wilson and Nina Bachkatov, *Russia and the Commonwealth: A to Z* (New York: HarperPerennial, 1992), s.v. "Putsch."

What are the names of the two divisions of China, and which one has a communist government?

China has been an officially divided country since 1949, when Nationalists under Chiang Kai-shek fled a takeover by Communists commanded by Mao Tse-tung. Mainland China, controlled by the Communists, was renamed the People's Republic of China. The Nationalists moved to Taiwan, a large island off China's coast, and it was rechristened the Republic of China. In addition to Taiwan, the Republic of China also governs some lesser islands in the region.

Arthur S. Banks, ed., *Political Handbook of the World, 1993* (Binghamton, NY: CSA Publications, 1993), 159.

What was Piccolo Peak?

During World War II (1939-45) an Allied regimental band was assigned to defend a hill in the battle for Salerno, Italy, dubbed Piccolo Peak. The orders came from General Mark Clark. The hill picked up the name after the troops took up their post.

Timothy B. Benford, *The World War II Quiz & Fact Book* (New York: Harper & Row, 1982), 55.

What was the German code name for the operation in which English-speaking German troops would penetrate U.S. lines?

The German SS Commando Otto Skorzeny was responsible for Greif—the code-name for the operation that was to ship German troops behind U.S. lines wearing U.S. uniforms. It was to be implemented in the Battle of the Bulge during World War II (1939-45).

Timothy B. Benford, *The World War II Quiz & Fact Book* (New York: Harper & Row, 1982), 45.

Which U.S. Supreme Court Justice resigned under fire?

Abe Fortas (1910-1982) resigned from the U.S. Supreme Court after a 1969 magazine article revealed that he had received a $20,000 fee three years earlier from a foundation with connections to financier Louis Wolfson, who was being investigated for securities fraud. With calls for his impeachment being made, Fortas resigned from the Supreme Court. He responded that he had returned the payment in 1966 when Wolfson was indicted and maintained that he had committed no wrong.

The Guide to American Law (St Paul, MN: West Publishing Co., 1984), s.v. "Fortas, Abe."

Who were the "Brown Shirts"?

"Brown Shirts" was the name coined for the private army of Nazi supporters that were organized in 1931 by Ernst Rhm (1887-1934) from the Nazi street fighters. The name is derived from the brown shirts the young men wore as uniforms. By 1932 these "storm troopers" or Sturmabteilung (SA) numbered almost half a million, and after 1933 they were sanctioned as a private Nazi police force. As Nazi leader Adolph Hitler (1889-1945) rose to power, the Brown Shirts grew to nearly two million, and they enforced the brutal policies of the Nazi, such as the "Kristallnacht" attack on German Jews on November 9, 1938.

In 1934, when Rhm pushed his plan to make the brown shirts part of the regular German army, Hitler, fearing Rhm as a potential rival, had Himmler's Schutzstaffel (SS) carry out a bloody purge of SA officers and men on the night of June 30, 1934-called the Night of the Long Knives. With the death of Rhm and many effective officers, the brown shirts, no longer powerful, were reorganized into an organization so ineffectual that the later Nuremburg War Crimes Military Tribunal would classify them as an association of unimportant Nazi hangers-on.

Norman Polmar, *World War II: America at War 1941-1945* (New York: Random House, 1991), s.v. "SA."

What was meant by the "policy of containment" developed by the Truman administration?

Just after the Second World War, President Harry S. Truman's administration, acting upon the belief that the Soviet Union was a totalitarian, imperialistic state bent upon spreading communism to other countries, proposed a "policy of containment." This became the official policy of the United States government toward the Soviet Union and its Eastern European satellite states throughout the 1950s, and it was the driving force behind the military buildup that became known as the "Cold War."

Walter J. Raymond, *International Dictionary of Politics* (Lawrenceville, VA: Brunswick Publishing Co., 1980), s.v. "containment."

What organization did Lech Walesa lead in the 1980s?

Lech Walesa rose from being an unknown electrician in the shipyards of Gdansk, Poland, to global prominence largely because of his leadership of Solidarity, an independent Polish trade union of the 1980s.

The International Who's Who 1993-94, 57th ed. (London: Europa Publications, 1993), s.v. "Walesa, Lech."

What were the circumstances surrounding the 1983 publication of diaries attributed to Adolf Hitler?

The German magazine *Stern* acquired 60 volumes purported to be the diary of Adolf Hitler (1889-1945) and published excerpts in April of 1983. Further examination of the documents resulted in a consensus that they were forged. The hoax, as reported in the *New York Times*, was said to have involved the exchange of "suitcases full of money." It may have cost the magazine as much as $3.7 million. Experts theorized that East German forgerers sprinkled authentic documents among the false, noting that forgery was a well-known money maker in that country. British historian Hugh Trevor-Roper was among those initially fooled by the documents; after confirming the authenticity of the diaries, he was forced to issue an apology in the *London Times*. Art dealer Konrad Kujau, who sold the forgeries to journalist Gerd Heidemann, was identified as the possible forgerer.

James M. Markham, "Stuttgart Man Named as Hitler Hoax Source," *New York Times* 10 May 1983. *New York Times* 15 May 1983. John Tagliabue, "The Diaries of Hitler Are Reported Found By German Weekly," *New York Times* 23 April 1983.

What was the Gaither Report, and what highly-charged information did it contain?

The Gaither Report, headed by H. Rowan Gaither, was commissioned during the administration of U.S. president Dwight D. Eisenhower (1890-1969) to compare the military strength of the Soviet Union with that of the United States. Eisenhower had been under pressure to approve $40 billion for the building of bomb shelters that would be used in case of Soviet atomic attack. Outraged at the expense, he commissioned the Gaither Report to determine the United States' strategic position.

When the report came out, it revealed that the United States lagged far behind the Soviet Union in weaponry and general military readiness. Eisenhower decided to re-allocate money in the budget to build-up military readiness.

John W. Finney, "Gaither Report Divides Leaders," *New York Times* 21 December 1957. E. W. Kenworthy, "The Gaither Report: What We Know of It," *New York Times* 29 December 1957. Jay Walz, "White House Says Gaither Report Found U.S. Strong," *New York Times* 29 December 1957.

What did the K.G.B. file "Black Bertha" indicate?

When Nazi deputy Rudolf Hess (1894-1987) parachuted into Scotland, in the hope of negotiating peace with England, the British government simply said he was crazy. Hess landed near the estate of Lord Hamilton on May 11, 1941, only to be taken as a prisoner of war. Some fifty years later, the K.G.B. released a file that documents how the British actually lured him into making the attempt. The file, labeled "Black Bertha," included a memo to Joseph Stalin. The memo asserts that Hess thought he was corresponding with the Duke of Hamilton, when he was in fact receiving letters faked by the British intelligence. Soviet evidence also included two reports from Englishman Kim Philby, the notorious Soviet spy. The file's name stems from K.G.B. reports that Hess was a homosexual and was known as "Black Bertha" in Berlin's homosexual community.

Craig R. Whitney, "Rudolf Hess's Daring Flight: K.G.B. Files Tell New Tales," *New York Times* 8 June 1991.

What was the U.S. cost for the Persian Gulf War?

According to a 1992 Pentagon report, the Persian Gulf War cost the United States $7.3 billion. In all, the war cost $61 billion, paid for with cash contributions and "in-kind" donations from U.S. allies. The largest of these contributions came from Kuwait, with $16.058 billion, and Saudi Arabia, which donated $16.839 billion along with troops and planes. The second greatest commitment of troops and pilots, after the United States, was made by Britain.

Laurence Jolidon, "USA's Bill for Gulf War: $7.3 Billion," *USA Today* 6 April 1992.

What is the Intifada?

The Palestinian uprising in the West Bank and Gaza Strip is commonly known as the Intifada. These areas have been occupied by Israel since 1967, and have been the site of violent Arab protests since 1987. Stone throwing and homemade explosives have been some of the weapons used by the Palestinians, the Israelis have responded with military force and economic isolation. In Arabic the word "intifada" means a "shaking off."

The Columbia Encyclopedia, 5th ed. (New York: Columbia University Press, 1993), s.v. "Intifada." *World Book Encyclopedia* (Chicago: World Book, 1993), s.v. "Gaza Strip."

How did the United Nations get its name?

President Franklin Delano Roosevelt (1882-1945) conceived the name United Nations during World War II (1939-45). Dissatisfied with phrases like Allied Nations or Associated Nations that the British prime minister Winston Churchill (1874-1965) used in his speeches, Roosevelt searched for a term that better expressed the common sense of purpose of those countries fighting against Germany and Japan. Immediately after thinking of United Nations, Roosevelt went to Churchill's room, interrupting him in his bath, and the two agreed on it right there. In 1945 it was used to designate the United Nations Organization.

William L. Safire, *Safire's Political Dictionary* (New York: Random House, 1978), s.v. "United Nations."

What defeat led to the French withdrawal from Indochina?

The French defeat at Dien Bien Phu in 1954 led to French withdrawal from Indochina. In 1953 Vietminh forces led by General Vo Nguyen Giap attacked the French military compound under the command of General Henri Navarre. The attack turned into a protracted siege marked by a continual and devastating artillery barrage. The loss was less of a strategic defeat then it was a major blow to French morale. Nevertheless Dien Bien Phu led to the French signing the Geneva Accord and subsequently leaving Indochina.

William J. Duiker, *Historical Dictionary of Vietnam* (Metuchen, NJ: Scarecrow Press, 1989), p. 46-7.

Was there a Nazi plot to kidnap the Pope?

A Rome-based Catholic magazine, *30 Giorni* claims that the Nazis had plans to invade the Vatican and kidnap and hold hostage Pope Pius XII (1876-1958) and his cardinals. The article is based on written statements of Rudolf Rahn, the wartime German ambassador to Italy. Fearful of the consequences of such an act Rahn claims to have persuaded Third Reich leaders to abandon their foolhardy plans.

Clyde Haberman, "Catholic Magazine Says Hitler Planned to Seize Pope Pius as Hostage," *New York Times* 21 July 1991.

Which U.S. president strongly supported the League of Nations and why did the United States not become a member?

The establishment of the League of Nations was one of U.S. president Woodrow Wilson's (1856-1924) "Fourteen Points" following the end of World War I (1914-18). His dream of American involvement in the league were dashed, however, when isolationist Henry Cabot Lodge (1850-1924) rallied the U.S. Senate to reject the Versailles Treaty and league membership.

Family Encyclopedia of American History (Pleasantville, NY: Reader's Digest Association, 1975), s.v. "League of Nations and U.S."

What was the Battle of the Bulge?

The Battle of the Bulge was a last-ditch effort by the German leader Adolph Hitler (1889-1945) to win World War II (1939-45). Hitler's attack began on December 16, 1944, in the Ardennes Forest in Luxembourg and southern Belgium. By the battle's conclusion in January of 1945, the Allied forces, led by U.S. General George S. Patton (1885-1945), defeated the Germans and succeeded in dissipating the "bulge" the Germans had created in the Allied line.

George C. Kohn, *Dictionary of Wars* (New York: Facts On File Publications, 1986), s.v. "Bulge, Battle of the."

What was the Abraham Lincoln Battalion?

The Abraham Lincoln Battalion was the name given to a group of American volunteers who fought on the side of the Republic against General Francisco Franco's Nationalist forces in the Spanish Civil War. Members of the Lincoln Battalion were generally young men between 21 and 28 years of age. They came from both white-collar and blue-collar backgrounds. Politically, they were idealistic radicals, and many were members of the Communist Party or Young Communist League. Most members of the battalion had very little prior military background or training.

On Christmas Day of 1936, the first contingent of the Lincoln Battalion set sail for Spain. They were soon followed by 3,000 other volunteers. Upon arrival in Spain, the battalion was soon involved in several major battles. Although the men fought bravely, they suffered tremendous casualties due to their insufficient military training. By the time the Spanish Civil War ended in 1939, over one-third of the Abraham Lincoln Battalion volunteers had lost their lives.

James W. Cortada, ed., *Historical Dictionary of the Spanish Civil War, 1936-1939* (Westport, CT: Greenwood Press, 1982), s.v. "Abraham Lincoln Battalion."

What happened in Tiananmen Square in Beijing, China, in June of 1989?

The year 1989 was a dramatic one for many of the world's Communist nations. Pro-democracy demonstrations in the countries of Eastern Europe had toppled many Communist regimes. The Soviet Union, under the leadership of Mikhail Gorbachev, continued to institute an increasing number of democratic reforms. The winds of democratic reform soon spread to Communist China.

On April 18, 1989, university students gathered in Tiananmen Square in China's capital, Beijing, to mourn the death of a popular Communist leader, Hu Yaobang. The gathering soon turned into a demonstration to demand democratic government reforms and an increase in personal freedoms. Student leaders of the demonstrations demanded an audience with China's hard-line leaders, led by Deng Xiaoping. Despite the presence of police and army troops, the demonstrators refused to leave Tiananmen Square. Throughout April and May of 1989, the demonstrators won the support of Beijing's citizenry. The size of the demonstrations in Tiananmen Square grew daily, and pro-democracy demonstrations began to form in other major cities throughout China.

China's hard-line Communist leaders realized that the demonstrators were growing stronger and bolder by the day and represented a serious challenge to their hold on power. On April 27 and May 20, they ordered army troops to enter Tiananmen Square and disperse the demonstrators. On both occasions, the army troops were convinced by the demonstrators and ordinary citizens not to disrupt the demonstrations. However, just after midnight on June 4, 1989, the demonstrators were attacked by tanks, armored personnel carriers, and troops loyal to the Communist government. The soldiers entered Tiananmen Square and brutally beat and shot many of the demonstrators as well as innocent civilians. Many of the student leaders of the demonstration were arrested and executed. The democracy movement had been savagely crushed. It is estimated that over 1,000 students and workers were massacred and more than 10,000 people injured.

Lee Davis, *Man-Made Catastrophes: From the Burning of Rome to the Lockerbie Crash* (New York: Facts on File, 1993), 62-66.

What was the "Final Solution"?

The term "Final Solution" ("Endlsung" in German) was often used by the German leader Adolf Hitler (1889-1945) and other high-ranking officials of the Nazi party when referring to the deportation and extermination of the Jews. Elite Nazi units known as the SS hunted down Jews and sent them to extermination camps that were built in areas captured by the Nazis during World War II (1939-1945). At these camps, Jews were often exterminated in elaborate gas chambers and their bodies burned in huge crematoriums. The "Final Solution" was a well-planned and well-executed government policy that was designed to eventually rid the world of Jews. The defeat of the Nazis in World War II ended these plans, but not before the "Final Solution" resulted in the deaths of almost six million Jews in Europe and many areas of the former Soviet Union.

Christian Zentner and Friedemann Bedurftig, eds., *The Encyclopedia of the Third Reich, trans. Amy Hacket* (New York: Macmillan, 1991), s.v. "final solution."

Who was Lon Blum?

Lon Blum (1872-1950) was the first socialist and Jew to hold the French national office of Premier (equivalent to the office of prime minister). His legacy was a social reform program he instituted in the 1930s that was similar to America's New Deal. Blum received liberal arts and law degrees and began working for the Conseil d'Etat (Council of State) which dealt with suits between citizens and the French government. In the 1890s Blum became involved on the side of the leftists in the "Dreyfus Affair" and following World War I (1914-18) he was active in the Socialist Party. The 1920s brought turbulence to both French society and the international socialist movement. From this era Blum emerged as the leader of moderate French socialism. Blum, as an intellectual turned politician, became premier of France in 1936 and held that office for 13 months. His term of office was clouded by the effects of the worldwide depression and the shadow of Adolph Hitler (1889-1945) coming to power in Germany. Blum's Popular Front government fell in June of 1937 but he regained the office of premier for a brief time in 1938. During World War II (1939-45) Blum was arrested by Vichy authorities and eventually was sent to the German concentration camp at Buchenwald. In August of 1944 his death was erroneously reported in the American press. Liberated by the American army in the closing days of the war, Blum returned to France and re-entered politics as a special ambassador to the United States. In the winter of 1946-47 he once again briefly held the post of premier. Blum died in Paris, the city of his birth, in 1950.

Anne Commire, ed., *Historic World Leaders* (Detroit: Gale Research, 1994), s.v. "Blum, Lon." Martin H. Greenberg, *The Jewish Lists* (New York: Schocken Books, 1979), 8.

When was the Republic of China established?

The Republic of China, more commonly known as Taiwan, was established in 1950 by Chiang Kai-shek. Chiang and his followers, the Kuomintang, fought a lengthy civil war against Mao Tse-tung's Communist forces. In 1949, the Communists had captured control of mainland China, and renamed it the People's Republic of China. Chiang and the nationalist remnants of the Kuomintang fled to the island of Formosa (Taiwan) and founded the Republic of China. The Taiwanese government, which is dominated by the Kuomintang, does not accept the legitimacy of mainland China's Communist government and considers itself the sole legal government of all of China. The United States government was a staunch supporter of Taiwan until 1979, when it established diplomatic relations with China's Communist government.

George C. Kohn, *Dictionary of Wars* (New York: Facts on File, 1986), s.v. "Chinese Civil War of 1945-49."

What were the meanings behind the markings and colors worn by inmates of concentration camps?

The concentration camps created by the Nazis during World War II (1939-45) housed people from a variety of political, religious, and ethnic groups. All inmates in the camp were categorized according to a color code system on their uniform. A red triangle designated political prisoners; homosexuals wore a pink triangle; Gypsies wore a brown triangle; criminals were designated with a green triangle; "shiftless elements" wore a black triangle; and Jews wore two overlapping yellow triangles, one pointing up and the other down, to resemble a Star of David. Inmates who were mentally retarded wore a label with the term *Bld* or "stupid," and those designated for slave labor wore the letter "A" for *Arbeit* or "work" on their uniform. Foreign prisoners were designated by an "F" for French, or "P" for Polish. War criminals were identified by the letter "K" on their uniform.

Louis L. Snyder, *Louis L. Snyder's Historical Guide to World War II* (Westport, CT: Greenwood Press, 1982), 162.

When did the Cold War officially end?

At the end of World War II (1939-45), tensions rose significantly between the Soviet Union and the United States. The Soviet Union and its allies formed the Eastern bloc, while the United States and its allies formed the Western bloc. For nearly 50 years, both sides built huge armies and possessed a massive arsenal of nuclear weapons that kept the world on the brink of nuclear war. However, the ending of Communism in Eastern Europe in 1989 caused a sea of change in attitudes between the Soviet Union and the United States. Both countries agreed to cooperate with each other rather than live as adversaries.

In November of 1990, representatives from the Soviet Union, the United States, and many of the countries in Europe met in Paris, France, for the Conference on Security and Cooperation in Europe. At the end of the conference on November 21, 1990, President Mikhail Gorbachev (1931-) of the Soviet Union and U.S. president George Bush (1924-) signed the Charter of Paris for a New Europe. By signing the charter, both countries declared an end to an era of confrontation in Europe and the beginning of a new era of democracy throughout Europe. The signing of the Charter of Paris for a New Europe is considered the official end of the Cold War.

Facts On File, 23 November 1990.

Who succeeded Leonid Brezhnev as the General Secretary of the Communist Party in the former Soviet Union?

After a bitter struggle with Konstantin Chernenko (1911-1985) following Leonid Brezhnev's death in 1982, former KGB man Yuri Andropov (1914-1984) assumed the General Secretaryship of the Communist Party in the former Soviet Union.

Ian Derbyshire, *Politics in the Soviet Union: from Brezhnev to Gorbachev* (Edinburgh: Chambers, 1987), 35-37.

Have the remains of Czar Nicholas II and his wife, Alexandra, ever been recovered?

In 1992 Soviet scientists claimed that two skeletons found in a pit in the Siberian city of Yekaterinburg were those of Czar Nicholas II (1868-1918) and his wife, Alexandra (1872-1918), who was the granddaughter of Queen Victoria of England. The determination was based on computer modeling which compared the skulls with photographs of the Czar and his wife. Nicholas, his wife, children, and entourage were in exile when they were executed on July 17, 1918, by a firing squad on Lenin's orders.

"Bones Are Identified as the Czar's," *New York Times* 23 June 1992.

Who was Lord Haw Haw?

Lord Haw Haw was the derisive name given to William Joyce (1906-1946), an Anglo-American turned propagandist for German leader Adolph Hitler's (1889-1945) Third Reich. Joyce, a member of the British Union of Facists, moved to Germany in 1939 where he quickly found employment with Paul Joseph Goebbels (1897-1945), the Minister for Public Enlightenment and Propaganda. Captured by British forces in 1945, Joyce was eventually tried and found guilty by the British courts. After an unsuccessful appeal, he was hanged in London on January 3, 1946, as a traitor.

Louis L. Snyder, *Louis L. Snyder's Historical Guide to World War II* (Westport, CT: Greenwood Press, 1982), s.v. "Joyce, William."

Were there any plans that used live bats as bomb carriers during World War II?

During World War II (1939-45) various branches of the U.S. military tested live bats as offensive weapons. The idea was that thousands of bats would be strapped with small incendiary devices and released by plane over Japanese cities. Many Japanese houses and buildings were constructed of wood and paper, making them extremely susceptible to fire. The plan, however, proved to be ill-conceived and fraught with problems. The project was finally canceled in August of 1944.

Norman Polmar and Thomas B. Allen, *World War II: America at War, 1941-1945* (New York: Random House, 1991), 135.

Which Supreme Court justice holds the record for the longest tenure on the court?

Former U.S. Supreme Court Justice William Douglas (1898-1980) holds the record for the longest tenure on the highest bench in the land. Douglas had served for 36 years and 7 months when he resigned in November of 1975. The previous record had been held by Justice Stephen Field (1816-99) who had served for 34 years and 9 months.

American Leaders, 1789-1987: A Biographical Summary (Washington, DC: Congressional Quarterly, 1987), 34.

Who were the members of the Warren Commission?

The Commission on the Assassination of President Kennedy is more commonly known as the Warren Commission. On September 24, 1964, it reported to U.S. president Johnson that Lee Harvey Oswald (1939-1963) had acted alone in John F. Kennedy's assassination.

The seven members of the Warren Commission, all appointed by U.S. president Lyndon B. Johnson (1908-1973) to investigate the 1963 assassination of U.S. president John F. Kennedy (1917-1963), were led by Earl Warren (1891-1974), chief justice of the United States Supreme Court. The other appointees to the team of inquiry— Hale Boggs, Gerald Ford, John Sherman Cooper, and Richard B. Russell—were an even bipartisan mix of members of the U.S. Congress. Onetime Central Intelligence Agency director Allen W. Dulles (1888-1959) was also on the Commission, as was John J. McCloy, former chair of Chase Manhattan Bank. Dulles' inclusion on the committee was questioned by critics, since Dulles was forced to sign by the slain president after the Bay of Pig's fiasco. Dulles headed the Central Intelligence Agency, which trained the operatives who failed to invade Cuba in 1961.

James P. Duffy and Vincent L. Ricci, *The Assassination of John F. Kennedy: A Complete Book of Facts* (New York: Thunder's Mouth Press, 1992), 492-93. Michael Nelson, ed., *The Presidency A to Z: A Ready Reference Encyclopedia* (Washington, DC: Congressional Quarterly, 1992), s.v. "Warren Commission."

With whom was U.S. representative Wilbur Mills linked in a 1974 scandal?

In 1974, U.S. representative Wilbur Mills became involved in an unusual scandal with a stripper named Fanne Foxe. The Arkansas Democrat, then chair of the powerful House Ways and Means Committee, was stopped by District of Columbia police in the early hours of October 8 of that year for having its lights off. Police followed it to the Tidal Basin, a shallow pool in the District of Columbia, where a woman had either fallen, jumped, or had been pushed from the vehicle into the water. All three occupants were brought into custody and their identities were revealed—Congressman Mills along with Foxe, a 38-year-old Argentine whose real name was Annabel Battistella, and a masseuse.

Media reports revealed that Mills had frequented the Silver Slipper, a strip club where Foxe worked, spending hundreds of dollars there over the last year. Despite the media attention and the fact that the married Mills publicly admitted to being involved with Foxe, he was re-elected by Arkansas voters a month later. Later the lawmaker entered Bethesda (Maryland) Naval Medical Center after he collapsed from "physical exhaustion" and after Mills lost his post as chair of the influential budget committee he retired from politics in 1975.

George C. Kohn, *Encyclopedia of American Scandal* (New York: Facts on File, 1989), s.v. "Wilbur Mills: the Tidal Basin incident."

What was the 1934 plot to overthrow the United States government?

A plot to overthrow the United States government was uncovered in 1934, involving members of the American Legion and Wall Street financiers who wished to restore the gold standard. Depression-era reactionary politics and the progressive policies of U.S. president Franklin D. Roosevelt (1882-1945) also entered into the motives of the plotters. The organizers of the alleged plan were associated with the American Liberty League, an anti-labor, anti-Semitic, and fascism-supporting organization. The trouble began when Gerald C. MacGuire, a Legionnaire and former Marine, and stockbroker Grayson M. P. Murphy requested that Major General Smedley D. Butler speak at the American Legion convention make a speech in favor of restoring the gold standard.

Butler, a Republican who had supported the Democrat Roosevelt, refused, but MacGuire and Murphy then began asking Butler to lead a group of Legionnaires in a march on the White House in Washington, DC. The veterans apparently planned to storm the White House while their leaders informed the public that Roosevelt was ailing. A cabinet minister would then be named interim president. The coup-plotters also had plans to remove the nation's numerous unemployed to labor camps. After MacGuire and others pestered Butler about 40 times with this request, the annoyed general told a newspaper reporter Paul Comly French about the nettlesome solicitations. The plot, as well as the activities of the well-connected American Liberty League, were revealed to the public by French's newspaper articles. The notoriety lead to congressional committee hearings, but they ended inconclusively.

Irving Wallace, David Wallechinsky and Amy Wallace, *Significa* (New York: E. P. Dutton, 1983), 78.

What were the six crises in the political career of former U.S. President Richard Nixon?

Former U.S. president Richard Nixon (1913-1994) had six crises in his political career:

The Alger Hiss case when as California's junior senator he stridently alerted the American public to the "communist menace."

The "Checkers speech" of 1952 when Nixon successfully defended his acceptance of $16,000 from California businessmen.

U.S. President Eisenhower's heart attack which produced profound feelings of inadequacy and humility in Nixon.

The Anti-American riots in Caracas directed at Nixon when he visited South America.

The "kitchen debate" with the Soviet Union's Nikita Khrushchev (1894-1971).

The presidential campaign of 1960 and his loss to John F. Kennedy (1917-1963) which left Nixon beaten but unbowed.

Pittsburgh Press 9 June 1973.

What was the name of the sailor that U.S. president-to-be John F. Kennedy rescued during World War II?

During World War II (1939-45), president-to-be John F. Kennedy (1917-63) was commander of PT-109, a patrol gunboat operating in and around the Solomon Islands in the Pacific Ocean. On the night of August 2, 1943, the boat was cut in two by a Japanese destroyer, *Amigiri* immediately killing two of the thirteen crewmen. Sailor Patrick Henry McMahon survived the crash but was badly burned about his face, chest, arms, and legs. Kennedy, then a Lieutenant (junior grade), took the injured sailor onto his back and gripping a strap from McMahon's life jacket between his teeth swam for four hours until reaching Plum Pudding Island. With no means of surviving on the desolate island, the 11 survivors rested a few days before undertaking a four-hour swim, again with Kennedy towing McMahon to Olasana Island where they were rescued by American forces. McMahon survived his severe injuries, was discharged from the navy in 1945 and was postmaster in Cathedral City, California, until his retirement in 1975. McMahon died in 1990 in Encinitas, California.

Years later Kennedy, during his presidency was asked by a young boy how he became a war hero. Kennedy replied, "It was absolutely involuntary. They sank my boat."

"Patrick H. McMahon Dead at 84. Burned Sailor Saved by Kennedy," *New York Times* 22 February 1990. Ralph Woods, ed., *A Third Treasury of the Familiar* (New York: Macmillan, 1970), 264. Fred L. Worth, *The Trivia Encyclopedia* (New York: Bell, 1974), 9.

What was the story behind the U.S. refusal to allow the German liner *St. Louis* dockage in 1939?

The German liner *St. Louis* was carrying 937 Jewish refugees from Nazi Germany in 1939 when it was refused dockage in New York. The Hamburg-American liner was the last vessel to leave Germany before the outbreak of World War II (1939-45), but its passengers were refused entry because U.S. policy restricted German emigration to the United States at 25,957. Although there was no official quota for Jewish emigres from Germany, that decision was largely left up to American consular officials in Germany. Germany only allowed refugees to take ten Reichsmarks (about four dollars) out of the country and the United States refused entry to anyone "likely to become a public charge." Although entry was officially refused on these grounds there were many charges of anti-Semitism. The president's wife Eleanor Roosevelt (1884-1962) favored letting the refugees in the country, but U.S. president Franklin Roosevelt (1882-1945) ultimately bowed to an isolationist public mood and refused to let the liner dock. The *St. Louis* then tried to set its passengers ashore in Cuba but was likewise rebuffed. Between May 27 and June 6 the ship steamed around the Caribbean and off the Florida coast before heading back to Europe. Eventually its passengers were allowed to disembark in various European ports including Antwerp and Rotterdam. From these cities some of the Jewish men, women, and children found their way to France and England. Many of the refugees, however, ended back in Hitler's Germany.

Gordon Thomas and Max Morgan Witts, *Voyage of the Damned* (New York: Stein and Day, 1974), 17-19, 287-93.

How many members of the U.S. Armed Forces lost their lives in hostile action during the Jimmy Carter administration?

During the Jimmy Carter (1924-) administration, eight members of the U.S. Armed Forces lost their lives in hostile action.

Parade 19 July, 1987.

Which U.S. general was courtmartialed for criticizing American defense policy?

General William (Billy) Mitchell (1879-1936) was courtmartialed in 1925 for his vociferous criticism of American defense policy following World War I (1914-18). Mitchell was a decorated hero in World War I and assistant chief of the Army Air Service from 1919 to 1925. He was a vocal proponent of the effectiveness of air power, called for the creation of an independent air corp and much to the chagrin of the navy, bombed and sunk a derelict warship in a staged air attack. Mitchell was also extremely critical of Pacific defense policy and foresaw a war with Japan. Mitchell accused the U.S. War Department of "incompetency, criminal negligence and almost treasonable administration of the national defense." He was subsequently courtmartialed for insubordination and forced to resign his Army commission. He died in 1936, but many critics claim he was vindicated by the events of World War II (1939-45).

Family Encyclopedia of American History, (Pleasantville, NY: Reader's Digest Association, 1975), s.v. "Mitchell, William (Billy)."

What were the results of a 1992 investigation into the 1935 assassination of Senator Huey Long of Louisiana?

A 1992 investigation of the 1935 assassination of Senator Huey Long of Louisiana (1893-1935) reached the same conclusion as the original investigation in 1935. Both concluded that Long was assassinated by Dr. Carl A. Weiss, who acted as the lone assassin, motivated by a personal grudge. Weiss had accused Long of depriving Weiss's father-in-law of a job and of spreading lies about the Weiss family lineage. Over the years conspiracy theorists believed that Long was assassinated because his growing political power threatened the reelection of U.S. president Franklin Roosevelt (1882-1945). Upon shooting Long at the Louisiana State Capitol, Weiss was immediately killed by Long's bodyguards. The conspiracy theory has been fueled over the years by the disappearance of many of the records relating to the assassination and the fact that an autopsy was not performed on either Long or Weiss.

Huey Long, who was nicknamed "the Kingfish," was a controversial politician who was as well known for his demagoguery as he was for his empathy for his poor Caucasian constituency.

McGraw-Hill Encyclopedia of World Biography (New York: McGraw-Hill, 1973), s.v. "Long, Huey P.." "Finding Confirmed in Huey Long Case," *New York Times* 6 June 1992.

When was the Lincoln copy of the Magna Carta returned to Great Britain?

The Lincoln copy of the Magna Carta was formally returned to Great Britain on January 11, 1946, having been kept safely in the United States for four years to avoid the perils of World War II (1939-45). The great charter, wrested from King John at Runnymede in 1215, was handed by Dr. Luther H. Evans, Librarian of Congress, to His Majesty's Minister, John Balfour, for return to the Dean and Chapter of Lincoln Cathedral.

"Magna Carta Copy Returned by U.S.," *New York Times* 12 January 1946.

What was the fate of the crew of the American B-24 Liberator bomber *Lady Be Good?*

The so-called "ghost" bomber of World War II (1939-45) got lost after a bombing raid on Naples, Italy, on April 4, 1943, running out of gas and crashing in the wastelands of Libya in the North African desert. It was not until February 19, 1960, however, that the details of the airplane's final flight became known, when the diary of the co-pilot was recovered from the desert. The diary was found deep in the Libyan wastelands, where the remains of five of the nine crew members of the four-engine B-24 Liberator *Lady Be Good* were recovered after 17 years. Second Lieutenant Robert F. Toner of North Attleboro, Massachusetts, bailed out with the rest of the crew after the ill-fated raid, and survived, walking about 85 miles from the downed aircraft, and making diary entries for eight days during which merciless heat alternated with bitter cold, little water, and no hope. The fliers' remains were found by American oilmen in 1960 in a spot 400 miles from the Mediterranean coast and hundreds of miles from regular caravan trails.

"Flier's Desert Diary Tells of '43 Ordeal," *New York Times* 21 February 1960.

What is the name of the airplane which carried the first atomic bomb?

During World War II (1939-1945), the *Enola Gay*, a modified Boeing B-29 bomber, dropped the first atomic bomb on Hiroshima, Japan, at 8:15 a.m. on August 6, 1945. It was piloted by Colonel Paul W. Tibbets, Jr. (b. 1915) of Miami, Florida. The bombardier was Major Thomas W. Ferebee of Mocksville, North Carolina. Bomb designer Captain William S. Parsons was aboard as an observer.

Three days later, another B-29 called *Bock's Car* dropped a second bomb on Nagasaki, Japan.

Facts On File News Digest with Index 1-7 August 1945. *Milestones of Aviation* (Washington, DC: Smithsonian Institution, 1989), 195.

What was the greatest loss ever suffered by a single family in American naval history?

Perhaps no family in American naval history has lost as many sons as those of Mr. and Mrs. Thomas Sullivan of Waterloo, Iowa. During World War II (1939-45) the cruiser *Juneau* was sunk during the battle for Guadalcanal on November 14, 1942. Although the Navy's policy was to separate members of the same family, the five sons of Mr. and Mrs. Thomas Sullivan had enlisted with the provision that they serve together. All five were on board the *Juneau* and died during its sinking.

Thomas Parrish, ed., *The Simon and Schuster Encyclopedia of World War II* (New York: Simon & Schuster, 1978), s.v. "Sullivan brothers."

When did World War II end?

In the European theater of war, on May 7, 1945, at 2:41 A.M. (8:41 P.M. Eastern Wartime, Sunday, May 6, in the United States), Colonel General Alfred Jodl, chief of staff of the German Armed Forces, signed a statement of unconditional surrender at General Eisenhower's headquarter in Reims, France, which was to be effective at 12:01 A.M. on May 9, 1945 (German time). Lieutenant General Walter Bedell signed for the United States and Major General Ivan Susloparav for the Soviet Union. Lieutenant General Sir Frederick Morgan of Britain and General Francois Sevez of France signed as witnesses. On hearing the news, Great Britain's Prime Minister Churchill and United States President Truman declared May 8 as Victory in Europe (V-E) Day. However, the Soviet Union's leader Stalin insisted on a second surrender ceremony in Berlin on that day (May 8 was premature, since the hostilities did not formally cease until that night.) In the Pacific theater of war Japan first offered to surrender, on August 10, 1945, but negotiations with the United States were not completed until August 14. On that day Japan agreed to an unconditional surrender by sending a note to the U.S. State Department in Washington, D.C. at 6:10 P.M. on Tuesday, August 14, 1945. On August 15, the Japanese Emperor Hirohito announced to the Japanese people that Japan had agreed to end the war. On September 2, 1945, aboard the battleship U.S.S. *Missouri* in Tokyo Bay, the official surrender took place with Foreign Minister Mamoru Shigemitsu and General Yoshijro Umezu signing for Japan and General Douglas MacArthur as Allied Supreme Commander, General Chester Nimitz signed for the United States, Admiral Bruce Fraser for Great Britain, and General Thomas Blamey for Australia. This is known as victory in Japan (V-J) Day. This signing signaled the end of World War II.

Barbara Berliner, *The Book of Answers* (New York: Prentice Hall Press, 1990), 286. *The World At Arms: The Reader's Digest Illustrated History of World War II* (London: Reader's Digest Association, 1989), 443-5.

What is the background of the false Knights of Columbus oath?

A document purporting to contain the oath of the Knights of Columbus, a Catholic organization, has resurfaced from time to time during political campaigns; it is a piece of anti-catholic propaganda intended to harm Catholic candidates. During a congressional election in 1912, the false oath was first circulated out of Aurora, Missouri. It read, "I do further promise and declare that I will, when opportunity presents, wage relentless war, secretly and openly, against all heretics, Protestants, and Masons, as I am directed to do, to extirpate them from the face of the whole earth." The oath was denounced as fake the following year by a congressional committee. It was used by the Ku Klux Klan against the Democratic presidential candidate Al Smith (1873-1944) in 1928 and reappeared during the presidential primary election between Hubert Humphrey (1911-78) and John F. Kennedy (1917-63) in 1960. Kennedy was a member of the Knights of Columbus.

Time 22 August 1960.

What did the Japanese signal "Tora! Tora! Tora!" signify the day of the attack on Pearl Harbor?

Since any false move could spoil the Japanese Navy's surprise attack on the U.S. naval base at Pearl Harbor, Hawaii, and other Pacific locations on December 7, 1941, all commanders had orders to refrain from any hostile act until the words "Tora! Tora! Tora!" ("Tiger! Tiger! Tiger!") were used to signal that the first wave of bombers had caught the Americans totally unaware.

Gordon W. Prange, *At Dawn We Slept* (New York: McGraw-Hill, 1981), 379, 504. Gordon W. Prange, *December 7, 1941: The Day the Japanese Attacked Pearl Harbor* (New York: McGraw-Hill, 1988), 108-10, 259.

Was Albert Einstein offered the presidency of Israel?

In 1952, after the death of Israel's first president, Chaim Weizmann (1874-1952), the position was offered to Albert Einstein (1879-1955) via a note sent by the Israeli ambassador. Einstein declined, citing his failing health and the fact that many years of abstract thinking prevented him from dealing properly with people.

Ronald W. Clark, *Einstein: The Life and Times* (New York: World Publishing, 1971), 617-19. Solomon Quasha, *Albert Einstein: An Intimate Portrait* (New York: Forest Publishing, 1980), 296-98.

When were women first admitted into West Point and other U.S. military academies?

U.S. Public Law 94-106, signed by the U.S. president Gerald Ford (1913-) on October 7, 1975, mandated that women could enter the Department of Defense service academies by the summer of 1976. Of the U.S. Military Academy (West Point) class of 1,480 that started on July 7, 1976, 119 were women. Eighty women were admitted to the U.S. Naval Academy on July 6 of that year. One hundred fifty-five enrolled at the Air Force Academy on June 28. This was the same day that 38 women enrolled in the U.S. Coast Guard Academy.

Angela Howard Zophy, ed., *Handbook of American Women's History* (New York: Garland, 1990), s.v. "United States Military Academy, The." Joseph Nathan Kane, *Famous First Facts, 4th ed.* (New York: H. W. Wilson, 1981), 9, 37, 176, 417. Joan McCullough, *First of All: Significant "Firsts" by American Women* (New York: Holt, Rinehart and Winston, 1980), 161. Judith Hicks Stiehm, *Bring Me Men and Women: Mandated Change at the U.S. Air Force Academy, 4th ed.* (California: University of California Press, 1981), 10-11.

Who were the American soldiers in the famous photograph of the flag-raising at Iwo Jima?

On February 23, 1945, during World War II (1939-45), several U.S. Marines were immortalized in a photograph while raising the American flag atop Mount Suribachi on Iwo Jima, an eight-mile island in the northwestern Pacific Ocean. The men who raised the flag were Private First Class Ira H. Hayes, a Pima Indian from Arizona; Private First Class Franklin R. Sousley from Kentucky; Sergeant Michael Strank from Pennsylvania; Pharmacist's Mate Second Class John Bradley from Wisconsin; Private First Class Rene A. Gagnon from New Hampshire; and

Corporal Harlon Block from Texas. Sousley, Strank, and Block were killed and Bradley was wounded and evacuated. Only Hay and Gagnon left the island unhurt.

The famous photograph of this incident was taken by Joe Rosenthal of the Associated Press, who won a Pulitzer Prize for it in 1945. The picture also served as a model for the Marine Corps War Memorial in Washington, DC.

Chronicle of America (Liberty, MO: JL International, 1993), 722. Bill D. Ross, *Iwo Jima: Legacy of Valor* (New York: Vanguard Press, 1985), 100-102.

What is the story behind the 1972 plane crash and subsequent cannibalism in the Andes Mountains?

An ill-famed case of modern cannibalism took place in 1972 as a result of an airplane crash in the 18,000-foot-high Andes Mountains in Chile. The plane crashed on October 13, killing 21 persons immediately. Eight were killed later in an avalanche. Two survivors found their way to safety on December 22, after climbing for ten days to reach civilization. The other 14 were then rescued. The survivors, having run out of food supplies, were forced to eat the remains of their dead companions in order to survive in the below-freezing weather. Some of the survivors were members of the Uruguayan Old Christian Brothers rugby team, which had chartered the flight. A 1974 book about the ordeal by Piers Paul Read entitled *Alive* was made into a movie of the same name in 1993.

Facts On File 24-31 December 1972. James Pallot, ed., *The Motion Picture Guide, 1994 Annual* (New York: CineBooks, 1994), 7-8. George E. Delury, ed., *The World Almanac and Book of Facts 1974* (New York: Newspaper Enterprise Association, 1973), 982.

Who were the first women generals in the United States armed forces?

The first woman to be named to the rank of major general in the United States Army was Mary Clarke (1924-) in June of 1978. She was promoted to this rank when the Women's Army Corps was dissolved and incorporated into the regular army.

The first woman to be appointed to the rank of admiral in the United States Navy was Alene B. Duerk (1920-) in 1972.

The first woman to be appointed to the rank of brigadier general in the United States Air Force was Jeanne M. Holm (1921-) in 1971. She was later promoted to major general.

The first woman to reach the rank of brigadier general in the United States Marine Corps was Margaret A. Brewer (c.1930-) in 1978. The Marine Corps was the last of the armed services to promote a woman to the rank of general.

Phyllis J. Read and Bernard L. Witlieb, *The Book of Women's Firsts* (New York: Random House, 1992), s.v. "Margaret A. Brewer," "Mary Clarke," "Alene B. Duerk," "Jeanne M. Holm."

Languages

How is the greeting "hello" and the salutation "goodbye" conveyed in other languages?

"Hello" and "goodbye" are expressed in some other languages in the following ways:

Language	Hello	Good-bye
French	Bonjour	Au revoir
German	Guten Tag	Auf Wiedersehen
Italian	Buon giorno	Arrivederci
Spanish	Buenos dias/Hola	Adios
Japanese	Arigato	Sayonara
Arabic	Salaam aleikum (peace to you)	Ila al-laqaa
Hebrew	Boker tov	Schalom
Swahili		Kwaheri

Graydon S. DeLand, *American Traveler's Companion* (New York: Fielding Publications, 1966), 108.

How are the expressions "thank you (very much)" and "you're welcome" conveyed in other languages?

"Thank you (very much)" and "you're welcome" are conveyed in some other languages in the following ways:

Language	Thank you	You're Welcome
German	Danke	Bitte
French	Merci	Je vous en prie; De rien
Italian	Grazie	Prego
Spanish	Gracias	No hay de que; De Nada

Graydon S. DeLand, *American Traveler's Companion* (New York: Fielding Publications, 1966), 252.

How is "Easter" or "Easter Sunday" translated into other languages?

"Easter" or "Easter Sunday" may be translated:
French—dimanche de Pques
German—Ostersonntag
Italian—domenica di Pasqua
Portuguese—Domingo da P scoa
Spanish—Domingo de Pascua

Graydon S. DeLand, *American Traveler's Companion* (New York: Fielding Publications, 1966), 72-73.

How is the phrase "I love you" translated into other languages?

The phrase "I love you" may be translated:
German-Ich liebe dich
French-Je t'aime
Italian-Ti voglio bene
Spanish-Yo te quiero

The American Heritage Larousse Spanish Dictionary (Boston: Houghton Mifflin, 1986), 425. Ken Noyle, *101 Ways to Say I Love You: Romance from Afghanistan to Zambia* (Los Angeles: Price, Stern, Sloan, 1983).

What are some examples of English words that are spelled differently in England than they are in the United States?

Words with the same meaning can be spelled differently in England than they are in the United States even though pronunciation is the same. One such word that is not quite so obvious is "gaol," which is a word for a British prison. It is pronounced the same as jail. Other examples of differences in spelling, with the American spelling listed first, are as follows:
center and centre
check and cheque
color and colour
curb and kerb
honor and honour
inquire and enquire
jewelry and jewellery
organization and organisation
pajamas and pyjamas
peddler and pedlar
program and programme
realize and realise
theater and theatre

The New York Public Library Desk Reference, 2d ed. (New York: Prentice Hall General Reference, 1993), s.v. "grammar and punctuation." *Random House Webster's College Dictionary,* (New York: Random House, 1992), s.v. "gaol."

What is the most frequently used letter and word in the English language?

The most frequently used letter in the English language is "e." The most frequently written word is "the"; the most frequently spoken word is "I."

Mark C. Young, ed., *The Guinness Book of Records 1995* (New York: Facts on File, 1994), 140.

Who invented the artificial language called "Esperanto"?

Ludwig Lazarus Zamenhof (1859-1917) invented what is the best-known artificial language, originally called "Lingro Internacia" but popularly known as "Esperanto." Zamenhof, a Polish oculist, first published Esperanto in Russian in 1887, calling it an international language. In 1966 the United Nations rejected a petition of nearly a million signatures requesting that Esperanto be officially designated an international language.

David Crystal, *The Cambridge Encyclopedia of Language* (Cambridge: Cambridge University Press, 1987), 354.

What is the etymology of the term "nincompoop"?

According to Samuel Johnson's (1709-1784) dictionary, "nincompoop," which meant fool or simpleton, derives from the Latin phrase "non compos mentis," or "not of sound mind." Another origin many have been "ninny," an abbreviation for "an innocent," meaning a silly fellow or simpleton. Another early form, "nickumpoop," suggests a French connection: in French, Nick was a name for "a fool" and poop was English slang for "to deceive, cozen, befool." Another derivation may be "noddy," meaning fool; "poopnoddy" and "noddypoop" were early synonyms for "nincompoop."

Craig M. Carver, *A History of English in Its Own Words* (New York: Harper Collins, 1991), 138-39.

What is a zeugma?

A zeugma is a figure of speech in which one word refers to two others in the same sentence. A zeugma can be achieved with a verb or preposition linking two objects. A zeugma might also link a verb with two subjects. According to *The Concise Oxford Dictionary of Literary Terms*, an example of a zeugma occurs in the final line of British poet William Shakespeare's (1564-1616) 128th sonnet: "Give them thy fingers, me thy lips to kiss."

Chris Baldick, *The Concise Oxford Dictionary of Literary Terms* (Oxford: Oxford University Press, 1990), s.v. "zeugma."

What is the longest word in the English language?

The longest word in the *Oxford English Dictionary (OED)* and others is pneumonoultramicroscopicsilicovolcanoconiosis. It has 45 letters and is defined as "a lung disease caused by the inhalation of a very fine silica dust." The *OED* editors state that the word is used "chiefly as an instance of a very long word."

Supercalifragilisticexpialidocious, with 34 letters, may be the longest, commonly used English word. It means the greatest, the best of all. This word is also the longest one-word title of a song. Written by Richard M. Sherman and Robert B. Sherman for the 1964 movie *Mary Poppins*, Dick Van Dyke and Julie Andrews sang the tune.

The longest printed word in the English language is a 1,185-letter word for tobacco mosaic virus that was created by stringing all the chemical names of its components together. Some would discount as real words such chemical names as well as words created only for the reason of length, such as the 100-letter word created by Irish author James Joyce in *Finnegan's Wake.*

Robert Hendrickson, *The Henry Holt Encyclopedia of Word and Phrase Origins* (New York: Henry Holt, 1987), 509. Dick Jacobs and Harriet Jacobs, *Who Wrote That Song?, 2nd ed.* (Cincinnati, OH: Writer's Digest Books, 1994), 227. Robert Jay Nash and Stanley Ralph Ross, *The Motion Picture Guide, 1927-1983* (Chicago: Cinebooks, 1986), 1893-94. *The Oxford English Dictionary* (Oxford: Clarendon Press, 1989), 11:1102. Mark C. Young, ed., *The Guiness Book of Records 1995* (New York: Facts on File, 1994), 152.

What is the correct spelling of Muammar Gaddafi's name?

No one standard spelling for the name of Libyan leader Muammar Gaddafi exists in English. The surname can be spelled Gaddafi, Qadhafi, Qaddafi, Kaddafi, and Khadafy. All are correct phonetic transliterations from the Arabic sound. Similarly the given name has been transliterated variously as Muammar, Mu'ammar, Moammar, and Moamar.

Beverly Baer and Neil E. Walker, *Almanac of Famous People, 5th edition* (Detroit: Gale Research, 1994), 854. Ken Gause, *Worldwide Government Directory* (Bethesda, MD: Belmont Publications, 1993), 659. *Time* 21 December 1981.

What is speedreading?

Speedreading involves the gaining of meaning from written material at up to four times the average reading rate (up to 1,000 to 1,200 words per minute as compared to 250 to 300 words per minute). Below are the ratings for reading speed.

Better than 600 words per minute-Superior
Between 300 and 600 words per minute-A little above average of college students
Between 180 and 300 words per minute-Average
Between 100 and 180 words per minute-Below average
Less than 100 words per minute-Poor

Franklin Agardy, *How to Read Faster and Better: How to Get Everything You Want from Anything You Read as Fast as You Can Think* (New York: Simon and Schuster, 1981), 43. Jay M. Shafritz, Richard P. Koeppe, and Elizabeth W. Soper, *The Facts On File Dictionary of Education* (New York: Facts on File, 1988), s.v. "speed reading."

How is the wish "Merry Christmas" and "Happy New Year" translated in other languages?

The wishes "Merry Christmas" and "Happy New Year" are said in some other languages:

Language	Merry Christmas	Happy New Year
German	Frohliche Weihnachten	Ein Gluckliches Neujahr
French	Joyeux Noel	Bonne Annee
Italian	Buon Natale	Felice Capo d'Anno
Portuguese	Feliz Natal	Feliz Ano Novo
Spanish	Feliz Navidad	Feliz Ano Nuevol

Graydon S. DeLand, *American Traveler's Companion* (New York: Fielding Publications, 1966), 106-7. *The World Book Encyclopedia* (Chicago: World Book, 1994), s.v. "Christmas."

What toast is equivalent to the phrase "To your health" in other languages?

The toast "To your health" may be translated:
German—Prosit!
French—A votre sant
Italain—Salute!
Spanish—Salud!

Charles Berlitz, *Around the World with 80 Words* (New York: G. P. Putnam's Sons, 1991), 27, 40, 53, 66.

What is "Plain English"?

"Plain English" is the goal of those wishing to uncomplicate the English language, especially in government and legal communications. Two examples of complicated language and their "Plain English" equivalents are "negative patient care outcome," which in Plain English means "death," and "revenue enhancement tax-base erosion control," which in Plain English means "tax increase."

David Crystal, *The Cambridge Encyclopedia of Language* (Cambridge: Cambridge University Press, 1987), 378.

Where is "Tamil" spoken?

"Tamil" is part of the Dravidian family of languages and is spoken by 60 million people, mostly in India. "Tamil" is the official language of Tamil Nadu, Sri Lanka, and Malaysia.

David Crystal, *An Encyclopedic Dictionary of Language and Languages* (Cambridge, MA: Blackwell, 1992), s.v. "Tamil."

Where is Krio spoken, and what are its components?

Krio, which is derived from the word *creole*, is a language that was developed by former slaves when they returned to West Africa. Although about 80 percent of the words have English roots, it is not a dialect but a language in its own right. There is a strong influence from West African languages, especially Yoruba, and a smattering of other elements, mainly Portuguese. Krio is spoken by perhaps two million people in Sierra Leone and is also present in Gambia, Nigeria, and Cameroon.

Robert McCrum, William Cran, and Robert MacNeil, *The Story of English* (New York: Viking, 1986), 320-22.

What is macaronic speech or writing?

"Macaronic" refers to a type of speech or writing that combines two languages. Since the term is usually applied when Latin is mixed with the vernacular, macaronic language has often been called Dog Latin. This genre has been known since the late Middle Ages and was a favorite with school children in the days when the study of classics was an important part of the curriculum. It may still be encountered in literature, like Umberto Eco's *The Name of the Rose.*

David Crystal, *An Encyclopedic Dictionary of Language and Languages* (Cambridge, MA: Blackwell Publishers, 1992), s.v. "macaronic."

How is the greeting "Welcome" translated into other languages?

The greeting "Welcome!" to a guest or foreigner may be translated:
German—Willkommen!
French—Bienvenu!
Italian—Benvenuto!
Spanish—Bienvenido!
Portuguese—Bem-vindo!

Graydon S. DeLand, *American Traveler's Companion* (New York: Fielding Publications, 1966), 282-83.

What is a good pronunciation guide for celebrities or other well known persons with difficult names?

A good pronunciation guide for celebrities or other well known persons with difficult names is Stephen Gilbar's *the BOOK book.* Some entries in his book are:

Name	Pronunciation
Sholom Aleichem	SHO-lem Ah-LAY-kem
Michael Crichton	CRY-tuhn
Thomas Mann	TOE-mass MAHN
Rainer Maria Rilke	RYE-nahr Ma-REE-ah RIHL-kuh
John LeCarre	Luh-car-RAY

Stephan Gilbar, *the BOOK book* (New York: St. Martin's Press, 1981), 29.

Do hoboes use a graphic sign language?

Hoboes do use a graphic language, which can be recognized and translated by hoboes around the world into their own languages. It consists of simple line-drawings, which can be chalked on a wall as warning or welcome to others about conditions ahead and the attitude of locals toward other hoboes.

Henry Dreyfuss, *Symbol Sourcebook* (New York: Van Nostrand Reinhold, 1984), 156.

What is the Gullah or Geechee dialect and where is it spoken?

The Gullah or Geechee dialect is a combination of dialects spoken among African Americans in Georgia and South Carolina. Some words, such as "vudu" or "voodoo," have made their way into the general American vocabulary. Linguists believe Gullah to be a simplified form of English, in which difficult sounds are omitted, words are shortened, and forms for person, number, case, and tense are minimized.

H.L. Mencken, *The American Language* (New York: Alfred A. Knopf, 1962), 265-70.

What are Venetian blinds called in Italy?

Since Venetian blinds originated in Persia, Italians refer to them as "persiana."

Piero Rebora, *Cassell's Italian Dictionary* (New York: Macmillan, 1977), 1060.

What are some Jewish words and phrases relating to death?

Frequently used Jewish words and phrases relating to death include the following:
Alav Hashalom—"Peace be upon him"
Alehaw Hashalom—"Peace be upon her"
Avelim—"mourners"
Hesped—eulogy delivered by rabbi
Kaddish—"holy" or "sanctification," a prayer of praise to God recited by mourners for eleven months from the date of burial
Keriah—"Rending," a custom in which a mourner rips a section of clothing or black ribbon to symbolize grief, with the tear made over the heart
Shiva—"seven," the first seven days of mourning after burial
Yahrzeit—anniversary of death

Earl A. Grollman, ed., *Concerning Death: A Practical Guide for the Living* (Boston: Beacon Press, 1974), 137-39.

Is the phrase "off of" ever correct?

The phrase "off of" is always improper English. "Get off of the jungle gym" is incorrect because the "of" idea is built into off.

"I borrowed the money off of my dad" is incorrect because "from" is the proper choice, not off.

Theodore M. Bernstein, Marylea Meyersohn, and Bertram Lippman, *Dos, Don'ts & Maybes of English Usage* (New York: Times Books, 1977), s.v. "off of."

When is the phrase "whether or not" used rather than "whether"?

The phrase "whether or not" is used rather than "whether" to give equal weight to alternatives. For instance, in the sentence, "The field trip will take place whether or not it rains," the "or not" is necessary. In another context, the "or not" is incorrect because the sentence already includes a negative, as in, "We don't know whether or not she is coming." "Or not" repeats the "not" understood in "don't," the contraction of "do not."

Theodore M. Bernstein, Marylea Meyersohn, and Bertram Lippman, *Dos, Don'ts & Maybes of English Usage* (New York: Times Books, 1977), s.v. "whether (or not)."

Why is Romanian a Romance language in isolation and how has it survived?

Romanian is an isolated Romance language that is separated from other Romance languages by hundreds of miles. For over 1,000 years that section of Europe north of the lower Danube had virtually no contact with speakers of other Romance languages and was periodically invaded by barbarian tribes such as the Goths and Magyars. How the Romanian language survived these hardships is a mystery.

One possible explanation is that the occupying Roman legions and settlers passed on the Latin language, the root of all Romance languages. However, the Roman troops remained for a relatively brief time, 165 years, and there was little to attract Roman colonists to the province. Therefore, some believe that the area was later repopulated by Romance language speakers. Another, more attractive, theory is that those who were left behind in Transylvania's mountains when the Roman troops evacuated kept the language of their Roman masters alive as all around them populations chaotically came and departed the lands surrounding the mountains. The existence of a variety of Transylvanian dialects supports this view.

Victor Stevenson, ed., *Words: The Evolution of Western Languages* (New York: Van Nostrand Reinhold, 1983), 114-15.

What are malapropisms and how did they get their name?

A malapropism is the humorous misuse of a word, especially when the speaker is trying to sound knowledgeable and important. The misused word usually sounds similar to the intended word but is hilariously out of place in the speaker's situation. The word comes from the name of Mrs. Malaprop, a character in Richard Sheridan's play, *The Rivals* (1775). Sheridan created the name from the French phrase "mal propos" meaning "out of place." Mrs. Malaprop's ludicrous statements include:

"She's as headstrong as an allegory on the banks of the Nile."

"He is the very pineapple of politeness."

"I would have her instructed in geometry, that she might know something of the contagious countries."

Other English fictional characters who mouth malapropisms are Mrs. Winifred Jenkins in Smollett's *Humphrey Clinker* (1771) and Mrs. Slipslop in Fielding's *Joseph Andrews* (1742).

Bryan A. Garner, *A Dictionary of Modern Legal Usage* (New York: Oxford University Press, 1987), 350. Robert Hendrickson, *The Literary Life and Other Curiosities* (New York: Viking Press, 1981), 398-99. *Webster's Ninth New Collegiate Dictionary* (Springfield, MA: Merriam-Webster, 1988), s.v. "malapropism."

What is a "spoonerism"?

A "spoonerism" is the unintentional transposition of syllables or letters within a spoken sentence. "Metathesis" is the technical term for a spoonerism, which takes its name from the Reverend William Archibald Spooner of New College, Oxford, who was well known for making these slips of the tongue in the pulpit, in his classes, and in speaking to the general public. Examples attributed to him include "the Lord is a shoving leopard" instead of "the Lord is a loving shepherd" and "Is the bean dizzy"? instead of "Is the dean busy"? He once referred to Queen Victoria as "our queer old dean." Spooner was an albino and it is possible that his difficulties arose from anxiety and impaired vision resulting from his condition.

Robert Hendrickson, *The Literary Life and Other Curiosities* (New York: Viking Press, 1981), 397-98.

What is a "pidgin" language and what is the origin of this word?

A "pidgin" language is a make-it-up-as-you-go language that is used by groups of people who do not speak a common language. "Pidgin" languages are usually used for commerce and trade and have a limited vocabulary and an informal grammatical structure. The word "pidgin" has murky origins but may derive from the Hebrew word "pidjom," which means to barter, or the English "pigeon," a method for carrying simple messages.

David Crystal, *The Cambridge Encyclopedia of Language* (Cambridge: Cambridge University Press, 1987), 334.

What is a bobche?

A bobche is a candlestick collar designed to catch dripping wax.

J. E. Mansion, *Harrap's New Standard French and English Dictionary, rev. ed.* (New York: Charles Scribner's Sons, 1972), s.v. "bobche."

What are some slang words and expressions from the counter-culture of the 1960s?

A list of slang words and expressions from the counter culture of the 1960s and their meanings would include:

Expression	Meaning
Blow your mind	Get high on drugs
Far out	Great
Psyshedelic	Pertaining to drugs
Out of sight	Terrific
Spaced out	Like Timothy Leary
Good vibes	Positive feelings
Be-in	Joyous gathering
Acid	LSD
Flower child	Hippie
Tune in	Take acid
Rap	Discuss
Roach	Butt of marijuana cigarette
Joint	Marijuana cigarette

Bread	Money
Groovy	Really fine

John Javna and Gordon Javna, *60s!* (New York: St. Martin's Press, 1988), 189.

How should an invitation be addressed to two women who use the title Ms.?

An invitation addressed to two women who use the title Ms. should read: Dear Ms. Smith and Ms. Jones. A formal invitation could read: Dear Mses. Smith and Jones or Dear Mss. Smith and Jones.

William A. Sabin, *Gregg Reference Manual,* (New York: Macmillan/ McGraw-Hill, 1992), 321.

How should an invitation to an unmarried couple living together be addressed?

An invitation to an unmarried couple living together should be addressed as follows:

Mr. John C. Scott
Ms. Melinda Southport
(followed by their address).

Points to remember include, one invitation should be sent, the names should be on separate lines, and there is no "and" linking their names together.

Letitia Baldridge, *Letitia Baldrige's Complete Guide to the Manners for the '90s* (New York: Rawson Associates, 1990), 593.

What is the derivation and English translation of the Yiddish word "gozlin" or "gozlen"?

"Gozlin" or "gozlen" is derived from the Hebrew word "gozlon," meaning "one who deprives others of their rightful possessions by force." The translation of the Yiddish term is thief, swindler, or an unethical person.

Leo Rosten, *The Joys of Yiddish* (New York: McGraw-Hill, 1968), 143.

Do prison inmates develop their own slang terms?

Prisoners do seem to develop a collection of slang terms which have meanings unique to their locations. At San Quentin, for instance, "across the street" means Warden's office, "clavo" means drugs, "shooting kites" is writing or mailing letters, and "tacks" are tattoos.

USA Today 28 September 1987.

What is the meaning of the French expression "embonpoint"?

"Embonpoint" is a French expression originating in the seventeenth century in reference to a plump or well nourished appearance. It is not necessarily used as a compliment.

A.J. Bliss, *A Dictionary of Foreign Words and Phrases in Current English* (London: Routledge & Kegan Paul, 1983), s.v. "embonpoint."

What does the exclamation point in front of a word represent?

The exclamation point in front of a word such as !Kung represents a unique speech sound used by the bushmen of southern Africa. The symbol "!" is representative of implosive consonants, which are achieved by a sharp inhalation of air. The "!k" sound is an implosive "k" click produced by the tongue moving quickly away from the palate as air is inhaled. According to Richard Leakey, an anthropologist who studies the !Kung and their language, simply saying a close approximation of the word using familiar speech sounds will effectively communicate meaning to the bushmen.

New York Times 17 July 1984.

What language's alphabet has the most letters?

The Cambodian alphabet has the most with 74 letters, including some that are not currently used. In contrast the Rotokas, living in Papua New Guinea, use an alphabet of only 11 letters: a, b, e, g, i, k, o, p, r, t, and u.

Mark C. Young, ed., *The Guinness Book of Records 1995* (New York: Facts on File, 1994), 139.

What is the correct pronunciation of the title "Ms."?

"Ms.," the preferred feminist title for married or unmarried women, is pronounced "Miz," according to Gloria Steinem, feminist leader and founding editor of *Ms.* magazine.

Time 8 November 1971.

Was Hebrew ever considered to become the national language of the United States?

Because of pervasive anti-British sentiment during the American Revolution Hebrew was briefly considered to replace English as the national language. Hebrew was viewed as the mother of all languages, the key to the scriptures, and the basis of a liberal education. The idea, however, never took hold.

Irving Wallace and David Wallechinsky, *Significa* (New York: E.P. Dutton, 1983), 194.

Why are ships affectionately referred to as "she"?

Undoubtedly ships are affectionately referred to as "she" because in the Romance languages all nouns have gender— masculine, feminine, or neuter—and the word for ship in these languages is always of the feminine gender.

William Morris and Mary Morris, *Morris Dictionary of Word and Phrase Origins* (New York: Harper & Row, 1977), 513.

What is the official language of Brazil?

A legacy of Portugal's colonial rule over Brazil, which lasted until 1815, Portuguese is the official language of Brazil. In all other South American countries Spanish is the official language.

Arthur S. Banks, ed., *Political Handbook of the World: 1993* (Binghamton, NY: CSA Publications, 1993), 99.

What is "Brooklynese"?

"Brooklynese" is a working-class dialect common to the Brooklyn, New York, area. It is characterized by substituting "oi" sounds for "er" or "ir" sounds ("boid" for bird), making an "r" sound at the end of words ending in a vowel ("idear" for idea), and locutions such as "pitcher" for picture. By 1974 the dialect was in its demise because of derision and the pervasive influence of the media, especially television.

Earl Lane, "Brooklynese Dialect Scholar Mourns Passing of Language," *Pittsburgh Press* 12 July 1974.

How is the wish "Happy Birthday" conveyed in foreign languages?

Here is a list of how to say "Happy Birthday" in various foreign languages:

Language	Translation of "Happy Birthday"
French	Bon anniversaire
German	Herzlichen Gluckwunsch zum Geburtstag
Italian	Buon compleanno
Portuguese	Feliz aniversario
Spanish	Feliz cumpleanos

Graydon S. DeLand, *American Traveler's Companion* (New York: Fielding Publications, 1966), 106.

What term is used to describe the misuse of words?

"Catachresis" is the term used to describe the incorrect or forced use of a word, phrase, or figure of speech. Examples include mixed or strained metaphors and the misapplication of terminology.

David B. Guralnik, ed., *Webster's New World Dictionary of the American Language* (New York: Simon and Schuster, 1980), s.v. "catachresis."

What is the meaning of the literary term "litotes"?

Litotes is a literary term that refers to the expression or affirmation of an idea through the denial of its opposite. In *Literary Terms: A Dictionary*, Karl E. Beckson noted: "Milton makes use of this device when, at the beginning of *Paradise Lost*, he asks the muse to aid his adventurous song 'That with no middle flight intends to soar,' indicating that in reality his poem will soar to the highest levels of imagination."

Karl E. Beckson, *Literary Terms: A Dictionary* (New York: Noonday Press, 1989), 146.

What Native American words are commonly used in the English language?

Many words in the English language have their origin in Native American languages and dialects. Several familiar words come from the Algonquian language, among them "caucus," "chipmunk," "hominy," "moccasin," "moose," "pecan," "podunk," "quahog," "succotash," "squash," "toboggan," and "wigwam." The words "bayou" and "catalpa" are derived from the Choctaw (Muskogean) language and the Creek (Muskogean) language respectively. "Kayak" and "igloo" are words used by the Inuits (Eskimos). The word "caribou" comes from the Micmac tongue; "klondike" from the Athabascan language; "maize" from the Arawak language; and "tipi" from the Siouan language.

Arlene Hirschfelder and Martha Kreipe de Montano, *The Native American Almanac: A Portrait of Native America Today* (New York: Prentice Hall General Reference, 1993), 85.

What is the difference between the United States and other parts of the world regarding the use of commas and periods in numbers?

Commas and periods are used to separate parts of a number. In some parts of the world, including the United States, commas are used to separate amounts of a thousand and periods to separate fractions. For example, two-thousand five-hundred dollars and fifty cents is written 2,500.00 in the United States. In the countries of Western Europe, this amount would be written 2.500,00.

Susan H. Munger, *The International Business Communications Desk Reference* (New York: American Management Association, 1993), 62.

When did the Chinese introduce the Pinyin system of writing?

The Chinese introduced the Pinyin system of writing in 1958, replacing the Wade-Giles system. The Wade-Giles system was introduced to China in the mid-nineteenth century by Sir Thomas Wade and Herbert Giles, two British Chinese scholars. Both systems romanized Chinese characters. Pinyin is a phonetic spelling method that was part of a program to reform the Chinese language and make it more consistent throughout the entire country. In 1978 the People's Republic of China mandated that all Chinese names used in English must be in Pinyin. The Wade-Giles "Peking" and "Mao Tse-tung" became "Beijing" and "Mao-Zedong" under Pinyin.

David Crystal, *An Encyclopedic Dictionary of Language and Languages* (Oxford: Blackwell Publishers, 1992), s.v. "Chinese." *World Book Encyclopedia* (New York: World Book, 1987), s.v. "Chinese language."

What is Dog-Latin?

Dog-Latin is a pretend "language" whereby for humorous effect English words are pronounced or spelled to imitate the Latin language. For example, in dog-Latin the English word saucepan would become "saucepannis." The "dog" in the term means something bad, spurious, bastard, or mongrel.

J. A. Simpson, *The Oxford English Dictionary, 2d ed.* (Oxford: Clarendon Press, 1989), s.v. "dog." Ivor H. Evans, *Brewer's Dictionary of Phrase and Fable, 14th ed.* (New York: Harper & Row, 1989), s.v. "Dog-Latin."

What is pig Latin?

Pig Latin is a gibberish in which the initial letter of an English word is transposed to the rear and "ay" is then added. The word "pig" thus becomes "igpay." One possible origin of the name given to this "language" is that when spoken rapidly, "pig Latin" resembles the grunting of hogs.

Reference Quarterly Fall 1974.

Poetry

What is the one word spoken and repeated by the Raven in Edgar Allan Poe's famous poem?

In American author Edgar Allan Poe's (1809-1849) famous poem *The Raven*, the one word spoken repeatedly by the Raven is "Nevermore."

Fred L. Worth, *The Trivia Encyclopedia* (Los Angeles: Brooke House, 1974), 183.

In whose honor was Edgar Allan Poe's poem "Annabel Lee" written?

The poem "Annabel Lee" was written by Edgar Allan Poe in 1849 in honor of his deceased wife, Virginia.

W.J. Burke and Will D. Howe, *American Authors and Books: 1640 to the Present Day, rev. ed. by Irving R. Weis* (New York: Crown, 1962), s.v. "Annabel Lee." Edward H. O'Neil, ed., *The Complete Tales and Poems of Edgar Allan Poe, with an introduction by Arthur Hobson Quinn* (New York: Dorset Press, 1989), 86.

What is a "dirge"?

A "dirge" is a song or hymn that is usually sung at funerals or in commemoration of the dead. It is a song of sorrow or mourning. The word "dirge" is derived from a prayer said in the monasteries of the Middle Ages. The most important of duty of the monks was to perform the "Opus Dei" (the work of God), which involved praying at seven specific times each day. On days that were devoted to a commemoration for the dead, the first prayer service, which was called Matins, began with a verse from Psalm 8. It started with the Latin word "dirige," from which "dirge" was derived, and the text of the first line read, "Dirige, Domine, Deus meus, in conspectu tuo viam meam," which translates, "Direct, O Lord, my God, my way according to thy sight."

Karl E. Beckson and Arthur Ganz, *Literary Terms: A Dictionary* (New York: Noonday Press, 1989)63. C.H. Lawrence, *Medieval Monasticism: Forms of Religious Life in Western Europe in the Middle Ages* (London: Longman, 1984) 234, 238-40. J.A. Simpson and E.S.C. Weiner, *The Oxford English Dictionary, 2d ed.* (Oxford: Clarendon Press, 1989), s.v. "dirge."

What happened to the Banbury Cross?

The Banbury Cross was a large elaborate monument with statues at its base and topped by a cross. The original cross is immortalized in the following famous nursery rhyme:

"Ride a cock-horse to Banbury Cross,
to see a blacklady ride on a white horse,
Rings on her fingers and bells on her toes,
That she will have music wherever she goes."

The cross was destroyed during an anti-Catholic Puritan riot in the English town of Banbury, Oxfordshire, England in 1601. A replica of it was erected in Banbury in 1859.

R. Chambers, *The Book of days: A Miscellany of Popular Antiquities* (Great Britain: J.B. Lippincott, n.d.). Lois H. Fisher, *A Literary Gazetteer of England* (New York: McGraw-Hill, 1980), 21.

What is John Hendrick Bangs' poem "The Little Elf" about?

John Hendrick Bangs' poem "The Little Elf" is about the irrelevant nature of physical size.

Edmund Clarence Stedman, ed., *An American Anthology, 1787-1900* (Boston: Houghton Mifflin Company, 1928).

Who wrote the famous line, "Do not go gentle into that good night"?

"Do Not Go Gentle Into That Good Night" is the title and the first line of the popular poem by Welsh poet Dylan Thomas (1914-53). The poem deals with the emotional affirmation of life as the inevitablility of death is at hand. It is assumed by most literary critics that the "wise men," "wild men," "good men," and "grave men" in the poem are metaphors for the Welsh poet's father.

Barbara Hardy, *The Advantage of Lyric: Essays on Feeling in Poetry* (Bloomington: Indiana Univeristy Press, 1977), 116-17. Michael W. Murphy, "Thomas' Do Not Go Gentle into that Good Night," *The Explicator* February 1970.

Who was Maxwell Bodenheim?

Maxwell Bodenheim was an American poet, novelist, and playwright. Born May 26, 1892, in Hermanville, Mississippi, Bodenheim was recognized as a minor literary figure during his day and was one of the great proletarian writers of the 1930s. He was published for the first time in 1914 when some of his poems were published in *Poetry*, and his first collection of poems, *Minna and Myself*, came out in 1918. Keeping company with such well-known American writers as Sherwood Anderson (1876-1941), Theodore Dreiser (1871-1945), and Carl Sandburg (1878-1967), Bodenheim's reputation remained strong throughout the 1920s. Six of his eleven volumes of verse were published during that decade: *Advice* (1920), *Introducing Irony* (1922), *Against This Age* and *The Sardonic Arm* (both 1923), *Returning to Emotion* (1927), and *The King of Spain* (1928).

Bodenheim was also the author of critical essays, several of which were produced by the Provincetown Players in 1917 and 1918, and approximately fourteen novels. He earned praise for his insight into the problem of women as victims in such novels as *Crazy Man* (1924); *Ninth Avenue* (1926); and *Georgie May* (1928). His more comic works include *Naked on Roller Skates* (1930) and *Duke Herring* (1931). In 1939, Bodenheim received *Poetry*'s Oscar Blumenthal Prize.

In his later years, Bodenheim lived a life of extreme poverty. On February 7, 1954, he was found dead of a gunshot wound in his skid-row flat.

Martin H. Greenberg, *The Jewish Lists* (New York: Schocken Books, 1979), 129. Hal May, ed., *Contemporary Authors* (Detroit: Gale Research, 1984), s.v. "Bodenheim, Maxwell."

What is the meaning of the literary term "refrain"?

In literary terms, "refrain" means the repetition of a phrase, line, or group of lines repeated at intervals throughout a poem. Refrains usually appear at the end of a stanza and are used to reinforce a mood or theme in the poem.

Kathleen Morner and Ralph Rausch, *NTC's Dictionary of Literary Terms* (Lincolnwood, IL: National Textbook Company, 1991), 183.

What is the "Jabberwock"?

The "Jabberwock" is a twenty-foot dragon created by Lewis Carroll, pseudonym of English writer Charles Dodgson (1832-1898). It appeared in a poem entitled "Jabberwocky" that was an integral part of Carroll's "Through the Looking Glass" (1871).

Jeff Rovin, *The Encyclopedia Of Monsters* (New York: Facts On File, 1989), 163.

What was the name of Percy Shelley's boat that sank and resulted in the poet's drowning?

On July 8, 1822, English poet Percy Shelley's boat, *Don Juan*, sank in the Gulf of Spezia off the Italian coast, resulting in the poet's drowning. Percy Bysshe Shelley was born on August 4, 1792, near Horsham, Sussex, England; he is regarded as one of the greatest lyric poets of the English language. Shelley led a tempestuous personal life and in 1818 he fled to the European continent with Mary Godwin and Mary's half-sister Claire Clarmont. He was never to return to England, and over the next four years of his life Shelley did most of his writing in Italy. The *Don Juan* was an open boat, twenty-four feet long and eight feet wide. Reportedly, the boat rode dangerously high and needed two tons of iron ballast to make it steady. It sank with two other people aboard and the three bodies were not recovered for ten days. Considerable controversy surrounds the drownings; some believe that the boat was swamped or run down by another vessel, while others contend that Shelley arranged his suicide to look like an accidental drowning. Some of the Romantic poet's best known works are *The Revolt of Islam* (1817), *Prometheus*

Unbound (1818-19), *The Masque of Anarchy* (1819), and *Hellas* (1821).

Kenneth Neill Cameron, *Shelley: The Golden Years* (Cambridge, MA: Harvard University Press, 1974), 98. *McGraw-Hill Encyclopedia of World Biography* (New York: McGraw-Hill, 1973), 30-33.

What is Vedic poetry?

Vedic poetry, the oldest surviving Indian poetry, was written in Sanskrit. The Vedas were probably composed in the second half of the second millennium B.C. and redacted around 1000 B.C. There are four Vedic collections, which contain hymns, prayers, spells, riddles, myths, and liturgical formulas. Vedic recurring themes of creation, birth, death, and sacrifice, have greatly influenced the Hindu religion and Indian culture. Because many of the poems are brilliant in their structure, sound, and phrasing, they helped establish literary norms for Indian poetry that lasted until the nineteenth century.

Alex Preminger and T. V. F. Brogan, eds., *The New Princeton Encyclopedia of Poetry and Poetics* (Princeton, NJ: Princeton University Press, 1993), 586-87.

What poem by Ariosto is the retelling of the Roland story?

Ludovico Ariosto (1474-1533) wrote an epic poem in Italian called *Orlando Furioso*, which some critics consider the finest poem written during the Italian Renaissance. This poem, whose title can be translated as "Mad Roland," has as its subject a genuine historical figure from the Carolingian period who takes on legendary qualities during the succeeding centuries. According to the story, Roland, the nephew of Charlemagne (742-814) and his bravest knight, was ambushed and killed by Moslem forces as he commanded the rear guard of Charlemagne's army. The legend was very popular during the crusading period and served as the basis for a great medieval French poem the *Chanson de Roland*. Ariosto's version blended medieval legends with works from classical authors like Virgil and Ovid and from works of his contemporaries like Dante and Petrarch. Ariosto departed from the medieval tale and introduced themes of love and magic. Although much of his material is borrowed, he has been praised as a story teller with great descriptive power, a painter with a pen. The work first appeared in 1516 and was republished by the author in an expanded edition in 1532.

Peter Bondanella and Julia Conaway Bondanella, eds., *Dictionary of Italian Literature* (Westport, CT: Greenwood Press, 1979), 22-24. A.J. Krailsheimer, *The Continental Renaissance, 1500-1600* (Middlesex, England: Penguin Books, 1978), s.v. "Ariosto, Ludovico."

What is the Poet's Corner in Westminster Abbey?

Part of the south transept of Westminster Abbey, the famous medieval church in London where the monarchs of Great Britain are crowned, is known as the Poet's Corner. It is an area filled with the tombs and monuments of the country's great literary figures. Among those buried here are the great English authors Geoffrey Chaucer, William Shakespeare, John Milton, and Charles Dickens.

Robert Hendrickson, *The Literary Life and Other Curiosities* (New York: Viking Press, 1981), 161.

What is a Spenserian stanza?

Sixteenth-century English poet Edmund Spenser (1552?-1599) invented what is known as the Spenserian stanza, a poetic form of nine iambic lines. The first eight lines of the stanza are pentameters, followed by a ninth line in iambic hexameter or an alexandrine. The form also requires a rhyme scheme of "ababbcbcc." More than one hundred years later, poets Baron George Gordon Byron, John Keats, and Percy Shelley revived the use of the Spenserian stanza in their own work.

Chris Baldick, *The Concise Oxford Dictionary of Literary Terms* (New York: Oxford University Press, 1990), 209.

What is haiku?

Haiku is a Japanese form of poetry. Haiku verses contain seventeen syllables within three lines. The syllables are arranged with five on the first line, seven on the second line, and five on the third line. By design, haiku expresses a single idea and must be complete on its own. Many modern poets, including Ezra Pound (1885-1972) and T.E. Hulme (1883-1917), have adopted this sixteenth-century form.

J.A. Cuddon, *A Dictionary of Literary Terms* (Garden City, NY: Doubleday, 1977), 294.

What poem did Maya Angelou read at the inauguration of President Bill Clinton?

At the inauguration of U.S. president Bill Clinton (1946-), Maya Angelou (1928-) read her poem "On the Pulse of Morning." Angelou, an acclaimed African-American author, poet, and performing artist was born Marguerite Johnson on April 4, 1928, in St. Louis. At the age of three she was sent to live with her paternal grandmother in Stamps, Arkansas, where she experienced racial bigotry and racial despair first hand. Angelou attended public schools in Arkansas and California and studied dance and drama. She was married to Tosh Angelou until their divorce in the early 1950s. Angelou toured in a production of *Porgy and Bess* which was sponsored by the U.S. State Department and had a wide variety of other theatrical experiences. Her acclaimed book *I Know Why the Caged Bird Sings* is based on her coming-of-age in Arkansas and was nominated for a National Book Award.

Michael LaBlanc, *Contemporary Black Biography* (Detroit: Gale Research, 1992), 1: 6-9. *USA Today* 20 September 1993.

Who was "Little Orphan Annie"?

The inspiration for "Little Orphan Annie" of James Whitcomb Riley's (1847-1916) famous 1883 poem was Mrs. Mary Alice Gray, who died March 7, 1924. As a child, Gray had lived at the Riley home in Greenfield, Indiana, leaving when she was twelve years old. For years Gray's grandchildren listened to Riley's poem without knowing that their grandmother was the little girl who "washed the cups an' saucers up, and brushed the crumbs away." Riley lost track of Gray for more than fifty years, although she was living on a farm outside Indianapolis, Indiana. Two years before Riley's death Gray was found, but Riley's illness prevented him from seeing her again.

Publishers' Weekly 22 March 1924.

What is the term for a poem in which letters of successive lines form a word or a pattern?

A poem in which the letters of successive lines make up a pattern or a word is called an "acrostic." To be considered a true acrostic, the initial letters must form the word or pattern; a "mesostich" utilizes the middle letters for the same purpose, while a "telestich" forms a word or pattern from the final letters in successive lines.

If the letters of the successive lines are in alphabetical order, the acrostic is called an "abecedarius." A "cross acrostic" forms the pattern from the first letter of the first line, second letter of the second line, third letter of the third line, and so on.

Karl E. Beckson and Arthur Ganz, *Literary Terms: A Dictionary* (New York: Farrar, Straus, and Giroux, 1960), 4. Dmitri A. Borgmann, *Language on Vacation: An Olio of Orthographical Oddities* (New York: Scribner, 1970), 152. Joseph T. Shipley, ed., *Dictionary of World Literary Terms, Forms, Technique, Criticism* (Boston: The Writer, 1965), 5.

Who wrote *The Canterbury Tales*?

Geoffrey Chaucer (c.1342-1400), England's first famous poet, wrote *The Canterbury Tales.* Although never completed, Chaucer's tales continue to influence the everyday speech of English-speaking people through such familiar phrases as "love is blind" and "through thick and thin." Chaucer died in 1400 at the age of sixty.

James Trager, *The People's Chronology: A Year-by-Year Record of Human Events from Prehistory to the Present, rev. ed.* (New York: Henry Holt, 1992), 138.

Who was the first female poet laureate of the United States?

Mona Van Duyn was named the first female poet laureate of the United States in 1992. Van Duyn, who also won the Pulitzer Prize for poetry in 1991, is known for her many works of poetry including *Letters from a Father and Other Poems.*

Van Duyn was born in Waterloo, Iowa, in 1921 and began writing creatively at a young age, her first poem being published in a newspaper when she was in the second grade. By the time she was in junior high she had compiled notebooks full of poems which she kept secret from her friends and family. In 1959 Van Duyn published *Valentines to the Wide World,* her first collection of poems. She has taught English at various colleges and universities and in addition to being named poet laureate Van Duyn has been the recipient of the National Book Award for *To See, To Take* (1971) and a Pulitzer Prize for *Near Changes* (1991).

James G. Lesniak and Susan M. Trosky, *Contemporary Authors, New Revision Series* (Detroit: Gale Research, 1993), s.v. "Van Duyn, Mona (Jane)." Irvin Molotsky, "Pulitzer-Winning Poet Is Named U.S. Laureate," *New York Times* 15 June 1992.

Who was the first African-American to be named poet laureate of the United States?

Rita Dove (1952-) an English professor at the University of Virginia in Charlottesville was named poet laureate of the United States in 1993, becoming the first African-American to hold that position. Recipient of the 1987 Pulitzer Prize for *Thomas and Beulah,* a collection of short lyric poems that interweave personal and social history, Dove focused on the tragedies, joys, and dreams of ordinary black people. In addition, Dove has written short stories and fiction.

Irvin Molotsky, "Rita Dove to Be Poet Laureate. First Black In the Post," *New York Times* 19 May 1993. Jessie Carney Smith, ed, *Notable Black American Women* (Detroit: Gale Research, 1992), s.v. "Rita Dove."

Who wrote the poem "The Barberry Tree"?

The poem "The Barberry Tree" is attributed to the English poet William Wordsworth (1770-1850) and, until recently, lay unknown among the papers of the English historian Henry Hallam (1777-1859). The poem, discovered in 1964 by a research student working with Hallam's papers, had gone unread since his death in 1859. The poem was attached to a letter written to Hallam's wife, Julia, by her brother, Charles Elton, who enclosed the poem to "awake his dormant intention of writing." The 113-line poem begins:

> "Late on a breezy vernal eve
> When breezes wheel'd their whirling flight;
> I wander'd forth;
> and I believe I never saw so sweet a sight."

Pittsburgh Post-Gazette 3 August 1964.

Which American poet laureate was a former inmate at a Soviet labor camp?

In 1991 Joseph Brodsky, a former Soviet labor camp inmate and Nobel Prize recipient was named poet laureate of the United States. Brodsky was incarcerated in the Soviet Union for "social parasitism" before coming to America in 1972.

Brodsky was born in Leningrad, Russia, in 1940 and even as a youth he was a dissenter against the Soviet Union's strict social norms. At fifteen he left school and worked at numerous jobs all the while studying literature and writing poetry. Much of his early work was published in fringe journals and Brodsky soon became known as a "street corner poet" or one whose reputation was earned at clandestine poetry readings and through the underground distribution of mimeographed copies of this writings. Although Brodsky was not a political dissident in the formal sense of the term he did challenge basic precepts of communist rule. Government newspapers were soon denouncing him as a writer of "pornographic and anti-Soviet poetry." In 1964 the state accused him of being a "social parasite" and sentenced him to five years of hard labor for not "...fulfilling the duties of a Soviet citizen." Brodsky left the Soviet Union in 1972 and his reputation quickly grew in western literary circles culminating in teaching positions at the University of Michigan, Columbia University, and New York University.

Irvin Molotsky, "A U.S. Poet Laureate From Russia," *New York Times* 11 May 1991. Charles Moritz, ed., *Current Biography Yearbook 1982* (New York: H. W. Wilson, 1982), s.v. "Brodsky, Joseph (Alexandrovich)."

What poem did President Ronald Reagan read after the explosion of the Space Shuttle *Challenger*?

After the explosion of the Space Shuttle *Challenger,* U.S. President Ronald Reagan (1911-) read the poem "Highflight" by John Gillespie Magee, which begins with the line:

> "Oh, I have slipped the surly bonds of earth"

> and ends with:

> "Put out my hand, and touched the face of God."

Sir Charles G.D. Roberts, ed., *Flying Colours* (Toronto: Ryerson Press, 1946), 115.

Was the nursery rhyme "Mary Had a Little Lamb" based on a true story?

The nursery rhyme "Mary Had a Little Lamb" was based on the early nineteenth century true-life adventures of Mary E. Sawyer of Sterling, Massachusetts. The poem was written by John Roulstone and later added to by a Mrs. Hale, both of whom evidently witnessed the events recorded in verse.

E.A. Warren, "The True Story of Mary and Her Little Lamb," *National Magazine* June, 1897.

What is "Raccontino"?

"Raccontino" is a form of poem written in couplets and invented by Etta Josephine Murfey. According to the *Poet's Handbook*, in this form of poetry the even number lines are on the same rhyming sound, the terminal words of the odd-numbered lines, taken with the title, tell a brief story. In the poem *Autumn Scherzo*:

When Autumn records
On the scroll of a leaf
The cycle of life
And a frost-gendered grief,
The tale of decay
Holds our senses in fief....
While we thrill to the pain
Of a beauty too brief.
The raccontino is "Autumn scherzo records life, decay, pain."

Clement Wood, *Poets' Handbook* (New York: Greenberg, 1940), 399.

Where did the phrase "splendor in the grass" originate?

The phrase "splendor in the grass" originated in a poem by British poet William Wordsworth (1770-1850) entitled "Intimations of Immortality from Recollections of Early Childhood."

The Oxford Book of English Verse, 1250-1918 (Oxford: Clarendon Press, 1939), 626-32.

Who authored the poem "Out in the Fields with God"?

Two poets have been attributed with authorship of the poem "Out in the Fields with God"—Louise Imogen Guiney and Elizabeth Barret Browning.

Caroline Miles Hill, *The World's Great Religious Poetry* (New York: Macmillan, 1954), 249. James Gilchrist Lawson, *The Best Loved Religious Poems* (Old Tappan, NJ: Fleming H. Revell, 1933), 214.

Which American poet was charged with treason?

Poet Ezra Pound, born in Hailey, Idaho, in 1885, was charged with treason following World War II (1939-45) broadcasts he made from Rome for the Axis powers. In November of 1945, Pound was declared unfit to stand trial by reason of insanity and was confined to St. Elizabeth's Hospital in Washington, DC, until 1958 when he was allowed to return to Italy. Pound died in Venice in 1972 at the age of 87.

Jack Salzman, ed., *The Cambridge Handbook of American Literature* (London: Cambridge University Press, 1986), 198-99.

Who was "Miss Phoebe Snow"?

"Miss Phoebe Snow" was celebrated in the following poem that was part of a 1904 Lackawanna Railroad advertisement:

Miss Snow draws near
The cab, to cheer
The level-headed
Engineer,
Whose watchful sight
Makes safe her flight
Upon the Road
Of Anthracite.

The advertisement featured "Miss Phoebe Snow" dressed in "spotless white" talking to the engineer.

Mark Sullivan, *Our Times: The United States, 1900-1925* (New York: Charles Scribner's Sons, 1927), 619.

What does the name Beowulf mean?

Beowulf, the hero of the epic Anglo-Saxon poem that is the oldest epic in the entire Germanic group of languages, including English, most probably derived his name from the Icelandic *Beadowulf*, or war-wolf, a complimentary term for a Nordic warrior of old. The Anglo Saxon *Beowulf* translates to bee-wolf, which some have equated to a fierce bear.

The poem appears to have originated around the time of the Danish conquest of the Cimbrian Peninsula (currently Denmark and part of northern Germany) in the early sixth century. The original Danish tale changed and grew and was presumably brought to England later in the 6th century by invading Angles, who had heard the story from their Danish neighbors. The version we know derives from an early eighth-century manuscript, which is housed in the Cottonian Library in the British Museum.

Wade Baskin, *The Sorcerer's Handbook* (New York: Philosophical Library, 1974), 81. Benjamin E. Smith, ed., *The Century Cyclopedia of Names* (New York: Century Company, 1902), 9:147.

What are the names of the frogs and mice from *The Battle of the Frogs and Mice*, a piece attributed to Homer?

The names of the frogs from *The Battle of the Frogs and Mice*, a piece attributed to Homer are: Borbocaetes, Calaminthius, Crambophagus, Hydrocharis, Hydromeduse, Hypsiboas, Lymnisius, Lymnocharis, Peleus, Pelion, Pelobates, Pelusius, Physignathus, Polyphonus, Prasseaeus, Prassophagus, and Seutlaens. The names of the mice are: Artophagus, Cnissodioctes, Crangasides, Meridarpax, Embasichytros, Lychenor, Lychomyle, Lychopinax, Psycarpax, Pternophaugs, Pternoglyphas, Pternotroctas, Sitophagus, Troglodytes, Troxartes, and Tyroglyphus.

Notes and Queries: A Monthly of History, Folk-Lore, Mathematics, Literature, Art, Arcane Societies, Etc. (Manchester, NH: S.C. & L.M. Gould, 1901), 203.

Was the poet Robert Browning of partial African descent?

The Academy, a 19th-century weekly review, claimed without offering substantiation that the father of poet Robert Browning (1812-1889) was "half creole."

The Academy: A Weekly Review of Literature, Science, and Art 19 April 1890.

What was George Washington's favorite poem?

U.S. President George Washington's (1732-1799) favorite poem was a couplet from English poet Alexander Pope's (1688-1744) "Essay on Man":

And spite of pride, in erring reason's spite,
One truth is clear, whatever is is right.

New York Times Magazine 9 December 1945.

What was U.S. president Franklin Delano Roosevelt's favorite poem?

U.S. president Franklin Delano Roosevelt's favorite poem was Rudyard Kipling's "The Ballad of East and West":

Oh, East is East, and West is West, and never the twain shall meet,
Till Earth and Sky stand presently at
God's great Judgment seat.
But there is neither East nor West, Border nor Breed nor Birth,

When two strong men come face to face, though they come from the ends of the earth.

"Presidents—Favorite White House Poems," *New York Times Magazine* 9 December 1945.

What was U.S. president Harry S. Truman's favorite poem?

U.S. president Harry S. Truman's (1884-1972) favorite poem is one by the English poet Alfred, Lord Tennyson (1809-1882):

For I dipt into the future, far as human eye could see,
Saw the Vision of the world, and all the wonder that would be;
Saw the heavens fill with commerce, argosies of magic sails,
Pilots of the purple twilight, dropping down with costly bales;
Heard the heavens fill with shouting, and there rain'd a ghastly dew
From the nations' airy navies grappling in the central blue;
Far along the world-wide whisper of the south-wind rushing warm,
With the standards of the peoples plunging thro' the thunder-storm;
Till the war-drum throbb'd no longer; and the battle-flags were furl'd
In the Parliament of man, the Federation of the World.

"Presidents—Favorite White House Poems," *New York Times Magazine* 9 December 1945.

What was the name of poet Baron George Gordon Byron's dog?

The English poet Baron George Gordon Byron (1788-1824) owned a beloved dog named Boatswain. On his pet's tombstone, Byron had the following words inscribed: "Near this spot are deposited the remains of one who possessed beauty without vanity, strength without insolence, courage without ferocity, and all the virtues of man without his vices. This praise, which would be unmeaning flattery if inscribed over human ashes, is but a just tribute to the memory of Botswain, a dog, who was born in Newfoundland May 1803 and died at Newstead Nov. 18th 1808."

George Gordon Byron, *"In my hot youth": Byron's Letters and Journals, edited by Leslie A. Marchand* (Cambridge, MA: Belknap Press of Harvard University Press, 1973), 176.

What was the route sailed by Homer's Greek hero Odysseus in the epic poem about his journey, the *Odyssey*?

The ancient Greek poet Homer's epic work, the *Odyssey*, describes hero Odysseus' sea journey home after his victory over the Trojans at Troy. Scholars chart the route beginning at the mouth of the Dardanelles, once the location of Troy, across the Mediterranean Sea to Tunis, on to the islands of Favignana and Lipari near Sicily, northward to Corsica and Capri, southward through the Strait of Messina to Syracuse and Corfu, then home to Ithaca and his faithful wife, Penelope. The legendary journey took ten harrowing, event-filled years to complete because of the malicious intervention of angry Greek gods.

The 1995 Grolier Multimedia Encyclopedia, (Danbury CT: Grolier Electronic Publishing, 1995), s.v. "Odysseus." *New York Times* 27 May 1968.

Who is known as "the father of American poetry"?

William Cullen Bryant (1794-1878) is known as "the father of American poetry," because his poetic voice produced the first "authentic" American poetry, utilizing native images, such as indigenuous birds, and geographical features in his poetry.

Charles B. Brown, *William Cullen Bryant* (New York: Charles Scribner's Sons, 1971), 2. Louis Untermeyer, *The Paths of Poetry: Twenty-Five Poets and Their Poems* (New York: Delacorte Press, 1966), 156.

What is William Butler Yeats' epitaph?

William Butler Yeats' (1865-1939), the Irish poet, epitaph reads:

Cast a cold eye On life, on death. Horseman, pass by!

Having died in France, where he lived due to poor health, at the beginning of World War II (1939-45), he was originally buried there. In 1948 his body was moved and buried in his native Ireland in a churchyard at Drumcliffe as he had wished.

Philip W. Goetz, ed. *The New Encyclopaedia Britannica, 15th ed., "Micropaedia"* (Chicago: Encyclopaedia Britannica, 1991), s.v. "Yeats, William Butler."

How did poet Robert Herrick begin his working life?

English poet and clergyman Robert Herrick (1591-1674) began his working life as a manufacturing jeweler. Later Herrick became known for his epigrams and elegant lyric poetry.

Louis Untermeyer, *The Paths of Poetry* (New York: Delacorte Press, 1966), 17.

Which poem by Robert Frost includes the line "Good fences make good neighbors"?

The poem "Mending Wall" by Robert Frost (1874-1963) includes the line "Good fences make good neighbors." The poem tells the story of a man and his neighbor; they are mending a stone wall that separates their properties. The narrator thinks "Something there is that doesn't love a Wall,/That wants it down." He wonders if perhaps they should give in to the forces that cause the rocks to fall and he wants to convince his neighbor that they need no barrier between them. But the other man simply repeats "Good fences make good neighbors."

Robert Frost, *Complete Poems of Robert Frost* (New York: Holt, Rinehart and Winston, 1949), 47.

What is the inscription over the Gate of Hell in Dante's *Divine Comedy*?

Readers of the Italian poet Alighieri Dante's (1265-1321) will find the following inscription carved into stone above the Gate of Hell.

I AM THE WAY INTO THE CITY OF WOE.
I AM THE WAY TO A FORSAKEN PEOPLE.
I AM THE WAY INTO ETERNAL SORROW.

SACRED JUSTICE MOVED MY ARCHITECT.
I WAS RAISED HERE BY DIVINE OMNIPOTENCE,
PRIMORDIAL LOVE AND ULTIMATE INTELLECT.

ONLY THOSE ELEMENTS TIME CANNOT WEAR
WERE MADE BEFORE ME, AND BEYOND TIME I STAND.
ABANDON ALL HOPE YE WHO ENTER HERE.

Alighieri Dante, *The Divine Comedy, translated by John Ciardi* (New York: W.W. Norton, 1977), 13.

What act of civil disobedience did Henry David Thoreau engage in to protest slavery and the Mexican War?

Henry David Thoreau (1817-1862), author of an essay later called "Civil Disobedience," was arrested in July of 1846 for refusing to pay poll tax. He took this stand to protest slavery and the Mexican War of 1846-1848.

Emory Elliott, ed., *Columbia Literary History of the United States* (New York: Columbia University Press, 1988), 411.

What Senegalese author who resided in Paris at the outbreak of World War II wrote a verse collection entitled *Black Victims?*

Lopold Sdar Senghor, a Senegalese author who was living in Paris when World War II (1939-45) began, wrote a collection of poems entitled *Black Victims* (*Hosties noires*), which reveal the war's impact on the poet.

Hans M. Zell, Carol Bundy, and Virginia Coulon eds., *A New Reader's Guide to African Literature* (New York: Africana Publishing, 1983), 271.

What was Byron's response to the success of *Childe Harold*?

The response of English poet Lord Byron (1788-1824) to the immediate success of his work *Childe Harold* was, "I awoke one morning and found myself famous."

Angela Partington, ed., *The Oxford Dictionary of Quotations, 4th edition* (Oxford: Oxford University Press, 1992), 174.

What are the "Kilkenny Cats"?

In Irish folkore there is the belief that once a year all neighborhood cats gather for a rousing, night long fight. The "Kilkenny Cats" were said to fight one night until nothing remained but their tails. This belief gave rise to the following poem:

There wanst was two cats in Kilkenny,
Aitch thought there was once cat too many;
So they quarrelled and fit,
They scratched and they bit,
Till, excepting their nails
And the tips of their tails,
Instead of the two cats, there wasn't any.

Mildred Kirk, *The Everlasting Cat* (Woodstock, NY: Overlook Press, 1977), 93-94.

Who was Thespis?

Thespis was a Greek poet who is credited with introducing the first actor in Greek tragedy around 543 B.C. Before this time performances were recited by a full chorus. Thespis chose a speaker to impersonate a specific character. Today *thespian* is a term that means actor, or an adjective to describe matters associated with dramatic arts.

Abraham H. Lass, David Kiremidjian, and Ruth M. Goldstein, *The Facts On File Dictionary of Classical, Biblical and Literary Allusions* (New York: Facts on File, 1987), 218.

Who wrote the famous inspirational poem, *If*?

British author Rudyard Kipling (1865-1936) wrote the famous inspirational poem, *If*, which ends with the notable following lines:

"If you can fill the unforgiving minute
With sixty seconds' worth of distance run,
Yours is the Earth and everything that's in it,
And -which is more -you'll be a Man, my son!"

Martin Gardner, ed., *Best Remembered Poems* (New York: Dover Publications, Inc., 1992), 78.

Which American poet was noted for his technical innovations, particularly in typography, such as frequent use of lower-case letters and extra spacing between words?

The poet e. e. cummings (1894-1962), author of 15 volumes of verse, was noted for his stylistic innovations, especially the use of lower case letters where capitals would normally be employed. Cummings, who received both bachelor's and master's degrees from Harvard University, and who worked as an ambulance driver in France during World War I, won the Bollingen Prize for poetry in 1957.

The Encyclopedia Americana, International Edition (Danbury, CN: Grolier, 1989), 8:323.

In poetry, what are "Bouts-rims"?

"Bouts-rims" are rhymed words or words with rhymed endings. A list of "Bout-rims" is used by poets who write "backwards," that is they start with the end words of each line and construct their poems around them. The use of "Bouts-rims" in writing poetry became a popular word game in eighteenth-century England with people sending each other lists of words. One Lady Ann Miller held weekly gatherings in her home where guests were given "Bout-rims" and challenged to writes poems around them. Horace Walpole (1717-1797), however, referred to such poetry as "a bouquet of artificial flowers."

Tony Augarde, *The Oxford Guide to Word Games* (Oxford: Oxford University Press, 1986), 135-38.

What is the verse written by Hilaire Belloc about a microbe?

Hilaire Belloc (1870-1953), a French-born British poet, essayist, and historian, wrote the following lines from the poem, "The Microbe" in his book, *Cautionary Verses*:

The Microbe is so very small
You cannot make him out at all.
But many people hope
To see him through a microscope.
His jointed tongue lies beneath
A hundred curious rows of teeth;
His seven tufted tails with lots
Of lovely pink and purple spots,
On each of which a pattern stands,
Composed of forty separate bands;
His eyebrows of a tender green;
But Scientists, who ought to know,
Assure us that they must be so...
Oh! let us never, never doubt
What nobody is sure about!

The Macmillan Dictionary of Quotations (New York: Macmillan, 1989), 501.

What did the poet Lord Byron write about gravity?

George Gordon Byron (1788-1824), the English poet known as Lord Byron, wrote the following lines:

When Newton saw an apple fall, he found...
A mode of proving that the earth turn'd round
In a most natural whirl, called "gravitation";

And thus is the sole mortal who could grapple,
Since Adam, with a fall or with an apple.

Isaac Asimov, *Isaac Asimov's Book of Science and Nature Questions* (New York: Grove Weidenfield, 1988), 113.

Who wrote the poem "Casey at the Bat"?

"Casey at the Bat" was first published in the San Francisco *Examiner* on June 3, 1888. It was written by Ernest Lawrence Thayer (1863-1940), who used the pseudonym "Phin." In the humorous poem, Mighty Casey, hero of the Mudville baseball team, strikes out and loses the game. The poem became famous when entertainer DeWolf Hopper began using it as part of his act.

George Perkins, Barbara Perkins, and Phillip Leininger, eds., *Benet's Reader's Encyclopedia of American Literature* (New York: HarperCollins, 1991), s.v. "Casey at the Bat."

What is *The Book of Counted Sorrows*, from which Dean Koontz draws poetry to use in his books?

If author Dean Koontz is unable to locate just the right bits of verse he would like to use to emphasize the themes of his stories, he writes the poetry himself and attributes it to *The Book of Counted Sorrows*. Koontz intends to actually publish a book by that name once he has composed enough verses.

Martin H. Greenberg, Ed Gorman, and Bill Munster, eds., *The Dean Koontz Companion* (New York: Berkley Books, 1994), 277-78.

Where did T.S. Eliot get the name "Prufrock," which he used in his famous poem "The Love Song of J. Alfred Prufrock"?

The Anglo-American poet T.S. Eliot (1888-1965), who won the Nobel Prize for literature in 1948, took the name "Prufrock" for his poem "The Love Song of J. Alfred Prufrock" (1917) from a St. Louis furniture company. The name was selected for its ironic effect. In "Prufrock's Dilemma," an essay written in 1949, American poet John Berryman states: "A man named J. Alfred Prufrock could hardly be expected to sing a love song; he sounds too well dressed. His name takes something away from the notion of love song." The poem is really about a timid, neurotic man who is incapable of love, and whose apprehensions reflect the sterile society that he inhabits.

James P. Draper, ed., *World Literature Criticism,* (Detroit: Gale Research, 1992), 2:1133-42.

Prose

What detective is featured in the novels of Walter Mosley?

The African American writer Walter Mosley (1952-) has written a series of detective stories set in the tough streets of black Los Angeles. These novels feature hard-boiled detective Ezekiel "Easy" Rawlins, who reluctantly finds himself drawn into morally ambiguous and dangerous situations. Rawlins first appeared in Mosley's award-winning *Devil in a Blue Dress* (1990).

Donna Olendorf, ed., *Contemporary Authors* (Detroit: Gale Research, 1994), 142:311.

What Virginia Woolf novel was inspired by Vita Sackville West?

English novelist Virginia Woolf (1882-1941), who experimented boldly in stream-of-conscious technique, used English poet and novelist Vita Sackville West (1892-1962) as the model for the character Orlando in the novel *Orlando* (1928).

Susan Mary Alsop, *Lady Sackville* (New York: Doubleday & Company, 1978), 228-29. Anne Olivier Bell, ed., *The Diary of Virginia Woolf* (New York: Harcourt Brace Jovanovich, 1980), 3: 156-57.

In what novel does Edward Casaubon appear and what qualities does he embody?

The Reverend Edward Casaubon is the creation of English novelist, Mary Ann Evans, who wrote under the name George Eliot (1819-80) and produced realistic novels like *Adam Bede* (1859) and *Silas Marner* (1861). The character appears in perhaps her finest work, *Middlemarch* (1871). The pedant archetypal know-it-all Casaubon is a self-centered, jealous, scholar, who is absolutely absorbed by his yet-to-be-written *Key to All Mythologies.*

Isadore G. Mudge and M. E. Sears, *A George Eliot Dictionary* (New York: Haskell House, 1972), s.v. "Casaubon, Reverend Edward."

According to Sir Thomas Malory, where did King Arthur find the sword Excalibur?

In the legend of King Arthur, the wizard Merlin lead the king to the lake of Avalon, where a mysterious hand, said to belong to the Lady of the Lake, reached out of the water and presented him with the sword Excalibur. It was to serve him for the rest of his life. Avalon was a magical place, surrounded by woods and meadows, where rain, snow, or hail have never fallen. In the version of the legend that Sir Thomas Malory recorded in his prose epic *Morte Darthur* (1485), at the end of his life, Arthur had to go back to Avalon and return the sword to the lake.

Alberto Manguel and Gianni Guadalupi, *The Dictionary of Imaginary Places* (San Diego: Harcourt Brace Jovanovich, 1987), s.v. "Avalon."

What work by Byron did Joyce consider turning into an opera?

The high-modernist Irish writer James Joyce (1882-1941), who created such masterpieces as *Ulysses* (1922) and *Finnegan's Wake* (1939), was fascinated by the symbolism that he found in the drama *Cain, A Mystery* (1821) by the English poet George Gordon, Lord Byron (1788-1824). Joyce attempted to interest the avant-garde American composer George Antheil (1900-1959) in collaborating with him to produce an opera based on the play. Antheil agreed initially but eventually grew uncomfortable with the idea, withdrawing from the project, which never reached fruition.

Richard Ellmann, *James Joyce* (New York: Oxford University Press, 1992), 640-41.

In what P.G. Wodehouse story did the characters Bertie and Jeeves make their first appearance?

English-born humorist P.G. Wodehouse (1881-1975) introduced his popular characters Bertie Wooster and his manservant Jeeves to his readers in a short story "Extricating Young Gussie" (1917).

David A. Jasen, *A Bibliography and Reader's Guide to the First Editions of P.G. Wodehouse* (n.p.: Archon Books, 1970), 57.

Who has been credited as the first professional English female author?

The first professional English female author was Aphra Behn. Details of her life are sketchy but her literary career began around 1666. Her writings include a play *The Forc'd Marriage* and a collection of poems entitled *Poems Upon Several Occasions.*

Cora Kaplan, *Salt and Bitter and Good: Three Centuries of English and American Women Poets* (London: Paddington Press, 1975), 49.

In which novel did P.G. Wodehouse introduce Blandings Castle?

British-born novelist P.G. Wodehouse (1881-1975) introduced Blandings Castle and its lord, Lord Emsworth, in *Something New* (1915), which appeared in England under the title *Something Fresh.* This was the beginning of the popular Wodehouse saga.

Wodehouse was born on October 15, 1881, in Guilford, Surrey, England. During a long and prolific career as a novelist, short story writer, and playwright, he carefully crafted comic tales that are quintessentially British. Wodehouse demonstrated his sense of humor while living in France at the outbreak of World War II (1939-45) when he found himself a prisoner of the invading Germans. He was taken to Berlin where he was put up in a nice hotel; he subsequently made a short radio broadcast during which he thanked the Germans for treating him so well. His fellow Englishmen were perturbed at what they viewed as consorting with the enemy, but all was forgiven when it was learned the Wodehouse, in his naivete, believed the war to be merely a "regrettable falling out between gentlemen." Wodehouse died February 14, 1975, in England.

David A. Jasen, *P.G. Wodehouse: A Portrait of a Master* (New York: Mason/Charter, 1974), 53. Stanley J. Kunitz and Howard Haycraft, eds., *Twentieth Century Authors* (New York: H.W. Wilson, 1942), 1538-39. James G. Lesniak, ed., *Contemporary Authors New Revision Series* (Detroit: Gale Research, 1991), 33:459.

What did William Shakespeare leave to his wife?

In his will, English dramatist William Shakespeare (1564-1646) left as his sole bequest to his wife: "I gy've unto my wief my second best bed with furniture." His principal heir was Susanna, his daughter.

Charles Hamilton, *In Search of Shakespeare,* (San Diego: Harcourt Brace Jovanovich, 1985), 83.

What San Francisco book store was intimately associated with the literature of the Beat Generation?

In 1955 Lawrence Ferlinghetti and Peter Martin established the City Lights Bookstore in San Francisco, which was intimately associated with the Beat Generation. In 1957 Ferlinghetti was put on trial for selling a book purported to be obscene, Allen Ginsberg's *Howl.*

Robert A. Hipkiss, *Jack Kerouac, Prophet of the New Romanticism* (Lawrence, KS: The Regents Press of Kansas, 1976), 86.

Through which war did Rip Van Winkle sleep?

After taking a magical draught from a flagon, American author Washington Irving's (1783-1859) fictional character Rip van Winkle slept in the Catskill Mountains for 20 years, through the entire war of the American Revolution (1775-1781).

Washington Irving, *The Complete Tales of Washington Irving, edited by Charles Neider* (Garden City, NY: Doubleday, 1975), 14.

Who was Nero Wolf, and where did he live?

Nero Wolfe, the rotund, orchid loving detective was created by mystery writer Rex Stout (1886-1975) and first appeared in *Fer de Lance* which was published in 1934. Wolfe always lived in New York, in a brownstone on West Thirty-Fifth Street although the street address varied from book to book.

Book title	Address on West Thirty-fifth St.
Over My Dead Body	506
Too Many Clients	618
Murder by the Book	902
Prisoner's Base	914
The Doorbell Rang	914
The Red Box	918
The Silent Speaker	922
Death of a Doxy	938

William S. Baring-Gould, *Nero Wolfe of West Thirty-fifth Street* (New York: Viking Press, 1969), 39.

How did Quasimodo get his name in Victor Hugo's *The Hunchback of Notre Dame*?

The name Quasimodo derives from the Latin form of the Introit, which is said at mass on the Sunday following Easter Day, known variously as Low Sunday, Low Easterday, and Quasimodo Sunday. The Introit begins "Quasi modo geniti infantes. . .," which translates "As newborn babes...." In Victor Hugo's (1802-1885) story *The Hunchback of Notre Dame,* it was on that day that a child was found abandoned and named Quasimodo to commemorate the fact. Marked by a physical deformity, that child was the title character in Hugo's novel.

Leslie Dunkling, *A Dictionary of Days* (New York: Facts on File, 1988), s.v. "Quasimodo Sunday."

In which of Shakespeare's plays do ghosts appear?

Ghosts appear in five of English dramatist William Shakespeare's (1564-1616) plays: *Hamlet, Macbeth, Julius Caesar, Richard III,* and *Cymbeline.*

Cumberland Clark, *Shakespeare and the Supernatural* (New York: Haskell House, 1971), 31-32.

What unfinished novel by Herman Melville was found in a tin box decades after the author's death?

Decades after the death of American novelist Herman Melville (1819-1891) the unfinished manuscript of *Billy Budd* was found in a tin box by Melville scholar Raymond Weaver.

Tyrus Hillway, *Herman Melville* (New York: Twayne Publishers, 1963), 65-66.

What is a "technothriller"?

A "technothriller" is an action-suspense novel noted for having high technology weapons systems and other sophisticated hardware integral to the plot. American writer Tom Clancy (1947-), author of *The Hunt For Red October,* is a master of the genre.

Stephen Glazier, *Random House Word Menu,* (New York: Random House, 1992), 541.

Who was the "man without a country"?

"The man without a country" was Philip Nolan, the main character in an 1863 short story of the same name by American clergyman and author E.E. Hale (1822-1909). The fictitious tale was written to inspire patriotism during the American Civil War. Philip Nolan, on trial for conspiracy, publicly damns the United States and states his wish that he would never hear of that place again. The court-martial grants that wish by sending him to sea where he is denied any news of his country. Nolan spends fifty-seven years in watery exile and eventually repents his traitorous statement. There was a real Philip Nolan, whose true story is told in *Philip Nolan's Friends* (1876), Hale's complementary novelette.

James D. Hart, *The Oxford Companion to American Literature, 5th edition* (New York: Oxford University Press, 1983), 468.

Is the Tom Clancy book *The Hunt for Red October* based on fact or fiction?

A story of international intrigue, American writer Tom Clancy's (1947-) *The Hunt for Red October* (1984) has created much speculation as to whether its events really happened. In the book, the captain of a Soviet submarine decides to use his vessel to defect to the West. With the help of U.S. intervention, he is successful. Soviet accounts from 1975, of mutiny and defection, have some resemblance to the story of Tom Clancy's novel. The Soviet newspaper *Izvestia* reported a near-mutiny on an anti-submarine frigate. The Soviets also related the attempted escape of navy captain Valeri Sablin, who, with a dozen others, tried to defect to Sweden. Aerial bombing was used to stop the group when it was 50 miles from Swedish waters. Sablin was court-martialed, found guilty, and executed.

Parade 24 June 1990.

What was the original title of Jane Austen's novel *Pride and Prejudice*?

The novel *Pride and Prejudice* by English writer Jane Austen (1775-1817) was originally titled *First Impressions.* Austen completed a book by the earlier title in 1797, which was not published. It is known to be the basis for *Pride and Prejudice,* which was published in 1813, although there is little evidence explaining what changes were made to the work. This is characteristic of the privacy maintained by the author.

David Louis, *Fascinating Facts* (New York: Ridge Press/Crown Publishers, 1977), 91. E. Rubinstein, ed., *Twentieth Century Interpretations of Pride and Prejudice* (Englewood Cliffs, NJ: Prentice-Hall, 1969), 1.

What kind of pipe was smoked by the fictional character Sherlock Holmes?

When Sir Arthur Conan Doyle (1859-1930) created the character of Sherlock Holmes he gave him three props that now instantly identify the famous detective. In illustrations, on the stage, and in films, Sherlock Holmes is known by his deerstalker hat, his magnifying glass, and his pipe. Curiously, the pipe has become further identified as a "meerschaum calabash" as the result of a 1904 illustration and a 1901 production of a Sherlock Holmes play in London. Doyle never named the type of pipe his character smokes in his books, but he did approve the use of a calabash in the plays *Sherlock Homes* and *The Speckled Band.*

Bill Blackbeard, *Sherlock Holmes in America* (New York: Harry N. Abrams, 1981), 15.

In which French cemetery are many famous literary people buried?

Many famous literary people are buried in the Pre Lachaise Cemetery in Paris, France. Included are Gertrude Stein, Abelard and Hlose, Appollinaire, Balzac, Colette, Constant, Daudet, Molire, Proust, Romains, and Wilde.

Robert Hendrickson, *The Literary Life and Other Curiosities* (New York: Viking Press, 1981), 115.

What English novelist, poet, and biographer lived in Sissinghurst Castle?

Vita Sackville-West (1892-1962), an English poet, novelist, and biographer, and her husband Harold Nicolson, a civil servant, moved into Sissinghurst Castle in 1930 where they jointly pursued an avid interest in gardening. At Sissinghurst, Sackville-West wrote *Sissinghurst* and *English Country Homes.* Although she was a lesbian and he was a homosexual, their unconventional marriage survived and is chronicled in their son Nigel's book, *Portrait of a Marriage.*

Claire Buck, ed., *The Bloomsbury Guide to Women's Literature* (New York: Prentice Hall, 1992), s.v. "Sackville-West, Vita."

Which female novelist used the pseudonym Tom Crampton?

English novelist Barbara Pym (1913-1980), first published in the 1950s, expressed ironic views of unrequited love, spinsters, provincial life, and the important role played by institutions, such as the Church, in the lives of educated women of the middle class. During the 1960s and 1970s she wrote under the name of Tom Crampton, but found that publishers rejected these works. Her popularity was renewed in the late 1970s.

Claire Buck, ed., *The Bloomsbury Guide to Women's Literature* (New York: Prentice Hall, 1992), 938-39.

Who were the *Prcieuses*?

The *Prcieuses* (meaning precious women in French) were a group of seventeenth-century literary women who emphasized refinement in and knowledge of society, literature, and language in an effort to improve the status of women. The *Prcieuses* highly valued independence from men and questioned the value of marriage. From 1650 to 1660 these women were closely linked to the salon movement. One of the women, Madeleine de Scudry, was noted for hosting *Samedis,* Saturday salons.

When first used the term bore a positive connotation. However, some of its luster was lost when the affectations and excesses of some of the women left all of the *Prcieuses* open to ridicule from the French playwright Molire (1622-1673) and others. Antoine Furetire's (1619-1688) dictionary refers to these women as "false" or "ridiculous" *Prcieuses.*

Claire Buck, *The Bloomsbury Guide to Women's Literature* (New York: Prentice Hall, 1992), 930.

What is a yahoo?

A yahoo is an uncouth or uncivilized person. The term was created by Jonathan Swift (1667-1745), an Anglo-Irish writer and clergyman who is considered the greatest satirist in the English language. In his most famous work, *Gulliver's Travels* (1729), a satire on the pretentiousness of public life, the Yahoos are irrational people who epitomize the worst aspects of humanity.

E.D. Hirsch Jr., Joseph F. Kett, and James Trefil, *The Dictionary of Cultural Literacy* (Boston: Houghton Mifflin, 1988), 139.

Who were the so-called "university wits" who challenged the literary canons of sixteenth-century Oxford?

The so-called "university wits" who challenged the literary canons of sixteenth-century Oxford were John Lyly (1554-1606), Thomas Lodge (1558-1625), George Peele (1556-1596), Robert Greene (1558-1592), and Thomas Nashe (1567-1601). In 1589, Thomas Brabine wrote the following line in reference to the group: "Come foorth you witts, that vaunt the pompe of speach."

A.W. Ward and A.R. Waller, eds., *The Drama to 1642, vol. 5 of The Cambridge History of English Literature* (Cambridge: Cambridge University Press, 1964), 121.

Who are the "big four" female writers of the English detective story?

According to some critics, Agatha Christie (1890-1976), Dorothy Sayers (1893-1957), Margery Allingham (1906-1966), and Ngaio Marsh (1889-1982) are the "big four" female writers of the classical English detective story.

Richard B. Gidez, *P.D. James* (Boston: Twayne Publishers, 1986), 7-8.

Which short story by Ernest Hemingway opens with a description of Africa's highest mountain?

"The Snows of Kilamanjaro," a short story by American Nobel Prize-winner Ernest Hemingway (1899-1961) opens with a description of Mt. Kilamanjaro, Africa's highest mountain.

Samuel Shaw, *Ernest Hemingway* (Frederick Ungar Publishing, 1973), 84-85.

In literature what is a "roman clef"?

In literature a "roman clef" is a novel about real persons and events but using fictional names.

Stephen Glazier, *Word Menu* (New York: Random House, 1992), 541.

Which play by T.S Eliot dramatizes the murder of Thomas Becket?

T.S. Eliot (1888-1976) was a poet, playwright, and literary critic, who won the Nobel Prize for Literature in 1948. Although his early success was as a poet, his conversion to the Church of England stimulated him to write drama as a means of spreading the Christian message to a wider audience than could be reached by his poetry. *Murder in the Cathedral* (1935) was the most successful of his verse dramas. It depicts the martyrdom of St. Thomas Becket (c. 1118-1170), an archbishop of Canterbury who was murdered by the vassals of King Henry II (1133-1189). Although he could have used the play to illustrate the conflict between church and state, Eliot emphasized the internal struggle of individual characters, especially that of the archbishop, who is able to triumph over his self-doubt and shape his destiny. The audience is brought into the action when the characters on stage address it directly and involve it in the moral questions that the play raises.

Stanley Weintraub, ed., *Dictionary of Literary Biography* (Detroit: Gale Research, 1982), 10:174-76.

In which of her novels did Agatha Christie introduce the fictional detective Hercule Poirot?

English novelist Agatha Christie (1890-1976) introduced the Belgian detective Hercule Poirot in her first mystery novel, *The Mysterious Affair at Styles* (1920).

Dilys Winn, *Murderess Ink: The Better Half of the Mystery* (New York: Workman Publishing, 1979), 52.

Which short story by author Alice Walker was banned in California?

Pulitzer Prize-winning American author Alice Walker's (1944-) short story "Roselily" was deleted from a California state tenth-grade English test after a Christian group protested what it called the work's anti-religious theme. "Roselily" is the story of a country woman who questions traditional views of marriage and religion.

USA Today 21 February 1994.

What is the general idea behind Mark Twain's short story "1601: A Tudor Fireside Conversation"?

The short story "1601" A Tudor Fireside Conversation" by American author Mark Twain (pseudonym of Samuel Clemens, 1835-1910) concerns a discussion between selected members of the court of Queen Elizabeth I. The group includes the Queen herself, several of her ladies-in-waiting, Sir Walter Raleigh, William Shakespeare, and other famous Elizabethan personalities. The humor lies in a contrast between their sophisticated reputations and the topic under discussion.

Anne Ficklen, ed., *The Hidden Mark Twain* (New York: Greenwich House, 1984), vii.

Which American novelist writes of life in Arkansas and was also an actress and singer?

African-American novelist and poet Maya Angelou (1928-) was an actress and singer before publishing her autobiographical novels. Her critically acclaimed novel *I Know Why the Caged Bird Sings* (1970) was a warm and humorous account of her early life in the segregated town of Stamps, Arkansas. Angelou has also published four sequels to her novel, plays, screenplays, and several volumes of poetry. In 1993, she read a poem she'd composed for U.S. president Bill Clinton at his inauguration ceremony.

The 1995 Grolier Multimedia Encyclopedia (Danbury, CT: Grolier Electronic Publishing, 1995), s.v. "Angelou, Maya." Carol DeKane Nagel, ed., *African American Biography* (Detroit: U*X*L, 1994), s.v. "Maya Angelou." Phyllis Rose, ed., *The Norton Book of Women's Lives* (New York: W.W. Norton, 1993), 41.

Who are some of the literary heroes of the "yuppie generation"?

A list of the literary heroes of the "yuppie generation" would certainly include Jay McInerney, Tama Janowitz, and Bret Easton Ellis, who share in their writings a common theme of social disenfranchisement amongst New Yorkers on the edge of intellectual and economic affluence.

McInerney was born in Hartford, Connecticut, on January 13, 1955, and is best known for his best-selling first novel *Bright Lights, Big City* (1984). Set in the early 1980s, it tells the story of an "angst-ridden, cocaine snorting preppie through the purgatory of Manhattan's downtown night life."

Tama Janowitz was born in San Francisco on April 12, 1957, and her 1986 *Slaves of New York* is set in New York's artsy SoHo district. Bret Easton Ellis, who was born in Los Angeles on March 7, 1964, published his first novel, *Less Than Zero*, in 1985. Like the other two members of this so-called "literary brat pack" Ellis writes of disenchanted youths, but wealthy ones. His 1991 novel, *American Psycho*, was extremely controversial for its horrifying and graphic presentation of a Wall Street investment banker turned serial killer who tortures and mutilates women. Pre-publication publicity caused Simon & Schuster to renege on its contract with Ellis which resulted in the prestigious book publisher being applauded by some and accused of intellectual cowardice and censorship by others.

Judith Graham, ed., *Current Biography Yearbook, 1994* (New York: H.W. Wilson, 1994), 170-73. Charles Moritz, ed., *Current Biography Yearbook, 1987* (New York: H.W. Wilson, 1988), 402-04. Charles Moritz, ed., *Current Biography Yearbook, 1989* (New York: H.W. Wilson, 1990), 278-81. "Yuppie Lit: Publicize or Perish, " *Time* 19 October 1987.

Who wrote *Mules and Men*?

African American author Zora Neale Hurston (1903-1960) wrote *Mules and Men*, a book centering on the folklore of Eatonville, Florida, an all-black community.

Rosemary M. Magee, *Friendship and Sympathy: Communities of Southern Women Writers* (Jackson, MS: University Press of Mississippi, 1992), 164.

Which American writer has written extensively on the history of food and its rituals?

American fiction writer M.F.K. (Mary Frances Kennedy) Fisher (1908-1992) was best known for her writings on the rituals of "sex, food, and shelter," having published a novel and numerous short stories. In addition, she translated Brillat-Savarin's *The Physiology of Taste*.

Charles Moritz, ed., *Current Biography Yearbook 1983* (New York: H.W. Wilson, 1983), 133-36. Mickey Pearlman and Katherine Usher Henderson, *Inter/View: Talks with America's Writing Women* (Lexington, KY: University Press of Kentucky, 1990), 80, 87.

Which Nobel Prize-winning author created the character "Gimpel the Fool" in the book of the same title?

Nobel Prize-winning Yiddish author Isaac Bashevis Singer (1904-1991) created the character "Gimpel the Fool" in his 1985 book of the same title.

Ruth S. Frank and William Wollheim, *The Book of Jewish Books* (New York: Harper & Row, 1986), 228.

What is the meaning of the title of Edward Albee's play *Who's Afraid of Virginia Woolf?*

American author Edward Albee is quoted in *Esquire* as saying, "Who's Afraid of Virginia Woolf? means Who's Afraid of the Big Bad Wolf? [or] Who's Afraid of Living Life without False Illusion." Virginia Woolf (1882-1941) was a culturally elite writer whose reputation was intimidating to the rest of the literary world. Albee believed life to be meaningless, and by stripping the intellectual characters in his play of all illusions, he challenges them to face and accept their fates. He wished them to view many of their fears as mere illusions.

Diana Trilling, "Who's Afraid of the Culture Elite," *Esquire* December 1963.

Who wrote the novel from which the film *Phantom of the Opera* was adapted?

The film *Phantom of the Opera* was adapted from a novel by the same name written by French novelist and author of detective and mystery stories Gaston Leroux (1868-1927).

Michael F. Blake, *Lon Chaney: The Man Behind the Thousand Faces* (Vestal, NY: Vestal Press, 1993), 132.

Which famous authors who have been accused of plagiarism?

Famous authors whose works have been cited for plagiarism include: Joseph Addison, Samuel Taylor Coleridge, Charles Dickens, F. Scott Fitzgerald, Robert Burns, Johann Wolfgang von Goethe, Ben Johnson, Stendhal, William Shakespeare, and Oscar Wilde.

William Fitzgerald, "Plagiarism, Naughtiest of Literary Vices, Has Had a Long, Dishonorable Career," *New York Times Magazine* 8 February 1953.

Which Hemingway novel has as its protagonist a successful American painter living in Bimini?

Islands in the Stream is the novel by Ernest Hemingway (1899-1961), which features Thomas Hudson as a successful American painter living in Bimini in the late 1930s and early 1940s. The novel was published posthumously in 1970.

Frank N. Magill, ed., *Cyclopedia of Literary Characters II* (Pasadena, CA: Salem Press, 1990), 780.

Who is the fictional police detective created by author Georges Simenon?

Inspector Jules Maigret is the fictional police detective created in 1929 by Belgian author Georges Simenon (1903-1988) and featured in nearly fifty of his novels. The pipe-smoking Maigret leaves no clue uninvestigated, and his loyal wife, Louise, realizes that Maigret places his work above all else in his life.

Michael R. Pitts, *Famous Movie Detectives II,* (Metuchen, NJ: Scarecrow Press, 1991), 33.

Who is author Raymond Chandler's fictional detective?

Philip Marlowe is the fictional detective created by American author Raymond Chandler (1888-1959) and featured in seven of his mystery novels, starting with *The Big Sleep* in 1939. Marlowe is ethical, honest, well educated, and enjoys literature and music.

Michael R. Pitts, *Famous Movie Detectives II* (Metuchen, NJ: Scarecrow Press, 1991), 91.

From where did Edgar Rice Burroughs derive the name "Tarzan" for his famous character?

According to the first published version of *Tarzan of the Apes* by Edgar Rice Burroughs (1875-1950), the protagonist's name meant "white-skin" in the language of the apes.

Gabe Essoe, *Tarzan of the Movies: A Pictorial History of More Than Fifty Years of Edgar Rice Burroughs' Legendary Hero* (New York: Citadel Press, 1968), 1.

What book helped bring an end to the corporal punishment of sailors?

American author Richard Henry Dana's (1815-1882) novel *Two Years Before the Mast* (1840) helped call attention to the inhumane treatment of common seamen aboard sailing vessels of his day, especially regarding the use of flogging as punishment. Dana had taken a break from his studies at Harvard University to work as a sailor, and the novel was based on his experiences as a seaman on the high seas around Cape Horn. Dana was also the author of *The Seaman's Friend* (1841), a reference classic on maritime legal issues.

Howard L. Hurwitz, *An Encyclopedic Dictionary of American History* (New York: Washington Square Press, 1968), s.v. "Dana, Richard Henry."

What was the name of Dashiell Hammett's handsome, hard-boiled private detective in his famous mystery *The Maltese Falcon*?

Sam Spade was the handsome, hard-boiled private detective in American writer Dashiell Hammett's (1894-1961) famous mystery *The Maltese Falcon* (1930).

Abraham H. Lass, David Kiremidjian, and Ruth M. Goldstein, *The Facts On File Dictionary of Classical, Biblical and Literary Allusions* (New York: Facts On File, 1987), s.v. "Spade, Sam."

What famous literary figure was imprisoned for nineteen years for stealing a loaf of bread?

The literary character Jean Valjean was imprisoned for 19 years for stealing a loaf of bread in Victor Hugo's *Les Misrables.* Victor Hugo (1802-1885) was a French poet, dramatist, and novelist whose great literary reputation continues to the present day. In *Les Misrables* (1862), Hugo realistically depicts the plight of the poor in nineteenth-century France. With the upheaval of French society as a backdrop Hugo paints a sympathetic portrait of the waif Gavroche and Jean Valjean, the escaped prisoner. Hugo presents a much less sympathetic view of Javert, the police agent who sets out to re-capture Valjean. Hugo's two other great works are *The Hunchback of Notre-Dame* (1831) and *Les Travailleurs de la mer* (1866).

McGraw-Hill Encyclopedia of World Biography (New York: McGraw-Hill, 1973), 5: 405. Justin Wintle, ed., *Makers of Nineteenth Centurt Culture, 1800-1914* (London: Routledge & Kegan Paul, 1982), 304-06.

Who was "George Spelvin"?

"George Spelvin" was the pseudonym of John Chapman who wrote for *Theater Arts*, a magazine of the 1940s. Chapman was a well known drama critic and his pseudonym, "George Spelvin" was often used in theater programs for a "double" actor, that is one who played more than one role in a single performance.

Pittsburgh Post-Gazette March 21, 1969.

In which Eugene O'Neill play does the character "Hickey" appear?

The character "Hickey" appears in *The Iceman Cometh* (1946) by American playwright Eugene O'Neill (1888-1953).

David Grote, *Common Knowledge: A Reader's Guide to Literary Allusions* (New York: Greenwood Press, 1987), s.v. "Hickey."

Which 1950's novel by Grace Metalious surpassed *Gone With The Wind* as the best-selling American novel?

Peyton Place by American author Grace Metalious (1924-64) was published in 1956 and became destined, largely through paperback editions, to surpass Margaret Mitchell's (1900-49) American Civil War novel *Gone With The Wind* (1936) in sales.

William Pratt, *Scarlet Fever: The Ultimate Pictorial Treasury of Gone With The Wind* (New York: Macmillan, 1977), 257.

Why was author Truman Capote's *Answered Prayers* so controversial?

Truman Capote's (1924-1994) *Answered Prayers* was controversial because of the transparent way he portrayed, satirized, and ultimately betrayed the sophisticated crowd that had supported him throughout his career as a writer. Chapters of his work-in-progress were originally published in *Esquire* in 1975 and 1976, and another chapter was published in Capote's *Music for Chameleons* (1980). In 1987 *Answered Prayers* was published by Random House as an unfinished novel.

Tina Brown, "Goodbye to the Ladies Who Lunch," *New York Times Book Review* 13 September 1987.

In what novel do three "witches" pool their psychic resources in an attempt to turn the tables on their errant lover-mentor?

In the horror novel, *The Witches of Eastwick* by John Updike, three "witches" pool their psychic resources in an attempt to turn the tables on their errant lover-mentor, Darryl Van Horne.

Neil Barron, ed., *Horror Literature: A Reader's Guide* (New York: Garland Publishing, 1990), 311.

Which mystery writer based a character in a novel on her second husband?

English mystery writer Agatha Christie (1890-1976) based a character in *Murder in Mesopotamia* after her second husband, Sir Max Mallowan (1904-1978), the eminent archaeologist and professor at the University of London,who directed the excavations at the Chaldean-Babylonian city of Ur with Sir Leonard Woolley in the 1920s. Christie often accompanied her husband to the Near East and used the area as the setting for several of her books.

William Amos, *The Originals: An A-Z of Fiction's Real-Life Characters* (Boston: Little, Brown, 1985), xiii.

Who was the real-life model for the title character in Lewis Carroll's *Alice's Adventures in Wonderland*?

Alice Liddell (1852-1934) was the model for the character of Alice in Lewis Carroll's *Alice's Adventures in Wonderland.* Lewis Carroll, a pseudonym of Charles Lutwidge Dodgson (1832-1898), was an instructor in mathematics at Christ Church College of Oxford University when classical scholar and father of Alice, Henry George Liddell, was appointed its dean. Carroll was also an an early devotee of photography, and it was through his camera that the fledgling author became acquainted with the Liddell family. *Alice's Adventures in Wonderland* was published in 1865, the same year Alice Liddell turned thirteen, and *Through the Looking-Glass* appeared in 1872. Alice's mother considered the relationship unhealthy and discarded the correspondence Carroll had sent to her daughter.

William Amos, *The Originals: An A-Z of Fiction's Real-Life Characters* (Boston: Little, Brown, 1985), s.v. "Alice."

What are Shakespeare's "Seven Ages of Man"?

In act II, scene vii of Shakespeare's *As You Like It* the "Seven Ages of Man"—infant, whining school-boy, lover, soldier, justice, a lean and slippered pantaloon, and second childhood—are recited by the character Jacques. A "pantaloon" is from the Italian "pantalone" and refers to a buffoon-like stock character in period Italian comedies. Shakespeare's "seven ages" has parallels in Palengenius' "Zodiacus Vitae" and the "Onomasticon" of

Julius Pollux and represent a cynical view of the folly of life's pageant. Jacques' recitation begins with the more familiar "All the world's a stage...."

Larry S. Champion, *The Essential Shakespeare* (New York: G.K. Hall & Co., 1993), 244. William Shakespeare, *As You Like It, edited by Albert Gilman* (New York: Signet, 1963), 77-78.

Who was the inspiration for the character Birkin in D.H. Lawrence's *Women In Love*?

The character Birkin in D.H. Lawrence's *Women in Love* was based on the author himself, according to Richard Aldington who wrote the introduction to a 1960 edition of the novel. David Herbert Lawrence (1885-1930) was a controversial English novelist, poet, essayist, short story writer, and playwright. Born in the village of Eastwood in Nottinghamshire, England, Lawrence grew up a brilliant but introspective child who doted on his mother and hated his drunkard father. Quitting his schoolmaster job because of health problems, Lawrence published his first novel *The White Peacock* in 1911, which was soon followed by *The Trespasser.*

Lady Chatterley's Lover was Lawrence's most controversial novel. Because of its "indecency" Lawrence had trouble getting it published; he also struggled to find someone to type it from his manuscript. Eventually the novel was printed privately in Florence, Italy, (1928) by a printer who was unable to read English. Although written in 1915, *Women In Love* was not printed until 1920 in New York by private subscription. Because of its controversial content, *Women In Love*, like *Lady Chatterley's Lover*, had been turned down by numerous London publishers. The author felt that *Women In Love* was the best work from what he called his "second phase."

Stanley J. Kunitz, ed., *Authors: Today and Yesterday* (New York, H.W. Wilson, 1933), 388-93. D.H. Lawrence, *Women In Love* (New York, Viking Press, 1960), xi.

Who was the inspiration for the character of Gudrun in D. H. Lawrence's *Women in Love*?

Richard Aldington, in his introduction to a 1960 edition of the novel, claims that the character of Gudrun in English author D.H. Lawrence's (1885-1930) *Women in Love* was based on the New Zealand novelist Katherine Mansfield (1888-1923).

D.H. Lawrence, *Women in Love* (New York: Viking, 1960), xi.

What is the name of Candide's tutor in the Voltaire novel of the same name?

Pangloss was the tutor of the title character in the work *Candide* by French satirist Voltaire, the pseudonym of Francois-Marie Arouet (1694-1778). The writer derived the loquacious instructor's name from the Greek phrase "all tongue."

Voltaire, *Candide, Zadig and Selected Stories* (Bloomington, IN: Indiana University Press, 1961), 4.

What was the real name of Voltaire?

The French satirist Voltaire (1694-1778) was born Francois-Marie Arouet. He took the nom de plume "de Voltaire" at the age of twenty-three. Voltaire is considered one of the most important figures of the French Enlightenment.

Voltaire, *Candide, Zadig, and Selected Stories* (Bloomington, IN: Indiana University Press, 1961), ix.

What novel foretold the 1924 sinking of the luxury liner *Titanic*?

Fourteen years before the sinking of the *Titantic*, Morgan Robertson published his novel, *Futility*, which featured an unsinkable, luxurious ocean liner that did sink after striking an iceberg in the cold April waters of the Atlantic Ocean. The name of Robertson's liner, the *Titan*, was closely prophetic.

Isaac Asimov, *Isaac Asimov's Book of Facts* (New York: Bell Publishing, 1981), 365.

What do the letters R.U.R. stand for in Karel Capek's melodrama about robots?

In Czech journalist and writer Karel Capek's (1890-1938) melodrama about robots, *R.U.R.*, the letters stand for Rossum's Universal Robots.

Karel Capek, *R.U.R. (Rossum's Universal Robots): A Fantastic Melodrama in Three Acts and an Epilogue* (New York: Doubleday, 1923). n.p.

What is the name of the novel by Alexandra Ripley that was written as a sequel to Margaret Mitchell's *Gone With the Wind*?

Scarlett is the name of the novel by Alexandra Ripley written as a sequel to Margaret Mitchell's *Gone With the Wind. Scarlett* was authorized by the estate of Margaret Mitchell, but some critics found that the sequel was not as good as the original.

Molly Ivins, "That O'Hara Woman,"*New York Times Book Review*27 October 1991.

Who was the wife of Nessim Hosnani in *The Alexandria Quartet* by Lawrence Durrell?

Justine was the wife of Nessim Hosnani in the four-part novel *The Alexandria Quartet* (1957-1961), written by English novelist Lawrence Durrell (1912-1970).

Martin Seymour-Smith, *Dictionary of Fictional Characters* (Boston: The Writer, 1992), s.v. "Justine."

How many words are there in a book?

Adult nonfiction books generally contain a minimum of 60,000 words or 200 typed pages. The maximum number of words practical for one volume is 500,000. Juvenile books are composed of between 30,000 and 60,000 words. Adult fiction runs between 50,000 and 300,000 words. Any adult book should have at least 60,000 words and a novice writer should submit 80,000 words or more.

Charles N. Heckelmann, *Writing Fiction for Profit* (New York: Coward-McCann, 1968), 40. David Raffelock, *Writing for the Markets* (New York: Funk & Wagnalls, 1969), 78. Paul R. Reynolds, *The Writing and Selling of Non-fiction* (Garden City, NY: Doubleday, 1963), 82.

In which horror novel does a governess, Morag MacLeod, come under Count Dracula's power?

In the horror novel *Dracula, My Love* by Peter Tremayne, governess Morag MacLeod comes under Count Dracula's power. In this story Dracula is characterized not as a villain but as a great romantic lover.

Neil Barron, ed., *Horror Literature: A Reader's Guide* (New York: Garland Publishing, 1990), 309.

Who was *Amadis of Gaul?*

Amadis of Gaul was the hero of a series of anonymous prose romances of chivalry written around 1400. These works made *Amadis* as popular in Spanish and Portugese romances as King Arthur was in English legend.

Grant Uden, *A Dictionary of Chivalry* (New York: Thomas Y. Crowell, 1968), s.v. "Amadis of Gaul."

What is unique about *Le Petit Prince* by Antoine De Saint-Exupry?

La Petit Prince by French author and aviator Antoine De Saint-Exupry (1900-1944) is unique because it is a versatile tool for French language instruction. The short novel can be used in elementary, intermediate, or advanced classes. It is suitable as an introductory reading text or in advanced courses dealing with French literary types, as well as with most levels in between.

Antoine De Saint-Exupry, *Le Petit Prince* (Cambridge, MA: Riverside Press, 1946), vii.

Who originated the detective story genre?

The detective story genre originated with the American poet and short-story writer Edgar Allen Poe's (1809-1849) *Murders in the Rue Morgue* (1841).

Dennis Sanders, *The First of Everything* (New York: Delacorte Press, 1981), 324.

What is "black humor" and who are some of its practitioners?

To paraphrase *Time Magazine*, black humor examines the megaton-megaopolis age and finds it funny in fearsome ways. Black humor is epitomized in Terry Southern's *Dr. Strangelove*, in which the world is destroyed in a nuclear holocaust amid bumbling characters and mis-understandings, Joseph Heller's classic novel *Catch-22*, and Bruce Jay Friedman's novel *Stern.*

Time 4 March 1966.

What was the name of the fictional character Tarzan's elephant?

Tantor was the name of Tarzan's elephant in the series of books created by adventure writer Edgar Rice Burroughs (1875-1950).

Philip Jos Farmer, *Tarzan Alive* (Garden City, NJ: Doubleday, 1972).

In which novel did F. Scott Fitzgerald make his oft-quoted observation about the rich being different from "you and me"?

In *The Rich Boy* American novelist F. Scott Fitzgerald (1896 1940) made his oft-quoted observation: "Let me tell you about the very rich. They are different from you and me."

Karen L. Rood, ed., *American Literary Almanac* (New York: Facts On File, 1988), 254.

What was the original title of *Pride and Prejudice* by Jane Austen?

Published in 1813, *Pride and Prejudice* by the English novelist of manners Jane Austen (1775-1817) was originally titled *First Impressions.*

Irving Wallace et al., *The Book of Lists #2* (New York: William Morrow, 1980), 227.

How many words are in Hervey Allen's novel *Anthony Adverse*?

There are an estimated 500,000 words in the lengthy novel *Anthony Adverse* (1933), written by the American writer Hervey Allen (1889-1949).

New Republic June 1933. *Saturday Review of Literature* June 1933.

In 1963, American novelist Ken Kesey published *One Flew Over the Cuckoo's Nest.* Kesey's title is similar to what line from a *Mother Goose* nursery rhyme?

The title of Kesey's novel *One Flew Over the Cuckoo's Nest* is remarkably similar to "And one flew over the Goose's nest," a line from a *Mother Goose* nursery rhyme.

Ken Elton Kesey was born in La Junta, Colorado, in 1935. His first novel, *One Flew Over the Cuckoo's Nest* is regarded by literary critics and cultural historians as representative of the psychedelic culture of the 1960s marked by the unrestrained use of mind-altering drugs. The novel is the story of one Patrick McMurphy, a criminal who feigns insanity in order to avoid jail and ends up in a mental institution. For his efforts to instill an awareness of the ludicrousness of the human condition on other patients McMurphy is eventually lobotomized. Much of the novel is based on Kesey's drug experimentations, his wanderings around the country in a wildly painted bus with a group calling themselves the Pranksters and his real life work as a night attendant in a mental hospital. *One Flew Over the Cuckoo's Nest* and other works by Kesey garnered a wide following and much acclaim. In 1975 Milos Forman directed a movie based on the novel starring Jack Nicholson as McMurphy. The movie won Oscars for Best Picture, Best Actor, Best Actress, Best Director, and Best Screenplay.

Charles Moritz, ed., *Current Biography Yearbook 1976* (New York: H. W. Wilson, 1976), s.v. "Kesey, Ken (Elton)." Jay Robert Nash and Stanley Ralph Ross, *The Motion Picture Guide* (Chicago: Cinebooks, 1986), s.v. "One Flew Over the Cuckoo's Nest." *Time for Poetry* (Glenview, IL: Scott, Foresman, 1961), 96.

What are some stories featuring the common apple?

The common apple is surrounded by many stories and much historical lore. The apple is purported to be the forbidden fruit Eve tasted in the Garden of Eden, an act that expelled her and Adam from paradise. One custom alleges that a girl may peel an apple in one long strip, toss it over her head, and decipher the initials of her lover in the peel's twists. In Scotland it is said that if a lass eats an apple in front of a mirror, the visage of her future husband will appear. In Arabian tales, the fruit possesses healing powers. William Tell, the hero of Swiss legend, shot an apple off of his son's head. American legendary figure Johnny Appleseed, the nickname of John Chapman, planted apple seeds along the American frontier so that orchards would greet pioneers heading westward.

"Applesauce: The Romance of a Fabled Fruit," *The Independent, A Weekly Journal of Free Opinion* 7 August 1926.

How long is Margaret Mitchell's novel *Gone with the Wind*?

Gone with the Wind, the novel by Margaret Mitchell (1900-1949), is approximately 400,000 words long, several times the average length of a novel.

Mitchell, who was born in Atlanta, Georgia, had a genteel upbringing and attended private schools where teachers praised her writing abilities. Her mother Maybelle often took the young

Margaret on carriage rides during which they viewed derelict plantations and the remaining ruins of "Sherman's March to the Sea." After attending Smith College, Mitchell completed her epic American Civil War novel in 1936. It was an immediate success selling over one million copies in the first six months and garnering Mitchell a Pulitzer Prize in 1937. Many critics feel that much of the novel is autobiographical. A main character in the novel, Ashley Wilkes, may have been modelled after Mitchell's fiance who was killed in World War I (1914-18). *Gone with the Wind* has become a permanent part of the American cultural scene. By the 1980s it had sold over sixteen million copies worldwide and continues to sell 250,000 paperback copies annually in the United States. The movie version (1939) received as much publicity as the novel and won ten Academy Awards.

On August 11, 1949, Mitchell was struck by a car and died five days later of brain injuries suffered in the accident.

Hal May and Susan M. Trosky, eds., *Contemporary Authors* (Detroit: Gale Research, 1989), 125: 340-48. *New Statesman & Nation* 3 October 1936.

What was the first work of fiction to be blessed by a pope?

The best-selling novel *Ben-Hur* (1880), written by American novelist Lew Wallace (1827-1905), received the blessing of Pope Leo XIII (1810-1902). The work, which is subtitled *A Tale of the Christ*, was well received by the Roman Catholic Church for its portrayal of Jesus Christ. The pope sanctioned an Italian translation in 1895 and later had his honorary chaplain Henry Salvadori prepare a special edition with "various modifications of ideas into the work in the interests of piety." Wallace's original novel has been translated into ten languages, re-written as a play, and produced as two classic films (1925 and 1959).

Isaac Asimov, *Isaac Asimov's Book of Facts* (New York: Bell Publishing, 1979), 311. John A. Garraty, ed., *Encyclopedia of American Biography* (New York: Harper & Row, 1974), 1144-45. Robert E. Morsberger and Katharine M. Morsberger, *Lew Wallace: Militant Romantic* (New York: McGraw-Hill, 1980), 448-49.

What book tells the story of Edward Rochester's first wife, who appeared in Charlotte Bronte's novel *Jane Eyre*?

Published in 1966, *Wide Sargasso Sea*, by Jean Rhys, pseudonym for English writer Ella Rees Williams (1894-1979), is the fictional "prequel" to Charlotte Bronte's (1816-53) classic nineteenth-century novel *Jane Eyre*. In *Jane Eyre*, the title character is hired by a Mr. Edward Rochester, with whom she eventually falls in love. But Miss Eyre is haunted by a madwoman who is kept locked away in the attic of Rochester's home, Thornfield Hall. It is later revealed that this woman is a Creole heiress Rochester married under his father's orders. When she is killed in a fire, Rochester and Miss Eyre become free to wed. Novelist Jean Rhys became fascinated by the shadowy figure of the first Mrs. Rochester and wrote an entire book about the childhood, marriage, and mental disintegration of the character she called Antoinette Bertha Cosway.

Jean Rhys, *Wide Sargasso Sea* (New York: W. W. Norton, 1966), dustwrapper.

What is the origin of "Mother Goose"?

"Mother Goose" is often romantically pictured as a benign, maternalistic figure reading nursery rhymes to children. Although her origins are murky, she is probably in some abstract way a variant of the Virgin Mary or Mary's mother, Saint Anne, a sacrificing mother figure.

Shari L. Thurer, *The Myths of Motherhood* (Boston: Houghton Mifflin, 1994), 193-94.

What was the name of the whaling ship in Herman Melville's *Moby Dick*?

In American author Herman Melville's (1819-91) famous novel *Moby Dick*, the great white whale was hunted from the decks of the *Pequod*.

James D. Hart, *The Oxford Companion to American Literature* (New York: Oxford University Press, 1983), s.v. "Pequod."

Did Frank R. Stockton ever write a conclusion or a sequel to his "The Lady or the Tiger?," a short story best known for leaving readers hanging?

Frank Stockton's 1882 short story *The Lady or the Tiger?* created a stir not only in literary circles, but also among the general public. Readers sent letters to the author, demanding that he write a sequel in order to provide a satisfactory conclusion, solving the dilemma faced by the man in the story who must choose between two doors, behind which he will find either a woman he must marry or a ferocious tiger. Readers submitted their own suggested solutions and the reasons behind them.

Stockton's *The Discourager of Hesitancy* was published in 1884 and although it may be called a sequel to *The Lady or the Tiger?* in the loosest sense of the word it does not answer the question as to what was behind the door, the lady or the tiger. Like its well known predecessor, *The Discourager of Hesitancy* is a psychological puzzler.

Fable and Fiction: Frank Stockton (Emmaus, PA: The Story Classics, 1949), 175. Frank R. Stockton, "The Lady or the Tiger: And What Came of Writing It," *Ladies Home Journal* November 1893. Susan M. Trosky and Donna Olendorf, eds., *Contemporary Authors* (Detroit: Gale Research, 1992), s.v. "Stockton, Francis Richard."

Where does the saying "cricket on the hearth" come from?

Seventeenth-century English poet John Milton's "Il Penseroso" contains the first appearance of the phrase "cricket on the hearth."

Douglas Bush, ed., *The Portable Milton* (New York: Viking Press, 1949), 68.

What is the Cradle of Securitie?

The Cradle of Securitie was an interlude mentioned in the manuscript tragedy of Sir Thomas More which was never printed and probably no longer exists. The date assigned to this interlude is somewhere between 1560 and 1570.

Stephen Jones, *Biographia Dramatica; or a Companion to the Playhouse, rev. ed.* (London: S. Gosnell, 1812), 2:140.

What is Cynewulf's *Elene*?

Cynewulf was an Anglo-Saxon poet who lived in the late eighth or early ninth century. He wrote in Old English, and his name is known because it was inscribed in runic characters after four poems that have been found in two ancient, hand-written anthologies, the *Exeter Book* and the *Vercelli Book*. The poems are, "The Ascension," which is part of a longer poem entitled *Christ, Juliana, The Fates of the Apostles*, and *Elene*, which is about Helen, the mother of the first Christian emperor Constantine. According to a legend that is recounted in the poem,

Helen discovered the cross on which Christ was crucified. *Elene* also is the only source of information about the life of the poet, who mentions in it a spiritual experience that transformed his life. Although many other poems have been attributed to Cynewulf, there is no hard evidence that he wrote any but the four mentioned above.

Margaret Drabble, ed. *The Oxford Companion to English Literature, 5th ed.* (Oxford: Oxford University Press, 1985), s.v. "Cynewulf."

What is a fable?

A fable is a moral tale that features animals endowed with human characteristics. Aesop's fables are the most famous fable collection in which the fable about the fox and the grapes, is the source of the saying "sour grapes."

Chris Baldick, *The Concise Oxford Dictionary of Literary Terms* (New York: Oxford University Press, 1990), s.v. "fable."

Who was the Japanese author who committed hari-kiri in 1970?

Born in 1925, Japanese author Yukio Mishima, a pseudonym for Kimitake Hiraoka, committed the ritualistic suicide known as hari-kiri after finishing his work *The Decay of the Angel*, the last installment of his literary cycle known as *Sea of Fertility*. The date of his death was November 25, 1970.

Peter Wolfe, *Yukio Mishima* (New York: Continuum Publishing, 1989), 7-9.

Who was the fictional detective character in the Raymond Chandler novels?

The name of the detective in the series of novels by Raymond Chandler (1888-1959) was Philip Marlowe. Marlowe, running a one-man detective agency was the epitome of what a 1930s-1940s private detective should be: well-educated, witty, honest, loyal, and urbane (being an art and classical music lover, a chess player). Chandler made Marlowe the chief character in *The Big Sleep* (1939), *Farewell, My Lovely* (1940), *The Lady in the Lake* (1943), and *The Long Goodbye* (1953).

Sylvia Cole and Abraham H. Lass, *The Facts On File Dictionary of 20th-Century Allusions: From Abbott and Costello to Ziegfeld Girls* (New York: Facts on File, 1991), s.v. "Marlowe, Philip."

Who is Sherlock Holmes?

The fictional character Sherlock Holmes, a brilliant but eccentric detective created by British novelist and physician, Sir Arthur Conan Doyle (1859-1930), first appeared in Doyle's short story *A Study in Scarlet*, which was published in the November 1887 issue of *Beeton's Christmas Annual* and later published as a novel. Holmes and his friend Dr. Watson, a bumbling physician, lived in London at 221B Baker Street. Their landlady was Mrs. Hudson. Mycroft Holmes was the detective's older brother by seven years.

The evil Professor James Moriarty, an art expert and criminal genius, was Holmes' arch enemy. Moriarty was modelled after Adam Worth (1844-1902), an international art thief also known as Henry Raymond who was famous for stealing, and then anonymously returning, Thomas Gainsborough's portrait of Georgiana, fifth Duchess of Devonshire, from William Agnew's London Gallery.

Encyclopedia Americana (Danbury, CT: Grolier, 1994), 24: 705. Allan Eyles, *Sherlock Holmes: A Centenary Celebration* (New York: Harper & Row, 1986), 128. *New York Times*, 31 July 1994. Michael Hardwick and Mollie Hardwick, *The Sherlock Holmes Companion* (New York: Doubleday & Co., 1963), 26, 29. *World Book Encyclopedia* (Chicago: World Book, 1994), 9: 295-96.

What was the first book manuscript to be produced on a typewriter?

The Adventures of Tom Sawyer by Mark Twain (1835-1910) was the first typewritten book manuscript. It was typed on a Remington typewriter in 1875. Twain's *Life on the Mississippi* was also typewritten later that year.

Joseph Nathan Kane, *Famous First Facts* (New York: H. W. Wilson, 1981), s.v. "typewritten book manuscript."

Has anyone ever written a book without using the letter "e"?

A 267-page book without the letter "e" in the text was published in 1939. Ernest Vincent Wright, a graduate of the Massachusetts Institute of Technology, tied down the "e" key on his typewriter and produced a credible 50,110-word novel, *Gadsby*, without the letter "e"—the most frequently used letter in the English language. Wright was 67 years old when he wrote his novel, which took 165 days to complete. He stated that his greatest problem was in avoiding verbs that ended with "ed" and pronouns such as he, she, or they. Although the work is a romance novel, Wright managed to avoid the word "love" as well. He died on the day of the book's publication. Originally priced at $3.00, the novel with a book jacket sold for $1,000 at rare-book dealers in 1983.

"No Page Goes Unturned in E-less Book Case," *USA Today* 24 February 1984. Amy Wallace, David Wallechinsky, and Irving Wallace, *The People's Almanac Presents The Book of Lists #3* (New York: William Morrow, 1983), 225-26.

How many characters appear in Leo Tolstoy's novel *War and Peace*?

The Russian novelist and count Leo Tolstoy (1828-1910) carefully rendered over 500 characters in what is regarded as his greatest work, *War and Peace*, originally entitled *All's Well That Ends Well*. The novel, which takes place in Russia during the Napoleonic Wars, contains more than 500,000 words. Reportedly Tolstoy's wife, Soph ia Behrs, copied the manuscript seven times for her husband.

Benet's Reader's Encyclopedia, 3d ed. (New York: Harper & Row, 1987), s.v. "War and Peace." Albert H. Morehead, ed., *The Illustrated Library of the Literary Treasures* (New York: Bobley Publishing, 1963), L-1228. Tikhon Polner, *Tolstoy and His Wife* (New York: Norton, 1945), 92. Irving Wallace, *The Book of Lists #2* (New York: William Morrow, 1980), 227.

Who created the original character of Tarzan?

American author Edgar Rice Burroughs (1875-1950), wrote 28 books about Tarzan. His first Tarzan story appeared in the magazine *The All-Story* in October 1912 under the title "Tarzan of the Apes." This was published in book form with the same title in 1914. Most associate Tarzan with the King of the Jungle of the movies who could speak very little English. The character in Burroughs's books was actually an intelligent man who spoke in several languages, had immense physical strength, and possessed the instinctive cunning of a wild jungle creature. Tarzan's real name in the books was John Clayton, Lord of Greystoke.

David Fury, *Kings of the Jungle: An Illustrated Reference to "Tarzan" on Screen and Television* (Jefferson, NC: McFarland, 1994), 1-9.

What is the real name of the author Trevanian?

Trevanian is the pseudonym of publicity-shy author and drama professor Rodney Whitaker, who also writes under the name of Nicholas Seare. Perhaps his best known suspense thriller is *The Eiger Sanction* (1972), which was made into a motion picture starring Clint Eastwood in 1975. Its protagonist is Jonathan Hemlock, a snobbish art history professor who is also a world-class mountain climber and an assassin for an American intelligence organization.

Donald McCormick and Katy Fletcher, *Spy Fiction: A Connoisseur's Guide* (New York: Facts on File, 1990), 246-47. Lesley Henderson, ed., *Twentieth-Century Crime and Mystery Writers, 3rd ed.* (Chicago: St. James Press, 1991), s.v. "Trevanian."

Who created the name Wendy?

The name Wendy was created by English author and playwright J.M. Barrie (1860-1937) as a name for a character in his children's classic *Peter Pan.* Wendy is a young girl who befriends Peter Pan and goes to Never-Neverland with him. In 1904 *Peter Pan* was brought to the stage with the character Wendy created in memory of a deceased daughter of Barrie's friend, W.E. Henley.

Stanley J. Kunitz and Howard Haycraft, eds., *Twentieth Century Authors* (New York: H.W. Wilson, 1942), s.v. "Barrie, James Matthew." David Pringle, *Imaginary People: A Who's Who of Modern Fictional Characters* (New York: World Almanac, 1987), s.v. "Darling, Wendy."

What are the titles of the various Dr. Dolittle books by Hugh Lofting?

Dr. John Dolittle, the doctor who is able to "talk to the animals," was the creation of English-born writer Hugh John Lofting (1886-1947). Lofting immigrated to the United States in 1912 after working in Africa, Cuba, and Canada. His famous character Dr. Dolittle who, after learning that he can converse with animals, gives up his human practice and starts caring for animals around the world and even on the moon. Lofting's series of children's books started with *The Story of Doctor Dolittle* (1920) and ran through 12 titles ending with *Doctor Dolittle's Puddleby Adventures* in 1952. Other titles include *The Voyages of Doctor Dolittle* (1922), *Doctor Dolittle's Post Office* (1923), *Doctor Dolittle's Circus* (1924), *Doctor Dolittle's Zoo* (1925), *Doctor Dolittle's Caravan* (1926), *Doctor Dolittle's Garden* (1927), *Doctor Dolittle in the Moon* (1928), *Gub Gub's Book* (1932), *Doctor Dolittle's Return* (1933), *Doctor Dolittle and the Secret Lake* (1948), and *Doctor Dolittle and the Green Canary* (1950). The last three books were published posthumously.

David Pringle, *Imaginary People: A Who's Who of Modern Fictional Characters* (New York: World Almanac, 1987), s.v. "Doolittle, John." Susan M. Trosky and Donna Olendorf, eds., *Contemporary Authors, Volume 137* (Detroit: Gale Research, 1992), s.v. "Lofting, Hugh John."

What are the titles of the various "Anne of Avonlea" books by Lucy Maud Montgomery?

When *Anne of Green Gables* by Lucy Maud Montgomery (1874-1942) was published in 1908, it became an overnight success but not before the manuscript had been rejected by numerous potential publishers over a number of years. Montgomery was born in Clifton, Prince Edward Island, Canada, and had a lonely but book-filled childhood. Her heroine Anne is much like her creator Lucy, sensitive and shy but embodied with imagination. Montgomery's first book was followed by nine other titles in the series: *Anne of Avonlea* (1909), *Chronicles of Avonlea* (1912), *Anne of the Island* (1915), *Anne's House of Dreams* (1917), *Rainbow Valley* (1919), *Further Chronicles of Avonlea* (1921), *Rilla of Ingleside* (1921), *Anne of Windy Poplars* (1936) (also published as *Anne of Windy Willows*), and *Anne of Ingleside* (1939). The series has been translated into more than 35 languages.

Susan M. Trosky and Donna Olendorf, eds., *Contemporary Authors, Volume 137* (Detroit: Gale Research, 1992), s.v. "Montgomery, L.M."

What are the various pen names of children's author Theodor Seuss Geisel?

Theodor Seuss Geisel (1904-1991), the immensely popular author of delightfully whimsical children's books, wrote under various pen names including Rosetta Stone and Theo LeSieg. He shall, however, always be remembered as Dr. Seuss, the author of *And To Think I Saw It On Mulberry Street, The Cat in the Hat, Green Eggs and Ham, Horton Hears A Who,* and *The Grinch Who Stole Christmas.* The full name of the pseudonymous Dr. Seuss was Dr. Theodophilus Seuss, Ph.D., I.Q. H2SO4.

Dr. Seuss from Then to Now: A Catalogue of the Retrospective Exhibition, San Diego Museum of Art (New York: Random House, 1986), 19. Donna Olendorf, ed., *Something About The Author, Vol. 67* (Detroit: Gale Research, 1992), s.v. "Geisel, Theodor Seuss."

Did Little Lord Fauntleroy have a real-life counterpart?

The model for the title character of *Little Lord Fauntleroy* (1885) was the son of the novel's author, Frances Hodgson Burnett (1849-1924). Like Fauntleroy, Vivian Burnett (1876-1937) addressed his mother as "Dearest" and wore a velvet knickerbocker suit. Overcoming the sissy image portrayed by his mother in her novel, Vivian went on to become a reporter for the Denver *Republican* and a magazine publisher. He died after he helped rescue four people in a boating accident.

William Amos, *The Originals: An A-Z of Fiction's Real-Life Characters* (Boston: Little, Brown, 1985), 178-79. Clarence L. Barnhart, ed., *The New Century Cyclopedia of Names* (New York: Appleton-Century-Croft, 1954), 2483.

Who gave the "Eulogy to a Dog"?

The "Eulogy to a Dog" was given by George Graham Vest when he was a young lawyer in Georgetown, Missouri, representing a plaintiff who was suing a neighbor for the killing of his dog. The case was said to have been won based on the emotional address to the jury on the steadfast faithfulness of dogs to their masters. West later served as a member of the Confederate Congress during the American Civil War and as a U.S. senator from Missouri from 1879-1903.

William Safire, comp., *Lend Me Your Ears: Great Speeches in History* (New York: W. W. Norton, 1992), s.v. "Vest, George Graham."

What is Dorothy's last name in the *Wizard of Oz*?

The full name of the chief character in L. Frank Baum's (1856-1919) tale *The Wizard of Oz* is Dorothy Gale.

L. Frank Baum, *Ozma of Oz* (Chicago: Reilly & Lee, 1907), p. 107.

Who practiced oratory with pebbles in his mouth?

Demosthenes (384 B.C.-322 B.C.) is considered to be the greatest of the Greek orators. An Athenian by birth, a city where all adult free males could attend the assembly and vote, Demosthenes became a dominant political figure because of his oratory skill. There are many legends about how Demosthenes developed his voice and later political power. According to one story, he was a stammerer, who learned to speak slowly by putting pebbles in his mouth.

Catherine B. Avery, ed., *The New Century Classical Handbook* (New York: Appleton-Century-Crofts, 1973, s.v. "Demosthenes." N.G.L. Hammond and H.H. Scullard, *The Oxford Classical Dictionary, 2nd ed.* (Oxford: Clarendon Press, 1970), s.v. "Demosthenes (2)."

What are the titles of the three volumes which comprise *The Lord of the Rings* by J.R.R. Tolkien?

The Fellowship of the Ring (1954), *The Two Towers* (1955), and *The Return of the King* (1955) are the three books in *The Lord of the Rings*, the three-volume fantasy work by English writer J.R.R. Tolkien (1892-1973). The books are a sequel to Tolkien's *The Hobbit* (1937). The trilogy chronicles the events in a fictional fantasy land called Middle Earth and is generally agreed to be the standard against which all fantasy works are now measured.

Marshall B. Tymn, *Fantasy Literature: A Core Collection and Reference Guide* (New York: R.R. Bowker, 1979), 163.

In what literary work were the magic words "open sesame" first used?

The magic words "open sesame" were first used by Ali Baba, hero of the story *Ali Baba and the Forty Thieves* in *Arabian Nights*. He overhears these magic words, which allow him entry into a cave laden with riches.

Abraham Lass, *The Facts on File Dictionary of Classical, Biblical, and Literary Allusions* (New York: Facts on File, 1987), s.v. "Ali Baba."

In Sir Walter Scott's *Ivanhoe*, what name did Robin Hood assume when he appeared as an archer at a tournament sponsored by his enemies?

Ivanhoe, by Sir Walter Scott (1771-1832), is just one of many novels featuring the Robin Hood character. In Scott's tale of chivalry and forbidden love, Robin Hood assumes the name Robin of Locksley in order to compete in a tournament. Locksley is said to have been the name of the village where the outlaw was born.

Benet's Reader's Encyclopedia, 3rd ed. (New York: Harper & Row, 1987), s.v. "Locksley."

In what form did Dickens's novels first appear?

Much of English author Charles Dickens's (1812-1870) fiction first appeared as serialized episodes in monthly magazines. In his lifetime Dickens became quite well-known for this sort of work, and he is said often to have written the next installment only when it was nearly due for publication.

Philip Gaskell, *A New Introduction to Bibliography* (New York: Oxford University Press, 1972), 302-03.

Which play by Shakespeare is never mentioned in the theatre because of a superstition of bad luck?

Of all plays in the English language, no other play has more bad luck associated with it than the play *Macbeth* by British playwright William Shakespeare (1564-1616). Personal and stage accidents, illnesses, and botched lines have all been attributed to the play. Consequently it has become a tradition never to utter the play's title in a stage dressing room. For hundreds of years, theatre folk have delicately referred to the Shakespearean tragedy as "The Scottish Play" or simply "That Play," rather than risk the curse associated with mentioning its title.

Norrie Epstein, *The Friendly Shakespeare: A Thoroughly Painless Guide to the Best of the Bard* (New York: Viking Penguin, 1993), 428.

What famous British playwright was imprisoned for killing an actor in a duel?

In 1598 Ben Jonson (c. 1573-1637), a member of Philip Henslowe'ss company serving as an actor and a playwright, was arrested for killing the actor Gabriel Spenser. Jonson escaped capital punishment (although his thumb was branded), by pleading "benefit of clergy," based on his ability to read the Bible in Latin.

Harold Bloom, ed., *Medieval Late Renaissance, vol. 1 of The Major Authors Edition of the New Moulton's Library of Literary Criticism* (New York: Chelsea House Publishers, 1985), 463.

What country lifted a ban on such western writers as Shakespeare, Cervantes, and Hugo in 1978?

China lifted a long-standing ban on western books in 1978. The political fall of the Gang of Four in October of 1976 resulted in the rerelease of books that had been banned during the country's Cultural Revolution. In December of 1977, China's official press agency announced the publication of plays by Shakespeare as well as works by Cervantes, Heine, Balzac, Hugo, and Tolstoy. The sale of a Chinese translation of *Hamlet* created lines up to one hundred yards long; it was the first time the work had been available in China in 23 years.

The New York Times 24 February 1978.

In what novel by Emile Zola does the character Anna Coupeau appear?

The character Anna Coupeau, a prostitute, appears in the novel *Nana* by Emile Zola. Published in 1880, the book is part of the "Rougon-Macquart" series.

David Pringle, *Imaginary People* (New York: World Almanac, 1987), 323.

Dashiell Hammett, Raymond Chandler, and many others wrote for which popular pulp mystery magazine?

Many American novelists who became famous for writing detective novels got their start working for "pulp" magazines, so-named because they were printed on coarse wood pulp. The top pulp magazine was *Black Mask*, which featured short stories by Dashiell Hammett (1894-1961) and Raymond Chandler (1888-1959) before they became famous novelists.

H.R.F. Keating, *Whodunit? A Guide to Crime, Suspense and Spy Fiction* (New York: Van Nostrand Reinhold, 1982), 37.

Ann Rampling and A.N. Roquelaure are the pen names of what contemporary horror novelist?

American novelist Anne Rice (1941-), author of *Interview with a Vampire*, *The Feast of All Saints*, *Cry to Heaven*, and other books, also writes under the names Anne Rampling and A.N. Roquelaure.

Anne Rice, *The Witching Hour* (New York: Ballantine Books, 1990).

What stories feature the character Natty Bumppo?

Author James Fenimore Cooper featured the character of Natty Bumppo in a series of five stories known as The Leatherstocking Tales. *The Last of the Mohicans*, and its several television and movie versions, is perhaps the best known of these stories. Bumppo is also known by many other names: Deerslayer, Hawkeye, La Longe Carabine, Leatherstocking, Pathfinder, and The Trapper.

Janet Husband, *Sequels, An Annotated Guide to Novels in Series* (Chicago: American Library Association, 1982), 54.

What are the two major literary awards for science fiction?

The Hugo and The Nebula are the two major literary awards for science fiction. The Hugo Awards were created by Hal Lynch as a promotional gimmick for the 1953 World Science Fiction Convention in Philadelphia. Prior to the convention, the awards, referred to as the Science Fiction Achievement Awards, received a lot of publicity in various science fiction magazines. The convention committee presented a list of nominees to the convention attendees who could then vote for their favorites. Shortly thereafter someone nicknamed the awards after Hugo Gernsback, founder of one of the early science fiction magazine *Amazing Stories*. The nickname has lasted over the years. Because there is no continuity of convention management, awarding The Hugo has been sporadic.

Nebula Award recipients are chosen by a mail ballot of members of the Science Fiction Writers of America. The awards are presented at an annual banquet. The Nebula started shortly after the founding of the Science Fiction Writers of America in 1956. Like the Hugo, the Nebula is awarded for a variety of categories but, unlike the Hugo, awarding of the Nebula is structured and disciplined. The Nebula winners are generally regarded as being chosen for literary merit, while the Hugo winners are chosen more on the basis of popularity.

Marshall B. Tymn, ed., *The Science Fiction Reference Book* (Mercer Island, WA: Starmont House, 1981), 154-56, 216-17.

What is a complete list of author Agatha Christie's fictional detectives?

In addition to the well-known Hercule Poirot, the list includes: Jane Marple, Tommy and Tuppence Beresford, (Christopher) Parker Pyne, Harley Quin, Superintendent Battle, Colonel John Race, Mark Easterbrook, Arthur Calgary, and Inspector Narracott.

Russell H. Fitzgibbon, *The Agatha Christie Companion* (Bowling Green, OH: Bowling Green State University□Popular Press, 1980), 44-80.

What was the name of the fictional French revolutionary character who knitted into her scarf the story of St. Evrmonde?

In Charles Dickens's (1812-1870) *A Tale of Two Cities* (1859), Madame DeFarge, a French revolutionary, sits outside her Paris wine shop knitting into a long scarf strange symbols which will later spell out a death list of hated aristocrats. Among the symbols is that of Monseigneur Marquis St. Evrmonde who, while driving in his carriage through the French countryside, carelessly killed the child of a peasant. The marquis was later murdered in his bed by persons unknown.

Frank N. Magill, ed., *Masterplots: 2,010 Plot Stories & Essay Reviews from the World's Fine Literature, rev. ed.* (Englewood Cliffs, NJ: Salem Press, 1976), 6373-74.

Who were the last of the Mohicans?

In *The Last of the Mohicans* (1826), an American novel by James Fenimore Cooper (1789-1851), the title refers to Chingachgook and Uncas, father and son, who become the sole remnants of the once numerous Delaware nation. As companions of the main character Hawk-eye, they are sympathetic characters—noble, loyal, dignified, and estimable.

Janet Mullane and Laurie Sherman, eds., *Nineteenth-Century Literature Criticism* (Detroit: Gale Research, 1990), 2:124.

What is the origin of the expression "salad days"?

The plays of English dramatist William Shakespeare (1564-1616) have enriched the English language with a wide range of colorful sayings and familiar phrases. Among these is "salad days," referring to a time of youth or inexperience. It comes from the historical *Antony and Cleopatra* (Act 1, Scene 5):

> My salad days,
> When I was green in judgment, cold in blood,
> To say as I said then!

Martin H. Manser, *The Guinness Book of Words* (Middlesex, England: Guinness Books, 1988), 89.

Who is Sancho Panza?

In Miguel de Cervantes's (1547-1616) classic novel *Don Quixote*, Sancho Panza is the squire and traveling companion of the title character.

Miguel de Cervantes Saavedra, *Don Quixote de la Mancha, translated by Charles Jarvis* (Oxford: Oxford University Press, 1992), ii.

Which two famous writers died within a few days of each other in 1616?

The great Spanish novelist Miguel de Cervantes (1547-1616) died within a few days of the great English dramatist William Shakespeare (1564-1616).

Miguel de Cervantes Saavedra, *Don Quixote de la Mancha, translated by Charles Jarvis* (Oxford: Oxford University Press, 1992), i.

From what novel did H. Rider Haggard derive *King Solomon's Mines*?

In writing the novel *King Solomon's Mines* (1886), English novelist H. Rider Haggard (1856-1925) drew upon Robert Louis Stevenson's *Treasure Island*. Both books feature a hidden treasure in a unknown part of the world, which can be located by a map which comes into the possession of one of the protagonists. The settings, however, are quite different. For example, Haggard's story is set in Africa, a continent about which he knew a good deal, whereas the Stevenson story takes place on an uninhabited Pacific island.

H. Rider Haggard, *She, introduction by Malcolm Elwin* (London: MacDonald, 1948), xiv.

What personal experience inspired F. Scott Fitzgerald's depiction of Gatsby's love affair in *The Great Gatsby*?

American writer F. Scott Fitzgerald (1896-1940) is known for his stories about life during the decade called the "Roaring Twenties." In *The Great Gatsby* (1925) Fitzgerald created Jay Gatsby, a rich racketeer who strives for acceptance by the monied elite of Long Island. He is obsessed with Daisy Buchanan, a poor-little-rich-girl with whom Gatsby had an earlier relationship and who is now married to a vulgar man. His passion for her is so strong that he takes responsibility for the death of a woman who Daisy killed in a hit-and-run accident. When Gatsby is murdered by the dead woman's husband, Daisy feels no remorse. Gatsby's powerful and largely unrequited love may reflect Fitzgerald's college romance with Ginevra King, a beauty from a rich Chicago family. Although according to Ginevra they spent no more than fifteen hours together, the affair had a lasting effect on Fitzgerald, for the thought of her could bring tears to his eyes even at the end of his life.

Thomas J. Stavola, *Scott Fitzgerald, Crisis in an American Identity* (n.p.: Vision and Barnes & Noble, 1980), 46.

What was F. Scott Fitzgerald's last novel, left unfinished at his death?

The Last Tycoon was the last novel of American novelist F. Scott Fitzgerald (1896-1940). He had been working on it steadily for over a year when he died of a heart attack on December 21, 1940. The book's central character is Monroe Stahr, a brilliant young film producer, who was killing himself with overwork in an effort to forget the death of his beloved wife. The story seems to focus on Stahr's love affair with Kathleen Moore, who reminded him of his dead wife. Because Fitzgerald had not completed the novel when he died, the novel has remained a source of conjecture with literary critics and the author's many readers.

Thomas J. Stavola, *Scott Fitzgerald, Crisis in an American Identity* (New York: Barnes & Noble, 1980), 70.

Who was Erle Stanley Gardner and under what pseudonym did he write?

Erle Stanley Gardner (1889-1970) was a flamboyant lawyer turned mystery writer, who is best known for the eighty-two Perry Mason stories, which made him one of the wealthiest writers of detective fiction ever. He also wrote under the names of Carleton Kendrake, Charles J. Kenny, and A.A. Fair. In fact many find his characterizations more vivid, the humor sharper, and the writing fresher in the twenty-nine books that he wrote using the name A.A. Fair, which feature the diminutive detective Donald Lam and his large partner Bertha Cool.

Lesley Henderson, ed., *Twentieth-Century Crime and Mystery Writers, 3d. ed.* (Chicago: St. James Press, 1991), 413-15.

Who was Thomas Gradgrind, and what does he symbolize?

Thomas Gradgrind was a character in English writer Charles Dickens'(1812-1870) *Hard Times* (1854), who exclaimed, "In this life, we want nothing but Facts, sir; nothing but Facts!" A retired hardware merchant, Gradgrind founded an experimental school where only facts and scientific laws were taught. Although he was essentially a good man, he caused a great deal of unhappiness because of his obsession with the scientific and the practical and his neglect of the imaginative and the speculative. Dickens used Gradgrind to criticize nineteenth-century industry and culture.

Charles Dickens, *Hard Times, reprint* (New York: New American Library, 1961), 12-13. Frank N. Magill, ed., *Masterplots: Cyclopedia of Literary Characters* (New York: Salem Press, 1963), 443.

How many authenticated signatures of William Shakespeare are known to exist?

Although British playwright and poet William Shakespeare (1564-1616) is considered by many to be the greatest writer in the English language, there exists very little written in his own hand. He left only six signatures and perhaps three pages of a promptbook.

Charles Hamilton, *In Search of Shakespeare* (San Diego: Harcourt Brace Jovanovich, 1985), 2.

By what name was author and British military officer T.E. Lawrence known during World War I?

During World War I (1914-1918), British military officer and author Thomas Edward (T.E.) Lawrence (1888-1935) came to be known as Lawrence of Arabia. Lawrence grew up with an abiding interest in archaeology and after much acclaimed studies in the field joined an expedition to Asia Minor. He soon developed a passion for Arab culture and readily adopted their language, food, and dress. When World War I broke out, Lawrence joined the British army and was assigned to the Military Intelligence Office in Cairo. With little supervision from his superiors, he began organizing an intelligence network and uniting irregular Arab forces to operate against Turkey, which was allied with Germany and the other Central Powers. Lawrence became a central figure in the Arab Revolt, which aided Allied efforts in the region. Some critics, however, claim he was better at self-promotion than military accomplishments. In 1927 Lawrence wrote *Revolt in the Desert* to critical acclaim and expanded it into *Seven Pillars of Wisdom* which was published posthumously in 1935.

Philip J. Haythornthwaite, *The World War One Sourcebook* (London: Arms and Armour, 1992), 335. *McGraw-Hill Encyclopedia of World Biography, Vol. 6* (New York: McGraw-Hill, 1973), s.v. "T.E. Lawrence."

What is the Newbery Medal for children's literature?

The Newbery Medal, which is awarded annually for the year's most distinguished contribution to children's literature, is named after John Newbery (1713-1767), a British writer and the first publisher of books for children. The medal is awarded by the Association for Library Services to Children, a division of the American Library Association. The award was donated by the Frederic G. Melcher family and only goes to a citizen or resident of the United States. Hendrik Willem Van Loon was the recipient of the first Newbery Medal in 1922 for *The Story of Mankind.*

Ray Prytherch, *Harrod's Librarians' Glossary, 6th ed.* (Brookfied, VT: Gower, 1987), 545.

What is the name of Jane Austen's satire on the Gothic romance, which was not published until after her death?

Jane Austen (1775-1817), who is considered to be the creator of the English novel of manners, wrote a satire on the Gothic romance called *Northanger Abbey*, which she sold to a publisher in 1803. Since it was never released, the family bought the manuscript back and had it published in 1818, a year after her death.

The Washington Post Book World, ed., *Book Bag Treasury of Literary Quizzes* (New York: Charles Scribner's Sons, 1984), 181-82.

In what Jane Austen novel does Fanny Price figure as a faultless heroine?

More of a perfect heroine than any other character created by the English novelist Jane Austen (1775-1817), Fanny Price appears in the novel *Mansfield Park.* Like Cinderella, she represents persecuted virtue that eventually rises above her family environment. Fanny was constantly reminded that she was a poor relation, but in the end she married a man of wealth and position.

Henrietta Ten Harmsel, *Jane Austen: A Study in Fictional Conventions* (London: Mouton, 1964), 95. Frank N. Magill, ed., *Masterplots: Cyclopedia of Literary Characters* (New York: Salem Press, 1963), 1:666-67.

What was the alternative title to Voltaire's *Candide?*

Voltaire was the assumed name of Francois-Marie Arouet (1694-1778), one of the most important figures of the French Enlightenment. Like many philosophes, Voltaire was a severe critic of his society, and in his satirical novella *Candide* (1759) he ridicules philosophical optimism—the assumption that we live in the best of all possible worlds. In this book, whose alternative title is *Optimism*, Candide, a naive young man who is accompanied at times by his Spanish valet Cacambo, travels the world and slowly grows to believe that this is not the best of all places, after witnessing such horrors as war, earthquake, and the Inquisition.

Frank N. Magill, ed., *Cyclopedia of Literary Characters* (New York: Salem Press, 1963), 144-46. Voltaire, *Candide and Other Writings* (New York: Modern Library, 1956), 134.

In Tolkien's Middle-earth what is an Ent?

J.R.R. Tolkien (1892-1973) was a scholar of medieval literature at the University of Oxford, but he is probably best known for a three-volume fantasy adventure *The Lord of the Rings* (1954-55) that takes place in an imaginary land called Middle-earth. Among the many fantastic creatures who inhabit that world are the Ents. They were half man and half tree, growing to a height of fourteen feet and living almost forever. They were wise beyond human ken and spoke a language that sounded like rolling thunder and that only they could master. Ents usually lived alone, often in mountain caverns close to spring water and surrounded by beautiful trees. They took no solid food but drank Ent-draughts, a magical fluid that glowed with green and gold light. Their participation in the War of the Ring was fundamental to the triumph of the forces of good over evil.

David Day, *A Tolkien Bestiary* (New York: Ballantine Books, 1979), s.v. "Ents."

In Tolkien's Middle-earth what were the Ringwraiths?

J.R.R. Tolkien (1892-1973) was a scholar of medieval literature at the University of Oxford, but he is probably best known for a three-volume fantasy adventure *The Lord of the Rings* (1954-55) that takes place in an imaginary land called Middle-earth. The story's plot centers on an epic struggle of good against evil. The forces of evil are lead by Sauron, the dark lord, who forged the Rings of Power and released into Middle-earth nine wraiths who were to be his chief servants and generals. These Black Riders brought terror even to the bravest in Middle-earth. In the Black Speech they were called NAZGUL, which translated to Ringwraiths in the common tongue.

David Day, *A Tolkien Bestiary* (New York: Ballantine Books, 1979), s.v. "Ringwraiths."

In Tolkien's Middle-earth where is the land of Moria?

J.R.R. Tolkien (1892-1973) was a scholar of medieval literature at the University of Oxford, but he is probably best known for a three-volume fantasy adventure *The Lord of the Rings* (1954-55) that takes place in an imaginary land called Middle-earth. According to Tolkien Moria is a vast underground city, the greatest of all the dwellings ever constructed by the dwarves, which lies deep beneath the Misty Mountains. It was a spectacular place, elaborately constructed by master craftsmen, but Moria had to be abandoned when it could no longer withstand attacks from the demon Balrog. Although they tried, the dwarves were never able to reestablish themselves there permanently, and Moria became a dangerous place, inhabited by the forces of evil.

Alberto Manguel and Gianni Guadalupi, *The Dictionary of Imaginary Places* (San Diego, CA: Harcourt Brace Jovanovich, 1987), s.v. "Moria."

What is a picaresque novel?

Picaresque is a type of fiction that is built around a dishonest or misbehaving character. The word is derived from the Spanish "pcaro," which means knavish or roguish, and it has been applied to a number of Spanish novels written in the first half of the seventeenth century. They usually recount the tales of men of humble parentage who face adversity and are driven to deceptions in order to improve their lot.

A.J. Krailsheimer ed., *The Continental Renaissance, 1500-1600* (Atlantic Highlands, NJ: Humanities Press, 1978), 333-34.

What is the title of Dickens' last unfinished novel?

The last unfinished novel of Charles Dickens (1812-1870) is entitled *The Mystery of Edwin Drood*, an outline of which he related to his friend and biographer John Forster. Shortly after murdering his nephew, an uncle discovers the futility of the crime and reviews his life from a jail cell as though it belonged to someone else. Dickens had completed about half the installments for the book when he died in 1870; although many volumes have been written in an effort to determine whether the author had decided to alter the plot, no definitive answer has been reached.

Michael D. Hardwick and Mollie Hardwick, *The Charles Dickens Encyclopedia* (New York: Charles Scribner's Sons, 1973), 29.

Travis McGee is the main character of what famous American mystery writer?

Prolific author John D. MacDonald's mysteries feature the cynical, philosophical Travis McGee, who lives on a houseboat in Florida and makes his living recovering stolen property.

Otto Penzler et al., *Detectionary* (Woodstock, NY: Overlook Press, 1977), s.v. "McGee, Travis."

What murder case provided Truman Capote with the story for his best-selling book *In Cold Blood?*

The book *In Cold Blood* by American author Truman Capote (1924-84) was inspired by the murder of a well-to-do Kansas rancher, Herbert W. Clutter, and his family in November of 1959 by two neurotic vagrants, Richard E. Hickock and Perry E. Smith. Believing that Clutter kept large amounts of money in his house, the thieves terrorized Clutter, his wife, and their two teenage children before killing them with a shotgun and a hunting knife. The murderers were trailed to Las Vegas, where they were arrested by the Nevada police. After a long trial a jury found both of them guilty, and they were hanged on April 14, 1965.

Jay Robert Nash, *Bloodletters and Badmen: A Narrative Encyclopedia of American Criminals from the Pilgrims to the Present* (New York: M. Evans, 1973), s.v. "Hickock, Richard E."

Who was Pierre de Coulevain?

Pierre de Coulevain was the pen name of Mlle. Fabre, a best-selling novelist during the early nineteenth century. The identity of the author of *Au Cour de la Vie, Sur la Branche*, and *L'Ille Inconnu* was hidden from the world until her death in 1913. In death, however, she remained almost as much a mystery as she had been in life. Serving as a governess for much of her life, she did not write her first novel, *Noblesse Americaine*, until she was 57. Upon death, she wished to be buried among exiles, wanderers, and forgotten ones because in the company of such people she would "never be entirely dead."

New York Evening Post 5 February 1921.

Where was Robinson Crusoe's island and are there maps of it?

There is a literary controversy over which island served as a model for English author Daniel Defoe's shipwrecked fictional hero Robinson Crusoe. Crusoe may have spent his 28 years on the island of Tobago in the Windward group of the West Indies or on the Island of Juan Fernandez in the Pacific Ocean off the coast of Chile. The skeleton of a goat found in a cave on Tobago Island was even exhibited at the World's Fair in Chicago in 1893. Claimants declared it to be the skeleton of Crusoe's goat-proof that the West Indies island had been Crusoe's home!

Clifford Howard, "Crusoe's Real Island," *Bookman* July 1914.

Who was mystery writer Sax Rohmer's ultimate villain?

The fictional character Dr. Fu Manchu, created by mystery writer Sax Rohmer, was the author's ultimate villain. Bent on conquering the world, Dr. Fu Manchu was a Chinese master criminal posessing untold wealth, intellect, and occult powers.

Chris Steinbrunner and Otto Penzler, *Encyclopedia of Mystery and Detection* (New York: McGraw-Hill, 1976), s.v. "Fu Manchu, Dr."

When Oscar Wilde was incarcerated at Reading Prison, what was his cell number?

When Irish poet and dramatist Oscar Wilde (1854-1900) was incarcerated for sodomy at Reading Prison in England, he was assigned to cell C.3.3.

Richard Ellman, *Oscar Wilde* (New York: Alfred A. Knopf, 1988), 496-97.

Who was the novelist of the Beat Generation who wrote *On The Road*?

Jack Kerouac (1922-1969) wrote *On the Road* (1957), an underground novel about a rebellious young man's cross-country journey in which he portrayed the life style of those who would later be called the Beat Generation. The term Beat Generation, coined by Kerouac in a 1959 conversation, epitomized a 1950s social and literary movement that Kerouac, poet Allen Ginsberg, and William Burroughs founded.

Ian Ousby, ed., *The Cambridge Guide To Literature in English* (Cambridge: Cambridge University Press, 1988). *The Oxford Dictionary of Quotations, 4th edition* (Oxford: Oxford University Press, 1992).

What were the names of the two future species in H.G. Wells' *The Time Machine*, and in what year did the Time Traveller find them?

In H.G. Wells' *The Time Machine*, the Eloi and the Morlocks are two human species that have evolved by the year 802701. The book's Time Traveller discovers these advanced human forms in conflict against each other. The soft, weak Eloi are preyed upon by the coarse Morlocks, who live under the earth.

I.F. Clarke, *Voices Prophesying War* (Oxford: Oxford University Press, 1992) 83.

Who was the publisher of James Joyce's *Ulysses*, and what was the name of her lending library and bookshop in Paris?

Sylvia Beach was the first publisher of James Joyce's novel *Ulysses*, one of the most influential works of modern fiction and, at the time of its publication, a highly controversial novel. Beach is also famous for being the owner of Shakespeare and Company, which was the first American lending library and bookshop in Paris. The shop also served as a gathering place for American authors such as Ernest Hemingway, F. Scott Fitzgerald, Katherine Anne Porter, and Sherwood Anderson. It also attracted other writers, including T.S. Eliot, Andr Gide, Samuel Beckett, and James Joyce.

Noel Riley Fitch, *Sylvia Beach and the Lost Generation* (New York: W.W. Norton & Co., 1983).

Who is Sweeney Todd?

Sweeney Todd is an infamous character from British folk tales that has been the inspiration for numerous books, plays, and films. Todd is a barber who kills his customers by slitting their throats, and who then makes them into meat pies as a means of getting rid of their corpses. This ghastly yet comic figure, who may actually have his origins in 14th-century French legend, was popularized by the novel *The String of Pearls*, written by Thomas Peckett Prest around 1840. One of the most recent reincarnations for the character was a 1979 Stephen Sondheim musical that was simply called *Sweeney Todd*.

David Pringle, *Imaginary People, A Who's Who of Modern Fictional Characters* (New York: World Almanac, 1987), 459.

Who was the real-life model for the Faust character?

Georg Faust (c.1480-c.1540) was a student at several German universities during the early 16th century, and was more than once expelled from his studies. Myths of his magical abilities were rampant during his lifetime, and he may have been the model for the character of Faust in literature.

Henry Garland, *The Oxford Companion to German Literature, 2d edition* (Oxford: Oxford University Press, 1986), 229.

What is a "Bildungsroman"?

A "Bildungsroman" is a German novel in which the hero achieves self-realization and maturity after several false starts or misguided choices in life.

Henry Garland, *The Oxford Companion to German Literature, 2d ed.* (Oxford: Oxford University Press, 1986), 87.

Which fictional detective is featured prominently in the novels of Dorothy L. Sayers, and what is his motto and coat of arms?

Lord Peter Wimsey is the aristocratic detective featured in mystery novels by Dorothy L. Sayers (1893-1957). Wimsey's coat of arms bears a cat crouched atop a knight's helmet and three running mice on a shield. His motto declares, "I hold by my whimsy."

Stefano Benvenuti and Gianni Rizzoni, *The Whodunit: An Informal History of Detective Fiction, translated by Anthony Eyre* (New York: Collier Books, 1979), 74-77.

Who were three outlaws whose lives might have influenced the Robin Hood stories?

Three outlaws whose tales paralleled the Robin Hood stories were Hereward the Wake, Eustace the Monk, and Fulk fitz Warin. Hereward was an 11th-century English hero who led a resistance against the Norman conquerors and inspired a book about his exploits, *De Gestis Herewardi Saxonis* or *The Deeds of Hereward the Saxon*, by Robert of Swaffham.

Eustace the Monk abandoned his French monastery around 1190 to avenge the murder of his father and became an outlaw, soldier of fortune, and naval commander. At various times he served kings of both England and France—a dangerous stance which eventually led to his beheading. His legend survives in a romance entitled, *Wistasse li Moine*.

Fulk fitz Warin was a Welsh baron who spent most of his life fighting for his family's claim to the barony and castle of Whittington, Shropshire. After being accused of the murder of the family's rival, he spent three years as an outlaw before gaining the king's pardon and possession of Whittington. His story is told in a prose romance, *Fouke le Fitz Waryn*.

J.C. Holt, *Robin Hood* (London: Thames and Hudson, 1989), 62-64.

Who was "Bulldog Drummond"?

"Bulldog Drummond" was a tough, boozing, crime-fighting adventurer created by English author Herman Cyril McNeile (1888-1937). McNeile had many adventures himself in World War I (1914-1918) and began writing in earnest following his retirement as a lieutenant-colonel from the Royal Engineers. It is probably more than a coincidence that "Bulldog" (his given name in the long running series of books was Captain Hugh Drummond, D.S.O., M.C., retired) was introduced to readers via a fictional newspaper advertisement which read: "Demobilised officer, finding peace incredibily tedious, would welcome diversion. Legitimate if possible, but crime, if of humorous description, no objection. Excitement essential. Would be prepared to consider permanent job if suitably impressed by applicant for services."

The ad was immediately answered by a beautiful young girl whose father was beset by evil doers. McNeile, known to his friends as "Sapper" churned out numerous "Bulldog" books including: *Bulldog Drummond* (1920), *Bulldog Drummond's Third Round* (1924), and *Bulldog Drummond Strikes Back* (1933). McNeile also authored adventure books featuring other characters but was working on a "Bulldog" play when he died at the age of forty-nine.

Stanley J. Kunitz and Howard Haycraft, eds., *Twentieth Century Authors* (New York: H.W. Wilson, 1942), 889-90. Otto Penzler, *The Private Lives of Private Eyes, Spies, Crimefighters, & Other Good Guys* (New York: Grosset & Dunlap, 1977), 59-60.

What are the origins of Inuit literature?

Inuktitut is the Inuit or "Eskimo" language. It did not develop as a written language on its own but rather was introduced by Christian missionaries in the early eighteenth century. Moravian missionaries in London began publishing the gospel in Labrador tracts as early as 1813 and there soon developed a demand for non-religious publications in Inuktitut. *The Odyssey* and *Pilgrim's Progress* were among the first Western classics translated into the language. By the 1980s literature by Inuit authors was being published in both Inuktitut and English. There are also many English/Inuktitut periodicals such as *Inuktitut, Inuit Today*, and *Igalaaq*.

William Toye, ed., *The Oxford Companion to Canadian Literature* (Toronto, Ontario: Oxford University Press, 1983), s.v. "Inuit literature."

What is cubist literature?

Cubist literature is an attempt to transpose the salient and defining features of cubism or cubist art into literature, especially poetry. The movement originated in the 20th century and presents words as "surprises" by "making the word-associations those of sound and suggestion rather than sense." Poets of the Cubist school include Apollinaire (1880-1918), Cendrars (1887-1961), Fargue, Jacob (1876-1944), Reverdy (1889-1960), and Salmon.

Joyce M.H. Reid, ed., *The Concise Oxford Dictionary of French Literature* (Oxford: Clarendon Press of Oxford University Press, 1976), 154.

Who is Nancy Drew?

Nancy Drew is the pretty, young, and immensely popular heroine of the long-running "Nancy Drew" series of adventure books for girls produced by the Stratemeyer Syndicate. The books are collectively written under the pseudonym Carolyn Keene. Since the late 1920s, Nancy has been solving crimes and collaring wrongdoers with the help of her lawyer father Carson Drew, her boyfriend Ned Nickerson, and friends George Fayne and Bess Marvin, all of River Heights (state unspecified). Nancy has been updated and modernized through the years as she has in the words of one critic "steered the Silent Generation, Woodstock Generation and Me Generation of women through their tender years as the model of a Junior Leaguer." She has been featured in hundreds of books with such formula titles as: *The Bungalow Mystery* (1930), *The Sign of the Twisted Candles* (1933), *The Secret of Lost Lake* (1963), and *The Clue of the Broken Locket* (1934).

Donna Olendorf, ed., *Something about the Author* (Detroit: Gale Research, 1991), 65: 94-99.

What was the first book written by children's book author Dr. Seuss?

The first book written by Dr. Seuss, a pseudonym of Theodor Seuss Geisel (1904-1991), was *And To Think That I Saw It On Mulberry Street*, published by Vanguard Press in 1937.

Dr. Seuss from Then to Now: A Catalogue of the Retrospective Exhibition, San Diego Museum of Art (New York: Random House, 1986), 94. Charles Moritz, ed., *Current Biography Yearbook, 1991* (New York: H.W. Wilson, 1991), s.v. "Geisel, Theodore Seuss."

What are the Narnia Chronicles?

Narnia Chronicles is the collective term given to a series of seven children's books by the prolific Irish author C.S. (Clive Staples) Lewis (1898-1963). The books concern the adventures of four English children, Peter, Susan, Edmund, and Lucy Pevensie, who discover the "other world" of Narnia while living in the country during the World War II (1939-45) bombing of London. A large wardrobe is soon discovered to be a doorway to Narnia, a fictional land replete with biblical metaphors.

The seven books in the series are: *The Lion, The Witch and the Wardrobe* (1950), *Prince Caspian* (1951), *The Voyage of the "Dawn Treader"* (1952), *The Silver Chair* (1953), *The Horse and His Boy* (1954), *The Magician's Nephew* (1955), and *The Last Battle* (1956). Lewis was also well known for his prodigious output of other children's books, adult fare, scholarly books, and literary criticism.

James G. Lesniak, ed., *Contemporary Authors, New Revision Series,* (Detroit: Gale Research, 1991), s.v. "Lewis, C.S.." David Pringle, *Imaginary People: A Who's Who of Modern Fictional Characters* (New York: World Almanac, 1987), s.v. "Atlan."

Which of British author Mary Norton's books featured a family of tiny people known as "The Borrowers"?

Mary Norton (1903-1992) is the highly acclaimed English author of a series of children's books which feature a family of tiny people known as "The Borrowers." The name refers to the practice these tiny people have of borrowing small everyday objects from full-sized people who assume they have been careless and lost them. The family of Borrowers— Homily, Pod, and Arriety— first appeared in *The Borrowers* (1952). Subsequent books in the series include: *The Borrowers Afield* (1955), *The Borrowers Afloat* (1959), *The Borrowers Aloft* (1961), and *The Borrowers Avenged* (1982). Norton received England's Carnegie Medal for the first volume.

Donna Olendorf, *Contemporary Authors, Volume 139* (Detroit: Gale Research, 1993), s.v. "Norton, Mary." David Pringle, *Imaginary People: A Who's Who of Modern Fictional Characters* (New York: World Almanac, 1987), s.v. "Borrowers, The."

Quotations

Where did the saying "the customer is always right" originate?

American department store magnate Marshall Field (1834-1906), originated the saying "the customer is always right" during the 1880s. This it on the customer signaled a change in business attitude. Prior to that time in rural, postcolonial America, the merchant enjoyed the advantage; now the customer had power.

Jane Polley, ed., *Stories Behind Everyday Things* (Pleasantville, NY: Reader's Digest Association, 1980), 105.

What was the memorable quote from the 1988 vice presidential debate?

When Senator Dan Quayle (1947-) compared himself to former U.S. president John F. Kennedy (1917-63), Senator Lloyd Bentsen (1921-) responded with the most memorable quote from the 1988 vice presidential debate. Bensten replied "Senator, I served with Jack Kennedy. I knew Jack Kennedy. Jack Kennedy was a friend of mine. Senator, you're no Jack Kennedy."

Michael Nelson, ed., *The Presidency A to Z* (Washington, DC: Congressional Quarterly, 1992), 29.

What does the phrase "Kemo Sabe" mean as spoken by Tonto, the faithful Native American companion of the Lone Ranger?

"Kemo Sabe," a favorite expression of the Lone Ranger's faithful Native American companion, Tonto, has a number of similar translations. A 1916 glossary of the Tewa of New Mexico lists the words "Kema" (friend) and "Sabe" (Apache). Another source translates the phrase as "Trusted scout."

Tom Ferrell and Virginia Adams, "What Means Kemo Sabe"? *New York Times* 18 September 1977. *TV Graphic (Pittsburgh Press)* 23 February 1958.

What was the famous quote of President John F. Kennedy, uttered during a White House dinner honoring Nobel Prize winners?

At a dinner held at the White House for Nobel Prize recipients, U.S. president John F. Kennedy (1917-63) stated that, "I think this is the most extraordinary collection of talent, of human knowledge, that has ever been gathered together at the White House-with the possible exception of when Thomas Jefferson dined alone."

Ralph L. Woods, *A Third Treasury of the Familiar* (New York: Macmillan, 1970), 264.

Who made the observation "War is hell"?

In a speech at the Michigan Military Academy on June 19, 1879, U.S. General William Tecumseh Sherman (1820-91) made the following statement: "I am tired and sick of war. Its glory is all moonshine. It is only those who have neither fired a shot nor heard the shrieks and groans of the wounded who cry aloud for blood, more vengeance, more desolation. War is hell."

Jay M. Shafritz, *Words on War: Military Quotations from Ancient Times to the Present* (New York: Prentice Hall, 1990), 457.

Who uttered the famous words, "I shall return"?

After leaving the Philippines and arriving in Australia to escape the invading Japanese army during World War II (139-45), U.S. General Douglas MacArthur (1880-1964) stated the following on March 17, 1942: "The President of the United States ordered me to break through the Japanese lines...for the purpose, as I understand it, of organizing the American offensive against Japan, a primary object of which is the relief of the Philippines. I came through and I shall return."

Jay M. Shafritz, *Words on War: Military Quotations from Ancient Times to the Present* (New York: Prentice Hall, 1990), 313.

Which author coined the expression "A confederacy of dunces"?

English churchman and writer Jonathan Swift (1667-1745), best known as the author of the political satire *Gulliver's Travels,* (1726) once stated that: "When a true genius appears in the world you may know him by this sign: that the dunces are all in confederacy against him."

Ralph L. Woods, ed., *A Third Treasury of the Familiar* (New York: Macmillan, 1970), 229.

What is the conservation pledge?

The conservation pledge is as follows: "I give my pledge as an American to save and faithfully to defend from waste the natural resources of my country-its soil and minerals, its forests, waters and wildlife."

Allen S. Hitch and Marian Sorenson, *Conservation and You* (Princeton, NJ: Van Nostrand, 1964), 110.

What is the source of the phrase "Big Brother is watching you" and what is its meaning?

The phrase "Big Brother is watching you" comes from the classic 1949 novel *1984* by English writer George Orwell, pseudonym of Eric Arthur Blair (1903-1950). The book describes a nightmarish totalitarian world of the future in which history is constantly rewritten. The world is in a state of perpetual warfare, and people are stripped of all individuality and doomed to a life of dreary service to the State. Ubiquitous placards serve as a constant reminder that "Big Brother is watching you"—meaning, quite literally, that private life is impossible. Even unsanctioned ideas are forbidden and can bring reprisals from the terrifying Thought Police. Orwell's satire was chiefly aimed at the Soviet Union and its brutal dictator Joseph Stalin (1879-1953).

Benet's Reader's Encyclopedia, 3rd ed. (New York: Harper & Row, 1987), 696.

Who said: "I'm just an average citizen. Many black people were arrested for defying the bus laws. They prepared the way"?

Civil rights activist Rosa Parks, whose refusal to surrender her bus seat precipitated the Civil Rights movement said in 1960: "I'm just an average citizen. Many black people were arrested for defying the bus laws. They prepared the way." Parks, who was born in Tuskegee, Alabama, on February 4, 1913, has been active in the struggle for civil rights since she was a young woman serving first as a youth adviser to the Montgomery, Alabama, National Association for the Advancement of Colored People (NAACP) and then as its secretary in the 1950s. In Alabama at that time black bus passengers were required by law to sit at the back of the bus and to surrender their seats to white passengers when there were no other seats available. In December of 1955 Parks refused to give her seat to a white man, was subsequently arrested, and fined $14. Her actions and the Montgomery bus boycott which followed were rallying cries for the southern civil rights movement. In 1957 Parks moved with her family to Detroit where she worked first as a seamstress and then as a staff assistant for U.S. congressman John Conyers. In 1956 the U.S. Supreme Court ruled that the infamous Montgomery bus laws were unconstitutional.

Darlene Clark Hine, ed., *Black Women in America: An Historical Encyclopedia* (Brooklyn, NY: Carlson Publishing, 1993), s.v. "Parks, Rosa." Dorothy Winbush Riley, ed., *My Soul Looks Back, 'Less I Forget* (New York: HarperCollins, 1993), 39.

Who said "I was free, but there was no one to welcome me to the land of freedom. I was a stranger in a strange land"?

The quotation is credited to Harriet Tubman (1820?-1913) who became a famous as a "conductor" of the Underground Railroad. She led over 200 slaves from the Southern slave states into the five northern states, along a dangerous and physically-taxing route. Her quotation reflected both her accomplishment of her escape to freedom as well as her loneliness and sorrow for her family she left behind.

Dorothy Winbush Riley, ed., *My Soul Looks Back, 'Less I Forget: A Collection of Quotations by People of Color* (New York: HarperCollins, 1993). Jessie Carney Smith, ed., *Notable Black American Women* (Detroit: Gale Research, 1992), s.v. "Harriet Tubman."

Where, when, and from whom did the expression "Heavens to Betsy!" originate?

The source of the expression "Heavens to Betsy!" is unknown. The expression is perhaps a hundred years old but its use can not be documented before 1940. It is used all over the United States but not in England. Therefore, this expression does not refer to Queen Elizabeth I of England, as was once suggested. In *Heavens to Betsy! and Other Curious Sayings*, Charles Funk writes, "Nor do I think...that it pertained in any way to the maker of the first American flag, Betsy Ross. It is much more likely to have been derived in some way from the frontiersman's rifle or gun which, for unknown reason, he always fondly called Betsy." However, such a derivation could not be verified.

Charles Earle Funk, *Heavens to Betsy!: and Other Curious Sayings* (New York: Harper & Brothers, 1955), ix-xi.

What does the expression "as dead as the dodo" mean?

The expression "as dead as the dodo" means done for, completely finished off, extinct. The dodo was a bird found on two islands east of Madagascar in the sixteenth and seventeenth centuries. It was a flightless bird, larger and heavier than a swan. Being defenseless, it was commonly killed and eaten, not only by early voyagers and settlers to the islands, but also by pigs introduced to the islands by the settlers. By the early eighteenth century, there were none left.

Charles Earle Funk, *Heavens to Betsy!: And Other Curious Sayings* (New York: Harper & Brothers, 1955), 182.

What is the term for the quotation found at the beginning of a written work?

An epigraph is the term for the quotation found at the beginning of a written work. It is meant to convey a main thematic idea. Sometimes referred to as an initial inscription, an epigraph may also be something other than a quotation.

J.A. Simpson and E.S.C. Weiner, eds., *The Oxford English Dictionary, 2nd ed.* (Oxford: Clarendon Press, 1989), s.v. "epigraph."

What was the motto of Italian Fascist students in the 1930s?

The motto "book and musket" was created by Italian Premier Benito Mussolini (1883-1945) as a calling cry for Italian Fascist college students in the 1930s. He encouraged the students to excel at their studies and to prepare themselves to defend Italy.

New York Times May 11, 1932.

What is meant by "big stick diplomacy"?

U.S. president Theodore Roosevelt (1858-1919) made a speech in 1912 that included the famous phrase "speak softly and carry a big stick and you will go far." The expression "big stick" has since been used to describe a style of foreign policy where larger, more powerful countries use their military strength and political influence to protect national interests in other countries.

Walter J. Raymond, *Dictionary of Politics, 6th ed.* (Lawrenceville, VA: Brunswick Publishing, 1980), 51.

What is the motto of "Canada Bill Jones"?

The anonymous motto of "Canada Bill Jones" is that: "It is morally wrong to allow suckers to keep their money."

Time 26 February 1979.

Who said, "If you haven't got anything good to say about anyone come and sit by me"?

The daughter of U.S. president Theodore Roosevelt, Alice Roosevelt Longworth (1884-1980) had embroidered on a pillow the line, "If you haven't got anything good to say about anyone come and sit by me."

Tony Augarde, ed., *The Oxford Dictionary of Modern Quotations* (Oxford: Oxford University Press, 1991), 139.

Which U.S. president was quoted as saying that he had often committed adultery in his heart?

U.S. president Jimmy Carter (1924-) stated in an interview in *Playboy* magazine: "I've looked on a lot of women with lust. I've committed adultery in my heart many times. This is something that God recognizes I will do—and I have done it—and God forgives me for it."

Tony Augarde, ed., *The Oxford Dictionary of Modern Quotations* (New York: Oxford University Press, 1991), 47.

What is Gumperson's Law?

Gumperson's Law is known as the rule of perverse opposites, or, according to *Changing Times Magazine*: "The contradictory of a welcome probability will assert itself whenever such an eventuality is likely to be most frustrating.... The outcome of a given desired probability will be inverse to the degree of desirability." The humorous law was named after the probably fictional Dr. R.F. Gumperson, who supposedly found that the scientific forecasts of the weather were not as accurate as that of The Old Farmer's Almanac.

Changing Times Magazine c. 1963. Kiplinger Washington Editors, *The Changing Times Calendar and Engagement Book, 1964* (Washington, DC: Changing Times, n.d.), 110.

Where did the phrase "warts and all" originate?

Although the story may be apocryphal, Oliver Cromwell (1599-1658), England's Lord Protector, is thought to have said to the artist painting his portrait, "I desire you would use all your skill to paint my picture truely like me.... Remark all these roughnesses, pimples, warts, and everything as you see me, otherwise I will never pay a farthing for it." It is from this remark that the phrase "warts and all" originates.

Robert Hendrickson, *The Henry Holt Encyclopedia of Word and Phrase Origins* (New York: Henry Holt, 1987), s.v. ""warts and all."

What is the origin of the lament "We wuz robbed!"?

The lament "We wuz robbed!" was heard by thousands of boxing fans following the 1932 heavyweight bout between Jack Sharkey and loser Max Schmeling. Schmeling's manager Joe Jacobs shouted the phrase into a radio microphone.

Stuart Berg Flexner, *Listening To America* (New York: Simon and Schuster, 1982), 545.

What is the origin of the phrase "tennis, anyone?"

The phrase "tennis, anyone"? was reportedly American actor Humphrey Bogart's (1899-1957) only line in his first but long since forgotten Broadway role.

William Morris and Mary Morris, *Morris Dictionary of Word and Phrase Origins* (New York: Harper & Row, 1977), 561.

Who coined the phrase "almighty dollar"?

The phrase "almighty dollar" was coined by American author Washington Irving (1783-1859) in "A Creole Village," which was published in *Knickerbocker Magazine* on November 12, 1836. He stated, "...the almighty dollar, that great object of universal devotion throughout our land...."

Stuart Berg Flexner, *Listening to America: An Illustrated History of Words and Phrases from our Lively and Splendid Past* (New York: Simon and Schuster, 1982), 181.

Who wrote the oft-quoted line "Fools rush in where angels fear to tread"?

The oft-quoted line "Fools rush in where angels fear to tread" does not originate from the Bible but was first written by the famous English poet Alexander Pope (1688-1744) in his *An Essay on Criticism* (1711).

Paul F. Boller Jr. andJohn George, *They Never Said It: A Book of Fake Quotes, Misquotes, and Misleading Attributions* (New York: Oxford University Press, 1989), 7.

Who is responsible for the line "then let them eat cake"?

Contrary to popular belief, the line "then let them eat cake" did not originate with the French queen Marie Antoinette (1755-1793) during the French Revolution. Before this event, the French social philosopher Jean-Jacques Rousseau (1712-1778) reported in his *Confessions* (1778) that a great princess was informed that the country people had no bread. "Then," she replied, "let them eat cake."

Paul Boller Jr. and John George, *They Never Said It: A Book of Fake Quotes, Misquotes, and Misleading Attributions* (New York: Oxford University Press, 1989), 98.

Who coined the 1950s political campaign slogan "I Like Ike," which was used by presidential candidate Dwight Eisenhower?

The 1950s political campaign slogan "I Like Ike," which was used by Dwight Eisenhower (1890-1969) during his presidential campaign, is attributed to Jacqueline Cochran (1910?-1980), an American aviator. Cochran was the first woman to break the sound barrier (1953) and set 200 other flying records including the fastest speed flown by a woman (1,429 miles per hour) in 1964. During World War II (1939-45), she was director of the Women's Air Force Service Pilots and a correspondent for *Liberty*; after the war she attained the rank of colonel in the Air Force Reserve. Cochran was a friend of Dwight Eisenhower and an early supporter of his bid for the White House. She credits herself with being instrumental in persuading "Ike" to seek the presidency.

Charles Moritz, ed., *Current Biography Yearbook, 1963* (New York: H.W. Wilson, 1964), 79. David Roberts, "The 99s: The right stuff then and now," *Smithsonian* August 1994.

What was U.S. president Ronald Reagan's favorite motto?

U.S. president Ronald Reagan (1911-) kept a plate on his Oval Office desk inscribed with the following unattributed quote: "There is no limit to what a man can do or where he can go if he doesn't mind who gets the credit."

Time 14 September 1981.

Where did the expression "eyes in the back of your head" originate?

The expression—"eyes in the back of your head"— comes from the play, *The Pot of Gold* (Act 1, scene 1, lines 60-64) by the Roman playwright Plautus (ca.244-184 B.C.). The old miser Euclio is determined to keep his gold hidden in his house, yet is bedevilled by the paranoid fantasy that everyone else knows about the gold and is plotting to take it. In particular, he is suspicious of his maid Straphyla, the "old hag" he accuses in this speech:

> I know for sure that I've never seen anyone more wicked
> Than this old hag; and I'm awfully afraid that,
> With some plot, she'll catch me unawares
> And detect the gold where it's hidden;
> She has eyes even in the back of her head, the wretch.

Michael Macrone, *It's Greek to Me!: Brush Up Your Classics* (New York: Cader Books, 1991), 124.

Whose motto was "Workers of all countries, unite"?

The Union of Soviet Socialist Republics (U.S.S.R.) had the motto "Workers of all countries, unite."

Laurence Urdang, Celia Dame Robbins, and Frank R. Abate, eds., *Mottoes* (Detroit: Gale Research, 1986), 539.

To whom was Winston Churchill referring when he said, "Never in the field of human conflict was so much owed by so many to so few"?

In a speech before the British House of Commons on August 20, 1940, British prime minister Winston Churchill (1874-1965) spoke in tribute to the Royal Air Force upon its victory over the German Air Force in the Battle of Britain, "Never in the field of human conflict was so much owed by so many to so few."

John Bartlett, *Familiar Quotations: A Collection of Passages, Phrases, and Proverbs Traced to Their Sources in Ancient and Modern Literature, 16th ed.* (Boston: Little, Brown, 1992), 620.

What did Winston Churchill describe as "a riddle, wrapped in a mystery, inside an enigma"?

When British soon-to-be prime minister Winston Churchill (1874-1965) declaired "It is a riddle, wrapped in a mystery, inside an enigma," he was referring to his inability to predict the actions of the Soviet Union during World War II. The phrase is a frequently-quoted passage from an October 1, 1939, radio broadcast.

John Bartlett, *Familiar Quotations: A Collection of Passages, Phrases, and Proverbs Traced to Their Sources in Ancient and Modern Literature, 16th ed.* (Boston: Little, Brown, 1992), 620.

What is the origin of the expression "there's more than one way to skin a cat"?

American humorist and author Samuel Clemens (1835-1910), writing under the pseudonym Mark Twain, adopted the popular expression in his *A Connecticut Yankee* (1889) where he wrote, "She knew more than one way to skin a cat." That followed a British version that appeared in *Westward Ho!* by Charles Kingsley (1819-1875), who wrote, "There are more ways of killing a cat than choking it with cream." The expression means that there are many different ways to reach the same end.

Christine Ammer, *Have a Nice Day—No Problem!: A Dictionary of Clichs* (New York: Dutton, 1992), 237.

What are some sayings relating to weather?

There are hundreds of weather sayings including:

As long as the sun shines one does not ask for the moon. (*Russian proverb*)

A man should learn to sail in all winds. (*Italian proverb)*

Winter comes fast on the lazy. (*Irish proverb)*

Some people are weather-wise, some are otherwise. (*Poor Richards Almanac*)

If you walk on snow you cannot hide your footrints. (*Chinese proverb*)

Sometime hath the brightest day a cloud. *(Shakespeare)*

Frances Bartlett Barhydt and Paul W. Morgan, *The Science Teacher's Book of Lists* (Englewood Cliffs, NJ: Prentice Hall, 1993), 334.

Who said "Damn the torpedoes!"?

During the American Civil War, Union Admiral David Farragut (1801-1870) is said to have exclaimed, "Damn the torpedoes! Go ahead!" It was August 5, 1864, when Farragut's forces, thirteen wooden ships and four ironclads, arrived in the harbor of Mobile, Alabama. The Union monitor *Tecumseh* sank when it hit a mine, which was called a torpedo at that time. After Farragut supposedly gave the famous order, the Union naval forces overwhelmed the Confederates.

Howard L. Hurwitz, *An Encyclopedic Dictionary of American History* (New York: Washington Square Press, 1968), 176.

Who said "If I owned Texas and Hell, I would rent out Texas and live in Hell"?

The quotation "If I owned Texas and Hell, I would rent out Texas and live in Hell" was uttered by American Civil War General Philip H. Sheridan (1831-88) at an officer's mess at Fort Clark, Texas, in 1855. Sheridan went on to achieve fame in the American Civil War, distinguishing himself at the battles of Chickamauga and Chattanooga. He is best remembered for revitalizing the Union's cavalry forces and making them an effective fighting force.

Patricia L. Faust, ed., *Historical Times Illustrated Encyclopedia of the Civil War* (New York: Harper & Row, 1986), s.v. "Sheridan, Philip Henry." Burton E. Stevenson, comp., *The Home Book of Quotations, 10th ed.* (New York: Dodd, Mead, 1967), s.v. "Hell."

Who coined the phrase "survival of the fittest"?

Although frequently associated with Darwinism, the phrase "survival of the fittest" was coined by Herbert Spencer, an English sociologist (1820-1903). It is the process by which organisms that are less well adapted to their environment tend to perish and better adapted organisms tend to survive.

Isaac Asimov, *Asimov's Biographical Encyclopedia of Science and Technology, 2d ed.* (Garden City, NY: Doubleday, 1982), 407. Peter J. Bowler, *Evolution, the History of an Idea* (Berkeley: University of California, 1984), 225. Elizabeth Toothill *The Facts On File Dictionary of Biology* (New York: Facts on File, 1988), 197.

Who used the phrase "a chicken in every pot"?

The phrase "a chicken in every pot" is generally attributed to then-presidential hopeful Herbert Hoover (1874-1964) although he certainly did not originate the phrase and it is questionable if he ever used it. Upon assuming the crown of France in 1589, King Henry IV (1553-1610) stated "...that there would not be a peasant so poor in all my realm who would not have a chicken in his pot every Sunday." Political pundit William Safire relates that Hoover never used the phrase although it was used in a Republican campaign flyer in 1928 entitled "A Chicken in Every Pot." Democratic opponent Al Smith (1873-1944) subsequently went on to say sarcastically that "...Republican prosperity has put a chicken in every pot..." which is how the phrase probably became attributed to Hoover.

Picturesque Expressions: A Thematic Dictionary, 2d ed. (Detroit: Gale Research, 1985), 539. William Safire, *Safire's New Political Dictionary* (New York: Random House, 1993), s.v. "chicken in every pot."

What is the motto of the Christopher Society?

"It is better to light one candle than to curse the darkness" is the motto of the Christopher Society. Based upon an old Chinese proverb, the motto was paraphrased in Adlai E. Stevenson's tribute to political activist and former first lady Eleanor Roosevelt after her death on November 7, 1952. The motto of the society is in accord with the Christophers' idea that each individual can make a difference by practicing Judeo-Christian values in all aspects of their lives, including their work life.

Suzy Platt, ed., *Respectfully Quoted: A Dictionary of Quotations Requested from the Congressional Research Service* (Washington, DC: Library of Congress, 1989), 89.

What is the Irish Blessing?

The Irish (or Gaelic) blessing is as follows:

> May the road rise to meet you,
> May the wind be always at your back,
> May the sun shine warm upon your face,
> and the rains fall soft upon your fields
> And, until we meet again,
> May God hold you in the palm of His hand.

Phyllis Fenner, *Something Shared: Children and Books* (New York: John Day, 1959), 233-34. *Irish Blessings* (New York: Kilkenny Press, 1990), 16.

Who said, "I have nothing to offer but blood, toil, tears, and sweat"?

Winston Churchill (1890-1965) made his first speech as Prime Minister of England in the House of Commons on May 13, 1940. Its most memorable line was, "I would say this to the house as I said to those who have joined my government, 'I have nothing to offer but blood, toil, tears, and sweat.'" Churchill had come to power in dire circumstances. The policy of appeasement that the previous prime minister Neville Chamberlain had exercised toward Adolf Hitler's Germany had failed, and Chamberlain's government resigned. On May 9, Churchill was selected to lead a new coalition, but Britain now found herself in a war without having made proper preparation. On May 10, the Germans had launched an invasion of Holland, Belgium, and Luxemburg. Their armies had moved more swiftly than the allies had imagined, and by May 12 they had crossed the French frontier. On May 13, when the House of Commons met to give the new government a vote of confidence, Churchill gave this rousing speech in which he pledged himself and the country to the defeat of Hitler. The address became so famous that later many people claimed to have heard it on the radio, although it was not broadcast.

Brian Gardner, *Churchill in His Time* (London: Methuen, 1968), 36-45.

What is Parkinson's Law?

Parkinson's Law states that "work expands so as to fill the time available for its completion." In 1957 British historian Cyril Northcote Parkinson originated this maxim to ridicule the excesses of bureaucracy.

Academic American Encyclopedia (Danbury, CT: Grolier, 1988), s.v. "Parkinson's law." Cyril Northcote Parkinson, *Parkinson's Law and Other Studies in Administration* (Boston: Houghton Mifflin, 1957), 33-35.

Who is the "Murphy" behind Murphy's Law?

The "Murphy" of Murphy's Law is unknown. There are actually three laws attributed to the elusive Murphy. The most popular is "If anything can go wrong it will." The others are "Everything will take longer than you think it will" and "Nothing is as easy as it looks."

Robert Hendrickson, *The Henry Holt Encyclopedia of Word and Phrase Origins* (New York: Henry Holt, 1990), s.v. "Murphy's Law." William Morris and Mary Morris, *Morris Dictionary of Word and Phrase Origins, 2nd ed.* (New York: Harper & Row, 1988), s.v. "Murphy's Laws."

What is the origin of the proverb "Don't judge a man until you have walked a mile in his shoes"?

The saying "Don't judge a man until you have walked a mile (or 100 miles) in his shoes" is a revised version of a Native American proverb. There are several versions of it, such as "Great Spirit, help me never to judge another until I have walked two months in his moccasins," or "Great Spirit, grant that I may not criticize my neighbor until I have walked a mile in his moccasins," or "Don't judge any man until you have walked two moons in his moccasins." The latter uses the word "moon" instead of "mile" since the word "mile" is not in the Indian vocabulary. "Day" is another option for "mile." Although several sources attribute it to Native Americans of the northern plains, the original author remains unknown.

RQ Summer 1974. *RQ* Winter 1974. *RQ* Summer 1983. *RQ* Winter 1983.

Did John F. Kennedy originate the saying "Ask not what your country can do for you; ask what you can do for your country"?

The now-famous quote from the January 20, 1961, inaugural speech of U.S. president John F. Kennedy (1917-1963)— "And so, my fellow Americans, ask not what your country can do for you; ask what you can do for your country"—originated with Kennedy. However, the sentiment has been expressed by others. For example, the American jurist Oliver Wendell Holmes, Jr. (1841-1935), speaking at Keene, New Hampshire, on May 30, 1884, said, "we pause to...recall what our country has done for each of us and to ask ourselves what we can do for our country in return."

Angela Partington, ed., *The Oxford Dictionary of Quotations, 4th ed.* (Oxford: Oxford University Press, 1992), 394.

Who originated the phrase "Praise the Lord and pass the ammunition"?

"Praise the Lord and Pass the Ammunition" was the title of a popular song during World War II (1939-1945). The words and the music were written by Frank Loesser (1910-1969). The phrase, however, came from American naval chaplain Howell Forgy (1908-1983). As he proceeded along a line of sailors who were passing ammunition by hand to the deck of a ship during the Japanese attack on Pearl Harbor, Hawaii, on December 7, 1941, he uttered these words which were to become the title and subject of Loesser's song.

Angela Partington, *The Oxford Dictionary of Quotations, 4th ed.,* (Oxford: Oxford University Press, 1992), 289. Ronny Schiff, ed., *A Selective Musical Collection of the World's Greatest Hits of the Forties* (Miami Beach, FL: Charles H. Hansen Music Corp., 1971), 71-73.

Where did the United States Postal Service maxim originate?

The saying most identified with the United States Postal Service mailcarriers is, "Neither snow, nor rain, nor heat, nor gloom of night stays these couriers from the swift completion of their appointed rounds." Inscribed on the facade of the New York City Post Office, this phrase describes the mounted couriers of the Persian King Xerxes the Great (519 B.C.?-465 B.C.) in the Greek historian Herodotus' *History*, Bk. VIII, section 98. This work, written around 445 B.C. is an account of the wars between the Greeks and the Persians.

The Macmillan Book of Proverbs, Maxims, and Famous Phrases (New York: Macmillan Publishing Co., 1976), 1386.

What was Albert Einstein's comment on science?

German-born American physicist Albert Einstein (1879-1955) said: "The whole of science is nothing more than a refinement of everyday thinking.... One thing I have learned in a long life is that all our science, measured against reality, is primitive and childlike—and yet it is the most precious thing we have."

Scientific Quotations: The Harvest of a Quiet Eye (New York: Crane, Russak, 1977), 52.

Who did Jonathan Swift call the best doctors in the world?

English churchman and writer Jonathan Swift (1667-1745) wrote, "The best doctors in the world are Doctor Diet, Doctor Quiet, and Doctor Merryman."

The Macmillan Dictionary of Quotations (New York: Macmillan, 1989), 166.

What did Plato have to say about mathematicians?

In the *Republic,* Book VII, the Greek philosopher Plato (ca. 428-348 B.C.E.) wrote, "I have hardly ever known a mathematician who was capable of reasoning."

John Bartlett, *Familiar Quotations* (Boston: Little, Brown, 1980), 84.

Who said "Wine is the most beautiful and most hygienic of beverages"?

French chemist Louis Pasteur (1822-1895) demonstrated that, in the fermentation of wines and beers, microorganisms were responsible for the substantive changes rather than spontaneous generation or chemical processes. Pasteur is quoted as saying, "Wine is the most beautiful and most hygienic of beverages." The scientific community, exemplified by the pre-eminent organic chemists in Europe, Justus von Liebig (1803-1873) and Friedrich Wohler (1800-1882), was convinced that fermentation was a purely chemical process. Early ridicule met theorists who proposed that living cells were involved in fermentation.

John Daintith and Amanda Isaacs, *Medical Quotes* (New York: Facts on File, 1989), 59.

Words and Symbols

What does the slang phrase "the cat's whiskers" mean?

The phrase "the cat's whiskers" came into use in the early 1950s as an equivalent to the phrase "the cat's meow," meaning something wonderful or "really neat."

Harold Wentworth and Stuart Berg Flexner, eds., *Dictionary of American Slang, 2nd ed.* (New York: Thomas Y. Crowell, 1975), s.v. "cat's whiskers, the."

What is the meaning of the slang term "brass ring"?

The term brass ring is a slang expression meaning a chance to accumulate wealth or achieve success. It can also refer to a reward or a prize.

The American Heritage Dictionary of the English Language, 3d edition, (Boston: Houghton Mifflin, 1992), s.v. "brass ring."

What is the meaning of the literary term "litotes"?

"Litotes" is a literary term that refers to the expression or affirmation of an idea through the denial of its opposite. In *Literary Terms: A Dictionary*, Karl E. Beckson noted that: "Milton makes use of this device when, at the beginning of *Paradise Lost*, he asks the muse to aid his adventurous song "'That with no middle flight intends to soar,' indicating that in reality his poem will soar to the highest levels of imagination." Or, as Wayne Campbell of the *Wayne's World* movies might say "Barry Manilow rocks-NOT!"

Karl E. Beckson and Arthur Ganz, *Literary Terms: A Dictionary, 3d ed.* (New York: Noonday Press, 1989), s.v. "litotes."

What is the meaning of the term "coup de grce"?

Translated literally, the French term "coup de grce" means "blow of mercy" and refers to the fatal blow that ends a person's life. While in modern times such an act may seem anything but merciful, to the medieval prisoners who were finally dispatched with a "coup de grce" after enduring agonizing tortures, the death stroke was cause for much relief indeed.

William Morris and Mary Morris, *Morris Dictionary of Word and Phrase Origins* (New York: Harper & Row, 1977), s.v. "coup de grce."

Who coined the expression "alternative future"?

John McHale originally coined the expression "alternative future." It has also been used by Robert Theobald, who said "We must invent an alternative future which will replace our current future by making it irrelevant." The phrase reflects the concept that current human behavior, due to its environmental and psychological impact, will lead to the destruction of the human race. Furthermore, it stresses that people can change attitudes and behaviors to bring a more desirable existence into being.

Center for Curriculum Design, *Somewhere Else: A Living-Learning Catalog* (Chicago: Swallow Press, 1973), 8.

What does the expression "from alpha to omega" signify?

The expression "from alpha to omega" has its origins in the book of Revelations from the Old Testament of the Bible and means "from beginning to end" or "the first and the last." In the Greek alphabet, Alpha is the first letter and Omega is the last.

Ivor H. Evans, *Brewer's Dictionary of Phrase and Fable, 14th ed.* (New York: Harper & Row, 1989), s.v. "Alpha."

What does "AWOL" stand for?

The military term "AWOL" means "Absent Without Leave." An acronym dating to the American Civil War (1861-65) or earlier, this offense assumes that the absentee will return. If a soldier is absent for 30 days or more, he or she is considered a deserter.

John R. Elting, Dan Cragg, and Ernest L. Deal, *A Dictionary of Soldier Talk* (New York: Scribner Press, 1984), s.v. "AWOL."

What is the symbolism of the colors red, white, and blue in the American flag?

There is no officially designated meaning for the red, white, and blue of the American flag. Current thought holds that the color red signifies bravery, white symbolizes purity, and blue stands for loyalty. Additional meanings for the colors in the flag have been suggested: red symbolizes blood shed in wars, white represents peace, and blue stands for faith in God. An earlier view, expressed by Charles Thomson who was secretary of the Continental Congress, was that red represented hardiness and valor, white symbolized purity and innocence, and blue stood for vigilance, perseverance, and justice.

William Rea Furlong and Byron McCandless, *So Proudly We Hail: The History of the United States Flag* (Washington, DC: Smithsonian Institution Press, 1981), 228. Robert Phillips, *The American Flag: Its Uses and Abuses* (Boston: 1930), 54-56.

What does a yellow butterfly symbolize?

In "Yellow Butterflies," a short story by Mary R. S. Andrews published in 1922, yellow butterflies are a symbol of immortality. In the story, a young mother is delighted when a pair of yellow butterflies light on her 5-year-old son's head one sunny day. Years later, after he has been lost in World War I (1914-18), she becomes obsessed with the notion that the body buried in the Tomb of the Unknown Soldier is her son's. Her belief is confirmed when she visits the site and yellow butterflies light on the flowers she leaves there.

Mary Raymond Shipman Andrews, "Yellow Butterflies," *Ladies Home Journal* November 1922.

What does the term "quid pro quo" mean?

The term "quid pro quo" means "what for what" or "something for something," as in giving one valuable thing for another.

Henry Campbell Black, *Black's Law Dictionary: Definitions of the Terms and Phrases of American and English Jurisprudence, Ancient and Modern, 6th ed.* (St. Paul, MN: West Publishing, 1990), s.v. "quid pro quo."

Who or what is a felinophile?

A person who has a love of cats is called a felinophile.

Celia Haddon, *An Illustrated Anthology about Cats and Their Companions* (New York: St. Martins Press, 1992), 9-10.

What is the origin of the phrase "kit and caboodle"?

The phrase "kit and caboodle" has a mixed origin. "Kit" means a collection of most anything, and its earliest use in England in 1785 is related to a soldier's kit bag. "Caboodle" undoubtedly comes from either the English "buddle," which means "bunch or bundle," or the Dutch "boedel," which means "property." "Caboodle" is most likely a corruption of "kit and boodle."

William Morris and Mary Morris, *Morris Dictionary of Word and Phrase Origins* (New York: Harper & Row, 1977), s.v. "kit and boodle."

In labor parlance, what is featherbedding?

Featherbedding is labor union insistence for work rules that safeguard the job security of its members at the cost of efficiency and innovation. The Taft-Hartley Act prohibited one form of featherbedding—that of paying for work that was not performed. Other forms include limiting the amount of labor done by each worker and requiring a prescribed number of workers for a particular job.

The Encyclopedic Dictionary of Economics (Guilford, CN: Dushkin Publishing Group, 1986), 84.

What was a stalag?

A stalag was a German detention camp for captured enemy personnel during World War II (1939-45). The term was an acronym for two other words of German origin-"stamm," meaning "stem" or "trunk," and "lager," meaning "camp." The prisoners of war held in the stalags were of numerous nationalities. The term entered the popular lexicon after the war in part because of a stage play and film called *Stalag 17* and later, the television series *Hogan's Heroes.*

Louis L. Snyder, *Louis L. Snyder's Historical Guide to World War II* (Greenwood Press, 1982), 665.

Why was the rattlesnake chosen an unofficial symbol of the American colonies in the years prior to the American Revolution?

The rattlesnake often appeared as a symbol of the American colonies in the years prior to the American Revolution. The snake, often accompanied with the words "Don't tread on me," appeared in colonial newspapers and on everything from paper money to buttons to military flags. In ancient cultures, serpents often symbolized wisdom and time without end. An anonymous writer to *Bradford's Pennsylvania Journal* declared in 1775 that the rattlesnake is bright of eye, ever vigilant, nevers attacks without being threatened, but once committed to battle never surrenders.

William Rea Furlong, *So Proudly We Hail: The History of the United States Flag* (Washington, DC: Smithsonian Institution Press, 1981), 71-75.

What is voguing?

Voguing is expressive African-American gay dancing. The term came into use in Harlem in the 1980s.

Clarence Major, *Juba to Jive: A Dictionary of African-American Slang* (New York: Penguin Books, 1994), s.v. "Voguing."

What is a Nefertiti flattop?

A Nefertiti flattop is a popular African-American male haircut of the 1990s.

Clarence Major, *Juba to Jive: A Dictionary of African-American Slang* (New York: Penguin Books, 1994), s.v. "Nefertiti flattop."

What are some good practice words for the first round of a national spelling bee?

Some good practice words for the first round of a national spelling bee are: accrue, anoint, argosy, baboon, caress, confetti, dulcet, effluent, fiasco, grammar, hideous, hopscotch, juror, ligature, mallet, phonics, proclivity, riffraff, shoddiness, shovel-like, snippet, stodgily, weevil, and zodiac.

David Grambs, *Death by Spelling: A Compendium of Tests, Super Tests, and Killer Bees* (New York: Harper & Row, 1989), 141.

What is a "lollapalooza"?

"Lollapalooza" is a slang word used in reference to an extraordinary or unusual thing, person, or event.

Random House Webster's College Dictionary (New York: Random House, 1991), s.v. "lollapalooza."

How long has the hexagram been a Jewish symbol?

The hexagram—also known as the Star of David, shield of David, and Magen David—has been a Jewish symbol since at least 30 B.C. During the Middle Ages, European Jewry used the hexagram on their banners and prayer shawls. The hexagram became popular during the nineteenth century to decorate newly-built synagogues. In Nazi Germany it was used in combination with the color yellow to distinguish Jews from Gentiles. It has appeared on the flag of Israel since 1948.

Carl G. Liungman, *Dictionary of Symbols* (Santa Barbara, CA: ABC-CLIO, 1991), 300-01.

How is the first name of novelist and diarist Anas Nin pronounced?

The first name of Spanish and French novelist and diarist Anas Nin (1903-1977) is pronounced: uh-nigh-is.

Wilfred J. McConkey, *Klee As in Clay: A Pronunciation Guide* (Lanham, MO: University Press of America, 1985), 21.

What is the meaning of the underworld phrase "park the biscuit"?

The underworld phrase "park the biscuit" means to get rid of a pistol or revolver that one is carrying. It can also mean to sit down.

Hyman E. Coldin, *Dictionary of American Underworld Lingo* (New York: Twayne Publishers, 1950), 152.

What is a "poodle faker"?

A "poodle faker" is British Navy slang for a ladies' man.

Edward Fraser and John Gibbons, *Soldier and Sailor Words and Phrases* (London: George Routledge and Sons, 1925), s.v. "Poodle Faker."

What is the origin of the word "leprechaun"?

"Leprechaun" is from the Gaelic *Leith bhrogan* and roughly translates as "one shoe maker." Leprechauns are debased Irish fairies who mischievously guard crocks of gold in deep forests while performing simple tasks such as shoe mending.

John P. Frayne, ed., *Uncollected Prose By W. B. Yeats* (New York: Columbia University Press, 1970), 135.

What is a "judas window" or a "judas-hole"?

A "judas window," which is sometimes called a "judas-hole," is a peep-hole in a door behind a small sliding panel. They are chiefly employed on the solid doors of prison cells to allow for inspections.

Webster's Third New International Dictionary of the English Language Unabridged (Springfield, MA: Merriam-Webster, 1986), s.v. "judas."

What is the origin of the word "curtsy"?

The word "curtsy" or "curtsey" was originally a form of the word "courtesy" that meant expression of courtesy or respect by a gesture or a bow. In modern usage, it describes a gesture of respect or reverence made by women by bending the knees with one foot forward and lowering the body.

Encyclopaedia Britannica, 11th ed. (England: University Press, 1910), s.v. "courtesy."

What is the origin of the word "debunk"?

The word "debunk" was originated by W. E. Woodward, an American historian and novelist, in 1923. He combined the word "bunk," meaning nonsense, with the prefix "de," meaning to remove, after reading the word "delouse" in a British newspaper during World War I (1914-18).

The Oxford English Dictionary, 2d ed. (Oxford: Clarendon Press, 1989), s.v. "debunk."

What is a kibitzer?

Kibitzer is a Yiddish word referring to someone who watches and interferes with things without becoming involved. Basically, the kind of person who keeps telling another individual where the card goes when that person is playing solitaire.

Eric Partridge, *A Dictionary of Slang and Unconventional English, 8th ed.* (New York: MacMillan, 1984), s.v. "kibitzer."

What is a fillip?

A fillip is the act of snapping one's fingers.

David Louis, *Fascinating Facts* (New York: Ridge Press/Crown Publishers, 1977), 82.

Where did the word "hangnail" originate?

The etymology of the word "hangnail" can be traced back to "agnail" or "angnail," which meant "a sore around a fingernail or toenail." The tenth century Old English word "agnail" or "angnail," however, meant "a corn on the foot." The first element, "ag-" or "ang-," was associated with "ange," which meant "painful." The second element, "-nail," meant an iron nail. Agnail therefore referred to a corn on the extremity that could be likened to the hard head of an iron nail.

By the sixteenth century, agnail referred to any number of ailments of the fingers or toes, which led to the acceptance of the "-nail" element dealing with the fingernail or toenail. At that time, the prefix to the word, "ag-," derived from the adjective "ange," was becoming obsolete. The compound was reforming to make sense to ordinary speakers, and by the last quarter of the seventeenth century, the term "hangnail" meant specifically, "a bit of skin hanging loose at the back or side of a fingernail."

Webster's Word Histories, (Springfield, MA: Merriam-Webster, 1989), s.v. "hangnail."

What does "hellacious" mean?

"Hellacious" is a slang term meaning overwhelming, really awful, or extreme. The word can also mean tremendous, formidable, or terrific.

John Ayto and John Simpson, *The Oxford Dictionary of Modern Slang* (Oxford: Oxford University Press, 1992), 100. Richard A. Spears, *Slang and Euphemism, 2nd edition* (New York: Signet Books, 1991), s.v. "hellacious."

What is the difference between an allegory and a symbol?

An allegory differs from a symbol in terms of the way it is understood. Although their meanings are similar-an image that represents one thing but means something else-an allegory differs in that it is complex, sometimes very complicated. It should preferably be understood or interpreted by everybody, and everybody should be able to agree on its meaning. A symbol, on the other hand, will be understood only by the initiated, and its meaning cannot be deduced. While its expression is generally simple and uncomplicated, its meaning cannot be arrived at by reasoning, it requires a previous knowledge. Even though certain symbols are so well known that everyone understands them, persons from another time would not be able to interpret their meaning because they lack the prior knowledge of the condition or situation the symbol represents.

Sven Tito Achen, *Symbols Around Us* (New York: Van Nostrand Reinhold, 1978), 11.

What do the colors red, yellow, blue, black, and white symbolize?

In Western cultures, the color red symbolizes "love" and all of its many facets—such as romantic love, platonic love, brotherly love, and the love of God. In Roman mythology, red is the color of Mars, the god of war. As a political symbol, red signifies communism, socialism, and revolution.

The color yellow is symbolic of many things for Western peoples. Yellow stands for wealth, royalty, divinity, and wisdom. Yellow is symbolic of the sun, for its light and warmth. By contrast, yellow also symbolizes deceit, malice, jealousy, treachery, cowardice, and disgrace.

The color blue, in Western cultures, is the color of "heaven," of God and of the celestial gods. In Greek and Roman mythology, the gods were often clad in blue. In Christendom, the Virgin Mary is depicted in blue. Blue is the color of royalty, nobility, excellence, distinction, and outstanding quality. It signifies honesty, fidelity, and chastity. Blue also symbolizes sadness and melancholy, from which the expression "the blues" is derived.

The color black is symbolically associated in Western societies with night, fear, evil, misfortune, and death; black is the color of mourning and grief. In many Western religions, black was viewed as a conscious expression of devotion, repentance, self-denial, and awareness of sin—wearing black demonstrated a person's piety, chastity, and rejection of vanity. In the 1960s, African-Americans, protesting the many negative associations with the color black and its symbolism, countered with the "pro-black" affirmations "Black is Beautiful" and "Say it Loud—I'm Black and I'm Proud!"

The Western interpretation of the color white is that it symbolizes purity, goodness, cleanliness, divinity, and peace. In many Western religions, white is the color of innocence, faith, and grace. A white flag can represent surrender or truce. Like the color black, white is also associated with death and mourning, feelings of loneliness and despair, possibly derived from its absence of color—its arid whiteness.

Sven Tito Achen, *Symbols Around Us* (New York: Van Nostrand Reinhold, 1978), 28-43.

How did policemen get their many nicknames?

Policemen have been labeled with many nicknames over the years—some not as nice as others-and most of these colorful descriptors find their origins in the early days of law enforcement. The term "bull" for example, is derived from a nineteenth-century Spanish Gypsy word for policeman-bul. A "harness bull" describes a uniformed policeman; a "cinder bull" is a railroad detective.

Police nicknames were often associated with their style of dress or their activity. The tags "flatfoot," "flatty," and "crusher" all identify the policeman walking a beat, and the perceived condition of his feet. The terms "cop" and "copper," probably the most widely used of all police nicknames, have more obscure origins. They may be derived from an old English verb, "cop," meaning to catch or hold, or from the attire of early nineteenth-century London officers, whose uniforms had large copper buttons. London policemen, known as "bobbies" and "peelers," were named so because their force was organized by Sir Robert Peel.

The term "fuzz" dates back to the 1920s and is possibly a variation of "feds," which is short for federal narcotic agents, or "fussytail," which describes a demanding person. "Pig," one of the more biting tags given to policemen, dates back to the 1840s. It was originally applied to police informers and stool pigeons who were paid to squeal on their cohorts, thus avoiding the "pen." Some of the more contemporary nicknames given to law enforcement include "smokey" or "bear," borne out of the CB-radio craze and given to highway patrolman who would "come out of the woods" to pursue speeding law breakers. The nickname "five-o," taken from the television series "Hawaii Five-O," finds its roots in rap music and the streets of urban America.

Jane Polley, ed., *Stories Behind Everyday Things* (Pleasantville, NY: Reader's Digest Association, 1980), 253.

What does "de facto" mean?

"De facto" is a term that means "in reality" or "actually," regardless of legal standards. For example, if two countries have severed diplomatic relations, closed their borders to citizens of the other countries, and imposed an economic embargo, they are considered in a "de facto" state of war, even though neither country has military attacked the other.

Robert L. Barker, *The Social Work Dictionary* (Silver Spring, MD: National Association of Social Workers, 1987), 38.

What does the "G" signify in abbreviations such as "G-5 nations"?

In abbreviations such as G-5, G-7, G-30, and so on, the "G" refers to the word "group." For example, the abbreviation G-7 refers to the Group of 7, or the seven major non-Communist economic powers: the United States, Great Britain, Canada, France, Japan, Italy, and Germany.

Department of State Library, *Dictionary of International Relations Terms* (Washington, DC: Government Printing Office, 1987), s.v. "Group of 5," "Group of 7," Group of 30."

What was a "beatnik"?

"Beatnik" was a term given to members of a self-marginalized social group of the late 1950s and early 1960s. Beatniks were usually identifiable by their unconventional dress, love of poetry and jazz, and indulgence in existential philosophy. Most beatniks were teens and young adults who were disillusioned with the existing social order in the United States.

Wayne R. Dynes, ed., *Encyclopedia of Homosexuality* (New York: Garland Publishing, 1990), 118-20.

What is the meaning of the word thanatology?

Thanatology is the study of death, particularly the philosophical, sociological, and psychological effects of death and the persons coping with it. The word is derived from *Thanatos*, the Greek word for death. Today thanatology has many close parallels with gerontology in that it is an interdisciplinary field lacking comprehensive theory and often sought to provide more information than can be drawn from the existing knowledge base.

George L. Maddox, ed., *The Encyclopedia of Aging* (New York: Springer Publishing, 1987), s.v. "Thanatology."

When was the term "gay" first used to mean homosexual?

The usage of the term "gay" to mean homosexual probably originated in France during the thirteenth and fourteenth centuries. The Provencal word "gai" referred to courtly love and its literature. "Gai saber" referred to "the art of poesy," "gaiol" meant lover, and "gai" designated an openly homosexual person. The poetry of courtly love and the troubadours, who were associated with southern French heretical Christian sects, especially the Cathars and Albigensians who most likely favored homosexuality, was often explicitly homosexual.

"Gay" became a code word for homosexual in early twentieth-cenhtury English homosexual subculture.

Robert T. Francoeur, Tomothy Perper, and Norman A. Scherzer, eds., *A Descriptive Dictionary and Atlas of Sexology* (New York: Greenwood Press, 1991), s.v. "gay."

How did the word "booze" become another word for alcohol?

In today's language, alcohol is often referred to as "booze." The origins of the word "booze" date back to the presidential campaign of 1840. Supporters of the Whig party candidate, William Henry Harrison (1773-1841), tried to portray their candidate as a hardworking common man. To reinforce this image, the Whig party adopted the campaign slogan "Log Cabin and Hard Cider Democracy." The slogan quickly caught on and log cabin facsimiles soon became the rage. In an attempt to cash in on the log cabin craze, the E.C. Booz Distillery manufactured a miniature log cabin filled with whiskey. The Booz log cabins were hugely popular, and the word "booze" was introduced into the English language. Harrison won the election, but died of pneumonia after only one month in office.

Eileen Shields-West, *The World Almanac of Presidential Campaigns* (New York: World Almanac, 1992).

What is the origin of the word "tipping"?

The concept of tipping people for the services they perform has been accepted for several centuries. The origin of the English word "tipping" is open to debate. Some people claim that the word "tip" is based on a slang term used by thieves in seventeenth-century England meaning "to hand something over," or based on the word "stipend," meaning a small fee. Others speculate that the word "tipping" was derived from containers found in eighteenth-century coffeehouses that were placed on the tables. The labels on these container read "To Insure Promptness"-TIP.

Jane Polley, ed., *Stories Behind Everyday Things* (Pleasantville, NY: Reader's Digest Association, 1980), 374.

How did the phrase "Adam's Apple" originate?

The term "Adam's Apple" is derived from the story that a piece of the forbidden apple lodged in Adam's throat. To this day all men have a distinctive "Adam's Apple" as a reminder of Adam's original sin.

Lillian Eichler, *The Customs of Mankind* (Garden City, NY: Nelson Doubleday, 1925), 666-67.

What does the slang expression "cockamamie" mean?

At one time "cockamamie" meant anything trifling or second-rate. This meaning comes from the word "decalcomania" which was the name for cheap dye transfers that children put on their arms and hands. The image left by these transfers was blurry and quickly wore off; hence "trifling" or "second-rate." Later the meaning referred to silly or laughable.

William Morris and Mary Morris, *Morris Dictinary of Word and Phrase Origins, 2d ed.* (New York: Harper & Row, 1988), s.v. "cockamamie."

Why were eighteenth-century British sailors called Limeys?

In the eighteenth century British sailors, while at sea, were given a daily serving of lime juice as a scurvy preventitive, since it contained vitamin C. So they were called "Limeys."

Irving Lewis Allen, *Unkind Words* (New York: Bergin & Garvey, 1990), 52.

What is Deux Ex Machina?

Deus or Deux Ex Machina is the occurrence or intervention of an unlikely providential event that rescues one from a difficult situation at exactly the right moment. It is largely a literary device employed mainly by playwrights and novelists. It literally means "a god let down upon the stage from the machine." The "machine" is a reference to stage equipment used in ancient Greek theaters.

Ivor H. Evans, *Brewer's Dictionary of Phrase and Fable, 14th ed.* (New York: Harper & Row, 1989), s.v. "Deus." Karl E. Beckson and Arthur Ganz, *Literary Terms: A Dictionary, rev. ed.* (New York: Noonday Press, 1989), s.v. "deux ex machina."

What does the word "Murgatroyd" from the expression "Heavens to Murgatroyd" mean?

The word "Murgatroyd" as in the expression "Heavens to Murgatroyd" comes from the game of Tiddlywinks and refers to a poorly manufactured wink that is flat on both sides.

Eric Partridge, *A Dictionary of Slang and Unconventional English, 8th ed.* (New York: Macmillan, 1984), s.v. "murgatroyd."

What does "humongous" mean?

The word "humongous" is a slang term possibly derived from a mixing of the words huge, enormous, tremendous, and monstrous. It connotes something of awe-inspiring size. The term first became popular on college campuses.

Jack Smith, "The Humongous Among Us," *Pittsburgh Press* 16 September 1979.

What is a "hodag"?

A hodag is a fictitious creature that lives in the swamps of Michigan's Upper Peninsula and Wisconsin. Both Michigan and Wisconsin natives claim to have originated this three-feet tall creature which has spikes running down its back. The argument even drew the attention of the states' governors.

USA Today 27 August 1984.

Where did the term "guerilla war" come from?

The term "guerilla war" was first used during the Peninsular Wars of 1808-1814. It refers to a war between a large, conventional army with superior weapons and numbers of troops and small, mobile armies of lightly armed partisans. The majority of guerilla wars have occurred in Latin America, Africa, and Asia. Although guerilla armies often lack sufficient weapons and manpower, they sometimes wear down and defeat a larger, better-equipped opponent because of stronger morale or a fervent commitment to a particular ideology.

Kofi Buenor Hadjor, *Dictionary of Third World Terms* (London: I. B. Tauris, 1992), s.v. "guerilla war."

What is the United States military's alphabet code?

The alphabet code adopted by the United States military, North American Treaty Organization, and the International Communications Aeronautical Organization is as follows: A (Alpha), B (Bravo), C (Charlie), D (Delta), E (Echo), F (Foxtrot), G (Golf), H (Hotel), I (India), J (Juliett), K (Kilo), L (Lima-pronounced LEE-MAH), M (Mike), N (November), O (Oscar), P (Popa), Q (Quebec), R (Romeo), S (Sierra), T (Tango), U (Uniform), V (Victor), W (Whiskey), X (X-Ray), Y (Yankee), and Z (Zulu).

Office of Naval Research, *Research Reviews* April 1956.

What is the origin of the pageant?

In the Middle Ages, plays were performed on scaffoldings referred to as "pageants" (variant spelling-pagiant). The scaffolding was sometimes on wheels, which allowed the play to move about in the streets. The plays themselves came to be known as pageants.

Karl Mantzius, *The Middle Ages and The Renaissance, vol. 2 of A History of Theatrical Art in Ancient and Modern Times* (London: Duckworth & Co., 1903), 82.

What is the origin of the phrase "mind your p's and q's" ?

Numerous explanations exist for the origins of the phrase "mind your p's and q's." Because the letters "p" and "q" so resemble one another teachers may have admonished their students to be particularly careful when writing them. English pubs used to keep blackboards to tally the number of pints and quarts, or p's and q's, that a patron drank. In the early years of the 20th century children were cautioned to "mind your pleases and excuses," which, if said quickly, could sound like "mind your p's and q's." Others maintain the phrase comes from the French custom of warning courtiers to "gardez votre pieds et queues" (mind your feet and wigs) when meeting royalty.

Word Ways: The Journal of Recreational Linguistics August 1977.

What is the origin of the word "nincompoop"?

The origin of the word "nincompoop" is cloudy at best. Dr. Samuel Johnson in 1755 suggested it comes from the Latin "non compos" which means "without ability," although Johnson's suggestion is regarded as tenuous at best. Others suggest "nincompoop" is an elaboration of the word "ninny." "Nincompoop" has been variously spelled "nicompoop," "nickumpoop," and "nincumpoop."

Charles Earle Funk, *Horsefeathers and Other Curious Words* (New York: Harper & Brothers, 1958), 150.

What is the origin of the word "laureate" as in "poet laureate"?

The title "poet laureate" comes from the ancient custom of crowning poets with bay or laurel. The first U.S. poet laureate was poet and novelist Robert Penn Warren (1905-1989), who was named to the post on February 26, 1986.

Kenneth Hopkins, *English Poetry: A Short History* (New York: Lippincott, 1962), 186-92. *The World Almanac and Book of Facts 1995* (Mahwah, NJ: World Almanac, 1994), 341.

What does the Irish euphemism "begorra" mean?

The Irish euphemism "begorra" translates into "by God"!

J.B. Sykes, ed., *The Concise Oxford Dictionary of Current English* (London: Oxford University Press, 1982), 80.

What is the origin of the word "bowdlerize"?

The word "bowdlerize," which denotes the act of expurgating (or censoring) portions of books thought to be objectionable, derives from the name of English doctor and editor Thomas Bowdler (1754-1825), who set out to rid English literature of "those words and expressions...which cannot with propriety be read aloud in a family."

David Loth, *The Erotic in Literature* (New York: Julian Messner, 1961), 123-24.

How did "XXX" come to symbolize kisses on cards and in letters?

The custom of using "XXX" to symbolize kisses on cards and in letters goes back to the early Christian era when "X" was a religious symbol for the cross and its use was as meaningful as a sworn oath. In later times people who could not write often made their "X" instead and kissed the "X" to show their sincerity.

Charles Panati, *Extraordinary Origins of Everyday Things* (New York: Harper & Row, 1987), 52-53.

What does the phrase "hanged, drawn, and quartered" mean?

Modern usage of the phrase "hanged, drawn, and quartered" is somewhat jocular and means to suffer greatly exaggerated consequences for an act or misdeed. Prior to the fifteenth century, however, its meaning was quite dire and referred to a criminal being drawn on a horse's tail or cart to an execution site, hanged by the neck until dead and his corpse cut into pieces and scattered around the English countryside.

Charles Earl Funk, *Heavens to Betsy! and Other Curious Sayings* (New York: Harper & Brothers, 1955), 50.

What is a "bolo" tie?

A bolo tie is a length of string, cord, or corded leather that is looped around the neck and held in place by an ornament known as a bolo or bola. The two ends of the tie or often tipped in silver. The original bolo tie was usually made of leather, silver, and turquoise by Southwest Native-American artisans.

New York Times 26 July 1987.

From where does the heliotrope, a plant with small purplish flowers, derive its name?

The name of the heliotrope, a plant with small purplish flowers, is derived from the Greek words "helios" (sun) and "tropos" (turn), and its origin was the subject of a mythological story that was recounted in Ovid's (43 B.C.-17 A.D.) *Metamorphoses.* A water nymph named Clyti fell madly in love with the sun god Helios, who was later identified with Apollo. Everyday she pined with unrequited love as she watched him traverse the sky, and so the gods changed her into a heliotrope, a flower whose petals follow the course of the sun.

Catherine B. Avery, ed., *The New Century Classical Handbook* (New York: Appleton-Century-Crofts, 1962), s.v. "Clyti." Ad de Vries, *Dictionary of Symbols and Imagery* (Amsterdam: North-Holland Publishing Company, 1974), 246.

What is the origin of the word "maverick"?

The word derives from the name of Samuel Maverick (1803-1870), a Texas rancher and politician, who was active in the movement that led to the independence of Texas from Mexico. He was a member of the convention that established the Republic of Texas, a mayor of San Antonio, and a member of the first legislature of the state of Texas. Since he was notorious for leaving his unbranded cattle free to range, the word "maverick" originally referred to a stray or unbranded cow or steer, usually a calf. In modern usage "maverick" also refers to a nonconformist.

Leslie Dunkling, *The Guinness Book of Names* (Middlesex, England: Guinness Books, 1986), 18.

What is the origin of the phrase "white elephant"?

"White elephant" refers to an item that is more trouble to keep around than the item is worth. The phrase originated in ancient Siam (now Thailand) where elephants born white were so rare that they immediately became property of the king. If a king's subject fell out of favor he would be given one of the white elephants to feed, care for, and house for the elephant's life.

Pittsburgh Post-Gazette 27 December 1975.

How many neologisms (new words) are attributed to Shakespeare?

The great English dramatist William Shakespeare (1564-1616) is credited with the first usage of over 1,700 words; such a newly coined word is known as a neologism.

Richard Lederer, *The Miracle of Language* (New York: Pocket Books, 1991), 93.

What does a unicorn symbolize when it appears on the scutcheon of a knight?

On the scutcheon of a knight, a unicorn symbolizes the courage and piety of the bearer. The imaginary unicorn, a medium sized horse-like animal with a single horn growing out of its forehead, has appeared in the mythology of many cultures since ancient times. It symbolizes supreme power because of the belief that vigour and virility is concentrated in its single horn. Reports of the unicorn appeared in India as early as 398 B.C., and its legend spread through much of Europe and Asia. Mystical powers were assigned to it; court physicians believed that scrapings from its horn cured many ills. It was also believed that a unicorn horn would "sweat" if filled with a poisonous drink, thus making the horn an ideal goblet for royalty who feared assasination by poisoned wine. Another belief held that a unicorn could only be tamed by a virgin holding a mirror to its face. Although unicorns are most often presented as being horse-like, many cultures described them as oxes, rams, goats, serpents, fish, or antelopes. The distinguishing feature of the unicorn was not its particular form but rather the single horn growing out of its forehead.

Rdiger Robert Beer, *Unicorn: Myth and Reality* (New York: Van Nostrand Reinhold, 1977), 137. Richard Cavendish, ed., *Man, Myth & Magic* (New York: Marshall Cavendish, 1983), 11: 2908-11.

What is the origin of the word "gossamer"?

The word "gossamer" is a contraction of the term "goose-summer," a reference to late October and early November. It is a time when geese are allowed to eat the stubble from harvested crops and "gossamer" spider webs can be readily seen hanging from the now bare branches.

John Train, *Remarkable Words with Astonishing Origins* (New York: Clarkson N. Potter, 1980), 42.

What is the origin of the term "male chauvinism"?

The term "male chauvinism" is derived from the name Nicholas Chauvin, a much-wounded French soldier in Napoleon's army. Upon retirement Chauvin became fanatical on the subject of the glory of France and the "Little Corporal." Eventually a number of French playwrights used Chauvin as a character in their comedies, and "Chauvin" entered the popular idiom as a zealot devoted to a cause or way of life.

Irving Wallace, David Wallechinsky, and Amy Wallace, *Significa* (New York: E.P. Dutton, 1983), 188.

What is the origin of the phrase "Blue Monday"?

The phrase "Blue Monday" probably has nautical origins in that Monday was usually reserved aboard ship for floggings. Another argument for a nautical origin refers to the custom of flying a blue flag at half-mast and painting blue stripes fore and aft when a captain or top officer died at sea.

Teri Degler, *Scuttlebut and Other Expressions of Nautical Origin* (New York: Henry Holt, 1989), 11-13.

What is a "devil's strip"?

If you were to visit Ohio, especially the Akron area, you would find residents using the term "devil's strip" to describe the grassy margin between streets and sidewalks. Residents of Toronto,

Ontario, however, use the same term to describe the dangerous center path between streetcar tracks.

William Morris and Mary Morris, *Morris Dictionary of Word and Phrase Origins* (New York: Harper & Row, 1977), 176.

What are the origins of the term "polka dot"?

The term "polka dot" originated with the nineteenth-century craze for dancing the polka. The clothing industry sought to capitalize on this fad by giving their products such names as "polka hats," "polka gauze," and "polka dots" for fabric printed with dots.

William Morris and Mary Morris, *Morris Dictionary Of Word And Phrase Origins* (New York: Harper & Row, 1977), 456.

What does the American slang word "torqued" mean?

The American slang word "torqued" means to be angry or "bent."

Richard A. Spears, *NTC's Dictionary of American Slang and Colloquial Expressions* (Lincolnwood, IL: National Textbook Company, 1989), 405.

What is the "Zeitgeist" theory of fashion?

"Zeitgeist" is a German word that means spirit of the times, and the "Zeitgeist" theory of fashion refers to the belief that the manner of dress reflects prevailing culture attitudes, including the attitude toward sexuality. For example, the modesty of the Victorian age was expressed by the multiplicity of women's petticoats, and the emancipation of the roaring twenties by short hair and short skirts.

Valerie Steele, *Fashion and Eroticism: Ideals of Feminine Beauty from the Victorian Era to the Jazz Age* (New York: Oxford University Press, 1985), 20-21.

What does veridical mean?

Veridical is a Latin-root word that means truthful or genuine, and it derives from the adjective *verus*, which means true or truthful, and the infinitive *dicere*, which means to speak.

Laurence Urdang, ed., *Everyday Reader's Dictionary of Misunderstood, Misused, Mispronounced Words* (New York: Quadrangle Books, 1972), s.v. "veridical."

Why does the ancient Irish kingdom of Ulster have a red hand on its coat of arms?

The ancient Irish kingdom of Ulster has a red hand on its coat of arms as a reminder of how the Ulster kings, the O'Neills, came to power. As a member of an invading Scottish force who agreed that the first hand to touch the soil would be made king, the original O'Neill drew his sword, cut off his own left hand, and threw it to shore in order to claim the throne.

William Eleroy Curtis, *One Irish Summer* (New York: Duffield & Company, 1909), 215.

On men's underwear, what do the initials BVD stand for?

On men's underwear, the initials BVD signify the surnames Bradley, Voorhies, and Day, early manufacturers of this product.

David Louis, *Fascinating Facts* (New York: Ridge Press/Crown Publishers, 1977), 112.

What does balkanization mean?

Balkanization refers to a continual state of mistrust, disharmony, and even war between countries which are usually characterized as being relatively small and if not sharing common borders then being in relatively close proximity to one another. The term originated in reference to the Balkan states, kingdoms, and principalities of eastern Europe, especially Serbia, Macedonia, Montenegro, Albania, Bulgaria, and Romania . These states fought continually among themselves and against the Ottoman Empire, which as it declined left a power vacuum in the region. Following the fall of Communism and another subsequent power vacuum, this area saw an almost immediate return of regional strife especially in the former Yugoslavia. In the 1990s many social observers claimed that the United States was becoming socially balkanized because of widespread minority, political, gender, and sexual group identification.

Walter J. Raymond, *International Dictionary of Politics, 6th ed.* (Lawrenceville, VA: Brunswick Publishing, 1980), s.v. "Balkanization."

Who coined the phrase "global village" to describe the world?

(Herbert) Marshall McLuhan (1911-1980), author, lecturer, college professor, and communications futurist coined the phrase "global village" when describing the world being created by the electronic communications revolution. He believed that one day everyone would be linked together in a worldwide communications network. McLuhan's other famous phrase was "The medium is the message."

E.D. Hirsch Jr., *The Dictionary of Cultural Literacy* (Boston: Houghton Mifflin, 1988), s.v. "Global village." Charles Moritz, ed., *Current Biography Yearbook, 1981* (New York: H.W. Wilson, 1981), s.v. "McLuhan, (Herbert) Marshall."

What is the history of the expression, "O.K."?

Most word authorities believe that "O.K." comes from the nickname of Martin Van Buren (1782-1862), who rose from potboy in a tavern to president of the United States. "O.K." was an abbreviation for "Old Kinderhook," a title bestowed upon Van Buren from the name of his birthplace in Kinderhook, N.Y. In order to counter strong political opposition, Van Buren's supporters formed the Democratic O.K. Club, the first two initials of which became a rallying cry and chant of approval among the candidate's supporters. A number of alternative theories has been advanced, over the years, but a consensus of lexicographers persists in attributing the origin of the expression to Van Buren's supporters.

Robert Hendrickson, *Human Words: The Compleat Unexpurgated, Uncomputerized Human Workbook* (Philadelphia: Chilton Book, 1972), 239-40.

What is the meaning of the expression, "oy vay!"?

According to author Leo Rosten, "oy" is not a word; it is a vocabulary, uttered in as many ways as the utterer's histrionic ability permits. It is a lament, a protest, a cry of dismay, and a reflex of delight. "Oy" is often used to lead off "oy vay!," which means, literally, "Oh, pain," but is used as an all-purpose ejaculation to express anything from trivial delight to abysmal woe. "Oy vay!" is the short form of "Oy vay iz mir!," an omnibus phrase for everything from personal pain to empathetic condolence. "Vay" comes from the German "Weh," meaning "woe."

Leo Calvin Rosten, *The Joys of Yinglish* (New York: McGraw-Hill, 1989), 399.

How did NASA come up with the name *Endeavour* for its new space shuttle?

The U.S. president George Bush selected the name *Endeavour* for NASA's newest space shuttle after it was the most popular name chosen in a national competition among American school children to name the craft. *Endeavour* was built to replace the *Challenger* shuttle, which was destroyed during a launch. It was named after the British sailing ship *Endeavour,* used by eighteenth century English explorer James Cook to explore the South Pacific from 1868 to 1772. The shuttle craft made its first space voyage in 1992.

Pittsburgh Post-Gazette 11 May 1989.

What is the origin of the expression "to be in a blue funk"?

The origin of the expression "to be in a blue funk" is uncertain. One theory holds that it comes from the Walloon expression "in de fonk zum," meaning "to be in the smoke." It may also have come from the Flemish word "fonck," which is translated "perturbation" or "disturbance." The expression has changed its meaning since the early eighteenth century when it meant to be nervous or terrified. It now means to be in a sad or dejected mood. The use of the word "blue" is considered a modern-day adaptation.

Christine Ammer, *Have a Nice Day—No Problem! A Dictionary of Clichs* (New York: Dutton, 1992), 35.

What is the meaning of jive?

Jive is a jargon that was popular during the 1940s. It was a combination of African-American slang from Harlem, terms used by drug addicts and petty criminals, and contributions from gossip columnists and high school students. It was spoken mainly by jazz musicians and jitterbug fans, and many of its terms refer to musical instruments, such as scratch-box for violin; skin or suitcase for a drum; and monkey-hurdler for an organist.

H.L. Mencken, *The American Language, Supplement II* (New York: Alfred A. Knopf, 1962), 704-05.

Is Arkansas pronounced differently in Kansas?

In 1881 the Legislature of Arkansas decided the name of their state, "should be pronounced in three syllables, with the final *s* silent, the *a* in each syllable with the Italian sound, and the accent on the first and last syllables." Residents of Kansas have a different slant on the subject. Once the Arkansas River crosses the border into the state of Kansas, it is called the Ar*kan*sas River with the accent on the second syllable. Ar*kan*sas City, which is in Kansas, is also pronounced with it on the second syllable.

H.L. Mencken, *The American Language* (New York: Alfred A. Knopf, 1962), 542-43.

What is "dj vu"?

The term "dj vu" is an expression that is used to describe the feeling of having seen or experienced something previously, without actual memory of having done so. It is also called "false memory" or "memory without recognition." Such an experience can be considered an illusion or it could imply precognitive or clairvoyant information. Dj vu translates from French to "already seen."

Michael A. Thalbourne, *A Glossary of Terms Used in Parapsycholgy* (London: William Heinemann, 1982), 19.

Where does the word "pandemonium" come from?

The word "pandemonium" was first coined by the English poet John Milton (1608-1674) in his poem *Paradise Lost.* Milton described the capital of Hell, which he called Pandemonium, as a council chamber filled with disorderly demons in concert with Satan. The term has since some to denote noisy confusion or wild tumult.

Robin Palmer, *A Dictionary of Mythical Places* (New York: Henry Z. Walck, 1975), s.v. "Pandemonium."

What does the phrase "Catch-22" mean?

The phrase "Catch-22" is taken from a satiric World War II novel bearing the same name by Joseph Heller (1923-). It has come to mean an "insoluble dilemma, a double bind" or a situation in which all alternatives are "no-win." In the novel, American pilots, forced to fly an unreasonable number of dangerous missions, could not be relieved of duty unless they were diagnosed insane. On the other hand, the same regulations stipulated that a pilot who refused to fly because of the danger could not be insane because he was thinking too rationally. The "Catch-22" was therefore a "no way out" situation. Originally Heller had called this situation and the book "Catch-18" but changed the number because *Mila-18* by Leon Uris (1924-) had just been published.

Robert Hendrickson, *The Henry Holt Encyclopedia of Word and Phrase Origins* (Detroit: Holt, 1987), 105.

What was the "Bloomsbury Group"?

In England's cultural history, the "Bloomsbury Group" was an informal coalition of intellectuals, authors, and artists who flourished in London between the two twentieth century world wars. Representative of the group were novelists Virginia Woolf and E. M. Forester, art critic Roger Fry, painter Duncan Grant, and economist John Maynard Keynes. While the group had no single philosophy, they appreciated "aesthetic excellence" and greatly valued their friendship. The name of the group comes from a London district where many of them lived.

John Drexel, ed., *The Facts On File Encyclopedia of the 20th Century* (New York: Facts On File, 1991), 110-11.

The 1920s are often called the "Roaring Twenties." What other phrases have been used to describe this decade?

In addition to being called the "Roaring Twenties," the decade of the 1920s, whose prosperity was chronicled by a rising stock market, was also known as the "Golden Twenties." The prohibition of alcohol lent it the title of the "Dry Decade." Fierce competition between gangsters dealing in illegal liquor earned it the name of the "Lawless Decade." It was also the "Age of the Flapper" when women began to experience the freedom of the post-World War I era as they danced the Charleston during the "Jazz Age."

Howard L. Hurwitz, *An Encyclopedic Dictionary of American History* (New York: Washington Square Press, 1968), 295.

Where did the term "diplomat" come from?

The term "diplomat" comes from the Greek word meaning "folded twice." Its meaning derives from papers that diplomats carried being so secret that they needed to be "folded twice."

John Train, *Remarkable Words with Astonishing Origins* (New York: Clarkson N. Potter, Inc., 1980), 19.

What is the origin of the word robot?

The word robot comes from the Slovene word "rbota" which means "compulsory service" or "forced labor."

Janko Kotnik, *Slovene-English Dictionary* (LJubljana: Izdala Drzavna Zalozba Slovenije, 1967), 574.

How and where did the word "brat" originate?

The word "brat" originally came from the Celtic (old Irish) language where it meant a cloth used as a covering for the body: a plaid, mantle, or cloak. In Old Welsh a similar word meant the swaddling clothes of an infant. Currently "brat" means a coarse or makeshift over-garment. "Brat," as it refers contemptuously to a child or suggests a spoiled, ill-mannered youth, is of uncertain origin. Some, but not all, scholars point to the origin described previously. In the sixteenth and seventeenth centuries, "brat" was sometimes used without contempt although the term has almost always implied insignificance, whether of an offspring or a product.

J.A. Simpson and E.S.C. Weiner, *The Oxford English Dictionary, 2nd edition* (Oxford, Clarendon Press of Oxford University Press, 1989), 2:495.

Where did the word "kangaroo" originate?

The word "kangaroo" is actually a phrase from the language of the aboriginal peoples of Australia that can be roughly translated as "what are you saying"? When English mariner Captain James Cook (1728-1779) first explored on the continent in the eighteenth century, members of his crew were perplexed by the unusual marsupial and its vertical maneuverings. They inquired as to its name and the native people replied "Kangaroo"?

John May et al., *Curious Trivia* (New York: Dorset Press, 1984), s.v. "Kangaroos."

What is meant by the term "Woopie"?

The term Woopie or Woopy is an informal acronym for a "well-off old(er) person." The term was first used in the late 1980s to describe affluent and active retired people who enjoy life.

John Simpson and Edmund Weiner, eds., *Oxford English Dictionary Additions Series* (Oxford: Clarendon Press, 1993), s.v. "woopie."

How did the word "rhubarb" come to be a synonym for "a heated argument"?

The word "rhubarb" does not merely designate a vegetable but is a synonym as well for a heated argument. This usage may have begun in the theater. When sound effects for a disgruntled, off-stage mob scene were needed, a group of actors would congregate behind the stage and loudly pronounce "rhubarb" over and over. Its origin as a synonym for argument has sometimes been misattributed to the sport of baseball.

Robert Hendrickson, *Grand Slams, Hat Tricks, and Alley-oops: A Sports Fan's Book of Words* (New York: Prentice Hall, 1994), 148.

What is manumission?

Manumission refers to the act of granting a slave his or her freedom. It can also mean releasing a person from the power or control of another.

Henry Campbell Black, *Black's Law Dictionary, 6th edition* (St. Paul, MN: West Publishing, 1990), s.v. "Manumission."

Where did the word "quisling" originate?

The term "quisling" was coined during World War II (1939-45) to refer to anyone or any group that collaborated with an occupying power. The name is derived from Norwegian prime minister Vidkun Quisling (1887-1945), who cooperated with Nazi Germany. The word quickly became synonymous for "traitor" and remains so to this day.

Graham Evans and Jeffrey Newnham, *The Dictionary of World Politics: A Reference Guide to Concepts, Ideas and Institutions,* (New York: Simon & Schuster, 1990), s.v. "Quisling."

What is a "junta"?

A word of Spanish derivation, "junta" is generally used to refer to a military government, especially, though not exclusively, in Latin America. The term originally referred to a ruling committee or administrative council but is now more commonly heard in reference to the dictatorial rule of a single military commander.

Graham Evans and Jeffrey Newnham, *The Dictionary of World Politics: A Reference Guide to Concepts, Ideas and Institutions* (New York: Simon & Schuster, 1990), s.v. "Junta."

What does the hammer, sickle, and five-pointed star represent on the flag of the former Soviet Union?

The hammer and sickle on the flag of the former Soviet Union represented the proletariat and the peasantry. The five-pointed star represented the unity of all people among the five continents.

Whitney Smith, *Flags and Arms Across the World* (New York: McGraw-Hill, 1980), 203.

What is a "Catherine wheel"?

A "Catherine wheel" is a large pinwheel-like firework named after St. Catherine, whose martyrdom upon a large wheel of torture was ordered by the Emperor Maximus in 309 A.D.

John Ciardi, *A Browser's Dictionary* (New York: Harper & Row, 1980), s.v. "Catherine wheel."

What is the symbolism of the olive branch?

According to Greek and Roman mythology, the olive branch symbolizes peace and serenity.

Laurence Urdang and Frederick G. Ruffner Jr., eds., *Allusions—Cultural, Literary, Biblical, and Historical: A Thematic Dictionary, 2nd ed.* (Detroit: Gale Research, 1986), s.v. "Peace."

What is the origin of the word "buddy"?

The word "buddy" probably arose as the result of childish mispronunciation of the word "brother." It is common for children to have trouble pronouncing the letter "r" when it appears with another consonant. Thus "brother" comes out "budda" or "buddy."

Webster's Word Histories (Springfield, MA: Merriam-Webster, 1989), s.v. "buddy."

What is the origin of the word "panic"?

The word "panic" has its origins in the ancient Greeks who were struck with terror at the prospect of the appearance of their mischievous god Pan. Unexplained stampedes and feelings of terror and alarm were attributed to Pan and referred to as a "panic."

Webster's Word Histories (Springfield, MA: Merriam-Webster, 1989), s.v. "Panic."

In American and British slang, what is pig heaven?

In American and British slang pig heaven refers to a police station.

Richard A. Spears, *Slang and Euphemism, 2d ed.* (New York: Signet, 1991), s.v. "Pig Heaven."

In American slang, what is a dudette?

In American slang, a dudette is a young woman.

Richard A. Spears, *Slang and Euphemism, 2d ed.* (New York: Signet, 1991), s.v. "Dudette."

What does the term "swatson" mean?

"Swatson" is a New England term meaning to engage in informal conversation, as in, "Let's *swatson* a while."

William Morris and Mary Morris, "Words and Wisdom," *Pittsburgh Post Gazette* 9 June 1970.

What is the meaning and origin of the phrase, "with a grain of salt"?

Statements that need be accepted "with a grain of salt" are considered to be at least partly untrue or exaggerated. The implication is that the information needs some "seasoning" before being "swallowed." The phrase originated with Pliny the Elder's (A.D. 23-79) stories about King Mithridates (120-63 B.C.). Mithridates so feared death by poisoning that he immunized himself by taking very small amounts of poison each day. Pliny wrote that the King managed to find an antidote against all poison but added that this fact was "to be taken with a grain of salt." Pliny himself was known to twist the truth for the sake of humor, so the phrase may have gained meaning through association with its author.

Bergen Evans, *Comfortable Words* (New York: Random House, 1962), 182-83.

Why is listening in to another's conversation called "eavesdropping"?

Listeners or snoopers to another's conversation could find a safe, dry spot for their pastime between the eaves of a house (the overhanging edge of a roof) and the place where rain fell from the roof, usually about two feet from the wall, called the "eavesdrop." At one time, eavesdroppers were enough of a nuisance to be cited in court if caught in the malicious act.

Bergen Evans, *Comfortable Words* (New York: Random House, 1962), 137.

Which novel by Hermann Hesse tells of a young Brahman's life-long pursuit of enlightenment?

Siddhartha is the novel by German author Hermann Hesse (1877-1962), published in 1922, which traces the young Brahman's life-long pursuit for enlightenment.

Frank N. Magill, ed., *Cyclopedia of Literary Characters II* (Pasadena, CA: Salem Press, 1990), 1400-01.

What is the meaning and origin of the term "pasquinade"?

"Pasquinade" means a satire, parody, or lampoon. Pasquino was an actual fifteenth-century Roman tailor known for his sarcastic wit. After his death, a mutilated statue was placed opposite his home and became known as "Pasquin." Irreverent Romans began the custom of attaching political flyers derogatory toward the Pope and other Italian leaders to the statue. Retaliatory answers to "pasquinades" were hung on Marforio, an ancient statue of Mars located in another area of Rome.

Nicholas Parsons, *The Book of Literary Lists: A Collection of Annotated Lists, Statistics, and Anecdotes Concerning Books* (New York: Facts on File, 1987), 170-71.

What is the meaning and derivation of the term blurb?

A blurb is the short summary of a book's contents printed on its jacket flap or cover. The term was coined by Gelett Burgess, editor of a review called *The Lark.* "A blurb," he once was quoted as saying, "is a check drawn on Fame, and is seldom honoured."

Nicholas Parsons, *The Book of Literary Lists* (New York: Facts on File, 1987), 168.

What is the origin of the title "She-Who-Must-Be-Obeyed"?

"She-Who-Must-Be-Obeyed" is the fictional character Ayesha, a supernatural white queen of a lost city in central Africa. Ayesha was the romantic heroine of H. Rider Haggard's (1856-1925) bestselling novel, *She* (1887). Although Ayesha actually perishes in *She*, her character proved popular enough to be resurrected in numerous prequels and sequels by Haggard and other authors. Ayesha was also the subject of several silent films and at least two sound films, including a 1965 version of *She* starring Ursula Andress.

David Pringle, *Imaginary People: A Who's Who of Modern Fictional Characters* (New York: World Almanac Pharos Books, 1987), s.v. "She-Who-Must-Be-Obeyed."

What is the meaning of the term "hot button"?

Created in the field of marketing to describe a consumer need waiting to be satisfied, the term "hot button" is now most frequently used in the field of politics to indicate an issue that arouses strong emotion in potential voters. A "hot button," according to *Newsweek* magazine, is "something a candidate says to instantly show that his values are the voters' values." The mention of certain controversial topics such as abortion, guns, welfare, or taxes would be "hot button" issues during political campaigns.

William Safire, *Quoth the Maven* (New York: Random House, 1993), 127-29.

What does the British slang term "twee" mean?

The British slang term "twee" implies an "affected daintiness," or "quaintness-for-quaintness' sake."

Norman W. Schur, *British English, A to Zed* (New York: Facts On File, 1987), s.v. "twee."

What does the Southern expression "you-all" mean?

The expression "you-all" and its contraction "y'all" is used by Southerners as a plural of "you." Southerners disagree among themselves, however, whether or not the expression is also used as a singular of "you." Many Southerners insist it is used only in the plural except by Northerners doing pitiable imitations of Southern speech. The American curmudgeon of letters H.L. Mencken (1880-1956) wrote a history of the dispute in his *The American Language* (1948).

Merriam-Webster's Dictionary of English Usage (Springfield, MA, Merriam-Webster, 1989), s.v. "you-all."

What is a "Hobson's choice"?

A "Hobson's choice" is a contradiction because no choice is involved. The phrase means taking what is offered or nothing at all as in "We are going to this movie or no movie at all." The phrase originates from one Tobias Hobson who although renting horses would only offer the horse closest to the stable door.

Longman Dictionary of English Idioms (London: Longman, 1979), 165.

What does the Yiddish expression "gevalt!" mean?

"Gevalt!" is a Yiddish expression that can be used as a cry of fear or astonishment, a cry for help or an utterance of protest. It can be used as an expletive or a noun as in: The man let out a gevalt! when the excited woman yelled "Gevalt! You frightened me!"

Leo Rosten, *The Joys of Yiddish* (New York: McGraw-Hill, 1968), 134.

What does the Italian word "pentimento" mean?

The Italian word "pentimento" has two meanings: repentance and a wiped-out detail that becomes more evident with time, such as a mark left by an artist's or printer's erasure.

Le Mot Juste: A Dictionary of Classical & Foreign Words & Phrases (New York: Vintage Books, 1981), 124.

How is the word "forte" pronounced, and what does it mean?

The word "forte" has two meanings and two different pronunciations. "Forte," referring to one's strong point, is pronounced "fort." Pronouncing the word "fortay" when the meaning is strong point is an often-used but incorrect pronunciation. "Forte," when used as a musical term meaning loud, is pronounced "fortay."

Theodore M. Bernstein, *Dos, Don'ts & Maybes of English Usage* (New York: Times Books, 1977), s.v. "forte."

What are the origins of the words "Eskimo" and "Inuit"?

The word "Eskimo" comes from the French word "Esquimau," which in turn comes from an Algonquian word meaning "eater of raw meat." "Inuit," which is the term preferred by the native Canadian people for themselves, means "mankind," "people," or "men."

Irving Lewis Allen, *Unkind Words: Ethnic Labeling from Redskin to WASP* (New York: Bergin & Garvey, 1990), 52.

When and how did the term "WASP" come into the English language?

In the mid-1950s, "WASP" was Chicago slang and Ohio Valley social worker's slang for "White Appalachian Southern Protestant." By 1960 the other, more familiar WASP—for "White Anglo-Saxon Protestant"—had arrived.

Irvin Lewis Allen, *Unkind Words: Ethnic Labeling from Redskin to WASP* (New York: Bergin & Garvey, 1990), 105-6.

What is a therblig?

Frank Bunker Gilbreth (1868-1924), the founder of modern motion study technique, called the fundamental motions of the hands of a worker therbligs (a variation of Gilbreth spelled backwards). He concluded that any and all operations are made up of series of these 17 motions: search, select, grasp, reach, move, hold, release, position, pre-position, inspect, assemble, disassemble, use, unavoidable delay, avoidable delay, plan, and test to overcome fatigue.

Benjamin W. Niebel, *Motion and Time Study, 7th ed.* (Homewood, IL: Irwin, 1982), 13, 165-66.

Which symbol is used to represent medicine?

The staff of Aesculapius has represented medicine since 800 B.C. It is a single serpent wound around a staff. The caduceus, the twin-serpent magic wand of the god Hermes or Mercury, came into use after 1800 and is commonly used today. The serpent has traditionally been a symbol of healing, and it is an old belief that eating part of a serpent would bring the power of healing to the ingester. Early Greeks saw in the serpent regenerative powers expressed by the serpent's periodic sloughing of its skin and venerated the serpent. Later the Greek god of medicine, Asklepius, or Asclepius, called Aesculapius by the Romans, performed his functions taking the form of a serpent. Sometimes this god is represented in art as an old man with a staff, around which is coiled a serpent.

The Journal of the American Medical Association 26 April 1985. Arnold Whittick, *Symbols, Signs and Their Meaning* (London: Leonard Hill Books, 1960), 258.

Why is the signal "SOS" used to indicate distress?

The distress signal "SOS," expressed in code as three dots, three dashes, three dots, was selected because of its simplicity to send and detect. The letters do not signify any particular words. The signal was adopted by international agreement in 1908. The first distress call was "CQD," CQ being the general call to alert other ships that a message is coming and D standing for "danger" or "distress."

Robert Hendrickson, *The Henry Holt Encyclopedia of Word and Phrase Origins* (New York: Henry Holt, 1990), 494. William Morris and Mary Morris, *Morris Dictionary of Word and Phrase Origins, 2d ed.* (New York: Harper & Row, 1988), 539.

What is the origin of the term "Dixieland"?

Although there are various stories about the source of the term "Dixieland," the most plausible is that the expression has its origins in the ten-dollar notes issued in Louisiana, which were popularly called dixies. The French-Creole word "dix" (ten) was on one side. The "land of dixies" or Dixieland became synonymous with the southern states and the south.

William Morris and Mary Morris, *Morris Dictionary of Word and Phrase Origins, 2nd ed.* (New York: Harper & Row, 1977), 181.

When was Chicago first dubbed "the windy city"?

Chicago received its nickname "the windy city" when it was one of four cities competing to be the site of the world's Columbian Exposition of 1893. In 1889, the U.S. Congress authorized the exposition and set hearings for the site. Competition was intense among the four cities vying for the trade fair. Charles A. Dana, owner and editor of the *New York Sun*, wrote of Chicago:

"Don't pay attention to the nonsensical claims of that windy city. Its people couldn't build a world's fair even if they won it."

Herman Kogan and Lloyd Wendt, *Chicago: A Pictorial History* (New York: E.P. Dutton and Co., 1958), 162.

What is the origin of the phrase "new deal"?

Although the phrase "new deal" had been used before, Franklin Delano Roosevelt (1882-1945) popularized it in a speech to the 1932 Democratic Convention, which had just nominated him as its presidential candidate. Roosevelt said: "I pledge you, I pledge myself, to a new deal for the American people." The actual originator of the expression as spoken by Roosevelt was Samuel Rosenman, who later wrote: "I had not the slightest idea it would take hold the way it did.... It was simply one of those phrases that catch public fancy and survive-short, concise, and yet comprehensive enough to cover a great many different concepts."

Without similar success, Woodrow Wilson (1856-1924) used the phrase in a 1910 speech, and in 1919 British statesman David Lloyd George (1863-1945) used it in his campaign slogan "A New Deal for Everyone." An even earlier use of the expression was in 1889 by American writer and humorist Mark Twain (1835-1910) in his book *A Connecticut Yankee in King Arthur's Court*, in which he wrote: "And now here I was, in a country where the right to say how the country should be governed was restricted to six persons in each thousand of its population.... It seemed to me that what the nine hundred and ninety-four dupes needed was a new deal."

William Safire, *Safire's New Political Dictionary: The Definitive Guide to the New Language of Politics* (New York: Random House, 1993), s.v. "new deal." Mark Twain, *A Connecticut Yankee In King Arthur's Court* (New York: Harcourt, Brace & World, 1962), 82.

Which words in the English language end in "dous"?

Some words ending in "dous" include: horrendous, hazardous, jeopardous, stupendous, pteropodous, and tremendous.

Merriam-Webster's Collegiate Dictionary, 10th edition (Springfield, MA: Merriam-Webster, Inc., 1993), 559. J. Walker, *The Rhyming Dictionary of the English Language, revised edition* (London: George Routledge), 475. Clement Wood, ed., *The Complete Rhyming Dictionary and Poet's Craft Book* (New York: Garden City Books, 1936), 251-52.

Are there any all-consonant, three-letter words?

One three-letter word without a vowel is "nth," which means extreme or utmost, such as "to the nth degree."

Dmitri A. Borgmann, *Language on Vacation* (New York: Charles Scribner's Sons, 1965), 177-79. *Merriam-Webster's Collegiate Dictionary, 10th ed.* (Massachusetts: Merriam-Webster, 1993), s.v. "nth."

What is the origin of the word "yankee"?

The appearance of the word "yankee" in early quotations (such as "Yankey Duch," 1683; "Captain Yankey," 1684) suggests its first use was as a nickname. It was also used as a term of contempt by General James Wolfe (1727-1759) in 1758 and as a general, though prideful, term for a native or inhabitant of New England around 1765. The word probably came from the Dutch. One explanation by Dutch linguist Henri Logeman is that the word may have been an alteration of "Jan Kees" (literally, John Cheese), a nickname for Dutchmen used by Flemings.

By about 1784 "yankee" was used by the British to apply to Americans in general; then from about 1812, and particularly since the American Civil War (1861-65) the name has been applied in the South to anyone from the northern states above the Mason-Dixon line.

Robert K. Barnhart, ed., *The Barnhart Dictionary of Etymology* (New York: H. W. Wilson, 1988), s.v. "Yankee."

Who are represented by the masks of tragedy and comedy?

The masks of tragedy and comedy are symbols of Thalia and Melpomene, two of the nine muses. The muses were first goddesses of memory but later became the divinities that presided over the arts and sciences. According to legend, Zeus, the chief god, and Mnemosyne, the goddess of memory, had nine daughters who learned the arts of singing, dancing, and poetry from the god Apollo. There are numerous myths about them judging or entering into musical competitions.

Melpomene was originally the patroness of song and musical harmony, but later she became the goddess of tragedy. She is usually depicted with a tragic mask and the club of Hercules. Her head is often wreathed with vine leaves to show her relationship to Dionysus, who was the god of wine, and at whose festival the first tragedies were performed. According to some accounts, she bore the Sirens, a group of sea-nymphs sired by the river god Achelous, whose singing lured sailors to their deaths.

Thalia, the muse of comedy, is represented by a comic mask, a shepherd's crook, and a wreath of ivy. According to some myths, she and Apollo were the parents of the Corybantes, priests of the Great Mother goddess in Phrygia who were known for their orgiastic dances.

Catherine B. Avery, ed., *The New Century Classical Handbook* (New York: Appleton-Century-Crofts, 1962), s.v. "corybantes, Melpomene, Mnemosyne, muses, sirens, Thalia."

What is the longest English word with only one vowel?

"Strengths" is the longest English word with only one vowel.

Dmitri A. Borgmann, *Language on Vacation: An Olio of Orthographical Oddities* (New York: Charles Scribner's Sons, 1965), 178.

Who was Kilroy in "Kilroy was here"?

"Kilroy was here" emerged as a famous graffiti from World War II (1939-45). It was found written on anything and everywhere. "Kilroy" was actually James J. Kilroy, a Bethlehem Steel Company inspector working at a Quincy, Massachusetts, shipyard who wrote the words on crates of equipment to indicate he had inspected them. The crates were shipped all over the world to military outposts and U.S. soldiers began copying the words on other items. Eventually with the graffiti appeared an ubiquitous, balding, long-nosed, pop-eyed graffiti character that was always drawn as though peering over a fence or wall. Along with his dome-shaped head only the top half of his face could be seen with his elongated nose draped over a fence gripped by bulbous fingers.

All kinds of theories emerged regarding the phrase. One serious one postulated that the graffiti was an anti-monarchial statement based on the division of the name Kilroy which could mean "kill" roi (king in French). After the war ended, the American Transit Association sponsored a contest to find out who originated this catchy phrase. Kilroy, still employed at the shipyard, won and was awarded a twenty-two ton trolley car. Kilroy died in 1962.

Robert Hendrickson, *The Henry Holt Encyclopedia of Word and Phrase Origins* (New York: Henry Holt, 1987), s.v. "Kilroy was here." *St. Louis Post-Dispatch* 26 November 1962. David Wallechinsky and Irving Wallace, *The People's Almanac* (New York: Doubleday, 1975), 755-57.

What is the meaning of the phrase "fifth column"?

The term "fifth column" means traitors; those within a country secretly working for the enemy. During the Spanish Civil War (1936-39) General Mola first uttered the phrase when he stated that he commanded four columns attacking Madrid from various directions and a "fifth column" within the city. However, author Ernest Hemingway permanently established the phrase in his play *The Fifth Column.*

Ivor H. Evans, *Brewer's Dictionary of Phrase and Fable, 14th ed.* (New York: Harper & Row, 1989), s.v. "Fifth Column." William Morris and Mary Morris, *Morris Dictionary of Word and Phrase Origins, 2d ed.* (New York: Harper & Row, 1963), s.v. "fifth column."

In travel guides what do the abbreviations AP, CB, DP, EP, FB, and MAP mean?

The abbreviations AP, CB, DP, EP, FB, and MAP refer to meal plans offered by hotels or other places of lodging. The American plan (AP) is a system of paying a single fixed rate that covers room and all meals. The modified American plan (MAP) covers room, breakfast, and one other meal, usually dinner. Demipension (DP) is an arrangement under which a fixed rate covers room, breakfast, and one other meal. A continental breakfast (CB) is a light breakfast usually consisting of coffee and rolls. A full American breakfast is represented by FB. Under the European plan (EP), a fixed rate covers only lodging.

Ralph De Sola, *Abbreviations Dictionary, 7th ed.* (New York: Elsevier, 1986), s.v. "fb." *The Random House Dictionary of the English Language, 2d ed.* (New York: Random House, 1983), s.v. "American plan, continental breakfast, demipension, European plan, modified American plan." Jennifer Mossman, ed., *Reverse Acronyms, Initialisms & Abbreviations Dictionary, 18th ed.* (Detroit: Gale Research, 1993), s.v. "Demi-Pension."

What do you call someone who is 40, 50, 60, 70, 80, 90, or 100 years old?

Someone who is 40 years old is a quadragenarian; 50, a quinquagenarian; 60, a sexagenarian; 70, a septuagenarian; 80, an octogenarian; 90, a nonagenarian; and 100, a centenarian.

Victoria Neufeldt, ed., *Webster's New World Dictionary of American English, 3d ed.* (New York: Webster's New World Dictionaries, 1988), s.v. "centenarian," "nonagenarian," "octogenarian," "quinquagenarian," "septuagenarian," "sexagenarian." *The World Book Dictionary* (Chicago: World Book, 1992), s.v. "quadragenarian."

What term describes the expression "the whole is greater than the sum of its parts"?

The word "synergy" or "synergism" means the combined effect of two or more forces is greater than the sum of their individual effects; the term is more popularly defined as "the whole is greater than the sum of its parts."

The American Heritage Dictionary of the English Language, 3d ed. (Boston: Houghton Mifflin, 1992), 1821. Clarence L. Barnhart and Robert K. Barnhart, eds., *World Book Dictionary* (Chicago: World Book, 1990), 2129.

When and where is the Nobel Prize for Literature announced?

Each December 10 since 1901, the Nobel Prize for Literature has been announced from Stockholm, Sweden. December 10 is the anniversary of Alfred Nobel's death. Five other Nobel Prizes are awarded for outstanding achievements in the fields of physics, chemistry, physiology or medicine, economics, and the promotion of world peace.

Jonathan Eisen and Stuart Troy, eds., *The Nobel Reader: Short Fiction, Poetry, and Prose by Nobel Laureates in Literature* (New York: Clarkson N. Potter, 1987), ix.

When were the characters of the Roman alphabet developed?

The development of most of the letters of the Roman alphabet began not in Rome but in the lands of the Semites along the eastern border of the Mediterranean Sea. Many cultures, including the Etruscans, Phoenicians, and Greeks, were part of this evolutionary process. The letter "f," for example, began as the Semitic latter *vau,* "hook," and later became the Greek letter *phi.* Originally, it sounded like a *w* but was changed to an *f* sound by the Etruscans and Romans.

Only a handful of the twenty-six letters used now did not have Semitic origins. The letter *w* was a Norman invention and the letters, *u, x,* and *y* are of Greek origin. The letter *v* came from the Romans; and the letter *j* was an medieval invention to differentiate the Roman vowel *I* from the Roman consonant *i.*

Barbara Berliner, *The Book of Answers: The New York Public Library Telephone Service's Most Unusual and Entertaining Questions* (New York: Simon & Schuster, 1992), 47. Victor Stevenson, ed., *Words: The Evolution of Western Languages* (New York: Van Nostrand, 1983), 70.

What is the symbolism of the 1913 Flag of Peace?

A flag symbolizing international peace was designed for the Hague peace palace in 1913. The design features seven rainbow-colored stripes that merge into white, a representation of separate nations joining together harmoniously. Presented by an American, the flag was hung in the peace palace in Berne, Switzerland.

New York Post 27 September 1913.

Who coined the term "Generation X"?

The term Generation X, used to describe people who are in their twenties during the 1990s, has been ascribed to the novelist Douglas Coupland.

Newsweek, 6 June 1994.

Who are the "granish" or "griners"?

Immigrants from the Slovenian province of Carniola (of the former Austrio-Hungarian Empire) were given the name "granish" or "griners" when they moved to the U.S. This appears to be a corruption of the German term Krainer, used for these people.

Emily Greene Balch, *Our Slavic Fellow Citizens* (New York: Charities Publication Committee, 1910), 148. *Pittsburgh Press* 7 July 1991.

What is the history of the word hello?

The word hello is a product of the telephone age, and the creation of Thomas Edison (1847-1931). Early telephone users struggled to find an appropriate and effective opening for speaking on the telephone. People initially answered the telephone by saying "What is wanted"? or "Are you there"? Edison first used the word in his laboratory in 1878 and "hello" found its way into the Oxford English Dictionary in 1883.

There are no records of exactly how Edison created the new word. He is known to have shouted "Halloo" on phonographic recordings, created during his experiments with recorded sound. "Halloo" is a traditional hunting call, used to gather the dogs for the chase. "Hallo" and its variations are also words used in England to greet someone from a distance. But Edison definitely created a new word, one that quickly came into frequent use. It was even used on name badges as early as 1880, at a convention of telephone companies, anticipating the ubiquitous "Hello, my name is..." used on name badges today.

New York Times 5 March 1992.

What are the origins of some Native American tribal names?

The names of Native American tribes come from a variety of sources. In some cases the tribes are known by names they gave themselves, but most frequently they been given names by other tribes or by white settlers and missionaries.

The name Apache is actually derived from the name given this group by the Zuni tribe: "Apachu," meaning "enemy." The Cherokee were probably named by the Creeks, from the word "Tciloki," which means "people of different speech." The Sioux are known by a French modification of a Chippewa word; the people we know as the Sioux consider this name derogatory and now call themselves the Dakotas. The Chippewa tribe, or the Ojibway, take their names from the Algonquin language. The Crow called themselves "Absaroka," which is actually a Sioux word meaning bird people; white settlers gave them the name of a well-known bird. Hopi is a shortened version of "Hopituh," the Hopi word meaning peaceful ones. The Algonquins named the Mohawk tribe, using a word that translates as "eaters of men."

Navajo is a name created by 17th-century Spanish missionaries from the Spanish "navaja" meaning "pocket knife"; the tribe hopes to someday to be known as the "Dine"' a word from their own language.

USA Today 15 December 1993.

What is a "big Kahuna"?

The original meaning of the word "kahuna" is "Hawaiian priest." In the 1990s, however, the slang expression "the big Kahuna" came to mean a person or thing that is impressive or powerful.

John Algeo and Adele Algeo, "Among the New Words," *American Speech* Fall 1993.

What is the origin of the phrase "dressed to the nines"?

The phrase "dressed to the nines" means to be elaborately fashionable. The expression in its original form may have been "dressed to the eyes," which written in Old English would have been "To then eyne."

William Morris and Mary Morris, *Morris Dictionary Of Word and Phrase Origins* (New York: Harper & Row, 1977), 193.

What does the phrase "to take the biscuit" mean?

"To take the biscuit" means to do something outrageous or to be an extremely bad example. It is the British equivalent of "to take the cake." In Great Britain "biscuit" refers to a cracker or, most probably in this case, a cookie.

David Grote, *British English for American Readers* (Westport, CT: Greenwood Press, 1992), 46.

What are the origins of the phrase "the lost generation"?

The phrase "the lost generation" was first used by one Monsieur Pernollet ("Une gnration perdue") in his description to Gertrude Stein (1874-1946) of the working-class French whose lives became disaffected by and after World War I (1914-1918). Stein applied the phrase to the young expatriate writers who settle in the artistic Left Bank area of Paris. One of these writers, Ernest Hemingway (1899-1961), used it in his novel *The Sun Also Rises* (1926), guaranteeing its place in the literary idiom.

Robert Hendrickson, *The Literary Life and Other Curiosities* (New York: Viking Press, 1981), 62.

What is the origin of the word classic?

The word classic was derived from the Latin word for class, a social and legal division of the Roman people that, according to legend, was developed in the sixth century B.C. by the king Servius Tullius. The word was particularly applied to the highest class and so became synonymous with what was considered most worthy or best. Therefore authors who were outstanding were called "classici auctores" (classic writers), meaning that they were of the first class, and eventually the word was applied to any work of great merit.

Stephen Gilbar, *The Book Book* (New York: St. Martin's Press, 1981), 7.

What is an "Ugly American"?

"Ugly American" is a derogatory term which refers to Americans traveling or living abroad who are ignorant of or condescending towards local cultures. The phrase is taken from the title of a book by Eugene Burdick and William Lederer.

E.D. Hirsch Jr., *The Dictionary of Cultural Literacy* (Boston: Houghton Mifflin Company, 1988), s.v. "Ugly American, the."

To what group of people does the term Creole refer?

The term Creole comes from the Spanish word *Criollo* and originally referred to people of European descent born in America in contrast to American nationals born in Europe. Eventually its use was restricted to describing people born in America of French, Spanish, or Portugese descent. Creoles of Latin America led revolts against Spanish authority in the early 1800s, and French Creoles have greatly influenced the culture and development of Louisiana.

Dictionary of American History, Vol. II, rev. ed. (New York: Charles Scribner's Sons, 1976), s.v. "Creoles."

Why is a fireplace sometimes called a mantlepiece?

A fireplace is sometimes called a mantlepiece because coats or "mantles" when wet often were hung there to dry.

David Louis, *Fascinating Facts* (New York: Ridge Press/Crown Press, 1977), 86.

Who were the "Boers"?

The term "Boers" is a Dutch/Afrikaner word meaning farmer, but over the decades the word has been used to describe a variety of peoples. In the 1700s it referred to Caucasian farmers or nomadic farmers known as "trekboers." By the 1800s usage of the term had expanded to include Afrikaners in general, Caucasian inhabitants of the Voortrekker republics in particular, and those who fought against the British in the South African War. Its use often had derogatory connotations, especially among English-speaking people.

Christopher Saunders, *Historical Dictionary of South Africa* (Metuchen, NJ: Scarecrow Press, 1983), 28.

What is the origin of the expression "Gordian knot"?

A "Gordian knot" is a baffling problem; to "cut the Gordian knot" is to solve the problem with a single bold act. The saying originates from the myth of Gordius, king of ancient Phrygia, who dedicated his wagon to the god Jupiter, tying it to the beam of Jupiter's temple with a strong knot. An oracle phrophesied that the person who untied this knot would rule Asia. According to the myth, the military leader Alexander the Great (356-323 B.C.) cut the knot in two with his sword and thus became ruler of the civilized world.

Robert Hendrickson, *Human Words: The Compleat Unexpurgated, Uncomputerized Human Wordbook* (Philadelphia: Chilton Book, 1972), 131.

What does the phrase "hole in the head" mean?

Yinglish is Leo Rosten's (1908-1997) coined phrase for words that are hybrids of English and Yiddish. The expression, "I need it like a hole in the head," common among Yiddish speakers (who actually call it "a loch in kop") was propelled into the American vernacular by the play *A Hole in the Head* by Arnold Schulman, which later became a popular movie starring Frank Sinatra. The meaning is that the speaker refers to something he or she definitely does not need.

Leo Calvin Rosten, *The Joys of Yinglish* (New York: McGraw-Hill Publishing, 1989), 247.

What is "Davy Jones' locker"?

When something is said to be in "Davy Jones' locker" it means that it is at the bottom of the ocean. The old sailor's expression has been in use for over 200 years, but its origin is uncertain. It may be a reference to some unknown, fearsome Davy Jones who made others walk the plank, sending them to a watery death.

William Morris and Mary Morris, *Morris Dictionary of Word and Phrase Origins* (New York: Harper & Row, 1977), 169.

What is the sandwich generation?

The term sandwich generation refers to a segment of American society in which adult children are finding themselves having to spend as much or more time caring for their aging parents as they spend caring for their own children. The term came into usage as the percentage of older Americans increased, and more middle-aged adults found themselves caring for both their children and their aging parents.

Scholastic Update 6 September 1991.

What are "cremains"?

The word "cremains" was first used in 1963, by combining "cremated" and "remains," thereby referring to the ashes produced by a cremation.

Robert K. Barnhart, Sol Steinmetz, and Clarence L. Barnhart, *The Third Barnhart Dictionary of New English* (New York: H.W. Wilson, 1990), 109.

What is the meaning and etymology of "schmoosing"?

"Schmoosing" is a slang term that means casual talking, or chat, particularly in a business setting. Its origin is the Yiddish word "schmus," or talk.

H.L. Mencken, *The American Language* (New York: Alfred A. Knopf, 1962), 754.

What is the origin of the word "phantasmagoria"?

A "phantasmagoria" was originally a modification of an old magic lantern machine, used to project pictures painted on glass onto a wall or screen. An inventor named Philipstal created a "phantasmagoria" which made the projected figures appear to grow, shrink, dissolve, and vanish. The word was a combination of terms from the Greek *agora*, place of assembly, to the Greek *phantasma*, image, and *phantos*, visible. The word came to mean "a constantly changing scene."

Craig M. Carver, *A History of English in its Own Words* (New York: HarperCollins, 1991), 153.

What is meant by the acronym RHIP?

The acronym RHIP, coined by soldiers, is short for Rank Has Its Privileges.

Source: John R. Elting, *A Dictionary of Soldier Talk* (New York: Charles Scribner Sons, 1984), s.v. "RHIP."

What is a villanelle?

An old French poetic form in six stanzas on two rhymes, the villanelle is usually written in iambic pentameter. The first and last lines of the opening tercet serve alternately as the closing line of the following four tercets. The two lines together conclude the final quatrain. An example of this form is Welsh poet Dylan Thomas's (1914-1953) poem, "Do No Go Gentle into That Good Night."

Richard Ellmann and Robert O'Clair, eds., *Modern Poems: A Norton Introduction* (New York: W.W. Norton, 1973), lxiv.

What is a pangram?

A pangram is a sentence that uses every letter of the alphabet. The perfect pangram, which remains elusive, would use all twenty-six letters only once and would contain no proper names, initials, or archaic words. "The quick brown fox jumps over the lazy dog" is a pangram but unfortunately totals thirty-three letters.

Tony Augarde, *The Oxford Guide to Word Games* (Oxford: Oxford University Press, 1986), 105. Gyles Brandreth, *The Book of Solo Games* (New York: Peter Bedrick Books, 1983), 146.

What was known as the field of honor?

The practice of dueling was considered an honorable way for gentlemen to settle disputes in the eighteenth and nineteenth centuries. Duels were known as affairs of honor and the field of honor was the location where the duel took place. In America, dueling was practiced until the late 1800s despite the fact that state laws made it a crime to participate.

Howard L. Hurwitz, *An Encyclopedic Dictionary of American History* (New York: Washington Square Press, 1968), s.v. "dueling."

What is High Technology or High Tech?

This buzz term used mainly by the lay media (as opposed to scientific, medical, or technological media) appeared in the late 1970s. It was initially used to identify the newest, "hottest" application of technology to fields such as medical research, genetics, automation, communication systems, and computers. It usually implied a distinction between technology to meet the information needs of society and traditional heavy industry which met more material needs. By the mid-1980s, the term had become a catch-all applying primarily to the use of electronics (especially computers) to accomplish everyday tasks.

Van Nostrand's Scientific Encyclopedia, 7th ed. (New York: Van Nostrand Reinhold, 1989), 1:1452. Connie Winkler, *Careers in High Tech* (Englewood Cliffs, NJ: Prentice Hall, 1987), 1.

What does the term ergonomics mean?

The study of human capability and psychology in relation to the working environment and the equipment operated by the worker is variously known as ergonomics, human engineering, human factors engineering, engineering psychology, or biotechnology. Ergonomics is based on the premise that tools humans use and the environment they work in should be matched with their capabilities and limitations, rather than forcing humans to adapt to the physical environment. Researchers in ergonomics try to determine optimum conditions in communication, cognition, reception of sensory stimuli, physiology, and psychology, and examine the effect of adverse conditions. Specific areas of study include design of work areas (including seats, desks, consoles, and cockpits) in terms of human physical size, comfort, strength, and vision; effects of physiological stresses such as work speed, work load, decision making, fatigue, and demands on memory and perception; and design of visual displays to enhance the quality and speed of interpretation.

The McGraw-Hill Dictionary of Scientific and Technical Terms, 4th ed. (New York: McGraw-Hill), 660. *McGraw-Hill Encyclopedia of Science and Technology, 7th ed.* (New York: McGraw-Hill, 1992), 8: 520-23.

What is the origin of the word "skosh"?

The term "skosh" means a little bit or a smidgen and derives from the Japanese word "sukoshi." Also spelled "scosh," the term was first used by the armed forces during the Korean conflict.

Robert L. Chapman, *New Dictionary of American Slang* (New York: Harper & Row, 1986), 393.

Where did the expression "the real McCoy" originate?

The origin of the term "the real McCoy" is unknown. Originally a Scottish phrase, "the real Mackay," designated the real or authentic thing. In the United States, this became "the real McCoy." The most popular attempt to account for the use of the phrase in the United States relates to a boxer, Kid McCoy (1873-1940), a former welterweight champion (1898-1900). It is speculated that while McCoy was champion his name was adopted to mean "the best" or "superior." Possibly there was a less talented boxer with the same surname and "the real McCoy" was used to indicate Kid McCoy, the genuine champion. Usage of the phrase gained during Prohibition when it was used to describe genuine, uncut whiskey.

Paul Beale, ed., *A Concise Dictionary of Slang and Unconventional English* (New York: Macmillan Publishing, 1989), s.v. "real Mackay, the. " Laurence Urdang, ed., *Picturesque Expressions: A Thematic Dictionary* (Detroit: Gale Research Co., 1985), s.v. "genuineness."

What does the "D" in "D-Day" mean?

The U.S. Army claims that the "D" in D-day is a simple alliteration. Some believe that the "D" stands for Day or Day of Decision. The term actually represents a secret date on which any military operation is to begin. Similarly, H-Hour designates the hour when an attack or movement is to begin, and Y-Day designates the target date for military operations.

The most famous D-Day was the beginning of Operation Overlord, the 1944 Allied landings in Normandy, France during World War II (1939-45).

William Morris and Mary Morris, *Morris Dictionary of Word and Phrase Origins* (New York: Harper & Row, 1988). Frederick G. Ruffner Jr. and Robert C. Thomas, eds., *Code Names Dictionary* (Detroit: Gale Research, 1963), s.v. "D day," "H hour," "Y day."

Do any words in the English language end in "cion"?

Words in English which end in the letters "cion" are: coercion, suspicion, internecion, and scion.

John Walker, *The Rhyming Dictionary of the English Language, rev. ed.* (New York: E. P. Dutton, 1936), 309.

Which word in the English language contains all five vowels in order?

A word containing all five vowels in order is "facetious." A word containing six vowels when "y" is considered a vowel is "facetiously."

Merriam-Webster's Collegiate Dictionary, 10th ed. (Springfield, MA: Merriam-Webster, 1993), s.v. "facetious."

What is the antonym of the word "euphemism"?

"Euphemism" is a mild or vague expression that substitutes for an expression thought to be too harsh or direct. Its antonym is "cacophemism" (a harsh or direct description or expression). Cacophemism derives from the word "cacophony," which means a harsh, discordant mixture of sound, while euphemism is based on "euphony," which means pleasantness of sound.

R. E. Allen, ed., *The Concise Oxford Dictionary of Current English* (Oxford: Clarendon Press, 1990), s.v. "cacophony, euphemism, euphony, -ism. *Mrs. Byrne's Dictionary of Unusual, Obscure, and Preposterous Words Gathered From Numerous and Diverse Authoritative Sources* (New Jersey: University Books, 1974), s.v. "cacophemism." Laurence Urdang, ed., *-Ologies & -Isms, 3d ed.* (Detroit: Gale Research, 1986), s.v. "euphony."

What are those things called...?

Some names for ordinary things:

Pointed garden tool used for boring holes for bulb and seed planting—dibble
The surrounding case into which the door opens and closes—door jamb
Device that shoe salespeople use to measure feet—Brannock device
Shaft on the top of an umbrella—ferrule
Metal hoop that supports a lampshade—harp
Two buttons a telephone receiver rests on—plungers
Vertical post that runs through a door hinge—pintle
Little plastic tip of a shoelace—aglet
Rim of a barrel—chimb

Wire handle of a bucket—bail
Decorative metal plate around a keyhole, drawer pull, or doorknob—escutcheon
Open-sided box in which a book is kept—forel
Thin end of a knife blade that fits into the handle— tang
Pointy, curved end of a wooden knife handle—neb
Loop on the front part of a belt that secures the tip— keeper
Ornamental piece that screws into the top of a lamp to help secure the shade—ferrule
Curved end on a suit hanger that forms a small loop— turnback
Holder for a paper cone coffee cup—zarf
Narrowest part of an hourglass—waist
Bar that holds typewriter paper in place—paper bail
Circular wax-catcher that fits over a candle—bobeche
Dock post that a boat is tied to—bollard
Frames for holding windowpanes—muntins
Ornate tiered centerpiece, often of wrought-iron that holds plates, candlesticks, vases—epergne
Small dots that are waste from the hole-punching process in computer paper, etc.—chad
Looped shoulder decorations on uniforms made of gilt cord that is usually braided—aiguilette

Reginald Bragonier Jr. and David Fisher, *What's What: A Visual Glossary of the Physical World, rev. ed.* (Maplewood, NJ: Hammond, 1990). Paul Dickson, *Words* (New York: Delacorte, 1982), 129-32. Richard Lederer, *The Play of Words: Fun & Games for Language Lovers* (New York: Pocket Books, 1990), 164-66, 212. Mary Brooks Picken, *The Fashion Dictionary* (New York: Funk & Wagnells, 1973), 2-3.

Which English words contain three consecutive pairs of letters?

Only a few words contain three consecutive pairs of letters. These include bookkeeper, bookkeeping, balloonnet (a gas-tight compartment within the interior of a balloon or airship used for controlling ascent or descent), and Moorreesburg (a town north of Capetown, South Africa).

Dmitri A. Borgmann, *Language on Vacation: An Olio of Orthographical Oddities* (New York: Charles Scribner's Sons, 1965), 166. *Webster's Third New International Dictionary of the English Language Unabridged* (Springfield, MA: Merriam-Webster, 1986), s.v. "balloonnet."

What is the significance of a yellow ribbon?

A yellow ribbon worn or displayed has for many years been a symbol of separated loved ones. The song, "Round Her Neck She Wore a Yellow Ribbon," was originally published in the 1830s and was popular in the United States as well as Europe. This song about a woman wearing the ribbon for her faraway lover became an army marching song with different titles and many parodies. In 1972 Irwin Levine and L. Russell Brown wrote the words and music to "Tie a Yellow Ribbon Round the Old Oak Tree," which was sung by Tony Orlando and Dawn. This touching song about an ex-convict returning home became a best-selling record and was nominated for a National Academy of Recording Arts and Sciences Award, Song of the Year, in 1973. In 1981 yellow ribbons became symbols for those waiting for the release of American Embassy hostages in Tehran, Iran. Again during the Persian Gulf War in 1991, citizens displayed yellow ribbons for the U.S. soldiers overseas.

Other colored ribbons, worn on lapels or tied on cars, represent an individual's support for various causes. Red, on a lapel, shows support for the fight against the disease AIDS; tied on a car, red symbolizes allegiance with Mothers Against Drunk Driving (MADD). The following colors demonstrate an individual's support for a variety of different causes: blue, to prevent child abuse; pink, to promote breast cancer research; green, to save the rain forests; and purple, to stop urban violence.

Leon Dallin and Lynn Dallin, *Folk Songster* (Dubuque, IA: Wm. C. Brown, 1967), 60-61. *Fortune* 11 March 1991. *1001 Jumbo Song Book* (New York: Charles Hansen Educational Sheet Music & Books, 1974), s.v. "Tie a Yellow Ribbon Round the Old Oak Tree." Nat Shapiro and Bruce Pollock, eds., *Popular Music, 1920-1979* (Detroit: Gale Research, 1985), s.v. "Tie a Yellow Ribbon Round the Old Oak Tree." *USA Today* 19 April 1993.

Why are spiderwebs called cobwebs?

The cob in cobweb may mean spider. Dating back to the early 1300s, cob is believed to be a form of the Middle English word cop or coppe meaning spider. However, cobweb could also be derived from an earlier meaning of cob or cop meaning head, as when people brush into spiderwebs with their heads or faces.

The Barnhart Dictionary of Etymology (New York: H. W. Wilson, 1988), 184. Robert Hendrickson, *The Henry Holt Encyclopedia of Word and Phrase Origins* (New York: Henry Holt, 1987), 123.

What is the difference between "affect" and "effect"?

As a verb "affect" means to "have an influence on," as in the example, The weather affects his health. As a verb "effect" means to "bring about" or to "cause." And example of this usage would be, The negotiators were not able to effect an agreement between labor and management. The noun form of "affect," rarely used, is a psychological term meaning "emotion." As a noun, "effect" means "result."

The American Heritage Dictionary of the English Language, 3rd ed. (Boston: Houghton Mifflin, 1992), 29. *The New York Public Library Writer's Guide to Style and Usage* (New York: HarperCollins, 1994), 29.

Why is the U.S. quarter called "two-bits"?

As early as the sixteenth century "bit" was British slang for any small coin. In the Southwest United States over two centuries ago, the term was applied to the Mexican "real" (worth about twelve and a half cents) which was used interchangeably with the local currency. The expression "two bits," two Mexican "reales," referred to twenty-five cents. When the United States quarter was coined, it was called "two bits"-a name that became popular throughout the century.

Robert Hendrickson, *The Henry Holt Encyclopedia of Word and Phrase Origins* (New York: Henry Holt, 1987), s.v. "two bits." William Morris and Mary Morris, *Morris Dictionary of Word and Phrase Origins, 2d ed.* (New York: Harper & Row, 1988), s.v. "two bits."

What does the Black Liberation Flag represent?

The Black Liberation Flag or Solidarity Flag is said to have first represented the Zingh Empire over 15,000 years ago. The emperor Tirus Afrik supposedly used this flag. American Black Nationalist leader Marcus Garvey (1887-1940), who founded the "Back to Africa" movement, used the flag to inspire followers in the 1920s and 1930s. It became popular again in the 1960s with the increased interest in African-American heritage and Black awareness. The black color in the flag symbolizes the association of Blacks of America with Blacks across the globe. The red reflects Black blood spilled in the quest for freedom. The green represents land and fertility, growth, and prosperity.

Whitney Smith, *The Flag Book of the United States, revised ed.* (New York: William Morrow, 1975), 274. *St. Louis Post-Dispatch* 11 March 1973.

What is an eponym?

An eponym is the real or legendary person whose name has become the name of a place, an event, an artifact, or a characteristic. Below are listed some examples.

(Giovanni Jacopo) Casanova	lover, adventurer
Croesus	wealth
(Gabriel Daniel) Fahrenheit	Fahrenheit degree
Goliath (of the Bible)	giant
Helen (of Troy)	beauty
Hercules	one of great physical strength
Jezebel	loose woman
Machiavelli	duplicity
(Jean) Martinet	strict disciplinarian
(Sir Robert) Peel	Bobby or peeler for policeman
Sherlock Holmes	detective

Hugh C. Holman and William Harmon, *A Handbook to Literature, 5th ed.* (New York: Macmillan, 1986), 184. James A. Ruffner, ed., *Eponyms Dictionaries Index* (Detroit: Gale Research, 1977), 70, 115, 210, 257, 300, 312, 436, 511, 607. Kenneth G. Wilson, *The Columbia Guide to Standard American English* (New York: Columbia University Press, 1993), 174.

Animal Care and Health

How can bluebirds be encouraged to nest in a particular location?

Bluebirds may be attracted by providing nesting boxes and perches, having an area of low or sparse vegetation, and planting nearby trees, vines, or shrubs such as blueberries, honeysuckle, and crabapples. Bluebirds prefer open countryside with low undergrowth. Parks, golf courses, and open lawns are their preferred habitats. In the last 40 years eastern bluebird populations have declined 90 percent coinciding with the disappearing farmland, widespread use of pesticides, and an increase in nest competitors (house sparrows and European starlings). Artificial nesting boxes sometimes provides more secure nesting places than do natural nest sites, because artificial structures can be built to resist predators. Bluebird boxes can be made with entrance holes (1.5 inches or 4 centimeters in diameter) small enough to exclude starlings and can have special raccoon guards on mounting poles. Mounted 3 to 6 feet (1 to 2 meters) above ground (to discourage predators) with the nesting boxes being no closer than 100 feet (30 meters). The box should have a tree within 50 feet (15 meters) so that the fledglings can perch. The box should have a 4 inch by 4 inch floor (11 by 11 centimeters), 8 to 12 inches (20 to 31 centimeters) in height, with the 1.5 inch hole 6 to 10 inches (15 to 25 centimeters) above the floor.

Stephen W. Kress, *The Audubon Society Guide to Attracting Birds* (New York: Charles Scribner's Sons, 1985), 183, 204-211. Donald Stokes, *The Bluebird Book* (Boston: Little, Brown, 1991), 30-34.

Besides humans, which animals are the most intelligent?

According to Edward O. Wilson, a behavioral biologist, the ten most intelligent animals ranked in descending order are the following:

Chimpanzees (two species)
Gorillas
Orangutans
Baboons (seven species, including drill and mandrill)
Gibbons (seven species)
Monkeys (many species, especially macaques, the patas, and the Celebes black ape)
Smaller toothed whales (several species, especially killer whales)
Dolphins (many of the approximately 80 species)
Elephants (two species)
Pigs

Wilson defined intelligence as the ability to learn a wide range of tasks with speed and skill. He took into account the ratio of the size of the brain to the size of the bulk of the body.

Russell Ash, *The Top Ten of Everything* (London: Dorling Kindersley, 1993), 35: Irving Wallace, The Book of Lists #2 (Morrow, 1980), 104.

Which plants are poisonous to cats?

Certain common houseplants are poisonous to cats and they should not be allowed to eat the following:

Caladium (Elephant's ears)
Dieffenbachia (Dumb cane)
Euphorbia pulcherrima (Poinsettia)
Hedera (True ivy)
Mistletoe
Oleander
Philodendron
Prunus laurocerasus (Common or cherry laurel)
Rhododendron (Azalea)
Solanum capiscastrum (Winter or False Jerusalem cherry)

David Taylor and Daphne Negus, *The Ultimate Cat Book* (New York: Simon and Schuster, 1989), 141. David Taylor, *You & Your Cat* (New York: Alfred Knopf, 1988), 147.

What is the proper size for the hole in a bird house for the purple martin?

The opening should be 2.5 inches in diameter (6 centimeters). Native Americans were the first to attract the martins to artificial nesting sites by hanging dried gourds from trees. In the southeastern United States today, this method remains popular. As with all martin houses, the nesting box or gourd should be mounted on a pole at least 15 feet (4.5 meters) from any buildings or overhanging branches. Purple martins avoid nests that are vulnerable to climbing predators. They like to be near water. Purple martins are highly social; they readily accept multiple housing units. In the eastern United States these units are popular structures to attract colonies of birds, but in the west these birds shun man-made structures.

Stephen W. Kress, *The Audubon Society Guide to Attracting Birds* (New York: Charles Scribner's Sons, 1985), 211. Walter E. Schutz, *How to Attract, House, and Feed Birds* (New York: Collier, 1974), 175.

Which types of birds make the best pets?

There are several birds that make good house pets and have a reasonable life expectancy:

Bird	Life expectancy in years	Considerations
Finch	2-3	Easy care
Canary	8-10	Easy care; males sing
Budgerigar	8-15	Easy care
Cockatiel	15-20	Easy care; easy to train
Lovebird	15-20	Cute, but not easy to care for or train
Amazon parrot	50-60	Good talkers, but can be screamers
African grey parrot	50-60	Talkers; never scream

Prevention's Giant Book of Health Facts (Emmaus, PA: Rodale Press, 1991), 463.

What kind of care do tadpoles need?

Tadpoles require special care. Keep the frog eggs and the tadpoles that hatch from them in water at all times, changing half of the water volume no more than once a week. The best diet is probably baby cereal having a high protein content, fresh greens, and bits of egg yolk. Provide a rock island when the legs of the tadpoles appear. A five-gallon (18.92-liter) tank is sufficient for a half dozen tadpoles. When they mature (lose their tails and have grown legs) they should be released in a pond or by the lake shore.

Emil P. Dolensek, *A Practical Guide to Impractical Pets* (New York: Viking Press, 1976), 67-68.

What are some high-tech medical treatments for pets?

Advanced medical treatments that are developed to save human lives are being used with increasing frequency on household pets. Procedures such as CAT scans, chemotherapy, and heart surgery are available at specialized veterinary centers. Local clinics are also providing more sophisticated medical care at the request of pet owners. While prize livestock and race horses have traditionally received advance medical care due to their high economic values, pet owners have limited the amount they are willing to spend on a sick animal. They turned to euthanasia rather than pay for expensive procedures. This practice appears to be on the wane, as spending on veterinary services increases. Pet owners are spending as much as $4,000 dollars on major surgery, a cost that is not covered by common insurance policies. This has stimulated debate over whether it is ethical to spend this kind of money on animals while many humans go without health care. On the other hand, many veterinarians are also beginning to question the right of pet owners to have a healthy animal euthanized.

Jon Nordheimer, "High-Tech Medicine At High-Rise Costs Is Keeping Pets Fit," *The New York Times* 17 September 1990.

When did "Butterfly Town U.S.A." formally provide a haven for its namesakes?

Pacific Grove, California, located on the Monterey peninsula, is also known as "Butterfly Town U.S.A." due to the fact that thousands of monarch butterflies migrate to the spot each year. In 1990, the town's residents voted on Measure G, a $1.2 million bond issue, for the purpose of establishing a protected area for the insects. The measure passed with 69 percent of the voters in favor of the sanctuary; 31 percent of voters opposed the bond issue. Pacific Grove was then able to purchase a 2.7 acre plot that would serve as a habitat for the butterflies.

The New York Times 8 November 1990.

How can pets be treated to remove skunk odor?

Purchase one of the products specifically designed to counteract skunk odor from a pet store. Most of these are of the enzyme or bacterial enzyme variety and can be used without washing the pet first.

Don Aslett, *Pet Clean-Up Made Easy* (Cincinnati: Writer's Digest Books, 1988), 14.

Where is Hawk Mountain Sanctuary?

Hawk Mountain Sanctuary, founded in 1934 as the first sanctuary in the world to offer protection to migrating hawks and eagles, is near Harrisburg, Pennsylvania, on the Kittatinny Ridge. Each year between the months of August and December, over 15,000 migrating birds pass by. Rare species such as Golden Eagles may be seen there.

Donald S. Heintzelman, *A Guide to Eastern Hawk Watching* (University Park: Pennsylvania State University Press, 1976), 57, 82-83.

When was the first zoo in the United States established?

The Philadelphia Zoological Garden, chartered in 1859, was the first zoo in the United States. The zoo was delayed by the American Civil War, financial difficulties, and restrictions on transporting wild animals. It opened in 1874 on 33 acres with 282 animals.

Victor J. Danilov, *America's Science Museums* (Westport, CT: Greenwood Press, 1990), 422.

Is there a recipe for homemade dog biscuits?

Homemade dog biscuits can be made by combining 31/2 cups all purpose flour, 2 cups whole wheat flour, 1 cup rye flour, 1 cup corn meal, 2 cups bulgur, 1/2 cup nonfat dry milk, and four teaspoons of salt. Cut in 2/3 cup of shortening, lard, bacon fat, or lard.

Dissolve one package of dry yeast in 1/4 cup of warm water. Combine the dissolved yeast, one pint of chicken stock, and the dry ingredients. Knead for approximately three minutes.

Roll the dough into a quarter-inch sheet. Cut with cookie cutters. Place on a baking sheet and brush with a wash of egg and milk.

Bake in a 300-degree oven for 45 minutes. Allow to stand in the oven overnight.

National Observer 23 November 1974.

What are the ten most trainable dog breeds?

The ten most trainable dog breeds, in order of ranking, are the Border Collie, Poodle, German Shepherd, Golden Retriever, Doberman Pinscher, Shetland Sheepdog, Labrador Retriever, Papillon, Rottweiler, and the Australian Cattle dog.

"How dogs rate in trainability," *USA Today* 28 March 1994.

Is there a national pet hot line for missing pets?

In 1992, the American Humane Association (AHA) set up a telephone system for reporting and identifying lost pets. The 24-

hour hot line features one number, 800-755-8111, for reporting stray animals and another, 900-535-1515, for registering a lost pet. The 900 number costs $1.95 per minute; the procedure of giving the pet's description and giving contact information takes about four minutes. Using Sprint's voice processing computer system, the service matches calls and gives owners an instant match if their pet has been found. Owners can call for status reports for two weeks. In this way, the AHA hopes to improve the chances of finding a lost pet; traditionally, only 16 percent of missing dogs are found and just two percent of lost cats are recovered. Profits from the service benefit the AHA.

Anita Manning, "Hot line helps trace stray pets," *USA Today* 10 August 1992.

Is it possible to adopt a wild horse or burro?

Under the Federal Wild Horse and Burro Act of 1971, it is possible to adopt a wild horse or burro. The act was passed in order to manage the growing populations of these animals; because of a lack of natural predators and increased federal protection, herds of wild horses and burros are outgrowing the ranges dedicated for their use. Since 1973 the U.S. Bureau of Land Management has removed excess animals from the herds and placed them in the Adopt-a-Horse-or-Burro Program. These animals are of no particular strain and are not totally acclimated to people when they are offered for adoption. Each year some 8,000 horses and 1,000 burros are available through the adoption program. There is a charge of $125 to adopt a horse and $75 to adopt a burro. The federal government also requires that a suitable home be provided upon adoption; the animals must be kept in an enclosed corral with a minimum of 400 square feet per animal. Exercising requirements and stable specifications are also made. When these conditions are met, a title is issued to the owner at the end of the first year of adoption.

Department of the Interior, *So You'd Like To Adopt: America's Wild Horses and Burros* (Washington, DC: Bureau of Land Management, 1995), 1-11. "Wild Horse Preserve Next Goal in Drive," *New York Times* 30 July 1971.

Is there a sanctuary for wild horses in the United States?

The U.S. Bureau of Land Management opened the first wild horse sanctuary on October 5, 1988, in the Black Hills of South Dakota. The 8,300-acre range was located at Hell's Canyon, southwest of the city of Hot Springs. Described as "an old-age home for wild horses" by wild horse specialist Donald Heinze, the sanctuary created a place for mustangs that are too old to be tamed. A federal adoption program places many wild horses with owners; unwanted horses were kept in pens under conditions that were criticized by animal rights groups. Such groups have also expressed concern about harsh South Dakota winters. The sanctuary is run by the non-profit Institute of Range and American Mustang.

Finding a place for wild horses became a problem when ranchers complained that mustangs overgrazed public lands used for livestock. The wild horse population has grown rapidly since 1971, when Congress passed the Wild Free-Roaming Horse and Burro Act, which protects the animals and keeps them from being captured and sold to slaughterhouses.

Dirk Johnson, "Nation's First Sanctuary for Wild Horse Opens," *New York Times* 6 October 1988.

Drugs and Medicinal Herbs

What is China white?

China white is a powerful synthetic heroin and even small amounts can be fatal. The chemical name is 3-methylfentanyl.

James E. Tunnell, *Latest Intelligence* (Blue Ridge Summit, PA: TAB, 1990), 39.

From what plant is taxol extracted?

Taxol is produced from the bark of the western or Pacific yew (*Taxus brevifolia*). It has been shown to inhibit the growth of HeLa cells (human tumor cells) and is a promising new treatment for several kinds of cancer. The bad news is that it is in short supply and may not be able to be synthesized on a commercial scale due to its molecular configuration.

Audubon Magazine March/April 1992.

What are monoclonal antibodies?

Monoclonal antibodies are artificially produced antibodies, designed to neutralize a specific foreign protein (antigen). Cloned cells (genetically identical) are stimulated to produce antibodies to the target antigen. Most monoclonal antibody work so far has used cloned cells from mice infected with cancer. In some cases they are used to destroy cancer cells directly; in others they carry other drugs to combat the cancer cells.

The American Medical Association Encyclopedia of Medicine (New York: Random House, 1989), 115. Anne Galperin, *Gynecological Disorders* (New York: Chelsea House, 1991), 85-86.

How is patient-controlled analgesia (PCA) administrated?

Patient-Controlled Analgesia (PCA) a drug-delivery system that dispenses a preset intravenous (IV) dose of a narcotic analgesic for reduction to pain when the patient pushes a switch on an electric cord. The device consists of a computerized pump with a chamber containing a syringe holding up to 60 milliliters of a drug. The patient administers a dose of narcotic when the need for pain relief arises. A lockout interval device automatically inactivates the system if the patient tries to increase the amount of narcotic within a preset time period.

Mosby's Medical, Nursing, and Allied Health Dictionary, 3d ed. (St. Louis, MO: Mosby, 1990), 888.

What is pharmacognosy?

Pharmacognosy is the science of natural drugs and their physical, botanical, and chemical properties.

Taber's Cyclopedic Medical Dictionary, 16th ed. (Philadelphia: Davis, 1989), 1380.

Where is marijuana grown legally in the United States?

The federal marijuana farm at the University of Mississippi was legally established in 1968. This farm supplies most of the marijuana (*Cannabis sativa*) used for official medical research.

Irving Wallace, *The Book of Lists #2* (New York: Morrow, 1980), 88.

How does RU-486, the abortion pill, cause a woman to abort a fetus?

A pill containing RU-486 (mifepristone) causes the abortion of a fetus by providing the fertilized embryo with an incompatible uterine environment to terminate the pregnancy within 45 days of fertilization. It is currently used in China and France.

Joe Graedon and Dr. Teresa Graedon, *Graedon's Best Medicine* (New York: Bantam Books, 1991), 355. *Science* 24 November 1989.

What does the phrase "balm of Gilead" mean?

The phrase "balm of Gilead" refers generally to any form of healing or solace. It has its origins in the biblical quotation (Jeremiah 8:22): "Is there no balm in Gilead..."? Gilead, an ancient Palestinian city, was known for its medicines and aromatic herbs.

Abraham H. Lass, David Kiremidjian, and Ruth M. Goldstein, *The Facts On File Dictionary of Classical, Biblical, and Literary Allusions* (New York: Facts on File, 1987), s.v. "Balm in Gilead."

What is the origin of the symbol "Rx" on prescriptions?

The symbol Rx, commonly seen on medical prescriptions, is a combination of the letter "R," for "recipe," and the symbol of Jupiter. It is an ancient reference, indicating that by the favor of the Greek god Jupiter, the patron god of medicine, the patient should take the following recommended dosage.

E. Cobham Brewer, *The Dictionary of Phrase and Fable,* (New York: Avenel Books, 1978), 1031.

What was laetrile?

Laetrile was an apricot-pit extract once believed to be a cure for cancer. Before its discredit by the U.S. National Cancer Institute in 1981, laetrile advocates had forced legalization of its use in 23 states.

Follow-Up, *Consumer Reports* July 1981. "Laetrile Flunks," *Time* 11 May 1981.

What are the common medication measures?

Approximate equivalents of apothecary volume measures are given below.

Volume	Equivalent
1 minim	0.06 milliliters
1 1/2 minim	1.00 milliliters
1 dram	4.00 milliliters
1 t (teaspoon)	60 drops
3 t (teaspoons)	1/2 ounce
1 T (tablespoon)	1/2 ounce
2 T (tablespoons)	1 ounce
1 C (cup)	8 ounces or 30 milliliters

Approximate equivalents of apothecary weight measures are given below.

Weight	Equivalent
1 grain	60 milligrams or 1/2 dram
60 grains	1 dram or 3.75 grams
8 drams	1 ounce or 30 grams

Lorrie N. Hegstad, *Essential Drug Dosage Calculations* (Bowie, MD: R.J. Brady, 1983), 23. Eldra Pearl Solomon and Gloria A. Phillips, *Understanding Human Anatomy and Physiology* (Philadelphia: W.B. Saunders, 1987), 369.

How deadly is strychnine?

The fatal dose of strychnine or deadly nightshade (the plant from which it is obtained) is 15 to 30 milligrams. It causes severe convulsions and respiratory failure. If the patient lives for 24 hours, recovery is probable.

Robert H. Dreisbach, *Handbook of Poisoning, 12th ed.* (Norwalk, CT: Appleton & Lange, 1987), 418-19.

How deadly is *Amanita phalloides*?

The poisonous mushroom *Amanita phalloides* has a fatality rate of about 50 percent. Ingestion of part of one mushroom may be sufficient to cause death. Over 100 fatalities occur each year from eating poisonous mushrooms, with more than 90 percent caused by the *Amanita phalloides* group.

Robert H. Dreisbach, *Handbook of Poisoning, 12th ed.* (Norwalk, CT: Appleton & Lange, 1987), 504-5. Sybil P. Parker, *Synopsis & Classification of Living Organisms* (New York: McGraw-Hill, 1982), 1:254.

What is the deadliest natural toxin to humans?

Botulinal toxin, produced by the bacterium *Clostridium botulinum,* is the most potent poison to humans. It has an estimated lethal dose in the bloodstream of 10-9 milligrams per kilogram. It causes botulism, a severe neuroparalytic disease that travels to the junctions of skeletal muscles and nerves, where it blocks the release of the neurotransmitter acetylcholine, causing muscle weakness and paralysis, and impairing vision, speech, and swallowing. Death occurs when the respiratory muscles are paralyzed; this usually occurs during the first week of illness. Mortality from botulism is about 25 percent.

Because the bacterium can form the toxin only in the absence of oxygen, canned goods and meat products wrapped in airtight casings are potential sources of botulism. The toxin is more likely to grow in low-acid foods, such as mushrooms, peas, corn, or beans rather than high-acid foods like tomatoes. However, some new tomato hybrids are not acidic enough to prevent the bacteria from forming the toxin. Foods being canned must be heated to a temperature high enough and for a long enough time to kill the bacteria present. Suspect food includes any canned or jarred food product with a swollen lid or can. Ironically, this dreaded toxin in tiny doses is being used to treat disorders that bring on involuntary muscle contractions, twisting, etc. The U.S. Food and Drug Administration (FDA) has approved the toxin for treatment of strabismus (misalignment of the eyes), blepharospasm (forcible closure of eyelids), and hemifacial spasm (muscular contraction on one side of the face).

Cecil Textbook of Medicine, 18th ed. (Philadelphia: Saunders, 1988), 1633. Harold Hillman, *Kitchen Science, rev. ed.* (Boston: Houghton Mifflin, 1989), 267-68. *New Scientist* 8 December 1990).

Which herbs are considered aphrodisiacs?

Several herbs have traditionally been considered to possess an aphrodisiac quality. Among these herbs are: anemone, black pepper, cardamom, cyclamen, jasmine, juniper, maidenhair fern, male fern, navelwort, pansy, periwinkle, rose, sandalwood, valerian, and wild poppy.

Harry E. Wedeck, *Dictionary of Aphrodisiacs* (New York: M. Evans, 1989), 75.

What does the term "backstabbing" refer to with regard to drug users?

"Backstabbing" is a phenomenon that occurs in the families of drug users. A drug user will borrow money from family members to support his or her habit. Eventually family members realize that the individual is using drugs and can become emotionally and financially drained or refuse to provide support. At this point, the user will often steal valuables from the household.

Department of Justice, *Drugs, Crime, and the Justice System: A National Report from the Bureau of Justice Statistics* (Washington, DC: Government Printing Office, 1992), 9.

Is there alcohol in mouthwash?

Many mouthwashes on the market contain alcohol. Some of these included Listerine, 26.9 percent; Cepacol, 14 percent; Scope, 18.5 percent; and Signal, 15.5 percent.

Robert O'Brien et al. , *The Encyclopedia of Drug Abuse, 2d ed.* (New York: Facts on File, 1992), s.v. "mouthwash."

What are the most popular over-the-counter medications in the United States?

The list of best-selling over-the-counter medications in the United States can be divided into three categories. Sales of pain relievers are led by Tylenol, Advil, Bayer, Excedrin, and Anacin. The most popular cold and cough remedies are Vicks, Robitussin, Halls, Sudafed, and Alka-Seltzer Plus. Americans with troubled stomachs turn first to Mylanta, then Tums, Maalox, and Rolaids; Pepto-Bismol and Alka-Seltzer are tied for the number-five slot in this category.

Superbrands 18 October 1993.

What were patent medicines of nineteenth-century America, and what were some of their ingredients?

In nineteenth-century America many home-mixed medicines were authoritatively called patent medicines. The free use of the term patent was, in fact, a ruse to lead the consumer into believing that the product had the approval of the federal government.

Strychnine was often used as an ingredient because it gave the consumers a feeling that they were getting their money's worth. Morphine and opium derivatives were used freely in painkillers, and petroleum advertised as Seneca or rock oil was also used. Tomato extracts were marketed as Phelps' Compound Tomato Pills and Dr. Miles's Compound Extract of Tomato.

Sarsaparilla was advertised to aid in the relief of "debility peculiar to the spring." Legislation, creating the U.S. Food and Drug Administration which regulated the production and advertising of medicinal products, put an end to these patent medicines.

Gerald Carson, *The Old Country Store* (New York: Oxford University Press, 1954), 238-39.

Why are anabolic steroids harmful?

Anabolic (protein-building) steroids are drugs that mimic the effects of testosterone and other male sex hormones. They can build muscle tissue, strengthen bone, and speed muscle recovery following exercise or injury. They are sometimes prescribed to treat osteoporosis in postmenopausal women and some types of anemia. Some athletes use anabolic steroids to build muscle strength and bulk, and to allow a more rigorous training schedule. Weight lifters, field event athletes, and body builders are most likely to use anabolic steroids. The drugs are banned from most organized competitions because of the dangers they pose to health and to prevent an unfair advantage.

Adverse effects include hypertension, acne, edema, and damage to liver, heart, and adrenal glands. Psychiatric symptoms can include hallucinations, paranoid delusions, and manic episodes. In men, anabolic steroids can cause infertility, impotence, and premature balding. Women can develop masculine characteristics, such as excessive hair growth, male-pattern balding, disruption of menstruation, and deepening of the voice. Children and adolescents can develop problems in growing bones, leading to short stature.

The American Medical Association Encyclopedia of Medicine (New York: Random House, 1989), 935, 940-41, 1049-50. Edward Edelson, *Sports Medicine* (New York: Chelsea House, 1988), 78. *Prevention's Giant Book of Health Facts* (Emmaus, PA: Rodale Press, 1991), 214.

What is meant by the term orphan drugs?

Orphan drugs are intended to treat diseases that affect fewer than 200,000 Americans. With little chance of making money, a drug company is not likely to undertake the necessary research and expense of finding drugs which might treat these diseases. The Orphan Drug Act of 1983 offers a number of incentives to drug companies to encourage development of these drugs. The act has provided hope for millions of people with rare and otherwise untreatable conditions.

Current Health April 1990.

How is the drug Clomid used to treat infertility?

In female infertility, Clomid acts by stimulating gonadotropin release, which then stimulates ovulation. In men, the drug is used to stimulate sperm production. Multiple births may occur as a result of the treatment.

The American Medical Association Encyclopedia of Medicine (New York: Random House, 1989), 284. *Current Medical Diagnosis and Treatment 1991, 30th ed.* (Norwalk, CT: Appleton & Lange, 1991), 524.

Which tests detect cocaine use?

Urine tests detect cocaine used by a person within the past 24 to 36 hours. Hair analysis can detect cocaine used more than a year ago because hair grows only about 0.5 inch (1.27 centimeters) per month.

U.S.A. Today 15 December 1989.

How long do chemicals from marijuana stay in the body?

When marijuana is smoked, tetrahydrocannabinol (THC), its active ingredient, is absorbed primarily in the fat tissues. The body transforms the THC into metabolites which can be detected by urine tests for up to a week. Tests involving radioactively labeled THC have traced the metabolites for up to a month. The retention of labeled THC in humans is about 40 percent at three days and 30 percent at one week.

U.S. Department of Health and Human Services, *Marijuana* (Washington, DC: U.S. Department of Health and Human Services, 1984), unpaged.

Who discovered the antibiotic streptomycin?

The Russian-born microbiologist Selman A. Waksman (1888-1973) coined the term antibiotic and subsequently discovered streptomycin in 1943. In 1944 Merck and Company agreed to produce it to be used against tuberculosis and tuberculosis meningitis. Because the drug can adversely affect hearing and balance, careful control of dosage is needed.

Dictionary of American Medical Biography, (Westport, CT: Greenwood, 1984), 2:769-70. Harry Harris, *Good Old-Fashioned Yankee Ingenuity* (Chelsea, MI: Scarborough House, 1990), 279-80.

How long can a prescription drug be kept?

Generally a prescription drug should not be more than one year old. Some over-the-counter medications have an expiration date on their box or container. A cream should not be used if it has separated into its components. Although some general guidelines are given below, when in doubt, throw it out.

Remedy	Maximum shelf life in years
Cold tablets	1 to 2
Laxatives	2 to 3
Minerals	6 or more
Nonprescription painkiller tablets	1 to 4
Prescription antibiotics	2 to 3
Prescription antihypertension tablets	2 to 4
Travel sickness tablets	2
Vitamins (protected from heat, light and moisture)	6 or more

New York Public Library Desk Reference (New York: Webster's New World, 1989), 616.

What is "free-basing"?

"Free-basing" is an extremely dangerous method of smoking cocaine. It is a refining process that extracts the drug from its hydrochloride salt base. The resulting granules are then smoked using a glass water pipe, sometimes using rum instead of water. A torch, lighter, or matches are used to burn the melting cocaine. The high produced by the technique is short and intense. Cocaine users who practice this smoking method are more likely to become addicted to the drug. Free-basing accidents are common; such an incident nearly killed comedian Richard Pryor in 1980.

"Melting Down," *Time* 11 April 1983.

Who discovered penicillin?

British bacteriologist Sir Alexander Fleming (1881-1955) discovered the bacteria-killing property of penicillin in 1928. Fleming noticed that no bacteria grew around bits of the *penicillium notatum* fungus that accidentally fell into a bacterial culture in his laboratory. However, although penicillin was clinically used, it was not until 1941 that Dr. Howard Florey (1898-1968) purified and tested it. The first large-scale plant to produce penicillin was constructed under the direction of Dr. Ernest Chain (1906-1979). By 1945 penicillin was commercially available. In that year, Chain, Florey, and Fleming received a joint Nobel Prize for their work.

Patrick Robertson, *The Book of Firsts* (New York: Clarkson N. Potter, 1974), 124-25. Dennis Sanders, *The First of Everything* (New York: Delacorte, 1981), 381.

How many of the medications used today are derived from plants?

Of the more than 250,000 known plant species, less than one percent have been thoroughly tested for medical applications. Yet out of this tiny portion have come 25 percent of our prescription medicines. The United States National Cancer Institute has identified 3,000 plants from which anti-cancer drugs are or can be made. This includes ginseng (*Panax quinquefolius*), Asian mayapple (*Podophyllum hexandrum*), western yew (*Taxus brevifolia*), and rosy periwinkle. 70 percent of these 3,000 come from rain forests, which also are a source of countless other drugs for diseases and infections. Rain forest plants are rich in so-called secondary metabolites, particularly alkaloids, which biochemists believe the plants produce to protect them from disease and insect attack.

McGraw-Hill Yearbook of Science and Technology 1991 (New York: McGraw-Hill, 1990), 202-3. *National Wildlife* April/May 1992. *New Scientist* August 1991.

Which part of mistletoe is poisonous?

The white berries of mistletoe contain toxic amines, which cause acute stomach and intestinal irritation with diarrhea and a slow pulse. Mistletoe should be considered a potentially dangerous Christmas decoration, especially if children are around.

Will H. Blackwell, *Poisonous and Medicinal Plants* (Englewood Cliffs, NJ: Prentice-Hall, 1990), 241-42.

What is the poison on arrows used by South American Indians to kill prey and enemies?

The botanical poison on arrows used by the Aucas and similar tribes in the South American jungles is curare. It is a sticky, black mixture with the appearance of liquorice and is processed from either of two different vines. One is a liana (*Chondodendron tomentosum*); the other is a massive tree-like vine (*Strychonos quianensis*).

Edward R. Ricciuti, *The Devil's Garden: Facts and Folklore of Perilous Plants* (New York: Walker, 1978), 119-20.

How is activated charcoal used medically?

Activated charcoal is an organic substance, such as burned wood or coal, that has been heated to approximately 1,000 degrees Fahrenheit (537 degrees Celsius) in a controlled atmosphere. The result is a fine powder containing thousands of pores that have great absorbent qualities to rapidly absorb toxins and poisons. Activated charcoal is used medically in the treatment of drug overdoses and poisonings.

William Tichy, *Poisons: Antidotes and Anecdotes* (New York: Sterling, 1977), 69.

How is a mustard plaster made?

To make a mustard plaster, mix 1 tablespoon of powdered mustard and 4 tablespoons of flour. Add enough warm water to make a runny paste. Put the mixture in a folded cloth and apply to the chest. Add olive oil first to the skin if the patient has a delicate skin.

Dian Dincin Buchman, *Dian Dincin Buchman's Herbal Medicine* (New York: Gramercy, 1980), 99-100.

What do the terms "false positive" and "false negative" mean?

Whenever tests measuring the presence or absence of a substance are conducted, there is always the possibility that they will reflect incorrect results. Sometimes a drug test will indicate the presence of a narcotic when none is present. This is called a "false positive" result. A "false negative" result can also occur if drugs are present in a person's system, but they are not discovered by the drug test. "False positive" and "false negative" results can occur as the result of improper handling of specimens, poorly conducted tests, or computer error.

Robert O'Brien et al. , *The Encyclopedia of Drug Abuse, 2d ed.* (New York: Facts on File, 1992), s.v. "false negative, false positive."

What is the history of amphetamines?

First synthesized in 1887, an amphetamine is a drug compound that acts as a stimulant to the central nervous system. When prescribed therapeutically, the physical effects include increased breathing and heart rate, rise in blood pressure, reduction in appetite, and dilation of the pupils. Psychological effects are feelings of euphoria, enhanced self-confidence, greater energy, and increased capacity for concentration. In 1927 amphetamines were first used medicinally as a stimulant and as a nasal decongestant, and they were marketed commercially under the trade name Benzedrine in 1932. The drug was first used to calm hyperactive children in 1937.

In the 1940s amphetamines were issued by the British, American, German, and Japanese governments to their troops during World War II (1939-45) to counteract fatigue, elevate mood, and increase endurance. Also at this time, use of amphetamines by athletes and businessmen was reported, and a black market emerged in which "pep pills" were sold to students and truck drivers.

The manufacture of Benzedrine inhalants was discontinued in 1949 due to the potential danger of overdoses.

The first "speedballs" were made by mixing amphetamines with heroin and used intravenously by American soldiers in Korea and Japan during the 1950s. While amphetamines continued to be prescribed therapeutically in the 1950s for narcolepsy, chronic fatigue, and as an anorectic, the abuse, whether the drug was obtained by prescription or on the black market, was becoming more widespread.

In the United States in the 1960s, amphetamine abusers became known as "speed freaks," injecting massive doses of methamphetamine, an extremely potent amphetamine derivative that causes a "rush" or a "flash."

Throughout the 1970s and 1980s, amphetamine abuse continued and increased. Studies show that amphetamine use by United States youth ages 18 years through 25 years was at 12 percent in 1972, 18 percent in 1982, and 11.4 percent in 1988. Amphetamines used commercially are regulated by the Controlled Substances Act of 1972. Illegal amphetamines and amphetamine derivatives are smuggled into the United States from Colombia and Mexico and sold on the black market or manufactured illicitly in the United States. Currently, phenolpropylenolamine is available without a prescription and heavily advertised in magazines that are youth oriented. Taken in large quantities, this drug mimics all the effects of amphetamines.

Robert O'Brien, et al. , *The Encyclopedia of Drug Abuse, 2d ed.* (New York: Facts on File, 1992), s.v. "amphetamines."

General Psychology

What is an anal personality?

An anal personality, also referred to an anal character, is said to be someone who remains fixated at the anal stage and who, therefore, displays characteristics developed at that stage. The anal retentive character is thought to be miserly, painstaking, and stubborn. The anal expulsive character is described as charitable, lackadaisical, and easygoing, while the anal aggressive character is characterized as mean and destructive. These descriptions are based on the work of psychoanalyst Sigmund Freud (1856-1939) who said that the anal stage is the second libidinal stage. He held that during this time a child from eighteen months to three years of age enjoys its urine and feces. In the anal explusive stage, the child enjoys expelling fees and in the anal retentive state, the child enjoys retaining feces. There is, however, no evidence that these characteristics are developed during the anal stage.

Stuart Sutherland, *The International Dictionary of Psychology* (New York: Continuum, 1989), s.v. "anal character."

Where did IQ tests originate?

The first Intelligence Quotient IQ tests were conducted in France by psychologist Alfred Binet (1857-1911) and his colleague Theodore Simon in an attempt to distinguish between normal and feebleminded children. Binet created 30 task-related problems involving repeating digits, word definition, comparison of line lengths, and naming objects. Using this criteria, Binet was able to determine whether a child had the learning capability of a two-year-old; five-year-old; or nine-year-old child. In 1908 Binet revised his test by dividing the mental age of test takers by their chronological age, coming up with an Intelligence Quotient of 100 as average for any given age.

Jane Polley, ed., *Stories Behind Everyday Things* (Pleasantville, NY: Reader's Digest Association, 1980), 193.

What is posttraumatic stress disorder?

When people undergo an extremely traumatic experience such as assault, rape, military combat, natural disasters, or witnessing atrocities committed by others, they often suffer a severe psychological reaction, which is referred to as posttraumatic stress disorder. People suffering from posttraumatic stress disorder may be plagued by sleeplessness, inability to concentrate, nightmares, flashbacks of the traumatic experience, or excessive nervousness.

Robert L. Barker, *The Social Work Dictionary* (Silver Spring, MD: National Association of Social Workers, 1987), s.v. "posttraumatic stress disorder."

What are the first and second laws of animal appeal?

The first law of animal appeal is that the popularity of an animal is directly correlated with the number of anthropomorphic features it possesses.

The second law of animal appeal is that the age of a child is inversely correlated with the size of the animals it prefers.

Harold Faber, *The Book of Laws* (New York: Times Books, 1979), 4.

What is school phobia?

School phobia is a fear of the school building and can be suffered by young children who are just beginning to go to school. It is associated with separation anxiety, the fear of leaving home and family. Going to school may be the first instance when a child is separated from their parents and home. A teacher can do several things to help a child suffering from school phobia: talk to the child about the fear; discuss the child's previous behavior with the parents; show respect for the child's fears; do not indulge fears, but give feedback that rewards independence; have a classmate serve as confidant to the child; let the child bring an object from home that will comfort them; and encourage classroom discussion about overcoming fears.

Mary Beth Spann, "Helping the Fearful Child Adjust to School," *Instructor* October 1993.

What is the new science of chaos?

Chaos or chaotic behavior is the behavior of a system whose final state depends very sensitively on the initial conditions. The behavior is unpredictable and cannot be distinguished from a random process, even though it is strictly determinate in a mathematical sense. Chaos studies the complex and irregular behavior of many systems in nature, such as changing weather patterns, flow of turbulent fluids, and swinging pendulums. Scientists once thought they could make exact predictions about such systems, but found that a tiny difference in starting conditions can lead to greatly different results. Chaotic systems do obey certain rules which mathematicians have described with equations, but the science of chaos demonstrates the difficulty of predicting the long-range behavior of chaotic systems.

The McGraw-Hill Dictionary of Scientific and Technical Terms, 4th ed. (New York: McGraw-Hill, 1989), 329. *World Book Encyclopedia* (Chicago: World Book, 1990), 3:376.

Who was the "Wild Boy of Aveyron"?

In the year 1800 a young boy, perhaps 11 or 12 years old, was found in the south of France who came to be known as the "Wild Boy of Aveyron." The child appeared to have lived in the countryside, without human contact for most of his short life. He was naked, scarred, and had absolutely no language skills. People who romanticized the idea of the "noble savage" brought him to Paris, where he was briefly treated as a celebrity. His uncivilized behavior soon prompted the decision that he was deaf, mute, and an "idiot." The boy was then sent to an institute for deaf-mutes, and he came under the care of Doctor Jean-Marc-Gaspard Itard (1775-1838). The doctor worked carefully with the boy, giving him the name Victor. Eventually, Victor learned to keep himself clean, to control his actions, and to say a few words. His development did not go beyond this, however, although he lived to the age of 40.

ABC's of the Human Mind (Pleasantville, NY: Reader's Digest Association, 1990).

What did Carl Jung mean by the terms "collective unconscious" and "archetypes"?

Swiss psychoanalytic theorist Carl Jung (1873-1961) believed that the unconscious mind played an important role in the formation of an individual's personality and that the roots of this unconscious mind went back to the beginning of human existence. The impersonal shared ancestral past that all human beings possess in the deepest layer of their individual unconscious minds is called the "collective unconscious." The common experiences or images from this ancestral past formed a deep impressions on the human mind. These experiences or images, Jung called archetypes. Some common archetypes are anima (feminine) and animus (masculine), the mandela (self) and the shadow (the darkside of human nature). These archetypes exist in all individuals and Jung called his type of psychology "depth psychology" because it delved into the top layer of the unconscious where archetypes derived.

John W. Santrock, *Psychology: The Science of Mind and Behavior, 3d ed.* (Dubuque, IA: Wm. C. Brown Publishers, 1991), 442.

What is the psychological definition of schizophrenia?

With one out of every 100 humans diagnosed with this condition, Schizophrenia can be described as a "severe psychological disorder in which the affected individual has distorted thoughts and perceptions, displays odd communication, and exhibits inappropriate emotion, abnormal motor behavior, and social withdrawal." Many schizophrenics can have delusions (false beliefs) or hallucinations in which they see, hear, feel, taste, and smell things that do not exist. Schizophrenia is divided into four main types: disorganized, paranoid, catatonic, and undifferentiated schizophrenia. The term "schizophrenia" comes from the Latin words "schizo" (meaning split) and "phrenia" (meaning mind). This does not imply a split personality but rather a split from reality.

John W. Santrock, *Psychology: The Science of Mind and Behavior, 3d ed.* (Dubuque, IA: Wm. C. Brown Publishers, 1991), 496.

Is there a correlation between personality traits and birth order?

Numerous psychologists support the contention that there is a correlation between personality traits and birth order. First-born children are often high achievers because of a hard work ethic and drive to succeed. The oldest children, although not necessarily smarter, begin reading earlier and score higher on aptitude tests. Psychologist Lucille Forer, in her book *The Birth Order Factor*, also notes a desire among first-born to conform because as children they were admonished to set a good example for their younger siblings. Second-born or middle children are apt to be better in interpersonal relationships because they are generally more open and easy-going. These children, however, can find their birth positions difficult to contend with, seemingly caught between the "eldest child" and the "cute baby," according to Jeannie Kidwell of the Child and Family Studies Department at the University of Tennessee. Youngest children are ambivalent about their birth positions because they are alternately teased and spoiled by older siblings and parents. They also have a tendency to develop a strong relationship with an older brother or sister. This can often hinder self-confidence and leadership development, according to Stephen P. Bank, a psychologist at Wesleyan University and the author of *The Sibling Bond*.

Barbara B. Raymond, "Our place among siblings affects our personalities," *USA Today* 1 November 1983.

What are the different styles of loving?

In their book *Styles of Loving* Marcia Lasswell and Norman Lobsenz define six different styles of love: best-friend's love, romantic love, logical love, game-playing love, unselfish love, and possessive love. These categories were determined by analyzing the attitude of the lover toward the beloved.

A best friend's lover seeks companionship, rapport, and mutual sharing but is seldom passionate or romantic.

Romantic lover wants a total emotional relationship and is apt to be in love with the idea of being in love.

A logical lover is pragmatic and looks for a fair exchange in the relationship.

A game-player wants to keep the other person off balance and rarely makes an emotional commitment.

The unselfish lover loves purely without any thought of return.

A possessive lover is dependant and demanding, placing great emotional burdens on partners.

Margaret DiCanio, *The Encyclopedia of Marriage, Divorce, and the Family* (New York: Facts on File, 1989), s.v. "love, styles of."

How does the psychological test known as the Szondi Personality Test work?

The Szondi Personality Test consists of a series of photographs of people which are shown to a subject. The subject selects which people in the photographs he or she would or would not care to be in contact with. Unknown to the subject the photographs are of mentally disturbed people with severe disabilities or anti-social tendencies. The choice, whether attraction or repulsion, supposedly provides insight into the mental state of the subject.

John May, *Curious Trivia* (New York: Dorset Press, 1984), 243-44.

What are feral children?

Children supposedly nurtured and raised in the wild by animals are commonly referred to as feral children. The term is sometimes used in relation to children who have managed to survive on their own in the wilds or children purposefully deprived of human contact. Although children raised by animals exist in literature and legend there is no conclusive proof that it has ever actually happened.

Academic American Encyclopedia (Danbury, CT: Grolier, 1988), s.v. "feral children."

What is Burton's *The Anatomy of Melancholy?*

The Anatomy of Melancholy, was written by Robert Burton as a medical treatise on depression. However, the work may be enjoyed on many levels because the author skillfully combined philosophy, wit, satire, and social and political commentary to such a degree that the literary aspects overpower the medical. Written almost four hundred years ago, *The Anatomy of Melancholy* is interesting, enlightening, and entertaining today.

A. W. Ward and A. R. Waller, eds., *Prose and Poetry: Sir Thomas North to Michael Drayton, vol. 4 of The Cambridge History of English Literature* (1909; reprint, Cambridge: University Press, 1964), 245.

What are the types of human body shapes?

The best known example of body typing (classifying body shape in terms of physiological functioning, behavior, and disease resistance), was devised by American psychologist William Herbert Sheldon (1898-1977). Sheldon's system, known as somatotyping, distinguishes three types of body shapes, ignoring overall size: endomorph, mesomorph, and ectomorph. The extreme endomorph tends to be spherical: a round head, a large fat abdomen, weak penguinlike arms and legs, with heavy upper arms and thighs but slender wrists and ankles. The extreme mesomorph is characterized by a massive cubical head, broad shoulders and chest, and heavy muscular arms and legs. The extreme ectomorph has a thin face, receding chin, high forehead, a thin narrow chest and abdomen, and spindly arms and legs. In Sheldon's system there are mixed body types, determined by component ratings. Sheldon assumed a close relationship between body build and behavior and temperament. This system of body typing has many critics.

Encyclopedia Americana (Danbury, CT: Grolier, 1990), 4:133.

How are IQ scores interpreted?

Intelligence quotient (IQ) test scores are interpreted through the use of a bell curve. About 68 percent of persons tested score between 85 and 115, and fewer than three percent of those tested score below 70 or above 130 points.

The results of IQ tests are often criticized because they tend to stereotype persons and may unfairly determine their placement in ability groups.

Jane Polley, ed., *Stories Behind Everyday Things* (Pleasantville, NY: Reader's Digest Association, 1980), 193-94.

What are some examples of "body language"?

It is sometimes said that "a picture is worth a thousand words." The way that persons position their bodies or the facial expressions they use can often reveal more about themselves than the words they use. Fidgeting excessively, jingling money or keys in the pocket, wringing hands, or clearing the throat are indications of nervousness. Standing with one's arms crossed, rubbing the eyes often, or giving sideways glances are ways of expressing defensiveness. Biting the fingernails or chewing on a pen or pencil expresses insecurity. Sitting on the edge of a chair, unbuttoning the coat, or using hand to face gestures expresses cooperation. A person's body language exudes confidence if he or she stands with back stiffened and hands behind back or on the lapels of coat. If a person breathes in short gasps, clenches the fists together tightly, rubs the neck, or wrings the hands, he or she is expressing frustration.

The Book of Inside Information (New York: Boardroom Classics, 1991), 192-93.

What are the signs of depression?

The Ohio State University Extension Service lists a number of physical, emotional, behavioral, and thought pattern changes that could indicate that a person is suffering from depression. Physical signs could include pains or complaints with no physical basis, sharp change in appetite, change in sleep patterns, and fatigue. Emotional clues are sadness, anxiety, apathy, and crying. Feelings and thoughts that indicate depression include feelings of hopelessness, helplessness, and guilt, as well as thoughts of death or suicide, forgetfulness, indecision, and impaired concentration. Depression is also marked by changes in behavior, such as loss of interest in favorite activities, neglected hygiene, the inability to perform ordinary tasks, withdrawal from social activity, increased use of alcohol or drugs, irritability, agitation, and verbalizing the wish to commit suicide as well as actual suicide attempts.

"News Notes: Signs of Depression, " *Aging* #365, 1993.

What is a Skinner box?

A Skinner box is an experimental enclosure for testing animal conditioning in which the subject animal performs a function (e.g., presses a bar or lever) to obtain a reward. By 1938 B.F. Skinner (b. 1904) worked out a technique for measuring the rewarding effect of a stimulus, or the effects of learning on voluntary behavior. The experimental animal (rat) was placed in a special box containing a lever that the animal could manipulate. When it pressed the lever small pellets of food would or would not be released, according to the experimental conditions. This box for animal conditioning has become known as a Skinner box.

Dorland's Illustrated Medical Dictionary, 27th ed. (Philadelphia: Saunders, 1988), 228. Cleveland P. Hickman, Jr., et al., *Integrated Principles of Zoology, 7th ed.* (St. Louis: Times Mirror/Mosby College Publishing, 1984), A-14.

Who was Christine Jorgenson?

Born George Jorgenson (1926-1989), Christine Jorgenson was the first American transsexual to publicly announce having undergone a sex-change operation. On December 15, 1952, she returned from Denmark after undergoing 2,000 hormone injections and six operations.

Chronicle of the 20th Century (Missouri: JL International Publishing, 1987), 727. John Drexel, ed., *The Facts On File Encyclopedia of the 20th Century* (New York: Facts on File, 1991), s.v. "Jorgensen, Christine."

What is a Rorschach test?

The Rorschach test is commonly known as the "ink blot test." Created by Hermann Rorschach (1884-1922), it is a technique in which the subject comments on what he or she sees in ten different, unstructured, ink blots. The subject's personality is projected into the answers. An examiner studies the responses for various factors, such as color, detail, form, and movement. Using these factors and a scoring system, the subject's personality is interpreted in terms such as emotionality, creativity, body image, orality, hypnotizability, and cognitive style. Initially, the test was considered a perfect measure of personality and an excellent means of predicting behavior. Experience eventually showed that the test was subject to situational and interpersonal variables that alter its results.

Raymond J. Corsini, ed., *Encyclopedia of Psychology* (New York: John Wiley & Sons, 1994), s.v. "Rorschach technique." Robert M. Goldenson, ed., *Longman Dictionary of Psychology and Psychiatry* (New York: Longman, 1984), s.v. "Rorschach test."

Who introduced the science of graphology and what are its analytical parameters?

Since its introduction by the French abbot Jean Hippolyte Michon (1806-81) graphology has attempted to show a relationship between a person's handwriting and his or her character and personality. When analyzing handwriting graphologists look at nine criteria: size, layout, line direction, connection, temporal features, regularity, letterforms, angle, and shading.

David Crystal, *The Cambridge Encyclopedia of Language* (Cambridge: Cambridge University Press, 1987), 32.

Who developed psychoanalysis?

Psychoanalysis was developed by Sigmund Freud (1856-1939), an Austrian medical doctor who specialized in neurology. He developed his psychoanalytic theories and techniques while working with patients with mental problems. Freud discovered a link between the early childhood experiences of his patients and their mental problems as adults. By probing into an individuals' memories and by uncovering their unconscious thoughts, often sexual in nature, Freud found a means for analyzing and relieving symptoms of mental illness.

John W. Santrock, *Psychology: The Science of Mind and Behavior, 3d ed.* (Dubuque, IA: Wm. C. Brown Publishers, 1991), 433-34.

What type of memory is retained best as one ages and what type declines most?

A study of normal mental decline in the elderly conducted by a psychologist at Pennsylvania State University reveals that as we age we experience differing rates of memory loss and memory retention. A study of more than 5,000 men and women over 35 years, in which they were tested regularly, considers everyone not classified as the 15 percent of the elderly who are "frail," to be "normal." The study looked at three key areas of mental ability: the spatial skills involved in, for example, assembling a piece of furniture from printed directions; the inductive reasoning used to read a bus timetable; and the verbal fluency that determines how readily you can think of a word. The study involved testing subjects regularly, but those who developed severely disabling diseases or senility were dropped from the study. One useful finding was that high blood pressure correlates with memory loss in older persons, and can lead to mental decline beyond that caused by the natural course of aging, researchers have found.

The study revealed different rates of decline. On average the decline in the basic mental abilities begins gradually in the middle to late 60s and accelerates in the late 70s, but the rate of decline differs for various mental faculties and differs in men and women. Results are inconclusive, however, because "there is a huge variation from person to person among older people, and the older a group gets, the less like each other they become."

Daniel Goleman, "Mental Decline in Aging Need Not Be Inevitable," *New York Times* 26 April 1994.

What does the term self-actualization mean?

The term self-actualization is associated with motivation and personality development in humanistic psychology. Abraham Maslow, American psychologist and founder of humanistic psychology in the 1940s, outlined four levels in his developmental motivational model of human needs. Sometimes these four levels are called Maslow's hierarchy of needs. At the first level behavior is driven by basic survival and psychological needs. At the second level security and safety are the driving forces of behavior. At the third level the individual focuses on meeting the needs for love and a sense of social belonging. At the fourth level the individual experiences the satisfaction of being respected and held in esteem. After these basic levels have been achieved the individual has reached the highest level of the motivational hierarchy when behavior is no longer driven by external needs. At this level the individual is self-motivated and self-actualized.

L. Dodge Fernald and Peter S. Fernald, *Introduction to Psychology, 5th ed.* (Dubuque, IA: W. C. Brown, 1985), 307-8. Robert T. Francoeur, *A Descriptive Dictionary and Atlas of Sexology* (Westport, CT: Greenwood Press, 1991), s.v. "self-actualization." Stuart Sutherland, *The International Dictionary of Psychology* (New York: Continuum, 1989), s.v. "need-hierarchy theory."

What is a "Boston marriage"?

A "Boston marriage" is a close and long-standing, but not necessarily sexual, relationship between two women.

Library Journal 1 October 1993.

Who was Alfred Charles Kinsey?

Alfred Charles Kinsey (1894-1956) was a famous researcher of human sexual behavior. After graduating from Bowdoin and Harvard, Kinsey began his sex research in 1938 and in 1947 his Institute for Sex Research was established as an affiliate of Indiana University. In 1948 and 1953 he published *Sexual Behavior in the Human Male* and *Sexual Behavior in the Human Female.* These are often referred to as the "Kinsey Reports."

David L. Sills, ed., *International Encyclopedia of the Social Sciences* (New York: Macmillan & The Free Press, 1968), s.v. "Kinsey, Alfred C."

Is one sex more likely to commit suicide than the other?

U.S. records show a 3:1 ratio of female to male suicide attempts.

U.S. News and World Report 25 October 1993.

Health Institutions and Practitioners

When was the first hospital ship built?

It is believed that the Spanish Armada fleet of 1587-1588 included hospital ships. England's first recorded hospital ship was the *Goodwill* in 1608, but it was not until after 1660 that the Royal Navy made it a regular practice to set aside ships for hospital use. The government outfitted six hospital ships, some of which were permanently attached to the fleet, during the Spanish-American War of 1898. The U.S. Congress authorized the construction of the USS *Relief* in August 1916. It was launched in 1919 and delivered to the Navy in December 1920.

Joseph N. Kane, *Famous First Facts, 4th ed.* (New York: Wilson, 1981), 575. John H. Plumridge, *Hospital Ships and Ambulance Trains* (London: Seeley, 1975), 13, 31.

Who was the first American-born winner of the Nobel Prize for physiology or medicine?

The American geneticist Thomas Hunt Morgan (1866-1945) was awarded the Nobel Prize in 1933 for his study on how chromosomes function in heredity.

Frank K. Magill, *Nobel Prize Winners: Physiology or Medicine* (Englewood Cliffs, NJ: Salem Press, 1991), 1:359.

Who was the first woman to be named to the National Inventors Hall of Fame?

Gertrude Belle Elion was named to the National Inventors Hall of Fame in 1991 for her research at the Burroughs Wellcome Company, which led to the development of the drug 6-Mercaptopurine which combats leukemia, septic shock, and tissue rejection in patients undergoing kidney transplants.

Otto Johnson, ed., *1995 Information Please Almanac, Atlas and Yearbook, 48th ed.* (Boston: Houghton Mifflin, 1995), 557. *Scientific American* October 1991.

For what is Percy Lavon Julian noted?

Dr. Percy Lavon Julian (1899-1975), a grandson of a former slave, is noted for his work on synthesizing hormones and medicinal substances, as well as for developing many industrial applications for plant products. He obtained 130 chemical patents in his lifetime. For instance, in 1935 he synthesized physostigmine, a powerful drug for the treatment of the disease glaucoma (build-up of pressure inside the eyeball that gradually destroys the retina, causing blindness). A year later, he isolated and prepared soybean protein to be used for paper coatings, textile sizing, and cold-water paints, and as a chemical fire-extinguishing foam. He also developed methods of synthesizing cortisone, used for treatment of rheumatoid arthritis and other inflammatory diseases, and the hormones progesterone and testosterone.

Louis Haber, *Odyssey Black Pioneers of Science and Invention* (San Diego, CA: Odyssey/Harcourt Brace Jovanovich, 1970), 131-33. Vivian O. Sammons, *Blacks in Science and Medicine* (New York: Hemisphere Publishing, 1990), 140.

What was the contribution of Dr. Gorgas to the building of the Panama Canal?

Dr. William C. Gorgas (1854-1920) brought the endemic diseases of Panama under control by destroying mosquito breeding grounds, virtually eliminating yellow fever and malaria. His work was probably more essential to the completion of the canal than any engineering technique.

Isaac Asimov, *Asimov's Biographical Encyclopedia of Science and Technology, 2d ed.* (Garden City, NY: Doubleday & Co., 1982), 453. Nigel Hawkes, *Structures* (New York: Macmillian, 1990), 139. Trevor Williams, *A Biographical Dictionary of Scientists* (London: Adam & Charles Black, 1969), 220.

Who was the first to use chemotherapy?

Chemotherapy is the use of chemical substances to treat diseases, specifically malignant diseases. The drug must interfere with the growth of bacterial, parasitic, or tumor cells, without significantly affecting host cells. Especially effective in types of cancer as leukemia and lymphoma, chemotherapy was introduced in medicine by the German physician Paul Ehrlich (1854-1915).

Encyclopedic Dictionary of Science (New York: Fact on File, 1988), 61, 84.

Does the healthy spouse have to use all joint family income and resources to pay for nursing home costs for an ailing spouse?

In the event of paying for nursing home costs, there are now rules that protect the healthy spouse from poverty. Each state sets a community spouse resource allowance and community spouse income allowance within federal guidelines. The healthy spouse must be allowed somewhere between approximately $900 and $1,700 a month in income and resources somewhere between about $12,000 and $67,000. These amounts must be considered in computing the sick spouse's eligibility for nursing home costs assistance.

Peter J. Strauss, Robert Wolf, and Dana Shilling, *What Every Caregiver Ought to Know* (Chicago: Commerce Clearing House, 1992), 15.

Who is considered the father of embryology?

Kaspar Friedrich Wolff (1733-1794), a German surgeon, is regarded as the father of embryology. Wolff produced his revolutionary work *Theoria generationis* in 1759. Until that time it was generally believed that each living organism developed from an exact miniature of the adult within the seed or sperm. Wolff introduced the idea that cells in a plant or animal embryo are initially unspecified, or undefined, but later differentiate to produce the separate organs and systems with distinct types of tissues.

The Biographical Dictionary of Scientists: Biologists (New York: Peter Bedrick Books, 1984), 138.

Is it illegal to give away funds in order to qualify for Medicaid?

There's nothing illegal about giving away funds in order to qualify for Medicaid, but the system has specific rules about what can and can't be done. States must impose a penalty period on asset transfers, such as gifts, with special rules for transfers of homes. The penalty period is a length of time between the application and the start of Medicaid benefits.

Peter J. Strauss, Robert Wolf, and Dana Shilling, *What Every Caregiver Ought to Know* (Chicago: Commerce Clearing House, 1992), 13-14.

What surgical procedures use the most Medicare dollars?

According to the Health Care Financing Administration, the surgical procedures that use the most Medicare dollars are as follows.

Procedure	Medicare costs
Cataract removal/lens insertation	$2 billion
Colonoscopy	$396.4 million
Knee arthroplasty	$265.3 million
Coronary angiography	$244.3 million
Prostatectomy	$214.7 million
Coronary angioplasty	$201.9 million

USA Today 22 March 1993.

What are the two parts of Medicare?

There are two parts to the Medicare program: hospital insurance (part A) helps pay for in-patient hospital care, in-patient care in a skilled nursing facility, home health care, and hospice care. Medical insurance (part B) helps pay for doctors' services, outpatient hospital services, durable medical equipment, and a number of other medical services and supplies that are not covered by the hospital insurance part of Medicare.

The Medicare 1994 Handbook (Washington, DC: Government Printing Office, 1994), 1, 39-40.

What are preferred ways of providing care when family members need assistance with everyday activities?

According to a telephone survey of a nationally representative sample of 723 adults age 45 and older, conducted in 1991, individuals of differing economic status (those whose income is under $25,000 per year vs. those whose income is $25,000 or more) prefer the following options for long-term care.

Preference	Age 45-64	Age 65+	Income under $25,000	Income over $25,000
Family/ friends/ at home	55%	44%	41%	30%
Paid home care	23%	32%	26%	44%
Nursing home or residential care	11%	14%	15%	18%
Don't know	11%	9%	18%	8%

Home Care: Attitudes and Knowledge of Retired Persons, (Washington, DC: American Association of Retired Persons, 1991), 6.

Is hospice care covered under Medicare?

Hospice care is a special way of caring for a patient whose disease cannot be cured. It is available as a benefit under Medicare Hospital Insurance (Part A). Medicare beneficiaries who choose hospice care receive non-curative medical and support services for their terminal illness. To be eligible, they must, among other things, be certified by a physician to be terminally ill with a life expectancy of approximately six months or less. Under Medicare, hospice is primarily a program of care delivered in a person's home by a Medicare-approved hospice.

Medicare covers the following hospice care services:
physicians' services
nursing care
medical appliances and supplies
outpatient drugs for symptom management and pain relief
short-term inpatient care, including respite care
home health aide and homemaker services
physical therapy, occupational therapy and speech/ language pathology services
counseling, including dietary counseling

Department of Health and Human Services, *Medicare Hospice Benefits: A Special Way of Caring for the Terminally Ill* (Washington, DC: Health Care Financing Administration, 1993), 1-2.

Who developed the raised-dot mathematical systems used by persons with visual disabilities?

Abraham Nemeth devised the *Nemeth Code of Braille Mathematics and Scientific Notation* in 1965. The code modifies the Braille literary raised-dot system by substituting mathematical and technical symbols for each Braille letter configuration of dots.

The New Encyclopaedia Britannica, 15th ed., "Micropedia" (Chicago: Encyclopaedia Britannica, 1993), s.v. "Braille."

Who founded Alcoholics Anonymous?

Alcoholics Anonymous (AA), a recovery program, was founded by a New York stockbroker and recovering alcoholic, William Griffith Wilson. His idea of a movement of recovered alcoholics who would help their still-suffering fellows came to fruition in 1935 when he met a fellow alcoholic, Dr. Robert Holbrook Smith, in Akron, Ohio. In 1941 the organization began its journey toward being an American institution when Jack Alexander wrote an article about AA for the *Saturday Evening Post.* Initially prepared to debunk the self-help society, Alexander ended up an enthusiastic believer.

Baz Edmeades, "Alcoholics Anonymous Celebrates its 50th Year," *Saturday Evening Post* July/August 1985.

Who was the first black surgeon to do heart surgery?

Dr. Daniel Hale Williams (1858-1931) was a pioneer in open heart surgery. In 1893, he was able to save a knifing victim by opening up the patient's chest with the help of a surgical team, exposing the beating heart. He sewed the knife wound a fraction of an inch from the heart without the aid of x-rays, blood transfusions, or anesthetics.

Hattie Carwell, *Blacks in Science: Astrophysicist to Zoologist* (Oakland, CA: Exposition Press, 1977), 57-58.

What is the La Leche League?

The La Leche League is an organization that offers encouragement and advice about breast-feeding to new mothers. Established in 1956 in Franklin Park, Illinois by seven mothers, it now has thousands of chapters around the world that conduct a monthly series of four meetings, where women learn breast-feeding techniques and provide one another with support. The league has a central office, which answers thousands of letters and calls each year, and a professional advisory board, which provides the organization with new information when it is available and monitors the league's publications.

Margaret DiCanio, *The Encyclopedia of Marriage, Divorce, and the Family* (New York: Facts on File, 1989), s.v. "La Leche League."

What is a dread disease insurance policy?

A dread disease policy (also known as specified disease insurance) is insurance that provides benefits for the treatment of the specific disease or diseases named in the policy.

MEDIGAP: Medicare Supplement Insurance: A Consumer's Guide, rev. ed. (Washington, DC: American Association of Retired Persons, 1992), 17.

Who is generally regarded as the father of medicine?

Hippocrates (ca.460-ca.377 B.C.), a Greek physician, holds this honor. Greek medicine, previous to Hippocrates, was a mixture of religion, mysticism, and necromancy. Hippocrates established the rational system of medicine as a science, separating it from religion and philosophy. Diseases had natural causes and natural laws: they were not the "wrath of the gods." Hippocrates believed that the four elements (earth, air, fire, and water) were represented in the body by four body fluids (blood, phlegm, black bile, and yellow bile) or "humors." When they existed in harmony within the body, the body was in good health. The duty of the physician was to help nature to restore the body's harmony. Diet, exercise, and moderation in all things kept the body well, and psychological healing (good attitude toward recovery), bed rest, and quiet were part of his therapy. Hippocrates was the first to recognize that different diseases had different symptoms; and he described them in such detail that the descriptions generally would hold today. His descriptions not only included diagnosis but prognosis.

Robert B Downs, *Landmarks in Science* (Littleton, CO: Libraries Unlimited, 1982), 21-24.

What documents should a caregiver of an elderly person have available?

The caregiver is responsible for careful record keeping, and should be able to find these documents relating to the person being cared for:

Will (if any)
Durable power of attorney (if any)
Life and health insurance
Living Will or proxy designation (if any)
Pension plan
Deeds to real estate
Banking records, including where any safe deposit boxes are kept
Brokerage and other investment records
Prepaid funeral plan (if any)
Evidence of financial obligations, e.g., mortgages, installation sales contracts, and evidence that obligations have been satisfied
Information about the individual's family tree, e.g., divorce records, addresses and telephone numbers of family members.

Peter J. Strauss, Robert Wolf, and Dana Shilling, *What Every Caregiver Ought to Know* (Chicago: Commerce Clearing House, 1992), 2-3.

What is the Hippocratic Oath?

The Hippocratic Oath is demanded of physicians who are entering practice. It can be traced back to the Greek physician and teacher, Hippocrates (ca.460-ca.377 B.C.). The oath reads as follows:

"I swear by Apollo the physician, by Aesculapius, Hygeia, and Panacea, and I take to witness all the gods, all the goddesses, to keep according to my ability and my judgement the following Oath:

To consider dear to me as my parents him who taught me this art; to live in common with him and if necessary to share my goods with him; to look upon his children as my own brothers, to teach them this art if they so desire without fee or written promise; to impart to my sons and the sons of the master who taught me and the disciples who have enrolled themselves and have agreed to rules of the profession, but to these alone, the precepts and the instruction. I will prescribe regiment for the good of my patients according to my ability and my judgement and never to harm anyone. To please no one will I prescribe a deadly drug, nor give advice which may cause his death. Nor will I give a woman a pessary to procure abortion. But I will preserve the purity of my life and my art. I will not cut for stone, even for patients in whom the disease is manifest; I will leave this operation to be performed by practitioners (specialists in this art). In every house where I come I will enter only for the good of my patients, keeping myself far from all intentional ill-doing and all seduction, and especially from the pleasures of love with women or with men, be they free or slaves. All that may come to my knowledge in the exercise of my profession or outside of my profession or in daily commerce with men, which ought not to be spread abroad, I will keep secret and will never reveal. If I keep this oath faithfully, may I enjoy life and practice my art, respected by all men and in all times; but if I swerve from it or violate it, may the reverse be my lot."

The oath varies slightly in wording among different sources.

Thomas Stedman, *Stedman's Medical Dictionary, 25th ed.* (Baltimore, MD: Williams and Wilkens, 1990), 716-17.

What is the difference between an ophthalmologist, optometrist, and optician?

An ophthalmologist is a physician who specializes in care of the eyes. Ophthalmologists conduct examinations to determine the quality of vision and the need for corrective glasses or contact lenses. They also check for the presence of any disorders, such as glaucoma or cataracts. Ophthalmologists may prescribe glasses and contact lenses, medication, or perform surgery, as necessary.

An optometrist is a specialist trained to examine the eyes and to prescribe, supply, and adjust glasses or contact lenses.

Because they are not physicians, optometrists may not prescribe drugs or perform surgery. An optometrist refers patients requiring these types of treatment to an ophthalmologist.

An optician is a person who fits, supplies, and adjusts glasses or contact lenses. Because their training is limited, opticians may not examine or test eyes or prescribe glasses or drugs.

The American Medical Association Encyclopedia of Medicine (New York: Random House, 1989), 745-46.

When was the first blood bank opened?

Several sites claim the distinction of opening the first blood bank. Some sources list the first blood bank as opening in 1940 in New York City under the supervision of Dr. Richard C. Drew (1904-1950). Others list an earlier date of 1938 in Moscow at the Sklifosovsky Institute (Moscow's central emergency service hospital) founded by Professor Sergei Yudin. The term "blood bank"was coined by Bernard Fantus who set up a centralized storage depot for blood in 1937 at the Cook County Hospital in Chicago, Illinois.

Barbara Berliner, *The Book of Answers* (Englewood Cliffs, NJ: Prentice-Hall, 1990), 77. Patrick Robertson, *The Book of Firsts* (New York: Clarkson N. Potter, 1974), 26.

Who was the father of modern medicine?

Thomas Sydenham (1624-1689), who was also called the English Hippocrates, reintroduced the Hippocratic method of accurate observation at the bedside and the recording of observations to build up a general clinical description of individual diseases. He is also considered one of the founders of epidemiology.

The Great Scientists (Danbury, CT: Grolier, 1989), 11:108.

What percentage of all days spent in the hospital are by Americans over age 65?

The 32 million Americans who are 65 years of age or older make up 13 percent of the population, but account for 44 percent of all days spent in the hospital, 40 percent of all visits to internists, and a third of the nation's health care expenditures.

Tamar Lewin, "As Elderly Population Grows, So Does the Need for Doctors," *New York Times* 31 May 1991.

What types of care are not covered by Medicare?

Among types of care not covered by Medicare are:
Custodial Care. Medicare does not pay for custodial care when that is the only kind of care needed. Care is considered custodial when it is primarily for the purpose of helping the individual with daily living or meeting personal needs and could be provided safely and reasonably by people without professional skills or training. Much of the care provided in nursing homes to people with chronic, long-term illnesses or disabilities is considered custodial care.
Care Not Reasonable and Necessary Under Medicare Program Standards. Medicare does not pay for services that are not reasonable and necessary for the diagnosis or treatment of an illness or injury, for example, drugs or devices that have not been approved by the Food and Drug Administration.
Care Outside the United States. Puerto Rico, the U.S. Virgin Islands, Guam, American Samoa, and the Northern Mariana Islands are considered part of the United States.

The Medicare 1994 Handbook (Washington DC: Government Printing Office, 1994), 12.

What is QMB?

QMB is short for "Qualified Medicare Beneficiary," a program run by the U.S. Department of Health and Human Services' Health Care Financing Administration and the state agency to provide medical assistance under the Medicaid program. The QMB program is important because it can save low-income beneficiaries at least $381 each year. The rules for qualification for the program vary slightly from state to state, but generally the criteria for assistance is the applicant has Medicare and has a yearly income of less than the national poverty guidelines of $6,810 for one person, or $9,190 for a couple or the applicant has Medicare and has "resources" no greater than $4,000 for one person, or $6,000 for a family of two.

Department of Health and Human Services, *You Should Know About QMB*, (Washington, DC: Social Security Administration, 1992), 1.

What is the Alcoholic Anonymous prayer?

The Alcoholics Anonymous prayer reads "God grant us the serenity to accept the things we cannot change, courage to change the things we can, and wisdom to know the difference." The prayer was originally part of a sermon by American theologian Reinhold Niebuhr (1892-1971) given at a small church near his summer home in Heath, Massachusetts, in 1934. A neighbor, Howard Chandler Robbins, published it as part of a pamphlet the following year. In addition to Alcoholics Anonymous, many others have used the prayer including the U.S.O., which distributed millions of copies to soldiers during World War II (1939-45).

The Little Red Book, rev. ed. (New York: Harper & Row/Hazelden Foundation, 1987), 58. James B. Simpson, comp., *Simpson's Contemporary Quotations* (Boston: Houghton Mifflin, 1988), 193.

What does the red and white striped barber pole represent?

In the days when few people could read, the spirally painted red and white striped pole was the emblem of barber-surgeons who extracted teeth, treated wounds, and bled patients, in addition to shaving and cutting hair. The white represented the bandage used in bloodletting, the red represented blood, and beneath the pole hung a brass basin used to receive the blood. After barbers and surgeons were separated into distinct professions in the 1700s, it was the barbers who retained the symbol.

George Stimpson, *A Book About a Thousand Things* (New York: Harper & Row, 1946), 95-6.

What are the main principles of a hospice?

Although the main principles of a hospice have been articulated in many ways, the basic tenets of the hospice program are: dying is a normal part of living, the goal of treatment is the control of pain and distressing symptoms; both patients and their closest companions-family and friends-need care; care should include support for survivors throughout their bereavement; and an interdisciplinary team, including volunteers, is best able to provide care.

Patricia Anderson, *Affairs in Order: A Complete Resource Guide to Death and Dying* (New York: Macmillan, 1991), 180.

What risk factors contribute to the likelihood that a person will become a resident of a nursing home?

Institutionalization in a nursing home is a common occurrence for many older Americans. Approximately one out of every two

Americans will spend at least some time as a resident in a nursing home during his or her lifetime. However, some risk factors make institutionalization more likely. Persons who spend time in a hospital or other health facility, have a high degree of chronic disability, and have an increased deterioration of cognitive functioning will often be institutionalized. Also, women tend to be admitted to nursing homes more often than men as they get older.

Elizabeth Vierck, *Fact Book on Aging* (Santa Barbara: ABC-CLIO, 1990), 121.

Who was Clara Louise Maass?

Nurse Clara Louise Maass (1876-1901) took part in a study of yellow fever that proved the disease was transmitted by mosquitos. Maass was among the volunteers who died in the study. She had seen the distressing details of the illness while working in army camps in Cuba and military hospitals in the Philippines and hoped to participate in the discovery of its prevention or cure. Maass was given full military honors for her act of courage.

Josephine A. Dolan, *History of Nursing* (Philadelphia: W. B. Saunders, 1963), 266.

Who was the first woman physician in the United States?

Elizabeth Blackwell (1821-1910) received her degree in 1849 from Geneva Medical College in New York. After overcoming many obstacles, she set up a small practice which expanded into the New York Infirmary for Women and Children, which featured an all-female staff.

Dennis Sanders, *The First of Everything* (New York: Delacorte, 1981), 156.

Health Care

Why are Robert Koch's scientific postulates significant?

The German bacteriologist, Robert Koch (1843-1910), developed four rules in his study of disease-producing organisms, which later investigators found useful. The following conditions must be met to prove that a bacterium causes a particular disease:

The microorganism must be found in large numbers in all diseased animals but not in healthy ones.

The organism must be isolated from a diseased animal and grown outside the body in a pure culture.

When the isolated microorganism is injected into other healthy animals, it must produce the same disease.

The suspected microorganism must be recovered from the experimental hosts (no. 3), isolated, compared to the first microorganism, and found to be identical.

Robert B. Downs, *Landmarks in Science* (Littleton, CO: Libraries Unlimited, 1982), 67. Leland G. Johnson, *Biology* (Dubuque, IA: Wm. C. Brown, 1983), 948.

Who was first to coin the word "virus"?

The English physician Edward Jenner (1749-1823), founder of virology and a pioneer in vaccination, first coined the word "virus." Using one virus to immunize against another one was precisely the strategy Jenner used when he inoculated someone with cowpox, a disease that attacks cows, to make them immune to smallpox. This procedure is called vaccination from vaccine (the Latin name for cowpox). Vaccines are usually a very mild dose of the disease-causing bacteria or virus (weakened or dead). These vaccines stimulate the creation of antibodies in the body that recognize and attack a particular infection. A virus is a minute parasitic organism that reproduces only inside the cell of its host. Viruses replicate by invading host cells and taking over the cell's machinery for DNA replication. Viral particles then can break out of the cells causing disease.

The Biographical Dictionary of Scientists: Biologists (New York: Peter Bedrick Books, 1984), 73-74. Richard P. Brennan, *Dictionary of Scientific Literacy* (New York: John Wiley & Sons, 1992), 315. *Encyclopedic Dictionary of Science* (New York: Facts On File, 1988), 247.

What is the meaning of the abbreviations often used by a doctor when writing a prescription?

Listed below are the meanings of the abbreviations often used by a doctor when writing a prescription.

Latin phrase	Shortened form	Meaning
quaque hora	qh	every hour
quaque die (de-uh)	qd	every day
bis in die	bid	twice a day
ter in die	tid	three times a day
quarter in die	qid	four times a day
pro re nata	prn	as needed
ante cibum	a.c.	before meals
post cibum	p.c.	after meals
per os	p.o.	by mouth
nihil per os	n.p.o.	nothing by mouth
signetur	sig	let it be
labeled statim	stat	immediately
ad libitum	ad lib	at pleasure
hora somni	h.s.	at bedtime
cum	c	with
sine	s	without
guttae	gtt	drops
semis	ss	a half
et	et	and

Rudolph Cartwright, *Doctors Are Easy to Understand If You Speak Their Language* (New York: Vantage Press, 1987), 7-8.

Is there a name for the heart-monitoring machine that people sometimes wear for a day or two while carrying on their normal activities?

The portable version of the electro-cardio-graph (ECG) designed by J.J. Holter is called a Holter monitor. Electrodes attached to the chest are linked to a small box containing a recording device. The device records the activity of the heart.

Mayo Clinic Family Health Book (New York: Morrow, 1990), 818.

What is the meaning of the numbers in a blood pressure reading?

When blood is forced into the aorta, it exerts a pressure against the walls; this is referred to as blood pressure. In the reading the upper number, the systolic, measures the pressure during the period of ventricular contraction. The lower number, the diastolic, measures the pressure when blood is entering the relaxed chambers of the heart. While these numbers can vary due to age, sex, weight, and other factors, the normal blood pressure is around 110/60 to 140/90 millimeters of mercury.

K. Melonakos, *Saunders Pocket Reference for Nurses* (Philadelphia: Saunders, 1990), 14. *Mosby's Medical, Nursing and Allied Health Dictionary, 3d ed.,* (St. Louis, MO: Mosby, 1990), 367, 1146.

How is blood pressure measured?

A sphygmomanometer is the device used to measure blood pressure. It was invented in 1881 by an Austrian named Von Bash. It consists of a cuff with an inflatable bladder that is wrapped around the upper arm, a rubber bulb to inflate the bladder, and a device that indicates the pressure of blood. Measuring arterial tension (blood pressure) of a person's circulation is achieved when the cuff is applied to the arm over the artery and pumped to a pressure which occludes or blocks it. This gives the systolic measure or the maximum pressure of the blood which occurs during contraction of the ventricles of the heart. Air is then released from the cuff until the blood is first heard passing through the opening artery (called Korotkoff sounds). This gives diastolic pressure, or the minimum value of blood pressure that occurs during the relaxation of the arterial-filling phase of the heart muscle.

The American Medical Association Encyclopedia of Medicine (New York: Random House, 1989), 927. Rudolf F. Graf and George J. Whalen, *The Reston Encyclopedia of Biomedical Engineering Terms* (New York: Reston Publishing, 1977), 107, 361, 373.

What is the instrument a doctor uses to check reflexes?

A plessor or plexor or percussor is a small hammer, usually with a soft rubber head, used to tap the body part directly. Also called a reflex hammer or a percussion hammer, it is used by a doctor to elicit reflexes by tapping on tendons. In the most common test, the patient sits on a surface high enough to allow his legs to dangle freely, and the physician lightly taps the patellar tendon, just below the kneecap. This stimulus briefly stretches the quadriceps muscle on top of the thigh. The stretch causes the muscle to contract, which makes the leg kick forward. The time interval between the tendon tap and the start of the leg extension is about 50 microseconds. That interval is too short for the involvement of the brain and is totally reflexive. This test indicates the status of an individual's reflex control of movement.

Neil R. Carlson, *Foundations of Physiological Psychology* (Needham Heights, MA: Allyn Bacon, 1988), 208-9. *Stedman's Medical Dictionary, 25th ed.* (Baltimore: Williams & Wilkins, 1990), 1215.

Was pellagra ever a common disease in the United States?

Pellagra, characterized by diarrhea, skin problems, and dementia, occurred frequently years ago in rural cotton mill towns, mining and sawmill camps, and in orphanages, prisons, and poorhouses. In these places, poverty and tradition reduced the diet to corn meal, fat salt pork, and carbohydrates with very few green vegetables especially during the winter months. Pellagra is brought on by an inadequate diet with not enough vitamins, especially vitamin B.

Louis I. Dublin, *Factbook on Man from Birth to Death, 2d ed.,* (New York: Macmillan, 1965), 348-49.

What is carpal tunnel syndrome?

Carpal tunnel syndrome occurs when a branch of the median nerve in the forearm is compressed at the wrist as it passes through the tunnel formed by the wrist bones (or carpals), and a ligament that lies just under the skin. The syndrome occurs most often in middle age and more so in women than men. The symptoms are intermittent at first, then become constant. Numbness and tingling begin in the thumb and first two fingers; then the hand and sometimes the whole arm becomes painful. Treatment involves wrist splinting, weight loss, control of edema; treatments for arthritis may help also. If not, a surgical procedure in which the ligament at the wrist is cut, could relieve pressure on the nerve.

Columbia University College of Physicians and Surgeons, *Complete Home Medical Guide* (New York: Crown, 1985), 599.

What is lactose intolerance?

Lactose, the principal sugar in cow's milk, found only in milk and dairy products, requires the enzyme lactase for human digestion. Lactose intolerance occurs when the lining of the walls of a person's small intestine does not produce normal amounts of this enzyme. Lactose intolerance causes abdominal cramps, bloating, diarrhea, and excessive gas when more than a certain amount of milk is ingested. Most people are less able to tolerate lactose as they grow older.

A person having lactose intolerance need not eliminate dairy products totally from the diet. Decreasing the consumption of milk products, drinking milk only during meals, and getting calcium from cheese, yogurt, and other dairy products having lower lactose values are options. Another alternative is to buy a commercial lactose preparation that can be mixed into milk. These preparations convert lactose into simple sugars that can be easily digested.

Mayo Clinic Family Health Book (New York: Morrow, 1990), 470, 623.

What is narcolepsy?

Although most people think of a narcoleptic as a person who falls asleep at inappropriate times, victims of narcolepsy also share other symptoms, including excessive daytime sleepiness, hallucinations, and cataplexy (a sudden loss of muscle strength following an emotional event). Persons with narcolepsy experience an uncontrollable desire to sleep, sometimes many times in one day. Episodes may last from a few minutes to several hours.

The Almanac of Science and Technology (San Diego: Harcourt Brace Jovanovich, 1990), 136. *Mosby's Medical, Nursing, and Allied Health Dictionary, 3d ed.* (St. Louis: Mosby, 1990), 792.

Who was Typhoid Mary?

Mary Mallon (1855-1938) who became known as Typhoid Mary, was a cook who worked in hotels and homes in New York around 1900, and was later identified as a chronic carrier of the typhoid bacilli. She was immune to the bacilli but passed it on to 51 people who contracted typhoid fever; three of them died. When the New York Health Department finally located her, she refused treatment and was confined. In 1910, she agreed never to work as a food handler or cook and to report frequently to the Health Department and was released. However, she disappeared and in 1915 caused an outbreak of the disease at the Sloan Hospital where she worked as a cook. She was arrested again and confined to the grounds of Riverside Hospital in New York after she again refused treatment. She remained there until she died in 1938 from a paralyzing stroke. The name "Typhoid

Mary" became known around the world as a symbol for the chronic carrier of disease.

Harry F. Dowling, *Fighting Infection* (Cambridge: Harvard University Press, 1977), 17-18. David Wallechinsky and Irving Wallace, *The People's Almanac #2* (New York: Bantam Books, 1978), 541-42.

How does jet lag affect one's body?

Jet lag is the term applied to the physiological and mental stress encountered by airplane travellers when crossing four or more time zones. Patterns of hunger, sleep, elimination, along with alertness, memory, and normal judgment, may all be affected. There are more than 100 biological functions that fluctuate during the 24-hour cycle (circadian rhythm) that can become desynchronized. Most humans adjust at a rate of about one hour per day. Thus after four time zone changes, the body will require about four days to return to its usual bio-rhythms. Flying eastward in which hours are lost affects the body more than flying westward (which adds hours to the day).

Mayo Clinic Family Health Book (New York: Morrow, 1990), 341-42. Frank E. Bair, *The Weather Almanac, 6th ed.* (Detroit, MI: Gale Research, 1992), 229.

What is the medical name for a sinking feeling in the pit of the stomach?

That sinking feeling in the pit of the stomach is called epigastric sensation.

Taber's Cyclopedia Medical Dictionary, 16th ed., (Philadelphia: Davis, 1989), 1658.

Why is the birth disorder once referred to as mongolism called Down Syndrome?

Down Syndrome was named after a British doctor, John Langdon Haydon Down, who first described the condition in 1866. Sources are divided as to whether it is properly referred to as "Down Syndrome" or "Down's Syndrome." It was once called "mongolism" because it was thought that the facial features of those with the disorder resembled those of Asians.

Charles B. Clayman, ed., *The American Medical Association Encyclopedia of Medicine* (New York: Random House, 1989), s.v. "Down's syndrome." David E. Larson, ed., *Mayo Clinic Family Health Book* (New York: William Morrow, 1990), 57. *The World Book Encyclopedia* (Chicago: World Book, 1994), s.v. "Down syndrome."

What are the average height and weight measurements for children at various ages?

The *1990 Physicians Handbook* lists the following measurements as the average heights and weights of American children. At birth, boys averaged one foot, eight inches and 7.5 pounds; the girls' averages were the same. At five years of age, boys averaged three feet, six inches and 39; five-year-old girls averaged three feet, five inches and 38 pounds. For children who were ten years old, boys averaged four feet, six inches and sixty-nine pounds; girls of the same age also averaged four feet, six inches and 69 pounds. At age fourteen, boys and girls also averaged the same heights and weights, at five feet, two inches and 107 pounds.

The World Almanac and Book of Facts 1995 (Mahwah, NJ: World Almanac, 1994), 972.

What percentage of people over age 95 are in nursing homes?

According to U.S. Census figures for elderly in nursing homes in 1990, 47.1 percent of the nation's elderly aged 95 and over resided in nursing homes. Comparable figures for other age groups are: 33.1 percent of those aged 90 to 94; 18.6 percent of those 85 to 89; 6.1 percent of those 75 to 84; and 1.4 percent of those age 65 to 74.

Profile of America's Elderly 1992 (Washington, DC: U.S. Bureau of the Census, 1993), 4.

What are some effective ways to deal with sleeplessness?

Sleeplessness can be combated with many techniques that offer an alternative to medications or sleeping pills. It is helpful to establish regular bedtimes and to avoid taking naps during the day. Just before going to bed, try taking a hot bath, drinking milk or herbal teas, or practice relaxation techniques. Do not exercise just before going to bed and do not go to bed hungry. Make sleeping conditions as comfortable as possible by adjusting the bed, temperature, humidity, sound, and light. Do not stay in bed if sleep does not come; get out of bed and try again later. Many people get less sleep as they get older; be sure to determine if you feel well with less sleep, rather than concentrating on the number of hours you are sleeping.

Paula B. Doress-Worters and Diana Laskin Siegal, *The New Ourselves, Growing Older: Women Aging with Knowledge and Power* (New York: Simon & Schuster, 1994), 33.

What was the contribution to medical science of a dog named Marjorie?

Marjorie was a diabetic black and white mongrel that was the first creature to be kept alive by insulin.

Wayne B. Eldridge, *The Best Pet Name Book Ever* (Hauppauge, NY: Barron, 1990), 31.

What is lithotripsy?

Lithotripsy is the use of ultrasonic or shock waves to pulverize kidney stones (calculi), allowing the small particles to be excreted or removed from the body. There are two different methods: extracorporeal shock wave lithotripsy (ESWL) and percutaneous lithotripsy. The ESWL method, used on smaller stones, breaks up the stones with external shock waves from a machine called a lithotripter. This technique has eliminated the need for more invasive stone surgery in many cases. For larger stones, a type of endoscope, called a nephroscope, is inserted into the kidney through a small incision. The ultrasonic waves from the nephroscope shatter the stones, and the fragments are removed through the nephroscope.

The American Medical Association Encyclopedia of Medicine (New York: Random House, 1989), 643-44.

What is the longest operation on record?

The longest surgical operation was performed on Mrs. Gertrude Levandowski of Burnips, Michigan, for removal of an ovarian cyst. She lost 308 pounds during the operation; her weight was 616 pounds before it started. The operation lasted 96 hours and took place from February 4 to February 8, 1951, in Chicago, Illinois.

Mark C. Young, ed., *Guinness Book of Records 1995* (New York: Facts on File, 1994), 19.

Who received the first heart transplant?

On December 3, 1967, in Capetown, South Africa, Dr. Christiaan Barnard and a team of 30 associates performed the first heart transplant. In a five-hour operation the heart of Denise Ann Darval, age 25, an auto accident victim, was transplanted into the body of Louis Washansky, a 55-year-old wholesale grocer. Washansky lived for 18 days before dying from pneumonia.

The first heart transplant performed in the United States was on a 2-week-old baby boy at Maimonides Hospital, Brooklyn, New York, on December 6, 1967, by Dr. Adrian Kantrowitz. The baby lived 6-hours. The first adult to receive a heart transplant in the United States was Mike Kasperak, age 54, at the Stanford Medical Center in Palo Alto, California, on January 6, 1968. Dr. Norman Shumway performed the operation. Kasperak lived 14 days. From then through 1993 there have been 16,378 heart transplants performed. In 1993, a record 2,293 transplants were done.

Dennis Sanders, *The First of Everything* (New York: Delacorte, 1981), 384. Mark Young, ed. *The Guinness Book of Records 1995* (New York: Facts on File, 1994), 20.

When was the first artificial heart used?

On December 2, 1982, Dr. Barney B. Clark (1921-1983), a 61-year-old retired dentist, became the first human to receive a permanently implanted artificial heart. It was known as the Jarvik-7 after its inventor, Dr. Robert Jarvik (b. 1946). The 7-hour operation was performed by Dr. William DeVries (b. 1943), a surgeon at the University of Utah Medical Center, in Salt Lake City, Utah. Dr. Clark died 112 days later, on March 23, 1983. In Louisville, Kentucky, William Schroeder (1923-1986) survived 620 days with an artificial heart (November 25, 1984 to August 7, 1986). On January 11, 1990, the U.S. Food and Drug Administration (FDA) recalled the Jarvik-7, the only artificial heart it had approved.

Mark Young, ed., *The Guinness Book of Records 1995* (New York: Facts on File, 1994), 20. G. J. Tortora, *Principles of Anatomy and Physiology, 4th ed.* (New York: Harper & Row, 1984), 462.

How many types of herpes virus are there?

There are five human herpes viruses all characterized by an eruption of small, usually painful, skin blisters:

Herpes simplex type 1—causes recurrent cold sores and infections of the lips, mouth, and face. The virus is contagious and spreads by direct contact with the lesions or fluid from the lesions. Cold sores are usually recurrent at the same sites and reoccur where there is an elevated temperature at the affected site; such as a fever or prolonged sun exposure. Occasionally this virus may occur on the fingers with a rash of blisters. If the virus gets into the eye, it could cause conjunctivitis, or even a corneal ulcer. On rare occasions, it can spread to the brain to cause encephalitis.

Herpes simplex type 2—causes genital herpes and infections acquired by babies at birth. The virus is contagious and can be transmitted by sexual intercourse. The virus produces small blisters in the genital area that burst to leave small painful ulcers, which heal within ten days to three weeks. Headache, fever, enlarged lymph nodes, and painful urination are the other symptoms.

Varicella-zoster (herpes zoster)—causes chicken pox and shingles. Shingles can be caused by the dormant virus in certain sensory nerves that re-emerge with the decline of the immune system (because of age, certain diseases, and the use of immunosuppressants), excessive stress, or use of corticosteroid drugs. The painful rash of small blisters dry and crust over, eventually leaving small pitted scars. The rash tends to occur over the rib area or a strip on one side of the neck or lower body. Sometimes it involves the lower half of the face and can affect the eyes. Pain that can be severe and longlasting affects about half of the sufferers and is caused by nerve damage.

Epstein-Barr—causes infectious mononucleosis (acute infection having high fever, sore throat and swollen lymph glands, especially in the neck, which occurs mainly during adolescence) and is associated with Burkitt's lymphoma (malignant tumors of the jaw or abdomen that occur mainly in African children and in tropical areas).

Cytomegalovirus—usually no symptoms but enlarges the cells it infects; it can cause birth defects when a pregnant mother infects her unborn child.

Herpes gestationis is a rare skin-blister disorder occurring only in pregnancy and is not related to the herpes simplex virus.

The American Medical Association Encyclopedia of Medicine (New York: Random House, 1989), 331, 415, 536-37, 693. Henry H. Balfour, *Herpes Diseases and Your Health* (Minneapolis, University of Minnesota Press, 1984), 3.

Which disease is the deadliest?

The most deadly infectious disease was the pneumonic form of the plague, the so-called Black Death of 1347-1351, with a mortality rate of 100 percent. Today, the disease with the highest mortality (almost 100 percent) is rabies in humans when it prevents the victim from swallowing water. This disease is not to be confused with being bitten by a rabid animal. With immediate attention, the rabies virus can be prevented from invading the nervous system and the survival rate in this circumstance is 95 percent. The virus AIDS (Aquired Immuno Deficiency Syndrome)1st reported in 1981, is caused by the HIV (Human Immunodeficiency Virus). The World Health Organization (WHO) reported 611,589 AIDS cases worldwide as of 1993, and estimated that there are 2.5 million actual cases of AIDS worldwide. In addition as of mid-1993, WHO estimated that there were 13 million people infected with HIV, of which one million were children. The United States had 328,392 cases of HIV positive with the number of deaths being 197,727 during the period of 1985-1993. In 1993 alone, there were 16,885 AIDS deaths and 83,814 AIDS cases. There has not been a case of recovery from AIDS yet.

Mark C. Young, *Guinness Book of Records 1995* (New York: Facts on File, 1994), 18-19. Robert Famighetti, ed., *The World Almanac and Book of Facts 1995* (Mahweh, NJ: World Almanac, 1994), 971-72.

How are the forms of cancer classified?

The many forms of cancer (malignant tumors) are classified into four groups: carcinomas, which involve the skin and skin-like membranes of the internal organs; sarcomas, which involve the bones, muscles, cartilage, and fat; leukemias, which involve the white blood cells; and lymphomas, which involve the lymphatic system.

Herman Schneider, *The Harper Dictionary of Science in Everyday Language* (New York: Harper & Row, 1988), 49.

What are HeLa cells?

HeLa cells, used in many biomedical experiments, were obtained from a cervical carcinoma in an African-American woman named Henriette Lacks. Epithelial tissue obtained by biopsy became the first continuously cultured human malignant cells.

Stedman's Medical Dictionary, 25th ed., (Baltimore: Williams & Wilkins, 1990), 268.

What is a negative ion generator?

A negative ion generator is an electrostatic air cleaner which sprays a continuous fountain of negatively charged ions into the air. Some researchers say that the presence of these ions causes a feeling of well-being, increased mental and physical energy, and relief from some of the symptoms of allergies, asthma, and chronic headaches. It may also aid in healing of burns and peptic ulcers.

Ellen J. Greenfield, *House Dangerous* (New York: Vintage Books, 1987), 104-5. B.G. Pearce, *Health Hazards of VDT's* (New York: John Wiley & Sons, 1984), 178.

What are the four humors of the body?

The four constituent humors of the body were identified as blood, phlegm, yellow bile, and black bile, originating in the heart, brain, liver, and spleen, respectively. Empedocles of Agrigentum (504-433 B.C.) probably originated this theory which he equates the body fluids to the four elements of nature: earth, fire, air, and water. These humors could determine the health of the body and the personality of the person as well. To be in good health the humors should be in harmony within the body. Ill health could be remedied by treatments to realign the humors and reestablish the harmony.

Erwin H. Ackerknecht, *A Short Story of Medicine* (New York: Ronald Press, 1955), 47.

Who is the heaviest person that ever lived?

John Brower Minnoch (1941-83) of Bainbridge Island, Washington, weighed 976 pounds (443 kilograms) in 1976 and was estimated to have weighed more than 1,387 pounds (630 kilograms) when he was rushed to the hospital in 1978 with heart and respiratory failure. Much of his weight was due to fluid retention. After two years on a hospital diet, he was discharged at 476 pounds (216 kilograms). He had to be readmitted, however, after reportedly gaining 197 pounds (89 kilograms) in seven days. When he died in 1983 Minnoch weighed 798 pounds (362 kilograms). The heaviest living male is Ken Nicholson (b. 1941) of Canton, Missouri, at 891 pounds (404 kilograms).

The heaviest woman ever recorded was American Rosalie Bradford (b. 1944) who weighed 1,200 pounds (545 kilograms) in January 1987. After suffering congestive heart failure, she dieted until she was 284 pounds (129 kilograms) in February of 1994.

Mark C. Young, ed., *Guinness Book of Records 1995* (New York: Facts on File, 1994), 8-9. *Prevention's Giant Book of Health Facts* (Emmaus, PA: Rodale Press, 1991), 546-47.

Who is the world's oldest person?

The greatest authenticated age to which any human has lived is 120 years 237 days in the case of Shigechiyo Izumi (1865-1986) of Japan.

Mark C. Young, ed., *The Guinness Book of Records 1995* (New York: Facts on File, 1994), 11.

Are more people nearsighted or farsighted?

About 30 percent of Americans are nearsighted to some degree; about 60 percent are farsighted. If the light rays entering the pupils of the eye converge exactly on the retina, then a sharply-focused picture is relayed to the brain. But if the eyeball is shaped differently, the focal point of the light rays is too short or too long, and vision is blurred. Convex lenses for farsightedness correct a too-long focal point. Concave lenses correct nearsightedness when the focal point of light rays, being too short, converge in front of the retina.

Prevention's Giant Book of Health Facts (Emmaus, PA: Rodale Press, 1991), 518.

What is dermatoglyphics?

Dermatoglyphics is the study of the skin ridge patterns on fingers, toes, palms of hands, and soles of feet. The patterns are used as a basis of identification and also have diagnostic value because of the association between certain patterns and chromosomal abnormalities.

Mosby's Medical, Nursing, and Allied Health Dictionary, 3rd ed., (St. Louis, MO: Mosby, 1990), 355.

Is it safer to ride an elevator or take the stairs?

According to one insurance company, walking up and down stairs is five times more hazardous than riding an elevator. Typically each year, the 345,000 elevators in the United States lift and lower approximately 43 billion passengers a distance of 1.5 billion miles with only 15 fatalities. Compared to other modes of transportation, elevators are the world's safest way to travel.

Jane Polley, ed., *Stories Behind Everyday Things* (Pleasantville, NY: Reader's Digest Association, 1980), 133.

What is the Kama Sutra?

The Kama Sutra is a manual dealing with various aspects of sex, love, and desire. It was written in Sanskrit by Vatsyayana and translated into English by Orientalist Sir Richard Burton (1821-90). The Kama Sutra offers information regarding the use of aphrodisiacs, advice on sexual problems, and ways of inducing desire. One of the underlying tenets of the Kama Sutra is that the person who is intelligent and prudent will become master of his senses and not succumb to mindless passion.

Harry E. Wedeck, *A Dictionary of Aphrodisiacs* (New York: M. Evans, 1989), 85-86.

What is progeria?

Progeria is premature old age. There are two distinct forms of the condition, both of which are extremely rare. In Hutchinson-Gilford syndrome aging starts around the age four, and by 10 or 12, the affected child has all the external features of old age, including gray hair, baldness, and loss of fat, resulting in thin limbs and sagging skin on the trunk and face. There are also internal degenerative changes, such as atherosclerosis (fatty deposits lining the artery walls). Death usually occurs at puberty. Werner's syndrome, or adult progeria, starts in early adult life and follows the same rapid progression as the juvenile form. The cause of progeria is unknown.

The American Medical Association Encyclopedia of Medicine (New York: Random House, 1989), 822-23.

Which medical condition is associated with Abraham Lincoln's awkward appearance?

The U.S. President, Abraham Lincoln (1809-1865), probably had Marfan's syndrome which abnormally lengthens the bones. It is a rare inherited degenerative disease of the connective tissue. Besides the excessively long bones, there are chest deformities, scoliosis (spine curvature), an arm span that can exceed height, eye problems (especially myopia or nearsightedness), abnormal heart sounds, and sparse subcutaneous fat. In 1991, researchers identified the gene causing the disease.

Diseases and Disorders Handbook (Springhouse, PA: Springhouse Corp., 1990), 467-68. Alice Loomer, *Famous Flaws* (New York: Macmillan, 1976), 145.

What is pelvic inflammatory disease?

Pelvic inflammatory disease (PID), a term used for a group of infections in the female organs, for example, inflammations of the Fallopian tubes, cervix, uterus, and ovaries. It is the most common cause of female infertility today. PID is most often found in sexually active women under the age of 25 and almost always results from gonorrhea or chlamydia, but women who have IUDs are also at risk. Aerobic or anaerobic organisms such as *Neisseria gonorrhoeae* that causes acute cervicitis, (a foul-smelling vaginal discharge accompanied by itching, burning, and pelvic discomfort, often resulting in infertility and spontaneous abortion) or common bacteria such as staphylocci, chlamydiae, and coliforms to produce acute endometritis (oozing vaginal discharge with ulteration, lower abdominal pain and spasms, fever, etc.) Chronic endometritis is becoming increasingly common because of the widespread use of IUDs. Untreated PID could be fatal.

Diseases and Disorders Handbook (Springhouse, PA: Springhouse Corp., 1990), 555-57. Anne Galperin, *Gynecological Disorders* (New York: Chelsea House, 1991), 75.

How are warts caused?

A wart is a lump on the skin produced when one of the 30 types of papillomavirus invades skin cells and causes them to multiply rapidly. There are several different types of warts: common warts, usually on injury sites; flat warts on hands, accompanied by itching; digitate warts having fingerlike projections; filiform warts on eyelids, armpits, and necks; plantar warts on the soles of the feet; and genital warts, pink cauliflowerlike areas that if occurring in a woman's cervix, could predispose her to cervical cancer. Each is produced by a specific virus and most usually symptomless. Wart viruses are spread by touch or by contact with the skin shed from a wart.

The American Medical Association Encyclopedia of Medicine (New York: Random House, 1989), 1069-70. *The American Medical Association Family Medical Guide, rev. ed.,* (New York: Random House, 1987), 252.

What are the symptoms and signs of AIDS?

The early symptoms (AIDS-related complex, or ARC, symptoms) include night sweats, prolonged fevers, severe weight loss, persistent diarrhea, skin rash, persistent cough, and shortness of breath. The diagnosis changes to AIDS (acquired immunodeficiency syndrome) when the immune system is affected and the patient becomes susceptible to opportunistic infections and unusual cancers, such as herpes viruses (herpes simplex, herpes zoster, cytomegalovirus infection), candida albicans (fungus) infection, cryptosporidium enterocolitis (protozoan intestinal infection), pneumocystis carinii pneumonia (PCP, a common AIDS lung infection), toxoplasmosis (protozoan brain infection), progressive multifocal leukoencephalopathy (PML, a central nervous system disease causing gradual brain degeneration), mycobacterium avium intracellulare infection (MAI, a common generalized bacterial infection), and Kaposi's sarcoma (a malignant skin cancer characterized by blue-red nodules on limbs and body, and internally in the gastrointestinal and respiratory tracts, where the tumors cause severe internal bleeding). More than 75 percent of AIDS victims die within two years of diagnosis.

The signs of AIDS are generalized swollen glands, emaciation, blue or purple-brown spots on the body, especially on the legs and arms, prolonged pneumonia, and oral thrush.

Diseases and Disorders Handbook (Springhouse, PA: Springhouse Corp., 1990), 11-17. Victor Gong, *AIDS: Facts and Issues* (New Brunswick, NJ: Rutgers University Press, 1980), 7.

If the sap of the poison ivy plant touches the skin, will a rash develop?

Studies show that 85 percent of the population will develop an allergic reaction if exposed to poison ivy, but this sensitivity varies with each individual according to circumstance, age, genetics, and previous exposure. The poison comes mainly from the leaves when the allergens touch the skin, a red rash with itching, and burning, will develop; skin blisters will develop usually within six hours to several days after exposure. Thorough washing of the affected area with mild soap within five minutes of exposure can be effective; sponging with alcohol and applying a soothing and drying lotion, such as calamine lotion, is the prescribed treatment for light cases. If the affected area is large, fever, headache, and generalized body weakness may develop. For severe reactions, a physician should be consulted, who may prescribe a corticosteroid drug. Clothing that touched the plants should also be washed.

American Academy of Dermatology, *Poison Ivy: First Aid Book* (Washington, DC: American Academy of Dermatology, 1990), 220-21.

How can a tick be removed?

A tick, common in woods and forests throughout the United States, fastens itself to a host with its teeth, then secretes a cementlike material to reinforce its hold. This flat brown speckled 0.25-inch insect can transmit diseases such as Rocky Mountain spotted fever and Lyme disease. To remove a tick, cover it with mineral, salad, or machine oil to block its breathing pores. If it does not disengage after about 30 minutes, use tweezers and grasp the tick as close to the skin as possible. Pull it away with a steady pressure, or lift the tick slightly upward and pull it parallel to the skin until the tick detaches. Do not twist or jerk the tick. Wash the bite site and hands well with soap and water and apply alcohol. If necessary apply a cold pack to reduce pain.

Diseases and Disorders Handbook (Springhouse, PA: Springhouse Corp., 1990), 412-13. Alton L. Thygerson, *First Aid Essentials* (Boston: Jones and Bartlett, 1989), 115-16.

How long does it take to bleed to death?

Serious bleeding requires immediate attention and care. If a large blood vessel is severed or lacerated, a person can bleed to death in one minute or less. Rapid loss of one quart or more of the total blood volume often leads to irreversible shock and death.

Lowell J. Thomas, *First Aid for Backpackers and Campers* (Fort Worth: Holt, Rinehart, and Winston, 1978), 7. Alton L. Thygerson, *First Aid Essentials* (Boston: Jones and Bartlett, 1989), 53.

Why do hangovers occur after some episodes of drinking alcohol?

Lowered blood sugar, dehydration, acidosis, and stress may all contribute to hangovers that occur eight to twelve hours after some episodes of drinking alcohol. Hangovers mimic hypoglycemia in that symptoms include general malaise; nausea and vomiting; dizziness; dry mouth and thirst; sensitivity to movement, bright lights, and loud sounds; a headache; anxiety; or depression. For heavy drinkers, there is speculation that hangovers are symptoms of early withdrawal from alcohol.

Robert O'Brien et al. , *The Encyclopedia of Drug Abuse, 2d ed.* (New York: Facts on File, 1992), s.v. "hangover."

Who are some famous snorers?

Twenty of the first 32 presidents of the United States were snorers. The loudest may have been Theodore Roosevelt (1858-1919), who once kept nearly a whole wing of a hospital awake all night with his snoring. Other famous snorers include British statesman Sir Winston Churchill (1874-1965), Italian dictator Benito Mussolini (1883-1945), Greek biographer Plutarch (ca.46-119), English politician Lord Chesterfield (1694-1773), George II (1683-1760) and George IV (1762-1830), Kings of Great Britain. It has been estimated that one out of every eight persons is a snorer.

Jane Polley, ed., *Stories Behind Everyday Things* (Pleasantville, NY: Reader's Digest Association, 1980), 317.

What are the most common disabilities in the U.S. and how many people are affected by them?

The most common disabilities in the U.S. and the number of people affected by them are:

Disability	**Number of Americans (in millions)**
Arthritis	30.8
Hearing impairments	23.3
Visual impairments	7.5
Speech impairments	2.3
Partial or complete paralysis	1.4
Epilepsy	1.2
Missing limbs	1.2

USA Today 22 July 1993.

How did the sled dog Balto earn the title "Hero Dog of Nome"?

In 1925 Balto was the lead canine on a dog sled team that carried a 20-pound parcel of antitoxin serum over 655 miles of rugged, frozen terrain from the railhead at Nenana to Nome, Alaska. The serum was urgently needed to combat an outbreak of malignant diptheria, then known as the "black death of the North." The desperate journey was made at the height of a 50 degrees below zero blizzard with gusts of wind up to 80 miles per hour.

"Racing the Black Death of Alaska for 1,000 lives," *Literary Digest* 21 February 1925.

What is the Alexander Technique of therapy?

The Alexander Technique is a kind of therapy that uses massage and manipulation of the neck combined with verbal instruction. It allows energy to flow from the spine to the head which controls body movement. Freeing this flow helps an individual to think, move and speak better. The Alexander Technique is named for F. Mathias Alexander, an Australian Shakespearean actor and monologist who developed these procedures in the late nineteenth century.

Rosemary Ellen Guiley, *Harper's Encyclopedia of Mystical & Paranormal Experience* (San Francisco: HarperCollins, 1991), s.v. "Alexander Technique."

How did the medical procedure known as a Caesarean section or Caesarean birth get its name?

The medical procedure known as a Caesarean section or Caesarean birth is named after the Roman emperor Julius Caesar (100-44 B.C.) who, according to legend, was born that way. A Caesarean section or "C-section," as it is commonly called, is the removal of the infant from the womb via an incision made in the mother's lower abdomen. The procedure, which is normally performed in a hospital by an obstetrician or a gynecologist, is used when labor will not progress to a normal vaginal delivery because of various factors, including the positioning of the infant or placenta, or severe stress on the infant or mother. The mortality rate of the C-section procedure is less than 0.1 percent but is still higher than the mortality rate for vaginal deliveries.

Charles B. Inlander, *Good Operations-Bad Operations* (New York: Viking, 1993), 125. Maria Leach, ed., *Standard Dictionary of Folklore Mythology and Legend* (New York: Funk & Wagnalls, 1972), s.v. "Caesarean birth."

Are left-handed children more prone to accidents?

Left-handed children are more prone to accidents according to a 1993 study by pediatrician Charles J. Graham of University of Arkansas for Medical Sciences. Graham's study evaluated 267 children who were brought to emergency rooms for accidents and 496 who were admitted for non-accident emergencies. Graham found that southpaws have a 1.8 greater risk of accidental injury. He also found that 18 percent of the injured children were left-handers, although as a group lefthanders make up only 10 percent of the population. Scientists speculated that differences in brain structure and the use of tools, implements, etc., that are designed for the right-handed majority might explain the higher injury rate.

Marilyin Elias, "Higher injury risk for young lefties," *USA Today* 9 December 1993.

When was the S.S. *Hope* retired?

The hospital ship S.S. *Hope* a worldwide symbol of United States medical aid to underdeveloped nations, was deliberately run aground in February of 1975, just south of Wilmington, Delaware, after a tug towing the ship to the scrap pile accidentally rammed her. The ship was beached in the Delaware River as a safety precaution after the tug put a hole in the starboard side near the waterline. The white ship had traveled over 250,000 miles during her career, promoting U.S. foreign aid and humanitarian assistance and was retired in 1974 after 11 voyages and nearly 14 years of roaming the globe. The world's first hospital ship was originally the mothballed navy ship *Consolation* which U.S. president Eisenhower donated to Project Hope (an acronym for "Health Opportunity for People Everywhere"), founded by Dr. William Walsh. The organization survives today as People-To-People Health Foundation, whose activities reach 26 countries on five continents.

Peggy K. Daniels and Carol A. Schwartz, eds., *Encyclopedia of Associations, 28th ed.* (Detroit: Gale Research, 1993), 1520. Holly G. Miller, "Thirty Years of Hope," *The Saturday Evening Post* April 1988. "S.S. Hope Beached to Prevent Sinking After Tug Ramming," *New York Times* 13 February 1995.

Prior to the condom, what was the main contraceptive practice?

Contraceptive devices have been used throughout recorded history, including the usual traditional sponge soaked in vinegar. The condom was devised by the personal physician to King Charles II (1630-1685), who used a sheath of stretched, oiled sheep intestine to protect the king himself from syphilis. Previously penile sheaths were used, such as the linen one made by Italian anatomist, Gabriel Fallopius (1523-1562), but they were too heavy to be successful.

The function of the condom was not for birth control but was a means of preventing venereal disease, especially when seeking sexual pleasure from prostitutes.

Janet Farrell Brodie, *Contraception and Abortion in Nineteenth-Century America* (Ithaca, NY: Cornell University Press, 1994), 204-7. Charles Panati, *Panati's Extraordinary Origins of Everyday Things* (New York: Perennial Library, 1987), 331-34. *Technology and Culture* January 1981.

What are the blood group combinations that can normally be used to prove that a man is not the father of a particular child?

The following table shows the blood combinations that can be used to prove that a man is not the father of a particular child.

Mother	Child	Father Yes	Father No
O	O	O, A, or B	AB
O	A	A or AB	O or B
O	B	B or AB	O or A
A	O	O, A, or B	AB
A	A	any group	
A	B	B or AB	O or A
A	AB	B or AB	O or A
B	O	O, A, or B	AB
B	B	any group	
B	A	A or AB	O or B
B	AB	A or AB	O or B
AB	AB	A, B, or AB	O

Anthony Smith, *The Body* (New York: Viking Press, 1986), 249.

What is the most commonly broken bone?

The clavicle (collar bone) is one of the most frequently fractured bones in the body. Fractured clavicles are caused by either a direct blow or a transmitted force resulting from a fall on the outstretched arm.

Alton L. Thygerson, *First Aid Essentials* (Boston: Jones and Bartlett, 1989), 162.

How many Americans wear hearing aids?

In 1990, more than 13.1 million Americans, or about 5.3 percent of the population, were using assistive technology devices to accommodate physical impairments. Of these, over 3.7 million were using hearing aids.

Department of Health and Human Services, National Center of Health Statistics, *Advance Data* (Hyattsville, MD: National Center for Health Statistics, 1992), 217:1, 6.

How is the term *zoonosis* defined?

A zoonosis is any infectious or parasitic disease of animals that can be transmitted to humans. Examples include cat-scratch fever, psittacosis from parrots, and trichinosis from pigs.

The American Medical Association Encyclopedia of Medicine (New York: Random House, 1989), 1088.

What is tango foot?

Officially known as *ibialis anticus*, tango foot is a strain of the leg muscles resulting from dancing the tango and maxixe.

Edward R. Plunkett, *Folk Name & Trade Diseases* (Stamford, CT: Barrett Book Co., 1978), 282.

What is Lou Gehrig's disease?

Sometimes called Lou Gehrig's disease, after the famous baseball player who had the disease, Amyotrophic Lateral Sclerosis (ALS) is a motor neuron disease of middle or late life. It results from a progressive degeneration of nerve cells controlling voluntary motor functions that ends in death three to ten years after its onset. There is no cure for it. At the beginning of the disease, the patient notices weakness in the hands and arms, with involuntary muscle quivering and possible muscle cramping or stiffness. Eventually all four extremities become involved. As nerve degeneration progresses, disability occurs and physical independence declines until the patient, while mentally and intellectually aware, can no longer swallow or move.

American Medical Association Encyclopedia of Medicine (New York: Random House, 1989), 696. Columbia University College of Physicians and Surgeons, *Complete Home Medical Guide* (New York: Crown, 1985), 599.

What is "Christmas factor"?

In the clotting of blood, factor IX, or the Christmas factor, is a coagulation factor present in normal plasma, but deficient in the blood of persons with hemophilia B or Christmas disease. It was named after a man called Christmas who, in 1952, was the first patient in whom this genetic disease was shown to be distinct from hemophilia (another genetic blood-clotting disease in which the blood does not have factor VIII).

The American Medical Association Encyclopedia of Medicine (New York: Random House, 1989), 277. *Mosby's Medical, Nursing, and Allied Health Dictionary, 3d ed.,* (St. Louis, MO: Mosby, 1990), 459.

What is the difference between homeopathy, osteopathic medicine, naturopathy, and chiropractic?

Developed by a German physician, Christian F.S. Hahneman (1755-1843), the therapy of homeopathy treats patients with small doses of two thousand substances. Based on the principle that "like cures like," the medicine used is one that produces the same symptoms in a healthy person that the disease is producing in the sick person.

Chiropractic is based on the belief that disease results from the lack of normal nerve function. Relying on physical manipulation and adjustment of the spine for therapy, rather than on drugs or surgery, this therapy, used by the ancient Egyptians, Chinese, and Hindus, was rediscovered in 1895 by Daniel David Palmer (1845-1913).

Developed in the United States by Dr. Andrew Taylor Still, osteopathic medicine recognizes the role of the musculoskeletal system in healthy function of the human body. The physician is fully licensed and uses manipulation techniques as well as traditional diagnostic and therapeutic procedures. Osteopathy is practiced as part of standard Western medicine.

Naturopathy is based on the principle that disease is due to the accumulation of waste products and toxins in the body. Practitioners believe that health is maintained by avoiding anything artificial or unnatural in the diet or in the environment.

The American Medical Association Encyclopedia of Medicine (New York: Random House, 1987), 270, 544, 716, 755. *The Guinness Book of Answers, 8th ed.* (Enfield, England: Guinness Publishing, 1991), 167-68.

Why does the risk of cancer diminish rapidly after one quits the cigarette smoking habit?

Exposure of a premalignant cell to a promoter converts the cell to an irreversibly malignant state. Promotion is a slow process, and exposure to the promoter must be sustained for a certain period of time. This requirement explains why the risk of cancer diminishes rapidly after one quits smoking; both cancer initiators and promoters appear to be contained in tobacco smoke.

Sigmund F. Zakrzewski, *Principles of Environmental Toxicology* (Washington, DC: American Chemical Society, 1991), 69.

What are the leading causes of stress?

In 1967, when they conducted a study of the correlation between significant life events and the onset of illness, Dr. Thomas H. Holmes and Dr. Richard H. Rahe from the University of Washington compiled a chart of the major causes of stress with assigned point values. They published their findings on stress effects as "The Social Readjustment Scale," printed in *The Journal of Psychosomatic Research.*

The researchers calculated that a score of 150 points indicated a 50-50 chance of the respondent developing an illness or a health change. A score of 300 would increase the risk to 90 percent. Of course, many factors enter into an individual's response to a particular event, so this scale, partially represented below, can only be used as a guide.

Event	Point value
Death of spouse	100
Divorce	73
Marital separation	65
Jail term or death of close family member	63
Personal injury or illness	53
Marriage	50
Fired at work	47
Marital reconcilation or retirement	45
Pregnancy	40
Change in financial state	38
Death of close friend	37
Mortgage over $10,000	31
Foreclosure of mortgage or loan	30
Outstanding personal achievement	28
Trouble with boss	23
Change in work hours or conditions or change in residence or school	20
Vacation	13
Christmas	12
Minor violation of the law	11

Christiaan Barnard, *The Body Machine* (New York: Crown, 1981), 166. *The World Almanac and Book of Facts 1992* (New York: World Almanac, 1991), 253.

Can owning a pet be beneficial to your health?

As a result of several studies, researchers now believe that regular contact with pets can reduce heart rate, blood pressure, and levels of stress in their human owners. In a study of 93 heart attack patients, only one of 18 pet owners died compared to one of three patients who did not have pets. A study of 1,000 Medicare patients showed that pet owners were less likely to visit the doctor. Dog owners, in particular, seemed to enjoy the greatest benefit; they visited the doctor 20 percent less than patients who did not have a pet. Pets offer constancy, stability, comfort, security, affection, and intimacy.

Linda Mason Hunter, *The Healthy Home* (New York: Pocket Books, 1989), 222-27. "Pet Owners Go to the Doctor Less," *New York Times* 2 August 1990. *Prevention's Giant Book of Health Facts* (Emmaus, PA: Rodale Press, 1991), 433.

How many school days and how many work days are missed annually because of allergies?

Because of allergies three million work days are missed annually while also accounting for two million missed school days every year.

U.S. News & World Report 4 April 1994.

Why do deep-sea divers get the bends?

Bends, also known as caisson disease, tunnel disease, and diver's paralysis, is a painful condition that develops in limbs and abdomen of the human body. It is caused by the formation and enlargement of bubbles of nitrogen in blood and tissues as a result of rapid reduction of air pressure. This condition can develop when a sea diver ascends too rapidly after being exposed to increased pressure. Severe pain will develop in the muscles and joints of the arms and legs. More severe symptoms include vertigo, nausea, vomiting, choking and shock, and sometimes death.

Taber's Cyclopedic Medical Dictionary, 16th ed. (Philadelphia: Davis, 1989), 203.

How are human body burns classified?

The following data gives the classifications of human burns, listed by type of burn and effects.

First-degree—Sunburn; steam. Reddening and peeling. Affects epidermis (top layer of skin). Heals within a week.
Second-degree—Scalding; holding hot metal. Deeper burns causing blisters. Affects dermis (deep skin layer). Heals in two to three weeks.

Third-degree—Fire. A full layer of skin is destroyed. Requires a doctor's care and grafting.
Circumferential—Any burns (often electrical) that completely encircle a limb or body region (such as the chest), which can impair circulation or respiration; requires a doctor's care; fasciotomy (repair of connective tissues) is sometimes required.
Chemical—Acid, alkali. Can be neutralized with water (for up to a half hour). Doctor's evaluation recommended.
Electrical—Destruction of muscles, nerves, circulatory system, etc., below the skin. Doctor's evaluation and ECG monitoring required.

If more than 10 percent of body surface is affected in second-and third-degree burns, shock can develop when large quantities of fluid (and its protein) are lost. When skin is burned, it cannot protect the body from airborne bacteria.

Jeff Rovin, *Laws of Order* (New York: Ballantine, 1992), 102.

What disease did Queen Victoria's children and grandchildren pass to many other royal families of Europe?

The descendants of Great Britain's Queen Victoria (1819-1901) carried the gene for hemophilia, a disease that disables blood clotting. As a result, hemophiliacs are in great danger when they receive the smallest of cuts and bruises. Such wounds do not heal normally and can result in death. Victoria's children and grandchildren married into other royal families in Europe, spreading the disease. The most notorious case was that of a great grandson, the heir to the Russian throne. The monk Rasputin (1871-1916) promised the boy's parents that he would provide a cure; in this vulnerable situation, the monarchy was weakened and soon fell from power during the Russian Revolution in 1917.

E. D. Hirsch, Joseph F. Kett, and James Trefil, *The Dictionary of Cultural Literacy* (Boston: Houghton Mifflin, 1988), s.v. "hemophilia."

How often should a person get periodic health exams?

It is recommended that healthy adults regularly visit their doctor for physical checkups as a means of detecting problems that could be prevented from becoming serious and even life-threatening. As a general rule, persons ages 20 to 40 should have a checkup every five years. From the ages 40 to 50, a visit to the doctor is recommended every three years. In the next twenty years, from ages 50 to 70, the suggested frequency is every two years. After age 70 an annual exam is advised.

"Health Watch" *Aging* #365, 1993.

What are some tips for talking with a person with a hearing loss?

Many factors can make it difficult for a person with a hearing loss to participate in a conversation. To improve the person's ability to understand what is said, avoid talking from another room or from behind. It is also helpful to cut down background noise and to try to speak more slowly and distinctly, without shouting. Try to stay in a lighted area; face the person, and do not obscure your face. Be sure that you have the person's attention before speaking and rephrase what you have said if it seems you are not understood. Be patient and, in turn, listen carefully to the person with a hearing loss.

Paula B. Doress-Wortersand Diana Laskin Siegal, *The New Ourselves, Growing Older: Women Aging with Knowledge and Power* (New York: Simon & Schuster, 1994), 397.

How much does the cardiac pacemaker weigh?

The modern pacemaker generator is a hermetically-sealed titanium metal can weighing from one to 4.5 ounces (30 to 130 grams) and powered by a lithium battery that can last two to 15 years. Used to correct an insufficient or irregular heartbeat, the cardiac pacemaker corrects the low cardiac rhythm through electrical stimulation, which increases the contractions of the heart muscle. The contraction and expansion of the heart muscle produces a heartbeat-one of three billion in an average lifetime-which pumps blood throughout the body. A pacemaker has gold or platinum electrodes, conducting wires, and a pacing box (miniature generator). In both kinds of pacemakers-those implanted in the chest or external-the electrode is attached to the heart's right ventricle (chamber), either directly through the chest or threaded through a vein.

Carol Sutton and Duncan M. Anderson, *How Do They Do That?* (New York: Quill, 1982), 28-30. *Van Nostrand's Scientific Encyclopedia, 7th ed.* (New York: Van Nostrand Reinhold, 1989), 1:220.

Why are eye transplants not available?

It is because the eye's retina is part of the brain, and the retina's cells are derived from brain tissue. Retinal cells and the cells that connect them to the brain are particularly difficult to manipulate outside the body.

The New York Times 17 December, 1991.

Who developed psychodrama?

Psychodrama is defined as a method of group psychotherapy in which personality makeup, interpersonal relationships, conflicts, and emotional problems are explored by means of special dramatic methods.

It was developed by Jacob L. Moreno, a psychiatrist born in Romania, who lived and practiced in Vienna until he came to the United States in 1925. He soon began to conduct psychodrama sessions and founded a psychodrama institute in Beacon, New York, in 1934. Largely because of Moreno's efforts it is practiced worldwide.

Comprehensive Textbook of Psychiatry, 5th ed. (Baltimore: Williams & Wilkins, 1989), 2:1531.

What is the longest coma on record?

Elaine Esposito (1934-1978) of Tarpon Springs, Florida, went into a coma after appendix surgery at age six. She died 37 years, 111 days later, without ever regaining consciousness.

Mark Young, ed., *The Guinness Book of Records 1995* (New York: Facts on File, 1994), 16.

How is Lyme disease carried?

The cause of Lyme disease is the spirochete *Borrelia burgdorferi* that is transmitted to humans by the small tick *Ixodes dammini* or other ticks in the Ixodidae family. The tick injects spirochete-laden saliva into the bloodstream or deposits fecal matter on the skin. This multisystemic disease usually begins in the summer with a skin lesion called erythema chronicum migrans (ECM), followed by more lesions, a molar rash, conjuctivitis, and urticaria. The lesions are eventually replaced by small red blotches. Other common symptoms in the first stage include fatigue, intermittent headache, fever, chills, and achiness.

In stage two, which can be weeks or months later, cardiac or neurologic abnormalities sometimes develop. In the last stage (weeks or years later) arthritis develops with marked swelling, especially in the large joints. If tetracycline, penicillin, or erythromycin is given in the early stages, the later complications can be minimized. High dosage of intravenously given penicillin can also be effective on the late stages.

Diseases and Disorders Handbook (Springhouse, PA: Springhouse Corp., 1990), 457-58.

What is Factor VIII?

Factor VIII is one of the enzymes needed for the clotting of blood. Hemophiliacs lack this enzyme and can bleed to death unless they receive supplemental doses of Factor VIII. The majority of bleeding episodes for hemophiliacs are hemorrhages into joints and muscles of the body. The lack of Factor VIII caused by a defective gene, that is affecting males—one in ten thousand; females can carry the gene this is a sex-linked inherited gene.

The Almanac of Science and Technology (San Diego: Harcourt Brace Jovanovich, 1990), 104. *The American Medical Association Encyclopedia of Medicine* (New York: Random House, 1989), 530.

What is the medical term for a heart attack?

Myocardial infarction is the term used for a heart attack in which part of the heart muscle's cells die as a result of reduced blood flow through one of the main arteries-many times due to atherosclerosis. The outlook for the patient is dependent on the size and location of the blockage and extent of damage, but 33 percent of patients die within 20 days after the attack; it is a leading cause of death in the United States.

Diseases and Disorders Handbook (Springhouse, PA: Springhouse corp., 1990), 491-96.

Which disease is the most common?

The most common noncontagious disease is periodontal disease, such as gingivitis, or inflammation of the gums. Few people in their lifetime can avoid the effects of tooth decay. The most common contagious disease in the world is coryza, or the common cold.

Guinness Book of Records 1995 (New York: Facts on File, 1994), 18.

How does a stroke occur?

A stroke, or cerebrovascular accident (CVA), is a medical emergency produced by a blood clot that lodges in an artery and blocks the flow of blood to a portion of the brain. It produces symptoms ranging from paralysis of limbs and loss of speech to unconsciousness and death. Less commonly, a stroke may be the result of bleeding into the substance of the brain. Strokes are fatal in about 33 percent to 50 percent of the cases and 500,000 cases a year make it the third most common cause of death. Certain factors increase the risk of stroke such as high blood pressure (hypertension), which weakens artery walls, and atherosclerosis (thickening of the lining of artery walls), which narrows arteries.

Diseases and Disorders Handbook (Springhouse, PA: Springhouse Corp., 1990), 128-32. *Mayo Clinic Family Healthbook* (New York: Morrow, 1990), 1328.

Which blood type is the rarest?

The rarest blood type is Bombay blood (subtype h-h), found only in a Czechoslovakian nurse in 1961 and in a brother and sister named Jalbert living in Massachusetts in 1968.

Prevention's Giant Book of Health Facts (Emmaus, PA: Rodale Press, 1991), 397.

Is it true that people need less sleep as they get older?

As a person ages, the time spent in sleeping changes. The following table shows how long a night's sleep generally lasts.

Age	Sleep Time in Hours
1 to 15 days	16 to 22
6 to 23 months	13.0
3 to 9 years	11.0
10 to 13 years	10.0
14 to 18 years	9.0
19 to 30 years	8.0
31 to 45 years	7.5
45 to 50 years	6.0
50 or more years	5.5

Frank Kendig and Richard Hutton, *Life-Spans* (New York: Holt, Rinehart and Winston, 1979), 25.

In the United States, what is the average height and weight for a man and a woman?

In the United States, the average female is 5 feet 3 and 3/4 inches (1.62 meters) tall and weighs 135 pounds (61.24 kilograms). The average male is 5 feet 9 inches (1.75 meters) tall and weighs 162 pounds (73.48 kilograms). Between 1960 and 1990 the average male became two inches (5.08 centimeters) taller and 27 pounds (12.25 kilograms) heavier, while the average woman grew two inches (5.08 centimeters) taller and gained one pound (0.45 kilograms).

Isaac Asimov, *The Human Body, rev. ed.* (New York: Mentor Book, 1992), 314. Diagram Group, *Comparisons* (New York: St. Martin's Press, 1980), 72-73.

How much of the body remains after cremation?

The solids left after cremation are about three percent of the former body weight, so a corpse weighing 150 pounds (68 kilograms) produces about five pounds (2 kilograms), or about 200 cubic inches, of remains.

William E. Phipps, *Cremation Concerns* (Springfield, IL: C. C. Thomas, 1989), 33.

Who invented bifocal lenses?

The original bifocal lens was invented in 1784 by Benjamin Franklin (1706-1790). At that time, the two lenses were joined in a metallic frame. In 1899, J.L. Borsch welded the two lenses together. One-part bifocal lenses were developed by Bentron and Emerson in 1910 for the Carl Zeiss Company.

Dictionary of Visual Science, 4th ed. (Radnor, PA: Chilton Trade Book, 1989), 388. Valerie-Anne Giscard-d'Estaing, *The World Almanac Book of Inventions* (New York: World Almanac Publications, 1985), 221.

How can a person register to become an organ donor?

Organ donor registration forms and information on organ donation are available from the Living Bank, a national organ and tissue donor registry and referral service that was founded in 1968. At the time of a donor's death, the Living Bank attempts to fulfill the donor's wishes by contacting the nearest transplant facility, organ or tissue bank, or medical school (in the case of body donation) according to the donor's wishes and physical condition at the time of death. The Living Bank also recognizes organ donations from persons who have registered with other organ banks or those who have indicated their wish to donate organs by signing the back of their driver's license. There is a Organ Donor Hotline that provides information on organ donations and waiting lists of transfer recipients through a twenty-four hour hotline.

Ken Skala, *American Guidance for Those Over 60, 2d ed.* (Falls Church, VA: American Guidance, 1990), 323-24. Barbara J. White and Edward J. Madara, eds., *The Self-Help Sourcebook, 4th ed.* (Denville, NJ: St. Clares-Riverside Medical Center, 1992), 167.

Which state has the highest percentage of physically active citizens, and which has the lowest?

Montana claims the highest percentage of physically active citizens at 82 percent while Washington, DC, has the lowest at 48 per cent.

Les Krantz, *America by The Numbers: Facts and Figures From the Weighty to the Way-Out* (Boston: Houghton Mifflin, 1993), 28.

What is quickening?

Quickening refers to movements of the fetus in the womb that first become noticeable to the mother between the sixteenth and twentieth week of pregnancy. In earlier periods of history abortion was considered more acceptable if it happened before quickening.

Margaret DiCanio, *The Encyclopedia of Marriage, Divorce, and the Family* (New York: Facts on File, 1989), s.v. "quickening."

What is monkey-paw?

Monkey-paw is a contracture of the hand resulting from median nerve palsy. The thumb cannot be opposed to the tips of the fingers.

Stedman's Medical Dictionary, 25th ed., (Baltimore: Williams & Wilkins, 1990), 977.

How is an iatrogenic illness defined?

An iatrogenic illness is an adverse mental or physical condition caused by the effects of treatment by a physician or surgeon. The term implies that it could have been avoided by judicious care on the part of the physician.

Taber's Cyclopedia Medical Dictionary, 16th ed., (Philadelphia: Davis, 1989), 885.

What is meant by *vectors* in medicine?

A vector is an animal that transmits a particular infectious disease. A vector picks up disease organisms from a source of infection, carries them within or on its body and later deposits them where they infect a new host. Mosquitoes, fleas, lice, ticks, and flies are the most important vectors of disease to humans.

The American Medical Association Encyclopedia of Medicine (New York: Random House, 1989), 1041.

What is dyslexia and what causes it?

Dyslexia covers a wide range of language and learning difficulties and affects millions of Americans. In general, a person with dyslexia cannot identify correctly letters and words, especially those having similar shapes. Persons suffering from dyslexia often have short attention spans and have difficulty expressing themselves. Dyslexic children may reverse letter and word order, make bizarre spelling errors, and may not be able to name colors or write from dictation. This condition may be caused by minor visual defects, emotional disturbance, or failure to train the brain, but new evidence indicates that a neurological disorder or irregularities in the left hemisphere of the brain which is responsible for language skills may be the underlying cause. Approximately 90 percent of dyslexics are male.

The term *dyslexia* is of Greek origin and was first suggested by Professor Rudolph of Stuttgart, Germany in 1887. The earliest references to the condition date as far back as 30 A.D. when Valerius Maximus and Pliny described a man who lost his ability to read after being struck on the head by a stone.

Although dyslexia is a challenging disorder to overcome, many famous dyslexics have gone on to lead very successful lives. Among them are inventor, Thomas Edison, U.S. Vice-President Nelson Rockefeller, U.S. General George Patton, Jr., fiction writer Hans Christian Andersen, athlete Bruce Jenner, and possibly Albert Einstein.

The American Medical Association Encyclopedia of Medicine (New York: Random House, 1989), 382-83. J. Gordon Millichap, *Dyslexia as the Neurologist and Educator Read It* (Springfield, IL: Thomas, 1986), 3. *The New Good Housekeeping Family Health and Medical Guide* (New York: Hearst Books, 1989), 141. *Pittsburgh Post-Gazette* 15 February 1984.

What is anorexia?

Anorexia simply means a loss of appetite. Anorexia nervosa is a psychological disturbance that is characterized by an intense fear of being fat. It usually affects teenage or young adult females. This persistent "fat image," however untrue in reality, leads the patient to self-imposed starvation and emaciation (extreme thinness) to the point where one-third of the body weight is lost. There are many theories on the causes of this disease, which is difficult to treat and can be fatal. Between five percent and 10 percent of patients hospitalized for anorexia nervosa later die from starvation or suicide. Symptoms include a 25 percent or greater weight loss (for no organic reason) coupled with a morbid dread of being fat, an obsession with food, an avoidance of eating, compulsive exercising and restlessness, binge eating followed by induced vomiting, and/or use of laxatives or diuretics.

The American Medical Association Encyclopedia of Medicine (New York: Random House, 1989), 112-13. *Diseases and Disorders Handbook* (Springhouse, PA: Springhouse Corp., 1990), 47-49.

Which first aid measures can be used for a bite by a black widow spider?

The black widow spider (*Latrodectus mactans*) is common throughout the United States. Its bite is severely poisonous, but no first aid measures are of value. Age, body size, and degree of sensitivity determine the severity of symptoms, which include an initial pinprick with a dull numbing pain, followed by swelling. An ice cube may be placed over the bite to relieve pain. Between 10 and 40 minutes after the bite, severe abdominal pain and rigidity of stomach muscles develops. Muscle spasms in the extremities, ascending paralysis, and difficulty in swallowing and breathing follow. The mortality rate is less than 1 percent; but anyone who has been bitten should see a doctor; the elderly, infants, and those with allergies are most at risk and should be hospitalized.

Diseases and Disorders Handbook (Springhouse, PA: Springhouse Corp., 1990), 412-16. *Merck Manual of Diagnosis and Therapy, 15th ed.* (West Pont, PA: Merck, Shark & Dohme, 1987), 2572.

What is the Heimlich maneuver?

The Heimlich maneuver is an effective first-aid technique to resuscitate choking and drowning victims, introduced by Dr. Henry J. Heimlich (b. 1920) of Xavier University, in Cincinnati, Ohio. It is a technique for removing a foreign body from the trachea or pharynx where it is preventing flow of air to the lungs. When the victim is in the vertical position, the maneuver consists of applying subdiaphragmatic pressure by wrapping one's arms around the victim's waist from behind, making a fist with one hand and placing it against the victim's abdomen between the navel and the rib cage, clasping one's fist with the other hand and pressing in with a quick, forceful thrust. Repeat several times if necessary. When the victim is in the horizontal position (which some experts recommend), the rescuer straddles the victim's thighs.

Harry Harris, *Good Old-Fashioned Yankee Ingenuity* (Chelsea, MI: Scarborough House, 1990), 143-44. *Taber's Cyclopedic Medical Dictionary, 16th ed.* (Philadelphia: Davis, 1989), 793-95.

How many people visit a dentist regularly?

Only about half the population visit a dentist as often as once a year.

Reader's Digest Consumer Adviser (Pleasantville, NY: Reader's Digest Association, 1989), 301.

What is amniocentesis?

Available since the 1930s, amniocentesis is a diagnostic procedure that can detect hereditary defects and chromosomal abnormalities in an unborn fetus. The procedure is performed by passing a needle through a pregnant woman's abdomen and uterine wall into the amnion, from which a small amount of amniotic fluid can be extracted. The procedure is performed when the mother is over 35 years of age; when either parent is known to have a transmissible genetic defect for certain diseases; when the mother has given birth to a child with a chromosomal or a neural-tube defect; or when the mother has a different Rh blood factor than the father. The last reason—possible Rh blood factor problems—was the original intent for the test.

Margaret DiCanio, *The Encyclopedia of Marriage, Divorce, and the Family* (New York: Facts On File, 1989), s.v. "amniocentesis."

What were the symptoms of the Black Death?

The term The Black Death refers to a plague epidemic that swept through most of Europe and Asia from 1348 to 1666. In some parts of Europe, as much as two-thirds of the population died from this disease. It is estimated that 25 million people died from the disease.

Two forms of the plague were responsible for the high death toll. One form, known as bubonic plague, was characterized by a high fever and the formation of large, bulbous abscesses, particularly in the armpit and groin area. Infected persons usually died five days after contracting the disease. The second type of plague was pneumonic plague, characterized by an intermittent fever and the spitting of black blood. Caused by the same bacteria as bubonic plague, this form was highly contagious because it was acquired by breathing the infected droplets coming from the lungs of a person with the disease. Persons infected with pneumonic plague died within three days of contracting the disease. The fact that many of the victims of the plague spit black blood earned the disease the nickname "Black Death."

The plague was believed to have originated in China and Turkestan and reached Genoa, Italy, in 1348 when cargo ships from Asia docked in the city's port. Disease-ridden rats from the ships escaped and spread throughout the town. In ten years, the plague spread across Europe, and cargo ships brought the disease to England. The population in some towns and villages was completely wiped out. Nine out of ten persons in London died of the disease and the entire populations of Cyprus and Iceland were killed. As sanitation and hygiene improved throughout Europe, the plague epidemic began to wane. By 1666, the Black Death disappeared.

Jay Robert Nash, *Darkest Hours: A Narrative Encyclopedia of Worldwide Disasters From Ancient Times to the Present* (Chicago: Nelson-Hall, 1976), s.v. "Black Death." James Trager, *The People's Chronology, rev. ed.* (New York: Henry Holt, 1992), 129

What caused a near panic among American parents of infants and school age children in the summer of 1949?

In the summer of 1949 a nationwide outbreak of polio, also known as infantile paralysis, caused a near panic among parents of infants and school age children. The epidemic claimed 42,033 victims and 2,720 fatalities between June and September of that year.

Woody Gelman and Barbara Jackson, *Disaster Illustrated: Two Hundred Years of American Misfortune* (New York: Harmony Books, 1976), 184.

When was the Band-Aid introduced?

The adhesive bandage called Band-Aid was introduced in 1920 by the Johnson & Johnson company of New Brunswick, New Jersey.

Dennis Sanders, *The First of Everything,* (New York: Delacorte Press, 1981, 13.

What percentage of the American population has regular medical checkups?

In 1994 *USA Today* reported that 32.4 percent of all Americans make routine checkup visits to the doctor every one to two years, and 38.8 percent get checkups more often than once a year. This compares to 14.2 percent of Americans who claimed to have checkups more than two years apart, and 13.3 percent who said they never visited a doctor for a checkup. Less than two percent of those surveyed—1.3 percent of the total—did not answer.

USA Snapshots *USA Today* 8 August 1994.

How many people died in the flu epidemic of 1918?

The influenza epidemic that spread throughout the world in the years 1918-1919 was the most deadly attack of disease since the Black Death plague of the 1300s. The epidemic, also known as the "Plague of the Spanish Lady," was estimated to have killed 21,642,274 people. More than a billion are thought to have suffered from the disease. Epidemiologists produced estimates for areas of Asia and Africa where there were no death records; in Australia and Oceania the total number of fatalities neared one million, while in Asia alone there were more than 15 million deaths.

It is impossible to say which virus caused the epidemic; scientific study has been unable to identify it despite arduous attempts to locate the virus. Doctors even exhumed the frozen bodies of Eskimos who died in the epidemic, hoping to find the virus intact. Experts believe that the 1918 virus is related to today's swine flu, also known as Swine "A," but are unable to explain why the virus has lost its deadly effect on humankind.

Richard Collier, *The Plague of the Spanish Lady: The Influenza Pandemic of 1918-1919* (New York: Atheneum, 1974), 305-6.

What common household products are harmful to children?

Many household products are harmful to children. These include: ammonia, insecticides, drain cleaner, rat poison, and gasoline. There are, however, many other products that are often viewed as being relatively benign but in fact can be dangerous. A list would include: aftershave lotion, air fresheners, arts-and-crafts supplies, automatic dishwasher detergent, bathtub and tile cleaner, bubble bath and salts, cologne, cosmetics, epsom salts, fabric softener, face cream, flea powder, ink, laxatives, meat tenderizers, mothballs and flakes, mouthwash, pens, peroxides, pet foods, plant seeds and bulbs, rug cleaner, shoe polish, soap, suntan lotion, toothpicks, vinegar, and window cleaner.

Jeanne E. Miller, *The Perfectly Safe Home* (New York: Fireside, 1991), 249-50.

How far back do health warnings concerning the effect of smoking on the lungs go?

Warnings go back one hundred years. In his *Annual Report* for 1894-95, the U.S. Commissioner of Indian Affairs included the following:

Cigarettes: In some report of mine to the Bureau I recommended that the Indian traders be enjoined specifically from selling tobacco and cigarettes to Indian youth. Any pathologist will tell you of the disastrous effects of tobacco smoke on a pair of lungs predisposed to tuberculosis . . . and the effect of inhaling the smoke of cigarettes is to disseminate the nicotine through the lung tissue, which, in combination with the gaseous carbon from the wrapper, produces a depressing, irritating, and biting effect on the delicate organs. It is greatly to be deplored that these Sioux have almost abandoned the use of the old-fashioned pipe and have taken to cigarette smoking, and the practice is almost as extensive with the children as with the adults.

1894-95 Annual Report of the U.S. Commission on Indian Affairs, (Washington, DC: Government Printing Office, 1894?), 290.

Which of the major blood types are the most common in the United States?

In the United States blood type O positive is the most common, with A positive a close second.

Blood type	Frequency in U.S.
0+	37.4%
0-	6.6%
A+	35.7%
A-	6.3%
B+	8.5%
B-	1.5%
AB+	3.4%
AB-	0.6%

In the world, the preponderance of one blood group varies greatly by locality. Group O is generally the most common with 46 percent of the population with this blood type, but in some areas such as Norway Group A predominates.

Mark Young, ed., *The Guinness Book of Records 1995* (New York: Facts on File), 15. *Current Health* October 1989.

What is cryonic suspension?

Cryonic suspension is the controversial process of freezing and storing bodies for later revival and has been practiced since the late 1960s. People are in most cases placed in cryonic suspension only after they are pronounced legally dead. Suspended animation, as the concept of long-term storage of humans is generally known, has been a topic of scientific speculation.

Search for Immortality (New York: TimeLife Books, 1992), 96-97.

What is color blindness?

Color blindness, also called daltonism, is the inability to tell colors apart. The two most common types of hereditary color vision deficiency are reduced discrimination of the colors green and red, which occur in the middle and long parts of the wavelengths of the visible spectrum. Very few people are truly blind to all colors, meaning they see only in shades of white, gray, and black. Among Caucasians of European origin, about eight percent of males and less than one percent of females have either green or red deficiency. The prevalence is generally lower in Asians and Native Americans, and even lower among African Americans. The defect is inherited and sex-linked, which means that the majority of sufferers are male, although women may carry the defect and pass it on to some of their children. There is no cure for color blindness.

Charles B. Clayman, ed., *The American Medical Association Encyclopedia of Medicine* (New York: Random House, 1989), s.v. "color vision deficiency." *World Book Encyclopedia* (Chicago: World Book, 1994), s.v. "color blindness."

What is the legal definition of blindness?

In determining whether or not an individual is eligible for federal or state benefits, the U.S. Internal Revenue Service, Social Security Administration, and other governmental agencies consider a person legally blind if the visual acuity of the better eye, with correction, is 20/200 or less. A loss of central (straight-ahead) vision is involved in such cases. An individual is also considered legally blind if the visual field of the better eye, even with 20/20 vision, is limited to 20 degrees or less. In such instances peripheral (side) or central vision loss is involved.

Legally blind people are not necessarily totally blind, and people who are blind in one eye are not necessarily legally blind since the classification is determined through measurement of the better eye.

Jill Sardegn and T. Otis Paul, *The Encyclopedia of Blindness and Vision Impairment* (New York: Facts on File, 1991), s.v. "blindness."

Who were the "Blue People" in Appalachia?

The "Blue People" were descendants of Martin Fugate, a French immigrant to Kentucky. He had a recessive gene that limited or stopped the body's production of the enzyme diaphorase. Diaphorase breaks down methemoglobin into hemoglobin in red blood cells. When the enzyme is not present, a disproportionate amount of methemoglobin remains in the blood, giving the cells a bluish tint, rather than the normal pink associated with Caucasians. The condition is strictly one of pigment and does not deprive the person of oxygen.

Despite bluish color, there are no known health risks associated with the deficiency. Fugate's family suffered from the condition because of excessive inbreeding. When both spouses had the recessive gene, their children would be blue. As the family became mobile following World War II (1939-45) and moved out of their Kentucky valley, the inbreeding ceased. As of 1982 there were only two or three members of the family with the condition.

Science 82 November 1982.

Why is neurofibromatosis called "Elephant Man's disease"?

Neurofibromatosis or Von Recklinghausen's disease (for the German doctor who first described the disease in detail) severely deformed the Englishman Joseph Merrick (1862-1889), who was referred to as "the Elephant Man." Neurofibromatosis is an uncommon inherited developmental disorder of the nervous system, bones, muscles, and skin. Occurring in one in every three thousand births, its symptoms generally appear during childhood or adolescence. It is characterized by numerous soft, fibrous swellings that grow on nerve trunks of the extremities, head, neck, and body; *cafe au lait* spots (pale, coffee-colored patches) on the skin of the trunk and pelvis; scoliosis; and short stature. In most cases, neurofibromatosis affects only the skin. But if the soft fibrous swellings occur in the central nervous system they can cause epilepsy, affect vision and hearing, and can also shorten life. Surgical removal of neurofibromas is necessary only if they are causing complications, or are likely to do so.

The American Medical Association Encyclopedia of Medicine (New York: Random House, 1989), 722-23. *Disease and Disorders Handbook* (Springhouse, PA: Springhouse Corp., 1990), 506-7. Frederick Drimmer, *The Elephant Man* (New York: Putnam, 1985), 138.

Why is Legionnaire's disease known by that name?

Legionnaire's disease was first identified in 1976 when a sudden, virulent outbreak of pneumonia took place at Bellevue Stratford Hotel in Philadelphia, Pennsylvania, where delegates to an American Legion Convention were staying; 29 of them died. The cause was eventually identified as a previously unknown bacterium that was given the name *Legionnella pneumophilia*. The bacterium probably was transmitted by an airborne route, possibly through the cooling tower or evaporation condensers in air-conditioning systems. It has been known to flourish in the soil and in excavation sites. Usually the disease occurs in late summer or early fall and its severity ranges from mild to life-threatening with a mortality rate as high as 15 percent. Symptoms include diarrhea, anorexia, malaise, headache, generalized weakness, recurrent chills and fever accompanied by cough, nausea, and chest pain. Antibiotics are administered along with other therapies (such as fluid replacement, oxygen, etc.) that treat the symptoms.

Diseases and Disorders Handbook (Springhouse, PA: Springhouse Corp., 1990), 439-41. *Mayo Clinic Family Health Book* (New York: Morrow, 1990), 921. James Trager, *The People's Chronology* (New York: Henry Holt, 1992), 1057.

Which name is now used as a synonym for leprosy?

Hansen's disease is the name of this chronic, systemic infection characterized by progressive lesions. Caused by a bacterium, *Mycabacterium leprae*, that is transmitted through airborne respiratory droplets, the disease is not highly contagious. Continuous close contact is needed for transmittal. Antimicrobial agents, such as sulfones (dapsone in particular), are used to treat the disease.

Diseases and Disorders Handbook (Springhouse, PA: Springhouse Corp., 1990), 440-41. *Merck Manual of Diagnosis and Therapy, 15th ed.* (West Point, PA: Merck, Shark & Dohme, 1987), 127.

Are men or women more accident-prone?

Women drive and even cross the street more safely than men. Men account for 70 percent of pedestrian fatalities since 1980. Between the ages of 18 and 45, males outnumber females as fatal crash victims by almost three to one according to the National Highway Traffic Safety Administration. Accidental deaths of all types-from falls, firearms, drownings, fires-are also more common among men than women.

McCall's December 1991.

Can ozone be harmful to humans?

Ozone in the lower atmosphere contributes to air pollution. It is formed by chemical reactions between sunlight and oxygen in the air in the presence of impurities. Such ozone can damage rubber, plastic, and plant and animal tissue. Exposure to certain concentrations can cause headaches, burning eyes, and irritation of the respiratory tract in many individuals. Asthmatics and others with impaired respiratory systems are particularly at risk. Exposure to low concentrations for only a few hours can significantly affect normal persons while exercising. Symptoms include chest pain, coughing, sneezing, and pulmonary congestion.

McGraw-Hill Encyclopedia of Science and Technology, 7th ed. (New York: McGraw-Hill, 1992), 12:637-38. *World Book Encyclopedia* (Chicago: World Book, 1990), 14:902.

How much radiation does the average dental x-ray emit?

Dental examinations are estimated to contribute 0.15 millirems per year to the average genetically significant dose, a small amount when compared to other medical x-rays.

Audrey S. Bomberger and Betty A. Dannenfelser, *Radiation and Health* (Gaithersburg, MD: Aspen Publishers, 1984), 58.

Games, Toys, and Hobbies

What do the different scales in model railroading represent?

The scales below indicate the size relationship between the model and a full-sized railroad.

Scale	Inches/Foot	Proportion
O	0.25	1:48
S	0.1875	1:64
OO	0.157 (4 mm)	1:76.2
HO	0.138 (3.5 mm)	1:87.1
TT	0.100	1:120
N	0.075	1:160

Jim Buehner, *The Complete Handbook of Model Railroading* (Blue Ridge Summit, PA: TAB Books, 1975), 20.

What is the world record for the fastest kite?

On May 17, 1987, Troy Vickstrom piloted a speeding ten-foot (3.05-meter) Flexifoil across the beach in Lincoln City, Oregon. Documentation of the record came from the local police, who issued Vickstrom a traffic citation for exceeding the beach's posted speed limit of 20 miles (32.18 kilometers) per hour. The fastest speed attained by a flying kite was 120 miles (193 kilometers) per hour on September 22, 1989, by Pete DiGiacomo at Ocean City, Maryland.

Mazwell Eden, *Kiteworks* (New York: Sterling, 1989), 93. *The Guinness Book of Records 1992* (New York: Bantam, 1992), 400. Mark C. Young, ed., *The Guinness Book of Records 1995* (New York: Facts On File, 1994), 197.

What is the "dead man's hand" in poker?

The poker hand consisting of one pair of black aces and one pair of black eights has been known as the "dead man's hand" since Wild Bill Hickok (1837-1876) supposedly held it in a poker game when he was killed by Jack McCall on August 2, 1876. The fifth card is disputed; it could have been a queen or jack of diamonds or a nine of diamonds.

Clarence L. Barnhart, ed., *The New Century Cyclopedia of Names* (New York: Appleton-Century-Crofts, Inc., 1954), 2005. Joseph G. Rosa, *They Called Him Wild Bill: The Life and Adventures of James Butler Hickok* (Norman, OK: University of Press, 1964), 216.

What is the origin of the joker in a deck of cards?

The first reference to the joker as a playing card dates from 1885. The card was invented in the United States for the game of euchre and it was originally called "best bower," which designated it as the highest trump card. Until that time, there were two bowers in euchre. The jack of the trump suite, the right bower, was the highest trump, and the jack of the suite of the same color, the left bower, was the second highest trump.

George Beal, *Playing Cards and Their Story* (New York: Arco Publishing, 1975), 58. Roger Tilley, *Playing Cards* (New York: G.P. Putmnam's, 1967), 86.

What is the order of winning hands in poker?

The nine classes of poker hands, in ascending order, are as follows:

Highest Card—any five odd cards
One Pair—two cards of the same rank and three odd cards
Two Pairs—two cards of the same rank, two other cards of the same rank, and an odd card
Threes—three cards of the same rank and two odd cards
Straight—any five cards in sequence, not of the same suit, aces are high or low
Flush—any five cards of the same suit
Full House—three cards of the same rank and two other cards of the same rank
Straight Flush—a sequence of five cards all of the same unit, aces are high or low.

George F. Hervey, *The Complete Illustrated Book of Card Games* (Garden City, NY: Doubleday & Company, 1973), 189-190.

What was the "Turk" machine, and who solved the mystery of how it worked?

The "Turk" was a chess automaton made by Kempelen and first shown at the court of Empress Maria Theresa in 1769. The machine was an expert opponent at the game, and consisted of a life-sized figure sitting at a desk which contained three doors and a lower drawer which ran the length of the desk. Kempelen and his machine toured Europe and were the subject of much speculation, and attempts to uncover their secrets. After Kempelen's death in 1804, the "Turk" was purchased by Johann Nepomuk Maelzel (1772-1838), who continued to operate the machine and amaze audiences and opponents with its skill in Europe and the United States until his death in 1838. Many attempts to analyze the machine uncovered isolated facts which explained its workings, and in 1820 Robert Willis published a book revealing how a man could be concealed within the desk and moves could be signaled by magnetically actuated levers. However, Edgar Allan Poe (1809-1849) was finally credited with publishing a complete revelation of its secrets in 1836. In

1838 the "Turk" was retired to a Philadelphia museum where it was destroyed by fire in 1854.

David Hooper and Kenneth Whyld, *The Oxford Companion to Chess,* (Oxford, NY: Oxford University Press, 1984), s.v. "Turk."

What is the recipe for homemade bubble blowing solution?

For homemade bubble blowing solution, mix 2/3 cup of clear, liquid dishwashing detergent with two tablespoons of glycerin and a scant gallon of warm water. An empty one-gallon milk jug can be used. Replace cap and shake gently. Allow the solution to sit awhile, pour some into a shallow tray, dip a wand into the mixture, and blow or wave to make bubbles.

"Homemake Bubbles," *Copycat* September/October 1994.

Who invented the Slinky?

Richard T. James was granted a patent in 1947 for his "toy and process of use." This helical spring toy tumbles smoothly down a flight of stairs when its free end is lifted, rotating about a diameter and quickly dropping to the step below. His invention was the result of a failed attempt to produce an antivibration device for ship instruments. Having built a spring that James hoped would instantaneously counterbalance wave motion on a ship, he accidentally knocked one off a shelf, and saw it literally crawl, coil by coil, to a lower shelf, onto a stack of books, down to the tabletop, and finally come to rest, upright, on the floor. James' wife, Betty, saw its potential as a toy and named it "slinky." Betty James still runs James Industries, the company she founded with her husband in 1946 to market the toy Slinky.

American Scientist, May/June 1987. Harry Harris, *Good, Old-Fashioned Yankee Ingenuity* (Chelsea, MI: Scarborough House, 1990), 267-68. Charles Panati, *Panati's Extraordinary Origins of Everyday Things* (New York: Perennial Library, 1987), 380-81. Bridget Travers, ed., *World of Invention* (Detroit: Gale Research Inc., 1994), 558.

How are collectible magazines graded and how should they be stored?

Collectible magazines are graded:

Magazine grades	Characteristics
Mint	Flawless; no subscription label
Fine	Sharp covers; no fading, stains, tears, or chipping
Good	Shows handling and wear
Poor	Clipped sections; pages or cover missing, defaced, stains—no collector's value

Collectible magazines should be stored in plastic magazine bags, backed by acid free cardboard inserts and stored in acid free boxes. Do not store them in areas of excessive humidity or dryness.

David K. Henkel, *Collectible Magazines: Identification & Price Guide* (New York: Avon Books, 1993), 3.

What is "scripophily"?

The practice of collecting dead stock certificates is called "scripophily." Dealers and hobbyists have discovered the appeal of this relatively new collectible, which started attracting public notice in the late 1970s. The old share certificates of long defunct companies and bonds that are no longer redeemable are now valued as antiques. The history behind a certificate, its rarity, and its beauty all contribute to the item's worth. A famous signature, such as the inventor Thomas Edison's or the industrialist John D. Rockefeller's, dramatically increases the value of a stock certificate. Many notes are admired for special and often elaborate artwork, for example a 1970s mint condition stock certificate from Ringling Brothers, Barnum & Bailey was valued at $500 in 1994. Scripophilists sometimes pay hundreds and even thousands of dollars for a special stock or bond.

Paul Lewis, "Dead Stocks Revive In Sales to Investors," *New York Times* 27 April 1981. "For The Circus Crowd," *USA Today* 14 March 1994.

Where can the actual streets and properties depicted in the Monopoly board game be found and are the names changed in the foreign language versions?

Charles Darrow who invented the Monopoly game based most of the streets and properties on memories of family vacations spent in the seaside resort town of Atlantic City, New Jersey. Marvin Gardens is the one exception: Darrow was short one name, so he borrowed this name from an area near his own Pennsylvania home called Margate. The Short Line Railroad was another example of creative license; Darrow named it for a bus company that maintained a freight depot in Atlantic City. In a move to upgrade the city in 1973, Atlantic City officials proposed changing the names of Baltic and Mediterranean Avenues. An uproar resulted, with protests heard from Monopoly loyalists around the country, and the city gave up on plans for modernization. By 1974, Parker Brothers began marketing the Monopoly game in 25 countries, and translating it into 15 languages: French, Italian, Spanish, German, Dutch, Flemish, Swedish, Danish, Norwegian, Greek, Portuguese, Japanese, Chinese, Hebrew, and British English. In most countries the properties take the name of foreign real estate, and the dollars are translated into local currency. However, the board design and colors remain much the same as in the original American version.

Currently the game is available in 23 languages and in 34 countries. Below are listed the most frequently landed-on squares on the Atlantic City board:

Illinois Avenue
Go
B & O Railroad
Free Parking
Tennessee Avenue
New York Avenue
Reading Railroad
St. James Place
Water Works
Pennsylvania Railroad

Russell Ash, *The Top 10 of Everything* (London: Dorling Kindersley, 1994), 281. Maxine Brady, *The MONOPOLY Book: Strategy and Tactics of the World's Most Popular Game* (New York: David McKay, 1974), 14-24.

What is the game of POG, and how did it originate?

POG is a game that dates back to the Great Depression in which youngsters played with the cardboard disks that capped glass milk bottles. Called Milk Caps, the object was to topple a pile of the disks with a thicker "slammer" disk. Points were scored for every disk that flipped over. The game was revived in 1991 in Hawaii, when school children began playing it with cardboard caps from a fruit juice drink named POG for its ingredients, passion fruit, orange, and guava. Toy companies seized on the fad and manufactured POGs decorated with pictures of superheroes and other popular characters. A trademark dispute has developed among competing companies over the name "POG," but players seem oblivious—a sign that the word has become a generic term for an accepted game.

The New York Times 9 September 1994.

What is the origin of the expression "olly, olly oxen free"?

"Olly, olly oxen free" is the chant used to call in the players at the end of a game of hide-and-seek. No one knows for sure where the expression comes from, but it is thought oxen (or octen) is a childish corruption of "all in."

Robert Hendrickson, *Grand Slams, Hat Tricks and Alley-oops: A Sports Fan's Book of Words* (New York: Prentice Hall General Reference, 1994), s.v. "olly, olly, oxen free."

What was the price of the golden spike used to complete the transcontinental railroad?

On May 10, 1869, a golden spike was used to drive in the last tie of the first transcontinental railroad at Promontory, Utah. The 18-ounce spike, which originally cost $350, had a gold value of $4,683 in 1993. The collector's value was estimated to be as much as $250,000.

USA Today 10 March 1993.

What kind of game is "Magic: The Gathering"?

"Magic: The Gathering" is the card game brainchild of Sunnyvale, California computer programmer Morgan Schweers. Wizards of the Coast, which is located in Renton, Washington distribute "Magic," which is sort of a card game version of Dungeons and Dragons. Over 1000 cards have been issued featuring such characters as "Lord of the Pit" and "Icy Manipulator." "Magic: The Gathering" can be complicated but one habitue likens it to the children's hand game of fist, rock, and scissors.

New York Times 14 August 1994.

How many different kinds of pieces are used in the game of chess and what are their names?

There are six different pieces used in the game of chess and each player has one king and queen, two bishops, knights and rooks, and eight pawns.

World Book Encyclopedia 1994. s.v. "chess."

What percentage of the population engages in various artistic activities as a hobby?

In the United States artistic hobbies are quite popular; 8.4 percent of the population is engaged in pottery/jewelry; 9.6 percent in painting; 11.6 per cent in photography/video; and 24.8 percent sew and do needlepoint.

USA Today 22 July 1994.

How did the Barbie doll get her name?

The teenage-fashion toy Barbie was named after the daughter of Eliot and Ruth Handler, the founders of the toy giant Mattel, Inc., who in 1959 introduced the best-selling doll in history.

John Javna and Gordon Javna, *60s!* (New York: St. Martin's Press, 1988), 204.

What are the oldest gaming instruments known to man?

Dice, small, hard cubes with one to six dots on each of its six sides, are the oldest known gaming instruments. They are rolled in numerous gambling and board games.

Academic American Encyclopedia (Danbury, CT: Grolier, 1989), s.v. "dice games."

What is "Trivial Pursuit"?

"Trivial Pursuit" is a board game based on knowledge of interesting facts, or trivia. Players roll a die to land on a space representing one of six categories: art and literature, entertainment, geography, history, science and nature, and sports and leisure. Opponents select a question-and-answer card to challenge the player on "trivial" information about the topic. Winners have to correctly answer a question in each category plus a final, extra question in a category chosen by opponents. "Trivial Pursuit" was invented and manufactured by Canadians Scott Abbott, Chris Haney, and John Haney. Introduced to the public in 1982, the game's popularity led to numerous spinoff editions based on such topics as sports, movies, and baby-boomers.

"The Newest Game in Town," *New York Times* 17 January 1983.

What is the highest price paid at auction for a postage stamp?

The highest price paid at auction for a postage stamp was 3,400,000 Swiss Francs (over $2.4 million). It was a Penny Black May 2, 1840 cover bought for a Japanese buyer on May 23, 1991, at Harmers in Lugano, Switzerland. The buyer's premium is included in the price.

Source: Mark C. Young, ed. *The Guinness Book of Records 1995* (New York: Facts On File, 1994), 174.

When did the United States produce the Silver Eagle coin?

In 1986, the United States introduced a new coin into the world bullion coin market. The coin, the Silver Eagle, is approximately one and one-half inches in diameter and contains one ounce of silver. The Silver Eagle has a value of one dollar but is valued for its silver content. It is not sold directly to the public but can only be obtained through authorized coin shops, banks, and other retail outlets. The Silver Eagle features a "Walking Liberty" design on the front and a "Heraldic Eagle with Shield" on the back.

"U.S. starts minting silver Eagle," *Pittsburgh Press* 30 October 1986. "Silver Eagle coin sales likely to soar," *Pittsburgh Press* 24 November 1986.

In international gambling parlance what is El Gordo?

In international gambling parlance El Gordo, or "the Fat One," is one of the world's oldest and reputedly the richest lotteries. It has been held annually in Spain since 1763 and in 1973 total prize money was $133 million. El Gordo was begun by King Carlos III and is a source of revenue for the Spanish government.

John May et al. , *Curious Trivia* (New York: Dorset Press, 1984), 97.

What is a "cruciverbalist"?

A "cruciverbalist" is one who works or creates puzzles, especially crossword puzzles.

Pittsburgh Post-Gazette 19 March 1981.

What is the distance between the stakes in the game of horseshoes?

In the game of horseshoes, the stakes should be placed 40 feet apart.

Fred L. Worth, *The Trivia Encyclopedia* (East Brunswick, NJ: Bell Publishing Co., 1974).

How many squares are on a chess board?

There are 64 squares on a chess board, with eight rows of eight squares. The eight rows that run horizontally are called ranks, while the eight rows that run vertically between players are called files.

The New York Public Library Desk Reference (New York: Stonesong Press, 1989), 594.

What is the highest recorded price paid for a coin?

A United States 1907 Double Eagle Ultra High Relief $20.00 gold piece was sold for 1.5 million dollars by MTB Banking Corporation of New York to a private investor on July 9, 1990. It is the most that has ever been paid for a single coin.

Mark C. Young, ed., *The Guinness Book of Records 1995* (New York: Facts on File, 1994,) 172.

What is the history of the game known "Chinese Checkers"?

The game now called "Chinese Checkers" originated in England in 1880 under the name "Halma." It is played on a perforated star-shaped board on which marbles are moved about, much like the game of checkers.

John Scarne, *Encyclopedia of Games* (New York: Harper & Row, 1973).

How is the condition of coins for collectors determined?

The American Numismatic Association has a grading system to determine the condition of coins, which are ranked by the amount of wear shown. The best have a brilliant mirror-like surface and are without blemish. These may be part of a proof set, which refers to the highly precise manner by which the coins were struck, and are considered to be in mint state or within the highest grade of uncirculated coins. The lowest grade is called About Good, and coins in this category are heavily worn with the date often barely legible.

R. S. Yeoman, *1994 Handbook of United States Coins* (New York: Western Publishing Co., 1993), 10.

What are Russian stacking dolls called?

The Russian stacking or nesting dolls are called *matreshka.* These traditional dolls, often painted to look like peasants, are made hollow, with a smaller doll fitting inside each larger one. A set is usually composed of four dolls, but sets of 12 or more are not uncommon.

World Book Encyclopedia (Chicago: World Book, 1992).

What is the origin of "knock-knock" jokes?

In Shropshire, England folklore, a character named Buff would begin humorous exchanges by thumping the floor with a stick and calling out "Knock, knock." Another character would cry, "Who's there"? and the response would be "Buff."

Alice Gomme, *The Traditional Games of England, Scotland, and Ireland* (David Nutt, 1894).

What is the Burlington Liar's Club?

The purpose of the Burlington Liar's Club is "To perpetuate the American heritage of telling humorous tall tales." It was originally founded in 1929 as the Liar's Club, which was disbanded in 1980 and was reestablished in 1981 under the current name. The address is: 149 Oakland Ave., Burlington, Wisconsin 53105.

Peggy Kneffel Daniels, ed., *Encyclopedia of Associations* (Detroit: Gale Research, 1994. Nino Lo Bello, "The Truth About the Liars Club," *American Mercury*June 1959.

How is the dice game called barbooth played?

Barbooth is a game played with a pair of dice and two cups. Two players stand at opposite ends of a long table with retaining walls, casting the pair of dice back and forth towards each other. Each try for the winning combinations of 3-3, 5-5, 5-6, and 6-6; losing combinations are 1-1, 1-2, 2-2, and 4-4. All other combinations have no significance and the players roll until a winning combination occurs. Other players frequently bet on the outcome of the game, for which the odds are always even, since there is an equal chance of throwing a winning roll as a losing roll.

Albert H. Morehead, *The Modern Hoyle: Rules and Instructions for All the Most Popular Games* (Philadelphia: John C. Winston Co., 1944), 232.

What is a "cinderella" in stamp collecting?

A "cinderella" is a term used by stamp collectors to describe bogus items, municipal issues, transportation stamps, phantoms, labels, fantasies, exhibition seals, poster stamps, local revenues, and the like. Some stamp collectors also consider forgeries, local postage issues, essays and proofs, and telegraph stamps as "cinderella" items.

William W. Cummings, ed., *1994 Standard Postage Stamp Catalogue, vol. 1,* (Sydney, OH: Scott Publishing Co., 1993).

What was the name of the bison that appeared on the Indian Head nickels issued in the United States?

The Indian Head or Buffalo Type nickel issued by the United States from 1913 to 1938 was designed by James E. Fraser. He modeled the bison after one in the New York Zoological Gardens named Black Diamond. The Indian portrait was based on three Indians named Irontail, Two Moons, and John Big Tree.

R.S. Yeoman, *1994 Handbook of United States Coins* (Racine, WS: Western Publishing, 1993), 67.

How can a collector tell if a coin is genuine?

Coin collectors often like to verify the authenticity of the coins they add to their collection. Two organizations offer coin authentication and certification services. They are:

American Numismatic Association, Certification Service, 818 N. Cascade Avenue, Colorado Springs, CO 80903

International Numismatic Society, Authentication Bureau, P.O. Drawer 33134, Philadelphia, PA 19142

Coins must not be submitted without first requesting mailing instructions and a schedule of fees charged for this service.

R. S. Yeoman, *1994 Handbook of United States Coins* (New York: Western Publishing Co., 1993).

What are the names for collectors of different things?

Collectors of specific items are known by distinctive names; a few are listed below.

Item collected	Name of collector
airmail stamps	aerophilatelist
writings by various authors	anthologist
aquariums	aquarist
teddy bears	arctophilist
books	bibliophile
shells	conchologist
key rings containing advertising	copoclephile
postcards	deltiologist
phonograph records	discophile or phonophile
herbs	herbalist
pictures, such as prints, engravings, lithographs	iconophilist
beer bottle labels	labeorphilist
coins or medals	numismatist
postage stamps	philatelist
matchbox labels and matchbook covers	phillumentist
dolls	planganologist
cardboard beer coasters	tegestologist
tokens used in buses and subways	vecturist
flags or banners	vexillologist

Clarence L. Barnhart and Robert K. Barnhart, eds., *The World Book Dictionary* (Chicago: World Book, 1990), s.v. "aerophilatelist," "aquarist," "bibliophile," "deltiologist," "discophile." Laurence Urdang, ed., *-Ologies & -Isms* (Detroit: Gale Research, 1986), s.v. "collections and collecting."

When and where did the first crossword puzzle appear?

The first crossword puzzle was published in the magazine section of the Sunday's New York *World* on December 21, 1913. It was originally called "word-cross" and developed by Arthur Wynne (sometimes spelt Winn), an American journalist born in England who worked for the *World.*

Wynne may have gotten his idea from the English children's puzzle activity called Magic squares or he might have seen a similar word puzzle earlier in the London Graphic. His first puzzles were diamond-shaped and contained all blanks. Wynne redesigned its shape and changed it to its current black-and-white format. The puzzles became very popular and by the 1920, other major newspapers started to feature them as well. The word "crossword" did not appear in the dictionary until 1930.

Cecil Adams, *More of The Straight Dope* (New York: Ballantine Books, 1988), 175-76. Roger Millington, *Crossword Puzzles: Their History and Their Cult* (Nashville: Thomas Nelson, 1974), 11-13. Charles Panati, *Extraordinary Origins of Everyday Things* (New York: Harper & Row, 1987), 375-76. J.A. Simpson and E.S.C. Weiner, eds., *The Oxford English Dictionary, 2d ed.* (Oxford: Clarendon Press, 1989), s.v. "crossword."

Who invented Monopoly?

During the early 1930s of the Great Depression, this high-stakes real estate game called Monopoly was invented by Charles B. Darrow (1889-1967) of Germantown, Pennsylvania. In 1934, he approached Parker Brothers, the Massachusetts-based game company, who rejected it as too dull, too complicated, and too time-consuming. When Darrow, after manufacturing five thousand sets, landed a sizable order from the John Wanamaker department store, Parker Brothers reconsidered and offered Darrow a contract, which eventually made him a millionaire. In 50 years, total sales exceeded 100 million. In 1970, shortly after Darrow's death, Atlantic City erected a plaque in his honor on Boardwalk near Park Place.

Maxine Brady, *The MONOPOLY Book* (New York: David McKay Co., 1974), 14-21. Harry Harris, *Good Old-Fashioned Yankee Ingenuity* (Chelsea, MI: Scarborough House, 1990), 193-94. Charles Panati, *Panati's Extraordinary Origins of Everyday Things*New York: Perennial Library, 1987), 379-80.

How many different bridge games are possible?

Roughly fifty-four octillion different bridge games are possible.

Isaac Asimov, *Asimov on Numbers* (New York: Doubleday, 1977), 39.

Which states have legalized lotteries?

As of 1994, these states, plus the District of Columbia, had legalized lotteries-Arizona, California, Colorado, Connecticut, Delaware, Florida, Georgia, Idaho, Illinois, Indiana, Iowa, Kansas, Kentucky, Louisiana, Maine, Maryland, Massachusetts, Michigan, Minnesota, Missouri, Montana, Nebraska, New Hampshire, New Jersey, New York, Ohio, Oregon, Pennsylvania, Rhode Island, South Dakota, Texas, Vermont, Virginia, Washington, West Virginia, and Wisconsin.

State Executive Directory (Washington: Carroll Publishing, 1994), 590.

Who invented the Hula-hoop toy?

The plastic Hula-hoop toy was introduced in 1958 by Richard P. Knerr and Arthur K. Melvin, owners of the Wham-O Manufacturing Company of San Gabriel, California. Basing the idea on the wooden exercise hoops used in Australian school gymnasiums, this fad eventually made $45 million for Wham-O.

Valerie-Anne Giscard d'Estaing, *The Second World Almanac Book of Inventions* (New York: Pharos Books, 1986), 49. Dennis Sanders, *The First of Everything* (New York: Delacorte Press, 1981), 37.

What is the ranking of card suits in the game of bridge?

In the game of bridge, card suits rank in the order of Spades, Hearts, Diamonds, and Clubs. Spades and Hearts are known as major suits, Diamonds and Clubs are known as minor suits. Within a suit, Aces are high, and the King, Queen, Jack, and Ten are known as honor cards.

George F. Hervey, *The Complete Illustrated Book of Card Games* (New York: Doubleday, 1973), 125.

How many dominoes are in a regular set of dominoes?

Dominoes are rectangular pieces of bone, ivory, wood, plastic, or other substances. Each piece is divided into two ends, and each end is marked by dots. There are 28 dominoes ("bones") in a regular set of dominoes. The game is most often played by two, but can also accommodate three or four players.

Richard L. Frey, ed., *According to Hoyle: Official Rules of More Than 200 Popular Games of Skill and Chance With Expert Advice on Winning Play* (New York: Fawcett Crest, 1970), 221.

How do boats get inside glass bottles?

The ship is built outside the bottle, with the masts laying down on the deck. A long cotton thread is attached to the rigging then the ship is pushed through the neck of the bottle. Pulling on the thread hoists the rigging and up comes the masts and the ship is miraculously in the bottle, in full sail.

The Bumper Book of Things a Boy Can Make (Blue Ridge, PA: TAB Books, 1978), 15.

Who invented Rubik's cube?

In 1974, a Hungarian chess fanatic and professor at the University of Budapest, Erno Rubik (b.1944), invented a cube puzzle brain-teaser. This game of logic first interested colleagues and mathematicians, but its popularity did not begin to grow until 1978, when it won a prize in the Budapest International Fair. In 1980, after Ideal Toys obtained the distribution rights, the craze came to the United States.

In May 1982 a patent infringement suit was filed by Arthur S. Obermayer, who claimed his company, Moleculon, held a 1972 United States patent based on the work of its chief research scientist, Larry D. Nichols, for the identical puzzle. In 1984 the court ruled in favor of Moleculon.

Valerie-Anne Giscard d'Estaing, *World Almanac Book of Inventions* (New York: World Almanac Publications, 1985), 132. Harry Harris, *Good Old-Fashioned Yankee Ingenuity* (Chelsea, MI: Scarborough House, 1990), 256. Don Taylor and Leanne Rylands, *Cube Games* (New York: Holt, Rinehart and Winston, 1981), 2. Bridget Travers, ed., *World of Invention* (Detroit: Gale Research, 1994), 530-31.

How did Silly Putty originate?

Silly Putty is just what its name implies-putty that acts in very silly ways. Although it is quite malleable when hit with a hammer, it shatters like a piece of glass. It can be molded into virtually any shape, but if left overnight, it reverts into a shapeless blob. Sold primarily as an amusement to children, it has applications in various technical fields, including geology and health care. Silly Putty was invented during World War II (1939-45) by James Wright, an engineer for General Electric who was experimenting with mixtures of boric acid and silicon oils. A one-time advertising copywriter, Peter C. Hodgson, heard of it and after the war he packaged the product in plastic eggs and sold it through specialized retail outlets. The rights to Silly Putty were bought by Binney & Smith, Inc., the manufacturers of Crayola crayons and, by the early 1990s over three thousand silly tons have been sold.

James Barron, "Silly Putty Celebrates Its 40th with Colors," *New York Times* 15 February 1990. Bridget Travers, ed., *The World of Invention* (Detroit: Gale Research, 1994), s.v. "Silly Putty."

Who is Vasily Ivanchuk, the 1994 winner of the Intel World Grand Prix?

In 1994, Vasily Ivanchuk beat Vishwanathan Anand in the chess tournament known as the Intel World Grand Prix. This placed the then 25 year old Ukrainian as a possible challenger to chess champion Gary Kasparov. Kasparov did not play in the September 3 Intel event because he was eliminated in the first round playing against the Pentium Genius 2 computer. Ivanchuk had refused to play with a computer and proceeded to the finals; Anand, Ivanchuk's final opponent, was in fact the first player to defeat the computer, doing so in the semi-finals.

New York Times 20 September 1994.

Who invented the jigsaw puzzle?

The first pictorial puzzle, a picture or map glued to wood or cardboard and cut into small pieces, was made by John Spilsbury, an eighteenth-century London mapmaker. Spilsbury marketed his jigsaw maps as educational tools for upper class children. The puzzles became very popular and by 1800 many other London mapmakers and publishers began to market the puzzles. Jigsaws were expensive because they were first constructed of fine woods, and engraved with hand-tinted prints.

Anne D. Williams, *Jigsaw Puzzles, An Illustrated History and Price Guide* (Radnor, PA: Wallace-Homestead Book Co., 1990), 4.

What is the game of sporting clays?

Sporting clays is a moving target game in which players use a shotgun to shoot clay birds which are released or thrown in pairs from a trap. The clay birds are launched in a way to imitate the flight patterns of real birds, presenting the player with real challenges. Game rules and scoring are set by the United States Sporting Clays Association and the National Sporting Clays Association which also sponsor championships.

Lionel Atwill, *Sporting Clays, An Orvis Guide* (New York: The Atlantic Monthly Press, 1990), 7-9.

What are the colors or markings on billiard balls?

The colors or markings on billiard balls are:
yellow
blue
red
purple
orange
green
maroon
black
yellow stripe
blue stripe
red stripe
purple stripe
orange stripe
green stripe
maroon stripe.

Diagram Group, *Rules of the Game* (New York: St. Martin's Press, 1990), 87.

Who popularized the game of billiards?

The game of billiards was popularized by French King Louis XIV (1638-1715). The king's physicians recommended the game to him as a beneficial form of exercise.

David Louis, *Fascinating Facts* (Santa Clarita, CA: Ridge Press/Crown Publishers, 1977), 67.

What is the origin of the trade name *Lego*?

The trade name *Lego* comes from the Danish *leg godt* which means "play well."

Leslie Alan Dunkling, *The Guinness Book of Names* (Middlesex, England: Guinness Superlatives, 1986), 157.

On a single number bet what is the payoff in roulette?

On a single number bet in roulette the payoff for winners is made at a rate of 35 to 1.

Carl Sifakis, *Encyclopedia of Gambling* (New York: Facts On File, 1990), 253.

What was the name of the controversial game that reached peak popularity in the 1980s and could conceivably last indefinitely?

"Dungeons and Dragons" was a controversial game that reached peak popularity in the 1980s and has been described as a "combination fantasy trip, war game exercise, drama workshop, and psychological work-out session" in Frank W. Hoffman's *Sports & Recreation Fads*. Game materials consisted of two booklets, with four other books needed to carry the game along. Being open-ended, a game could last indefinitely. The game was invented by Gary Gygax, an insurance underwriter with a penchant for writing war games.

Frank W. Hoffman and William G. Bailey, *Sports & Recreation Fads* (New York: Harrington Park Press, 1991), 109-110.

Which civilization played an ancient board game, "Hounds and Jackals"?

The ancient Egyptians played a board game called "Hounds and Jackals" an example of which was found in the tomb of Renseneb who died around 1800 B. C. The game resembles a modern cribbage board but is curved at one end. Pegs with jackal and hound like heads, whose movements were probably determined by the casting of sticks, advance along points or holes in the board. Some of the opposing points are connected by lines evidently allowing lucky players shortcuts to advanced positions.

Jack Botermans, *The World of Games*, (New York: Facts On File, 1989), 19. Frederick V. Grunfeld, *Games of the World*, (Zurich: Swiss Committee for UNICEF, 1982), 8.

What is the highest price paid for a presidential document or letter?

In 1986 an unidentified buyer paid $396,000 for a letter written by U.S. president Thomas Jefferson (1743-1826), the highest price paid for a presidential document. In this letter written to Jewish diplomat Mordecai Noah, the President commented on anti-Semitism. The buyer purchased the letter from the heirs of Charles J. Rosenbloom of Pittsburgh and donated it to New York's Yeshiva University Museum.

"A Jeffersonian Record," *USA Today* 30 October 1986.

How did the sport of duckpin bowling get its name?

Duckpin bowling got its start in Baltimore in 1900 as a scaled down variation of from regular bowling using smaller pins and a six-inch ball. When the pins were struck, they literally went flying and reminded the game's originators, baseball Hall of Famers John J. McGraw and Wilbert Robinson, of flying ducks. Baltimore sportswriter Bill Clarke came up with the term duck pins for the new game after a conversation with McGraw and Robinson.

Harvey Frommer, *Sports Roots: How Nicknames, Namesakes, Trophies, Competitions, and Expressions in the World of Sports Came to Be*, (New York: Atheneum, 1979), "s.v. "duckpin bowling."

What was the first book written about coins?

The earliest book devoted to coins—distinct from the economic aspects of money—was *Illustrium Imagines*, by Andrea Fulvio. The work was first published in Rome in 1517.

Richard G. Doty, *The Macmillan Encyclopedic Dictionary of Numismatics* (New York: Macmillan Publishing Co., 1982), ix.

What terms are used in describing the physical condition of paper money?

In describing the physical condition of paper money, the following terms are used:
New and Uncirculated (used interchangeably, currency may show evidence of bank teller handling but no folds, tears or creases)
Extremely Fine (very crisp with possible center or light corner folds only)
Very Fine (some crispness, two to four folds, corner folds, limited stains are permitted but no tears)
Fine (well defined vertical and horizontal folds, increased limpness, minor tears)
Very Good (well worn, considerable folds and limpness, dirty, fading print at fold lines)
Good (ragged and dirty, holes, large tears, degradation at corners.)

Beth Deisher, ed., *Coin World Almanac: A Handbook for Coin Collectors, 5th ed.* (Sidney, OH: Amos Press, 1987).

How did the teddy bear get its name?

The teddy bear was named in questionable homage to U.S. President Theodore "Teddy" Roosevelt (1858-1919), who served from 1901 to 1909. During a hunting expedition Roosevelt refused to shoot a bear cub—an act that was mocked in a political cartoon. The popular reprinted image of Roosevelt's encounter with the cub gave an entrepreneur an idea, and soon a new stuffed toy named after the president was on the market.

Sid Frank and Arden Davis Melick, *The Presidents: Tidbits & Trivia* (Maplewood, NJ: Hammond, 1980), 131. Russell Ash, *The Top 10 of Everything* (London: Dorling Kindersley, 1994), 281.

What is the origin of the "Raggedy Ann" and "Raggedy Andy" dolls?

"Raggedy Ann" was a life-sized doll created by artist Johnny Gruelle in 1918. She was based on a rag doll made by Gruelle's mother and later found in the attic of her home. After Gruelle's death in 1938, his wife began marketing a scaled down "Raggedy Ann" and a newly introduced "Raggedy Andy" doll.

Ruth Freeman, *American Dolls* (Watkins Glen, NY: Century House, 1952), 62.

What is boccie?

Boccie is an Italian bowling game that is simple enough to attract all ages. Although there are no regulations about the boccie ball court, the game is usually played on a field 60 feet long and 10 feet wide with 10-or 12-inch sides and slightly higher backstops. On some fields there are gutters at the backstops to prevent out-of-bounds balls from returning to the field. For light recreation, boccie is often played on lawns, not courts. The game is played with eight balls, each having a diameter of 4 1/2 inches, and a smaller jack ball, also known as a *pallino*, of 2 3/4 inches in diameter. Four of the balls are marked to distinguish teams.

The play is divided between two teams of one, two, or four players. The teams are stationed at opposite ends of the court. The side that begins play tosses out the jack ball, then tosses one of the balls as close to the jack ball as possible. The starting team then waits until the opposing team has gotten one of its balls closest to the jack or has run out of balls. The balls must be delivered underhanded. The jack ball can be hit as well as the opponents' balls. Points are awarded for each ball closer than those of the opponents to the jack ball. The game is played up to 12 points, but there must be a two-point difference for a team to win, so the limit may be exceeded and play continued until one side has a two-point advantage. A match is the best two of three games.

Frank G. Menke, *The Encyclopedia of Sports, 6th rev. ed.* (A.S. Barnes, 1978), s.v. "Boccie."

What is Hacky Sack?

Hacky-Sacking is a game where the players use a small plastic pellet-filled pigskin ball called a footbag and attempt to keep it from hitting the ground. To complicate matters, only the feet, legs, head, and derriere can be used. The game was originally developed by a physical therapist in Oregon to help with rehabilitating a patient's knee. The Kenn Corp. of Portland and Wham-O bought out the company and product in 1983. With Wham-O's distribution and marketing power, the Hacky Sack footbag became a phenomenally successful product.

Gabriel Ireton, "People are Getting the Knack of Hacky Sack," *Pittsburgh Post Gazette* 11 August 1984.

Who was the inventor of bingo?

Bingo, a popular game in the United States, was invented by Hugh J. Ward, a sometime air-brakeman, cab driver, concessionaire, and trucking operator from Pittsburgh. Ward got his concept for bingo from horsey-horsey, a similar game played by Canadian soldiers with numbered squares on cards. Ward modified the game by reducing the number combinations. He called the game "bingo" and operated it at carnivals. In 1924, several Chicago companies made bingo equipment. In 1933, Ward wrote and published a rule book. Despite copyrighting his book, Ward never collected any money for his invention.

The Bulletin Index 5 December 1935. *Pittsburgh Post-Gazette* 5 September 1980.

How much money does each player start out with in the game of Monopoly?

In the real estate game Monopoly, each participant begins play with $1500: Two $500 bills, two $100 bills, two $50 bills, six $20 bills, and five each of ten dollars, five dollars, and one dollar bills.

Maxine Brady, *The Monopoly Book: Strategy and Tactics of the World's Most Popular Game* (New York: David McKay, 1974), 139.

What do the four suites of standard playing cards represent?

The four suites of a standard deck of 52 playing cards represent the four classes of French society. In 1392 French court painter Jacques Gringonneur designed the playing cards which remain in use today. Spades represents pikemen or soldiers; clubs, farmers and husbandmen; diamonds, artisans; and hearts, the clergy.

James Trager, *The People's Chronology: A Year-by-Year Record of Human Events from Prehistory to the Present* (New York: Henry Holt, 1992).

What is China's oldest game?

The oldest game existing in China today is Mah-Jong. Mah-Jong means "sparrow" and was invented in 550 B.C., probably in Canton. Mah-Jong is a complicated game having elaborate rules and penalties. It is played with tiles called "pai" (pronounced "pie").

Lillian Eichler, *The Customs of Mankind* (Garden City, NY: Nelson Doubleday, 1925), 720-21.

How many slots are on a roulette wheel?

On the American roulette wheel there are 38 slots or pockets for numbers 1 thru 36 plus 0 and 00. On some European wheels 00 is omitted. Roulette wheels are three feet in diameter and free-spinning. Each wheel has horizontal and vertical buffers which slow the rotation of the plastic ball, which is rolled in the opposite direction of the spin of the wheel. Each of the 38 pockets are separated from their neighbors by a metal divider. The 0 and 00 pockets are opposite one another and number slots alternate red and black except the pockets 0 and 00, which are green.

Peter Arnold, ed., *The Illustrated Book of Games* (New York: St. Martin's Press, 1975), 190-92. Edwin Silberstang, *The New American Guide to Gambling Games* (New York: New American Library, 1987), 398-99.

What is the game Killer?

The game Killer was introduced in 1976 by mathematics student Lenny Pape at the University of Michigan, Ann Arbor, to relieve the tensions during the period between midterms and Thanksgiving. The game is played by assigning each player a victim and a dart gun with suction-cup darts. The object is to "kill" one's victim using the dart gun and then to kill the victim's assigned victim. The victim may kill the assassin in self-defense. There must be two witnesses in order for the kill to be valid. The game lasts until only one person remains, and he or she must then commit "suicide."

"Object of Popular Game on Campuses Is to 'Assassinate' Opponents," *New York Times* 9 May 1980.

What is an Aerobie?

An Aerobie, invented by Alan Alder, is a Frisbee-style disc with a hole in the middle. When thrown, the aerodynamically-sophisticated Aerobie can travel as far as 1,257 feet. This distance is the farthest that any man-made object has been thrown.

USA Today 1 May 1987.

What was the subject of the first special issue stamp printed in the United States?

The printing of special issue stamps by the United States government began in 1893 with the release of a stamp commemorating Christopher Columbus's discovery of America. Generally, up until 1890 most governments issued portrait stamps, with George Washington appearing on the common U.S. stamp. Many governments saw an interest in collecting stamps as an opportunity to turn a hobby into a big government business. It was felt that colorful and pictorial stamps might attract the interest of stamp collectors.

Handbook of American Popular Culture Greenwood Press, 1981.

How can one preserve a coin?

According to most numismatists, a coin should never be cleaned, as this will reduce the value of the coin. The tarnish that forms on older coins is oxidation acting on the metal.

To keep uncirculated or proof coins bright, they should not come in contact with ordinary paper due to its sulphur content. Only sulphur-free paper should be used to store coins. They should also not come in contact with rubber (for example, rubber bands), as prolonged contact will leave a black mark on the coin. The best protection is obtained by storing the coins in airtight boxes.

Coins are often marred by improper handling. One should always hold a coin by its edges and not come in contact with its faces. Even if the coins are not proof or uncirculated pieces, they should be handled in this manner. It is considered numismatic etiquette to hold another collector's coin by its edges.

R. S. Yeoman, *1994 Handbook of United States Coins* (Racine, WI: Western Publishing, 1993), 11.

What were the first United States commemorative coins to be issued?

The first commemorative coin issued in the United States was the Isabella Quarter. It was issued in 1892 to commemmorate the World's Columbian Exposition in Chicago.

R. S. Yeoman, *1994 Handbook of United States Coins* (New York: Western Publishing Co., 1993).

Individual Awards

What are the dimensions of an Olympic-size swimming pool?

For Olympic Games, the swimming pool must be 50 meters long and at least 21 meters wide. The overall depth must be 1.8 meters. Ropes divide the pool into eight lanes, each measuring 2.5 meters wide with a space at least 50 centimeters wide outside lanes one and eight.

Diagram Group, *The Rule Book: The Authoritative, Up-to-Date, Illustrated Guide to the Regulations, History, and Object of All Major Sports* (New York: St. Martin's Press, 1983), 350-51.

Is Minnesota Fats a real person?

Minnesota Fats, played by Jackie Gleason in the movie *The Hustler*, is a real person. Also known as New York Fats, his real name is Rudolph Wanderone, Jr. (1913-1996). He chose not to play professional pool but to earn money in pool halls.

Jay Robert Nash and Stanley Ralph Ross, *The Motion Picture Guide 1927-1983* (Chicago: Cinebooks, 1986), s.v. "hustler, the." George Sullivan, *The Complete Beginner's Guide to Pool and Other Billiard Games* (Garden City, NY: Doubleday, 1979), 15-17.

Which horse races constitute the Triple Crown, and when did they originate?

The three horse races referred to as the Triple Crown are the Belmont stakes, first run in 1867, a 1-mile race; the Preakness Stakes, begun in 1873, a 1 3/16-mile race; and the Kentucky Derby, inaugurated in 1875, a 1-mile race.

American Racing Manual, 1991 ed., (Hightstown, NJ: Daily Racing Form, 1991), 679, 827, 923.

What do the different colors of karate sashes represent?

Karate sashes are differently colored to distinguish between the various levels of proficiency attained for this Japanese martial art. The present ranking system used in the United States is as follows:

White—novice
Yellow—basic blocks, stances, kicks, and punches
Green—all basic techniques have been mastered
Purple—most intermediate-level techniques have been mastered
Brown—all intermediate-level techniques have been mastered
Black—most of the advanced techniques have been mastered (There are ten degrees to a black belt, with ten being the most proficient.)

Lisbeth Mark, *The Book of Hierarchies* (New York: William Morrow, 1984), 127.

Has a filly ever won the Kentucky Derby?

The only fillies to have won the Kentucky Derby are Regret in 1915, Genuine Risk in 1980, and Winning Colors in 1988.

Robert Famighetti, ed., *World Almanac and Book of Facts 1995* (Mahwah, NJ: World Almanac, 1994), 864.

When did the Olympic torch relay make its debut?

The torch relay was introduced at the 1936 Olympic Games in Berlin. It symbolized a connection between the ancient games in Olympia, Greece, and modern time. The torch is first lit by the sun's rays in Olympia and then carried by a relay of runners to the Olympic site. Ships and planes are used when necessary.

Academic American Encyclopedia (Danbury, CT: Grolier, 1988), s.v. "Olympia." *The Encyclopedia Americana, international ed.* (Danbury, CT: Grolier, 1994), 20:715. David Wallechinsky, *The Complete Book of the Olympics* (New York: Penguin Books, 1988), xxii.

What are the Dinnie Stones of Scotland?

The 800-pound Dinnie Stones are two irregularly weighted rocks that are the center of an event at Scotland's Highland Games. The boulders are named after Donald Dinnie, the last man who was able to pick them up and walk with them. Since the turn of the century, not one of the athletes participating in the festival of traditional Scottish athletic games has been able to lift and carry them at the same time. A television program challenged a triumvirate of the world's strongest men to the task in September of 1987, but none succeeded.

Simon Welfare and John Fairley, *The Cabinet of Curiosities* (New York: St. Martin's, 1992), 185.

How many horses have won the Preakness and Belmont Stakes without sweeping the Triple Crown?

The following 16 horses have won the Preakness and Belmont Stakes but failed to sweep the Triple Crown:

Cloverbrook -1877
Duke of Magenta -1878
Grenada -1880
Saunterer -1881
Belmar -1895

Man O' War -1920
Pillory -1922
Bimelech -1940
Capot -1949
Native Dancer -1953
Nashua -1955
Damascus -1967
Little Current -1974
Risen Star -1988
Hansel -1991
Tabasco Cat -1994.

The first seven horses did not run in the Kentucky Derby.

USA Today 13 June 1994.

Who was the first non-Asian to win the World Martial Arts Championship?

In 1978 Peter Ralston of San Francisco won the World Martial Arts Championship making him the first non-Asian to do so.

Irving Wallace, David Wallechinsky, and Amy Wallace, *Significa* (New York: E.P. Dutton, 1983), 294-95.

Who holds the record for the most completed marathons?

62 year old Norm Frank of Rochester, N.Y. holds the record for most completed marathons at 525. The previous record of 524 was held by Sy Mah of Toledo, Ohio.

USA Today 2 May 1994.

Who was the first woman jockey to compete in the Kentucky Derby?

The first woman jockey in the Kentucky Derby was Diane Crump. She finished fifteenth in May of 1970.

New York Times 3 May 1970.

In rodeo competition, how long must a cowboy aboard a "bucking bronco"?

A rider must remain aboard a "bucking bronco" at least eight seconds in rodeo competition.

Joseph A. DeBartolo, *In Further Pursuit of Trivial Pursuit* (Chicago: Sarsaparilla, 1984), 399.

Who were some well known athletes and coaches who died in airplane crashes?

Numerous athletes, coaches and sports officials have died in airplane crashes while still active in their athletic endeavors. A list would include the following: Notre Dame football coach Knute Rockne—Kansas, March 31, 1931; 18 members of the United States figure skating team— Belgium, February 16, 1961, Pittsburgh Pirates outfielder Roberto Clemente—from San Juan, Puerto Rico enroute to Nicaragua, December 31, 1972; New York Yankees catcher Thurman Munson—Canton, Ohio, August 2, 1979; NASCAR driver Davey Allison—Birmingham, Alabama, July 13, 1993.

USA Today 14 July 1993.

What was boxing champ Muhammad Ali's career record?

In 59 bouts Heavyweight champ Muhammad Ali had 37 knockouts, won 19 decisions and lost 3 times in his illustrious but controversial boxing career. Ali, born Cassius Marcellus Clay, Jr. on January 17, 1942 in Louisville, Kentucky, grew up in a poor neighborhood, where he learned to use his fists at an early age. By the age of twelve he was boxing in sanctioned matches, and at the age of eighteen he won a gold medal in the 1960 Rome Olympics as a light heavyweight. Turning professional he "shocked" the boxing world on February 25, 1964 with a seventh round technical knockout of the heavily favored heavyweight champ Charles "Sonny" Liston. Although his boxing technique was generally held in high regard, Clay became controversial for what he did outside the ring. A braggart and a narcissistic self-promoter he loudly proclaimed himself as the "world's greatest" and predicted the outcome of fights in doggerel verse. Clay maintained *ad nauseam* that in the ring he would "float like a butterfly, but sting like a bee." The day after he gained the heavyweight title from Liston, the new champion announced that he had joined the Black Muslims (a black nationalistic and separatist religious/social movement) and changed his name to Muhammad Ali. By 1964 Ali was in and out of court claiming religious exemption from the draft. The World Boxing Association subsequently stripped him of his title, which he had defended nine times, and a Houston federal court sentenced him to five years in prison for refusing induction. Nonetheless he regained his title in 1974 by defeating George Forman, but lost it again the novice Leon Spinks in 1978. After retiring in 1979, he made two unsuccessful attempts at a comeback, before he permanently gave up boxing in 1981.

"Muhammad Ali's Ring Record," *New York Times*, 1 July 1979. Michael W. Williams, ed., *The African American Encyclopedia* (New York: Marshall Cavendish, 1993) 50-54.

Who was the first female skater since Sonja Henie to win gold medals in successive Olympics?

Katarina Witt (1965-) of the former East Germany was the first female figure skater since Sonja Henie—over 50 years before—to win successive Olympic gold medals. Witt captured the gold in the 1984 and 1988 Olympics.

Lincoln Library of Sports Champions (Galveston, TX: Frontier Press, 1989), 64.

How many gold medals did Olympic swimmer Mark Spitz win in 1972 ?

In the 1972 Olympics champion swimmer Mark Spitz (1950-) won seven gold medals in the 100-meter-and 200-meter-freestyle and butterfly races and in the 400-meter-and 800-meter-freestyle relay and in the 400-meter medley relay. In the 1968 Olympics Spitz won a silver (100-meter butterfly) and a bronze (100-meter freestyle) as well as two gold medals in the relays. In 1988 Matt Biondi (USA) tied Spitz's records for the most medals (seven) in one Olympic game and most total Olympic medals (eleven), but Spitz still hold the record for most gold medals (nine).

Lincoln Library of Sports Champions (Galveston, TX: Frontier Press, 1989), 28. Mark C. Young, ed., *The Guinness Book of Records, 1995* (New York: Facts on File, 1994), 276.

Where and when were the first modern Olympic games held?

The first modern Olympic games were held in Athens, Greece, April 6-15, 1896. Three hundred eleven male athletes from thirteen countries compete in a stadium that has been designed for 50,000 spectators.

David Wallechinsky, *The Complete Book of the Olympics* (Boston: Little, Brown and Company, 1991).

How many dimples are on the average golf ball?

In 1974, Titleist set an industry standard for design of golf ball dimple patterns with its "icosahedral" pattern. It consists of 20 equal triangular dimple groups and totals 384 dimples per ball. Previously, most golf balls had 324 dimples, based on the straight-line "octahedral" design.

Golf ball manufacturers are constantly redesigning the dimple pattern on the ball, which causes the number to fluctuate. However, the icosahedral pattern is used on approximately 90 percent of all golf balls sold today. Dimples allow the ball to travel twice as far as a ball without dimples.

John Stravinsky, *The Complete Golfers Catalog* (Los Angeles: Price Stern Sloan, 1989).

Did anyone ever finish the Boston Marathon with a broken leg?

In 1982, Guy Gertsch of Salt Lake City ran at least 19 miles of the Boston Marathon with a broken leg. About seven miles into the race, Gertsch felt what he thought was a cramp in his leg. He continued the race, however, and finished No. 985 at 2.47. Doctors who set his leg theorized his powerful thigh muscles acted as a splint.

Time Magazine 3 May 1982.

Who was the first female million-dollar earner in professional tennis?

The first million-dollar earner in women's tennis was Chris Evert Lloyd (1954-). The American-born player began competing on the pro circuit in the early 1970s when she was just out of her teens. During her career Evert captured most of the top titles in the sport, including two victories at Wimbledon in 1976 and 1981.

Goton Carruth and Eugene Ehrlich, *Facts & Dates of American Sports* (New York: Harper & Row, 1988), 195.

How did professional sports in the United States react to World War II?

World War II affected professional sports in the United States in many ways including:

When the war began hundreds of NFL players enlisted or were drafted into military service.

Of the 5,700 professional baseball players in the U.S. 4000 were called up by the military.

Although night games were banned, some games began as early as 10:30 A.M. to accommodate shift workers.

The 1945 All-Star game was canceled as was most spring training.

By the end of the war 32 of the 41 minor leagues had shut their doors.

The Indianapolis 500 and the Henley Regatta were canceled.

More than 80 National Hockey League players joined the military. Bauer, Dumart and Schmidt, the so-called "Kraut Line" of the Boston Bruins, were called up by the Canadian Armed Forces.

USA Today 6 December 1991.

Who won the 1976 Olympic gold medal for the women's figure skating competition?

In 1976 American figure skater Dorothy Hamill (b. 1956) brought home the Olympic gold medal from the 1976 Winter Olympics at Innsbruck. Turning professional in April 1976, Hamill began skating in the Ice Capades.

World Almanac, eds., *The Good Housekeeping Woman's Almanac* (New York: Newspaper Enterprise Association, 1977), 434.

Who was the youngest person to be honored in the National Racing Hall of Fame?

Jockey Steve Cauthen was the youngest person to be inducted into the National Racing Hall of Fame. He is well known for being the youngest jockey to win thoroughbred racing's Triple Crown, riding Affirmed at the age of 18. Cauthen was inducted into the Hall of Fame on August 8, 1994, 16 years after his Triple Crown victory.

USA Today 8 August 1994.

What is the heaviest recorded weight lifted by a single person?

On June 12, 1957 at an exhibition in Toccoa, Georgia, 24-year-old Paul Anderson lifted carefully calibrated weights totaling 6,270 pounds off the ground. Anderson had previously won the Olympic gold medal for weight lifting in 1956. Born in Toccoa, Georgia in 1933, Anderson died in 1994 at the age of 61.

New York Times 16 August 1994.

How old is the game of golf?

The game of golf dates at least to the fifteenth century, since the first written reference to it is found in a decree of the Scottish king James II (1430-1460) dating from March of 1457. In this edict the king declared the game to be illegal because it interfered with the archery practice of his citizen army, which was then engaged in a long war with England. Since a similar ban against football (probably an early form of soccer), issued in 1424, does not mention golf, it has been conjectured that the sport became popular in the intervening years. It origin, however, would have been earlier and cannot be precisely determined.

Charles Price, *The World of Golf: A Panorama of Six Centuries of the Game's History* (New York: Random House, 1962), 10.

Is bullfighting a sport?

Bullfighting is not a sport in the American sense of the word. It is more a spectacle that seems related to an ancient religious ceremony. The bull will be sacrificed, and the outcome is never in doubt. Yet, the skill and courage with which the torero dispatches the animal is meant to be a tribute to the nobility of the beast, as well as to the man who is facing a creature that is faster and stronger than he is. Bullfighting's defenders would call it a demonstration of human excellence not a game. Some of the famous bullfighters of the past were Joselito (1895-1920), Belmonte (1892-1962), Manolete (1917-1947), and El Cordobs.

Rafael Millan, trans., *Bulls & Bullfighting: History, Techniques, Spectacle* (New York: Crown Publishers, 1970), 28-29.

Which professional boxer held championship titles in three different weight categories simultaneously?

Henry Armstrong won boxing championships in three weight categories within a ten-month period: featherweight, October 29, 1937; welterweight, May 31, 1938; and lightweight, August 17, 1938.

"Pryor Stops Argello in 14th," *New York Times* 13 November 1982.

Who was Ayrton Senna?

Ayrton Senna was the youngest race car driver to win the Formula One world championship three times, in 1988, 1990, and 1991. Born in 1960 to a wealthy family in Brazil, he began racing in competition as a teenager. He was Pan American champion by 1977 and moved to Europe in 1981, where he captured 41 Grand Prix victories. Senna combined a successful business career as an Audi representative with his racing. He was launching a comic book for children just before his death in 1994 of injuries sustained in a crash at Imola, Italy.

"The Senna File," *USA Today* 2 May 1994.

What real-life event does the *Iditarod*, an Alaskan sled dog race commemorate?

The *Iditarod*, a grueling Alaskan sled dog race commemorates the 650-mile emergency mid-winter run which carried life-saving serum from Nenana to Nome, Alaska, during a diphtheria epidemic in 1925. The race, named for deserted mining town along the routes began in 1973 and is the world's toughest and longest dog-sled competition, usually about 70 teams participate in the 1157 mile round trip. The first woman, Libby Riddles, won it in 1985, finishing the trip in eighteen days.

Sue Ellen Thompson and Barbara W. Carlson, comps., *Holidays, Festivals and Celebrations of the World Dictionary* (Detroit: Omnigraphics, 1994), s.v. "Iditarod Trail Sled Dog Race." "Mushmash," *USA Today*, 25 April 1994. Mark Young, ed., *The Guinness Book of Sports Records 1994-1995* (New York: Facts On File, 1994), 179.

Who was the self-proclaimed "clown prince of tennis" who challenged a famous female tennis player to a match in 1973?

Bobby Riggs was the self-proclaimed "clown prince of tennis." He challenged Margaret Court, the Australian winner of three Wimbledon and five U.S. championships, to a match in order to find out if women tennis players were as "good" as the men. Court lost to Riggs in the "Mother's Day Massacre" in May of 1973. To redeem the situation, the reigning U.S. tennis champion, Billie Jean King, stepped in to face Riggs in a "battle of the sexes." In September of 1973 Riggs lost the much-publicized televised match with King before millions of worldwide viewers.

Allen Guttmann, *Women's Sports* (New York: Columbia University Press, 1991), 210.

What is the "delayed death touch" in the martial arts?

The "delayed death touch," known in Chinese martial arts as *dim mok*, reputedly enables its user to slay an opponent days, weeks, or even months after the technique has been applied to the victim. While some kung-fu experts claim to possess the ability to perform the *dim mok*, no established proof of its existence has surfaced.

Emil Farkas and John Corcoran, *The Overlook Martial Arts Dictionary* (New York: Overlook Press, 1983), s.v. "delayed death touch," "dim mok."

Are there any restrictions on naming a thoroughbred horse that will be registered?

Before the name of a thoroughbred can become "official" it must be submitted to the Jockey Club for approval. Certain kinds of names are not permissible. Listed below are kinds of names which are not eligible:

Names consisting of more than 18 letters (spaces and punctuation marks count as letters).

Initials (e.g. F.O.B.).

Names that end in a horse-related term, e.g. "filly," "colt," "stud," "mare," or "stallion."

Names having the repeated use of a similar prefix or suffix, etc. which would cause confusion with a previously named horse.

Names consisting entirely of numbers below 30; numbers above 30 may be used, but they must be spelled out.

Names ending with a numerical designation such as "2nd" or "3rd," whether or not such a designation is spelled out.

Names of living persons without their written permission.

Names of "famous" deceased people, without approval from the Jockey Club.

Names of "notorious" people no longer living.

Names of racetracks or races.

Assumed names or stable names or any kind of recorded name.

Names with a commercial significance (e.g. trade names).

Names of copyrighted materials (that have not been "abandoned"), titles of books, plays, motion pictures, popular songs, etc.

Suggestive, vulgar, or obscene names.

Names that are currently active in the stud or on the turf, and names similar in spelling or pronunciation to such names.

Permanent names (or names similar in spelling or pronunciation) to horses in racing's Hall of Fame; horses that have won an Eclipse Award; horses that have been voted Horse of the Year, Champion Older Horse or Mare, or Champion Three-Year-Old Colt or Filly; horses elected to the Gallery of Champions; annual leading money winners; Canadian champions; cumulative money winners of $750,000 or more; horses included on the International List of Protected Names; and horses that have won the Kentucky Derby, the Preakness, the Belmont Stakes, the Jockey Club Gold Cup, or the Breeder's Cup Classic.

The American Racing Manual, 1991 ed. (Chicago: Daily Racing Form, 1991), 566-67. O.E. Pettingill, *Born to Run*, (New York: Arco, 1973), 33.

Why do golf balls have dimples?

The dimples on a golf ball minimize the drag—a force that makes a body lose energy as it moves through a fluid—allowing the ball to travel further than a smooth ball would. In a dimpled ball the air, as it passes a ball, tends to cling to the ball longer, reducing the eddies or wake effect that drain the ball's energy. The dimpled ball can travel up to 300 yards (275 meters) but a smooth ball only goes as far as 70 yards (65 meters). A ball can have 300 to 500 dimples which can be 0.01 inch (0.25 millimeters) deep. Another effect to increase distance is to give the ball a backspin. With a backspin there is less air pressure on the top of the ball, so the ball stays aloft longer—much like an airplane does.

Ira Flatow, *Rainbows, Curve Balls and Other Wonders of the Natural World Explained* (New York: Harper & Row, 1988), 80-82. *How in the World* (Pleasantville, NY: Reader's Digest Association, 1990), 432.

Who was the first woman to referee a heavyweight championship fight?

Eva Shain is the first woman to referee a heavyweight championship fight she did so in the 15-round Muhammad Ali-Earnie Shavers prizefight on September 29, 1977, at Madison Square Garden in New York City.

Joseph Nathan Kane, *Famous First Facts: A Record of First Happenings, Discoveries, and Inventions in American History, 4th ed.* (New York: H.W. Wilson, 1981), 509.

How many balls are used in bumper pool?

Bumper pool is played with ten balls, five to each player or team. One five-ball set is red, with one red ball marked as a cue ball, and the other set is white, with one marked as a cue ball.

Billiards: The Official Rules & Records Book, 1990, (Iowa City, IA: Billiard Congress of America, 1990), 74-75.

In what sport is a half-shoe worn?

A half-shoe is worn for rhythmic gymnastics, and consists of the front half of a shoe held in place by elastic around the heel.

Jenny Bott, *Rhythmic Gymnastics, The Skills of the Game* (Marlborough, UK: The Crowood Press, 1989), 116.

What is the Tour de France?

The Tour de France, began in 1903, is considered the most important annual bicycle race in the world. Its course traverses nearly 4,000 kilometers, or 2,500 miles, over public roads throughout parts of France, Belgium, Germany, Italy, Spain, and Switzerland. The race is held in 21 daily, timed stages, and the competitor with the lowest combined score wins. The Tour was begun in 1903.

Webster's Sports Dictionary, (Springfield, MA: G. & C. Merriam Company, 1976), s.v. "Tour de France."

Who was the first American skier to win a medal in Olympic or World competition?

William Winston "Billy" Kidd (born August 13, 1943) was the first American skier to win an Olympic medal in Alpine skiing. He was also named Athlete of the Year in 1964 by the U.S. skiers. Kidd, who was born in Burlington, Vermont, won the silver medal in the slalom ski event and the bronze in the combined standings in Alpine Olympic skiing at the 1964 Olympic Games at Innsbruck, Austria. He won a slew of medals, but was plagued by ankle injuries for much of his career. He once said: "One of the reasons I was a good ski racer was because I had a chronically sprained ankle. I had to figure out how to ski race without falling down because, as soon as I'd fall, I'd sprain my ankle."

David L. Porter, ed., *Biographical Dictionary of American Sports: Outdoor Sports* (New York: Greenwood Press, 1988), 281.

Who was the first American woman to sail around the world alone?

Tania Aebi was the first American woman to sail around the world alone. The 18-year-old from New York City was also the youngest person ever to complete a solo circumnavigation. Aebi was an teen-age dropout, night spot habitue and Manhattan bicycle messenger when her father issued an ultimatum: get back in school or sail around the world alone. She chose the latter and sailed out of New York Harbor on a course set for Bermuda on May 30, 1985. On November 6, 1987 she returned to New York by way of Gibraltar having sailed 27,000 solo miles in two and a half years. Her adventures are set down in her book *Maiden Voyage.*

Tania Aebi and Bernadette Brennan, *Maiden Voyage* (New York: Simon and Schuster, 1989), jacket.

When was the last bare-knuckle championship bout in boxing?

The last bare-knuckle championship bout under the London Prize Ring Rules took place between heavyweight contenders John L. Sullivan (1858-1918) and Jake Kilrain on February 7, 1882 at Richburg, Mississippi. Sullivan defeated Kilrain in the seventy-fifth round.

Frank W. Hoffmann and William G. Bailey, *Sports & Recreation Fads* (New York: Harrington Park, 1991), 355.

What two cities usually mark the ends of the course used when swimming across the English Channel?

The course most frequently used by swimmers attempting to cross the English Channel is from Shakespeare Beach in Dover, England to Cap Gris Nez in Calais, France. The 22-mile swim is notoriously difficult; only about 20 percent of all attempts are successful. The cold salt water, unpredictable weather conditions, and shifting tides make the crossing extremely perilous. It is the ultimate challenge for marathon swimmers.

Tom Slear, "A Record Unbroken," *Women's Sports & Fitness* August/September 1988.

Who was the first athlete from a Communist country to be named as the Associated Press Female Athlete of the Year?

Soviet gymnast Olga Korbut was the first athlete from a Communist country to win the Associated Press award for Female Athlete of the Year. She received the award after winning three gold medals at the 1972 Olympic Games in Munich, Germany. With these victories the diminutive Russian gymnast drew unprecedented attention to her sport.

The Lincoln Library of Sports Champions (Columbus, OH: Frontier Press, 1989), 16.

Are there any official rules regarding the velocity of a golf ball?

According to the United States Golf Association rules, a golf ball must be built so that it cannot exceed 250 feet per second.

United States Golf Association, *Rules of Golf for 1992 and the Rules of Amateur Status* (Far Hills, NJ: United States Golf Association, 1992), 88-89.

Has a man with one leg ever played major league baseball?

In 1945, near the end of World War II (1939-45), one-legged ex-fighter pilot Bert Shepard pitched for the Washington Senators. Injured while flying a mission north of Berlin, Shepard's right leg was amputated between the knee and the ankle. Shepard did, however, play with an artificial limb.

Richard Goldstein, *Spartan Seasons: How Baseball Survived the Second World War* (New York: Macmillan, 1980), 210-3.

Which pool player has held the world title the most?

For 14.1 continuous pool, also known as American straight pool, Ralph Greenleaf and Willie Mosconi (1913-), both of the United States, have won the world title six times and defended it thirteen times. Mosconi also holds the record for the longest consecutive run recognized by the Billiard Congress of America. His record of 526 balls was set in March of 1954 in Springfield, Ohio.

Mark Young, ed., *The Guinness Book of Sports Records, 1994-1995* (New York: Facts on File, 1994), 166.

What are the historical highlights of hot-air ballooning?

Hot-air ballooning began in 1709 when Father Bartolomeu de Gusmo (1685-1724) launched a model balloon indoors at Casa da India, Terreiro do Pao, Portugal. Near the end of the century, in 1783, Jacques and Joseph Montgolfier constructed the first hot-air balloon capable of carrying a man, and the first free flight, a journey of six miles, took place in France that same year. Balloons were used for military purposes as early as 1794, when the French army employed them to observe the Austrians at the battle of Fleurus. They were used extensively in World War I and World War II as observation platforms and as barrage balloons, which were a series of balloons connected by steel cable that prevented enemy aircraft from flying low enough to drop their bombs accurately. First the use of balloons filled with hydrogen or helium and then the development of satellites and modern aircraft technology have largely made hot-air balloons commercially and militarily obsolete. There has been some discussion about using them again to transport heavy materials, but nothing has come of it. Besides being used to study the weather, hot-air balloons today are a means of advertising, recreation, and setting a distance, endurance, or accuracy records.

Dick Brown, *Hot Air Ballooning* (Blue Ridge Summit, PA: Tab Books, 1979), 9-10. Paul Garrison, *The Encyclopedia of Hot Air Balloons* (New York: Drake Publishers, 1978), 13-15. Dennis Sanders, *The First of Everything* (New York: Delacorte Press, 1981), 85-88.

Who was the first man to run the mile in less than four minutes?

Sir Roger Bannister (1929-), an English athlete, ran the mile in 3 minutes and 59.4 seconds at Oxford, England, on May 6, 1954. He was also *Sports Illustrated*'s first Sportsman of the Year.

Don Bowden was the first American to break the 4-minute mile. He did it in 3:58.7 at Stockton, California, in 1957. The first American to break the 4-minute mile indoors was Jim Beatty in 1962. He was clocked at 3:58.9 in Los Angeles, California.

Norm Hitzges, *The Norm Hitzges Historical Sports Almanac* (Dallas, TX: Taylor Publishing, 1991), 127. Dennis Sanders, *The First of Everything: A Compendium of Important, Eventful, and Just-Plain-Fun Facts About All Kinds of Firsts* (New York: Delacorte Press, 1981), 337. *World Book Encyclopedia* (Chicago: World Book, 1993), s.v. "Bannister, Sir Roger."

Who was Man O'War?

Man O'War, also known as "Big Red" for his size and color, is considered the greatest thoroughbred racehorse ever. Winning won 20 of 21 races, in the two years he raced (1919-1920), he only lost to Upset on August 13, 1919, at Saratoga, when he came in second. He was faced the wrong way at the start, it took him a mile to catch up, and after getting blocked on the rail, his jockey had to pull him out and around the other horses. Nevertheless, some consider this his best race, because despite the bad start and inept ride, Man O'War lost by only a half-length. Because he never ran the Kentucky Derby-it was not considered an important race then, he is not listed as a Triple Crown winner. One of his foals, War Admiral, won the Triple Crown in 1937. He died in November 1947 at the age of 26.

Gorton Carruth and Eugene Ehrlich, *Facts & Dates of American Sports* (New York: Harper and Row, 1988), 107. Ruthven Tremain, *The Animals' Who's Who* (New York: Charles Scribner's Sons, 1982), s.v. "Man O'War." Terri A. Wear, *The Horse's Name Was . . .: A Dictionary of Famous Horses from History, Literature, Mythology, Television and Movies,* (New Jersey: Scarecrow Press, 1993), s.v. "Man O'War."

What is the greatest distance traveled on water skis?

Steve Fontaine of the United States holds the record for the longest run on water skis, with a distance of 1,321.16 miles. He performed this feat in Florida in October of 1988.

Mark C. Young, ed., *The Guinness Book of Records 1995* (New York: Facts On File, 1994), 297.

What was the classic "long count" moment in boxing when Gene Tunney returned to emerge victorious over Jack Dempsey?

The "long count" fight took place on September 22, 1927, between Jack Dempsey (1895-1983) and Gene Tunney (1898-1978) in Chicago. In the seventh round of the heavyweight championship bout, Dempsey knocked Tunney down. After the knockdown the referee asked Dempsey to go to the neutral corner. Dempsey waited a few seconds before doing so, thereby delaying the count. This enabled Tunney to get back up and win the fight.

Mel Heimer, *The Long Count* (New York: Atheneum, 1969), jacket. Herbert G. Goldman, ed., *The Ring: 1985 Record Book and Boxing Encyclopedia* (New York: Ring Publishing, 1985), 50-51. Gerald Suster, *Champions of the Ring: The Lives and Times of Boxing's Heavyweight Heroes* (London: Robson Books, 1992), 93-95.

Who are the oldest and youngest persons to swim across the English Channel?

Swimming across the English Channel is one of the world's most challenging tests of physical endurance. As of July 1993, approximately 4,300 people have made the attempt, but only 426 people have succeeded, and three have drowned trying. In 1987, 67-year-old Clifford Batt of Australia became the oldest person to complete the swim across the English Channel. One year later, 11-old Thomas Gregory of England became the youngest person to do so.

New York Times 5 August 1993.

What was the *Bluenose*?

During the 1920s and 1930s the *Bluenose* was a 143-foot schooner that was the pride of Nova Scotia for the excitement it brought to racing. The word "bluenose" is a nickname for a Nova Scotian. The vessel was designed by William Roue, a marine architect from Halifax, and captained by Angus Walters, a colorful character, one of the "iron men" who sailed the last of the wooden ships.

"They Couldn't Beat Bluenose" Reader's Digest, October, 1966.

Who was the first Native American to compete in the Olympics?

The first Native American to compete in the Olympics was Jim Thorpe (1887-1953), who won the pentathlon and decathlon at the 1912 Stockholm games. Thorpe's mother was a descendant of the lauk and Fox chief, Black Hawk, who was a renowned warrior and athlete, and Thorpe had been a three-time all-American football player before he went to the Olympics. Six months after Thorpe returned to the United States, his amateur status was questioned; at that time only amateur athlete's could participate in those games. Thorpe had to relinquish his medals because he had played semiprofessional baseball in 1909-10. Thorpe went on the play professional baseball in the major and minor leagues and was also in football as a player and later as a coach. In 1950, twenty years after he left sports the

Associated Press still selected him greatest male athlete and the greatest football player in the first-half of the twentieth century. In 1982, the International Olympic Committee agreed to return the medals posthumously to Thorpe after revising the definition of amateurism. Thorpe died in 1953; the medals were returned to Thorpe's daughter in a Los Angeles ceremony in 1983.

Gerald Eskenazi, "Jim Thorpe's Olympic Medals Are Restored," *New York Times* 14 October 1983. Sharon Malinowski, ed., *Notable Native Americans* (Detroit: Gale Research, 1995), 434-37. Dennis Sanders, *The First of Everything: A Compendium of Important, Eventful, and Just-Plain-Fun Facts About All Kinds of Firsts* (New York: Delacorte Press, 1981), 237.

Who was one of the most successful women runners in 1993?

Wang Junxia of China was one of the most successful women runners of 1993. She set world records at 3,000 and 10,000 meters, had the year's fastest marathon and the second fastest time in the 1,500. All of her feats were accomplished in China.

USA Today 1 February 1994.

What is a caber tossed by Scottish athletes?

"Tossing the caber" is a popular Scottish sport in which contestants hurl a caber, a long pole of unspecified dimensions made from a tree trunk. The caber is presented vertically to the competitor, who forms a platform with his interlocked hands in front of him to take the caber's weight. The athlete will run a few paces with the caber resting on his shoulder, then proceed to "toss" the pole directly in front of himself so that it revolves longitudinally, with the base pointing away from him.

While the size of the caber is not specific, it cannot be altered during competition once it has been tossed. The participant has three trials for tossing in competition, but there are no restrictions on the length of his run or from what point he must make the throw.

John Arlott, ed., *The Oxford Companion to World Sports and Games* (London: Oxford University Press, 1975), s.v. "caber, tossing the."

Why are horse races run counterclockwise?

The direction in which horses run in the United States follows a precept from ancient Rome, but the connection is indirect at best. In the second century, the emperor Hadrian decreed that all horse races were to be run counterclockwise, and one may suppose that races in the ancient and early medieval world were run in that direction. But at some indeterminate point of time and for reasons that are not entirely clear, the English decided to run their horses clockwise. The change may have stemmed from a superstition that to walk counterclockwise around a church would bring bad luck and evoke the devil. In the United States horse racing reverted to Roman tradition because a Kentucky horseman so hated the English and their customs that when he built a track in the early 1800s, he declared that no race would be run clockwise. Other tracks simply followed suit.

Andrew Bernhard, "Going Around In Circles..." *Pittsburgh Post Gazette* 14 September 1975.

What Roman Emperor competed in the ancient Olympics?

The ruthless Roman Emperor Nero (37-68 A.D.) competed in chariot racing events in the 66 A.D. Olympics in Greece.

Irving Wallace et al. , *The Book of Lists #2* (New York: William Morrow and Company, 1980), 356.

Who was the only amateur golfer to win the U.S. Open?

Francis Ouimet was the only amateur golfer ever to win the U.S. Open Championship, which he did in 1913. Ouimet had grown up across the road from The Country Club in Brookline, Massachusetts, where the championship was held. He was a Massachusetts Amateur champion at the time he entered the Open. In winning the cup, he defeated British champions Harry Vardon and Ted Ray. Ouimet never turned professional, but he did go on to twice win the U.S. Amateur title, as well as the French Amateur, the Massachusetts Open, and five additional Massachusetts Amateur championships. His victory in the Open changed golfing's image forever. The sport had traditionally been seen as a pastime restricted to the elite classes, but its popularity among the masses soared after Ouimet's win at Brookline. In 1913, there were just 350,000 golfers in the United States. Ten years later, that number had risen to over two million.

George Peper, ed., *Golf in America: The First One Hundred Years* (New York: Harry N. Abrams, 1988), 129-30.

What famous American doctor competed in the 1924 Olympics?

Dr. Benjamin Spock (1903-1998), the noted American pediatrician, author, and political activist, competed in the 1924 Paris Olympics with the rowing team.

Irving Wallace et al., *The Book of Lists #2* (New York: William Morrow and Company, 1980), 356.

What is Kung-Fu?

Kung-Fu is an ancient form of Oriental self-defense. Its actual name is Kung-Fu, Wu Su, which loosely translated means "discipline and martial arts training." Kung-Fu refers to the fine arts (music, painting, philosophy, history) aspect of the discipline, while Wu Su refers to the martial arts side. The ideal Kung-Fu adherent is a man of culture as well as a deadly fighter.

Mechanix Illustrated April 1970.

Who was named female athlete of the half-century by Associated Press in 1950?

Mildred "Babe" Didrikson (Mrs. Zaharias) (1914-1956) was named female athlete of the half-century by Associated Press in 1950 and will arguably go down in sports history as the best female athlete of the twentieth century. Didrikson excelled at basketball, softball, track and field, but especially professional golf. She died of cancer in 1956 at the age of 42.

Ralph Hickok, *The Encyclopedia of North American Sports History* (New York: Facts On File, 1992), 136.

Who was the first drag racer in history to win three National Hot Rod Association world championships in the Top Fuel category?

Not only was Shirley "Cha Cha" Muldowney (1940-) the first woman to be licensed as a Top Fuel driver by the National Hot Rod Association (NHRA), she was also the first drag racer ever to win three championships in this category.

The Lincoln Library of Sports Champions (Galveston, TX: The Frontier Press Company, 1989), 120.

What does the golf term "gimmie" mean?

In golf a "gimmie" is an easy putt of less than 18 inches that is conceded to the player without actually having to be made.

It is a recent corruption of the phrase "give it to me," which has been in use for probably less than fifty years.

Robert Hendrickson, *Grand Slams, Hat Tricks and Alley-oops* (New York: Prentice Hall General Reference, 1994), 73.

What is the John L. Sullivan Belt?

The John L. Sullivan Belt is a gold-plated, diamond-studded belt that was awarded to the boxing great in 1887. Sullivan, however, eventually pawned the belt, made at a cost of over $10,000, to support his drinking habit. Over the years, the belt or dubious copies of it have disappeared and re-appeared numerous times. In the 1950s, Melvin Herman, an 84-year-old man who did not recall how he came by it, offered to sell the belt for $5,000.

New York Times 3 December 1957.

What sport uses the terms "kaboom" and "swivel hips"?

A trampolinist would be likely to use terms like "kaboom" and "swivel hips" in describing the various exercises involved in this sport.

Laurence V. Griswold and Glenn Wilson, *Trampoline Tumbling Today, 2d ed.* (New York: A.S. Barnes, 1970), 71-72.

When was baseball legend Harold Joseph "Pie" Traynor born?

Harold Joseph "Pie" Traynor (1899-1972), the legendary baseball player, manager, sportscaster and scout was born November 11, 1899, in Framingham, Massachusetts. Traynor grew up with a love of sports and by the age of twelve was an ardent supporter of the Boston Braves and the Boston Red Sox. When he started playing sandlot ball, Harold would come home so dirty that his father, a printer, would complain that his soiled appearance reminded him of pied type. Eventually this description was shortened into his nickname. In 1920 he was offered a contract by Portsmouth, a team in the Virginia League. In Traynor's first year he played 104 games and hit a respectable .270. His beloved Red Sox made an offer, but Traynor had already been signed by the Pittsburgh Pirates. "Pie" had both batting and fielding problems during his first year in the majors and was sent to Birmingham to play in the Southern Association. In 1922 he was back with Pittsburgh, and his career began to skyrocket. For ten seasons Traynor hit over .300 and during his career he led his team to two pennants and one World Series victory. In 1934 "Pie" was named player-manager, a testament to his leadership abilities. Between 1936 and 1939 he was the bench manager for Pittsburgh and in 1948 he was inducted into the National Baseball Hall of Fame.

Great Athletes (Pasadena, CA: Salem Press, 1992), s.v. "Pie Traynor." David L. Porter, *Biographical Dictionary of American Sports, Baseball* (New York: Greenwood Press, 1987), s.v. "Traynor, Harold Joseph 'Pie'."

Who was named Rolex Yachtsman and Yachtswoman of the Year?

Cam Lewis of Lincolnville, Maine was named Rolex Yachtsman of the Year in 1994-the first time that an offshore sailor was honored with the title. Lewis was watch captain on the record-breaking French catamaran *Commodore Explorer* when it sailed around the world in 79 days, 6 hours. Betsy Alison of Newport, Rhode Island became the first four-time winner of the Rolex Yachtswoman of the Year designation after she won the 1993 Rolex International Women's Keelboat championship.

USA Today 11-13 February 1994.

Who was *Sports Illustrated*'s first Sportsman of the Year?

In 1954, the first year that *Sports Illustrated* presented an award for Sportsman of the Year, English athlete Roger Bannister (1929-) received the award for "pure excellence" in his sport of track and field. That year Bannister became the first person to run a mile in less than four minutes. It had been generally believed that it was humanly impossible to run the distance in so short a time. Bannister, medical student, used advanced training methods and did his own research on the mechanics of running.

The New Encyclopedia Britannica, 15th ed., "Micropaedia" (Chicago: Encyclopedia Britannica, 1994), s.v. "Bannister, Sir Roger (Gilbert)." Claire Walter, *Winners, The Blue Ribbon Encyclopedia of Awards* (New York: Facts on File, 1982), 690.

What was the shortest world title boxing match?

The shortest boxing match for a world title was the 20-second WBC middleweight bout between the winner Gerald McClellan and loser Jay Bell at Bayamon Puerto Rico on August 7, 1993.

Mark Young, ed., *The Guinness Book of Records 1994* (New York: Facts On File, 1994), 62.

What are picadores?

In a bullfight the matador, the one who kills the bull, and has a number of assistants, among whom are the picadores. Mounted on horseback, they carry a lance, with which they jab the bull to weaken its neck and shoulder muscles and so lessen the threat of its lethal horns. Although there are usually two for each fight, a number of extras will be kept in reserve in case a horse or rider is injured.

John Leibold, *This is the Bullfight* (South Brunswick, NJ: A.S. Barnes, 1971), 90, 322-23.

Which Russian female athlete was suspended by the International Amateur Athletic Federation in 1994?

In 1994 Russian pentathlete Irina Belova was suspended for four years by the International Amateur Athletic Federation after testing positive for testosterone during the 1993 World Indoor Championships.

USA Today 18-20 March 1994.

What is the Grand Slam of professional tennis, and who are its winners?

The Grand Slam of professional tennis is accomplished by players who win the English championship at Wimbleton, as well as the Australian, French, and U.S. Opens, during the same calendar year. Only five players who have achieved this distinction—two men and three women: Don Budge of the United States of America in 1938; Rod Laver of Australia, twice, in 1962 and 1969; Maureen Connolly of the United States of America in 1953; Margaret Smith Court of Australia in 1970; and Steffi Graf of West Germany in 1988.

USA Today 1 June 1994.

What are the Queensberry Rules?

The Queensberry Rules were boxing rules codified in England in 1867. By 1889 they had become the standard for boxing matches. The rules were devised by John Sholto Douglas (1844-1900), the eighth marquis of Queensberry, and boxer John Graham Chambers in an effort to make the sport of boxing more humane.

Harvey Frommer, *Sports Roots: How Nicknames, Namesakes, Trophies, Competitions, and Expressions in the World of Sports Came to Be* (New York: Atheneum, 1979), s.v. "Queensbury Rules."

Who was the first woman to win an Olympic marathon?

After a quick recovery from knee surgery, Joan Benoit won the first women's marathon in Olympic history during the games that were held at Los Angles in 1984. She was a graduate of Bowdoin College in Brunswick, Maine, and represented the United States.

Allen Guttmann, *Women's Sports History* (New York: Columbia University Press, 1991), 246.

What world middleweight boxing champion regained his title for an unprecedented fifth time when he defeated Carmen Basilio in 1958?

On March 25, 1958, Sugar Ray Robinson (1920-1989) defeated Carmen Basilio in 15 rounds in Chicago; this fight made Robinson the middleweight champion for an unprecedented fifth time. Overall, in a 25-year boxing career, Robinson's record was 174-19-6 with 109 knock-outs.

Mike Meserole, ed., *The 1991 Information Please Sports Almanac* (New York: Houghton Mifflin, 1990), s.v. "Sugar Ray Robinson." Gorton Carruth, *What Happened When: A Chronology of Life and Events in America* (New York: Signet, 1989), 879.

What is a "perfect game" in bowling?

When a player bowls 12 consecutive strikes in a single game, the result is a "perfect game." A perfect game scores 300 points.

The New York Public Library Desk Reference (New York: Stonesong Press, 1989), 579.

What is a bungee cord?

A bungee is an elasticized cord, and the kind with which most people are familiar has with a hook at each end and is used to bind a suitcase to a wheeled carrier. The modern-day craze of bungee jumping had its origins in 1979. Jumpers leap headfirst from bridges, cranes, and hot-air balloons, from 90 to 300 feet (27.4 to 91.4 meters) above the ground, with only a long nylon-cased rubber bungee cord to break their fall. Anchored around the ankles or to a body harness, the wrist-thin cord is long enough to allow a few seconds of free fall before it stretches, dampening the force of the plunge. The diver sometimes hurtles to within a few feet of the ground before rebounding skyward like a yo-yo.

Time , 23 April 1990. *Merriam-Webster's Collegiate Dictionary* (Springfield, MA: Merriam-Webster, 1993), s.v. "bungee cord."

When was the first soap box derby held?

The first soap box derby was held on Saturday, August 19, 1933, in Dayton, Ohio. Sponsored by the Dayton *Daily News*, its photographer, Myron E. Scott, came up with the idea, when he saw three boys racing soap-box cars down one of Dayton's steep streets. One girl, Alice Johnson entered the race; she lost to Randall Custer.

In August, 1934, under the joint sponsorship of Chevrolet and the newspaper, the race became a national event, when 34 cities sent contestants to Dayton. In 1935, the race was moved to Akron, Ohio. Currently the contest is for young people aged 10 to 15 who design, build, and drive their own motorless race cars. Cars must be built according to strict rules and pass an official inspection before being admitted to the competition. Site of the final race is a 975.4-foot coasting course known as Derby Downs where racers compete for trophies and scholarship prizes totaling $10,000. The race is organized by the International Soap Box Derby, Inc., a nonprofit public charity in Akron, Ohio.

Collier's Encyclopedia (New York: Macmillan Educational Company, 1991), s.v. "Soap Box Derby." Sylvia A. Rosenthal, *Soap Box Derby Racing* (New York: Lothrop, Lee & Shepard Books, 1980), 23-27.

What was the shortest heavyweight title fight on record?

The shortest heavyweight title fight on record took place in 1908 in Dublin, when champion Tommy Burns (1881-1955) knocked out Irish Jem Roche at 1:28 of the first round.

Norm Hitzges, *The Norm Hitzges Historical Sports Almanac* (Dallas TX: Taylor Publishing, 1991), 77.

What are komats, and in what sport are they performed?

A komat is a jump from one foot to the other with knees bent up in front. A komat is also called a cat leap, and is performed in rhythmic gymnastics.

Jenny Bott, *Rhythmic Gymnastics, The Skills of the Game* (Marlborough, UK: The Crowood Press, 1989), 117.

What are the three weapons used in fencing?

The three weapons used in fencing are the foil, the epee, and the sabre. They all must have a flexible steel blade, and hilt with a guard. Foils and epees have a button at the end of their blades.

E.D. Morton, *Martini A-Z of Fencing* (London: Queen Anne Press, 1988) 61. Sylvia Worth, ed., *Rules of the Game* (New York: St. Martin's Press, 1990), 63.

What are the odds of a professional golfer sinking a hole-in-one in a single round of golf?

According to the Professional Golfers Association (PGA), the odds are 3,708 to one that a professional golfer will sink a hole-in-one in a single round of golf.

Les Krantz, ed. *What the Odds Are: A-to-Z Odds on Everything You Hoped or Feared Could Happen* (New York: HarperPerennial, 1992), s.v. "hole-in-one."

When was the first women's air race?

The first women's air race was billed as the "Women's Air Derby" and was a nine-day contest stretching from Santa Monica, California to Cleveland, Ohio. The 1929 event was won by Louise Thaden who had already set numerous women's air records.

David Roberts, "The 99s: the right stuff then and now," *Smithsonian* August 1994.

In golf what are the designations given to one-, two-, and three-woods?

In the game's early years, centuries ago, the one-, two-, and three-wood clubs acquired the nicknames "driver," "brassie," and "spoon," respectively.

Charles Price, *The World of Golf: A Panorama of Six Centuries of the Game's History* (New York: Random House, 1962), 201.

Why was George H. Willig fined $1.10 in May of 1977?

George H. Willig paid the City of New York $1.10 to settle a $250,000 court case that resulted from his successful attempt to scale the South Tower of the World Trade Center. The sum represented one penny for each floor of the building. Willig was described as a folk hero by the press and was congratulated by the city's mayor, who accepted the out of court settlement. Mayor Abraham Beame convinced the city's prosecutors that the suit was inappropriate and initiated talks between the city and Willig. The court case had been filed to discourage other "human flies" from making similar attempts and to pay for the cost ($250,000) of deploying city helicopters and police officers. The climb, which lasted three and a half hours, was seen by thousands of onlookers and was viewed on television by millions. Willig agreed to assist the city by providing suggestions on how to prevent copycat incidents; he noted that others might not be as skilled or as lucky as he was.

The New York Times 28 May 1977.

Which heavyweight boxing champion won all of his professional bouts?

Rocky Marciano, the world heavyweight boxing champion from 1952 until his retirement in 1956, was also famous for having won all of his professional fights. In 43 of 49 bouts, his opponents could not finish the fight. Only two other boxing champions come close to this record: Gene Tunney, who was undefeated as champion but had one professional loss, and Joe Louis, who was unbeaten until he tried a comeback against, of all people, Rocky Marciano.

Gilbert Odd, *Encyclopedia of Boxing* (New York: Crescent Books, 1983), 77.

Outdoor Activities

What services do U.S. national parks offer to disabled travelers?

U.S. national parks have developed several means to accommodate disabled travelers. Ramps are used to make the parks more accessible, and in some instances, free wheelchairs are available. Information provided at visitor's centers is available in braille, large print, and audio recordings. A free "Golden Access Passport" allows people who are permanently disabled to visit all of the national parks at no charge.

Fodor's National Parks of the West (New York: Fodor's Travel Publications, 1992), 1213.

Who invented the Ferris Wheel?

Originally called pleasure wheels, the first such amusement rides were described by English traveller Peter Mundy in 1620. In Turkey he saw a ride for children consisting of two vertical wheels, 20 feet (6.1 meters) across, supported by a large post on each side. Such rides were called ups-and-downs at the St. Bartholomew Fair of 1728 in England, and in 1860 a French pleasure wheel was turned by hand and carried sixteen passengers. They were also in use in the United States by then, with a larger, wooden wheel operating at Walton Spring, Georgia.

Wanting a spectacular attraction to rival that of the 1889 Paris Centennial celebration-the Eiffel Tower-the directors of the 1893 Columbian Exposition had a design competition. The prize was won by the American bridge builder George Washington Gale Ferris (1859-1896). In 1893 he designed and erected a gigantic revolving steel wheel whose top reached 264 feet (80.5 meters) above ground. The wheel-825 feet (251.5 meters) in circumference, 250 feet (76.2 meters) in diameter, and 30 feet (9.1 meters) wide-was supported by two 140-foot (42.7 meters) towers. Attached to the wheel were 36 cars, each able to carry 60 passengers. Opening on June 21, 1893, at the exposition in Chicago, Illinois, it was extremely successful. Thousands lined up to pay 50 cents for a 20-minute ride-a large sum in those days, considering that a merry-go-round ride cost only four cents. In 1904 it was moved to St. Louis, Missouri, for the Louisiana Purchase Exposition. It was eventually sold for scrap. The largest-diameter Ferris wheel currently operating is the Cosmoclock 21 at Yokohama City, Japan. It is 344.48 feet (105 meters) high and 328 feet (100 meters) in diameter.

Norman D. Anderson and Walter R. Brown, *Ferris Wheels* (New York: Pantheon Books, 1983), 7-23. Mark C. Young, ed., *The Guinness Book of Records 1995* (New York: Facts On File, 1994), 99. Harry Harris, *Good Old-Fashioned Yankee Ingenuity* (Chelsea, MI: Scarborough House, 1990), 125-26.

What natural attractions in the United States are the most popular?

Some of the most popular natural attractions in the United States are:

The Grand Canyon, Arizona
Yellowstone National Park, Wyoming
Niagara Falls, New York
Mount McKinley, Alaska
California's "Big Trees": the sequoias and redwoods
Hawaii's volcanoes
Florida's Everglades

David Wallechinsky, *The Book of Lists* (New York: Morrow, 1977), 25.

Is there an admission charge for national parks?

Almost all national parks in the United States have an entrance fee, ranging from three to ten dollars per vehicle. The entrance fee is valid for seven consecutive days.

Paula Consolo, ed., *Fodor's National Parks of the West* (New York: Fodor's Travel Publications, 1992), 5.

How can one obtain tickets to tour the White House?

Free tickets for special tours of the White House can be obtained by writing to one's Senator or Congressperson, in care of the Senate or the House of Representatives Office Building, Washington, DC 20510.

U.S. and World Wide Travel Accommodations Guide, 13th ed. (Fullerton, CA: Campus Travel Service, 1993), 87.

What are the most popular names for boats?

Thirty percent of all pleasure boats share five names. In descending order of popularity the five names are: *Serenity* (12 percent), *Obsession* (7 percent), *Osprey* (6 percent), *Fantasea* (5 percent), and *Liquid Asset* (4 percent).

USA Today 2 July, 1993.

What is the origin of the phrase "to skin the cat"?

The phrase "to skin the cat" refers to a children's exercise in which youngsters hang from a branch by their hands and draw their legs up through their arms until they have pulled themselves into a sitting position. It may have been so named because of the resemblance to removing a pelt from an animal by starting at the forelegs and then going down over the body.

Charles Earle Funk, *A Hog on Ice and Other Curious Expressions* (Harper & Brothers Publishers, 1948), 112.

According to a survey, what are the three most desirable travel destinations of Americans?

The three places in the world that Americans most want to visit, according to a survey conducted by Holiday Inns, are Hawaii, with over 50 percent, London, with 15 percent, and Paris, with 14 percent. Eight hundred people were polled.

Modern Maturity April-May, 1988.

Which European countries have mandated vacations periods for workers?

Workers in most European countries have fixed, longer vacations than do their American counterparts. Here are the specifics.

Country	Vacation time by law	Vacation time by agreement
Austria	5 weeks	
Belgium	4 weeks	5 weeks
Denmark		5 weeks
Finland	5 weeks	5 to 6 weeks
France	5 weeks	5 to 6 weeks
Germany	3 weeks	5 1/2 to 6 weeks
Great Britain		4 to 6 weeks
Greece	4 weeks	
Iceland	4 weeks, 4 days	
Ireland	3 weeks	+/-4 weeks
Italy		4 to 6 weeks
Luxembourg	5 weeks	25 to 30 days
Malta	4 weeks	
Netherlands	4 weeks	4 to 5 weeks
Norway	4 weeks, 1 day	
Portugal	30 civil days	4 1/2 to 5 weeks
Spain	30 civil days	4 1/2 to 5 weeks
Sweden	5 weeks	5 to 8 weeks
Switzerland	4 weeks	4 to 5 weeks

Escape Winter 1994.

What is a rain fly and what purpose does it serve on a tent?

A rain fly is a waterproof tarp stretched over a tent's frame, staked to the ground or bottom of the tent, so it protects the tent canopy from rain. The canopy is air-permeable so that moisture can rise out of a tent, condense on the underside of the fly, and trickle down to the ground. The dead air space formed between the rain fly and canopy also serves as an insulator, helping to maintain a comfortable tent temperature.

Andrew Sugar, *The Complete Tent Book* (Chicago: Contemporary Books, 1979, 42.

How many roller coasters are there in the United States, and how many people ride them?

There were 164 roller coasters in the United States in 1989 and an estimated 214 million people rode them during that year. Roller coasters have had a long history in thrill-giving. During the fifthteenth and sixteenth centuries, the first known gravity rides were built in St. Petersburg and were called Russian Mountains. A wheeled roller coaster, called the Switchback, was used as early as 1784 in Russia. By 1817 the first roller coaster with cars locked to the tracks operated in France. The first U.S. roller coaster patent was granted to J.G. Taylor in 1872, and LaMarcus Thompson built the first known roller coaster in the United States at Coney Island, Brooklyn, New York, in 1884. Until recently, the longest roller coaster in the world was The Beast at Kings Island, Ohio, which has a run of 1.4 miles (2.25 kilometers) with 800 feet (243.84 meters) of tunnels. The current record holder is the Ultimate at Lightwater Valley, Ripon, Great Britain, with a run of 1.42 miles (2.28 kilometers).

Robert Cartnell, *The Incredible Scream Machine: A History of the Roller Coaster* (Fairview Park, OH: Amusement Park Books, 1987), 4-5, 19-34. Mark C. Young, ed., *The Guinness Book of Records 1995* (New York: Facts On File, 1994), 100. *Smithsonian* August 1989.

Which national park is America's oldest?

Hot Springs National Park in Hot Springs, Arkansas, is the oldest national park but not the first. It was established as a reservation by an act of the U.S. Congress on April 20, 1832, but not designated as a national park until March 4, 1921. The park consists of 911 acres and 46 hot springs. The first national park was Yellowstone National Park, authorized on March 1, 1872.

Russell Ash, *The Top 10 of Everything* (London: Dorling Kindersley, 1994), 104. Joseph Nathan Kane, *Famous First Facts: A Record of First Happenings, Discoveries, and Inventions in American History, 4th ed.* (New York: H.W. Wilson, 1981), s.v. "park."

How long is the Appalachian National Scenic Trail?

The Appalachian National Scenic Trail, which begins at Mt. Katahdin, Maine and runs to Springer Mountain, Georgia, is over 2,000 miles long. The highest point in the trail is Clingmans Dome in the Great Smoky Mountains at 6,643 feet.

Webster's New Geographical Dictionary (Springfield, MA: Merriam-Webster, 1984), 62.

What are some sites in the nation's capital that are open to the public?

Some of the tourist attractions inside Washington, D.C.'s corridors of power are the Capitol Building, the Supreme Court, the White House, the State Department, and the Pentagon. In most cases, official tours conducted by trained professionals must be undertaken by those wishing to enter. The Lincoln, Jefferson, and Vietnam War Memorials, the Library of Congress, the National Archives, the museums, and Arlington National Cemetery are also popular with visitors and usually do not require formal tours.

The World Almanac of U.S. Politics (New York: World Almanac, 1989), 73.

What is a vomitorium?

The term vomitorium (from the Latin *vomere,* to discharge, vomit) refers to a large opening in a stadium or auditorium through which large numbers of people may enter or leave quickly.

Mario A. Pei, et al., eds., *Dictionary of Foreign Terms* (New York: Delacorte Press, 1975), s.v. "Vomitorium."

Team Sports

When was the first Rose Bowl game played?

The Tournament of Roses in Pasadena, California, began in 1889 as a parade and sports activities. In 1902, a football game was added. In that first game, Michigan beat Stanford 49-0. The next game was not played until 1916 when Washington State defeated Brown 14-0. Thereafter games were held annually, with the name "Rose Bowl" being officially adopted in 1923.

Gorton Carruth and Eugene Ehrlich, *Facts & Dates of American Sports* (New York: Harper & Row, 1988), 65, 96, 112. Ralph Hickock, *The Encyclopedia of North American Sports History* (New York: Facts on File, 1992), 389.

Who was Pete Gray?

During the 1945 season Pete Gray, a one-armed outfielder, played for the St. Louis Browns. Born Peter Wyshner in 1916 in Pennsylvania, Gray fell off a milk truck at the age of six and mangled his right arm, which had to be amputated. Naturally right-handed, he learned to throw and bat from the opposite side. He entered professional ball in 1942 and won national attention in 1944 when he played for Memphis in the Southern Association. In that year he batted .333, hit five home runs, and tied a league record by stealing 68 bases. That showing earned Gray the spot with the St. Louis Browns, but he was overmatched in spite of the all-time low quality of major league play due to the World War II player shortage. In 1946 Gray was sent back to the minors when baseball once again returned to full strength and there he played until the early 1950s.

Bill Borst, *Still Last in the American League: The St. Louis Browns Revisited* (West Bloomfield, MI: Altwerger and Mandel Publishing, 1992), 123-24. Mike Shatzkin, ed., *The Ballplayers: Baseball's Ultimate Biographical Reference* (New York: William Morrow, 1990), s.v. "Pete Gray."

When did colleges begin charging admission to football games?

The first instance at which an admission fee was charged at a college football game was on May 14, 1874, when McGill University of Montreal, Canada, played Harvard University in Cambridge, Massachusetts. Harvard won 3-0.

Thomas G. Bergin, *The Game: The Harvard-Yale Football Rivalry, 1875-1983,* (New Haven, CT: Yale University Press, 1984), 4-5. Norm Hitzges, *The Norm Hitzges Historical Sports Almanac* (Dallas, TX: Taylor Publishing, 1991), 135. Richard Whittingham, *Saturday Afternoon: College football and the men who made the day* (New York Workman Publishing, 1985), 16.

Did twin brothers ever play in baseball's major Leagues?

Two sets of twin brothers played in the major baseball leagues. Eddie O'Brien played for the Pirates while his twin brother, Johnny, played for the Pirates, Cardinals, and Braves. The Havana-born brothers, Jose and Ozzie Canseco, are the other pair.

Mike Shatzin, ed., *The Ballplayers: Baseball's Ultimate Biographical Reference* (New York: Arbor House, 1990), s.v. "Eddie O'Brien," "Johnny O'Brien." *The Baseball Encyclopedia: The Complete and Definitive Record of Major League Baseball, 9th ed.* (New York: Macmillan Publishing, 1993), s.v. "Jose Canseco," "Ozzie Canseco."

Was there ever a father-son combination in major league baseball that has played for the same team at the same time?

Both Ken Griffey, Jr. and Sr. played for the Seattle Mariners in the American League on August 31, 1990, the Griffeys had been the first father-son combination to play in the Major leagues at the same time in 1989.

Mark Young, ed., *The Guinness Book of Sports Records 1994-1995* (New York: Facts On File, 1994), 23.

Who is the home run king of japan?

Sadaharu Oh is the home run king of Japan, if not the world. By the time he retired from baseball in 1980, Sadaharu had hit 868 home runs (with 2,170 RBI's and a career batting average of .301.) Sadaharu was born May 10, 1940, in Tokyo and after the war enjoyed watching the increasingly popular game of baseball in Japan. He played baseball in junior high and, after failing to get a seat in an engineering high school which would prepare him for a future university degree in mechanical engineering, he attended a commercial high school with a strong baseball program. After attracting the attention of baseball scouts, Sadaharu signed with the Yomiuri Giants of Tokyo. His first few seasons were mediocre at best, but under the tutelage of a patient batting coach his batting prowess became widely respected as his yearly stats began to climb. In 1976 he broke Babe Ruth's homerun record of 714 and in 1977 Sadaharu topped Hank Aaron's score of 755 homers. Some critics claim that had Sadaharu played major league ball in the U.S. his record would have been diminished due to longer fences. Others say that had Sadaharu played major league ball in the U.S. his record would have been greater due to a longer season than that played in Japan.

Great Athletes (Pasadena, CA: Salem Press, 1992), 13:1881-84.

Who pitched baseball's most bittersweet no hitter?

On May 26, 1959, while playing against Milwaukee, pitcher Harvey Haddix of the Pittsburgh Pirates threw 12 perfect innings only to lose the game 1-0 in a very confusing and controversial thirteenth inning.

Lee Allen, *The National League Story* (New York: Hill & Wang, 1965), 266-67.

Who was the first woman to do the play-by-play reporting for a National Football League game?

In 1987, Gayle Sierens became the first woman to anchor a play-by-play telecast of a National Football League game between the Kansas City Chiefs and the Seattle Seahawks.

Pittsburgh Press 28 December 1987.

What National Football League teams have retired numbers and which ones were retired?

Only five National Football League teams have not retired any of their numbers: the Buffalo Bills, the Pittsburgh Steelers, the

Los Angeles Raiders, the Dallas Cowboys, and the San Diego Chargers.

Those that retired only one include the Cincinnati Bengals, which retired Bob Johnson's number 54; the Miami Dolphins, Bob Griese's 12; the Seattle Seahawks, 'The Fans' 12; the Atlanta Falcons, Tommy Nobis' 60; the Minnesota Vikings, Fran Tarkenton's 10; the Tampa Bay Bucanneers, Lee Roy Selmon's 63; and the Washington Redskins, Sammy Baugh's 33.

The teams that retired only two players' numbers include the Denver Broncos, which retired Frank Tripucka's 18 and Floyd Little's 44; the New York Jets, Joe Namath's 12 and Don Maynard's 13; the Los Angeles Rams, Bob Waterfield's 7 and Merlin Olsen's 74; and the New Orleans Saints, Jim Taylor's 31 and Doug Atkins' 81.

The teams with three numbers retired include the Houston Oilers, with Earl Campbell's 34, Jim Norton's 43, and Elvin Bethea's 65; and the New England Patriots, with Gino Cappelletti's 12, Jim Hunt's 20 and Bob Dee's 79.

There are only two teams with four numbers retired. The Green Bay Packers retired Tony Canadeo's 3, Don Hutson's 14, Bart Starr's 15, and Ray Nitschke's 66; and the Phoenix Cardinals retired Larry Wilson's 8, Stan Mauldin's 77, J.V. Cain's 88, and Marshall Goldberg's 99.

Three teams have retired five numbers. The Cleveland Browns retired Otto Graham's 14, Jim Brown's 32, Ernie Davis' 45, Don Fleming's 46, and Lou Groza's 76; the Kansas City Chiefs have retired Len Dawson's 16, Abner Haynes' 28, Stone Jackson's 33, Mack Lee Hill's 36, and Bobby Bell's 78; and the Philadelphia Eagles have retired Steve Van Buren's 15, Tom Brookshier's 40, Pete Retzlaff's 44, Chuck Bednarik's 60, and Al Wistert's 70.

The teams that retired six players' numbers are the Detroit Lions, which retired Dutch Clark's 7, Bobby Layne's 22, Doak Walker's 37, Joe Schmidt's 56, Chuck Hughes' 85, and Charlie Sanders' 88; and the San Francisco 49ers, which retired John Brodie's 12, Joe Perry's 34, Jimmy Johnson's 37, Hugh McElhenny's 39, Charlie Krueger's 70, and Leo Nomellini's 73.

There are two teams with seven numbers retired. The Indianapolis Colts retired Johnny Unitas's 19, Buddy Young's 22, Lenny Moore's 24, Art Donovan's 70, Jim Parker's 77, Raymond Berry's 82, and Gino Marchetti's 89; the New York Giants retired Ray Flaherty's 1, Mel Hein's 7, Y.A. Tittle's 14, Al Blozis' 32, Joe Morrison's 40, Charlie Conerly's 42, and Ken Strong's 50.

The Chicago Bears have retired the most players' numbers: These numbers include Bronko Nagurski's 3, George McAfee's 5, Willie Galimore's 28, Walter Payton's 34, Brian Piccolo's 41, Sid Luckman's 42, Bill Hewitt's 56, Bill George's 61, Bulldog Turner's 66, and Red Grange's 77.

"Of the numbers," *USA Today* 22 July 1988.

What is the two-point conversion in football?

The two-point conversion in football gives the team an option, after scoring a touchdown, to go either for a one-point kick or a two-point pass or run from the three-yard line. The option was created to lessen the reliance on kickers in the game.

USA Today 17 March 1994. *USA Today* 24 March 1994.

What percentage of professional football players graduated from college?

A 1986 *Dallas Times Herald* study revealed that only about 41 percent of professional football players graduated from college. Thirty-three percent of black players and 50 percent of white players earned degrees. The only group of schools with a 100 percent graduation rate was the Ivy League. The worst record went to the Big Eight and Southeast conferences, where only 34 percent graduated.

"NFL fails," *Pittsburgh Press* 26 January 1986.

What major league baseball players have been physically handicapped?

The first physically handicapped baseball players to join the major leagues were Pete Gray and Bert Shepard in 1945. Gray, who had one arm, played for the St. Louis Browns after becoming the Southern Association's Most Valuable Player in 1944. He lost his arm when he was six years old and taught himself to bat, catch, and throw. Bert Shepard was a World War II veteran who overcame the loss of his lower right leg, amputated due to wounds received when his plane was shot down. Shepard received a prosthesis and, within a week, was trying out for the Washington Senators. Team management had Shepard pitch batting practice until late July, when he made his first and only major league appearance. Put in as a relief pitcher against the Boston Red Sox, he pitched four-and-one-third innings, allowing only three hits and one run. Complications with his leg ended Shepard's pitching career.

In 1989, one-armed pitcher Jim Abbott (1967-) became the number one draft choice of the California Angels. After playing for the University of Michigan, Abbott has no qualms about his fielding abilities and does not consider his missing hand to be a detriment. He does not wear a prosthesis, he has said "If I don't make it there'll be nothing or no one to blame it on except my own absence of pitching ability."

John Thorn, *A Century of Baseball Lore* (New York: Hart Publishing Company, 1974), 145-46. *Pittsburgh Press* 5 February 1989.

Who were "the Black Sox"?

In 1919 eight members of the Chicago White Sox baseball team accepted bribes from New York gambler Arnold Rothstein to throw the World Series. The players—Joseph Jefferson "Shoeless Joe" Jackson, Charles "Swede" Risberg, Oscar "Happy" Felsch, Arnold "Chick" Gandil, George "Buck" Weaver, Fred McMullin, Eddie Cicotte, and Claude "Lefty" Williams—were banned from baseball forever, and their team was nicknamed "the Black Sox."

Jay Robert Nash, *Crime Chronology: A Worldwide Record, 1900-1983* (New York: Facts on File, 1984), 51.

What was the nickname of baseball legend Lou Gehrig?

Baseball great Lou Gehrig's (1903-1941) nickname was the "Iron Horse." The nickname came from his durability; he played 2,130 consecutive games and won the Most Valuable Player (MVP) award in 1927 and 1936. Gehrig wore number four.

Richard G. Hubler, *Lou Gehrig: The Iron Horse of Baseball* (Boston: Houghton Mifflin Company, 1941), 189. Chuck Wielgus and Alexander Wolff, *From A-Train to Yogi: The Fan's Book of Sports Nicknames* (New York: Harper & Row, 1987), 103.

What was the highest college football score ?

Dickinson beat Haverford Gr. School 227 to 0 in 1900, while in 1916, Georgia Tech beat Cumberland (Tennessee) 222 to 0 but the playing time was reduced to 45 minutes.

Frank G. Menke, *Encyclopedia of Sports, 5th ed.* (New York: A.S. Barnes and Company, 1975), 461.

Has a U.S. baseball team ever played a team from Russia?

On June 1, 1988, the baseball team from Johns Hopkins University traveled to Moscow to play a team from Russia's D.I. Mendeleyev College of Chemical Technology. It was the first known organized game between teams from the two countries and was won handily by the Americans, 15-2. When in the fifth inning Aleksei Koshevoy became the first Soviet baseball player to score a run against an American team, he immediately asked to renegotiate his contract.

Felicity Barringer, *New York Times* 2 June 1988.

Who made the first unassisted triple play in major league history?

The first unassisted triple play in the history of major league baseball was recorded by Cleveland Indians shortstop Neal Ball in the 1909 season. In a July game against the Boston Red Sox, Ball made a leaping catch of a line drive with runners on first and second bases. He touched second to force out the lead runner, then caught the other runner between first and second bases for the third out.

Patrick Clark, *Sports Firsts* (New York: Facts on File, 1981), 15.

What does the baseball term "fungo" mean and how is it used?

The word "fungo" is a baseball term in use since as early as 1867. It can be used as both a noun and a verb. A fungo is a fly ball hit to baseball players during fielding practice. The batter, frequently a coach, throws the ball up into the air and hits it as it descends. A fungo bat is often used, a light, long bat that gives the batter greater accuracy in directing the ball. There is a designated fungo circle on the baseball field, located near the batter's box, where the fungo batter stands. The fungo batter can be referred to as the "fungoer," and the term is also used as a verb, "to fungo" or "to fungo bat," as in "I will fungo bat for the other players." The term also describes a weak style of batting; a fungo hit is a high fly ball that looks as if it was hit with a fungo bat.

The etymology of the word is subject to much debate and even some humorous conjecture, most notably in William Safire's *What's the Good Word.* One theory is that the word is derived from a chant used in street games: "One goes, two goes, fun goes." Others speculate that it comes from either the German "fangen," meaning to catch, or the Scottish "fung," meaning to toss, pitch, or fling. It may also take its meaning from the word "fungible," meaning something that can be substituted, referring to the special bat used. Fungo may even refer to the sound or feel of the fungo bat being like soft fungus.

Paul Dickson, *The Dickson Baseball Dictionary* (New York: Facts on File, 1989), 172.

Who was the first pitcher to throw a no-hit game in the World Series?

On October 8, 1956, New York Yankee Don Larsen threw 97 pitches for a perfect game against the Brooklyn Dodgers, in the first World Series no-hitter. The game ended in a 2-0 victory for the Yankees.

The Baseball Encyclopedia: The Complete and Definitive Record of Major League Baseball, 9th ed. (New York: MacMillan, 1993), 2737.

Who holds the record for the most points scored in a single basketball game?

On March 2, 1962, Wilt Chamberlain scored 100 points--the all-time pro basketball record—to lead the Philadelphia Warriors to a 169-147 victory over the New York Knicks. In setting the mark, Chamberlain hit 36 field goals and 28 (of 32) free throws.

New York Times 3 March 1962.

Who was the first woman to play professional basketball?

Lusia "Lucy" Harris Stewart, a standout 6-foot 3-inch center at Delta State University and a member of the 1976 U.S. Olympic Team, became the first woman to join the ranks of the National Basketball Association (NBA) when she was selected in the seventh round of the 1977 draft by the New Orleans Jazz. The following year she became the number-one free agent signed by the Houston Angels of the Women's Professional Basketball League (WPBL). Her uniform was placed in the Naismith Memorial Basketball Hall of Fame.

David L. Porter, ed., *Biographical Dictionary of American Sports: Basketball and Other Indoor Sports* (New York: Greenwood Press, 1989), 289-90.

What is the name of the National Basketball Association's expansion franchise in Toronto?

The name of Toronto's National Basketball Association expansion franchise is the Raptors.

USA Today 16 May 1994.

Are the baseballs used in the major leagues being "juiced"?

A sharp increase in opposite-field home runs and a dramatic rise of 13.2 percent in the number of runs per game in the first month of the 1994 season as compared to that of the 1987 season, when runs scored were the highest since 1950, raised the question of whether baseballs used in the major leagues are being "juiced," that is, tampered with in order to improve the ball's performance. The issue has not been resolved, however, since estimates of the distance of home runs have not risen sharply, and tests done on the elasticity of baseballs in 1987 and 1994 revealed that there has been virtually no increase from 1987 to 1994 in the distance a batted ball travels. Other tests, however, indicate that a heated ball bounces higher than a cold ball. A regulation baseball is constructed out of cork, rubber, four different types of yarn, and a cowhide cover that is hand-stitched with 88 inches of waxed thread.

USA Today 10 May 1994

What are the origins of the nicknames of the National and American League baseball teams?

In baseball's National League, the St. Louis Cardinals were named in 1900, supposedly by a woman spectator who referred to the red trim on their away uniforms as being a lovely shade of "cardinal." Sports reporter Billy McHale heard the remark and used it in a story, and the name stuck.

Chicago's team was dubbed the Cubs in 1901 by Fred Hayner, then sports editor of the Chicago *Daily News*.

The Brooklyn Dodgers acquired that name from baseball writers in the late 1880s, when residents of Brooklyn were known as "trolley-dodgers." The team has also been known as the Superbas, the Robins, and the Kings, but the name Dodgers has always come back into favor.

The New York Giants took their name from a chance remark made in 1888, when the team's manager asserted that his players were giants in stature and in ability.

The Philadelphia Phillies borrowed their home town's nickname when they entered the National League in 1883. They had previously been called the Quakers by out-of-town writers, but never by the fans.

The Pittsburgh Pirates were so named after the baseball war of 1890. In that year, players seceded from the National League and the American Association—forerunner of the American League—to form the short-lived Players League. When the conflict ended, there was some confusion as to the status of certain players. Louis Bierbauer, a star of the Philadelphia Athletics, was snapped up by the Pittsburgh club, an act the Philadelphia press derided as comparable to piracy. The Pittsburgh team was thereafter branded the Pirates.

The Cincinnati Reds were organized as the Red Stockings in 1869, but their name was immediately shortened to Reds.

In the American League, the Philadelphia Americans nicknamed themselves the Athletics after one of the country's original teams. Athletics is often shortened to A's, and the club has also been tagged the Elephants.

The St. Louis Browns were so named in 1875 when the club entered the National League (the American League had not yet been formed). Like several other clubs, they were named after the color of their stockings.

Two explanations are put forth for the naming of the Cleveland Indians. One states that the title was chosen by a group of baseball writers. The other says that the team members acted so wild at a party that it was decided to call them Indians. The team had previously been called the Blues, after the blue in their uniforms, and the Naps, after one of their stars, Napoleon Lajoie.

The Boston Red Sox were named in 1904 by the son of their team's owner, Charles H. Taylor.

The Washington Senators were originally called the Nationals, but later christened the Senators because they represented the nation's capital.

The Detroit Tigers were originally known as the Wolverines. In 1901, when they first appeared in new uniforms including blue-and-orange-striped stockings, sportswriter Phil J. Reid noted the similarity to the colors of the Princeton team, which was known as the Tigers, and that nickname was adopted.

The Chicago White Sox were tagged the White Stockings by Charles A. Comiskey when he bought the club. That name had previously been used by Chicago's National League team, and although it had since been discarded, the National League objected to its use for an American League organization. Comiskey sidestepped the issue by shortening the name to White Sox.

Previous to 1909, New York's American League team had been nicknamed the Hilltoppers and the Highlanders. *New York Press* sports editor Jim Price tired of these cumbersome titles and in 1909 referred to the team as the Yankees. Other sportswriters, pleased with a nickname that could be further shortened to Yanks, picked up on the name, and it soon became official.

American Speech April 1941.

Did a midget ever play major league baseball?

Edward Gaedel was the only midget ever to play major league baseball. He made history in the sport on August 19, 1951, when he popped out of a huge cake set up in St. Louis Sportsman's Park as part of a between-games show at a doubleheader between St. Louis and Detroit. Gaedel, who was 3 feet 7 inches tall, had been signed to the St. Louis Browns by the team's president, Bill Veeck. He was allowed to play and was walked by the Tigers's pitcher, Bob Cain, but it was Gaedel's only appearance with the Browns. His contract was ruled invalid just a few days later. In June of 1961, the 36-year-old man was found beaten to death in his apartment on Chicago's South Side.

New York Times 20 June 1961.

How do the rules of football differ between the National Football League and the Canadian Football League?

There are ten significant differences in the rules of the National Football League (NFL) and the Canadian Football League (CFL). They are as follows:

NFL teams have 11 players; CFL teams have 12.

The official size for an NFL field is 100 yards long and 53 and a half yards wide, with two 10-yard end zones; a CFL field is 110 yards long and 65 yards wide, with two 20-yard end zones.

The NFL requires 4 downs to get 10 yards; the CFL requires just 3 downs for 10 yards.

In the area of points after touchdowns, both leagues allow 1 point for a kick, 2 points for a run/pass; but the CFL also gives 1 point for a single (rouge).

In the NFL, the offense has 45 seconds to put the ball in play; in the CFL, the offense has just 20 seconds to accomplish this.

Each team has 3 timeouts per half in the NFL, while in the CFL, each team has just 1 timeout per half.

In the NFL, only one player is allowed to be in motion when the ball is snapped, but in the CFL, all players in the backfield may be in motion in any direction before the ball is put into play.

In an NFL scrimmage, the linemen are just off the end of the ball, whereas in the CFL, the offense line is on the ball, with the defensive line 1 yard back.

In the area of punt returns, the NFL requires a fair catch, calls a kick into the end zone a touchback, and does not allow the kicking team to recover unless the receiving team fumbles. In the CFL, there is no fair catch; tacklers give the receiver five yards; the punter may recover the kick; and the punt must be run out of the end zone or concede a rouge. The same is true on a missed field goal.

In the NFL, penalties are given at 5, 10, and 15 yards; in the CFL, at 5, 10, 15, and 25 yards.

U.S.A. Today July 6, 1994.

Who were the first players elected to the Baseball of Fame?

On February 2, 1936, baseball writers voted for the first players to be named to the new Baseball Hall of Fame. Ty Cobb, Babe Ruth, Honus Wagner, Christy Mathewson, and Walter Johnson each received the requisite 75 percent of ballots cast.

James Charlton, ed., *The Baseball Chronology: The Complete History of the Most Important Events in the Game of Baseball* (New York: Macmillan, 1991), 289.

Which country won the first World Cup soccer competition in 1930?

Uruguay defeated Argentina to win the first World Cup soccer competition in 1930, capturing an emotional and controversial victory. Three players, dubbed the "Iron Curtain," led the team to its victory. They were halfbacks Jose Andrade, Lorenzo Fernandez, and Alvaro Gestido.

Jack Rollin, *The World Cup 1930-1990: Sixty Glorious Years of Soccer's Premier Event* (New York: Facts On File, 1990), 9.

What American professional baseball player was also a scholar and World War II spy?

Catcher Moe (Morris) Berg (1902-1972) played for the Dodgers, White Sox, Indians, Senators, and Red Sox ball clubs in the 1920s and 1930s. Called "the strangest man ever to play baseball" by Casey Stengel, Berg was an alumnus of three universities and was a scholar of mathematics, linguistics, and law. He was something of an eccentric, keeping piles of "special" newspapers and books in his hotel rooms and spouting mystical phrases in the bullpen. In the 1930s Berg traveled with Babe Ruth (1895-1948) Lou Gehrig (1903-1941), and others to Japan and the Axis countries, ostensibly as a ballplayer. In fact he served as a spy for the American military, particularly in the field of atomic armaments. Berg later declined the Medal of Merit for his wartime service and refused to write his memoirs. Once asked why he wasted his time playing baseball rather than using his vast education, Berg replied: "I'd rather be a ballplayer than a justice on the U.S. Supreme Court."

Mike Shatzkin, ed., *The Ballplayers: Baseball's Ultimate Biographical Reference* (New York: Arbor House, 1990), s.v. "Moe Berg."

In baseball parlance what is a "corked bat"?

In baseball parlance a "corked bat" is one that has been partially hollowed out at the heavy end and filled with cork, rubber or other similar substances. It is thought that the filling adds a "springiness" to the bat which makes it more effective or the change in weight and balance accomplishes the same. The practice is not uncommon but is expressly illegal.

Paul Dickson, *The Dickson Baseball Dictionary* (New York: Facts On File, 1989), 111.

What is the origin of baseball?

Baseball descended from an English game called rounders, base ball, or goal ball. Forms of the game were played in the United States as early as 1778, but the first group to play regularly was the Knickerbocker Base Ball Club of New York City. The first recorded game among members was October 7, 1845, with the first game against another team on June 19, 1846, between the Knickerbockers and the New York Club. Most of the early teams were composed of wealthy young men. The game gradually spread through the Northern states and, although slowed down by the American Civil War (1861-65), spread to the South during the war via Union prisoners. The first all-professional team was the Cincinnati Red Stockings, formed in 1869. By the 1880s, baseball was so popular that it was being called "the national game."

Ralph Hickok, *The Encyclopedia of North American Sports History* (New York: Facts on File, 1992), s.v. "baseball."

Was the forward pass first used in the 1913 football game between Notre Dame and Army?

Underdog Notre Dame University coached by Kenneth "Knute" Rockne (1888-1931) routed Army at Westpoint in 1913 utilizing the forward pass. However, this was not the first time the forward pass was used. It was legalized in 1906 and used by many teams over the objections of conservative opinion. Strict rules as that time also limited its use. Failure to complete a forward pass drew a 15-yard penalty from the line of scrimmage and a loss of one down.

Tom Burnam, *More Misinformation* (New York: Lippincott & Crowell, 1980), 99-100.

How did former professional baseball player Lawrence Berra get the nickname "Yogi"?

Former professional baseball catcher/manager Lawrence Berra (1925-) was tagged with the nickname "Yogi" at age 15, when his St. Louis friends thought he looked like a squatting yogi, one who practices the Hindu discipline of Yoga, which they had seen in a movie. The new nickname quickly replaced his real name.

Chuck Wielgus, Alexander Wolff, and Steve Rushin, *From A-Train to Yogi* (New York: Harper & Row, 1987), 176.

What is a Baltimore chop?

Baltimore chop is a baseball term for a batted ball that hits the ground close to home plate and bounces so high that the batter can reach first base safely. Also it has been sometimes described as a batted ball that hits home plate.

Paul Dickson, *The Dickson Baseball Dictionary* (New York: Facts on File, 1989), 26.

How is a forfeited baseball game scored?

A forfeited baseball game is scored 9-0. A forfeit occurs when a team acts in an illegal manner, such as refusing to play, delaying the game, or failing to remove an ejected player. The decision to call a forfeiture rests with the chief umpire.

Paul Dickson, *The Dickson Baseball Dictionary* (New York: Facts On File, 1989), 166.

What is the Wade Trophy?

The Wade Trophy is presented by the National Association of Girls and Women in Sports to the top senior woman college basketball player-scholar.

USA Today 15 April 1994.

Who were the most recent football players inducted into the Football Hall of Fame?

In 1994, three former Dallas Cowboys were among six football greats inducted into the Football Hall of Fame. The former Dallas Cowboys were Tony Dorsett, third in NFL rushing records; Randy White; and Jackie Smith, who played 15 years for the Cardinals before the Cowboys. Bud Grant was named for his distinguished coaching career for the Minnesota Vikings. Also inducted were Jimmy Johnson, San Francisco 49ers; and Leroy Kelly, Cleveland Browns.

In 1995, the five football players honored were Steve Largent, former Seattle Seahawk wide receiver and Oklahoma congressmen, the late Jim Finks, Sports executive in the Minnesota Vikings, Chicago Bears, and New Orleans Saints, Lee Roy Selmon, former Tampa Bay Buccaneer defensive end the late Henry Jordan and Kellen Winslow.

David Leon Moore, "Dorsett, Grant Lead a Class of Six into Hall of Fame," *USA Today* 31 January 1994. Leonard Shapiro, "Football Hall of Fame Take 5," *Washington Post* 29 January 1995.

What is the 46 Defense?

In the game of football, the 46 Defense is a special formation of the defensive team consisting of four defensive linemen, two linebackers at the line of scrimmage, two linebackers/defensive backs, a free safety, and two cornerbacks. It was developed by defensive coordinator Buddy Ryan of the Chicago Bears in the 1980s when National Football League rules changed so as to benefit offensive linemen and wide receivers. The formation was named after Bears safety Doug Plank, who wore the number 46.

Pittsburgh Press 24 January 1986.

Who was "The Golden Boy" of football?

During his nine-year career with the Green Bay Packers, Paul Hornung was known as "The Golden Boy" for a number of reasons. He was able to handle the chores of quarterback, kicker, receiver, and blocking halfback. He was also quite popular with women and moviemakers due to his blond hair, blue-eyed good looks. He led the National Football League in scoring from 1959 to 1961, including a record-setting 176 points in 1960. In 1963, Hornung was suspended from the NFL for gambling. He was inducted into the Pro Football Hall of Fame in 1986.

The Lincoln Library of Sports Champions (Columbus, OH: Frontier Press, 1989), 8:92.

In professional football what was the instant replay?

The instant replay was used in the National Football League (NFL) games between 1986 and 1991 on questionable referee rulings. A videotape replay was shown to those officiating the game in the hopes of doing away with missed or questionable calls. While the instant replay worked in some cases it also was causing officials to become overly cautious in making calls, game delays which subsequently caused teams to lose their momentum and viewers to become more interested in the call than in the play and the action. In March of 1992 NFL owners voted against continued use of the instant replay.

Jim Baker, "No second guesses for football referees," *TV Guide* 5-11 September 1992. Norman Chad, "The play stand," *Sports Illustrated* 3 February 1992.

Who was the first woman to play on the legendary Harlem Globetrotters basketball team?

In 1985, 5-feet, 11-inch Lynette Woodard, a 1981 graduate of the University of Kansas, became the first female member of the famed Harlem Globetrotters. Woodard was also the captain of the 1984 gold medal-winning U.S. Olympic women's basketball team. She scored 3,649 points in her career at University of Kansas.

Sports Illustrated 6 January 1986. *Time* 21 October 1985.

What were the dates and ticket prices of the 1996 Olympics held in Atlanta, Georgia?

The 1996 Olympic summer games were held in Atlanta, Georgia, from July 19 to August 4. There were 558 sessions in 37 sports, and ticket prices ranged from $6.00 to $250.00. The average ticket price was $39.72. The estimated average daily expense for Olympic attendees was $150.00.

USA Today 27 June 1994.

What is the logo for the 1996 Summer Olympic Games?

The logo for the 1996 Summer Olympic Games to be held in Atlanta consists of the five Olympic rings and the numeral 100 forming a base for a torch with red and orange flames topped by three multicolored stars. Underneath the logo are the words "Atlanta 1996." The logo symbolizes the centennial of the modern Olympics.

USA Today 14 February 1992.

Who was the first athlete to have his uniform number retired?

Harold Grange (1903-1991), who played football for the University of Illinois, is probably the first athlete to have his uniform number retired. Also known as "Red," "77," and the "Galloping Ghost," a term bestowed in 1920 by sportswriter Grantland Rice, Grange went on to play professional football and later became a television sportscaster.

Robert Hendrickson, *Grand Slams, Hat Tricks and Alley-oops: A Sports Fan's Book of Words* (New York: Prentice Hall, 1994), 148.

What was the "Gashouse Gang"?

"Gashouse Gang" was the sobriquet of the 1930's St. Louis Cardinals. Some of its more notable members were "the Dazzling Deans" (Paul and Dizzy), Pepper Martin, Joe "Ducky" Medwick (a.k.a. the "Hungarian Rhapsody"), and Leo Durocher. They played the game of baseball with such "wild abandon" that someone remarked, "it appeared as if they worked in a gashouse and not a ball park."

Harvey Frommer, *Sports Roots* (New York: Atheneum, 1979), 63.

Which Division I college football team has the record for the most consecutive losses?

Between 1983 and 1988 the Columbia University Lions lost 44 straight football games, the most consecutive losses ever for a Division I college football team. The old record of 34 had been held by the 1979-82 Northwestern University Wildcats. A Division III school, Macalester College, which lost 50 games between 1974 and 1980, holds the overall record.

Gorton Carruth and Eugene Ehrlich, *Facts & Dates of American Sports* (New York: Harper & Row, 1988) 299-300. Mike Meserole, ed., *The 1994 Information Please Sports Almanac* (Boston: Houghton Mifflin Company, 1994), 185.

What is FIFA?

FIFA is the acronym for the Federation Internationale de Football Association or, in English, the International Federation of Association Football, which is the Zurich-based, governing body of international soccer. Comprised of 191 countries, it is larger than the United Nations, which has only 184 members.

USA Today 31 August 1994.

When and where was the first major league All-Star Game played?

The first All-Star Game in major league history was played in Comiskey Park, home of the Chicago White Sox, on July 6, 1933. The American League defeated the National League with a score of 4-2.

Craig Carter, ed., *The Sporting News Complete Baseball Record Book, 1994 Edition* (St. Louis: Sporting News Publishing, 1993), 494.

Who was the first left-handed catcher in the major leagues?

The first left-handed catcher in major league baseball was William Arthur Harbidge of the Hartford Blues of the National League in 1876. Harbidge, who also played first base and outfield, spent eight years in the National League. Left-handed catchers are rare because of the difficulty of throwing to second base with a right-handed batter at the plate.

Patrick Clark, *Sports Firsts* (New York: Facts on File, 1981), 7.

When was the first time a National Basketball Association game was postponed in progress?

On January 5, 1986, the first National Basketball Association game to be postponed in progress took place under the leaky roof of the Seattle Coliseum in Seattle, Washington. Referee Mike Mathis stopped play in the second quarter of a game between the Seattle SuperSonics and the Phoenix Suns when water on the floor made play too hazardous. The game had to be rescheduled.

Pittsburgh Press 6 January 1986.

Who was the first African-American woman to play baseball in the old Negro League?

The first African-American woman to play baseball in the old Negro League was Marcenia "Toni" Stone who played second base for the Indianapolis Clowns from 1951-53. In 1954 she played for the Kansas City Monarchs, also of the Negro League.

USA Today 2 July 1992.

What baseball star was nicknamed the "Georgia Peach"?

Baseball great Ty Cobb (1886-1961), who was born in Narrows, Georgia, was nicknamed the "Georgia Peach." Georgia is known as the Peach State; Cobb was also dubbed "a peach" of a player by more than one critic. In twenty-four seasons of professional baseball, Cobb's batting average was less than .320 only once—his rookie year. His career batting average was .367.

Louis Phillips and Burnham Holmes, *Yogi, Babe and Magic* (New York: Prentice Hall, 1994), 67.

How did Babe Ruth get his nickname, and what was his real name?

Babe Ruth (1895-1948) got his nickname when he was a new prospect for the Baltimore Orioles. The first time manager Jack Dunn brought him into the clubhouse, "some guy named Steinam," as Ruth would recall, said, "Here comes Dunnie with his newest babe." Although Babe is his best known nickname, George Herman Ruth was also called The Bambino, Jedge, The Sultan of Swat, and Babe Ruth of Murderers' Row of the Bronx Bombers. Babe's bat even had a nickname—Black Betsy.

Chuck Wielgus, Alexander Wolff, and Steve Rushin, *From A-Train to Yogi: The Fan's Book of Sports Nicknames* (New York: Harper & Row, 1987), 20.

Who was the first African-American quarterback in the National Football League?

Willie Thrower was the first African-American quarterback in pro football. He spent a single season on the roster of the Chicago Bears in 1953.

Patrick Clark, *Sports Firsts* (New York: Facts on File, 1981), 50.

What seven members of the Pro Football Hall of Fame also played major-league baseball?

Jim Thorpe, Paddy Driscoll, Red Badgro, Ernie Nevers, George Halas, Greasy Neale, and Ace Parker are members of the Pro Football Hall of Fame who also played major-league baseball.

Pittsburgh Press 6 March 1988.

What was the average cost of preparing American stadiums to host the 1994 World Cup soccer games?

The average cost to prepare American stadiums to host the 1994 World Cup soccer games was $2 million per stadium. The nine American stadiums selected to host the games were the Silverdome Stadium in suburban Detroit, the Citrus Bowl in Orlando, the Cotton Bowl, the Foxboro (Massachusetts) Stadium, RFK Stadium in Washington, the Rose Bowl in Pasadena, Soldier Field in Chicago, Giants Stadium in New Jersey, and Stanford Stadium in Palo Alto.

New York Times 20 March 1983. Hank Hersch, "Setting Sites," *Sports Illustrated* 30 March 1992.

What is lawn bowling?

Lawn bowling is a form of outdoor bowling in which wooden or plastic balls are rolled over a level, smooth, grassy plot of lawn called a "green." The balls are rolled towards a smaller target ball called a "jack." The object of the game is for a player to get his or her ball closest to the jack while knocking opponent's balls away from the jack. The game may be played singly or in teams of up to four members.

Lawn bowling is a game of great antiquity that probably originated in ancient Egypt, eventually spreading to Greece and Rome. Lawn bowling as it is played today, however, can be traced directly to England and Scotland of the twelfth century where it was called "bowles." Today's formal lawn bowling is sanctioned by the International Bowling Board and is played on a flat green measuring approximately 120 feet by 120 feet which is divided into six rinks the length of the lawn and 14 to 19 feet wide. The green is surrounded by a ditch two inches deep and twelve inches wide.

The ancient Roman variation of lawn bowling was called "boccie" as it is still called today. Popular in Italy and in Italian communities around the world, boccie is played on a court of hard-packed dirt or clay which measures approximately 60 feet by 10 feet.

Frank G. Menke, *The Encyclopedia of Sports* (New York: A.S. Barnes, 1977), 693-94, 712-13. John Arlott, *The Oxford Companion to World Sports and Games* (London: Oxford University Press, 1975), 94-95.

Who holds the all-time high school record for kickoffs returned for touchdowns in a football game?

Roger Maris holds the high school record for kickoffs returned for touchdowns, with four in one game while playing in Fargo, North Dakota, in 1951.

USA Today 3 August 1994.

What is the origin of the term southpaw?

The term southpaw originally meant a left-handed pitcher, but today it describes anyone who is left-handed. The term originated with Finley Peter Dunne, an 1880's sportswriter for the *Chicago News.* In the Chicago ballpark of the time home plate faced east, thus the "paw" of left-handed pitcher would be on his south side.

John Ciardi, *A Browser's Dictionary* (New York: Harper & Row, 1980), 369.

Which basketball player played in all three leagues?

Thomas Thacker played basketball in all three leagues. He played for Cincinnati from 1962 to 1967 (NCAA), Boston in 1968 (NBA), and Indiana in 1969 and 1970 (ABA).

Zander Hollander, ed., *The Modern Encyclopedia of Basketball, 2d ed.* (Garden City, NY: Dolphin Books, 1979), s.v. "Thacker, Tom."

Who was the first woman to pitch on a men's college baseball team?

Amid much derision and many catcalls, Ila Borders became the first woman pitcher on a men's college baseball team in 1994. She pitched at Southern California College in Costa Mesa, California.

Sports Illustrated 7 March 1994.

In 1994, who was the tallest player on the NBA roster?

In 1994 the tallest player on the NBA roster was Romanian-born Gheorghe Muresan at 7 feet 7 inches.

USA Today 8 February 1994.

How did baseball pitcher "Three Finger Brown" get his nickname?

Baseball pitcher "Three Finger Brown" once worked as a coal miner but lost part of his right hand index finger in an accident while operating a cornshredder. Because of the missing finger, he was able to deliver an unorthodox and baffling curveball which helped him win 239 major league games with an ERA of 2.06. He was born Mordecai Peter Centennial Brown and pitched from 1903 to 1916.

James K. Skipper, Jr., *Baseball Nicknames: A Dictionary of Origins and Meanings* (Jefferson, NC: McFarland & Company, 1992), 33.

Why is baseball exempt from antitrust laws?

Baseball enjoys an exemption from antitrust laws because in 1922, in a case before the U.S. Supreme Court Justice Oliver Wendell Holmes (1841-1935), Holmes wrote a majority opinion stating that baseball was not engaged in trade or commerce in the usual sense, and so its owners are free to engage in monopolistic practices.

New York Times 20 August 1994.

Which countries have participated in all the modern Summer Olympics since 1896?

Just four countries—Greece, Australia, Great Britain, and Switzerland—have participated in all the Summer Olympics since 1896. Of those four, only Great Britain has been present at all the Winter Olympics as well.

Stan Greenberg, *The Guinness Book of Olympics Facts and Feats* (Enfield, England: Guinness Superlatives Limited, 1983).

What is the largest crowd on record for a National Football League game?

When the Dallas Cowboys and the Houston Oilers traveled to Mexico City to play a preseason game, they set a record for the largest crowd in National Football League (NFL) history. On August 15, 1994, the two teams played before 112,376 spectators in Azteca Stadium. Attendance surpassed a 1947 record of 105,840, that was set at an exhibition game at Soldier Field between the Chicago Bears and The College All-Stars. The game in Mexico was marred by poor field conditions; Dallas coach Barry Switzer benched some star players in order to prevent injuries.

USA Today 12 August 1994, 16 August 1994.

When was the first intercollegiate baseball game played?

On July 1, 1859 in Pittsfield, Massachusetts, the first intercollegiate baseball game was played between Amherst College and Williams College. After 26 innings, Amherst won, beating Williams, 73 to 32.

Joseph Nathan Kane, *Famous First Facts: A Record of First Happenings, Discoveries, and Inventions in American History, 4th ed.* (New York: H.W. Wilson, 1981), 99.

What are the average 1990 salaries for the major league baseball players?

In 1991, the average salary for a baseball player was $891,188 and the average series share for those eligible was $119,579 per series player.

Kathleen Droste, ed., *Gale Book of Averages* (Detroit: Gale Research, 1994), 377.

Which stadium sporting event has attracted the largest crowd?

The largest stadiums in the world are generally those designed for soccer games, with the exception of the Indianapolis Motor Speedway, which has a seating capacity of 250,000 and has had an estimated crowd of 425,000 for the Indianapolis 500 in 1994. The largest soccer stadium is the Mario Filho (Maracana) in Rio de Janeiro, Brazil, with seating capacity of 155,000 and a total capacity of 205,000 to 220,000. Its largest crowd was 199,854 on July 16, 1950.

Although a stadium may have a large capacity, the number of people allowed inside may be much lower for safety reasons. The capacity figure includes standing numbers, but revised Federation Internationale de Football Association (FIFA) rules limit attendance to actual seats following the Hillsborough Stadium tragedy. Ninety-five people were killed in Sheffield, England, on April 15, 1989, when too many people tried to crowd into a section of the stadium that allowed spectators to stand to watch a soccer match.

Michael L. LaBlanc and Richard Henshaw, *The World Encyclopedia of Soccer* (Detroit: Visible Ink, 1994), 28, 413-15. Peter Matthews, ed., *The Guinness Book of Records 1995* (New York: Facts on File, 1994), 97. John Sonderegger, "New Breed Taking over at Indy: Ex-Champs Retiring Instead of Re-Tiring," *St. Louis Post-Dispatch* 29 May 1994.

Who were the "Four Horsemen" associated with football?

The "Four Horsemen" were Jim Crowley, Elmer Layden, Don Miller, and Harry Stuldreher, who all played the backfield for the University of Notre Dame in 1924-25. The name was the idea of George Strickler, a student sports publicist who had a publicity photograph taken of the four on horseback. The concept was made famous, however, by Grantland Rice, a syndicated sportswriter. With Knute Rockne (1888-1931) as their coach, the "Four Horsemen" helped lead Notre Dame's 1924 squad to an unbeaten season.

Ralph Kickok, *The Encyclopedia of North American Sports History* (New York: Facts on File, 1992), s.v. "Four Horsemen, Rockne, Knute."

Has anyone broken Babe Ruth's career home run record?

Hank Aaron (1934-), playing for the Atlanta Braves, tied Babe Ruth's (1895-1948) career home run record of 714 in Cincinnati, Ohio, on April 4, 1974, at the beginning of the baseball season. He broke the record at his home park on April 8, 1974, with a pitch from Al Downing of the Los Angeles Dodgers. His career total was 755 homers.

Joe Marcin et al. , eds., *Official Baseball Guide for 1975* (St. Louis, MO: The Sporting News, 1975), 305. Mike Shatzkin, ed., *The Ballplayers: Baseball's Ultimate Biographical Reference* (New York: William Morrow, 1990), s.v. "Hank Aaron." John Thorn and Pete Palmer, eds., *Total Baseball, 2d ed.* (New York: Warner Books, 1991), 699.

When and where was the first major league baseball game played inside?

The first inside major league baseball game was played in the Houston Astrodome on April 25, 1965. The Houston Astros beat the Pittsburgh Pirates 5-4 in 11 innings.

Pittsburgh Post-Gazette 26 April 1965.

When did Babe Ruth hit the final home run of his career?

Babe Ruth hit the last three home runs of his career on May 25, 1935, while playing for the Boston Braves against Pittsburgh. The "Sultan of Swat" homered in the first inning off Red Lucas and in the third and seventh innings off Guy Bush. Ruth also hit a single in the 5th inning. Pittsburgh won, however, 11-7.

Pittsburgh Press 26 May 1935.

In major league baseball, when was the pitching distance lengthened to 60 feet 6 inches?

On March 7, 1893, the pitching distance in major league baseball was lengthened from 50 feet to 60 feet 6 inches. At this time the pitcher's box was eliminated as well.

James Charlton, *The Baseball Chronology* (New York: Macmillan, 1991), 96.

What are the average salaries of football players?

As of 1993 the average National Football League (NFL) player's salary had risen to $737,850. Unrestricted free agents had an average salary of $1,125,000. Those who stayed with their own teams averaged $896,000.

Larry Weisman, "Union reports player salaries rose 51% in '93," *USA Today* 28 January 1994.

What is a "taxi squad" in professional football and where did the term come from?

The "taxi squad" in professional football refers to players who are not on the official active roster. The term originated with the founder of the Cleveland Browns, Arthur McBride, who wanted to form the perfect football team. This entailed picking up every potential talent whether there was room on the roster or not. He also owned a taxicab company, so he would pay his extra players as taxicab employees.

Pittsburgh Post Gazette 27 October 1977.

Was there ever an effort under way to start an international football league?

The World League of American Football began playing spring football in March 1991 with ten teams (three of them in Europe. Seven in North America). After two seasons, the playing was suspended, with the hope that it could be revived only with six teams in Europe in 1995.

Information Please Almanac, Atlas & Yearbook 1995, 48th ed. (Boston: Houghton Mifflin, 1995), 907.

Which player has played for the National Football League (NFL), United States Football League (USFL), and the World Football League?

Glenn Hyde is the only person to have played in three different football leagues. He has played for the National Football League (NFL), United States Football League (USFL), and the World Football League, as well as in college.

Pittsburgh Press 2 December 1986.

Who was the first baseball player to be used as a pinch hitter?

John Joseph "Dirty Jack" Doyle was baseball's first pinch hitter in a game played on June 7, 1892. Cleveland Spider's manager Oliver Wendell "Patsy" Tebeau put Doyle up to bat in the ninth inning of play against the Brooklyn Ward's Wonders. Doyle hit a single. The game was being played according to rules established in 1891, which allowed substitutions at any position, at any time during the game.

Joseph Nathan Kane, *Famous First Facts: A Record of First Happenings, Discoveries, and Inventions in American History, 4th ed.* (New York: H.W. Wilson, 1981), 102.

Which baseball player was the first to hit 500 home runs and get 3,000 hits?

In 1970, Hank Aaron (1934-) became the first baseball player to hit 500 home runs and get 3,000 hits.

Sports Illustrated 25 May 1970.

What is unique about the Colorado Silver Bullets baseball team?

The Colorado Silver Bullets is the first all-female professional baseball team. Organized in 1994, approximately 1,300 athletes tried out for 24 team slots.

USA Today 13 April 1994.

Where is the National High School Football Hall of Fame?

The National High School Football Hall of Fame is planned for Valdosta, Georgia, 225 miles south of Atlanta. Completion of the facility is expected before the August 1996 Olympics, which will be hosted by the city of Atlanta.

USA Today 2 February 1994.

When did the custom of the "seventh-inning stretch" originate?

The custom of baseball fans rising and stretching when their teams come to bat at the seventh inning has come to be known as the "seventh-inning stretch." There is debate as to the origin of the popular tradition that still continues today. In a letter written in 1869 by Harry Wright of the Cincinnati Red Stockings observes: "The spectators all arise between halves of the seventh inning, extend their legs and arms and sometimes walk about. In so doing they enjoy the relief afforded by relaxation from a long posture upon hard benches."

Manhattan college in New York City claims the term originated there in 1882 when Brother Jasper was the school's first Moderator of Athletics and Prefect of Discipline. While coaching a game on a hot spring day, he noticed his students in the stands, becoming restless. When the team was coming to bat in the seventh inning he told the student fans to stand and stretch and walk about. It seemed to ease the unrest and he continued to have the students "...give it the old seventh inning stretch."

Another story claims the custom originated at a ball game in Pittsburgh in 1910 when U.S. President Taft (1857-1930) stood in the seventh inning. The crowd also stood in deference to his office.

The first time the term was used by the press can only be traced to October 10, 1920, when it was used in a *New York Times* article.

Paul Dickson, *The Dickson Baseball Dictionary*, (New York: Facts on File, 1989), s.v. "seventh-inning stretch." *USA Today* 19 July 1991.

Who was the youngest player to make it to the major leagues in baseball?

The youngest player in major league baseball was Joe Nuxhall. At the age of 15, Nuxhall made his major league debut with the Cincinnati Reds. On June 10, 1944, he was used as a relief pitcher against the St. Louis Cardinals, when the Reds were losing 13-0. Nuxhall was not effective against the Cardinals, who scored another six runs while he was pitching. Joe Nuxhall did not play in another major league game until eight years later.

Jesse Jacobs, *A Century of Baseball Lore* (New York: Hart Publishing, 1974), 144.

Which teams played the longest professional baseball game?

The longest professional baseball game took place on April 18 and April 19, 1981, between two International League teams. The Pawtucket Red Sox and the Rochester Red Wings battled for 32 innings, only to have the game postponed, when they were tied at 2-2. That was after eight hours and seven minutes of play; the game's officials called league president Harold Cooper at 4 a.m. asking how to proceed. Pawtucket first baseman Dave Koza felt that the game could have been completed in the standard nine innings if there had not been a strong wind. When the game was continued on June 23, Pawtucket won in the thirty-third inning, 3-2. The longest major league baseball game in innings took place on May 1, 1920; it was a 26-inning game between the Brooklyn Dodgers and the Boston Braves. The longest major league baseball game in elapsed time was the eight-hour, six-minute-game when the Chicago White Socks beat Milwaukee 7-6 in the 25th inning on May 9, 1984.

Mark C. Young, ed., *The Guinness Book of Records 1995* (New York: Facts On File, 1994), 220-21.

Who was the baseball player who died after being hit by a pitched ball during the 1920 pennant race?

Raymond Johnson Chapman, shortstop for the Cleveland Indians, died after being hit by a pitched ball on August 16, 1920. The incident took place during a pennant race game against the New York Yankees. Chapman was known to crowd the plate but was also said to have a good eye. When the ball was thrown by pitcher Carl Mays, Chapman ducked but did not evade the pitch. Chapman's skull was fractured, and he died the next day. He was not wearing a batting helmet, nor did it become common practice for professional baseball players to wear helmets until many years later.

Ray Chapman was in his ninth season in the American League when he died. He was a well-rounded player: a good fielding shortstop, a fast runner, and a solid hitter. He had 233 steals during his major league career and a .278 lifetime batting average. Chapman was popular among other players, liked to dress well, and often performed humorous skits. Married for a year at the time of his death, Chapman was reportedly planning to retire at the end of the season.

Gene Karst and Martin J. Jones, Jr., *Who's Who in Professional Baseball* (New York: Arlington House, 1973),158.

What is bicycle polo?

Bicycle polo is played just like regular polo, except the four players on each team are mounted on bicycles. The players use croquet mallets and a solid rubber ball between 6-10 inches in diameter.

E.O. Harbin, *The Fun Encyclopedia* (New York: Abingdon Press, 1940), 183.

Who was major league baseball's first designated hitter?

On April 6, 1973 Ron Blomberg of the New York Yankees became major league baseball's first official designated hitter. Blomberg walked with the bases loaded. He was 1 for 3 in that game which the Yankees lost to the Red Sox with a score of 15-5. Luis Tiant pitched to Blomberg.

James Charlton, ed., *The Baseball Chronology: The Complete History of the Most Important Events in the Game of Baseball* (New York: Macmillan, 1991), 528.

Who played in the most World Series games?

The player who appeared in the most World Series—14 total—was New York Yankees catcher Yogi (Lawrence) Berra (1925-), who appeared in the post-season classic in 1947, 1949, 1950, 1951, 1952, 1953, 1955, 1956, 1957, 1958, 1960, 1961, 1962, and 1963. In all, Berra played in 75 World Series games (65 consecutive).

Craig Carter, ed., *The Sporting News Complete Baseball Record Book, 1994 Edition* (St. Louis: Sporting News Publishing, 1993), 414.

Which players have had the longest tenures in each major professional team sport?

The "iron men" of sports—those players with the longest careers in each of the major professional team sports—are Gordie Howe, Nolan Ryan, George Blanda, and Kareem Abdul-Jabbar. Howe played hockey for 32 seasons, from 1946 to 1980, with the Detroit Red Wings, Houston Aeros, New England Whalers, and Hartford Whalers. Ryan played baseball for 27 seasons, beginning in 1966, then continuing after a year's interruption from 1968 to 1993. He was associated variously with the New York Mets, California Angels, Houston Astros, and Texas Rangers. Blanda played 26 seasons of professional football, from 1949 to 1958 and then from 1960 to 1975. He was a member of the Chicago Bears, Baltimore Colts, Houston Oilers, and Oakland Raiders. Abdul-Jabbar put in 20 seasons of professional basketball from 1969 to 1989, with the Milwaukee Bucks and Los Angeles Lakers.

"The Iron Men of Sports," *USA Today* 24 September 1993.

In the game of baseball, when does a batter become a runner?

According to the rules of baseball, a batter becomes a runner and gains the right to attempt to score when he hits a fair ball; when he is charged with a third strike (if the third strike is caught, he is out the instant after he becomes a runner); when an intentional base on balls is awarded, or a fourth ball is called by the umpire; when a pitched ball hits his person or clothing, provided he does not strike at the ball; or when the catcher or any infielder interferes with him.

Jay Baum, *Umpiring Baseball* (Chicago: Contemporary Books, 1979), 115-16.

What were the most home runs hit by a player in his first major league game?

In baseball history, three players share the record for hitting the most home runs in their first major league game. Each player hit two home runs.

Charles T. Reilly, playing for Columbus on October 9, 1889 (third and fifth at bat).

Robert C. Nieman, playing for St. Louis on September 14, 1951 (first two at bat).

Bert Campaneris, playing for Kansas City on July 23, 1964 (first and fourth at bat).

Seymour Siwoff, ed., *The Book of Baseball Records* (New York: Seymour Siwoff, 1994), 230.

What are the specifications for pucks used by the National Hockey League?

Rule 25 of the National Hockey League specifies that the puck must be made of vulcanized rubber, with the dimensions one inch thick and three inches in diameter. Its weight must be between five and a half and six ounces. The NHL Rules Committee approves all pucks to be used in league competition.

Zander Hollander, *The Complete Encyclopedia of Hockey, 4th ed.* (Detroit: Gale Research, 1993), 569.

Who was the first black heavyweight champion?

Jack Johnson, a fighter from Galveston, Texas, was the first heavyweight champion of the world. Johnson's race proved to be a disadvantage to him in the face of prejudice. For example, fight promoters refused to let him fight for the heavyweight title until they had no other alternative—he had beaten all the other opponents. Johnson held the title longer than any other individual except Joe Louis.

Patrick Clark, *Sports Firsts* (New York: Facts On File, 1981), 170.

What baseball team had the nickname "Dem Bums"?

"Dem Bums" is a traditional nickname given to the American baseball team, the Brooklyn Dodgers. The name was established and characterized by a cartoon tramp drawn by Willard Mullin.

Paul Dickson, *The Dickson Baseball Dictionary* (New York: Facts on File, 1989), 126.

What are the odds against a triple play?

The odds against a triple play in a game of baseball are 1,400 to one.

The Odds on Virtually Everything (New York: G.P. Putnam's Sons, 1980), 50.

Who was the first African American to play major league baseball?

Jackie Robinson (1919-1972) was the first African-American player in major league baseball. He played for the Brooklyn Dodgers from 1947 to 1956, was the National League's Most Valuable Player in 1949, and was elected to the Baseball Hall of Fame in 1962.

Charles Moritz, ed., *Current Biography Yearbook 1972* (New York: H.W. Wilson, 1973), s.v. "Robinson, Jackie." John Thorn and Peter Palmer, *Total Baseball, 2d ed.* (New York: Warner Books, 1991), s.v. "Jackie Robinson."

When was the first African-American baseball league formed?

Because most college and professional sports were segregated in 1920, Andrew "Rube" Foster formed the National Negro Baseball League. This became the first truly successful African-American professional league. The league included six Midwestern cities and lasted through 1930 when the stock market crashed. The Eastern Colored League was formed in 1923 by six Eastern clubs and lasted until 1929. Between 1924 and 1927 the winners of the two leagues met in a World Series.

In 1933 the Negro National League was established and for the next four years the winners of two half-seasons met in a championship series.

In 1937, with the establishment of the Negro American League, two regional leagues reappeared (the Negro National League in the East, and Negro American League in the West). Each league had six teams, and the winners of each met in an annual World Series.

In 1946, when Jackie Robinson (1919-1972) became the first African-American to play with a major league team, the Black Leagues began losing their stars to previously all-white teams. From 1954 to 1964 African-American talent dominated the formerly all-white National League. African-Americans led in batting average seven of eleven seasons and in homeruns eight of eleven seasons. As all-white professional teams recruited their players the leagues were eventually forced to disband.

The Baseball Encyclopedia: The Complete and Definitive Record of Major League Baseball, 9th ed. (New York: Macmillan, 1993), 2611-12. W. Augustus Low, ed., *Encyclopedia of Black America* (New York: McGraw-Hill,

1981), s.v. "Athletes." John Torn and Pete Palmer, eds., *Total Baseball, 2d ed.* (New York: Warner Books, 1991), 551-66.

When was the last time a major league baseball team had to forfeit a game for stalling?

On July 18, 1954, the St. Louis Cardinals forfeited a game to the Philadelphia Phillies—the last time a major league baseball team was thus penalized for stalling. The Cardinals were losing 8-1 in the second game of a doubleheader at Philadelphia's Sportsman's Park when their manager Eddie Stanky tried to dodge defeat by changing pitchers three times in the fifth inning even though the Phillies had made only one hit. Stanky hoped to stall until the game could be called because of darkness, but umpires lost patience with his tactics.

David Nemec, *The Rules of Baseball: An Anecdotal Look at the Rules of Baseball and How They Came to Be* (New York: Lyons & Burford, Publishers, 1994), 76.

What does the baseball slang phrase "next stop Peoria" mean?

In baseball slang, the phrase "next stop Peoria" is used in reference to a player who is in a prolonged slump and is on the verge of being sent to the minor leagues, which is usually considered a setback for a major league player. The phrase started with the St. Louis Cardinals, which had a minor league franchise in Peoria.

Paul Dickson, *The Dickson Baseball Dictionary* (New York: Facts On File, 1989), 274.

Where did lacrosse originate?

In 1705 French cleric Pierre de Charlevoix observed a game played by Algonquin Indians called baggataway. The webbed stick the Indians used to carry and throw the ball reminded Charlevoix of a bishop's crozier or cross. The sport became popular amongst the French who eventually changed the name to lacrosse.

Harvey Frommer, *Sports Roots: How Nicknames, Namesakes, Trophies, Competitions, and Expressions in the World of Sports Came to Be* (New York: Atheneum, 1979), s.v. "lacrosse."

Which professional sports teams have been most frequently featured on Wheaties cereal boxes?

In addition to sports figures, professional sports teams are often featured on Wheaties (The Breakfast of Champions) cereal boxes. Those teams featured most often have been the Chicago Bulls (three times) and the Dallas Cowboys, Minnesota Twins, Washington Redskins, and Pittsburgh Penguins (twice each).

"Breakfast (boxes) of champions," *USA Today* 8 February 1994.

How did the television special "Heidi" upset football fans in 1968?

On November 17, 1968, NBC was broadcasting the football game between the Oakland Raiders and the New York Jets when the station had to decide whether or not to start a special dramatization of "Heidi" at its scheduled time. At this point, the game had two minutes remaining with a score of 32-29 in favor of the Jets. NBC decided to show "Heidi." To make matters worse, the Raiders staged a comeback, scoring two touchdowns in the remaining time and winning the game 43-32. NBC was deluged with so many angry phone calls from football fans who wanted to see the game's outcome that the network vowed it would never again interrupt a football game.

David S. Neft, *The Sports Encyclopedia: Pro Football* (New York: Grosset & Dunlap, 1974), 350.

What was Fordham's "Seven Blocks of Granite"?

The Fordham Seven Blocks of Granite was the defensive line of the 1937 Fordham football team. The tackle and guard was Ed Franco; center, Alex Wojciechowicz; tackles, Al Babartsky and Paul Berezney; guard, Michael Kochel; and ends, Henry Jacunski and Johnny Druze. This defensive line was noted for its ability to fend off almost any offense.

Allison Danzig, *History of American-Football* (New York: Prentice-Hall, 1956), 337-38.

Which football team was the first to implement the forward pass?

The forward pass in football was legalized in 1906, although it was used sparingly for the first few years. A number of claims have been made by various coaches as to who was the first to implement the pass with his team.

Henderson E. Van Surdam, coach at Marietta College in Ohio, claimed that his team was the first to use the forward pass in 1906, gaining 47 yards and a touchdown against Ohio University. St. Louis University coach Eddie Cochems also claimed to have used the pass in September of 1906. Wesleyan University made a similar claim, stating that on October 3, 1906, quarterback Sammy Moore threw to Irvin Van Tassell for a gain of 18 yards against Yale.

The most famous early use of the forward pass occurred in 1913 by Notre Dame during its rivalry game against Army. Quarterback Gus Dorias successfully threw to Knute Rockne a number of times during the game, which led to the Fighting Irish becoming the trailblazers on use of the forward pass.

Allison Danzig, *Oh, How They Played the Game: The Early Days of Football and the Heroes Who Made It Great* (New York: Macmillan, 1971), 177.

Who was Morris "Red" Badgro?

Morris "Red" Badgro was one of the few athletes who was able to play on both a professional football and baseball team. He played for the New York Giants from 1930 to 1935, as well as a year each on two now-defunct football teams, the New York Yankees in 1927 and the Brooklyn Dodgers in 1936. During that time period, he also played for the St. Louis Browns baseball team. Badgro was inducted into the Pro Football Hall of Fame in 1981.

New York Times 2 August 1981.

Who were the first American Football League players inducted into the Pro Football Hall of Fame?

The first original American Football League player inducted into the Pro Football Hall of Fame was Lance Alworth. Alworth played pro ball from 1962 to 1972 and was inducted into the Hall of Fame in 1978 after the mandatory five year wait. Alworth was followed by AFL players Ron Mix, who played football from 1960 to 1969 and again in 1971, and Jim Otto who played from 1960 to 1975. Mix was inducted in 1979 and Otto in 1980.

The American Football League of the "Modern Era" was established in 1960 with an Eastern and Western Division of four teams each. In 1970 the National Football League and the American Football League merged into a single major league called the National Football League. The new league has two conferences, the National Football Conference and the American Football Conference with three divisions each. Ground was broken on August 11, 1962 in Canton, Ohio for the Pro Football Hall of Fame. The Hall of Fame underwent expansions in 1970 and 1977.

Great Athletes (Pasadena, CA: Salem Press, 1992), 1:39-40, 12: 1735-36, 13: 1908-09. Mike Rathet and Don R. Smith, *Their Deeds and Dogged Faith* (New York: Balsam Press, 1984). Roger Treat, *The Encyclopedia of Football* (New York: A.S. Barnes, 1976), 147, 638.

Who achieved the first perfect score in modern Olympic competition?

Ulise "Pete" DesJardins, who was born in St. Pierre, Manitoba, Canada, but raised in Miami Beach, Florida, was the first competitor in modern Olympic history to receive a perfect score. Competing as a United States citizen, the five foot, three inch DesJardins won a perfect score of ten points in the 1928 Olympic springboard competition. He also won a gold medal in the same Olympics for highboard diving.

Lord Killanin and John Rodda, eds., *The Olympic Games* (New York: Macmillan, 1976), 205-06. David Wallechinsky, *The Complete Book of the Olympics* (New York: Viking, 1988), 451.

What is the current Olympic Summer Game—Winter Game cycle?

In 1986 the International Olympic Committee voted to alternate the Summer and Winter Games every two years, beginning in 1994. The plan called for the Summer Games to be held in 1992 and 1996. The Winter Games were to be held in 1992, again in 1994, and then every four years after that.

New York Times 15 October 1986.

What was the 1994 grievance involving the United States Olympic bobsled team?

In January of 1994, a grievance was filed with the United States Bobsled and Skeleton Federation charging a member of the U.S. Olympic bobsled team with using stolen sled runners during qualification trials.

USA Today 28 January 1994.

Who sang the national anthem the night Hank Aaron hit his 715th home run?

Pearl Bailey (1918-1990) sang the national anthem the night baseball great Hank Aaron (1934-) hit his record-breaking 715th home run in Atlanta, Georgia.

Frank W. Hoffman and William G. Bailey, *Sports & Recreation Fads* (New York: Harrington Park Press, 1991), 3.

When was the first officially recorded baseball game?

On June 19, 1846, the first officially recorded baseball game took place, when the New York Club defeated the Knickerbockers 23-1 at the Elysian Fields in Hoboken, New Jersey. It was played by the rules of Alexander Joy Cartwright (1820-1892), who helped found the Knickerbocker Baseball Club of New York in 1845. He also established a set of rules that included such provisions as tagging a runner out rather than hitting him with a thrown ball. In addition, Cartwright is credited with fixing the base paths at 90 feet and adopting the first baseball uniforms. In 1938 he was elected to the Baseball Hall of Fame. At least 14 games were played according to his rules in the fall of 1845 before the first officially recorded game. The sport itself is clearly much older, because in 1845 the New York *Morning News* reported that New York beat Brooklyn 24-4 in a "friendly match of the time honored game of Baseball."

James Charlton, ed., *The Baseball Chronology: The Complete History of the Most Important Events in the Game of Baseball* (New York: Macmillan Publishing Company, 1991), 13.

Who was the first African American to play in the National Basketball Association (NBA)?

In the spring of 1950, the Boston Celtics drafted Charles "Chuck" Cooper of Duquesne University, who became the first African American to play in the National Basketball Association (NBA).

Gorton Carruth and Eugene Ehrlich, *Facts & Dates of American Sports* (New York: Harper & Row, 1988), 182.

What were some Little League World Series "firsts" for female participants?

The Little League World Series saw its first female players and its first female umpire in the 1980s. In 1984, Victoria Roche, playing as a substitute for the European Championship team from Brussels, Belgium, became the first girl to play in the baseball tournament. The first American girl to play in the Little League World Series was Victoria Brucker; in 1989 she played first base for the San Pedro team, the West U.S. regional champion. Brucker was also the leading home run hitter for her team. That same year, Betty Speziale became the first woman to umpire in the Little League World Series. Although Speziale never played organized baseball during her childhood, she was determined to become involved as an adult. At age 35 she reached her goal of becoming the first female official at the Little League tournament.

USA Today 22 August 1989.

In sports, what is the "sixth man"?

The "sixth man" is a basketball term for the player who normally is the first to enter the game as a substitute when one of the starters needs a rest or is in foul trouble. The sixth man also becomes involved when a team needs a psychological lift or a change in game plan.

Tim Considine, *The Language of Sport* (New York: Facts on File, 1982), 76.

Who is the all-time leading scorer in college basketball history?

On February 24, 1994, Lipscomb University (Tennessee) center John Pierce became college basketball's all-time leading scorer in a victory over Cumberland (Kentucky). Pierce's 33 points gave him a career total of 4,110—four points more than previous record holder Phil Hutcheson, his ex-roommate.

USA Today 25 February 1994.

Who was the first U.S. president to throw out the first ball at a season opening major league baseball game?

William Howard Taft (1857-1930) was the first U.S. president to throw out the first ball at a major league baseball game. Taft attended the season opening game between the Washington Senators and Philadelphia Athletics on April 14, 1910, and threw out the first ball to dedicate the start of a new season. The Senators won, 3-0. Woodrow Wilson (1856-1924) became the first president to throw out the first ball at a World Series game on October 9, 1915, when he attended the second game of the series between Boston and Philadelphia, which the Boston Red Sox won, 2-1. The first president to throw out the opening ball at a World Series opener was Calvin Coolidge (1872-1933) at the October 4, 1924, game between the Washington Senators and New York Giants. The Giants prevailed, 4-3.

Patrick Clark, *Sports Firsts* (New York: Facts on File, 1981), 15.

What is the chronology of major league baseball's labor problems through the early 1980s?

A brief chronology of major league baseball's labor strife shows that:

The baseball player's union was formed in 1953.

A basic agreement was not signed until 1968.

The first major league baseball strike lasted for 13 days at the beginning of the 1972 season.

In 1980 there was an eight day strike during the exhibition season.

The longest strike through the early 1980s was the 49 day strike (June 12-July 31) in 1981 that resulted in the cancellation of 712 games.

Facts On File 7 August 1981. *New York Times* 13 June 1981.

Who was the first African-American baseball umpire in the major leagues?

The first African-American baseball umpire in the major leagues was Emmett Ashford. Emmett Littleton Ashford made history on April 11, 1966, in Washington D.C., when he umpired an American League game in which the Cleveland Indians beat the Washington Senators, 5-2. Ashford had trouble getting into the stadium that day because U.S. the Secret Service was out in force to protect U.S. vice president Hubert Humphrey (1911-1978), who was going to throw out the first ball. As Ashford related to Larry Gerlach in *The Men in Blue*, the driver of the taxicab Ashford rode in was stopped at a Secret Service command post going into the stadium. When the cab driver told the agent that he was bringing in an umpire, the agent replied that, "There are no Negro umpires in the major leagues." Ashford spoke up, "Well, there will be a Negro umpire in the American League if you will let me into the park." Emmett Ashford was admitted to the park and he umpired for the American League with boundless energy and unique style until 1970.

Art Williams in 1975 became the first African-American umpire in the National League.

Larry R. Gerlach, *The Men in Blue: Conversations with Umpires* (New York: The Viking Press, 1980), 276.

Why did relief pitchers David Nen and Dave Otto make baseball history?

David Nen of the Florida Marlins and Dave Otto of the Chicago Cubs made baseball history when they became the first two palindromic names to pitch in the same game. This was a first-time occurrence in the 125-year annals of baseball. A palindrome is a word that is spelled the same backward as it is forward.

Pittsburgh Post-Gazette 7 August 1994.

Who is Pele?

Pele (1940-) is a Brazilian soccer star of international acclaim. Born Edson Arantes do Nascimento, he began playing professionally in the mid-1950s when he was just 15 years old. With the help of Pele's talents, the Brazilian National Team captured three World Cup victories in 1958, 1962, and 1970. The athlete was the first in the sport to score 1000 career goals, a record he achieved in 1969.

The Lincoln Library of Sports Champions (Columbus, OH: Frontier Press, 1989), 76.

Are there plans for a football league owned entirely by corporate advertisers?

Former NFL and World League executive Mike Lynn has tried to start a football league, called "A League," with the participating teams being owned entirely by corporate advertisers. According to Lynn's plan, the $120 million start-up cost for the eleven national teams and one overseas team will be paid by corporate owners-advertisers and CBS which is searching for a sport to sponsor after losing its 38-year run of NFL broadcasts. Lynn calls the new league a "sponsors dream."

USA Today 3 May 1995.

In the National Hockey League (NHL) Stanley Cup finals, in which a Canadian team opposed a U.S. team, which country has had the most wins?

Canadian and U.S. teams have battled for the National Hockey League (NHL) Stanley Cup 44 times since 1927. Canadian teams were the victors 33 times; U.S. teams trail with 11 wins.

USA Today 9 June 1994.

What are the differences between indoor volleyball and beach volleyball?

There are a number of differences between indoor volleyball and beach volleyball. The latter will be introduced at the Summer Olympics in 1996. For beach volleyball, players may wear non-matching shorts or bathing suits and must play barefoot; the ball may be brightly colored and must have an 8-inch diameter and low pressure; the court is sand; there are two players on a team; no substitutions and two timeouts are allowed. Beach volleyball matches are won by the team that wins two out of three sets. Indoor volleyball players must wear matching jerseys, shorts, and sports shoes; the court is a hard surface; the ball must be white and have an 8-inch diameter but with higher pressure; there are six players on a team; six substitutions and four time-outs are allowed; and a match is won by winning three out of five sets.

USA Today 21 July 1994.

What are the distances of the three-point lines in the various basketball associations?

In the National Collegiate Athlete Association (NCAA) in basketball the three-point field-goal line is 19 feet, 9 inches as opposed to 22 feet in the National Basketball Association

(NBA) and 21 feet, 9 inches in International basketball. The distance is measured from the center of the basket to the baseline.

"Three-point field goal lines," *Pittsburgh Press* 30 November 1986. *Information Please Almanac, Atlas & Yearbook 1995, 48th ed.* (Boston: Houghton Mifflin Company, 1995), 1004.

In college basketball, what is the Extra Point Club All-Americans?

In college basketball, the Extra Point Club All-Americans is an eleven-member team of players from historically black colleges and universities.

USA Today 12 April 1994.

Between 1951 and 1994 who won more All-Star basketball games, the East or the West?

Between 1951 and 1994 the East won twenty-eight All-Star basketball games while the West has won sixteen.

USA Today 14 February 1994.

In the 1994 NBA season, who were the Long-Distance Shootout and Slam-Dunk Contest champions?

In the 1994 NBA season, Mark Price of Cleveland and Isiah Rider of Minnesota were the respective Long-Distance Shootout and Slam-Dunk Contest champions.

USA Today 14 February 1994.

Which baseball player was a pinch runner for Babe Ruth and was thus nicknamed "Babe Ruth's Legs"?

From 1929 to 1934, Samuel Dewey Byrd often pinched for Babe Ruth as a base-runner and in the outfield, thus earning him the nickname "Babe Ruth's Legs."

James K. Skipper, Jr., *Baseball Nicknames: A Dictionary of Origins and Meanings* (Jefferson, NC: McFarland & Company, 1992), 37.

Who was "Shoeless Joe" Jackson?

"Shoeless Joe" Jackson played major league baseball from 1908 to 1920. Because of blistered feet caused by ill-fitting shoes, Jackson chose one day to play the game barefoot, thus earning the sobriquet "Shoeless Joe." Jackson was involved in the so-called "Black Sox" scandal in 1919 in which the Chicago White Sox threw the World Series, and he was banned from baseball for life. Jackson's story was retold in W.P. Kinsella's 1982 novel *Shoeless Joe* and the subsequent 1989 movie *Field of Dreams.* There is also a Jackson biography, *Say It Ain't So, Joe*, by Donald Gropman.

James K. Skipper, Jr., *Baseball Nicknames: A Dictionary of Origins and Meanings* (Jefferson, NC: McFarland & Company, 1992), 136.

What was unique about Princeton's 1899 football players called the Poes of Princeton?

The Poes of Princeton were six members of Princeton's college football team of 1899. They all bore the name of Poe and were great-nephews of the famed American poet and short story writer, Edgar Allan Poe (1809-1849). The famed Poe had been an excellent athlete. While Poe was a student at West Point, he long-jumped 21 feet. A good swimmer, Poe once swam seven- and one-half miles against the tide. However Poe was only at that military academy for a short time, from July 1830 until February of 1831. Since he could not leave the school without the consent of his foster father, John Allan, Poe purposefully provoked his expulsion by not obeying the rules and not doing the duties required of cadets.

Robert Hendrickson, *Grand Slams, Hat Tricks and Alley-oops: A Sports Fan's Book of Words* (New York: Prentice Hall General Reference, 1994), s.v. "Poes of Princeton." Arthur Hobson Quinn, ed., *The Complete Tales and Poems of Edgar Allan Poe: With Selections From His Critical Writings* (New York: Dorset Press, 1989), 6.

Who was the "Grand Old Man of Football"?

Amos Alonzo Stagg (1862-1965) was know as the "Grand Old Man of Football." In 75 years of coaching, he coached for only two teams, the University of Chicago and the College of the Pacific. His contributions to the sport of football are as impressive as his longevity: he introduced the huddle, single and double wingbacks, the man in motion, the end run, tackling dummies, and the practice of awarding letters to athletes. In 1943, at the age of 81, Stagg was named the college coach of the year. The award was a good indication of his vigor; Amos Alonzo Stagg continued to coach until he was 98 years old.

Robert Hendrickson, *Grand Slams, Hat Tricks and Alley-oops: A Sports Fan's Book of Words* (New York: Prentice Hall, 1994), 76.

Occult

What are the signs in the Chinese zodiac and their characteristics?

There are 12 signs in the Chinese zodiac; each sign represents one year. These signs are named after animals and correspond to birth year, recurring every 12 years in the same order. They include:
The Rat (1924, 1936, etc...)—characterized by physical beauty and charm; are also hard workers and active socially, as well as highly emotional.
The Buffalo (1925, 1937, etc...)—characterized by perfectionism; tend to be good with their hands and often hold a grudge if opposed.
The Tiger (1926, 1938, etc...)—a hard worker and usually does well financially; tend to be physically big and well-liked yet doubt their own worth.
The Rabbit (1927, 1939, etc...)—conservative in nature and usually upholds traditional values and morals; tend to seek knowledge to impress others and, as result, do not make friends easily.
The Dragon (1928, 1940, etc...)—characterized by being internally miserable despite having many desirable qualities, such as being orderly, honest, intelligent, stable, patient, generous, and clean.
The Snake (1929, 1941, etc...)—glamorous and chic, yet deeply emotional and can be easily hurt; enjoy helping others but tend to fall victim to hasty judgement.
The Horse (1930, 1942, etc...)—the life of the party, and as such is often physically beautiful; tend to be easy to anger and are frequently quite impatient.
The Goat (1931, 1943, etc...)—extremely sensible, sincere, devout, and capable; tend to be insecure and consequently settle for their lot in life.
The Monkey (1932, 1944, etc...)—a worldly and social animal; tend to have a lively sense of humor but will give up on something if not immediately successful.
The Rooster (1933, 1945, etc...)—a strong intellect and imagination; tend to be frank and subsequently offend their friends.
The Dog (1934, 1946, etc...)—socially gracious and loyal; docile but make quick judgements, exhibit dreaminess, and are needlessly worrisome.
The Boar (1935, 1947, etc...)—the most favorable sign of the Chinese zodiac; studious, kind, generous, affectionate, honest, pragmatic, loyal, chivalrous, complaisant, and possesses of all the most desirable traits of human nature.

McCall's March 1976. An Nguyen, *Chinese Astrology* (New York: Arbor House, 1980), 7-15.

What other names are used for the "Abominable Snowman"?

Throughout the Himalayas and mountainous regions of northeastern and central Asia, reports abound of a large, hairy, humanlike creature. This creature is referred to by many names, the most common being the "Abominable Snowman," which is a rough translation of a Tibetan term "metoh kangmi." The Sherpa, a tribe of people living in the mountains of Nepal, call the creature "Yeti." The word Yeti means "all-devouring creature" and probably originated in response to an old legend that the creature attacks and devours humans. Since the late 1890s, explorers and scientists have periodically discovered unusually large footprints, which has prompted some to call the creature "Bigfoot."

Although sightings of this unusual creature are often reported, explorers and scientists have found no conclusive proof that it exists.

The World Book Encyclopedia (Chicago: World Book, 1987), vol. 1, 13-14.

What amazing coincidence involved the burial of actor Charles Coghlan?

The veteran actor Charles Coghlan wished to be buried on Prince Edward Island in Canada, where he grew up, and his wish came true but in an amazing way. Since he died suddenly in 1899 in Galveston, Texas, two thousand miles from his home, it was too expensive to send his body back to Canada. The next year a hurricane hit Galveston and washed up Coghlan's coffin, which floated into the Gulf of Mexico and gradually up the east coast of the United States. Months after he had been disinterred, his coffin came ashore on Prince Edward Island, on a beach where Coghlan had played as a boy. It was reburied in a local churchyard.

Pittsburgh Press 10 May 1969.

What is rhabdomancy, or divination by rods or wands?

Rhabdomancy, or divination by rods or wands, is used to foretell future events or locate hidden treasures, ores, or water. The term comes from Greek words meaning "a rod" and "divination." The practice was probably started by the Chaldeans and Scythians and passed onto the Germanic tribes. Many different kinds of wood have been used in the practice of rhabdomancy, including branches from fruit trees as well as myrtle and sallow. In divination, staffs are allowed to stand upright, and verses and incantations are recited. The direction and the manner in which the staffs fall are said to be controlled by demons.

Lewis Spence, *An Encyclopedia of Occultism* (New York: University Books, 1974).

What is the "evil eye"?

Superstitious people have believed for thousands of years that certain of their brethren possess the powers of an "evil eye." One who has such powers is able with a glance to cast a spell or a miasma of bad luck and misfortune over individuals. Occurrences of the belief in the evil eye have appeared in ancient Egypt, Babylonia, Greece, Rome, and especially in Europe during the Middle Ages. There was even thought to be a connection between those who succumbed to the Black Death and the evil eye. In modern times, belief in the evil eye continues, particularly in Greece, Italy, and Spain as well as Great Britain and the Scandinavian countries.

Frederick Thomas Elworthy, *The Evil Eye: The Origins and Practices of Superstition* (London: Collier Books, 1970).

What superstitions surround elephants?

Elephants have inspired many superstitions around the world. These animals are noted for their intelligence and long memories. In Thailand, Cambodia, and other countries it is believed that the elephant, especially a white elephant, may be an incarnation of a divine soul. Hindus believe that an elephant supports the world and thus is quite as advanced as human beings are. Because of this, the white elephant must be revered and maintained.

Elephant figurines are considered to be good luck. If the figurine has its trunk held up, it is holding in the good luck. If the trunk is held down, the elephant is pouring good fortune into the dwelling. The figurine is often placed facing a door so that those with the "evil eye" or evil intent cannot enter.

Elephants do not go to a special elephant graveyard in order to die. Like human beings they die wherever they die. The reason their remains are not found is that the wilderness reclaims the corpse quite quickly through insects, carrion eating animals and birds, and plant life.

Claudia de Lys, *A Treasury of American Superstitions,* (The Philosophical Library, 1948).

What is tea leaf reading?

The reading of tea leaves is an old divining art. The shapes of patterns of the tea leaves are used to interpret the future. The subject is expected to drink freshly brewed tea and then hold the cup in the left hand, swirling the dregs around at least three times and then turning the cup over to rid it of any excess liquid. If any liquid runs out of the cup when it is given to the reader, tears will fall in the subject's life.

There are many set patterns to tea leaves, most of which are animals. A snake represents evil. A cat represents an untrue friend and a dog, loyalty. A mouse indicates financial crisis and a rat, personal danger. A horse indicates a lover is on the horizon. Initials and numbers also appear frequently in tea leaves, which the subject is often asked to interpret.

In the United States the Gypsy Tearooms are where readers can be found. In Ireland tea leaf reading is widespread, and even the local priest may occasionally have his leaves read.

Sybil Leek, *The Sybil Leek Book of Fortune Telling* (New York: MacMillan, 1969), 11-21.

What is the origin of the witch's cape and pointed hat?

A modern representation of a witch pictures a woman in a cape and pointed hat. In the latter half of the seventeenth century in England and America, capes and steeple-crowned hats were quite fashionable among both men and women. Coincidentally, it was during this period that witchcraft trials reached their peak, and the costume has carried down through the centuries.

Alice Morse Earle, *Two Centuries of Costume in America, MDCXX-MDCCCXX* (1903; reprint, Williamstown, MA: Corner House Publishers, 1974), 234.

What is a Grimoire?

The grimoires are instructional books of European magic. They contain directions on how to summon spirits, make talismans, and how to perform other magical acts. Although most are from the sixteenth through eighteenth centuries, they contain older material. The most famous is called the *Key of Solomon.*

Richard Cavendish, ed., *Man, Myth & Magic: An Illustrated Encyclopedia of the Supernatural* (New York: Marshall Cavendish Corp., 1970), s.v. "Grimoire."

What is the history of the process of channeling?

Channeling is a process in which individuals, called channelers, acquire and express information that does not come from their own consciousness, but from a consciousness outside of themselves. Communication methods include automatic writing, telepathy, and through the assumption by the channeler of another's voice and mannerisms. A channeler's state may range from complete consciousness to a full trance.

In ancient Egypt priests and priestesses believed that they communicated with the gods during trances induced with the help of statues. In China early historical records indicate that a type of divining rod was used by those wishing to communicate with disembodied souls. In fact, messages purportedly received by an emperor from a dead princess became the foundation of the legal system of that time. In Japan the Shintoist shamans of the eighth century were believed to have induced the presence of the god by using a lightning-shaped wand prior to channeling. Some ancient Greek oracles apparently entered trances in order to communicate with spirits.

J. Gordon Melton, Jerome Clark, and Aidan A. Kelly, *New Age Almanac* (New York: Visible Ink Press, 1991), 45-46.

Among vampire believers is there an association between vampires and cats?

It is believed by some that vampires can turn themselves into cats; others believe that a dead cat is a deterrent to vampires entering a house.

Matthew Bunson, *The Vampire Encyclopedia* (New York: Crown Trade Paperbacks, 1993), 42.

What is lycanthropy?

Lycanthropy is an ancient belief that human beings can be transformed into animals. The term is derived from a combination of the Greek word for wolf, "lukos," and for man, "anthropos." This belief involves wolves only in countries with large wolf populations. For example, in Africa these tales concern leopards; in India, tigers; in Russia, bears. The nature of the transformation also varies a great deal. They could be voluntary or involuntary, temporary or permanent. The human spirit could enter the animal or the human body itself could be transformed. Magicians were often believed to possess the power to transform themselves or others into animals.

Leslie Shepard, ed., *Encyclopedia of Occultism & Parapsychology* (Detroit: Gale Research, 1991), s.v. "lycanthropy."

What is the etheric world?

In the parlance of parapsychology the word "etheric" refers to the invisible. The etheric world is the place where humans or human spirits reside in their post-earthly transition. Varied life forms reside in the etheric world and are able to communicate under certain conditions with those still earth bound. Residents of the etheric world are often referred to as "soul-minds," both advanced and inferior. Inferior soul-minds, with evil intent purposefully harangue earthlings; while superior or advanced soul-minds communicate with earthlings via psychics.

Arthur S. Berger and Joyce Burger, *The Encyclopedia of Parapsychology and Psychic Research* (New York: Paragon House, 1991), s.v. "etheric." June G. Bletzer, *The Donning International Encyclopedic Psychic Dictionary* (Norfolk, VA: Donning Co., 1986), s.v. "etheric world."

In parapsychology parlance what is a "channel" and what is "channeling"?

In parapsychology parlance a "channel" is a person who allows those residing in the etheric or invisible world to use his or her body as a means for communicating with earthlings. Psychic information is transmitted while the "channel" is in a semi-trance. The word "channeling" describes this activity.

June G. Bletzer, *The Donning International Encyclopedic Psychic Dictionary* (Norfolk, VA: Donning, 1986), s.v. "channel" and "channeling."

What are the largest ground figures found on the earth's surface?

The earth's largest ground figures can be found in the Nacza Desert about 200 miles south of Lima, Peru. They include geometric shapes, outlines of animals and plants, and straight lines, one of which measures longer than seven miles. Although it is not known which people drew the figures, they were most likely drawn between 100 B.C. and 600 A.D. possibly for astronomical, religious, or economic reasons.

Mark Young, ed., *The Guinness Book of Records 1995* (New York: Facts on File, 1994), 136-7.

What is unusual about the Winchester House in San Jose, California?

Winchester House, a rambling estate in San Jose, California, was built by Sarah L. Winchester, heir to the Winchester Arms fortune. Sarah believed she would not die while the house was under construction, so she continuously added to it. The house has 160 rooms, 200 doors, 10,000 windowpanes, and 47 fireplaces. To this day people call it the "mystery house" due to its labyrinth-like structure.

Fred L. Worth, *The Trivia Encyclopedia* (New York: Bell Publishing Co., 1974), 296.

What strange event betook the buried remains of Roger Williams, the great seventeenth-century religious emancipator?

After the burial of the great seventeenth-century religious emancipator Roger Williams (1603-1683), the ramifying roots of an apple tree consumed his remains. An 1860 disinterment revealed that the root of an apple tree had entered Williams's skull, and guided by the contours of his body, inched down the side of his head, backbone, hips, and legs, all the while absorbing his corpse into the tree.

Irving Wallace and David Wallechinsky, *Significa* (Bergenfield, NJ: E.P. Dutton, 1983).

What strange and still unexplained disappearance took place in Anjikuni, Canada, in 1930?

In 1930 a Canadian trapper entered the Eskimo village of Anjikuni only to find it totally deserted. Its approximately 30 inhabitants abandoned the village never to be seen or heard from again, leaving behind clothing, food, hunting and cooking utensils, kayaks, sleds, and starving dogs. A contingent of the Royal Canadian Mounted Police investigated the strange disappearance, but remain at a loss for an explanation.

Woody Gelamn and Barbara Jackson, *Disaster Illustrated* (New York: Harmony Books, 1976).

What special significance did the Chinese once believe jade to possess?

The ancient Chinese believed that jade was a source of life and gave off masculine vibrations that could only be sensed by the purest of women. The semi-precious stone was used as thumb rings by Chinese archers, cures for certain diseases, a mark of nobility for the living, and a talisman for the dead.

John May, *Curious Trivia* (New York: Dorset Press, 1984).

When will the Age of Aquarius begin?

Although the 1960s counter culture-based rock musical *Hair* declared that the Age of Aquarius was dawning, many find that the beginning of a new age is yet to become a reality. The Age of Aquarius is one of twelve successive 2150-year periods that the planet Earth is passing through. Each 2150-year period corresponds to one of the twelve zodiac signs.

Although a popular date for the beginning of the Aquarian Age is the year 2000, many claim that the year should be closer to 2150. This claim is based on the assumption that the Age of Pisces began with the ministry of Jesus Christ.

The Age of Aquarius is characterized as a time when the materialistic civilization will begin to be spiritualized. Aeronautical and scientific achievement will be great and the mysteries of time and space will be understood. It is also predicted that during this age, humankind will create permanent, enduring institutions and there will be an increased separation between progressives (the Uranians) and conservatives (the Saturnians).

Manly P. Hall, *Astrological Keywords* (New York: Philosophical Library, 1959), 217. James R. Lewis, *The Astrology Encyclopedia* (Detroit: Gale Research, 1994), 7.

What is the origin of the "bed of nails" used by Indian sadhus/fakirs?

The "bed of nails"-as it is known in the West-is used by Indian sadhus/fakirs to afflict and subdue the body. The modern term in India for the bed is "Kantaka-sayya," which translates as "thorn couch." It originated from the ancient Bhishma term "sara-sayya," which means "arrow bed."

John Campbell Oman, *The Mystics, Ascetics, and Saints of India* (London: T. Fisher Unwin, 1905), 45.

Who are the Children of God?

The Children of God are members of a nomadic religious commune which claimed 2,500 members by the early 1970s. They originally called attention to themselves by standing stoically, dressed in sack cloth with ashes on forehead and staff and scroll in hand. This stance was taken to symbolize that the end of mankind was near.

John W. Drakeford, *Children of Doom: A Sobering Look at the Commune Movement Nashville* TN: Broadman Press, 1972), 23-26.

What was a Ren or cartouche to the ancient Egyptians?

Among the ancient Egyptians a Ren or cartouche was an amulet that appeared to be made out of a piece of cord with a knot on the end. The amulet contained inscriptions of the name of a king, which protected his soul from evil.

Migene Gonz lez-Wippler, *The Complete Book of Amulets Talismans* (St. Paul, MN: Llewellyn Publications, 1991), 22-23.

What is a banshee?

A banshee is an Irish harbinger of imminent death. The banshee or "bean si" is always a woman and appears just prior to a death in an Irish family. Sometimes the banshee appears as a young and beautiful woman and at other times it appears as an old crone. Weeping and wailing in an unintelligible language, the "bean-nighe," as she is known in Scotland, is often believed to be the spirit of an already deceased family member.

Peter Haining, *A Dictionary of Ghost Lorel* (Englewood Cliffs, NJ: Prentice-Hall, 1984), 12-13.

What is Rosicrucianism ?

Rosicrucianism was a seventeenth and eighteenth century religious secret society that laid claim to various forms of occult knowledge and power. It was named after Rosenkreuz, the supposed fifteenth century founder of the movement who was born in 1378. The cult also professed esoteric principles of religion. In America the movement exists as the Ancient Mystic Order Rosae Crucis.

Jess Stein, *The Random House Dictionary of the English Language* (Manchester, NH: Random House, 1973), 18.

What does the expression "PSI" stand for?

The expression "PSI" refers collectively to psychic phenomena, which generally means phenomena that cannot be explained through the conventional physical sciences. It is pronounced "sigh" and comes from the first letter of the Greek word "psyche" which means soul. PSI is divided into three categories: Extrasensory perception (ESP); psychokinesis (PK), or mind over matter; and survival phenomena (symbol of theta), which are events controlled by deceased humans or spirits.

Saturday Review 22 February 1975.

Who was the medieval astrologer that offered predictions in rhymed verse?

Nostradamus (1503-1566) was a physician and astrologer in France who became famous for his predictions, which were written in rhymed verse for a 1555 tome entitled *Centuries*. This book excited the interest of the French queen, Catherine de Mdicis (1519-1589), because it correctly foretold the death of her husband, Henry II (1519-1559). Through her influence Nostradamus became physician to her son, Charles IX (1550-1574).

Leonard R. N. Ashley, *The Wonderful World of Superstition, Prophecy, and Luck* (New York: Dembner Books, 1984), 91.

What is divination?

According to William Perkins in 1608, divination was "a part of witchcraft, whereby men reveal strange things, either past, present, or to come, *by the assistance of the devil.*" Primarily used to uncover hidden treasure or predict future events, divination used an array of methods, including astrology, the disemboweling of animals, or the conjuring up of the dead. Its roots were traced to pagans rites of the classical Mediterranean world. In medieval times Christian authorities had declared some types of divination heretical.

Rossell Hope Robbins, *The Encyclopedia of Witchcraft and Demonology* (New York: Crown, 1972), s.v. "Divination."

What is special about the number six?

Because the number six is the only perfect number (a number which equals the sum of its divisors other that itself, i.e. 1+2+3 = 6) among the first ten numerals (the next is 28), it has been credited throughout history with many associations and powers. In the Bible, God completed creation in six days, and on the sixth day He created man and woman. Six is a number of balance, symmetry, and the harmony of opposites as evidenced by the six points of a hexagram which consists of one triangle superimposed on another. Since one triangle points up and the other down, the hexagram has come to symbolize opposites such as man and woman, God and man, fire and water, or spirit and matter. Six is also considered the number of love. The Tarot trump numbered six is The Lovers, sixth card of the Tarot pack. The number six signifies peaceful, married love.

Richard Cavendish, ed., *Man, Myth & Magic* (New York: Marshall Cavendish, 1983), s.v. "Six."

How many different kinds of witches are there?

According to William West, author of *Simboleography*, published in 1594, there are six kinds of witches: magicians (who act as conjurers), soothsaying wizards(who foretell the future), divinators (who find what has been lost), jugglers (curers of sickness through words, spells, and charms), enchanters and charmers (who use trickery, words, and herbs to effect what they said they can do), and witches (who with the aid of the devil can do evil and cause unnatural things). However, others like John Wycliffe, Thomas Ady, and John Gaule distinguished eight or more varieties of witches that also were divided along functional lines, such as diviner, or along methodologies, such as a geomancer, who can foretell the future using figures and lines. Gaule's eight classes in 1616 included the fortunetelling witch (a diviner or gypsy); a star-gazing witch (an astrologer); the chanting witch (venefial witch); the exorcist or conjuring witch; the gastronomic witch and the magical witch.

Rossell Hope Robbins, *The Encyclopedia of Witchcraft and Demonology* (New York: Crown Publishers, 1972), 545.

Why would someone wear the first chapter of St. John's gospel around their neck?

The practice of wearing the first chapter of St. John gospel around the neck is said to protect the wearer from witchcraft. A small copy of the chapter, having been consecrated in a mass, has been used as an amulet to prevent fevers, as a cure for disease, and as a protection from all evil.

Reginald Scot, *The Discoverie of Witchcraft* (Lanham, MD: Rowman & Littlefield, 1973), 220.

Why is the number nine mystical?

Throughout history there have many mystical associations with the number nine including:

Nine is a multiple of three and thus is the "trinity of trinities."

There were nine muses and nine virgin priestesses of the ancient Gallic oracle.

Hydra had nine heads.

Hell has nine rivers.

The Styx River encompassed Hell in nine circles.

In William Shakespeare's *Macbeth* the witches sang: "Thrice to thine, and thrice to mine, and thrice again to make up nine."

The number nine is also regarded as mystical because the human gestation period is nine months. Furthermore, the number nine is the "highest" number, numbers 10 and beyond being mere repetitions of the single digits. Nine also marks the end of number series, (1-9, 11-19, etc.), and when multiplied by another single digit it reproduces itself (3 x 9 = 27, 2 + 7 = 9).

Richard Cavendish, *Man, Myth & Magic* (New York: Marshall Cavendish, 1983), 7:2003. Ivor H. Evans, *Brewer's Dictionary of Phrase and Fable* (New York: Harper & Row, 1989), s.v. "nine."

What is the legend of the Hope Diamond?

The Hope Diamond, the famous gem currently owned by the Smithsonian Institution, has allegedly been accompanied by a legendary curse. Tragedy and even violent death are said to come to the owners of this 45.52 karat diamond. The Smithsonian has published a history of the gem that tries to discredit the curse by reviewing the lives of past owners. Jean Baptiste Tavernier, a French diamond trader, is said to have stolen the diamond from the eye of a Hindu idol, smuggling it out of India in 1642. Contrary to stories that Tavernier was killed by a pack of wild dogs, records indicate that he died at the age of 83. French King Louis XIV was the next owner of the Hope Diamond. It is believed that the gem was stolen during the French Revolution, only to reappear in a smaller form in London in 1830. The stone then changed hands many times in Europe, and, according to legend, several owners met untimely deaths and one was dethroned. In 1911, jeweler Pierre Cartier sold the diamond to millionairess Evalyn Walsh McLean. Upon her death, jeweler Harry Winston donated it to the Smithsonian. The museum asserts that there have been no unusual or tragic occurrences, although it has received letters attributing the Watergate scandal to the stone's curse.

Mindy Yochelson, "New Study Debunks Hope Diamond 'Curse'," *Pittsburgh Press* 4 January 1976.

What is the "Hatteras Hexagon"?

The Hatteras Hexagon is an appropriately hexagon-shaped area in the Atlantic Ocean just off of Cape Hatteras on the North Carolina coast. The area is distinguished for its history of shipwrecks, and the name is an attempt to put it in the same league as the Bermuda Triangle. Records show that a thousand ships have fallen victim to the perils of the Hatteras Hexagon, and 697 wrecks have been identified on its ocean floor. Other records, however, indicate that this may not be an exceptionally problematic area and that a sea-going life is simply dangerous everywhere. The U.S. Hydrographic Office has cited an average of 2,172 ships sinking each year throughout the world.

New York Times 5 April 1975.

What is the significance of "The Man in Gray" to London's Drury Lane Theatre?

"The Man in Gray" is the most famous ghost, though not the only one, to haunt London's Drury Lane Theatre. Unlike other ghosts, the Man in Gray is considered good luck and is well loved by actors and theater management. He is described as a "dignified ghost, a handsome and elegantly dressed young man, apparently from the eighteenth century." His popularity stems from the fact that he is most often seen during the rehearsal of shows that prove to be very successful. This ghost is most often seen in the empty seats of the house or on the balcony, and he is, therefore, not thought to have been an actor. An old story hints at a possible reason for his ghostly presence. It is said that a skeleton, with a knife in its ribs, was found during renovation work in the theater; the discovery happened more than a hundred years ago.

Daniel Cohen, *The Encyclopedia of Ghosts* (New York: Dodd, Mead & Co., 1984), s.v. "Hauntings."

Which of King Henry VIII's wives have been sighted as ghosts?

England's King Henry VIII (1457-1509) is thought to be resting peacefully in his grave, unlike several of his six wives. No sightings have reported Henry's ghost, however, Hampton Court is said to be visited by the ghosts of three of his wives. Jane Seymour (1509?-1537), who died after bearing the king's only son, was his third wife; her likeness has been seen gliding through the castle's Clock Court, always carrying a lighted candle. Lady Catherine Howard (1520?-1542), his fifth wife, was executed after the king heard rumors of her infidelity. When she was arrested, Catherine was dragged away screaming. Reports say she can still be heard on the anniversary of the arrest. Henry's second wife, Anne Boleyn (1507?-1536), was beheaded; her ghost has been spotted at Hampton Court as well as at the Tower of London.

Daniel Cohen, *The Encyclopedia of Ghosts* (New York: Dodd, Mead & Co., 1984), s.v. "Hauntings."

In astrology what is a "significator" and a "co-significator"?

In astrology a "significator" is a planet which signifies those aspects of the house in which it is located or the house it rules. In this regard every planet is a "significator." The term "co-significator," which is quite similar, refers to a planet that relates "to the matter under consideration by virtue of certain traditional astrological associations." These terms are most often used by practitioners of horary astrology.

James R. Lewis, *The Astrology Encyclopedia* (Detroit: Gale Research, 1994), s.v. "Co-significator" and "Significator."

What is "Obeah"?

"Obeah" is a cult originating with the Ashantis in Africa but transported to Jamaica during the slave trade. Its followers make use of sorcery, magic rituals, poisonous herbs, and fear to cast spells and cause sickness and accidents, employing in their ceremonies such items as feathers, blood, shells, wooden images, and grave dirt.

Wade Baskin, *The Sorcerer's Handbook* (New York: Philosophical Library, 1974), 423-24.

Did the ancient Egyptians believe in astrology?

According to Herodotus (ca. 484 B.C.-420 B.C.), the ancient Greek historian who wrote an account of his visit to Egypt, the Egyptians considered horoscopes to be very important. Each day and month belonged to a special god, and the fate of people was determined by the day of birth. Egyptian astrology borrowed many ideas from Mesopotamian or Babylonian astrology, including the zodiac signs and the prophecy aspect of the stars and planets.

James R. Lewis, *The Astrology Encyclopedia* (Detroit: Gale Research, 1994), 184, 364. Sir Flinders Petrie, *Religious Life in Ancient Egypt* (Boston: Houghton Mifflin Company, 1924), p. 204.

What is phrenology?

Phrenology is the study of the shape of the human skull, which, it claims, is the key to mental capabilities and personality. Like other theories developed in the nineteenth century, it considers the body as a reflection of the soul, and maintains that one's character is determined by the interaction of 33 "organs," each of which have a specific location in the brain, and can be detected by a phrenologist's touch. For example, by determining the development of the "organ of combativeness," the phrenologist can decide whether the subject will have an aggressive or passive personality.

Richard Cavendish, ed., *Man, Myth & Magic: An Illustrated Encyclopedia of the Supernatural* (North Bellmore, NY: Marshall Cavendish, 1970), 2188-90.

How was the phrase hocus-pocus coined?

Hocus pocus refers to tricks and magicians' illusions and the words said while effecting them. "I will speake of one man. . ." wrote Thomas Ady in *A Candle in the Dark* (1656), "that went about in King James his time. . .who called himself, The Kings Majesties most excellent Hocus Pocus, and so was called, because that at the playing of every trick, he used to say, "Hocus Pocus, tontus talontus, vade celeriter jubio," a dark composure of words, to blinde the eyes of the beholders, to make his trick pass the more currantly without discovery."

The words, which have become a symbol of illusion and deceit, may come from a perversion of the sacramental blessing, reinforced by the nickname that the ancient juggler assumed from his diverting pseudo-Latin patter, and further strengthened by the names of other successful jugglers and magicians named after him. From Hocus Pocus came, in all probability, such current words as hoax, hokum, and hokey-pokey.

Robert Hendrickson, *Human Words: The Compleat Unexpurgated, Uncomputerized Human Wordbook* (Philadelphia: Chilton, 1972), 144-45.

Where is the Bermuda Triangle located?

The Bermuda Triangle, sometimes known as the Devil's Triangle, is an area of the Atlantic Ocean with the corners of the triangle being at the southern Virginia coast, the Bermuda Islands, and the Florida Keys, covering about 14,000 square miles. On a number of occasions ships and airplanes have vanished in this area, often without a trace.

The first known navigator of the Burmuda Triangle, Christopher Columbus, reported on September 15, 1492, seeing "a remarkable bolt of fire fall into the sea." While sailing in that area, there was also a baffling disturbance of the ship compass. Other reported incidents included the disappearance of four American Naval vessels between 1781 and 1812; the 1918 disappearance of the *U.S.S. Cyclops*, a Navy collier; the December 6, 1945 disappearance of five Navy torpedo bomber planes and the disappearance of a Martin Marine flying boat that was searching for the missing bombers; and the 1963 disappearances of an American merchant ship, a fishing boat, and two Air Force tanker jets.

Explanations for these disappearances have ranged from the plausible (extreme air turbulence, powerful ocean currents, waterspouts, magnetic anomalies, electromagnetic storms) to the absurd (kidnappings by alien flying saucers, gateways to other dimensions). However, scientific studies have revealed no significant peculiarities about the area. Many of the so-called incidents within the Bermuda Triangle can be attributed to other causes including bad weather, malfunctioning instruments, and faulty navigation. It is also not the only part of the ocean where ships and planes have disappeared.

Academic American Encyclopedia (Danbury, CT: Grolier, 1991), 3:219. Robert B. Downs, *Scientific Enigmas* (Littleton, CO: Libraries Unlimited, 1987), 96-101. "Ocean Triangle Retains Mystery," *New York Times* 21 May 1968.

Does dowsing have any scientific basis?

Dowsing is searching for water, metal ores, or other materials hidden beneath the earth's surface by using a divining rod or dowsing rod. These rods are usually forked or Y-shaped and can be made of wood or metal. The rods are carried by their tips and are believed to bend downward when they pass over hidden materials. Although studies have failed to explain scientifically the basis for dowsing, the practice is still popular throughout the world. Some civil engineering companies use dowsers to locate existing pipelines or cables when making site surveys, because often the companies find the results more reliable than those from standard detectors.

Kenneth L. Roberts, *How In the World?* (Pleasantville, NY: Reader's Digest Association, 1990), 1. *The Seventh Sense* (New York: Doubleday, 1953), 316. *Science and Technology Illustrated* (Chicago: Encyclopaedia Britannica, 1984), 8:1012.

What is pyramid power?

An interesting belief about the strange power of pyramids was popular during the 1970s. The power of the pyramid is based on the belief that a pyramid shaped like that of the Great Pyramid of Giza could focus an unspecified energy in a mystical way to bring about a beneficial result, and by placing the item under study inside a hollow pyramid, will benefit the item. Some of the claims of its power include keeping food fresh, making meat tender, improving the taste of wine and tobacco, purifying water, curing headaches, shortening healing time, making plants grow better, and keeping razor blades sharp. A physicist and "pyramidologist," Dr. G. Pat Flanagan describes experiments he conducted in his book *Pyramid Power.* Later researchers have debunked this theory.

Human Behavior April 1979. *Mechanix Illustrated* April 1977.

How many people died because of the Salem witch trials?

The witch trials took place in Salem, Massachusetts, a city about 30 miles north of Boston, between May and October of 1692. A few girls were influenced by Tituba, a West Indian slave, who had told them voodoo tales from the Caribbean. They claimed that they were possessed by the devil and charged Tituba and two other Salem women with witchcraft. When the accused were intimidated to implicate others, hysteria gripped Massachusetts Bay Colony, and a special court was established to try those suspected of being witches. In all twenty-four people died as a result of these trials. Nineteen were hanged: Bridget Bishop, George Burroughs, Martha Carrier, Martha Cory, Mary Easty, Sarah Good, Elizabeth Howe, George Jacobs, Sr., Susannah Martin, Rebecca Nurse, Alice Parker, Mary Parker, John Procter, Ann Pudeator, Wilmot "Mammy" Redd, Margaret Scott, Samuel Wardwell, Sarah Wildes, and John Willard. Four died in prison: Lydia Dastin, Ann Foster, Sarah Good's unnamed infant, and Sarah Osborne. Giles Corey was crushed to death by heavy weights being placed on his chest in a futile effort to extract a confession. In fact, of those hanged only Samuel Wardwell confessed to witchcraft, and he later denied his guilt before execution. In 1711, the Massachusetts General Court (legislature) reversed all the convictions, and compensation was paid to the heirs of those who were put to death.

Tom Burnam, *The Dictionary of Misinformation* (New York: Harper & Row, 1975), s.v. "witchcraft trials in Salem." Katherine W. Richardson, *The Salem Witchcraft Trials* (Salem, MA: Essex Institute, 1983), 21.

Which element is associated with each of the signs of the zodiac?

Elements associated with the zodiac are:
Air signs—Libra, Aquarius, Gemini
Earth signs—Capricorn, Taurus, Virgo
Fire signs—Aries, Leo, Sagittarius
Water signs—Cancer, Scorpio, Pisces

Eleanor Bach, *Astrology From A to Z* (New York: Allied Books, 1990), 8, 57, 66, 213.

Is there more violence on the streets and in mental institutions when there is a full moon?

A review of 37 studies that attempted to correlate the phases of the moon with violent crime, suicide, crisis center hotline calls, psychiatric disorders, and mental hospital admissions found that there is absolutely no relation between the moon and the mind.

Prevention's Giant Book of Health Facts (Emmaus, PA: Rodale Press, 1991), 87.

What do the terms "chiromancy" and "chirognomy" mean?

The terms "chiromancy" and "chirognomy" are used in palmistry. Chiromancy is translated "fortune telling by the hand" and refers to the practice of predicting the future and reading an individual's character by the lines on the hand. Later, when the form of the hand was also considered important to study, the term "chirognomy" came into being.

Fred Gettings, *The Book of Palmistry* (London: Triune Books, 1974), 10.

Who was John Dee?

Dr. John Dee (1527-1608) was a spiritualist who claimed he could communicate with the dead through crystallomancy. Author of *Liber Mysteriorum,* Dee traveled throughout Europe studying astrology, alchemy, and the occult. At one point he was imprisoned by Queen Mary of England on the charge of "practicing enchantments."

Harry E. Wedeck, *Dictionary of Spiritualism* (New York: Philosophical Library, 1971), 99.

What is the origin of the belief that breaking a mirror brings bad luck?

The belief that breaking a mirror brings bad luck goes back to the ancient Greeks and the practice of catoptromancy, which predicted one's future from gazing into a glass or earthenware bowl of water. The Romans referred to a such a glass bowl as a "miratorium." If the container happened to break it was believed that the gods wanted to shield the person from insight into horrendous or heartbreaking future events. By the fifteenth century glass mirrors were in use although they were extremely expensive. Servants were warned that to break a mirror during cleaning would bring them seven years of bad luck.

Charles Panati, *Extraordinary Origins of Everyday Things* (New York:Harper & Row, 1987), 11.

What twentieth century psychic was called "the sleeping prophet"?

Edgar Cayce (1877-1945) was an American psychic known as "the sleeping prophet." Born in Kentucky, Cayce was reputed to have psychic powers from an early age. He is reputed to have cured people from throughout the world of a variety of illnesses by going into a trance and prescribing appropriate medications. He died in 1945.

Rosemary Ellen Guiley, *Harper's Encyclopedia of Mystical and Paranormal Experience San Francisco: Harper San Francisco* 1991), s.v. "Cayce, Edgar."

Philosophy

What is karma?

In Hindu and Buddhist philosophy, karma is the total of one's actions and experiences from all previous earthly existences. The sum total of one's Karma strongly influences each succeeding existence or incarnation.

Abraham H. Lass, *Dictionary of Classical, Biblical, and Literary Allusions* (New York: Facts On File, 1987).

Who was Diogenes?

Diogenes of Sinope (c.400 B.C.-325 B.C.) was a founder of the Cynic school of Greek philosophy. He taught that people should find happiness by satisfying their natural needs in a cheap and easy way. Diogenes maintained that what is natural cannot be indecent and so should be done in public. Yet he was not recommending a sensual life, for he claimed that one should train the body to have as few needs as possible. By all accounts, Diogenes lived a rigorously ascetic life, true to the principles that he advocated, but in his opinion society was filled with hypocrites, who only talked about living virtuously. His views and behavior earned him the contempt of the Athenians, who called him "dog." It is from the Greek word for dog (kon) that the term "cynic" is derived.

Because of his caustic wit and his nonconformist life style, many legendary stories arose about him, making it difficult for modern scholars to separate the facts of his life and teaching from fiction. The most famous of these tales, whether true or not, certainly reflects a cynical attitude. It was said that Diogenes went about in daylight with lighted lamp, seeking an honest man.

Catherine B. Avery, *The New Century Classical Handbook* (New York: Appleton-Century-Crofts, 1962), s.v. "Diogenes." N.G.L. Hammon and H.H. Scullard, *The Oxford Classical Dictionary, 2d ed.* (Oxford: The Clarendon Press, 1970), s.v. "Diogenes (2)."

What is Marshall's Generalized Iceberg Theorem?

Marshall's Generalized Iceberg Theorem states: "Seven-eights of everything can't be seen." The source of this expression is anonymous.

Time 26 February 1979.

What are the Cardinal or Seven Virtues?

The origin of the idea of cardinal virtues comes from Book Four of *The Republic* by the ancient Greek philosopher Plato. Plato listed four: "prudence," or practical wisdom; "justice, temperance," or self-control; "fortitude," or courage. These principal virtues are tied to the three dimensions of the soul (reason, spirit, and desire) as well as to the three parts of the polity (the philosopher-kings, the guardians, and the artisans). Plato's four cardinal virtues migrated into early Church doctrine to which were added the three theological virtues of faith, hope, and charity. The importance of the cardinal virtues has been a topic of prolonged debate among theologians, especially during the Middle Ages.

James F. Childress and John Macquarrie, eds., *The Westminster Dictionary of Christian Ethics* (Philadelphia: Westminster Press, 1986). William H. Gentz, ed., *The Dictionary of Bible and Religion* (Nashville: Abingdon Press, 1986), s.v. "seven virtues."

Who was Hypatia?

Hypatia (ca. 370-415) was a Neoplatonic philosopher and mathematician in Alexandria. She was an exponent of Platonic, Neoplatonic, and Aristotelian philosophy, and her brilliant reputation earned her the admiration of many students. It is believed that she was probably murdered for political and religious reasons by a group of monks under the orders of Cyril (ca. 375-444 A.D.), Archbishop of Alexandria. The feminist philosophy journal, *Hypatia*, is named after her.

Ethel M. Kersey, *Women Philosophers: A Bio-Critical Source Book* (New York: Greenwood Press, 1989), s.v. "Hypatia of Alexandria."

What is another name for the *I Ching*?

The *I Ching*, also called the *Book of Changes*, is a classical Chinese philosophy text attributed to Emperor Fo-Hi in 3468 B.C. The text explains the dynamic principles of the Yin and Yang as well was gives interpretations for a divination process that uses sticks to form hexagrams.

Leslie Shepard, ed.*Encyclopedia of Occultism & Parapsychology, 3d ed.* (Detroit: Gale Research, 1991), s.v. "I Ching (Yi King or Y-Kim)."

What famous Greek philosopher was the first to write about the legendary land of Atlantis?

The first written references to Atlantis are in the ancient Greek philosopher Plato's dialogues *Timaeus* and *Critias*, written in 350 B.C. They include the story of how this highly advanced civilization was swallowed up by a geological catastrophe. Plato wrote of the Atlantis legend as a parable about "the fall of man," rather than as a real place or series of events. Modern accounts of Atlantis such as Ignatius Donnelly's "non-fiction" work *Atlantis: the Antediluvian World* (1882) have tried to prove that Atlantis really did exist.

Peter Nicholls, ed., *The Science Fiction Encyclopedia* (Garden City, NY: Doubleday & Co., 1979), 49.

What are the origins of the term "ubermensch"?

"Ubermensch" is German for "overman" or "superman." The term was first used by Goethe in *Faust* to describe his exceptional hero. Ubermensch is also a central concept in Nietzsche's philosophy, which was subsequently distorted by Adolph Hitler (1889-1945) and the Nazis to justify their belief in Aryan supremacy.

Abraham H. Lass, David Kiremidjian, and Ruth M. Goldstein, *The Facts On File Dictionary of Classical, Biblical and Literary Allusions* (New York: Facts On File, 1987), s.v. "Ubermensch."

What is the meaning of Plato's image of the cave?

In the seventh book of his work *Republic*, the ancient Greek philosopher Plato (428 B.C.-348 B.C.) used the image of a cave to illustrate the difference between reality and illusion. Plato described men in a cave who were chained so that they could only see a blank wall. Men in this position, if there were to be a fire burning behind them, would mistake the shadows cast upon the blank wall for real objects. If any of the men were released from the cave and saw real objects bathed by the light of the sun, not only would it be difficult for them to return to the darkened cave, it would be even more of a challenge to convince the men who had never left the cave that what they were seeing on the blank wall were shadows of a real world.

Jennifer Speak, ed., *A Dictionary of Philosophy, rev. 2nd ed.*, (New York: St. Martin's Press, 1984), s.v. "cave, image of the."

Which ancient Greek philosopher carried out his death sentence by drinking a cup of hemlock?

When the ancient Greek philosopher Socrates (469 B.C.-399 B.C.) killed himself by drinking a cup of hemlock, he was accepting a death sentence issued by the city-state of Athens. Socrates had been convicted of not believing in the gods of Athens and of corrupting the city's youth. His accusers, Anytus, Meletus, and Lycon probably did not expect him to comply with the death penalty. Socrates could have gone into voluntary exile before the end of the trial, or could have asked for banishment as an alternative sentence. The philosopher had to accept the hemlock after his own proposals were rejected. He had asked to be dined for life, at public expense, or that a fine should be issued, to be paid by his friends. The nature of these proposals indicates that Socrates did not believe that he had done any harm to Athens.

M. C. Howatson, *Oxford Companion to Classical Literature* (New York: Oxford University Press, 1989), 529.

What philosophical movement did Ayn Rand inspire?

The Objectivism movement was inspired by author Ayn Rand, and is based on the philosophy she promoted in books such as the novel *The Fountainhead.* These works champion a life that is guided purely by reason and not by personal or emotional feelings. One of Rand's "disciples," Nathaniel Branden, helped to formalize the Objectivism movement by first developing a series of lectures in 1958, and then by creating an institute to teach her philosophy. The Nathaniel Branden Institute received Rand's reluctant approval and the author took part in the institute's seminars. Those who followed the Institute's course of study, which included reading all of Rand's books, and who believed in and promised to follow Rand's philosophy were known as the Senior Collective.

James T. Baker, *Ayn Rand* (Boston: Twayne Publishers, 1987), 18.

Religion and Mythology

What is the Decalogue or the Ten Commandments?

One of the hallmarks of the Jewish religion are the ten commandments given to Moses by God on Mt. Sinai. These commandments, known collectively as the Decalogue, form the basis of Jewish law. The first five commandments in the Decalogue focus on God's relationship with man while the final five commandments deal with man's relations with his fellow human beings.

The Jewish Decalogue and the Protestant and Eastern Orthodox version of the ten commandments is based on Deuteronomy 5:6-21 and is as follows:

I am the Lord thy God. Thou shalt have no other gods before me.
Thou shalt not make any graven images.
Thou shalt not take the name of the Lord in vain.
Remember the Sabbath day, to keep it holy.
Honor thy father and thy mother.
Thou shalt not kill.
Thou shalt not commit adultery.
Thou shalt not steal.
Thou shalt not bear false witness against thy neighbor.
Thou halt not covet thy neighbor's house.

Roman Catholics and some Lutherans follow the enumeration based on Exodus 20:1-17. The first commandment combines the first and second commandments in the above version, and these denominations make the prohibition, "Thou shalt not covert thy neighbor's wife," the ninth commandment. So this version becomes the following:

I, the Lord, am your God.... You shall not have other gods besides me.
You shall not take the name of the Lord, your God, in vain.
Take care to keep holy the sabbath day as the Lord, your God, commanded you.
Honor your father and your mother.
You shall not kill.
You shall not commit adultery.
You shall not steal.
You shall not bear dishonest witness against your neighbor.
You shall not covet your neighbor's wife.
You shall not desire your neighbor's house or field, nor his male or female slave, nor his ox or ass, nor anything that belongs to him.

Felician A. Foy, ed., *1993 Catholic Almanac* (Huntington, IN: Our Sunday Visitor, 1992), 200. Charles M. Laymon, ed., *The Interpreter's One-volume Commentary on the Bible* (Nashville: Abington Press, 1971), 53.

How tall was Jesus Christ?

If the controversial Shroud of Turin is to be considered as the authentic burial cloth of Jesus Christ, then his height can be estimated at 5 feet, 8 inches tall. The linen of the shroud is 14 feet, 3 3/5 inches by 3 feet, 7-inches. It bears a faint image of the front and back of a man who had been whipped, crowned with thorns, and crucified. Wounds on the image correspond to the details of the death of Jesus Christ as described in the Bible. Tests have proven that the blood stains are human and that the image could not have been painted on the cloth, but experts still dispute the age of the shroud. In 1988, the Vatican gave scientists around the world the opportunity to study the Shroud of Turin in order to document its authenticity. Radiocarbon dating revealed that the cloth was probably made in 1350 A.D., although some dispute the test results. The first official record of the shroud was in 1354 in Lirey, France. The earliest known mention of it was by a crusader, Robert of Clari, in 1203, who saw the cloth at the imperial palace in Constantinople.

Due to the carbon dating, the Roman Catholic Church announced that the Shroud of Turin is not the burial shroud of Jesus Christ, but that it should be treated as an icon. The Church claims that there have been documented cases of healing and other miracles related to the Shroud.

Kazimir de Proszynski, *The Authentic Photograph of Christ* (London: Search Publishing, 1932), 44. *World Book Encyclopedia* (Chicago: World Book, 1994), 17:442. Roberto Suro, "Church Says Shroud of Turin Isn't Authentic," *New York Times* 14 October 1988. "Face Cloth likened to Christ's Shroud of Turin," *USA Today* 19 April 1984. "Tests Say Shroud of Turin is 600 Years Old," *Pittsburgh Press* 28 September 1988.

Are the names known of the men who were crucified with Jesus?

Dismas (sometimes spelled as Dysmas, Demas, or Damachus) is the traditional name of the penitent thief who was crucified beside Jesus on Good Friday. He is also known as "The Good Thief." The other thief is usually referred to as Gestas (or Gesmas) Apocryphal. Longfellow, in his *Golden Legend,* referred to the thieves as Titus and Dumachus, whom Jesus first met as a child during the flight into Egypt. At that time Jesus foretold their deaths.

Herbert Thurston and Donald Attwater, eds., *Butler's Lives of the Saints* (New York: P.J. Kenedy & Sons, 1956), 1:676-77. Alfred Edersheim, *The Life and Times of Jesus the Messiah* (New York: E.R. Herrick, n.d.), 2:598. Adam Fahling, *The Life of Christ* (St. Louis: Concordia Publishing House, 1936), 671. William Rose Benet, *The Reader's Encyclopedia: An Encyclopedia of World Literature and the Arts* (n.p.: Thomas Y. Crowell Co., 1955), s.v. "Dismas or Dysmas."

What is the Swiss Guard?

The security of the Pope is entrusted to the Swiss Guard. The Vatican is the only "foreign government" where a Swiss soldier can enlist, according to the Swiss constitution since 1874. In fact, the members of the Swiss Guard cannot be actively recruited in Switzerland but usually join based upon "word of mouth" information. Mercenary Swiss soldiers have served the papacy since the end of the fourteenth century, but the first organized corps directly dependent upon the pope was not formed until 1505 under Pope Julius II (1443-1513). The term of service is two years, with half-salary pension after 18 years, two-thirds after 25, and full-salary pension after 30 years. Recruits must be Swiss, Catholic, unmarried, under 25 years of age, and take an oath to protect the pope and the college of cardinals. The Swiss Guard consists of four officers, a chaplain, four lesser officers, two drummers, and 70 guards.

New Catholic Encyclopedia (New York: McGraw-Hill, 1967), s.v. "Swiss Guards." Jerrold M. Packard, *Peter's Kingdom: Inside the Papal City* (New York: Charles Scribner's Sons, 1985), 137.

Who was St. Laura?

St. Laura was born in Cordova, Spain, and became a nun at Cuteclara after becoming a widow. Little is known of her life. Captured by the Moors, she was then martyred by scalding in 864 A.D. Her feast day is October 19.

John J. Delaney and James Edward Tobin, *Dictionary of Catholic Biography* (Garden City, NY: Doubleday & Co., 1961), s.v. "Laura, St."

What Greek mythological figures were associated with rocks?

Rocks played a punitive role in several Greek myths. For angering Zeus, king of the Greek gods, Sisyphus was struck with a thunderbolt and hurled to the Underworld. There he was condemned to eternally roll an enormous rock up a hill. As soon as he reached the top, the rock rolled down and Sisyphus had to begin again.

For murdering his son, Tantalus was placed under a massive stone which was always on the point of falling. In other versions of the myth, Tantalus is described as being placed in water up to his neck but unable to drink and within reach of a fruit-laden branch which sprang away whenever he reached toward it.

Pierre Grimal, *The Dictionary of Classical Mythology* (New York: Basil Blackwell, 1951), s.v. "Sisyphus," "Tantalus." Anthony S. Mercatante, *The Facts On File Encyclopedia of World Mythology and Legend* (New York: Facts on File, 1988), s.v. "Sisyphus," "Tantalus."

Who were the four U.S. chaplains who sacrificed their lives for others when their ship was torpedoed during World War II?

On February 3, 1943, the U.S. troopship *Dorchester* was torpedoed off Greenland during World War II (1939-45). Four chaplains, who gave their lifebelts to others, went down with the ship. They were Clark A. Poling of Schenectady, New York, and George L. Fox of Sharon, Vermont, both Protestants; John P. Washington of Newark, New Jersey, a Roman Catholic priest; and Alexander D. Goode of York, Pennsylvania, a rabbi. Each were posthumously awarded the Distinguished Service Cross.

Facts on File 2-8 February 1951. *Time* 11 December 1944.

What is the difference between All Saints' Day and All Souls' Day?

The Roman Catholic Church and the Church of England honor the dead on the first two days of November. November 1 is All Saints' Day, which celebrates all the departed who have entered heaven and not just those whom the church has officially declared to be saints. Feasts honoring all of the saints originate in the fourth century when they were commemorated on various dates in May or early June. Orthodox Christians still mark this day on the first Sunday after Pentecost. In A.D. 609 or 610, the bones of those who had been buried in the catacombs were transported by the cart load to Rome to be interred under a pagan temple called the Pantheon. The building was then dedicated as a church to the Virgin Mary and the martyrs (later all saints), and the anniversary of this dedication, which took place on May 13, was celebrated with great pomp. Many scholars find the origin of All Saints' Day, as it is observed in the West, in this commemoration, but there is no consensus on the matter. How the feast was moved to November 1 has never been adequately explained, but it occurred during the eighth or ninth century. According to John Beleth, who died around 1135, Pope Gregory IV (827-844) moved the date from May 13 to November 1 because there were more provisions for pilgrims in Rome after the fall harvest.

All Souls' Day is observed on November 2 and celebrates all the faithful members of the church who have died. It is distinguished from All Saints Day because it particularly commemorates the souls in purgatory. According to Catholic theology, purgatory is a place of expiation for the dead who have been saved, but whose souls need to be purified before they can come before the presence of God in heaven. Their purgation can be shortened by the prayers of the living, and a special day is set aside to remember the souls. The feast and the date on which it is celebrated was first proposed by St. Odilo of Cluny in A.D. 998. It was adopted by Rome in the fourteenth century. Orthodox Christians honor all souls on the Saturday before Pentecost and on the three Saturdays prior to the beginning of Lent.

The Catholic University of America, *New Catholic Encyclopedia* (New York: McGraw-Hill, 1967), s.v. "all saints, feast of," "all souls, feast of." Felician Foy, ed., *1994 Catholic Almanac* (Huntington, IN: Our Sunday Visitor Publishing Division, 1993), 246. Sue Ellen Thompson and Barbara W. Carlson, eds., *Holidays, Festivals, and Celebrations of the World Dictionary* (Detroit: Omnigraphics, 1994), s.v. "all saints' day," "all souls' day."

Has the snake always been a symbol of evil?

In mythology and folklore the snake, or serpent, is sometimes a symbol of good and sometimes of evil. The snake often symbolizes rebirth and healing, perhaps because of the parallel between man's shaking off disease and the snake's casting off its skin. Yet the snake can also be the vehicle of disease, death, and such human frailties as falsehood and greed.

In most of today's religions the snake is usually associated with evil. Not only did St. Patrick drive the snakes from Ireland, but the snake is often depicted under the foot or power of the Virgin Mary.

Anthony A. Mercatante, *The Facts On File Encyclopedia of World Mythology and Legend* (New York: Facts on File, 1988), s.v. "snake." H.M. Raphaelian, *Signs of Life: A Pictorial Dictionary of Symbols* (New York: Anatol Sivas, 1957), 99-102.

What have been the nationalities of the Roman Catholic popes?

Including John Paul II, there have been 263 Roman Catholic popes. Two hundred nine of them Italians; 15 were Frenchmen; 12, Greeks; 6, Germans; 6, Syrians; 3, Africans; 3, Spaniards; 2, Dalmatians; and 1 Dutch, English, Polish, Portuguese, and Jewish (St. Peter, the first pope). The nationality of two popes is unknown.

Ivor H. Evens, *Brewer's Dictionary of Phrase and Fable* (New York: Harper & Row, 1989), s.v. "pope."

What is an "ayatollah" and when did the Iranian leader Khomeini receive this title?

"Ayatollah" is an honorific title for a Shiite Moslem religious leader, especially in Iran. Ayatollah is a Persian word meaning reflection or sign of Allah (God) on earth. A person who carries the title is one who through his learning and probity is qualified to be followed in all points of religious practice and law by the generality of Shiites. Ayatollahs are also known as "marja' at-taqlid" or "mujtahids," although not all mujtahids are ayatollahs. There is no formal appointment as a mujtahid, rather, gradual public recognition through prestige among fellow religious students, family connections, and the ability to preach and communicate with the people results in the status as a religious leader. Recognition among other mujtahids, which is dependent upon public acclaim of one's piety and learning, and also the death of more prominent mujtahids, results in a rise to greater prominence in the unofficial religious ranks. The title of ayatollah was not used until the twentieth century, and after the 1979 revolution in Iran the title proliferated, thus diluting its importance. in 1980 there were 50-60 ayatollahs. In the 1950s this honorific title was added to Iranian leader Ruholla Khomeini's name by his followers. Born Ruholla (meaning soul of God) Hendi, the name Khomeini was added to his name around 1930. Ruholla derived the name "Khomeini" from the name of the town Khomein, in which he was born.

Moojan Momen, *An Introduction to Shi'i Islam: The History and Doctrines of Twelver Shi'ism* (New Haven, CT: Yale University Press, 1985), xix-xxii, 150-1, 203-6, 340. J. D. Douglas, *New 20th-Century Encyclopedia of Religious Knowledge, 2d ed.* (Grand Rapids, MI: Baker Book House, 1991), s.v. "Shi'ism." *The Oxford English Dictionary, 2d ed.* (Oxford: Clarendon Press, 1989), s.v. "ayatollah."

What is the Stone of Unction?

The Stone of Unction or Stone of Anointment is the stone upon which the body of Jesus Christ is said to have lain when anointed by Nicodemus. It is located in the Church of the Holy Sepulchre in Jerusalem.

K. Baedeker, *Palestine and Syria: Handbook for Travelers* (London: Dulau, 1876), 194.

What are the Biblical references to "Watergate"?

Five verses in the book Nehemiah of the Bible contain the words "water gate," apparently in reference to a section of the city walls of Jerusalem. The references are: chapter 3, verse 26; chapter 8, verses 1, 3, and 16; and chapter 12, verse 37.

Alexander Cruden, *Cruden's Complete Concordance to the Old and New Testaments* (Grand Rapids, MI: Zondervan Publishing House, 1968), s.v. "gate," "water gate." John W. Ellison, *Nelson's Complete Concordance of the Revised Standard Version Bible* (Nashville, TN: Thomas Nelson, 1957), 2048. *The Holy Bible* (London: Cambridge University Press, 1937), Nehemiah 3:36, 8:1, 3, 16, 12:37.

What is the legend of the dogwood tree?

The dogwood tree, with the spectacular blossoms it produces every spring, became associated with the belief in the passion and resurrection of Jesus Christ, which Christians commemorate during the same season. According to the legend, the dogwood tree grew a straight, tall trunk before the crucifixion of Jesus, and for that reason it was chosen for the cross. Having participated in so great a crime, the tree became twisted and gnarled that it could never again be used as a cross. Yet on the morning of the first Easter, the dogwood was able to participate in the glory of the resurrection by bringing forth beautiful white blossoms. The passion was also recalled by its flower's center, which resembles a crown of thorns, its four petals, which together form the shape of a cross, and singly-edged with dark spots resembling nail prints.

Jessie Eubank Harris, *Legends and Stories of Famous Trees* (Philadelphia: Dorrance and Co., 1963), 41-42.

What is the longest name in the Bible?

Isaiah's son, Maher-shalal-hash-baz, has the longest name in the Bible.

Holy Bible: (Authorized or King James Version) The New Standard Alphabetical Indexed Bible, School and library ref. ed. (Chicago: John A. Hertel, 1955), 116.

Who pierced Jesus Christ's side as he was dying on the cross?

Longinus was the name of the soldier who pierced Jesus Christ's side with a spear at the Crucifixion. He later came to believe in the divinity of Jesus, preached the gospel, suffered martyrdom, and was proclaimed a saint.

Herbert Thurston and Donald Attwater, eds., *Butler's Lives of the Saints* (New York: P.J. Kennedy & Sons, 1956), 594-95. Peter Calvocoressi, *Who's Who in the Bible* (London: Viking, 1987), s.v. "Longinus."

What are the nine choirs of angels?

The word "angel" comes from the Greek word for "messenger," and according to the Bible, angels are heavenly beings who oversee God's will on earth. In the Old Testament, the greatest angels were the seven archangels, whose names varied according to the source used. The angels most cited are Micael (Mikael), Gabriel, Uriel, and Raphael. Ragriel, Sariel, and Jeremial, as well as others, serve with these great angels. Early Christians derived four types of angels from Judaic literature (angels, archangels, seraphim and cherubim) and another five from the epistles of Paul (virtues, powers, principalities, dominions, and thrones). Around A.D. 500, these nine types or choirs of angels were arranged in celestial hierarchy by an anonymous author who probably lived in Syria and who claimed to be Dionysius the Areopagite, an Athenian philosopher whom Paul converted to Christianity. Pseudo-Dionysius wrote *The Celestial Hierarchy*, which ranks the nine different types of angels into three orders. Each order purifies, illuminates, and perfects the rank below. The first order consists of those angels who are closest to God: seraphim, cherubim, and thrones. The second order is composed of the priest-princes of the court of heaven: dominions, virtues, and powers. The third order comprises ministering angels, those who are closest to humans: principalities, archangels, and angels.

Philip W. Goetz, ed., "Micropaedia," *The New Encyclopedia Britannica, 15th ed.* (Chicago: Encyclopedia Britannica, 1991), s.v. "angel." Joseph

Strayer, ed., *Dictionary of the Middle Ages* (New York: Charles Scribner's Sons, 1982), s.v. "angel/angelology," "Pseudo-Dionysius the Areopagite." Gustav Davidson, *A Dictionary of Angels* (New York: The Free Press, 1967), 51, 338.

Did horses play any significant role in Greek mythology?

Horses have played important roles in Greek mythology. One Greek legend states that Poseidon, god of the sea, and Athena, goddess of war, agreed that the one who created the most useful gift for humankind would rule Athens. Poseidon produced the horse and Athena the olive tree. Athena won because her gift was a symbol of peace while Poseidon's was a symbol of war.

Pegasus, a winged horse, played a part in several Greek myths. When Perseus killed the Gorgon Medusa, Pegasus sprang from her mutilated head. After his birth Pegasus flew to Olympus to serve Zeus, to whom he brought thunderbolts. Thanks to Pegasus, Bellerophon was able to kill the Chimaera-a monster with the forequarters of a lion, the hindquarters of a dragon, and flame-breathing goat's head.

Another winged horse, Arion, enabled Adrastus to escape destruction during a war to capture Thebes.

Boreas, god of the North Wind, assumed the form of a horse to sire twelve colts so fast that they could not be overtaken.

Centaurs, monstrous creatures with the appearance of being half horse and half human, played parts in several myths. They lived in the mountains and forests, ate raw flesh, and generally demonstrated monstrous behavior. However, the most famous and wisest of the Centaurs was Chiron, who shunned violence.

Pierre Grimal, *The Dictionary of Classical Mythology* (New York: Basil Blackwell, 1951), 15, 75, 77, 94, 200, 349, 360, 532.

Which human figures in Greek mythology were able to fly?

In several Greek myths humans had the ability to fly. To escape the labyrinth, Daedalus made sets of wings for himself and his son, Icarus, and fixed them to their shoulders with wax. Icarus flew so close to the sun that the wax melted and he fell into the sea. When he slew the Gorgon Medusa, Perseus rose up in the air on winged sandals. Hermes, messenger to Zeus, not only had winged shoes but a winged helmet as well.

Pierre Grimal, *The Dictionary of Classical Mythology* (New York: Basil Blackwell, 1951), s.v. "Hermes," "Icarus," "Perseus."

What is the significance of the number "666"?

The number "666" or the terms "Great Beast" or "Great Beast of the Apocalypse" refer to the devil or to the Antichrist and originate in chapter 13 of the book of Revelation in the Bible. Six hundred sixty-six is a number riddle; the Great Beast's name or title will add to 666 if its letters are turned into numbers (Hebrew and Greek alphabets also stood for numbers).

Man, Myth & Magic: The Illustrated Encyclopedia of Mythology, Religion and the Unknown (New York: Marshall Cavendish, 1983), 4:1074, 1157-58.

Who were the three wise men who visited the baby Jesus at the manger?

The three wise men who paid homage to Jesus Christ as an infant were as follows:
Melchior—King of Arabia, who brought a gift of gold.
Gaspar—King of Tarsus, who brought a gift of myrrh.
Balthasar—King of Ethiopia or Saba, who brought a gift of frankincense.

Alfred Carl Hottes, *1001 Christmas Facts and Fancies* (New York: A.T. De La Mare Co., 1954), 24.

According to the Bible, what did God create on each of the first seven days?

The seven days of creation (Genesis 1:1-31, 2:1-2) are as follows:
First day—light and darkness, or day and night
Second day—the firmament separating earthly and heavenly waters
Third day—dry land and vegetation
Fourth day—heavenly luminaries (sun, moon, stars)
Fifth day—water creatures and birds
Sixth day—land creatures and man
Seventh day—God rested

The Holy Bible: Containing the Old and New Testaments (Cambridge: Cambridge University Press, 1937), 1.

How many books are there in the Bible?

The number of books in the Bible depends upon the version in question. The Hebrew Bible has 24 books and is divided into three sections. The Torah (The Law) comprises the five books that were traditionally believed to have been written by Moses. The Nevi'im (Prophets) has eight books, including Joshua, Judges, Samuel, Kings and the writings of the prophets. The Ketuvim (Writings) consists of eleven books of religious poetry and wisdom literature. The Hebrew Bible used by Christians, called The Old Testament is, however, slightly different. These books derive from a Greek version of the Hebrew scriptures that is called the Septuagint. It was redacted in the second and third centuries B.C. by Jewish scholars and adopted by the Christian Church in the first centuries after Jesus Christ. The Septuagint reorders the Hebrew Bible and divides it into 39 books. Also it adds seven books or parts of books not found in the original. The Roman Catholic Church has accepted these additional books as genuine and refers to them as Deuterocanonica (The Second Canon). On the other hand, Protestants reject these books, referring to them as Apocrypha (fictitious writings). Therefore the Protestant Old Testament has 39 books and the Catholic version, 46.

Catholics and Protestants both accept the 27 books of the New Testament as canonical. These books were written between 50 and 100 A.D. and cover the period from the birth of Jesus Christ to the spread of Christianity through the Roman Empire. They are divided into four parts. The Gospels consist of four books that narrate the life of Christ. The Acts of the Apostles is a single book that describes the spread of Christianity from Rome to Jerusalem. The Epistles are 21 books of letters to churches and individuals. The Apocalypse or Book of Revelation is a series of prophecies about the end of the world.

Therefore, there are 24 books in the Hebrew Bible, 73 in the Roman Catholic, and 66 in the Protestant.

Clive Carpenter, ed., *The Guinness Book of Answers, 9th ed.* (New York: Facts on File, 1993), 342-43.

Why are some editions of the Bible given strange names?

Some early editions of the Bible are named for the typographical or editorial errors found in them. For example, a 1717 Oxford printing uses the title "The parable of the Vinegar," instead of

"The parable of the Vineyard." It is known as the Vinegar Bible. The Wife-hater Bible (1810) misquotes *Luke* xiv, 26: "If any man come to me, and hate not his father and mother . . . yea, and his own wife." The last word should be "life." The Wicked Bible exhorts the faithful to be unfaithful by omitting the word "not" from the seventh commandment. It reads, "Thou shalt commit adultery." This edition was printed in 1631 by Barker and Lucas, the king's printers, who were ruined by the 300 pound fine that this act of negligence had cost them. Among other celebrated printer's errors, *Coverdale's Bible* is sometimes known as the Bug Bible because it reads "Thou shalt not need to be afraid for any bugs by night" in a passage from *Psalms*, using "bugs" instead of terrors in the sentence. The *Unrighteous Bible*, which says that "the unrighteous shall inherit the Kingdom of God"; and the Sin On Bible, which in the book of *John* reads "sin on more" instead of "sin no more." There is even a vegetarian Bible and one with no references to sex.

Robert Hendrickson, *Human Words: The Compleat Unexpurgated, Uncomputerized Human Wordbook* (Radnor, PA: Chilton Book Co., 1972), 28-29. Ivor H. Evans, *Brewer's Dictionary of Phrase and Fable 14th ed.* (New York: Harper & Row, 1989), 110.

According to the Bible, what is the full and proper name of God?

According to Hebrew Scriptures, the full and proper name of God is written with four consonants YHWH. Known as the Tetragrammaton, it is probably pronounced Yahweh. The name was considered so sacred that often the word "Adonai," which means lord, or "Elohim," which is the plural form of the word "majesty," was substituted for it. Because Yahweh was rarely spoken, the proper way of vocalizing it was forgotten. The pronunciation Jehovah, which is common in many older translations, is wrong and is based on a misunderstanding of ancient scribal practices. Although there is some dispute as to its meaning, Yahweh is probably an abbreviated form of "He brings into being whatever exits." The name is used 6,855 times in the Bible.

The Catholic University of America, *The New Catholic Encyclopedia* (New York: McGraw-Hill, 1967), s.v. "Elohim, Yahweh." Ivor H. Evans, *Brewer's Dictionary of Phrase and Fable, 14th ed.* (New York: Harper & Row, 1989), s.v. "Bible."

In what year did Jesus Christ die?

Although the exact year is not known, it is reasoned that Jesus Christ died sometime between 26 and 36 A.D. Those are the years that the Roman procurator Pontius Pilate governed Judea. During this period he tried and condemned Jesus Christ.

ABC's of the Bible (Pleasantville, NY: Reader's Digest Association, 1991), 257. Paul J. Achtemeier, ed., *Harper's Bible Dictionary* (San Francisco, CA: Harper & Row, 1985), s.v. "New Testament."

What was the outcome of Vatican Council II?

Vatican Council II was the 21st ecumenical or general council of the Roman Catholic Church. It was called by Pope John XXIII (1881-1963) and was held in four sessions in Rome between October 1962 and December, 1965. The goal of Vatican II was to spiritually renew the Church, ease reunification efforts with Christians separated from Roman Catholicism, and update its church practices while remaining consistent with its historic tradition. For example, it allowed its major liturgical ceremony, the mass, to be offered in the vernacular instead of Latin, but it kept the doctrine that the mass was a sacrifice in which bread and wine are transformed into the body and blood of Christ. The previous ecumenical council, Vatican I, met in Rome in late 1869 and lasted through most 1870.

An important outcome of Vatican II were the four *Constitutions*. The *Dogmatic Constitution of the Church* dealt with the hierarchical, triumphal, clerical, and judicial structure of the church. The *Dogmatic Constitution on Divine Revelation* focused on the history of the Gospel, and Church tradition and its relation to Scripture. The *Constitution on the Sacred Liturgy* dealt with the Biblical foundation of the liturgy. The *Pastoral Constitution on the Church in the World of Today* was a treatise on the relationship between the Church and a host of temporal activities. These activities included the conflict between good and evil, the role of women, and the effects of the Church on racism, poverty, Marxism, freedom, culture and scholarly research.

New Catholic Encyclopedia (Washington, DC: Catholic University of America, 1967), s.v. "Vatican Council II." Philip W. Goetz, ed., *The New Encyclopedia Britannica, 15th ed.* (Chicago: Encyclopedia Britannica, 1991), s.v. "Vatican Council, second."

Is the often published 1934 photograph of Scotland's Loch Ness monster a hoax?

The Loch Ness monster of Scotland may or may not exist, but the famous photograph of this reputed beast is definitely a fake. In 1994, Christian Spurling on his deathbed described his role in the 1934 published photograph of "Nessie," as the Loch Ness monster was affectionately known. Experts have described the murky image on the photograph as being everything from an otter to a log to a plesiosaur, a dinosaur long thought to be extinct. Spurling claimed he was approached in 1934 by Marmaduke "Duke" Wetherell, a filmmaker and adventurer who persuaded him to mold the fake dinosaur out of a 14-inch toy submarine and plastic wood. The photograph was taken by Wetherell's son Ian.

"Creature May Be Real, But This Photo Wasn't," *Pittsburgh Post-Gazette* 13 March 1994.

What is Valhalla in Teutonic mythology?

Valhalla comes from the Icelandic term, *valhall*, hall of the slain. In Teutonic mythology, it is the dwelling place of heroes after death.

Mario A. Pei, et al., *Dictionary of Foreign Terms* (New York: Delacorte Press, 1975), s.v. "Valhalla."

What was the name of the mythological three-headed dog who guarded the entrance to Hades?

On guard before the gate of Hades, the mythical city of the Underworld, stands Cerberus, the three-headed, dragon-tailed dog, who permits all spirits to enter but none to return.

Edith Hamilton, *Mythology* (Boston: Little, Brown and Co., 1942), 43.

In mythology, what were the five rivers of Hades?

According to the Roman poet Virgil (70 B.C.-19 B.C.), Hades has five rivers, each named for the condition it represents. Acheron, the river of woe, pours into Cocytus, the river of lamentation, where Charon, an aged boatman, ferries the souls of the dead across the water to the farther bank and the adamantine gate. Three other rivers separate the underworld from the world above: Phlegethon, the river of fire; Styx, the river of the unbreakable oath by which the gods swear; and Lethe, the river of forgetfulness.

Edith Hamilton, *Mythology* (Boston: Little, Brown and Co., 1942), 43.

How long did the biblical Methuselah live?

Methuselah (meaning in Hebrew, "man of the deity") was the eighth patriarch listed in the genealogy of the *Bible's* Genesis 5. The son of Enoch and grandfather of Noah, he is said to have lived to the great age of 969 years.

J. D. Douglas, ed., *The Illustrated Bible Dictionary, Part 2* (Sydney: Inter-Varsity Press, 1980), 996.

In the Jewish faith, what is a Shofar, and when is it used?

A Shofar is a ram's horn which is sounded as a call to prayer before or during some Jewish services and feasts. It should be curved in shape and decorated with carvings, but not painted. It may be covered on the outside with gold, as long as the gold does not interfere with its natural sound. The horn is symbolic of the ram tha Abraham sacrificed in place of his son Isaac. When the Shofar is blown by a good and righteous person, it is a sign that the present world order ends and the time of God's order, reign, or presence begins.

Isaac Klein, *A Guide to Jewish Religious Practice* (New York: The Jewish Theological Seminary of America, 1979), 192-94.

Who was Lilith?

Lilith was a sensuous Sumerian "bird-woman" who represented uncontrolled sexuality. Her image appeared on terracotta plaques; she evidently had royal status but was not regarded as a benevolent figure. According to rabbinic legend Lilith was Adam's first wife, who was created simultaneously with him. Because she would not consider him her superior, she was driven out of Eden and fled into the air as a hybrid bird-woman. In medieval times she became a famous witch who was dangerous to children and pregnant women during stormy weather. In Arabic mythology Lilith became the mother of witches when she married the devil.

Elinor W. Gadon, *The Once and Future Goddess* (New York: Harper & Row, 1989), 123-24.

Is a shaman or "medicine man" always a male?

A shaman or "medicine man" may be either male or female. Religions which incorporate the concept of a shaman into their practices are predominantly from the Siberian and Ural-Altaic cultures of the Arctic and central Asia. Elements of shamanism, however, can be found in the cultures of southeast Asia, Oceania, and the aboriginal tribes of North and South America. A shaman, who is sometimes referred to as a medicine man, cures sickness, supervises sacrifices, and is believed to direct the souls of departed to the "other world." Many shamanistic cultures believe that illness is caused by the victim's soul either having wandered away or having been stolen. The shaman thus must either recapture the stolen soul or persuade the errant soul to return to the sick person's body. The procedures by which one becomes a shaman can be quite complex but usually involves an extreme illness or crisis bordering on madness for the would-be shaman, which he or she is able to overcome. Maintaining an environment in which a shaman can continue his or her legitimacy can also be quite complex and is deeply rooted in the mythology, traditions and group psychology of the culture.

Richard Cavendish, ed., *Man, Myth & Magic* (New York: Marshall Cavendish, 1983), 9:2546-49. Rosalie Magio, *The Nonsexist Word Finder: A Dictionary of Gender-Free Usage* (Phoenix, AZ: Oryx Press, 1987), s.v. "shaman."

In Greek legend what was the name of Odysseus' dog?

In Greek legend Argos was the name of Odysseus' dog. However, in the anonymous poem entitled *Ulysses' Dog Aryus*, the spelling of the dog's name varies. The poem related how the aged worn out dog is the first to recognize his long-awaited master when Odysseus returns to Ilion.

Allen Mandelbaum, trans., *The Odyssey of Homer* (Berkeley, CA: University of California Press, 1990), 355. *Notes and Queries: A Monthly of History, Folk-Lore, Mathematics, Literature, Art, Arcane Societies, Etc.* 1901.

Do Chinese legends include vampires?

In China vampires are known as "kuang-shi" or "chiang-shi." The most fearsome ones are described as demons with red glaring eyes, white or greenish hair, and sharp fangs and talons. Like their western counterparts Chinese vampires can fly, appear as a mist or fog, and are allergic to garlic.

Matthew Bunson, *The Vampire Encyclopedia* (New York: Crown Trade Paperbacks, 1993), 46-47.

What is the origin of the Jewish menorah?

Under the direction of Moses, the first menorah was crafted by the artist Bezalel for use in the Tabernacle of the Wilderness. Exodus 37:17 of the Bible describes the shape and details of this work. A menorah holds seven lamps or candles, one on the central stem and three on foliating branches on each side. Light has a significant symbolic meaning in the Jewish religion. It is with light that God is seen and the soul of man is associated with light. As to the significance of seven lamps, there are varying interpretations. Lohar believed that the light signified divine presence; the oil, the Torah; the wick, Israel. The Jewish historian Josephus thought the seven lamps stood for the seven planets that are lit by God. Some thought the seven lights were symbolic of the seven days of the week.

Nathan Ausubel, *The Book of Jewish Knowledge* (New York: Crown Publishers, 1964), 276-77.

What did the goddess Minerva represent?

To the ancient Romans, Minerva was the goddess of wisdom and the patron of crafts and intellectual activity. She was represented holding in her hand an owl, also a symbol of wisdom in her hand.

Veronica Ions, *The World's Mythology in Colour* (London: Hamlyn, 1974), 126.

Who was the first canonized saint from the New World?

The first canonized saint from the New World was St. Rose of Lima. She was born in Lima, Peru, in 1586, died in 1617, and was canonized by Pope Clement X in 1671.

Herbert Thurston and Donald Attwater, eds., *Butler's Lives of the Saints* (New York: P.J. Kenedy & Sons, 1956), 3:444-43.

What are the symbolic representations or attributes of the four evangelists?

The four evangelists are the writers of the first four books of the New Testament, narrating the life of Jesus Christ. They are depicted by symbols that are meant to reflect their messages. John the Evangelist is represented by an eagle because his gospel emphasizes Christ's divine nature, and because the evangelist is often identified with St. John the Apostle, who was especially close to Jesus.

Since in medieval mythology the eagle was able to stare at the sun without blinking, the eagle was considered a fitting symbol for one so close to God. Mark is represented by a winged lion because the lion was a symbol of the Resurrection, the episode with which his gospel ends. Luke's gospel stressed Jesus' sacrifice, so he is represented by an ox, an animal that was used for religious sacrifices in the ancient world. Matthew is represented by a man because in his gospel he gave Jesus' genealogy and thus emphasized the human side of Jesus.

J. C. J. Metford, *Dictionary of Christian Lore and Legend* (London: Thames and Hudson, 1983), s.v. "John the Evangelist," "Luke, St.," "Mark, St.," "Matthew, St."

What legends are associated with Pope Joan?

The legendary Pope Joan supposedly reigned during the ninth century, although written legends (with many variations) about her did not appear until the thirteenth century. She was supposedly an English girl, though born in Mainz, who fell in love with an English monk, disguised herself as a man and followed him to Athens. Later she moved to Rome and worked first as a scribe, then a papal notary to Pope Leo IV, as a cardinal, then Pope when Leo died in 855. There are two legends about Pope Joan's reign—in one she rules for two years and her sex is only discovered after her death. In another, she is pregnant during her election, gives birth during her coronation procession, and is stoned to death by an irate Roman crowd. In yet another version her gender is discovered and she is murdered at the Lateran Palace by a furious crowd.

During the ninth century, there were 24 Italian popes who reigned as head of the Roman Catholic Church. This was a period of moral decline within the Church, and many of these popes ruled for short, nondescript periods of time. Few reliable records were kept regarding the papacy, and since the moral character of some members of the Church hierarchy was questionable, many stories and legends circulated. It is unlikely that Pope Joan existed, even her name is in dispute. Some variations of the story name her Agnes, others call her Ghiberta. One possible source of the stories is the existence of the Theophylact family whose women held some influence over the Bishops of Rome during this time. Despite her shaky status, a statue of Pope Joan was erected in the Siena cathedral around 1400.

Michael Walsh, *An Illustrated History of The Popes* (New York: St. Martin's Press, 1980), 83.

Who are some of the lesser-known patron saints in the Roman Catholic Church?

The saints have long been regarded by Roman Catholics as patrons and intercessors for groups of people, causes, nations, or countries. For example, the patron saint of artists is St. Luke; fathers, St. Joseph; mothers, St. Monica; lost articles, St. Anthony of Padua; skiers, St. Bernard; Americas, St. Rose of Lima; Asia Minor, St. John the Evangelist; workers, St. Rita; astronomers, St. Dominic; bakers, St. Nicholas of Myra; farmers, St. Isidore; natural sciences, St. Albert the Great; tax collectors, St. Matthew (the apostle).

John J. Delaney, *Dictionary of Saints* (Garden City, NY: Doubleday & Co., 1980), 601-3. Don Sharkey, *Popular Patron Saints* (Milwaukee, WI: Bruce Publishing, 1960), 223-26.

What is voodoo and where is it practiced today?

Voodoo is a religion that originated in Africa, probably with the Dahomey or Togo tribes, and traveled to the Americas along with African slaves. It arrived in Saint-Dominique in the late 1600s. The practice of voodoo involves the worship of African gods and spirits through rituals of music, dance, and animal sacrifice. The word "voodoo" may be a corruption of "vaudois," a twelfth-century religious sect founded by Father Valdesius; voodoo is used to describe a god, spirit, or sacred object. The priestess is a "mambo," a priest is a "hungan," meaning "master of the god." African slaves managed to keep the voodoo culture alive in their new homes despite often being forced to accept Christianity through merging identities of a number of African gods with those of acceptable Roman Catholic saints. Thus, Oxossi, the god of the hunt, shares his identity with St. Sebastian; Damballah, god of fertility, is St. Patrick; and Erzulie, the goddess of love, is the Virgin Mary. Because of the negative publicity the sect attracted, voodoo is practiced quietly under various other names in a number of countries today. Brazilians practice several versions of voodoo they call macumba, candomble, and umbanda. In Trinidad the cult is known as shango. Throughout the Caribbean it is known as santeria, and African Americans in the United States call it simply "the religion." There is no international voodoo organization or leader. Communities form locally and informally around a leader/priest.

Pittsburgh Press 4 August 1984. *New York Times* 2 December 1979. Alfred Mtraux, *Voodoo in Haiti* (New York: Schocken Books, 1972), 25-31, 60.

Who was Saint Valentine?

Valentine was a Roman priest who was martyred and killed on February 14, circa 270 A.D. Coincidentally, in mid February the Romans celebrated Lupercalia, a festival held to insure the fertility of people, fields, and animals. Christians countered the pagan festival with one more religious but various legends and customs with fertility overtones continued to surround the date.

Herbert Thurston and Donald Attwater, eds., *Butler's Lives of the Saints, rev. ed.* (New York: P.J. Kenedy & Sons, 1956) 1:332-34. *Good Housekeeping* February 1965.

What are the names and meanings of common Roman Catholic rituals relating to illness, death, and burial?

A number of Roman Catholic rituals relate to illness, death and burial.

"Anointing of the Sick" is a Roman Catholic ritual in which oil is applied to the body of a sick person and prayers are offered. Formerly this ritual was provided at the hour of impending death and was called last rites. After Vatican II (1962-65) it was done at the early stage of a severe illness.

The funeral mass or the Mass of the Resurrection is a worship service of celebration in the Roman Catholic church, usually on the day of burial. Scripture readings are offered on the Christian meaning of death, followed by a Eucharistic prayer and the communion rite. The mass starts with a rite of greeting the body of the deceased and concludes with a rite of commendation. Formerly this rite was sometimes referred to as a "requiem mass." "Month's Mind Mass" is a worship service conducted a month after a funeral mass or the Mass of the Resurrection. Anniversary masses may be held annually in remembrance of the dead. "Pall" refers to the covering placed over the casket at the introduction to the Mass of the Resurrection. The ensuing prayer connects the white garment given a Christian at baptism with the pall provided at death. "Paschal Candle" is a special candle that is lit during the Easter vigil and whose flame symbolizes new life in Jesus Christ. This candle stands prominently in the church throughout the year and is lit at funerals and baptisms to symbolize oneness with the dead and risen Jesus Christ and to signify that in those two events, humans also pass with Jesus Christ from death to life. "Viaticum" is the last communion given to the dying, in which the sacrament of communion is the consecrated bread eaten during the celebration of mass, which becomes the body of Jesus Christ. Special formulas are used to aid the person at the hour of death. "Wake" is the period of time from death until the funeral mass or the mass of the Resurrection. It is usually a special period of hours during which friends visit the family of the deceased and offer prayers at the casket.

Earl A. Grollman, ed., *Concerning Death: A Practical Guide for the Living* (Boston: Beacon Press, 1974), 111-112.

What are the titles and order of the books of the Old Testament?

These are the books of the Old Testament of the Bible derive from the Septuagint, which is the Greek version of the Hebrew scriptures. Both Roman Catholics and Protestants accept these books. In addition, the Catholics accept seven more books from the Septuagint as genuine parts. These seven books together are called the Deuterocanonica by the Catholics and Apocrypha by the Protestants, who believe them to be nongenuine.

The books common to both Catholics and Protestants are:

Genesis
Exodus
Leviticus
Numbers
Deuteronomy
Joshua (called Josue by Catholics)
Judges
Ruth
1 Samuel (called First Book of Kings by Catholics)
2 Samuel (called Second Book of Kings by Catholics)
1 Kings (called Third Book of Kings by Catholics)
2 Kings (called Fourth Book of Kings by Catholics)
1 Chronicles (called First Book of Paralipomenon by Catholics)
2 Chronicles (called Second Book of Paralipomenon by Catholics)
Ezra (called First Book of Esra by Catholics)
Nehemiah (called Second Book of Esra by Catholics)
Esther
Job
Psalms
Proverbs
Ecclesiastes
Song of Solomon (called Canticle of Canticles by Catholics)
Isaiah (called Isaias by Catholics)
Jeremiah (called Jeremaias by Catholics)
Lamentations
Ezekiel (called Ezechiel by Catholics)
Daniel
Hosea (called Osea by Catholics)
Joel
Amos
Obadiah (called Abdias by Catholics)
Jonah (called Jonas by Catholics)
Micah (called Micheas by Catholics)
Nahum
Habakkuk (called Habacuc by Catholics)
Zephaniah (called Sophonias by Catholics)
Haggai (called Aggeus by Catholics)
Zechariah (called Zacharias by Catholics)
Malachi (called Malachias by Catholics)

The seven books that the Roman Catholics believe to be part of the Old Testament are Tobias, Judith, Wisdom of Solomon, Sirach, Baruch, and the First and Second Books of Machabees.

The Holy Bible: Revised Standard Version (New York: Collins, 1973), xiii. Clive Carpenter, ed., *The Guinness Book of Answers, 9th ed.* (New York: Facts on File, 1993), 342-43.

Why is there a ban on Catholics becoming Freemasons?

Pope John Paul II (1920-) reaffirmed the ban on becoming Freemasons that is imposed on all Roman Catholics. Disobeying the ban invites excommunication from the church. The Freemasons, which were formed in Florence, Italy, in 1732, is a secret society that the Vatican fears could take the place of religion.

Peter Hebblewaite, "Pope, Masons Debate Who is Most Occult," *National Catholic Reporter* 24 May 1991. *New York Times* 3 March 1981.

How did the Nation of Islam evolve?

The first Nation of Islam temple was established in Detroit in the 1920s. Founded by Wallace Delaney Fard, it marked the birth of the Black Muslim sect known as the Nation of Islam. Fard taught his followers that Islam was the true religion of all blacks, and introduced them to orthodox Islamic teachings. He also preached that whites were evil, that blacks would come to have power over whites, and that he was the messiah. In 1934, Fard disappeared and Elijah Muhammad (1897-1975), the former Robert Poole, became the head of the Black Muslim movement.

Over the course of the next 30 years, a following grew in Chicago, Detroit, and New York, as well as in the nation's prisons. During that time ex-convict Malcolm Little joined the Detroit temple, became known as Malcolm X (1925-1965), and was made a national spokesman for the Nation of Islam. He became a more popular figure than Elijah Muhammad in the early 1960s. When U.S. President John F. Kennedy (1917-1963) was assassinated, he made comments such as "The old devil is dead," putting himself in the national spotlight and alienating himself from Muhammad. He left the organization in 1964, to establish his own Muslim Mosque Inc. and to participate in the civil rights movement. On February 21, 1965, Malcolm X was killed by Nation of Islam gunmen. Ten years later, Elijah Muhammad died and was succeeded by his aide Louis Farrakhan, who drew new media attention to the group. Muhammad's son, Warith Deen, had meanwhile left the movement to start his own sect, following more traditional Muslim teachings.

USA Today 18 November 1992.

What is galgal?

Galgal, or gilgal, is the site of an early Israelite sanctuary in the area of the eastern limits of Jericho. It was the site of Israel's encampment across the Jordan River and the place from which Israel set out to conquer the Holy Land.

The Hebrew name "gilgal" means "circle" of stones, indicating a sanctuary that was already in existence before the arrival of Israel.

New Catholic Encyclopedia (Washington, DC: Catholic University of America, 1967), s.v. "Galgal."

What are the four major groups within Buddhism?

The four major groups within Buddhism and their basic precepts are as follows:

Hinayana or Theravada which stresses monastic discipline and the attainment of *Nirvana* through meditation.

Mahayana in which virtue, wisdom and idealism is emphasized by its adherents.

Mantrayana which has a structure of spiritual leaders and disciples who believe in evil spirits and deities. Its secret rituals often include magic.

Zen has a more informal structure of leaders and disciples who seek enlightenment through introspection and intuition.

Poughkeepsie Journal 8 July 1994.

Who were the Gorgons?

In classical mythology, the three Gorgons were snake-haired monsters named Stheno, Euryale, and Medusa. The classical Greek dramatist Euripides (ca. 484 B.C.-406 B.C.), in his *Ion* writes that the goddess Ge brought forth the Gorgon to help her children, the Giants, in their battles with the gods. Other tales have the Gorgons springing forth from the union of the ancient sea god Phorcys and his sea monster sister Ceto.

The hideous Gorgons are said to have brazen hands and wings of gold. They have red tongues and tusks. Of the three, only Medusa was mortal. She was murdered by Perseus.

Edward Tripp, *Crowell's Handbook of Classical Mythology* (New York: Thomas Y. Crowell, 1970), s.v. "Gorgons."

What was a centaur?

In Greek mythology, a centaur was a creature with the chest, arms, and head of a man but the body and legs of a horse. Centaurs lived on Mount Pelion in Thessaly and symbolized hedonism bordering on barbarism.

M. C. Howatson, ed., *The Oxford Companion to Classical Literature, 2d ed.* (Oxford: Oxford University Press, 1989), s.v. "centaurs."

What did the Egyptian goddess Isis personify?

The Egyptian goddess Isis personified the female creative power from which all living things spring forth. She was viewed as a kind and beneficent earth-mother whose love and influence was pervasive throughout the universe and the afterlife. She was also the best example of a faithful, loving wife and mother.

Anthony S. Mercatante, *Who's Who In Egyptian Mythology* (New York: Clarkson N. Potter, 1978), s.v. "Isis."

What was the "tree of life" from which the dead received nourishment in Paradise?

In Paradise, the dead received nourishment from the sycamore fig, also known as the "tree of life."

Donald A. Mackenzie, *The Migration of Symbols and their Relations to Beliefs and Symbols* (1926; reprint, Detroit, MI: Gale Research, 1968), 159.

In the Roman Catholic Church, when does "Spy Wednesday" occur?

In the Roman Catholic Church, "Spy Wednesday" is the Wednesday during Holy Week. It is traditionally believed that during this time Judas Iscariot was "spying" on Jesus Christ to betray Him. The Passion of the Mass on this day makes reference to the betrayer Judas.

Albert J. Nevins, ed., *The Maryknoll Catholic Dictionary* (New York: Dimension Books, 1965), s.v. "Spy Wednesday."

Which nineteenth-century British theologian was central to the development of fundamentalism?

The nineteenth-century British theologian John Nelson Darby (1800-1882) became important in the development of fundamentalism. When he broke with the Church of England in 1827 he founded small religious communities that were independent of allegiance to any one church.

J. Gordon Melton, *Encyclopedia of American Religions, 4th ed.* (Detroit, MI: Gale Research Inc., 1993), 107.

How did the Ukrainian independence affected religion and religions practices?

The very religious people of the Ukraine had, under the auspices of communism, been grouped into one church-Russian Orthodox. When independence came, this situation changed. The Russian Orthodox church split into three different denominations: the Ukranian Catholic Church, the Ukranian Orthodox branch of the Russian Orthodox Church and the Ukranian Autocephalous Orthodox Church.

The Ukranian Catholic Church (UCC) had been in existence since 1596, and was a popular religion among Eastern Christians. The Ukranian Autocephalous Orthodox Church (UAOC) had been born during the Ukranian independence movement (1917-21), but was squashed when the Ukraine joined the Soviet Union. The UAOC had experienced a rebirth during the German occupation of World War II (1939-45), but it was crushed when the Ukraine again became part of the Soviet Union.

Stephen K. Batalden and Sandra L. Batalden, *The Newly Independent States of Eurasia: Handbook of Former Soviet Republics* (Phoenix, AZ: Oryx, 1993), 75-77.

Who are the Falashas?

The Falashas are the black Jews of Ethiopia, who call themselves Beth Israel, or in English, House of Israel. Officially affirmed as Jewish by the Israeli religious authorities, the Falashas claim to be descendants of King Solomon and the Queen of Sheba. Most historical authorities do not verify this union, however, but do date that the Falashas may be descendants of the tribe of Dan.

Falasha is an Amharic word. Amharic is a Semitic language and the official language of Ethiopia. The word has a negative connotation and is given to many different shades of meaning. In the mildest sense it can be translated as meaning stranger.

Others translate it as outcast or outsider. For many, however, the word means illegitimate or bastard.

New York Times Magazine 27 January 1985.

What is the original name of the leader of the Nation of Islam, Louis Farrakhan?

Nation of Islam leader Louis Farrakhan was born Louis Eugene Walcott in New York City in 1933. Educated at the Winston-Salem Teachers College in North Carolina, Farrakhan was performing in a Caribbean-style night club act when he came to the attention of Malcolm X who was then a minister for Elijah Muhammad. Muhammad was a controversial Black leader who advocated separatism and conversion to the Muslim religion for Black Americans. Malcolm X was assassinated in 1965 and Farrakhan replaced him as the head of the Harlem mosque and has since become the leader of the Nation of Islam. Farrakhan has created controversy with his inflammatory rhetoric punctuated by what his critics call strident anti-Semitism. Farrakhan has at times worked closely with mainstream Black leaders such as Jesse Jackson and has been active in the fight against drugs and crime in the Black community. Louis Farrakhan is his Muslim name.

Barbara Carlisle Bigelow, ed., *Contemporary Black Biography* (Detroit: Gale Research, 1992), 2:70-74. *Life* August 1984.

Which Aztec god is the guardian of the milk-yielding tree of Paradise?

Texcatlipoca, the god of the north, is the Aztec guardian of the milk-yielding tree of Paradise. The tree is mentioned in the Hindu sacred book, *Mah bh rata.*

Donald A. Mackenzie, *The Migration of Symbols* (New York: Alfred A. Knopf, 1926), 169.

What are the Sirens?

In legend Sirens are women of the underworld who are particularly dangerous to men. Their first appearance is in Book 12 of *The Odyssey* where they were portrayed as beautiful women who would lure sailors into abandoning ship and swimming ashore. Once ashore, the men were doomed to a miserable death surrounded by the bones and rotting corpses of other luckless sailors.

Richard Cavendish, ed., *Man, Myth, and Magic* (New York: Marshall Cavendish, 1983), s.v. "Sirens."

What are carlings and when is Carling Sunday?

Carlings are gray peas which are soaked in water and then fried in butter. This is a culinary dish from the north of England, often served on the fifth Sunday of Lent, which is known as Palm Sunday or Carling Sunday. Carlings are also termed parched peas.

Priscilla Sawyer Lord and Daniel J. Foley, *Easter Garland* (Philadelphia: Chilton, 1963), 52.

For what is Saint Brendan of Ireland best known?

Brendan, a popular Irish saint and patron saint of sailors, was probably born near Tralee, Kerry, Ireland, circa 484. He was sent to St. Jarlath's monastic school in Tuam and eventually founded numerous monasteries in Ireland. Best known for his seven-year voyage in a hide-covered boat in which he journeyed in the middle of the sixth century to the Land of Promise, he later wrote of his adventures in *Navigatio Sancti Brendani Abbatis.* This epic saga, very popular in the Middle Ages, was translated into most European languages. Although many scholars doubted the veracity of Brendan's voyages, in 1976 Tim Severin, an expert on exploration, traveled over many of Brendan's claimed routes in a "curragh," a hide-covered boat. Severin demonstrated the accuracy of the directions and descriptions of the places cited by Brendan.

John J. Delaney, *Dictionary of Saints* (Garden City, NY: Doubleday & Co., 1980), 117-18.

Who was the only twentieth century pope to be made a saint?

Pope Pius X (1835-1914) was the only pope in the twentieth century to be made a saint. Born Giuseppe Melchiorre Sarto in the village of Riese in Northern Italy, he attended a seminary in Padua and, after ordination in 1858, spent the next seventeen years as a parish priest in the diocese of Treviso. As a man of outstanding ability, he was made bishop of Mantua in 1884 and patriarch of Venice in 1893, before being elected pope on August 4, 1903. He was very interested in social issues, particularly in relieving the miserable conditions of the poor. In addition, he began reforms in church music and ecclesiastical laws. Pius X denounced anti-Catholic legislation in France and South America and upheld the rights of the church in Italy. Known as the "Pope of the Eucharist," he fostered devotion to the Catholic belief that Jesus is physically present in liturgically consecrated bread and wine. His decree of December 20, 1905, entitled *Tridentina Synodus,* recommended that the faithful partake of the sacrament more frequently. He also encouraged children to receive it, although previous practice had restricted its reception to adults. Heartbroken over the outbreak of World War I (1914-18), he died of congestion on August 20, 1914. He was canonized a saint on May 29, 1954.

The Catholic University of America, *The New Catholic Encyclopedia* (New York: McGraw-Hill, 1967), s.v. "Pius X, Pope, St."

Who was the first non-Italian Pope of recent history?

Pope John Paul II (1920-) was the first non-Italian Pope in the Roman Catholic Church since the death of Pope Hadrian VI, a Dutchman in 1523. In 1942 Karol Wojtyla enrolled in a seminary in Krakow, Poland, which was operating illegally under the Nazi occupation of Poland during World War II (1939-1945). Wojytla was ordained a priest in 1946 and in 1978 became the 264th bishop of Rome.

Pittsburgh Post-Gazette 17 October 1978.

What is "Maundy Thursday"?

"Maundy Thursday" is the Thursday before Easter. The word "Maundy" comes from a French word that has its origins in the Latin *mandatum* or "commandment." It refers to when Jesus Christ washed the feet of his disciples, telling them "A new commandment I give to you..." The Roman Catholic Church still observes the ceremonial custom of the washing of the feet on Maunday Thursday, also called Holy Thursday.

Leslie Dunkling, *A Dictionary of Days* (New York: Facts On File, 1988), 74.

What is a will-o'-the-wisp?

In folklore a will-o'-the-wisp is a flame carried by an elfin creature. In many folk tales, however, the creature carrying the flame more resembles a ghost than an elf. Depending on the country in which the particular legend is being told, the elf or ghost-like creature is usually inhabited by the soul of a still-born and unbaptized child, a boundary-stone mover, a swindler, or a usurer. The will-o'-the-wisp stories originated to explain the phosphorescent lighting often seen in swampy areas after dark. At sea this phenomenon is known as St. Elmo's fire. It is also called ignis fatuus, wildfire, friar's lantern, Jack-o'-Lantern, foxfire, and fair maiden of Ireland.

Nancy Arrowsmith, *Field Guide to the Little People* (New York: Hill and Wang, 1977), 34-36. Ad de Vries, *Dictionary of Symbols and Imagery* (Amsterdam: North-Holland, 1974), s.v. "will o' the wisp."

Did many Popes have relatively brief reigns?

Quite a number of Popes had relatively short reigns. Of the 262 Popes since Linus I, who succeeded Peter in 67 A.D., 45 have died less than a year after their elections. Although technically not a Pope, in 752 a priest named Stephen died three days after his election (but prior to his consecration).

Time 9 October 1978.

What is the name of the prayer shawl worn by Jewish men at their weddings?

The prayer shawl worn by Jewish men at their weddings is called a "tallith." Jewish men are also buried with their tallith over their shoulders.

Anita Compton, *Marriage Customs* (New York: Thomson Learning, 1993), 220.

What was the origin of the "Black Mass"?

The "Black Mass" describes a "mass" held to mock the real Roman Catholic ceremony. in which the Lufibel is honored. Black Masses were reportedly held as early as the fifteenth century, according to trial records of Brescia in Lombardy, and by so-called degenerates of the court of Louis XIV (1638-1715) during the Chambre Ardente affair. The Black Mass is often associated with the Witch Sabbat, or Witches Sabbath.

Wade Baskin, *The Sorcerer's Handbook* (New York: Philosophical Library, 1974), 92-93.

What influence did the Bible have on early American history?

The beginnings of European settlements along the Atlantic seaboard of America coincided with the publication of one of the first English translations of the Bible. Appearing in 1560 the Genevan Bible was popular because of its size, price, and Calvinistic notes. Between 1560 and 1640 it went through 160 editions and came to be regarded as the "Puritan's Bible." The King James version which appeared in 1611 was likewise popular. These two books had tremendous influence, both moral and cultural, on colonial settlers.

Following the American Revolution there was little doubt that the new nation would be largely Christian. The American Bible Society, the American Tract Society, and the American Sunday School Union all promoted Christianity by distributing Bibles to westward-bound pioneers and in frontier settlements. Many historians feel that the Bible played a great role in the many reform movements, such as anti-slavery and temperance, that shaped the American social landscape.

Dictionary of American History, rev. ed. (New York: Charles Scribner's Sons, 1973), s.v. "Bible." John Shea, "The Bible in American History," *American Catholic Quarterly Review* 3 January 1878.

What is the Ghost Dance?

The Ghost Dance is a Native American religious movement that was popular in the late 1800s. Although the beliefs and rituals were not identical in each tribe, there were common beliefs in the white man's disappearance, the return of the dead and the buffalo, and the Indians' reclamation of their land. During the ritual dances it was not uncommon for a dancer to enter a trance during which the dancer envisioned a reunion with deceased relatives. The practice died out after the U.S. Army's massacre of the Indians at Wounded Knee, South Dakota.

The Encyclopedia Americana (Toronto: Grolier, 1990).

Which Egyptian pharaoh promoted the idea of monotheism?

Akhenaten, originally named Amenhotep IV (1353-1335 B.C.), was called the "heretic pharaoh" in some contemporary chronicles because he insisted upon exclusive worship of Aten, the sun god. Soon after beginning his 18-year reign, Akhenaten repudiated his allegiance to the god Amon and moved the court site to Middle Egypt along the Nile River where he ordered a new capital city to be built. He called it Akhetaten (meaning "the Horizon of Aten"); its modern-day name is el-Armana.

Akhenaten's name meant "He Who is of Service to Aten," and he tried to prove himself worthy of the title. His insistence upon the sole cult of Aten brought radical changes in Egyptian religious life. The great temples of Thebes, Memphis, and Heliopolis were deprived of their income-producing estates, with the money reverting to the crown. Akhenaten, whose most famous wife was Nefertiti, was so unpopular that after his death, his mummified remains were destroyed and almost all other traces of his reign were abolished.

Margaret Bunson, *The Encyclopedia of Ancient Egypt* (New York: Facts On File, 1991), 11-12.

Who were the "Ten Lost Tribes," and what happened to them?

The "Ten Lost Tribes" is the name given to ten major Jewish tribes who ruled the northern kingdom of Israel during biblical times. The members of these tribes were enslaved by the Assyrians between 721 B.C. and 715 B.C. During this time, they were exiled from Israel and dispersed throughout the world. The ultimate fate of the Ten Lost Tribes is uncertain. Scholars have debated and theorized about the existence of the Ten Lost Tribes, suggesting that peoples throughout the globe, such as the Japanese and the British, may be descendants. Many Jews believe that the redemption of the world will occur when all of the tribes of Israel, including the Ten Lost Tribes, are reunited.

Geoffrey Wigoder, ed., *Encyclopedic Dictionary of Judaica* (New York: Leon Amiel Publisher, 1974), s.v. "ten lost tribes." Geoffrey Wigoder, ed., *The New Standard Jewish Encyclopedia, 7th ed.* (New York: Facts on File, 1992), s.v. "tribes, lost ten."

In the Islamic world what is the significance of the Hegira?

In the Islamic world the Hegira, or Hejira (taken from the Arabic word "Higrah" or "Hijrah" meaning flight or emigration) was the Prophet Muhammad's 622 A.D. journey from Mecca to Medina to avoid persecution. This event represents the beginning of the Muslim era, which is abbreviated in dates as A.H. (for Anno Hegirae, meaning in the year of the Hegira). Caliph Umar I introduced this new commemorative dating system, having the first year A.H. correspond to the first day of the lunar month of Muharram (i.e. July 16, 622 A.D.).

Philip W. Goetz, ed., *Encyclopedia Britannica, 15th ed., "Micropedia"* (Chicago: Encyclopedia Britannica, 1989), s.v. "hegira."

What is the Egyptian Book of the Dead?

The Egyptian Book of the Dead refers to various mortuary texts of spells and magic incantations that were placed in tombs with the belief that they would aid the deceased in the afterlife. Books of the Dead, including the Coffin and Pyramid texts, date from 2400 B.C. to 2000 B.C. The various texts, including hymns to Re, the Sun god, were written or compiled by various authors.

Encyclopedia Britannica (Chicago: Encyclopedia Britannica, 1989), s.v. "Book of the Dead."

What ironic fact added to the tragedy of the panic and stampede at the Shiloh Baptist Church in Birmingham, Alabama, in 1902?

At the Shiloh Baptist Church in Birmingham, Alabama, in 1902, a panic and stampede led to the death of 115 people who mistakenly believed the church was on fire. Tragically and ironically there was no fire. Someone yelled the word "fight" during an altercation in the choir, but the church attendees thought they heard the word "fire."

Woody Gelman and Barbara Jackson, *Disaster Illustrated* (New York: Harmony Books, 1976), 50.

What does the bear represent to Native Americans?

The bear represents immortality and the self-existent to Native Americans. This belief stems from the animal's winterly hibernation habits-it was originally thought to rise from the dead each spring.

Gertrude Jobes, *Dictionary of Mythology, Folklore and Symbols* (New York: Scarecrow Press, 1962), 1:189.

What was the Great Awakening?

The Great Awakening was a religious revival that occurred in the American colonies during the 1740s. Jonathan Edwards (1703-1758), a Massachusetts clergyman and theologian, was one of the main leaders of the crusade to restore stricter, fundamentalist Protestant values to an increasingly prosperous and secular population. Edwards "became famous for his fire-and-brimstone, pit-of-hell sermons, which provoked near hysteria in his listeners." Edwards influenced another cleric, George Whitefield (1714-1770), whose name is also associated with the Great Awakening. Thousands attended Whitefield's outdoor declamations, and even noted cynic Benjamin Franklin was said to have been impressed by Whitefield's oratory talents.

Kenneth C. Davis, *Don't Know Much About History* (New York: Crown Publishers, 1990), 39.

Was Noah of biblical fame known by any other names?

Noah of Biblical fame was called that name by his grandfather Methuselah. Methuselah used that name because "the earth was appeased" by his grandson's later activities. Among other theories to the name's significance include "he that caused rest," "the pleasant one," or "he that will comfort the earth after all of the destruction." Noah's father Lemach, however, referred to his son as Menahem.

Louis Ginzberg, *The Legends of the Jews* (Philadelphia: Jewish Publication Society of America, 1925), 168.

In classical mythology who was the queen of the Amazons?

In classical mythology Hippolyte was the queen of the Amazons, a race of female warriors who were said to dwell near the Black Sea.

Robert E. Bell, *Women of Classical Mythology* (Santa Barbara, CA: ABC-CLIO, 1991), 30.

Who was the first African American admitted to priesthood in the Mormon Church?

Joseph Freeman Jr. was the first African American admitted to priesthood in the Mormon Church. The 26-year-old telephone repairman was ordained on June 11, 1978, in Salt Lake City.

Pittsburgh Post-Gazette 12 June 1978.

What were the labors of Hercules?

In order to achieve immortality, Hercules was required to successfully perform twelve difficult tasks that are commonly known as the "twelve labors of Hercules." The first was to slay the Nemean lion, a monstrous animal immune to weapons. Hercules strangled the animal with his bare hands. The second labor was to kill the Hydra, a hideous, many-headed creature that was related to the Nemean lion. Hercules drove the Hydra from its lair with burning arrows and began hacking at its heads with his sword, only to find that each time he cut off a head, two more popped up to replace it. Hercules called out for help to his friend Iolaus, who came with burning brands; thereafter, each time Hercules chopped off a head, Iolaus cauterized the wound so that more were unable to grow. In this way, the two slowly destroyed the Hydra. Hercules was next required to capture a golden-horned deer, the Cerynitian hind, that was sacred to Artemis. After a year of stalking the animal, he caught it—some accounts say through the use of nets, while others state that he approached it while it slept. As his fourth labor, Hercules was told to capture alive yet another animal, the Erymanthian boar. He trapped the huge creature in the deep snows of Mount Erymanthus.

After capturing the boar, Hercules was briefly distracted by the quest of Jason and the Argonauts for the golden fleece. He joined their expedition for a time, and when he returned to his labors, he was punished for his lack of attention with the assignment of the most humiliating task of his career: that of cleaning out the incredibly filthy Augeian stables in a single day. Hercules broke down the walls of the corral near the stables and diverted the rivers Alpheius and Peneius to sweep away the immense deposits of dung. For his sixth labor, he was told to chase away the Stymphalian birds, which had become so numerous on Lake Stymphalus that they were considered a nuisance. Hercules used some type of noisemaker to frighten the birds into flight. He shot great numbers of them, and the remainder were scared away. Hercules next captured the Cretan bull—the father of the Minotaur. His eighth labor was to catch the mares of Diomedes. Diomedes was a savage king who fed these four mares on human flesh. Hercules overpowered the king's groom, drove the wild mares into the sea, and then calmed them by feeding Diomedes to them.

For his ninth labor, Hercules was told to fetch the belt of Hippolyte, queen of the Amazons. After a long voyage, he reached Hippolyte's kingdom, and she agreed to give him her belt. The goddess Hera was angry that Hercules had had so little difficulty with this labor, so she posed as an Amazon and told Hippolyte's subjects that Hercules was kidnapping the queen. In the ensuing confusion, Hercules killed Hippolyte and took the belt. The tenth labor was to capture the cattle of Geryon, king of Erytheia. The herd was guarded by a herdsman named Eurytion and his two-headed hound, Orthus. Hercules slew them both with his club and made off with the cattle. His eleventh labor was to take possession of the apples of the Hesperides, a golden fruit that grew somewhere at the ends of the earth. Hercules eventually gained his prize and proceeded to undertake his twelfth and final labor: to bring up from Hades Cerberus, a many-headed hound with a snake's tail, who was brother to the Hydra and the Nemean lion. After many adventures in the underworld, Hercules dragged the hellhound to the surface, successfully completing his twelve labors.

Edward Tripp, *Crowell's Handbook of Classical Mythology* (n.p.: Thomas Y. Crowell, 1970).

Which gemstone is the emblem of the Muslim faith?

The semi-precious gemstone known as carnelian-a reddish-colored variety of chalcedony-is the emblem of the Muslim faith. It is sometimes called the rattatua.

P. N. Scherman, *Gems and Their Occult Powers, 3d ed.* (Kanpur, India: Self-published, 1979), 68.

What is the meaning of the term "Ishmaelite"?

"Ishmaelite" is a term that refers specifically to the descendants of Ishmael, but it is also applied in a broader sense to all members of Middle Eastern desert tribes. In Chapter 17 of the book of Genesis, God informs Abraham that He will establish His covenant with Isaac-who will be born to Abraham's wife Sarah-and with Isaac's descendants. Referring to Ishmael, the son of Abraham and the slave-woman Hagar, God promises only that He will beget twelve princes that will form the foundation of a great nation.

Ishmael's sons are later listed in Genesis as Nebajoth, Kedar, Adbeel, Mibsam, Mishma, Dumah, Massa, Hadar, Tema, Jetur, Naphish, and Kedemah. Each became the patriarch of a great desert tribe. Thus, Arabs were originally close kin to the Hebrews, but from the earliest days, the relationship between the two groups was often hostile. In Genesis 16:12, Ishmael himself is referred to as "a wild man; his hand shall be against every man, and every man's hand against him." Eventually, the term "Ishamelite" came to be used to describe any desert nomad or bedouin, not just those with traceable lineage to Ishmael himself.

Geoffrey W. Bromiley et al., *The International Standard Bible Encyclopedia* (Exeter: Paternoster Press, 1982), 2:906. *Holy Bible, New King James Version* (Nashville, TN: Thomas Nelson, 1982), 14, 23. Paul Kevin Meagher, Thomas C. O'Brien, and Sister Consuelo Maria, eds., *Encyclopedic Dictionary of Religion* (Philadelphia: Corpus Publications, 1979), 1:241.

What religious sects may be described as being fundamentalist?

The term "fundamentalist," as it refers to religious sects, became popular in America in the 1920s as a Protestant reaction to "modernism." Fundamentalists meant to protect their perception of the basic fundamentals of the Christian faith and Biblical doctrine. Much importance was placed on the literal interpretation of the Bible in terms of doctrinal infallibility. The roots of this movement, however, can be traced to the nineteenth century when evolution, biblical criticism, comparative religion, and other "modernist" movements began. In 1910 a group of conservative scholars wrote a series of publications called "The Fundamentals" in opposition to "modernism" and other avant-garde theological movements.

During the latter half of the twentieth century, however, the term "fundamentalist" was being used to describe any religious group which interprets religious text literally and imposes rigorous daily regulations on its followers. Often grouped under this latter definition are Moslems, Orthodox Jews, and other non-Protestant sects.

Irving Hexham, *Concise Dictionary of Religion* (Downers Grove, IL: Inter-Varsity Press, 1993), s.v. "fundamentalism." Marilyn Elias, "Strict Religious Faith Lifts Mind As Well As Spirit," *USA Today* 2 August 1993.

What are the largest cathedrals in the world?

The six largest cathedrals in the world are St. Peter's in Rome, with 227,069 square feet; the Seville in Spain, with 128,570 square feet; St. John the Divine in New York, with 121,000 square feet; Liverpool Cathedral in England, with 101,000 square feet; the Milan Cathedral in Italy, with 92,600 square feet; and the National Cathedral in Washington, D.C., with 83,012 square feet.

USA Today 20 June 1990.

Who is the Roman Catholic patron saint of the United States?

In 1846 at the Sixth Provincial Council of Baltimore, the American Roman Catholic bishops made Mary, the mother of Jesus and under her title the Immaculate Conception, the patroness of the United States. The Immaculate Conception, which is often confused with the virgin birth, refers to the Roman Catholic belief that Mary was born without the stain of original sin. According to Catholic theology, all human beings have inherited a proclivity toward sin that would make their redemption impossible, if it were not for the merits that Jesus earned for them through his passion and death. Only Mary, who by giving birth to Jesus was the vehicle through whom God became man, was exempted from that condition. Although it is based on a tradition of the early church, the doctrine of the Immaculate Conception did not become Catholic dogma until it was proclaimed by Pope Pius IX (1792-1878) in 1854.

The Catholic University of America, *The New Catholic Encyclopedia* (New York: McGraw-Hill, 1967), s.v. "immaculate conception."

What is the name of the oldest and most flourishing Christian communal group in North America?

The Hutterian Brethren is the oldest and most flourishing of all family-type Christian communes in North America. Also known as the Hutterites, this branch of Anabaptist Christians trace their beginnings to Jacob Hutter and a founding date of 1528. Unlike their Anabaptist counterparts, the Amish and Mennonites, the Hutterites hold "all things common." The group underwent much persecution in the 1600s and 1700s and were forced to move eastward through Moravia, Transylvania, Slovakia, and the Ukraine. Living in Russia until 1870 they began leaving en masse to the United States between 1874 and

1877. The group settled in South Dakota but during World War I their unpopular pacifist stance forced them to move once again, this time to Canada. After the war, however, many returned to the United States. By the 1980s there were 250 Bruderhofs or colonies in Canada and the midwestern United States with a total population of 30,000. All Hutterite property is held in common by the Bruderhof, most of which allow a maximum number of 150 members. Administration of each Bruderhof is the responsibility of five or six men who are elected for life. Each Bruderhof has a minister with both secular and spiritual responsibilities.

Mircea Eliade, *The Encyclopedia of Religion* (New York: Macmillan, 1987), s.v. "Hutterian Brethren." John A. Hostetler, *Hutterite Life* (Scottdale, PA: Herald Press, 1983), 3.

What does "hare" stand for in the Hare Krishna movement?

In the Hare Krishna movement "hare" represents the god Krishna's energy. The Hare Krishna movement is more formally known as the International Society For Krishna Consciousness (ISKCON). It is a proselytizing, missionary form of devotional Hinduism that was brought to the United States in 1965 by devotees of Krishna. Their purpose is to convert the world and particularly the English-speaking peoples to "God-consciousness." One of their hallmarks is the public chanting of the Hare Krishna mantra. It is believed that this constant repetition of God's name is an aid to salvation.

Mircea Eliade, *The Encyclopedia of Religion* (New York: Macmillan, 1987), s.v. "International Society for Krishna Consciousness." Judah J. Stillson, *Hare Krishna and the Counterculture* (New York: John Wiley & Sons, 1974), 96-97.

Has the resting site of Noah's Ark ever been found?

In 1984 explorers from the United States found a boat-shaped impression on Mount Ararat, Turkey, that is believed to be the resting site of Noah's Ark. The impression matches biblical measurements of the ark as they are given in Chapter 6 of the Book of Genesis. The expedition that found the site 5,200 feet up the southern slope of Mount Ararat included former U.S. astronaut James Irwin.

Pittsburgh Press 26 August 1984. *USA Today* 28 August 1984.

What are symbolic foods served at the Passover Seder meal?

The six symbolic foods included on a Passover Seder tray include maror, bitter herbs often in the form of horseradish; karpas, a vegetable such as lettuce, parsley, or potato; chazeret, a more bitter vegetable such as radish, cucumber, or watercress; charoset or charoses, a mixture of apples and nuts; zeroa, usually a roasted shankbone of a lamb or chicken; and baytza, a roasted hard boiled egg. Each item has significance for the Passover, which commemorates the escape of the Jews from Egypt.

The maror and chazeret symbolize the bitterness of the Israelites existence as slaves in Egypt. The karpas are there by custom. The charoset is a remembrance of the mortar that was made by the Jews during their captivity in Egypt. Zeroa represents the arm of God that delivered the Israelites out of pharoah's hands. Baytza represents either the sacrifice or the mourning for the loss of the two temples in Jerusalem.

In addition to the foods of the Seder Tray, matza is eaten. Matza, or mazzah, is an unleavened bread that is eaten in remembrance of the quick escape from Egypt, which left no time for the breads to rise.

The middle of the three portions of the matza on the Seder Tray is the "afikoman," of which all who participate in the Passover service will partake. The leader of the service will hide the afikoman in a napkin during the service, and it is customary for the children attending to find it and be rewarded.

Alfred J. Kolatch, *The Jewish Book of Why* (New York: Jonathan David Publishers, 1981), 190-201. *A Passover Haggadah* (New York: Central Conference of American Rabbis, 1975), 26.

What is the "Holy See"?

The word "see" derives from the Latin "sedes," which means seat or residence, and the term "Holy See" designates Rome as the bishopric of the pope. According to Roman Catholic theology, the pope is the successor of the apostle Peter, whom Christ made head of the church. Peter died at Rome, and Catholics believe that he transmitted his authority to those who succeeded him as leader (bishop) of the Christian community there. Thus Rome is considered the holy or apostolic see, which means that it is the residence of the bishop whose authority derives from Christ through St. Peter, the Apostle.

Tim Guyse Williams, ed., *BBC World Service Glossary of Current Affairs* (Chicago: St. James Press, 1991), 696. R.H.C. Davis, *A History of Medieval Europe from Constantine to Saint Louis, 2d ed.* (London: Longman, 1988), 65.

What are Judaizers?

In Russia during the fifteenth century, a religious sect of people known as Judaizers developed. They are non-Jews who embrace the laws and practices of Judaism. Following the fifteenth century, Judaizers seemed to disappear from Russia. They reappeared in the eighteenth century, and sects of Judaizers sprang up throughout the country. In the early nineteenth century, the Judaizer movement again waned throughout Russia, but by the end of the century, Judaizers began to appear in greater numbers.

Geoffrey Wigoder, ed., *Encyclopedic Dictionary of Judaica* (New York: Leon Amiel Publisher, 1974), s.v. "Judaizers."

What are some of the African names for God?

Africa is a continent with a myriad of cultures. While most of these cultures are quite religious, their versions of God are as diverse as the continent that gave rise to them. Generalizations concerning their perception of God are thus difficult if not impossible to make. Some cultures have personal names for their deity while others have descriptive names. The roots of personal names, mostly ancient in origin, have been lost over the millennium. The meanings of descriptive names, however, are readily apparent. Many African cultures view God as having pre-eminence and greatness. The Akan refer to him as "Grandfather God who alone is the Great One" while the Shona seek comfort from "the Great One of the Sky." Other cultures view their God as the source of all things. Zulus refer to God as "the One who sprang up first"; the Ngoni believe God to be the "the Original Source" and the "beginning of all things."

The following African names for God do not easily lend themselves to translation:

Angola-Kalunga, Nzambi, Suku
Burundi-Imana

Ivory Coast-Nyame, Onyankopon
Malawi-Cauta, Chiuta, Leza, MuLungu
South Africa-Inkosi, Khuzwane, Modimo, Mwari
Sudan-Ajok, Bel, Dyong, Elo, Jok
Zambia-Chilenga, Chiuta, Nyambe, Nzambi, Tilo

John S. Mbiti, *Concepts of God in Africa* (London: S.P.C.K., 1970), 20-21. John S. Mbiti, *Introduction to African Religion* (New York: Praeger. 1975), 42-43.

What is the meaning of the Hindu holiday Diwali?

The Hindu holiday Diwali is referred to as the Festival of Lights and is held in celebration of the New Year in India. The holiday falls on the last day of the waning half of Kartika, which occurs sometime in October or November. It celebrates the movement of the human spirit from the darkness of ignorance into the light of truth. The holiday is also associated with the triumph of Lord Rama over Ravana, a Sri Lankan ruler who kidnapped Rama's wife. Rama is an epic but secular hero of ancient India whose exploits are heralded in music, art, and literature throughout the Indian sub-continent.

Just prior to the Diwali holiday houses, courtyards, and places of worship are meticulously cleaned in anticipation of the celebration. On the day of Diwali sweets are exchanged and people ask forgiveness for past wrongs. Diwali also marks the sowing of the new year's crop.

Mircea Eliade, ed.*The Encyclopedia of Religion* (New York: Macmillan, 1987), s.v. "Rama." Aidan Kelly, Peter Dresser, and Linda M. Ross, *Religious Holidays and Calendars* (Detroit: Omnigraphics. 1993), 71-72.

What may have been the exact cause of Jesus Christ's death?

Although it is generally believed that Jesus Christ died by crucifixion, the exact cause of death may have been a heart attack. A Mayo Clinic autopsy pathologist believes that the physical horrors of crucifixion may have caused asphyxia and a diaphragm-crushing suffocation which led to heart failure.

Pittsburgh Press 21 March 1986.

How is Hanukkah observed in Jewish homes and what is a *dreydl*?

Hanukkah, also known as the Feast of Lights, is a joyous holiday celebrated with games, plays, gifts, and meals featuring *latkes*, or potato pancakes. In Jewish homes, candles or small oil lamps in a menorah are lighted, one on the first evening, and the number increasing by one each night of the eight-day festival. A *dreydl* is a four-sided top used in a popular game played at Hanukkah.

Robert J. Myers, *Celebrations: The Complete Book of American Holidays* (New York: Doubleday & Co., 1972), 307. Hennig Cohen and Tristram Potter Coffin, eds., *The Folklore of American Holidays* (Detroit: Gale Research, 1987), 355.

What is the "lion-lamb" quote from the Bible?

In the Bible, the "lion-lamb" quote, symbolizing peace, appears in Isaiah II, verse 6: "The wolf also shall dwell with the lamb, The leopard shall lie down with the young goat, the calf and the young lion and the fatling together; And a little child shall lead them."

Holy Bible: The New King James Version (Nashville, TN: Thomas Nelson Publishers, 1982).

How many people took refuge on Noah's Ark?

During the great flood described in the Book of Genesis of the Bible, eight people took refuge on Noah's ark. They were Noah and his wife Naamah (meaning "the lovely one"), their three sons Ham, Shem, and Japheth, and their three sons' wives.

Joseph A. DeBartolo, *In Further Pursuit of Trivial Pursuit* (Sarsaparilla Ltd., 1984), 254. Louis Ginzberg, *The Legends of the Jews* (Philadelphia: Jewish Publication Society of America, 1925), 172.

What did the mark of Cain signify?

It is commonly believed that the mark placed on Cain was meant to identify him as the murderer of his brother, Abel. A close reading of Genesis 4:13-15, however, reveals just the opposite. The mark placed upon Cain following Abel's murder was meant to protect him from those who, in Cain's words, "shall slay me."

Tom Burnam, *The Dictionary of Misinformation* (New York: Thomas Y. Crowell, 1975), s.v. "Cain, mark of."

Which three angels appear most often in the Bible?

The three angels most frequently mentioned in the Bible are Michael, Gabriel, and Raphael.

New Catholic Encyclopedia (Washington, DC: Catholic University of America, 1967), 513. Allen C. Myers, ed., *The Eerdman's Bible Dictionary* (Grand Rapids, MI: William B. Eerdmans Publishing Co., 1987), 56-57.

Who wrote the Dead Sea Scrolls?

The consensus of biblical scholars is that the Dead Sea Scrolls, collections of manuscript material discovered in 1947 and the years following, were written by numerous people, not a single author. No particular authors have been identified. There are in fact three separate and unrelated groups of Dead Sea Scrolls: the Qumran texts, the texts of the Bar-kokhba War, and the Khirbet Mird.

The Illustrated Bible Dictionary (Downers Grove, IL: InterVarsity Press, 1980), 372-73.

What were Ezekiel's wheels?

According to Biblical scholars, the wheels in the book of Ezekiel were those of the chariot of the sun-god.

The Interpreter's Bible: The Holy Scriptures (Nashville, TN: Abingdon Press, 1935), 72.

Who were some of the incestuous couples mentioned in the Bible?

Some incestuous couples mentioned in the Bible include Lot and his daughters, Abraham and Sarah, Nahor and Milcah, Amram and Jochebed, Amnon and Tamar.

Irving Wallace et al., *The Book of Lists #2* (New York: William Morrow, 1980), 310.

What is the Druze religion?

With approximately 550,000 followers, mostly in Lebanon, Syria, and Israel, the Druze religion is a mix of Greek philosophy and Muslim mysticism revering Jesus Christ, Moses, and Muhammad. The movement was founded in Cairo, Egypt, in 1017 and gradually spread to the Levant. Although many of the Druze beliefs are secret, it is known that followers adhere to the unity of all things under a single entity. Man is constantly being reborn and with each new life moves closer to perfection. As only a limited number of Druze followers will be admitted into Paradise, intermarriages and conversions are frowned on. Although a minority religion, the Druze have at various times been a powerful political, social, and even violent force in the Middle East.

Time 3 October 1983.

How did the wall of Jericho fall?

Jericho was a town under an Israelite siege. On the seventh day of the siege, according to the Bible, the Israelite priests blew their ram's horn trumpets, the whole people of the Israelites uttered a mighty war cry, and the wall of Jericho came tumbling down.

The Jerusalem Bible (New York: Doubleday & Co., 1966), 280-81.

Which rivers are frequently mentioned in the Bible?

Rivers frequently mentioned in the Bible include the Euphrates, Nile, Tigris, Jordan, Abanah, Ahava, Chebar, Gihon, Gozan, Hiddekel, Jabbok, Kishon, Pharpar, Pishon, Ulai, and the River of Egypt.

Interpreters Dictionary of the Bible (Nashville, TN: Abingdon Press, 1962), 100-1.

What is the Divine Light Mission?

The Divine Light Mission is an Eastern religious movement that gained acceptance worldwide but was short-lived in the United States. The Mission was founded in 1960 by Sri Hans Maharaj Ji, who was a follower of the Sant Mat tradition. Following Sri Hans Maharaj Ji's death in 1966, his eight-year-old son, Prem Pal Singh Rawat, became the leader of the Mission and soon took the title Maharaj Ji. A number of Americans living in India became involved with the movement and prevailed on the young Maharaj Ji to come to the United States. A 1971 American tour attracted attention and followers, but by 1973 enthusiasm was waning. Family problems over control of the Mission forced the Maharaj Ji to return to India, where he was forced to relinquish control of the movement. A 1975 lawsuit won him back control of the Mission outside of India. A small following of adherents continues in the United States.

Rosemary Guiley, *Harper's Encyclopedia of Mystical & Paranormal Experience* (San Francisco: HarperSanFrancisco, 1991), 12-13.

What is the significance of Christ's disciples?

There are several meanings to the religious term "disciple." Etymologically, the word "disciple" in early Greek and Latin meant "learner." Colloquially, however, the terms "disciple" and "apostle" are often used interchangeably. In Biblical scripture the term is used in three ways: one who is distinguishable from a teacher, one who follows a great leader or movement, or one who believes in the doctrine of Jesus Christ. It is also applied to a select group of 70 or 72 individuals who followed Jesus Christ with greater fervor than most of his followers, but with less fervor than the twelve apostles. Jesus Christ did specify that disciples must dedicate their lives to the Kingdom of God. Disciples must renounce material possessions as well as family and friends, must be willing to suffer and die for their spiritual beliefs, and must accept Jesus as their spiritual leader and not as their political messiah.

New Catholic Encyclopedia (Washington, DC: Catholic University of America, 1967), s.v. "disciples."

What is the significance of the practice of circumcision in Judaism?

In Judaism, the practice of circumcision is known as a Brith. This practice has its roots in the Biblical account of a covenant made between God and Abraham. All of Abraham's sons were circumcised on their eighth day, and the ceremony symbolized their entry into the Jewish fold. In modern times, circumcisions are performed by a certified Mohel.

Brith Milah Board of New York, *A Vital Message to Jewish Parents* (Pittsburgh: Public Service Division of the Prise Institute of Continuing Jewish Education).

What is the significance of the vestment colors worn by Roman Catholic priests?

Color is used in the Roman Catholic liturgical vesture to convey the mood or spirit of the feast day or church season. The liturgical colors of white, red, green, black, and violet were mandated for the Roman rite by Pope Innocent III, who reigned from 1198 to 1216. White is worn on feasts of Jesus Christ, Mary, confessors, and virgins and on Sundays during paschal time. Red is used for the Pentecost and for the feasts of the apostles and martyrs. Violet is worn for the seasons of Advent and Lent and for certain feast day vigil. Green is used on Sundays after the Epiphany and the Pentecost. Black is worn for masses of the dead and on Good Friday. Since the thirteenth century, rose vesture has been worn on the third Sunday of Advent and the fourth Sunday of Lent. For the Feast of the Immaculate Conception, blue has been worn in Spain only during the nineteenth century.

Catholic University of America, *New Catholic Encyclopedia* (New York: McGraw-Hill, 1967), s.v. "colors, liturgical."

Who was Aphrodite?

In Greek mythology, Aphrodite is the goddess of love, beauty, and sexuality. She is considered one of the most sensual figures in Greek mythology and served as a symbol of sexuality and female beauty for Renaissance and later Western artists. Aphrodite's name serves as the basis for the term "aphrodesiac," which is a substance that is said to increase sexual arousal. In Roman mythology, Aphrodite is known as Venus.

Robert T. Francoeur, ed., *A Descriptive Dictionary and Atlas of Sexology* (Westport, CT: Greenwood Press, 1991), 41.

What is the Vulgate?

The Vulgate version is the Latin translation of the Bible, prepared in large part by the Church father Jerome (*ca.* 347-419 or 420) between 382 and 405 A.D. and authorized by Pope Damasus I. It was written to replace the *Itala*, an old Latin translation of the Greek version. The Vulgate was popular with Roman Catholics from the fifth to the sixteenth centuries, and the Council of Trent declared it the Roman Catholic biblical Latin authority in 1546. The Vulgate went virtually unchanged until a commission was appointed by the Second Vatican Council in 1965 to revise it.

George C. Kohn, *Dictionary of Historic Documents* (New York: Facts on File, 1991), 355.

Who was the first black cardinal of the Roman Catholic church?

The first black cardinal ordained in the Roman Catholic church was Laurian Cardinal Rugambwa of Tanganyika (now Tanzania). He was ordained in 1960 by Pope John XXIII.

New York Times 29 March 1960.

What was Vatican I?

Called by Pope Pius IX (1792-1878), Vatican I was the nineteenth ecumenical council of the Roman Catholic Church. It was held in St. Peter's Basilica in the Vatican in 1869-70 and was the first council held since the Council of Trent in the sixteenth century. Vatican I was meant to evaluate the intellectual, social, and political movements that had developed in contemporary society, including modern science, nationalism, and democracy. Much of its work, however, was never completed, because the council was cut short by the collapse of the papacy as an independent political power and the absorption of the papal states by the Italian kingdom. Vatican I did produce the doctrine of papal infallibility, by which popes are declared to be incapable of error in matters of faith and morals when they officially proclaim the church's teaching.

The Catholic University of America, *New Catholic Encyclopedia* (New York: McGraw Hill Book Company, 1967), s.v. "Vatican Council I."

To whom did the Greeks dedicate the Parthenon?

One of the most recognizable examples of Greek architecture is the Parthenon. Located in Athens on a hill known as the Acropolis, the Parthenon is a temple dedicated to the goddess Athena. Constructed between 447 and 432 B.C., the Parthenon is 237 feet long, 110 feet wide, and 60 feet high.

The World Book Encyclopedia (Chicago: World Book, 1987), s.v. "parthenon."

What are the twelve tribes of Israel?

The twelve tribes of Israel are groups who trace their descent to the sons of Jacob, one of the patriarchs of the Jewish faith. The twelve tribes of Israel are: Reuben, Simeon, Levi, Judah, Zebulun, Issachar, Dan, Gad, Asher, Naphtali, Joseph, and Benjamin.

The World Book Encyclopedia (Chicago: World Book, 1987), s.v. "Jews."

Which emperor introduced Buddhism to China?

In 517 A.D., Emperor Wu-Ti converted to Buddhism and introduced the new religion to central China.

Bernard Grun, *The Timetables of History* (New York: Simon & Schuster, 1991), 36.

According to Jewish tradition, how long did Adam, Noah, and the patriarchs live?

According to Jewish tradition, the principal figures of early biblical history lived extremely long lives. Adam is reputed to have lived 930 years and Noah 950 years. Abraham died at 175 and Moses at 120.

Nissan Mindel and Gershon Kranzler, *Who, What, When, Where: Interesting Facts from Jewish History* (n.p., n.p., 1967), 9, 12.

What does the Ankh symbolize?

The ancient Egyptian symbol Ankh, the crux ansata (or ansated cross), is a tau cross with a ring at the top that serves as a handle. The symbol is formed by combining the male and female symbols, the Egyptian deities Osiris and Isis respectively, equating the principles of heaven and earth. The cross portion represents immortality and life in general, while the circle at the top is symbolic of the eternal preserver of the world. The "T" forming the body of the cross is the monogram of Thoth, who represents wisdom. The Goddess of Truth, Maat, has been depicted holding the Ankh.

J. C. Cooper, *An Illustrated Encyclopedia of Traditional Symbols* (New York: Thames and Hudson, 1978), s.v. "Ankh." Ivor H. Evans, *Brewer's Dictionary of Phrase and Fable* (New York: Harper & Row, 1989). Heather Child, *Christian Symbols: Ancient and Modern* (New York: Charles Scribner's Sons, 1971). *New Catholic Dictionary* (n.p.: Universal Knowledge Foundation, 1929).

Who was the first convert to Judaism?

The first convert to Judaism was Ruth, who was not born a Jew. The Book of Ruth is read on the Shavuot, the Festival of Weeks, to celebrate her story and subsequent conversion which occurred during the harvest season.

Stephen J. Einstein and Lydia Kukoff, *Every Person's Guide to Judaism* (New York: UAHC Press, 1989), 55.

What is the Dome of the Rock?

The Dome of the Rock is a Moslem shrine in Jerusalem on the Temple Mount. The shrine is built over a rock from which Moslems believe Mohammad ascended into heaven. Jews believe, however, that the rock was the altar on which Isaac was to be sacrificed by Abraham. The shrine was built by Caliph Abd Al-Malik in 691 at the site of an earlier wooden structure. It is known in Arabic as *Haram ash-Sharif,* or the Noble Temple.

Aryeh Grabois, *The Illustrated Encyclopedia of Medieval Civilization* (New York: Octopus, 1980), s.v. "Dome of the Rock."

What are the "Seven Deadly Sins"?

The concept of seven categories of sinful behavior came from the writings of medieval Christian theologians Evagrius Ponticus, John Cassian, and Gregory the Great. The "seven deadly sins," or Cardinal sins, are pride (in Latin, *superbia*), envy (*invidria*), anger (*ira*), sloth (*acedia*), avarice (*avaritia*), gluttony (*gula*), and (*lust*). These sins are sometimes called capital sins because they lead to other sins; they are the sources of all sins. The term capital derives from the Latin word *caput,* which menas "source."

The seven categories were never ranked by theologians, nor were they standardized in name or number (originally there were eight). The adjective "deadly" is used within the context of mortal sin, in which the sinner suffers spiritual death.

William H. Gentz, ed., *The Dictionary of Bible and Religion* (Nashville, TN: Abingdon Press, 1986), s.v. "cardinal sins/cardinal virtues." Joseph R. Strayer, ed., *Dictionary of the Middle Ages* (New York: Charles Scribner's Sons, 1988), 11:211-12.

What is the largest number mentioned in the Bible?

The largest number specifically named in the Bible is a thousand thousand; i.e., a million. It is found in 2 Chronicles 14:9.

Isaac Asimov, *Asimov on Numbers* (New York: Doubleday, 1977), 60.

What special significance does the passionflower have?

Most species of passionflower are native to the tropical areas of the Western Hemisphere and it was the Spanish friars of the sixteenth century who first gave the name to this flower because they saw in the form of the passionflower (*Passiflora*) a representation of the passion of Jesus Christ. The flowers have five petals and five sepals, which to the friars symbolized the ten faithful apostles present at Jesus' crucifixion; the corona of five filaments was thought to resemble Jesus' crown of thorns; the five stamens represented the five wounds in Jesus's body, and the three stigmas symbolized the nails driven into his hands and crossed feet.

Encyclopedia Americana (Danbury, CT: Grolier, 1990), 21:512. Arnold Whittick, *Symbols, Signs and their Meaning* (London: Leonard Hill Books, 1960), 234-35.

What is the Black Madonna and where is it located?

The Black Madonna of Czestochowa (Poland) is a 4-foot by 2--foot painting of the Virgin Mary and the Christ child that serves as both religious icon and symbol of Polish historical continuity. According to legend, the portrait was executed by St. Luke the Evangelist on a table top from the home of Mary, Jesus, and Joseph in Nazareth. Art historians believe the gilt-and-tempera depiction of Madonna and child, painted in extremely dark skin tones, dates to 6th century Greece or Byzantium.

The first historical account of the icon dates to 1382, when it found its way to the Jasna Gora (Mountain of Light) monastery in Czestochowa, 140 miles south of Warsaw. During the Swedish invasion of 1655 the monastery was under siege for 40 days while the monks prayed to the icon for help. When the siege, and ultimately the invasion failed, Polish ruler Jan Kazimierz attributed his country's deliverance to the intercession of the Virgin Mary and named her Queen of Poland. An annual pilgrimage to Czestochowa dates to 1711, when the grateful citizens of Warsaw walked to the monastery to give thanks for sparing their city from a bubonic plague epidemic that was sweeping the countryside.

Time 27 June 1983.

Where did the custom of the Advent wreath originate?

The Advent wreath, used to mark the time from the fourth Sunday before Christmas to Christmas day, was originally a Lutheran custom that originated in Germany. The wreath, made of evergreen branches or laurel, is adorned with four candles, one for each of the Sundays of Advent. On the first Sunday one candle is lit, on the second Sunday two candles are lit, and so forth. The Advent wreath has been adopted by many other religious groups. In some countries, Advent candles are burned, but are not set in a wreath.

Gerard Del Re and Patricia Del Re, *The Christmas Almanack* (Garden City, NY: Doubleday, 1979), 40. Elizabeth Hough Sechrist, *Christmas Everywhere: A Book of Christmas Customs of Many Lands, rev. ed.* (Philadelphia: Macrae Smith, 1962), 111.

In what year did the Vatican permit girls to become altar servers?

The Vatican announced in 1994 that both girls and boys would be allowed to act as altar servers at Roman Catholic Masses. However, individual bishops have the authority to decide whether or not to allow girls to serve in their dioceses.

USA Today 14 April 1994.

What was the name of Adam's first wife in Hebrew legend as well as the Devil's wife in Arabic mythology?

According to Hebrew legend, Lilith was Adam's first wife while in Arabic mythology, Lilith was married to the Devil.

Benet's Reader's Encyclopedia (New York: Harper & Row, 1987).

How is St. Agnes' Day celebrated in Rome?

Every year on St. Agnes' Day (January 21) in Rome, two lambs are blessed by the Pope in the church of St. Agnus after mass is celebrated. St. Agnus is the patron saint of purity and virginity, and she is often represented with a lamb by her side.

William S. Walsh, *Curiosities of Popular Customs and of Rites, Ceremonies, Observances, and Miscellaneous Antiques* (Philadelphia: J. B. Lippincott, 1897), 16.

What is the meaning of agoga and amoma?

Agoga is a type of Sunday school class organization for Baptist men from ages 16 to 21 in which they are trained to live as young Christians. The first class was organized by the Rev. H. E. Tralle on March 9, 1905 at the Third Baptist Church in St. Louis, Missouri. Amoma is the agoga equivalent for young women.

John T. McFarland, et al., eds., *The Encyclopedia of Sunday Schools and Religious Education* (Nashville, TN: Thomas Nelson & Sons, 1915), 21.

What religious denomination was the first African-descendant church in the United States?

The first African American church in America was the Bethel African Methodist Episcopal Church, established in 1793 by Richard Allen (1760-1831), an African American, in Philadelphia, Pennsylvania.

The church was opened for public worship on July 17, 1794, and dedicated that same month by Bishop Francis Asbury. On October 12, 1794, it was announced from the pulpit by the Reverend Robert Blackwell that the congregation was received in full fellowship in the Methodist Episcopal Church.

Joseph Nathan Kane, *Famous First Facts, 4th ed.* (New York: H. W. Wilson Company, 1981), 5.

In Sikhism, what does "Guru" mean?

In Sikhism, "Guru" comes from two terms: "Gu," which means darkness, and "Ru," which means light. "Guru" thus represents the light which dispels darkness. The Guru is a perfect messenger of God in whom the Light of God shines fully.

Sikh Religion (Detroit: Sikh Missionary Center, 1990), 7.

What does "Tao" mean and what do Taoists believe?

In Chinese *tao* means "the way" and specifically refers to the way of nature. Taoists believe that the cycles in nature and changes in the physical world are apparent signs of the great but unseen force known as Tao.

Tao is the presence that existed before the universe was formed, and continues to guide the world and everything in it. Taoism has no founder. Its followers do not worship one god, but focus instead on coming into harmony with Tao.

Paula R. Hartz, *Taoism* (New York: Facts On File, 1993), 8.

What is an incubus?

An incubus is an angel fallen from grace because of a lust for sexual intercourse with women. Many western European countries have incorporated the *incubus* into their folklore where they are regarded as a lewd demon or goblin.

Rossell Hope Robbins, *The Encyclopedia of Witchcraft and Demonology* (New York: Crown Publishers, 1972), 254-59.

What are straw dogs?

"Straw dogs" are Chinese artifacts from the third century B.C. They were made of straw because they were first worshiped and then sacrificially burned. Controversial movie director Sam Peckinpah titled one of his movies *Straw Dogs.*

Time 20 December 1971.

Why is salt important in Jewish tradition?

Its preservative qualities gives salt symbolic importance in Jewish tradition. Leviticus 2:13 of the Bible commands that "on all your meal offerings shall you sprinkle salt." The Talmud required salt to all sacrifices, especially if the sacrifice was not to be immediately consumed. In much of the Middle East, salt is used today as a symbol of greeting and a sign for the sealing of contracts and agreements.

Alfred J. Kolatch, *The Second Jewish Book of Why* (Middle Village, NY: Jonathan David Publishers, 1985), 328.

What is Pope John Paul II's stand on women as priests?

In his apostolic letter entitled "On Reserving Priestly Ordination to Men Alone," Pope John Paul II (1920-) stated that women will not be ordained in the Roman Catholic Church and that the issue will not be open for debate. In his 1994 address, the Pope said that priesthood should be reserved for men based on the fact that Jesus chose only male apostles.

Alan Cowell, "Pope Rules Out Debate on Women as Priests," *New York Times* 31 May 1994.

What is the origin of the phrase "odour of sanctity"?

The phrase "odour of sanctity" originated from the Bible passage II Corinthians 2:15: "...we are the good odour of Christ to God." Many have come to interpret this passage literally and often associate fragrance with various religious experiences. Examples include Christian martyrs, Teresa De Jesus's account of Catalina de Cardona, and Sister Giovanna Maria della Croce of Roveredo.

John Ferguson, *An Illustrated Encyclopedia of Mysticism and the Mystery Religions* (New York: Seabury Press, 1977), 135.

Who ordered Uriah into battle so as to have him die and free his wife to marry another?

In the book II Samuel of the Old Testament of the Bible, King David ordered Uriah into the forefront of a battle in hopes that he would be killed so as to free his wife, Bathsheba, for marriage. Uriah was killed, and David married his mistress Bathsheba, who bore him a son named Solomon.

Abraham H. Lass, *Dictionary of Classical, Biblical and Literary Allusions* (New York: Facts On File, 1987), 25.

Where and when was the Church of Jesus Christ of Latter-Day Saints first organized?

Mormonism is a popular name for a religious movement made up of several denominations including the Church of Jesus Christ of Latter-Day Saints which was formally organized by Joseph Smith Jr. in Manchester, New York on April 6, 1830. It is the largest denomination of Mormonism today and is headquartered in Salt Lake City, Utah. The second largest denomination is the Re-organized Church of Jesus Christ of Latter Day Saints in Independence, Missouri. All denominations of the Mormon religion claim origination with Joseph Smith Jr.

Mormonism had its unofficial beginnings in western New York State in the early 1820s with the family of Joseph and Lucy Mack Smith, who emigrated there from New England in search of economic opportunity. Although a religious family, the Smiths did not feel entirely comfortable with the various religious denominations of the day. It is claimed by subsequent followers of Mormonism that in 1820 Joseph Smith Jr. was praying for divine guidance when he experienced a visitation from God the Father and Jesus Christ, telling him the denominations of the day were "all wrong" and to join none. Further visions convinced Smith Jr. that he had been chosen as a "divine instrument" of God and that he was guided by an angel. He uncovered a set of "golden records" on the family farm which he subsequently published in 1830 as the *Book of Mormon.* This tract relates the "sacred history" of pre-Columbian migrants to America. The Smith family, convinced of their divine mission, began to proselytize and attract converts.

Smith's Mormonism gradually became radicalized and divisive and his relations with non-Mormons and Mormon converts became strained. Plural marriage for "time and eternity" and baptism of the dead caused dissent both in and out of the movement. In 1844 Smith and his brother Hyrum were killed by an anti-Mormon mob. In 1840 Brigham Young had become an influential member of the Church and he would eventually lead followers west to the Rocky Mountains following Smith's death. In 1860 Smith's son Joseph became president of the Reorganized Church in Missouri.

Mircea Eliade, *The Encyclopedia of Religion* (New York: Macmillan, 1987), s.v. "Mormonism."

What is the origin of the term "abracadabra"?

The term "abracadabra" is considered a charm against evil and illness, first used by a physician during the second century A.D. There are several explanations for its origin. The word may be a combination of initials of the Hebrew words for "Father, Son, and Holy Ghost," (the Holy Trinity); or it may be a version of the Hebrew words for "blessing" and "word"-*bracha* and *dabar.* Another theory is that abracadabra is the name of an ancient demon. Some cultures consider knowledge of the name of supernatural being to impart special powers for good or evil, so speaking the name or wearing a badge with Abracadabra's name was believed to be a magic formula against disease.

One more explanation can be found in the practice of a Persian cult which worshiped 365 different gods. Reciting the names of all the gods was necessary to earn their help. To facilitate the task, priests invented a charm which used a combination of Greek letters whose numerical value replaced the 365 names. In this charm, which could be worn like a talisman, the word "ABRACADABRA" was written repeatedly in the shape of an inverted triangle: the complete word was on the first line, and each succeeding line omitted one letter until the triangle was complete. In recent times the term has been used by stage magicians as a magic word to complete their tricks.

Rudolph Brasch, *How Did It Begin?* (n.p.: n.p., 1966), 163-65. T. A. Waters, *The Encyclopedia of Magic and Magicians* (New York: Facts on File, 1988), s.v. "abracadabra."

What name is given to the worship sites of Jehovah's Witnesses?

Jehovah's Witnesses worship and hold meetings in Kingdom Halls, which they usually build themselves, since all of the Witnesses' activities are supported by volunteer workers. Founded by Charles Taze Russell (1852-1916) as the Bible Students, the sect uses the Bible as the basis for their beliefs. Rejecting the concepts of the Trinity, immortality of the soul, and Hell, Witnesses believe that Jesus Christ, along with 144,000 co-rulers taken from the earth, will rule the earth after its transformation into a paradise during the Millennium. In 1931 the sect's name was changed to Jehovah's Witnesses.

J. Gordon Melton, *Encyclopedia of American Religions, 4th ed.* (Detroit: Gale Research, 1993), 581-82.

What is the Old Testament counterpart to the New Testament story about Jesus feeding the multitudes?

An Old Testament counterpart to the New Testament story of Jesus Christ feeding the multitudes can be found in the Bible in 2 Kings, chapter 4, verses 42-45, in which Elisha feeds 100 men from twenty loaves of bread.

Holy Bible: The New King James Version (Nashville, TN: Thomas Nelson Publishers, 1982), 376.

How did the Vatican officially acknowledge the Holocaust?

In 1994 the Vatican officially acknowledged the Holocaust with a papal concert featuring London's Royal Philharmonic Orchestra and the Choir of St. Peter's Basilica singing in Hebrew. American actor Richard Dreyfuss (1947-) read Kaddish, the Jewish Prayer for the Dead.

USA Today 7 April 1994.

What is the origin of the custom of kissing the Pope's toe?

Kissing the Pope's toe is a custom that originates with several early cultures as a sign of deference or respect. Orientals honored a person by kissing the hands, feet, or hem of his clothing. Egyptians, Greeks, and Romans also practiced these customs. Mary Magdalene kissed the feet of Jesus as a penance. Mohammedans may wash and kiss the feet of a guest who has traveled a long distance. The Pope himself washes and kisses the feet of pilgrims as part of Holy or Maundy Thursday services. Today the Pope wears a slipper decorated with a cross over the toe, to defer the honor to Christ.

William S. Walsh, *Curiosities of Popular Customs* (Philadelphia: J. B. Lippincott, 1925), 603-4.

Who was president of the Lutheran Church-Missouri Synod at the time of its schism, and what was the name of the church formed by the dissidents?

The Reverend Jacob A. O. Preus (1920-1994) was president of the Lutheran Church-Missouri Synod from 1969 to 1981, during its schism. Preus was a leader of the fundamentalists and insisted on the historical truth of Bible stories. Dissidents were considered liberals and broke away to form the Association of Evangelical Lutheran Churches. In 1988, this group merged with two others to form the Evangelical Lutheran Church in America.

New York Times 15 August 1994.

What are the writings or scriptures of the Spiritualist churches?

The written teachings or scriptures of Spiritualist churches are contained in *Oahspe* (1882) and the *Urantia* book (1955).

Diane Choquette, comp., *New Religious Movements in the United States and Canada: A Critical Assessment and Annotated Bibliography* (Westport, CT: Greenwood Press, 1985), 7.

What is the Coptic Gospel of Thomas?

The Coptic Gospel of Thomas is a collection of 114 sayings, "logia," attributed to Jesus. The work was written around A.D. 140 in the Greek language. "Coptic" is derived from the Greek word for Egyptian. Its contents were unknown until the Coptic version was discovered in Egypt in 1946. Many of the sayings are variations of Jesus' words as already recorded in the New Testament, but about 40 were previously unknown sayings.

Allen C. Myers, *The Eerdmans Bible Dictionary* (Grand Rapids, MI: William B. Eerdmans Publishing Co., 1987), s.v. "Thomas, Coptic Gospel of."

What is the Gospel of Judas?

The Gospel of Judas is an apocryphal text that was probably written in the second century A.D. There is no surviving record of this gospel, which is attributed to a Gnostic sect and supposedly portrayed Jesus' betrayer, apostle Judas Iscariot, as an enlightened and noble character.

Allen C. Myers, *The Eerdmans Bible Dictionary* (Grand Rapids, MI: William B. Eerdmans Publishing Co., 1987), s.v. "Judas, Gospel of."

What are the seven works of mercy?

According to the Roman Catholic Church, the seven works of mercy are: the conversion of sinners, the instruction of the ignorant, the counseling of the doubtful, the comfort of the sorrowful, bearing ills patiently, forgiving wrongs, and praying for the living and the dead.

William H. Gentz, ed., *The Dictionary of Bible and Religion* (Nashville, TN: Abingdon Press, 1986), s.v. "seven works of mercy."

Who were the nine Muses?

Sometimes named the Pierides after their home in Macedonia called Pieria, the nine Muses were Greek goddesses who performed at all major celebrations of the gods of mythology. They were generally considered to be the daughters of Zeus and Mnemosyne. The Muses were a source of inspiration to writers and poets and were each associated with a field of study or fine art: Calliope was the Muse of epic poetry; Clio, of history; Erato, of love and lyric poetry; Euterpe, of music and the flute; Melpomene, of tragedy; Polyhymnia, the Muse of songs, hymns to the gods, and mime; Terpsichore, of dance and light verse; Thalia, of comedy; and Urania, of astronomy.

Pierre Grimal, *The Dictionary of Classical Mythology* (New York: Basil Blackwell, 1986), 297-98.

Which groups constitute the largest part of the American Pentecostal movement, and where did they originate?

The largest part of the American Pentecostal movement are those groups believing in two-stage salvation, although there is a significant contingent professing three-stage salvation. The principal group is the Churches of God, among them very large and significant African-American denominations. Most of the Pentecostal churches bearing the name "Church of God" can be traced to a holiness revival in the mountains of northeast Georgia and eastern Tennessee, although other Churches of God originated independently of the Church of God (Cleveland). Another major group in the Pentecostal family is the Pentecostal Holiness Church.

W.J. Hollenweger, *The Pentecostals: The Charismatic Movement in the Churches* (Minneapolis: Augsburg Publishing House, 1972), 47-50. J. Gordon Melton, *The Encyclopedia of American Religions, 2d ed.* (Detroit, MI: Gale Research, 1987), 310.

What is meant by the term "Ragnarok"?

The term "Ragnarok" derives from Scandinavian mythology. It is a name for the anticipated day of doom, when the world and its inhabitants will be destroyed. The myth teaches that only Vidar of Vali will survive to reconstruct a lasting universe.

E. Cobham Brewer, *The Dictionary of Phrase and Fable* (New York: Avenel Books, 1978), s.v. "Ragnarok."

In Greek mythology, what Trojan woman was granted the gift of prophecy but was never believed?

Greek mythology tells the tragic story of Cassandra, also known as Alexandra, the beautiful daughter of Queen Hecuba of Troy. A priestess of the sun, she became the object of the god Apollo's desire. He promised her that he would grant any wish if she would sleep with him. Cassandra asked for the power of prophecy, but after the wish was granted, she refused to complete the bargain. Apollo then wet her lips with his tongue, thereby cursing her; even though she could foretell the future, not one person would believe her. She tried to stop the Trojans from waging war with Greece and foretold of Greek soldiers in a wooden horse. After the Trojan defeat, she was made a concubine of the Greek King Agamemnon.

Patricia Monaghan, *The Book of Goddesses and Heroines* (New York: E.P. Dutton, 1981), s.v. "Cassandra, Alexandra."

In Scandinavian mythology, who are the Berserks?

The Berserks were warriors in the service of the god Odin, according to Scandinavian mythology. They wore bear skins and howled like animals when in battle. They may have been a model for the bodyguards of ancient kings, who were also known for their wild fighting behavior. Their name is the source of the modern English word "berserk."

Michael Senior, *The Illustrated Who's Who in Mythology* (New York: Macmillan Publishing Company, 1985), s.v. "Berserks."

In Scandinavian mythology, who is Freya?

The Scandinavian goddess Freya, also known as Frejya, was the mistress of all gods and the ruler of death. She wore a feathered cloak and a magic amber necklace, and drove a chariot drawn by cats, or rode on a golden-bristled boar. Her powers and influences were widespread: she lead the Valkyries, the maiden goddesses who carried fallen war heroes to Valhalla; she was the spirit of fertility and the recipient of love prayers; and she was the goddess of magic, who gave sorcery to those on earth. Some call another aspect of Freya the goddess Frigg.

Patricia Monaghan, *The Book of Goddesses and Heroines* (New York: E.P. Dutton, 1981), s.v. "Freya, Frejya."

Who are the Valkyries?

The Valkyries are the fierce maiden goddesses of Scandinavian mythology who chose fallen war heroes, bringing them back to the god Odin. They were helmeted and flew on supernatural horses. The Valkyries were sometimes said to have the power to determine the outcome of a battle, using the image of a bloody web of war that was woven with severed human heads, spears, and arrows. Such stories draw a far more bloodthirsty picture of the Valkyries, who are otherwise seen as the obedient servants of Odin. Some stories also tell of half-human Valkyries or Vaetter-maidens, who could be seen by humans with second sight.

Patricia Monaghan, *The Book of Goddesses and Heroines* (New York: E. P. Dutton, 1981), s.v. "Valkyries, Valkyrjr."

What is Swedenborgianism?

Swedenborgianism is a doctrine derived from in the writings of Emmanuel Swedenborg (1688-1772). He claimed that he received a number of visions of Jesus Christ in 1745 during which Christ imparted new insights into biblical scripture and appointed Swedenborg to spread them. He rejected certain central Christian beliefs including the Resurrection, the Trinity, and original sin. He also held that there were only two sacraments, baptism and the Eucharist. Today's adherents to Swedenborgianism belong to the Church of the New Jerusalem or the New Church.

Felician A. Foy, ed., *1993 Catholic Almanac* (Huntington, IN: Our Sunday Visitor, 1992), 329.

What is the Fifth Heaven?

According to Ptolemy of ancient Egypt, the Fifth Heaven is the dwelling of God and the angels. The Hebrews saw it as the land of the fallen angels and, according to the lost *Apocalypse of Zephaniah*, in its northern region as the home of enthroned angels whose crowns shone brighter than the sun. Moslems call it "the seat of Aaron and the Avenging Angel."

Gustav Davidson, *A Dictionary of Angels, Including the Fallen Angels* (New York: The Free Press, 1967), s.v. "Fifth Heaven."

In Arthurian legend who imprisoned Merlin?

In Arthurian legend the enchanter Merlin was imprisoned under a great stone by Nimue, sometimes called Vivianne, who was the daughter of Dionas. Merlin became infatuated with Nimue and thus susceptible to capture after which she adopted his magical powers.

John Matthews, *The Elements of the Arthurian Tradition* (Dorset, Engl.: Element, 1991), 102.

What are Judaism's ideas about life after death?

There are a number of approaches to life-after-death in the Jewish tradition, although the Old Testament says little about it, and concentrates instead on what one should do while alive. The Old Testament explains how to live in this world, not what is going to happen to us after we die. Centuries ago, the Baal Shem Tov, the father of the Chasidic movement and a believer in life-after-death, said "If I love God here and now, why do I need to worry about the life of the world-to-come?" A statement from the Book of Job (7:9) seems to rule out life-after death: "As a cloud fades away and disappears, so a person that goes down to the grave will not come up from it." The book of Daniel (12:2-3), however, tells of a different fate for mankind. It says that when the people of Israel are saved, "many of those who 'sleep' in the dust of the earth shall awaken, some to everlasting life and some to criticism and everlasting rejection," depending on the lives they led prior to death. The beliefs of the Pharisees also became widely accepted among Jews. One such belief taught "resurrection," such that, when the Messiah came, the graves of the dead would open and the bodies would be made perfect and pure. They would then rise, redeem their souls from Heaven, and come before God for judgment. Those deemed righteous would go straight into the life of the world-to-come, while the wicked would be punished until they were purified.

Eugene B. Borowitz, *Understanding Judaism* (New York: Union of American Hebrew Congregations, 1979), 218-20.

When Palm Sunday is celebrated in Russia what is substituted for palms?

Because of a scarcity of palms in Russia, pussy-willows are substituted in Palm Sunday celebrations.

Henry Dreyfuss, *Symbol Sourcebook* (1972; reprint, New York: Van Nostrand Reinhold, 1984), 139.

In voodoo what is a lao?

In voodoo a lao is a supernatural being. Voodoo adherents believe in endless numbers of these supernatural beings with new ones being constantly created by "faith and fantasy." Laos are often referred to as "mysteries" and sometimes as "saints" and "angels" but regardless of their demeanor they are an integral part of voodoo and monopolize all aspects of the religion. They can be benevolent and compassionate but a "diab" or "devil spirit" can be violent and cruel.

The word voodoo probably comes from the Fon language group of Africa meaning "god" or "spirit" but would translate into western languages as "fetish."

Alfred Metraux, *Voodoo in Haiti* (New York: Schocken Books, 1972), 27, 82-83, 376.

What are yin and yang in Chinese cosmology?

Yin and yang are the two basic elements that make up the universe. According to traditional Chinese cosmology, yin is feminine and passive. It is of the earth, embracing all that is dark, cold, and wet. Yang is active, masculine, and of the heavens. It includes light, heat, and dryness. They are supposed to complement each other and work in harmony. Through their interaction all that exists has been created.

Richard Cavendish, ed., *Man, Myth & Magic: An Illustrated Encyclopedia of the Supernatural* (NY: Marshall Cavendish, 1970), 457, 459.

Who was the founder of Christian Science?

Christian Science, one of several indigenous American religious denominations, was founded by Mary Baker Eddy (1821-1910). An invalid, she became interested in different types of healing, both physical and mental. Eddy eventually turned to the Bible during a recovery from a severe fall and developed a spiritual and metaphysical system known as Christian Science. She defined her teachings of harmonialism in *Science and Health with Key to the Scriptures* (1875), and she started the Church of Christ Scientist in 1879.

Charles H. Lippy and Peter W. Williams, eds., *Encyclopedia of the American Religious Experience* (New York: Charles Scribner, 1988), 2:901.

What is a good source of prayers appropriate for funerals or vesper services?

A good source of prayers appropriate for funerals or vesper services is *The Book of Common Prayer* published by the Episcopal Church.

Episcopal Church, *The Book of Common Prayer* (New York: Church Hymnal Corporation, 1979), 833.

Who was Aimee Semple McPherson?

Aimee Semple McPherson (1890-1944) was a charismatic preacher who settled in Los Angeles and started the Angelus Temple, a religious cult that sponsored revivalist meetings throughout the United States and in several foreign countries. Known for her flamboyant style of preaching, "Sister Aimee," as she was called, also had a radio show and rubbed shoulders with many of the important people of her day. A controversial figure, she was often involved in law suits and disappeared mysteriously for five weeks in 1926.

E. Randall Floyd, *Great American Mysteries* (Little Rock, AR: August House, 1991), 123-24.

What are some of the superstitions about ocean waves?

There are many superstitions about ocean waves. According to some primitive people the sea was considered an animate being, and waves were a result of its voluntary movement. The ancient Greeks and Romans believed the god Poseidon (Neptune) produced the waves and also made them subside. The Vikings maintained that the waves were daughters of the goddess Rana, and that the gods or genii were responsible for the movements of the sea. In Saint Malo, a coastal town in Brittany, it is told that waves are caused by a sorcerer who lost his magic mill in the ocean and now plunges in to find it. According to another legend, witches can take the form of waves and destroy ships carrying people with whom they are angry. In Brittany it is said that the sound of the tossing sea is really the cry of drowned men who are restless and agitated because their bodies have not been buried in consecrated ground.

Angelo S. Rappoport, *Superstitions of Sailors* (London: Stanley Paul & Co., 1928), 32-34.

What are some of the superstitions about the phosphorescence of the sea?

There are many legends about the phosphorescence of the sea. sometimes called Saint Elmo's fire. Sailors on the coast of the English Channel say that it is caused by small fishes turned blue by the stars. There is also the tradition that it emanates from the lantern of a sorcerer who is searching for his magic handmill. Breton sailors believe that a big bottom-dwelling fish, which is called the devil of the sea, breathes out flames through his nostrils to destroy his enemies. In Pomerania the phosphorescence of the sea is said to issue from a burning cask of tar on which the devil is sailing. It is also claimed that the glow is caused by the jewels of nymphs and sirens, or by diamonds and precious stones that ornament a garden at the bottom of the sea where the souls of the just who have drowned are living.

Angelo S. Rappoport, *Superstitions of Sailors* (London: Stanley Paul & Co., 1928), 51-52.

Who was the first native-born American to be declared a saint in the Roman Catholic Church?

Elizabeth Ann Bailey Seton (1774-1821), who is better known as Mother Seton, was the first native-born American to be named a saint. She came from a distinguished New York family; her father was the first professor of anatomy at Columbia University. In 1794 she married William Seton, and in the years when New York was the capital of the United States, the Setons were friends with men such as George Washington (1732-1799) and Thomas Jefferson (1743-1826). Left a widow with five children at age twenty-nine, she was drawn to the Roman Catholic church, which she entered in 1805. She started an elementary school in Baltimore and laid the foundation of the Catholic parochial system. In 1809 she established a religious order, the Sisters of Charity of Saint Joseph. She was canonized in 1975 by Pope Paul VI. Seton Hall University in South Orange, New Jersey is named in her honor. Although Mother Seton is the first native-born American saint, Francis Cabrini (1850-1917), born in Italy, was the first American citizen to become a saint.

Leonard Feeney, *Mother Seton: Saint Elizabeth of New York* (Cambridge: Ravengate Press, 1975).

What was the main target of theologian Martin Luther's 95 Theses?

Theologian Martin Luther (1483-1546) disapproved of granting indulgences. The Roman Catholic Church teaches that indulgences are a means by which a penitent receives remission from the temporal punishment caused by sin (time spent in Purgatory) by undertaking some pious act like saying a prayer or making a pious bequest. The indulgence against which Luther reacted was being used as a means of raising funds for the building of St. Peter's cathedral in Rome. The faithful were required to go to Confession and to make a money offering, and in exchange they or, if they so intended, a departed loved one would receive a plenary indulgence (all time in Purgatory would be erased). The indulgence was preached in a most unscrupulous way by John Tetzel, who implied that one could buy God's mercy. Luther, who saw salvation as a free gift of God, reacted against the notion that it could be compelled by our actions. True penance, according to Luther, is a permanent interior attitude, which has been given and could never be bought.

Martin Luther, *Luther's Ninety-five Theses, trans. C.M Jacobs, rev. Harold J. Grimm* (Philadelphia: Fortress Press, 1957), 6

What tragedy occurred near Jonestown, Guyana?

Jonestown, Guyana became well known following the slaying of a U.S. congressman and the mass suicide of hundreds of Americans at the religious commune. On November 18, 1978, members of the People's Temple religious cult gunned down U.S. Representative Leo J. Ryan and four others. Ryan had come to Guyana to investigate allegations that cult members were being held against their wishes. Jim Jones, the founder of the People's Temple, had previously left San Francisco in 1977 to escape abuse allegations there by former cult members and build a commune in the South American country. The violence erupted when Ryan, reporters, relatives of cult members, and some residents who had elected to leave the commune prepared to board a plane. Many were wounded in random fire, but Ryan, NBC-TV reporter Don Harris, *San Francisco Examiner* photographer Gregory Robinson, and NBC cameraman Robert Brown were killed at point blank range. Cult member Patricia Parks also died of gunshot wounds.

Guyanese troops did not arrive at the scene until the next morning, since the airstrip was unlit. They were soon met by a man from Jonestown who reported the mass suicide. When the soldiers reached the village they discovered hundreds of bodies. Some had been shot in the head, while many had killed themselves by drinking Kool-Aid mixed with cyanide. Jim Jones was found dead near an altar with a bullet wound to the head. The number of dead totaled 780. It was estimated that only 35 cult members survived by escaping into the surrounding jungle. The survivors related that Jones became despondent during the congressman's visit, feeling betrayed by the departing members. After the airport shooting he urged the Jonestown residents to end their lives using his preplanned method. One of the survivors also gave details of how Jones had directed the gunmen to kill the pilot of Ryan's plane after it was in the air. The failure to kill all witnesses led to the second tragedy.

Facts on File (New York: Facts on File, 1978), 889.

In the Old Testament, who is the "Avenger of Blood?"

The Old Testament identifies the "Avenger of Blood" as the closest relative of a murdered person. It is this individual's responsibility to avenge the death of their kinsman by killing a member of the murderer's family. Patterns of kinship and specific responsibilities are defined in the books Numbers and Deuteronomy. The ancient law discriminates between murder and unintentional manslaughter, and allows for the killer's exile in the second case. One example of blood vengeance in the Old Testament is in the Book of Judges, when Gideon avenged the death of his brothers by killing the Midanites who were responsible for their murders; another such example is in the Second Book of Samuel, in the account of how the Gibeonites avenged murders caused by Saul.

Allen C. Myers, ed., *The Eerdmans Bible Dictionary* (Grand Rapids, MI: William B. Eerdmans Publishing, 1987), 109.

What pope died 33 days after his election?

Pope John Paul I (1912-1978) died 33 days after he was elected Pope of the Roman Catholic Church. He was elected Pope on August 26, 1978 and died of heart attack on September 28. He was the first Pope to use two names, taking them from his two predecessors, John XXIII and Paul VI.

Joseph A. DeBartolot, *In Further Pursuit of Trivial Pursuit* (Chicago: Sarsaparilla, 1984), 196.

What role did Tom s de Torquemada play in the Spanish Inquisition?

Tom s de Torquemada (1420-1498) was inquisitor-general, or chief official, of the Spanish Inquisition for 15 years (1482-98). During his period of office, some 2,000 people were executed by the Inquisition for heresy (beliefs contrary to those of the Catholic church). Torquemada was the head of the Inquisition under Ferdinand (1452-1516) and Isabella (1451-1504) when Christopher Columbus (1451-1506) discovered America.

World Book Encyclopedia (Chicago: World Book, 1994), s.v. "Torquemada, Tom s de."

What are the Orphic Hymns?

The name Orphic Hymns has been given to a collection of 87 hymns that are believed to have been composed between 200 and 100 B.C. The hymns address well-known Greek gods and goddesses such as Dionysus and Demeter. They presumably were chanted during the Orphic Mysteries, initiation ceremonies for a religion sometimes called Orphism.

Rufus C. Camphausen, *The Divine Library: A Comprehensive Reference Guide to the Sacred Texts and Spiritual Literature of the World* (Rochester, VT: Inner Traditions International, 1992), 71-72.

Can a note be faxed to Jerusalem's Wailing Wall?

Every day hundreds of notes from people seeking divine intervention are stuffed into cracks in Jerusalem's Wailing Wall, one of Judaism's most sacred shrines. A fax, transmitted to Israel's national telephone company, will be taken to the wall by company employees. The number, which is not toll-free, is 972-2-612222.

USA Today 21 January 1993.

When did the Huguenots come to America?

Escaping religious persecution, the first Huguenots-the name given to French Protestants-settled in Florida but were killed by the Spanish in 1565 at Fort Caroline. Following further religious persecutions during 1685 in France under Louis XIV, Huguenots who came to the colonies were from France's upper classes and were quickly assimilated into the general population. One exception to this is the town of New Rochelle, New York, which Huguenots established it in 1688. The only remaining Huguenot church in America today is in Charleston, South Carolina. U.S. presidents George Washington, John Adams, John Quincy Adams, James Garfield, and Theodore Roosevelt have claimed some Huguenot ancestry.

Family Encyclopedia of American History (Pleasantville, NY: Reader's Digest Association, 1975), s.v. "Huguenots in America."

Who is St. Expeditus?

St. Expeditus, "the patron of haste," is among the saints whose existence has been disputed. For the cult that grew up around him, it was believed that invoking his assistance in those matters requiring haste would guarantee a good outcome. Many scholars believe that this saint grew out of a misspelling on the rolls of martyrs.

Herbert Thruston and Donald Attwater, eds., *Butler's Lives of the Saints* (P.J. Kenedy & Sons, 1956), 128-29.

What is the meaning of the story of the blind men and the elephant?

The Indian story of the blind men and the elephant is told as an example of how narrow-mindedness can lead to false conclusions. The blind men each took to examining a different aspect of the elephant, becoming convinced that his view was the correct one. Touching the animal's trunk, one man believed the elephant was much like a snake; another thought it was similar to a fan because he happened to touch the elephant's ear; and on it went. It never dawned on any of the men to share their observations with the others and accept the others' viewpoints so that they could come to a more complete idea of what the elephant was. The story has been used by theologians to teach that the great truths cannot be understood by those who approach them from a single perspective.

John Arnott MacCulloch, ed., *The Mythology of All Races* (n.p., Marshall Jones Co., 1928). Burton Egbert Stevenson, ed., *The Home Book of Verse* (New York: Holt, 1962).

How many times does the Lord's Prayer occur in the Bible?

The Lord's Prayer occurs twice in the New Testament of the Bible, in the books of Matthew (Chapter VI) and Luke (Chapter XI).

David Louis, *2201 Fascinating Facts* (Old Lyme, CT: Greenwich House, 1983), 21.

How many popes have been murdered?

There have been twenty-six popes murdered.

John May, *Curious Trivia* (New York: Dorset Press, 1984), 198.

What is a millennium?

A millennium is a one thousand year period. Christians believe that Jesus Christ will rule for a millennium on earth. Some people believe that at the end of the millennium there will be a significant occurrence, such as a final judgement or redemption of the world. Those who believe in the significance of the millennium are called millenarians.

Herbert Kohl, *From Archetype to Zeitgeist* (Boston: Little, Brown and Co., 1992).

What is a Kakure Kirishitan?

Kakure Kirishitan is a unique religion existing in Japan. The term translates into "crypto-Christian," and the religion consists of rituals borrowed from Christianity and Buddhism.

The history of the sect can be traced back to the arrival of Jesuit missionary Francis Xavier (1506-1552), who brought Roman Catholicism to Japan in 1549. The creed soon grew to 300,000 followers, but Japanese rulers feared its strength and mounted a terror campaign. The faithful soon learned to adapt much of their Christian rituals while praying in Buddhist temples or secretly praying at home. The Kakure survived secretly until 1865, when Japan allowed the Catholic church on its soil. The Vatican took a strong stance against the Kakure, and many returned to their own way of worship. Today there are approximately 10,000 followers of Kakure Kirishitan.

Time 11 January 1992.

Who were the twelve apostles to Jesus in Christianity?

The following is a list of the twelve disciples to Jesus Christ in the Christian religion:

Simon, also called Peter
Andrew, his brother
James, son of Zebedees
John, his brother
Philip
Bartholomew
Thomas
Matthew, the tax collector

James, son of Alphaeus
Thaddaeus
Simon the Canaanite
Judas Iscariot, who betrayed Jesus

The Holy Bible, New King James Version (Nashville, TN: Thomas Nelson, 1982), 940.

What do the four Horsemen of the Apocalypse represent?

The four Horsemen of the Apocalypse represent war, force, famine, and death. They are referred to in the Bible in the book of Revelation 6:1-8. War is represented by a rider with a bow on a white horse. His purpose is to overthrow anything that would challenge divine will. A red horse carrying a rider with a sword represents force resulting in civil war or the principle that evil is inherently self-destructive. Famine is represented by a black horse and a rider carrying a balance. An evil society that survives attack and civil war will succumb to starvation. The last horse is greenish yellow and the rider is Death. Vincente Blasco Ibanez, a Spanish author, wrote an anti-war story about family members who fight on different sides during World War I (1914-18) entitled *Four Horsemen of the Apocalypse.* It has been twice produced as a motion picture: first as a silent film in 1921 starring Rudolph Valentino, and later in 1962 with Glenn Ford, Charles Boyer, and Lee J. Cobb.

The Interpreter's Bible: The Holy Scriptures in the King James and Revised Standard Versions with General Articles And Introduction, Exegesis, Exposition for Each Book of the Bible (Nashville, TN: Abingdon Press, 1957). *Benet's Reader's Encyclopedia, 3d ed.* (New York: Harper & Row, 1987), s.v. "four horsemen of the apocalypse." *The Holy Bible* (New York: Cambridge University Press, 1937), Revelations 6:1-8. Leonard Maltin, ed., *Leonard Maltin's Movie and Video Guide* (New York: Penguin, 1992), s.v. "Four Horsemen of the Apocalypse."

Which of the nine Muses is depicted with a tablet and stylus, and sometimes with a scroll?

Calliope is the Muse of epic poetry and as such, is depicted with a tablet and stylus, and sometimes with a scroll. She is one of the nine Muses in mythological literature and was said to be the mother of several famous poets and musicians. Her children include Corybantes by Zeus; Hymen, Ialemus, and Linus by Apollo; and Orpheus by Oeargus.

Robert E. Bell, *Women of Classical Mythology: A Biographical Dictionary* (Santa Barbara, CA: ABC-CLIO, 1991), s.v. "Calliope."

What is Scientology and who was its founder?

Scientology is a religious philosophy which has spread throughout the world. It is promoted by the Church of Scientology which was founded by L. (Lafayette) Ron Hubbard (1911-1986) in 1953. Scientology teaches therapeutic techniques and regimens to help individuals overcome the negative effects of their present and previous lives. This overcoming process is called "auditing" and it achieves a condition known as "clear." According to Scientology, if all people were "clear," the world would be relieved of all problems, such as war, crime, drugs, pollution, and disease. Scientology and Hubbard, before his death in 1986, have been involved in many controversies and disputes with numerous governments.

Rosemary Ellen Guiley, *Harper's Encyclopedia of Mystical & Paranormal Experience* (San Francisco: HarperSanFrancisco, 1991), s.v. "Church of Scientology."

What is the Serenity Prayer?

The Serenity Prayer, written by Reinhold Niebuhr, offers: "God, give us grace to accept with serenity the things that cannot be changed, courage to change the things which should be changed, and the wisdom to distinguish the one from the other." Its origins date to 1943, when Niebuhr penned it for a Congregational service in Heath, Massachusetts. The prayer later appeared in the monthly publication of the Federal Council of Churches.

John Bartlett, *Familiar Quotations* (Boston: Little, Brown, 1980), 823.

Who was the goddess Cybele?

Cybele was a goddess who personified the earth in a primitive state, and in her native province of Phrygia in Anatolia (modern-day Turkey) she was worshiped on mountain tops in the form of a black meteorite. She was brought to Rome in 205 B.C. during the Second Punic War to save the city from Hannibal's invading army. The Romans gave her a woman's body and established her temple close to the seat of government on the Capitoline Hill. They called the Great Mother (magna mater), and she became one of the most important deities in the city.

Elinor W. Gadon, *The Once and Future Goddess,* (New York: Harper & Row, 1989), 197.

What were Mahatma Gandhi's Seven Sins?

Mahatma Gandhi (1869-1948), the Indian nationalist and spiritual leader, is considered to be the father of his country for his leadership in ending British colonial rule in India. Because of his insistence on nonviolence and passive resistance, he earned the admiration of many people outside of his own country. On the wall of the memorial built on the spot where he was cremated, there are inscribed his seven deadly sins: wealth without works, pleasure without conscience, knowledge without character, commerce without morality, science without humanity, worship without sacrifice, and politics without principle.

Presidential Documents 23 January 1978.

What is the history of Black Judaism?

The history of Black Judaism evolved from several sources. To begin with, freed slaves were welcome at American synagogues during the early nineteenth century. Next, many West Indians converted to Judaism when they worked for Jewish plantation owners on the islands. As the West Indians migrated to American cities they began their own synagogues. The Moorish Zionist Temple in New York City, founded in 1899, was one of the first such congregations. Another impetus for African-Americans to convert to Judaism came in the later decades of the nineteenth century. A group of long-lost Jews known as the Falashas, possibly descendants of a queen mentioned in the Old Testament of the Bible, were discovered in Ethiopia. During the early twentieth century, Black Judaism gained more adherents as a black consciousness movement also grew. Some Jewish African-American leaders argued that Christianity was an unacceptable choice of creed for blacks since its tenets had sometimes been utilized as a basis for their oppression by whites.

J. Gordon Melton, *Encyclopedia of American Religions, 4th ed.* (Detroit: Gale Research, 1993), 189.

Who was the founder of the Quakers?

A mystic and physic, George Fox (1624-1691) founded the Quaker religious movement in the mid-seventeenth century. As a young minister in England, Fox began preaching a doctrine of piety and sober living, and his teachings served as the basis for the group known formally as the Society of Friends.

J. Gordon Melton, *Encyclopedia of American Religions, 4th ed.* (Detroit, MI: Gale Research Inc., 1993), 90.

What did the scarab symbolize to the ancient Egyptians?

The scarab was an ancient Egyptian representation of a dung-eating beetle and a symbol of the god of creation. The scarab represented the gathering of life and strength by the living. They were often made of black basalt, green stone, or hematite. Amulet scarabs were half an inch to two inches in length. They were popular during the XIth or XIIth dynasties, but by 550 B.C. lost their appeal.

Migene Gonz lez-Wippler, *The Complete Book of Amulets & Talismans* (St. Paul, MN: Llewellyn Publications, 1991), 18-19.

Who were the *Essenes?*

The *Essenes* were a Jewish ascetic sect who dwelled on the shores of the Dead Sea during the time of Jesus Christ. Generally they rejected marriage and lived segregated and dedicated lives, striving to become pure temples of the Holy Spirit. They readily received Jesus of Nazareth and openly shared their secrets with him. During the time of Christ the order was an important representative of ascetic occultism.

Lionel Stebbing, *A Dictionary of the Occult Sciences* (New York: Gordon Press, 1976), 5-30.

What is Zen?

Zen is a form of Buddhism based on the teachings of Bodhidharma, who taught in China circa A.D. 520. The word derives from the Japanese equivalent of the Chinese Ch'an, which translates as "meditation." Zen has been described as "the revolt of the Chinese mind against the intellectual Buddhism of India."

Christmas Humphreys, *A Popular Dictionary of Buddhism* (London: Curzon Press, 1976), 222-23.

What famous lexicographer censored the Bible?

Famed American lexicographer Noah Webster (1758-1843) once published a version of the Bible from which he had eliminated all references to sex and what might be deemed "vulgar passages."

Irving Wallace, *Significa* (New York: E.P. Dutton, 1983), 178.

What happened to 200 Roman Catholic saints in 1969?

In 1969 the Roman Catholic Church removed more than 200 saints from its official liturgical calendar. Affected by the reform move, which was ordered by the Ecumenical Council Vatican II (1962-65), were such well-known saints as St. Valentine and St. Christopher. Some of them, however, will still remain saints, but without a feast day.

"200 Catholic Saints Lose Their Feast Day," *New York Times* 10 May 1969.

Who was the first male American saint named so by the Roman Catholic Church?

The first male American saint named by the Roman Catholic Church was Father John Nepomucene Neuman, a Redemptorist Priest. Father Neuman served in the Pittsburgh area in the 1840s.

Pittsburgh Advertiser 18 August 1976.

Who was the Emperor of Ethiopia and the Rastafarian Messiah?

Haile Selassie (1892-1975), who was born Tafari Makonnen, was the Emporer of Ethiopia from 1930 to 1974. He was forced to abdicate following widespread political discontent, a famine in the Wello province, and rising oil prices following the 1973 Arab-Israeli War which had a devastating effect on Ethiopia's economy. Selassie will be best remembered for his 1936 impassioned plea before the League of Nations calling for an end to Facist Italy's invasion of his country.

As Emperor of Ethiopia Selassie was also believed to be the Rastafarian Messiah. Rastafarianism is an Afro-Caribbean religious movement which is especially prominent in Jamaica and holds that the Messiah will come from Ethiopia. This belief is largely based on *Psalms* 68:31: "Princes come out of Egypt; Ethiopia shall soon stretch out her hands unto God." The word "rastafarian" is derived from the Ethiopian "Ras" (Prince) and "Tafari," which was Selassie's former name. Following his abdication, Selassie was held under house arrest; the leftist revolutionary government issued a terse statement of his demise but refused to reveal the burial site of the man who served as Ethiopia's leader for sixty years.

Anne Commire, ed., *Historic World Leaders* (Detroit: Gale Research, 1994), 1:192-96. Mircea Eliade, *The Encyclopedia of Religion* (New York: Macmillan, 1987), 3:95-96.

Who were the Horae?

Horae is the collective name for the goddesses of the seasons. They signified continuity and dependability. Because of the regular recurrence of the seasons, these goddesses also came to personify justice and law. They could be called upon to bring order, fairness, and peace to the activities of humankind. Various writers offer different interpretations of the concept of the Horae. Homer depicted them as ministers of Zeus guarding the doors of Olympus and as divinities of weather providing the earth with the changing seasons essential to fertility. Eunomia (Discipline), Dice (Justice), and Eirene (Peace) were names attributed to them by Hesiod. In Athens the Horae, Thallo and Carpo, were worshiped in relation to the birth and maturation of living things and Thallo came to be seen as the protectress of youth. Other authors offered additional interpretations which may have included parts of the seasons or the hours as Horae.

Robert E. Bell, *Women of Classical Mythology: A Biographical Dictionary,* (Santa Barbara, CA: ABC-CLIO, 1991), s.v. "horae."

When did Buddhism officially come to Japan?

Buddhism officially came to Japan on October 13, 552 during the reign of Emperor Kimmei, the 29th mikado of Japan. This is according to the *Nihonshoki*, an official history of Japan that dates to 720, although many scholars think the religion probably came earlier.

Shinsho Hanayama, *A History of Japanese Buddhism* (Tokyo: Bukkyo Dendo Kyokai, 1966).

What superstitions do sailors attach to waterspouts?

Waterspouts, which are rotating columns of cloud-filled wind that extend from the base of a cloud to the mist above the surface of the sea, are the subject of many sailors' legends. In Brittany it is said that waterspouts are sent by God for the purpose of feeding the clouds. They can sweep away everything in their path and even sink a ship. The Arabs, Japanese, and Chinese have identified them with dragons. It was often believed that by making a great deal of noise one could frighten off the dragon. In Western culture reciting Scripture and cutting the spout with a black-handled knife were deemed effective ways of dealing with waterspouts.

Angelo S. Rappoport, *Superstitions of Sailors* (London: Paul Stanley & Co., 1928), 47-50.

What is the ancient Egyptian equivalent of the River Styx?

The ancient Egyptians shared a belief in an afterlife, but they often differed as to its exact nature. According to one version the deceased would to travel east to the Lily Lake, which had to be crossed to reach the land Ra. There was a regular boatman, but he was reluctant and had to be cajoled to do his job. As a last resort one could fly over the lake as a bird or be transported on a cloud of incense.

Flinders Petrie, *Religious Life in Ancient Egypt* (Boston: Houghton Mifflin, 1924), 118-19.

What was the Social Gospel movement?

The Social Gospel movement was a late nineteenth-century attempt by Protestants to apply principles of Christianity to the social and economic problems caused by an increasingly industrialized society. Forefront in the movement were such noted Protestant churchmen as Washington Gladden, Lyman Abbott and Charles Sheldon. The movement strived for improved working conditions for women, the abolition of child labor, and a good working wage. The precepts of the movement were adopted in 1908 by the Federal Council of the Churches of Christ in America. Allied in principle with the movement was the Society of Christian Socialists, founded in 1889.

Family Encyclopedia of American History (Pleasantville, NY: Reader's Digest Association, 1975), 1040.

Why did King James have his version of the Bible translated, and who are some others who have their own translations?

Numerous editions of the Bible have been named for their translators or patrons, the most famous being the *King James* or *Authorized Version,* which was prepared by a group of British scholars working at the command of King James I from 1604 to 1611. James commissioned this version mainly because other Bibles of the time had marginal notes questioning the divine right of kings. *Coverdale's Bible, Cranmer's Bible, Cromwell's Bible, Matthew's Bible, Matthew Parker's Bible, Taverner's Bible, Tyndale's Bible* and *Wycliffe's Bible* are all famous in history.

Robert Hendrickson, *Human Words: The Compleat Unexpurgated, Uncomputerized Human Wordbook* (Radnor, PA: Chilton Book Co., 1972), 28-29.

Where is the Hill of Evil Counsel?

The Hill of Evil Counsel is located in Jerusalem. It is also known as Givat Hananiah to Jews, and as Abu Tor to Moslems. Christian tradition identifies the site as the summer home of the High Priest Caiaphas, and the place where he asked Jesus if he was the "Christ." Jesus answered that he was the Christ, which meant that he was the anointed one, the Messiah who had come to save the human race. To a pious Jew this response seemed to be blasphemy, and for this reason the site was called the hill of Evil Counsel. The location is significant in Jewish tradition, as the burial place of the High Priest Hananiah in the Second Temple Period. Moslems know the hill as a monument to Saladin, a warrior who helped defeat the Crusaders in 1187. He was given the hill and it was named after his practice of riding a bull; Abu Tor means "father of the bull."

Nitza Rosovsky, *Jerusalemwalks* (New York: Holt, Rinehart and Winston, 1982), 177.

What was the Delphic oracle?

The Delphic oracle was an ancient shrine at Delphi, on the southern slope of Mount Parnassus. Revelations, or oracles from the gods, were mouthed by a priestess and interpreted by a priest. There were many oracles in the Greek world, but the Delphic oracle was considered the final authority in religious matters, and was the source of many famous Greek myths.

Benet's Reader's Encyclopedia, 3d ed. (New York: Harper & Row, 1987), s.v. "Delphic Oracle."

What character in Greek mythology had snakes for hair and the particular quality of turning to stone those who looked at her face?

Medusa is the character from Greek mythology who had snakes for hair. She was one of the three Gorgons, and had the ability to turn to stone those who looked at her face. She was finally defeated by Perseus, who used his shield as a mirror to avoid looking directly into her face while cutting off her head.

Michael Senior, *The Illustrated Who's Who in Mythology* (New York: Macmillan Publishing Co., 1985), s.v. "Medusa."

What is meant by the phrase "fiddler's green"?

The term "fiddler's green," coined by soldiers, is a region between heaven and hell to which some souls go after death. The concept of a fiddler's green was particularly popular among hard-living military men who felt that after suffering through warfare they had earned some respite from the rigors of hell.

John R. Elting, *A Dictionary of Soldier Talk* (New York: Charles Scribner's Sons, 1984), s.v. "Fiddler's (Fiddlers') Green."

What is meant by the concept "justification by faith"?

The concept of "justification by faith" is central to the Christian religion. Christian teachers, including St. Paul and St. James, explained that salvation is the result of a complete act of justification, in which the sinner repents and accepts God's grace. Full assurance of salvation therefore rests wholly upon God's word which accomplishes what it says, and not on a series of good deeds or pious activities. In the Christian religion, one does not become good by doing good, but rather must *be* good before he or she can *do* good. Grace flows from God into humanity, and through the Christian disciple out into the world at large. The fuller phrase "justification by grace alone, for Christ's sake, through faith active in good works" provides a more comprehensive explanation of the tenet.

James Childress and John Macquarrie, eds., *The Westminster Dictionary of Christian Ethics* (Philadelphia: Westminster Press, 1986), s.v. "justification by faith."

How many wives did Mormon leader Brigham Young have?

Mormon leader Brigham Young (1801-1877) left the Methodist Church to join the Mormon Church, as did several of his family members. He was appointed an apostle in 1835 and was elected church president in 1847. Young proceeded to follow the Mormon practice of plural marriage; he had 27 wives and fathered 56 children.

The Encyclopedia Americana, International Edition (Danbury, CT: Grolier, 1994), s.v. "Young, Brigham."

What is involved in the Catholic rite of exorcism?

The Catholic rite of exorcism, consisting of 11 parts, is performed by a priest following strict guidelines outlined by the Vatican. Scripture readings, prayers, and admonitions for the demon to leave the "child of God" are included in the service, during which holy water is sprinkled on the possessed person and those attending the exorcism and signs of the cross are made on the forehead of the possessed. In the past, flagellation and fumigation were used to torture the demon into leaving the possessed.

Rossell Robbins, *Encyclopedia of Witchcraft and Demonology* (New York: Crown Publishers, Inc., 1972).

Biology, Zoology, Botany, Anatomy

Why does a wet beard ensure a closer shave?

Scientists say that the hairs in a man's beard can expand as much as thirty-four percent when wet with warm water, which makes them softer and easier to cut.

Jane Polley, ed., *Stories Behind Everyday Things* (Pleasantville, NY: Reader's Digest Association, 1980), 273.

Which blood type was not present in the pre-Columbian Native American population?

Pre-Columbian Native Americans were type A or type O blood. They had no type B.

Isaac Asimov, ed., *Isaac Asimov's Book of Facts* (New York: Bell Publishing, 1981), 29.

What is the origin of the word dandelion?

The word "dandelion" is a corruption of the French *Dent de lion* (meaning tooth of the lion), and refers to the resemblance between the plant's jagged leaf and the jaw of a lion. Dandelion seeds blown into the wind carry with them thoughts of love, its dried roots make a passable coffee, and its tender young leaves grace many a salad. It has been stated that when their crops failed, the Minorca inhabitants lived on this plant for weeks.

A. Stoddard Kull, *Secrets of Flowers* (Brattleboro, VT: Stephen Greene Press, 1976), 80.

What percentage of people are left-handed?

It is estimated that ten percent of the population is left-handed.

John Powers, "The Left Stuff," *Reader's Digest* August 1992.

How large was Tyrannosaurus Rex?

Tyrannosaurus Rex, long been regarded as the greatest predator of the Late Cretaceous Period, is the largest carnosaur and the largest terrestrial carnivore yet discovered. The average "T Rex" was 39 feet (12 meters) long, 20 feet (6 meters) tall and probably weighed around 8 tons. The head was over four feet long, was armed with fangs that measured six inches in length. The dinosaur roamed over much of what is now Alberta, Montana, Saskatchewan, Texas, Wyoming, and Mongolia. The long standing belief that Tyrannosaurus was a predator was seriously questioned by paleontologists in the 1960s who suggested that it may have been nothing more than a large scavenger. Paleontologists have since gone back to viewing Tyrannosaurus as a predator because of the large flat area behind the skull which probably anchored massive and powerful jaw muscles. Tyrannosaurus's brain was also quite developed in those areas usually associated with smell and sight, and, in fact, it may have had binocular vision. These physiological developments are characteristic of a predator. If so, Tyrannosaurus probably ambushed and fed on hadrosaurs, the duckbilled dinosaurs.

Dougal Dixon et al., eds, *Macmillan Illustrated Encyclopedia of Dinosaurs and Prehistoric Animals: A Visual Who's Who of Prehistoric Life* (New York: Macmillan Publishing, 1988), 121.

How are coral reefs formed?

Coral reefs grow only in warm, shallow water. The calcium carbonate skeletons of dead corals serve as a framework upon which layers of successively-younger animals attach themselves. Such accumulations, combined with rising water levels, slowly lead to the formation of reefs that can be hundreds of feet deep and long. The coral animal, or polyp, has a columnar form; its lower end is attached to the hard floor of the reef; the upper end is free to extend into the water. A whole colony consists of thousands of individuals.

There are two kinds of corals, hard and soft, depending on the type of skeleton secreted. The polyps of hard corals deposit around themselves a solid skeleton of calcium carbonate (chalk), thus, most swimmers see only the skeleton of the coral; the animal is in a cup-like formation into which it withdraws during the daytime.

Eugene H. Kaplan, *Field Guide to Coral Reefs* (Boston: Houghton Mifflin Co., 1982), 78-79. *Nature* 23 April 1993. *The New Book of Popular Science* (Danbury CT: Grolier, 1988), 2:270.

Do all birds fly?

There are flightless birds, among which the penguins and the ratites are the best known. Ratites includes emus, kiwis, ostriches, rheas, and cassowaries. They are called ratite, because they lack a keel on the breastbone. All of these birds have wings but lost their power to fly millions of years ago. Many birds that live isolated on oceanic islands (for example, the great auk) apparently became flightless in the absence of predators and the consequent gradual disuse of their wings for escape.

Bernhard Grzimek, *Grzimek's Animal Life Encyclopedia* (New York: Van Nostrand Reinhold Company, 1973), 7:89. Ephram L. Palmer, *Fieldbook of Natural History, 2d ed.* (New York: McGraw-Hill, 1974), 550. John K.

Terres, *The Audubon Society Encyclopedia of North American Birds* (New York: Wings Books, 1991), 379.

What is the name of the bird that perches on the black rhinoceros' back?

The bird, a relative of the starling, is called an oxpecker (a member of the Sturnidae family). Found only in Africa, the yellow-billed oxpecker (*Buphagus africanus*) is widespread over much of western and central Africa, while the red-billed oxpecker (*Buphagus erythrorhynchus*) lives in eastern Africa from the Red Sea to Natal. Seven to eight inches (17 to 20 centimeters) long with a coffee-brown body, the oxpecker feeds on more than 20 species of ticks that live in the hide of the black rhinoceros (*Diceros bicornis*), also called the hook-lipped rhino. The bird spends most of its time on the rhinoceros or on other animals, such as the antelope, zebra, giraffe, buffalo, etc. The bird has been known to even roost on the body of its host. The relationship between the oxpecker and the rhinoceros is a type of symbiosis (a close association between two organisms in which at least one of them benefits) called mutualism. The rhinoceros' relief of its ticks and the bird's feeding clearly demonstrates mutualism (a condition in which both organisms benefit). In addition, the oxpecker, having much better eyesight than the nearsighted rhinoceros, alerts its host with its shrill cries and flight when danger approaches.

Maurice Burton, *Encyclopedia of Animals in Colour* (London: Octopus Books, 1972), 209-10. Malcolm Penny, *Rhinos: Endangered Species* (New York: Facts on File, 1988). 32.

What is the most destructive insect in the world?

The most destructive insect is the desert locust (*Schistocera gregaria*), the locust of the Bible, whose habitat ranges from the dry and semi-arid regions of Africa and the Middle East, through Pakistan and northern India. This short-horn grasshopper can eat its own weight in food a day, and during long migratory flights a large swarm can consume 20,000 tons (18,160,000 kilograms) of grain and vegetation a day.

Gerald L. Wood, *The Guinness Book of Animal Facts and Feats, 3d ed.* (London: Guinness Superlatives, 1982), 174.

Do male mosquitoes bite humans?

No, male mosquitoes live on plant juices, sugary saps, and liquids arising from decomposition. They do not have a biting mouth that can penetrate human skin. But the females do. In some species, the females need blood to lay their eggs. Blood lipids are converted into the needed iron and protein to produce great numbers (200) of eggs.

David Feldman, *Do Penguins Have Knees?* (New York: Harper Perennial, 1991), 190. d'Entreves P. Passarin, *The Secret Life of Insects* (New York: Chartwell, 1976), 28.

How many eggs does a spider lay?

The number of eggs varies according to the species. Some larger spiders lay over 2,000 eggs, but many tiny spiders lay one or two and perhaps no more than a dozen during their lifetime. Spiders of average size probably lay a hundred or so. Most spiders lay all their eggs at one time and enclose them in a single egg sac. Others lay eggs over a period of time and enclose them in a number of egg sacs.

Richard Headstrom, *Spiders of the United States* (Stamford, CT: A.S. Barnes, 1973), 34.

How long does it take the average spider to weave a complete web?

The average orb-weaver spider takes 30 to 60 minutes to completely spin its web. The order Araneae (the spiders) constitutes the largest division in the class Arachnida, containing about 32 thousand species. These species of spiders use silk to capture their food in a variety of ways ranging from the simple trip wires used by the large bird-eating spiders to the complicated and beautiful webs spun by the orb spiders. Some species produce funnel-shaped webs and there are also communal webs built by communities of spiders.

The completed web has several spokes leading from the initial structure. The number and nature of the spokes depend on the species. The spider replaces any damaged threads by gathering up the thread in front of it and producing a new one behind it. The orb web must be replaced every few days because it loses its stickiness (and its ability to entrap food).

The largest aerial webs are spun by the tropical orb weavers of the genus *Nephila*, measuring up to 18 feet 9 inches (5.72 meters) in circumference. The smallest webs are done by the *Glyphesis cottonae* which covers about 0.75 square inches (4.84 square centimeters).

The Guinness Book of Records 1992 (New York: Bantam Book, 1992), 98. *The Illustrated Encyclopedia of Wildlife* (Lakeville,CT: Grey Castle Press, 1991), 9:2264-5. *Scientific American* April 1960.

How do fleas jump so far?

The jumping power of fleas comes both from strong leg muscles and from pads of a rubber-like protein called resilin. The resilin is located above the flea's hind legs. To jump, the flea crouches, squeezing the resilin, and then it relaxes certain muscles. Stored energy from the resilin works like a spring, launching the flea. A flea can jump well both vertically and horizontally. Some species can jump 130 times their own length. To match that record, a human would have to spring over the length of 2 football fields-or the height of a 100-story building-in a single bound. The common flea (Pulex irritans) has been known to jump 13 inches (33 centimeters) in length and 7 inches (18 centimeters) in height.

Mark C. Young, ed., *The Guinness Book of Records, 1995* (New York: Facts on File, 1994), 38. *National Geographic World* July 1990.

How is the light in fireflies produced?

The light produced by fireflies (*Photinus pyroles*) or lightning bugs, is a kind of heatless light called bioluminescence caused by a chemical reaction in which the substance, luciferin, undergoes oxidation, when the enzyme luciferase is present. The flash is a photon of visible light that radiates, when the oxidating chemicals produce a high-energy state, and revert back to their normal state. The flashing is controlled by the nervous system and takes place in special cells called photocytes. The nervous system, photocytes, and the tracheal end organs control the flashing rate. Scientists are uncertain as to why this occurs. The rhythmic flashes could be a means of attracting prey or enabling mating fireflies to signal in heliographic codes (that differ from one species to another) or perhaps even be a warning signal. The air temperature seems to be correlated with the flashing rate. The higher the temperature, the shorter the interval between flashes-8 seconds at 65 degrees Fahrenheit (18 degrees Celsius) and 4 seconds at 82 degrees Fahrenheit (28 degrees Celsius).

Edward Duensing, *Talking to Fireflies, Shrinking the Moon* (New York: Penguin, 1990), 44. Peter Farb, *The Insects* (Alexandria, VA: Time-Life Books, 1977), 119. Caroline Sutton and Duncan M. Anderson, *How Do They Do That?* (New York: Quill, 1982), 206-7.

What causes the Mexican jumping bean to move?

The bean moth (*Carpocapa saltitans*) lays its eggs in the flower or in the seed pod of the spurge, a bush known as *Euphorbia sebastiana*. The egg hatches inside the seed pod producing a larva or caterpillar. The jumping of the bean is caused by the active shifting of weight inside the shell as the caterpillar moves. The jumps of the bean are stimulated by sunshine or by heat from the palm of the hand.

Nature Magazine 1945.

How many horses are there in the world?

According to Dr. D. Fielding of the Edinburgh School of Agriculture (in Edinburgh, United Kingdom) the number of horses worldwide is 65,292,000, the number of donkeys is 41,599,000, and the number of mules is 15,462,000.

Cornell Animal Health Newsletter March 1992.

What is chamois?

The chamois (of the family Bovidae) is a goat-like animal living in the mountainous areas of Spain, central Europe (the Alps and Apennines), south central Europe, the Balkans, Asia Minor, and the Caucasus. Agile and surefooted, with acute senses, it can jump 6.5 feet (2 meters) in height and 19.7 feet (6 meters) in distance, and run at speeds of 31 miles (50 kilometers) per hour. Its skin has been made into "shammy" leather for cleaning glass and polishing automobiles; although now, many times the shammy or chamois skins sold are specially treated sheepskin.

Robert M. Nowak, *Walker's Mammals of the World, 5th ed.* (Baltimore: The Johns Hopkins University Press, 1991), 2:1446.

What are some animals that have pouches?

Marsupials (meaning "pouched" animals) differ from all other living mammals in their anatomical and physiological features of reproduction. Most female marsupials-kangaroos, bandicoots, wombats, banded anteaters, koalas, opossums, wallabies, tasmanian devils, etc.—possess an abdominal pouch (called a marsupium), in which their young are carried. However in some small terrestrial marsupials the marsupium is not a true pouch but merely a fold of skin around the mammae (milk nipples).

The short gestation period in marsupials (in comparison to other similarly-sized mammals) allows their young to be born in an "undeveloped" state. Consequently, these animals have been viewed as "primitive" or second-class mammals. However, some now see that the reproductive process of marsupials has an advantage over that of placental mammals. A female marsupial invests relatively few resources during the brief gestation period, more so during the lactation (nursing period) when the young are in the marsupium. If the female marsupial loses its young, it can sooner make a second attempt than a placental mammal in a comparable situation.

The Illustrated Encyclopedia of Wildlife, (Lakeville, CT: Grey Castle Press, 1991), 607-44. Robert M. Nowak, *Walker's Mammals of the World* (Baltimore: Johns Hopkins University Press, 1991), 1:10-11.

What is the chemical composition of a skunk's spray?

The chief odorous components of the spray have been identified as crotyl mercaptan, isopentyl mercaptan, and methyl crotyl disulfide in the ratio of 4:4:3. The liquid is an oily, pale-yellow, foul-smelling spray which can cause severe eye inflammation. This defensive weapon is discharged from two tiny nipples located just inside the skunk's anus—either as a fine spray or a short stream of rain-sized drops. Although the liquid's range is 10 to 15 feet (3 to 4.5 meters), its smell can be detected one mile (1.6 kilometers) downwind.

Encyclopedia Americana (Danbury, CT: Grollier, 1994), 25:12. Ronald M. Nowak, *Walker's Mammals of the World* (Baltimore: The Johns Hopkins University Press, 1991), 2:1131.

Which mammals lay eggs and suckle their young?

The duck-billed platypus (*Ornithorhynchus anatinus*) and the echidna or spiny anteater (family Tachyglossidae), indigenous to Australia, Tasmania, and New Guinea, are the only two species of mammals that lay eggs (a non-mammalian feature) but suckle their young (a mammalian feature). These mammals (order Monotremata) resemble reptiles in that they lay rubbery shell-covered eggs that are incubated and hatched outside the mother's body. In addition they resemble reptiles in their digestive, reproductive, and excretory systems, and in a number of anatomical details (eye structure, presence of certain skull bones, pectoral (shoulder) girdle and rib and vertebral structures). However they are classed as mammals because they have fur and a four-chambered heart, nurse their young from gland milk, are warm-blooded, and have some mammalian skeletal features.

Nicole Duplaix and Noel Simon, *World Guide to Mammals* (New York: Crown Publishers, 1976), 20. George Stimpson, *Information Roundup* (New York: Harper, 1948), 114.

Do camels store water in their humps?

The hump or humps do not store water, since they are fat reservoirs. The ability to go long periods without drinking water, up to ten months if there is plenty of green vegetation and dew to feed on, results from a number of physiological adaptations. One major factor is that camels can lose up to 40 percent of their body weight with no ill effects. A camel can also withstand a variation of its body temperature by as much as 14 degrees Fahrenheit (-10 degrees Celsius). A camel can drink 30 gallons of water in ten minutes and up to 50 gallons over several hours. A one-humped camel is called a dromedary or Arabian camel; a Bactrian camel has two humps and lives in the wild on the Gobi desert. Today, the Bactrian is confined to Asia, but most of the Arabian camels are on African soil.

Marshall Cavendish International Wildlife Encyclopedia (London: Marshall Cavendish, 1989), 5:484, 488. William Voelker, *The Natural History of Living Mammals* (Medford, NJ: Plexus, 1986), 272-73.

Which animals spend part of the winter in hibernation?

To avoid the harsh winter conditions, some animals migrate, while others build special nests, hide away in caves and burrows and enter a sleep-like state called hibernation. In hibernation heart rate and respiration slow and body temperature drops. Being so inactive, for several months these animals use little energy and can survive on the fat stores they built up earlier. Hibernators include certain birds, such as nighthawks and swifts; mammals, such as bats, chipmunks, ground squirrels, hamsters, hedgehogs, lemurs, groundhogs, marmots and picket mice; amphibians such as frogs and toads; and reptiles such as lizards, snakes, and turtles. The longest hibernator with nine months rest is the Burrow ground squirrel (*Spermophilus parryl barrowensis*) of Point Barrow, Alaska.

Some animals like dormice became active at times and feed on nut and seed caches they stored away in the autumn. They are not true hibernators; nor are bears, skunks and opossums. Although these animals lapse into prolonged sleep, they wake from time to time and do not undergo the extreme metabolic changes that true hibernators do.

Some animals go underground and become inactive to avoid the harsh summer conditions; this is called aestivation (estivation). For example, some lungfish will burrow into the dried-up mud of the river or lake bottoms and wait for more water to come.

Charles J. Cazeau, *Science Trivia* (New York: Berkley Books, 1986),108. Mark C. Young, *The Guinness Book of Records, 1995* (New York: Facts on File, 1994), 26. Harrison L. Matthews, *The Life of Mammals* (New York: Universe Books, 1971), 1:97, 293-5, 300, 2:148.

What is the difference between a reptile and an amphibian?

Reptiles are clad in scales, shields, or plates and their toes have claws. Young reptiles are miniature replicas of their parents in general appearance if not always in coloration and pattern. Reptiles include alligators, crocodiles, turtles, and snakes. Amphibians have moist, glandular skins, and their toes lack claws. Their young pass through a larval, usually aquatic stage before they metamorphose (change in form and structure) into the adult form. Amphibians include salamanders, toads, and frogs.

Roger Conant, *A Field Guide to Reptiles and Amphibians: Eastern and Central North America, 3d ed.* (Boston: Houghton Mifflin, 1991), 1.

How is the age of a cat computed in human years?

When a cat is one year old, it is about 20 years old in human years. Each additional year is multiplied by four. Another source counts the age of a cat slightly differently. At age one, a cat's age equals 16 human years. At age two, a cat's age is 24 human years. Each additional year is multiplied by four.

Cats Magazine March 1982. David Taylor, *You & Your Cat* (New York: Alfred Knopf, 1988), 35.

Which canine breed is known as the "wrinkled dog"?

The shar-pei, or Chinese fighting dog, is covered with folds of loose skin as if its coat is in need of ironing. It stands 18 to 20 inches (46 to 51 centimeters) and weighs up to 50 pounds (22.5 kilograms). Its solid-colored coat can be black, red, fawn, or cream. The dog originated in Tibet or the northern provinces of China some 2,000 years ago. The People's Republic of China put such a high tax on shar-peis that few people could afford to keep them and the dog was in danger of extinction. However, a few specimens were smuggled out of China and the breed has made a comeback in the United States, Canada, and the United Kingdom. Although bred as a fighting dog, the shar-pei is generally an amiable dog.

Joan Palmer, *Dog Facts* (New York: Dorset Press, 1991), 74.

What is the world's oldest breed of dog?

The Saluki is believed to be the world's oldest pure-bred dog. Sumerian rock carvings in Mesopotamia that date to about 7000 B.C. depict dogs bearing a striking resemblance to the Saluki. The dogs are 23 to 28 inches (58.4 to 71 centimeters) tall with a long, narrow head. The coat is smooth and silky and can be white, cream, fawn, gold, red, grizzle (bluish-gray) and tan, black and tan, or tricolor (white, black, and tan). The tail is long and feathered. The Saluki is an excellent hunter, having remarkable sight and tremendous speed. The Greyhound has an almost as equally long pure-bred lineage as the Saluki. Carvings in the tomb of Amten in the Valley of the Nile made about 2900-2751 B.C. depict a Greyhound-type dog in relief.

The oldest American pure-bred dog is the American Foxhound. It descends from a pack of foxhounds belonging to an Englishman named Robert Brooke who settled in Maryland in 1650. These dogs were crossed with other strains imported from England, Ireland, and France to develop the American Foxhound. This dog stands 22 to 25 inches (55.9 to 63.5 centimeters) tall. It has a long, slightly domed head, with a straight, squared-out muzzle. The coat is of medium length and can be any color. They are used primarily for hunting.

American Kennel Club, *The Complete Dog Book* (New York: Howell Book House, 1985), 182, 210-42, 246-48. Joan Palmer, *Dog Facts*, (New York: Dorset Press, 1991), 9-11, 144-45.

How many bones are in the tail of a cat?

The number of bones in the tail of a cat can vary a great deal depending on the length of the tail, but usually the minimum number is 20.

Robert B. Chiasson, *Laboratory Anatomy of the Cat, 6th ed.* (Dubuque, IA: Wm. C. Brown, 1977), 12.

What is the original breed of domestic cat in the United States?

The American shorthair is believed by some naturalists to be the original domestic cat in America. It is descended from cats brought to the New World from Europe by the early settlers. The cats readily adapted to their new environment. Selective breeding to enhance the best traits began early in the twentieth century.

The American shorthair is a very athletic cat with a lithe, powerful body, excellent for stalking and killing prey. Its legs are long, heavy, and muscular, ideal for leaping and for coping with all kinds of terrain. The fur, in a wide variety of color and coat patterns, is thick enough to protect the animal from moisture and cold but short enough to resist matting and snagging.

Although this cat makes an excellent house pet and companion, it remains very self-sufficient. Its hunting instinct is so strong that it exercises the skill even when well-provided with food. The American shorthair is the only true "working cat" in the United States.

Ulrike Mller, *The New Cat Handbook* (Woodbury, NY: Barron, 1984), 125. David Taylor and Daphne Negus, *The Ultimate Cat Book* (New York: Simon and Schuster, 1989), 102-3. David Taylor, *You & Your Cat* (New York: Alfred Knopf, 1988), 90-91.

Why do cats have whiskers?

The function of a cat's whiskers or vibrissae is not fully understood. They are thought to be sensory organs that had keen nerves at their ends. Removing them can disturb a cat for some time. The whiskers may act as antennae in the dark, enabling the cat to identify things it cannot see and to walk confidently when blindfolded. The whiskers may help the cat to pinpoint the direction from which an odor is coming. In addition, the cat is thought to point some of its whiskers downwards to guide it when jumping or running over uneven terrain at night.

William H. Carr, *The New Basic Book of the Cat* (New York: Charles Scribner's Sons, 1978), 102. Michael W. Fox, *Understanding Your Cat* (New York: Bantam, 1974), 182-83. David Taylor, *You & Your Cat* (New York: Alfred Knopf, 1988), 35.

How much does an average adult Chinese potbellied pig weigh compared to a regular farm pig?

The adult Chinese potbellied pig usually weighs about 70 to 150 pounds (31.75 to 68 kilograms); adult farm pigs may weigh 1,200 to 1,500 pounds (544.32 to 680.4 kilograms). Chinese potbellies are an ancient breed that stand only 16 inches (40.64 centimeters) tall. They are very intelligent, easily housebroken, and reportedly make affectionate pets.

Kayla Mull, *Pot-Bellied Pet Pigs* (Orange, CA: ALL Publishing, 1990), 6-7. *People Weekly* 15 February 1988.

What is the best way to remove a skunk that stays near the house?

Skunks are beneficial animals; they are great rodent hunters and eat lots of insects (cutworms, army worms, grubs, and potato beetles). They can be caught in cages, placed inside plastic bags, and baited with cat kibbles.

Hilary D. Klein, *Tiny Game Hunting* (New York: Bantam, 1991), 190-91.

Any suggestions for keeping mosquitoes away from an outdoor patio in the summertime?

To keep mosquitoes away from an outdoor patio, one idea is to keep a 12-inch oscillating electric fan operating to make it difficult for the mosquitoes to land. Although this is not 100 percent effective, it helps. Another idea comes from Spain. Plant basil all around the patio; mosquitoes do not like basil.

New York Times Book of Indoor and Outdoor Gardening Questions (New York: Quadrangle, 1975), 84.

What are the five kingdoms presently used to categorize living things?

Carolus Linnaeus (1707-1778) in 1735 divided all living things into two kingdoms in his classification system that was based on similarities and differences of organisms. However, since then, fungi seemed not to fit nicely into either kingdom. Although fungi were generally considered plants, they had no chlorophyll, roots, stems, or leaves, and hardly resemble any true plant. They also have several features found in the animal kingdom, as well as unique features characteristic of themselves alone. So fungi was considered the third kingdom. In 1959, R.H. Whittaker proposed the current five kingdom system, based on new evidence from biochemical techniques and electron microscope observations that revealed fundamental differences among organisms. Each kingdom is listed below:

Monera—One-celled organisms lacking a membrane around the cell's genetic matter. Prokaryote (or procaryote) is the term used for this condition where the genetic material lies free in the cytoplasm of the cell without a membrane to form the nucleus of the cell. The kingdom consists of bacteria and blue-green algae (also called blue-green bacteria or cyanobacteria). Bacteria do not produce their own food but blue-green algae do. Blue-green algae, the primary form of life 3.5 to 1.5 billion years ago, produce most of the world's oxygen through photosynthesis.

Protista—Mostly single-celled organisms with a membrane around the cell's genetic material called eukaryotes (or eucaryotes) because of the nucleus membrane and other organelles found in the cytoplasm of the cell. Protista consists of true algae, diatoms, slime molds, protozoa, and euglena. Protistans are diverse in their modes of nutrition, etc. They may be living examples of the kinds of ancient single cells that gave rise to the kingdoms of multicelled eukaryotes (fungi, plants, and animals).

Fungi—One-celled or multicelled eukaryotes (having a nucleus membrane or a membrane around the genetic material). The nuclei stream between cells giving the appearance that cells have multiple nuclei. This unique cellular structure, along with the unique sexual reproduction pattern, distinguish the fungi from all other organisms. Consisting of mushrooms, yeasts, molds, etc., the fungi do not produce their own food.

Plantae—Multicellular organisms having cell nuclei and cell walls, which directly or indirectly nourish all other forms of life. Most use photosynthesis (a process by which green plants, containing chlorophyll, utilize sunlight as an energy source to synthesize complex organic material, especially carbohydrates from carbon dioxide, water, and inorganic salts) and most are autotrophs (produce their own food from inorganic matter).

Animalia—Multicellular organisms whose eukaryotic cells (without cell walls) form tissues (and from tissues form organs). Most get their food by ingestion of other organisms; they are heterotrophs (cannot produce their food from inorganic elements). Most are able to move from place to place (mobile) at least during part of the life cycle.

Cesare Emiliani, *The Scientific Companion* (New York: Wiley Science Editions, 1988), 149-55. Lynn Margulis, *Five Kingdoms* (New York: Witt, Freeman and Co., 1988), 3. Cecie Starr and Ralph Taggart, *Biology, 6th ed.* (Belmont, CA: Wadsworth Publishing, 1992), 347, 385, 406.

What is Batesian mimicry?

In 1861 Henry Walter Bates (1825-1892), a British naturalist, proposed that a nontoxic species can evolve (especially in color and color pattern) to look like a toxic or unpalatable species, or to act like a toxic species to avoid being eaten by a predator. The classic example is the viceroy butterfly which resembles the unpalatable monarch butterfly. This is called Batesian mimicry. Subsequently, Fritz Mller (1821-1897), a German-born zoologist, discovered that all the species of similar appearance were distasteful to predators; this phenomenon is called Mllerian mimicry.

The Biographical Dictionary of Scientists: Biologists (New York: Peter Bedrick Books, 1984), 15. W.F. Bynum et al., *Dictionary of the History of Science* (Princeton, NJ: Princeton University Press, 1985), 149. *Discover* January 1992.

When was the Scopes (monkey) trial?

John T. Scopes (1900-1970), a high-school biology teacher, was brought to trial by the State of Tennessee in 1925 for teaching the scientific theory of evolution. This was illegal because Tennessee had passed a law making it unlawful to teach in a public school any theory that denied the divine creation of man. Famed lawyer Clarence Darrow (1857-1938) was one of three lawyers who represented Scopes and William Jennings Bryan (1860-1925) represented the religious Fundamentalist viewpoint as a member of the prosecution team. Scopes was convicted and sentenced to pay a fine of one hundred dollars, but the decision was later reversed and the law repealed in 1967.

At the present, pressure against school boards still affects the teaching of evolution today. Recent drives by anti-evolutionists have tried to either ban the teaching of evolution or have demanded "equal time" for "special creation" as described in the biblical Book of Genesis. This has raised many questions about the separation of church and state, the teaching of controversial subjects in public schools, and the ability of scientists to communicate with the public. The gradual improvement of the fossil record, the result of comparative anatomy, and many other developments in biological science contributed toward making evolutionary thinking more palatable.

Encyclopedia Americana (Danbury, CT: Grolier, 1990), 24:397. Edward W. Knappman, ed. *Great American Trials* (Detroit: Gale Research, 1994), 312-18. Lois N. Magner, *A History of the Life Sciences* (New York: Marcel Dekker, 1979), 395.

Who is generally known as the father of genetics?

The English biologist William Bateson (1861-1926) coined the term *genetics* as the study of the causes and effects of heritable characteristics, and was a leading proponent of Mendelian views. Although Gregor Mendel (1822-1884) is considered the founder of genetics, there are other contenders such as William Bateson to share the honor with Mendel.

Isaac Asimov, *Asimov's Chronology of Science and Discovery* (New York: Harper & Row, 1989), 346. *Encyclopedic Dictionary of Science* (New York: Facts On File, 1988), 38. Peter Gray, *The Dictionary of the Biological Sciences* (New York: Van Nostrand Reinhold, 1970), 224.

Are there stone-eating bacteria?

Stone-eating bacteria belong to several families in the genus *Thiobacillus.* They can cause damage to monuments, tombs, buildings, and sculptures by converting marble into plaster. The principal danger seems to come from *Thiobacillus thioparus.* This microbe's metabolic system converts sulfur dioxide gas, found in the air, into sulfuric acid and uses it to transform calcium carbonate— marble into calcium sulfate—plaster. The bacilli draw their nutrition from carbon dioxide formed in the transformation. *Nitrobacter* and *Nitrosomonas* are other stone-eating bacteria that use ammonia from the air to generate nitric and nitrous acid, and there are still other kinds of bacteria and fungi producing organic acids (formic, acetic, and oxalic acids), which can attack the stone as well. The presence of these microbes was first observed by a French scientist, Henri Pochon, at Angkor Wat, Cambodia, during the 1950s. The increase of these bacteria and other biological-damaging organisms that threaten tombs and buildings of antiquity are due to the sharp climb in the level of free sulfur dioxide gas in the atmosphere from automotive and industrial emissions.

Science 80 September-October 1980.

Who were the founders of modern bacteriology?

The German bacteriologist Robert Koch (1843-1910) and the French chemist Louis Pasteur (1822-1895) are considered the founders of modern bacteriology. Pasteur devised a way to heat food or beverages at a temperature slow enough not to ruin them, but high enough to kill most of the microorganisms that would cause spoilage and disease. This process is called pasteurization. By demonstrating that tuberculosis was an infectious disease caused by a specific bacillus and not by bad heredity, Koch laid the groundwork for public health measures that would significantly reduce such diseases. His working methodologies for isolating microorganisms, his laboratory procedures, and his four postulates for determination of disease agents gave medical investigators valuable insights into the control of bacterial infections.

The Biographical Dictionary of Scientists: Biologists (New York: Peter Bedrick Books, 1984), 77, 103. Cecie Starr and Ralph Taggart, *Biology, 6th ed.* (Belmont, CA: Wadsworth, 1992), 680.

What is a lichen?

Lichens are organisms which grow on rocks, tree branches, or bare ground. They are composed of a green algae and a colorless fungus living together symbiotically. They do not have roots, stems, flowers, or leaves. The fungus, having no chlorophyll, cannot manufacture its own food, but can absorb food from the algae which it enwraps completely, providing protection from the sun and moisture.

This relationship between the fungus and algae is called symbiosis, a close association of two organisms not necessarily to both their benefits. Lichens were the first recognized and are still the best examples of this phenomenon. An unique feature of lichen symbiosis is that it is so perfectly developed and balanced as to behave as a single organism.

Mason E. Hale, Jr., *The Biology of Lichens, 2d ed.* (London: Edward Arnold, 1974), 69. Eleanor Lawrence, *Henderson's Dictionary of Biological Terms, 10th ed.* (New York: John Wiley & Sons, 1989), 532. *The Wise Garden Encyclopedia* (New York: HarperCollins, 1990), 581.

What is the scientific study of fungi called?

Mycology is the science concerning fungi. In the past, fungi have been classified in other kingdoms, but currently they are recognized as a separate kingdom based on their unique cellular structure and their unique pattern of sexual reproduction.

Fungi are heterotrophs; they cannot produce their own food from inorganic matter. They secrete enzymes that digest food outside their bodies and their fungal cells absorb the products. Their activities are essential in the decomposition of organic material and cycling of nutrients in nature.

Some fungi, called saprobes, obtain nutrients from non-living organic matter. Other fungi are parasites; they obtain nutrients from the tissues of living host organisms. The great majority of fungi are multicelled and filamentous. A mushroom is a modified reproductive structure in or upon which spores develop. Each spore dispersed from it may grow into a new mushroom.

Elizabeth Moore-Landecker, *Fundamentals of the Fungi, 3d ed.* (Englewood Cliffs, NJ: Prentice-Hall, 1990), 1-2. Cecie Starr and Ralph Taggert, *Biology, 6th ed.* (Belmont, CA: Wadsworth Publishing, 1992), 373.

Who is regarded as the father of biochemistry?

Jan Baptista van Helmont (1577-1644) is called the father of biochemistry because he studied and expressed vital phenomena in chemical terms. The term biochemistry, coined by F. Hoppe-Seyler in 1877, is the science dealing with the dynamics of living chemical processes or metabolism. It was formed from both the chemists' animal and vegetable chemistry, and the biologists' and doctors' physiological, zoological, or biological chemistry.

Johannes Baptista van Helmont devoted his life to the study of chemistry as the true key to medicine and is considered one of the founders of modern pathology because he studied the external organs of diseases, as well as the anatomical changes caused by diseases.

W.F. Bynum et al., *Dictionary of the History of Science* (Princeton, NJ: Princeton University Press, 1985), 42. *Encyclopedic Dictionary of Science* (New York: Facts On File, 1988), 116. *World Who's Who in Science* (Chicago: Marquis-Who's Who, 1968), 782.

What is the difference between DNA and RNA?

DNA (deoxyribonucleic acid) is a nucleic acid formed from a repetition of simple building blocks called nucleotides. The nucleotides consist of phosphate, a sugar called deoxyribose, and a base which is either adenine (A), thymine (T), guanine (G), or cytosine (C). In a DNA molecule, this basic unit is repeated in a double helix structure made from two chains of nucleotides linked between the bases. The links are either between A and T or between G and C. The structure of the bases does not allow other kinds of links. The famous double helix structure resembles a twisted ladder. The 1962 Nobel Prize in physiology or medicine was awarded to James Watson (b. 1928), Francis Crick (b. 1916), and Maurice Wilkins (b. 1916) for determining the molecular structure of DNA.

RNA (ribonucleic acid) is also a nucleic acid, but it consists of a single chain and the sugar is ribose rather than deoxyribose. The bases are the same except that the thymine (T) which appears in DNA is replaced by another base called uracil (U), which links only to adenine (A).

Frank N. Magill, *Nobel Prize Winners: Physiology or Medicine* (Englewood Cliffs, NJ: Salem Press, 1991), 2:853. James Trefil, *1001 Things Everyone Should Know About Science* (New York: Doubleday, 1992), 260-61.

What are the stages in the type of cell division called mitosis?

Cell division in eukaryotes (higher organisms) consists of two stages, mitosis, the division of the nucleus, and cytokinesis, the division of the whole cell.

The first process in the actual division of the cell is mitosis. In mitosis, the replicated chromosomes are maneuvered so that each new cell gets a full complement of chromosomes-one of each. The process is divided into four phases: prophase, metaphase, anaphase, and telophase.

Nuclear division of sex cells is called meiosis. Sexual reproduction generally requires two parents and it always involves two events (meiosis and fertilization).

Joseph E. Armstrong, *Science in Biology* (Prospect Heights, IL: Waveland Press, 1990), 64. Helena Curtis and N. Sue Barnes, *Invitation to Biology, 4th ed.* (New York: Worth Publishing, 1985), 92, 155. Norman Maclean, *Dictionary of Genetics and Cell Biology* (New York: New York University Press, 1987), 255.

What is a biome?

A biome is a plant and animal community that covers a large geographical area. Complex interactions of climate, geology, soil types, water resources, and latitude all determine the kinds of plants and animals that thrive in different places. Fourteen major ecological zones, called "biomes," exist over five major climatic regions and eight zoo geographical regions. Three types of biomes are desert, tropical rain forest, and tundra.

Geoffrey Lean, Don Hinrichsen, and Adam Markham, *WWF Atlas of the Environment* (Boston: Willard Grant Press, 1991), 11. *World Book Encyclopedia* (Chicago: World Book, 1990), 2:322-23.

Who coined the term "Spaceship Earth"?

American inventor and environmentalist, Buckminster Fuller (1895-1983), coined the term "Spaceship Earth" as an analogy of the need for technology to be self-contained and to avoid waste.

William Ashworth, *The Encyclopedia of Environmental Studies* (New York: Facts on File, 1991), 155. Bernard J. Nebel, *Environmental Science* (Englewood Cliffs, NJ: Prentice-Hall, 1990), 11.

What is a quagga?

The quagga, a native of South Africa, was basically a brown, rather than striped, zebra with white legs and tail. In the early nineteenth century, it lived in the wild in great herds and was tamed to become a harness animal or was killed for its skin. The species became extinct in 1883.

David Day, *The Doomsday Book of Animals* (New York: Viking, 1983), 207-9.

Why did dinosaurs become extinct?

There are many theories as to why dinosaurs disappeared from the earth about 65 million years ago. Scientists argue over whether the dinosaurs became extinct gradually or all at once. The gradualists believe that the dinosaur population steadily declined at the end of the Cretaceous Period. Numerous reasons have been proposed for this. Some claim the dinosaurs' extinction was caused by biological changes which made them less competitive with other organisms, especially the mammals who were just beginning to appear. Overpopulation has been argued, as has the theory that mammals ate too many dinosaur eggs for the animals to reproduce themselves. Others believe that disease-everything from rickets to constipation-wiped them out. Changes in climate, continental drift, volcanic eruptions, and shifts in the earth's axis, orbit, and/or magnetic field have also been held responsible.

The catastrophists argue that a single disastrous event caused the extinction, not only of the dinosaurs, but also of a large number of other species that coexisted with them. In 1980, American physicist Luis Alvarez (1911-1988) and his geologist son, Walter Alvarez (b. 1940), proposed that a large comet or meteoroid struck the earth 65 million years ago. They pointed out that there is a high concentration of the element iridium in the sediments at the boundary between the Cretaceous and Tertiary Periods. Iridium is rare on earth, so the only source of such a large amount of it had to be outer space. This iridium anomaly has since been discovered at over 50 sites around the world. In 1990, tiny glass fragments, which could have been caused by the extreme heat of an impact, were identified in Haiti. A 110-mile-wide (177-kilometer) crater in the Yucatan Peninsula, long covered by sediments, has been dated to 64.98 million years ago, making it a leading candidate for the site of this impact.

A hit by a large extraterrestrial object, perhaps as much as six miles (9.3 kilometers) wide, would have had a catastrophic effect upon the world's climate. Huge amounts of dust and debris would have been thrown into the atmosphere, reducing the amount of sunlight reaching the surface. Heat from the blast may also have caused large forest fires which would have added smoke and ash to the air. Lack of sunlight would kill off plants and have a domino-like effect on other organisms in the food chain, including the dinosaurs.

It is possible that the reason for the dinosaurs' extinction may have been a combination of both theories. The dinosaurs may have been gradually declining, for whatever reason. The impact of a large object from space merely delivered the coup de grce.

The fact that dinosaurs became extinct has been cited as proof of their inferiority and that they were evolutionary failures. However, these animals flourished for 150 million years. By comparison, the earliest ancestors of humanity appeared only about three million years ago. Humans have a long way to go before they can claim the same sort of success as the dinosaurs.

The Almanac of Science and Technology (San Diego: Harcourt Brace Jovanovich, 1990), 73-84. Jean-Guy Michard, *The Reign of the Dinosaurs* (New York: Harry N. Abrams, 1992), 88-94. David Norman, *Dinosaur!* (New York: Prentice-Hall, 1991), 144-59.

How does a mastodon differ from a mammoth?

Although the words are sometimes used interchangeably, the mammoth and the mastodon were two different animals. The mastodon seems to have appeared first and a side branch may have led to the mammoth.

The mastodon lived in Africa, Europe, Asia, and North and South America. It appears in the Oligocene (25 to 38 million years ago) and survived until less than one million years ago. It stood a maximum of ten feet (three meters) tall and was covered with dense woolly hair. Its tusks were straight forward and nearly parallel to each other.

The mammoth evolved less than two million years ago and died out about ten thousand years ago. It lived in North America, Europe, and Asia. Like the mastodon, the mammoth was covered with dense, woolly hair, with a long, coarse layer of outer hair to protect it from the cold. It was somewhat larger than the mastodon, standing 9 to 15 feet (2.7 to 4.5 meters). The mammoth's tusks tended to spiral outward, then up.

The gradual warming of the earth's climate and the change in environment were probably primary factors in the animals' extinction. But early man killed many of them as well, perhaps hastening the process.

Ronald M. Nowak, *Walker's Mammals of the World, 5th ed.* (Baltimore: Johns Hopkins University Press, 1991), 2:1277-78. Marcus Schneck, *Elephants: Gentle Giants of Africa and Asia* (Stamford, CT: Longmeadow, 1992), 91-94.

Who was the first American woman to win a Nobel prize?

For work on glycogen conversion, this Czechoslovakian-born biochemist, Gerty T. Cori (1896-1957), who shared the 1947 Nobel Prize for Physiology and Medicine with her husband, Carl Cori (1896-1984), became the first American winner. The first native-born American woman to be honored was Rosalyn S. Yallow, who shared the 1977 prize in Physiology and Medicine with two male associates. The award was given for their work on hormones in body chemistry.

Dennis Sanders, *The First of Everything* (New York: Delacorte, 1981), 167.

When was the first patent covering an animal issued?

On April 12, 1988, patent history was made when a patent was issued covering specifically genetically engineered mice for cancer research. Philip Leder and Timothy Stewart of Harvard University had developed this mouse by inserting a human cancer gene into mouse egg cells. The U.S. Patent and Trademark Office granted the standard chemical utility patent to the "Harvard mouse" because it satisfied the primary criteria of a patent in its novelty and usefulness.

Timothy Lee Wherry, *Patent Searching for Librarians and Inventors* (Chicago: American Library Association, 1995), 69.

Which species of mosquito causes malaria and yellow fever in humans?

The bite of the female mosquito of the genus *Anopheles* can contain the parasite of the genus *Plasmodium*, which causes malaria, a serious tropical infectious disease affecting 200 to 300 million people worldwide. More than one million African babies and children die from the disease annually. The *Aedes aegypti* transmits yellow fever—a serious infectious disease characterized by jaundice, giving the infected person yellowish skin; ten percent of those infected die.

Guinness Book of Records 1992 (New York: Bantam Book, 1992), 52. P. Passarin d'Entreves, *The Secret Life of Insects* (New York: Chartwell, 1976), 29-30.

How much blood is in the average human body?

A man weighing 154 pounds (69.8 kilograms) would have about 5.5 quarts of blood. A woman weighing 110 pounds (49.8 kilograms) would have about 3.5 quarts.

Neil McAleer, *The Body Almanac* (New York: Doubleday, 1985), 143.

Who were the original Siamese twins?

Siamese twins are twins physically joined at birth as a result of the incomplete separation of a single ovum that has split in the process of twinning. The term "Siamese twins" originated with the appearance of Chang and Eng Bunker (1811-1874), conjoined Chinese twins born in Siam (now Thailand) and used as a circus attraction by P.T. Barnum.

Siamese twins may be joined at various parts of the body. Many have lived far into adulthood without being separated, but most doctors will separate twins if possible. If certain organs are shared, both individuals may not survive a surgical separation.

James Wynbrandt and Mark D. Ludman, *The Encyclopedia of Genetic Disorders and Birth Defects* (New York: Facts on File, 1991), 80-81. Mark Young, ed., *The Guinness Book of Records 1995* (New York: Facts on File, 1994), 10.

How loud can a snore sound?

Research has indicated that a snore can reach 69 decibels as compared to 70 to 90 decibels for a pneumatic drill.

Neil McAleer, *The Body Almanac* (New York: Doubleday, 1985), 178.

What are endorphins?

Endorphins are chemical substances called polypeptides, produced in the brain. They act as opiates, in that they produce an absence to the sensation of pain by binding to opiate receptor sites involved in pain perception. This action increases the threshold for pain.

Taber's Cyclopedic Medical Dictionary, 16th ed. (Philadelphia, Davis, 1989), 593.

Who coined the term *homeostasis*?

Walter Bradford Cannon (1871-1945) who elaborated on Claude Bernard's (1813-1878) concept of the *milieu intrieur* (interior environment) used the term *homeostasis* to describe the body's ability to maintain a relative constancy in its internal environment.

Dictionary of Scientific Biography (New York: Charles Scribner, 1973), 15: 73.

How many muscles does it take to produce a smile and a frown?

There are 17 muscles that are used in smiling. The average frown uses 43 muscles.

Gyles Brandreth, *Your Vital Statistics* (New York: Citadel, 1986), 17. Neil McAleer, *The Body Almanac* (New York: Doubleday, 1985), 111.

Why does excessive exercise cause muscles to become stiff and sore?

If muscles are worked too hard, the cells run out of oxygen. This starts a fermentation process which produces lactic acid. The build-up of lactic acid in the muscles causes soreness and stiffness.

James Trefil, *1001 Things Everyone Should Know About Science* (New York: Doubleday, 1992), 95.

What is the largest nerve in the body?

The sciatic nerve is the largest in the human body-about as thick as a lead pencil-0.78 inches (1.98 centimeters). It is a broad, flat nerve composed of nerve fibers, and it runs from the spinal cord down the back of the each leg.

Neil McAleer, *The Body Almanac* (New York: Doubleday, 1985), 79.

How much force does a human bite generate?

All the jaw muscles working together can close the teeth with a force as great as 55 pounds (25 kilograms) on the incisors or 200 pounds (90.7 kilograms) on the molars. A force as great as 268 pounds (122 kilograms) for molars has been reported.

Charles H. Best, *Best and Taylor's Physiological Basis of Medical Practice* (Baltimore: Williams & Wilkins, 1985), 642. Arthur C. Guyton, *Basic Human Physiology* (Philadelphia: Saunders, 1977), 659.

What regulates body temperature in humans?

The hypothalamus gland controls internal body temperature. The gland responds to sensory impulses from temperature receptors in the skin and in the deep body regions. The hypothalamus establishes a "set point" for the internal body temperature, then constantly compares this with its own actual temperature. If the two do not match, the hypothalamus activates either temperature-decreasing or temperature-increasing procedures to bring them into alignment.

Arthur C. Guyton, *Textbook of Medical Physiology, 8th ed.,* (Philadelphia: Saunders, 1991), 802. Ewald E. Selkurt, *Physiology, 5th ed.* (Boston: Little, Brown, 1984), 169.

What is the basic constituent unit of the brain?

Neurons are the nerve cells that are the major constituent of the brain. At birth the brain has the maximum number of neurons-20 billion to 200 billion. Thousands are lost daily, never to be replaced and apparently not missed, until the cumulative loss builds up in very old age.

The Human Brain (Englewood Cliffs, NJ: Prentice-Hall, 1977), 16-17.

What is the largest organ in the human body?

The largest and heaviest human organ is the skin, with a total surface area of about 20 square feet (1.9 square meters) for an average person or 25 square feet (2.3 square meters) for a large person and an average weight of 5.6 pounds (2.7 kilograms). Although generally it is not thought of as an organ, medically it is so by definition: an organ is a collection of various tissues integrated into a distinct structural unit and performing specific functions. The second largest and heaviest organ is the liver, weighing 2.5 to 3.3 pounds (1.1 to 1.5 kilograms).

The liver is seven times larger than it needs to be to perform its estimated 500 functions. It is the main chemical factory of the body and regulates the levels of most of the body's chemicals. A ducted gland that produces bile to break down fats and reduce acidity in the digestive process, the liver is also a part of the circulatory system. It cleans poisons from the blood and regulates blood composition.

The American Medical Association Encyclopedia of Medicine (New York: Random House, 1989), 749. Mark C. Young, ed., *The Guinness Book of Records 1995* (New York: Facts On File, 1994), 18. Neil McAleer, *The Body Almanac* (New York: Doubleday, 1985), 100.

How hard does the heart work?

The heart squeezes out about 2-ounces (70.8 grams) of blood at every beat. Daily it pumps at least 2,500 gallons (9,450 liters) of blood, which weigh 20 tons (18,144 kilograms). On the average the adult heart beats 70 to 75 times a minute. The rate of the heartbeat is determined in part by the size of the organism. Generally the smaller the size, the faster the heartbeat. Thus a woman's heart has six to eight beats more than a man's heart has. At birth the heart of a baby has as many as 130 beats per minute.

Isaac Asimov, *The Human Body, rev. ed.* (New York: Mentor Books, 1992), 167. Gyles D. Brandreth, *Your Vital Statistics* (New York: Citadel, 1986), 53. Arthur Fisher, *The Healthy Heart* (New York: Time-Life Books, 1981), 11.

What are phosphenes?

If the eyes are shut tightly, the lights seen are phosphenes. Technically, the luminous impressions are due to the excitation of the retina caused by pressure on the eyeball.

David Wallechinsky et al. *The Book of Lists* (New York: Morrow, 1977), 163.

What does it mean to have 20/20 vision?

Many people think that with 20/20 vision the eyesight is perfect, but it actually means that the eye can see clearly at 20 feet what a normal eye can see clearly at that distance. Some people can see even better-20/15, for example. With their eagle eyes, they can view objects from 20 feet away with the same sharpness that a normal-sighted person would have to move in to 15 feet to achieve.

Prevention's Giant Book of Health Facts (Emmaus, PA: Rodale Press, 1991), 519.

Can a person get a suntan through a window?

No. The ultraviolet radiation which causes suntan does not pass through glass. A tan is the skin's natural defense against these harmful sun rays; pigment cells in the lower skin level make more pigment and melanin to absorb the ultraviolet rays. As this pigment spreads into the top layer of the skin, it becomes darker.

Ira Flatow, *Rainbows, Curve Balls, and Other Wonders of the Natural World Explained* (New York: Harper & Row, 1988), 36-39. *Science Digest* January 1985.

What is the purpose of goose-bumps?

The puckering of the skin that takes place when goose-flesh is formed is the result of contraction of the muscle fibers in the skin. This muscular activity will produce more heat, and raise the temperature of the body.

Marshall Cavendish Illustrated Encyclopedia of Family Health, (London: Marshall Cavendish, 1984), 19:2052.

How fast do fingernails grow?

Healthy fingernails grow about 0.8 inches (2 centimeters) each year. The middle fingernail grows the fastest, because the longer the finger, the faster its nail growth. Fingernails grow four times as fast as toenails.

Harvard Medical School Health Letter May 1984. Frank Kendig and Richard Hutton *Life Spans* (New York: Holt, Rinehart and Winston, 1979), 24. C. Van Amerogen, *The Way Things Work Book of the Body* (New York: Simon and Schuster, 1979), 416.

How much does human hair grow in a year?

Each hair grows about 5 inches (12.7 centimeters) every year.

Neil McAleer, *The Body Almanac* (New York: Doubleday, 1985), 106.

Does any wood sink in water?

Ironwood is a name applied to many hard, heavy woods. Some ironwoods are so dense that their specific gravity exceeds 1 and they are therefore unable to float in water. North American ironwoods include the American hornbeam, the mesquite, the desert ironwood, and leadwood (Krugiodendron ferreum), which has a specific gravity of 1.34-1.42 making it the heaviest in the United States.

The heaviest wood is black ironwood (Olea laurifolia), also called South African ironwood. Found in the West Indies, it has a specific gravity of 1.49 and weighs up to 93 pounds (42.18 kilograms) per foot. The lightest wood is Aeschynomene hispida, found in Cuba, with a specific gravity of 0.044 and a weight of 2-pounds (1.13 kilograms) per foot. Balsa wood (Ochroma pyramidale) varies between 2-(1.13 kilograms) and 24 pounds (10.88 kilograms) per foot.

Encyclopedia Americana (Danbury, CT: Grolier, 1990), 15:467. *Guinness Book of Records 1992* (New York: Bantam Books, 1992), 140.

How old are fossils?

The oldest known fossils are of single-celled organisms, blue-green algae, found in 3.2 billion-year-old cherts, shales, and sandstone from the Transvaal of South Africa. Multicellular fossils dating from about 700 million years ago are also known. The largest number of fossils come from the Cambrian period of 590 million years ago, when living organisms began to develop skeletons and bony hard parts. Since these parts tended to last longer than tissue, they were more likely to be preserved in clay and became fossilized.

Carroll L. Fenton, *The Fossil Book* (New York: Doubleday, 1989), 91, 93. James Trefil, *1001 Things Everyone Should Know About Science* (New York: Doubleday, 1992), 59-61.

Where are living stones found?

Living stones is a name given to various succulent plants from the stony deserts of South Africa, which mimic their surroundings. Each shoot or plant is made up of two grossly swollen leaves virtually fused together and colored to resemble a pebble. Large daisy-like flowers are borne from between the leaf pair.

Illustrated Dictionary of Botany (Chesnut Ridge, NY: Triune Books, 1979), 144.

What is wormwood?

Artemisia absinthium, known as wormwood, is a hardy, spreading, fragrant perennial, 2 to 4 feet (61-122 centimeters) tall. It is native to Europe but widely naturalized in North America. The liqueur absinthe is flavored from this plant.

Thomas H. Everett, *New York Botanical Garden Illustrated Encyclopedia of Horticulture,* (Hamden, CT: Garland, 1981), 1: 255. *Stedman's Medical Dictionary, 25 ed.* (Baltimore, MD: Williams & Wilkins, 1990), 6.

Who is known as the father of botany?

Theophrastus (ca.372-ca.287 B.C.E.), is known as the father of botany. His two large botanical works, *On the History of Plants* and *On the Causes of Plants* were very comprehensive in the scope of plants covered. He integrated the practice of agriculture into botany and established a theory of plant growth and the analysis of plant structure. He related plants to their natural environment and identified, classified, and described 550 different plants.

The Biographical Dictionary of Scientists: Biologists (New York: Peter Bedrick, 1984), 127. Robert B. Downs, *Landmarks in Science* (Littleton, CO: Libraries Unlimited, 1982), 30-33.

What is the greatest number of leaves a clover can have?

A fourteen-leafed white clover (Trifolium repens) and a fourteen-leafed red clover (Trifolium pratense) have been found in the United States.

Mark C. Young, ed., *The Guinness Book of Records 1995* (New York: Facts on File, 1994), 42.

What is meant by the chilling requirement for fruit trees?

When a fruit tree's fruiting period has ended, there must follow a dormant period during which the plant rests and regains strength for another fruit set the following year. The length of this set is measured in hours between 32 degrees Fahrenheit and 45 degrees Fahrenheit (0 degrees Celsius and 7.2 degrees Celsius). A cherry tree requires about 700 hours of chilling time.

Fruits and Vegetables: 1001 Gardening Questions Answered (Pownal, VT: Storey Communications, 1990), 2-3.

How many chloroplasts are there in plant cells?

Functional units where photosynthesis takes place. Chloroplasts contain the green pigments chlorophyll a and b, which trap light energy for photosynthesis (the process whereby green plants use light energy for the synthesis of sugar from carbon dioxide and water, with oxygen released as a by-product). A unicellular plant may have only a single large chloroplast, whereas a plant leaf cell may have as many as 20 to 100.

Plants: Their Biology and Importance (New York: Harper & Row, 1989), 17, 127. Claude A. Villee, et al. *Biology* (CBS College Publishing, 1985), 107.

What is a banyan tree?

The banyan tree (*Ficus benghalensis*), a native of tropical Asia, is a member of the *Ficus* or fig genus. It is a magnificent evergreen, sometimes 100 feet (30.48 meters) in height. As the massive limbs spread horizontally, the tree sends down roots that develop into secondary, pillar-like supporting trunks. Over a period of years a single tree may spread to occupy a tremendous area, as much as 2,000 feet (609.6 meters) around the periphery.

Thomas H. Everett, *The New York Botanical Garden Illustrated Encyclopedia of Horticulture* (Hamden, CT: Garland, 1981), 4:1363.

How can a spruce tree be distinguished from a fir tree?

The best way to tell the difference between the two trees is by the cones and leaves. On a fir tree the cones are upright (erect) and the needles flat, while spruces have pendulous (hanging) cones and very angular, four-sided needles.

Melanie Choukas-Bradleyand Polly Alexander, *City of Trees, rev. ed.* (Baltimore: Johns Hopkins University Press, 1987), 86. *The Wise Garden Encyclopedia* (New York: HarperCollins, 1990), 1.

Are there any natural predators of gypsy moth caterpillars?

About 45 kinds of birds, squirrels, chipmunks, and white-footed mice eat this serious insect pest. Among the 13 imported natural enemies of the moth, two flies, *Compislura concinnata* (a tachnid fly) and *Sturnia scutellata*, parasitize the caterpillar. Other parasites and various wasps have also been tried as controls, as well as spraying and male sterilization. Originally from Europe, this large moth (*Porthetria dispar*) lays its eggs on the leaves of oaks, birches, maples, and other hardwood trees. When the yellow hairy caterpillars hatch from the eggs, they devour the leaves in such quantities that the tree becomes temporarily defoliated. Sometimes this causes the tree to die. The caterpillars grow from one eighth of an inch (three millimeters) to about two inches (5.1 centimeters) before they spin a pupa in which they will metamorphose into adult moths.

William Ashworth, *The Encyclopedia of Environmental Studies* (New York: Facts on File, 1991), 176. *The Wise Garden Encyclopedia* (New York: HarperCollins, 1990), 470.

What percentage of the population is left-handed?

Approximately 10 percent of the population is left-handed. One in seven children are left-handed, but many change over as they become older.

"The Perils of Being a Lefty," *Time* 15 April 1991. Les Krantz, *What the Odds Are: A-to-Z Odds on Everything You Hoped or Feared Could Happen* (New York: HarperCollins, 1992), 15.

What are the odds of having naturally blonde hair?

The odds are 1 in 4 that a child will have one of the parent's overall hair color if the parents are Caucasians of European origin. The odds that a Caucasian American will have brown hair are 7 in 10; blonde hair, 1 in 7; black hair, 1 in 10; or red hair, 1 in 16. Hair color is almost invariably very dark brown or black in other racial groups.

Les Krantz, *What the Odds Are* (New York: HarperCollins, 1992), s.v. "hair color."

How many puppies were in the largest known litter?

The largest known litter of puppies is 23. There have been three recorded cases: an American Foxhound from Ambler, Pennsylvania, on June 19, 1944; a St. Bernard from Lebanon, Missouri, on February 6-7, 1975; and a Great Dane from Little Hall, Great Britain, in June of 1987. Only 14 survived of the St. Bernard's litter, and only 16 survived of the Great Dane's litter.

Mark C. Young, ed., *The Guinness Book of Records 1995* (New York: Facts on File, 1994), 34.

Are zebras white-on-black or black-on-white?

Zebras usually have a white background with black or dark brown stripes, although occasionally there might be a black zebra with white stripes. These stripes run all over the body, meeting diagonally down the sides of the head. The lines may appear on the ears, mane, and down its tail. Each zebra's stripe design is different.

David Macdonald, ed., *The Encyclopedia of Mammals* (New York: Facts on File, 1984), 486-87.

How long can humans live without sleep?

While there are a few, extremely rare individuals who sleep very little without ill effects, sleep is a fundamental human need. Even though it is not known exactly how sleep is beneficial, studies have shown that irritability and shortened attention spans occur after less than three hours of sleep. After longer periods without sleep, individuals become increasingly unable to concentrate and task performance deteriorates as they continually slip into short periods of "microsleep." Insomnia, or problems with falling or staying asleep, is considered a transient condition lasting anywhere from several nights to two or three weeks.

The American Medical Association, *Encyclopedia of Medicine* (New York: Random House, 1989), 914-16.

Can any bird fly backwards?

The only bird that can fly backwards is the minute hummingbird. It can also fly sideways, straight up, straight down, or hover in mid-air. Hummingbirds can accomplish these amazing maneuvers because their wings can swivel in all directions from the shoulder. To fly backwards, the wings are tilted slightly so air is forced forwards as well, and the hummingbird is driven back.

Philip Whitfield, ed., *Macmillan Illustrated Animal Encyclopedia* (New York: Macmillan, 1984), s.v. "hummingbirds." *The Marshall Cavendish International Wildlife Encyclopedia* (New York: Marshall Cavendish, 1989), s.v. "hummingbird." Hilda Simon, *Wonders of Hummingbirds* (New York: Dodd, Mead & Co., 1964), 40-47.

What are the parts of a flower?

Sepal—Found on the outside of the bud or on the underside of the open flower. It serves to protect the flower bud from drying out. Some sepals ward off predators by their spines or chemicals.
Petals—Serve to attract pollinators and are usually dropped shortly after pollination occurs.
Nectar—Contains varying amounts of sugar and proteins that can be secreted by any of the floral organs. It usually collects inside the flower cup near the base of the cup formed by the flower parts.
Stamens—The male part of a flower and consists of a filament and anther where pollen is produced.
Pistil—Is the female part which consists of the stigma, style, and

ovary containing ovules. After fertilization the ovules mature into seeds.

Practical Botany (Reston, VA: Reston Publishing, 1983), 6.

How many whiskers does the average man shave during his lifetime?

The average male lops off over nine yards, or 27-feet, of beard in a lifetime by shaving his face.

Jane Polley, ed., *Stories Behind Everyday Things* (Pleasantville, NY: Reader's Digest Association, 1980), 273.

What is the multiple birth of nine babies called?

Nine babies born in a multiple birth are referred to as "nontuplets." The first such birth ever recorded happened in Australia in 1971 to a woman taking a fertility drug. Sadly, only one of the nontuplets survived by the end of the first week after the multiple birth.

"How to Have a Baby or Nine," *New York Times* June 14, 1971.

What is the may apple?

The may apple (*Podophyllum peltatum*) is a plant that is indigenous to the deciduous forests of eastern North America. Indians used it as a purgative, an anthelmintic and an abortifacient. The rootstock was also thought to have magical powers and often was used as an amulet, earning the name mandrake by European settlers.

Christian Rtsch, *The Dictionary of Sacred and Magical Plants* (Santa Barbara: ABC-CLIO, 1992), 116-19.

What causes blushing?

Blushing is a physiological reaction to anxiousness, cold temperatures, increased physical activity, or nervousness and is characterized by a sudden redness and warmth of the face and neck. It is caused by stimulation of the *vasodilator* nerves, which cause the blood vessels or *capillaries* in these areas to suddenly swell with blood.

World Book Encyclopedia (Chicago: World Book, 1993), s.v. "blushing."

Which dog breeds were crossed to produce the Miniature Schnauzer?

The Miniature Schnauzer was originally bred by crossing the black Poodle, the gray Wolfspitz, and possibly the Affenpinscher.

Arthur S. Lockley, *Giant Schnauzers* (Neptune City, NJ: T. F. H. Publications, 1993), 6.

Is there anything to the myth that New York City's sewer system is the home to crocodiles and alligators?

A persistent myth of the 1980s was the belief that New York City's 6,500 miles of underground sewers was home to crocodiles and alligators. John T. Flaherty, chief of design in the New York City Bureau of Sewers, claims he's never seen any animal larger than a rat. The myth purports that tourists return from Florida with baby alligators and crocodiles which are eventually flushed down toilets only to grow to immense size in the sewer system.

Anna Quindlen, "About New York: Debunking the Myth of Subterranean Saurians," *New York Times* 19 May 1982.

What are the most recognizable odors?

A Yale University study has ranked eighty common odors; the twenty most recognizable scents were placed in the following descending order: coffee, peanut butter, Vicks VapoRub, chocolate, wintergreen oil, baby powder, cigarette butts, mothballs, dry cat food, beer, Ivory bar soap, Juicy Fruit gum, orange, cinnamon, lemon, tuna, banana, crayons, cheese, and bleach.

"Making sense out of scents," *USA Today* 2 October 1992.

How is the age of fish determined?

One way to determine the age of a fish is by its scales, which have growth rings just as trees do. Scales have concentric bony ridges or "circuli," which reflect the growth patterns of the individual fish. The portion of the scale that is embedded in the skin containing clusters of these ridges (circuli) are called "annuli"; each cluster marks one year in the growth cycle.

Academic American Encyclopedia (Danbury CT: Grolier, 1991), 8:113. Bernard Grzimek, *Grzimek's Animal Life Encyclopedia* (New York: Van Nostrand Reinhold Company, 1973), 4:49.

How much electricity does an electric eel generate?

An electric eel (*Electrophorus electricus*) has current-producing organs made up of electric plates on both sides of its vertebral column running almost its entire body length. The charge-on the average of 350 volts, but as great as 550 volts-is released by the central nervous system. The shock consists of four to eight separate charges, which last only two-to three-thousandths of a second each. These shocks, used as a defense mechanism, can be repeated up to 150 times per hour without any visible fatigue to the eel. The most powerful electric eel, found in the rivers of Brazil, Colombia, Venezuela, and Peru, produces a shock of 400 to 650 volts.

Bernhard Grzimek, *Grzimek's Animal Life Encyclopedia* (New York: Van Nostrand Reinhold Company, 1973), 4:296-97. Mark C. Young, ed., *The Guinness Book of Records, 1995* (New York: Facts on File, 1994), 36. Robert W. Taber, 1001 *Questions Answered About the Oceans and Oceanography* (New York: Dodd Mead, 1972), 143.

Which birds lay the largest and smallest eggs?

The elephant bird (Aepyornis maximus), an extinct flightless bird of Madagascar, also known as the giant bird or roc, laid the largest known bird eggs. Some of these eggs measured as much as 13.5 inches (34 centimeters) in length and 9.5 inches (24 centimeters) in diameter. The largest egg produced by any living bird is that of the North African ostrich (Struthio camelus). The average size is six to eight inches (15 to 20 centimeters) in length and four to six inches (5 to 15 centimeters) in diameter.

The smallest mature egg, measuring less than 0.39 inches (one centimeter) in length, is that of the vervain hummingbird (Mellisuga minima) of Jamaica.

Allan D. Cruickshank, *1001 Questions Answered About Birds* (New York: Dodd, Mead, 1958), 174. Gerald L. Wood, *The Guinness Book of Animal Facts and Feats, 3d ed.* (London: Guinness Superlatives, 1982), 90-91. Mark C. Young, ed., *The Guinness Book of Records 1995* (New York: Facts on File, 1994), 30.

Why do geese fly in formation?

Aerodynamicists have suspected that long-distance migratory birds, such as geese and swans, adapt the "V" formation in order to reduce the amount of energy needed for such long flights.

According to theoretical calculations, birds flying in a "V" formation can fly some 10% farther than a lone bird can. Formation flying lessens the drag (the air pressure that pushes against the wings). The effect is similar to flying in a thermal upcurrent, where less total lift power is needed. In addition, when flying, each bird creates behind it a small area of disturbed air. Any bird flying directly behind it would be caught in this turbulence. In the "V" formation of the Canadian geese, each bird flies not directly behind the other, but aside or above the bird in front.

Philip S. Callahan, *Bird Behavior* (New York: Four Winds Press, 1975), 133-34. John K. Terres, *Audubon Society Encyclopedia of North American Birds* (New York: Wings Books, 1991), 377.

Who discovered the "dance of the bees"?

In 1943 Karl von Frisch (1886-1982) published his study on the dance of the bees. It is a precise pattern of movements performed by returning forager (worker) honeybees in order to communicate the direction and distance of a food source to the other workers in the hive. The dance is performed on the vertical surface of the hive and two kinds of dances have been recognized: the round dance (performed when food is nearby) and the waggle dance (done when food is further away). In the waggle dance the bee moves in a figure 8. The angle between the figure 8 and the vertical indicates the direction. Since then, some doubt has been cast on the interpretation of the dance.

Elizabeth Toothill, *The Facts On File Dictionary of Biology* (New York: Facts On File, 1988), 83.

What is a "daddy longlegs"?

The name applies to two different kinds of invertebrates. The first is a harmless, non-biting long-legged arachnid which preys on small insects, dead insects, and fallen fruit. Also called a harvestman, it is often mistaken for a spider, but it lacks the segmented body shape that a spider has. Although it has the same number of legs (eight) as a spider, the harvestman's legs are far longer and thinner. These very long legs enable it to raise its body high enough to avoid ants or other small enemies. The term "daddy longlegs" also is used for a cranefly-a thin-bodied insect with long thin legs that has a snout-like proboscis with which it sucks water and nectar.

Maurice Burton and Robert Burton, *Encyclopedia of Insects and Arachnids* (New York: Crescent Books, 1975), 63. Ephram L. Palmer, *Fieldbook of Natural History* (New York: McGraw-Hill, 1974), 433. *World Book Encyclopedia* (Chicago: World Book, 1990), 5:3

Which is stronger-steel or silk from a spider's web?

The only man-made material that comes close to matching the strength of a spider's silk is steel, but the strongest silk has a tensile strength five times greater than that of steel having the equivalent weight. Tensile strength is the longitudinal stress that a substance can bear without tearing apart.

How Things Work: Structures (New York: Time-Life Books, 1991), 32.

How long have cockroaches been on the earth?

The earliest cockroach fossils are about 280 million years old. Some cockroaches measured 3 to 4 inches (8 to 10 centimeters) long. Cockroaches (order Dictyoptera) are nocturnal scavenging insects, that eat not only human food but book-bindings, ink, and whitewash as well.

Carroll L. Fenton, *The Fossil Book* (New York: Doubleday, 1989), 234. *Marshall Cavendish International Wildlife Encyclopedia* (London: Marshall Cavendish, 1989), 6:606-7.

How fast is a snail's pace?

The speed of a land snail was recorded in 1970 as 0.00758 miles (40 feet or 12.2 meters) per hour. The fastest moving species of land snail is probably the common garden snail (*Helix aspersa*) which moves at 0.03 miles (158.5 feet or 48.3 meters) per hour.

The Guinness Book of Records 1992 (New York: Bantam Book, 1992), 57, 106. Irving Wallace, *The Book of Lists #2* (New York: Morrow, 1980), 142.

How many quills does a porcupine have?

For its defensive weapon, the average porcupine has about 30 thousand quills or specialized hairs, comparable in hardness and flexibility to slivers of celluloid and so sharply pointed, they can penetrate any hide. The quills that do the most damage are the short ones that stud the porcupine's muscular tail. With a few lashes, the porcupine can send a rain of quills that have tiny scale-like barbs into the skin of its adversary. The quills work their way inward because of their barbs and the involuntary muscular action of the victim. Sometimes the quills can work themselves out, but other times the quills pierce vital organs, and the victim dies.

Slow-footed and stocky, porcupines spend much of their time in the trees, using their formidable incisors to strip off bark and foliage for their food, and supplement their diets with fruits, grasses, etc. Porcupines have a ravenous appetite for salt; as herbivores (plant-eating animals) their diets have insufficient salt. So natural salt licks, animal bones left by carnivores (meat-eating animals), yellow pond lilies, and other items having a high salt content (including paints, plywood adhesives and sweated-on clothing, etc. of humans) have a strong appeal to porcupines.

David F. Costello, *The World of the Porcupine,* (Philadelphia: Lippincott, 1966), 13. *Smithsonian* May 1992.

How long do wombats live and what do they eat?

Native to Australia and Tasmania, the common wombat or coarse-haired wombat (*Vombatus ursinus*) lives between 5 and 26 years (26 years in zoos). It dines mostly on grasses, roots, mushrooms, fresh shoots, and herbaceous plants. A wombat looks like a small bear in appearance, has a thick heavy body ranging from 2.3 to 4 feet (0.7 to 1.2 meters) and weighs 33 to 77 pounds (15 to 35 kilograms). This marsupial resembles a rodent in its manner of feeding and in its tooth structure—all its teeth are rootless and ever growing to compensate for their wear. Shy, it lives in a burrow and is an active digger, and its rough fur ranges from yellowish buff, gray, to dark brown or black.

The Complete Encyclopedia of the Animal World (London: Octopus Books, 1980), 261. Bernard Grzimek, *Grzimek's Encyclopedia of Mammals* (New York: McGraw-Hill, 1990), 1:342-43.

Are there any mammals that fly?

Bats (order Chiroptera with 986 species) are the only truly flying mammals, although several gliding mammals are referred to as "flying" (such as flying squirrel and flying lemur). The "wings" of bats are double membranes of skin stretching from the sides of the body to the hind legs and tail, and are actually skin extensions of the back and belly. The wing membranes are supported by the elongated fingers of the forelimbs (or arms). Nocturnal (active at night), ranging in length from 1.5 inches to 1.33 feet (25 to 406 millimeters), living in caves or crevices, bats inhabit most of the temperate and tropical regions of both hemispheres. The majority of species feed on inserts and fruit, and some tropical species eat pollen and nectar of flowers and insects found inside them. Moderate size species usually prey on small mammals, birds, lizards, and frogs, and some eat fish. But true vampire bats (three species) eat the blood of animals by making an incision in the animal's skin—from these bats, animals can contract rabies. Most bats do not find their way around by sight but have evolved a sonar system, called "echolocation," for locating solid objects. Bats emit vocal sounds through the nose or mouth while flying. These sounds, usually above the human hearing range, are reflected back as echoes. This method enables bats, when flying in darkness, to avoid solid objects and to locate the position of flying insects. Bats have the most acute sense of hearing of any land animal, hearing frequencies as high as 120 to 210 kilohertz. The highest frequency humans can hear is 20 kilohertz.

William Henry Burt, *A Field Guide to the Mammals, 3d ed.* (Boston: Houghton Mifflin Company, 1976), 21. Robert M. Nowak, *Walker's Mammals of the World* (Baltimore: The Johns Hopkins University Press, 1991), 1:190-92.

Which bear lives in a tropical rain forest?

The Malayan sun bear (*Ursus malayanus*) is one of the rarest animals in the tropical forests of Sumatra, Malay Peninsula, Borneo, Burma, Thailand, and southern China. The smallest bear, with a length of 3.3 to 4.6 feet (1 to 1.4 meters) and weighing 59.5 to 143.3 pounds (27 to 65 kilograms), it has a black strong, stocky body. With powerful paws having long, curved claws to help it climb trees in the dense forests, it is an expert tree climber. The sun bear tears at tree bark to expose insects, larvae, and the nests of bees and termites. Fruit, coconut palm, and small rodents, too, are part of its diet. Sleeping and sunbathing during the day, it is active at night. Unusually shy and retiring, cautious and intelligent, it is declining in population as the forests are being destroyed.

Macmillan Illustrated Animal Encyclopedia (New York: Macmillan, 1984), 82. Robert M. Nowak, *Walker's Mammals of the World, 5th ed.* (Baltimore: Johns Hopkins University, 1991), 2:1084, 1094.

What is the name of the seal-like animal in Florida?

The seal-like West Indian manatee (*Trichechus manatus*), in the winter, moves to more temperate parts of Florida, such as the warm headwaters of the Crystal and Homosassa rivers in central Florida or the tropical waters of southern Florida. When the air temperature rises to 50 degrees Fahrenheit (10 degrees Celsius), it will wander back along the Gulf coast and up the Atlantic coast as far as Virginia. Long-range offshore migrations to the coast of Guyana and South America have been documented. This large, plant-eating, water mammal may have been the inspiration for the mermaid legend. In 1893 when the population of manatees in Florida was reduced to several thousand, the state gave it legal protection from being hunted or commercially exploited. However, many animals continue to be killed or injured by the encroachment of humans. Entrapment in locks and dams, collisions with barges and power boat propellers, etc., cause at least 30 percent of the manatee deaths (125 to 130 total annual number of deaths).

New York Times, 8 December, 1991. Ronald M. Nowak, *Walker's Mammals of the World, 5th ed.* (Baltimore: Johns Hopkins University Press, 1991), 2:1300-2. *The Universal Almanac 1992* (Kansas City, MO: Andrews and McMeel, 1991), 544.

What is the difference between porpoises and dolphins?

The chief differences between dolphins (family Delphinidae) and porpoises (family Phocoenidae) occur in the snout and teeth. True dolphins have a beak-like snout and cone-shaped teeth. True porpoises have a rounded snout and flat or spade-shaped teeth.

Macmillan Illustrated Animal Encyclopedia (Mew York: Macmillan, 1994), 112, 114. Ronald M. Nowak, *Walker's Mammals of the World, 5th ed.* (Baltimore: Johns Hopkins University Press, 1991), 2:969-82.

What names are used for groups of animals?

Below are listed some names used for groups of animals:
Ants—Nest, army, colony, state or swarm
Bees—Swarm, cluster, nest, hive, or erst
Caterpillars—Army
Eels—Swarm or bed
Fish—School, shoal, haul, draught, run, or catch
Flies—Business, hatch, grist, swarm, or cloud
Frogs—Arm
Gnats—Swarm, cloud, or horde
Goldfish—Troubling
Grasshoppers—Cloud
Hornets—Nest
Jellyfish—Smuck or brood
Lice—Flock
Locusts—Swarm, cloud, or plague
Minnows—Shoal, steam, or swarm
Oysters—Bed
Sardines—Family
Sharks—School or shoal
Snakes—Bed, knot, den, or pit
Termites—Colony, nest, swarm, or brood
Toads—Nest, knot, or knab
Trout—Hover
Turtles—Bale or dole
Wasps—Nest, herd, or pladge

Clive Carpenter, ed., *The Guinness Book of Answers* (New York: Facts on File, 1993), 147-48. Robert Famighetti, ed. *The World Almanac and Book of Facts 1995* (Mahwah, NJ: World Almanac, 1994), 594. *1995 Information Please Almanac, Atlas and Yearbook* (Boston: Houghton Mifflin Company, 1994), 573. Peter Gray, *The Encyclopedia of the Biological Sciences* (New York: Van Rostrand Reinhold, 1970), 594. Ivan G. Sparkes, *Dictionary of Collective Nouns and Group Terms, 2d ed.* (Detroit: Gale Research, 1985).

Do all animals have red blood?

The color of blood is related to the compounds which transport oxygen. Hemoglobin, containing iron, is red and is found in all vertebrates (animals having a backbone) and a few invertebrates (animals lacking a backbone). Annelids (segmented worms) have either a green pigment chlorocruorin or a red pigment, hemerythrin. Some crustaceans (arthropods having divided bodies and generally having gills) have a blue pigment, hemocyanin, in their blood.

New Encyclopedia Britannica (Chicago: Encyclopedia Britannica, 1990), 2:290.

Can animals regenerate parts of their bodies?

Regeneration does occur in animals; however, it progressively declines the more complex the animal species becomes. Among primitive invertebrates (lacking a backbone), regeneration frequently occurs. For example, a planarium (flatworm) can split symmetrically, each being a clone of the other. In higher invertebrates regeneration occurs in echinoderms (such as starfish) and arthropods (such as insects and crustaceans). Regeneration of appendages (limbs, wings, and antennae) occurs in insects (such as cockroaches, fruitflies, and locusts) and in crustaceans (such as lobsters, crabs, and crayfish). For example, regeneration of the crayfish's missing claw occurs at its next molt (shedding of its hard cuticle exterior shell/skin in order to grow and the subsequent hardening of a new cuticle exterior). However, sometimes the regenerated claw does not achieve the same size of the missing claw. But after every molt (occurring 2 to 3 times a year) it grows, it eventually will be nearly as large as the original claw. On a very limited basis, some amphibians and reptiles can replace a lost leg or tail.

Mary S. Gardiner, *The Biology of Invertebrates* (New York: McGraw-Hill, 1972), 872-74. Thomas H.Huxley, *The Crayfish* (Cambridge, MA: MIT Press, 1974), 38-39. Frank N. Magill, *Magill's Survey of Science: Life Science Series* (Englewood Cliffs NJ: Salem Press, 1991), 5:2311.

What are a turtle's upper and lower shell called?

The turtle (order Testudines) uses its shell as a protective device. The upper shell is called the *dorsal carapace* and the lower shell is called the *ventral plastron.* The shell's sections are referred to as *the scutes.* The carapace and the plastron are joined at the sides.

Roger Conant, *A Field Guide to Reptiles and Amphibians: Eastern and Central North America, 3d ed.* (Boston: Houghton Mifflin Company, 1991), front end paper.

Which poisonous snakes are native to the United States?

Copperheads, rattlesnakes, water moccasins (cottonmouths), and coral snakes are all poisonous. Copperheads (*Agkistrodon contortex*) tend to inhabit areas in the southeastern United States, Texas, and the lower Ohio Valley. Rattlesnakes (genus *Crotalus*) range throughout the United States, and cottonmouths (*Agkistrodon piscivorus*) range from Texas across to North Carolina. Coral snakes (*Microrus fulvius*), the most venomous snakes in the United States, tend to inhabit the southeastern States and Texas.

Roger Conant and Joseph T. Collins, *A Field Guide to Reptiles and Amphibians* (Houghton Mifflin Company, 1991), 188-201.

Do dogs and cats dream?

Dogs have REM (rapid eye movement) sleep periods, which are associated with dreaming in humans. Therefore, it is assumed that dogs dream. Movements of the eyeballs, lip trembling, twitching of the extremities, and vocalizations have been observed during these sleep periods. Sleeping cats have been studied with electroencephalograms (EEG) which read their brain activity.

Thirty percent of the cats' sleep time were deep sleep times or REM (rapid eye movement) sleep periods accompanied by changes in body posture, paw and claw movements, whisker twitching, ear flicking and, in some cases, vocalization. It could be assumed, as well, that cats dream or at least have semiconscious experiences similar to human dreams.

Fernand Mery, *The Life, History, and Magic of the Dog* (New York: Grosset & Dunlap, 1970), 181. William H. Moorcroft, *Sleep, Dreaming, and Sleep Disorders* (Lanham, MD: University Press of America, 1989), 80. Marcus Schneck and Jill Caravan, *Cat Facts* (New York: Dorset Press, 1990), 24-25.

What is the rarest breed of dog?

The Tahltan bear dog, of which only a few remain, is thought to be the rarest dog. It is in danger of extinction. It was once used by Tahltan Indians of western Canada to hunt bear, lynx, and porcupine.

Joan Palmer, *Dog Facts* (New York: Dorset Press, 1991), 16.

Which breed is known as the "voiceless dog"?

The basenji dog does not bark. When happy, it will make an appealing sound described as something between a chortle and a yodel. It also snarls and growls on occasion. One of the oldest breeds of dogs and originating in central Africa, the basenji was often given as a present to the Pharaohs of ancient Egypt. Following the decline of the Egyptian civilization, the basenji was still valued in central Africa for its hunting prowess and its silence. The dog was rediscovered by English explorers in the nineteenth century, although it was not widely bred until the 1940s.

The basenji is a small, lightly built dog with a flat skull and a long rounded muzzle. It measures 16 to 17 inches (40 to 43 centimeters) in height at the shoulder and weighs 22 to 24 pounds (10 to 11 kilograms). The coat is short and silky in texture. The feet, chest, and tail tip are white; the rest of the coat is chestnut red, black, or black and tan.

American Kennel Club, *The Complete Dog Book* (New York: Howell Book House, 1985), 156-59. *The New Dog Encyclopedia* (Harrisburg, PA: Stackpole, 1970), 505-6. Joan Palmer, *Dog Facts* (New York: Dorset Press, 1991), 150.

Where did the pug dog originate?

The pug's true origin is unknown, but it has existed in China, its earliest known source, for 1,800 years. A popular pet in Buddhist monasteries in Tibet, it next appeared in Japan and then in Europe. It probably was introduced into Holland by the traders of the Dutch East India Company. The name "pug dog" may have come from the dog's facial resemblance to a marmoset monkey. This popular pet in the 1700s was called a "pug." So the term "pug dog" distinguished the dog from the "pug" monkey.

A pug has a square, short compact body, either silver or apricot-fawn in color. Its muzzle is black, short, blunt, and square; its average weight is 14 to 18 pounds (6.4 to 8.2 kilograms). The pug is often described by the motto "Multum in Parvo"-a lot of dog in a small space.

American Kennel Club, *The Complete Dog Book* (New York: Howell Book House, 1985), 477-79. Louise L. Gore, *Meet the Pug* (Wilsonville, OR: Doral, 1990), 3.

What controls the formation of the color "points" in a Siamese cat?

The color points in a Siamese cat are due to the presence of a recessive gene which operates at cooler temperatures, limiting the color to well-defined areas-the mask, ears, tail, lower legs, and paws-the places at the far reaches of the cardiovascular system of the cat. There are four classic varieties of Siamese cats. Seal-points have a pale fawn to cream colored coat with seal-brown markings. Blue-points are bluish-white with slate blue markings. Chocolate-points are ivory colored with milk-chocolate brown colored markings. Lilac-points have a white coat and pinkish-gray markings. There are also some newer varieties with red, cream, and tabby points. The Siamese originated in Thailand (once called Siam) and arrived in England in the 1880s. They are medium-sized and have long, slender, lithe bodies, with long heads and long tapering tails. Extroverted and affectionate, Siamese are known for their loud, distinctive voices which are impossible to ignore.

Cat Fancy April 1991. *Standard Guide to Cat Breeds* (New York: McGraw Hill, 1979), 41. David Taylor and Daphne Negus, *The Ultimate Cat Book* (New York: Simon and Schuster, 1989), 108-9.

Why and how do cats purr?

Experts cannot agree on how or why cats purr, or on where the sound originates. Some think that the purr is produced by the vibration of blood in a large vein in the chest cavity. Where the vein passes through the diaphragm, the muscles around the vein contract, nipping the blood flow and setting up oscillations. These sounds are magnified by the air in the bronchial tubes and the windpipe. Others think that purring is the vibrations of membranes, called false vocal cords, located near the vocal cords. No one knows for sure why a cat purrs, but many people interpret the sound as one of contentment.

Marcus Schneck and Jill Caravan, *Cat Facts* (New York: Dorset Press, 1990), 26. David Taylor, *You & Your Cat* (New York: Alfred Knopf, 1988), 35.

Why do cats' eyes shine In the dark?

A cat's eyes contain a special light-conserving mechanism called the tapetum lucidum, which reflects any light not absorbed as it passes through the retina of each eye. The retina gets a second chance (so to speak) to receive the light, aiding the cat's vision even more. In dim light, when the pupils of the cat's eyes are opened the widest, this glowing or shining effect occurs when light hits them at certain angles. The tapetum lucidum, located behind the retina, is a membrane composed of fifteen layers of special glittering cells, that all together act as a mirror. The color of the glow is usually greenish or golden, but the eyes of the Siamese cat reflect a luminous ruby red.

Faith McNulty, *Wholly Cats* (New York: Bobbs-Merrill, 1962), 17. Marcus Schneck and Jill Caravan, *Cat Facts* (New York: Dorset Press, 1990), 40. David Taylor, *You & Your Cat* (New York: Alfred Knopf, 1988), 28.

What is a "tabby" cat?

"Tabby," the basic feline coat pattern, goes back to when cats were wild. The tabby coat is an excellent form of camouflage. Each hair has two or three dark and light bands with the tip always dark. There are four variations on the basic tabby pattern.

The mackerel (also called striped or tiger) tabby has a dark line running down the back from the head to the base of the tail with several stripes branching down the sides. The legs have stripes and the tail has even rings with a dark tip. There are two rows of dark spots on the stomach. Above the eyes is a mark shaped like an "M" and dark lines run back to the ears. Two dark necklace-like bands appear on the chest.

The blotched, or classic, tabby markings seem to be the closest to those found in the wild. The markings on the head, legs, tail, and stomach are the same as the mackerel tabby. The major difference is that the blotched tabby has dark patches on the shoulder and side rimmed by one or several lines.

The spotted tabby has uniformly shaped round or oval dark spots all over the body and legs. The forehead has a "M" on it and a narrow dark line runs down the back.

The Abyssinian tabby has almost no dark markings on its body; they appear only on the forelegs, the flanks, and the tail. The hairs are banded except on the stomach where they are light and unicolored.

Ulrike Mller, *The New Cat Handbook* (Woodbury, NY: Barron, 1984), 114-15.

Has there ever been a pet alligator in the White House?

In 1825 the Marquis de Lafayette (1757-1834) toured America and was given an alligator by some grateful citizen. While Lafayette was the guest of U.S. President John Quincy Adams (1767-1848), the alligator took up residence in the East Room of the White House for several months. When Lafayette departed, he took his alligator with him.

Niall Kelly, *Presidential Pets* (New York: Abbeville Press, 1992), 17. Margaret Truman, *White House Pets* (New York: David McKay, 1969), 4, 169.

How can bats be removed from the house?

To rid an attic or other part of a house of a bat colony, seal, caulk, weatherstrip, or screen all exterior openings greater than inch wide-except one, through which the bats can escape. Wait three days; then, about -hour after dark (when the bats are outside feeding), seal the last opening. If an area can not be sealed, install a light that would shine directly on the roosting area. In confined areas, suspend mothballs in porous bags as a repellent. Avoid exterminating bats; they are desirable as insect eaters. If a single bat strays into a room, after dark open the windows and any outside doors and turn off all the lights. The bat will fly outside. Never touch a bat; it can be a carrier of rabies. If bitten, go to a hospital immediately.

How to Do Just About Anything (Pleasantville, NY: Reader's Digest Association, 1986), 28.

Who coined the term biology?

Biology was first used by Karl Burdach (1776-1847) to denote the study of man. Jean Baptiste Pierre Antoine de Monet Lamarck (1744-1829) gave the term a broader meaning in 1812. He believed in the integral character of science. For the special sciences, chemistry, meteorology, geology, and botany zoology he coined the term biology.

Lamarckism epitomizes the belief that changes acquired during an individual's lifetime as the result of active, quasi-purposive, functional adaptations can somehow be imprinted upon the genes, thereby becoming part of the heritage of succeeding generations. Today, very few professional biologists believe that anything of the kind occurs-or can occur.

Biology is the science that deals with living things (from the Greek word *bios* meaning life). Formerly broadly divided into two areas, zoology (from the Greek word *zoon* meaning animal), the study of animals, and botany (from the Greek word *botanes* meaning plant), the study of plants, biology is now divided and sub-divided into hundreds of specialized fields involving the structure, function, and classification of the forms of life such as anatomy, ecology, embryology, evolution, genetics, paleontology, and physiology.

W.F. Bynum et al., *Dictionary of the History of Science* (Princeton, NJ: Princeton University Press, 1985), 43. P.B. Medawar and J.S. Medawar, *Aristotle to Zoos* (Cambridge: Harvard University Press, 1983), 166. Herman Schneider and Leo Schneider, *The Harper Dictionary of Science in Everyday Language* (New York: Harper & Row, 1988), 41.

What is meant by Mendelian inheritance?

Mendelian inheritance refers to genetic traits carried through heredity, described by the Austrian monk, Gregor Mendel (1822-1889). Mendel was the first to deduce correctly the basic principles of heredity. Mendelian traits are also called single gene or monogenic traits because they are controlled by the action of a single gene or gene pair. More than 4,300 human disorders are known or suspected to be inherited as Mendelian traits, encompassing autosomal dominant (e.g., neurofibromatosis), autosomal recessive (e.g., cystic fibrosis), sex-linked dominant and recessive conditions (e.g., color-blindness and hemophilia).

Overall, incidence of Mendelian disorders in the human population is about one percent. Many nonanomalous characteristics that make up human variation are also inherited in Mendelian fashion.

The Biographical Dictionary of Scientists: Biologists (New York: Peter Bedrick Books, 1984), 93-94. James Wynbrandt, *The Encyclopedia of Genetic Disorders and Birth Defects* (New York: Facts On File, 1991), 205.

What is the significance of *The Origin of Species*?

Charles Darwin (1809-1882) first proposed a theory of evolution based on natural selection in his treatise on *The Origin of Species.* The publication of *The Origin of Species* ushered in a new era in our thinking about the nature of man. The intellectual revolution it caused and the impact it had on man's concept of himself and the world were greater than those caused by the works of Newton and others. The effect was immediate, the first edition being sold out on its day of publication on November 24, 1859. The *Origin* has been referred to as "the book that shook the world." Every modern discussion of man's future, the population explosion, the struggle for existence, the purpose of man and the universe, and man's place in nature rests on Darwin.

The work was a product of his analyses and interpretations of his research findings made during his voyages on the H.M.S. *Beagle.* Charles Darwin served on the H.M.S. *Beagle* as a naturalist, setting sail on December 27, 1831, for South America. This five-year journey was the starting point of Darwin's career as a scientist. During the trip, Darwin studied fossilized remains of animals and observed the vegetation and animal species in South America, and most importantly, in the Galapagos Islands. In Darwin's day, the prevailing explanation for organic diversity was the story of creation in the Book of Genesis in the Bible. The *Origin* was the first publication to present scientifically sound, well-organized evidence for evolution. Darwin's theory of evolution was based on natural selection in which the best, the fittest, survive, and if there is a difference in genetic endowment among individuals, the race will, by necessity, steadily improve. It is a two-step process: the first consists of the production of variation, and the second, of the sorting of this variability by natural selection in which the favorable variations tend to be preserved.

Charles Darwin, *On the Origin of Species* (Cambridge: Harvard University Press, 1964), vii-xvi. William Irvine, *Apes, Angels, and Victorians,* (New York: McGraw-Hill, 1955), 46-47.

Can human beings be cloned?

In theory, human beings can be cloned. There are, however, many technical obstacles to human cloning, as well as moral, ethical, philosophical, religious, and economic issues to be resolved before a human being could be cloned.

A clone is a group of cells derived from the original cell by fission—one cell dividing into two cells—or by mitosis—cell nucleus division with each chromosome splitting into two. It perpetuates an existing organism's genetic make-up. Gardeners have been making clones of plants for centuries by taking cuttings of plants to make genetically identical copies. For plants, that refuse to grow from cuttings or for the animal world, modern scientific techniques have greatly extended the range of cloning. The technique for plants starts with taking a cutting of a plant, usually the best one in terms of reproductivity or decorativeness or other standard. Since all the plant's cells contain the genetic information from which the entire plant can be reconstructed, the cutting can be taken from any part of the plant. Placed in a culture medium having nutritious chemicals and a growth hormone, the cells in the cutting divide, doubling in size every six weeks until the mass of cells produces small white globular points called embryoids. These embryoids develop roots, or shoots, and begin to look like tiny plants. Transplanted into compost, these plants grow into exact copies of the parent plant. The whole process takes 18 months. This process, called tissue culture, has been used to make clones of oil palm, asparagus, pineapples, strawberries, brussels sprouts, cauliflower, bananas, carnations, and ferns. Besides making high productive copies of the best plant available, this method controls viral diseases that are passed through seed generations.

For animals, a technique called nuclear transfer enables up to 32 clones to be produced at one time. An embryo at the 32-cell stage of development is split up using tiny surgical tools. Each of the 32 cells then are combined with single cell embryos (from the same species) from which the nucleus has been removed. This method has been used on mice, frogs, sheep, and cattle. Ultimately, there seems to be no biological reason why human beings could not be cloned, sometime in the future.

How in the World (Pleasantville, NY: Reader's Digest Association, 1990), 188. Robert G. McKinnell, *Cloning of Frogs, Mice, and Other Animals, rev. ed.* (Minneapolis: University of Minnesota Press, 1985), 95-107. *Scientific American* May 1989.

What are petite yeasts?

In certain yeasts, abnormally small colonies occur. The cells which form petite colonies are mutants which lack certain components for respiration, therefore they exhibit a reduced growth rate. Mutations occur in nuclear DNA or in mitochondrial DNA. Mitochondria are "organelles" found in most eukanyotic (complex) cells. They are the sites for cellular respiration and other cellular processes. Occurrence is one in 500.

Paul Singleton and Diana Sainsbury, *Dictionary of Microbiology* (New York: John Wiley & Sons, 1978), 300.

What are diatoms?

Diatoms are microscopic algae in the phylum *bacillarrophyte* of the protista kingdom. Yellow or brown in color, almost all diatoms are single-celled algae, dwelling in fresh and salt water, especially in the cold waters of the North Pacific Ocean and the Antarctic. Diatoms are an important food source for marine plankton—floating animal and plant life—and many small animals.

Diatoms have hard cell walls; these shells are made from silica that they extract from the water. It is unclear how they accomplish this. When they die, their glassy shells, called frustules, sink to the bottom of the sea, which hardens into rock called diatomite. One of the most famous and accessible diatomites is the Monterrey Formation along the coast of central and southern California.

Neil A. Campbell, *Biology, 2d ed.* (Redwood, CA: Benjamin/Cummings, 1990), 549. *Encyclopedic Dictionary of Science* (New York: Facts On File, 1988), 77. Ira Flatow, *Rainbows, Curve Balls and Other Wonders of the Natural World Explained* (New York: Harper & Row, 1988), 16-17.

How is a fairy ring formed?

A fairy ring, or fungus ring, is found frequently in a grassy area. There are three types: those which do not affect the surrounding vegetation, those that cause increased growth, and those that damage the surrounding environment. The ring is started from a mycelium, the underground, food-absorbing part of a fungus. The fungus growth is on the outer edge of the grassy area because the inner band of decaying mycelium "use-up" the resources in the soil at the center. This creates a ring effect. Each succeeding generation is farther out from the center.

G.C. Ainsworth, *Ainsworth's & Bisby's Dictionary of the Fungi, 5th ed.* (London: Commonwealth Agricultural Bureaau, 1961), 148.

What is a biological clock?

First recognized by the Chinese in the third century B.C., the biological clock is an intrinsic mechanism that controls the rhythm of various metabolic activities of plants and animals. Some functions, such as mating, hibernation, and migration have a yearly cycle; others, such as ovulation and menstrual cycles of women, follow a lunar month. The majority, however, have a 24-hour, day-night or light-dark cycle called circadian rhythm. This day-night cycle, first recognized in plants over 250 years ago and existing in virtually all species of plants and animals, regulates the metabolic functions of organisms such as plants opening and closing their petals or leaves, germination and flowering functions, changes in human body temperature, hormone secretion, blood sugar and blood pressure levels, and sleep cycles.

Research in chronobiology-the study of these daily rhythms-reveals that many accidents occur between 1 a.m. and 6 a.m., that most babies are born in the morning hours, that heart attacks tend to occur between 6 a.m. and 9 a.m., and that most Olympic records are broken in the late afternoon. The clock regulator may be the pineal gland located in the head of an animal.

Richard P. Brennan, *Dictionary of Scientific Literacy* (New York: John Wiley & Sons, 1992), 25, 49. *Encyclopedic Dictionary of Science* (New York: Facts on File, 1988), 42. Robert Temple, *The Genius of China* (New York: Simon and Schuster, 1986), 124.

What does "ontogeny recapitulates phylogeny" mean?

Ontogeny is the course of development of an organism from fertilized egg to adult; phylogeny is the evolutionary history of a group of organisms. So the phrase, originating in nineteenth-century biology means that, as an embryo of an advanced organism grows, it will pass through stages that look very much like the adult phase of less advanced organisms. For example, at one point the human embryo has gills and resembles a tadpole.

Elizabeth Toothill, *The Facts On File Dictionary of Biology* (New York: Facts On File, 1988), 210, 235. James Trefil, *1001 Things Everyone Should Know About Science* (New York: Doubleday, 1992), 23.

How many mitochondria are there in a cell?

The number of mitochondria varies according to the type of cell, but each cell in the human liver has over one thousand mitochondria. A mitochondrion (singular form) is a self-replicating double-membraned body found in the cytoplasm of all eukaryotic (having a nucleus) cells. The number of mitochondria per cell varies between one and 10,000, and averages about 200. The mitochondria are the sites for much of the metabolism necessary for the production of ATP, lipids, and protein synthesis.

W.F. Bynum et al., *Dictionary of the History of Science* (Princeton, NJ: Princeton University Press, 1985), 149. Norman Maclean, *Dictionary of Genetics and Cell Biology* (New York: New York University Press, 1987), 254. James Trefil, *1001 Things Everyone Should Know About Science* (New York: Doubleday, 1992), 101.

How does the process work in a food chain?

A food chain is the transfer of food energy from the source in plants through a series of organisms with repeated eating and being eaten. The number of steps or links in a sequence is usually four to five. The first trophic, or group of organisms that get their energy the same way is plants; the animals that eat plants, called herbivores, form the second trophic level. The third level consists of primary carnivores-animal-eating animals like wolves-who eat herbivores, and the fourth level are animals that eat primary carnivores. Food chains overlap because many organisms eat more than one type of food, so that these chains can look more like food webs. In 1891 German zoologist Karl Semper introduced the food chain concept.

Eugene Odum, *Fundamentals of Ecology, 3rd. ed.* (Philadelphia: W. B. Saunders, 1971), 63. James H. Otto, *Modern Biology* (Fort Worth, TX: Holt, Rinehart and Winston, 1981), 666. James Trefil, *1001 Things Everyone Should Know About Science* (New York: Doubleday, 1992), 43.

What is eutrophication?

Eutrophication is a process in which the supply of plant nutrients in a lake or pond is increased. In time, the result of natural eutrophication may be dry land where water once flowed, caused by plant overgrowth.

Natural fertilizers, washed from the soil, result in an accelerated growth of plants, producing overcrowding. As the plants die off, the dead and decaying vegetation depletes the lake's oxygen supply causing fish to die. The accumulated dead plant and animal material eventually changes a deep lake to a shallow one, then to a swamp, and finally it becomes dry land.

While the process of eutrophication is a natural one, it has been accelerated enormously by human activities. Fertilizers from farms, sewage, and industrial wastes and some detergents all contribute to the problem.

Herman Schneider, *The Harper Dictionary of Science in Everyday Language* (New York: Harper & Row, 1988), 113.

What was the first animal on the U.S. endangered species list?

The peregrine falcon was the first animal to be listed on the U.S. endangered species list in the late 1970s.

Barbara Berliner, *The Book of Answers* (Englewood Cliffs, NJ: Prentice-Hall, 1990), 32.

How did the dodo become extinct?

The dodo became extinct around 1800. Although thousands were slaughtered for meat, pigs and monkeys, which destroyed dodo eggs, were probably most responsible for the dodo's extinction. They were native to the Mascarene Islands in the Central Indian Ocean. They became extinct on Mauritius Island soon after 1680 and on Reunion Island about 1750. They remained on Rodriguez until 1800.

Encyclopedia Americana (Danbury, CT: Grolier, 1990), 232-33.

What was the life span of a dinosaur?

The lifespan of a dinosaur has been estimated at 75 to 300 years. Such estimates are educated guesses. From examination of the microstructure of dinosaur bones, scientists have inferred that they matured slowly and probably had proportionately long lifespans.

John N. Wilford, *The Riddle of the Dinosaur* (New York: Knopf, 1986), 249.

Under what conditions is a species considered "endangered"?

The determination to list a species as endangered is a complex process that has no set of fixed criteria that can be applied consistently to all species. The known number of living members in a species is not the sole factor. A species with a million members known to be alive but living in only one small area could be considered endangered, whereas another species having a smaller number of members, but spread out in a broad area, would not be considered so threatened. Reproduction data-the frequency of reproduction, the average number of offspring born, the survival rate, etc.-enter into such determinations. In the United States, the director of the Fish and Wildlife Service (within the Department of the Interior) determines which species are to be considered endangered, based on research and field data from specialists, biologists, botanists, and naturalists.

According to the Endangered Species Act of 1973, a species can be listed if it is threatened by any of the following:

The present or threatened destruction, modification, or curtailment of its habitat or range. Utilization for commercial, sporting, scientific, or educational purposes at levels that detrimentally affect it. Disease or predation. Absence of regulatory mechanisms adequate to prevent the decline of a species or degradation of its habitat. Other natural or man-made factors affecting its continued existence.

If the species is so threatened, the director then determines the "critical habitat," that is the species' inhabitation areas that contain the essential physical or biological features necessary for the species' preservation. The critical habitat can include non-habitation areas, which are deemed necessary for the protection of the species.

Caroline Sutton and Duncan M. Anderson, *How Do They Do That?* (New York: Quill, 1982), 92-93.

What is a jackalope?

The "jackalope" is said to be a rare, nearly extinct antlered species of rabbit. Pictures of it abound, and stuffed specimens of the creature can sometimes be found on display in Western states, especially in bars. The "creature" is in fact an elaborate hoax played on unsuspecting tourists. It is in fact a stuffed jackrabbit with a pair of horns or antlers glued onto its head.

Daniel Cohen, *The Encyclopedia of Monsters* (New York: Dodd, Mead, 1982), 254.

What are dust mites?

Dust mites are microscopic arachnids (members of the spider family), commonly found in house dust. An allergy to dust mites is probably one of the leading causes of asthma-breathlessness and wheezing caused by the narrowing of small airways of the lungs-in North America, as well as the major cause of common allergies (exaggerated reactions of the immune system to exposure of offending agents).

Thad Godish, *Indoor Air Pollution Control* (Chelsea, MI: Lewis Publishers), 55-56.

How many miles of blood vessels are contained in the body?

If they could be laid end to end, the blood vessels would total about 60 thousand miles (97 thousand kilometers).

World Book Encyclopedia (Chicago: World Book, 1990) 2: 424.

What is the amount of carbon dioxide found in normal blood?

Carbon dioxide normally ranges from 19 to 25 mm per liter in arterial blood and 22 to 30 mm per liter in venous blood.

Cathey Pinkney, *The Patient's Guide to Medical Tests, 3d ed.* (New York: Facts on File), 72.

Why do people snore?

Snoring is produced by vibrations of the soft palate, usually caused by any condition that hinders breathing through the nose. It is more common while sleeping on the back.

The American Medical Association Encyclopedia of Medicine (New York: Random House, 1989), 922.

What is REM sleep?

REM sleep is rapid eye movement sleep. It is characterized by faster breathing and heart rates than NREM (nonrapid eye movement) sleep. The eyes move rapidly, and dreaming, often with elaborate story lines, occurs. The only people who do not have REM sleep are those who have been blind from birth. REM sleep usually occurs in about four or five periods, varying in length from five minutes to about an hour, growing progressively longer as sleep continues.

Scientists do not understand why dreaming is important, but they think the brain is either cataloging the information it picked up during the day and throwing out the data it does not want, or is creating scenarios to work through situations causing emotional distress.

The American Medical Association Encyclopedia of Medicine (New York: Random House, 1989), 915. Jeff Rovin, *Laws of Order* (New York: Ballantine, 1992), 112.

How does the immune system work?

The immune system has two main components: white blood cells and antibodies circulating in the blood. The antigen-antibody reaction forms the basis for this immunity. When an antigen (*anti*body *gen*erator), such as a harmful bacterium, virus, fungus, parasite, or other foreign substance invades the body, a specific antibody is generated to attack the antigen. The antibody is produced by beta-lymphocytes (B-cells) in the spleen or lymph nodes. An antibody may either destroy the antigen directly or it may "label" it so that a white blood cell (called a microphage, or scavenger cell) can engulf the foreign intruder. After a human has been exposed to an antigen, a later exposure to the same antigen will produce a faster immune system reaction. The necessary antibodies will be produced more rapidly and in larger amounts. Artificial immunization uses this antigen-antibody reaction to protect the human body from certain diseases, by exposing the body to a safe dose of antigen to produce effective antibodies as well as a "readiness" for any future attacks of the harmful antigen.

Mayo Clinic Family Healthbook (New York: Morrow, 1990), 448-49. *Oxford Illustrated Encyclopedia of Invention and Technology*, (Oxford, England: Oxford University Press, 1992), 177. *Taber's Cyclopedic Medical Dictionary, 16th ed.* (Philadelphia: Davis, 1989), 113.

How long does it take food to digest?

The stomach holds just under two quarts (1.9 liters) of semi-digested food that can stay in the stomach for a period of three to five hours. The stomach releases this food slowly to the rest of the digestive tract. Fifteen hours or more after the first bite started down the alimentary canal the final residue of the food is passed along to the rectum and is excreted through the anus as feces.

Neil McAleer, *The Body Almanac* (New York: Doubleday, 1985), 186.

How many chromosomes are there in a human body cell?

A human being normally has 46 chromosomes (23 pairs) in all but the sex cells. Half of each pair is inherited from the mother's egg; the other, from the father's sperm. When the sperm and egg unite in fertilization, they create a single cell, or zygote, with 46 chromosomes. When cell division occurs, the 46 chromosomes are duplicated and this process is repeated billions of times over, with each of the cells containing the identical set of chromosomes. Only the gametes, or sex cells, are different. In their cell division, the members of each pair of chromosomes are separated and distributed to different cells. Each gamete has only 23 chromosomes.

Chromosomes contain thousands of genes, each of which have information for a specific trait. That information is in the form of a chemical code, and the chemical compound that codes this genetic information is *d*eoxyribo*n*ucleic *a*cid or DNA. A gene can be seen as a sequence of DNA that is coded for a specific protein. These proteins determine specific physical traits (such as height, body shape, color of hair, eyes, skin, etc.), body chemistry (blood type, metabolic functions, etc.), and some aspects of behavior and intelligence. More than 150 human disorders are inherited, and genes are thought to determine susceptibility to many diseases.

Eldra Pearl Soloman and Gloria A. Phillips, *Understanding Human Anatomy and Physiology* (Philadelphia: W.B. Saunders, 1987), 358-59. *World Book Encyclopedia* (Chicago: World Book, 1990), 3: 538.

How many cells are in the human body?

Sources give figures that vary from 50 to 75 trillion cells.

Isaac Asimov, *The Human Body, rev. ed.* (New York: Mentor Book, 1992), 79. *New Encyclopaedia Britannica, 15th ed.* (Chicago: Encyclopaedia Britannica, 1990), 6:134. C. Van Amerogen, *The Way Things Work Book of the Body* (New York: Simon and Schuster, 1979), 13.

In addition to left or right-handedness, what other preferences do people have?

Most people have a preferred eye, ear, and foot. In one study, for example, 46 percent were strongly right-footed, while 3.9 percent were strongly left-footed; furthermore 72 percent were strongly right-handed and 5.3 percent strongly left-handed. Estimates vary about the proportion of left-handers to right-handers, but it may be as high as one in ten. Some 90 percent of healthy adults use the right hand for writing; two-thirds favor the right hand for most activities requiring coordination and skill. There are no male-female difference in these proportions.

The American Medical Association Encyclopedia of Medicine (New York: Random House, 1989), 506. Gyles D. Brandreth, *Your Vital Statistics* (New York: Citadel, 1986), 84. Sally P. Springer, *Left Brain, Right Brain, rev. ed.* (New York: W.H. Freeman, 1985), 137, 140.

Why do humans have wisdom teeth?

Although they are useless to humans now, they must have had some purpose in the past. Nature rarely produces extraneous features. Perhaps when primitive man ate tough meats, the extra molars in the mouth, now known as wisdom teeth, helped to chew up the meat fibers. As humans evolved, the brain became larger and the face position moved further downward and inward. Also the protruding jawbones of early humans gradually moved backward, leaving no room for these third molars or wisdom teeth.

David Feldman, *Why Do Clocks Run Clockwise? and Other Imponderables* (New York: Perennial Library, 1988), 137.

What was the likely purpose of the human appendix?

Experts can only theorize on the purpose of the human appendix. It may have had the same purpose it does in present-day herbivores, where it harbors colonies of bacteria that help in the digestion of cellulose in plant material. Another theory suggests that tonsils and the appendix might manufacture the antibody-producing white blood cells called B-lymphocytes; however B-lymphocytes could also be produced by the bone marrow. The third theory is that the appendix may "attract" body infections to localize the infection in one spot that is not critical to body functioning. The earliest surgical removal of the appendix was by Claudries Amyand (1680-1740) in England in 1736. The first American to have her appendix removed was Mary Gartside of Davenport, Iowa, on January 4, 1885.

Christiaan Barnard, *The Body Machine* (New York: Crown, 1981), 127. David Feldman, *Do Penguins Have Knees?* (New York: Harper Perennial, 1991), 152-53. Laurence J. Peters, *Peter's Almanac* (New York: William

Morrow, 1982). Mark C. Young, ed., *Guinness Book of Records, 1995* (New York: Facts on File, 1994), 187.

Are the human lungs identical?

The human lungs are not identical. The right lung tends to be shorter than the left by one inch (2.5 centimeters); however, its total capacity is greater. The right lung has three lobes, the left lung has two.

Isaac Asimov, *The Human Body, rev. ed.* (New York: Mentor Book, 1992), 145. Henry Gray, *Anatomy of the Human Body, 28th ed.* (Malvern, PA: Lea & Febiger, 1966), 1148.

Whose brain is larger: Neanderthal man or modern man?

The capacity of the skull of "classic" Neanderthal man was often larger than that of modern man. The capacity was between 1,350 to 1,700 cubic centimeters with the average being 1,400 to 1,450 cubic centimeters. The mean cranial capacity of modern man is 1,370 cubic centimeters, with a range of 950 to 2,200 cubic centimeters. However, brain size alone is not an index of intelligence.

Jan Jelinek, *The Pictorial Encyclopedia of the Evolution of Man* (London: Hamlyn, 1975), 92-93. Kenneth A. R. Kennedy, *Neanderthal Man* (Minneapolis: Burgess, 1975), 40.

What are the seven endocrine glands?

The major endocrine glands include the pituitary, thyroid, parathyroids, adrenals, pancreas, testes, and ovaries. These glands secrete hormones into the blood system, which generally stimulate some change in metabolic activity:

Pituitary—secretes ACTH to stimulate the adrenal cortex; produces aldosterone to control sodium and potassium reabsorption by the kidneys; FSH to stimulate gonad function and prolactin to stimulate milk secretion of breasts; TSH to stimulate thyroid gland to produce thyroxin; LH to stimulate ovulation in females and testerone production in males; GH to stimulate general growth. Stores oxytocin for uterine contraction.

Thyroid gland—secretes thyroxine and triiodothyronine to stimulate metabolic rate, especially in growth and development, and secretes calcitonin to lower blood-calcium levels.

Parathyroids—secrete hormone PTH to increase blood-calcium levels; activates vitamin D and stimulates calcium reabsorption in kidneys.

Adrenals—secrete epinephrine and norepinephrine to help the body cope with stress, raise blood pressure, heart rate, metabolic rate, raise blood sugar levels, etc. Aldosterone secreted by the adrenal cortex maintains sodium-phosphate balance in kidneys and cortisol helps the body adapt to stress, mobilizes fat, and raises blood sugar level.

Pancreas—secretes insulin to control blood sugar levels, stimulates glycogen production, fat storage, and protein synthesis. Glucagon secretion raises blood sugar level and mobilizes fat.

Ovaries and testes—secrete estrogens, progesterone, or testosterone to stimulate growth and reproductive processes.

Science and Technology Illustrated (Chicago: Encyclopaedia Britannica, 1984), 9:1136. Eldra PearlSolomon and Gloria A. Phillips, *Understanding Human Anatomy and Physiology* (Philadelphia: W. B. Saunders, 1987), 178-79.

Why do all newborn babies have blue eyes?

The color of the iris gives the human eye its color. The amount of dark pigment, melanin, in the iris is what determines its color. In newborns the pigment is concentrated in the folds of the iris. When a baby is a few months old, the melanin moves to the surface of the iris and gives the baby his or her permanent eye color.

Neil McAleer, *The Body Almanac* (New York: Doubleday, 1985), 41.

What are the floaters that move around on the eye?

Floaters are semi-transparent specks perceived to be floating in the field of vision. Some originate with red blood cells that have leaked out of the retina. The blood cells swell into spheres, some forming strings, and float around the areas of the retina. Others are shadows cast by the microscopic structures in the vitreous humor, a jellylike substructure located behind the retina. A sudden appearance of a cloud of dark floaters, if accompanied by bright light flashes, could indicate retinal detachment.

The American Medical Association Encyclopedia of Medicine (New York: Random House, 1989), 458-59. *Scientific American* April 1981.

What are the primary sensations of taste?

The four primary categories are sweet, sour, salty and bitter. The sensitivity and location of these areas on the tongue varies from person to person. Some of the nine thousand taste buds are located in the other areas of the mouth as well—the lips (usually very salt-sensitive), the inner cheeks, the underside of the tongue, the back of the throat, and the roof of the mouth. The sense of taste is intimately associated with the sense of smell, so that foods taste bland to someone suffering from a cold. Also related are the appearance, texture, and temperature of food.

The American Medical Association Encyclopedia of Medicine (New York: Random House, 1989), 965. Arthur C. Guyton, *Textbook of Medical Physiology, 8th ed.* (Philadelphia: Saunders, 1991) 581. Harold Hillman, *Kitchen Science, rev. ed.* (Boston: Houghton-Mifflin, 1989), 283-84.

How much skin does an average person have?

There are about 20 square feet or 2 square meters of skin covering the average human body. Weighing 6 pounds (2.7 kilograms), the skin is composed of two main layers: the epidermis (outer layer) and the dermis (inner layer). The epidermis layer is replaced continually as new cells that are produced in the stratum basale, mature and are pushed to the surface by the newer cells beneath; the entire epidermis is replaced in about 27 days. The dermis, the lower layer, contains nerve endings, sweat glands, hair follicles, and blood vessels. The upper portion of the dermis has small fingerlike projections called "papillae" which extend into the outer layer. The patterns of ridges and grooves visible on the skin of the soles, palms, and fingertips are formed from the tops of the dermal papillae. The capillaries in these papillae deliver oxygen and nutrients to the epidermis cells and also function in temperature regulation.

Neil McAleer, *The Body Almanac* (New York: Doubleday, 1985), 100, 103. Eldra Pearl Solomon, and Gloria A. Phillips, *Understanding Human Anatomy and Physiology* (Philadelphia, PA: W.B. Saunders, 1987), 60-61.

Do the nails and hair of a dead person continue to grow?

Between 12 and 18 hours after death, the human body begins to dry out. That causes the tips of the fingers and the skin of the face to shrink, creating the illusion that the nails and hair have grown.

Prevention's Giant Book of Health Facts (Emmaus, PA: Rodale Press, 1991) 156.

How many hairs does the average person have on their head?

The amount of hair covering varies from one individual to another. An average person has about 100,000 hairs on their scalp. Most redheads have about 90,00 hairs, blonds have about 140 thousand, and brunettes fall in between these two figures. Most people shed between 50 to 100 hairs daily.

Gyles D. Brandreth, *Your Vital Statistics* (New York: Citadel, 1986), 22. Margo, *Growing New Hair!* (Brookline, MA: Autumn Press, 1980), 40.

What is ambergris?

Ambergris, a highly odorous waxy substance found floating in tropical seas, is a secretion from the sperm whale (*Physeter catodon*). The whale secretes ambergris to protect its stomach from the sharp bone of the cuttlefish, a squid-like sea mollusk, which it ingests. Ambergris is used in perfumery as a fixature to extend the life of a perfume and as a flavoring for food and beverages. Today ambergris is synthesized and used by the perfume trade, which has voluntarily refused to purchase ambergris to protect sperm whales from exploitation.

Charles Panati, *Panati's Browser's Book of Beginnings* (Boston: Houghton Mifflin, 1984), 24. Paul W. Thrush, *Dictionary of Mining, Mineral and Related Terms* (Washington, DC: U.S. Bureau of Mines, 1968), 33. Ruth Winter, *A Consumer's Dictionary of Cosmetic Ingredients, 3d ed.* (New York: Crown, 1989), 32.

Where does a luffa sponge come from?

Luffas are nonwoody vines of the cucumber family. The interior fibrous skeletons of the fruit are used as sponges. The common name is sometimes spelled loofah. Dishcloth gourd, rag gourd, and vegetable sponge are other popular names for this sponge.

Thomas H. Everett, *The New York Botanical Garden Illustrated Encyclopedia of Horticulture* (Hamden, CT: Garland, 1981), 6:2068. *The Wise Garden Encyclopedia* (New York: Harper Collins, 1990), 602.

How are fossils formed?

Fossils are the remains of animals or plants that were preserved in rock before the beginning of recorded history. It is unusual for complete organisms to be preserved, and fossils usually represent the hard parts such as bones or shells of animals and leaves, seeds, or woody parts of plants.

Some fossils are simply the bones, teeth, or shells themselves, which can be preserved for a relatively short period of time. Another type of fossil is the imprint of a buried plant or animal which decomposes, leaving a film of carbon which retains the form of the organism.

Some buried material is replaced by silica and other materials which permeate the organism and replace the original material in a process called petrification. Some woods are replaced by agate or opal so completely that even the cellular structure is duplicated. The best examples of this can be found in the Petrified Forest National Park in Arizona.

Molds and casts are other very common fossils. A mold is made from an imprint, such as a dinosaur footprint, in soft mud or silt. This impression may harden, then be covered with other materials. The original footprint will have formed a mold and the sediments filling it will be a cast of the footprint.

William R. Hamilton, *The Henry Holt Guide to Minerals, Rocks, and Fossils* ((New York: Henry Holt, 1989), 210. Herbert S. Zim and Paul Shaffer, *Rocks and Minerals* (New York: Golden Press, 1957), 130-32.

How are carnivorous plants categorized?

Carnivorous plants, numbering between 450-500 species and 12 genera, are classified according to the nature of their trapping mechanisms. Active traps display rapid motion in their capture of prey. The Venus fly trap (*Dionaea muscipula*) and the bladderwort (*Utricularia vulgaris*) are active traps. Semi-active traps employ a two-stage trap in which the prey is caught in the trap's adhesive fluid. As it struggles, the plant is triggered to slowly tighten its grip. The sundew (species *Drosera*) and butterwort (*Pinguicula vulgaris*) are semi-active traps. Passive traps entice insects by nectar. The insects fall into a reservoir of water and drown. An example of the passive trap is the pitcher plant (5 genera).

F.N. Howes, *A Dictionary of Useful and Everyday Plants and Their Common Names* (Cambridge, England: Cambridge University Press, 1974), 47. Randall Schwartz, *Carnivorous Plants* (New York: Praeger, 1974), 9.

What is unique about the water-lily *Victoria amazonica*?

It is very big! Found only on the Amazon River, this water-lily has leaves that are up to six feet in diameter. The 12-inch flowers open at dusk on two successive nights.

Donald Wyman, *Wyman's Gardening Encyclopedia, 2d ed.* (New York: Macmillan, 1986), 1162-63.

What is a dwarf conifer?

The conifers are evergreen shrubs and trees with needle-shaped leaves, cones, and resinous wood, such as the pines, spruces, firs, and junipers. After 20 years, dwarf or slow-growing forms of these otherwise tall trees are typically about three feet (91 centimeters) tall.

Donald Wyman, *Wyman's Gardening Encyclopedia, 2d ed.* (New York: Macmillan, 1986), 251, 331, 364.

What is the difference between container-grown, balled-and-burlapped, and bare-rooted plants?

Container-grown plants have been grown in some kind of pot-usually peat, plastic, or clay-for most or all of their lives. Balled-and-burlapped plants have been dug up with the soil carefully maintained around their roots in burlap. Bare-rooted plants have also been dug from their growing place but without retaining the root ball. Typically plants from a mail-order nursery come bare-rooted with their roots protected with damp sphagnum moss. Bare-rooted plants are the most susceptible to damage.

Fruits and Vegetables: 1001 Gardening Questions Answered (Pownal, VT: Storey Communications, 1990), 5.

What is the best type of pollination?

Effective pollination occurs when viable pollen is transferred to plant's stigmas, ovule-bearing organs, or ovules (seed precursors). Without pollination, there would be no fertilization. Since plants are immobile organisms, they usually need external agents to transport their pollen from where it is produced in the plant to where fertilization can occur. This situation produces cross-pollination wherein one plant's pollen is moved by an agent to another plant's stigma. Some plants are able to self-pollinate-transfer their own pollen to their own stigmas. But of the two methods, cross-pollination seems the better, for it allows new genetic material to be introduced.

The cross-pollination agents include insects, wind, birds, mammals, or water. Many times flowers offer one or more "rewards" to attract these agents-sugary nectar, oil, solid food bodies, perfume, a place to sleep, or sometimes, the pollen itself. Other times the plant can "trap" the agent into transporting the pollen. Generally plants use color and fragrances as attractants to lure these agents. For example, a few orchids use a combination of smell and color to mimic the female of certain species of bees and wasp so successfully that the corresponding males will attempt to mate with them. Through this process (pseudo-copulation) the orchids achieve pollination. While some plants cater to a variety of agents, other plants are very selective and are pollinated by a single species of insect only. This extreme pollinator specificity tends to maintain the purity of a plant species.

Plant structure can accommodate the type of agent used. For example, plants whose pollen is carried by the wind, tend to have a simple structure lacking petals, with freely exposed and branched stigmas, and dangling anthers (pollen-producing parts) on long filaments. This type of anther allows the light round pollen to be easily caught by the wind. These plants are found in areas, such as prairies and mountains, where insect agents are rare. In contrast, semi-enclosed, nonsymmetrical, long-lived flowers (such as iris, rose, and snapdragon) have a "landing platform," and nectar in the flower base to accommodate insect agents such as the bee. The sticky abundant pollen can easily become attached to the insect to be borne away to another flower.

Sybil P. Parker, *McGraw-Hill Concise Encyclopedia of Science & Technology, 2d ed.* (New York: McGraw-Hill, 1982), 146. *Practical Botany* (Reston, VA: Reston Publishing, 1983), 7-11.

How are tree rings used to date historical events?

Tree fragments of unknown age and the rings of living trees can be compared in order to establish the date when the fragment was part of a living tree. Thus, tree rings can be used to establish the year in which an event took place as long as the event involved the maiming or killing of a tree. Precise dates can be established for the building of a medieval cathedral or an American Indian pueblo; the occurrence of an earthquake, landslide, volcanic eruption, or a fire; and even the date when a panel of wood was cut for a Dutch painting.

Every year, the tree produces an annular ring composed of one wide, light ring and one narrow, dark ring. During spring and early summer, tree stem cells grow rapidly and are larger to produce the wide, light ring. In winter cell growth is greatly reduced and cells are much smaller in size; this produces the narrow, dark ring. In the coldest part of winter or the dry heat of summer, no cells are produced.

Harold C. Fritts, *Tree Rings and Climate* (New York: Academic Press, 1976), 1-2. Charles E. Roth, *The Plant Observer's Guidebook* (Englewood Cliffs, NJ: Prentice-Hall, 1984), 150-51.

Does the rose family produce any trees?

The apple, pear, peach, cherry, plum, mountain ash, and hawthorn trees are members of the rose family (Rosaceae).

D.J. Mabberley, *The Plant Book* (New York: Cambridge University Press, 1987), 507. Rutherford Platt, *1001 Questions Answered About Trees* (New York: Dodd, Mead, 1959), 40.

Who introduced the gypsy moth in the United States?

In 1869, Professor Leopold Trouvelot brought gypsy moth egg masses from France to Medford, Massachusetts. His intention was to breed the gypsy moth with the silkworm to overcome a wilt disease of the silkworm. He placed the egg masses on a window ledge, and evidently the wind blew them away. About ten years later these caterpillars were numerous on trees in that vicinity, and in 20 years, trees in eastern Massachusetts were being defoliated. A contaminated plant shipment from Holland in 1911 also introduced the gypsy moth to that area. These pests have now spread to 25 states, especially in the northeastern United States. Scattered locations in Michigan and Oregon have also reported occurrences of gypsy moth infestations.

William Ashworth, *The Encyclopedia of Environmental Studies* (New York: Facts on File), 176. Robert E. Pfadt, *Fundamentals of Applied Entomology, 3d ed.* (New York: Macmillan, 1978), 553. *The Wise Garden Encyclopedia* (New York: HarperCollins, 1990), 469.

Are there many famous left-handed celebrities?

The following celebrities are just a few of many famous left-handed people:

Alexander the Great
Dan Aykroyd
F. Lee Bailey
Bill the Kid
Robert Blake
Lenny Bruce
Carol Burnett
George Burns
George Bush
Ruth Buzzi
Peggy Cass
Julius Caesar
Charlie Chaplin
Charlemagne
Prince Charles
Natalie Cole
Clarence Darrow
Olivia De Havilland
Leonardo da Vinci
John Dillinger
Bob Dylan
Albert Einstein
Queen Elizabeth
W. C. Fields
Gerald Ford
Henry Ford II
Benjamin Franklin
Judy Garland
Errol Garner
Lou Gehrig
Euell Gibbons
Paul Michael Glaser
Betty Grable

Cary Grant
Dorothy Hamill
Goldie Hawn
Jimi Hendrix
Herbert Hoover
Rock Hudson
Daniel Inouye
Bruce Jenner
Danny Kaye
Michael Landon
Paul McCartney
Harpo Marx
James Michener
Marilyn Monroe
Edward R. Murrow
Anthony Newley
Pablo Picasso
Cole Porter
Richard Pryor
Robert Redford
Jack the Ripper
Babe Ruth
Mark Spitz
Ringo Starr
Casey Stengel
Harry Truman
Dick Van Dyke
Joanne Woodward

Jesse Birnbaum, "The Perils of Being a Lefty," *Time,* 15 April 1991. Jean R. Komaiko, "Lefties Are All Right," *Parents Magazine,* July 1963. Ed Lucaire, *The Celebrity Almanac* (New York: Prentice-Hall, 1991), 135-36.

Do the branches of trees rise higher from the ground as the tree grows taller?

The branches of the tree may appear to rise higher from the ground as the tree matures, but it is an illusion. This illusion occurs as a result of the tree's lower branches dying and dropping off, while new branches are growing at the top of the tree.

McGraw-Hill Encyclopedia of Science & Technology, 7th ed. (New York: McGraw-Hill, 1992), s.v. "tree."

Who was the tallest documented human?

The tallest documented human was Robert P. Wadlow (1918-1940) of Alton, Illinois, who reached a height of 8 feet, 11 inches, and a weight of 491 pounds before he died at age 22. His arm span was 9 feet, 53/4 inches, his hands measured 123/4 inches from the wrist to tip of the middle finger, and he wore size 37AA (18 inches) shoes. Wadlow suffered from gigantism, or excessive growth (especially height), resulting from overproduction of growth hormone by a tumor of the pituitary gland. His death was a result of a septic blister on his right ankle.

Charles B. Clayman, M.D., ed., *The American Medical Association Encyclopedia of Medicine* (New York: Random House, 1989), s.v. "Gigantism." Mark C. Young, ed., *The Guinness Book of Records 1995* (New York: Facts on File, 1994), 58-59.

Do animals sleep?

Brain-wave studies indicate that only animals with highly developed brains sleep. For example, a butterfly's inactivity during the night is called dormancy rather than sleep since no brain-wave patterns typical of sleep can be detected. Shallow torpor, a somewhat more sleeplike condition, is typical of some small mammals and birds when both their activity and body temperature considerably decreases. Hibernation, or deep torpor, protects small animals from cold.

Edward Edelson, *Sleep* (New York: Chelsea House, 1992), 15.

What is the heaviest weight on record for a gorilla?

In the wild, gorillas average 310 to 400 pounds. Gorillas in captivity are often obese. One gorilla attained a recorded weight of 750 pounds. It was claimed that "Phil" at the St. Louis Zoo weighed 776 pounds at death, but there is some dispute that he could have been that heavy. Other large gorillas were "N'gagi" at 683 pounds and "Mbongo" at 660 pounds in the San Diego Zoo, and "Bushman" at 565 pounds in Chicago's Lincoln Park Zoo.

David Macdonald, ed., *Encyclopedia of Mammals* (New York: Facts on File, 1984), s.v. "Gorilla." Ruthven Tremain, *The Animals' Who's Who* (New York: Charles Scribner's Sons, 1982), s.v. "Bushman." David P. Willoughby, *All About Gorillas* (South Brunswick, NJ: A. S. Barnes, 1978), 199-201. Mark C. Young, ed., *The Guinness Book of Records 1995* (New York: Facts on File, 1994), 31.

Chemistry, Physics, Astronomy

What is the Night of the Shooting Stars?

August 11, the Night of the Shooting Stars, is actually a meteor shower that has lit up the Earth's atmosphere every year since 830. Skywatchers on much of the planet can observe the fusillade of meteor fragments in the sky on this night. The meteor shower is also known as the Perseids, since it is believed to come from the constellation of Perseus.

Sue Ellen Thompson and Barbara W. Carlson, comps., *Holidays, Festivals, and Celebrations of the World Dictionary* (Detroit: Omnigraphics, 1994), s.v. "Night of the Shooting Stars."

What famous Greek astronomer and geographer put forth the theory of an earth-centered universe?

Ptolemy, a second-century Greek astronomer and geographer, believed that the earth was a motionless body at the center of the universe and that all other celestial bodies revolved around it. Ptolemy's theory was accepted until 1543 when the Polish astronomer Nicolaus Copernicus (1473-1543) formulated his theory of the planets, in which they including the earth, revolved around the sun.

World Book Encyclopedia (Chicago: World Book, 1987), s.v. "Ptolemy."

What is a "Gibbous Moon"?

A "Gibbous Moon" is a moon that is between its quarter and full phase. It originates from the Latin word *gibbosus* which means humped or hunched, and it can also used in describing the planets.

Mario Pei, *Language of the Specialists* (Funk & Wagnalls, 1966), 13.

Which elements are the noble metals?

The noble metals are gold (Au, element 79), silver (Ag, element 47), mercury (Hg, element 80), and the platinum (Pt, element 78) group (including palladium (Pd, element 46), iridium (Ir, element 77), rhodium (Rh, element 45), ruthenium (Ru, element 44), and osmium (Os, element 76)). The term noble metals refers to those metals highly resistant to chemical reaction. In contrast to base metals which are not so resistant. The term has its origins in ancient alchemy in which properties of metals and chemicals were explored in its goal to transform baser metals into gold. The term is not synonymous with precious metals, although a metal, like platinum, may be both.

George S. Brady, *Materials Handbook, 12th ed.* (New York: McGraw-Hill, 1986), 644. Paul W. Thrush, *A Dictionary of Mining, Mineral, and Related Terms* (Washington, DC: U.S. Bureau of Mines, 1968), 753.

What were the proposed names for elements 104 and 105 in use before their official names were chosen by the International Union of Pure and Applied Chemistry?

Rutherfordium (Rf) and kurchatovium (Ku) were the names proposed by rival groups for element 104 (unnilquadium (Unq)). Hafnium (Ha) and nielsbohrium (Ns) were proposed for element 105 (unnilpentium (Unp)).

American Scientist May/June 1980. Jeff Rovin, *Laws of Order* (New York: Ballantine, 1992), 181. *Science 80* January/February 1980.

What is superconductivity?

Superconductivity is a condition, occurring in many metals, alloys, etc., usually at low temperatures, in which there is zero electrical resistance and perfect diamagnetism. In such a material an electric current will persist indefinitely without any driving voltage, and applied magnetic fields are exactly canceled out by the magnetization they produce. Superconductivity was discovered by Heike Kamerlingh Onnes (1853-1926) in 1911.

Encyclopedic Dictionary of Science (New York: Facts On File, 1988), 231.

Who is the father of magnetic science?

Called the father of magnetic science, the English scientist William Gilbert (1544-1603) regarded the earth as a giant magnet, and investigated its magnetic field in terms of dip and variation and he explored many other magnetic and electrostatic phenomena. The Gilbert (symbol Gb), a unit of magnetism, is named for him.

Encyclopedic Dictionary of Science (New York: Facts On File, 1988), 108.

What is Harkin's rule?

Harkin's rule states: atoms having even atomic numbers are more abundant in the universe than are atoms having odd atomic numbers. Chemical properties of an element are determined by the element's atomic number-the number of protons in the atom's nucleus or the number of electrons revolving around this nucleus.

David J. Fisher, *Rules of Thumb for Engineers and Scientists* (Houston, TX: Gulf, 1991), 85. *A New Dictionary of Physics* (Bristol, England: Longman Group, 1975), 33.

Which chemical element is the most abundant on earth?

Oxygen (symbol O, element 8) is the most abundant element in the earth's crust, waters, and atmosphere. It composes 49.5 percent of the total mass of the earth.

Nicholas D. Tzimopoulos et al. , *Modern Chemistry* (Fort Worth, TX: Holt, Rinehart and Winston, 1990), 289.

Which elements have the most isotopes?

There are 2,550 or more isotopes and cesuim (Cs) with one stable isotope (identified in 1921) and 36 radioactive isotopes (identified from 1935 to 1983) has the most isotopes. Xenon (Xe) is next with 36 isotopes, 9 of which are stable (identified from 1920 to 1922) and 27 of which are radioactive (identified from 1939 to 1981).

The element with the least number of isotopes is hydrogen (H), with three isotopes, including two stable ones-protium (identified in 1920) and deuterium (identified in 1931)-and one radioactive isotope-tritium (first identified in 1934, but later considered a radioactive isotope in 1939).

Guinness Book of Records 1992 (Bantam Books, 1992), 262. Mark C. Young, ed., *Guinness Book of Records 1995* (New York: Facts On File, 1994), 75.

Why are the rare earth elements?

Elements numbered 58 through 71 in the periodic table plus yttrium (Y, element 39) and thorium (Th, element 90) are called rare earths because they are difficult to extract from monazite ore, in which they occur. The term has nothing to do with scarcity or rarity in nature.

George S. Brady, *Materials Handbook, 12th ed.* (New York: McGraw-Hill, 1986), 661-62.

What is the composition of house dust?

Dust is particles of less than one millimeter in diameter, regardless of its content. A significant portion of dust is dead skin fragments from human bodies, tobacco smoke, and airborne particles (pollen or other plant particles, industrial smoke particles, etc.) and clay and other mineral (soil) matter, that is "tracked" into the house. Major volcanic eruptions produce thousands of tons of dust, and dust from outer space can be another source. Over 43 million tons (38.8 metric tons) of dust settle over the United States each year. This includes 31 million tons (28.1 metric tons) from natural sources, with the remainder coming from sources of human activity.

Charles J. Cazeau, *Science Trivia,* (New York: Berkley Books, 1986), 130-31.

What is radiocarbon dating?

Radiocarbon dating is a process for determining the age of a prehistoric object by measuring its radiocarbon content. The technique was developed by an American chemist, Dr. Willard F. Libby (1908-1980), in the late 1940s. All living things contain radiocarbon (carbon 14), an isotope that occurs in a small percentage of atmospheric carbon dioxide as a result of cosmic ray bombardment. After an animal or plant dies, it no longer absorbs radiocarbon and the radiocarbon present begins to decay (break down by releasing particles) at an exact and uniform rate. Its half-life of 5,730 years made it useful for measuring prehistory and events occurring within the past 35,000 to 50,000 years. A recent development, called the Accelerated Mass Spectrometer, which separates and detects atomic particles of different mass, can establish more accurate dates with a smaller sample. The remaining radiocarbon can be measured and compared to that of a living sample. In this way, the age of the 50,000 year old or less animal or plant (or more precisely the elapsed time since its death) can be determined.

Since Libby's work other isotopes having longer half-lives have been used as "geologic clocks" to date very old rocks-at least 100 thousand years old to use the isotope potassium-argon dating. The isotope Uranium-238 (decaying to Lead-206) has a half-life of 4.5 billion years, Uranium-235 (decaying to Lead-207) has a value of 704 million years, Thorium-232 (decaying to Lead-278) has a half-life of 14 billion years, Rubidium-87 (decaying to Stronium-87) has a half-life value of 48.8 billion years, Potassium-40 (decaying to Argon-40) has a value of 1.25 billion years and Samarium-147 (decaying to Neodymium-143) has a value of 106 billion years. These isotopes are used in dating techniques of gas formation light emission (called thermoluminescence). Other ways to date the past is dating by tree rings (counting its annual growth rings), and dating by thermoremanent magnetism (the magnetic field of the rock is compared to a date chart of changes in the earth's magnetic field).

The Biographical Dictionary of Scientists: Chemists (New York: Peter Bedrick Books, 1983), 84-85. Peter Gray, *The Encyclopedia of the Biological Science* (New York: Van Nostrand Reinhold, 1970), 141.

What is meant by Group I elements?

Group I elements are these elements on the left side of the chemical periodic table: lithium (Li, element 3), potassium (K, element 19), rubidium (Rb, element 37), cesium (Cs, element 55), francium (Fr, element 87), and sodium (Na, element 11). They are alkali metals, sometimes called the sodium family of elements. Because of their great chemical reactivity (easily form positive ions), none exist in nature in the elemental state.

The Facts On File Dictionary of Chemistry, rev. ed. (New York: Facts On File, 1988), 7. Nicholas D. Tzimopoulos et al., *Modern Chemistry* (Fort Worth, TX: Rinehart and Winston, 1990), 713.

What are the transition elements?

The transition elements of the chemical periodic table are the ten subgroups of elements between group II and group III, starting with period 4. They include gold (Au, element 79), silver (Ag, element 47), platinum (Pt, element 78), iron (Fe, element 26), copper (Cu, element 29), and other metals. The transition elements or metals are so named because they represent a gradual shift from the strongly electropositive elements of Group I and II to the electronegative elements of Groups VI and VII of the chemical periodic table.

Clifford A. Hampel, *Glossary of Chemical Terms, 2nd. ed.* (New York: Holt, Rinehart and Winston, 1982), 98, 288. Nicholas D. Tzimopoulos et al. , *Modern Chemistry* (Fort Worth, TX: Rinehart and Winston, 1990), 729.

What is "earthshine"?

A spacecraft in orbit around the Earth is illuminated by sunlight and "earthshine." Earthshine consists of sunlight reflected by the Earth and thermal radiation emitted by the Earth's surface and atmosphere.

Joseph A. Angelo, *The Extraterrestrial Encyclopedia, rev. ed.* (New York: Facts on File, 1991), 33.

What is a light year?

A light year is a measure of distance, not time. It is the distance that light, which travels in a vacuum at the rate of 186,000 miles (300,000 kilometers) per second, can travel in a year (or 365 1/4 days). This is equal to 5,870 billion miles or 9,460 billion kilometers.

Other astronomical measures include the astronomical unit (AU) which is often used to measure distances within the solar system. One AU is equal to the average distance between the earth and the sun or 92,955,630 miles (149,597,870 kilometers). The parsec is equal to 3.26 light years, or about 19,180 billion miles (30,820 billion kilometers).

Valerie Illingworth, *The Facts On File Dictionary of Astronomy* (New York: Facts On File, 1979), 235-36. Patrick Moore, *International Encyclopedia of Astronomy* (New York: Orion Books, 1987), 231. Jeff Rovin, *Laws of Order* (New York: Ballantine, 1992), 213. *The Universal Almanac 1992* (Kansas City, MO: Andrews and McMeel, 1991), 569.

Who is considered the father of systematic astronomy?

The Greek scientist, Hipparchus (fl. 146-127 B.C.), is considered to be the father of systematic astronomy. He measured as accurately as possible the directions of objects in the sky. He compiled the first catalog of stars, containing about 850 entries, and designated each star's celestial coordinates, indicating its position in the sky. Hipparchus also divided the stars according to their apparent brightness or magnitudes.

George O. Abell, *Realm of the Universe* (New York: Holt, Rinehart and Winston, 1976), 16. *Dictionary of Scientific Biography,* (New York: Charles Scribner's Sons, 1973), 16, 207-9.

When was spontaneous combustion first recognized?

Spontaneous combustion is the ignition of materials stored in bulk. This is due to internal heat build-up caused by oxidation (generally a reaction in which electrons are lost, specifically when oxygen is combined with a substance, or when hydrogen is removed from a compound). Because this oxidation heat cannot be dissipated into the surrounding air, the temperature of the material rises until the material reaches its ignition point and bursts into flame.

A Chinese text written before 290 A.D. recognized this phenomenon in a description of the ignition of stored oiled cloth. The first Western recognition of spontaneous combustion was by J.P.F. Duhamel in 1757, when he discussed the gigantic conflagration of a stack of oil-soaked canvas sails drying in the July sun. Before spontaneous combustion was recognized, such events were usually blamed on arsonists.

Sybil P. Parker, *McGraw-Hill Concise Encyclopedia of Science and Technology, 2nd ed.* (New York: McGraw-Hill, 1989), 1765. Robert K.G. Temple, *The Genius of China* (New York: Simon and Schuster, 1986), 166-67.

Who is generally regarded as the father of quantum mechanics?

The German mathematical physicist, Werner Karl Heisenberg (1901-1976), is regarded as the father of quantum mechanics which is the theory of small-scale physical phenomena. His theory of uncertainty in 1927 overturned traditional classical mechanics and electromagnetic theory in relation to energy and motions in subatomic particles such as electrons and parts of atomic nuclei. The theory limits specify the impossibility of specifying precisely both the position and the simultaneous momentum (mass times volume) of a particle, but they could only be predicted. This meant that a result of an action can only be expressed in terms of probability that a certain effect will occur, not certainty.

The Biological Dictionary of Scientists: Physicists (New York: Peter Bedrick Books, 1984), 79-81. *Encyclopedic Dictionary of Science* (New York: Facts On File, 1988), 116.

Why is John H. Van Vleck considered to be one of the fathers of modern magnetic theory?

Awarded the Nobel Prize in 1977, American physicist John H. Van Vleck (1899-1980) made significant contributions in the field of magnetism. He explained the magnetic, electrical, and optical properties of many elements and compounds with the ligand field theory, demonstrated the effect of temperature on paramagnetic materials (called Van Vleck paramagneticism), and developed a theory on the magnetic properties of atoms and their components.

The Biographical Dictionary of Scientists: Physicists (New York: Peter Bedrick Books, 1984), 164.

What is the fourth state of matter?

Plasma, a mixture of free electrons and ions or atomic nuclei, is sometimes referred to as a fourth state of matter. Plasmas occur in thermonuclear reactions as in the sun, in fluorescent lights, and in stars. When gas temperature is raised high enough the collision of atoms become so violent that electrons are knocked loose from their nuclei. The result of a gas having loose negatively charged electrons and heavier positively-charged nuclei is called a plasma.

All matter is made up of atoms. Animals and plants are organic matter; minerals and water are inorganic matter. Whether matter appears as a solid, liquid, or gas depends on how the molecules are held together in their chemical bonds. Solids have a rigid structure in the atoms of the molecules; in liquids the molecules are close together but not packed; in a gas, the molecules are widely spaced and move around, occasionally colliding but usually not interacting. These states-solid, liquid, and gas-are the first three states of matter.

Robert K. Barnhart, *American Heritage Dictionary of Science* (Boston: Houghton Mifflin, 1986), 385. John Daintith, *The Facts On File Dictionary of Physics* (New York: Facts On File, 1988), 154. James Trefil, *1001 Things Everyone Should Know About Science* (New York: Doubleday, 1992), 201.

What substance, other than water, is less dense as a solid than as a liquid?

Only bismuth and water share this characteristic of density. Density, which is the mass per unit volume refers to how compact or crowded a substance is. For instance the density of water is one gram per cubic centimeter or one kilogram per liter; the density of a rock is 3.3 grams per cubic centimeter; pure iron is 7.9 grams per cubic centimeter; and the earth (as a whole) is 5.5 grams per cubic centimeter (average). Water as a solid (i.e. ice) floats; which is a good thing, otherwise ice would sink to the bottom of every lake or stream, which would result in great flooding.

Tom Burnam, *The Dictionary of Misinformation* (New York: Perennial Library, 1986), 281. James T. Shipman and Jerry D. Wilson, *An Introduction to Physical Science, 6th ed.* (Lexington, MA: D.C. Heath & Co., 1990), 10.

Who is known as the father of crystallography?

The French priest and mineralogist, Rene-Just Hay (1743-1822), is called the father of crystallography. In 1781 Hay had a fortunate accident when he dropped a piece of calcite and it broke into small fragments. He noticed that the fragments broke along straight planes that met at constant angles. He hypothesized that each crystal was built up of successive additions of what is now called a unit cell to form a simple geometric shape with constant angles. An identity or difference in crystalline form implied an identity or difference in chemical composition. This was the beginning of the science of crystallography.

Isaac Asimov, *Asimov's Biographical Encyclopedia of Science and Technology, 2nd ed.* (Garden City, NY: Doubleday, 1982), 221. James Berry, *Exploring Crystals* (New York: Crowell-Collier Press, 1969), 4.

Who made the first organic compound to be synthesized from inorganic ingredients?

Urea was synthesized by Friedrich Wohler (1800-1882) in 1828 from ammonia and cyanic acid. The creation of this synthesis dealt a deathblow to the vital-force theory, which had assumed the existence of a mysterious "vital force," that was necessary for the formation of compounds. Therefore, the preparation of compounds in the laboratory could hardly have been expected.

Encyclopedia of Chemical Technology, 3rd ed. (New York: Wiley, 1978), 23:548. J.R. Partington, *A Short History of Chemistry, 3rd ed.* (New York: Dover, 1989), 221.

Who was the father of analytical chemistry?

Rene Descartes' (1596-1650) reform of science was the establishment of a mechanical philosophy, which sought to explain the properties and actions of bodies in terms of the parts of which they are composed. He proposed the use of mathematical methods to investigate scientific problems. Descartes rejected all untested ancient and medieval authority as opinion that must be subjected to objective scientific analysis to test its validity. Honored in physics and mathematics, he is also considered one of the foremost philosophers of the modern era. Descartes believed in a firm unity of all knowledge, scientific and philosophical, which he symbolized in the metaphor of a tree whose roots are metaphysics, whose trunk is physics, and whose branches are specific topics (such as medicine, mechanics, and morality).

I. Bernard Cohen, *Revolution in Science* (Cambridge, MA: Belknap Press, 1985), 146. Robert B. Downs, *Landmarks in Science* (Littleton, CO: Libraries Unlimited, 1982), 117-19. *The Great Scientists* (Danbury, CT: Grolier, 1989), 4:13.

What is the Guzman prize?

It is a prize offered in France in 1901 to the first person to make contact with beings from another planet. Mars is excluded as being "too easy." The prize is as yet unclaimed.

International Encyclopedia of Astronomy (New York: Orion, 1987), 176.

For what accomplishments did Marie Curie receive a Nobel Prize?

Marie Curie (1867-1934) received two Nobel Prizes-one in physics in 1903 and one in chemistry in 1911. She and her husband Pierre (1859-1906), along with A.H. Becquerel (1852-1908), were awarded the prize in 1903 for their work on radioactivity. They separated minute amounts of two new highly radioactive chemical elements from uranium ore. The Curies named the elements "radium" and "polonium." In 1911, Marie Curie won the Nobel Prize for Chemistry for her discovery of the new elements, and for work in isolating and studying the chemical properties of radium.

World Book Encyclopedia (Chicago: World Book, 1990), 1194.

What quick way can a chemist be identified from a non-chemist?

Science and fiction writer Isaac Asimov suggests that the person be shown the word "unionized." The non-chemist will pronounce the word "YOON-yun-ized." The chemist, however, will say without a moment's hesitation "un-EYE-on-ized."

Isaac Asimov, *Asimov on Chemistry* (New York: Anchor Books, 1975), 90.

What is the chemical composition of kidney stones?

The chemical composition of kidney stones is about 80 percent are calcium, mainly calcium oxalate and/or phosphate; five percent are uric acid; two percent are amino acid cystine; the remainder are magnesium ammonium phosphate. About 20 percent of these stones are infective stones, linked to chronic urinary infections, and contain a combination of calcium, magnesium, and ammonium phosphate produced from the alkalinity of the urine and bacteria action on urea (a substance in urine).

The American Medical Association Encyclopedia of Medicine (New York: Random House, 1989), 225. *Merck Manual of Diagnosis and Therapy, 15th ed.,* (West Point, PA: Merck, Shark & Dohme, 1987), 1641.

What is the composition of cigarette smoke?

Cigarette smoke contains about 4,000 chemicals. Carbon dioxide, carbon monoxide, methane, and nicotine are some of the major components, with lesser amounts of acetone, acetylene, formaldehyde, propane, hydrogen cyanide, toluene, and many others.

Involuntary Smoking (Washington, DC: U.S. Public Health Service, 1979), 6. *Mayo Clinic Family Health Book* (New York: Morrow, 1990), 409. *Prevention's Giant Book of Health Facts* (Emmaus, PA: Rodale Press, 1991), 198.

What is "aqua regia"?

"Aqua regia," also known as nitrohydrochloric acid, is a mixture of one part concentrated nitric acid and three parts concentrated hydrochloric acid. The chemical reaction between the acids makes it possible to dissolve all metals except silver. The reaction of metals with nitrohydrochloric acid typically involves oxidation of the metals to a metallic ion and the reduction of the nitric acid to nitric oxide. The term comes from Latin and means royal water. It was named by the alchemists for its ability to dissolve gold, sometimes called the royal metal.

McGraw-Hill Encyclopedia of Science and Technology, 7th ed. (New York: McGraw-Hill, 1992), 2:1. *Van Nostrand Reinhold Encyclopedia of Chemistry, 4th ed.* (New York: Van Nostrand Reinhold, 1984), 94. *World Book Encyclopedia* (Chicago: World Book, 1990), 1:578.

Who discovered deuterium?

American chemist Harold C. Urey (1893-1981), 1934 winner of the Nobel Prize for chemistry, discovered deuterium (heavy hydrogen, symbol D) in 1931 with F.G. Brickwedde and G.M. Murphy. This isotope (a form of an element that differs in the number of neutrons and atomic weight) has twice the weight of hydrogen, while all the other isotopes differed slightly in their atomic weights. Deuterium and its oxide make heavy water, which is used to slow down the neutrons in atomic piles of nuclear reactors.

Richard Earl Dickerson, *Chemical Principles, 3rd ed.* (Menlo Park, CA: Benjamin/Cummings Publishing, 1979), 4. Edward Farber, *Nobel Prize Winners in Chemistry, 1901-1961, rev. ed.* (New York: Ablard-Schuman, 1963), 137. *The Great Scientists* (Danbury, CT: Grolier, 1989), 11:203.

Why are essential oils called "essential"?

Called essential oils because of their ease of solubility in alcohol to form essences, essential oils are used in flavorings, perfumes, disinfectants, medicine, and other products. They are naturally occurring volatile aromatic oils found in uncombined forms within various parts of plants (leaves, pods, etc.). These oils contain as one of their main ingredients a substance belonging to the terpene group. Examples of essential oils include bergamot, eucalyptus, ginger, pine, spearmint, and wintergreen oils. Extracted by distillation or enfleurage (extraction using fat) and mechanical pressing, these oils can now be made synthetically.

Oxford Illustrated Encyclopedia of Invention and Technology (Oxford, England: Oxford University Press, 1992), 123.

What is rosin?

Rosin is the resin produced after the distillation of turpentine, obtained from several varieties of pine trees, especially the longleaf pine (*Pinus palustris*) and the slash pine (*Pinus caribaea*). Rosin is used in varnishes, paint driers, soluble oils, paper sizing, belt dressings, and for producing many chemicals.

George S. Brady, *Materials Handbook, 12th ed.* (New York: McGraw-Hill, 1986), 685. John N. Winburne, *A Dictionary of Agricultural and Allied Terminology* (East Lansing: Michigan State University Press, 1962), 651.

An asteroid came close to hitting the earth sometime in 1989. How much damage might it have done?

Asteroid 1989 FC passed within 434 thousand miles (700 thousand kilometers) of the earth on March 22, 1989. The impact, had it hit the earth, would have delivered the energy equivalent of more than 1 million tons of exploding TNT and created a crater up to 4.3 miles (7 kilometers) across.

Sky and Telescope, vol. 79, no. 3 (March 1990), 261.

When will Halley's comet return?

Halley's comet returns about every 76 years. It was most recently seen in 1985/1986 and is predicted to appear again in 2061, then in 2134. Every appearance of what is now known as Comet Halley has been noted by astronomers since the year 239 B.C.

The comet is named for Edmund Halley (1656-1742), England's second Astronomer Royal. In 1682 he observed a bright comet and noted that it was moving in an orbit similar to comets seen in 1531 and 1607. He concluded that the three comets were actually one and the same and that the comet had an orbit of 76 years. In 1705 Halley published *A Synopsis of the Astronomy of Comets* in which he predicted that the comet seen in 1531, 1607, and 1682 would return in 1758. On Christmas night, 1758, a German farmer and amateur astronomer named Johann Palitzsch spotted the comet in just the area of the sky that Halley had foretold.

Prior to Halley, comets appeared at irregular intervals and were often thought to be harbingers of disaster and signs of divine wrath. Halley proved that they are natural objects subject to the laws of gravity.

Patrick Moore, *International Encyclopedia of Astronomy* (New York: Orion Books, 1987), 177. Carl Sagan and Ann Druyan, *Comet* (New York: Random House, 1985), 364.

When do meteor showers occur?

There are a number of groups of meteoroids circling the sun just as the earth is. When earth's orbit intercepts the path of one of

these swarms of meteoroids, some of them enter earth's atmosphere. When friction with the air causes a meteoroid to burn up, the streak, or shooting star, that is produced is called a meteor. Large numbers of meteors can produce a spectacular shower of light in the night sky. Meteor showers are named for the constellation that occupies the area of the sky from which they originate. Listed below are ten meteor showers and the dates during the year during which they can be seen:
Quadrantids—January 1-6
Lyrids—April 19-24
Eta Aquarids—May 1-8
Perseids—July 25-August 18
Orionids—October 16-26
Taurids—October 20-November 20
Leonids—November 13-17
Phoenicids—December 4-5
Geminids—December 7-15
Ursids—December 17-24

Jeff Rovin, *Laws of Order* (New York: Ballentine, 1992), 217.

Who invented the telescope?

Hans Lippershey (ca. 1570-1619), a German-Dutch lens grinder and spectacle maker, is generally credited with inventing the telescope in 1608 because he was the first scientist to apply for a patent. Two other inventors, Zacharias Janssen and Jacob Metius, also developed telescopes. Modern historians consider Lippershey and Janssen as the two likely candidates for the title of inventor of the telescope, with Lippershey possessing the strongest claim.

The Great Scientists, (Danbury, CT: Grolier, 1989), 7: 162.

What are the phases of the moon?

The phases of the moon are changes to the moon's appearance during the month, which are caused by the position of the illuminated hemisphere of the moon in relation to the earth. When the moon is between the earth and the sun, its daylight or illuminated side is turned away from the earth, so it is not seen. This place is called new moon. As the moon continues its revolution around the earth, more and more of its illuminated surface becomes visible. This is called the waxing crescent phase. About a week after the new moon, half the moon becomes visible-the first quarter phase. During the following week, more than half of the moon is seen; this is called waxing gibbous phase. Finally about two weeks after the new moon, the moon and sun are on opposite sides of the earth. The side of the moon facing the sun is also facing the earth, and all the moon's illuminated side is seen on earth as a full moon. In the next two weeks the moon goes through the same phases, but in reverse from a waning gibbous to third or last quarter to waning crescent phase. Gradually, less and less of the moon is visible until a new moon occurs again.

George O. Abell, *Realm of the Universe* (New York: Holt, Rinehart and Winston, 1976), 72-73. Donald H. Menzel, and Jay M. Pasachoff, *A Field Guide to Stars and Planets, 2d ed.,* (Boston: Houghton Mifflin, 1990), 318-22.

Is the moon really blue during a blue moon?

A blue moon is the phenomenon of having a second full moon in a single month. The phrase does not refer to the color of the moon, but rather to the infrequency of the occasion. It occurs, on average, every 2.72 years. Since 29.53 days pass between full moons or a synodial month, there can never be a blue moon in February since it has at most 29 days during a leap year. The last blue moon occurred on August 31, 1993, the next one, June 30, 1996. Every 19 years there will be two such months having blue moons. The next time for this event is in the year 1999.

A bluish-looking moon can be seen, however, and it is the result of atmospheric effects. For example, this phenomenon was widely observed on September 26, 1950, after Canadian forest fires which had scattered high altitude dust. More recently, some observers reported seeing a blue-colored moon on August 27, 1991, and scientists explained that this was a result of the eruption of Mount Pinatubo in the Philippines, which spread ash into the atmosphere. P. Egan's work, *Real Life in London* states, "Haven't seen you this blue moon" which coined the phrase, blue moon, in the English vocabulary in 1821.

Country Journal, May 1988. Patrick Moore, *International Encyclopedia of Astronomy* (New York: Orion Books, 1987), 83. *USA Today* 31 August 1993.

Which planets are the so-called inferior planets and which are the so-called superior planets?

An inferior planet is one whose orbit is nearer to the sun than Earth's orbit is. Mercury and Venus are the inferior planets. Superior planets are those whose orbits around the sun lie beyond that of the earth. Mars, Jupiter, Saturn, Uranus, Neptune, and Pluto are the superior planets. The terms have nothing to do with the quality of an individual planet.

Patrick Moore, *International Encyclopedia of Astronomy* (New York: Orion Books, 1987), 192, 423.

Is it true that the rotation speed of the earth varies?

The rotation speed is at its maximum in late July and early August and at its minimum in April; the difference in the length of the day is about 0.0012 seconds. Since about 1900 the earth's rotation has been slowing at a rate of approximately 1.7 seconds per year. In the geologic past the earth's rotational period was much faster; days were shorter and there were more days in the year. About 350 million years ago, the year had 400-410 days; 280 million years ago, a year was 390 days long.

McGraw-Hill Encyclopedia of Science and Technology, 7th ed. (New York: McGraw-Hill, 1992), 5: 483.

Is there life on Mars?

Three experiments on the composition of the Martian soil and atmosphere were carried out by the Viking Lander in July 1976 offered no evidence of life on Mars.

Irwin W. Sherman, *Biology: A Human Approach, 4th ed.* (New York: Oxford University Press, 1989), 4.

What is Planet X?

Astronomers have observed perturbations, or disturbances, in the orbits of Uranus and Neptune since the discoveries of both planets. They speculated that Uranus and Neptune were being influenced by the gravity of another celestial body. Pluto, discovered in 1930, does not appear to be large enough to cause these disturbances. The existence of another planet, known as Planet X, orbiting beyond Pluto, has been proposed. As yet there have been no sightings of this tenth planet but the search continues. There is a possibility that the unmanned space probes *Pio-*

neer 10 & *11* and *Voyager 1* & *2*, now heading out of the solar system, will be able to locate this elusive object.

The Almanac of Science and Technology (San Diego: Harcourt Brace Jovanovich, 1990), 82. Patrick Moore et al., *The Atlas of the Solar System* (New York: Crescent Books with the Royal Astronomical Society, 1990), 397.

Which star is the closest to earth?

The sun, at a distance of 93 million miles (150 million kilometers), is the closest star to the earth. After the sun, the closest stars are the members of the triple star system known as Alpha Centauri (Alpha Centauri A, Alpha Centauri B, and Alpha Centauri C, sometimes called Proxima Centauri). They are 4.3 light years (LY) away.

Richard Flaste, *The New York Times Book of Science Literacy* (New York: Orion Books, 1987), 19. Patrick Moore, *International Encyclopedia of Astronomy* (New York: Random House, 1991), 22.

What is the Big Dipper?

The Big Dipper is a group of seven stars which are part of the constellation Ursa Major. They appear to form a sort of spoon with a long handle. The group is known as The Plough in Great Britain. The Big Dipper is almost always visible in the northern hemisphere. It serves as a convenient reference point when locating other stars; for example, an imaginary line drawn from the two end stars of the dipper leads to Polaris, the North Star.

Nicholas Booth, *The Concise Illustrated Book of Planets and Stars* (New York: Gallery Books, 1990), 30.

What is the Milky Way?

The Milky Way is a hazy band of light that can be seen encircling the night sky. This light comes from the stars that make up the Milky Way galaxy, the galaxy to which the sun and the earth belong. Galaxies are huge systems of stars separated from one another by largely empty space. Astronomers estimate that the Milky Way galaxy contains at least 100 billion stars and is about 100 thousand light years in diameter. The galaxy is shaped like a phonograph record with a central bulge, or nucleus, and spiral arms curving out from the center.

Valerie L. Illingworth, *The Facts On File Dictionary of Astronomy* (New York: Facts On File, 1979), 130.

When will the sun die?

The sun is approximately 4.5 billion years old. About 5 billion years from now, the sun will have burned all of its hydrogen fuel into helium. As this process occurs, the sun will change from the yellow dwarf we know it as to a red giant. Its diameter will extend well beyond the orbit of Venus, and even possibly beyond the orbit of Earth. In either case, the earth will be burned to a cinder.

Jay M. Pasachoff, *Contemporary Astronomy* (Philadelphia: W. B. Saunders, 1977), 205-6. John Wright, ed., *The Universal Almanac 1994* (Kansas City, MO: Andrews and McNeel, 1993), 519.

What is the ecliptic?

Ecliptic refers to the apparent yearly path of the sun through the sky with respect to the stars. In the spring, the ecliptic in the northern hemisphere is angled high in the evening sky. In fall, the ecliptic lies much closer to the horizon.

Terence Dickinson and Alan Dyer, *The Backyard Astronomer's Guide* (Ontario: Camden House, 1991), 141. *World Book Encyclopedia* (Chicago: World Book, 1990), 1:835.

What is the Maunder minimum?

It was the time between 1645 and 1715 when sunspots were very scarce or missing entirely. From studying old solar records in 1890, E. Walter Maunder observed that sunspot activity during these years was at a minimum. This observation was confirmed in 1976 by John Eddy.

Patrick Moore, *International Encyclopedia of Astronomy* (New York: Orion Books, 1987), 247.

Who is Stephen Hawking?

Hawking, a British physicist and mathematician, is considered to be the greatest theoretical physicist of the late twentieth century. In spite of being severely handicapped by Amyotrophic Lateral Sclerosis (ALS), he has made major contributions to scientific knowledge about black holes and the origin and evolution of the universe though his research into the nature of space-time and its anomalies. For instance, Hawking proposed that a black hole could emit thermal radiation and predicted that a black hole would disappear after all its mass has been converted into radiation (called *Hawking's radiation*). A current objective of Hawking is to synthesize quantum mechanics and relativity theory into a theory of quantum gravity. He is also the author of several books including the popular best-selling work *A Brief History of Time*.

The Biographical Dictionary of Scientists: Astronomers (New York: Peter Bedrick Books, 1984), 67-68. David F. Iver, *Dictionary of Astronomy, Space, and Atmospheric Phenomena* (New York: Van Nostrand Reinhold, 1979), 32. Sheridan Simon, *Stephen Hawking* (New York: Dillon, 1991), 9-10, 93-94.

What are quasars?

The name quasar is short for *quasi*-stellar Radio source. Quasars appear to be stars, but they have large red shifts in their spectra indicating that they are receding from the earth at great speeds, some at up to 90 percent of the speed of light. Their exact nature is still unknown, but many believe quasars to be the cores of distant galaxies, the most distant objects yet seen. Quasars were first identified in 1963 by astronomers at the Palomar Observatory, near San Diego, California.

William Hartmann and Ron Miller, *Cycles of Fire* (New York: Workman Publishing, 1987), 154-57. James Trefil, *1001 Things Everyone Should Know About Science* (New York: Doubleday, 1992), 259.

What is the origin of the Brown Mountain Lights of North Carolina?

For a period of some thirty years the "lights" seen at Brown Mountain could not be explained. In 1922, the United States Geological Survey studied the mystery. The area has extraordinary atmospheric conditions and automobile, locomotive, and fixed lights from miles away are reflected in the atmosphere.

George Rogers Mansfield, *Origin of the Brown Mountain Light in North Carolina* (Washington, DC: U.S. Geological Survey, 1971), 15-18.

What is the atmospheric phenomenon called a bishop's ring?

It is a ring around the sun, usually with a reddish outer edge. It is probably due to dust particles in the air as it is seen after all great volcanic eruptions.

Gershom Bradford, *A Glossary of Sea Terms* (New York: Dodd, Mead, 1942), 43.

Why was *De Revolutionibus Orbium Coelestium* written by Copernicus so controversial?

De Revolutionibus Orbium Coelestium was written by Nicolaus Copernicus, a sixteenth-century Prussian-Polish astronomer. In it he claimed that the earth was not the center of the universe, but that the earth rotated daily on its axis while orbiting the sun as did the other planets. However, at that time, the Catholic Church would not relinquish its strongly held belief that the earth was the center of the universe. Consequently, Copernicus did not allow the work to be published immediately. It was not until he lay upon his deathbed that he saw the first published copy. He died on May 24, 1543.

James Trager, *The People's Chronology: A Year-by-Year Record of Human Events from Prehistory to the Present, rev. ed.* (New York: Henry Holt, 1992), 183.

What were the provisions of Albert Einstein's will?

Following the death of famed physicist Dr. Albert Einstein (1879-1955), the conditions of his will were revealed. All of Einstein's books and personal effects, as well as $20,000, was bequeathed to his housekeeper and personal secretary, Helene Dukas. Margot Einstein, his stepdaughter, received $20,000 and his household furniture and effects. Einstein's son, Eduard, was awarded $15,000. Another son, Hans Albert, received $10,000. Einstein's violin was bequeathed to his grandson, Bernhard. Einstein's literary property and rights, including copyrights and royalties were to be held in trust for the benefit of Helene Dukas and Margot Einstein. After their deaths, the remaining property would pass to Israel's Hebrew University.

"$65,000 Legacies Left By Einstein," *New York Times* 1 May 1955.

Where did the word "atom" originate?

The word "atom" is derived from the Greek term "atomos," meaning indivisible. The idea of a particle being the smallest unit of matter, thus something considered indivisible, was first proposed by the Greek philosopher Democritus (*ca.* 460 B.C. -*ca.* 370 B.C.). By the late sixteenth century the shortened form of "atom" was found in the work of English writers. Etymologists have noted the use of the phrase "atomic bomb." The English science fiction writer H. G. Wells (1866-1946) coined the term in 1914 in his book *The World Let Free*, in an issue of the *Yale Review* in 1917, yet this device was not developed and tested until the mid-1940s. The science of atomic energy, sometimes called "atomistics" in its early years, required several new dictionary entries during the 1930s, including "atomic energy" itself, "atomerg," and "atomic ray." *Newsweek* in May of 1944 was the first general news source to use the term "atom," when it referred to a bomb of devastating explosive power that Nazi Germany was thought to possess. When the United States dropped the first atomic bomb on Japan in August of 1945, the word and its compounds entered the domain of public usage almost instantly.

"The Linguistic Fission of the Atom," *Word Study* April 1955.

Why do whips make a cracking sound when snapped?

When a whip is snapped, it can attain a speed of more than 700 miles per hour, breaking the sound barrier.

David Feldman, *Why Do Clocks Run Clockwise and other Imponderables* (New York: Harper & Row, 1987), 74.

What is oobleck?

Oobleck is a homemade concoction that flows like a liquid but under sudden force behaves like a solid. It can be made by mixing 16 oz. of cornstarch with 1 1/2 to 1 2/3 cups of water. If desired five drops of food coloring may be added. Combine the water and cornstarch and lift the oobleck from the bottom to top with your fingers in a stirring motion. Let the oobleck sit for 30 minutes. If too thin allow some water to evaporate or if the mixture becomes too dry after storing covered in a refrigerator more water may be added. Do not dispose of the mixture in the sink as it will clog the drain. The word comes from *Bartholomew and the Oobleck* by Dr. Seuss.

Cary I. Snelder, "Teacher Resource," *Book Links* July 1993, 19.

Which chemical element is the most abundant one in the universe?

Hydrogen (H, element 1) is the most abundant element; it makes up about 75 percent of the mass of the universe. It is estimated that more than 90 percent of all atoms in the universe are hydrogen atoms. Most of the rest are helium (He, element 2) atoms.

Science and Technology Illustrated 6:659.

Does hot water freeze faster than cold?

A bucket of hot water will not freeze faster than a bucket of cold water. However, a bucket of water that has been heated or boiled, then allowed to cool to the same temperature as the bucket of cold water, may freeze faster. Heating or boiling drives out some of the air bubbles in water because air bubbles cut down thermal conductivity, they can inhibit freezing. For the same reason, previously heated water forms denser ice than unheated water, which is why hot-water pipes tend to burst before cold-water pipes.

Tom Burnam, *The Dictionary of Misinformation* (New York: Perennial Library, 1986), 112.

What is inertia?

Inertia is a tendency of all objects and matter in the universe to remain at rest, or if moving, to continue moving in the same direction, unless acted on by some outside force. This forms the first law of motion formulated by Isaac Newton (1642-1727). To move a body at rest, enough external force must be used to overcome the object's inertia; the larger the object is, the more force is required to move it. In his *Philosophae Naturalis Principia Mathematica*, published in 1687, Newton sets forth all three laws of motion. Newton's second law is that the force to move a body is equal to its mass times its acceleration (F = MA), and the third law states that for every action there is an equal and opposite reaction.

Robert K. Barnhart, *The American Heritage Dictionary of Science* (Boston: Houghton Mifflin, 1986), 316. *The Biographical Dictionary of Scientists: Physicists* (New York: Peter Bedrick Books, 1984), 119-21. James Trefil, *1001 Things Everyone Should Know About Science* (New York: Doubleday, 1992), 146-47.

What is Maxwell's demon?

Maxwell's demon is an imaginary creature who, by opening and shutting a tiny door between two volumes of gases, could, in principle, concentrate slower molecules in one volume (making it colder) and faster molecules in the other volume (making it hotter), thus breaking the second law of thermodynamics-heat cannot by its own accord flow from a colder to a hotter body. This hypothesis was formulated in 1871 by James C. Maxwell (1831-1879), who is considered to be the greatest theoretical physicist of the nineteenth century. Maxwell discovered that light consists of electro-magnetic waves, proved the nature of Saturn's rings, set forth the principles of color vision and established the kinetic theory of gases, in which heat resides in the motion of the molecules.

The Biographical Dictionary of Scientists: Physicists (New York: Peter Bedrick Books, 1984), 109-11.

What is the second most abundant chemical element on earth?

Silicon (symbol Si, element 14) is the second most abundant element. Silicon dioxide and silicates make up about 87 percent of the materials in the earth's crust.

Nicholas D. Tzimopoulos et al. , *Modern Chemistry* (Fort Worth, TX: Holt, Rinehart and Winston, 1990), 758.

Why is Jns Jakob Berzelius considered one of thc founders of science in its modern form?

Swedish chemist Jns Jakob Berzelius (1779-1848) devised chemical symbols, determined atomic weights, contributed to the atomic theory, and discovered several new elements. Between 1810 and 1816, he described the preparation, purification, and analysis of 2,000 chemical compounds. Then he determined atomic weights for 40 elements. He simplified chemical symbols, introducing a notation which is still used today-letters with numbers-that replaced the pictorial symbols his predecessors used. He discovered cerium (in 1803, with Wilhelm Hisinger), selenium (1818), silicon (1824), and thorium (1829).

The Biographical Dictionary of Scientists: Chemists (New York: Peter Bedrick Books, 1983), 17.

Who developed the periodic table?

Dmitri Ivanovich Mendeleyev (1834-1907) was a Russian chemist whose name will always be linked with this outstanding achievement-the development of the periodic table. He was the first chemist to fully understand that all elements are related members of a single ordered system. He changed what had been a highly fragmented and speculative branch of chemistry into a true, logical science. His nomination for the 1906 Nobel Prize for Chemistry failed by one vote, but his name became recorded in perpetuity 50 years later when element 101 was called mendelevium in his honor.

According to Mendeleyev, the properties of the elements, as well as those of their compounds, are periodic functions of their atomic weights (in the 1920s, it was discovered that atomic number was the key rather than weight). Mendeleyev compiled the first true periodic table listing all the then-known 63 elements. In order to make the table functional, Mendeleyev had to leave gaps, and he predicted that further elements would eventually be discovered to fill them. Three were discovered in Mendeleyev's lifetime: gallium, scandium, and germanium. Of the 109 currently-known elements, 94 (elements 1 to 94) are naturally-occurring; the others were created in a laboratory.

The Biographical Dictionary of Scientists: Chemists (New York: Peter Bedrick Books, 1983), 91. John W. Wright, ed., *The Universal Almanac 1994* (Kansas City, MO: Andrews and McMeel, 1993), 543. Mark C. Young, ed., *The Guinness Book of Records 1995* (New York: Facts on File, 1994), 260. 505.

Is vinegar a good cleaner?

Vinegar is not a good cleaner. It does not break down dirt and grease like a detergent. Most common household soils such as oils, fats, and grease are acidic, as is vinegar, and alkaline cleaners work best to remove them. Vinegar is a good rinsing agent; it neutralizes soap residue left by floor cleaners or clothing detergents. It is also good for brightening stained aluminum cookware, removing tarnish from brass and copper, and dissolving hard water spots on dishes and glassware.

Don Aslett, *How Do I Clean the Moosehead?* (New York: New American Library, 1989), 137-38.

Who is Melvin Calvin?

Calvin (b. 1911) is an American chemist who won the 1961 Nobel Prize for Chemistry for his achievement of working out the chemical reaction cycles (called biosynthetic pathways) in photosynthesis. Photosynthesis is the process by which green plants use the energy of the sunlight to convert water and carbon dioxide into carbohydrates and oxygen. This cycle of reactions is now called the Calvin cycle. Calvin also conducted research in organometallic chemistry, the chemical origin of life, and taught chemistry at the University of California at Berkeley.

The Biographical Dictionary of Scientists. Chemists (New York: Peter Bedrick Books, 1983), 24. Edward Farber, *Nobel Prize Winners in Chemistry 1901-1961, rev. ed.* (New York: Ablard-Schuman, 1963), 307.

Which elements are called Group II elements?

Group II elements of the chemical periodic table are beryllium (Be, element 4); magnesium (Mg, element 12); calcium (Ca, element 20); strontium (Sr, element 38); barium (Ba, element 56); and radium (Ra, element 88). They are known as the alkaline-earth metals. Like the alkali metals, they are never found as free elements in nature and are moderately reactive metals. Harder and less volatile than the alkali metals, Group I, these elements all burn in air.

The Facts On File Dictionary of Chemistry, rev. ed. (New York: Facts On File, 1988), 7. Nicholas D. Tzimpoulos et al., *Modern Chemistry* (Fort Worth, TX: Rinehart and Winston, 1990), 717.

Which elements are liquid at room temperature?

Mercury (liquid silver, Hg, element 80) and bromine (Br, element 35) are liquid at room temperature 68 degrees to 70 degrees Farenheit (20 degrees to 25 degrees Centigrade). Gallium (Ga, element 31) with a melting point of 85.6 degrees Farenheit (29.8 degrees Centigrade) and cesium (Cs, element 55) with a melting point of 83 degrees Farenheit (28.4 degrees Centigrade), are liquids at slightly above room temperature.

Theodore L. Brown, *Chemistry, 4th ed.* (Englewood Cliffs, NJ: Prentice-Hall, 1988), 140, 143. Ingo W.D. Hackh, *Grant & Hackh's Chemical Dictionary, 5th ed.* (New York: McGraw-Hill, 1987), 96, 362. *Science and Technology Illustrated* (Chicago: Encyclopedia Britannica, 1984), 6:658.

What did NASA mean by *Voyager 1* and *2* taking a "grand tour" of the planets?

Once every 176 years the giant outer planets-Jupiter, Saturn, Uranus, and Neptune-align themselves in such a pattern that a spacecraft launched from Earth to Jupiter at just the right time might be able to visit the other three planets on the same mission. A technique called "gravity assist" used each planet's gravity as a power boost to point *Voyager* toward the next planet. 1977 was the opportunity for the "grand tour."

Joseph A. Angelo, *The Extraterrestrial Encyclopedia, rev. ed.* (New York: Facts on File, 1991), 219.

What is meant by the phrase *"greening of the galaxy"*?

The expression means the spreading of human life, technology, and culture through interstellar space and eventually across the entire Milky Way galaxy, the earth's home galaxy.

Joseph A. Angelo, *The Extraterrestrial Encyclopedia, rev. ed.* (New York: Facts on File, 1991), 59.

What is an astrolabe?

Invented by the Greeks or Alexandrians in about 100 B.C. or before, an astrolabe is a two-dimensional working model of the heavens, with sights for observations. It consists of two concentric flat disks, one fixed, representing the observer on earth, the other moving which can be rotated to represent the appearance of the celestial sphere at a given moment. Given latitude, date, and time, the observer can read off the altitude and azimuth of the sun, the brightest stars and the planets. By measuring the altitude of a particular body, one can find the time. The astrolabe can also be used to find times of sunrise, sunset, twilight, or the height of a tower or depth of a well. It was replaced by the sextant and other more accurate instruments.

The Illustrated Science and Invention Encyclopedia, International ed. (Westport, CT: H.S. Stuttman Publishers, 1983), 2: 168-169. *World Book Encyclopedia,* (Chicago: World Book, 1990) 1: 826.

How are new celestial objects named?

Many stars and planets have names that date back to antiquity. The International Astronomical Union (IAU), the professional astronomers organization, has attempted, in this century, to standardize names given to newly discovered celestial objects and their surface features.

Stars are generally called by their traditional names, most of which are of Greek, Roman, or Arabic origin. They are also identified after the constellation in which they appear, designated in order of brightness by Greek letters. Thus Sirius is also called alpha Canis Majoris, which means it is the brightest star in the constellation Canis Major. Other stars are called by catalog numbers which include the star's coordinates. To the horror of many astronomers, several commercial star registries exist, and for a fee, one can submit a star name to them. These names are not officially recognized by the IAU.

The IAU has made some recommendations for naming the surface features of the planets and their satellites. For example, features on Mercury are named for composers, poets, and writers; the features of Venus for women; Saturn's moon Mimas for people and places in Arthurian legend.

Comets are named for their discoverers. Newly discovered asteroids are first given a temporary designation consisting of the year of discovery plus two letters. The first letter indicates the half month of discovery and the second the order of discovery in that half month. Thus asteroid 1991BA was the first asteroid (A) discovered in the second half of January (B) in 1991. After an asteroid's orbit is determined it is given a permanent number and its discoverer is given the honor of naming it. Asteroids have been named after such diverse things as mythological figures (Ceres, Vesta), an airline (Swissair), and the Beatles (Lennon, McCartney, Harrison, Starr).

The Planetary Report November/December 1991. Carl Sagan, *Broca's Brain* (New York: Random House, 1979), 160-175. *Science News* 18 February, 1984).

What is phlogiston?

Phlogiston was a name used in the eighteenth century to identify a supposed substance given off during the process of combustion. The phlogiston theory was developed in the early 1700s by the German chemist and physicist, Georg Ernst Stahl (1660-1734).

In essence, Stahl held that combustible material such as coal or wood was rich in a material substance called "phlogiston." What remained after combustion was without phlogiston and could no longer burn. The rusting of metals also involved a transfer of phlogiston. This accepted theory explained a great deal previously unknown to chemists. For instance, metal smelting was consistent with the phlogiston theory. Charcoal in burning lost weight. Thus the loss of phlogiston either decreased or increased weight.

The French chemist Antoine Lavoisier (1743-1794) demonstrated that the gain of weight when a metal turned to a calx was just equal to the loss of weight of the air in the vessel. Lavoisier also showed that part of the air (oxygen) was indispensable to combustion, and that no material would burn in the absence of oxygen. The transition from Stahl's phlogiston theory to Lavoisier's oxygen theory marks the birth of modern chemistry at the end of the eighteenth century.

The Biographical Dictionary of Scientists: Chemists (New York: Peter Bedrick Books, 1983), 131-32. W.F. Bynum, *Dictionary of the History of Science* (Princeton, NJ: Princeton University Press, 1985), 322-23. Robert B. Downs, *Landmarks in Science* (Littleton, CO: Libraries Unlimited, 1982), 170-72.

Does water running down a drain rotate in a different direction in the Northern and Southern Hemispheres?

If water runs out from a perfectly symmetrical bathtub, basin, or toilet bowl, in the Northern Hemisphere it would swirl counterclockwise; in the Southern Hemisphere, the water would run out clockwise. This is caused by the Coriolis effect-the earth's rotation influencing any moving body of air or water. However, some scientists believe that the effect does not work on small bodies of water. Exactly on the equator of the earth, the water would run straight down a drain.

Tom Burnam, *The Dictionary of Misinformation* (New York: Perennial Library, 1986), 27. Ira Flatow, *Rainbows, Curve Balls and Other Wonders of the Natural World Explained* (New York: Harper & Row, 1988), 151-53. Charles A. Schweighauser, *Astronomy from A to Z* (Springfield, IL: Illinois Issues, 1991), 27.

How did the quark get its name?

The quark is a mathematical particle considered to be the fundamental unit of matter named by Murray Gell-Mann (b. 1929) an American theoretical physicist and Nobel Prize winner. Its name was initially a playful tag that Gell-Mann invented, sounding something like "kwork." Later Gell-Mann came across the line "Three quarks for Master Marks" in James Joyce's *Finnegan's Wake*, and the tag became known as a quark. There are six kinds or "flavors" (up, down, strange, charm, bottom, and top) of quarks, and each "flavor" has three varieties or "colors" (red, blue, and green). All eighteen types have different electric charges-a basic characteristic of all elementary particles. Three quarks form a proton (having one unit of positive electric charge) or a neutron (having zero charge), and two quarks (a quark and an antiquark) form a meson. Like all known particles, a quark has its anti-matter opposite, known as an antiquark-having the same mass but with an opposite charge.

Isaac Asimov, *Asimov's Chronology of Science and Discovery* (New York: Harper and Row, 1989), 606. *Biographical Encyclopedia of Scientists* (New York: Facts On File, 1981), 1:310. Cesare Emiliani, *The Scientific Companion* (New York: Wiley Science Editions, 1988), 11-13. *Science News* 12 September 1992.

Who is generally regarded as the discoverer of the electron?

In 1897, the British physicist, Sir Joseph John Thomson (1856-1940) researching electrical conduction in gases discovered that cathode rays consisted of negatively charged particles called electrons. This important discovery of the electron inaugurated the electrical theory of the atom, and this with other work entitled Thomson to be regarded as the founder of modern atomic physics.

Encyclopedic Dictionary of Science (New York: Facts On File, 1988), 238. A. Hechtlinger, *Modern Science Dictionary* (London: W. & R. Chambers, 1955), 124, 308. A.V. Howard, *Chamber's Dictionary of Scientists, 2nd ed.* (Palisade, NJ: Franklin, 1975), 435.

Why is liquid water more dense than ice?

Pure liquid water is most dense at 39.2 degrees Farenheit (3.98 degrees Centigrade) and decreases in density as it freezes. The water molecules in ice are held in a relatively rigid geometric pattern by their hydrogen bonds, producing an open, porous structure. Liquid water has fewer bonds; therefore, more molecules can occupy the same space, making liquid water more dense than ice.

Luna B. Leopold, *Water* (New York: Time, 1966), 30.

What does half-life mean?

Half-life is defined as the time it takes for the number of radioactive nuclei originally present in a sample to decrease to one half of the original number. For example, if a sample has a half-life of one year, its radioactivity will be reduced to half its original amount at the end of a year and to one quarter at the end of two years. The half-life of a particular radionuclide is always the same, independent of temperature, chemical combination, or any other condition.

Robert K. Barnhart, *The American Heritage Dictionary of Science* (Boston: Houghton Mifflin, 1986), 273. *Encyclopedia Americana* (Danbury, CT: Grolier, 1990), 13:712.

Who is considered the father of modern chemistry?

Several contenders share this honor. Robert Boyle (1627-1691), a British natural philosopher, is considered one of the founders of modern chemistry. Best known for his discovery of Boyle's Law (which is the volume of a gas is inversely proportional to its pressure at constant temperature), he was a pioneer in the use of experiments and the scientific method. A founder of the Royal Society, he worked to remove the mystique of alchemy from chemistry-elevating it to a pure science.

The French chemist Antoine-Laurent Lavoisier (1743-1794) is regarded as another founder of modern chemistry. His wide-ranging contributions include the discrediting of the phlogiston theory of combustion, which had been for so long a stumbling block to a true understanding of chemistry. He established modern terminology for chemical substances and did the first experiments in quantitative organic analysis. He is sometimes credited with having discovered or established the law of conservation of mass in chemical reactions.

Encyclopedic Dictionary of Science (New York: Facts On File, 1988), 50. *The Great Scientists* (Danbury, CT: Grolier, 1989), 7:84.

What are the Van Allen belts?

The Van Allen belts (or zones) are two regions of highly charged particles above the earth's equator trapped by the magnetic field which surrounds the earth. Also called the magnetosphere, the first belt extends from a few hundred to about 2,000 miles (3,200 kilometers) above the earth's surface and the second is between 9,000 and 12,000 miles (14,500 to 19,000 kilometers). The particles, mainly protons and electrons, come from the solar wind and cosmic rays. The belts are named in honor of James Alfred Van Allen (b. 1914), the American physicist who discovered them in 1958 and 1959, with the aid of radiation counters carried aboard the artificial satellites, *Explorer I* (1958) and *Pioneer 3* (1959).

The Biographical Dictionary of Scientists: Astronomers (New York: Peter Bedrick, 1984), 154-55. Patrick Moore and Garry Hunt, *The Atlas of the Solar System* (New York: Crescent Books with the Royal Astronomical Society, 1990), 140-41. Adrlan Room, *Dictionary of Astronomical Names* (New York: Routledge, 1988), 160.

What were the discoveries of John Bardeen, the only person to win two Nobel prizes in the same field?

In 1956 John Bardeen (1908-1991) won the Nobel Prize for Physics for his research on semiconductors and discovery of the transistor effect. His second prize, awarded in 1972, was for the microscopic theory of superconductivity.

Physics Today April 1992.

Who was the first American to receive a Nobel Prize?

Albert Abraham Michelson (1852-1931), a German-born American physicist, received the 1907 Nobel Prize in Physics, becoming the first American to win the award. The prize recognized both his design of extremely sensitive precise optical instruments to measure the velocity of light and the resulting accurate measurements he made with them. With Edward Morley (1838-1923), Michelson performed the classic Michelson-Morley experiment for light waves to determine very precisely light's velocity.

The Biographical Dictionary of Scientists: Physicists (New York: Peter Bedrick Books, 1984), s.v. "Michelson, Albert Abraham."

What is holography?

Hungarian-born scientist, Dennis Gabor, invented the technique of holography (image in the round) in 1947, but it was not until 1961 when Emmet Leith and Juris Upatnieks produced the modern hologram using a laser, which gave the hologram the strong, pure light it needed. Three-dimensions are seen around an object because light waves are reflected from all around it, overlapping and interfering with each other. This interaction of these collections of waves, called wave fronts, give an object its light, shade, and depth. A camera cannot capture all the information in these wave fronts, so it produces two dimensional objects. Holography captures the depth of an object by measuring the distance light has travelled from the object.

A simple hologram is made by splitting a laser light into two beams through a silvered mirror. One beam, called the object beam, lights up the subject of the hologram. These light waves are reflected onto a photographic plate. The other beam, called a reference beam, is reflected directly onto the plate itself. The two beams coincide to create, on the plate, an "interference pattern." After the plate is developed, a laser light is projected through this developed hologram at the same angle as the original reference beam, but from the opposite direction. The pattern scatters the light to create a projected, three-dimensional, ghost-like image of the original object in space.

How in the World? (Pleasantville, NY: Reader's Digest Association, 1990), 229.

How can the amount of lead in tap water be reduced in an older house having lead-containing pipes?

To reduce the amount of lead in tap water in an older house with lead-containing pipes let the tap run until the water becomes very cold before using it for human consumption. By letting the tap run, water that has been in the lead-containing pipes for awhile is flushed out. Also, cold water, being less corrosive than warm, contains less lead from the pipes. Lead accumulates in the blood, bones, and soft tissues of the body as well as the kidneys, nervous system, and blood-forming organs. Excessive exposure to lead can cause seizures, mental retardation, and behavior disorders. Infants and children are particularly susceptible to low doses of lead and suffer from nervous system damage.

Another source of lead poisoning is old flaking lead paint. Lead oxide and other lead compounds were added to paints before 1950 to make the paint shinier and more durable. 14 percent of the lead ingested by humans comes from the seam soldering of food cans, according to the U.S. Food and Drug Administration (FDA). The FDA has proposed a reduction in this lead to 50 percent over the next five years. Improperly glazed pottery can be a source of poisoning. Acidic liquids such as tea, coffee, wine, and juice can break down the glazes so that the lead can leak out of the pottery. The lead is ingested little by little over a period of time. People can be exposed to lead in the air. Lead gasoline additives, nonferrous smelters, and battery plants are the most significant contributors of atmospheric lead emissions.

Linda Mason Hunter, *The Healthy Home* (New York: Pocket Books, 1989), 108-10. *Current Health* 2 February 1992.

What is buckminsterfullerene?

It is a large molecule in the shape of a soccer ball, containing 60 carbon atoms, whose structure is the shape of a truncated icosahedron (a hollow, spherical object with 32 faces, 12 of them pentagons and the rest hexagons). This molecule was named buckminsterfullerene because of the structure's resemblance to the geodesic domes designed by American architect R. Buckminster Fuller (1895-1983). The molecule was formed by vaporizing material from a graphite surface with a laser. Large molecules containing only carbon atoms have been known to exist around certain types of carbon-rich stars. Similar molecules are also thought to be present in soot formed during the incomplete combustion of organic materials. Chemist Richard Smalley identified buckminsterfullerene in 1985 and speculated that it may be fairly common throughout the universe. Since that time, other stable, large, even-numbered carbon clusters have been produced. This new class of molecules has been called "fullerenes" since they all seem to have the structure of a geodesic dome. Buckministerfullerene seems to function as an insulator, conductor, semi-conductor, and superconductor in various compounds.

The Almanac of Science and Technology (San Diego: Harcourt Brace Jovanovich, 1990), 209-10.

What is the lightest solid material?

The lightest substance is silica aerogels, made of tiny spheres of bonded silicon and oxygen atoms linked together into long strands separated with air pockets. They appear almost like frozen wisps of smoke. In February, 1990, the lightest of these aerosols, having a density of only 5 ounces per cubic foot was produced at the Lawrence Livermore Laboratory in California. It will be used in window insulation, as traps for sampling cosmic dust in space, and in liquid rocket fuel storage.

Britannica Book of the Year 1991 (Chicago: Encyclopaedia Britannica, 1991), 141. Mark C. Young, ed., *Guinness Book of Records 1995* (New York: Facts On File, 1994),75.

What is technetium?

Technetium (Tc, element 43) is a radioactive metallic element that does not occur naturally either in its pure form or as compounds; it is produced during nuclear fission. A fission product of molybdenum (Mo, element 42), Tc can also occur as a fission product of uranium (U, element 92). It was the first element to be made artificially in 1937 when it was isolated and extracted by C. Perrier and Emilio Segre (1905-1989).

Tc has found some application in diagnostic medicine. Ingested soluble technetium compounds tend to concentrate in the liver and are valuable in labeling and in radiological examination of that organ. Also, by technetium labeling of blood serum components, diseases involving the circulatory system can be explored.

American Medical Association Encyclopedia of Medicine (New York: Random House, 1989), 966. Isaac Asimov, *Asimov's Biographical Encyclopedia of Science and Technology, 2d ed.* (Garden City, NY: Doubleday, 1982), 803-4. *Van Nostrand Reinhold Encyclopedia of Chemistry, 4th ed.* (New York: Van Nostrand Reinhold, 1984), 926.

Where does isinglass come from?

Isinglass is the purest form of animal gelatin. It is manufactured from the swimming bladder of the sturgeon. It is used in the clarification of wine and beer as well as in the making of some cements, jams, jellies, and soups.

Encyclopedia of Chemical Technology, 3d ed. (New York: Wiley, 1978), 11:911. *World Book Encyclopedia* (Chicago: World Book, 1990), 10:463.

Where are the asteroids found?

The asteroids, also called the minor planets, are smaller than any of the nine major planets in the solar system and are not satellites of any major planet. The term asteroid means "starlike" because asteroids appear to be points of light when seen through a telescope.

Most asteroids are located between Mars and Jupiter, between 2.1 and 3.3 astronomical units (AUs) from the sun. Ceres, the largest and the first to be discovered, was found by Giuseppe Piazzi, on January 1, 1801, and has a diameter of 582 miles (936 kilometers). A second asteroid, Pallas, was discovered in 1802. Since then, over 18 thousand asteroids have been identified and astronomers have established orbits for about five thousand of them. Some of these have diameters of only 0.62 miles (one kilometer). Originally, astronomers thought the asteroids were remnants of a planet that had been destroyed; now they believe asteroids to be material that never became a planet, possibly because it was affected by Jupiter's strong gravity.

Not all asteroids are in this main asteroid belt. Three groups reside in the inner solar system. The Aten asteroids have orbits that lie primarily inside Earth's orbit. However, at their farthest point from the sun, these asteroids may cross Earth's orbit. The Apollo asteroids cross Earth's orbit; some come even closer than the moon. The Amor asteroids cross the orbit of Mars and some come close to Earth's orbit. The Trojan asteroids move in virtually the same orbit as Jupiter but at points 60 degrees ahead or 60 degrees behind the planet. In 1977 Charles Kowal discovered an object now known as Chiron orbiting between Saturn and Uranus. Originally cataloged as an asteroid, Chiron was later observed to have a coma (a gaseous halo) and it may be reclassified as a comet.

Donald H. Menzel and Jay M. Pasachoff, *A Field Guide to Stars and Planets* (Boston: Houghton Mifflin, 1990),243-45. *The Planetary Report* November/December 1991. *Scientific American* October 1991.

What was the Tunguska Event?

On June 30, 1908, a violent explosion occurred in the atmosphere over the Podkamennaya Tunguska river, in a remote part of central Siberia. The blast's consequences were similar to an H-bomb going off, leveling thousands of square miles of forest. The shock of the explosion was heard over 600 miles (960 kilometers) away. A number of theories have been proposed to account for this event.

Some people thought that a large meteorite or a piece of anti-matter had fallen to earth. But a meteorite, composed of rock and metal, would have created a crater and none was found at the impact site. There are no high radiation levels in the area which would have resulted from the collision of anti-matter and matter. Two other theories include a mini-black hole striking the earth and the crash of an extraterrestrial spaceship. However, a mini-black hole would have passed through the earth and there is no record of a corresponding explosion on the other side of the world. As for the spaceship, no wreckage of such a craft was ever found.

The most likely cause of the explosion was the entry into the atmosphere of a piece of a comet which would have produced a large fireball and blast wave. Since a comet is composed primarily of ice, the fragment would have melted during its passage through the earth's atmosphere, leaving no impact crater and no debris. Since the Tunguska Event coincided with the earth's passage through the orbit of Comet Encke, the explosion could have been caused by a piece of that comet.

Joseph A. Angelo, *The Extraterrestrial Encyclopedia, rev. ed.* (New York, Facts On File, 1991), 220. Nigel Calder, *The Comet Is Coming* (New York: Penguin Books, 1982), 124-26.

From where do comets originate?

According to a theory developed by Dutch astronomer Jan Oort, there is a large cloud of gas, dust, and comets orbiting beyond Pluto out to perhaps 100,000 astronomical units (AU). An occasional passing star close to this cloud disturbs some of the comets from their orbits. Some fall inwards towards the sun.

Comets, sometimes called "dirty snowballs," are made up mostly of ice, with some dust mixed in. When a comet moves closer to the sun, the dust and ice of the core, or nucleus, heats up, producing a tail of material which trails along behind it. The tail is pushed out by the solar wind and almost always points away from the sun.

Most comets have highly elliptical orbits that carry them around the sun and then fling them back out to the outer reaches of the solar system, never to return. Occasionally however, a close passage by a comet near one of the planets can alter a comet's orbit making it stay in the middle or inner solar system. Such a comet is called a short-period comet because it passes close to the sun at regular intervals. The most famous short-period comet is Comet Halley which reaches perihelion (the point in its orbit that is closest to the sun) about every 76 years. Comet Encke, with an orbital period of 3.3 years, is another short-period comet.

Ron Miller and William K. Hartmann, *The Grand Tour: A Traveler's Guide to the Solar System* (New York: Workman Publishing, 1981), 173-79. Carl Sagan and Ann Druyan, *Comet* (New York: Random House, 1985).

How does a meteorite differ from a meteoroid?

A meteorite is a natural object of extraterrestrial origin that survives passage through the earth's atmosphere and hits the earth's surface. A meteorite is often confused with a meteoroid or a meteor. A meteoroid is a small object in outer space, generally less than 30 feet (10 meters) in diameter. A meteor (sometimes called a shooting star) is the flash of light seen when an object passes through earth's atmosphere and burns as a result of heating caused by friction. A meteoroid becomes a meteor when it enters the earth's atmosphere; if any portion of a meteoroid lands on earth, it is a meteorite.

There are three kinds of meteorites: irons contain 85-95 percent iron; the rest of their mass is mostly nickel; stony irons are relatively rare meteorites composed of about 50 percent iron and 50 percent silicates; and stones are made up mostly of silicates and other stony materials.

Patrick Moore et al., *The Atlas of the Solar System* (New York: Crecent Books with the Royal Astronomical Society, 1990), 406-7. *The Planetary Report* November/December 1991.

Why does the moon always keep the same face toward the earth?

Only one side of the moon is seen because it always rotates in exactly the same length of time that it takes to revolve about the earth. This combination of motions (called "captured rotation") means that it always keeps the same side toward the earth.

Patrick Moore et al., *The Atlas of the Solar System* (New York: Crescent Books with the Royal Astronomical Society, 1990), 147. James S. Pickering, *1001 Questions Answered About Astronomy* (New York: Dodd, Mead, 1958), 23.

What is the difference between a hunter's moon and a harvest moon?

The harvest moon is the full moon nearest the autumnal equinox. It is followed by a period of several successive days when the moon rises soon after sunset. In the southern hemisphere the harvest moon is the full moon closest to the vernal equinox (on or about March 17). In this period farmers have extra hours of light for harvesting crops. The next full moon after the harvest moon is called the hunter's moon.

Astronomical Almanac 1992 (Washington, DC: Government Printing Office, 1991), D1. Robert Famighetti, ed., *The World Almanac and Book of Facts 1995* (Mahwah, NJ: World Almanac, 1994), 269.

Astronomers have discovered that the moon has a tail. What does this mean?

A glowing 15 thousand mile (24 thousand kilometers) long tail of sodium atoms streams from the moon. The faint, orange glow of sodium cannot be seen by the naked eye but it is detectable by instruments. Astronomers are not certain of the source of these sodium atoms.

The Planetary Report September/October 1991.

Which planets have rings?

Jupiter, Saturn, Uranus, and Neptune all have rings. Jupiter's rings were discovered by *Voyager 1* in March, 1979. The rings extend 80,240 miles (129,130 kilometers) from the center of the planet. They are about 4,300 miles (7,000 kilometers) in width and less than 20 miles (30 kilometers) thick. A faint inner ring is believed to extend to the edge of Jupiter's atmosphere.

Saturn has the largest, most spectacular set of rings in the solar system. That the planet is surrounded by a ring system was first recognized by the Dutch astronomer Christiaan Huygens (1629-1695) in 1659. Saturn's rings are 169,980 miles (273,550 kilometers) in diameter, but less than 10 miles (16 kilometers) thick. There are seven different rings, the largest of which appear to be divided into thousands of ringlets, but this may be an optical illusion. The rings appear to be composed of pieces of water ice ranging in size from tiny grains to blocks several tens of yards in diameter.

In 1977 when Uranus occulted (i.e. passed in front of) a star, scientists observed that the light from the star flickered or winked several times before the planet itself covered the star. The same flickering occurred in reverse order after the occultation. The reason for this was determined to be a ring around Uranus. Nine rings were initially identified and *Voyager 2* observed two more in 1986. The rings are thin, narrow, and very dark.

Observations on Earth suggested that there were rings around Neptune but it was not until *Voyager 2* flew by the planet in 1989 that their existence was confirmed. Neptune has at least three narrow rings. The outer ring is unique in that the material in it is not spread out uniformly throughout the ring. Instead there are three arc-like areas where particles are concentrated. Scientists suspect that the gravity of tiny, as yet undiscovered moonlets among the rings is responsible for this bunching up effect.

Clive Carpenter, ed., *The Guinness Book of Answers, 9th ed.* (New York: Facts on File, 1993), 23-26. Ron Miller and William K. Hartmann, *The Grand Tour: A Traveler's Guide to the Solar System, rev. ed.* (New York: Workman Publishing, 1993), 39. *The Planetary Report* March/April 1992.

What are the Jovian and terrestrial planets?

Jupiter, Saturn, Uranus, and Neptune are the Jovian (the adjectival form for the word "Jupiter"), or Jupiter-like, planets. They are giant planets, composed primarily of light elements such as hydrogen and helium.

Mercury, Venus, Earth, and Mars are the terrestrial (derived from *terra*, the Latin word for "earth"), or earth-like planets. They are small in size, have solid surfaces, and are composed of rocks and iron. Pluto appears to be a terrestrial-type planet as well, but it may have a different origin from the other planets.

McGraw-Hill Encyclopedia of Science and Technology, 7th ed. (New York: McGraw-Hill, 1992), 13: 602. *Webster's Ninth New Collegiate Dictionary* (Springfield, MA: Merriam-Webster, 1989), 652, 1218.

What is the circumference of the earth?

The earth is an oblate ellipsoid-a sphere that is slightly flattened at the poles and which bulges at the equator. The distance around the earth at the equator is 24,902 miles (40,075 kilometers). The distance around the earth through the poles is 24,860 miles (40,008 kilometers).

Philip W. Goetz, ed., *New Encyclopaedia Britannica, 15th ed.* (Chicago: Encyclopaedia Britannica, 1990), 4:320. *Science and Technology Illustrated* (Chicago: Encyclopaedia Britannica, 1984), 9:1049.

Is it true that Pluto is not always the outermost planet in the solar system?

Pluto's very eccentric orbit carried it inside Neptune's orbit on January 23, 1979, where remained until March 15, 1999. During this time, Neptune was the outermost planet in the solar system. However, because the planets are so far apart, they are in no danger of colliding with one another.

Pluto, discovered in 1930 by American astronomer Clyde Tombaugh (b. 1906), is the smallest planet in the solar system. It is composed of rock and ice, with methane ice on the surface and a thin methane atmosphere. Pluto's single moon, Charon, discovered by James Christy in 1978, has a diameter of 741 miles (1,192 kilometers). This makes Charon, at half the size of Pluto, a very large moon relative to the planet. Some astronomers consider Pluto and Charon to be a double planet system.

The Guinness Book of Answers, 8th ed. (Enfield, England: Guinness Publishing, 1991), 22. Ron Miller and William K. Hartmann, *The Grand Tour: A Traveler's Guide to the Solar System* (New York: Workman Publishing, 1981), 126-27. Patrick Moore et al. , *The Atlas of the Solar System* (New York: Crescent Books with the Royal Astronomical Society, 1990), 396-97.

What is a binary star?

A binary star is a pair of stars revolving around a common center of gravity. About 50 percent of all stars are members of either binary star systems or multiple star systems which contain more than two stars.

The bright star Sirius, about 8.6 light years away, is composed of two stars, one about 2.3 times the mass of the sun, the other a white dwarf star about 980 times the mass of Jupiter. Alpha Centauri, the nearest star to Earth after the sun, is actually three stars: Alpha Centauri A and Alpha Centauri B, two sunlike stars, orbit each other, and Alpha Centauri C, a low mass red star, orbits around Centauri A and B.

Encyclopedic Dictionary of Science, (New York: Facts On File, 1988), 79. William K. Hartmann, and Ron Miller *Cycles of Fire* (New York: Workman Publishing, 1987), 100-101.

Where is the North Star?

If an imaginary line is drawn from the North Pole into space, there is a star called Polaris, or the North Star, less than one degree away from the line. As the earth rotates on its axis, Polaris acts as a pivot-point around which all the stars visible in the northern hemisphere appear to move, while Polaris itself remains motionless.

George Abell, *Realm of the Universe* (New York: Holt, Rinehart, and Winston, 1976), 11. Nicholas Booth, *The Concise Illustrated Book of Planets and Stars* (New York: Gallery Books, 1990), 30.

How hot is the sun?

The center of the sun is about 27,000,000 degrees Fahrenheit (15,000,000 Celsius). The surface, or photosphere, of the sun is about 10,000 degrees Fahrenheit (5,500 Celsius). Magnetic anomolies in the photosphere cause cooler regions which appear to be darker than the surrounding surface. These sunspots are about 6,700 degrees Fahrenheit (4,000 Celsius). The sun's layer of lower atmosphere, the chromosphere, is only a few thousand miles thick. At the base, the chromosphere is about 7,800 degrees Fahrenheit (4,300 Celsius), but its temperature rises with altitude to the corona, the sun's outer layer of atmosphere, which has a temperature of about 1,800,000 degrees Fahrenheit (1,000,000 Celsius).

Isaac Asimov, *Isaac Asimov's Guide to Earth and Space* (New York: Random House, 1991), 159-61. Patrick Moore et al. , *The Atlas of the Solar System* (New York: Crescent Books with the Royal Astronomical Society, 1990), 19.

How long does it take light from the sun to reach the earth?

Sunlight takes about 8 minutes and 20 seconds to reach the earth, traveling at 186,282 miles (299,792 kilometers) per second.

World Book Encyclopedia (Chicago: World Book, 1990), 18: 972.

What is a pulsar?

A pulsar is a rotating neutron star that gives off sharp regular pulses of radio waves at rates ranging from 0.001 to 4 seconds. Stars burn by fusing hydrogen into helium. When they use up their hydrogen, their interiors begin to contract. During this contraction energy is released and the outer layers of the star are pushed out. These layers are large and cool; the star is now a red giant. A star with more than twice the mass of the sun will continue to expand, becoming a supergiant. At that point, it may blow up, in an explosion called a supernova. After a supernova, the remaining material of the star's core may be so compressed that the electrons and protons become neutrons. A star 1.4 to 4 times the mass of the sun can be compressed into a neutron star only about 12 miles (20 kilometers) across. Neutron stars rotate very fast. The neutron star at the center of the Crab Nebula spins 30 times per second.

A pulsar is formed by the collapse of a star with 1.4 to 4 times the mass of the sun. Some of these neutron stars emit radio signals from their magnetic poles in a direction that reaches earth. These signals were first detected by Jocelyn Bell (b. 1943) of Cambridge University in 1967. Because of their regularity some people speculated that they were extraterrestrial beacons constructed by alien civilizations. This theory was eventually ruled out and the rotating neutron star came to be accepted as the explanation for these pulsating radio sources, or pulsars.

Astronomy November 1991. Donald H. Menzel, and Jay M. Pasachoff *A Field Guide to Stars and Planets, 2d ed.* (Boston: Houghton Mifflin, 1990), 112-4.

How old is the universe?

The universe is believed to be somewhere between 15 billion and 20 billion years old. The figure is derived from the concept that the universe has been expanding at the same rate since its birth at the Big Bang. The rate of expansion is a ratio known as Hubble's Constant. It is calculated by dividing the speed at which the galaxy is moving away from the earth by its distance from the earth. By inverting Hubble's Constant, that is dividing the distance of a galaxy by its recessional speed, the age of the universe can be calculated. The estimates of both the velocity and distance of galaxies from the earth are subject to uncertainties and not all scientists accept that the universe has always expanded at the same rate. Therefore, many still hold that the age of the universe open to question.

Richard P. Brennan, *Dictionary of Scientific Literacy* (New York: John Wiley, 1992), 310-11. Tjeerd H. Van Andel, *New Views on an Old Planet* (New York: Cambridge University Press, 1985), 28.

What is a syzygy?

A syzygy is a configuration that occurs when three celestial bodies lie in a straight line, such as the sun, earth, and moon during a solar or lunar eclipse. The particular case when a planet is on the opposite side of the earth from the sun is called an opposition.

Valerie Illingworth, *The Facts On File Dictionary of Astronomy* (New York: Facts On File, 1979), 335.

How often does an aurora appear?

The auroras, occurring in the polar regions, are broad displays of usually colored light at night. Because it depends on solar winds (electrical particles generated by the sun) and sunspot activity, the frequency of an aurora cannot be determined. Auroras usually appear two days after a solar flare (a violent eruption of particles on the sun's surface) and reach their peak two years into the 11-year sunspot cycle. The Northern polar aurora is called Aurora Borealis or Northern Lights and the Southern polar aurora is called the Aurora Australis.

Jeanne Hopkins, *Glossary of Astronomy and Astrophysics* (Chicago: University of Chicago, 1976), 10. *World Book Encyclopedia* (Chicago: World Book, 1990), 1:895-96.

Geology, Meteorology, Oceanography

What is the theory of the "hollow earth"?

The "hollow earth" theory is often attributed to John Cleves Symmes, a decorated War of 1812 veteran. According to Symmes' theory, the earth is composed of hollow, concentric spheres that could support life forms such as plants, humans, and animals. This hollow interior could be accessed by sailing into a 6,000-mile diameter opening in the South Pole and a 4,000-mile diameter opening in the North Pole. Symmes was such a staunch believer in the "hollow earth" theory that he contacted his Congressman, Richard Johnson, in 1823 and requested that the U.S. Congress fund an expedition to the center of the earth. Johnson, who would later serve as Vice President in the administration of Martin Van Buren (1782-1862), brought the request before the Congress, which vetoed the bill. Since Symmes' time, scientists have discovered that the interior of the earth is composed of solid rock and iron, while the center core is composed of nickel and molten iron.

"The Hollow Earth," *Parade* 2 August 1981.

What are the "Barisal Guns," and where can they be heard in the United States?

Occurring off the southeastern shore of North Carolina, the "Barisal Guns" are mysterious noises that begin like a low rumble of thunder and then become louder to sound like an artillery shell. There is no confirmed scientific explanation for these noises, but it has been postulated that they are caused by chunks of the continental shelf dropping from a cliff under the Atlantic Ocean. The phenomenon is named after the city of Barisal in Bangladesh, where similar sounds are heard.

E. Randall Floyd, *Great American Mysteries* (Little Rock, AR: August House, 1991), 114.

Who originated the idea called panspermia?

Panspermia is the idea that microorganisms, spores, or bacteria attached to tiny particles of matter have travelled through space, eventually landing on a suitable planet and initiated the rise of life there. The word itself means "all-seeding." The British scientist Lord Kelvin (1824-1907) suggested, in the nineteenth century, that life may have arrived here from outer space, perhaps carried by meteorites. In 1903 the Swedish chemist Svante Arrhenius (1859-1927) put forward the more complex panspermia idea that life on Earth was seeded by means of extraterrestrial spores, bacteria, and microorganisms coming here on tiny bits of cosmic matter.

Joseph A. Angelo, *The Extraterrestrial Encyclopedia, rev. ed.* (New York: Facts On File, 1991), 127.

Why is the sky blue?

The sunlight interacting with the earth's atmosphere makes the sky blue. In outer space the astronauts see blackness because outer space has no atmosphere. Sunlight consists of light waves of varying wavelengths, each of which is seen as a different color. The minute particles of matter and molecules of air in the atmosphere intercept and scatter the white light of the sun. A larger portion of the blue color in white light is scattered, more so than any other color because the blue wavelengths are the shortest. When the size of atmospheric particles are smaller than the wavelengths of the colors, selective scattering occurs-the particles only scatter one color and the atmosphere will appear to be that color. Blue wavelengths especially are affected, bouncing off the air particles to become visible. This is why the sun looks yellow (yellow equals white minus blue). At sunset, the sky changes color because as the sun drops to the horizon, sunlight has more atmosphere to pass through and loses more of its blue wavelengths (the shortest of all the colors). The orange and red, having the longer wavelengths and making up more of sunlight at this distance, are most likely to be scattered by the air particles.

Ira Flatow, *Rainbows, Curve Balls, and Other Wonders of the Natural World Explained* (New York: Harper & Row, 1988), 33-35. Frank H. Forrester, *1001 Questions Answered About the Weather* (New York: Grosset & Dunlap, 1957), 167. James Trefil, *1001 Things Everyone Should Know About Science* (New York: Doubleday, 1992), 113.

How many layers are there in the earth's atmosphere?

The atmosphere, the "skin" of gas that surrounds the earth, consists of five layers that are differentiated by temperature:

The troposphere is the lowest level; it averages about seven miles (11 kilometers) in thickness, varying from five miles (eight kilometers) at the poles to 10 miles (16 kilometers) at the equator. Most clouds and weather form in this layer. Temperature decreases with altitude in the troposphere.

The stratosphere ranges between seven miles (11 kilometers) to 30 miles (48 kilometers) above the earth's surface. The ozone layer, important because it absorbs most of the sun's harmful ultraviolet radiation, is located in this band. Temperatures rise slightly with altitude to a maximum of about 32 degrees Fahrenheit (0 degrees Celsius).

The mesosphere (above the stratosphere) extends from 30 miles (48 kilometers) to 55 miles (85 kilometers) above the earth. Temperatures decrease with altitude to -130 degrees Fahrenheit (-90 degrees Celsius).

The thermosphere (also known as the hetereosphere) is between 55 miles (85 kilometers) to 435 miles (700 kilometers). Temperatures in this layer range to 2696 degrees Fahrenheit (1475 degrees Celsius).

The exosphere beyond the thermosphere, applies to anything above 435 miles (700 kilometers). In this layer, temperature no longer has any meaning.

The ionosphere is a region of the atmosphere that overlaps the others, reaching from 30 miles (48 kilometers) to 250 miles (402 kilometers). In this region, the air becomes ionized (electrified) from the sun's ultraviolet rays, etc. This area affects the transmission and reflection of radio waves. It is divided into three regions: the D region (at 35 to 55 miles, or 56 to 88 kilometers), the E Region (Heaviside-Kennelly Layer, 55 to 95 miles, or 56 to 153 kilometers), and the F Region (Appleton Layer, at 95 to 250 miles, or 153 to 402 kilometers).

The Guinness Book of Answers, 8th ed. (Enfield, England: Guinness, 1991), 96. Jeff Rovin, *Laws of Order* (New York: Ballantine, 1992), 91. *The Universal Almanac 1992* (Kansas City, MO: Andrews and McMeel, 1991), 494.

What is a tufa?

Tufa is a general name for calcium carbonate deposits or spongy porous limestone found at springs in limestone areas, or in caves as massive stalactite or stalagmite deposits. Tufa, derived from the Italian word for "soft rock," is formed by the precipitation of calcite from the water of streams and springs.

Encyclopaedic Dictionary of Physical Geography (London: Blackwell, 1985), 445. L. Don Leet and Sheldon Judson, *Physical Geology, 4th ed.* (Englewood Cliffs, NJ: Prentice-Hall, 1971), 143.

What is the difference between spelunking and speleology?

Spelunking, or sport caving, is exploring caves as a hobby or for recreation. Speleology is the scientific study of caves and related phenomena, such as the world's deepest cave, Rseau Jean Bernard, Haute Savoie, France, with a depth of 5,256 feet (1,602 meters), or the world's longest cave system, Mammoth Cave in Kentucky, with a length of 348 miles (560 kilometers).

William R. Halliday, *Depths of the Earth* (New York: Harper, 1976), 407.

What are the LaBrea tar pits?

The La Brea tar pits are located in an area of Los Angeles, California, formerly known as Rancho LaBrea. Heavy, sticky tar oozed out of the earth, the scum from great petroleum reservoirs far underground. The pools were cruel traps for uncounted numbers of animals. Today the tar pits are a part of Hancock Park. In the park, many fossil remains are displayed along with life-sized reconstructions of these prehistoric species.

Cities of the United States: The West (Detroit: Gale Research, 1989), 66. *Natural History* December 1940.

What is the composition of the Rock of Gibraltar?

The Rock of Gibraltar is composed of gray limestone, with a dark shale overlay on parts of the western slopes. Located on a peninsula at the southern extremity of Spain, the Rock of Gibraltar is a mountain at the east end of the Strait of Gibraltar, the narrow passage between the Atlantic Ocean and the Mediterranean Sea. "The Rock" is 1,398 feet (426 meters) tall at its highest point.

Encyclopedia Americana (Danbury, CT: Grolier, 1990), 12:734. *Webster's New Geographical Dictionary* (Springfield, MA: Merriam-Webster, 1988), 442.

What is a hoodoo?

A hoodoo is a fanciful name for a grotesque rock pinnacle or pedestal, usually of sandstone, that is the result of weathering in a semi-arid region. An outstanding example of hoodoos occurs in the Wasatch Formation at Bryce Canyon, Utah.

George A. Goulty, *A Dictionary of Landscape* (Brookfield, VT: Gower, 1991), 135.

Are there tides in the solid part of the earth as well as in its waters?

The solid earth is distorted about 4.5 to 14 inches (11.4 to 35.6 centimeters) by the gravitational pull of the sun and moon. It is the same gravitational pull that creates the tides of the waters. When the moon's gravity pulls water on the side of the earth near to it, it pulls the solid body of the earth on the opposite side away from the water to create bulges on both sides, and causing high tides. These occur every 12.5 hours. Low tides occur in those places from which the water is drained to flow into the two high-tide bulges. The sun causes tides on the earth that are about 33 to 46 percent as high as those due to the moon. During a new moon or a full moon when the sun and moon are in a straight line, the tides of the moon and the sun reinforce each other, to make high tides higher; these are called spring tides. At the quarter moons, the sun and moon are out of step (at right angles), the tides are less extreme than usual; these are called neap tides. Smaller bodies of water, such as lakes, have no tides because the whole body of water is raised all at once, along with the land beneath it.

Source: Isaac Asimov, *Isaac Asimov's Guide to Earth and Space* (New York: Random House, 1991), 97-98. David Feldman, *Do Penguins Have Knees?* (New York: Harper Perennial, 1991), 138-39. James S. Pickering, *1001 Questions Answered About Astronomy* (New York: Dodd, Mead, 1958), 41.

When was the Ice Age?

Ice ages, or glacial periods, have occurred at irregular intervals for over 2.3 billion years. During an ice age, sheets of ice cover large portions of the continents. The exact reasons for the changes in the earth's climate are not known, although some think they are caused by changes in the earth's orbit around the sun.

The Great Ice Age occurred during the Pleistocene Epoch which began about 2 million years ago and lasted until 11 thousand years ago. At its height, about 27 percent of the world's present land area was covered by ice. In North America, the ice covered Canada and moved southward to New Jersey; in the Midwest, it reached as far south as St. Louis. Small glaciers and ice caps also covered the western mountains. Greenland was covered in ice as it is today. In Europe, ice moved down from Scandinavia into Germany and Poland; the British Isles and the Alps also had ice caps. Glaciers also covered the northern plains of Russia, the plateaus of Central Asia, Siberia, and the Kamchatka Peninsula.

The glaciers' effect on the United States can still be seen. The drainage of the Ohio River and the position of the Great Lakes were influenced by the glaciers. The rich soil of the Midwest is mostly glacial in origin. Rainfall in areas south of the glaciers formed large lakes in Utah, Nevada, and California. The Great Salt Lake in Utah is a remnant of one of these lakes. The large ice sheets locked up a lot of water; sea level fell about 450 feet (137 meters) below what it is today. As a result, some states, such as Florida, were much larger during the ice age.

The glaciers of the last ice age retreated about 11 thousand years ago. Some believe that the ice age is not over yet; the glaciers follow a cycle of advance and retreat many times. There are still areas of the earth covered by ice and this may be a time in between glacial advances.

L. Don Leet and Sheldon Judson, *Physical Geology, 4th ed.* (Englewood Cliffs, NJ: Prentice-Hall, 1971), 304-5. U.S. Geological Survey, *Our Changing Continent* (Washington, DC: U.S. Geological Survey, 1991), 11.

Are all craters part of a volcano?

No, not all craters are of volcanic origin. A crater is a nearly circular area of deformed sedimentary rocks, with a central vent-like depression. Some craters are caused by the collapse of the surface when underground salt or limestone dissolves. The withdrawal of ground-water and the melting of glacial ice can also cause the surface to collapse, forming a crater.

Craters are also caused by large meteorites, comets, and asteroids which hit the earth. A notable impact crater is Meteor Crater near Winslow, Arizona. It is 4,000 feet (1,219 meters) in diameter, six hundred feet (183 meters) deep and is estimated to have been formed 30 thousand to 50 thousand years ago.

Robert I. Tilling, *Volcanoes* (Washington, DC: U.S. Geological Survey, 1992), 21.

Who was the first person to map the Gulf Stream?

In his travels to and from France as a diplomat, Benjamin Franklin (1706-90) noticed a difference in speed in the two directions of travel between France and America. He was the first to study ships' reports seriously to determine the cause of the speed variation. As a result, he found that there was a current of warm water coming from the Gulf of Mexico that crossed the North Atlantic Ocean in the direction of Europe. In 1770, Franklin mapped it.

Isaac Asimov, *Asimov's Chronology of Science and Discovery* (New York: Harper & Row, 1989), 215-16.

What are the highest and lowest points on earth?

The highest point on land is the top of Mt. Everest (in the Himalayas on the Nepal-Tibet border) at 29,028 feet (8,848 meters) above sea level, plus or minus 10 feet (3 meters) because of snow. This height was established by the Surveyor General of India in 1954 and accepted by the National Geographic Society. Prior to that the height was taken to be 29,002 feet (8,840 meters). Satellite measurements taken in 1987 indicate that Mt. Everest is 29,864 feet (9,102 meters) high but this measurement has not been adopted by the National Geographic Society.

The lowest point on land is the Dead Sea between Israel and Jordan which is 1,312 feet (399 meters) below sea level. The lowest point on the earth's surface is thought to be in the Marianas Trench in the western Pacific Ocean extending from southeast of Guam to northwest of the Marianas Islands. It has been measured as 36,198 feet (11,034 meters) below sea level.

Richard Ojakangas, *Schaum's Outline of Theory and Problems of Introductory Geology* (McGraw-Hill, 1991), 5. Robert Famighetti, ed., *The World Almanac and Book of Facts 1995* (New York: World Almanac, 1994), 546,552,555.

Of what magnitude was the earthquake that hit San Francisco on April 18, 1906, on the Richter scale?

The historic 1906 San Francisco earthquake took a mighty toll on the city and surrounding area. Over 700 people were killed; the newly-constructed $6 million city hall was ruined; the Sonoma Wine Company collapsed, destroying 15 million gallons of wine. The quake registered 8.3 on the Richter scale and lasted seventy-five seconds total. Many poorly-constructed buildings built on landfills were flattened and the quake destroyed almost all of the gas and water mains. Fires broke out shortly after the quake, and when they were finally eliminated, 3,000 acres of the city, the equivalent of 520 blocks, were charred. Damage was estimated to be $500 million, and many insurance agencies went bankrupt after paying out the claims.

Again on October 17, 1989, an earthquake hit San Francisco, measuring 7.1 on the Richter scale, killing 67 people, and causing billions of dollars worth of damage.

Clive Carpenter, ed., *The Guinness Book of Answers* (New York: Facts on File, 1993), 95. Jay Robert Nash, *Darkest Hours* (Chicago: Nelson-Hall, 1976), 490-507. *The Public Health Consequences of Disasters 1989* (Atlanta, GA: Centers for Disease Control, 1989). John W. Wright, ed., *The Universal Almanac 1994* (Kansas City, MO: Andrews and McMeel, 1993), 534.

When did Mount St. Helens erupt?

Mount St. Helens, located in southwestern Washington state in the Cascades mountain range, erupted on May 18, 1980. Sixty one people died as a result of the eruption. This was the first known eruption in the 48 contiguous United States to claim a human life. Geologists call Mount St. Helens a composite volcano (a steep-sided, often symmetrical cone constructed of alternating layers of lava flows, ash, and other volcanic debris). Composite volcanoes tend to erupt explosively. Mount St. Helens and the other active volcanoes in the Cascade Mountains are a part of the "Ring of Fire"-the Pacific zone having frequent and destructive volcanic activity.

Volcanoes have not only been active in Washington, but also in three other U.S. states: California, Alaska, and Hawaii. Lassen Peak is one of several volcanoes in the Cascade Range. It last erupted in 1921. Mount Katmai in Alaska had an eruption in 1912 in which the flood of hot ash formed the Valley of Ten Thousand Smokes 15 miles (24 kilometers) away. And Hawaii has its famed Mauna Loa, which is the world's largest volcanoe, being 60 miles (97 kilometers) in width at its base.

Great Disasters (Reader's Digest Association, 1989), 272. Robert I. Tilling, *Eruptions of Mount St. Helens* (U.S. Department of the Interior, 1990), 3. *World Book* (Chicago: World Book, 1987), s.v. "Volcanoes."

How many kinds of volcanoes are there?

Volcanoes are usually cone-shaped hills or mountains built around a vent connecting to reservoirs of molten rock, or magma, below the surface of the earth. At times the molten rock is forced upwards by gas pressure until it breaks through weak spots in the earth's crust. The magma erupts forth as lava flows or shoots into the air as clouds of lava fragments, ash, and dust. The accumulation of debris from eruptions cause the volcano to grow in size. There are four kinds of volcanoes:

Cinder cones—built of lava fragments. They have slopes of 30 degrees to 40 degrees and seldom exceed 1,640 feet (500 meters) in height. Sunset Crater in Arizona and Paricutin in Mexico are examples of cinder cones.

Composite cones made of alternating layers of lava and ash. They are characterized by slopes of up to 30 degrees at the summit, tapering off to 5 degrees at the base. Mount Fuji in Japan and Mount St. Helens in Washington are composite cone volcanoes.

Shield volcanoes built primarily of lava flows. Their slopes are seldom more than 10 degrees at the summit and 2 degrees at the base. The Hawaiian Islands are clusters of shield volcanoes. Mauna Loa is the world's largest active volcano, rising 13,653 feet (4,161 meters) above sea level.

Lava domes made of viscous, pasty lava squeezed like toothpaste from a tube. Examples of lava domes are Lassen Peak and Mono Dome in California.

L. Don Leet and Sheldon Judson, *Physical Geology, 4th ed.* (Englewood Cliffs, NJ: Prentice-Hall, 1971), 74-5. Frank E. Bair, *The Weather Almanac, 6th ed.* (Detroit: Gale Research, 1992), 200-204.

Is the Dead Sea really dead?

The Dead Sea, on the boundary between Israel and Jordan, is called "dead" because nothing but bacteria and halophites—plants that can withstand high saline levels—can live in it. Fish entering the sea from the Jordan River die instantly. It has a salt content of 25 percent. Because it is the lowest body of water on the earth's surface, any water that flows into the Dead Sea has no outflow. As the water evaporates, dissolved minerals are left in the sea. The Great Salt Lake in Utah is similar in composition and also contains only minor life forms.

Charles J. Cazeau, *Science Trivia* (New York: Berkley Books, 1986), 58-59. *The New Encyclopaedia Britannica, 15th ed.,* (Chicago: Encyclopaedia Britannica, 1990), 3:448.

What is an aquifer?

Some rocks of the upper part of the earth's crust contain many small holes, or pores. When these holes are large or are joined together so that water can flow through them easily, the rock is considered to be permeable. A large body of permeable rock in which water is stored and flows through is called an aquifer (from the Latin for "water" and "to bear"). Sandstones and gravels are excellent examples of permeable rock.

As water reservoirs, aquifers provide about 60 percent of American drinking water. The huge Ogallala Aquifer, underlying about two million acres of the Great Plains, is a major source of water for the central United States. It has been estimated that after oceans (containing 1,370 million cubic kilometers of water), aquifers, with an estimated 50 million cubic kilometers, are the second largest store of water. Water is purified as it is filtered through the rock, but it can be polluted by spills, dumps, acid rain, and other causes. In addition, recharging of water by rainfall often cannot keep up with the volume removed by heavy pumping. The Ogallala Aquifer's supply of water could be depleted by 25 percent by the year 2020.

Nigel J. Hopkins, John W. Mayne, and John R. Hudson, *The Numbers You Need* (Detroit: Gale Research, 1992), 112. *The 1992 Information Please Environmental Almanac* (Boston: Houghton-Mifflin, 1992), 92. *New Scientist* 16 February 1991).

How far can sunlight penetrate into the ocean?

Because seawater is relatively transparent, approximately 5 percent of sunlight can penetrate clean ocean water to a depth of 262 feet (80 meters). When the water is turbid (cloudy) due to currents, mixing of silt, increased growth of algae, or other factors, the depth of penetration is reduced to less than 164 feet (50 meters).

Alyn C. Duxbury and Alison Duxbury, *An Introduction to the World's Oceans* (Reading, MA: Addison-Wesley Publishing, 1984), 382-83.

What is the difference between an ocean and a sea?

There is no neatly defined distinction between ocean and sea. One definition terms the ocean as a great body of interconnecting salt water that covers 71 percent of the earth's surface. There are three distinct oceans-the Atlantic, Indian, and Pacific-the Arctic and Antarctic are now considered marginal seas. The terms "ocean" and "sea" are often used interchangeably, but a sea is generally considered to be smaller than an ocean. The name is often given to salt-water areas on the margins of an ocean, such as the Mediterranean Sea.

Susan Mayhew and Anne Perry, *The Concise Oxford Dictionary of Geography* (New York: Oxford University Press, 1992), 164. *The Guinness Book of Answers, 8th ed.* (Enfield, England: Guinness Publishing, 1991), 62-65. John Wright, ed., *The Universal Almanac 1994* (Kansas City, MO: Andrews and McNeel, 1993), 311.

When will Niagara Falls disappear?

The water dropping over Niagara Falls digs great plunge pools at the base, undermining the shale cliff and causing the hard limestone cap to cave in. Niagara has eaten itself seven miles (11 kilometers) upstream since it was formed 10 thousand years ago. At this rate, it will disappear into Lake Erie in 22,800 years. The Niagara River connects Lake Erie with Lake Ontario, and marks the U.S.-Canada boundary (New York-Ontario).

Luna B. Leopold, *Water* (New York: Time, 1966), 94.

Where are the world's highest tides?

The Bay of Fundy (New Brunswick, Canada) has the world's highest tides. Burncoat Head in the Minas Basin has the greatest mean spring range at 47 feet 6 inches (14.6 meters). But in general the tides average about 45 feet (14 meters) high in the northern part of the bay, far surpassing the world average of 2.5 feet (0.8 meter).

Mark C. Young, ed., *The Guinness Book of Records 1995,* (New York: Facts on File, 1994), 59-60. *World Book Encyclopedia,* (Chicago: World Book, 1990), 14: 181.

How and when was coal formed?

Coal is formed from the remains of plants and trees that have undergone a series of far-reaching changes, turning into a substance called peat, which subsequently was buried. Through millions of years, the earth's crust buckled and folded, subjecting the peat deposits to very high pressure and temperature, which changed the peat chemically into lignite and eventually changed the deposits into coal. The Carboniferous, or coal-bearing period, occurred about 250 million years ago. Geologists in the United States sometimes divide this period into the Mississippian and the Pennsylvanian periods. Most of the high-grade coal deposits are to be found in the strata of the Pennsylvanian period.

The New Book of Popular Science (Danbury, CT: Grolier, 1988), 320-321.

How does ozone benefit life on earth?

Ozone in the upper atmosphere (stratosphere) is a major factor in making life on earth possible. The ozone belt shields the earth from excessive ultraviolet radiation generated by the sun. Scientists predict that depletion of this layer could lead to increased health problems for humans and disruption of sensitive terrestrial and aquatic ecosystems. Ozone, a form of oxygen with three atoms instead of the normal two, is highly toxic; less than one part per million of this blue-tinged gas is poisonous to humans. While beneficial in the stratosphere, near ground level it is a pollutant that helps form photochemical smog and acid rain.

Geoffrey Lean, Don Hinrichsen, and Adam Markham, *WWF Atlas of the Environment* (Boston: Willard Grant Press, 1991), 97-98. Glenn E. Schweitzer, *Borrowed Earth, Borrowed Time* (New York: Plenum, 1991), 214, 218.

What are the components of smog?

Photochemical air pollution, commonly known as smog, is the result of a number of complex chemical reactions. The hydrocarbons, hydrocarbon derivations, and nitric oxides emitted from such sources as automobiles are the raw materials for photochemical reactions. In the presence of oxygen and sunlight, the nitric oxides combine with organic compounds, such as the hydrocarbons from unburned gasoline, to produce a whitish haze, sometimes tinged with a yellow-brown color. In the process, a large number of new hydrocarbons and oxyhydrocarbons are produced. These secondary hydrocarbon products may compose as much as 95 percent of the total organics in a severe smog episode.

E. Willard Miller, *Environmental Hazards: Air Pollution* (Santa Barbara, CA: ABC-CIO, 1989), 77.

What is the Flat Earth Society?

The Flat Earth Society International, founded in 1800, is composed of individuals characterized by a seeking for truth and the denial of "imaginary" theories. They believe the "spinning ball" theory of the earth is absurd, and that the earth is a flat, infinite world.

Charles J. Cazeau, *Science Trivia* (New York: Berkley Books, 1986), 56. *Encyclopedia of Associations, 27th ed.* (Detroit: Gale Research, 1993), 1:727.

Which metallic element is the most abundant?

Aluminum is the most abundant metallic element on the surface of the earth and moon; it composes more than 8% of the earth's crust. It is never free in nature, combining with oxygen, sand, iron, titanium, etc.; its ores are mainly bauxites (aluminum hydroxide). Nearly all rocks, particularly igneous rocks, contain aluminum as aluminosilicate minerals. Napoleon III (1808-1883) recognized that the physical characteristic of its lightness could revolutionize the arms industry, so he granted a large subsidy to French chemist Sainte-Claire Deville (1818-1881) to develop a method to make its commercial use feasible. In 1854, Deville obtained the first pure aluminum metal through the process of reduction of aluminum chloride. In 1886, the American Charles Martin Hall (1863-1914) and the Frenchman Paul Heroult (1863-1914) independently discovered an electrolytic process to produce aluminum from bauxite. Because of aluminum's resistance to corrosion, low density, and excellent heat-conducting property, it is used in cookware manufacturing and can-making industries. It is a good conductor of electricity and is widely used in overhead cables. Aluminum alloys, such as duralumin, have high tensile strengths and are of considerable industrial importance, especially in the aerospace industry.

Encyclopedia of Chemical Technology, 3d ed. (New York: Wiley, 1978), 2:129. Valerie-Anne Giscard d'Estaing, *The World Almanac Book of Inventions* (New York: World Almanac, 1986), 256. *Oxford Illustrated Encyclopedia of Invention and Technology* (Oxford: Oxford University Press, 1992), 12.

Is lodestone a magnet?

Lodestone is a magnetic variety of natural iron oxide. It was used as a magnet by early mariners to find the magnetic north. Lodestone is frequently called a natural magnet.

Paul W. Thrush, *Dictionary of Mining, Mineral, and Related Terms* (Washington, DC: U.S. Bureau of Mines, 1968), 655.

Which diamond is the world's largest?

The Cullinan Diamond, weighing 3,106 carats, is the world's largest discovered diamond. Found on January 25, 1905, at the Premier Diamond Mine in Transvaal, South Africa, it was named for Sir Thomas M. Cullinan, chairman of the Premier Diamond Company. It was cut into nine major stones and 96 smaller brilliants; the total weight of the cut stones was 1,063 carats, only 35 percent of the original weight.

Cullinan I, also known as the "Greater Star of Africa" or the "First Star of Africa," is a pear-shaped diamond weighing 530.2 carats. It is 21/8 inches (5.4 centimeters) long, 13/4 inches (4.4 centimeters) wide, and 1 inch (2.54 centimeters) thick at its deepest point. It was presented to Britain's King Edward VII in 1907, and was set in the British monarch's scepter with the cross. It is still the largest cut diamond in the world.

Cullinan II, also know as the "Second Star of Africa," is an oblong stone which weighs 317.4 carats. It is set in the British Imperial State Crown.

The largest cut diamond is the "Unnamed Brown" a 545.67-carat gem that had been part of an original 775.5-carat rough diamond found at the Premier Diamond Mine in Transvaal, South Africa.

Victor Argenzio, *Diamonds Eternal* (New York: David McKay, 1974), 40-43. Leslie Field, *The Queen's Jewels* (New York: Harry N. Abrams, 1987), 72-75. *How In the World* (Pleasantville, NY: Reader's Digest Association, 1990), 144-45. Mark C. Young, ed., *The Guinness Book of Records 1995* (New York: Facts On File, 1994), 61.

What are Cape May diamonds?

They are quartz pebbles, found in the vicinity of the Coast Guard station in Cape May, New Jersey. The pebbles are polished, faceted, and sold to tourists as "Cape May diamonds."

Edward Fletcher, *Pebble Collecting and Polishing* (New York: Sterling, 1973), 21.

What are Indian Dollars?

They are six-sided disk-shaped twin crystals of aragonite which have altered to calcite but retained their outer form. They occur in large numbers in northern Colorado where they are known as Indian Dollars. In New Mexico they are called Aztec Money and in western Kansas they are called Pioneer Dollars.

Richard M. Pearl, *1001 Questions Answered About the Mineral Kingdom* (New York: Dodd, Mead, 1959), 14. Richard M. Shipley, *Dictionary of Gems and Gemology, 6th ed.* (Santa Monica: Gemological Institute of America, 1974), 12.

What is a geode?

A geode is a hollow, stone-like formation lined inside with inward projecting, small crystals. Geodes are frequently found in limestone beds and occur in many parts of the world. They average two to six inches (5 to 15 centimeters) in diameter.

American Geological Institute, *Dictionary of Geological Terms, rev. ed.* (Garden City, NY: Anchor Press, 1976), 181. *The McGraw-Hill Dictionary of Scientific and Technical Terms, 4th ed.* (New York: McGraw-Hill, 1989), 800.

What is petrology and what does a petrologist do?

Petrology is the science of rocks. A petrologist is a person who is interested in the study of the mineralogy of rocks. From these rocks, a petrologist can learn about past climates and geography, past and present composition of the earth , and the conditions which prevail within the interior of the earth.

W. R. Hamilton, *The Henry Holt Guide to Minerals, Rocks, and Fossils* (New York: Henry Holt, 1989), 146.

What is fool's gold?

Iron pyrite is a mineral popularly known as "fool's gold." Because of its metallic luster and pale brass yellow color it is often mistaken for gold. Real gold is much heavier, softer, not brittle, and not grooved.

Robert L. Bates and Julia A. Jackson, *Glossary of Geology, 3d ed.* (Alexandria, VA: American Geological Institute, 1987), 540. Eva Fejer and Cecilia Fitzsimons, *An Instant Guide to Rocks and Minerals* (Stamford, CT: Longmeadow Press, 1988), 104.

What is galena?

Galena is a lead sulphide (PbS) and the most common ore of lead, containing 86.6 percent lead. Lead-gray in color, with a brilliant metallic luster, galena has a specific gravity of 7.5 and a hardness of 2.5 on the Mohs scale, and usually occurs as cubes or a modification of an octahedral form. Mined in Australia, it is also found in Missouri, Kansas, Oklahoma, Colorado, Montana, and Idaho.

The American Geological Institute, *Dictionary of Geological Terms, rev. ed.* (Garden City, NY: Anchor Press, 1976), 177. Sybil P. Parker, *McGraw-Hill Concise Encyclopedia of Science and Technology, 2d ed.* (New York: McGraw-Hill, 1989), 826. Paul W. Thrush, *Dictionary of Mining, Mineral, and Related Terms* (Washington, DC: U.S. Bureau of Mines, 1968), 475.

Who is regarded as the father of modern mineralogy?

Georg Bauer (1495-1555) was a German mineralogist, physician, and scholar. Also known by the Latin name Georgius Agricola, he studied mining methods and mining ores, and wrote on the classification of minerals, mineral extraction, and geological phenomena. *De re metallica*, his major work, covered the entire field of mining and metallurgy in a systematic and comprehensive manner. Bauer was one of the first to base his writings on observation and scientific inquiry.

Robert B. Downs, *Landmarks in Science* (Littleton, CO: Libraries Unlimited, 1982), 75-77. *The Great Scientists* (Danbury, CT: Grolier, 1989), 1:29.

What is meant by the term *strategic minerals*?

Strategic minerals are minerals essential to the national defense-the supply of which a country uses but cannot produce itself. 33 percent to 50 percent of the 80 minerals used by industry could be classed as strategic minerals. Wealthy countries, such as the United States, stockpile these minerals to avoid any crippling effect on their economy or military strength if political circumstances were to cut off their supplies. The United States, for instance, stockpiles bauxite (14-million tons), manganese (2.2 million tons), chromium (1.8 million tons), tin (185 thousand tons), cobalt (19 thousand tons), tantalum (635 tons), palladium (1.25 million troy ounces), and platinum (453 thousand troy ounces).

William Cunningham and Barbara Woodhouse Saigo, *Environmental Science: A Global Concern* Dubuque, IA: Wm. C. Brown, 1990), 152-53. Paul W. Thrush, *Dictionary of Mining, Mineral, and Related Terms* (Washington, DC: U.S. Bureau of Mines, 1968), 1086.

When and by whom were clouds first classified?

The French naturalist Jean Lamarck (1744-1829) proposed the first system for classifying clouds in 1802; however, his work did not receive wide acclaim. A year later the Englishman Luke Howard (1772-1864) developed a cloud classification system that has been generally accepted and is still used today. Clouds are distinguished by their general appearance ("heap clouds" and "layer clouds") and by their height above the ground. Latin names and prefixes are used to describe these characteristics. The shape names are *cirrus* (curly or fibrous), *stratus* (layered), and *cumulus* (lumpy or piled). The prefixes denoting height are *cirro* (high clouds with bases above 20,000 feet or 6.1 kilometers) and *alto* (mid-level clouds from 6,000 to 20,000 feet or 1830 to 6,100 kilometers). There is no prefix for low clouds. *Nimbo* or *nimbus* is also added as a name or prefix to indicate that the cloud produces precipitation.

C. Donald Ahrens, *Meteorology Today, 2d ed.*, (St. Paul, MN: West Publishing, 1985), 163. Jack Williams, *The Weather Book* (New York: Vintage Books, 1992), 160-61.

What are the four major cloud groups and their types?

The four major cloud groups are as follows:

High Clouds are composed almost entirely of ice crystals. The bases of these clouds start at 16,500 feet (5,032 meters) and reach 45,000 feet (13,725 meters). *Cirrus* (from Latin, "lock of hair") are thin feather-like crystal clouds in patches or narrow bands. The large ice crystals that often trail downward in well-defined wisps are called "mares tails." *Cirrostratus* is a thin, white cloud layer that resembles a veil or sheet. This layer can be striated or fibrous. Because of their ice content, these clouds are associated with the halos that surround the sun or moon. *Cirrocumulus* are thin clouds that appear as small white flakes or cotton patches and may contain super-cooled water.

Middle Clouds are composed primarily of water. The height of the cloud bases range from 6,500 to 23,000 feet (1,983 to 7,015 meters). *Altostratus* appears as a bluish or grayish veil or layer of clouds that can gradually merge into altocumulus clouds. The sun may be dimly visible through it, but flat, thick sheets of this cloud type can obscure the sun. *Altocumulus* is a white or gray layer or patches of solid clouds with rounded shapes.

Low Clouds are composed almost entirely of water that may at times be super-cooled; at subfreezing temperatures, snow and ice crystals may be present as well. The bases of these clouds start near the earth's surface and climb to 6,500 feet (1,982 meters) in the middle latitudes. *Stratus* are gray uniform sheet-like clouds with a relatively low base or they can be patchy, shapeless, low gray clouds. Thin enough for the sun to shine through, these clouds bring drizzle and snow. *Stratocumulus* are globular rounded masses that form at the top of the layer. *Nimbostratus* are seen as a gray or dark relatively shapeless massive cloud layer containing rain, snow, and ice pellets.

Clouds with Vertical Development contain super-cooled water above the freezing level and grow to great heights. The cloud bases range from 1,000 feet (305 meters) to 10,000 feet (3,020 meters). *Cumulus* are detached, fair weather clouds with relatively flat bases and dome-shaped tops. These usually do not have extensive vertical development and do not produce precipitation. *Cumulonimbus* are unstable large vertical clouds with dense boiling tops that bring showers, hail, thunder, and lightning.

C. Donald Ahrens, *Meteorology Today* (New York: Grossett & Dunlap, 1978), 164. Frank E. Bair, *The Weather Almanac, 6th ed.* (Detroit: Gale Research, 1992), 289-94.

How hot is lightning?

The temperature of the air around a bolt of lightning is about 54,000 Fahrenheit (30,000 Celsius), which is six times hotter than the surface of the sun, yet many times people survive a bolt of lightning. American park ranger Roy Sullivan was hit by lightning seven times between 1942 and 1977. In cloud-to-ground lightning, its energy seeks the shortest route to earth, which could be through a person's shoulder, down the side of the body through the leg to the ground. As long as the lightning does not pass across the heart or spinal column, the victim usually does not die.

How in the World (Pleasantville, NY: Reader's Digest Association, 1990), 298. Frank N. Magill, *Magill's Survey of Science: Earth Science Series* (Englewood Cliffs, NJ: Salem Press, 1990), 3:1374.

Does lightning ever strike in the same place?

It is not true that lightning does not strike twice in the same place. In fact, tall buildings, such as the Empire State Building in New York City, can be struck several times during the same storm. For instance, during one storm, lightning struck the Empire State Building 12 times.

Barbara Tufty, *1001 Questions Answered About Hurricanes, Tornadoes, and Other Natural Air Disasters* (New York: Dover, 1987), 126.

How long is a lightning stroke?

The visible length of the streak of lightning depends on the terrain and can vary greatly. In mountainous areas where clouds are low, the flash can be as short as 300 yards (174 meters); whereas in flat terrain, where clouds are high, the bolt can measure as long as 4 miles (6.5 kilometers). The usual length is about 1 mile (1.6 kilometers), but streaks of lightning up to 20 miles (32 kilometers) have been recorded. The stroke channel is very narrow-perhaps as little as -inch (1.3 centimeters). It is surrounded by a "corona envelope" or a glowing discharge that can be as wide as 10 to 20 feet (3 to 6 meters) in diameter. The speed of lightning can vary from 100 to 1,000 miles (161 to 1,609 kilometers) per second for the downward leader track; the return stroke is 87,000 miles (139,983 kilometers) per second (almost half the speed of light).

Guinness Book of Records 1992 (New York: Bantam Books, 1992), 43.

What is the order of colors in a rainbow?

Red, orange, yellow, blue, indigo, and violet are the colors of the rainbow, but these are not necessarily the sequence of colors that an observer might see. Rainbows are formed when raindrops reflect sunlight. As sunlight enters the drops, the different wavelengths of the colors that compose sunlight are refracted at different lengths to produce a spectrum of color. Each observer sees a different set of raindrops at a slightly different angle. Drops at different angles from the observer send different wave lengths (i.e., different color) to the observer's eyes. Since the color sequence of the rainbow is the result of refraction, the color order depends on the viewer's angle of perception.

Vincent J. Schaefer and John A. Day, *A Field Guide to the Atmosphere* (Boston: Houghton Mifflin, 1981), 163. *World Book Encyclopedia* (Chicago: World Book, 1990), 16:130.

When does frost form?

A frost is a crystalline deposit of small thin ice crystals formed on objects that are at freezing or below freezing temperatures. This phenomenon occurs when atmospheric water vapor condenses directly into ice without first becoming a liquid; this process is called sublimation. Usually frost appears on clear, calm nights especially during early autumn when the air above the earth is quite moist. A light frost damages only the most tender plants and vines, whereas a heavy frost (a heavy deposit of crystallized water) might kill plants that were not sturdy. A killing frost may do that to sturdy plants. Black frost (or hard frost) occurs in late autumn when both objects and air are at temperatures below freezing. Leaf edges and leaf tips turn black from this frost. Hoar or hoarfrost is the term for frost in Europe. Finally, permafrost is ground permanently frozen that never thaws out completely.

Barbara Tufty, *1001 Questions Answered About Hurricanes, Tornadoes, and Other Natural Air Disasters* (New York: Dover, 1987), 276-78.

Where is the rainiest place on earth?

The wettest place in the world is Tutunendo, Colombia, with an average annual rainfall of 467.5 inches per year. With 56 inches of rain annually, the wettest state is Louisiana. The place that has the most rainy days per year is Mount Wai-'ale'ale on Kauai, Hawaii. It has up to 350 rainy days annually.

In contrast the longest rainless period in the world was from October 1903 to January 1918 at Arica, Chile-a period of 14 years. In the United States the longest dry spell was 767 days at Bagdad, California, from October 3, 1912, to November 8, 1914. The longest drought occurred in Chile's Atacama Desert, which went without water from 1570-1971 -401 years. In the United States the longest drought of 57 months occurred in Western Kansas, lasting from May of 1952 to March of 1957.

Mark Young, ed., *Guinness Book of Records 1995* (New York: Facts On File, 1994), 44. Jack Williams, *The Weather Book* (New York: Vintage Books, 1992), 89. John W. Wright, ed., *The Universal Almanac 1991* (Kansas City, MO: Andrews and McMeel, 1991), 317.

How does dew form?

At night, as the temperature of the air falls, the amount of water vapor the air can hold also decreases. Excess water vapor then condenses as very small drops on whatever it touches.

Richard Bamberger, *Physics Through Experiment* (New York: Sterling, 1969), 104.

How large can hailstones become?

The average hailstone is about inch (0.63 centimeters) in diameter. However, hailstones weighing up to seven and a half pounds (3.4 kilograms) are reported to have fallen in Hyderabad state in India in 1939, although scientists think these huge hailstones may be several stones that partly melted and stuck together. On April 14, 1986, hailstones weighing two and a half pounds (one kilogram) were reported to have fallen in the Gopalgang district of Bangladesh.

The largest hailstone ever recorded in the United States fell in Coffeyville, Kansas on September 3, 1970. It measured 5.57 inches (14.1 centimeters) in diameter and weighed 1.67 pounds (0.75 kilograms).

Hail is precipitation consisting of balls of ice. Hailstones usually are made of concentric, or onion-like, layers of ice alternating with partially melted and refrozen snow, structured around a tiny central core. It is formed in cumulonimbus or thunderclouds when freezing water and ice cling to small particles in the air, such as dust. The winds in the cloud blow the particles through zones of different temperatures causing them to accumulate additional layers of ice and melting snow and to increase in size.

Louis J. Battan, *Weather in Your Life* (New York: W. H. Freeman, 1983), 56-57. Barbara Tufty, *1001 Questions Answered About Hurricanes, Tornados, and Other Natural Air Disasters* (New York: Dover, 1987), 151-53.

Are all snowflakes shaped alike?

Although no two snowflakes are identical, they all have six sides or six prongs. The many forms that a snow crystal can have are explained by the number of water molecules involved and the different ways that the molecules can arrange themselves in a three-dimensional hexagonal pattern. Temperature may be the key to the crystal's shape-flat, plate-like forms, long columnlike forms or prismlike forms. Snow crystals are classified into ten categories in the International Snow Classification. Half are symmetrical and include plates, stellars, columns, needles, and capped columns. Columns and capped columns occur at temperatures colder than 12 Fahrenheit (-10 Celsius). Needles occur at the warmest temperatures. Plates and stellars, the most beautiful of the snow crystals, are rare and occur under special weather conditions. Very plentiful are the asymmetrical snow crystals, the spatial dendrites (three-dimensional irregular stellar-or plate-like crystals occurring in high-moisture clouds) and the irregular crystals (ice prisms called diamond dust).

James Berry, *Exploring Crystals* (New York: Crowell-Collier Press, 1969), 7. Vincent J. Schaefer and John A. Day, *A Field Guide to the Atmosphere* (Boston: Houghton Mifflin, 1981), 246-47. Jack Williams, *The Weather Book* (New York: Vintage Books, 1992), 98-100.

Is it ever too cold to snow?

No matter how cold the air gets, there is still some moisture in it, and this can fall out of the air in the form of very small snow crystals. Very cold air is associated with no snow because these invasions of air from northerly latitudes are associated with clearing conditions behind cold fronts. Heavy snowfalls are associated with relatively mild air in advance of a warm front. The fact that snow piles up, year after year, in Arctic regions illustrates that it is never too cold to snow.

Frank Forrester, *1001 Questions Answered About the Weather* (New York: Grosset & Dunlap, 1957), 286. Ti Sanders, *Weather* (South Bend, IN: Icarus Press, 1985), 165.

How much water is there in an inch of snow?

On the average ten inches (25 centimeters) of snow is equal to one inch (2.5 centimeters) of water. Heavy, wet snow has a high water content; four to five inches (10 to 12.5 centimeters) may contain one inch (2.5 centimeters) of water. A dry, powdery snow might require 15 inches (37.5 centimeters) of snow to equal one inch (2.5 centimeters) of water.

Mineral Information Service September 1970.

How far away can thunder be heard?

Thunder is the crash and rumble associated with lightning. It is caused by the explosive expansion and contraction of air heated by the stroke of lightning. This results in sound waves that can be heard easily six to seven miles (9.7 to 11.3 kilometers) away. Occasionally such rumbles can be heard as far away as 20 miles (32.1 kilometers). The sound of great claps of thunder are produced when intense heat and the ionizing effect of repeated lightning occurs in a previously heated air path. This creates a shock wave that moves at the speed of sound.

Barbara Tufty, *1001 Questions Answered About Hurricanes, Tornadoes, and Other Natural Air Disasters* (New York: Dover, 1987), 132.

How can the temperature be determined from the frequency of cricket chirps?

Count the number of cricket chirps in 14 seconds and add 40.

Nature and Science 4 April 1966.

What are the highest and lowest recorded temperatures on earth?

The highest temperature in the world was recorded as 136 degrees Fahrenheit (58 degrees Celsius) at Al Aziziyah (el-Azizia), Libya, on September 13, 1922. The highest temperature recorded in the United States was 134 degrees Fahrenheit (56.7 degrees Celsius) in Death Valley, California, on July 10, 1913. The lowest temperature was -128.6 degrees Fahrenheit (-89.6 degrees Celsius) at Vostok Station in Antarctica on July 21, 1983. The record cold temperature for an inhabited area was -90.4 degrees Fahrenheit officially and 98 degrees unofficially (-68 degrees Celsius) at Oymyakon, Siberia (population 4,000), on February 6, 1933. The lowest temperature reading in the United States was -79.8 degrees Fahrenheit (-62.1 degrees Celsius) on January 23, 1971 in Prospect Creek, Alaska; for the contiguous 48 states, the coldest temperature was -69.7 degrees Fahrenheit (-56.5 degrees Celsius) at Rogers Pass, Montana, on January 20, 1954.

Mark Young, ed., *Guinness Book of Records 1995* (New York: Facts On File, 1994), 69, 71.

What is nowcasting?

Nowcasting is a form of very short-range weather forecasting. The term is sometimes used loosely to refer to any area-specific forecast for the period up to twelve hours ahead that is based on very detailed observational data. However, nowcasting should probably be defined more restrictively as the detailed description of the current weather along with extrapolated forecasts for the next few hours.

McGraw-Hill Encyclopedia of Science and Technology, 7th ed. (New York: McGraw-Hill, 1992), 12:116.

What is barometric pressure and what does it mean?

Barometric, or atmospheric, pressure is the force exerted on a surface by the weight of the air above that surface, as measured by an instrument called a barometer. Pressure is greater at lower levels because the air's molecules are squeezed by the weight of the air above. So while the average air pressure at sea level is 14.7 pounds per square inch, at one thousand feet above sea level, the pressure drops to 14.1 pounds per square inch, and at 18,000 feet the pressure is 7.3 pounds, about half of the figure at sea level. Changes in air pressure bring weather changes. High-pressure areas bring clear skies and fair weather, low pressure areas bring wet or stormy weather. Areas of very low-pressure have serious storms, such as hurricanes.

Sally Lee, *Predicting Violent Storms* (New York: Franklin Watts, 1989), 16-17. Barbara Tufty, *1001 Questions Answered About Hurricanes, Tornadoes, and Other Natural Air Disasters* (New York: Dover, 1987), 316. Jack Williams, *The Weather Book* (New York: Vintage Books, 1992), 30.

When did weather forecasting begin?

On May 14, 1692, a weekly *A Collection for the Improvement of Husbandry and Trade*, gave a seven-day table with pressure and wind readings for the comparable dates of the previous year. Readers were expected to make up their own forecasts from the data. Other journals soon followed with their own weather features. In 1771, a new journal, called the *Monthly Weather Paper*, was completely devoted to weather prediction. In 1861, the British Meteorological Office began issuing daily weather forecasts. The first broadcast of weather forecasts was done by the University of Wisconsin's station 9XM at Madison, Wisconsin on January 3, 1921.

Patrick Robertson, *The Book of Firsts* (New York: Clarkson N. Potter, 1974), 200.

Why are the horse latitudes called by that name?

The horse latitudes are two high-pressure belts characterized by low winds about 30 degrees north and south of the equator. Dreaded by early sailors, these subtropical atmospheric belt areas have undependable winds with periods of calm. In the northern hemisphere, particularly near Bermuda, sailing ships carrying horses from Spain to the New World were often becalmed. When water supplies ran low, these animals were the first to be rationed water. Dying from thirst or tossed overboard, the animals were sacrificed to conserve water for the men. Explorers and sailors reported that the seas were "strewn with bodies of horses." This may be why the areas are called the horse latitudes. The term might also be rooted in the complaints by sailors who were paid in advance and received no overtime when the ships slowly transversed this area. During this time they are said to be "working off a dead horse."

Encyclopedic Dictionary of Science (New York: Facts on File, 1988), 121. Jeff Rovin, *Laws of Order* (New York: Ballantine, 1992), 87. Barbara Tufty, *1001 Questions Answered About Hurricanes, Tornadoes, and Other Natural Disasters* (New York: Dover, 1987), 189-90.

Who is associated with developing the concept of wind chill?

The Antarctic explorer Paul A. Siple coined the term in his dissertation "Adaptation of the Explorer to the Climate of Antarctica," (1939). Siple was the youngest member of Admiral Byrd's Antarctica expedition in 1928-1930, and later made other trips to the Antarctic as part of Byrd's staff and for the U.S. Department of the Interior assigned to the U.S. Antarctic Expedition. He also served in many other endeavors related to the study of cold climates.

Weatherwise December 1981. *Who Was Who in American History: Science and Technology* (Wilmette, IL: Marquis Who's Who, 1976), 557.

How does a cyclone differ from a hurricane or a tornado?

All three wind phenomena are rotating winds that spiral in toward a low-pressure center as well as upward. Their differences lie in their size, wind velocity, rate of travel, and duration. Generally, the faster the winds spin, the shorter (in time) and smaller (in size) the event becomes.

A cyclone has rotating winds from 10 to 60 miles (16 to 97 kilometers) per hour can be up to 1,000 miles (1,609 kilometers) in diameter, travels about 25 miles (40 kilometers per hour, and lasts from one to several weeks. A hurricane (or typhoon, as it is called in the Pacific Ocean area) has winds that vary from 75 to 200 miles (121 to 322 kilometers) per hour, moves between 10 to 20 miles (16 to 32 kilometers) per hour, can have a diameter up to 600 miles (965 kilometers), and can exist from several days to more than a week. A tornado can reach a rotating speed of 300 miles (423 kilometers) per hour, travels between 25 to 40 miles (40 to 64 kilometers) per hour and generally lasts only minutes, although some have lasted for five to six hours. Its diameter can range from 300 yards (274 meters) to one mile (1.6 kilometers) and its average path length is 16 miles (26 kilometers), with a maximum of 300 miles (483 kilometers).

Typhoons, hurricanes, and cyclones tend to breed in low-altitude belts over the oceans generally from five degrees to fifteen degrees latitude north or south. A tornado generally forms several thousand feet above the earth's surface usually during warm, humid weather; many times it is in conjunction with a thunderstorm. Although a tornado can occur in many places, the continental plains of North America (i.e., from the Plains States eastward to western New York and the southeastern Atlantic states) is where most tornadoes happen. Eighty-two percent of them materialize during the warmest hours of the day (noon to midnight) with 23 percent of all tornado activity taking place between 4 p.m. and 6 p.m.

Vincent J. Schafer and John Day, *A Field Guide to the Atmosphere* (Boston: Houghton Mifflin, 1981), 198. Barbara Tufty, *1001 Questions Answered About Hurricanes, Tornadoes, and Other Natural Disasters* (New York: Dover, 1987), 58-60.

Which states have never experienced earthquakes?

Only the state of Wisconsin and the District of Columbia have never experienced an earthquake, although shocks from nearby states have been felt by residents in both areas.

Department of Commerce, National Oceanic and Atmospheric Administration, Department of the Interior, Geological Survey, *Earthquake History of the United States, rev. ed. reprinted with supplement* (1971-1980), (Washington, DC: Government Printing Office, 1982), 191-207. Department of the Interior, Geological Survey, *Seismicity of the United States, 1568-1989, rev. ed.* (Washington, DC: Government Printing Office, 1993), 1.

What are the "Seven Seas"?

The "Seven Seas" refers to all the navigable waters of the world; for example, "sail the seven seas." Most believe the seven refers to the Arctic, Antarctic, North and South Pacific, North and South Atlantic, and Indian oceans. The phrase has been in existence, however, before all of these bodies of water were identified.

Philip Babcock Gove, ed., *Webster's Third New International Dictionary of the English Language Unabridged* (Springfield, MA: Merriam-Webster, 1986), s.v. "seven seas." *The World Book Encyclopedia* (Chicago: World Book, 1994), s.v. "seven seas."

How many times has Mt. Vesuvius erupted since 79 A.D.?

In 79 A.D. the 4,000-foot-high volcano Mt. Vesuvius near current day Naples, Italy, erupted, spewing ash, stones, and noxious gases over the cities of Pompeii and Herculaneum. Many residents were caught by surprise and buried alive under tons of hot ash, cinders, and stone. Others were killed by the poisonous fumes. Over 16,000 people were killed.

Mt. Vesuvius is one of the world's most active volcanoes and has erupted many times since 79 A.D. Mt. Vesuvius has erupted in 203 A.D.; 472 A.D.; 512 A.D.; 685 A.D.; 993 A.D.; 1036; 1049; 1139; 1198; 1302; 1306; 1500; 1538; 1631; 1707; 1737; 1760; 1766; 1779; 1793-94; 1822; 1855; 1872; 1879; 1900; 1903; 1905-06; 1929; and 1944.

Jay Robert Nash, *Darkest Hours* (Chicago: Nelson-Hall, 1976), s.v. "Vesuvius."

What is the climate of Finland?

Since one third of Finland lies within the Arctic Circle, temperatures in the far north range from a general low of -22 degrees Fahrenheit (-30 degrees Celsius) to the high of 81 degrees Fahrenheit (27 degrees Celsius). In the southern part of the country, temperature variations are less marked.

Europe's Business Cities of The Economist Business Traveller's Guides (New York: Prentice Hall, 1989), 42.

What was the Washoe zephyr?

The Washoe zephyr was an imaginary wind of great force that became part of the nineteenth-century folklore of the American West. The Washoe zephyr was raised from local to national consciousness in the 1870s when American author Mark Twain wrote about it in his book on Washoe, the early popular name for western Nevada.

Richard G. Lillard, "Evolution of the Washoe Zephyr," *American Speech* December 1943.

What is the earth's axis?

The earth's axis is an imaginary line running through the center of the earth and joining North and South Pole. The earth rotates on its axis once every 24 hours and its inclination is fixed at 66-degrees to the plane of the earth's orbit.

W. G. Moore, *A Dictionary Of Geography, rev. ed.* (New York: Frederick A. Praeger, 1967), s.v. "axis, earth's."

What has traditionally been the only source of water for the city of San Antonio?

San Antonio, Texas, has always relied on the Edwards Aquifer as its sole water source. In 1993, however, the city received a court order from U.S. District judge Lucius Bunton to find other means of meeting its water needs. San Antonio had been pumping 250 million gallons of water from the aquifer each day. As a result, the ground water source was showing signs of overuse at two cold water springs that are fed by the aquifer. These springs are home to four endangered species: the fountain darter, the San Marcos gambusia fish, the Texas blind salamander, and Texas wild rice. The status of these species reflects the health of the Edwards Aquifer.

USA Today 12 August 1994.

What is the composition of the earth's atmosphere?

The earth's atmosphere, apart from water vapor and pollutants, is composed of 78 percent nitrogen, 20 percent oxygen, and less than one percent each of argon and carbon dioxide. There are also traces of hydrogen, neon, helium, krypton, xenon, methane, and ozone. The earth's original atmosphere was probably composed of ammonia and methane; 20 million years ago the air started to contain a broader variety of elements.

Richard P. Brennan, *Dictionary of Scientific Literacy* (New York: John Wiley & Sons, 1992), 18.

What is the density of dry air?

The density of dry air is 1.29 grams per liter at 32 degrees Fahrenheit (0 degrees Celsius) at average sea level. Average sea level, measured by the height of a column of mercury in a barometer, is 29.92 inches (760 millimeters).

Hawley's Condensed Chemical Dictionary, 11th ed. (New York: Van Nostrand Reinhold), 29.

How does a stalactite differ from a stalagmite?

A stalactite is a conical or cylindrical calcite formation hanging from a cave roof. It forms from the centuries-long buildup of mineral deposits resulting from the seepage of water from the limestone rock above the cave. This water containing calcium bicarbonate evaporates, losing some carbon dioxide, to deposit small quantities of calcium carbonate (carbonate of lime), which eventually forms a stalactite.

A stalagmite is a stone formation which develops upward from the cave floor and resembles an icicle upside down. Formed from water containing calcite which drips from the limestone walls and roof of the cave, it sometimes joins a stalactite to form a column.

Robert L. Bates and Julia A. Jackson, *Glossary of Geology, 3d ed.* (Alexandria, VA: American Geological Association, 1987), 640. L. Don Leet and Sheldon Judson, *Physical Geology, 4th ed.* (Englewood Cliffs, NJ: Prentice-Hall, 1971), 269-70.

How is speleothem defined?

Speleothem is a term given to those cave features that form after a cave itself has formed. They are secondary mineral deposits that are created by the solidification of fluids or from chemical solutions. These mineral deposits usually contain calcium carbonate or limestone, but gypsum or silica may also be found. Stalactites, stalagmites, soda straws, cave coral, boxwork and cave pearls are all types of speleothems.

Susan Mayhew and Anne Penny, *The Concise Oxford Dictionary of Geography* (New York: Oxford University Press, 1992), 28. Sharon H. Silverman, *Going Underground* (Philadelphia: Camino Books, 1991), 14-25.

How tall is a sand dune?

Dunes can range from three feet (one meter) to greater than 650 feet (200 meters) in height. Star dunes (having one central peaked mound with radiating ridges) can grow as high as 1,000 feet (300 meters).

McGraw-Hill Encyclopedia of Science and Technology, 7th ed. (New York: McGraw-Hill, 1992), 5: 433-34.

From what type of stone was Mount Rushmore National Monument carved?

Mount Rushmore National Monument was carved from granite. The monument, in the Black Hills of southwestern South Dakota, depicts the 60-foot-high (18-meter-high) faces of four U.S. presidents: George Washington, Thomas Jefferson, Abraham Lincoln, and Theodore Roosevelt. Sculptor Gutzon Borglum (1867-1941) designed the monument, but died before the completion of the project; his son, Lincoln, finished it. From 1927 to 1941, 360 people, mostly construction workers, drillers, and miners, "carved" the figures using dynamite.

How in the World (Pleasantville, NY: Reader's Digest Association, 1990), 362-64. Charles Panati, *Panati's Extraordinary Origins of Everyday Things* (New York: Perennial Library, 1987), 282-84. *The World Almanac and Book of Facts 1992* (New York: World Almanac, 1991), 646.

Do the continents move?

In 1912 a German geologist, Alfred Lothar Wegener (1880-1930), theorized that the continents had drifted or floated apart to their present locations and that once all the continents had been a single land mass near Antarctica, which is called *Pangaea* (from the Greek word meaning all-earth). Pangaea then broke apart some 200 million years ago into two major continents called Laurasia and Gondwanaland. These two continents continued drifting and separating until the continents evolved their present shapes and positions. Wegener's theory was discounted but it has since been found that the continents do move sideways (not drift) at an estimated 0.75 inch (1.9 centimeters) annually because of the action of plate tectonics. American geologist, William Maurice Ewing (1906-1974) and Harry Hammond Hess (1906-1969) proposed that the earth's crust is not a solid mass, but composed of eight major and seven minor plates that can move apart, slide by each other, collide, or override each other. Where these plates meet are major areas of mountain-building, earthquakes, and volcanoes.

Isaac Asimov, *Isaac Asimov's Guide to Earth and Space* (New York: Random House, 1991), 42-43. W.F. Byrum et al. , *Dictionary of the History of Science* (Princeton, NJ: Princeton University Press, 1985), 78. Cesare Emiliani, *Scientific Companion* (New York: Wiley Science Editions, 1988), 177-93, 203-5.

How thick is the ice that covers Antarctica?

The ice that covers Antarctica is 15,700 feet (4,785 meters) in depth at its thickest point. This is about ten times taller than the Sears Tower in Chicago, the world's tallest building. However, the average thickness is 7,100 feet (2,164 meters).

World Book Encyclopedia (Chicago: World Book, 1990), 1:530, 532.

Who is regarded as the father of American geology?

Born in Scotland, the American William Maclure (1763-1840) was a member of a commission set up to settle claims between the United States and France during 1803-1807. In 1809 he made a geographical chart of the United States in which the land areas were divided by rock types. In 1817 he revised and enlarged this map. Maclure wrote the first English language articles and books on United States geology.

Dictionary of Scientific Biography (New York: Charles Scribner's Sons, 1973), 8:615-17. *Encyclopedic Dictionary of Science* (New York: Facts on File, 1988), 155.

How much does the earth weigh?

Weight has no meaning outside of a gravity field, but the mass of the earth has been estimated at 6 sextillion, 588 quintillion short tons (6.6 sextillion short tons) or 5.97 x 1024 kilograms with the earth's mean density being 5.515 times that of water (the standard). This is calculated from using the parameters of an ellipsoid adopted by the International Astronomical Union in 1964 and recognized by the International Union of Geodesty and Geophysics in 1967 in which the area of the ellipsoid is 196,938,800 square miles.

Issac Asimov, *Asimov's Guide to the Earth and Space* (New York: Random House, 1991), 34-35. Cesare Emiliani, *The Scientific Companion* (New York: Wiley Science Editions, 1988), 167. Robert Famighetti, ed., *The World Almanac and Book of Facts, 1995* (Mahwah, NJ: World Almanac, 1994), 269.

Who invented the first earthquake detector?

The detector, invented by Zhang Heng (78-139 A.D.) around 132 A.D., was a copper domed urn with dragons' heads circling the outside, each containing a bronze ball. Inside the dome was suspended a pendulum that would swing when the earth shook, and knock a ball from the mouth of a dragon into the waiting open mouth of a bronze toad below. The ball made a loud noise and signaled the occurrence of an earthquake. Knowing which ball had been released, one could determine the direction of the earthquake's epicenter (the point on the earth's surface directly above the quake's point of origin).

Robert K. G. Temple, *The Genius of China* (New York: Simon & Schuster, 1986), 162-63. Barbara Tufty, *1001 Questions About Earthquakes, Avalanches, Floods, and Other Natural Disasters* (New York: Dover Publications, 1987), 44-45.

When did the most severe earthquake in American history occur?

The New Madrid earthquakes (a series of quakes starting on December 16, 1811 and lasting until March 1812) is considered to be the most severe earthquake event in United States history. It shook more than two-thirds of the United States and was felt in Canada. It changed the level of land by as much 20 feet, altered the course of the Mississippi River, and created new lakes, such as Lake St. Francis west of the Mississippi River and Reelfoot Lake in Tennessee. Because the area was so sparsely populated, there was no known loss of life.

Barbara J. Tufty, *1001 Questions Answered About Earthquakes, Avalanches, Floods, and Other Natural Disasters* (New York: Dover Publications, 1978), 9-10.

How does a seismograph work?

A seismograph is an instrument that records vibrations within the earth usually caused by earthquakes. A typical seismograph contains three supported pendulums that are connected to recorders, one pendulum records vertical movement, or waves; the other two, horizontal movements or waves. The first true seismograph was constructed by the Italian scientist Luigi Palmieri in 1855; the first accurate seismograph was developed in Japan in 1880 by the British geologist John Milne, who is often called the father of seismology.

When an earthquake occurs, the vibrations are recorded on moving tape. These three waves from a quake arrive at different times and by comparing the arrival times of the waves at different seismographs throughout the world, it is possible to determine exactly where the earthquake took place.

Frank H.T. Rhodes, *Geology* (New York: Golden Press, 1972), 126-27. Neil Schlager, ed., *How Products Are Made* (Detroit: Gale Research, 1994), 1:400.

Why is the sea blue?

There is no single explanation for the colors of the sea. What is seen depends in part on when and from where the sea is observed. Eminent authority can be found to support almost any explanation. Some explanations include absorption and scattering of light by pure water; suspended matter in sea water; the atmosphere; and color and brightness variations of the sky.

For example, one theory is that when sunlight hits seawater, part of the white light, composed of different wavelengths of various colors, is absorbed, and some of the wavelengths are scattered after colliding with the water molecules. In clear water, red and infrared light supposedly are greatly absorbed but blue is least absorbed, so that the blue wavelengths are reflected out of the water. This blue effect requires a minimum depth of ten feet (three meters) of water.

Craig F. Bohren, *Clouds in a Glass of Beer* (New York: Wiley, 1987), 155. David Feldman, *Why Do Clocks Run Clockwise and Other Imponderables* (New York: Harper Perennial, 1991), 213.

What causes waves in the ocean?

The most common cause of surface waves is air movement (the wind). Waves within the ocean can be caused by tides, interactions among waves, submarine earthquakes or volcanic activity, and atmospheric disturbances. Wave size depends on wind speed, wind duration, and the distance of water over which the wind blows. The longer the distance the wind travels over water, or the harder it blows, the higher the waves. As the wind blows over water it tries to drag the surface of the water with it. The surface cannot move as fast as air, so it rises. When it rises, gravity pulls the water back, carrying the falling water's momentum below the surface. Water pressure from below pushes this swell back up again. The tug of war between gravity and water pressure constitutes wave motion. Capillary waves are caused by breezes of less than two knots. At 13 knots the waves grow taller and faster than they grow longer, and their steepness cause them to break, forming whitecaps. For a whitecap to form, the wave height must be 1/7 the distance between wave crests.

Tidal waves are really seismic waves or tsunamis. A tsunami is a giant wave set in motion by a large earthquake occurring under or near the ocean which causes the ocean floor to shift vertically. This vertical shift pushes the water ahead of it and starts a tsunami. These are very long waves-100 to 200 miles (161 to 322 kilometers) with high speeds (500 miles, or 805 kilometers, per hour)-that, when approaching shallow water, can grow into a 100-foot-high (30.5-meter) wave as its wavelength is reduced abruptly. Ocean earthquakes below a magnitude of 6.5 on the Richter scale, and those that shift the sea floor only horizontally, do not produce these destructive waves.

Diagram Group, *Comparisons* (New York: St. Martin's Press, 1980), 187. Ira Flatow, *Rainbows, Curve Balls, and Other Wonders of the Natural World Explained* (New York: Harper & Row, 1988), 28-32. Don Groves, *The Ocean Book* (New York: Wiley, 1989), 29. Sally Lee, *Predicting Violent Storms* (New York: Franklin Watts, 1989), 99-100.

What is the world's highest waterfall?

Angel Falls, named after the explorer and bush pilot, Jimmy Angel, on the Carrao tributary in Venezuela is the highest waterfall in the world. It has a total height of approximately 3,212 feet (979 meters) with its longest unbroken drop being 2,648 feet (807 meters).

It is difficult to determine the height of a waterfall because many are composed of several sections rather than one straight drop. The highest waterfall in the United States is Yosemite Falls on a tributary of the Merced River in Yosemite National Park, California, with a total drop of 2425 feet (739 meters). There are three sections to the Yosemite Falls: Upper Yosemite is 1,430 feet (435 meters); Cascades (middle portion), 675 feet (205 meters); and Lower Yosemite, 320 feet (97 meters).

Tom Burnam, *Dictionary of Misinformation* (New York: Perennial Library, 1986), 8. Clive Carpenter, ed., *The Guinness Book of Answers, 8th ed.* (Enfield, England: Guinness, 1991), 83. Mark C. Young, ed., *The Guinness Book of Records 1995* (New York: Facts on File, 1994), 64. Otto Johnson, ed., *1995 Information Please Almanac* (Boston: Houghton Mifflin, 1994), 488-89.

What is a tidal bore?

Tide bore is a wave which moves inland or upriver as the incoming tidal current surges against the flow of river water. A tidal bore occurs in a river that flows into an estuary or in a long narrow estuary—the area of a river mouth that empties into a sea and is affected by the ebb and flow of the tide.

Robert K. Barnhart, *The American Heritage Dictionary of Science* (Boston: Houghton Mifflin, 1986), 670. Susan Mayhew and Anne Penny *The Concise Oxford Dictionary of Geography* (New York: Oxford University Press, 1992), 78.

What causes the most forest fires in the U.S. western states?

Lightning is the single largest cause of forest fires in the U.S. western states.

The Odds on Virtually Everything (New York: G. P. Putnam's Sons, 1980), 181.

How harmful are balloon releases?

Both latex and metallic balloons can be harmful. A latex balloon can land in water, lose its color, and resemble a jellyfish, which if eaten by sea animals can cause their death because they cannot digest it. A metal balloon can get caught in electric wires and cause power outages.

50 Simple Things You Can Do to Save the Earth (Berkeley, CA: Earth Works Press, 1989), 58.

What was the world's greatest fraud?

Piltdown, the name given to the remains of a supposed prehistoric man, was "discovered" in a gravel formation at Piltdown Commons, near Lewes, in southern England in 1912. The unknown person combined an ape jaw with skull fragments of a modern man so skillfully that scientists argued over Piltdown for about 40 years. The forger filed the teeth in the ape jaw to give them the appearance of a human wear pattern. Many anatomists of the day accepted Piltdown as a primitive form of man but chemical investigations during the 1950s showed the cranium and jaw were of different ages.

Charles J. Cazeau, *Science Trivia* (New York: Berkley Books, 1986), 167. *The New Encyclopaedia Britannica, 15th ed.* (Chicago: Encyclopaedia Britannica, 1989), s.v. "Piltdown."

What is a nuclear winter?

The phrase "nuclear winter" was coined by American physicist Richard P. Turco in a 1983 article in the journal *Science*, in which he describes a hypothetical post-nuclear war scenario having severe world-wide climatic changes: prolonged periods of darkness, below-freezing temperatures, violent windstorms, and persistent radioactive fallout. This would be caused by billions of tons of dust, soot, and ash being tossed into the atmosphere, accompanied by smoke and poisonous fumes from firestorms. In the case of a severe nuclear war, within a few days, the entire northern hemisphere would be under a blanket so thick that as little as one tenth of one percent of available sunlight would reach the earth. Without sunlight, temperatures would drop well below freezing for a year or longer, causing dire consequences for all plant and animal life on earth.

Reaction to this doomsday prediction lead critics to coin the term "nuclear autumn," which downplayed such climatic effects and casualties. In January 1990, the release of *Climate and Smoke: An Appraisal of Nuclear Winter*, based on five years of laboratory studies and field experiments, reinforced the original 1983 conclusions.

Sheikh R. Ali, *The Peace and Nuclear War Dictionary* (Santa Barbara, CA: ABC-Clio, 1989), 202-03. Richard P. Brennan, *Dictionary of Scientific Liter-*

acy (New York: John Wiley & Sons, 1992), 220-21. Gene B. Williams, *Nuclear War, Nuclear Winter* (New York: Franklin Watts, 1987), 11-14.

Which countries have uranium deposits?

Uranium, a radioactive metallic element, is the only natural material capable of sustaining nuclear fission. But only one isotope, uranium-235, which occurs in one molecule out of 40 of natural uranium, can undergo fission under neutron bombardment. Mined in various parts of the world, it must then be converted during purification to uranium dioxide. Uranium deposits occur throughout the world. The United States (especially Arizona, Colorado, New Mexico, North Carolina, and Utah), Canada, France, South Africa, Zaire, Australia, and the former Soviet Union have significant uranium resources. Canada and Zaire provide the best sources.

Eva Fejer and Cecilia Fitzsimons, *An Instant Guide to Rocks and Minerals* (Stamford, CT: Longmeadow Press, 1988), 54. *Hawley's Condensed Chemical Dictionary, 11th ed.* (New York: Van Nostrand Reinhold, 1987), 1207. *Oxford Illustrated Encyclopedia of Invention and Technology* (Oxford: Oxford University Press, 1992), 369.

What is diatomite?

Diatomite (also called diatomaceous earth) is a white or cream-colored, friable, porous rock composed of the fossil remains of diatoms (small water plants with silica cell walls). These fossils build up on the ocean bottoms to form diatomite, and in some places, these areas have become dry land or diatomacceous earth. Chemically inert and having a rough texture and other unusual physical properties, it is suitable for many scientific and industrial purposes, including use as a filtering agent; building material; heat, cold, and sound insulator; catalyst carrier; filler absorbent; abrasive; and ingredient in pharmaceutical preparations. Dynamite is made from it by soaking it in the liquid explosive nitroglycerin.

Robert K. Barnhart, *American Heritage Dictionary of Science* (Boston: Houghton Mifflin, 1986), 161. Sybil P. Parker, *McGraw-Hill Concise Encyclopedia of Science & Technology, 2d ed.* (New York: McGraw-Hill, 1989), 574.

Other than the Cullinan Diamond, what are the largest precious stones?

The largest ruby is a 8,500 carat stone that is 5-inches (14 centimeters) tall, carved to resemble the Liberty Bell. The largest star ruby is the 6,465 carat "Eminent Star" from India which has a six-line star. The largest cut emerald, of 86,136 carats, was found in Carnaiba, Brazil, in August 1974. A 2,302 carat sapphire from Anakie, Queensland, Australia, was carved into a 1,318 carat head of Abraham Lincoln, making it the largest carved sapphire. "The Lone Star," at 9,719.5 carats, is the largest star sapphire. The largest natural pearl is the "Pearl of Laotze," also called the "Pearl of Allah." Found in May 1934 in the shell of a giant clam at Palawan, Philippines, the pearl weighs 14 pounds, 1 ounce (6.38 kilograms).

Guinness Book of Records 1992 (New York: Bantam Books, 1992), 48-50. Mark C. Young, ed. *The Guinness Book of Records 1995* (New York: Facts On File, 1994), 61.

How can a genuine diamond be identified?

There are several tests that can be performed without the aid of tools. A knowledgeable person can recognize the surface luster, straightness and flatness of facets, and high light reflectivity. Diamonds become warm in a warm room and cool if the surroundings are cool. A simple test that can be done is exposing the stones to warmth and cold and then touching them to one's lips to determine their appropriate temperature. This is especially effective when the results of this test are compared to the results of the test done on a diamond known to be genuine. Another test is to pick up the stone with a moistened fingertip. If this can be done, then the stone is likely to be a diamond. The majority of other stones cannot be picked up in this way.

The water test is another simple test. A drop of water is placed on a table. A perfectly clean diamond has the ability to almost "magnetize" water and will keep the water from spreading. An instrument called a diamond probe can detect even the most sophisticated fakes. Gemologists always use this as part of their inspection.

Marc Hudgeons, *The Official Investors Guide* (Orlando, FL: House of Collectibles, 1981), 166-67.

How does the emerald get its color?

Emerald is a variety of green beryl that is colored by a trace of chromium (Cr), which replaces the aluminum (Al) in the beryl structure. Other green beryls exist; but if no chromium is present, they are, technically speaking, not emeralds.

Joel E. Arem, *Color Encyclopedia of Gemstones* 2d ed. (New York: Van Nostrand Reinhold), 1987, 51-52.

How do rocks differ?

Rocks can be conveniently placed into three groups-igneous, sedimentary, and metamorphic.

Igneous rocks, such as granite, pegmatite, rhyolite, obsidian, gabbro, and basalt, are formed by the solidification of molten magma that emerges through the earth's crust via volcanic activity. The nature and properties of the crystals vary greatly, depending in part on the composition of the original magma and partly on the conditions under which the magma solidified. There are thousands of different igneous rock types. For example, granite is formed by slow cooling of molten material (within the earth). It has large crystals of quartz, feldspars, and mica.

Sedimentary rocks, such as brecchia, sandstone, shale, limestone, chert, and coals, are produced by the accumulation of sediments. These are fine rock particles or fragments, skeletons of microscopic organisms, or minerals leached from rocks that have accumulated from weathering. These sediments are redeposited under water, and are then compressed in layers over time. The most common sedimentary rock is sandstone, which is predominantly quartz crystals.

Metamorphic rocks, such as marble, slate, schist, gneiss, quartzite, and hornsfel, are formed by the alteration of igneous and sedimentary rocks through heat and/or pressure. These transformations are exemplified by marble which is formed by thermal changes occurring in limestone.

Eva Fejer and Cecilia Fitzsimons, *An Instant Guide to Rocks and Minerals* (Stamford, CT: Longmeadow Press, 1988), 16-43. W.R. Hamilton, *The Henry Holt Guide to Minerals, Rocks and Fossils* (New York: Henry Holt, 1989), 146.

Who was the first person to attempt a color standardization scheme for minerals?

The German mineralogist Abraham Gottlob Werner (1750-1817) devised a method of describing minerals by their external characteristics, including color. He worked out an arrangement of colors and color names, illustrated by an actual set of minerals.

A. Maerz, *A Dictionary of Color, 2d ed.* (New York: McGraw-Hill, 1950), 137.

How does a rock differ from a mineral?

Mineralogists use the term mineral for a substance that has all four of the following features: it must be found in nature; it must be made up of substances that were never alive (organic); it has the same chemical makeup wherever it is found; and its atoms are arranged in a regular pattern and form solid crystals.

While rocks are sometimes described as an aggregate or combination of one or more minerals, geologists extend the definition to include clay, loose sand and certain limestones.

American Geological Institute, *Dictionary of Geological Terms, rev. ed.*, (Garden City, NY: Anchor Press, 1976), 282, 369. Robert K. Barnhart, *The American Heritage Dictionary of Science* (Boston: Houghton Mifflin, 1986), 566.

What is pitchblende?

Pitchblende is a massive variety of uraninite or uranium oxide found in metallic veins. The most important ore of uranium and a radioactive material, pitchblende is the original source of radium.

The American Geological Institute, *Dictionary of Geological Terms, rev. ed.* (Garden City, NY: Anchor Press, 1976), 450. *Hawley's Condensed Chemical Dictionary, 11th ed.* (New York: Van Nostrand Rinehold, 1987), 923.

What is stibnite?

Stibnite is a lead-gray mineral with a metallic luster. It is the most important ore of antimony, and is also known as antimony glance. One of the few minerals that fuses easily in the match flame (977 degrees Fahrenheit or 525 degrees Celsius), stibnite has the hardness of 2 on the Mohs scale and a specific gravity of 4.5-4.6. It is commonly found in hydrothermal veins or hot springs deposits. Stibnite is mined in Germany, Rumania, France, Bolivia, Peru, and Mexico. The Yellow Pine mine at Stibnite, Idaho, is the largest producer in the United States, but California and Nevada also have deposits.

Sybil P. Parker, *McGraw-Hill Concise Encyclopedia of Science and Technology, 2. ed.* (New York: McGraw-Hill, 1989), 1788. Stella E. Stiegeler, *A Dictionary of Earth Sciences* (London: Pan Books, 1978), 263. Paul W. Thrush, *Dictionary of Mining, Mineral, and Related Terms* (Washington, DC: U.S. Bureau of Mines, 1968), 1077.

What is Saint Elmo's fire?

Saint Elmo's fire has been described as a corona from electric discharge produced on high grounded metal objects, chimney tops, and ship masts. Since it often occurs during thunderstorms, the electrical source may be lightning. Another description refers to this phenomenon as weak static electricity formed when an electrified cloud touches a high exposed point. Molecules of gas in the air around this point become ionized and glow. The name originated with sailors who were among the first to witness the display of spearlike or tufted flames on the tops of their ships' masts. Saint Elmo (which is a corruption of Saint Ermo) is the patron saint of sailors, so they named the fire after him.

Frank Forrester, *1001 Questions Answered About the Weather* (New York: Grosset & Dunlap, 1957), 182-83. Vincent J. Schaefer and John A. Day, *A Field Guide to the Atmosphere* (Boston: Houghton Mifflin, 1981), 196

What are fulgurites?

Fulgurites (from the Latin word "fulgur," meaning lightning) are petrified lightning, created when lightning strikes an area of dry sand. The intense heat of the lightning melts the sand surrounding the stroke into a rough glassy tube forming a fused record of its path. These tubes may be one-half to two inches (one and a half to five centimeters) in diameter, and up to ten feet (three meters) in length. They are extremely brittle and break easily. The inside walls of the tube are glassy and lustrous while the outside is rough, with sand particles adhering to it. Fulgurites are usually tan or black in color, but translucent white ones have been found.

New Encyclopaedia Britannica, 15th ed. (Chicago: Encyclopaedia Britannica, 1990), 5:43. Barbara Tufty, *1001 Questions Answered About Hurricanes, Tornadoes and Other Natural Air Disasters* (New York: Dover, 1987), 128-29.

What color is lightning?

Lightning is often seen as white or white-yellow, although it may appear to have other colors depending on the background against which it is seen.

Frank Field, *Doctor Frank Field's Weather Book* (New York: Putnam, 1981), 201.

What is ball lightning?

Ball lightning is a rare form of lightning in which a persistent and moving luminous white or colored sphere is seen. It can last from a few seconds to several minutes, and travels at about a walking pace. Spheres have been reported to vanish harmlessly, or to pass into or out of rooms leaving, in some cases, sign of their passage such as a hole in a window pane. Sphere dimensions vary but are most commonly from four to eight inches (10 to 20 centimeters).

Other types of lightning include the common streak lightning (a single or multiple zigzagging line from cloud to ground); forked lightning (lightning formed two branches simultaneously); sheet lightning (a shapeless flash covering a broad area); ribbon lightning (streak lightning blown sideways by the wind to make it appear like parallel successive strokes); bead or chain lightning (a stroke interrupted or broken into evenly-spaced segments or beads); and heat lightning (lightning seen along the horizon during hot weather and believed to be a reflection of lightning occurring beyond the horizon).

Frank E. Bair, *The Weather Almanac, 6th ed.* (Detroit: Gale Research, 1992), 121. Great Britain Meteorological Office, *Meteorological Glossary* (New York: Chemical Publishing, 1972), 37.

How is the distance of a lightning flash calculated?

Count the number of seconds between seeing a flash of lightning and hearing the sound of the thunder. Divide the number by five to determine the number of miles away that the lightning flashed.

World Book Encyclopedia (Chicago: World Book, 1990), 19:272.

How many volts are in lightning?

A stroke of lightning discharges from 10 to 100 million volts of electricity. In an average lightning stroke there are 30 thousand amperes.

Barbara Tufty, *1001 Questions Answered About Hurricanes, Tornadoes, and Other Natural Air Disasters* (New York: Dover, 1987), 126.

What is the difference between freezing rain and sleet?

Freezing rain is rain that falls as a liquid but turns to ice on contact with a freezing object to form a smooth ice coating called "glaze." Usually freezing rain only lasts a short time, because it either turns to rain or to snow. Sleet is frozen or partially frozen rain in the form of ice pellets. Sleet forms as falling rain from a warm layer of air passes through a freezing air layer near the earth's surface to form hard, clear, tiny ice pellets that can hit the ground so fast that they bounce off with a sharp click.

Barbara Tufty, *1001 Questions Answered About Hurricanes, Tornadoes, and Other Natural Air Disasters* (New York: Dover, 1987), 275.

How fast can rain fall?

The speed of rainfall varies with drop size and wind speed. A typical raindrop in still air falls about 600 feet (183 meters) per minute or about seven miles (11 kilometers) per hour.

Frank Field, *Dr. Frank Field's Weather Book* (New York: Putnam, 1981), 196. Frank H. Forrester, *1001 Questions Answered About the Weather* (New York: Grosset & Dunlap, 1957), 53.

What is the shape of a raindrop?

Although a raindrop has been illustrated as being pear-shaped or tear-shaped, high-speed photographs reveal that a large raindrop has a spherical shape with a hole not quite through it (giving it a doughnut-like shape). Water surface tension pulls the drop into this shape. As a drop larger than 0.08 inches (two millimeters) in diameter falls, it will become distorted. Air pressure flattens its bottom and its sides bulge. If it becomes larger than 0.25 inches (6.4 millimeters) across, it will keep spreading crosswise as it falls and will bulge more at its sides, while at the same time, its middle will thin into a bow-tie shape. Eventually in its path downward, it will divide into two smaller spherical drops.

Barbara Tufty, *1001 Questions Answered About Hurricanes, Tornadoes, and Other Natural Disasters* (New York: Dover, 1987), 247. Jack Williams, *The Weather Book* (New York: Vintage Books, 1992), 63.

What causes exceptionally large snowflakes?

Giant snowflakes, four to six inches (10 to 15 centimeters) in diameter, have been verified. Large flakes are probably aggregations of smaller flakes created by collisions and/or electrostatic attraction.

William R. Corliss, *Tornadoes, Dark Days, Anomalous Precipitation, with Related Weather Phenomena* (Glen Arm, MD: Sourcebook Project, 1983), 99-100.

How does snow form?

Snow is not frozen rain. Snow forms by sublimation of water vapor (the turning of water vapor directly into ice, without going through the liquid stage). High above the ground, chilled water vapor turns to ice when its temperature reaches the dew point. The result of this sublimation is a crystal of ice. Snow begins in the form of these tiny hexagonal ice crystals in the high clouds. As water vapor is pumped up into the air by updrafts, more water is deposited on the ice crystals, causing them to grow. Soon some of the larger crystals fall to the ground as snowflakes.

Jerome Spar, *The Way of the Weather* (Mankato, MN: Creative Educational Society, 1967), 103.

What is the record for the greatest snowfall in the United States?

The record for the most snow in a single storm is 189 inches (480 centimeters) at Mount Shasta Ski Bowl in California from February 13-19, 1959. For the most snow in a 24-hour period, the record goes to Silver Lake, Colorado, on April 14-15, 1921, with 76 inches (193 centimeters) of snow. The year record goes to Paradise Ranger Station, Mount Rainier, in Washington with 1,224.5 inches (3,110 centimeters) from February 19, 1971, to February 18, 1972. The highest average annual snowfall was 241 inches (612 centimeters) for Blue Canyon, California. In March 1911, Tamarack, California, had the deepest snow accumulation-over 37.5 feet (11.4 meters).

Mark Young, ed., *Guinness Book of Records 1995* (New York: Facts on File, 1994),72. Russell Ash, *The Top Ten of Everything* (London: Dorling Kindersley, 1994), 27. *Information Please Almanac, Atlas & Yearbook 1995, 48th ed.* (Boston: Houghton-Mifflin, 1995), 395.

What would cause frogs and toads to fall from the sky like a rain shower?

Documented cases of showers of frogs have been recorded since 1794, usually during heavy summer rainstorms. Whirlwinds, waterspouts, and tornadoes are given as the conventional explanation. Extensive falls of fish, birds, and other animals have also been reported.

William R. Corliss, *Tornadoes, Dark Days, Anomalous Precipitation, with Related Weather Phenomena* (Glen Arm, MD: Sourcebook Project, 1983), 72-74.

When do thunderstorms occur?

In the United States, thunderstorms usually occur in the summertime, especially from May through August. Thunderstorms tend to occur in late spring and summer when large amounts of tropical maritime air move across the United States. Storms usually develop when the surface air is heated the most from the sun (2 to 4 p.m.). Thunderstorms are relatively rare in the New England area, North Dakota, Montana, and other northern states (latitude 60 degrees) where the air is often too cold. These storms are also rare along the Pacific Ocean, because the summers there are too dry for them to occur. Florida, the Gulf states, and the southeastern states tend to have the most storms, averaging 70 to 90 annually. The mountainous southwest averages 50 to 70 storms annually. In the world, thunderstorms are most plentiful in the areas between latitude 35 degrees north and 35 degrees south where there can be as many as 3,200 storms within a 12 hour nighttime period. There can be as many as 1,800 storms occurring at once throughout the world.

Lightning performs a vital function; it returns to the earth much of the negative charge the earth loses by leakage into the atmosphere. The annual death toll in the United States from lightning is greater than the annual death toll from tornadoes or hurricanes-150 Americans die annually from lightning and 250 are injured.

Guinness Book of Records 1992 (New York: Bantam Books, 1992), 46. Vincent J. Schaefer and John A. Day, *A Field Guide to the Atmosphere* (Boston: Houghton Mifflin, 1981), 196. Barbara Tufty, *1001 Questions Answered About Hurricanes, Tornadoes, and Other Natural Air Disasters* (New York: Dover, 1987), 115-17.

Why was 1816 known as the "year without a summer"?

In 1815, the eruption of Mount Tambora, a volcano in Indonesia, threw billions of cubic yards of dust over 15 miles into the atmosphere. Because the dust penetrated the stratosphere, wind currents spread it throughout the world. As a consequence of this volcanic activity, in 1816 normal weather patterns were greatly altered. The sun "arose each morning as though in a cloud of smoke, red and rayless, shedding little life or warmth." Some parts of Europe and the British Isles experienced average temperatures 2.9 degrees Fahrenheit to 5.8 degrees Fahrenheit (1.6 degrees Celsius to 3.2 degrees Celsius) below normal. In New England heavy snow fell between June 6 and June 11, the summer had ice and hail storms, and frost occurred every month of 1816. A Connecticut minister's diary tells of ice thick enough to stand on in Massachusetts, and a foot of snow in the Berkshires. Sheep froze to death. Unless a cornfield was near a source of water, its entire corn crop failed. An enterprising Vermont farmer saved his corn crop by burning fires that he and his men tended each night to ward off the frost. Crop failures were experienced in Western Europe and Canada as well as in New England. In 1817, the excess dust had settled and the climate returned to more normal conditions.

Eugene W. Miller, *Environmental Hazards; Air Pollution: A Reference Handbook* (Santa Barbara, CA: ABC-CLIO, 1989), 6.

Why are the hot humid days of summer called "dog days"?

This period of extremely hot, humid, sultry weather that traditionally occurs in the northern hemisphere around July 3 through August 11 received its name from Sirius, called the dog star, of the constellation Canis Major. At this time of year, Sirius, the brightest visible star, rises in the east at the same time as the sun. Ancient Egyptians believed that the heat of this brilliant star added to the sun's heat created this hot weather and named this period "dog days." Sirius was blamed for the withering droughts, sickness and discomfort that occurred during that year.

Barbara Tufty, *1001 Questions Answered About Hurricanes, Tornadoes, and Other Natural Air Disasters* (New York: Dover, 1987), 311-12.

Is a halo around the sun or moon a sign of rain or snow approaching?

The presence of a ring around the sun or, more commonly, the moon in the night sky betrays very high ice crystals composing cirrostratus clouds. The brighter the ring, the greater the odds of precipitation and the sooner it may be expected. Rain or snow will not always fall, but two times out of three, precipitation will start to fall within twelve to eighteen hours. These cirroform clouds are a forerunner of an approaching warm front and an associated low pressure system.

Ti Sanders, *Weather* (South Bend, IN: Icarus Press, 1985), 160.

Can weather be predicted from the stripes on a wooly-bear caterpillar?

It is an old superstition that the severity of the coming winter can be predicted by the width of the brown bands or stripes around the wooly-bear caterpillar in the autumn. According to the belief if the brown bands are wide, then the winter will be mild; but if the brown bands are narrow, a rough winter is ahead. Studies at the American Museum of Natural History in New York failed to verify any connection between the weather and the caterpillar's stripes. This belief has no basis in scientific fact.

Frank H. Forrester, *1001 Questions Answered About the Weather* (New York: Grosset & Dunlap, 1957), 281.

What are halcyon days?

This term is often used to describe a time of peace or prosperity. It is the two-week period of calm weather approximately before and after the shortest day of the year, about December 21. The phrase is derived from the halcyon-the name the ancient Greeks gave to the kingfisher, which would breed around the winter solstice (about December 21). According to legend, the halcyon built its nest on the ocean water and would charm the waves and quiet the winds while its eggs were hatching. Eighteenth-century poet William Shenstone described it thus,

> There came the halcyon, whom the sea obeys,
> When she her nest upon the water lays.

Leslie Dunkling, *A Dictionary of Days* (New York: Facts on File, 1988), s.v. "Halcyon days." *World Book Encyclopedia* (Chicago: World Book, 1990), 9:18.

What is meant by the wind chill factor?

The wind chill factor or wind chill index is a number, which expresses the cooling effect of moving air at different temperatures. It indicates in a general way how many calories of heat are carried away from the surface of the body.

Scientists have devised an equivalent temperature scale which makes it easy to determine the wind chill factor. The accompanying chart is used for that purpose. Find the wind speed in the column on the left and find the temperature reading in the horizontal row at the top. The intersection of these two points gives the corresponding wind chill factor. For example, a temperature of 10 Fahrenheit along with a wind speed of 29 to 32 miles per hour corresponds to a wind chill factor of -35 Fahrenheit

William Vergara, *Science in Everyday Life* (New York: Harper & Row, 1980), 168-69.

When was the jet stream discovered?

A jet stream is a flat and narrow tube of air that moves more rapidly than the surrounding air. Discovered by World War II bomber pilots flying over Japan and the Mediterranean Sea, jet streams have become important with the advent of airplanes capable of cruising at over 30,000 feet (9,144 meters). The currents of air flow from west to east and are usually a few miles deep, up to 100 miles (160 kilometers) wide and well over 1,000 miles (1,600 kilometers) in length. The air current must flow at over 57.5 miles (92 kilometers) per hour.

There are two polar jet streams, one in each hemisphere. They meander between 30 and 70 degrees latitude, occur at altitudes of 25,000 to 35,000 feet (7,620 to 10,668 meters), and achieve maximum speeds of over 230 miles (368 kilometers) per hour. The subtropical jet streams-again one per hemisphere-wander between 20 and 50 degrees latitude. They are found at altitudes of 30,000 to 45,000 feet (9,144 to 13,715 meters), and have speeds of over 345 miles (552 kilometers) per hour.

Encyclopedia of Aviation (New York: Scribners, 1977), 107. *Van Nostrand's Scientific Encyclopedia, 7th ed.* (New York: Van Nostrand Reinhold, 1989), 1:1631-32.

Which year had the most tornadoes?

From the period 1916 (when records started to be kept) to 1989, more tornadoes occurred in 1973 than in any other year. That year 1,102 tornadoes struck in 46 states, killing 87 persons. From 1980-1989, an average of 820 tornadoes occurred each year. The largest outbreak of tornadoes occurred on April 3 and 4, 1974. 127 tornadoes were recorded in this "Super Outbreak" in the Plains and midwestern states. Six of these tornadoes had winds greater than 26 miles (420 kilometers) per hour and some of them were the strongest ever recorded.

Frank E. Bair, *The Weather Almanac, 6th ed.* (Detroit: Gale Research, 1992), 85, 88. Jack Williams, *The Weather Book* (New York: Vintage Books, 1992), 111.

What was the greatest natural disaster in United States history?

The greatest natural disaster in terms of loss of human life was the hurricane that struck Galveston, Texas, on September 8, 1900, killing over 6,000 people. The costliest national disaster to date was Hurricane Andrew which hit Florida on August 31, 1992, and Louisiana on September 1, 1992. Early warning kept the death toll low, but total property damage is estimated at $30 billion, of which $15.5 billion were insured losses.

Information Please Almanac, Atlas and Yearbook 1995, 48th ed. (Boston: Houghton Mifflin, 1995), 404-5. *Nature on the Rampage* (Washington, DC: National Geographic Society, 1986), 122. *Newsweek* September 7, 1992.

Is the water deeper in the north or south polar regions?

The south polar waters are deeper then the north. The deepest recorded depth in the Arctic Ocean (north) is 17,880 feet with an average depth of 4,300 feet. The deepest depth in the Antarctic Regions (south) is 21,043 feet.

Webster's New Geographical Dictionary (Springfield, MA: Merriam-Webster, 1988), s.v. "Antarctic Regions," "Arctic, The," "Arctic Ocean."

Mathematics

What is the ancient Greek problem of squaring the circle?

This problem was to construct, with a straight edge and compass, a square having the same area as a given circle. The Greeks were unable to solve the problem because the task is impossible, as was shown by the German mathematician Ferdinand von Lindemann (1852-1939) in 1882.

Yearbook of Science and the Future 1991 (Chicago: Encyclopaedia Britannica, 1990), 377.

How is the "rule of 70" used?

This rule is a quick way of estimating the period of time it will take a quantity to double given the percentage of increase. Divide the percentage of increase into 70. For example, if a sum of money is invested at six percent interest, the money will double in value in 70 / 6 = 11.7 years.

Robert L. Hershey *How to Think With Numbers* (Los Altos, CA: William Kaufmann, 1982), 22.

What is Zeno's paradox?

Zeno of Elea (*ca.*490-*ca.*425 B.C.), a Greek philosopher and mathematician, is famous for his paradoxes which deal with the continuity of motion. One form of the paradox is: if an object moves with constant speed along a straight line from point zero to point one, the object must first cover half the distance (1/2), then half the remaining distance (1/4), then half the remaining distance (1/8), and so on without end. The conclusion is that the object never reaches point one. Because there is always some distance to be covered, motion is impossible. In another approach to this paradox, Zeno used an allegory telling of a race between a tortoise and Achilles (who could run 100 times as fast), where the tortoise started running ten rods in front of Achilles. Because the tortoise always advanced 1/100 of the distance that Achilles advanced in the same time period, it was theoretically impossible for Achilles to pass him. The English mathematician and writer Charles Dodgson (1832-1898), better known as Lewis Carroll, used the characters of Achilles and the tortoise to illustrate his paradox of infinity.

Dictionary of Scientific Biography (New York: Charles Scribner's Sons, 1973), 14:607-8. Douglas R. Hofstadter, *Gdel, Escher, Bach: An Eternal Golden Braid* (New York: Vintage Books, 1979), 28-32. Lloyd Motz and Jefferson Hane Weaver, *Conquering Mathematics* (New York: Plenum Press, 1991), 47-48.

What is the value of pi out to 30 digits past the decimal point?

Pi represents the ratio of the circumference of a circle to its diameter, used in calculating the area of a circle and the volume of a cylinder or cone. It is a "transcendental number," an irrational number with an exact value that can be measured to any degree of accuracy, but that can not be expressed as the ratio of two integers. In theory, the decimal extends into infinity, though it is generally rounded to 3.1416. Rounded to 30 digits past the decimal point, it equals 3.141592653589793238462643383279. In 1991, Gregory David Volfovich Chudnovsky, in New York City, calculated the value of pi to 2,260,321,336 decimal places.

William H. Beyer, *CRC Standard Mathematical Tables, 28th ed.* (Boca Raton, FL: CRC Press, 1987), 5. Carol Gibson, *The Facts On File Dictionary of Mathematics, rev. ed.* (New York: Facts On File, 1988), 139. Mark Young, ed., *The Guinness Book of Records 1995,* (New York: Facts On File, 1994), 80.

What are Fibonacci numbers?

Fibonacci numbers are a series of numbers where each, after the second term, is the sum of the two preceding numbers-for example, 1, 1, 2, 3, 5, 8, 13, 21 .... They were first described by Leonard Fibonacci (*ca.*1180-*ca.* 1250), also known as Leonard of Pisa, as part of a thesis on series in his most famous book *Liber abaci* (*The Book of the Calculator*), (1202). In addition to their function as recreational mathematics (providing entertainment to mathematicians who enjoy calculating series), Fibonacci numbers have proved useful in describing the positioning of leaves around plant stems, the spiral patterns in the heads of sunflowers, and the genealogy of honeybees.

The Biographical Dictionary of Scientists: Mathematicians (New York: Peter Bedrick Books, 1986), 51-52. Glenn James, *Mathematics Dictionary, 4th ed.* (New York: Van Nostrand Reinhold, 1976), 151. David A. Thomas, *Math Projects for Young Scientists* (New York: Franklin Watts, 1988), 41-42.

What are the Roman numerals?

Roman numerals are symbols that stand for numbers. They are written using seven basic symbols: I (1), V (5), X (10), L (50), C (100), D (500), and M (1,000). Sometimes a bar is place over a numeral to multiply it by 1,000. For example, 5,000 may be written V. A smaller numeral appearing before a larger numeral indicates that the smaller numeral is subtracted from the larger one. This notation is generally used for numeral four and numeral nine, for example, 4 is written IV, 9 is IX, 40 is XL, and 90 is XC.

World Book Encyclopedia (Chicago: World Book, 1990), 16:413-14.

What is a polygon?

A polygon is a plane figure bounded by line segments call sides.

A polygon with three sides is called a triangle; with four, a quadrilateral; with five, a pentagon; with six, a hexagon; with seven, a heptagon or septagon; with eight, an octagon; with nine, a nonagon; with ten, a decagon; with eleven, a hendecagon; with twelve, a dodecagon; with fifteen, a pentadecagon.

Academic American Encyclopedia (Danbury, CT: Grolier, 1988), s.v. "polygon." A. M. Welchons, W. R. Krickenberger, and Helen R. Pearson, *Plane Geometry* (New York: Ginn, 1965), 201. *The World Book Encyclopedia* (Chicago: World Book, 1994), s.v. "polygon."

How much is a billion?

A billion is a number so large that it is quite difficult to visualize. The distance between the earth and moon is only slightly more than a billion and one-quarter feet. Counting at a rate of 3,000 bills an hour, it would take 124 years working eight hours a day to count out one billion one-dollar bills. To live a billion seconds, one would be just over thirty years old. To live a billion days, one would be 2,740,000 years old.

"What is a Billion"? *Pittsburgh Press* 17 September 1961.

What is an algorithm?

An algorithm is a set of clearly defined rules and instructions for the solutions of a problem. It is not necessarily applied only in computers, but can be a step-by-step procedure for solving any particular kind of problem. A nearly four-thousand-year-old Babylonian banking calculation inscribed on a tablet is an algorithm, as is a computer program which consists of the step-by-step procedures for solving a problem.

The term is derived from the name of Muhammad ibn Musa al Kharizmi (ca. 780-ca. 850), a Baghdad mathematician who introduced Hindu numerals (including zero) and decimal calculation to the west. When his treatise was translated into Latin in the 12th century, the art of computation with Arabic (Hindu) numerals became known as *algorism*.

Isaac Asimov, *Asimov's Biographical Encyclopedia of Science and Technology, 2d ed.* (Garden City, NY: Doubleday, 1982), 48. *Understanding Computers: Computer Languages* (New York: Time-Life Books, 1986), 17-19. *Understanding Computers: Illustrated Chronology and Index* (New York: Time-Life Books, 1989), 8.

If 30 people are chosen at random, what is the probability that at least two of them have their birthday on the same day?

The probability that at least two people in a group of 30 share the same birthday is about 70 percent.

Harold R. Jacobs, *Mathematics: A Human Endeavor* (San Francisco: W.H. Freeman, 1970), 380.

How is percent of increase calculated?

To find the percent of increase, divide the amount of increase by the base amount. Multiply the result by 100 percent. For example, a raise in salary from $10,000 to $12,000 would have percent of increase = (2,000 / 10,000) * 100 percent = 20 percent.

Stanley Kogelman and Barbara R. Heller, *The Only Math Book You'll Ever Need* (New York: Facts On File, 1986), 3-4.

What is a Mbius strip?

A Mbius strip is a surface with only one side, usually made by connecting the two ends of a rectangular strip of paper after putting a half-twist (180 degrees relative to the opposite side) in the strip. Cutting a Mbius strip in half down the center of the length of the strip results in a single band with four half-twists. Devised by the German mathematician August Ferdinand Mbius (1790-1868) to illustrate the properties of one-sided surfaces, it was presented in a paper that was not discovered or published until after his death. Another nineteenth-century German mathematician, Johann Benedict Listing, developed the idea independently at the same time.

The Biographical Dictionary of Scientists: Mathematicians (New York: Peter Bedrick-Books, 1986), 92-93. William Karush, *Webster's New World Dictionary of Mathematics* (Englewood Cliffs, NJ: Webster's New World, 1989), 172-73. *Mathematics Encyclopedia* (New York: Doubleday, 1977), 127.

When was a symbol for the concept "zero" first used?

Hindu mathematicians are usually given credit for developing a symbol for the concept "zero"; it appears in an inscription at Gwalior dated 870 A.D. It is certainly older than that; it is found in inscriptions dating from the seventh century in Cambodia, Sumatra, and Bangka Island (off Sumatra). While there is no documentary evidence for the zero in China before 1247, some historians believe that it originated there, and arrived in India via Indochina.

Max S. Shapiro, *Mathematics Encyclopedia* (New York: Doubleday, 1977), 214. Robert Temple, *The Genius of China* (New York: Simon and Schuster, 1986), 140.

Is it possible to count to infinity?

No. Very large finite numbers are not the same as infinite numbers. Infinite numbers are defined as being unbounded, or without limit. Any number that can be reached by counting or by representation of a number followed by billions of zeroes is a finite number.

Lloyd Motz and Jefferson Hane Weaver, *Conquering Mathematics* (New York: Plenum Press, 1991), 17.

Weights, Measures, and Times

What is the difference between the United States and other parts of the world regarding the ways dates are written?

Dates are written in various ways throughout the world. In the United States, the month of the year is written first. For example, June 12 is written 6/12/96. In other parts of the world, the day is written first. June 12 is written 12/6/96. In the United

States, a date is often written with the use of slashes, such as 7/25/92. Periods are used in other parts of the world: 25.7.92.

Susan H. Munger, *The International Business Communications Desk Reference* (American Management Association, 1993), 59.

Who developed the first calendar and upon what was it based?

The Egyptians developed the first calendar, and it was based upon observation of one cycle of the moon's phases. For example, it might measure the period from one full moon to the next, about 29.5 days by solar reckoning. Since a lunar year of 12 such months was shorter than a solar year, it was not a reliable guide for planting or harvesting. In the third millennium B.C. the Egyptians changed to a solar calendar of 365 days, having twelve 30-day months. However, because it was a quarter of a day shorter than the actual year, over a long period of time this calendar, too, became out of sequence with the seasons.

Laurence Urdang, Christine N. Donohue, and Frank R. Abate, eds., *Holidays and Anniversaries of the World* (Detroit: Gale Research , 1985), viii.

How is the Hebrew calendar structured?

The Hebrew calendar was supposed to have begun with the creation of man, approximately 3,760 years and three months before the birth of Jesus Christ. To determine the year in the Hebrew calendar, one must add 3,760 to the date in the Gregorian calendar. Thus, the year 2000 A.D. will be the year 5760 according to the Hebrew calendar. However, the beginning of the year on the Hebrew calendar is in the autumn, not in midwinter.

The Hebrew calendar consists of 12 months of either 29 or 30 days. Seven times during every 19-year period, an embolismic, or extra 29-day month, is added to the cycle.

The World Book Encyclopedia (Chicago: World Book, 1993), s.v. "calendar."

What is meant by Universal Time?

On January 1, 1972, Universal Time (UT) replaced Greenwich Mean Time (GMT) as the time reference coordinate for scientific work. Universal Time is measured by an atomic clock and is seen as the logical development of the adoption of the atomic second in 1968. An advantage of UT is that the time at which an event takes place can be determined very readily without recourse to the time-consuming astronomical observations and calculations which were necessary before the advent of atomic clocks. Universal Time is also referred to as International Atomic Time. GMT is measured according to when the sun crosses the Greenwich Meridian (0 degrees longitude when passes through the Greenwich Observatory).

H. G. Jerrard, *A Dictionary of Scientific Units, 4th ed.* (New York: Chapman and Hall, 1980), 148.

What is the Julian Day Count?

The Julian Day Count is a system of counting days rather than years, developed by Joseph Justus Scaliger (1540-1609) in 1583. Still used by astronomers today, the count (named after Scaliger's father, Julius Caesar Scaliger) Julian Day (JD) 1 was January 1, 4113 B.C. On this date the Julian calendar, the ancient Roman tax calendar, and the lunar calendar all coincided. This event would not occur again until 7,980 years later. Each day within this 7,980 year period is numbered. December 31, 1994 at noon is the beginning of JD 2,449,718. The figure reflects the number of days that have passed since the JD inception. Simple JD conversion tables have been devised for astronomers, to convert Gregorian calendar dates into Julian Day.

Jay M. Pasachoff, *Contemporary Astronomy* (Philadelphia: W. B. Saunders, 1977), 101. Robert Famighetti, ed., *The World Almanac and Book of Facts 1995* (Mahwah, NJ: World Almanac, 1994), 289.

How were the months of the year named?

The English names of the months of the current (Gregorian) calendar derive from the Latin words for the Roman gods and rulers. Each month is given below with its derivation.

January (Januarius in Latin)—named after Janus, a Roman two-faced god: one looking into the past, the other into the future.

February (Februarium)—He guarded the gates of heaven: named after Februus or Faunus, the god of purification and fertility. At this time of year, the Romans performed religious rites to purge themselves of sin.

March (Martius)—is named in honor of Mars, the god of war.

April (Aprilis)—after the Latin word Aperio , meaning to open because plants begin to grow in this month.

May (Maius)—after the Roman goddess of spring Maia Majestas as well as from the Latin word Maiores meaning elders, who were celebrated during this month.

June (Junius)—after the goddess of marriage, Juno and Latin word iuniores , meaning youth.

July (Iulius)—was, at first, known as Quintilis from the Latin word meaning five, since it was the fifth month in the early ten-month Roman calendar which started in March. Its name was changed to July, as an honor to Julius Caesar (100 B.C.-44 B.C.).

August (Augustus)—is so named in honor of the Emperor Octavian (63 B.C.-14 B.C.), first Roman emperor, known as Augustus Caesar. Originally the month was known as Sextilis (sixth month of early Roman calendar).

September (September)—was first the seventh month and accordingly took its name from septem, meaning seven.

October (October)—takes its name from octo (eight) from the time it was the eighth month.

November (November)—from novem, meaning nine from the ninth month of the early Roman calendar.

December (December)—from decem, meaning ten from the tenth month of the early Roman calendar.

William J. Fielding, *Strange Superstitions and Magical Practices* (Philadelphia: The Blakiston Company, 1945), 84-86. William Markowitz, *Grolier's Electronic Encyclopedia* (Grolier Electronic Publishing, 1995). *The New Encyclopaedia Britannica, 15th ed.* (Chicago: Encyclopaedia Britannica, 1990), 8:292. *Stories Behind Everyday Things,* (Pleasantville, NY: Reader's Digest, 1980), 54.

How long has the abacus been used? Is it still used?

The abacus grew out of early counting boards, with hollows in a board holding pebbles or beads used to calculate. It has been documented in Mesopotamia back to around 3500 B.C. The current form, with beads sliding on rods, dates back at least to fifteenth-century China. Before the use of decimal number systems, which allowed the familiar paper-and-pencil methods of calculation, the abacus was essential for almost all multiplication and division. The abacus is still used in many countries where modern calculators are not available. It is also still used in countries, such as Japan and China, with long traditions of abacus use. As recently as the mid-1970s, most Japanese shopkeepers used abaci for totaling customers' bills. While the calculator is now more widely used, many people still prefer to check the results on an abacus. At least one manufacturer offers calculators with small, built-in abaci.

Discover May 1985. *Oxford Illustrated Encyclopedia of Invention and Technology* (Oxford: Oxford University Press, 1992), 1. *Science and Technology Illustrated* (Chicago: Encyclopaedia Britannica, 1984), 20-21.

How are diamonds weighed?

The basic unit is a carat, which is 200 milligrams or 1/142 of an avoirdupois ounce. Another unit commonly used is the point, which is one hundredth of a carat. A stone of one carat weighs 100 points.

Victor Argenzio, *Diamonds Eternal* (New York: David McKay, 1974), 9, 230.

Is it possible for a calendar month to pass without a full moon?

Yes, a calendar month can have no full moon. February is the only month that may not have a full moon. This occurred in 1866, 1893, 1915, and 1980, and will happen again in 1999 and 2066.

Science News-Letter 4 February 1961.

What is the 24-hour or military time system?

With the 24-hour time system, all time references are given in four figures, from 0000 to 2359. The day begins at midnight. Thus, 1:00 a.m. is written 0100 and spoken as oh-one hundred (the hundred indicating an even hour; 1:36 a.m. is written 0136 and spoken as oh-one hundred thirty-six. 1:00 p.m. is written as 1300, 2:00 p.m. is written as 1400, and so on. Noon becomes 1200; midnight becomes 2400.

To translate 24-hour time into familiar time, the a.m. times are obvious. For p.m. times, subtract 1200 from numbers larger than 1200, e.g. 1900 minus 1200 is 7:00 p.m.

The system is widely used in scientific work throughout the world. In the United States it is also used by the armed forces. In Europe it is frequently used by transportation systems.

Mary Blocksma, *Reading the Numbers* (New York: Penguin, 1989) 124. Harrison J. Cowan, *Time and Its Measurement* (Cleveland: World Publishing Co., 1958), 52. Robert Famighetti, ed., *The World Almanac and Book of Facts 1995* (Mahwah, NJ: World Almanac, 1994), 290.

How much does a cubic foot of books weigh?

A cubic foot of books weighs 65 pounds (29.48 kilograms). This does not take into consideration any type of variation in paper quality or binding.

David Kent Ballast, *Architects' Handbook of Formulas, Tables and Mathematical Calculations* (New York: Prentice-Hall, 1988), 461.

How far can a Pershing missile travel?

The surface-to-surface nuclear missile, which is 34.5 feet long (10.5 meters) and weighs ten thousand pounds (4,536 kilograms), has a range of about 1,120 miles (1,800 kilometers). It was developed by the United States Army in 1972. Other surface-to-surface missiles are the Polaris, with a range of 2,860 miles (4,600 kilometers); the Minuteman, with a range of 1,120 miles (1,800 kilometers); the Tomahawk, 2,300 miles (3,700 kilometers); the Trident, 4,600 miles (7,400 kilometers); and the Peacemaker, 6,200 miles (10 thousand kilometers).

Barbara Berliner, *The Book of Answers* (Englewood Cliffs, NJ: Prentice-Hall, 1990), 20. *Oxford Illustrated Encyclopedia of Invention and Technology* (Oxford: Oxford University Press, 1992), 230.

What is Hopper's rule?

Electricity travels one foot in a nanosecond (a billionth of a second). This is one of a number of rules compiled for the convenience of computer programmers. This is also considered to be a fundamental limitation on the possible speed of a computer: signals in an electrical circuit cannot move any faster.

David J. Fisher, *Rules of Thumb for Engineers and Scientists* (Houston: Gulf, 1991), 87. James Trefil, *1001 Things Everyone Should Know About Science* (New York: Doubleday, 1992), 129.

What were the longest and shortest years on record?

The longest year was 46 B.C. when Julius Caesar (100-44 B.C.) introduced his calendar, called the Julian calendar, which was used until 1582. He added two extra months and 23 extra days to February to make up for accumulated slippage in the Egyptian Calendar. Thus, 46 B.C. was 455 days long. The shortest year was 1582, when Pope Gregory XIII (1502-1585) introduced the Gregorian calendar. He decreed that October 5 would be October 15, eliminating 10 days, to compensate for the accumulated error in the Julian calendar. Not everyone changed over to this new calendar at once. Catholic Europe adopted it within two years of its inception. Many Protestant continental countries did so in 1699-1700; England imposed it on its colonies in 1752 and Sweden in 1753. Many non-European countries adopted it in the nineteenth century, with China doing so in 1912, Turkey in 1917, and Russia in 1918. To change from the Julian to the Gregorian calendar, 10 days are added to dates October 5, 1582, through February 28, 1700; after that date 11 days are added through February 28, 1800; 12 days, through February 28, 1900; and 13 days, through February 28, 2100.

Robert Famighetti, ed., *The World Almanac and Book of Facts 1995* (Mahwah, NJ: World Almanac, 1994), 288. James Trefil, *1001 Things Everyone Should Know About Science* (New York: Doubleday, 1992), 138.

What is the United States Time Standard signal?

The most-used high-frequency reference signals are the U.S. Time Standard signals from radio stations WWV, Fort Collins, Colorado, and WWVH, Kauai, Hawaii. These stations transmit standard "tic" pulses each second with minute announcements and special bulletins periodically. They transmit 1.5, 5, 10, 15, and 20 megahertz signals with very precise time and frequency stability. The first radio station to transmit time signals regularly was the Eiffel Tower Radio Station in Paris in 1913.

The ARRL Handbook for Radio Amateurs, 68th ed. (Newington, CT: American Radio Relay League, 1991), 12-22. Patrick Robertson, *The Book of Firsts* (New York: Clarkson N. Potter, 1974), 149.

How many time zones are there in the world?

There are 24 standard time zones that serially cover the earth's surface at coincident intervals of 15 degrees longitude and 60 minutes Universal Time (UT), as agreed at the Washington Meridian Conference of 1884, thus accounting, respectively, for each 24 hours of the calendar day.

Van Nostrand's Scientific Encyclopedia, 7th ed. (New York: Van Nostrand Reinhold, 1989), 2:2833.

What do the initials a.m. and p.m. mean?

a.m. stands for ante meridiem, Latin for "before noon." p.m. stand for post meridiem, Latin for "after noon."

Acronyms, Initialisms & Abbreviations Dictionary 1993, 17th ed. (Detroit: Gale Research, 1992), 1:178, 2716.

How is time denoted at sea?

The day is divided into watches and bells. A watch equals four hours except for the time period between 4 p.m. and 8 p.m., which has two short watches. From midnight to 4 a.m. is the middle watch; from 4 a.m. to 8 a.m., the morning watch; 8 a.m. to noon, the forenoon watch; noon to 4 p.m., afternoon watch; 4 p.m. to 6 p.m., first dog watch; 6 p.m. to 8 p.m., second or last dog watch; 8 p.m. to midnight, first watch. Within each watch there are eight bells-one stroke for each half hour, so that each watch ends on eight bells except the dog watches which end at four bells. New Year's Day is marked with 16 bells.

The Guinness Book of Answers, 8th ed. (Enfield, ENG: Guinness Publishing, 1991), 43-44. Jeff Rovin, *Laws of Order* (New York: Ballantine, 1992), 203.

How was the length of a meter originally determined and how is it calculated?

The meter is equal to 39.37 inches. It was originally intended that the meter should represent one ten-millionth of the distance along the meridian running from the North Pole to the equator through Dunkirk, France, and Barcelona, Spain. French scientists determined this distance, working nearly six years to complete the task in November of 1798. They decided to use a platinum-iridium bar as the physical replica of the meter. Although the surveyors made an error of about two miles, the error was not discovered until much later. Rather than changing the length of the meter to conform to the actual distance, in 1889 the platinum-iridium bar was chosen as the international prototype and was used until 1960. There are numerous copies of it in other parts of the world, including the U.S. National Bureau of Standards. From 1960 to 1983, the length of a meter had been defined as 1,650,763.73 times the wavelength of the orange light emitted when a gas consisting of the pure krypton isotope of mass number 86 is excited in an electrical discharge. It is presently defined as the distance traveled by light in a vacuum during 1/299,792,458 of a second.

CRC Handbook of Chemistry and Physics, 72d ed. (St. Louis, MO: CRC Press, 1991), 1-14. Richard Deming, *Metric Power* (Nashville: Nelson, 1974), 49, 67-68. *The McGraw-Hill Dictionary of Scientific and Technical Terms, 4th ed.* (New York: McGraw-Hill, 1989), 1186. Frank Xavier Ross, *The Metric System-Measures for All Mankind* (New York: Phillips, 1974), 57-58.

Who was the first person to date events from the time of the birth of Jesus?

The Venerable Bede, an Anglo-Saxon priest, theologian, chronologist, and historian who lived from 672 or 673 to 735, is thought to be the first person to date events from the time of the birth of Jesus Christ. He used this method-A.D., i.e. Anno Domini, "in the year of the Lord"-in two chronologies and in his *Historia ecclesiastica gentis Anglorum* (Ecclesiastical History of the English People). It was the popularity of these works that brought the practice into general use. *Historia ecclesiastica,* a lengthy work that traces events in Britain from the Roman invasions of 55-54 B.C. to St. Augustine's arrival in A.D. 597, is indispensable to the study of the conversion of England's Anglo-Saxon tribes to Christianity.

Bede's other works included hymns, scripture commentaries, and biographical studies. He was canonized a saint by the Roman Catholic Church in 1899.

The New Encyclopaedia Britannica, Micropaedia, 15th ed. (Chicago: Encyclopaedia Britannica, 1989), s.v. "Bede the Venerable, Saint."

Which two counting devices use beads?

Beads are used as a counting device in both the abacus and the rosary. The abacus was a Chinese invention and is still used throughout Asia. The rosary is a religious device for counting prayers.

Joan Mowat Erikson, *The Universal Bead* (New York: W. W. Norton, 1993), 78-79.

How was the calendar changed during the French Revolution?

The French Revolution brought the most radical calendar reform in modern history. On September 22, 1792, when France was proclaimed a republic, the revolutionaries believed that a new era of history had begun, and so a new calendar was needed. It was to be more rational, secular, and harmonious with nature than the Gregorian calendar then in use. Year one started in 1792, which implied that the establishment of the republic was more important than the birth of Jesus Christ. There were to be twelve months of thirty days each, which were to named after the natural phenomena that occurred around Paris at that time. They were Vendmiaire (vintage), Brumaire (fog), Frimaire (frost), Nivse (snow), Pluvise (rain), Ventse (wind), Germinal (budding), Floral (flowering), Prairial (meadows), Messidor (harvest), Thermidor (heat), and Fructidor (fruit). Extra days were added to make the calendar coincide with the solar year. The calendar showed the influence of the decimal system. Each month was to have three ten-day weeks; each day ten hours: each hour one hundred minutes; each minute one hundred seconds.

The calendar lasted only through 1805, and the reasons for its failure are many. There had never been a general demand for a calendar revision, and with longer weeks people resented waiting longer for a day off. Religious feeling was stronger than the revolutionaries had thought, and when Napoleon reconciled with the Roman Catholic Church, the new calendar was doomed.

Samuel F. Scott and Barry Rothaus, eds., *Historical Dictionary of the French Revolution, 1789-1799* (Westport, CT: Greenwood Press, 1985), s.v. "calendar of the French Republic."

How is a ship's tonnage calculated?

Tonnage of a ship is not necessarily the number of tons that the ship weighs. Although there are as many as six different methods of rating ships, the most common are as follows:

Displacement tonnage—used especially for warships and U.S. merchant ships-is the weight of the water displaced by a ship. Since a ton of sea water occupies 35 cubic feet, the weight of water displaced by a ship can be determined by dividing the cubic footage of the submerged area of the ship by 35. The result is converted to long tons (2,240 pounds). Loaded displacement tonnage is the weight of the water displaced when a ship is carrying its normal load of fuel, cargo, and crew. Light displacement tonnage is the weight of water displaced by the unloaded ship.

Gross tonnage (GRST) or gross registered tonnage (GRT)—used to rate merchant shipping and passenger ships-is a measure of the enclosed capacity of a vessel. It is the sum in cubic feet of the vessel's enclosed space divided by 100 (100 such cubic feet is considered one ton). The result is gross (registered) tonnage. For example, the old *Queen Elizabeth* did not weigh 83,673 tons, but had a capacity of 8,367,300 cubic feet.

Deadweight tonnage (DWT)—used for freighters and tankers-is the total weight in long tons (2,240 pounds) of everything a ship can carry when fully loaded. It represents the amount of cargo, stores, bunkers, and passengers that are required to bring a ship down to her loadline, i.e., the carrying capacity of a ship.

Net registered tonnage (NRT)—used in merchant shipping-is the gross registered tonnage minus the space that cannot be utilized for paying passengers or cargo (crew space, ballast, engine room, etc.)

Mary Blocksma, *Reading the Numbers* (New York: Penguin, 1989), 160. Tom Burnam, *The Dictionary of Misinformation* (New York: Perennial Library, 1986), 228. *The Guinness Book of Answers, 8th ed.* (Enfield, ENG: Guinness Publishing, 1991), 281.

What was unusual about the original Celsius temperature scale?

In 1742 the Swedish astronomer Anders Celsius (1701-1744) set the freezing point of water at 100 degrees Centigrade and the boiling point of water at 0 degrees Centigrade. It was Carolus Linnaeus (1707-1778) who reversed the scale, but a later textbook attributed the modified scale to Celsius and the name has remained.

American Scientist March/April 1992.

What is the abbreviation STP?

The abbreviation STP is often used for standard temperature and pressure. As a matter of convenience, scientists have chosen a specific temperature and pressure as standards for comparing gas volumes. The standard temperature is 0 degrees Celsius (273 degrees Kelvin) and the standard pressure is 760 torr (one atmosphere).

Jacqueline I. Kroschwitz, *Chemistry* (New York: McGraw-Hill, 1990), 212.

What abbreviations can be used to indicate 12:00 midnight and 12:00 noon?

Twelve o'clock midnight can be indicated by 12 a.m. (ante meridiem) 12 M, 12 MDNT, 12 MID, 12 MIDN, or 12 MN, or M (meridies). Twelve o'clock noon can also be indicated by 12 p.m. (post meridiem), 12 M, and by 12 N or 12 MN or M (meridies). However, each style manual differs in its interpretation of which abbreviations are acceptable.

The Chicago Manual of Style, 14th ed. (Chicago: University of Chicago Press, 1993), 469. Jennifer Mossman, ed., *Reverse Acronyms, Initialisms & Abbreviations Dictionary, 18th ed.* (Detroit: Gale Research, 1993), 2188, 2439. *Webster's Standard American Style Manual* (Springfield, MA: Merriam-Webster, 1985), 129.

Why do American shoe sizes differ from those in other countries?

The American shoe sizing system has its roots in fourteenth-century England, when King Edward II established the inch to be the length of three barley corns. Shoemakers found that the longest normal foot was about equivalent to 39 barley corns in a row, exactly 13 inches. They named this largest shoe a size 13. A variation of this system was developed in the United States by Edwin B. Simpson of New York. With this system, the sizing for men, women, and children do not correspond. For example, a man's size 8 is about the equivalent of a woman's size 9-. Most countries use a less complicated metric shoe-sizing system with no half sizes and the same size number for male and female feet.

Mary Blocksma, *Reading the Numbers: A Survival Guide to the Measurements, Numbers, and Sizes Encountered in Everyday Life* (New York: Penguin Books, 1989), s.v. "shoes."

How did the Gregorian calendar get its name and how long has it existed?

The Gregorian calendar, formulated by the Renaissance astronomer, Christoph Clavius, was adopted by the Roman Catholic church in 1582. Because it was put into effect by Pope Gregory XIII, it is known as the Gregorian calendar. The calendar was meant to correct the Julian calendar, which had been established by Julius Caesar in 46 B.C. The Julian calendar was 11 minutes and 14 seconds longer than the solar year (the amount of time the earth takes to revolve completely around the sun); so by 1580 it had accumulated ten additional days. In 1582 Pope Gregory eliminated ten days from the month of October to remedy the cumulative error and thereafter the calendar has operated on the principle of the leap year. Every year divisible by four is a leap year, which means that an extra day is added to February that year to keep the calendar in accord with the solar year. However, years that end in two zeros are leap years only if they are divisible by 400. For example, 1900, 1800, and 1700 were not leap years, but 1600 was. Although the calendar is now used in all Western countries and several others, it was at first met with some resistance. Great Britain, for example, did not adopt the calendar until 1751 and Russia did not adopt it until the Bolshevik Revolution in 1917.

Tom Ferrell, "Gregorian Calendar Marks 400th Year of Its Adoption," *The New York Times* 15 October 1982. *The World Book Encyclopedia* (Chicago: World Book, 1994), s.v. "Gregorian calendar."

What terms are used to describe a period of a specific number of years?

Words used to describe a period of years begin with a numerical designation and end with the suffix -ium, as in biennium, meaning a period of two years; sexennium, a period of six years; decennium, a period of ten years; centennium, a period of 100 years; and millennium, a period of 1000 years. The suffix can be changed to -ary to designate an anniversary, such as centenary, meaning a 100th anniversary; bicentenary, a 200th anniversary; and tercentenary, a 300th anniversary. An adjective is created by adding -ial, as in sesquicentennial, pertaining to a period of 150 years; quadricentennial, 400 years; and quincentennial, 500 years.

Lois Irene Hutchinson, *Standard Handbook for Secretaries* (New York: McGraw-Hill Book Company, 1956), 594.

In what order did Western calendars evolve?

Since the beginning of recorded history, human beings have tried to develop a useful way to keep track of time and commemorate important events. In the Western world, the Egyptians were one of the first civilizations to create an organized calendar. This calendar eventually formed the basis for the Roman calendar, which in turn created the foundation for the Julian calendar. The Julian calendar proved to be very useful and was utilized for approximately 1,500 years. It was eventually replaced by the Gregorian calendar, which is currently used throughout most of the world. The Gregorian calendar is extremely valuable for dating seasonal activities based on solar motion and religious holidays.

Frank Parise, ed., *The Book of Calendars* (New York: Facts on File, 1982), 294.

How did the Aztec calendar system work?

The Aztec calendar system was based on one used by the Mayans. There were two calendars that worked in conjunction with each other and that were organized around a concept of endlessly repeating cycles. A ritual calendar was used by the Aztec priests to forecast the best time to undertake important events, such as war or marriage. Because the ritual calendar took only 260 days to complete a cycle, it did not correspond very well to the length of the solar year. In addition the Aztecs also employed a 365-day solar calendar of 18 months, each of which had 20 days, and added five extra "unlucky" days at the end of the year. The 260-day and 365-day cycles were combined to form a giant cycle of 18,980 days or 52 years.

The Aztec Calendars (Denver: Denver Museum of Natural History, 1992).

Is there a year "0" between the years 1 B.C. and A.D. 1?

According to chronologers, the beginning of the Christian Era on January 1, A.D. 1, was directly preceded by the year 1 B.C. Astronomers, however, denote the year preceding the dawn of the modern era as 0, and the year previous to that as 1 B.C.

Encyclopaedia Britannica, 11th ed. (New York: Encyclopaedia Britannica, 1910-11), s.v. "Chronology."

What is a leap second?

The earth's rotation is slowing down and to compensate for this, June 1992 was one second longer than normal. This leap second, announced in February 1992 by the International Earth Rotation Service, will keep calendar time in close alignment with international atomic time. To accomplish this change, 23h 59m 59s Universal Time on June 30, 1992, was followed by 23h 59m 60s, and this in turn followed by 0h 0m 0s on July 1.

Astronomy June 1992.

Where did the concept of the seven day week originate?

The ancient Babylonians, a Semitic people, are thought to be the first people to use a seven-day week. This week concept apparently was patterned after the periods between the distinct phases of the moon, which roughly correspond to seven days. The Babylonians also regarded the number seven as sacred, probably because they observed this recurring number in relation to other astronomical phenomena; for instance, they observed seven principal heavenly bodies: the sun, moon, and the planets, Mars, Mercury, Jupiter, Venus, and Saturn. The days of the week were named for these principal heavenly bodies.

The ancient Hebrews may have adopted the practices and observance of a seven-day week from the Babylonians, probably during the time of Jewish captivity in Babylon beginning in 586 B.C. Christians continued to use the concepts of the week and the month cycle that they inherited from the Jewish calendar in the first century A.D. and both traditions were officially adopted by the Roman emperor Constantine in the fourth century A.D.

Christine N. Donohue, ed., *Holidays and Anniversaries of the World, 1st ed.* (Detroit: Gale Research, 1985), ix.

When traveling from Tokyo to Seattle and crossing the international date line, what day is it?

Traveling from west to east (Tokyo to Seattle), the calendar day is set back, i.e., Sunday becomes Saturday. Traveling east to west, the calendar day is advanced, i.e., Tuesday becomes Wednesday. This is the result of crossing the International Date Line.

The International Date Line is an imaginary line that was established by major countries and that runs from the North Pole to the South Pole in a zigzag fashion, marking where each new day begins. It runs roughly along the 180-degree line of longitude through the Pacific Ocean. It zigzags past land areas such as the Aleutian Islands, Siberia, and the Fiji Islands so that all the people of a particular area will be on the same day of the week. For instance, some of the Fijis are exactly on the 180-degree parallel. If the International Date Line did not zigzag, then it could be Tuesday on part of the Fijis and Wednesday on another part.

Gary L. Fitzpatrick, *International Time Tables* (Metuchen, NJ: Scarecrow Press, 1990). *The New Encyclopaedia Britannica, 15th ed.* (Chicago: Encyclopaedia Britannica, Inc., 1993), 6:349. *World Book Encyclopedia* (Chicago: World Book, 1994), 10:339.

Who set a doomsday clock for nuclear annihilation?

The doomsday clock first appeared on the cover of the magazine *Bulletin of the Atomic Scientists* in 1947 with its time set at 11:53 p.m. The symbolic clock, appearing in subsequent issues of the magazine, was created by the magazine's board of directors, to dramatize the threat of nuclear holocaust with midnight representing the time of destruction. Just after the United States tested the hydrogen bomb in 1953, the clock was set at 11:58 p.m., the closest to midnight ever. Disarmament negotiations between the United States and the former Soviet Union during the 1960s and 1970s pushed the clock back periodically. In 1991, in response to the fall of Communism in the Eastern bloc, the clock was moved back to 11:43 p.m., the farthest from midnight it has ever been.

Buzzworm: The Environmental Journal January/February 1992. *Pittsburgh Press* 7 March, 1990. *USA Today* 26 November, 1991.

What is a Foucault pendulum?

An instrument devised by Jean Foucault (1819-1868) in 1851 to prove that the earth rotates on an axis, the pendulum consisted of a heavy ball suspended by a very long fine wire. Sand beneath the pendulum recorded the plane of rotation of the pendulum over time.

A reconstruction of Foucault's experiment is located in Portland, Oregon at its Convention Center. It swings from a cable 90 feet (27.4 meters) long, making it the longest pendulum in the world.

The Cambridge Dictionary of Science and Technology (New York: Cambridge University Press, 1988), 362, 812. John Daintith, *The Facts on File Dictionary of Physics* (New York: Facts on File, 1988), 78. Mark Young, ed., *The Guinness Book of Records 1995* (New York: Facts on File, 1994), 86.

Who invented the slide rule?

The slide rule is based on the use of logarithmic scales, which were invented by John Napier (1550-1617), Baron of Merchiston, and published in 1614. In 1620, Edmund Gunter (1581-1626) of Gresham College, London, England, described an immediate forerunner of the slide rule, his "logarithmic line of numbers." William Oughtred (1574-1660), Rector of Aldbury, England, made the first rectilinear slide rule in 1621. This slide rule consisted of two logarithmic scales that could be manipulated together for calculation. His former pupil Richard Delamain published a description of a circular slide rule in 1630, three years before Oughtred published a description of his invention (at least one source says that Delamain published in 1620). Oughtred accused Delamain of stealing his idea, but evidence indicates that the inventions were probably arrived at independently. The earliest existing straight slide rule using the modern design of a slider moving in a fixed stock dates from 1654. A wide variety of specialized slide rules were developed by the end of the seventeenth century, for trades such as masonry, carpentry, and excise tax collecting. Peter Mark Roget (1779-1869), best known for his *Thesaurus of English Words and Phrases*, invented a log-log slide rule for calculating the roots and powers of numbers in 1814. While the slide rule was popular as a calculating tool for several centuries, it has largely been superseded by the electronic calculator.

Edward De Bono, *Eureka!* (New York: Holt, Rinehart and Winston, 1974), 210. Ellis Mount and Barbara A. List, *Milestones in Science and Technology* (Phoenix: Oryx Press, 1987), 76. *The New Encyclopaedia Britannica, 15th ed.* (Chicago: Encyclopaedia Britannica, 1990), 10:140.

When does a century begin?

A century has 100 consecutive calendar years. The first century consisted of years 01 through 100. The twentieth century started with 1901 and will end with 2000. The twenty-first century will begin January 1, 2001. The year 2001 is the beginning of the Third Millennium of the Christian Era.

Fred L. Worth, *The Trivia Encyclopedia* (New York: Bell Publishing, 1974), 130.

Who establishes the correct time in the United States?

The U.S. National Institute of Standards and Technology, Time and Frequency Division in Boulder, Colorado, uses an atomic clock accurate to 3 millionths of a second per year to establish the correct time. The atomic clock was constructed at the U.S. Bureau of Measures in Washington, DC, in 1948. American physicist W. Libby formulated the principle of this extremely accurate clock.

Passport to World Band Radio (Penn's Park, PA: International Broadcasting Services, 1992), 70.

When does leap year occur and why does it occur?

Because it takes almost 365 1/4 days for the earth to revolve around the sun, every fourth year, known as a leap year, has an extra day added to it in February-the 29th. A leap year occurs when the year is exactly divisible by four except centenary years. A centenary year must be divisible by 400 to be a leap year. For example, there was no February 29 in 1900, which was not a leap year. The next centenary year, 2000, is divisible by 400 so it will have a February 29.

The leap year concept is the result of using a solar calendar, which began in 46 B.C. when Roman general and stateman Julius Caesar (100 B.C.-44 B.C), on the advice of the astronomer Sosigenes, created a solar calendar of 365 days, with an extra day added every four years. The number of days in each month was rearranged. January, March, May, July, September, and November were given 31 days. All other months except February were given 30 days. In a common year, February contained 29 days and 30 days in a leap year.

Following the death of Caesar in 44 B.C., the Julian calendar was amended. September and November were reduced to 30 days, and August, October and December were given 31 days. February was reduced to 28 days, but in a leap year, it received an extra day.

Tom Burnam, *The Dictionary of Misinformation* (New York: Perennial Library, 1986), 136. Frank Parise, ed., *The Book of Calendars* (New York: Facts On File, 1982), 294.

Why do clocks and watches with the Roman numerals on their faces use "IIII" for the number 4, rather than "IV"?

A clock with a "IV" has a somewhat unbalanced appearance. Thus tradition has favored the strictly incorrect "IIII," which more nearly balances the equally heavy "VIII."

Frederick J. Britten, *Britten's Old Clocks and Watches and Their Makers, 8th ed.* (New York: Dutton, 1973), 88.

When is Daylight Savings Time observed in the United States?

In 1967 all states and possessions of the United States began observing Daylight Savings Time (DST) at 2 A.M. on the first Sunday in April of every year. The clock would advance one hour at that time until 2 A.M. of the last Sunday of October when the clock then would be turned back one hour. In the intervening years, the length of this time period was changed, but on July 8, 1986, the original states and ending dates were reinstated. An amendment in 1972 allowed some areas to be exempt; Arizona, Hawaii, Puerto Rico, the Virgin Islands, American Samoa, and part of Indiana do not follow DST.

This time change was enacted to provide more light during the evening hours. The phrase "fall back, spring forward" indicates the direction in which the clock setting is moved during these seasons. Other countries have adopted DST as well. For instance, in western Europe the period is from the last Sunday in March to the last Sunday in September, with the United Kingdom extending the range to the last Sunday in October. Many countries in the Southern Hemisphere generally maintain DST from October to March; countries near the equator maintain standard time.

Jay M. Pasachoff, *Contemporary Astronomy* (Philadelphia: W. B. Saunders, 1977), 87. Robert Famighetti, ed., *The World Almanac and Book of Facts 1995* (Mahwah, NJ: World Almanac, 1994), 290.

Where did the term "grandfather clock" come from?

The weight-and-pendulum clock was invented by Dutch scientist Christian Huygens (1629-1695) around the year 1656. In the United States, Pennsylvania German settlers considered such clocks, often called long-case clocks, to be a status symbol. In 1876 American songwriter Henry Clay Work (1832-1884) referred to long-case clocks in his song "My Grandfather's Clock," and the nickname stuck.

David Feldman, *Why Do Dogs Have Wet Noses?* (New York: Harper Perennial, 1991), 178.

What is the SI system of measurement?

French scientists as far back as the seventeenth and eighteenth centuries questioned the hodge-podge of the many illogical and imprecise standards used for measurement, and began a crusade to make a comprehensive logical, precise, and universal measurement system called Systme Internationale d'Units, or SI. It uses the metric system as its base. Since all the units are in multiples of ten, calculations are simplified. Today all countries except the United States, Burma, South Yemen, and Tonga use this system. However, elements within American society use SI-scientists, exporting/importing industries, and federal agencies (as of November 30, 1992).

The SI or metric system has seven fundamental standards: the meter (for length), kilogram (for mass), second (for time), ampere (for electric current), kelvin (for temperature), candela (for luminous intensity), and mole (for amount of substance). In addition, two supplementary units, the radian (plane angle) and steradian (solid angle) and a large number of derived units compose the current system, which is still evolving. Some derived units, which use special names, are the hertz, newton, pascal, joule, watt, coulomb, volt, farad, ohm, siemens, weber, tesla, henry, lumen, lux, becquerel, gray, and sievert. Its unit of volume or capacity is the cubic decimeter, but many still use "liter" in its place. Very large or very small dimensions are expressed through a series of prefixes, which increase or decrease in multiples of tens. For example, a decimeter is 1/10 meter; a centimeter is 1/100 of a meter, and a millimeter is 1/1000 of a meter. A dekameter is 10 meters, a hectometer is 100 meters, and a kilometer is 1,000 meters. The use of these prefixes enable the system to express these units in an orderly way, and avoid inventing new names and new relationships.

Robert J. Cone, *How the New Technology Works* (Phoenix: Oryx Press, 1991), 99-103. *The Oxford Dictionary for Scientific Writers and Editors* (Oxford: Oxford University Press, 1991), 382-83.

How is the distance to the horizon measured?

Distance to the horizon depends on the height of the observer's eyes. To determine that, take the distance (in feet) from sea level to eye level and multiply by three, then divide by two and take the square root of the answer. The result is the number of miles to the horizon. For example, if eye level is at a height of six feet above sea level, the horizon is almost three miles away. If eye level were exactly at sea level, there would be no distance seen at all; the horizon would be directly in front of the viewer.

Science Digest February 1984.

What is the difference in meaning between the words "carat" and "karat"?

The word "karat" is used to describe the fineness of gold. "Carat" is used to describe not only the fineness of gold but also that of pearls and precious stones.

Theodore M. Bernstein, *Dos, Don'ts & Maybes of English Usage* (New York: Times Books, 1977), 36-37.

How much does a denier weigh?

Denier is the international textile and hosiery unit of measurement to denote the thickness of silk and man-made filament yarns. The low numbers represent finer yarns, the higher numbers the heavier or coarser yarns. Originally the word was taken from the Roman coin *denarius.* The measurement was first established in France in the sixteenth century. One denier equals 0.05 grams. One pound of one-denier yarn would measure about 4-million yards in length; a gram of one-denier yarn would measure 900 meters.

Charlotte M. Calasibetta, *Fairchild's Dictionary of Fashion* (New York: Fairchild Publications, 1988), 158. *Encyclopedia of Textiles* (Englewood Cliffs NJ: Prentice-Hall, 1980), 316-17, 536.

Where does the term "mark twain" originate?

Mark twain is a riverboat term meaning 2 fathoms (a depth of 12 feet or 3.65 meters). A hand lead is used for determining the depth of water where there is less than 20 fathoms. The lead consists of a lead weight of 7 to 14 pounds (3.17 to 6.35 kilograms) and a line of hemp or braided cotton, 25 fathoms (150 feet or 46 meters) in length. The line is marked at 2, 3, 5, 7, 10, 15, 17, and 20 fathoms. The soundings are taken by a leadsman who calls out the depths while standing on a platform projecting from the side of the ship, called "the chains." The number of fathoms always forms the last part of the call. When the depth corresponds to any mark on the lead line, it is reported as "By the mark 7," "By the mark 10," etc. When the depth corresponds to a fathom between the marks on the line, it is reported as "By the deep 6," etc. When the line is a fraction greater than a mark, it is reported as "And a half 7," "And a quarter 5"; a fraction less than a mark is "Half less 7," "Quarter less 10," etc. If bottom is not reached, the call is "No bottom at 20 fathoms."

"Mark Twain" was also the pseudonym chosen by American humorist Samuel L. Clemens. Supposedly, he chose the name because of its suggestive meaning, since it was a riverman's term for water that was just barely safe for navigation. One implication of this "barely safe water" meaning was, as his character Huck Finn would later remark, "Mr. Mark Twain ... he told the truth, mostly." Another implication was that "barely safe water" usually made people nervous, or at least uncomfortable.

Felix Cornell, *American Merchant Seaman's Manual* (Centreville, MD: Cornell Maritime, 1964), 433. James M. Cox, *Mark Twain: The Fate of Humor* (Princeton, NJ: Princeton University Press, 1966), 22-24. *World Book Encyclopedia* (Chicago: World Book, 1990), 19:528.

How did the term horsepower originate?

Horsepower is the unit of energy needed to lift 550 pounds the distance of one foot in one second. Near the end of the eighteenth century the Scottish engineer James Watt (1736-1819) made improvements in the steam engine and wished to determine how its rate of pumping water out of coal mines compared with that of horses, which had previously been used to operate the pumps. In order to define a horsepower, he tested horses and concluded that a strong horse could lift 150 pounds 220 feet in one minute. Therefore, one horsepower was equal to 150 x 220/1 or 33,000 foot pounds per minute (also expressed as 745.2 joules per second, 7,452 million ergs per second, or 745.2 watts).

The term horsepower was frequently used in the early days of the automobile because the horseless carriage was generally compared to the horse-drawn carriage. Today this inconvenient unit is still used routinely to express the power of motors and engines, particularly of automobiles and aircraft. A typical automobile requires about 20 horsepower to propel it at 50 miles (80.5 kilometers) per hour.

Isaac Asimov, *Understanding Physics* (New York: Dorset Press, 1988), 1:93. Richard P. Brennan, *Dictionary of Scientific Literacy* (New York: John Wiley

& Sons, 1992), 144. G. J. Davis, *Automotive Reference* (Boise, ID: Whitehorse, 1987), 209-10.

Who invented the thermometer?

The Greeks of Alexandria knew that air expanded as it was heated, and it is known that Hero of Alexandria (1st century B.C.) and Philo of Byzantium made simple thermometers or thermoscopes, but they were not real thermometers. In 1592 Galileo (1564-1642) made a kind of thermometer which also functioned as a barometer, but in 1612, his friend Santorio Santorio (1561-1636) first adapted the air thermometer (a device in which a colored liquid was driven down by the expansion of air) to measure the body's temperature change during illness and recovery. Still, it was not until 1713 that Daniel Fahrenheit (1686-1736) began developing a thermometer having a fixed scale. He worked out his scale from two fixed points: the melting point of ice and the heat of the healthy human body. He realized that the melting point of ice was a constant temperature, whereas the freezing point of water varied. Fahrenheit put his thermometer into a mixture of ice, water, and salt (which he marked off as zero degrees) and using this as a starting point, marked off melting ice at 32 degrees and blood heat at 96 degrees. In 1835, it was discovered that normal blood measured 98.6 degrees Farenheit. Sometimes, Fahrenheit used spirit of wine as the liquid in the thermometer tube, but more often he used specially purified mercury. Later, the boiling point of water (212 degrees Farenheit) became the upper fixed point.

Edward De Bono, *Eureka!* (New York: Holt, Rinehart and Winston, 1974), 194. Meredith Hooper, *More Everyday Inventions* (London: Angus and Robertson, 1974), 112-16.

How does gram atomic weight differ from gram formula weight?

Gram atomic weight is the amount of an element (substance made up of atoms having the same atomic number) equal to its atomic weight, the number of protons, in grams. Gram formula weight is an amount of a compound, a combination of elements, equal to its formula weight in grams.

Charles H. Henrickson, *Chemistry for the Health Professions* (New York: Van Nostrand, 1980), 65. *McGraw-Hill Dictionary of Physics and Mathematics* (New York: McGraw-Hill,1978), 59, 316.

What is meant by DIN standards?

They are German standards for products and procedures, covering a wide range of engineering and scientific fields. The German Institute for Standardization (Deutsches Institut fr Normung) is the publisher of the DIN standards and also represents Germany in the International Organization for Standardization (ISO).

English Translations of German Standards Catalog (Braintree, MA: Beuth Verlag Gmbh., 1991), R112.

Who published the first calendar?

Cneius (or Gneius) Flavius of Rome, the son of a freed slave, published the first calendar in book form in 304 B.C. Flavius' calendar allowed ordinary citizens to know what legal acts were required or forbidden to be done on a specified day. With a calendar individuals would not have to pay tribute to priests and lawyers to discover such information.

Anges Kirsopp Michels, *The Calendar of the Roman Republic* (New Jersey: Princeton University Press, 1967), 106-119. P.W. Wilson, *The Romance of the Calendar* (New York: W.W. Norton, 1937), 97-101.

How is typing speed calculated?

Gross production rate per minute is determined by dividing the gross (total) words typed by the total number of minutes.

Net production rate (in which errors are corrected) per minute is determined by deducting ten words for each uncorrected error from the gross (total) words typed. The adjusted gross is then divided by the total number of minutes.

D.D. Lessenberry, S.J. Wanous, and C.H. Duncan, *College Typewriting: Intermediate and Advanced Course, 7th ed.* (Cincinnati, OH: South-Western Publishing, 1965), 134, 152.

Community Services

What famous Americans were once Boy Scouts?

Some of the now-famous Americans whose lives were influenced at least in some part by scouting include names like former U.S. President Gerald Ford, Senator Hubert H. Humphrey, actors Henry Fonda, Jimmy Stewart, Bob Hope, Paul Winfield, Arthur Godfrey, and Rich Little. In sports there are men like Hank Aaron, Mark Spitz, Bruce Jenner, and Willis Reed. Nobel Peace Prize winner Dr. Ralph J. Bunche, Jr., bandleader Kay Kyser, cartoonists Milton Caniff, and the great Walt Disney, were all Boy Scouts.

Will Oursler, *The Boy Scout Story* (Garden City, NY: Doubleday, 1955), 233-4. *Parade* 9 September 1978.

When did the Boy Scouts of America decide to redefine its literature concerning God?

The Boy Scouts of America made the decision to change its rules on religion after an incident in which a Scout was denied the rank of Life Scout and his membership revoked because he did not believe in God or a supreme being. The teenager was later readmitted and the organization agreed to remove language from its literature that defines God as a supreme being. In a resolution approved by its national executive board, the organization reaffirmed the Boy Scout Oath. The resolution read: "While not intending to define what constitutes belief in God, the Boy Scouts of America is proud to reaffirm the Scout Oath and its declaration of duty to God." Raul Chavez, a spokesman for the Boy Scouts, said, "What it boils down to, the reason this young man was denied his life Scout badge was that he could not adhere to the term supreme being. That was the terminology that he and his family . . . could not adhere to. We have since learned that many other people out there interpreted the term 'supreme being' as a definition of God, describing God and that was not the intent. . . ."

New York Times 13 October 1985.

What is the Make-A-Wish Foundation of America?

Founded in 1980, the Make-A-Wish Foundation of America grants the wishes of children with life-threatening illnesses, thereby providing these children and their families with special memories and a welcome respite from the daily stress of their situation. The Make-A-Wish Foundation of America considers the wish of any child with a life-threatening illness up to the age of 18. All expenses incurred during the fulfillment of wishes are covered by the foundation.

Peggy Kneffel Daniels and Carol A. Schwartz, eds., *Encyclopedia of Associations, 28th ed.* (Detroit: Gale Research, 1994), 1:1235.

What is the origin of Freemasonry and what role did it play in early America?

An international quasi-religious, service-based social organization, Freemasonry originated in the Middle Ages in England and Scotland when freestone craftsman established meeting places close to their place of work to discuss their trade. Often voiced in these discussions were complaints about their working conditions, and their employers. Out of this grew the Freemason penchant for secrecy. In the 1600s people employed outside of the freestone craft were allowed to join the lodges and by the 1700s lodges were being established for those not employed in the masonry crafts. Freemasonry became established in America in the 1730s by English, Irish and Scotch Masons. By the mid-1730s it is estimated that there were six thousand Masons along the Atlantic seaboard. Many heroes of the American Revolution were Masons including General George Washington, Samuel Adams and fifty of the fifty-six signers of the Declaration of Independence. In 1775 a number of Blacks were initiated into a lodge in Boston and later that year a lodge of "Colored Masons" was established in that city. Black lodges soon increased especially into the border states and as far south as Louisiana. In 1826 the death of William Morgan, a Mason who allegedly threatened to reveal lodge secrets, caused a decline in membership and a public outcry against Freemasonry. The notoriety passed however and by the 1840s membership began to rise again. By the mid-20th century there were an estimated four million Masons in the United States.

Dictionary of American History (New York: Charles Scribner's Sons, 1976), 108-09. *Encyclopedia Americana* (Danbury, CT: Grolier, 1990), s.v. "Masons."

What was Hands Across America?

On May 25, 1986 the group Hands Across America attempted to create a human chain from New York to Los Angeles. With each participant paying ten dollars, the event was planned to raise $100 million to support the hungry and homeless. Since the chain was to cover a distance of 4,000 miles, it required some six million participants. Organizers claim nearly 6 million people did participate, and $28 million was donated.

Pittsburgh Post Gazette 10 March 1986.

What were some of the activities of Red Cross volunteers during World War II?

Many Americans contributed to the war effort during World War II (1939-1945) by volunteering for the Red Cross. Such volunteer participation peaked in 1942-1943, when 256,491,827 hours of service were given. More than three thousand chapters were involved, with volunteers serving in many different "Special Corps" activities: Canteen, Home Service, Motor, Braille, Production, Arts and Skills, Dietician's Aide, Hospital and Recreation, and Nurse's Aid Corps.

Red Cross Service Record, Accomplishments of Seven Years, July 1, 1939 -June 30, 1946, (Washington, D.C., American National Red Cross, 1946), 9.

Who played a major role in the founding of the Boy Scouts and what exciting career had he previously enjoyed?

Robert Stephenson Smyth Baden-Powell (1857-1941) was born on February 22, 1857, at Oxford, England, and had an illustrious career with the British Army, retiring with the rank of General. Stationed at numerous British outposts in their colonies, he fought in many wars and uprisings against British rule including the Fourth Ashanti War (1895-96) and the Boer War (1899-1902). Baden-Powell was particularly adept at military scouting and reconnaissance and published a number of small books on the subject including *Aids To Scouting* (1898). While an army captain in South Africa he made numerous scouting and mapping forays disguised as a journalist and in 1890 he headed British intelligence efforts in the entire Mediterranean area. While operating undercover he would often make freehand sketches of butterflies and surreptitiously incorporate the plans for military emplacements and deployments as part on the wing pattern. In 1907 Baden-Powell set up a trial boy scout camp at a military compound after learning the scouts were using his books as a basis for many of their activities. After retirement he devoted himself fully to the burgeoning Boy Scout movement over which he had tremendous influence. In 1910 he helped organize the Girl Guides, which became known in the United States as the Girl Scouts.

Trevor N. Dupay, Curt Johnson, and David L. Bongard, *The Harper Encyclopedia of Military Biography* (New York: HarperCollins, 1992), 58-9. Amy Wallace, David Wallechinsky, and Irving Wallace, *The Book of Lists #3* (New York: William Morrow, 1983), 100.

What is the origin of the term "community chest"?

Harry P. Wareham originated the term "community chest" which means "a fund of money given voluntarily by people to support charity and welfare in their community." Wareham organized and directed 131 financial campaigns for various philanthropic and educational organizations, netting more than $250,000,000 in contributions.

Clarence L. Barnhart and Robert K. Barnhart, *The World Book Dictionary* (Chicago: World Book, 1992), 1:420. *Who Was Who in America* (Chicago: Marquis-Who's Who, 1963), 3:890.

Was Neil Armstrong a Boy Scout?

Neil Armstrong (1930-), the first man to walk on the moon, was an Eagle Scout. Of the 195 pilots and scientists serving as astronauts from 1959 through 1992, more than 123 were Scouts or have been active in scouting. Thirty-one had been Eagle Scouts; 21, Life Scouts; 11, Star Scouts; 17, First Class Scouts; 13, Second Class Scouts; 7, Tenderfoot Scouts; 2, Explorers; 13, Cub Scouts; and 8 had unknown ranks.

Fact Sheet (Texas: Boy Scouts of America, 1992), 3.

When was the term "March of Dimes" first used?

U.S. President Franklin D. Roosevelt (1882-1945), founder of the National Foundation for Infantile Paralysis, credited entertainer Eddie Cantor (1892-1964) with coining the phrase "March of Dimes," which symbolized the fight against polio. Cantor first spoke the words on a radio show in January of 1938, in a fund-raising effort.

Current Biography: Who's News and Why 1954 (New York: H. W. Wilson, 1954), s.v. "Cantor, Eddie." Carol A. Schwartz and Rebecca L. Turner, eds., *Encyclopedia of Associations 1995, 29th ed.* (Detroit: Gale Research, 1994), 1601. *Woman's Home Companion* February 1948.

What were the "Gold Star Mothers"?

The "Gold Star Mothers" was an organization founded in 1928 by the mothers of men or women who died in military service during wartime. The name stems from the service flags displayed by families and organizations to which soldiers and sailors belonged during the world wars. Blue stars denoted men and women in the service, and gold stars denoted those who had died.

Concise Dictionary of American History (New York: Charles Scribner's Sons, 1983), s.v. "Gold Star Mothers."

What are the qualities of a Boy Scout?

The Boy Scouts of America look for the following qualities, as outlined in the Scout Law: a Boy Scout is trustworthy, obedient, loyal, cheerful, helpful, thrifty, friendly, brave, courteous, clean, kind, and reverent.

Fred L. Worth, *The Trivia Encyclopedia* (New York: Bell Publishing, 1974), s.v. "Scout Law, The."

Who founded Hull House in Chicago?

Jane Addams (1860-1935) was born in Cedarville, Illinois, and is best known as a social reformer and the founder of Hull House in Chicago in 1889. She graduated from Rockford Seminary in 1881 and briefly attended the Women's Medical College in Philadelphia before dropping out for health reasons. In London she became attracted to the social reform movement and the Whitechapel settlement house Toynbee Hall. With like-minded friend Ellen Gates Starr, Addams returned to the United States and in 1889 founded Hull House which soon became a sanctuary for the poor, the homeless, and those with seemingly unresolvable problems. Hull House eventually grew to 13 buildings with a staff of 65. A political activist, Addams also helped pass the Child Labor Law of 1903. She was also the author of *Democracy and Social Ethics* (1902) and *Twenty Years at Hull House* (1910).

John A. Garraty, *Encyclopedia of American Biography* (New York: Harper & Row, 1974), s.v. "Addams, Jane." *The World Book Encyclopedia* (Chicago: World Book, 1987), s.v. "Hull House."

Who was the first African-American member of the Daughters of the American Revolution?

The first African-American member of the Daughters of the American Revolution (DAR) was Karen Farmer of Detroit, Michigan. Farmer was admitted to the DAR in 1977 after tracing her mother's family back to William Hood, a native of Ireland, who came to America and served in the American Revoutionary War as a private 6th class in the Lancaster (Pennsylvania) County Militia.

New York Times 28 December 1977.

What is the official name of the philanthropic service organization known as the Shriners?

The official name of the Shriners is the Ancient Arabic Order of the Nobles of the Mystic Shrine for North America. Founded in 1872 as a fraternal order, the Shriners are a philanthropic service organization.

The Encyclopedia Americana, international ed. (Danbury, CT: Grolier, 1989), s.v. "shriners."

What do the four "H"s stand for in the 4-H Clubs?

Originally developed in 1902 in rural America, the Four-H clubs now can be found in urban and suburban areas as well. Membership includes individuals ages nine to nineteen from different cultures, ethnic groups, and economic strata. Each one of the leaves on the four-leaf clover that is the emblem of the clubs represents one of the four "H"s: Head, Heart, Health, and Hands. The emblems reflect the club's goal of helping young people gain practical knowledge and skills through real-life learning opportunities. There is a total of over three and a half million members throughout the United States. Projects often vary according to location. In rural areas projects may be done in the fields of conservation, farming, forestry, or livestock. In urban and suburban areas projects may include money management, food, clothing, and automobiles.

The Encyclopedia Americana, international ed. (Danbury, CT: Grolier, 1994), s.v. "Four-H Clubs." Timothy T. Fullerton, *Triviata: A Compendium of Useless Information* (New York: Bell Publishing, 1975), 158.

On what date were women allowed to become Boy Scout leaders?

In February of 1988 officials of the Boy Scouts of America voted to allow women in leadership positions, including scoutmaster, bringing an end to the longstanding male-only policy. The change was voted by the national executive board in a meeting held in Washington, D. C., according to *The St. Paul Pioneer Press-Dispatch*. Previously, the Boy Scouts had successfully defended legal challenges over its policy of allowing men in leadership positions but decided not to continue the restrictions because court challenges had become too expensive.

New York Times 14 February 1988.

Has membership in the Boy Scouts increased or decreased over the years?

During the early 1970s membership in the Boy Scouts of America peaked at almost 4.9 million. Those numbers began to dwindle slightly and in 1980, membership numbers fell to about 3.2 million. Membership began to increase through the mid-1980s and in 1990 the organization recorded membership at 4.3 million.

USA Today 13 June 1991.

What is Parents Without Partners?

Founded in 1957, Parents Without Partners is an educational non-profit organization designed to offer support for single parents. Although the organization is composed primarily of parents who are divorced, some chapters offer discussion groups for widowed parents as well. Parents Without Partners has over 700 chapters located throughout the United States.

Barbara J. White and Edward J. Madara, eds., *The Self-Help Sourcebook, 4th ed.* (Denville, NJ: St. Clares-Riverside Medical Center, 1992), 127.

Who was the first president of the American Red Cross?

The first president of the American Red Cross was Clara Barton (1821-1912), a schoolteacher and humanitarian who became famous for her care of wounded soldiers during the American Civil War and the Franco-Prussian War. Under Barton's leadership (1882-1904), the Red Cross became an organization that offered assistance to victims of peacetime disasters.

Howard Hurwitz, *An Encyclopedic Dictionary of American History* (New York: Washington Square Press, 1968), 55-6.

When did the Friar's Club admit its first women members?

The Friar's Club ended a long-term policy of men only when it admitted several honorary female members in 1988, including Barbara Sinatra, Lucille Ball, Carol Burnett, Eydie Gorme, Barbra Streisand, Elizabeth Taylor, Dinah Shore, Phyllis Diller, and Martha Raye. Liza Minnelli applied for, and received, a regular membership.

USA Today 1 July 1988.

What is the largest organization of American veterans?

The largest organization of American veterans is the American Legion, open to those who participated in World Wars I (1914-1918) and II (1939-1945) and the Korean (1950-1953) and Vietnam (1961-1975) conflicts. The American Legion is politically active and generally conservative.

E.D. Hirsch, Jr., *The Dictionary of Cultural Literacy* (MA: Houghton Mifflin, 1988), s.v. "American Legion."

In 1977 why did the German Red Cross give money to the American Red Cross?

In 1977 the German Red Cross donated $475,000 to the American Red Cross to be used to help Americans suffering from a particularly bitter winter. The project was started by Peter Lorenz, the president of the West Berlin Assembly. Lorenz felt that the American people were owed thanks for their help to Berlin, particularly in the bleak days following World War II (1939-1945).

"West Berliners Donate $475,000 for U.S. Aid," *New York Times* 22 February 1977.

What are some types of community services available for the aged?

There are numerous types of community services available for the aged, including:

Case Management Services -A health care or social worker evaluates the needs of the aged on an individual basis.

Adult Day-Care and Day Health Centers -These community centers offer a variety of supervised social, recreational, educational, and therapeutic services.

Respite Care Service -This is short-term institutional care designed to provide temporary relief for home care providers.

In-Home Care Services -These services include daily visits which provide in home nursing, physical, occupational, speech/

therapy, social work, case management, and mental health assessment services.

Homemaker Services -Personal care and household tasks are taken care of under these programs allowing individuals to be maintained in their own homes.

Friendly Visitors -These visitors write letters, make telephone calls, play cards, and chat with homebound people.

Hospice Services -These services provide care and counseling for the terminally ill and their families.

Meals On Wheels -One hot meal a day is provided for the homebound. Special meals for vegetarians are often available.

Telephone Reassurance -A daily telephone call is made to the homebound.

American Red Cross -This organization has many programs for the aged including medical supplies and equipment such as wheel chairs, crutches.

Transportation Services -These include such programs as "Dial-A-Car, Dial-A-Ride."

Congregate Meals -One hot meal a day is provided in a school, senior center, or other community setting.

Paula B. Doress-Wortersand Diana Laskin Siegal, *The New Ourselves, Growing Older* (New York: Touchstone, 1994), 216-17.

What is the history of Easter Seals?

The history of Easter Seals began in 1907, when a wealthy Ohio entrepreneur, Edger "Daddy" Allen, quit his business to focus on philanthropy after his son was killed in a streetcar accident. In 1915 he opened Gates Hospital for Crippled Children, the first facility in the United States devoted solely to the care of children with disabilities. In 1919 he and the Ohio Rotarians organized a state Society for Crippled Children, which became a national society in 1921. In 1934, with the country in a depression, contributions fell off. To raise funds, the society sold "penny seals" with the theme of Easter, which was chosen because it represented new growth and renewed life. In 1951 the society adopted the lily as its symbol and began referring to affiliates as Easter Seal Societies. In 1967 the society incorporated the words "Easter Seal" into its official title. Easter Seals are still distributed every year around February through a direct-mail program.

Peggy Kneffel Daniels and Carol A. Schwartz, eds., *Encyclopedia of Associations, 1994, 28th ed.* (Detroit: Gale Research, 1993), s.v. "National Easter Seal Society. " National Easter Seal Society, *Annual Report* (Chicago: National Easter Seal Society, 1992), 5, 7, 9, 13.

Which American city was the first to have an actual Y.M.C.A. building?

While the Young Men's Christian Association (Y.M.C.A.) was founded in London in 1844, the organization did not reach America until 1851. The first Y.M.C.A. building was erected in Chicago with funds donated by John V. Farwell (1825-1908), a Chicago businessman.

Abby Farwell Ferry, *Reminiscences of John V. Farwell, by His Elder Daughter* (Chicago: Ralph Fletcher Seymour, 1928), 86. Lewis Nordyke, *Cattle Empire* (New York: William Morrow and Co., 1949), 27. David Wallechinsky and Irving Wallace, *The People's Almanac #2* (New York: Bantam Books, 1978), 415.

How many people headed the National Urban League?

Founded in 1910, the National Urban League is a voluntary nonpartisan community service agency that aims to eliminate racial segregation and discrimination in the United States and to achieve parity for blacks and other minorities in every phase of American life.

Carol A. Schwartz and Rebecca L. Turner, eds. *Encyclopedia of Associations 1995, 29th ed.* (Detroit, MI: Gale Research 1994), 1939-40.

Who was the founder of Boys Town?

Father Edward Joseph Flanagan (1886-1948), a Roman Catholic Irish priest, started Boys Town near Omaha, Nebraska in 1917. Flanagan was a parish priest in Omaha when he began his Home For Homeless Boys with $90 and a rented house. Originally housing five boys, in three months he had 30 wards and by 1918 he had moved to the outskirts of the city and Boys Town as it became known was founded. By the 1940s Boy Town had room for 525 homeless boys and was known worldwide. Flanagan's famous motto was "Remember, there are no bad boys." After World War II (1939-45) Boys Towns were founded in Italy and Israel. The home and Flanagan received much favorable publicity from the 1938 movie *Boys Town* starring Spencer Tracy (1900-67) as Father Flanagan and Mickey Rooney (1920-)as a troubled but good-at-heart runaway.

Maxine Block, ed., *Current Biography: Who's News and Why, 1941* (New York: H. W. Wilson, 1941), s.v. "Flanagan, Edward Joseph, Mgr.." *Encyclopedia Americana, intern. ed.* (Danbury, CT: Grolier, 1990), s.v. "Boys Town." Jay Robert Nash, *The Motion Picture Guide A-B 1927-1983* (Chicago: Cinebooks, 1985), s.v. "Boys Town."

What is the Midland Community Spirit Award?

The Midland Community Spirit Award is presented every year by the people of Midland, Texas, to a community who best represents the idea of coming together to help others in need. Any community in the United States is eligible for the award. In the past, the presentation of the Midland Community Spirit Award has taken place at the White House and is conferred by the President of the United States.

Pittsburgh Press 20 June 1990.

What are the five levels of Girl Scouts?

The five levels of Girl Scouts, which are separated by age, are: Daisy, Brownie, Junior, Cadette and Senior Girl Scout. The organization is aimed at strengthening values of citizenship and personal development in girls aged 5-17 years.

E.D. Hirsch, Jr., Joseph F. Kett and James Trefil, *Dictionary of Cultural Literacy*, (Boston: Houghton Mifflin, 1988), s.v. "Girl Scouts of America."

Crime and Criminals

What is the origin and symbolism of the "Jolly Roger" pirate flag?

One of the most easily recognizable features of a pirate ship is the black flag with a skull and crossbones. Known as the "Jolly Roger," it was first used in 1700 by the French pirate Emanuel Wynne. The skull and crossbones on the flag symbolize death and were meant to intimidate intended victims. Some versions of the "Jolly Roger" also included an hourglass, which was meant to indicate that the pirates were willing to consider dialogue with their victims. If the "Jolly Roger" was lowered and replaced with a red flag, it indicated that the pirates were intent on attacking the opposing ship and its crew.

The origin of the term "Jolly Roger" is uncertain. Some experts contend that the term is a version of the French term "joli rouge," which French pirates used to describe the red flag mentioned above. Others claim that the term "Roger" is derived from the English word "rogue," which means vagabond. The first reference to the term "Jolly Roger" was included in the *Oxford English Dictionary* in 1724.

Patrick Pringle, *Jolly Roger: The Story of the Great Age of Piracy* (New York: W.W. Norton and Co., 1953), 123-25.

What kind of doctor was "Doc" Holliday?

"Doc" (John Henry) Holliday (1852-1887) a hired-gun, the infamous contemporary of the legendary lawman Wyatt Earp, studied dentistry and on occasion practiced it.

Jay Robert Nash, *Encyclopedia of Western Lawmen & Outlaws* (New York: Paragon House, 1992), 162.

Who was the first person in the U.S. executed as the result of a conviction based on DNA-matching technology?

Timothy W. Spencer was the first person in the United States executed as the result of a conviction based on DNA-matching technology often referred to as "genetic fingerprinting." The 32-year-old Spencer was executed April 27, 1994, in Virginia for the rape and murder of four women in 1987. DNA is the body's genetic code.

New York Times 29 April 1994.

Which United States cities are considered the safest places to live?

In terms of the violent crime rates for United States cities, the metropolitan area of Bismarck, North Dakota, is considered the safest place to live, followed by: State College, Pennsylvania; Parkersburg, West Virginia; Marietta, Ohio; Fargo, North Dakota; Moorhead, Minnesota; and Eau Claire, Wisconsin. For cities with low property crime rates, the Johnstown, Pennsylvania, metropolitan area tops the list of safest places to live, followed by: Wheeling, West Virginia; Steubenville, Ohio; Weirton, West Virginia; Sharon, Pennsylvania; Scranton, Wilkes-Barre, and Hazleton, Pennsylvania. The violent crime rate is the sum of rates for murder, robbery, and aggravated assault, and the property crime rate is the sum of rates for burglary, larceny-theft, and motor-vehicle theft.

David Savageau and Richard Boyer, *Places Rated Almanac: Your Guide to Finding the Best Places to Live in North America* (New York: Prentice Hall, 1993) 216.

Are there any states that authorize hanging or a firing squad as a method of execution?

Of the 37 states that have death penalties, five use hanging or a firing squad as an authorized method of execution. In the states of Delaware, Montana, and New Hampshire, hanging is an authorized method as well as lethal injection. Idaho and Utah are the only states to utilize a firing squad as a method of execution; both also authorize lethal injection. The remaining 31 state use lethal gas or injection and electrocution as the means of execution. Kansas has the death penalty on its books, but currently has no death sentence for any felonies.

David Savageau and Richard Boyer, *Places Rated Almanac: Your Guide to Finding the Best Places to Live in North America* (New York: Prentice Hall, 1993), 231. Richard Leiter, ed. *National Survey of State Laws* (Detroit, MI: Gale, 1993), 59-73.

What percentage of individuals arrested for property crimes tested positive for drugs?

According to a U.S. Bureau of Justice Statistics State Prison Inmate Survey conducted in 1986, approximately 39 percent of individuals who committed property crimes did so while under the influence of a drug, and 48 percent reported daily use of any drug in the month before the conviction offense.

Drugs, Crime, and the Justice System: A National Report from the Bureau of Justice Statistics (Washington, DC: Government Printing Office, 1992), 7.

In what period of American history were no executions performed in the United States?

From 1968 to 1976 no executions were performed in the United States.

Les Krantz, *America by the Numbers* (Boston: Houghton Mifflin, 1993), 41.

What was the Black Dahlia murder case, and how did it get its name?

On January 15, 1947, the nude, mutilated body of Elizabeth Ann Short, a 22-year-old would-be starlet who had supplemented her income as a prostitute, was discovered in a vacant, weed-choked lot in Los Angeles, California. An autopsy indicated that Short had been hung upside down and tortured before being killed. Her body had then been bisected at the waist and scrubbed meticulously before being dumped at the scene.

Bevo Means, a reporter covering the case for the now-defunct *Los Angeles Express*, nicknamed Short "the Black Dahlia" because the victim tended to dress entirely in black to accentuate her milk-white complexion. The nickname captured the public's imagination and gained the case nationwide attention.

Within days police began receiving some of Short's personal possessions in the mail, including her address book and birth certificate. An anonymous male caller claiming to be the killer contacted the *Los Angeles Examiner* with details only the killer could have known and indicated that he would give himself up once he was certain he had outwitted the police. As if to taunt police, he continued to mail Short's personal items to them. Twenty-seven men subsequently confessed to the murder; all were discounted as the real killer. More disturbing, a half dozen "copycat" murders were recorded in Los Angeles alone. Despite exhaustive efforts by the Los Angeles Police Department and its chief homicide inspector, Harry "Red" Hansen, the case was never solved. A generation later, some researchers noted a similarity between the Black Dahlia case and a string of murders that took place in Cleveland, Ohio, during the late 1930s, but no positive connection was ever established.

Cosmopolitan, September 1977. *Time* 24 March 1948. Colin Wilson, *A Criminal History of Mankind* (New York: Carroll & Graf, 1990), 614.

What are the chances that a person will become a victim of auto theft?

With over 600,000 automobiles stolen annually, a person has a 50-50 chance that he or she will become a victim of auto theft in his or her lifetime.

Les Krantz, *America by the Numbers: Facts and Figures from the Weighty to the Way-Out* (Boston: Houghton Mifflin, 1993), 17.

Has the number of jail inmates in the United States increased over the past 20 years?

According to the United States Bureau of Justice Statistics, there has been a marked increase in inmate population in American jails since 1970. In 1970 there were 196,429 federal and state prisoners; by 1980 this figure had leaped to 315,974, and in 1991, 789,347 inmates were housed in federal and state institutions.

Bureau of the Census, *Statistical Abstract of the United States, 1993, 113th ed.* (Washington, DC: Government Printing Office, 1993), 210.

Do most murder victims know their assailants?

According to figures provided by the U.S. Federal Bureau of Investigation, the percentage of murder victims in 1992 who were acquainted with their assailants was 35 percent. Twelve percent of murder victims were related to their assailants. Only 14 percent of victims were murdered by strangers. For 39 percent of murders, the victim/offender relationship was unknown.

Uniform Crime Reports for the United States 1992 (Washington, DC: Government Printing Office, 1992), 17.

What is a Ponzi scheme?

Ponzi schemes are originated by embezzlers who pay interest to early investors with subsequent investors' money. The swindler pockets the remaining money when he or she decides to no longer pay interest to investors. Schemes can masquerade as tax shelters or deals in precious metals, gold, diamonds, real estate, and collectibles. When there is a guarantee of interest rates that are much higher than the prevailing market, a buyer should be cautious.

Nancy Dunnan, *Dun & Bradstreet Guide to Your Investment $. 1994* (New York: HarperPerennial, 1994), 248.

Where do illicit drug dollars go?

Drug traffickers often launder their money through foreign exchange houses. Legitimate exchange houses make money by charging a commission for the conversion of currency. Some exchange houses which operate illegally will exchange American dollars from drug traffickers with local currency, which can be used locally. American dollars can be sold to local businessmen who wish to do business in the United States.

Legal and illegal currency exchangers in South America are called "casas de cambio." The "hawala" or "hundi" systems were established centuries ago in Southwest Asia as an informal banking system. The "hui kuan" is an ethnic Chinese underground banking system which centers around gold and jewelry shops.

Money facilitation centers for drug dollars have been identified as operating in Vancouver, Toronto, and Montreal in Canada; New York, Los Angeles, Houston, and Miami in the United States; the Bahamas; the Cayman Islands; Mexico; Panama; Colombia; Ecuador; Uruguay; Luxembourg; London, England; the Channel Islands; Germany; Switzerland; Spain; Andorra; the United Arab Emirates; Hong Kong; Singapore; and Japan.

U.S. Department of Justice, Bureau of Justice Statistics, *Drugs, Crime, and the Justice System: A National Report from the Bureau of Justice Statistics* (Washington, DC: U.S. Government Printing Office, 1992), 66-67.

Who was Harry "Happy" Maione?

Killer-for-hire, Harry "Happy" Maione was a member of Murder, Inc., which was employed by the national crime syndicate in the 1930s to carry out contract killings. He was credited with killing at least a dozen men. Abe "Kid Twist" Reles, also a member of Murder, Inc., witnessed murders committed by Maione and provided testimony that led to Maione's conviction. Maione died in the electric chair in 1942.

Jay Robert Nash, *World Encyclopedia of Organized Crime* (New York: Paragon House, 1992), s.v. "Maione, Harry."

How prevalent is the rape of males?

Male rape is a sexual act by a male imposed upon an unwilling male victim. Most often violence is involved, although there may also be threats, intimidation, or abuse of positions of authority. Misunderstood as the crime of rape is, when the victim is male, the misconceptions are rampant. In the past, victims remained silent and the crime was thought to be confined to penal institutions. There is still a strong sigma surrounding male rape that comes from the mistaken notion that a "real man" cannot be raped.

Studies conducted in the 1980s show that boys and girls up to the early teen years have an equal chance of being sexually assaulted. While young girls are usually victimized by a relative or family friend, young boys are most likely to be sexually assaulted by strangers or authority figures in church, school, athletics, or scouting.

For later teens and adult males, it is estimated that approximately one-seventh to one-fourth of all rapes involve male victims, or as many as 12,300 rapes of males a year. The most common sites for male rape involving older teens are outdoors in remote areas and in automobiles, usually in relation to hitchhiking.

Contrary to popular myth, most rapes of males are perpetrated by men who are heterosexual, not homosexual, in their consensual sexual preference and self-identity. Further, anywhere from 80 to 100 percent of adult male rapists of women have themselves a history of childhood sexual victimization.

Wayne R. Dynes, ed., *Encyclopedia of Homosexuality* (New York: Garland Publishing, 1990), 2:1094-96.

Was Frank Sinatra Jr. kidnapped?

On December 8, 1964, 19-year-old Frank Sinatra, Jr., was abducted by Joseph C. Amsler, John W. Irwin, and Barry Keenan. The kidnappers received from his father, a famous singer and movie actor, the $240,000 in ransom that they demanded. Eventually they were caught and sent to prison for long terms.

Jay Robert Nash, *Crime Chronology: A Worldwide Record, 1900-1983* (New York: Facts on File, 1984), 169.

Who was Jimmy Blue Eyes?

Although his eyes were brown, the mobster Vincent Alo was known as Jimmy Blue Eyes. Working for the mobster Lucky Luciano, Alo was the Mafia connection to the syndicate's banker Meyer Lansky, who became his close friend. Through Lansky and other criminal connections, Alo was able to amass a fortune of tens of millions of dollars. He eventually became the overlord for the Brooklyn Mafia family of Joe Adonis, where he further enriched himself through fostering prostitution, drugs, and gambling. Although he attempted to avoid publicity, he was brought before the Crime Committee headed by Senator Estes Kefauver and closely questioned by the United States Attorney's office in a failed effort to apprehend Lansky. There was enough evidence, however, to convict Alo of obstruction of justice and send him to prison.

Jay Robert Nash, *World Encyclopedia of Organized Crime* (New York: Paragon House, 1992), 18-19.

What were murderer Gary Gilmore's last words before he was executed?

The last words of Gary Mark Gilmore (1941-1977) were "Let's do it!" The convicted murderer, whose life was chronicled in Norman Mailer's best-selling book *The Executioner's Song*, shouted this phrase to his firing squad at the Utah State Prison on January 18, 1977.

Jay Robert Nash, *Crime Chronology: A Worldwide Record, 1900-1983* (New York: Facts on File, 1984), 191.

Which gangster survived the most bullet wounds?

Known as the "Clay Pigeon of the Underworld," Jack or "Legs" Diamond, born John T. Nolan (1837-1931) survived the most bullet wounds during the bootlegging 1920s. He was a lieutenant in Little Augie Orgen's gang, which fought to control bootlegging in Manhattan.

Jay Robert Nash, *World Encyclopedia of Organized Crime* (New York: Paragon House, 1992), 134.

What was the relationship between outlaw Henry Starr and President Theodore Roosevelt?

Henry Starr was serving 15 years for robbery and murder in the Ohio State Penitentiary when he was pardoned by U.S. President Theodore Roosevelt (1858-1919), who wired Starr in prison the message, "Will you be good if I set you free"? Starr promised, was released, but continued his robbing spree.

Starr was the first felon to use an automobile in a bank robbery. He was killed during a bank robbery in Arkansas in 1921.

Jay Robert Nash, *Crime Chronology: A Worldwide Record, 1900-1983* (New York: Facts on File, 1984), 10.

How was Richard Speck, the mass murderer, identified?

Richard Franklin Speck (1941-), who murdered eight student nurses in Chicago during the night of July 13, 1966, was identified by the sole survivor of the massacre, Corazon Amurao. Amurao, also a student nurse living in the same building, was able to hide under a bed while her friends were taken to other rooms, one or two at a time, and murdered. Her accurate description enabled the police artist to draw a realistic portrait of the killer, and at his trial she was able to identify Speck. He also left a T-shirt and numerous fingerprints at the scene of the crime.

Jay Robert Nash, *Bloodletters and Badmen: A Narrative Encyclopedia of American Criminals from the Pilgrims to the Present* (New York: M. Evans, 1973), 511-6.

What mobster in the 1930s was declared "Public Enemy Number One" by the FBI?

John Dillinger (1903-1934) was a bank robber and murderer who formed a gang in 1933 that robbed more than ten banks in the Midwest. Finally caught in Arizona, he was reputed to have pulled a "wooden gun" escape from the Crown Point, Indiana, jail to which he had been extradited. His gang, now strengthened by the addition of such hardened criminals as George "Baby Face" Nelson and Homer Van Meter, conducted a series of spectacular jail breaks, fought itself out of many police traps, and murdered 16 persons. The FBI then declared Dillinger "Public Enemy Number One." The gang began to break apart as various members died in gun fights with the police. Dillinger underwent plastic surgery to evade arrest, but having been betrayed by the friend of the waitress with whom he was romantically involved, the mobster was shot to death by the FBI as he and his date left a movie theater in Chicago on July 22, 1934.

George C. Kohn, *Dictionary of Culprits and Criminals* (Metuchen, NJ: Scarecrow Press, 1986), 110.

Who was Bruno Richard Hauptmann?

On March 1, 1932, Bruno Richard Hauptmann (1900-1936) kidnapped Charles Lindbergh, Jr., the 20-month-old son of the famous aviator. Hauptmann murdered the child but was still able to collect $50,000 in ransom before the body was discovered. He was eventually caught and executed.

Jay Robert Nash, *Crime Chronology: A Worldwide Record, 1900-1983* (New York: Facts on File, 1984), 91.

How much money is derived annually from illegal drug sales in the United States?

A 1992 government report estimated that the illegal drug trade in the United States generates $40 to $50 billion a year in sales, mostly in cash.

U.S. Department of Justice, Bureau of Justice Statistics, *Drugs, Crime, and the Justice System: A National Report from the Bureau of Justice Statistics* (Washington, DC: U.S. Government Printing Office, 1992), 62.

What percentage of bank robbers are apprehended?

Approximately 75 percent of bankrobbers are caught. Those convicted of the crime face up to 25 years in prison, a few years less if they committed the robbery unarmed.

Les Krantz, *America by the Numbers* (Boston: Houghton Mifflin, 1993), 21.

What are some safety tips for adults to avoid becoming a victim of crime?

Crime can strike anyone at anytime. However, there are some safety tips that can reduce the likelihood that a person will become a crime victim. When at home, make sure that the door is securely fastened with a deadbolt or chain-type safety lock. When someone rings the doorbell or knocks on the door, look through the peephole or out a window before opening the door. Always check the credentials of repairmen or other strangers before allowing entry into the home. When leaving the home for vacation or overnight trips, inform neighbors and have them pick up any mail or deliveries. Use timers on lights, radios, or televisions.

In order to discourage crime while driving or riding in a car, lock all doors and keep the windows closed. Keep all packages in the trunk or out of sight. Use well-traveled roads and, if possible, avoid traveling alone. If the car should break down, raise the hood and tie a white handkerchief to the antenna. Do not accept rides or offers of help from strangers.

A person should be especially alert when walking or traveling alone. If a stranger is following, find a police station or a well-populated area for help. Travel only on well-lit and well-traveled streets. In order to foil pickpockets, men should carry their wallet in their front pocket and women should carry their purse with the clasp facing their person. Never carry large amounts of cash, take shortcuts through dimly lit areas, or accept rides from strangers.

Ted L. Gunderson, *How to Locate Anyone Anywhere* (New York: Plumb Books, 1989), 99-100.

How can an individual assume a new name and identity illegally and not be discovered?

Throughout the United States there are people who, for whatever reason, are trying to change their names and identities. Some people go to cemeteries, choose a name from one of the tombstones, and apply for a driver's license, Social Security number, or birth certificate using this name. Because most employers do background checks on prospective employees, however, it would be very difficult for a person to find a decent job using an assumed name.

It is possible for a person to illegally change his or her name or identity by hiring a company that offers to falsify birth certificates, Social Security numbers, trade certificates, or a driver's license. However, it should be noted that if a person uses one of these companies and is caught with false identity papers, a jail sentence for fraud may be the penalty.

Most persons who change their names and wish to remain anonymous usually settle in a large or medium-size city where a large population makes it easier to get lost in the crowd. Small towns are not considered good places to hide because a new person usually attracts suspicion or unwanted attention. Resort towns such as Las Vegas, Nevada, are considered risky because of the large number of bounty hunters and law-enforcement personnel in these areas.

Ted L. Gunderson, *How to Locate Anyone Anywhere without Leaving Home* (New York: Plume, 1989), 80-1.

Were there any female pirates?

Not all of the pirates who have sailed the seven seas were men. Two notable exceptions were Anne Bonny and Mary Read.

Anne Bonny was born in Ireland to a successful attorney and his wife. When her father's flourishing law practice fell on hard times, Anne accompanied her father to the United States. While in America, Anne's father soon became a rich plantation owner and sought a suitable mate for his daughter. However, Anne fell in love with a sailor and secretly married him. When her father found out about the marriage, he disowned her. When Anne's new husband discovered that she would likely not be receiving a handsome inheritance, he quickly abandoned her. Undaunted, Anne soon fell in love with John Rackam, a pirate known as "Calico Jack." Anne accompanied Rackam on his pirate expeditions and soon became an active participant. In October of 1720, Rackam's ship was intercepted off the coast of Jamaica by an armed sloop sent by the Governor of Jamaica. Although Rackam and most of his men refused to fight, Anne Bonny and Mary Read, another female pirate, battled fiercely until they were finally taken prisoner. Anne Bonny, John Rackam, and other members of their party were taken to Jamaica, tried, and convicted of piracy on November 28, 1720. Although Anne Bonny was not hanged with other members of the crew, the circumstances of her death are unknown.

Mary Read was born in London, although very little is known about her parents. At the age of 13, Mary ran away and, disguised as a boy, joined the crew of a British warship. She deserted several years later and became a soldier, fighting in Flanders and exhibiting great bravery. She became a member of a cavalry regiment, where she met a fellow soldier and fell in love. After she revealed to this soldier that she was a woman, Mary and the soldier were married. They left the army and opened a restaurant together. After her husband died, Mary reenlisted in the army disguised as a man and spent time in Holland. She soon grew restless, left the army again, and boarded a ship for the West Indies. The ship was captured by pirate John Rackam, and Mary decided to become a member of his crew. During one of her ship's pirate expeditions, Mary fell in love with a man that her crew had taken prisoner. The prisoner soon became involved in an argument with one of the pirates. According to pirate law, the two men had to fight to the death. In an attempt to protect her lover, Mary purposely involved herself in a fight with the same pirate and killed him. Mary and her lover were then married. Shortly after the marriage, John Rackam, Anne Bonny, Mary Read, and other crew members on their pirate ship were taken prisoner. Although she was convicted of piracy and sentenced to hang in Jamaica on November 28, 1720, Mary Read died in prison of a fever.

Philip Gosse, *The Pirates' Who's Who* (New York: Burt Franklin, 1968), 55-7, 255-6.

For what was John Wayne Bobbitt-who became famous in June of 1993 when his wife cut off his penis-arrested in July of 1994?

John Wayne Bobbitt gained international attention in June of 1993 when his wife, Lorena, severed his penis as he slept, following a sexual assault on her. Bobbitt, whose penis was reattached surgically, was brought up on marital sexual abuse charges but acquitted in November of 1993. Lorena Bobbitt was then tried for the mutilation of her husband, but in January of 1994, she was found innocent by reason of insanity. John Wayne Bobbitt enjoyed a brief, strange celebrity, even making a personal-appearance tour. While on that tour, he met and became engaged to Kristina Elliott, a topless dancer. On May 6, 1994, he allegedly assaulted Elliott and was charged with domestic battery. Then, in July of 1994, Bobbitt, Elliott, and their mutual friend Todd Biro were all arrested on charges of domestic battery. Elliott said that she was beaten by the two men after an evening spent drinking and driving around Las Vegas. Bobbitt countered that he had been struck by Elliott and bitten on the chest by her. The police report confirmed that Bobbitt had a bite mark on his chest, while Elliott had two bumps on the back of her head, bruises on her nose, and redness on her arms.

New York Newsday 5 July 1994.

What was the largest mass execution in United States history?

The largest number of executions to take place at one time in the United States happened late in 1862 when 38 Native Americans were hanged in Minnesota. In August of that year, members of the Dakota Sioux, plagued by large debts, out of food, and unable to obtain credit from merchants, went on a rampage throughout the state. What began as a series of raids on food storehouses turned bloody, and in the end 307 Sioux were given the death sentence by a local military court. Most of the sentences were commuted by U.S. President Abraham Lincoln (1809-1865), but 38 warriors were publicly executed in Mankato on December 26. The incident ignited a three-decade battle between Native Americans and settlers.

Publishers Weekly 13 January 1992. Duane Schultz, *Over the Earth I Come: The Great Sioux Uprising of 1862* (New York: St. Martin's Press, 1992), 2, 259.

What are some of the penalties in countries outside the United States for drunk driving?

Penalties for drunk driving in foreign countries are often quite severe in comparison to those in the United States, according to information gathered by Mothers Against Drunk Driving (MADD) for the year 1988. In Bulgaria or El Salvador, an offender could receive the death penalty. Scandinavian countries were also rather serious about the matter: in Sweden and Finland, the penalty was a year's hard labor; neighboring Norway granted the convicted drunk driver three weeks of hard labor but also suspended the license for a year. The Soviet Union (now the Commonwealth of Independent States revoked the license permanently. Drivers caught under the influence in South Africa faced either a ten-year prison sentence or $10,000 fine, but sometimes both. A $1,000 fine was levied in France along with a one-year jail term and three-year license suspension. In England, offenders could also look forward to a year in jail, a fine of $250, and a one-year suspension. Jail terms were obligatory for drunk drivers in Malaysia, and if married, their spouses were also incarcerated.

Parade 9 October 1988.

Who were Leopold and Loeb?

On May 21, 1924, Nathan Leopold and Richard Loeb murdered 14 year-old Bobbie Franks in an attempt to commit the perfect crime. Evidence left at the crime scene, however, quickly led police to the killers. Despite negative public reaction to the defendants' family wealthy and their unremorseful courtroom demeanor, they were not sentenced to death. Defense lawyer Clarence Darrow (1857-1938) portrayed Leopold as a paranoid and Loeb as a dangerous schizophrenic; he obtained a sentence of life plus 99 years for each of them.

Jay Robert Nash, *Bloodletters and Badmen: A Narrative Encyclopedia of American Criminals from the Pilgrims to the Present* (New York: M. Evans, 1991), 319-20. Jay Robert Nash, *World Encyclopedia of 20th Century Murder* (New York: Paragon House, 1992), 354. Carl Sifakis, *The Encyclopedia of American Crime,* (New York: Facts on File, 1982), s.v., "Leopold and Loeb."

Who discovered the Watergate break-in?

Frank Wills, a security guard at the Watergate building complex, discovered the break-in which occurred on June 17, 1972, at 2:00 A.M. in the headquarters of the Democratic National Committee in Washington, D.C.

Jet 22 June 1992. *Jet* 8 March 1993.

What was the St. Valentine's Day Massacre?

The St. Valentine's Day Massacre was one of the most notorious episodes of homicidal gangland warfare in history. On February 14, 1929, five men (three dressed in police uniforms) entered a garage at 2122 North Clark Street in Chicago, Illinois. Six men who worked for the gangster George "Bugs" Moran (1893-1957) were waiting inside for a delivery of hijacked liquor. Adam Heyer, John May, brothers Frank and Pete Gusenberg, Al Weinshank, and James Clark, along with Dr. Reinhardt H. Schwimmer, an optometrist and something of a "gangster groupie," were lined up against a wall and shot to death with Thompson submachine guns. Moran, who arrived at the garage as the men entered, escaped without notice. Although the crime was never solved, the St. Valentine's Day Massacre was blamed on Chicago gangster Al "Scarface" Capone (1899-1947), who was trying to eliminate Moran and his men, the North Side Gang, as competition for control of illegal activities in the area.

Jerome Burne, ed., *Chronicle of the World* (Mount Kisco, NY: Ecam Publications, 1990), 1093. Carl Sifakis, *The Encyclopedia of American Crime* (New York: Facts On File, 1982), 636-7, 497-9. *World Book Encyclopedia* (Chicago: World Book, 1994), 3:197, 436.

Did the Supreme Court rule that capital punishment was illegal?

On June 29, 1972, the United States Supreme Court ruled that capital punishment was unconstitutional because it was, in practice, being imposed both arbitrarily and inconsistently on the state and federal levels. While this ruling voided all death penalties on the books, it left the way open for states to write new death penalty statutes that were not per se unconstitutional. The first execution to take place after the Supreme Court's decision was that of Gary Gilmore, which took place in Utah on January 17, 1977.

Presently, 35 of the 50 states have the death penalty. Of those not having the death penalty, the first state to abolish capital punishment was Michigan, in 1847. Following is a list of states that do not have the death penalty.

Alaska
District of Columbia
Hawaii
Iowa
Kansas
Maine
Massachusetts
Michigan
Minnesota
New York
North Dakota
Rhode Island
Vermont
West Virginia
Wisconsin

Academic American Encyclopedia (Danbury, CT: Grolier, 1987), s.v. "capital punishment." Dennis Sanders, *The First of Everything* (New York: Delacorte Press, 1981), 177. *The World Almanac and Book of Facts, 1995* (Mahwah, NJ: Funk & Wagnalls, 1994), 956-6.

What is a yegg?

A yegg is underworld slang for a safecracker. The term supposedly originates from the name of an alleged safecracker, John Yegg.

John Ciardi, *A Browser's Dictionary and Native's Guide to the Unknown American Language* (New York: Harper & Row, 1980), s.v. "yegg."

What are some statistics regarding gun ownership and homicides involving guns in the United States?

Public interest in the issues of gun ownership and crime involving firearms has uncovered many eye-opening statistics. Figures from 1993 show that there were 211 million firearms in the

United States, "enough to arm every adult, and more than half the children," reported USA Today. In 1992 the total number of firearm deaths in the United States was 15,377. Statistics from the previous year showed that even more people—18,562—committed suicide using a gun. Numbers also indicate that the risk of being shot and killed is 15 times greater in the United States than in Europe.

USA Today 29 December 1993.

What are the statistics regarding violent attacks at abortion clinics?

Attacks against abortion providers have increased sharply in recent years according to statistics compiled by the National Abortion Federation. During the years between 1977 and 1983 the number of violent incidents totaled 149. From 1984 to 1994 the number of incidents jumped to 1,460.

USA Today 3 August 1994.

What gangster's business card read "Second Hand Furniture Dealer"?

The Chicago Prohibition gangster Alphonse "Scarface" Capone (1899-1947) maintained the front that he was a "Second Hand Furniture Dealer." At least, that is what Capone's business card said; it also listed the address 2222 South Wabash in Chicago. The only other attempt to maintain this identity was the use of broken down furniture, which was placed in the windows of the brothels that he managed for mob bosses Big Jim Colosimo and Johnny Torrio. As Capone became more powerful in the Chicago crime scene of prostitution, extortion, and bootlegging, he found little need to keep up the front. The police were known to protect Capone in his brushes with the law and witnesses at the murders he committed unfailingly lost their memories. It is thought that Capone had some 500 men killed, and that more than 1,000 died in the bloody war that erupted between his gang and other Chicago bootleggers. The U.S. Internal Revenue Service proved to be the one power that Capone could not beat; he was finally jailed in 1932 for tax evasion.

Jay Robert Nash, *Bloodletters and Badmen* (New York: M. Evans, 1973), 99.

When was a speed trap first employed to apprehend speeding automobile drivers?

In 1905, William McAdoo, police commissioner of New York City, was stopped for traveling at 12 miles per hour in an 8 mile per hour zone in rural New England. The speed detection device consisted of two lookout posts, camouflaged as dead tree trunks, spaced one mile apart. A deputy with a stopwatch and a telephone kept watch for speeders. When a car appeared to be traveling too fast, the deputy pressed his stopwatch and telephoned ahead to his confederate who immediately consulted a speed-mileage chart and phoned ahead to another constable manning a road block to apprehend the speeder. McAdoo invited the New England constable to set up a similar device in New York City.

One of the most famous speed traps was in the Alabama town of Fruithurst on the Alabama-Georgia border. In one year, this town of 250 people collected over $200,000 in fines and forfeitures from unwary "speeders."

The Inventive Yankee (Camden, ME: Yankee Books, 1989), 186-87. Rex Power, *How to Beat Police Radar* (New York: Arco Publishing, 1977), 13.

Who were Butch Cassidy and the Sundance kid?

Butch Cassidy was born Robert LeRoy Parker in Circleville, Utah, in 1866. As a teenager he came under the influence of an old-time rustler named Mike Cassidy, whose last name he later took as his own. The nickname "Butch" is believed to be associated with his employment in a butcher shop in 1884.

Born in 1863, Harry Alonzo Longbaugh was arrested for horse stealing at the age of fourteen and spent 18 months in jail in Sundance, Wyoming. As a result he was dubbed "the Sundance Kid."

The fate of these outlaws is open to conjecture. Some believe they died in 1908 in San Vicente, Bolivia, after robbing the payroll of a tin mine; others claim the year to be 1911. However, Cassidy's sister reported that Cassidy returned to the United States and lived until 1937. There are accounts that the Sundance Kid later turned up in Utah and that he eventually lived in Mexico City with his mistress, Etta Place.

Lula Parker Betensen, *Butch Cassidy, My Brother* (Provo, UT: Brigham Young University Press, 1975), 69-70. George C. Kohn, *Dictionary of Culprits and Criminals* (Metuchen, NJ: Scarecrow Press, 1986), 70, 343. Jay Robert Nash, *Bloodletters and Badmen: A Narrative Encyclopedia of American Criminals from the Pilgrims to the Present* (New York: M. Evans and Co., 1991), 114-18. Carl Sifakis, *The Encyclopedia of American Crime* (New York: Facts On File, 1982), 129-30, 694-95.

What is extradition?

Extradition is defined as the surrender by one state or country to another of an individual accused or convicted of a crime outside its own territory and within the territorial jurisdiction of the other. The surrender must be demanded by the state or country in which the offense was committed.

Henry Campbell Black, *Black's Law Dictionary, 6th ed.* (St. Paul, MN: West Publishing, 1990), s.v. "Extradition."

What contemporary British female mystery writer served a prison term for murder?

British novelist, Anne Perry, author of numerous mysteries set in Victorian England, actually committed a murder for which she served five and a half years in prison. Perry was sent to New Zealand at age 15 to recover from an illness. There she helped kill the mother of a friend, after the friend threatened suicide. Perry claimed she was taking a medication that impaired her judgment at the time, and remembers little of the crime. Today Perry lives in Scotland with her mother. Her shocking past was revealed when a film about the murder was released and journalists contacted her for interviews.

Sarah Lyall, "Uncovering a Mystery Writer's Hidden Past," *The New York Times* 17 August 1994.

What does SWAT stand for?

The police acronym SWAT stands for "Special Weapons and Tactics."

Stuart W. Miller, *Concise Dictionary of Acronyms and Initialisms,* (New York: Ballantine Books, 1988), s.v. "SWAT."

What is the average prison sentence served by persons who have been convicted of not filing income tax forms?

People who were jailed for not filing an income tax report served an average prison sentence of 28.5 months in 1993. That was more than double the average time served in 1992. The stiffer sentences reflected the fact that the average amount of tax not paid had also jumped from an average of $45,000 in 1992 to $108,000 in 1993.

USA Today 18 April 1994.

Who was the Boston Strangler?

Albert DeSalvo (1933-1973) was the "Boston Strangler," who between June of 1962 and January of 1964 sexually assaulted and strangled 13 women in the Boston area. He was finally apprehended in the fall of 1964 when he was identified by a woman he molested but did not kill, and he subsequently confessed. DeSalvo was committed to Boston State Hospital as a schizophrenic and judged incompetent to stand trial for the murders. Eventually he was given a life sentence for sex offenses and robberies he had committed earlier. DeSalvo was stabbed to death on November 26, 1973, by unknown convicts at the Massachusetts Walpole State Prison.

George C. Kohn, *Dictionary of Culprits and Criminals* (Metuchen, NJ: Scarecrow Press, 1986), s.v. "Boston strangler, DeSalvo, Albert Henry. " Carl Sifakis, *The Encyclopedia of American Crime* (New York: Facts on File, 1982), s.v. "DeSalvo, Albert H." J. H. H. Gaute and Robin Odell, *The Murderers' Who's Who* (New York: Methnen, 1979), s.v. "Boston strangler."

What was the Alger Hiss case all about?

In 1948 Whittaker Chambers (1901-1961), a confessed Communist spy, accused Alger Hiss, a former official in the U. S. Department of State, of having given him secret government documents in the 1930s. Chambers produced microfilms of the documents that he had hidden in a pumpkin on his Maryland farm. Since too much time had passed, Hiss could not be charged with spying, but in 1949 he was convicted of perjury for denying accusations that he gave away secret documents and for claiming that he had not seen Chambers since January 1, 1937. Hiss served three years and eight months of a five-year prison term.

John Chabot Smith, *Alger Hiss: The True Story* (New York: Holt, Rinehart, and Winston, 1976), 255. *The World Book Encyclopedia* (Chicago: World Book Inc., 1994), s.v. "Hiss, Alger."

Were there eight or seven persons charged with causing a riot in Chicago in 1968?

The Chicago Eight were persons indicted under the Anti-Riot Provisions of the 1968 U.S. Civil Rights Act for conspiring to cause riots during the 1968 Democratic convention in Chicago. Many of the protests organized by the National Mobilization Committee to End the War in Vietnam were related to the U.S. involvement in the war. The trial began on September 24, 1969, for Rennie Davis (1941-), David Dellinger (1915-), John Froines (1939-), Tom Hayden (1939-), Abbie Hoffman (1936-1989), Jerry Rubin (1938-1994), Bobby Seale (1936-), and Lee Weiner. They asserted they were being tried for their political views. There were numerous outbursts by the defendants, and Judge Julius J. Hoffman ordered Seale bound and gagged on October 29, then sentenced him to four years in prison on 16 counts of contempt and separated his case from the others, who then became the Chicago Seven.

On February 18, 1970, the defendants were acquitted of conspiracy charges in connection with riots but five were found guilty of crossing a state line with intent to incite a riot. Froines and Weiner were acquitted. On February 20, they were sentenced to the maximum five year prison terms. These convictions were later overturned during the appeal process. At the end of the trial the judge charged all the defendants and defense lawyers with contempt of court and sentenced them to four years for contempt. On December 4, 1973, Dellinger, Hoffman, Rubin, and attorney William Kunstler were convicted of the contempt charge, but no sentence was imposed because of time already served and because of the improper conduct of the original judge, Julius Hoffman.

Gorton Carruth, *The Encyclopedia of American Facts and Dates, 9th ed.* (New York: HarperCollins, 1993), 666, 671, 698. *Chronicle of the 20th Century* (St. Louis: JL International, 1992), 1017. *Facts On File,* December 2-8, 1973. Charles Moritz, ed., *Current Biography Yearbook 1976* (New York: H. W. Wilson, 1976), 183.

What sentence did Governor Gifford Pinchot of Pennsylvania hand down in 1924 to a neighbor's dog for killing Mrs. Pinchot's cat?

"Pep," a male Labrador Retriever, was sentenced in 1924 to life imprisonment for killing a cat in Pike County, Pennsylvania. Unfortunately, the cat belonged to Mrs. Gifford Pinchot, the wife of the Governor. The Pinchots were neighbors of Pep's owner. Governor Pinchot held an immediate hearing, sentenced Pep to life imprisonment and sent the dog to the state penitentiary in Philadelphia. The dog was photographed for his mug shot wearing I.D. No. C2559 and soon became a beloved pet of the inmates and, after six years, died in prison of old age.

Amy Wallace et al., *The Book of Lists #3,* (New York: William Morrow, 1983), 63-64.

When was the last escape attempt made from Alcatraz Federal Penitentiary?

The last escape attempt from Alcatraz Federal Penitentiary was made on December 16, 1962, by convicted bank robbers Darl Parker and Paul Scott. Aided by surgical gloves inflated as water wings, the pair jumped into San Francisco Bay and began their swim for freedom. Parker, soon exhausted, was forced to stop at Little Alcatraz, a rocky islet where he was picked up by authorities a few hours later. Scott made it to the mainland but, cold and exhausted, he immediately fell asleep only to awake surrounded by law officers. Although both were returned to prison, Scott dispelled the myth that Alcatraz was inescapable. Scott's feat then raised doubts concerning the fate of five other escapees who subsequently disappeared and were presumed drowned. U.S. Attorney General Robert Kennedy (1925-1968) closed the federal prison on March 21, 1963.

Amy Wallace et al., *The Book Of Lists #3* (New York: William Morrow, 1983), 85.

In medieval and Renaissance England, why did people who were condemned to die by the axe tip their executioner?

In medieval and Renaissance England, people who were condemned to die by beheading often tipped their executioners to insure the swing of the axe would be swift. The condemned undoubtedly wished to avoid the fate of Mary Queen of Scots (1542-1587) whose neck took fifteen blows of the executioner's axe before her head was completely severed from her body.

David Louis, *Fascinating Facts* (New York: Ridge Press/Crown, 1977), 48.

What was keel-hauling in the early navy?

Keel-hauling was a form of punishment that involved weighing down the man's body, and hauling him down under the ship's keel and up again on the other side of the boat.

Gershom Bradford, *A Glossary of Sea Terms* (New York: Dodd, Mead, 1942), s.v. "keel-haul."

Which Mafia chief was known as "The Lord High Executioner"?

Albert Anastasia was a mafia chief in New York and New Jersey, who was also known as "The Lord High Executioner." The name, taken from a character in the Gilbert and Sullivan operetta *The Mikado*, was a very literal title for Anastasia. As the head of "Murder, Inc." he handed out many death sentences in the form of murder contracts. Anastasia is even known to have directed the killing of a man he saw on the television; he did not like the fact that the man, Arnold Schuster, had turned in a bank robber. Mob gunmen killed Schuster on March 8, 1952. Such behavior earned Anastasia his other nickname, "The Mad Hatter." On October 25, 1957, Albert Anastasia was himself killed by the order of his Mafia rival, Vito Genovese. He was shot to death by Genovese's gunmen as he sat in a barber's chair. His murderers were later identified as Carlo Gambino and Joseph Biondo, but they were never apprehended.

Jay Robert Nash, *Bloodletters and Badmen* (New York: M. Evans, 1973), 21.

What machine did Joseph Guillotin invent?

Joseph Ignace Guillotin (1738-1814) was a physician who became chief doctor of the medical faculty at Paris. A supporter of the French Revolution, he was the first to demand a doubling of the representatives of the common people at the assembly of the Estates-General in 1789. Considering himself a philanthropist who wanted to decrease the amount of human suffering, he devised a machine, which now bears his name, to cut off heads in a quick, efficient manner, and so to lessen the pain of the condemned, who would otherwise have been dependent on the axman's skill.

Chronicle of the French Revolution, 1788-1799 (London: Chronicle Publications, 1989), 24.

What percentage of rape perpetrators in 1991 were strangers to their victims?

Investigation in 1991 showed that 11 percent of rapists were strangers to their victims.

Mademoiselle December 1991.

What was Charles Manson's name at birth?

Convicted murderer, Charles M. Manson, born November 12, 1934, in Cincinnati, was identified at birth as "no name Maddox," the illegitimate child of a sixteen-year old.

Vincent Bugliosi and Curt Gentry, *Helter Skelter: The True Story of the Manson Murders* (New York: Bantam Books, 1974), 184.

Who was the "Lady in Red"?

One of the most notorious American gangsters of the 1930s was John Dillinger (1902-1934). Police organizations throughout the United States desperately wanted to capture him. In 1934 Martin Zarkovich, an East Chicago, Indiana, police officer with secret ties to organized crime, approached the U.S. FBI and unveiled a plan that he claimed would entrap and kill Dillinger. The FBI agreed enthusiastically to Zarkovich's proposal.

On the evening of July 27, 1934, Anna Sage, a friend of Zarkovich and a whorehouse madam known as the "Lady in Red," met a man believed to be John Dillinger in front of the Biograph Theater in Chicago. The FBI and Zarkovich watched and waited nearby. As the man left his meeting with Sage, he was shot by Zarkovich. The FBI quickly announced to the press that John Dillinger had been killed. However, an autopsy of the dead man indicated that he was not John Dillinger, but a man known as Jimmy Lawrence. Further investigation revealed that Sage and Zarkovich had hatched the phony assassination plot as part of a plan by organized crime to help Dillinger escape justice. The FBI was deeply embarrassed by its error and was forced to resume its search for Dillinger.

Jay Robert Nash, *Bloodletters and Badmen: A Narrative Encyclopedia of American Criminals from the Pilgrims to the Present* (New York: M. Evans and Co., 1973), s.v. "Dillinger, John."

Who were the Black September terrorists?

In September of 1972, Munich, West Germany, was the setting of the twentieth summer Olympic Games. The Games were intended to be a peaceful competition between athletes from countries worldwide. However, this particular Olympiad would be marked by a horrible massacre.

On the morning of September 5, 1972, eight terrorists from Black September, a fanatical splinter group within the Palestine Liberation Organization, snuck into the Olympic village complex that housed the athletes. They located the Israeli team and, in a surprise attack, killed a coach and a referee and took 9 Israeli athletes hostage. Negotiations between the Black September terrorists and West German officials began a few hours later. The terrorists demanded the release of 200 prisoners held in Israeli jails and a plane to carry the terrorists and their Israeli hostages to an Arab country. West German officials agreed to these demands and provided two helicopters to transport the terrorists and their hostages from the Olympic village to Furstenfeldbruck Field and another helicopter to carry German officials and Israeli intelligence officers. At Furstenfeldbruck Field, a team of German sharpshooters awaited to attempt a rescue of the hostages. The three helicopters landed at the field, and the terrorists exited and proceeded toward a Lufthansa 727 jumbo jet. As the terrorists neared the plane the sharpshooters opened fire, killing two of the terrorists. A fierce gun battle ensued. Five of the eight terrorists were killed and the other three were captured. Unfortunately, all 9 Israeli athletes were killed by their captors. The Olympic Games were postponed temporarily but resumed after a memorial service to honor the Israeli athletes.

Lee Davis, *Man-Made Catastrophes: From the Burning of Rome to the Lockerbie Crash* (New York: Facts on File, 1993), 98-100.

Who was the first person in the United States convicted of burning his draft card?

The 1960s were a very turbulent time in the United States, as many people protested U. S. involvement in the Vietnam Conflict. To symbolize their opposition to the war, many draft-age men publicly burned their draft cards. In response, the federal government passed a law that made the burning of draft cards a criminal offense. The first person convicted of burning his draft card was David J. Miller in 1966. He admitted to the act because the draft board in Syracuse, New York, had reclassified his status from a student deferment to 1-A. Miller's attorneys appealed his conviction on the grounds that the federal law violated Miller's constitutional right to free speech. The Federal law carried a maximum penalty of five years in prison and a $10,000 fine.

Douglas Robinson, "Pacifist Is Convicted of Burning His Draft Card," *The New York Times* 11 February 1966.

What two notorious criminals of the 1930s wrote unsolicited testimonials to Henry Ford?

John Dillinger (1902-1934) and Clyde Barrow (1909-1934), two of the 1930's most notorious criminals, wrote unsolicited testimonials to Henry Ford in praise of the Ford as a getaway car.

Irving Wallace and David Wallechinsky, *Significa* (New York: E.P. Dutton, 1983), 215-6.

Who are the most frequent victims of serial killers?

The most frequent victims of serial killers are prostitutes.

U. S. News and World Report 2 May 1994.

Which United States cities have the highest crime rates?

In terms of violent crime in metropolitan areas, Miami, Florida, has the highest crime rate followed by New York, New York; Los Angeles-Long Beach, California; Tallahassee, Florida; and Jacksonville, Florida. The United States city with the highest rate of property crime is the metropolitan area of Baton Rouge, Louisiana, followed by Miami, Florida; San Antonio, Texas; Dallas, Texas; Atlantic City, New Jersey; and Cape May, New Jersey. The violent crime rate is the sum of rates for murder, robbery, and aggravated assault, and the property crime rate is the sum of rates for burglary, larceny-theft, and motor-vehicle theft.

David Savageau and Richard Boyer, *Places Rated Almanac: Your Guide to Finding the Best Places to Live in North America* (New York: Prentice Hall, 1993), 216.

How can a merchant spot a fake ID?

There are several things to look for when trying to verify the authenticity of a piece of identification. Merchants are instructed to check ID cards for signs of tampering such as flaws in laminated cards, raised edges around photographs, no signs of wear around the edges of supposedly old cards, a mismatch in the typewriter face on different sections, and typographical errors. Other suggestions include asking the holder to repeat or recite information listed on the ID such as the address or birth date and checking the user's signature against the signature on the ID card.

Experts suggest that the best identification contains a photograph, physical description, and signature. All these facts can be compared against the holder. For these reasons, a birth certificate is a poor ID because it contains no description of the user.

The Book of Inside Information (New York: Boardroom Classics, 1991), 10-11.

Who was known as America's most expert pickpocket?

Eddie Jackson (1873-1932), a pickpocket who worked in Chicago's Loop area from the 1890s until the early 1930s, is considered America's most expert pickpocket. Jackson's favorite pickpocketing technique was called "kiss-the-sucker." This technique involved bumping a victim directly in front while deftly lifting the person's wallet in one quick movement.

George C. Kohn, *Dictionary of Culprits and Criminals* (Metuchen, NJ: Scarecrow Press, 1986), 187.

What was the Everleigh Club?

On February 1, 1900, Ada and Minna Everleigh opened the most lavish brothel in the United States on South Dearborn Street in Chicago. The sisters called it the Everleigh Club and were able to earn millions of dollars from it until their retirement 11 years later.

Robert Jay Nash, *Crime Chronology: A Worldwide Record, 1900-1983* (New York: Facts on File, 1984), 3.

If a person becomes a victim of auto theft, what are the chances that the automobile will be recovered?

A victim of automobile theft has a two in three probability of having the property recovered.

Les Krantz, *America by the Numbers: Facts and Figures from the Weighty to the Way-Out* (Boston: Houghton Mifflin, 1993), 17.

Do most burglaries occur during the day or at night?

Burglaries for which time of occurence is reported are committed evenly between day and night.

Uniform Crime Reports for the United States 1992 (Washington, DC: Government Printing Office, 1992), 39.

What are some common characteristics of arsonists?

The National Center for Analysis of Violent Crime, arson and bombing unit, established a profile of a serial arsonist through interviews with 83 convicted arsonists. The average number of fires set by each arsonist was 31.5. The average age at which the arsonists set their first fire was 15 years old. Of those interviewed, 94 percent were male, 82 percent were white, 66 percent were single, and the average educational level was tenth grade. Eighty-seven percent had prior arrests for a felony, 63 percent for multiple felonies, and 24 percent for arson. Most lived near the arson scene, with 29.7 percent living within 1-miles, 20.3 percent living between one and two miles, 20.3 percent living from zero through five blocks, 16.3 percent living two miles or more away from the scene, and 6.8 percent committing arson at their home or institution. Of the arsonists interviewed, 54 percent at one time had been placed in juvenile detention, 46 percent in a mental health institution, and 28 percent in foster homes. Motives cited by the arsonists included: revenge, 41 percent; excitement, 30 percent; mixed motives, including psychological problems, 12 percent; vandalism, 7 percent; profit, 5 percent; and concealment of another crime, 5 percent. Of those arsonists who cited revenge as a motive, 59 percent said they were retaliating against society, 20 percent against an institution, 15 percent against a person, and 16 percent against a group.

USA Today 24 March 1994.

What is money laundering?

Money laundering is the concealment of income and its conversion to other assets in order to disguise its illegal source or use. There are three basic steps to money laundering. Placement is the conversion of cash into other negotiable instruments, such as money orders or checks, which can then be used in the financial system. Layering could be done by wire transfers, which separate the proceeds from the source. Integration provides an apparent legitimate explanation for the illicit proceeds. Money laundering schemes may involve transactions with foreign banks and a variety of financial instruments.

While primarily associated with illicit funds, money laundering is also used by tax evaders, corporations setting up slush funds for bribes and kickbacks, and foreign nationals avoiding currency restrictions at home. It is estimated by the Internal Revenue Service that tax evaders skim as much as $50 billion per year from their tax bills.

U.S. Department of Justice, Bureau of Justice Statistics, *Drugs, Crime, and the Justice System: A National Report from the Bureau of Justice Statistics* (Washington, DC, U.S. Government Printing Office, 1992), 62.

What is forfeiture?

Forfeiture is the surrender of property deemed by the government to be derived from or used in criminal activity. It aims to reduce the profitability of illegal activity and permanently curtail the financial ability of criminal organizations to continue illegal operations.

U.S. Department of Justice, Bureau of Justice Statistics, *Drugs, Crime, and the Justice System: A National Report from the Bureau of Justice Statistics* (Washington, DC: U.S. Government Printing Office, 1992), 156.

What is the "twinky defense" and where and why was it used?

The "twinky defense" was used in a San Francisco murder trial to claim that the defendant, Dan White, had eaten so much junk food that his judgment was impaired. Dan White, a rival politician and defender of "family values," murdered Mayor Moscone of San Francisco and Harvey Milk (1930-1978), member of the San Francisco Board of Supervisors, on November 27, 1978. The judge sentenced White to only seven years and eight months for voluntary manslaughter. Harvey Milk was an acknowledged homosexual and the lenient verdict set off a major riot in the San Francisco gay community.

Wayne R. Dynes, ed., *Encyclopedia of Homosexuality,* (New York: Garland Publishing, 1990), 2:818. Jay Robert Nash, *Crime Chronology: A Worldwide Record, 1900-1983,* (New York: Facts On File, 1984), 194.

Did millionaire Harry K. Thaw spend time in prison for the murder of architect Stanford White?

Harry K. Thaw (1871-1947), the heir of an American multimillionaire railroad tycoon, shot and killed world-renowned architect Stanford White (1853-1906) in cold blood on June 25, 1906. Thaw's wife, Evelyn Nesbit, had been White's mistress before she married Thaw. After their marriage, Thaw whipped his wife until she described her sexual relationship with White, which created intense jealousy in Thaw.

At the trial, Thaw's lawyer, Delphin Delmas, said in Thaw's defense, that Thaw temporarily suffered from "dementia Americana," a neurosis that makes an American male believe that his wife is sacred. Thaw was found not guilty on the grounds of insanity at the time of the murder. He was imprisoned in the asylum at Matteawan, New York. In 1915, a court declared Thaw sane and he left the asylum. He divorced his wife and in 1916 was returned to Matteawan for horsewhipping a teenaged boy. After his release in 1922, Thaw became an international playboy with the help of his inheritance.

George C. Kohn, *Dictionary of Culprits and Criminals* (Metuchen, NJ: Scarecrow Press, 1986), 350.

Who was Joe Adonis?

Joe Adonis was the nickname of handsome Giuseppe Doto (1902-1972), one of the most powerful crime figures in the United States and a member of the board of the national syndicate in New York. Involved in bootlegging, gambling, bribery, prostitution, and murder, Adonis also participated in legitimate businesses and became a multimillionaire long before he was deported to Italy in 1956.

Jay Robert Nash, *World Encyclopedia of Organized Crime* (New York: Paragon House, 1992), 8-12.

What happened to J. Paul Getty III after he as kidnapped?

Sixteen-year-old J. Paul Getty III was kidnapped near his residence in Rome, Italy, on June 10, 1973. His grandfather, American oil magnate J. Paul Getty (1892-1976), refused to pay his ransom, believing that the young man had concocted a scheme to obtain more spending money. However, when the kidnappers sent a severed ear and a picture of the mutilated boy to a Rome newspaper, the elder Getty paid $2.9 million to them. The captive was released, but the criminals were never apprehended.

Jay Robert Nash, *Crime Chronology: A Worldwide Record, 1900-1983* (New York: Facts on File, 1984), 185-6.

What was the Dead Rabbits riot of 1857?

In the 1840s and 1850s, New York City contained large gangs of pickpockets, robbers, and killers with colorful names like the Bowery Boys, the Plug Uglies, and the Roach Guards who inhabited the lower east side. Among the fiercest of these was the Dead Rabbits, a group of Irish and Welsh immigrants, whose battle emblem was a dead rabbit impaled on a spear. On July 4, 1857, a two-day gang fight broke out in the Bowery. Although it originally involved only the Dead Rabbits, Plug Uglies, and Bowery Boys, it spread to the others gangs in the area, and over 5,000 thugs, 100 of whom may have been slain, took part. The police were incapable of handling the situation, and the disturbance known as the Dead Rabbits Riot was not quelled until three regiments of soldiers were called out.

Jay Robert Nash, *World Encyclopedia of Organized Crime* (New York: Paragon House, 1992), 129.

Who was Virginia Hill?

Virginia Hill (1916-1966) was a notorious mobster moll, courier for the national crime syndicate, and girlfriend of Benjamin "Bugsy" Siegel (1906-1947). She was born to poverty in 1916. In Chicago, Illinois, where she worked as a waitress, she met Joseph Epstein, a lieutenant of Jake Guzik's of the racing wire racket. Through her association with him, she was introduced to key mobsters of the crime syndicate and became a courier, establishing what eventually became drug smuggling routes with Mexico.

Hill's notoriety rose during her 1940s affair with Bugsy Siegel, owner of the Flamingo Club, a casino in Las Vegas, Nevada. Concerned about their investments in the fledgling gambling business, the Chicago and New York mobs called in their loans in 1945 only to be rebuffed by Siegel. Hill fled to Paris on June 10, 1947, ten days before Siegel was shot to death.

The Kefauver Rackets Committee summoned Hill in 1951. She testified that her lifestyle was supported by "gifts" from boyfriends. However, the Internal Revenue Service determined that she owed $500,000 in back taxes. Hill married a ski instructor and fled to Europe, where she lived in exile until she overdosed on sleeping pills on the ski slopes of Salzburg, Austria, in March of 1966. At the time of her death she was being supported by her 15-year-old son, who was working as a waiter.

Jay Robert Nash, *World Encyclopedia of Organized Crime* (New York: Paragon House, 1992), 203-4.

Who shot Jesse James?

The notorious train and bank robber Jesse James (1847-1882) was treacherously murdered for a reward by Robert Ford, a member of his gang, in 1882. James was killed in his home in St. Joseph, Missouri, where Ford, who was accompanied by his brother Charles, waited until James had removed his gun belts and turned his back to them to adjust a picture on the wall. Then the assassin fired several rounds into his back at a distance of about six feet and ran from the house shouting, "I have killed Jesse James! I killed him! I killed him! I have killed Jesse James!"

Jay Robert Nash, *Bloodletters and Badmen: A Narrative Encyclopedia of American Criminals from the Pilgrims to the Present* (New York: M. Evans, 1973), 282.

Who was Ruth Ellis?

Ruth Ellis (1927-1955) was the last woman hanged by the state in the United Kingdom. On April 10, 1955, Ellis shot her lover, a race car driver named David Blakely, because he was seeing another woman. At her trial the judge declared that romantic rejection was not a valid excuse for murder and sentenced her to death. Although she was executed, there was a significant protest against this verdict both in Britain and abroad. The House of Commons voted the next year to abolish the death penalty, but the motion was overturned in the House of Lords.

Jay Robert Nash, *Look for the Woman: A Narrative Encyclopedia of Female Poisoners, Kidnappers, Thieves, Extortionists, Terrorists, Swindlers and Spies from Elizabethan Times to the Present* (New York: M. Evans, 1981), 140-3.

Was Jack the Ripper apprehended?

Jack the Ripper, the infamous murderer, was never apprehended. Between August 6, and November 9, 1888, he killed at least seven prostitutes in the Whitechapel district of London's East End. After having been brutally stabbed, all his victims had their throats cut by a knife with a long blade. From the way in which the last body was mutilated, it has been conjectured that the culprit had medical training. The police received half a kidney in the mail and numerous notes of ridicule from someone calling himself Jack the Ripper, but in spite of a vociferous public outcry, they were never able to identify the killer.

George C. Kohn, *Dictionary of Culprits and Criminals* (Metuchen, NJ: Scarecrow Press, 1986), 186-7.

Who was the first woman executed in San Quentin's gas chamber?

On November 21, 1941, Ethel Leta Juanita "Duchess" Spinelli became the first woman executed in San Quentin's gas chamber. Leader of a gang during the 1930s, she was condemned for ordering the death of a gang member whom, she feared, would inform on her.

Jay Robert Nash, *Crime Chronology: A Worldwide Record, 1900-1983* (New York: Facts on File, 1984), 118.

What is a lockdown?

A lockdown in the criminal justice system is when all inmates of a prison are kept in their cells 24 hours a day. The term came from an incident in 1973, when California director of corrections Raymond K. Procunier ordered all prisoners in four of the state's correctional facilities to be "locked down" due to the rise in assaults by prisoners on fellow inmates and staff members. All work assignments, recreational activities, and rehabilitation programs were canceled, affecting 9,000 inmates.

Vergil L. Williams, *Dictionary of American Penology* (Westport, CT: Greenwood Press, 1979), 131.

What is recidivism?

In the field of criminal justice, recidivism refers to when a criminal offender fails to avoid further problems with the law after serving a prison sentence. The subsequent rearrest and conviction of these felons is often blamed on the failure of the rehabilitation programs in the prison systems.

Vergil L. Williams, *Dictionary of American Penology* (Westport, CT: Greenwood Press, 1979), s.v. "recidivism."

Who was "God's Banker"?

Roberto Calvi, the head of Italy's Banco Ambrosiano, was often dubbed "God's Banker" because of his close ties to the Vatican. In June of 1982, Calvi's body was found hanging under the Blackfriars Bridge in London, England. The cause of his death was a subject of considerable debate. Some investigators believed that Calvi committed suicide. However, a Mafia informer in Italy revealed in a 1983 statement to five Rome magistrates that Calvi was murdered on the orders of Pippo Calo, a notorious Mafia crime boss in retaliation for Calvi embezzling money from Calo and another Mafia crime boss, Licio Gelli. Calvi's alleged murderer, Francesco Di Carlo, was sentenced in 1981 to serve 25 years in prison for heroin smuggling.

Wall Street Journal 30 July 1991.

How many women did Ted Bundy kill?

Serial killer Ted Bundy, who was executed in Florida on January 24, 1989, was linked to the deaths and disappearances of 36 women, ranging in ages from 12 to 26. His victims were found in six states of Florida, Idaho, Colorado, Oregon, Utah, and Washington. He may, however, have been responsible for many more deaths.

USA Today 24 January 1989.

What were the names of Jack the Ripper's victims?

From December 26, 1887, through February 13, 1891, 13 women were believed to have been murdered or attacked in and around the Whitechapel area of London, by one individual called Jack the Ripper. The victims were as follows: the woman known as "Fairy Fay," found off Commercial Street on December 26, 1887; Emma Elizabeth Smith, found on Osborn Street on April 3, 1888; Martha Tabram, found at 37 George Yard on August 7, 1888; Mary Ann Nichols, found on Buck's Row on August 31, 1888; Annie Chapman, found at 29 Hanbury Street on September 8, 1888; Elizabeth Stride, found on Berner Street on September 30, 1888; Catharine Eddowes, found on Mitre Square also on September 30, 1888; Mary Jane Kelly, found at Miller's Court, Dorset Street on November 9, 1888; Annie Farmer, found at 19 George Street on November 21, 1888; Rose

Mylett, found at Clarke's Yard, Poplar High Street on December 20, 1888; Alice McKenzie, found in Castle Alley on July 17, 1889; an unidentified woman (possibly Lydia Hart), found on Pinchin Street on September 10, 1889; and Frances Coles, found in Swallow Gardens on February 13, 1891. Three of the women, Stride, Eddowes, and Kelly, may not have been victims of the Ripper.

Paul Begg, Martin Fido, and Keith Skinner, *The Jack the Ripper A to Z* (London: Headline Book Publishing, 1992), 2.

Who were the Watergate Seven?

The Watergate Seven were E. Howard Hunt, James W. McCord, G. Gordon Liddy, Jr., Eugenio R. Martinez, Bernard L. Barker, Virgilio R. Gonzalez, and Frank A. Sturgis. They were arrested on June 17, 1972, for breaking into the Democratic party's campaign headquarters in the Watergate building in Washington, D.C. The Nixon administration attempted to cover up the incident, but failed. The ensuing crisis resulted in the resignation of U.S. president Richard Nixon (1913-1994) on August 9, 1974.

Fred L. Wirth, *The Trivia Encyclopedia* (New York: Bell Publishing, 1974), 290.

Which nations allow corporal punishment?

There are several nations with laws permitting corporal punishment of criminal offenders. The judicial systems in many of these countries follow Islamic law, which permits a variety of sentences that include stoning, flogging, caning, whipping, and amputation of hands or feet. Nations with such laws on the books are Afghanistan, Bangladesh, Brunei, parts of the English-speaking Caribbean, Iran, Libya, Malaysia, Pakistan, Qatar, Saudi Arabia, Singapore, South Africa, Sudan, Swaziland, United Arab Emirates, Yemen, and Zimbabwe. The Isle of Man, part of the United Kingdom, has a statute permitting caning but had plans to abolish it in 1994. Additionally, 27 American states permit educators to punish students corporally, usually by paddle; however, many local municipalities have passed laws prohibiting corporal punishment that override the state statutes.

New York Times 26 June 1994. *Newsweek* 18 April 1994.

What was the nickname of convicted criminal George Nelson?

George Nelson (1908-1934), the infamous American bank robber, murderer, and gangster, was born Lester J. Gillis in Chicago, Illinois. He changed his birth name because he felt it sounded effeminate and insisted on being called "Big George" Nelson. However, because of his short stature and schoolboy looks most of his associates called him "Baby Face" behind his back. "Baby Face" quickly became Nelson's nickname.

In 1931, Nelson was sentenced to one year to life at the State Penitentiary in Joliet, Illinois, for robbing a Chicago jewelry store. However, Nelson escaped one year later. In 1933 he and several other criminals went on a bank-robbing spree throughout Nebraska, Iowa, and Wisconsin and in early 1934 Nelson robbed two banks with another notorious gangster, John Dillinger. Nelson's crime sprees quickly made him one of the FBI's Most Wanted criminals. In a shootout with FBI agent W. Carter Baum on April 23, 1934, Nelson killed Baum. Later that year, on November 27, Nelson had another shootout with FBI agents Sam Cowley and Herman Hollis. All three were killed.

George C. Kohn, *Dictionary of Culprits and Criminals* (Metuchen, NJ: Scarecrow Press, 1986), s.v. "Nelson, George. " Jay Robert Nash, *Bloodletters and Badmen* (New York: M. Evans, 1973), s.v. "Nelson, George."

When did the FBI's "Ten Most Wanted Fugitives" program begin, and how does the FBI decide who to list?

The U.S. Federal Bureau of Investigation (FBI), under the direction of J. Edgar Hoover (1895-1972), inaugurated its "Ten Most Wanted Fugitives" program officially on March 14, 1950. Criteria for listing includes the outlaw's record, his/her potential as a public menace, and the estimated contribution of publicity toward his/her apprehension. During 1950 to 1989 there has been 420 fugitives on the list; 391 have been apprehended; 15 were deleted for various reasons, and 4 have been dropped for no longer meeting the criteria. Seven women have made the list. The average time between listing and apprehension is 157 days, with the shortest time being two hours and the longest being 18 years, 4 months, and 9 days. Six men have made the list twice. Under special circumstances the list of ten has been expanded. In October of 1970, the greatest number of fugitives, 16, were listed during this time of radical unrest.

Michael Newton and Judy Ann Newton, *The FBI Most Wanted: An Encyclopedia* (New York: Garland Publishing, 1989), xiii-xvi.

When was the gas chamber first used to execute convicts?

In 1921 Nevada approved the "Humane Death Bill" to provide for execution of a sleeping prisoner in his cell without warning by a lethal dose of gas. Nevada governor Emmet Boyle, an opponent of capital punishment, signed the bill, expecting that it would be overturned "cruel and unusual punishment" by the courts. Its constitutionality was upheld, and a gas chamber was built because the original idea was not feasible. On February 8, 1924, convicted murderer Gee Jon became the first person to be executed by a lethal dose of cyanide gas.

Hugo Adam Bedau, ed., *The Death Penalty in America, 3d ed.* (New York: Oxford University Press, 1982), 16-17.

Which U.S. Senate committee investigated organized crime in the 1950s?

In 1950 the United States Senate established the Senate Special Committee to Investigate Organized Crime in Interstate Commerce, better known as the Kefauver Committee. The committee originated with a bill sponsored by Democratic Senator Estes Kefauver (1903-1963) of Tennessee. During 1950-1951, the committee's intensive investigations into crime in the nation's major cities, coupled with the use of television coverage, made the public aware of the extensive nature of organized crime, spurred prosecutions, and made Kefauver a national figure. The other members of the committee were Herbert R. O'Conor from Maryland, Lester C. Hunt from Wyoming, Charles W. Tobey from New Hampshire, and Alexander Wiley from Wisconsin.

Concise Dictionary of American Biography, 4th ed. (New York: Charles Scribner's Sons, 1990), 587. *Concise Dictionary of American History* (New York: Charles Scribner's Sons, 1983), s.v. "Kefauver, (Carey) Estes. *"U.S. Congress Official Congressional Directory* (Washington, DC: Government Printing Office, 1951), 199.

How did Bonnie and Clyde die?

Passionate about guns and killing, Bonnie Parker (1911-1934) and Clyde Barrow (1909-1934), known for their small-time but violent robberies in the 1930s, were ambushed on May 23, 1934, in Gibland, Louisiana, near the Texas state line. They were supposed to meet their friend Henry Methvin at this site, but he had informed the law of the imminent rendezvous. With the trap set, Captain Frank Hamer of the Texas Highway Patrol and five other lawmen opened fire, shooting Clyde 25 times and Bonnie 23 times.

Jay Robert Nash, *Bloodletters and Badmen: A Narrative Encyclopedia of American Criminals from the Pilgrims to the Present* (New York: M. Evans, 1991), s.v. "Barrow, Clyde. " Carl Sifakis, *The Encyclopedia of American Crime* (New York: Facts On File, 1982), s.v. "Bonnie and Clyde: public enemies."

Who was the first person to be executed in the electric chair?

On August 6, 1890, William Kemmler of Buffalo, New York became the first person to be executed in the electric chair, following his conviction of murdering his mistress with an axe.

Carl Sifakis, *The Encyclopedia of American Crime,* (New York: Facts On File, 1982), s.v. "Kemmler, William."

What is bid-rigging?

Even though bid-rigging is a felony, it still occurs at auctions. A ring of dealers will meet before an auction to agree which merchandise they will bid on. They agree not to bid against one another. Each member is responsible for acquiring one or more specific items-known as lots-at the auction. In this way they can acquire the goods cheaply and the seller or the auction house loses money because the sale of the item is less than its actual value. Bid-rigging may be obvious at the auction if winking or hand signals are apparent among audience members, or the auctioneer does not seem very interested in moving the prices up, or audience members seem quite friendly with one another either before or after the sale.

George C. Chelekis, *The Official Government Auction Guide* (New York: Crown Publishers, 1992), 73-75.

What was the Gulag?

The word Gulag is an abbreviation for the Russian phrase, Glavnoye Upravleniye Ispravitelno-Trudovykh Lagerey, which translates in English to: Chief Administration of Corrective Labor Camps. The Gulag was a system of Soviet detention camps that operated from 1930 to 1955. Founded by the secret police, it was used to imprison millions of people, including dissident intellectuals, political outcasts, members of ethnic groups that were deemed disloyal, and common criminals.

The New Encyclopaedia Britannica (Chicago: Encyclopaedia Britannica 1989), s.v. "Gulag."

Who are the major mob families in New York and New Jersey?

Seven families have been identified by law enforcement officials as the major leaders of organized crime in New York and New Jersey. The Bonanno clan is made up of 50 to 75 members and is one of the weaker mob families; government infiltration has limited their influence. The smallest crime family is the Bruno-Scarfo group which was decimated by internal wars as well as by jail terms. The Colombo family, believed to have some 75 to 100 members, is split into two factions. Colombo activities include drug trafficking, gambling, loan sharking and activity in labor rackets. The small DeCavalcante family, once active in New Jersey, has lost most of its turf to the Gambino family, which numbers around 300. Private carting, extortion, bid rigging in the construction and garment industries, gambling and loan sharking are included in Gambino activities. Gambino boss John Gotti is said to run the operation from his federal prison cell. The other large crime family, the Genovese clan, has been identified as being active in gambling, loan sharking, narcotics, construction, private sanitation, and extortion. Labor racketeering has been the specialty of the Lucchese crime family, which lost "business" in the garment district to the Gambino family.

"Who's Who in the Mob," *The New York Times* 29 May 1994. "Who's Who in the Underworld," *USA Today* 2 April 1993.

Who first used fingerprints as a means of identification?

It is generally acknowledged that Francis Galton (1822-1911) was the first to classify fingerprints. However, his basic ideas were further developed by Sir Edward Henry (1850-1931), who devised a system based on the pattern of the thumb print. In 1901 in England, Henry established the first fingerprint bureau with Scotland Yard called the Fingerprint Branch.

E.B. Block, *Fingerprinting: Magic Weapon Against Crime* (New York: McKay, 1969), 7.

When and where did the Birdman of Alcatraz die?

Robert Stroud known as the "Birdman of Alcatraz," died on November 21, 1963, at the Medical Center for Federal Prisoners in Springfield, Missouri. Stroud had become an authority on birds and their diseases while serving a life prison term for murder. At the time of his death, Stroud had spent 42 of his 54 prison years in solitary confinement.

Facts on File (New York: Facts on File, 1963), 498.

What does the phrase "Murder will out" mean?

The phrase "Murder will out" suggests that all crimes and wrongdoings will eventually become known.

E.D. Hirsch, Jr., F. Kett, and James Trefil, *The Dictionary of Cultural Literacy* (Boston: Houghton Mifflin, 1988), 53.

Who are the most frequent targets of bias attacks?

In its first report on bias crimes, the FBI revealed that the majority of such crimes are motivated by racial hatred. The study of 1991 crime statistics showed that 6 out of 10 offenses showed racial bias, 2 of 10 showed religious bias, and ethnic and sexual orientation each accounted for 1 of 10. African Americans were the race most frequently targeted, in 36 percent of all cases, whites were targeted in 19 percent, and Jews were the victims in 17 percent.

Time 18 January 1993.

What is a Black Maria?

A Black Maria, which is pronounced Mah-rye'-ah, is a police patrol wagon, a vehicle used to transport persons under arrest. It may owe its origin to an African American woman, Maria Lee, who ran a lodging house for sailors in Boston in the early 1800s, and who, because of her large size, would assist police in the removal of her unruly guests. The term, however, was first applied to a prison van in London in 1847.

Charles Earle Funk, *A Hog on Ice and Other Curious Expressions* (New York: Harper & Brothers, 1948), 164.

What was the Symbionese Liberation Army?

The Symbionese Liberation Army (SLA) was a band of terrorists who had declared war on "the fascist state of Amerikka." In February of 1974 the group kidnapped Patricia Hearst of the Hearst newspaper dynasty, with the intention of using her as a hostage to secure the release of two incarcerated SLA members. During her one-and-one-half year with the SLA, Hearst was brainwashed and converted to the cause of her abductors. She was captured in September of 1975 and sentenced to seven years in prison for taking part in a bank robbery. On January 29, 1979, her sentence was commuted by U.S. President Jimmy Carter.

The SLA was founded in Berkeley, California, in 1973 by former police informant and escaped convict Donald Defreeze (Swahili name Cinque Mtume), who was killed in 1974 in a shootout between police and six members of the SLA in Los Angeles. Other members carried on the "mission," which included robbery, kidnapping, and assassination. The arrest of Hearst and others in 1975 essentially ended the organization.

Charles Moritz, ed., *Current Biography Yearbook 1982* (New York: H. W. Wilson, 1983), s.v. "Hearst, Patricia (Campbell)."

What was the real name of the pirate Blackbeard?

English pirate Edward Teach (1680?-1718) received the name of Blackbeard from his habit of braiding his beard and tying it with ribbons. Known as "the scourge of the Spanish Main" because of his audacity and ferocious cruelty, he operated from the Bahamas on a captured French merchantman, the *Queen Anne's Revenge*. Blackbeard died on November 2, 1718, when H.M.S. *Pearl*, sent by the Virginia governor, caught him of the coast of North Carolina. He is said to have had 14 wives.

Clarence L. Barnhart, ed., *The New Century Cyclopedia of Names* (New York: Appleton-Century-Croft, 1954), s.v. "Blackbeard." *World Book Encyclopedia* (Chicago: World Book, 1994), s.v. "Blackbeard."

For whom is the Miranda Rule named?

The Miranda Rule, also referred to as "being Mirandized," or reading a suspect his/her rights, was named after Ernesto Miranda. Convicted of kidnapping and rape in Arizona, he challenged his conviction on the basis that he had not been advised of his right to remain silent and to consult an attorney. The U.S. Supreme Court ruled in his favor in 1966. Miranda was retried later and sent to prison. Released in 1972, he died in 1976 as a result of stab wounds sustained in a bar fight in Phoenix.

Henry Campbell Black, *Black's Law Dictionary, 6th ed.* (St. Paul: West Publishing, 1990), s.v. "Miranda Rule." *Newsweek*, 9 February 1976. Elder Witt, , *Congressional Quarterly's Guide to the U.S. Supreme Court, 2d ed.* (Washington, DC: Congressional Quarterly, 1990), 556.

What was Gary Gilmore's last meal before he was executed at Utah State Prison?

Gary Gilmore was the first person to be executed following the reinstatement of the death penalty by the U.S. Supreme Court in 1976. Gilmore ate a hamburger, eggs, and potatoes, and he drank two small bottles of bourbon before being executed by a firing squad at Utah State Prison on January 17, 1977.

Amy Wallace et al., *The Book Of Lists #3* (New York: William Morrow, 1983), 87.

What did the 1993 report by the Milton S. Eisenhower Foundation say about urban violence?

The 1993 study by the Milton S. Eisenhower Foundation looked for causes underlying the Los Angeles riots that took place in April of 1992. The study found that the kinds of racial and economic discrimination present in 1992 were matched by the conditions that have been blamed for riots by inner-city blacks throughout the century. Riots dating back to 1919 have been created by the despair of people living in black ghettos. The foundation also cited inadequate and misdirected federal efforts to solve this problem. It recommended a program including job training, improved housing, and inner-city banks to finance new development.

Sonya Ross, "Report says U.S. hasn't learned how to respond to urban riots," *Pittsburgh Post Gazette* 28 February 1993.

Who were the first people to be executed for espionage during peacetime in the United States?

On April 5, 1951, Ethel and Julius Rosenberg received the death sentence for espionage. They were the first convicted spies to receive the death sentence in peacetime. The sentences were imposed by U.S. District Court judge Irving Robert Kaufman. The Rosenbergs were electrocuted on June 19, 1953, at Sing Sing Prison in Ossining, New York. Morton Sobell was also convicted by the same jury, but he received a 30-year prison sentence.

Joseph Nathan Kane, *Famous First Facts*, (New York: H.W. Wilson, 1981), 607.

Who was Black Francis?

Black Francis was an Irish highwayman in the late seventeenth century, who like Robin Hood robbed the rich and gave to the poor. Various legends about his chivalrous behavior and hidden treasure have risen up around him.

Henry H. Glassie, *Irish Folk History: Texts from the North* (Philadelphia: University of Pennsylvania Press, 1982), 47-51.

What is the chronology of the so-called Navy Tailhook Scandal?

The chronology of the so-called Navy Tailhook Scandal begins September 5-7, 1991 at the 35th annual Tailhook Association convention in Las Vegas. 26 women, half of them naval officers were allegedly forced to run a gauntlet of drunken U.S. Navy and Marine officers in a hotel hallway. While "running the gauntlet" many of the women charged they were groped, fondled and otherwise sexually harassed. Other ensuing developments:

October 10, 1991 -A female officer files a complaint which is referred to the Naval Investigative Service.

October 11, 1991 -Tailhook president Capt. F.G. Ludwig Jr. notifies Navy Secretary Lawrence Garrett 3d that he has received five reports of sexual harassment in relation to the incident.

October 29, 1991 -Garrett asks the Navy Inspector General to investigate incident and states the Navy has severed all ties with the Tailhook Association.

April 30, 1992 -The Inspector General and the Navy Investigative Service concurs as to much of what happened but amidst uncooperative witnesses names only two suspects.

June 2, 1992 -The Navy sends the names of 60 officers to their commanding officers for possible disciplinary action.

June 18, 1992 -Garrett asks the Pentagon to investigate charges.

June 26, 1992 -Taking full responsibility for the incident Garrett resigns.

September 24, 1992 -The Pentagon Inspector General issues a report highly critical of the Navy's handling of the incident.

April 23, 1993 -The Pentagon Inspector General implicates 140 officers in the incident.

October 1, 1993 -Navy Secretary John H. Dalton calls for the resignation of Admiral Kelso for shirking proper leadership over the incident.

October 21, 1993 -The Marine Corps drops charges against a Marine captain charged in the scandal.

February 8, 1994 -A Navy judge dismisses all charges against three officers charged in the incident but says they are still subject to future administrative discipline.

New York Times 9 February 1994.

Are privately run prisons on the rise in the United States?

Because of greater efficiency, profitability, and low operating costs privately run prisons are on the rise in the United States. In 1986 there were only three companies running prisons but by the end of 1993 there were an estimated 24. In 1992 alone the number of privately managed prisons rose by 25 percent.

Financial World 3 August 1993.

Why do members of the Royal Canadian Mounted Police wear red jackets?

Royal Canadian Mounted Police wear red jackets because the color red signifies law and authority.

R.G. Macbeth, *Policing the Plains* (London: Hodder and Stoughton, 1922), 26.

Cultures and Customs

What is Chusok?

Chusok is a Korean holiday that is held on the fifteenth of the Eighth Moon which is considered to be the fairest of the twelve full moons. It is celebrated by families going into the countryside for outdoor sports, visiting shrines and graves of loved ones and reveling in the harvest by consuming wine, cakes and fresh fruits. Chusok is also known as Hangawi.

Margaret Read MacDonald, ed., *The Folklore of World Holidays* (Detroit, MI: Gale Research, 1991), 430.

Which celebrities are buried in London's Westminster Abbey?

London's Westminster Abbey is the burying place of many of England's kings and queens as well as famous commoners. The first royal graves are those of King Sebert and his queen. Many succeeding monarchs and their families are also buried there, some in elaborate tombs and chapels. When King Richard II ordered the burials of John of Waltham, Bishop of Salisbury, and Sir John Galoppe, he was the first to permit the burial of commoners in the Abbey. Many famous British statesmen are now entombed or memorialized in the Abbey, including Benjamin Disraeli (1804-1881) and Sir Winston Churchill (1874-1965). Franklin D. Roosevelt (1882-1945) is one of the few foreigners to be memorialized in the church. Westminster Abbey is well known for its Poet's Corner, where many famous writers and poets lie. Geoffrey Chaucer (1310?-1400) was the first to be buried there; he was followed by many others, although often these memorials were placed long after the writer's death. Famous scientists and soldiers also have their place in the Abbey. Perhaps the most famous tomb is that of the Unknown Warrior, which holds the body of a soldier from World War I. There is now only one family to hold the right of burial at Westminster Abbey, the Percy family has a private vault. The Abbey now only accepts ashes for internment.

Ben Weinreb and Christopher Hibbert, ed., *The London Encyclopaedia* (Bethesda, MD: Adler & Adler, 1986), s.v. "Westminster Abbey." *USA Today* 20 July 1989.

What is the proper way to dispose of a U.S. flag?

When a U.S. flag is no longer in a condition to be displayed, it should be destroyed. U.S. Code specifies that a dignified manner of destroying the flag is by burning.

United States Code, vol. 14 (Washington, DC: United States Government Printing Office, 1989), 64.

When do the swallows come back to Capistrano in California?

According to legend, every year the swallows are expected to return to the Mission San Juan Capistrano, California, on St. Joseph's Day, March 19, and depart on October 23, when they immigrate to the Southern Hemisphere. The birds can actually arrive anytime during the month of March and leave in October to migrate to the Southern Hemisphere. The number that return each year has been declining, with the growth of the town and the large number of tourists blamed for the decrease. The legend began when a local innkeeper who considered the birds a nuisance destroyed their nests as an attempt to drive the birds away. One of the Mission fathers called the swallows to the mission for shelter and the swallows have returned every year since then.

Encyclopedia Americana (Danbury, CT: Grolier, 1990), 24:210. Hennig Cohen and Tristram Potter Coffin, eds., *The Folklore of American Holidays, 2d ed.,* (Detroit: Gale Research, 1991), 133-35.

Why and how did the ancient Egyptians practice mummification?

Ancient Egyptians embalmed their dead because they believed that the eternal survival of each person's "life forces," ka and ba was dependent on these forces returning periodically to the corpse thus it needed to be preserved. The word "mummy" derives from the Arabic/Persian word "moumiya," which is the name of a black resinous crusty substance that encoats Egyptian mummies. It is formed by the interaction of oils, perfumes, unguents, and resins with which the wrappings are coated.

Three levels of mummification were perfected during the New Kingdom, the highest level being the most costly and the most sophisticated. At this level the internal organs were removed from the corpse including the brain which was scooped out via the nostrils. The viscera was subsequently embalmed and wrapped in separate parcels. At various times the organs were either placed in the chest cavity or in canopic jars. The embalmed corpse was usually wrapped with household linen, although the finest burials called for linen woven specifically for this purpose. The linen strips were first wrapped around the extremities and then around the whole body, binding the arms and legs to the torso. Amulets were often placed on specific points of the body as it was being wrapped. At every step of the bandaging process oils and perfumes were brushed on the body resulting in the above-mentioned black, crusty coating. The mummy was then placed in an anthropomorphic coffin for burial in a tomb.

Christine Hobson, *The World of the Pharaohs* (New York: Thames and Hudson, 1987), 152-54.

What unusual substances were used in nineteenth-century America as hair preparations?

According to Mrs. Lydia Child, who published *The Frugal Housewife* in 1829, New England rum was a good hair cleaner. If hair roots needed strengthening, brandy was suggested.

Isaac Asimov, *Isaac Asimov's Book of Facts* (New York: Grosset & Dunlap, 1979), 115.

What are Blue Laws, and how did they come to be so named?

Blue Laws are laws that regulate personal behavior especially on Sundays. They were quite prevalent in colonial America but not restricted to Puritan New England. Regulations forbidding Sunday kissing, outdoor recreation and work, and the selling of alcohol and cigarettes are typical Blue Laws, some of which are still on the books in various regions of the country. The term comes from a book by the Reverend Samuel A. Peters that gave an account of Connecticut Blue Laws, entitled *A General History of Connecticut, by a Gentleman of the Province* (1781).

Dictionary of American History, vol. I, Rev. ed. (New York: Charles Scribner's Sons, 1976), s.v. "Blue Laws."

What was Mrs. Santa Claus's maiden name?

According to at least one scholar, Mrs. Santa Claus was a member of New York City's Grundy family of Fifth Avenue.

Robert Haven Schauffler, ed., *Christmas: Its Origin, Celebration and Significance as Related in Prose and Verse* (New York: Dodd, Mead, 1930), 214.

Is it possible to be buried in space?

In 1985, the Celestis Group of Melbourne, Florida, made plans to bury people in space, after cremation. For $3,900 (1985 dollars) Celestis planned to offer cremation (a special process reduces the usual two to four pounds of ash to a mere handful), a small titanium urn the size of a lipstick complete with social security number, and religious symbols if desired. Space Services Inc. of Houston will transport the remains into the heavens in a privately developed rocket.

Phil Musick, *Pittsburgh Press* 7 February 1985.

What is the history of beards and shaving?

In early civilizations, men considered their beards to be a sign of virility, and since hair grew out of his body, to hold his personality or spirit. Allowing clippings from one's beard to fall into the hands of an enemy was very dangerous. Cutting off a beard was considered abnormal, and shaving was used as a punishment or as a sign of illness, mourning, or disgrace. The Samson legend, or the beard as a sign of strength, was accepted because the weak—women, young boys, and eunuchs—were beardless.

Beard shape and length usually related directly to the hierarchy of a society. The aristocracy generally mimicked their king's style of beard or lack of one. Alexander the Great departed from tradition during the fourth century B.C. when he ordered his soldiers to shave as a precaution. He considered beards to be an obvious handle for enemies to grip. On the other hand, soldiers fighting in the Crimean War, 1853-56, pampered their beards because they believed them to guard against cold and pain. During the nineteenth century, doctors wore beards as a trademark of their profession.

Rudolph Brasch, *How Did It Begin?* (New York: David Mc Kay, 1966), 136-39.

What is the origin of the custom of dressing boys in blue and girls in pink?

Ancient fears of evil spirits menacing infants in the nursery led to the wearing of blue by babies. Certain colors were considered powerful repellents of evil; because the heavens were blue, that hue was thought to be particularly powerful in warding off evil spirits. In some cultures boy babies were much superior to girl babies, the boys were dressed in blue, while any color would do for the girls.

Another explanation for the blue-is-for-boys, pink-is-for-girls tradition comes from a European legend. It explained that boy babies were found under cabbages, which were mostly blue in Europe, while girls were born inside a delicate pink rose.

Rudolph Brasch, *How Did It Begin?* (New York: David Mc Kay, 1966), 22-23.

What is the origin of the phrase "beyond the pale"?

The expression "beyond the pale" refers to behavior outside of society's jurisdiction and mores. In the past, the "pale" referred to a region enclosed by a fence or other boundary marker over which a governing body had authority and control. The most famous of these territories was the English Pale, the region around Dublin over which England had power.

Bergen Evans, *Comfortable Words* (New York: Random House, 1962), 272.

What is Belsnickling?

Belsnickling is the term for a nineteenth-century Pennsylvania custom in which costumed, singing revelers paraded through residential areas on Christmas Eve. The practice was a combination of two older folk traditions of the region. The first of these, mumming, involved informal groups of entertainers performing short theatrical skits for Philadelphia residents on Christmas Eve, in hopes of receiving a bit of food or money. Elsewhere, in the Pennsylvania countryside, a lone performer known as the belsnickel went about bestowing small gifts on obedient children and punishing the naughty. The two traditions merged over the years and mask-wearing youths began an annual night of serenading townspeople that continued until the early decades of the twentieth century. The practice also spread to other areas of North America when Pennsylvanians migrated.

Alfred L. Shoemaker, *Christmas in Pennsylvania: A Folk-Cultural Study* (Kutztown: Pennsylvania Folklife Society, 1959), 73.

What is Kwanzaa?

Kwanzaa is an annual seven-day African-American festival of heritage occurring between December 26 and January 1. It is thought to be celebrated by about 15 million people of African ancestry around the world. The origins of Kwanzaa date back to 1966, when California State University Black Studies professor Maulana Karenga founded the holiday whose name is the Swahili word for "first fruits of the harvest." The festival is a composite of various African harvest festivals. Each of its seven days pays homage to a different principle: the first is "umoja (unity); second, kujichagulia (self-determination); third, ujima (collective work and responsibility); fourth, ujamaa (cooperative economics); fifth, nia (purpose); sixth, kuumba (creativity); and seventh, imani (faith)." Three red candles (representing blood), one black candle (representing skin color); and three green (representing homeland) are lit each successive night in a special seven-candle-holder known as a kinara. A community-wide celebration, karamu, is held on December 31.

Karen S. Peterson, "A Celebration of African Heritage," *USA Today,* 26 December 1989. Sue Ellen Thompson and Barbara W. Carlson, comps., *Holidays, Festivals, and Celebrations of the World Dictionary* (Detroit, MI: Omnigraphics, 1994), s.v. "Kwanzaa."

What was the mystery of "Little Miss 1565," a victim of the Ringling Brothers Circus Fire of 1944?

In 1944 a Ringling Brothers Circus tent caught fire in Hartford, Connecticut, and 168 people were trampled or burned to death trying to escape. One of the bodies was never claimed-she was a blonde, blue-eyed girl whose features were not changed in the fire. After months of trying, no one claimed her as family. She was named after her morgue number and "Little Miss 1565" was inscribed on her tombstone.

Woody Gelman and Barbara Jackson, *Disaster Illustrated: Two Hundred Years of American Misfortune* (New York: Harmony Books, 1976), 59. Gary Smith, "The Little Girl in Grave 1565," *Life* November, 1991.

What was the Jekyll Club?

During the 1890s, millionaires such as J. Pierpont Morgan, Henry Clay Frick, Joseph Pulitzer, E. H. Goodyear and J. D. Rockefeller met to hunt and fish at the exclusive Jekyll Club on Georgia's Jekyll Island. The state of Georgia purchased the island in 1947.

John May, *Curious Trivia* (New York: Dorset Press, 1984), 52.

What are the original title and words to the poem popularly known as "The Night Before Christmas"?

The holiday poem known to most people as "The Night Before Christmas," by Clement C. Moore (1779-1863), was originally published in 1823 under the title "A Visit from St. Nicholas." The text is as follows:

'Twas the night before Christmas, when all through the house
Not a creature was stirring, not even a mouse;
The stockings were hung by the chimney with care,
In hopes that St. Nicholas soon would be there;
The children were nestled all snug in their beds,
While visions of sugar-plums danced through their heads;
And mamma in her kerchief, and I in my cap,
Had just settled our brains for a long winter's nap,—
When out on the lawn there arose such a clatter,
I sprang from my bed to see what was the matter.
Away to the window I flew like a flash,
Tore open the shutters and threw up the sash.
The moon, on the breast of the new-fallen snow,
Gave a lustre of midday to objects below;
When what to my wondering eyes should appear,
But a miniature sleigh and eight tiny reindeer,
With a little old driver, so lively and quick
I knew in a moment it must be St. Nick.
More rapid than eagles his coursers they came,
And he whistled and shouted and called them by name:
"Now, Dasher! now, Dancer! now, Prancer and Vixen!
On, Comet! on, Cupid! on, Donder and Blitzen!
To the top of the porch, to the top of the wall!
Now, dash away, dash away, dash away all!"
As dry leaves that before the wild hurricane fly,
When they meet with an obstacle, mount to the sky,
So, up to the house-top the coursers they flew,
With a sleigh full of toys,—and St. Nicholas too.
And then in a twinkling I heard on the roof
The prancing and pawing of each little hoof.
As I drew in my head and was turning around,
Down the chimney St. Nicholas came with a bound.
He was dressed all in fur from his head to his foot,
And his clothes were all tarnished with ashes and soot;
A bundle of toys he had flung on his back,
And he looked like a peddler just opening his pack.
His eyes how they twinkled! his dimples how merry!
His cheeks were like roses, his nose like a cherry;
His droll little mouth was drawn up like a bow,
And the beard on his chin was as white as the snow.
The stump of a pipe he held tight in his teeth,
And the smoke it encircled his head like a wreath.
He had a broad face, and a little round belly
That shook, when he laughed, like a bowl full of jelly.
He was chubby and plump,—a right jolly old elf—
And I laughed when I saw him, in spite of myself.
A wink of his eye and a twist of his head
Soon gave me to know I had nothing to dread.
He spoke not a word, but went straight to his work,
And filled all the stockings; then turned with a jerk,
And laying his finger aside of his nose,
And giving a nod, up the chimney he rose.
He sprang to his sleigh, to his team gave a whistle,
And away they all flew like the down of a thistle;
But I heard him exclaim, ere he drove out of sight:
"Happy Christmas to all, and to all a good-night!"

Florence Adams and Elizabeth McCarrick, *Highdays & Holidays* (New York: E.P. Dutton, 1955), 307-11.

Who started the celebration of Arbor Day?

In 1872 Julius Sterling Morton (1832-1902) introduced a resolution into the Nebraska state legislature that April 10 of that year be dedicated to tree planting in the State of Nebraska, and that the day should be called Arbor Day. Morton, who later from 1893 to 1897 served as U.S. Secretary of Agriculture under President Grover Cleveland (1837-1908), got the idea for Arbor Day while watching a group of Russian immigrants who, upon settling the equally treeless land around Lincoln, Nebraska, began planting trees to prevent soil erosion and to serve as windbreakers. Convinced that the so-called "civilization" of the prairie states would be severely limited as long as the region lacked trees, he made it his personal mission to encourage their planting. Morton's 1872 resolution was adopted because at this time Americans realized that their country's natural resources were finite, and the idea of Arbor Day quickly spread throughout the nation. By the end of the century, nearly every state and territory of the United States observed the holiday, although the date for doing so varied widely from one location to another. Today, Arbor Day is most often held in cooperation with schools, in order to impress children with the importance of conservation efforts.

The Conservationist, May-June 1982. The Encyclopedia Americana, international ed (Danbury, CT: Grolier, 1989), 2:179-80.

To various Indian tribes, what was a "potlatch"?

A potlatch was a winter festival celebrated by Indian tribes along the Pacific coast from Alaska to Oregon. The word comes from the Nootka word patshatl for "gift" or "giving." Although specific aspects of the celebration varied in different locations, they were all characterized by the giving away of large numbers of goods, usually blankets. Some people, however, gave away almost all of their possessions, with the exception of their homes. Consequently, they were held in high esteem by their neighbors and often received even greater gifts when others "potlatched."

Singing, dancing, and feasting figured prominently. Some specific practices included inducting children of the chiefs into secret societies, raising houses and carved poles, and selling copper plates which played a role in the local economy. The Haida also tattooed their children at this time.

Frederick Webb Hodge, ed., *Handbook of American Indians North of Mexico* (New York: Pageant Books, 1959), 293.

What are the origins of the "crossing the line" ceremony among sailors aboard a ship traversing the Equator?

The "crossing the line" ceremony among sailors aboard ships traversing the Equator was derived from medieval religious observances of Northern European sailors. When a famous landmark was passed-such as the Pointe du Raz near the northwest coast of France-French, Dutch, or Hanseatic seamen held a religious service. The first known reference to an observance marking an equatorial crossing dates back to 1529, when a French ship bound for Sumatra had a ceremony for the men who were crossing it for the first time. According to the ship's journal, a mass was held and a tuna stew served. However, such sober celebrations soon evolved into equatorial-related pranks, carousing, and general drunken mayhem among ships of many nationalities. In nautical slang, those who have made the crossing are referred to as shellbacks, while the uninitiated remain pollywogs.

Samuel Eliot Morison, *The European Discovery of America: The Southern Voyages, A.D. 1492-1616* (New York: Oxford University Press, 1974), 167-69.

How did the custom of eating hot cross buns on Good Friday originate?

The custom of eating hot cross buns on Good Friday traces its origin to pre-Christian societies. Ancient Egyptians, in devotion to Isis the Mother Goddess, ate small loaves of bread stamped with symbolic horns. Greeks cross-marked their cakes in honor of Diana, and in the ancient Roman city of Herculaneum, loaves of bread with the familiar cross have been unearthed. Early Christians ate unleavened loaves in imitation of Passover bread eaten by Jesus before His death on the cross.

Robert J. Myers, *Celebrations: The Complete Book of American Holidays,* (New York: Doubleday, 1972), 96-97.

What is the Gimmal Ring?

Serving as a love token for a betrothed couple, the Gimmal Ring consisted of two bands that could be joined together by fitting into each other with little teeth. This was meant to take the place of the broken coin, in which the two lovers split a coin, with each one keeping one half of the coin.

Source: Leopold Wagner, *Manners, Customs, and Observances: Their Origin and Signification (1894 reprint)* Detroit: Gale Research, 1968), 91.

Is the Fourth of July celebrated outside of the United States?

In Denmark the United States' Independence Day is celebrated. In 1912 some Danish-born United States citizens bought a tract of land near the village of Rebild and gave it to the Danish government with the stipulation that the Fourth of July be commemorated every year. Over time a replica of Abraham Lincoln's log cabin and exhibits of early American life were built on the land and the area became known as Rebild National Park.

Source: H. Dennis-Jones, *Your Guide to Denmark* (New York: Funk & Wagnalls, 1969), 172.

What is the earliest recorded account of the bride's wedding veil?

The earliest recorded account of the bride's wedding veil is the biblical story as recorded in the Book of Genesis of Jacob who loved his cousin, Rachel. Jacob asked his uncle Laban for permission to marry his beautiful daughter. Laban agreed, but only if Jacob consented to work in his servitude for seven years. When Jacob fulfilled his duty, he asked for Rachel again. Laban complied and arranged for the wedding. At the ceremony, Laban managed to successfully deceive Jacob. Wearing a veil over her face, the bride was actually Laban's first-born daughter, Leah, and not Rachel. To guarantee that a bride is the correct person the groom intended to marry, a practice was begun whereby the groom and witnesses confirmed the bride's identity and then placed a veil over her head. Today the veil has become part of traditional wedding apparel.

The Interpreter's Bible: The Holy Scriptures (New York: Abingdon-Cokesbury Press, 1952), 700. Abraham J. Klausner, *Weddings: A Complete Guide to All Religious and Interfaith Marriage Services* (New York: Signet, 1986), 128-29.

How many members are there in the Ku Klux Klan?

Because of internal difficulties as well as vigorous civil and criminal prosecutions against them, membership in the Ku Klux Klan has been shrinking for many years. According to an Anti-Defamation League (ADL) report issued in 1991, the "combined total membership of all Klans today is approximately 4,000."

John George and Laird Wilcox, *Nazis, Communists, Klansmen, and Others on the Fringe: Political Extremism in America* (Buffalo, NY: Prometheus Books, 1992), 411.

What were molly houses?

Found in eighteenth-century London, molly houses were gathering places for male homosexuals. They were sometimes informal public houses with a special back room for "mollies" or else more elaborate establishments catering exclusively to homosexuals, with perhaps 20 to 40 patrons at the busiest time of the week, Sunday night, the homosexuals' "night out." In 1726, a wave of prosecuting zeal caused the authorities to raid at least 20 such houses, a number of whose owners were convicted and made to stand in the pillory, while three individuals were hanged for the crime of sodomy.

Wayne R. Dynes, ed., *Encyclopedia of Homosexuality* (New York: Garland Publishing, 1990), 2:827-8.

Where are canine mascots of university football teams often buried?

Many canine mascots of university football teams are buried in their respective football stadiums. Interred in such places are Ugas I, II, and III, the bulldog mascots for the University of Georgia, and Reveilles I, II, III, and IV, all female collies and mascots at Texas A&M.

Pittsburgh Press 14 January 1990.

Who asked the question, Is there a Santa Claus?

Perplexed by her friends disbelief in Santa Claus, eight-year-old Virginia O'Hanlon wrote to the *New York Sun* in 1897 inquiring about the reality of Santa. She wrote to the newspaper because her father claimed that "If you see it in the *Sun*, it's so." The reply by editor Frank Church written on its editorial page is given below:

"Virginia, your little friends are wrong. They have been affected by the skepticism of a skeptical age. They do not believe except [what] they see. They think that nothing can be which is not comprehensible by their little minds. All minds, Virginia, whether they be men's or children's are little. In this great universe of ours man is a mere insect, an ant, in his intellect, as compares with the boundless world about him, as measured by the intelligence capable of grasping the whole truth and knowledge. Yes, Virginia, there is a Santa Claus. He exists as certainly as love and generosity and devotion exist, and you know that they abound and give to your life its highest beauty and joy. Alas! how dreary would be the world if there were no Santa Claus! It would be as dreary as if there were no Virginias. There would be no childlike faith then, no poetry, no romance to make tolerable this existence. We should have no enjoyment except in sense and sight. The eternal light with which childhood fills the world would be extinguished. Not believe in Santa Claus! You might as well not believe in fairies! You might get your papa to hire men to watch in all the chimneys on Christmas Eve to catch Santa Claus, but even if they did not see Santa Claus coming down, what would that prove? Nobody sees Santa Claus, but that is no sign that there is no Santa Claus. The most real things in the world are those that neither children nor men can see. Did you ever see fairies dancing on the lawn? Of course not, but that's no proof that they are not there. Nobody can conceive or imagine all the wonders there are unseen and unseeable in the world. You tear apart the baby's rattle to see what makes the noise inside, but there is a veil covering the unseen world which not the strongest man, nor even the united strength of all the strongest men that ever lived, could tear apart. Only faith, fancy, poetry, love, romance, can push aside that curtain and view and picture the supernal beauty and glory beyond. Is it all real? Ah, Virginia, in all this world there is nothing else real and abiding.

"No Santa Claus! Thank God! he lives and he lives forever. A thousand years from now, Virginia, nay, ten times ten thousand years from now, he will continue to make glad the heart of childhood."

New York Sun 21 September 1897.

Which months have the highest number of births?

The months having the highest number of births are September, with 11.6 thousand births per day; August, with 11.4 thousand; July, with 11.2 thousand; June, with 11.0 thousand; and October, with 10.7 thousand.

USA Today 20 September 1990.

What is the purpose of a milk bath or buttermilk bath?

People throughout history have bathed in milk or buttermilk for various reasons. According to Arab custom, persons who wash their genitals in the milk of an ass will increase their sexual prowess. In Hindu tradition, if a woman wants to eliminate the unwanted attention of a man, she should bathe in the buttermilk of a female buffalo mixed with yellow amarinth, banupadika plant, and goplike powder.

Source: Harry E. Wedeck, *A Dictionary of Aphrodisiacs* (New York: M. Evans, 1989), 33, 98-9.

What is the preferred size of the American family?

According to the Gallup Poll Monthly of June 1990, 57 percent of Americans thought that two was the ideal number of children in a family, while 29 percent felt that three or more children constituted the ideal American family. Only three percent of Americans polled felt that one child or no children comprised the ideal family.

Margaret Ambry and Cheryl Russell, *The Official Guide to the American Marketplace* (Ithaca, NY: New Strategist Publications and Consulting, 1992).

In what foreign country are most of the American deceased servicemen buried?

Over 130,000 United States war dead are buried in 24 federally maintained cemeteries in various countries throughout the world. Of these, France has the most deceased American servicemen with 60,509. The Philippines has 17,206, followed by Belgium with 13,685, Italy with 12,264, and Luxembourg with 5,076.

USA Today 24 May 1991.

Who was the first Miss America?

In 1921 sixteen-year-old Margaret Gorman, a 108 pound "bathing beauty" won the first Miss America title. This national beauty pageant continues to be held every September in Atlantic City, New Jersey.

Debra M. Kirby, ed., *Awards, Honors, & Prizes 1995-95, 11th ed.* (Detroit, MI: Gale Research, 1994), 1:749. Dennis Sanders, *The First of Everything: A Compendium of Important, Eventful, and Just-Plain-Fun Facts About All Kinds of Firsts* (New York: Delacorte Press, 1981), 168.

How many Native American tribes are recognized by the United States government?

According to the U. S. Bureau of Indian Affairs, 515 Indian tribes were recognized by the federal government as of January 1993. This number includes 318 "tribal entities" in the lower

48 states, which are described as Indian tribes, bands, villages, communities, and pueblos. The remaining 197 recognized entities are in Alaska.

Approximately 200 or more Native American tribal entities are not recognized by the United States government. Some tribes have purposely isolated themselves from federal authorities and never sought federal recognition. Other tribes maintained peaceful relations with federal authorities throughout history and never had to obtain recognition through a peace treaty. Some groups were so small that they escaped the attention of the federal government. In other cases, tribes may have been recognized by the federal government at one time but had this recognition revoked by Congress.

Jack Utter, *American Indians: Answers to Today's Questions* (Lake Ann, MI: National Woodlands Publishing, 1993), 32-3.

What is the Blarney Stone?

The Blarney Stone, which is two-and-one-half-feet long and nine-to twelve-feet high, is located in a wall of Blarney Castle in Ireland. According to tradition, anyone who kisses the Blarney Stone is rewarded with marvelous gifts of verbal persuasion. The Blarney Stone is considered one of Ireland's most famous tourist attractions.

New York Times Magazine 30 April 1952.

What was the greatest contributor to the decline of the Native North American population during the conquest era?

Historians believe that the major cause of the Native North American population decline during the conquest era was the introduction of disease by European explorers and settlers, not military conflict. Diseases that commonly caused high mortality among Native North Americans at that time included smallpox, measles, whooping cough, chicken pox, bubonic plague, typhus, diphtheria, amoebic dysentery, influenza, and parasitic worms.

Jack Utter, *American Indians: Answers to Today's Questions* (Lake Ann, MI: National Woodlands Publishing, 1993), 24.

According to the Chinese, when is a child one year of age?

The Chinese consider a child to be one year old at the time of its birth. An additional year is added to the child's age on the Chinese New Year, not on the child's birthday. Thus, a child born on the last day of the Chinese year would celebrate its second birthday when it was only two days old.

Adelin Linton and Ralph Linton, *The Lore of Birthdays* (New York: Schuman, 1952), 31.

What are the origins and symbolism of Christmas candles?

Traditionally, candles have played a variety of roles in Christmas decorations and celebrations. Although the exact date of the first use of candles at Christmas cannot be determined, it is likely that they were burning in the halls of England's King Arthur in 521 when supposedly he celebrated the first Christmas feast. Most notably, candles have served to symbolize Jesus Christ as the light of the world and Christmas as the day of his birth. In earlier days it was the custom in the Church of England to burn two small candles in the church on Christmas Eve, one candle representing Christ's human nature and the other his divine nature.

Superstitions have sometimes arisen concerning Christmas candles. For example, they were used as protection from evil spirits when burned on Christmas, as Shakespeare noted, and in West Jutland, to determine whose life would last longer—the householder's or his wife's. In Norway objects of pewter and silver were placed so that they would reflect the rays of the candle because candle rays on Christmas were said to bring blessings to the home. There is a legend that says burning a "Christ child" candle in the window on Christmas Eve light the way for Jesus Christ and to make amends for his first visit when there was no room at the inn in Bethlehem.

Legends also surround the fragrant bayberry candles, often lit on Christmas and made by the Puritans from bayberries when other forms of wax to make candles were not available. Supposedly a lit bayberry candle brought good fortune to the home in which it burned. If two lovers, separated from one another on Christmas Eve, were to light bayberry candles, each would detect the sweet aroma of the other's candle, if their love was true.

"A Bayberry candle burned to is socket
Brings food to the larder,
Health to the home,
And wealth to the pocket."

Horace Gardner, *Let's Celebrate Christmas* (New York: A.S. Barnes, 1950), 74. *"Good Luck Candles,"* St. Nicholas, December 1935. Mildred Kenney Rost, *Candles of Christmas* (Oceanside, CA: Mildred Kenney Rost, 1947), 5-7.

What is the etymology of the word "Christmas," and what is the origin of the use of "X-mas" for "Christmas"?

The word "Christmas" finds its origin in an Old English phrase, "Cristes Maesse," that is, a mass or festival for Christ, the Lord's anointed. While many believe that the abbreviation "X-mas" is disrespectful, it is true that the Greek letter "X" is the first letter in the Greek word for Christ, *Christos.* The earliest identified use of the abbreviation is in 1551, when it appeared as *X'temmas.*

C. T. Onions, ed., *The Oxford Dictionary of English Etymology* (Oxford: Oxford at the Clarendon Press, 1966), s.v. "Christmas," "Christ."

Where did luminaria originate and how are they made?

Luminaria originated in the old Southwest, where it was believed that the Christ Child wandered softly throughout Christmas Eve night, blessing all who had placed a light to help the child find his way. At first the luminaria were small wood fires. Later, a more practical method of putting a candle in a paper bag replaced the wood fires. The bags were introduced into the area when the first American traders, traveling on the old Santa F Trail, brought with them the brown paper bags that merchants used to package their customers' purchases.

The materials needed to make a luminaria are: a brown grocery sack, some sand, and a plumber's candle or votive candle. To begin, fold down the top inch and a half or two inches of the bag so that the bag will stay open. Next, pour two inches of sand into the bag. This weighs down the bag, provides a base for the candle, and snuffs the candle out when it has burned down to the bottom. Place the candle in the bag. Lit luminarias are often put along lawns, sidewalks, and patio walls. They should be placed two or three feet apart.

Gilbert Love, "Luminaria: Silent Night Silent Lights," *Pittsburgh Press* 23 December 1970.

Where did Groundhog Day originate?

Groundhog Day celebrated on February 2 annually is the day when the groundhog emerges from the ground to predict when spring will come. First celebrated in Germany, the farmers would watch for a badger to emerge from winter hibernation. If the day was sunny, the sleepy badger would be frightened by his shadow and duck back for a six week nap. If it were a cloudy day the badger would stay out, to enjoy an early spring. German farmers who emigrated to Pennsylvania brought the celebration to the United States. Finding no badgers in Pennsylvania, they chose the groundhog as a substitute. "Punxsutawney Phil" is or was the legendary weather forecaster who lived in a groundhog hole in north-central Pennsylvania and appeared every Groundhog Day to predict by the presence or absence of his shadow how long or short the winter will be. Over a 60-year period "Phil" has been right only 28 percent of the time.

Barbara Berliner, *The Book of Answers* (Englewood Cliffs, NJ: Prentice-Hall, 1990), 92. Dennis Sanders, *The First of Everything* (New York: Delacorte, 1981), 369-70. Sue Ellen Thompson, ed., *Holidays, Festivals, and Celebrations of the World Dictionary* (Detroit: Omnigraphics, 1994), 127.

Who can be buried in a national cemetery?

In order to be buried in a national cemetery, a person must have served in the Armed Forces of the United States or in active duty or related duty with the Reserves of the Armed Forces; been a citizen of the United States who fought in the service of an allied country when the United States was at war; or been a spouse or dependent child of any of the above.

Burial in Arlington Nation Cemetery is more restrictive because there are a limited number of available full-casket gravesites. To be buried there, the deceased must meet one of the following criteria:

A veteran of the armed forces who dies while on active duty

Recipient of the Medal of Honor, Distinguished Service Cross, Air Force Cross, Navy Cross, Distinguished Service Medal, Silver Star, or Purple Heart

An individual who performed honorable military service and who held an elective office in the U.S. Government (or the Supreme Court, the Cabinet, or in offices compensated at Level II under the Executive Security Act)

A former member of the armed forces who was separated because of a 30 percent or greater physical disability before October 1, 1949 and who served on active duty (other than training)

A retired military personnel included in an official service retired list who is eligible to receive compensation stemming from military services

A spouse, minor child, or dependent adult child (including spouses and children of individual already buried in the cemetery) of a veteran who meets the preceding requirements

Ken Skala, *American Guidance For Those Over 60, 2nd ed.* (Falls Church, VA: Sharff Publications, 1990), 348. Department of Veteran Affairs, Veterans Benefits Administration, *Book A-General, Code of Federal Regulations, Title 38,* (Austin, TX: Jonathan Publishing, 1992), 1.620-1 -1.620-2.

How many cigarettes does the average smoker smoke per day?

In 1980, the average American smoker smoked 31 cigarettes a day. In 1993, the average smoker smoked a pack of cigarettes a day, most of which contain 20 cigarettes.

Mike Feinsilber and William B. Mead, *American Averages: Amazing Facts of Everyday Life* (Garden City, NY: Doubleday, 1980), 61. *The Most Often Asked Questions About Smoking, Tobacco, and Health and ... The Answers* (Atlanta, GA: American Cancer Society, 1993), pamphlet.

What is the origin of the European ceremony of "hunting the wren"?

"Hunting the wren" is a European ceremony that exemplifies a shared communion by first sacrificing and then taking a sacred animal from house to house so that all may share in the animal's "divine influence." The wren has long been regarded in much of Europe as the king of birds. In eighteenth century France and England (especially on the Isle of Man), a wren was killed on Christmas Eve and carried from house to house hanging from a long pole with its wings extended while townspeople chanted:

> "We hunted the wren for Robin the Bobbin,
> We hunted the wren for Jack of the Can,
> We hunted the wren for Robin the Bobbin,
> We hunted the wren for every one."

James George Frazer, *The New Golden Bough* (New York: Criterion Books, 1959), 482.

What is a "husking bee"?

A husking bee is a social event where friends and neighbors gather to help a farmer husk his corn. The task is made less like work by dividing the participants into teams, competing to see who can husk the fastest. The loud, joyous competition is followed by a banquet.

E. Custead, *Rose and Elza: Songs and Stories of Bygone Days in Fayette County and Elsewhere* (New York: Edward O. Jenkins' Sons, n.d.), 309.

What are the top greeting card holidays?

Christmas tops the list with over 2.3 billion Christmas cards being sold in 1993. It is followed by Valentine's Day, with 1 billion cards sold; Easter, with 165 million; Mother's Day, with 150 million; and Father's Day, with 101 million cards sold.

Arsen J. Darnay and Marlita A. Reddy, *Market Share Reporter: An Annual Compilation of Reported Market Share Data On Companies, Products, and Services 1995* (Detroit, MI: Gale Research, 1995), 146.

Who introduced Sadie Hawkins Day?

Sadie Hawkins Day, celebrated on November 9, was introduced by Al Capp in his *Li'l Abner* comic strip in 1938. On this day the maids and spinsters of Dogpatch, Capp's invented rural town, were given the legal right to chase after unmarried males. Any such bachelor who was caught by a woman was obliged to marry her. Capp's holiday resulted in the creation of Sadie Hawkins Day dances; schools and clubs sponsor these events for which girls issue invitations to boys.

Leslie Dunkling, *A Dictionary of Days* (New York: Facts On File, 1988), s.v. "Sadie Hawkins Day."

When does the Chinese New Year begin?

The Chinese New year begins between January 20th and February 19th with the first moon. Celebration of the Lunar New

Year, as the holiday is called in China and much of Asia dates from pre-history and marks the beginning of a new lunar cycle. In China everyone become a year older during the Lunar New Year as age is calculated by the year, not by the date of birth. The Lunar New Year is China's longest and most important celebration. Houses are cleaned, financial activities are brought up to date, special meals are prepared and windows and homes are decorated with red paper which signifies good fortune. Fireworks are an integral part of the holiday as it is believed that the exploding firecrackers and whistling rockets will scare away evil spirits. Once called *Yuan Tan* (First Morning) the lunar celebration is now called Ch'un Chieh (Spring Festival). The change was made in 1912 with China's adoption of the Gregorian calendar.

Sue Ellen Thompson and Barbara W. Carlson, comp., *Holidays, Festivals, and Celebrations of the World Dictionary* (Detroit, MI: Omnigraphics, 1994), 187-89.

What was the Memorial Day first celebrated in the United States?

Memorial Day was originally celebrated to honor soldiers who died in the Civil War. The first such observance took place on May 5, 1866, in Waterloo, New York. However, it was in 1868 that Major John A. Logan declared May 30 as a special day for decorating the graves of Union soldiers, and for many years that date was regarded as the traditional Memorial Day, also known as Decoration Day. Today, the holiday pays tribute to all persons who have died in wars in which the United States has been involved. Since 1971, Memorial Day has been a Federal public holiday observed on the last Monday in May. Many Southern states continue to celebrate Confederate Memorial Day on a separate date.

Chase's 1995 Calendar of Events (Chicago: Contemporary Books, 1994), 227-8. *World Book Encyclopedia* (Chicago: World Book, 1991), 392.

Where and when did the "New Year's Baby" originate?

The "New Year's Baby" in swadling clothes originated in ancient Greece during the festival of Dionysus, when a babe in a basket was paraded through town accompanied by two men—one young and the second older and bearded. The babe symbolized the rebirth of the god Dionysus as a symbol of fertility. Christianity took over this custom with the babe representing the infant Jesus Christ, the new light of the world. As early as the fourteenth century, the newborn one made its appearance in a German folksong as a metaphor for the New Year.

Theodor Gaster, *New Year: Its History, Customs and Superstitions* (New York: Abelard-Schuman, 1955), 67-70.

What is the oldest known greeting card?

Throughout history people have exchanged gifts and greetings during holidays, especially around New Year's celebrations which are indigenous to most cultures. The first known greeting card appeared around 1450 in Germany. The woodcut card carried the following New Year's message, "Here I come from Alexandria and bring many good years to give generously. I will give them for almost no money and have only God's love for my reward." Following 1450 and well into the 1500s holiday greeting cards became quite popular, especially those with religious themes. By about 1770 woodcut cards were being replaced with engraved ones and these were likewise popular around the Christmas holidays and also carried a religious themes.

James D. Chamberlain, ed., *The Romance of Greeting cards* (Cambridge: University Press of Cambridge, 1956), 10-12.

Why does the U.S. Surgeon General wear a uniform?

The U.S. Surgeon General heads the Public Health Service, whose roots predate the American Revolutionary War. By law the U.S. Surgeon General holds the same rank as the surgeon generals of the navy, army, and air force. The official uniform is patterned after that of navy officers, but has distinct seals, insignia, buttons, and tags.

Parade Magazine 27 March 1994.

What is the origin of Labor Day?

The American tradition of celebrating Labor Day began on September 5, 1882, in New York City. Labor Day celebrations spread to other cities and states, and the holiday gained national recognition in 1894, when U.S. President Grover Cleveland signed a bill. Just who came up with the idea of honoring the nation's workers is a matter of debate. Peter J. McGuire, a founder of the United Brotherhood of Carpenters and Joiners, is credited by some, including the Department of Labor. Matthew Maguire, a leader in the International Association of Machinists, is identified by others. Canada also celebrates Labor Day on the first Monday in September, while other nations follow a tradition of honoring workers on May 1.

Pittsburgh Post Gazette 5 September 1994.

What is the origin of the visiting card used to announce one's presence?

The visiting card, which is used to announce one's presence, has its origins in the ancient if not prehistoric custom of loudly announcing one's coming so as not to be taken for an enemy. The visiting card first appeared in the late seventeenth or early eighteenth century and was especially used in France.

Lillian Eichler Watson, *The Customs of Mankind* (Garden City, NY: Garden City Publishing, 1924), 317-20.

In a traditional Polish wedding celebration, what is the capping ceremony?

One of the most important parts of a traditional Polish wedding celebration is the "oczepiny," the moment that the "czepek" or cap is placed on the head of the bride. "Oczepiny" usually takes place at the height of revelry during the celebration. The cap is a sign of a married woman.

The marriage cap was usually a gift to the bride from her godmother. Sometimes the bride made her own cap or had someone else make it. This first cap was held as special for wearing to church, for folk festivals, and for her burial.

Along with the capping ceremony, other associated customs included the symbolic removal of the Lair wreath worn by the bride that symbolized her virginity, the unbraiding of her hair, and cutting it.

Sophie Hodorowicz Knab, *Polish Customs, Traditions and Folklore* (New York: Hippocrene Books, 1993), 210-3.

When do Canadians celebrate Thanksgiving?

Canadians celebrate Thanksgiving on the second Monday of October. Canadians contend that the first Thanksgiving service was celebrated in Newfoundland in 1578 by Sir John Frobisher when the first immigrants settled there. It wasn't until 1879 that they began celebrating Thanksgiving as an annual event. Canadians also contend that the last Thursday in November, when Americans give thanks, is too late in the year for an authentic harvest celebration.

Robert Meyer, *Festivals: U.S.A. & Canada* (New York: Ives Washburn, 1970), 152-53.

What is a "galette des rois"?

A "galette des rois" or cake of kings, is an elaborate and traditional Epiphany cake made of puff pastry. It is a Parisian tradition to bake the cake with a single almond inside and whomsoever shall find it in their serving is king or queen for 24 hours and must bake the next cake.

Maria Robbins and Jim Charlton, *A Christmas Companion: Recipes, Traditions and Customs From Around the World* (New York: Perigree, 1989), 56.

Who were the "Black Irish"?

The phrase "Black Irish" refers to the children resulting from the taking of West African slaves as wives and mistresses by Irish planters on the Caribbean island of Montserrat.

Robert McCrum, *The Story of English,* (New York: Elisabeth Sifton Books, 1986), 180.

Among Hispanic-Americans what is a quince?

Among Hispanic-Americans, especially Cuban exiles in Florida, a quince is a combination of a Sweet-fifteen and coming-out party. The celebration marks a girl's passage into adulthood and the moment a girl could start dating. The party can be an extremely elaborate affair, often requiring bank loans and outlays of up to $15 thousand dollars.

"Sweet 15—Latin Style," *Newsweek* 28 August 1978.

What is aromatherapy?

Aromatherapy was first introduced as a treatment including aromatic facials of floral and herbal masks that were meant to either energize or calm the skin and mood. It has since grown to include fragrances that affect people's moods.

Harold LeMay, Sid Lerner, and Marian Taylor, *The Facts On File Dictionary of New Words* (New York: Facts on File, 1985), s.v. "aromatherapy."

Who is a "Chicano"?

A "Chicano" is an American of Mexican descent. Some, but not all, citizens prefer this term over Mexican-American. It has connotations of political activism.

Paul Dickson, *What Do You Call A Person From. . .?: A Dictionary of Resident Names* (New York: Facts on File, 1990), s.v. "Chicano."

How many U.S. presidents are buried at Arlington National Cemetery?

Only two U.S. presidents have been buried at Arlington National Cemetery, in Arlington, Virginia. They are William Howard Taft (1857-1930), who died at the age of 72, and John F. Kennedy (1917-1963), who died at the age of 46.

Joseph Nathan Kane, *Facts About the Presidents, 6th ed.* (New York: H.W. Wilson, 1993), 346-7.

What is the "wave" and where did it originate?

The "wave" is a "wave-like effect produced in a grandstand or stadium by successive sections of the crowd of spectators standing up, raising their arms, and sitting down again," according to the *Oxford English Dictionary.* It first became popular at University of Washington football games in the late 1970s or early 1980s. Then the National Football team, the Seattle Seahawks, was one of the first professional teams to introduce it to a wider national television audience. International attention was drawn to this phenomena at the World Cup football competition held in Mexico City in 1986.

The Oxford English Dictionary, 2d ed. (Oxford: Clarendon Press, 1989), s.v. "wave." "Tony's Gone, But Panthers Aren't Out of the Woods Yet," *Pittsburgh Post Gazette* 17 August 1987.

What is the oldest Valentine card still in existence?

Now in the British Museum, the oldest existing valentine was sent in 1415 by Charles (1394-1465), Duke of Orleans, to his wife while he was a prisoner in the Tower of London.

Charles Panati, *Extraordinary Origins of Everyday Things,* (New York: Harper & Row, 1987), 51.

How is the date of Mardi Gras determined?

Mardi Gras, French for Fat Tuesday, is a day of feasting before the Lenten fasting begins on Ash Wednesday. It occurs on Shrove Tuesday, which is always 46 days before Easter. Easter is always on the first Sunday after the full moon following the Spring Equinox. The name Shrove Tuesday comes from the custom of "shriving" or purification through confession of one's sins prior to Lent. In New Orleans, Carnival, the joyous season preceding Mardi Gras, has been celebrated from the 1800s. It includes parades, music, masquerade balls, and pageantry. It starts on Twelfth Night, January 6, and ends at midnight on Mardi Gras day.

Hennig Cohen and Tristram Potter Coffin, *The Folklore of American Holidays, 2d ed.* (Detroit: Gale Research, 1991), 84. *New Orleans Mardi Gras Guide* (New Orleans: Arthur Hardy, 1985), 15.

What was considered an appropriate amount of makeup for married women in the Edwardian period?

Although many people living around the turn of the century were suspicious of what they called "deceits," it was generally conceded that the married woman could use cosmetics to make herself more attractive. A modest amount of powder, rouge, and lipstick were acceptable, as well as the use of hair dye, wigs, and corset.

Valerie Steele, *Fashion and Eroticism: Ideals of Feminine Beauty from the Victorian Era to the Jazz Age* (New York: Oxford University Press, 1985), 215-16.

Who were the flappers?

Flappers were women of the 1920s whose general demeanor was marked by sexual and social liberation. A hallmark of flappers were their avant-garde fashion statements. A flapper usually wore flesh-colored stockings, relatively short hemlines and low pumps which showed off their ankles. Bobbed hair and a slender boyish figure completed the look.

James S. Olson, *Historical Dictionary Of The 1920s,* (CT: Greenwood Press, 1988), s.v. "Flapper."

How do people celebrate New Year's Eve?

According to a 1991 survey 45 percent of people spend New Year's Eve quietly with friends, 25 percent go to a party, 28 percent don't celebrate at all, and 9 percent find other ways to welcome in the New Year.

USA Today 31 December 1991.

What is the origin of the pigtail traditionally worn by Chinese men?

For hundreds of years Chinese men wore their hair in long pigtails. Surprisingly, the style began as a sign of Chinese subjection to the conquering Manchus, who took power in 1644. The Manchus forced Chinese men to shave the front of their heads and to grow long hair that was exhibited in a long braided pigtail. When the Manchus were defeated in 1912, the style had become so widely accepted that many men continued to wear pigtails.

David Louis, *Fascinating Facts* (New York: Ridge Press/Crown, 1977), 49.

What does the custom of throwing rice at weddings mean?

Rice thrown at the couple at the end of weddings signifies a prayer for fertility; a wish for many children. Similar customs include throwing other types of grain, throwing nuts (in ancient Roman times), throwing sweets, throwing paper confetti (in modern times), breaking oatcake over the bride's head (in Scotland), throwing fruit such as figs (in southern Europe), and breaking and scattering pomegranates (in Greece).

Gertrude Jobes, *Dictionary of Mythology, Folklore and Symbols* (New York: Scarecrow Press, 1962), s.v. "rice." Ethel L. Urlin, *A Short History of Marriage, 1913 reprint* (Detroit: Singing Tree Press, 1969), 234.

What is the origin of kissing under mistletoe?

In second century B.C. Britain, the Druids celebrated the beginning of winter by gathering mistletoe and burning it in sacrifice to their gods. Sprigs of the plant were also hung in homes to work miracles of healing, to protect against witchcraft, and to bring fertility to the land and the people. Guests to the house were embraced under the mistletoe's good auspices. Kissing beneath it may have been prompted by the Druids' belief in the plant's powers of fertility. Mistletoe also was hung outside a house to welcome travelers, and if enemies chanced to meet under a tree in which it grew, they were expected to forget their differences for a day. Druids as well as many other cultures had specific rules on the time and the technique of cutting the mistletoe. According to Druid custom, this parasitic plant with white berries had to be cut down on the sixth day of the moon. Other cultures waited for a full March moon or the waning moon of winter.

For the Scandinavians the mistletoe was also a plant of hope, peace and harmony. It belonged to Frigga, the goddess of love, and kissing under the mistletoe may have been derived from this association.

James Frazer, *The New Golden Bough* (New York: Criterion Books, 1959), 590-92. Frank Muir, *Christmas Customs & Traditions* (New York: Taplinger Publishing Co., 1975), 45. Charles Panati, *Extraordinary Origins of Everyday Things* (New York: Harper & Row, 1987), 68-69.

Which U.S. government officials are entitled to a state funeral?

The only individuals entitled to a state funeral are the President of the United States, an ex-president of the United States, the president-elect of the United States, and any other person specifically designated by the President of the United States. Among those who have been designated by the president as being worthy of a state funeral include the Unknown Soldiers and Generals John J. Pershing and Douglas MacArthur.

State funerals are held at the Rotunda of the U.S. Capitol. Burial is not necessarily conducted at a national cemetery.

Mary Jane McCaffree and Pauline Innis, *Protocol: The Complete Handbook of Diplomatic, Official and Social Usage* (Washington, DC: Devon Publishing, 1985), 342. B. C. Mossman and M. W. Stark, *The Last Salute: Civil and Military Funerals 1921-1969* (Washington, DC: Government Printing Office, 1971), vii-viii.

What are the Santa Claus traditions in other countries?

Santa Claus has various names in different countries. Examples include the following:

Czechoslovakia—"Svaty Mikulas" slides down from heaven on a golden cord. An angel and an evil spirit called "Cert" leads him.

Italy—"Befana," a kindly witch, flies through the air on a broom leaving gifts for children and looking for the Christ child.

Russia—"Baboushka" performs the same function as does Befana in Italy.

France—"Tante Aria," or Mother Air, rides on a donkey accompanied by Father Star bringing gifts.

Holland—"Sinterklaas" arrives on a white horse, wearing a bishop's robe, miter, and white gloves. He is accompanied by "Swarte Piet," or Black Peter, who carries switches for bad children.

Germany—"Weihnachtsman" arrives on foot carrying gifts for good children and sticks for bad children.

Belgium—"Sint Nicholaas."

Switzerland—"Samichlaus."

Irena Chalmers et al. , *The Great American Christmas Almanac* (New York: Penguin Group, 1988), 147. Lavinia Dobler, *Customs and Holidays Around the World* (New York: Fleet Press, 1962), 127-9.

When was the Thanksgiving holiday first celebrated in America?

Thanksgiving was first celebrated in 1621 by the colonists in Plymouth, Massachusetts, with Chief Massasoit and 90 braves of the Wampanoag tribe. The dinner included venison, duck, goose, fish, eels, corn bread, wild plums, and wine made from wild grapes. The first official celebration was proclaimed on Thursday, November 26, 1789, by U.S. President George Washington (1732-1799). It was first made a national holiday by President Abraham Lincoln (1809-1865) on November 26, 1863, at the urging of Sarah Josepha Hale, editor of *Godey's Lady's Book and Magazine*, who felt the last Thursday in November should always be a day of national unity and thanksgiving in the United States.

Godey's Lady's Book and Magazine, July-December 1863. Dennis Sanders, *The First of Everything* (New York: Delacorte Press, 1981), 36

Where was Mardi Gras first celebrated in America?

Mardi Gras, in one form or another, has been celebrated in Louisiana ever since 1699. On Tuesday, March 3, of that year, while camping on a bayou adjacent to the Mississippi River, the French explorer Pierre Le Moyne, Sieur d'Iberville, realized it was Mardi Gras and named his campsite "Point du Mardi Gras." He then declared an impromptu celebration during which he and his men sang and drank wine. Mardi Gras was a popular celebration in France. It is the last day of the period of carnival before Ash Wednesday, which marks the arrival of the fasting days of Lent.

However, the way in which Mardi Gras is celebrated today has its roots in Mobile, Alabama, where each New Year's Eve since 1830 a group called "The Cowbellion de Rakin Society" sponsored a celebration that included a parade with floats and costumed participants, followed by a ball. In 1857 six men, once members of the Mobile society who were working in New Orleans, created the "Krewe of Comus," arranged to borrow floats from Mobile, and made arrangements for costumes, flambeaux, and music. Comus is the Greek god of revelry. The success of the two-float parade was phenomenal and went on to become an annual event.

Myron Tassin and Gaspar Stall, *Mardi Gras and Bacchus: Something Old, Something New* (New Orleans: Pelican Publishing, 1984), 19, 23-25.

When did people begin wearing hose?

Hose can be traced back to ancient times. They were originally worn by men. In Northern Europe, Germanic tribes wore loose-fitting trousers that went from waist to ankle and were called *heuse.* The fabric was commonly crisscrossed with rope from the ankle to the knee to reduce air drafts. The Roman legions of the first century B.C. wore hosa, which were gathered leg coverings of cloth or leather worn beneath the short military tunic. However, these did not cover the foot.

The Romans had a cloth foot sock called an *udo* or *udones* by the first century A.D. As tailors extended these further and further up the leg, effeminacy became attached to men who wore them without boots. But by the fifth century full-length stockings were popular for clergy and laymen. "Skin-tights" became the vogue for men by the year 1000, then fell in to some disrepute if the stockings were too tightly worn.

It is not exactly known when women began wearing stockings, as it was not proper to mention women's legs. By the sixteenth and seventeenth century stockings had become accepted apparel for women also.

Charles Panati, *Extraordinary Origins and Everyday Things* (New York: Harper & Row, 1987), 343-46.

What is the mark called that often appears on the foreheads of Indians?

The mark on the forehead of persons from India or members of the Hindu religion is called a tilak (tilaka, tilka) or tika (tikka). Among Hindus, the mark originally indicated caste, status, or sectarian affiliation; more recently it is worn simply as a decoration. In some areas the mark on a Hindu woman had indicated that she was married. Kumkum (kum-kum, kunku) is a red powder used ceremonially by the Hindus to make the mark. Sometimes the mark itself is also referred to as "kum-kum." A caste mark also can be made in other colors, worn on the chest or arms, and created in different sizes or shapes to signify the caste.

George Thomas Kurian, *Historical and Cultural Dictionary of India* (Metuchen, NJ: Scarecrow Press, 1976), 52. Jean Lyon, *Just Half a World Away* (New York: Thomas Y. Crowell Co., 1954), 371. *The Oxford English Dictionary, 2nd ed.,* (Oxford, England: Clarendon Press, 1989), 8:544, 18:85.

What fashion custom do the Padaung people of Burma observe?

The Padaung, a tribal people living in eastern Burma, have a very unique custom. Women in the tribe wear brass coils around their necks that measure nearly one foot high and weigh over 20 pounds. These coils are usually adorned with coins and silver chains. The purpose of the coils is meant to convey wealth, status, and elegance. Women are usually fitted with their first brass ring around the age of five. Additional rings are added at later dates. Many women in the Padaung tribe also wear successive bands of brass coils around their arms and legs.

The Padaung custom of placing successive brass rings around the neck alters the women's physiological makeup. The collarbone and ribs are gradually pushed down into the chest cavity. This phenomenon makes the neck look abnormally long. The brass rings also give the voices of the women a very hollow quality. Liquids must be swallowed through the use of a straw, as the rings prevent the women from tilting their heads back. This custom is on the decline among the Padaung.

John M. Keshishian, "A Clinical Look at Burma's Long-necked Women," *National Geographic* June 1979.

What are South American cowboys called?

The cowboy is one of the most recognizable symbols of the Old West. However, cowboys live in places other than the United States. South American cowboys, known as gauchos, roam the prairies or pampas of Argentina and Uruguay. Like cowboys of the United States, gauchos in earlier times were skilled horsemen who caught and raised wild cattle. The gaucho's favorite weapon was the bola, a cord with round weights attached to the ends. When a bola is thrown, it wraps itself around the legs of the animal and entraps it.

Gauchos, like their North American counterparts, have been romanticized in many literary and musical works. Unfortunately, they are a dying breed. Many of the duties once performed by the gauchos are now handled by day laborers.

The World Book Encyclopedia (Chicago: World Book, 1987), s.v. "gaucho."

What does a knight's suit of armor weigh?

A complete suit of armor can weigh anywhere from 41 to 90 pounds, depending upon where it was made and what its intended use was. German field armor was the lightest at nearly 42 pounds, while German jousting armor is among the heaviest at just over 90 pounds. English field armor weighed almost 72 pounds and Italian field armor was lighter at 57 pounds. It was said that King Edward I (1239-1307) of England could leap into the saddle of a horse without stirrups while wearing his armor.

Grant Uden, *A Dictionary of Chivalry* (New York: Thomas Y. Crowell, 1968), 7-9.

What is the history of the English celebration known as Guy Fawkes Day?

Guy Fawkes Day has been celebrated on November 5th in England ever since 1605 when the English conspirator Guy Fawkes and a band of cohorts were discovered with explosives in the cellars underneath the Houses of Parliament. Fawkes had planned to blow up the building in retaliation for the penal laws enacted against Roman Catholics. The present celebrations usually include bonfires and fireworks at night.

David Grote, *British English for American Readers* (Westport, CN: Greenwood Press, 1992), 259.

When did Christmas stockings first appear as an American custom?

The custom of putting Christmas gifts in a stocking grew out of a Scandinavian tradition in which all of the members of a family would place their shoes together at Christmastime as a sign of good will. Gifts were then placed in the shoes. Being more flexible and stretchable than shoes, stockings eventually became the preferred gift receptacle. The hanging of stockings for the same purpose appeared as an American tradition in the last two centuries. Washington Irving, in *Knickerbocker History of New York* (1809), referred to hanging up stockings on the chimney on Christmas Eve. Artists' rendering of stockings on the mantel appeared shortly thereafter. Toward the end of the nineteenth century the now-familiar bright red, gaily decorated Christmas stockings, ranging in size from 8 inches to 30 inches, appeared for sale along with pre-filled stockings.

Irena Chalmers et al. , *The Great American Christmas Almanac* (New York: Penguin Group, 1988), 90-93. *The Scholastic* 15 December 1928.

From where did the universal custom of closing the eyes of the dead come from?

Closing the eyes of the dead is a nearly universal practice, which most likely originated out of the fear of being hurt if a dead person gazed upon an individual. The notion of the "evil eye" of the dead has long been potent. If a person dies with eyes open and is not found for more than 12 hours, the muscles may tighten, making it difficult to close the eyes. In different cultures throughout the ages, people have then weighted down the open eyes to keep them closed.

Webb Garrison, *How it Started,* (TN: Abington Press, 1972), 216.

What was the meaning of a symbolic hand painted on a Sioux warrior's body or clothing?

When a Sioux warrior displayed a painted hand on his body or clothing, it indicated that he had killed a man in hand-to-hand combat.

John Pimlott, *The Military Quiz Book* (Harrisburg, PA: Greenhill Books and Stackpole Books, 1993), 33.

In South Africa what was the practice of necklacing?

In the mob violence that preceded the abolishment of apartheid in South Africa, the practice of necklacing was a trademark means of killing those who cooperated with the Caucasian government. The gruesome method utilizes a tire filled with gasoline, which is thrown over the victim and set on fire.

Martin Meredith, *In the Name of Apartheid* (New York: Harper & Row, 1988), 201.

Who are some celebrities who renounced their U.S. citizenship?

The following celebrities renounced their U.S. citizenship:
Josephine Baker—Singer and dancer
Jefferson Davis—President of the Confederate States of America
W.E.B. Du Bois—Civil rights activist
T.S. Eliot—Poet and playwright
John Huston—Movie producer and director
Henry James—Novelist
Lee Harvey Oswald—Accused assassin of President John F. Kennedy
Elizabeth Taylor—Actress

Amy Wallace, et al., *The Book of Lists #3* (New York: William Morrow, 1983), 40-41.

After his death how were the remains of Alexander the Great preserved?

Alexander the Great (356 B.C.-323 B.C.), the renowned military figure and Macedonian king, had at a relatively young age conquered much of the known world of his time.

At the age of 33 he died suddenly in his sleep in Babylon (the former capital of the Persian Empire). His body was probably preserved in a large crock of honey, as was the practice among ancient Egyptians, before being buried in a gold coffin in Alexandria, Egypt.

Anne Commire, ed., *Historic World Leaders, vol. 2* (Detroit, MI: Gale Research, 1994), 20-24. David Louis, *Fascinating Facts* (New York: Ridge Press/Crown Publishers, 1977), 41.

In the absence of soap in the ancient Mediterranean world, what was used for bathing?

In the absence of soap in the ancient Mediterranean world, olive oil was often used for bathing.

Isaac Asimov, *Isaac Asimov's Book of Facts* (New York: Grosset & Dunlap, 1979), 172.

Who originated the idea that Santa Claus lives at the North Pole?

Thomas Nast (1840-1902), a German born illustrator and New York political cartoonist, and the man who gave the world the symbol of the Republican elephant and the Democratic donkey, was responsible for revealing to children of the world that Santa Claus lives at the North Pole.

Nast did much to popularize the present-day image of Santa Claus—a jolly, chubby individual with a full white beard, carrying an overflowing bag of toys. Nast created Santa's North Pole workshop, toy factory, and book in which all children's names were recorded. He made a series of Christmas drawings that appeared in *Harper's Weekly* for 23 years.

Patricia Bunning Stevens, *Merry Christmas!: A History of the Holiday* (New York: Macmillan Publishing, 1979), 87.

When finished with a meal, how should the used cutlery be left on the plate?

When finished with a meal, used cutlery should be joined together at the 4 o'clock position on the plate. The crumpled napkin should be placed on the left side of the plate.

"Making the Proper Moves at the Table," *USA Today* 16 February 1994.

What is the origin of the custom of christening a ship with champagne?

The custom of christening a ship with champagne began with the Vikings, who launched their war ships by running them down to the sea over rollers to which sacrificial victims were tied. By the time the ships reached the water, they were sprinkled with blood. The practice was called hlunn-rod or "roller reddening." They believed that the sacrificial victim was necessary so that the spirit of the victim would guard the ship from harm. Red wine became the humane substitute for blood, and finally in modern times, champagne replaced red wine.

Other ancient christening customs included decorating the bow with flowers, making crowns for the sailors, and having a priest perform a purification or consecration ceremony to honor a specific god. Greek captains baptize their ships by sipping from a jug of wine, then pouring the remainder onto the deck.

David Louis, *Fascinating Facts* (New York: Ridge Press/Crown Publishers, 1977), 74. *Notes & Queries* 9th Series, vol. 1, 1898, 317-18, 373.

What are some superstitions associated with moles or birthmarks?

There are numerous superstitions associated with moles, which are birthmarks caused by changes in skin pigment. Greeks considered moles to be a sign of luck and throughout the ages man has assigned significance to mole placement. Some of these are: a mole on the temple signals happiness in love; a nose mole signals success in the business world; chin moles signal luck in choice of friends; and leg moles signal a strong will.

Other mole myths include a theory about mole color and placement in association with the planets as an early sign of a person's character and personality. Facial moles were also considered a sign of beauty on a woman. A beauty patch worn on the face was an artificial mole. Throwing black pepper on an expectant mother was one way of wishing for lucky moles on her child.

Claudia De Lys, *A Treasury of Superstitions* (New York: Philosophical Library, 1957), 198-200.

What is "feng shui"?

"Feng shui," which translates as "wind" and "water," refers to an ancient Chinese practice that uses the location of cultural and physical features of the landscape to predict health, luck and prosperity. "Feng shui" purports that those who are healthy and prosperous are in harmony with their natural surroundings and receive benefits via "ch'i," an all-encompassing life principle that uses nature as a conduit.

Rosemary Ellen Guiley, *Harper's Encyclopedia of Mystical & Paranormal Experience* (San Francisco: HarperSanFrancisco, 1991), s.v. "feng shui."

What is the custom of "barring out the schoolmaster"?

The custom of barring out the schoolmaster was practiced in Pennsylvania during the early period of one-room schools. A few days before Christmas, and in some places, on Shrove Tuesday, children would literally lock their teacher out of the school building until the teacher promised, usually in writing, to give them a present of candy or cookies. Frequently they also extorted that day, and perhaps several others, as a holiday from school.

Alfred L. Shoemaker, *Christmas in Pennsylvania: A Folk-Cultural Study* (Kutztown: Pennsylvania Folklife Society, 1959), 24.

How do Brazilian believers in Umbanda celebrate New Year's Eve?

Believers in Umbanda, the religious affiliation of Rio de Janeiro's poor, offer supplication to a goddess of the ocean known as Iemanj on New Year's Eve. In the hours before midnight, thousands of Umbanda celebrants arrive at the city's Copacabana Beach. They wear white and bring flowers, candles, and other offerings to be set on tablecloths along the beach. Sometimes animals are sacrificed. At midnight revelers run with their gifts into the ocean, making a great deal of noise; if the tide carries the offerings out, it is thought to be a sign that Iemanj is pleased.

Sue Ellen Thompson and Barbara W. Carlson, comps., *Holidays, Festivals, and Celebrations of the World Dictionary* (Detroit: Omnigraphics, 1994), s.v. "New Year's Eve in Brazil."

What is the custom of bundling?

The European practice of bundling became common in the poorer quarters of seventeenth and eighteenth-century America, and refers to the custom of allowing fully-clothed courting couples to share a bed. Despite the absence of a matrimonial certificate, such permissiveness was tolerated among families of courting couples because homes were often overcrowded and underheated.

Howard L. Hurwitz, *An Encyclopedic Dictionary of American History* (New York: Washington Square Press, 1968), s.v. "bundling."

What is the symbolism of eating fish on New Year's Day?

Fish are a symbol of teeming abundance, and it is customary in Mecklenburg, Germany, and in other parts of the world to eat fish on New Year's Day in hopes of a prosperous future.

Theodor Gaster, *New Year: Its History, Customs, and Superstitions* (New York: Abelard-Schuman, 1955), 81.

What are the names of St. Nicholas's reindeer?

According to the poem "A Visit from St. Nicholas," by Clement C. Moore (popularly known as "The Night Before Christmas"), the sleigh of St. Nicholas is pulled by eight reindeer: Dasher, Dancer, Prancer, Vixen, Comet, Cupid, Donder, and Blitzen. In the original poem, "Donner" was "Donder" (meaning thunder in German and "Blitzen" meant lightning in German). Later editions changed the name to Donner.

Florence Adams and Elizabeth McCarrick, *Highdays & Holidays* (New York: Dutton, 1955).

What is the legend of the Christmas rose?

According to legend, the shepherds who went to pay homage to Jesus after the angels announced His birth in Bethlehem were accompanied by a little shepherd girl. All the shepherds carried gifts with them, but this child had nothing to offer. She lagged behind the others, feeling troubled. Suddenly, an angel appeared to her alone, bathed in a glow of light. This celestial being scattered beautiful white roses across the path of the little girl, who gathered them in her arms to lay at the manger when she reached the birthplace of Jesus.

Herbert H. Wernecke, *Christmas Customs Around the World* (Philadelphia: Westminster Press, 1959), 20.

What is the British version of the United States' Uncle Sam?

John Bull is England's Uncle Sam, a fictitious character who represents his country and his fellow citizens. His name, John Bull, was first used in the 1600s but the nickname was not popular until 1712 when John Arbuthnot's pamphlets, calling for an end to the War of the Spanish Succession, were republished as the book, *The History of John Bull.*

John Bull's appearance has undergone a few metamorphoses over the years. In Arbuthnot's book John Bull is a jovial upright farmer with a hot-temper. In the 1800s the famous cartoonist, Sir John Tenniel, portrayed him as a distinguished gentleman in the magazine, Punch. Later, in the Westminster Gazette, Sir Francis Carruthers Gould dressed him in a swallow-tailed coat and a "tile" hat, and tucked his trousers into his boots. At times he wore the British flag as a waistcoat or vest. This is still the way that John Bull is portrayed.

World Book Encyclopedia (Chicago: World Book, 1987),11:111.

Where did the jack-o'-lantern originate?

The Halloween jack-o'-lantern originated in the Celtic countries of Scotland and Ireland where children carved out large rutabagas, turnips, and potatoes and placed candles in the hollow centers, on October 31st, which was called All Souls Day in the Roman Catholic Church and Sambain (summer's end). In the Celtic tradition, the souls of everyone who died during the year reappeared on Sambain as witches, ghosts, and hobgoblins. A long time ago, Druids lit bonfires to frighten away these spirits; the lit candles in jack o' lanterns and the scary faces carved into the vegetables are a reminder of the Sambain spirits and bonfires. As for the reason why these pumpkins are called jack o'lanterns, no one knows for certain. But there is an Irish legend about a miser named Jack who outsmarted the devil. When he died, Jack was not admitted to either heaven or hell, but wanders in his afterlife without a home, but with a carved turnip containing a burning coal to light his way. Irish immigrants brought the Halloween tradition to the United States in the 1840s, where pumpkins were used since they were abundant at this time of year.

Robert J. Myers, *Celebrations: The Complete Book of American Holidays* (New York: Doubleday, 1972). David Feldman, *Why Do Dogs Have Wet Noses? and Other Imponderables of Everyday Life* (New York: HarperCollins, 1990), 180-81.

What is the Japanese tea ceremony?

The formal Japanese tea ceremony, known as *chanoyu*, or "hot water for tea," can be traced back to the twelfth century, when Japanese students brought green tea from China. The ceremony takes about 40 minutes and is usually preceded by the *kaiseki*, a multicourse meal of simple dishes. This is followed by the serving of sweets and then *koicha*, or thick tea. The ceremony finishes with the serving of *usucha*, or foamy thin tea.

Cuisine, January 1984.

When is Grandparents Day?

The holiday of National Grandparents Day was established in 1979 by Presidential Proclamation 4679 to fall on the first Sunday of September following Labor Day.

Chase's Annual Events: The Day-by-Day Directory to 1994, (Chicago: Contemporary Books, 1993), 366.

What is the name given to the tall, black fur cap worn by some soldiers and drum majors?

The tall, black fur cap worn by some British army soldiers and drum majors is called a bearskin. The bearskin is worn by the household troops of the British sovereign as part of their dress uniform.

Clarence L. Barnhart and Robert K. Barnhart, eds., *The World Book Dictionary* (Chicago: World Book, 1990), 1:177.

What does the phrase "taking your night feet for a walk" mean?

"Taking your night feet for a walk" is an English translation of a phrase that describes a Scandinavian courtship tradition. In Scandinavia, single eligible women would move to the loft of the barn for the summer. The ladder to the loft would be left down at night as an invitation to young men seeking a bride, who were said to "take their night feet for a walk."

Robert T. Francoeur, Timothy Pepper, and Norman A. Scherzer, eds., *A Descriptive Dictionary and Atlas of Sexology* (New York: Greenwood Press, 1991), s.v. "taking your night feet for a walk."

Where is the national Christmas tree located?

Contrary to popular belief, the national Christmas tree is not located in Washington, DC. Rather, the official national Christmas tree is an ancient giant sequoia located in the Sierra Nevada. Dubbed the "General Grant," the sequoia, is believed to be over 2,000 years old, is 267.4 feet tall and 107.5 feet in circumference at the base, and has a volume of 46,608 cubic feet.

In 1926 the Chamber of Commerce of Sanger, a small town located near Fresno, California, petitioned U. S. President Calvin Coolidge (1872-1933) to name the "General Grant" the national Christmas tree. Coolidge agreed to the petition, and every year the citizens of Sanger hold a small worship service near the tree to kick off the holiday season. The service draws about 1,000 people every year.

New York Times 24 December 1989.

What is the origin of the Christmas terms "yule," "yuletide," and "yule-log"?

The Christmas term "yule" probably comes from the Icelandic "yol," which was a pagan festival celebrating the winter solstice. "Yuletide" is related to the practice of using an extra large log as the base of a holiday fire, hence the "yule-log."

Pittsburgh Post Gazette 24 December 1968.

Who was the first man arrested for wearing a beard?

Joseph Palmer was arrested in Fitchburg, Massachusetts, in May of 1830 for wearing a beard—the first American to be incarcerated for such an "offense." At that time no Americans wore beards. After Mr. Palmer spent some time in jail in Worcester, Henry Thoreau, Bronson Alcott, and Ralph Waldo Emerson rallied to his cause. He was finally released after a year, still sporting a beard.

Parade 10 May 1981.

What are some benefits and disadvantages of staying at home with young children instead of returning to the paid workforce?

When a woman gives birth to a new baby, she often faces the dilemma of returning to the workforce or staying home full-time

with the child. Many women-and some men-decide to stay home full-time with their children. Among the reasons cited by full-time mothers for their decision are the following:
Staying home fosters a deeper relationship with the child
Raising a child is more fulfilling than having a full-time job
Staying home ensures that the child receives proper guidance and the family's own values
Staying home offers a parent unlimited time to spend with the child
A reluctance to allow others to care for the child

Full-time parenting offers rewards far greater than obtaining more money or material possessions; and if a career is already established, the parent can reenter the workforce after a few years without irreparably harming career prospects. However, some are reluctant to remain at home for the following reasons:
A perception of having traded a challenging career for the daily routine of housework, running chores, and other tedious albeit necessary mothering activities
The loss of a structured workday to the more unstructured daily life of a stay-at-home mom filled with constant interruptions
Feelings of inadequacy in motherhood because few previous job skills can be transferred to the new role
No paycheck, advancements, promotions, and accompanying social accolades
Questioning of one's identity, worth, and self-esteem
Concerns of decreasing intellectual activity; increasing isolation
Feelings of entrapment and the distancing of former friends and co-workers
Feelings of being powerless and viewing of the new role as lacking in measurable rewards, recognition, and respect
Feelings of financial dependence and financial insecurity
May become a 24-hour job with little free time for outside activities

Many of these problems can be dealt with by emphasizing the shared responsibility of child rearing, structuring free and quality time for oneself, networking with others and continually emphasizing the importance and worthiness of the stay-at-home mother.

Darcie Sanders and Martha M. Bullen, *Staying Home: From Full-Time Professional to Full-Time Parent* (Boston: Little, Brown and Company, 1992), 5-15.

Is cremation common in the United States?

In the United States cremation is becoming an increasingly popular means of disposing of corpses. Cremation, which was the interment choice in only eight percent of all deaths in 1977, had risen to over fifteen percent in 1991. The increase in the use of cremation can be attributed to a lack of available land for cemetery plots; the need for clean, safe disposal of corpses; and the fact that cremation is generally cheaper than earth burial.

Patricia Anderson, *Affairs in Order: A Complete Resource Guide to Death and Dying* (New York: Macmillan, 1991), 45.

Where is the oldest known cemetery located?

In southeastern Iran a cemetery containing approximately 100,000 skeletons and dating back to 5,000 B.C. is considered the oldest cemetery in the world. It predates the pyramids of ancient Egypt by about 2,000 years.

New York Times 3 November 1992.

How is Twelfth Night celebrated in France, and what is it called?

Twelfth Night, which is the last or twelfth night of the Christmas season, is called the "fte des Rois" in France. In the United States it is called the Epiphany and celebrates the visit of the magi or kings to the Christ Child. To celebrate, French merchants give gifts to their customers. The grocer may leave some fruit, or the laitier may leave some cream. The baker sends a galette, a flaky pastry which is used to celebrate this season. Inside the cake a small china sabot, a tiny doll, or a bean has been baked into the cake for luck.

Elizabeth Hough Sechrist, *Christmas Everywhere: A Book of Christmas Customs of Many Lands, new rev. ed.,* (Philadelphia: Macrae Smith, 1962), 107.

What percentage of Native Americans live on Indian land?

Approximately 685,000 Indians or 35 percent of Native Americans in the United States lived on Indian lands (reservations, rancherias, trust lands, native Alaskan villages, etc.) in 1990. This total is down slightly from 1980, when roughly 37 percent lived on Indian land.

Arlene Hirschfelder and Martha Kreipe de Montao, *The Native American Almanac: A Portrait of Native America Today* (New York: Prentice Hall, 1993), 40.

What percentage of children are read to every day?

According to statistics compiled by the United States Department of Education, the percentage of children between the ages of three years old and eight years old that are read to every day is 35 percent.

U.S. Department of Education, *Digest of Education Statistics, 1993* (Washington, DC: National Center for Education Statistics, 1993), 136.

What and when is Juneteenth?

Juneteenth, one of a number of freedom day celebrations, marks the date—June 19, 1863—when Union General Gordon Granger arrived in Texas to enforce U.S. President Lincoln's January 1, 1863, Emancipation Proclamation. To commemorate the freeing of former slaves, June 19 has been observed in Texas, Arkansas, Oklahoma, and other areas with all-day picnics, parades, games and other festivities.

Hennig Cohen and Tristram Potter Coffin, eds., *The Folklore of American Holidays, 1st ed.* (Detroit: Gale Research, 1987), 213-14.

What colors are used for decorating during the Christmas season?

Although red and green have long been the most frequently used colors for Christmas decorations, no definitive reason can be found for their use. The red and green of the holly leaf and berry are thought to be the source of the colors. Many other colors are now used at Christmas, including dark blue, silver, white, and red gold.

Gerard Del Re and Patricia Del Re, *The Christmas Almanack* (Garden City, NY: Doubleday, 1979), 127. Alfred Carl Hottes, *1001 Christmas Facts and Fancies* (New York: A. T. De La Mare, 1944), 84.

Where did the custom of decorating a birthday cake with candles originate?

Decorating a birthday cake with candles is a custom that originated in Germany, where it was thought that the celebrant's wishes would be granted if all the candles could be extinguished with one breath. This practice is also common in the United States. The roots of this custom go back to the early Greeks and Romans, who ascribed magical powers to burning candles, believing that the flames would carry their requests to the gods.

Ralph Linton and Adelin Linton, *The Lore of Birthdays* (New York: Henry Schuman, 1952) 16. Barbara Rinkoff, *Birthday Parties Around the World* (New York: M. Barrows and Co., 1967).

What is the French Christmas Eve celebration called?

After returning from Christmas Eve's Midnight Mass, the French celebrate with a late supper called *le rveillon.* It is from this word that the army takes its name for the bugle call that signals the start of the day-reveille. Various parts of France favor certain dishes for this celebration. In Burgundy, turkey and chestnuts are traditional; whereas in Alsace, a roasted goose takes center stage, while the Bretons enjoy buckwheat cakes with sour cream.

Gerard Del Re and Patricia Del Re, *The Christmas Almanack* (Garden City, NY: Doubleday, 1979), 128. Daniel J. Foley, *Christmas the World Over: How the Season of Joy and Good Will Is Observed and Enjoyed By Peoples Here and Everywhere* (Philadelphia: Chilton, 1963), 43-44. Elizabeth Hough Sechrist, *Christmas Everywhere: A Book of Christmas Customs of Many Lands, rev. ed.* (Philadelphia: Macrae Smith, 1962), 110.

What is the "topping out" party that an iron worker does?

When the last beam is placed on a new bridge, skyscraper, or building, ironworkers hoist up an evergreen tree, attach a flag or a handkerchief, and brightly paint the final beam and autograph it. This custom of raising an evergreen tree, called "topping out," goes back to Scandinavia in 700 when attaching the tree to the building's ridge pole signaled to all who helped that the celebration of its completion would begin.

Stone Winter 1971.

When did January 1 become the first day of the new year?

When Julius Caesar (100 B.C.-44 B.C.) reorganized the Roman calendar and based it on a solar year rather than a lunar one in the year 45 B.C., he standardized the beginning of the year as January 1. However, after the Roman Empire crumbled, no standardized date was observed. The New Year was usually celebrated near March 25, the date of the spring equinox, during medieval times. In 1582 Catholic areas of the world adopted the Gregorian calendar, which standardized January 1 as New Year's Day and recognized it as the first day of the year in most places. However, in England and the American colonies, the beginning of the year remained March 25. Under this system, March 24, 1700, was followed by March 25, 1701. In 1752, the British government changed the beginning date of the year to January 1.

Isaac Asimov, *Asimov on Numbers* (New York: Doubleday, 1977), 159. Frank Parise, ed., *The Book of Calendars* (New York: Facts on File, 1982), 377.

How did eggs and rabbits become associated with Easter?

The egg symbolized fertility and the start of spring in ancient pre-Christian pagan rites. As these rites occurred at the same time of the year as the Christian celebration of the Resurrection of Christ, the two gradually merged. Decorated eggs have been exchanged as gifts since ancient times. Some of the most famous Easter eggs are the ones made by Peter Carl Faberg, which were commissioned by Czar Alexander III of Russia for his wife.

In mythology, hares were the escorts of the pagan goddess of spring Ostara or Eostre; hence the Easter rabbit. The word "Easter" is derived from her name. German immigrants brought the tradition of the Easter bunny to America in the eighteenth and nineteenth centuries. Children would anticipate visits from the bunny on Easter evening. If the children were good, according to the legend, the bunny would leave colored eggs.

Charles Panati, *Extraordinary Origins of Everyday Things* (New York: Harper & Row, 1987), 55-57. Dennis Sanders, *The First of Everything* (New York: Delacorte Press, 1981), 371-72. *World Book Encyclopedia* (Chicago: World Book, 1994), s.v. "Easter."

What is Martin Luther King, Jr., Day, and when is it celebrated?

Martin Luther King, Jr., Day is a federal holiday honoring the birthday of slain civil rights leader Martin Luther King, Jr. (1929-1968). It is celebrated on the third Monday in January. The law making it a federal holiday was passed in 1983, with the first observance on January 20, 1986. Since federal passage, all states but one have passed legislation in observance of this holiday. New Hampshire's legislature has not passed the law to specifically honor the civil rights leader. Rather New Hampshire celebrates Civil Rights Day on the third Monday in January. The governor has recognized the King holiday through executive order.

Facts On File, 29 July 1993. World Book Encyclopedia (Chicago: World Book, 1994), s.v. "Martin Luther King, Jr., Day."

What is Remembrance Sunday?

Remembrance Sunday is the British equivalent of America's Veterans Day. Remembrance Sunday (formerly Remembrance Day) falls on the Sunday nearest November 11. The day of remembrance originated as Armistice Day in both countries and honored those who died in World War I (1914-1918). Following World War II (1939-1945), the name of the celebration was changed in both countries in order to include in remembrance those who gave their lives in World War II.

Norman W. Schur, *British English, A to Zed* (New York: Facts On File, 1987), 303.

What is the origin of the word "wedding"?

The word "wedding" originated from the ancient practice of purchasing a wife with "wed"—money or its equivalent in animals or other property. The groom or his father exchanged "wed" with the bride's father to secure the deal. Later the Anglo-Saxons accepted a bridegroom's pledge of marriage to their daughter in the form of a security, or "wed," provided by the groom's father. So "wedding" meant the pledging of a woman to a man who was gaining her by contract or cash.

William J. Fielding, *Strange Superstitions and Magical Practices* (Philadelphia: Blakiston, 1945), 242.

What is the proper order in which to fly state flags?

The flags of the 50 U.S. states should be flown in chronological order of the dates they were admitted into the Union; however, it is also correct to fly the state flags in alphabetical order.

RQ Summer 1970.

Who was dubbed "The Hobo King"?

Jefferson (Jeff) Davis formed the Hobos of America in 1908, and reigned as "The Hobo King" until he retired in 1964. Davis traveled the country educating people on the issue of hobos, explaining how hobos were different from bums or tramps. Hobos, he claimed, were able to make a living, but because of an incipient wanderlust, were forced to be itinerant workers for their whole life. Hobos, unlike tramps, did not feel that the world owed them a living.

New York Times 6 April 1968.

What is a kaffiyeh?

A kaffiyeh, or keffiyeh, is an Arab and Bedouin headdress for men made of cotton, linen, or silk, plain or striped in pattern, and of various colors. It is folded into a triangle and put on the head; two points drape over the shoulders creating a tie, if desired, and one hangs down the back to protect the neck. A skull cap may be worn underneath and an agal is wound around the head several times to hold it in place. This headdress has been worn for thousands of years for all occasions and is often times worn with Western attire.

R. Turner Wilcox, *The Dictionary of Costume* (New York: Charles Scribner's Sons, 1969), s.v. "kaffiyeh."

What is a May-pole and how was May Day celebrated in Elizabethan England?

A May-pole is a high thin pole usually decorated with flowers, ribbons and gaily painted designs. It serves as a focal point for dancing and other activities associated with May Day festivities. The custom of a May-pole is an integral part of May Day celebrations and probably originated in England.

In Elizabethan England, May Day was celebrated towards the end of April or the beginning of May. Peasants and shopkeepers would walk through the woods and fields gathering spring flowers and hawthorn branches in anticipation of the celebration. These gathering activities were often referred to as "going a-Maying" or "bringing home the May." There was often a "Queen of the May" and festivities centered around the May-pole.

R. Chambers, *The Book of Days* (J.B. Lippincott, 1940), 570-74.

Why is the New Year "brought in with a bang"?

The custom of bringing in the New Year "with a bang" has its origins in the ancient belief that loud noises would scare away lurking demons and evil spirits at this critical time of the calendar. All over the world bells ring, gongs clash, whistles blow, horns toot and guns or rockets are fired. Perhaps this is one way that nine percent of the respondents of a 1989 Roper survey meant when they indicated "other." Forty-five percent spent New Year's Eve quietly with friends; 25 percent, at parties or clubs; and 28 percent did not celebrate at all. Respondents could choose more than one category.

Theodor Gaster, *New Year: Its History, Customs and Superstitions* (New York: Abelard-Schuman, 1955), 45-46. "USA Snapshot," *USA Today* 31 December 1991.

What is the origin of the New Year's pretzel?

The New Year's pretzel has its origins in the German custom of bringing one's girlfriend a coffee ring or twisted loaf on New Year's Eve. It is kept until the twelfth night when the pair partake of the treat together.

Theodor Gaster, *New Year: Its History, Customs and Superstitions* (New York: Abelard-Schuman, 1955), 90-91.

What is the derivation and history of the term Mausoleum?

When King Mausolus of Caria (now southwestern Turkey) died in 353 B.C., his wife Artemesia was beside herself with grief. She built an expensive and ostentatious monument in his memory. From the Greek word Mausoleion came the English mausoleum, now used to refer to any commemorative burial place.

Michael Macrone, *It's Greek to Me: Brush Up Your Classics* (New York: Cader Books, 1991), 41.

Who receives our valentine cards?

According to a Hallmark Cards survey of 1,500 American households, 20 percent of valentines are given or sent go to spouses, 15 percent to children, 14 percent to friends, which includes boyfriends and girlfriends; 13 percent to parents, 11 percent to grandchildren, and 27 percent to others.

USA Today 14 February 1995.

Who was feted by New York City's first ticker-tape parade?

The first ticker-tape parade in New York history occurred on June 18, 1910, when the city created a paper blizzard to welcome U.S. president Theodore Roosevelt (1858-1919) back from an African hunt and European tour.

Pittsburgh Press 1 March 1962.

Why are the rules of the road different in America and England?

The rules of the road are different in American and England. One theory is that the English drive to the left because early horsemen passed each other to the right in order to draw swords quickly if needed. Americans drive to the right because Conestoga wagon drivers rode the left lead horse of teams and could better gauge passing distance on the left. Another answer has to do with the customs of horse-or ox-drawn traffic on the roads. The English rule recognized that most people are righthanded, and favored that arm for guiding dray animals, thus the wagoner walked beside his team on the left side, so that he would be both safely out of the path of oncoming traffic and at liberty to use his right hand to guide his horse or team. In America and on the Continent, where custom favored the use of reins to guide animals, the ordinary preference for the right hand dictated that traffic would proceed on the right.

The New York Times 24 April 1966. *Notes & Queries* 6th series, vol. 4, 29 August 1881.

Where did the fable that storks deliver babies originate?

Legends surrounding the stork go back to ancient Rome, but the belief that storks deliver babies is mostly of German origin. Bavarians believe that good baby boys ride on the back of the stork, while naughty boys are delivered hanging from its bill. In Holland and Germany, children sing to the stork to bring them a brother or sister. The stork is associated with water, which contributes to the fertility theme. The stork was also the messenger of Athene, who in some places, is associated with childbirth.

Richard Cavendish, ed., *Man, Myth and Magic* (New York: Marshall Cavendish, 1983), s.v. "Stork."

What is the tradition of "jumping the broom"?

The tradition of "jumping the broom" originated as a marriage ritual among Africans, whereby the couple would literally jump over a broom and into matrimony. The broom held spiritual significance for many African peoples, representing the beginning of homemaking. For the Kgatla tribe of southern Africa, it is traditional for the bride to help the other females in the family to sweep the courtyard clean. This symbolizes her obligation to do housework at her in-laws' residence until the newlyweds moved to their own home. The African-American community has adopted this tradition, helping to bond them and their cultural heritage.

Harriette Cole, *Jumping the Broom: The African-American Wedding Planner* (New York: Henry Holt, 1993), 16-20.

Where can one find a spa in the United States that gives "brain tune-ups"?

Paradise Shopping Center in the town of Corte Madera in California's Marin County, just north of San Francisco, is the home of Universe of You, a self-discovery spa that provides "brain tune-ups." For $12.00 (1988 dollars) a customer can listen to New Age piano music and nature sounds, wear goggles that flash pattern of colored lights, and use Synchro-Energizer headphones. Denis E. Gorges, the inventor of the Synchro-Energizer, claims his machine uses light and sound to attract the brain's attention in order to create a "harmonic."

New York Times 27 October 1988.

Why is fish a special Christmas Eve dish in many regions of Italy?

In many regions of Italy, Christmas Eve has been a religious fast day, when eating meat has been prohibited. So fish has traditionally been served and often seven different kinds of fish are served in seven different ways, to symbolize the seven sacraments of the Catholic Church.

Maria Robbins and Jim Charlton, *A Christmas Companion: Recipes, Traditions and Customs from Around the World* (New York: Perigee, 1989).

What is the Amen Corner?

The first reference to Amen Corner is a location in London, England, along Paternoster Row. In pre-Reformation England on Corpus Christi Day an annual procession to St. Paul's Cathedral would recite the prayer the Our Father (Pater noster). The ending to the prayer—Amen—was said at the corner of Pater Noster Row and Maria Lane. This spot soon was referred to as Amen Corner.

The second Amen Corner was located in a meeting place in New York City. During the 1890s, Republican Congressman Thomas Collier "Boss" Platt would hold political rallies in a corner of the Fifth Avenue Hotel in New York City. Followers would often shout "Amen!" after hearing his remarks; thus, the press tagged the location "Amen Corner."

Howard L. Hurwitz, *An Encyclopedic Dictionary of American History* (New York: Washington Square Press, 1968), 16. William S. Walsh, *Curiosities of Popular Customs,* (Philadelphia: J.B. Lippincott, 1925), 38.

Why is a bride advised to wear "something blue"?

The custom of a bride wearing "something blue" at her wedding ceremony comes from a similar custom among the ancient Israelites, who regarded blue as representing purity, love, and fidelity.

Lillian Eichler, *The Customs of Mankind* (Garden City, NY: Nelson Doubleday, 1925), 237.

In Jewish wedding ceremonies why is a napkin-wrapped wine glass crushed under the groom's foot?

In Jewish wedding ceremonies the groom crushes a napkin-wrapped wine glass under his foot to symbolize the destruction of the Holy Temple in Jerusalem and other calamities that have befallen the Jewish people.

Editors of Bride's Magazine, *Bride's All New Book of Etiquette* (New York: Perigee Book, 1993), 156.

Who is a Latino?

A Latino is a male Latin American. He is from or his ancestors are from Latin America, the countries of the Western Hemisphere south of the United States, having Spanish, Portuguese, or French as their official language. A Latina is a female Latin American. Latino may also be used as an adjective synonymous with Latin American. The word Hispanic is also used as a synonym, but that usage is incorrect; Hispanic designates Spanish-speaking ancestry, including Spain.

Paul Dickson, *What Do You Call A Person From. . .?: A Dictionary of Resident Names* (New York: Facts On File, 1990), s.v. "Latino."

What is the origin of Father's Day?

The first Father's Day was celebrated in Spokane, Washington, on June 19, 1910. It was the idea of Mrs. John Bruce Dodd and promoted by the Ministerial Association and the YMCA of Spokane. In 1924 U.S. President Calvin Coolidge (1872-1933) officially approved the day. Father's Day is now observed on the third Sunday of June.

Ruth W. Gregory, *Anniversaries and Holidays, 4th ed.* (Chicago: American Library Association, 1983), 82.

Who originated the Christmas card?

The origin of the Christmas card is in dispute. Some believe a sixteen-year-old English engraver's apprentice, William Maw Egley, designed the first card and sent it to his friends in 1842. Others claim that Sir Henry Cole (1808-1882), founder of the Victoria and Albert Museum in England, commissioned John Calcott Horsley to design the first card in 1843; 1,000 cards were printed. In 1874 Louis Prang, a German-born Boston printer, manufactured the first card in the United States from the designs of Mrs. O. E. Whitney.

George Bunday, *The History of the Christmas Card* (London: Spring Books, 1964), 6-8, 14-15, 20. Katharine Morrison McClinton, *The Chromolithographs of Louis Prang* (New York: Clarkson N. Potter, 1973), 73-74. James Meyers, *Eggplants, Elevators, Etc.: An Uncommon History of Common Things* (New York: Hart Publishing, 1978), 56-61.

What is a "zoot suit?"

A style that peaked in the early years of World War II (1939-45), the "zoot suit's" knee-length baggy jacket had wide lapels with a long, narrow "reet" pleat, heavily padded shoulders, multibutton sleeves, and a tight waist. It was worn with high-waisted trousers cut full in the thigh and tapering to ankle-hugging tightness called the "peg leg." The suit was often worn with a wide-brimmed fedora hat, brightly patterned fish-tail tie, and a long length of curving key chain. Whether the fashion originated in America or England is disputed. One claim is that the suit is an adaptation of British Guards officers' oversized greatcoats designed by a British tailor named F.P. Scholte. Another claim is that the suit was designed by Louis Lettes, a white tailor in Memphis, Tennessee, for black students attending Booker T. Washington High School. The outfit was worn by teenagers, gangsters, and Harlem "hipsters," and it was popularized by singer Frank Sinatra. Condemned by many states, the zoot suit inspired riots between those wearing them and those not, especially servicemen. With the wartime restrictions on fabric, the suit went out of style. "Zoot" is assumed to be a jive rhyme pronunciation of "suit."

Charles Panati, *Panati's Parade of Fads, Follies, and Manias* (New York: HarperCollins, 1991), 198-99. John Ciardi, *A Browser's Dictionary,* (New York: Harper & Row, 1989), s.v. "zoot suit."

Which American president started the tradition of the National Christmas Tree?

The first Christmas tree in the White House was erected during the administration of U.S. President Franklin Pierce (1804-1869) in 1853. He and the First Lady invited the Sunday school class of the New York Avenue Presbyterian Church to join them for a holiday celebration. Even though in mourning for their son who was killed in a railway accident, the Pierces insisted on making the occasion a happy one for their visitors.

The lighting of the first National Community Christmas Tree did not take place until 1923 during the administration of President Calvin Coolidge (1872-1933).

Albert J. Menendez, *Christmas in the White House* (Philadelphia: Westminster Press, 1983), 39-40.

What are the origins of tattooing?

Tattooing is a form of body art and body alteration done by inserting various pigments, usually ink, under the skin in some sort of decorative pattern. Tattooing may have started during the Stone Age as is evidenced by carved European figures dating from 6000 B.C. which are marked with what is believed to be representations of tattoos. Tattooing was definitely practiced by the ancient Egyptians but only among women. Tattooed dots and geometric patterns appear on women's mummified remains and are thought to be fertility symbols. Around that same period (2000 B.C.) the practice probably began spreading from the Middle East to India, China, Japan, and finally the Pacific Islands. Other historians of the art, however, believe that tattooing reached the Pacific Islands via western explorers who learned the practice from the Aztec, Inca, and Mayan cultures. Ancient tribal groups in Britain such as the Picts practiced tattooing and passed the art on to invading Roman soldiers. The first professional tattooist in the United States was Martin Hildebrand, who by the 1890s, claimed to have tattooed thousands of soldiers and sailors at his New York location. The 1920s showed a shift in attitude toward tattooing, which had become a distasteful and freakish practice to the upper classes. By the 1960s, however, tattooing began a renaissance amongst the middle class, marked by highly stylized artistry.

Clinton R. Sanders, *Customizing the Body: The Art and Culture of Tattooing,* (Philadelphia: Temple University Press, 1989), 9-19.

What festival is associated with the running of the bulls in Pamplona, Spain?

The famous running of the bulls takes place during the week of July 7-14 to celebrate the festival of St. Fermin in Pamplona in northern Spain. Every morning at 8:00 a.m. young bulls are set loose in the narrow streets of the old city, and men run before them, attempting to evade their horns.

Cristina Garca Rodero, *Festivals and Rituals of Spain* (New York: Harry N. Abrams, 1994), 285.

When did the custom of standing during the playing of the American national anthem, "Star Spangled Banner" begin?

The custom of standing during the playing of the "Star-Spangled Banner" began in Tacoma, Washington, in 1893 at a meeting of the Military Order of the Loyal Legion. Rossell Galbraith O'Brien, a Union veteran of the American Civil War (1861-1865) presented a resolution to the Commandery of the Loyal Legion requiring that all members of the organization stand whenever the National Anthem is played. The Commandery concurred and the custom soon spread nationwide.

American Legion Magazine January 1976.

What is Santa Claus's zip code?

The U.S. Postal Service and Coca-Cola USA agreed to give Santa Claus his own zip code in 1989. The nine-digit code, 30351-1989, directs cards and letters to an address in Atlanta and the soda manufacturer rather than to the North Pole. Coca-Cola offered to read all of the mail sent to Santa with this zip code and to forward letters from needy children to local charities and welfare offices. The company also committed to donating five cents to the Toys for Tots program for each card they received.

James Cox, "Coke gives ZIP to Santa," *USA Today* 2 November 1989.

How did candy canes originate?

Candy canes were originally sugar sticks used to placate crying babies. In 1670 a choirmaster in Cologne, Germany, curved the end of the white sugar stick to resemble shepherds' crooks. The use spread throughout Europe, and candy canes became gifts accompanying Nativity plays. Records show a German-Swedish immigrant to America used the white candy canes to decorate a spruce tree for Christmas in the 1850s. Red stripes were added with the peppermint flavor at the turn of the century.

Patricia Dreame Wilson, ed., *American Country Christmas 1990* (Alabama: Oxmoor House, 1990), 74.

What does it mean when a Polynesian woman wears a flower behind her left ear?

In Polynesia, a woman who wears a flower behind her left ear is "happily taken." However, if the flower is worn behind her right ear, she is still available.

David Stanley, *Tahiti-Polynesia Handbook,* (California: Moon Publications, 1992), 11.

What is the origin of the Christmas tree?

One of the earliest stories traces the origin of the Christmas tree to the eighth century, when British monk St. Boniface cut down an oak tree to convince a group of Germanic Druids that the tree was not sacred and inviolable. In one version of the story, the oak crushed everything in its path except for a small fir sapling, while in another version, as the oak fell a young fir tree appeared in its place. In both versions, Boniface declared the fir's survival or appearance a miracle and proclaimed it the tree of the Child, Jesus Christ.

By 1604, small fir trees-both indoors and outdoors-were being decorated in celebration of Christmas in Germany, and it is believed that the sixteenth-century Protestant reformer Martin Luther was the first to add lighted candles.

From Germany the custom spread to other parts of Western Europe, becoming popularized in England in the nineteenth century by Prince Albert, who brought the custom with him from Germany when he married Queen Victoria of England.

Hessian soldiers used during the American Revolution could have introduced the tree custom to America at that time, but the popularization of the custom did not occur until the nineteenth century when the tradition became firmly established in America by the immigrating Pennsylvania Germans. The Puritans had frowned upon such "pagan" customs, and in 1659 the colony of Massachusetts had imposed a fine for hanging any Christmas decorations.

Frank Muir, *Christmas Customs & Traditions* (New York: Taplinger Publishing, 1975), 45-47. Charles Panati, *Extraordinary Origins of Everyday Things* (New York: Harper & Row, 1987), 69-71.

What is the origin of Santa Claus?

There are different stories about the origin of Santa Claus. The current image of a roly-poly, jolly man with a white beard is basically American. The idea of Santa Claus is said to have originated from a combination of St. Nicholas and "Father Christmas." St. Nicholas, the patron saint of children and sailors, was the Bishop of Myra in the third century and known for his concern and gifts for the poor. The Dutch called St. Nicholas "Sinterklaas," which evolved into the name Santa Claus. Father Christmas came from the Roman god Saturn, who presided over the winter feast of Saturnalia. When Roman soldiers occupied England in A.D. 43, they brought the holiday tradition with them. After they left, the Saturn figure evolved into a gigantic man in a scarlet robe lined with fur who wore a crown of holly, ivy, or mistletoe on his head and was a symbol of feasting, drinking, and other holiday merriment.

James Cross Giblin, *The Truth About Santa Claus* (New York: Thomas Y. Crowell, 1985), 32-41. Elizabeth Hough Sechrist, *Red Letter Days: A Book of Holiday Customs, rev. ed.* (Philadelphia, PA: Macrae Smith, 1965), 195-202. *World Book Encyclopedia* (Chicago: World Book, 1994), s.v. "Santa Claus."

When was Mother's Day first observed in the United States?

Mother's Day was founded by Anna M. Jarvis of Philadelphia in May of 1907. It started as a special service in her church. The next year more churches held special services honoring mothers on the second Sunday in May. The practice became so popular that by 1911 every U.S. state and other countries had some sort of Mother's Day celebration. In 1912 a Mother's Day International Association was formed to urge more recognition for the day. On May 9, 1914, President Woodrow Wilson (1856-1924) issued a proclamation encouraging people to fly a flag on the second Sunday of May as "a public expression of our love and reverence for the mothers of our country." Proclamations are issued each year by the president for Mother's Day.

For those who wear flowers on Mother's Day, white signifies that the person's mother is deceased, while red indicates one's mother is still living.

George William Douglas, *The American Books of Days* (New York: H. W. Wilson, 1938), 263-5.

What is the origin of Veterans Day, and when is it celebrated?

Armistice Day acknowledges the cessation of hostilities that ended World War I (1914-1918) at 11:00 A.M. on November 11, 1918. In 1954, the United States changed the name from Armistice to Veterans Day by U.S. Public Law 83-380 in order to honor veterans of other wars. In 1971, the "Monday Holiday Law" (Public Law 90-363) changed the observance of Veterans Day from November 11 to the fourth Monday in October, but the moveable observance that separated Veterans Day from Armistice Day was so unpopular that Public Law 94-97 of September 18, 1975, changed the date back to November 11, effective January 1, 1978.

Chase's Annual Events: The Day-By-Day Directory to 1994 (Chicago: Contemporary Books, 1993), 438-39. Ruth W. Gregory, *Anniversaries and Holidays, 4th ed.* (Chicago: American Library Association, 1983), 145. Laurence J. Peter, *Peter's Almanac* (New York: William Morrow, 1982), s.v. "November 11."

When did the custom of exchanging engagement and wedding rings originate?

Available evidence suggests that betrothal rings were in use before wedding rings, and that if a ring was part of the wedding ceremony, it was the same betrothal ring. The practice of presenting betrothal rings could have begun with the Phoenicians, the Egyptians, the Greeks, or the Romans. The Egyptians, it is said, were the first to believe that the ring was a sign that life, happiness, and love had no beginning or end. The first rings were probably iron, replaced by gold in the second century. Gems were used during the Middle Ages and the Renaissance, when the rings took on beauty as well as meaning. It was the Venetians who introduced the diamond engagement ring around 1500. About the time of the Reformation the betrothal ring probably became a wedding ring. Later still came the custom of giving the prospective bride a ring at the time of the proposal, followed by a plain band of holy union when the actual wedding took place.

James R. McCarthy, *Rings Through the Ages: An Informal History* (New York: Harper & Brothers, 1945), 152-6. Charles Panati, *Extraordinary Origins of Everyday Things* (New York: Harper & Row, 1987), 22-24.

What flowers are associated with each of the twelve calendar months?

The following flowers are associated with the calendar months:
January—Snowdrop
February—Primrose
March—Violet
April—Daisy
May—Hawthorn
June—Rose
July—Water Lily
August—Poppy
September—Morning Glory
October—Hops

November—Chrysanthemum
December—Holly

The New York Public Library Desk Reference (New York: Simon & Schuster, 1989), 51.

What are dowry deaths?

Dowry deaths occur primarily in India when grooms and their families who are dissatisfied with financial arrangements about the marriage kill the new wives. Hindu law prohibits women from inheriting property or money, so the custom arose that the bride's family would give a monetary or other type of gift to the groom and his family in an arranged marriage. Dowries were officially outlawed in 1960, but the practice did not abate, partly because of consumer demand for material goods. For some without the necessary purchasing power, an unofficial dowry is a way of obtaining gifts like television sets or sums of cash. Some brides' families are unable to meet the financial obligation, and the groom or his family have murdered the young woman in anger, in some cases setting her on fire. Women's advocacy groups say that those responsible for what may be hundreds of deaths each year often go unpunished, because witnesses are unwilling to testify in court for fear of reprisals.

New York Times 12 September 1982.

What was particularly unique about the arrangement of Victorian households?

The Victorian household was unique in the way its living spaces were strictly divided or segregated. In it were zones for public and private use, for males and females, and zones for children, adults, and servants.

Shari L. Thurer, *The Myths of Motherhood: How Culture Reinvents the Good Mother* (Boston: Houghton Mifflin, 1994), 189-90.

What is the difference between archaeology and anthropology?

Archaeology is that branch of learning and investigation concerned with the material remnants of man's past and is usually divided into geographical areas such as ancient Greece or Rome and historical periods such as the archaeology of the Middle Ages. Anthropology, on the other hand, is the study of man and is usually divided into physical anthropology and cultural anthropology. Physical anthropology is the description of humankind as a unique physical entity, while cultural anthropology deals with the many diverse cultures and societies that have appeared throughout the world.

The New Encyclopaedia Britannica, 15th ed. (Chicago: Encyclopaedia Britannica, 1989), s.v. "anthropology," archaeology."

What is the history of the poinsettia?

Variously known as the Easter flower, Christmas flower, Mexican flame leaf, and lobster flower, the plant, with the brilliant red bracts, is still most popularly known as the poinsettia. It is named after Joel Poinsett, who first became familiar with the plant while serving as U.S. Minister to Mexico. In 1828, when Poinsett returned home, he brought specimens of the flower with him to his South Carolina greenhouse where he cultivated them. Its popularity as a Christmas plant soon spread along with Poinsett's name.

The poinsettia's association with Christmas has its roots in Mexican folklore. A Mexican legend has it that a poor village lad knelt before a creche on Christmas Eve and said a prayer, since he had no other gifts to offer. In the snow where the boy had knelt, a beautiful plant with scarlet leaves soon flowered and he presented it as his gift to the infant Jesus.

Robert J. Myers, *Celebrations: The Complete Book of American Holidays* (Garden City, NY: Doubleday, 1972), 338. *Phipp's Folio* Fall/Winter 1982.

General Sociology

What was "The Problem That Has No Name"?

In 1963, American feminist author Betty Friedan (1921-) published *The Feminine Mystique* with the first chapter entitled "The Problem That Has No Name." The problem, she explained, was that for many years women had been led to believe that femininity, motherhood, and homemaking were the pinnacle of female achievement. But her observation was that millions of American women were withering away because they had shed their career ambitions to become what was in society's eyes "the perfect housewife." In the fifties, women were dropping out of college in record numbers either to marry or because they were afraid to become too educated to marry. Women were dying their hair blonde, going on severe diets, and even refusing a cancer drug-all out of the need to be more feminine.

Betty Friedan, *The Feminine Mystique* (New York: W. W. Norton, 1963), 15-18.

What is ethnocentrism?

Ethnocentrism is the tendency to evaluate matters by reference to values proposed and shared by an individual's own ethnic group. Ethnocentrists operate from the point of view that their ethnic group is the center of everything.

Michael Mann, ed., *The International Encyclopedia of Sociology* (New York: Continuum Publishing, 1984), s.v. "ethnocentrism."

What are the ten most popular sources of solace?

The ten most popular sources of solace or comforts are:
Being with someone else
Listening to music
Watching TV
Eating
Reading
Talking to oneself
Prayer
A special book, such as the Bible
Recalling pleasant memories
Walking.

New York Times 4 February 1988.

How are the various degrees of cousins in a family determined?

A cousin is a relative descended from a common ancestor such as a grandparent, with the degree of "cousinship" dependent on how the grandparent is shared. First cousins are children of brothers and sisters. Children of first cousins are second cousins to each other. Children of second cousins are third cousins to each other.

Relationships between cousins of different generations are indicated with the word "removed." A person whose first cousin has children is a first cousin once removed to the children. One is a first cousin twice removed to the grandchildren of one's first cousin. The reverse is true also; a person's first cousin's grandchildren are one's first cousins twice removed.

Jackie Smith Arnold, *Kinship: It's All Relative* (Baltimore, MD: Genealogical Publishing, 1990), 24-25.

What is a simple way to locate a missing person?

One way to locate a missing person is to contact motor vehicle departments and request the subject's driving record. It is easier to find men because they change their names less frequently than women, but some departments keep records of the previous surnames for years. It is helpful to have a date of birth, but if this is unknown, the date may be located through an alpha search.

Joseph J. Culligan, *You, Too, Can Find Anybody* (North Miami, FL: Hallmark Press, 1993), 1-1, 1-2.

What is the six-and-six technique?

The six-and-six technique is a way of generating ideas and participation at a meeting of almost any size. Members divide into groups of six, and have six minutes to discuss the given topic. The six choose a member to take notes of their discussion and conclusions. Either a written or oral report is then submitted to the chair of the meeting by the recorder.

Marjorie Mitchell Cann, *Cann's Keys to Better Meetings: Parliamentary Procedure Simplified,* (Mobile, AL: HB Publications, 1990), 60-61.

What is known about the white supremacist group called the Phinehas Priesthood?

The Phinehas Priesthood was described as "a little-known racist group whose members are said to consider themselves 'God's executioners,'" by *The New York Times* in October of 1991. The group's name surfaced when prosecutors in Jackson, Mississippi indicted Byron de la Beckwith for the 1963 murder of civil rights leader Medgar Evers. Beckwith was involved in two mistrials in 1964. The case was reopened in 1991 based on the discovery of witnesses who placed Beckwith in Jackson at the time of the murder.

The Phinehas Priesthood was not well known by police officials or by experts who monitor hate groups. The group could not be linked to any violent crimes. They were identified as not only believing that the Bible forbids racial integration but as also being "...devoted to punishing people who violate their concept of God's law as found in the Bible," according to the *The New York Times.*

"Suspect in Slaying of Evers is Linked to Racist Group," *The New York Times* 30 October 1991.

What is an "old boy network"?

An "old boy network" is a relationship between various people based on past acquaintances and friendships. It usually exists for the benefit of those in the network and often at the expense of those who operate in official channels.

E.D. Hirsch, Jr., Joseph F. Kett, and James Trefil, *Dictionary of Cultural Literacy,* (Boston: Houghton Mifflin, 1988), s.v. "old boy network."

What is the organization known as Brothers to the Rescue?

The organization known as Brothers to the Rescue is a group of pilots that assist Cuban refugees who are trying to make the 90-mile crossing to Florida. A group of some 24 pilots, they search for the often dangerous boats and rafts that carry the refugees. When a craft is sighted, the U.S. Coast Guard is alerted using orange flares. The group was founded in 1991 by two Cuban-Americans; by early 1994, the Brothers had saved 1,286 refugees. In the process, three planes have crashed and one pilot was paralyzed.

Kathy Booth, "Desperate Straits," *Time* 7 March 1994.

Social Issues

What are the economic incentives for a single parent with two children receiving public assistance to get a job or to get married?

According to a 1991 report by the National Commission on Children, a single parent with two children who is receiving AFDC and food stamps has ample incentive to get off of public assistance. By obtaining a minimum wage job, a single parent could increase the family income by $2,720. Obtaining a $15,000 per year job would yield $5,670 in additional income. Conversely, marriage would be an economic disincentive to that same parent. If the new spouse held a minimum wage job, the loss of welfare benefits would yield a 19 percent penalty; if the spouse earned $15,000 per year, the penalty would be 20 percent.

Leon Ginsberg, *Social Work Almanac* (Washington, DC: NASW Press, 1992), 169.

What should the first step be when searching for a parent who refuses to pay child support?

Many steps can be taken at both the federal and state levels to track down delinquent parents who do not pay child support as required. The first step involves contacting the Child Support Enforcement office, which has an office in each state and the District of Columbia. The Child Support Enforcement office will then use a free service known as the State Parent Locator Service, which will try to track down the delinquent parent by using records from other agencies such as state income tax, correctional facilities, motor vehicle registration, and unemployment insurance. If this search proves ineffective, the Federal Parent Locator Service will access federal records to find the parent.

Joseph J. Culligan, *You, Too, Can Find Anybody* (Hallmark Press, 1993), 11-1-6.

Are children in joint custody situations better off than those in single parent custody situations?

There seems to be no psychological benefit in joint custody households for the children of divorced parents. It does not seem to help mitigate the negative impact of the divorce on the children either, at least in the first two to three years following the divorce. There is not yet sufficient research to analyze the long-range effects of the two types of custody.

Judith S. Wallerstein and Sandra Blakeslee, *Second Chances: Men, Women, and Children A Decade After Divorce* (New York: Ticknor & Fields, 1989), 271.

Do men do more housework if their wives earn more on the job?

Only one study found a relationship between how much a man earned and how much he helped around the house. If a man made more or roughly the same amount of money as his wife, he was more likely to assist with the housework. If he made substantially less than his wife, he would not help at all. This may be related to a tendency to try and balance power in the relationship. Because the husband's manhood is threatened by his wife earning more, he cannot afford to invest time in "women's work."

Arlie Russell Hochschild, *The Second Shift: Working Parents and the Revolution at Home* (New York: Viking, 1989), 220-21.

What happened during the Kent State University demonstrations of 1970?

Student antiwar disturbances had already occurred in Ohio during April of 1970 in Cleveland, Oxford, and Sandusky, when on May 1 demonstrations that would last for three days erupted in Kent, Ohio, and on the campus of Kent State University. The protesters were reacting to the April 30, 1970, announcement by then U.S. President Richard M. Nixon (1913-1994) of the U.S. invasion of Cambodia.

On May 1, 1970, students buried the U.S. Constitution. The students stopped traffic, climbed lamp posts, started fires, broke windows, and spread false fire alarms, bomb threats, and rumors of further turbulence. Tensions worsened on May 2 as students burned down the ROTC building and battled fire fighters trying to quench the blaze. The riot spread to downtown Kent. As it had been during April's demonstrations in other cities, the Ohio National Guard was called in. The Guard was able to bring the situation under control but by the evening of May 3 confrontations again erupted. Unfortunately, by this time the students had been erroneously informed by one student that there was an agreement that the National Guard would now be kept off campus. Feeling betrayed, the students escalated their violence. By approximately 11:30 p.m. the Guard had the campus secured.

On May 4, in spite of a ban on outdoor demonstrations, student leaders called for a rally at noon. The Guard was ordered to disperse the crowd of students. The students retaliated by throwing objects such as gas cans and rocks at the Guard. The Guardsmen responded with tear gas. Suddenly, at approximately 12:30 p.m., a group of Guardsmen halted, turned, and fired at some students who were about 200 yards away from the soldiers and could not have hurt them. In thirteen seconds sixty-seven shots were fired. One student was dead, three more were fatally injured, and nine others were wounded. It is not known who started the shooting. There were 113 Guardsmen and approximately 1,100 student on campus at the time. The student-led antiwar movement, which had occurred on campuses across the country, virtually came to an end after this incident.

Source: Lee Davis, *Man-Made Catastrophes: From the Burning of Rome to the Lockerbie Crash,* (New York: Facts On File, 1993), 92-94.

How many American women are battered by a male partner?

Domestic abuse is one of the most pressing problems in the United States. According to the American Psychological Association, approximately one out of every three American women is physically abused by a male partner during her lifetime. Roughly 28 percent of married women are abused by their husbands. The degree of abuse varies, from hitting to assault with weapons. Several studies suggest that nearly 40 percent of unmarried women who are dating or living with a male partner are victims of abuse.

Many reasons can be cited for domestic violence. The principal reasons why men abuse women is fear of abandonment and the need to control. Abuse is usually heightened when a woman rebels against male control or threatens to leave the relationship.

Marilyn Elias, "A third of women hit by male partner," *USA Today* 7 July 1994.

What is the average length of a marriage that ends in divorce?

The average length of a U.S. marriage that ends in divorce is 7.1 years, increasing from the 6.6-year-average length 20 years ago.

U.S. News & World Report 6 June 1994.

What is food insecurity?

As many as 4.9 million elderly Americans go hungry or worry about how they'll afford their next meal, a condition dubbed by the Urban Institute as food insecurity. The condition persists, even among those above the poverty line-around $6,700 yearly for a senior citizen living alone-leaving many ineligible for food stamps and largely ignored in the battle against hunger, the institute's study says. The study is based on a national questionnaire and surveys in 16 communities, and is the first comprehensive look at the problem of food insecurity.

Alan Bash, "Millions of Elderly Fear Going Hungry," *USA Today* 16 November 1993.

What is the basic premise of the pro-life position?

The basic premise of the pro-life position is four-pronged. First, the pro-life position holds that an unborn embryo or fetus is fully human from the moment of conception. Second, it is self-evident that it is morally wrong to kill any fully human entity. Third, the primary intention of most abortions is to kill the unborn, except when the abortion is performed in order to save the life of the mother. Therefore, in almost every case, it is self-evident that abortions are morally wrong.

Francis J. Beckwith, *Politically Correct Death: Answering the Arguments for Abortion Rights* (Grand Rapids, MI: Baker Books, 1993), 153-54.

What kinds of adoptions are available?

Adopters, that is, prospective adoptive parents, have four types of adoptions available to them: public and private agency adoptions, independent adoptions, international adoptions, and foster adopt programs. Public agencies offer low to no-fee adoptions and can often provide subsidies for medical care and other adoption expenses. In the case of special needs adoptions, public agencies are more likely to provide support after the adoption. In a private agency adoption, the agency is responsible for the entire process which means that the number of organizations and people that the adopters must deal with is minimized. Some fees may be refundable or payable in the event that the adoption is successful.

Independent, or private, adoptions account for approximately two-thirds of the adoptions of newborn infants in the United States. Most adopters hire an attorney or a facilitation service to locate and screen birth parents and to mediate contact between the birth and adoptive parents. Only a few states have banned independent adoptions. The placing of advertisements by adopters seeking pregnant women is the most common method of locating birth parents. Many states have restricted or banned adoption advertising, however.

International adoptions, which involve foreign travel, can be exciting and enriching. They are almost always, however, very time consuming. Adopters must collect many documents and then make sure that they are notarized, verified, translated, authenticated by the country's consulate or embassy, and received by the intermediary in the child's country. Adopters can end up waiting months or years before bringing home a child. In some cases, they return empty-handed.

Foster adopt programs, also known as permanency planning programs, combine the adoption and foster care processes. Once the foster parents, who must be properly trained and licensed, accept a child they work with the agency staff and the birth parents to form a parenting plan. At this stage the child's natural family receives counseling on parenting. If these efforts are successful, and occasionally they are, the child is returned to its biological family. Conversely, if the foster care placement does not work out for the adopters, they are able to more easily end a foster care relationship than an adoptive relationship.

Nancy Thalia Reynolds, *Adopting Your Child: Options, Answers, and Actions* (North Vancouver, BC, Canada: Self-Counsel Press, 1993), 91-97.

What name was given to the U.S. civil rights leader Martin Luther King, Jr., at his birth?

The male child born to Alberta (Williams) King and the Rev. Michael Luther King, Sr., on January 15, 1929, was named Michael Luther King, Jr. (1929-1968). At the age of six his name was changed to Martin Luther, at about the time that Michael Luther King, Sr., also changed his name.

Current Biography Yearbook 1965 (New York: H. W. Wilson, 1966), s.v. "King, Martin Luther, Jr."

What is meant by the terms "nuclear" and "extended" family?

Terms such as "nuclear" and "extended" are sociological attempts to define basic types of family structure among human societies. According to this field of study, there are three types of family: nuclear, extended, and polygamous. The nuclear unit is characterized by one husband and one wife. They may or may not have offspring. An extended family is one with three or more generations living under the same roof. The third type of family structure is the polygamous, with one husband with more than one wife, or one wife with more than one husband.

Margaret DiCanio, *The Encyclopedia of Marriage, Divorce, and the Family* (New York: Facts On File, 1989), s.v. "family forms."

What is the legend of the thorn bird?

The thorn bird legend describes a bird who sings only once. Its sole purpose in life is to find a thorn tree and impale itself on the longest, sharpest spine. The thorn bird's song, a death song, is so beautiful it causes God and the world to stop and listen. The legend's lesson is that greatness is only achieved through the endurance of great pain.

Colleen McCullough, *The Thorn Birds,* (New York: Harper & Row, 1977).

Are baby boomers better off financially than their parents were at the same age?

Baby boomers, people born from 1946 to 1964, are better off financially than their parents were at the same age, at least for the time being. An increase in real wages has occurred since baby boomers entered the work force. This group also enjoys a higher level of education, resulting in higher income. Many baby boomers live in two income households; more women are working outside the home than in previous generations. What remains to be seen is if baby boomers will continue to enjoy financial security in their own retirement years. Economic growth and the status of the Social Security and Medicare programs will be two factors. Current studies also show that baby boomers are not yet saving the money needed to maintain their current standard of living during retirement.

Secure Retirement November/December 1993.

Why was age 65 selected to be the age of retirement?

Otto von Bismarck (1815-1898), Germany's chancellor over a century ago, selected the age 65 when he was asked to establish a pension system for his government's service. Bismarck was said to have looked at the amount of money in the treasury, the age of the people in the country, and selected 65 as the age at which people could start collecting a pension.

Pittsburgh Press 8 October 1989.

Into what classes have Western societies traditionally been divided?

Western societies generally recognize the existence of three classes: upper, middle, and lower. These divisions mark levels of social, economic, and occupational standing, and their accompanying privileges and powers. Marxist theory, however, only recognizes the existence of two significant classes, the upper class, or bourgeoisie, and the working class or proletariat.

E.D. Hirsch, Joseph F. Kett, and James Trefil, *The Dictionary of Cultural Literacy,* (New York: Houghton Mifflin, 1988), 394.

What are perceived to be the most stressful situations and common troubles in the United States?

The National Opinion Research Center asked 1,700 individuals to identify the most stressful events in life. This was done by ranking 58 events according to the level of misery they cause. The death of a child was rated as the worst experience in life, followed by the death of a spouse. Not having money to purchase food was third on the list; the death of a parent was fourth; and losing your home in a disaster was fifth. Participants were also asked what kinds of troubles they had experienced in the last year. Health related problems were the most common, affecting 73 percent of adults. Other common troubles and the percentage of adults who suffered from them were: work related difficulties, 29 percent; financial, 26 percent; housing, 22 percent; family/personal, 22 percent; material hardship, 20 percent; and law/crime, 14 percent.

USA Today 30 August 1993.

What percentage of individuals arrested for prostitution tested positive for drugs?

In 1990, the National Institute of Justice's Drug Use Forecasting Program determined that there is a direct correlation between drug use and prostitution. Approximately 81 percent of the females and 49 percent of the males arrested for prostitution and being held in jail tested positively for drugs.

Drugs, Crime, and the Justice System: A National Report from the Bureau of Justice Statistics (Washington, DC: Government Printing Office, 1992), 7.

What is gentrification?

Many people are interested in restoring decayed neighborhoods in communities throughout the United States. One way in which a depressed neighborhood can be revived is through gentrification. Gentrification involves the purchase and renovation of dilapidated homes in poor neighborhoods by more affluent persons as an investment or personal dwelling. The results of gentrification are mixed. Although gentrification tends to increase the desirability of a particular neighborhood, it also increases the neighborhoods property values, tax rates, and rents. As a result, families who can no longer afford to live in the gentrified neighborhood are displaced and crowd into other neighborhoods, which in turn decline further.

Robert L. Barker, *The Social Work Dictionary* (Silver Spring, MD: National Association of Social Workers, 1987), 63.

Which sex has the higher remarriage rate among the older population?

A study has shown that older men remarry at a rate seven times greater than older women.

Elizabeth Vierck, *Fact Book on Aging* (Santa Barbara, CA: ABC-CLIO, 1990), 47.

What are the four types of child abuse?

Child abuse, one of the most pressing problems in contemporary American society, can be classed into four general types: physical abuse, sexual abuse, emotional abuse, and neglect.

Physical abuse is defined as a consistent pattern of inflicting physical harm on a child for the purposes of discipline or releasing anger. Among the types of physical abuse are beating with fists, slapping, or whipping.

Sexual abuse involves any type of sexual contact between children and adults.

Child welfare experts have a difficult time defining what constitutes emotional abuse. Among the behaviors cited by experts as emotional abuse are berating a child consistently, being aloof or unresponsive to a child's emotional needs, withholding praise and constructive criticism, and making a child feel inferior or unloved.

Neglect is often defined as failing to provide children with adequate food, medical care, shelter, clothing, or educational opportunities.

New York Times 8 January 1989.

What are the three stages of divorce?

The first or acute stage of divorce usually involves escalating fighting and sometimes physical violence between the two partners until one leaves. There seems to be a return to adolescence and an obsession with sexual fantasies. Some individuals start behaving in a sexually irresponsible manner.

The second or transitional stage is a period of flux as the adults and children experiment with new lifestyles in new settings. Many families move during this time.

The third stage is a return to stability. The divorced family is established as a new unit.

Judith S. Wallerstein and Sandra Blakeslee, *Second Chances: Men, Women, and Children a Decade After Divorce* (New York: Ticknor & Fields, 1989), 8-10.

What are the orders of knighthood in Great Britain?

The orders of knighthood in Great Britain begin with the Garter which is of royalty or peerage. The next order is Thistle which is for Scottish nobles. The third order is that of St. Patrick which is for Irish nobles. The fourth order is of Bath which has three classes. The fifth order is Star of India which has three classes. The sixth order is of St. Michael and St. George with three classes. The seventh order is the Order of the Indian Empire with three classes. Only the eighth and ninth orders are open to women. The eighth order is the Victorian Order with five classes. The ninth order is the Order of the British Empire with five classes. Baronets rank below Knights of the Bath. The Knights Bachelor are not part of any order.

Fred L. Worth, *The Trivia Encyclopedia* (New York: Bell Publishing, 1974), 140.

How much money do delinquent dads in the United States owe to their children?

The trauma of divorce for a couple with children or an unplanned pregnancy for an unmarried couple is compounded when delinquent dads do not pay child support. According to *U.S. News and World Report*, approximately 75 percent of single mothers do not receive regular child support payments from the fathers of their children. More than 20 billion dollars in child support was owed in 1993 by absent fathers to single mothers and their children.

Database, *U.S. News & World Report* 6 September 1993.

Who described herself as "God's vessel" in a crusade against homosexuality?

Conservative activist Anita Bryant described herself as "God's vessel" in a 1970s crusade against homosexuality. The singer and former runner-up in the 1959 Miss America pageant was a well-known national spokesperson for the Florida Citrus Commission when she spearheaded a group called "Save Our Children" in 1977. That year, the Dade County (Florida) Commission approved an ordinance barring discrimination on the basis of sexual orientation. Bryant and the "Save Our Children" group launched a crusade to repeal the civil rights law, arguing that it made homosexuality socially acceptable and with it the "recruitment of our children." During her crusade Bryant cited Biblical references to homosexuality and asserted that her outspoken public campaign was indeed God's own campaign and she was His "vessel." Voters in Dade County overturned the ordinance, but the gay community both in Florida and the rest of the country became politically galvanized as a result. A few years later, Bryant fell from grace among the more conservative elements in the United States when she ended her 20 year marriage through divorce. She later went into the fashion business.

George C. Kohn, *Encyclopedia of American Scandal* (New York: Facts on File, 1989), 50-1.

To what factors do Americans over 90 years of age attribute their long lives?

Living right may mean living longer, according to the results of a lifestyle survey by the nonprofit Humana Seniors Association of Louisville, Kentucky. Humana sent surveys to 1,500 hundreds of Americans 90 years old or older, and received more than 375 responses. The survey found the following:
96% of respondents do not smoke
89% do not drink
58% "eat whatever I want." Almost none are on vegetarian, low-fat, or low-salt diets, but 53% eat balanced meals.
80% exercise regularly; walking was the favorite form of exercise
72% believe that the right career had a positive effect on their lives
31% believe that their religious faith keeps them healthy and happy

USA Today 20 January 1992.

What percentage of elderly care funding comes from the recipients' own families?

According to Children of Aging Parents, a national support group, 80 to 90 percent of elderly care for older Americans comes from their own families. That includes personal care, help with household tasks, transportation, some medical assistance, and help shopping. Only 5 percent of those 65 or older are in nursing homes, but by age 80, the numbers increase to 20-25 percent.

USA Today 1 November 1990.

What were some reproductive control methods in colonial America?

The common methods of birth control used by some colonial Americans were withdrawal, breast-feeding, and abortion. Although contemporary medicine does not fully understand how it is that lactation renders a woman less fertile, it is known that breast-feeding reduces the probabilities of pregnancy perhaps by as much as 25 percent. It lengthens the duration of the suppression of menstruation after giving birth.

Nicholas Culpeper's books *The English Physician* and *Complete Herbal* suggested six to twelve botanical preparations that he thought induced abortion. These included sage, pennyroyal, brake fern, honeysuckle, gladwin, and snakeweed. Native Americans also used pennyroyal as an abortive. Some of the methods used were not only dangerous but ineffective. For example, some herbs were poisonous including castor bean, foxglove, white hellebore, boneset herb, mayapple, bloodroot, and mistletoe. Women who used these herbs were taking a risk when they tried to kill the life within them without killing themselves. Cathartics were also widely used based on the belief that severe intestinal cramping would induce an abortion. Aloe was the most commonly used cathartic for abortions.

Janet Farrell Brodie, *Contraception and Abortion in Nineteenth-Century America,* (Ithaca, NY: Cornell University Press, 1994), 41-45.

What is the difference between bigamy and polygamy?

Bigamy is the practice of having two spouses at the same time. It is illegal and usually punished by a prison term unless the person who has taken two wives or two husbands can prove that he or she did not know the first marriage was valid or the first spouse was still alive. In the American colonies, bigamy was punishable by death. Polygamy is the practice of having multiple spouses at the same time. The terms polyandry and polygyny are not used as often but relate to the same topic. Polyandry is the practice of having more than one husband at one time. Polygyny is the practice of having two or more wives at one time.

Robert K. Barnhart, ed., *The Barnhart Dictionary of Etymology* (New York: H. W. Wilson, 1988), s.v. "bigamy," "polyandry," "polygamy." Henry Campbell Black, *Black's Law Dictionary, 6th ed.* (St. Paul: West Publishing, 1990), s.v. "bigamy," "polygamy." *The World Book Encyclopedia* (Chicago: World Book, 1994), s.v. "bigamy."

Which president signed the Americans with Disabilities Act into law?

President George Bush (1924-) was responsible for signing the Americans with Disabilities Act (ADA) into law on July 26, 1990. This act is the world's first comprehensive civil rights statute of its kind. It guarantees the disabled "equal access to employment. The employer must consider whether reasonable accommodation could remove the barrier created by the individual disability.

Department of Justice, U.S. Equal Employment Opportunity Commission, *Americans with Disabilities Act Handbook,* (Washington, DC: Government Printing Office, 1992), I-1.

What is a binuclear family?

A binuclear family is one in which a legal separation or divorce of a married couple with children creates two households.

David K. Barnhart, *Neo-Words: A Dictionary of the Newest and Most Unusual Words of Our Times* (New York: Collier Books, 1991), 8.

What are the major events of the gay-rights movement?

Protests and policy changes mark a chronology of events in the gay rights movement. Public consciousness of the gay community increased greatly after a 1969 riot in New York City's Greenwich Village; after a police raid of the Stonewall Inn, a gay nightclub, more than 4,000 people were involved in a riot lasting several days. In 1970, the University of Chicago was the site of the first public gay dance. Two years later, Ann Arbor, Michigan passed the first law against discrimination based on sexual preference. The next major policy change came in 1974, when the American Psychiatric Association eliminated its references to homosexuality as a mental disorder. That same year, Massachusetts legislator Elaine Noble was successful in her bid to become the first openly gay person in a high elected office. In 1975, the U.S. government lifted its ban of homosexuals in the civil service. A highly publicized protest against laws favoring gays took place in 1977, led by singer Anita Bryant. The year 1981 saw the first reports of a disease that was killing gay men, later known to be AIDS. In 1984, Wisconsin became the first state to include gays in their anti-discrimination laws. Hundreds of thousands of gay-rights demonstrators marched on the U.S. capitol in 1987. Voters in Colorado passed an amendment to the state constitution in 1992, banning gay rights legislation. And in 1993, the U.S. Defense Department revises its policy regarding gays, instituting what is known as the "don't ask, don't tell" policy.

USA Today 24 June 1994.

Who is Norma McCorvey?

Norma McCorvey was the plaintiff "Jane Roe" in the Roe v. Wade U.S. Supreme Court case. Because of the controversial case, abortion procedures were decriminalized and McCorvey and Roe v. Wade are assured a place in U.S. judicial history.

Norma McCorvey, *I Am Roe: My Life, Roe v. Wade, and Freedom of Choice,* (New York: HarperCollins, 1994), 1.

Does the practice of slavery still exist?

The country of Mauritania in northwest Africa is still home to slavery although it has been outlawed three times. As a French colony, Mauritania forbid slavery in 1905; upon gaining independence in 1960, it constitutionally abolished slavery; and in 1980 a law was passed prohibiting the practice. It was the last country on earth to institute such a policy. Ten years later reports indicated that slavery still existed; open slave markets had been closed but gifts and exchanges of slaves continued.

The white slave owners are Arab and Berber descendants, known as Beydanes, a racial minority that has political power in Mauritania. The persecution of Haratines, freed slaves and their descendants, has been severe. Many have become refugees in Senegal and Mali, rather than be victim to human rights abuses. The Haratines have seen mass arrests followed by torture, rape, and sometimes death. International response to events in this country of some two million people has been minimal. Despite this brutality, Mauritania remained a member in good standing of the United Nations.

Aryeh Neier, "Watching Rights," *The Nation* 8 July 1991. B.J. Cutler, "Mauritania Still Practices Slavery," *Pittsburgh Press* 5 September 1990.

Which occupational group is the most trusted by the American public?

Pharmacists are the most trusted occupational group in America. Polls show that they gained this distinction in 1988, when they bypassed the clergy as the most ethical profession. The clergy still ranked highly, however, as did college teachers. The worst ratings were given to car salesmen, closely followed by lawyers.

USA Today 2 July 1993.

What was the Crop Club?

The Crop Club was a group of men who followed the lead of the Duke of Bedford in his protest of a tax on hair-powdering in 1795. The Englishmen thwarted the crown's efforts to restore the wearing of wigs among men by keeping their hair cut short, and unpowdered.

John Woodforde, *The Strange Story of False Hair* (New York: Drake Publisher, 1972), 57-58.

Social Statistics

How accurate are opinion polls?

Opinion polls, scientifically designed to gauge the mood to the populace, have become increasingly more accurate since they first appeared in the 1930s; for example, the Gallup Poll's margin of error in 1936 was 2.3 percent, and by 1976 that figure had dropped to just over one percent. In a typical survey, a random sample is computer selected and then compared to census reports to verify that it accurately reflects society as a whole, if this is the desired population. Top pollsters such as Gallup rely primarily on person-to-person interviews for canvassing because telephone interviews inject a prejudice against the poor and prohibits in-depth questioning. Accuracy increases by the number of interviews conducted. However, after 500 people are interviewed the margin of error decreases on slightly even if millions more are interviewed.

Jane Polley, ed., *Stories Behind Everyday Things* (Pleasantville, NY: The Reader's Digest Association, 1980), 234-5.

What is the cost of conducting the U.S. Census?

Per capita, the estimated cost of counting the estimated 250 million people in the United States in 1990 was $10.55. The cost of the 1980 Census $7.53. The 1970 Census cost $3.66 per capita, while the 1960 Census cost $2.58. The Census of 1950 figured in at $2.43. All figures are converted to 1990 constant dollars.

USA Today 28 August 1990.

What was the return rate of U.S. Census questionnaires for 1980 and 1990?

The rate of return on questionnaires for the 1990 U.S. Census was 74 percent, compared to 81 percent in 1980. This caused a cost increase in 1990 of 25 percent over 1980.

Les Krantz, *America by the Numbers* (Boston: Houghton Mifflin, 1993), 43.

Has the number of senior citizens in the United States increased since the late nineteenth century?

There has been a thirtyfold increase in the number of senior citizens-defined as those 65 years of age or older-in the United States since the late nineteenth century. In 1870 there were one million seniors in the United States; in 1900, three million; and according to the 1990 U.S. census, there were over 30.6 million. The growth rate continues at a rapid pace, since the number of seniors is expected to more than double by 2030.

Elizabeth Vierck, *Fact Book on Aging* (Santa Barbara, CA: ABC-CLIO, 1990), 3.

Are there more men or women in the world?

United Nations Statistics indicate that there were more men than women in the world as of 1990. Of the 5.3 billion people in the world, fewer than half, 2.63 billion, were women. More males are born into the world than females, but females usually have lower mortality rates than males at all ages. In developed regions of the world, the ratio of women to men is 106 to 100. In some countries, there are fewer than 95 women to 100 men. Reasons for a lower ratio of females to males include denial of equivalent health care and nutrition to girls and women, dowry deaths, female infanticide, and abortion on the basis of male preference.

The World's Women 1970-1990: Trends and Statistics (New York: United Nations, 1991), 11.

How is the composition of American households changing?

According to the United States Bureau of the Census, the composition of the American family in 1990 was characterized by proportionately more people living alone, fewer married-couple households, and more single-parent households than in the past. Married couples with children accounted for 26.3 percent of households in 1990, compared to 40.3 percent of households in 1970. The number of single-person households increased from 17.1 percent in 1970 to 24.6 percent in 1990.

Leon Ginsberg, *Social Work Almanac* (Washington, DC: NASW Press, 1992), 5.

What is the status of small towns in the United States?

According to the 1990 United States census, only one in ten persons lived in a city with fewer than 10,000 residents-the lowest percentage in at least 100 years. Small towns in the United States with a population between 100 and 999 residents lost nearly five percent of their residents. The population of cities with fewer than 100 residents tumbled nearly 30 percent between the years 1980 and 1990.

USA Today 6 January 1992.

What are the social standings of different ethnic groups in the United States?

Adults in the United States are becoming more tolerant of different ethnic groups. The study of polls conducted over several years by seven national polling organizations evaluating the changes in ethnic social standing over the course of 25 years was sponsored by the American Jewish Committee. The Japanese have made the greatest advance followed by African-Americans, Chinese, and Jews. Almost every one of 58 designated groups received higher scores when comparing two surveys, the first done in 1964 and the second in 1989.

European groups were ranked with the highest social standing, roughly in the order of their immigration to this country. The British and Protestants received the top social standings, while Mexicans, Puerto Ricans, and Gypsies received the lowest rankings.

Tamar Lewin, "Study Points to Increase in Tolerance of Ethnicity," *The New York Times* 5 January 1992.

What is Africa's most populated country?

With an estimated population of between 116.5 and 120 million people, the Federal Republic of Nigeria is Africa's most populated country.

Pierre Etienne Dostert, *Africa 1993,* (Washington, DC: Stryker-Post Publications, 1993), 74.

What changes in the U.S. household population were shown between the 1980 and 1990 censuses?

A comparison of 1980 and 1990 census figures shows the biggest change in household demographics to be the number of married couples who have children at home. That number dropped from 32 to 27 percent of the population. Another decrease was the percentage of married couples with no children at home. The average household size also dropped, from 2.8 to 2.6. Increases were seen in the following categories: single person households, people over 65 living alone or with non-relatives, singles with children at home, stepfamilies, and unmarried couples of the opposite sex. There was no change in the percentage of same sex couples, but reporting in this category is considered less reliable, because gay couples may fear discrimination based on their response to the census. The total number of households grew from 79 million in 1980 to 93 million in 1990.

Pittsburgh Press 29 January 1992.

In what places have blacks reported a higher median income than whites?

Analysis of the 1990 U.S. census has shown that 130 cities and counties reported a higher median income for black households than for white households. In the majority of these cases the median income was below the national average, or blacks accounted for a very small minority or a great majority of the population. Communities containing military bases were also among those listed.

Ten of the 130 communities, however, did have a racially diverse population of more than 50,000: Carson, Rialto and Vacaville, California; Southfield, Michigan; Vineland, New Jersey; Brentwood, New York; Queens, New York; Cleveland Heights, Ohio; Penn Hills, Pennsylvania; and Dale City, Virginia. A detailed study of the Queens' census data showed the median income for blacks was $34,300, while the median income for non-Hispanic whites was $34,000. Blacks in Queens had a higher median income than blacks elsewhere because the households included a greater number of married couples. When compared to married white couples in Queens, blacks worked longer hours, and black wives were more likely to work outside the home.

Sam Roberts, "Where Median Income of Blacks Leads That of White Households," *The New York Times* 6 June 1994.

How much is the population of the United States expected to grow during the next century?

U.S. population figures depend upon projected life expectancy during the next century. If life expectancy in the year 2080 is 77.4 years, the population is expected to grow from 266,497 in the year 2000; 296,454 in 2080. If life expectancy is projected at 81 years, the population should grow from 267,955 in the year 2000; 310,762 in 2080. If life expectancy is assumed to be 85.9 in the year 2080, the population of the U.S. should grow from 269,576 in the year 2000; 328,983 in 2080.

Gregory Spencer, *Current Population Reports: Population Estimates and Projections* (Washington, DC: Government Printing Office, 1984), 18.

What did Americans see in 1994 as serious threats to their rights and freedoms?

According to a 1994 Gallup Poll 83 percent of Americans saw crime as a threat to their rights and freedoms. Lack of opportunity was seen as a threat by 47 percent of the people interviewed while 41 percent feared government regulation.

USA Today 19 August 1994.

What is the estimate of the number of older Americans who may be victims of elder abuse?

The term "elder abuse" generally refers to the abuse, neglect, or exploitation of people aged 60 and older. It may include physical, psychological, and sexual abuse; material or financial exploitation; and neglect and self-neglect. The precise number of elder abuse incidents in the United States each year is unknown because no standard definition of abuse exists and a significant proportion of incidents never come to public attention. However, various experts estimate that as many as 1.5 to 2.0 million older Americans may be victims of elder abuse each year, and the number is expected to increase as the nation's elderly population continues to grow.

Elder Abuse: Effectiveness of Reporting Laws and Other Factors (Washington, D.C.: U.S. General Accounting Office, 1991), 1.

Which cities in the United States are most conducive to marriage?

A 1987 survey ranked Orlando as the American city most conducive to marriage, followed closely by Philadelphia, Pittsburgh, Cleveland, and Tampa-St. Petersburg. The worst cities for marriage included Los Angeles, New York, and Albuquerque.

Pittsburgh Press 16 April 1987.

What was the distribution of ethnic groups at the time of the first U.S. Census in 1790?

At the time of the first U.S. Census in 1790, the majority of foreign-born citizens came from European countries. Sixty percent had immigrated from England; 9.5 percent, from Ireland; 8.6 percent, from Germany; 8.1 percent, from Scotland; 3.1 percent, from the Netherlands; 2.3 percent, from France; 0.7 percent, from Sweden; 0.8 percent, from Spain; and another 0.8 percent were termed "unclassified."

Stephanie Bernardo, *The Ethnic Almanac* (Garden City, NY: Doubleday, 1981), 18.

What different ethnic populations live in Siberia?

Siberian citizens are 95 percent Russian, but there are a wide variety of other nationalities that make a home there. The reindeer-herding tribes of the Chukchi (population 14,000), the Koriak (8,000), the Eskimos (1,500), and the Iukagirs (800) live along with the Itelmen (1,300), the Nivkh (4,400) and the Lower Amur people. Other nationalities include the Nenets (29,000), the Selkup (3,500), the Nganasan (860), the Khanti (21,000), the Mansi (7,500), the Orok (1,200), the Ainu (1,500), the Evenk (27,500), the Even (12,500), the Negidal, the Nanai, the Udegei, the Sakha (328,000), the Dolgan (5,000), the Siberian Tatars, the Shor, the Khakass, the Altai, the Tuvinian, the Kazakh, the Buriat (353,000), and the Ket (1,200).

Stephen K. Batalden and Sandra L. Batalden, *The Newly Independent States of Eurasia: Handbook of Former Soviet Republics* (Phoenix: Oryx Press, 1993), 28-50.

Have childhood deaths from poisoning decreased since the introduction of child-proof containers?

After child-proof packaging was required on all drugs and medications beginning in 1973, the childhood poisoning death rate declined dramatically. A 50 percent decrease was noted in 1973-1976 and the decline has continued. Other factors in this decline have been the development of poison control centers, changes in products to reduce poisonous agents, and the introduction of single-dose packages.

Susan P. Baker et al. , *The Injury Fact Book, 2d ed.* (New York: Oxford University Press, 1992), 207-8.

Who has fathered the most children?

Ismail Ibn Sharif (1645-1727), ruler of the 'Alawi dynasty of Morocco from 1672 to 1727, was reported to have fathered 700 sons and over 340 daughters, the greatest number on record.

Mark C. Young, ed., *The Guinness Book of Records 1995* (New York: Facts On File, 1994), 10. *The New Encyclopaedia Britannica, 15th ed.* (Chicago: Encyclopaedia Britannica, 1993), s.v. "Ishmail."

What is the estimated number of refugees worldwide?

A November 9, 1993, report by the United Nations High Commissioner for Refugees stated that 19.7 million people had been forced to leave their home countries in 1992. Yet another 24 million were displaced within their own countries. These numbers indicated that, among the world's entire population, one in 130 had been driven from their homes by civil war, persecution, or violence. The areas that were hardest hit by the increased refugee population were the country of Afghanistan, with 4.5 million refugees, and the continent of Asia, with 7.2 million refugees.

Facts on File 25 November 1993.

What percentage of people are adopted?

In the United States and Canada, about two percent of all people are adopted; that impacts about 20 percent of all families. In 1993, the typical number of adoptions per year in North America was 150,000.

Nancy Thalia Reynolds, *Adopting Your Child, Options, Answers, and Actions* (Bellingham, WA: Self-Counsel Press, 1993), 1.

Who are some renowned redheads?

A list of renowned redheads would include:
Lucille Ball—Screen TV comedienne
Lizzie Borden—Alleged hatchet murderess
Emily Dickinson—Poet
Harold "Red" Grange—Football hero
Judas Iscariot—Christ's betrayer
Thomas Jefferson—U.S. President
Rod Laver—Tennis champion
Sinclair Lewis—Author
Walter Reuther—Labor leader
Margaret Sanger—Feminist
George Bernard Shaw—Playwright
Svetlana Stalin—Stalin's daughter
Mark Twain—Author
Martin Van Buren—U.S. President

David Wallechinsky and Irving Wallace, *The People's Almanac* (Garden City, NY: Doubleday & Co., 1975), 1227.

Which workers in the United States are most likely to be murdered on the job?

According to the Census of Fatal Occupational Injuries by the U.S. Bureau of Labor Statistics, taxi drivers, food retailers, especially convenience store workers, and security guards are the occupations that experienced the most on-the-job violence in 1994. Of the 6,588 people killed on-the-job, 20 percent were violence-related. Ninety-one percent of the homicides were committed by co-workers, customers, or clients; 73 percent of the homicides were done during robberies.

"On the Job Deaths: Homicide No. 2 Cause," *USA Today* 4 August 1995.

How many times a day does sexual intercourse occur?

The World Health Organization has estimated that sexual intercourse takes place more than 100 million times each day. A 1992 report showed that 910,000 of these cases resulted in conception and that in 350,000 instances a sexually-transmitted disease was contracted. Additional information told of 150,000 abortions per day and one death per minute as a result of pregnancy or childbirth. Contraception greatly increased in the thirty-year period prior to the study, which revealed that 381 million people were practicing birth control, up from only 31 million during the 1960-65 period.

"U.N. Agency on Sex: Pitfalls and Promise," *The New York Times* 25 June 1992.

How has the average poverty threshold in the United States risen in the last thirty years?

The average poverty threshold in the United States grows with the rate of inflation according to the Consumer Price Index. For a family of four it has risen $2,973 in 1959 to $14,335 in 1992. The threshold is determined by adding money wages to the income derived from self-employment and from sources other than earnings.

Department of Commerce, Economics and Statistics Administration, *Poverty in the United States: 1992,* (Washington, DC: Government Printing Office, 1992), A6-A7.

What guidelines does the U.S. federal government give to states to assist them in determining the poverty level?

The federal government gives guidelines to states in order to allow them to determine the poverty level, which in turn determines many of the social services for which people living below that line are eligible. The level varies by the number of persons in the family and whether the family resides in Alaska or Hawaii, where the cost of living is higher, or in the contiguous forty-eight states and the District of Columbia.

Federal Register 10 February 1994.

What are the fastest growing areas in the United States?

The fastest growing places in the United States are rural areas that are close enough to big cities to allow its residents to commute and yet far enough from the congestion, crime, and high prices of urban areas. The fastest growing community is Chandler, Arizona, which expanded by 184.7 percent in the decade that stretched from 1980 to 1990. From downtown Phoenix it is about one hour by car, roughly the same distance as Sandoval County, New Mexico, which had the second fastest growth rate at 80.3 percent, is from Albuquerque.

USA Today 12 December 1990.

What percentage of people includes their pets in their wills?

27 percent of dog owners bequeath their pets in their wills while 21 percent of cat owners do the same.

USA Today 28 June 1993.

Which city had the fastest growth rate in the early 1990s?

According to the U. S. Census Bureau, Las Vegas, Nevada was the fastest growing metropolitan area in America during the early 1990s. From 1990 to 1992, Las Vegas' population increased 13.9 percent to 971,169. Laredo, Texas, was the second fastest growing metropolitan, experiencing an 11.4 percent population growth.

Pittsburgh Post-Gazette 8 February 1994.

What will families spend to raise a child to age 17?

Raising a child is a very expensive proposition. According to the Family Economic Research Group of the U.S. Department of Agriculture, families with an income of less than $29,000 will spend $86,100 to raise a child born in 1990 to age 17. Families with an income of between $29,000 and $48,300 will spend $120,150. Families with an income of over $48,300 will spend $168,480.

USA Today 27 January 1992.

Are most inmates in maximum- or minimum-security prisons?

In 1991 there were 196,546 inmates in minimum-security prisons, over twice the 88,060 who could have been found in maximum-security facilities.

Juvenile & Adult Correctional Departments, Institutions, Agencies & Paroling Authorities (Laurel, MD: American Correctional Association, 1992), xxx-xxxi.

What is the largest Indian tribe in the United States?

Determining the Indian population by tribe, as opposed to reservation, is difficult. During the 1990 census, the U.S. Census Bureau counted as "Indian" everyone who stated he or she was Indian, and then the individual was asked for tribal affiliation. Using this self-reporting method alone, the Cherokee Nation would be the largest tribe with 308,132 individuals identifying themselves as members in 1990. However, its official tribal enrollment is less than that of the Navajo, and tribal officials acknowledge the Navajo Nation as the largest tribe in the United States; the Navajo reservations's population was 143,405 in 1991. Since not all people who qualify for enrollment live on the reservation or are registered with the tribe, the actual number of Navajo Indians living in the United States is undoubtedly higher.

Jack Utter, *American Indians: Answers to Today's Questions* (Lake Ann, MI: National Woodlands Publishing Company, 1993) 37-38.

How many non-Indians live on reservations?

The total population (all races) for Indian reservations and trust lands in the United States is 808,163. Non-Indians account for 370,732 or 45.9 percent, of the total. This high percentage of non-Indians can be attributed to intermarriage, various land-leasing programs, and the employment of non-Indians on reservations.

Jack Utter, *American Indians: Answers to Today's Questions* (Lake Ann, MI: National Woodlands Publishing, 1993), 21.

What percentage of U.S. workers drive alone to work?

In 1990, 73.2 percent or 84,215,298 of U.S. workers drove alone to work, according to the Bureau of Census, United States Department of Commerce. In 1980, the figure was 64.4 percent or 62,193,449. However in 1990, 13.4 percent or 15,377,634 of U.S. workers car pooled compared to 19.7 percent or 9,065,947 in 1980.

Robert Famighetti, ed., *The World Almanac and Book of Facts 1995* (Mahwah, NJ: World Almanac, 1994), 210.

What percentage of adult Americans read at least one book per year?

Despite the proliferation of cable television, video games, computer software, and other electronic marvels, Americans still enjoy reading. According to *Newsweek* magazine, 81 percent of American adults read at least one book in 1991. Fifty-eight percent of Americans gave or received books at Christmas that year, and consumers spent $7.9 billion on books as compared to $4.9 billion on going to the movies.

Les Krantz, *America by the Numbers: Facts and Figures from the Weighty to the Way-out* (Boston: Houghton Mifflin, 1993), 36.

How many people move to another state each year?

Approximately eight million North Americans move to another state or province each year. While most persons change their address 11 times during their lifetime, they usually move to another location within the same city or metropolitan area.

David Savageau and Richard Boyer, *Places Rated Almanac* (New York: Prentice Hall Travel, 1993), 1.

What are the primary sources of food for the homeless?

According to homeless shelter providers, the primary source of food for the homeless is provided by the private sector meals available at the shelters. Soup kitchens (when accessible), other free food sites, and dumpsters also provide food.

Fifty-two percent of the shelters do not provide two main meals daily. Two main meals is defined as lunch and dinner which contain at least one-half of a person's daily nutritional requirements.

Mary Ellen Hombs, *American Homelessness: A Reference Handbook* (Santa Barbara, CA: ABC-Clio, 1990), 36.

What is the life expectancy of males living in Harlem compared to men living in Bangladesh?

Men living in Harlem, New York have a very poor life expectancy. A study has shown that only 40 percent of Harlem males lived to age 65 while 55 percent of men living in Bangladesh, one of the world's poorest countries, reached age 65.

Elizabeth Vierck, *Fact Book on Aging* (Santa Barbara, CA: ABC-CLIO, 1990), 14.

What percentage of American women are satisfied with their marriages, their financial security, the balance of work and home life, and their physical fitness?

In 1994, *USA Today* reported that 85 percent of American women surveyed said they were satisfied with their marriage; 78 percent said they were satisfied with their financial security; 75 percent expressed comfort with their balance of work and home life; and 72 percent said they were satisfied with their level of physical fitness.

"USA Snapshots," *USA Today* 4 August 1994.

According to the "Human Suffering Index," what countries have the best and worst living conditions?

Denmark and Mozambique mark the ends of the spectrum of human suffering in our world, according to the Population Crisis Committee. The group's "Human Suffering Index" measures indicators such as life expectancy and diet, as well as political and civil rights. Denmark is followed by the Netherlands, Belgium, Switzerland, and Canada as nations where people suffer the least. Mozambique is joined by Somalia, Afghanistan, Haiti, and the Sudan as countries that are home to the greatest suffering. In the world as a whole, the index shows that for 73 percent of the world population suffering is extreme. The U.S. scored high marks in life expectancy, which is 75 years, while in Afghanistan it is only 41 years. The lowest U.S. scores came in the categories of political and civil rights.

USA Today 18 May 1992.

How many Gypsies are living in Europe?

European Gypsies are primarily concentrated in Romania, with 3.5 million currently living in that country. Slovakia, Bulgaria, Bosnia and Herzegovina, have 750,000 each; Hungary 900,000, Spain has 650,000, and France and Russia have 500,000.

Henry Kamm, "In New Eastern Europe, an Old Anti-Gypsy Bias," *New York Times* 17 November 1993.

Are Native Americans living on reservations U.S. citizens?

All Native Americans are U.S. citizens. They were given full citizenship status by a 1924 act of Congress. Court decisions in 1948 were needed, however, to gain full voting rights for Native Americans in Arizona and New Mexico.

Pittsburgh Post Gazette 1 June 1988.

What was the mortality rate for African slaves in transit to the United States during the eighteenth century?

The mortality rate for African slaves in transit to America varied from less than five percent on British slave ships to about ten percent among other European slavers by the end of the eighteenth century. This was an improvement upon earlier statistics that averaged thirteen percent. Ship captains took pains to treat the slaves humanely because a healthy cargo drew greater profits. Slave mortality was also affected by the travel conditions to the coast of Africa before the slaves reached the ships, and their condition and treatment once they arrived in America.

Terence Brady and Evan Jones, *The Fight Against Slavery* (New York: W. W. Norton, 1977), 25. James Walvin, *Slavery and the Slave Trade* (Jackson: University Press of Mississippi, 1983), 56.

Is there an index of leading cultural indicators?

Former U.S. Secretary of Education William Bennett created an index of leading cultural indicators which rates the quality of the American culture. The indicators are the daily number of television viewing hours, the percent of illegitimate births, the percent of children on welfare, SAT scores, the percent of children with single mothers, teen suicide rate, violent crime rate, and median prison sentences. Bennett was Secretary of Education from 1985 to 1988 and is the co-director of Empower America and a fellow at the Heritage Foundation.

Wall Street Journal 15 March 1993.

During the peak decades of immigration, from which countries did most of the new arrivals to the United States come?

Over the years, the majority of immigrants to the United States have come from European nations. Of the millions who entered the country between 1820 and 1975, the highest number emigrated from Germany with 14.8 percent, followed by Italy, with 11.1 percent, Great Britain with 10.3 percent, Ireland with 10.0 percent, the former Austro-Hungarian Empire with 9.2 percent, Canada with 8.6 percent, Russia with 7.1 percent, Mexico with 4.1 percent, the West Indies with 3.0 percent, and Sweden with 2.7 percent.

Stephanie Bernardo, *The Ethnic Almanac* (Garden City, NY: Dolphin Books, 1981), 24.

What percentage of fireworks-related injuries are sustained by children 14-years-old and younger?

The greatest number of injuries caused by fireworks happen to children ages 5 to 14. In 1992 the Consumer Products Safety Commission found that this age group received 44 percent of such injuries. Children age 4 and under suffered another 9 percent of total fireworks injuries.

USA Today 1 July 1992.

What are the odds against being struck by lightning?

The odds against being struck by lightning are 606,944 to 1 against.

The Odds on Virtually Everything (New York: G.P. Putnam's Sons, 1980), 181.

How has the world's population grown since 1500?

The world population around 1500 was estimated at 450 million. By 1900 the number had risen to 1.5 billion, with 2 billion by 1930, 4 billion by 1975, and 5.5 billion by 1993.

The World Almanac and Book of Facts 1994 (Mahwah, NJ: Funk & Wagnalls, 1993), 499, 828. *World Book Encyclopedia* (Chicago: World Book, 1994), s.v. "World, History of the."

What percentages of men and women over age 85 are currently married?

According to a U.S. government's census report, *Marital Status and Living Arrangements, March 1992*, 50.1 percent of American males age 85 years and older are currently married, with spouse present, while only 9.5 percent of American females are in the same category.

Profile of America's Elderly 1992 (Washington, DC: U.S. Bureau of the Census, 1993), 2.

What is the nationality of most illegal immigrants to the United States?

In 1993, it was estimated that 3.2 million illegal immigrants were living in the United States, accounting for 1.3 percent of the country's population. According to the Immigration and Naturalization Service, the leading country of origin was Mexico; 31 percent of illegal immigrants were thought to be Mexican. This figure had been greatly reduced by the U.S. Immigration Reform and Control Act of 1986, which resulted in the legalization of 3 million people.

USA Today, September 1993.

What is the average entry age into prostitution?

The average entry age into prostitution in the United States is 14 years old. The estimated number of prostitutes is one-half to two million, with 47,526 women and 24,401 men arrested (in 1992) for prostitution or commercialized vice. Estimated daily spending on prostitution is assessed at 40 million.

U.S. News & World Report 22 November 1993.

How do South Americans identify themselves according to their ancestry?

Many people in South America have a mixed racial ancestry, a combination of Caucasian, Indian, and African. Often these people are simply identified as "mestizo," a word used for any combination of racial backgrounds. In the first half of the century, there was a practice of using separate names that distinguished the ratio of the different races, but this has been abandoned. In Bolivia, the name "cholo" is used to identify Indian-Caucasian people as well as Indians who have adopted a Caucasian life-style and mode of dress. Africans who speak an Indian language are also included in this group. In the Portuguese-speaking country of Brazil, several racial distinctions are made: "mestizo" means Caucasian and Indian; "mulatto" indicates Caucasian and African ancestry; "mameluco," Portuguese and Indian; and "cafuso," Indian and African.

Emil L. Jordan, *Americans: A New History of the Peoples Who Settled the Americas* (New York: W. W. Norton, 1939), 389. Amiram Gonen, ed., *The Encyclopedia of the Peoples of the World* (New York: Henry Holt, 1993), s.v. "Bolivians," "Brazilians."

What are the poorest counties in the United States?

The poorest counties in the United States in 1980 and 1990 according to the Census Bureau were Tunica County in Mississippi, which in 1980 had 52.9 percent of its people living beneath the federal poverty line, and Shannon County in South Dakota, which in 1990 had 63.1 percent of its people in that category. Most of the twenty-five poorest counties in both 1980 and 1990 census belong to states that were members of the old confederacy. The exceptions were counties from Kentucky, Wisconsin, North Dakota, and South Dakota.

USA Today 11 November 1992.

What percentage of people in the United States live in the suburbs?

According to the 1990 U.S. census, 46.2 percent of the people in the continental United States live in the suburbs, the highest percentage in the nation's history. In 1900 only 5.8 percent of the population lived there. On the other hand, central cities claimed 19.7 percent of the population in 1900, expanded to 32.8 percent in 1950, and declined to 31.3 percent by 1990. Rural living has declined steadily since the turn of the century, when three out of every four Americans lived in the countryside.

New York Times 11 June 1992.

Where do most teen-agers get their spending money?

A 1992 survey by Teenage Research Unlimited revealed that 48 percent of teen-agers get spending money from their parents(as needed), 43 percent from occasional jobs, 33 percent receive a regular allowance, 30 percent from part-time jobs and 13 percent from full-time jobs. In 1991 teens spent an estimated $82 billion.

USA Today 4 February 1992.

What was the percentage of working mothers in East and West Germany prior to reunification?

Prior to the reunification of Germany, 90 percent of East German women with children worked outside the home in 1989. This rate was one of the highest in the world. In comparison, only 38 percent of West German women with children under the age of ten worked outside the home in 1988.

Paula Snyder, *The European Women's Almanac* (New York: Columbia University Press, 1992), 144.

How many cheerleaders by grade level are there in the United States?

Cheerleaders are people who add a great deal of team spirit to any sport. According to the International Cheerleading Foundation, in 1991 there were 460,000 junior high school cheerleaders in the United States; 290,000 senior high school cheerleaders; 120,000 combined K-8/K-12 school cheerleaders; and 105,000 college and university cheerleaders.

USA Today 17 September 1991.

How much money will middle-income families need to raise a child born in 1992 to age 18?

According to the Family Economics Research Group of the United States Department of Agriculture, middle-income couples who had a child in 1992 will spend an average of $128,670 by the time the child reaches the age of 18. An average of $6,810 per year will be spent on the child between ages zero and five; $6,865 between the ages of six and 11; $7,540 between the ages of 12 and 14; and $8,000 between the ages of 15 and 17.

USA Today 28 July 1993.

Agriculture

Who first took tobacco to England?

Sir John Hawkins, an English naval commander, first brought tobacco to England from Florida in 1565.

The Encyclopedia Americana, intern. ed. (Danbury, CT: Grolier, 1990), s.v. "tobacco."

How much of the agricultural land in the United States is foreign-owned?

Roughly 14.8 million acres of the total 978 million acres of agricultural land in the United States is owned by foreigners. Of that figure, Canadians possess the largest share with 2 million acres. The British are next with 1.8 million acres. Europeans account for the rest with Germans possessing 757,000 acres; the Dutch, 367,000; and the Swiss, 300,000.

Robert Famighetti, ed., *The World Almanac and Book of Facts 1995* (Mahwah, New Jersey: World Almanac, 1994), 134. *USA Today* 10 February 1993.

What is a "scratching post"?

"Scratching posts" are often erected in Scottish pastures and used by cattle to brush off flies or scratch themselves. Some have claimed however that the posts more often used by Scotsmen than by cattle!

"Grandmother Carty Told Us," *New Yorker* 24 September 1955. *New Yorker* 8 October 1955.

What program promotes tree planting in national forests?

Since 1982, the Plant-A-Tree program has improved U.S. national forests. The National Forest Service plants ten to fifteen seedlings on behalf of donors who contribute ten dollars. The seedlings are planted in the 156 U.S. national forests. In return, the donor receives a certificate commemorating the gift. Some donors have taken part in the program as a way to celebrate a holiday or birthday, or to create a memorial to a loved one.

"Gift Idea: Plant Tree in National Forest," *USA Today* 8 August 1991.

What is the Wawona Tunnel Tree?

The Wawona Tunnel Tree was a 234-foot Sequoia in the Mariposa Grove in California's Yosemite National Park. In 1881, the tree was turned into a tourist attraction when the entrepreneurial Washburn brothers carved a large tunnel through its base. Millions of people, first in horse-drawn coaches and then in cars, rode through the tree's 26 foot tunnel. Some called the Wawona Tunnel Tree the most famous tree in the world. But the tunnel that made Wawona famous also proved to be its downfall. Weakened over time, the tree toppled in 1969 after having lived some 2000 years.

Nancy Gray, *American House* September 1969.

Who was the father of conservation?

American naturalist John Muir (1838-1914) was the father of conservation and the founder of the Sierra Club. He fought for the preservation of the Sierra Nevada Mountains in California, and the creation of Yosemite National Park. He directed most of the Sierra Club's conservation efforts and was a lobbyist for the Antiquities Act.

William Ashworth, *The Encyclopedia of Environmental Studies* (New York: Facts on File, 1991), 248. *Buzzworm: The Environmental Journal* March/April 1992.

What products come from the tropical forests?

Products that come from the tropical forest are listed below.

Woods
Balsa
Mahogany
Rosewood
Sandlewood
Teak

Fibers
Bamboo
Jute/Kenaf
Kapok
Raffia
Ramie
Rattan

Gums, resins
Chicle latex
Copaiba
Copal
Gutta percha
Rubber latex
Tung oil

Houseplants
Anthurium
Croton
Dieffenbachia

Dracaena
Fiddle-leaf fig
Mother-in-law's tongue
Parlor ivy
Philodendron
Rubber tree plant
Schefflera
Silver vase bromliad
Spathiphyllum
Swiss cheese plant
Zebra plant

Oils, etc.
Camphor oil
Cascarilla oil
Coconut oil
Eucalyptus oil
Oil of star anise
Palm oil
Patchouli oil
Rosewood oil
Tolu balsam oil
Annatto
Curare
Diosgenin
Quinine
Reserpine
Strophanthus
Strychnine
Yang-Yang

Spices
Allspice
Black pepper
Cardamom
Cayenne
Chili
Cinnamon
Cloves
Ginger
Mace
Nutmeg
Paprika
Sesame seeds
Turmeric
Vanilla bean

Foods
Avocado
Banana
Coconut
Grapefruit
Lemon
Lime
Mango
Orange
Papaya
Passion fruit
Pineapple
Plantain
Tangerine
Brazil nuts
Cane sugar
Cashew nuts
Chocolate
Coffee
Cucumber
Heart of palm
Macadamia nuts
Manioc/tapioca
Okra
Peanuts
Peppers
Cola beans
Tea

The 1992 Information Please Environmental Almanac (Boston: Houghton Mifflin, 1992), 284.

What is meant by espaliering a fruit tree and why is it done?

To espalier a fruit tree means to train it to grow flat against a surface. It can be grown in small places such as against a wall, and it will thrive even if its roots are underneath sidewalks or driveways. Since many fruit trees must be planted in pairs, espaliered fruit trees can be planted close together, providing pollen for each other, yet taking up little space.

Rodale's Illustrated Encyclopedia of Gardening and Landscaping Techniques (Emmaus, PA: Rodale Press, 1990), 282-85.

What is the best soil pH for growing plants?

Nutrients such as phosphorous, calcium, potassium, and magnesium are most available to plants when the soil pH is between 6.0 and 7.5. Under highly acid (low pH) conditions, these nutrients become insoluble and relatively unavailable for uptake by plants. High soil pH can also decrease the availability of nutrients. If the soil is more alkaline than pH 8, phosphorous, iron, and many trace elements become insoluble and unavailable for plant uptake.

Wise Garden Encyclopedia (New York: HarperCollins, 1990), 728.

What is meant by the term "double-digging"?

Double-digging produces an excellent deep planting bed for perennials, especially if the area is composed of heavy clay. It involves removing the top ten inches of soil and moving it to a holding area, then spading the next ten inches, and amending this layer with organic matter and/or fertilizer. Then the soil from the "first" digging is replaced after it, too, has been amended.

A. Cort Sinnes, *All About Perennials* (San Ramon, CA: Ortho Books, 1981), 31.

Which type of fence protects a garden from deer?

A post and wire mesh fence with a sharp angled, narrow gate, which people and small animals can navigate, but deer cannot, plus the installation of a standard motion-sensing security light with a beeper helps keep deer away.

Fine Gardening November/December 1991.

How can squirrels be kept away from vegetable and flower gardens?

Squirrels like to take a bite out of tomatoes, cucumbers, and melons, dig up bulbs, and ruin anything colorful in the flower garden. The traditional recommendation of spreading mothballs around has apparently not been too successful. A better method is laying down 1-to 2-inch (2.5-to 5-centimeter) mesh sheets of chicken wire. Squirrels will avoid the mesh, apparently because they fear getting their toes stuck in it. Another method to try is sprinkling hot pepper around the plants, renewing it after it rains.

Horticulture April 1991.

What is meant by *xeriscaping*?

A xeriscape, a landscape of low water-use plants, is the modern approach to gardening in areas that experience water shortages. Taken from the Greek word *xeros*, meaning dry, this type of gardening utilizes drought-resistant plants and low maintenance grasses, which require water only every 2 to 3 weeks. Drip irrigation, heavy mulching of plant beds, and organic soil improvements are other xeriscape techniques that allow better water absorption and retention which in turn decrease garden watering time.

Flower and Garden May 1990.

Is there a "best" time to weed in the vegetable garden?

Weeding is usually the most unpopular and the most time-consuming garden chore. Some studies (using weeding with peas and beans as examples) have shown that weeding done during the first three to four weeks of vegetable growth produced the best crops and that unabated weed growth after that time did not significantly reduce the vegetable yields.

Robert B. Thomas, *The Old Farmer's Almanac 1988 Dublin* NH: Yankee Publishing, 1989), 172-73.

What does the term *hydroponics* mean?

This term refers to growing plants in some medium other than soil; the inorganic plant nutrients (such as potassium, sulphur, magnesium, and nitrogen) are continuously supplied to the plants in solution. Hydroponics is mostly used in areas where there is little soil or unsuitable soil. It is a much-used method of growing plants in research, but for the amateur, it has many limitations and may prove frustrating. Hydroponics was developed in 1959 by two Soviet research scientists at the University of Leningrad.

Valerie-Anne Giscard d'Estaing, *The World Almanac Book of Inventions* (New York: World Almanac Publicatons, 1985), 67. Donald Wyman, *Wyman's Gardening Encyclopedia, 2d ed.* (New York: Macmillan, 1986), 549-50.

What is the secret of bonsai-the Japanese art of growing dwarf trees?

These miniature trees with tiny leaves and twisted trunks can be centuries old. To inhibit growth of the plants, they have been carefully deprived of nutrients, pruned of their fastest-growing shoots and buds, and kept in small pots to reduce the root systems. Selective pruning, pinching out terminal buds, and wiring techniques are devices used to control the shape of the trees. Bonsai possibly started during the Chou dynasty (900-250 B.C.) in China, when emperors made miniature gardens that were dwarf representations of the provincial lands that they ruled.

Can Elephants Swim? (New York: Time-Life Books, 1969), 27. Sybil P. Parker, *McGraw-Hill Concise Encyclopedia of Science and Technology, 2d ed.* (New York: McGraw-Hill, 1989), 267.

How can a Christmas tree be made fire-resistant?

Mix in a bucket:

2 cups corn syrup
2 ounces liquid chlorine bleach
2 pinches Epsom salts
1/2 teaspoon borax
1 teaspoon chelated iron
2 gallons hot water

Use the solution to water the tree every day. Chelated iron is available at garden supply centers.

Blair & Ketchum's Country Journal December 1985

What is a five-in-one-tree?

These very curious trees consist of a rootstock with five different varieties of the same fruit-usually apples-grafted to it. The blooming period is usually magnificent with various colors of blooms appearing on the same tree.

Fruits and Vegetables: 1001 Gardening Questions Answered (Pownal, VT: Storey Communications, 1990), 7.

What is the railroad worm?

The apple maggot (*Rhagoletis pomonella*), which becomes the apple fruit fly, is frequently called the railroad worm. Inhabiting orchards in Eastern United States and Canada, the larvae feed on the fruit pulp of apples, plums, cherries, etc., and cause damage to fruit crops.

Thomas H. Everett, *The New York Botanical Garden Illustrated Encyclopedia of Horticulture* (Hamden, CT: Garland, 1981), 6:2096.

How are seedless grapes grown?

Since seedless grapes cannot reproduce in the conventional way that grapes usually do (i.e., dropping seeds), growers have to take cuttings from other seedless grape plants and root them. Although the exact origin of seedless grapes is unknown, they might have first been cultivated in present-day Iran or Afghanistan thousands of years ago. Initially the first seedless grape was a genetic mutation in which the hard seed casing failed to develop-the mutation is called stenospermoscarpy. One modern seedless grape commonly bought today is the green Thompson seedless grape from which 90 percent of all raisins are made.

David Feldman, *Why Do Clocks Run Clockwise? And Other Imponderables* (New York: Perennial Library, 1988), 218-19. Caroline Sutton and Duncan M. Anderson, *How Do They Do That?* (New York: Quill, 1982), 98-100.

When was the first practical greenhouse built?

French botanist Jules Charles constructed one in 1599 in Leiden, Holland in which tropical plants for medicinal purposes were grown. The most popular plant there was the Indian date, the tamarind, whose fruit was made into a curative drink.

T. Jeff Williams, *Greenhouses* (San Ramon, CA: Ortho Books, 1991), 7.

How much of a tree that is cut down is sold as timber?

For the average hardwood tree cut down to make lumber, half the total wood volume is left in the woods as tops, limbs, and logging residue; about a quarter is lost as sawdust, slabs, and edgings in the sawmill; one-eighth disappears as shavings and machining residues, leaving about one-eighth of the original volume to be sold as timber.

Pennsylvania Woodland News January/February 1991.

How are cashews grown?

Cashews, bean-shaped nuts that are popular as a snack food, grow on tropical evergreen trees. The nut is attached to the lower end of the fruit of the tree. The nut is detached from the fruit, and the two outer shells and skin are removed before eating. The first shell contains a poisonous oil which can blister the skin and cause eye irritation from the fumes if burned. The trees originally grew in South America. They can reach a height of 40 feet and have large, leathery, green leaves up to six inches long and four inches wide. Each fruit of the cashew contains one nut. The trees were imported by India and other countries. The United States grows some in Florida but imports the majority of its cashews from India.

David Wallechinsky and Irving Wallace, *The People's Almanac* (Garden City, NY: Doubleday, 1975), 1027. *The World Book Encyclopedia* (Chicago: World Book, 1994), s.v. "cashew."

What did Joseph F. Glidden do to improve ranch farming in the United States?

In 1874 Illinois farmer and inventor Joseph F. Glidden developed an improvement on barbed wire so that it could be easily manufactured in factories. This resulted in a drastic change in ranching. Private ranches could now be enclosed, lessening thievery, ending animal straying, and improving breeding.

Howard L. Hurwitz, *An Encyclopedic Dictionary of American History* (New York: Washington Square Press, 1968), s.v. "barbed wire."

What was a collective farm called in the Soviet Union?

In the Soviet Union a collective farm was called a kolkhoz, an abbreviation for the Russian Kollektivnoye Khozyaynstvo. Originally a kolkhoz was conceived as a voluntary agrarian union of peasants who worked state owned land and were paid as salaried employees based on the quality and quantity of their labor. The state began expropriating private holdings in 1929, and collective farming became the dominant form of agricultural enterprise in the Soviet Union.

The New Encyclopaedia Britannica (Chicago: Encyclopaedia Britannica 1989), s.v. "kolkhoz."

What is a sharecropper?

A sharecropper is a tenant farmer, that is one who pays a portion of the crop he raises, usually half, to the landowner. Sharecropping originated in the post-American Civil War South and was an economic and social response to low liquidity and the need for a steady supply of cheap farm labor to replace slavery. Sharecropping, which was on the lowest rung of the social ladder was shared by poor Caucasians and African-Americans alike. The sharecropper was forever dependent on the landlord and landlord-owned commissary which supplied the seed, implements, and fertilizer on credit at interest rates varying from ten to sixty percent. As security, the sharecropper could only put up his future crop. In the 1930s government programs such as the U.S. Bankhead-Jones Farm Tenant Act helped sharecroppers purchase their own land.

Dictionary of American History, rev. ed. (New York: Charles Scribner's Sons, 1976), s.v. "sharecropper."

Can the dollar value of a tree be calculated?

The International Society of Arborculture has created a formula for judging the value of a tree. According to this standard, a tree's size, hardiness, location, and condition determine its worth. A four-step process is used to calculate dollar value:

Measure the tree's circumference four and a half feet from the ground, and use this figure to determine its radius

Figure the area of the cross section, which equals pi times the radius squared

Multiply the area of the cross section by the current standard value, a dollar figure per square inch for the particular species, to determine the tree's base value

The base value is then adjusted according to three variables: species, location, and condition. This rather sophisticated formula is most often used by certified arborists and tree estimators.

Pittsburgh Post Gazette 18 July 1989.

What role did Chico Mendes play in the environmental movement?

Francisco Mendes Filho, better known as Chico Mendes, was an activist in the fight to save Brazil's Amazon rain forests. Mendes lost his life in the process, murdered by a hit man who was hired by a cattle rancher's son. The assassination, which took place on December 22, 1988, came after numerous death threats to Mendes. As an environmentalist, Chico Mendes won the United Nations Global 500 ecology prize in 1987; he also served as president of a union for itinerant rubber tappers in the Xapuri region of Brazil.

Facts on File 31 December 1988.

What are Operation Ranch Hand and Agent Orange?

Operation Ranch Hand was the tactical military project for the aerial spraying of herbicides in South Vietnam during the Vietnam Conflict (1961-75). In these operations Agent Orange, the collective name for the herbicides 2,4-D and 2,4,5-T, was used for the defoliation. The name derives from the color-coded drums in which the herbicides were stored.

Agent Orange and Its Associated Dioxin: Assessment of a Controversy (New York: Elsevier, 1988), 10. E. Willard Miller, *Environmental Hazards: Toxic Waste and Hazardous Material* (Santa Barbara: ABC-CLIO, 1991), 13.

How is petrified wood formed?

Water containing dissolved minerals such as calcium carbonate and silicate infiltrates the wood, and the minerals gradually replace the organic matter. The process takes thousands of years. After a time, the wood seems to have turned to stone because the original outer form and structure are retained during this process of petrification. The wood itself does not turn into stone.

George Stimpson, *Information Roundup* (New York: Harper, 1948), 457.

How can garden soil be used as potting soil?

The garden soil must be pasteurized and then mixed with coarse sand and peat moss. Soil may be pasteurized by putting the soil in a covered baking dish in the oven. When a meat thermometer stuck in the soil has registered 180 degrees Fahrenheit (82 degrees Celsius) for 30 minutes, the soil is done.

James U. Crockett, *Crockett's Indoor Garden* (Boston: Little, Brown, 1978), 35.

When is the best time to work the soil?

Although it is possible to prepare the soil at any time of year, fall digging is the best time. Dig in the fall and leave the ground rough. Freezing and thawing during winter breaks up clods and aerates the soil. Insects that otherwise "overwinter" are mostly turned out. The soil settling during winter will lessen the likelihood of air pockets in the soil when planting the following spring. Fall preparation provides time for soil additives such as manure and compost to break down before planting time.

Fruits and Vegetables: 1001 Gardening Questions Answered (Pownal, VT: Storey Communications, 1990), 63. *Rodale's Illustrated Encyclopedia of Gardening and Landscaping Techniques* (Emmaus, PA: Rodale Press, 1990), 4.

How are seedlings hardened off before planting?

Hardening off is a gardening term for gradually acclimatizing seedlings raised indoors to the outdoor environment. Place the tray of seedlings outdoors for a few hours each day in a semi-protected spot. Lengthen the amount of time they stay out by an hour or so each day; at the end of the week, they will be ready for planting outdoors.

Ortho's Complete Guide to Successful Gardening (San Ramon, CA: Ortho Books, 1983), 70.

Which flowers should be planted in the garden to attract hummingbirds?

Scarlet Trumpet Honeysuckle, Weigela, Butterfly Bush, Beardtongue, Coralbells, Red-Hot-Poker, Foxglove, Beebalm, Nicotiana, Petunia, Summer Phlox, and scarlet sage provide brightly colored shades of red and orange, nectar-bearing attractants for the hummingbirds.

Joan Beth Erickson, *Flower Garden Plans* (San Ramon, CA: Ortho Books, 1991), 68-69.

What was a victory garden?

During World War I (1914-1918), patriots grew "liberty gardens." In World War II (1939-1945), these gardens were called victory gardens. U.S. Secretary of Agriculture Claude R. Wickard encouraged householders to plant vegetable gardens wherever they could find space. By 1945 there were said to be 20 million victory gardens producing about 40 percent of all American vegetables in many unused scraps of land. Such sites as the strip between a sidewalk and the street, town squares, and the land around Chicago's Cook County jail were used. The term "victory garden" dates back to Elizabethan England in a book by that title (1603) written by Richard Gardner.

Gerry Schremp, *Kitchen Culture* (New York: Pharos, 1991), 14.

What size vegetable garden is recommended for the beginner?

It really depends on the amount of space available, how much produce is desired from a garden, and how much work a person is willing to put into it. A modest-sized, 10-by-20 foot (3-by-6 meter) plot, laid out in traditional rows, is quite manageable in terms of weeding, cultivating, planting, and harvesting. Even a 10-by-10 foot (3-by-3 meter) plot will suffice for a salad or "kitchen" garden, with plenty of greens and herbs for salads and seasonings on a daily basis. "Intensive" gardening methods where plants are arranged in blocks rather than rows, allow for increased yield in an even smaller space. One 4-by-4 foot (1-by-1 meter) block, with a vertical frame at one end, can provide salad vegetables for one person throughout the growing season, though two blocks would provide a wider variety of vegetables.

Mel Bartholomew, *Square Foot Gardening* (Emmaus, PA: Rodale Press, 1981), 29-30. *Fruits and Vegetables: 1001 Gardening Questions Answered* (Pownal, VT: Storey Communications, 1990), 55.

How can geraniums be kept indoors from fall year to the next spring?

While they must be kept from freezing, geraniums can survive the winter happily in a cool sunny spot, such as a cool greenhouse, a bay window, or a sunny unheated basement. They need only occasional watering while in this semi-dormant state. Cuttings from these plants can be rooted in late winter or early spring for a new crop of geraniums (some sources suggest rooting in the fall). In homes without a suitable cool and sunny spot, the plants can be forced into dormancy by allowing the soil to dry completely, then gently knocking the soil off of the roots. While the plants can simply be hung from the rafters in a cool (45 to 50 degrees Fahrenheit; 7 to 10 degrees Celsius), slightly humid room, they will do better if put into individual paper bags, with the openings tied shut. The plants should be checked regularly. The leaves will dry and shrivel, but if the stems shrivel, the plants should be lightly misted with water. If any show mold or rot, cut off the affected sections, move the plants to a drier area, and leave the bags open for a day or two. In the early spring, prune the stems back to healthy green tissue and pot in fresh soil.

Horticulture April 1992. *Rodale's Illustrated Encyclopedia of Gardening and Landscaping Techniques* (Emmaus, PA: Rodale Press, 1990), 110-11.

How can poison ivy, poison oak, and poison sumac be eliminated from the garden?

First, choose a moist, cool day in early spring or late fall when the plant is less armed with irritant. Wear thick leather or cotton gloves (but not rubber); cut the vines near the base and apply an herbicide to kill the roots. Handle the vines carefully, and dispose of them by burying them in a biodegradable container. *Do not burn* the plants; smoke and ash may cause the rash on exposed parts of the body, eyes, nasal passages, and lungs.

All parts of poison ivy (*Rhus radicans*) and poison oak (*Rhus toxicodendron*) can cause serious dermatitis. These North American woody plants grow in almost any habitat and are quite similar in appearance. Each has alternating compound leaves of three leaflets each, berrylike fruits, and rusty brown stems. But poison ivy acts more like a vine than a shrub at times and can grow high into trees. Its grey fruit is not hairy, and its leaves are slightly lobed. On the other hand, poison oak is often shrubby, but it can climb. Its leaflets are lobed and resemble oak leaves; its fruit is hairy. Poison sumac (*Rhus vernix*) grows only in North American wet acid swamps. This shrub can grow as high as 12 feet (3.6 meters). The fruit it produces hangs in a cluster and is grayish-brown in color. Poison sumac has dark green sharply-pointed compound, alternating leaves, and greenish-yellow inconspicuous flowers.

Edward Frankel, *Poison Ivy, Poison Oak, Poison Sumac, and Their Relatives* (Pacific Grove, CA: Boxwood Press, 1991), 81-83.

Is there a way to preserve a cut Christmas tree long?

Soak the tree trunk in a solution containing:

1 gallon warm water
4 tablespoons chelated iron (available at garden supply centers)
4 tablespoons Karo syrup
4 tablespoons household bleach

Meg Crager, *Christmas Trees* (New York: Grove Weidenfeld, 1986), 32.

Did Johnny Appleseed really plant apple trees?

John Chapman (1774?-1845), called Johnny Appleseed, established nurseries of apple seedlings and planted orchards from the Allegheny River in Pennsylvania to Indiana. He did not prowl the countryside scattering seeds at random from a bag slung over his shoulders, as artists like to depict him, but rather established trees along the rivers in the Midwest states of Ohio, Indiana, and Illinois where he worked as a missionary and returned to these sites year after year to care for the trees he planted.

Waverly L. Root, *Food* (New York: Simon and Schuster, 1980), 10.

Can a branch of the dogwood tree be forced into bloom?

Forcing dogwood (genus *Cornus*) into bloom is similar to forcing forsythia. Bring the dogwood branch indoors when the buds begin to swell. Put the branch in water and set it in a sunny window.

New York Times Book of Indoor and Outdoor Gardening Questions (New York: Quadrangle, 1975), 199.

How did the navel orange originate?

Every navel orange is derived from a mutant tree that appeared on a plantation in Brazil in the early nineteenth century. A bud from the mutant tree was grafted onto another tree, whose branches were then grafted onto another, and so forth.

James Trefil, *1001 Things Everyone Should Know About Science* (New York: Doubleday, 1992), 4.

What were some of the accomplishments of Dr. George Washington Carver?

Because of the work of noted African American Dr. George Washington Carver (1864-1943) in plant diseases, soil analysis, and crop management, many Southern farmers have greater crop yields and profits. He eventually made 118 products from sweet potatoes, 325 from peanuts, and 75 from pecans. He promoted soil diversification and the adoption of peanuts, soybeans, and other soil-enriching crops. During his lifetime, he only applied for three patents, because he believed that his inventions were a gift from God that should not be subject to financial gain.

The Great Scientists (Danbury, CT: Grolier, 1989), 3:67, 70. Vivian O. Sammons, *Blacks in Science and Medicine* (New York. Hemisphere Publishing, 1990), 50.

Who developed DDT?

Although DDT was synthesized as early as 1874 by Othmar Zeidler, it was the Swiss chemist Paul Mller (1899-1965) who recognized its insecticidal properties in 1939. He was awarded the 1948 Nobel Prize in Medicine for his development of *d*ichloro-*d*iphenyl-*tr*ichloro-ethene or DDT. This substance killed insects quickly but seemed to have little or no poisonous effect on plants and animals, unlike the arsenic-based compounds then in use. In the following twenty years it proved to be effective in controlling disease-carrying insects and in killing many plant crop destroyers. Increasingly DDT-resistant insect species and the accumulative hazardous effects of DDT on plant and animal life cycles led to its disuse in many countries during the 1970s.

The Biographical Dictionary of Scientists: Chemists (New York: Peter Bedrick Books, 1983), 99-100.

How many eggs does the average hen lay in a year?

In the United States, commercial laying hens produce an average of 245 eggs a year.

World Book Encyclopedia (Chicago: World Book, 1994), s.v. "chicken."

Buildings, Bridges, and Other Structures

Which Central American country was considered as a site for a canal that would connect the Atlantic and Pacific oceans before Panama was finally chosen?

Plans to create a canal in Central America that would connect the Atlantic and Pacific oceans were considered as early as the 18th century by Spain, which had colonized heavily in that area. When its colonies revolted in the early 19th century, Spain gave up all thoughts of a canal. The United States promptly stepped in declaring through President James Monroe's Monroe Doctrine that any canal should be under its control. At first a proposed Nicaraguan route received the most attention. In 1846, however, the United States and the Republic of New Granada, which later became Columbia, agreed to a treaty in which the United States would be granted free use of the proposed canal across the Isthmus of Panama in the Republic of New Granada in exchange for which the United States promised to guarantee the isthmus' neutrality.

Construction of a canal began in 1878 but was abandoned in 1889 due illness and financial difficulties. A Nicaraguan canal figured prominently once again in 1901 and 1902. In 1901 the United States' first Isthmian Canal Commission recommended a Nicaraguan canal. Then in 1902 the commission recommended a canal in Panama provided Columbia would grant the United States permanent control over the land needed for a canal and if the $40 million in assets of the New Panama Canal Company could be obtained by the United States. On June 28, 1902 the Spooner Act adopted the commission's recommendations and further stipulated that if these conditions were not met, the canal was to be built in Nicaragua. Although Colombia and the United States signed a treaty fulfilling the Spooner Act's requirements, Colombia balked at ratifying the treaty. After Colombia rejected the treaty, Panama revolted, proclaimed its independence on November 3, 1903, and on November 13 signed a treaty with the United States for the construction of a canal in Panama.

Dictionary of American History, rev. ed. (New York: Charles Scribner's Sons, 1976), s.v. "Panama Canal."

What did the Spanish call the sun-dried bricks from which they made their homes?

Throughout parts of Mexico and southwestern parts of the United States, homes and other buildings are made of sun-dried bricks. These bricks are known as adobe and were first used by Pueblo Indians and Spanish settlers. Adobe bricks were used by the ancient Babylonians and Egyptians to build many of their structures. Modern adobe structures are often covered with a layer of stucco.

Adobe is a mixture of water, sandy clay, and a small quantity of grass or straw. This mixture is placed in forms, shaped into bricks, and allowed to dry. When the bricks dry, they are removed from the forms. The newly formed bricks are placed in the sun and allowed to bake for a period of ten days to two weeks.

The World Book Encyclopedia (Chicago: World Book, 1987), s.v. "adobe."

What is a widow's walk?

A widow's walk is a railed platform found on the roof of many imposing American colonial homes. They were usually built close to chimneys and accessible through an upstairs room. Stocked with pails of water, they also provided quick access for extinguishing chimney and roof fires. Wives of sea captains were said to anxiously pace the widow's walk in hopes of getting a reassuring glimpse of their husbands' incoming vessels. Although a widow's walk is a popular feature of many colonial-era coastal houses, they are also found on similar houses far inland.

John Ciardi, *A Browser's Dictionary and Native's Guide to the Unknown American Language* (New York: Harper & Row, 1980), s.v. "Widow's walk."

Where is the longest suspension bridge in the United States?

Spanning New York (City) Harbor, the Verrazano-Narrows Bridge is the longest suspension bridge in the United States. With a span of 4,260 feet (1,298.5 meters) from tower to tower, its total length is 7,200 feet (2,194.6 meters). Named after Giovanni da Verrazano (1485-1528), the Italian explorer who discovered New York Harbor in April of 1524, it was erected under the direction of Othmar H. Ammann (1879-1965), and completed in 1964. To avoid impeding navigation in and out of the harbor, it provides a clearance of 216 feet (65.8 meters) between the water level and the bottom of the bridge deck. Like other suspension bridges, the bulk of the load of the Verrazano-Narrows Bridge is carried on cables anchored to the banks.

Donald C. Jackson, *Great American Bridges and Dams* (Washington, DC: Preservation Press, 1988), 138. Mark C. Young, ed., *The World Almanac and Book of Facts 1995* (New York: Facts ON File, 1994), 104.

What are the various types of bridge structures?

There are four basic types of structures that can be used to bridge a stream or similar obstacle: rigid beam, cantilever, arch, and suspension systems.

The rigid beam bridge, the simplest and most common form of bridging, has straight slabs or girders carrying the roadbed. The span is relatively short and its load rests on its supports or piers. The arch bridge is in compression, and thrusts outward on its bearings at each end. In the suspension bridge, the roadway hangs on steel cables with the bulk of the load carried on cables anchored to the banks. It can span a great distance without intermediate piers. Each arm of a cantilever bridge is, or could be, free-standing, with the load of the short central truss span pushing down through the piers of the outer arms and pulling up at each end. The outer arms are usually anchored at the abutments and project into the central truss.

The Illustrated Science and Invention Encyclopedia, intern. ed. (Westport, CT: H. S. Stuttman, 1983), 3:353, 357-59. *Oxford Illustrated Encyclopedia of Invention and Technology* (Oxford: Oxford University Press, 1992), 48, 57. John H. Stephens, *The Guinness Book of Structures* (London: Guinness Superlatives, 1976), 11-15.

What is a "kissing bridge"?

Covered bridges with roofs and wooden sides are called "kissing bridges," because people within the bridge could not be seen from outside. Such bridges can be traced back to the early nineteenth century. Contrary to folk wisdom, they were not designed to produce rural "lovers' lanes," but were covered to protect the structures from deterioration.

Donald C. Jackson, *Great American Bridges and Dams* (Washington, DC: Preservation Press, 1988), 20. C.J. Maginley, *Models of America's Past* (San Diego: Harcourt, Brace & World, 1969), 100.

How many covered bridges are there in the United States?

There were more than 10,000 covered bridges built across the United States between 1805 (when the first was erected in Philadelphia) and the early twentieth century. As of January 1980, only 893 of these covered bridges remain-231 in Pennsylvania, 157 in Ohio, 103 in Indiana, 100 in Vermont, 54 in Oregon, and 52 in New Hampshire. Three interstate bridges link New Hampshire and Vermont. The remainder are scattered throughout the country. Non-authentic covered bridges-built or covered for visual effect-appear in each state.

Richard T. Donovan, *World Guide to Covered Bridges, rev. ed.* (Worcester, MA: National Society for the Preservation of Covered Bridges, 1980), 1.

What is the world's longest road tunnel?

The two-lane road tunnel at St. Gotthard Pass between Gschenen, Switzerland, and Airolo, Italy, constructed between 1970 and 1980, is 10.1 miles (16.3 kilometers) long. The Mont Blanc tunnel, completed in 1965, is the next longest road tunnel. Its two lanes connect the 7.2 miles (11.6 kilometers) between Chamonix, France, and the Valle d'Aosta, Italy. The longest road tunnel in the United Kingdom is the four-lane Mersey Tunnel, joining Liverpool and Birkenhead, Merseyside. It is 2.13 miles (3.43 kilometers) long. In the United States, the longest road tunnel is the 2.5 mile (4.02 kilometer) Lincoln tunnel, connecting New York City and New Jersey, and constructed under the Hudson River in 1937.

Nigel Hawkes, *Structures* (New York: Macmillan, 1990), 160. John H. Stephens, *The Guinness Book of Structures* (London: Guinness Superlatives, 1976), 113. Mark C. Young, ed., *Guinness Book of Records 1995* (New York: Facts on File, 1994), 104.

Why are manhole covers round?

Circular covers are almost universally used on sewer manholes because they cannot drop through the opening. The circular cover rests on a lip that is smaller than the cover. Any other shape-such as square or rectangle-could slip into the manhole opening.

Harold E. Babbitt, *Sewage and Sewage Treatment, 8th ed.* (New York: Wiley, 1958), 127.

Which building has the largest nonair-supported clear span roof?

The Suncoast Dome in St. Petersburg, Florida, completed in 1990, has a nonair-supported clear span roof of 688 feet (209.7 meters). Covering an area of 372,000 square feet (34,570.1

square meters), the fabric-covered dome is a cable roof structure-the newest structural system for trussed domes. Its structural behavior is exactly opposite that of the traditional dome: the base ring is in compression rather than tension, and the ring at the crown is in tension rather than compression. Also, the space enclosed is not totally free and unobstructed, but includes structural, top-to-bottom members. To retain its characteristic lightness, the roofing surface employs flexible fabric membranes. These must be flexible since cable structures undergo major structural distortions, and they actually change shape under different load conditions. The largest air-supported building is the 80,600-capacity octagonal Pontiac Silverdome Stadium in Pontiac, Michigan. 522 feet (159.1 meters) wide and 722 feet (220.1 meters) long, it is supported by a 10 acre (1.62 hectare) translucent fiberglass roof.

Michele Melaragno, *An Introduction to Shell Structures* (New York: Van Nostrand Reinhold, 1991), 322-24. *Yearbook of Science and the Future 1991* (Chicago: Encyclopaedia Britannica, 1990), 286-87. Mark C. Young, ed., *Guinness Book of Records 1995* (New York: Facts on File, 1994), 99.

When was the first skyscraper built?

Designed by William Le Baron Jenney (1832-1907), the first skyscraper, the ten-story Home Insurance Company Building in Chicago, Illinois, was completed in 1885. A skyscraper-a very tall building supported by an internal frame (skeleton) of iron and steel rather than by load-bearing walls-maximizes floor space on limited land. Three technological developments made skyscrapers feasible: a better understanding of how materials behave under stress and load (from engineering and bridge design); the use of steel or iron framing to create a structure, with the outer skin "hung" on the frame; and the introduction of the first "safety" passenger elevator, invented by Elisha Otis (1811-61).

Philip Bagenal and Jonathan Meades, *The Illustrated Atlas of the World's Great Buildings* (London: Salamander Books, 1980), 161. Barbara Berliner, *The Book of Answers* (Englewood Cliffs, NJ: Prentice-Hall, 1990), 72.

What causes formaldehyde contamination in homes?

Formaldehyde contamination is related to the widespread construction use of wood products bonded with urea-formaldehyde resins and products containing formaldehyde. Major formaldehyde sources include subflooring of particle board; wall paneling made from hardwood plywood or particle board; and cabinets and furniture made from particle board, medium density fiberboard, hardwood plywood, or solid wood. Urea-formaldehyde foam insulation (UFFI) has received the most media notoriety and regulatory attention. Formaldehyde is also used in drapes, upholstery, carpeting, and wallpaper adhesives, milk cartons, car bodies, household disinfectants, permanent-press clothing, and paper towels. In particular, mobile homes seem to have higher formaldehyde levels than houses do. Six billion pounds of formaldehyde are used in the United States each year.

The release of formaldehyde into the air by these products (called outgassing) can develop poisoning symptoms in humans. The Environmental Protection Agency classifies formaldehyde as a potential human carcinogen (cancer-causing agent).

Thad Godish, *Indoor Air Pollution Control* (Chelsea, MI: Lewis Publishers, 1989), 37-39, 336-37. Linda Mason Hunter, *The Healthy Home* (New York: Pocket Books, 1989), 75-80.

What is a bench mark?

A bench mark is a permanent, recognizable point that lies at a known elevation. It may be an existing object, such as the top of a fire hydrant, or it may be a brass plate placed on top of a concrete post. Surveyors and engineers use bench marks to calculate the elevation of objects by reading, through a level telescope, the distance a point lies above some already established bench mark.

World Book Encyclopedia (Chicago: World Book, 1990), 2:247.

What are the Seven Modern Wonders of the World?

There is a diversity of opinion as to what technological achievements should be on such a list as well as what constitutes the time period modern. Below is one sample list of the so-called modern wonders:

Suez Canal, in northeast Africa, connecting the Red Sea with the Mediterranean Sea
Dneproges Dam on the Dnepr River in Russia
Atomic Energy Research Establishment at Harwell, England
Alaska (or Alcan) Highway, connecting Alaska with Canadian and other United States highways
Golden Gate Bridge in San Francisco, California
Eiffel Tower in Paris, France
Empire State Building in New York City, New York

Others would substitute the Taj Mahal of Agra, India (completed about 1648); the Washington Monument in Washington, D.C. (completed in 1885), the Panama Canal, or the still standing structures created much earlier of the Great Pyramid of Egypt and the Great Sphinx; the sixth-century cathedral Hagia Sophia in Istanbul, Turkey, the Leaning Tower of Pisa, the Greek Pantheon in Athens, Greece, and St. Peter's Basilica in Rome, Italy.

World Book Encyclopedia (Chicago: World Book, 1971), s.v. "Seven Wonders of the World." *Webster's New Geographical Dictionary* (Springfield, MA: Merriam-Webster, 1972), s.v. "Suez Canal."

Where is the largest U.S. artificial reservoir located?

Lake Mead in Nevada is the largest wholly artificial reservoir in the United States. Formed by Hoover Dam the lake has a capacity of 1,241,445 million cubic feet and a surface area of 28,255,000 acre-feet.

Bratskoye reservoir on the Angara River in Siberia, Russia is the largest man-made reservoir in the world. Its volume is 40.6 cubic miles and its area is 2,111 square miles. It took six years (1961-67) to fill.

Mark C. Young, ed., *The Guinness Book of Records 1995*, (New York: Facts on File, 1994), 103.

Why is London Bridge famous?

From A.D.43, when it was first built by the Romans, until 1750, London Bridge was the only bridge across the Thames River at London. The early structures were made of wood, and were destroyed many times. Perhaps the most famous incident its early history was when it was attacked and pulled down by an Anglo-Saxon fleet in 1014. The event was memorialized by an Norse poet and became the source of the seventeenth-century nursery rhyme "London Bridge is Falling Down."

The first stone bridge was built by Peter de Colechurch between 1176 and 1209. It was a masterpiece of medieval engineering and became center of city life. By 1358, 138 separate buildings were constructed on the bridge, some of which were seven stories high. Because its 20 piers impeded the river's flow, cold winters would cause the Thames to freeze, and frost fairs with dancing and entertainment were held on the ice.

The medieval bridge was torn down and replaced by one that was built between 1823 and 1831 by Sir John Rennie. In 1968 an American oil millionaire Robert P. McCulloch purchased 10,000 tons of the granite facing of the nineteenth-century bridge and moved it to Lake Havasu City, Arizona, where the bridge was rebuilt and opened to the public as a tourist attraction on October 10, 1971.

The present London Bridge is a modern three-span structure, made of prestressed concrete, which was opened in stages between 1970 and 1972. It is one of 31 bridges, including railroad bridges, that cross the Thames at London. It not as architecturally striking as Tower Bridge, whose two Gothic towers grace the London skyline, and with which London Bridge is often confused. The Albert Bridge with its web-like cantilever suspension system is also more beautiful. London Bridge's fame rests on its history or rather on the history of its two predecessors.

Paul Murphy, *The Guinness Guide to Superlative London* (London: Guinness Publishing, 1989), 211-12.

What was the first bridge across the Mississippi River?

The first bridge to span the Mississippi River was a railroad bridge built by Rock Island Railroad that was completed in 1855. It connected Rock Island, Illinois, and Davenport, Iowa. River pilots called it "Hell-gate" ..."the invention of Satan and the Rock Island Railroad Company" because of the number of boats that crashed into the bridge's piers and sank. The owners of the *Effie Afton* brought suit against the railroad after the boat struck the bridge and burned in 1856. Abraham Lincoln represented the railroad and asserted the steamboat's starboard wheel had gone dead before the crash. The jury deadlocked and the suit was dropped.

Illinois: A Descriptive and Historical Guide, rev. ed. (Chicago: A. C. McClurg, 1947), 378.

Why was the Great Wall of China built?

Although the Great Wall of China attracts thousands of tourists every year it was originally meant to deter invaders. Various sections of the wall were built over many centuries by different rulers beginning around 400 B.C. The concept of a unified "Great Wall" originated during the Qin Dynasty (221-206 B.C.) with the Emporer Shi Huangdi who began linking together walls constructed during earlier dynasties. Work continued over the centuries and much of the Great Wall as it stands today was built and linked up during the Ming Dynasty (1368-1644). The Great Wall runs through northern China between the east coast and the north central provinces.

China's Great Wall is the longest structure ever built. Although once believed to be 6,200 miles (9,978 kilometers) long, 4,000 miles (6,440 kilometers) remain today. The main wall is 2,150 miles (3,460 kilometers) long with branches and spurs accounting for the remaining distance. The Great Wall is 25 feet (7.6 meters) high and measures 25 feet at its base and 15 feet (4.6 meters) along its walkway.

World Book Encyclopedia (Chicago: World Book, 1994), s.v. "great wall of china." Luo Zewen et al., *The Great Wall* (New York: McGraw-Hill, 1981), 187.

Who created the Coral Castle in Florida?

A Latvian immigrant, Edward Leedskalnin single-handedly quarried and set in place coral rock segments up to 35 tons to create the Coral Castle, now a tourist attraction near Homestead, Florida. In 1918 he settled in Florida and began building the castle that would take years to complete. Everything in the castle and its surrounding grounds is made of rock-tables, chairs, bathtub-without a trace of cement. Leedskalnin died in 1951 at the age of 64. Many of the techniques he used in constructing his creations remain mysteries.

William Kofoed, "Wizard of Coral Castle," *Coronet* February 1958.

Where is the world's largest pyramid?

The world's largest pyramid is in Mexico. It is the temple of Quetzalcoatl-Kukulcan at Cholula de Rivadabia, 63 miles southeast of Mexico City. The pyramid is 177 feet tall, has a base of 45 acres, and its volume is estimated to be 116.5 million cubic feet. In comparison, the Egyptian Pyramid of Khufu or Cheops, a fourth dynasty pharaoh has only 88.2 million cubic feet. Originally built ca. 6-12 A.D. the pyramid subsequently was expanded at various periods in its history.

Gilbert Charles-Picard, ed., *Larousse Encyclopedia of Archeaology* (New York: G. P. Putnam's Sons, 1972), 364. Mark C. Young, ed., *The Guinness Book of Records 1995* (New York: Facts on File, 1994), 107.

How many square feet does a gallon of paint usually cover?

One gallon of paint usually covers 400 to 500 square feet of surface. This figure can vary depending on the condition of the surface and the various types of paints.

Lois Libien, *Paint It Yourself* (New York: Morrow, 1978), 21. Richard V. Nunn, *Home Paint Book* (Birmingham, AL: Oxmoor House, 1976), 13.

What unusual method of testing was used to prove the safety of the first bridge across the Mississippi River at St. Louis?

According to a historical appraisal of the bridge by Howard Miller in 1874:

"Progressively heavier trains shuttled back and forth across the bridge as its engineer, James B. Eads, took meticulous measurements. However, the general public was probably more reassured by a nonscientific test. Everyone knew that elephants had canny instincts and would not set foot on an unsound bridge. The crowd cheered as a great beast from a local menagerie mounted the approach without hesitation and lumbered placidly across to the Illinois side."

American Scientist March/April 1992.

Are there any floating bridges in the United States?

There are three floating pontoon bridges in the United States, all located in the state of Washington. The Evergreen Point (or Second Lake) Bridge (1963) and the Lacey V. Murrow-Lake Washington Bridge (1993) in Seattle are 7,518 feet and 6,543 feet long respectively. The Hood Canal Bridge (1961) in Port Gamble is 6,471 feet long.

Robert Famighetti, ed., *The World Almanac and Book of Facts 1995* (Mahwah, NJ: World Almanac, 1994), 692.

Why are Phillips screws used?

The recessed head and cross-shaped slots of Phillips screws are self-centering and allow a closer, tighter fit than conventional screws. Straight slotted screws can cause the screwdriver to slip out of the groove and ruin the wood.

Screws were used in carpentry as far back as the sixteenth century, but slotted screws with a tapering point were made at the beginning of the nineteenth century. The great advantage of screws over nails is that they are extremely resistant to longitudinal tension. Larger-size screws that require considerable force to insert have square heads that can be tightened with a wrench. Screws provide more holding power than nails and can be withdrawn without damaging the material. Types of screws include wood screws, lag screws (longer and heavier than wood screws), expansion anchors (for masonry usually), and sheet metal screws. The screw sizes vary from quarter inch to six inches.

David Feldman, *Why Do Clocks Run Clockwise? and Other Imponderables* (New York: Perennial Library, 1988), 206-7. Pedro Guedes, *The Macmillan Encyclopedia of Architecture and Technological Change* (London: Macmillian Press, 1979), 209. Department of the Army, Headquarters, *Carpenter* (Washington, DC: U.S. Department of the Army, Headquarters, 1971), 3-6 to 3-8.

Why is the term "penny" used in nail sizes?

The term "penny" is a measurement relating to the length of nails, originating in England. One explanation is that it refers to cost, with the cost of 100 nails of a certain size being 10 pence or 10d ("d" being the British symbol for a penny). Another explanation suggests that the term refers to the weight of 1,000 nails, with "d" at one time being used as an abbreviation for a pound in weight.

Mankind has been using nails for the last 5,000 years or so. Nails are known to have been used in Ur (ancient Iraq) to fasten together sheet metal. Before 1500, nails were made by hand by drawing small pieces of metal through a succession of graded holes in a metal plate. In 1741, there were 60,000 people employed in England making nails.

The first nail-making machine was invented by the American Ezekiel Reed. In 1851, Adolphe F. Brown of New York invented a wire-nail-making machine. This enabled nails to be mass-produced cheaply.

E.F. Carter, *Dictionary of Inventions and Discoveries* (New York: Crane Russak, 1974), 122. Meredith Hooper, *Everyday Inventions* (London: Angus & Robertson, 1972), 3-5. Robert Putnam, *Builder's Comprehensive Dictionary, 2d ed.* (Carlsbad, CA: Craftsman Book, 1989), 290.

How does a chimney differ from a flue?

A chimney is a brick and masonry construction which contains one or more flues. A flue is a passage within a chimney through which smoke, fumes, and gases ascend. A flue is lined with clay or steel to contain the combustion wastes. By channeling the warm, rising gases, a flue creates a draft that pulls the air over the fire and up the flue. Each heat source needs its own flue, but one chimney can have several flues.

How Things Work in Your Home (New York: Holt, Rinehart and Winston, 1985), 299.

What name is given to the covering at the top of a concrete wall?

A coping is the protective covering over any vertical construction, such as a concrete wall or chimney. A coping may be made of masonry, metal, or wood and is usually sloping or beveled to shed water in such a way that it does not run down the vertical face of the wall.

Means Illustrated Construction Dictionary (Kingston, MA: R. S. Means, 1985), 121.

How many acres of trees are used in the construction of a single-family home?

On the average, an acre of softwood forest is used for a typical 2,000 square-foot house.

Harrowsmith Country Life January/February 1992.

Will building a seawall protect a beach?

Building a seawall may protect a beach for a while, but during a storm the sand cannot follow its natural pattern of allowing waves to draw the sand across the lower beach making the beach flatter. With a seawall, the waves carry off more sand, dropping it into deeper water. A better alternative to the seawall is the revetment. This is a wall of boulders, rubble, or concrete block, tilted back away from the waves. It imitates the way a natural beach flattens out under wave attack.

Wallace Kaufman, *The Beaches Are Moving* (New York: Anchor Press, 1979), 207-8, 211.

How big is the Hoover Dam?

Formerly called Boulder Dam, the Hoover Dam is located between Nevada and Arizona on the Colorado River. The highest concrete arch dam in the United States, the dam is 1,244 feet (379 meters) long and 726 feet (221 meters) high. It has a base thickness of 660 feet (201 meters) and a crest thickness of 45 feet (13.7 meters). It stores 21.25 million acre-feet of water in the 115-mile-long (185-kilometer) Lake Mead reservoir.

The dam was built because the Southwest was faced with constantly recurring cycles of flood and drought. Uncontrolled, the Colorado River had limited value, but once regulated, the flow would assure a stabilized, year-round water supply and the low-lying valleys would be protected against floods. On December 21, 1928, the Boulder Canyon Project Act became law, and the project was completed on September 30, 1935-two years ahead of schedule. For 22 years, Hoover Dam was the highest dam in the world.

U.S. Department of the Interior, *The Story of the Hoover Dam* (Washington, DC. Department of Interior, 1971), 8, 15, 35.

How is asbestos removed from existing sites?

There are three acceptable procedures to use in removing asbestos from existing sites: removal, encapsulation, and enclosure. In the removal process, asbestos is stripped from the underlying surface, collected, and placed in containers for burial in an approved site. Encapsulation, the quickest and least expensive method, coats the asbestos material with a sealant. This is often used when the asbestos is not readily accessible. In the enclosure process, a barrier is placed between the asbestos and the building environment. This is rarely used because the asbestos remains in place and has the potential for exposure during routine maintenance.

E. Willard Miller, *Environmental Hazards: Toxic Waste and Hazardous Material* (Santa Barbara, CA: ABC-CLIO,1991), 84.

Why are barns and schoolhouses traditionally painted red?

Farmers in the late 1700s began to use a homemade wood preservative on their barns that they could make cheaply. The mixture of red iron oxide, skim milk, and linseed oil produced a red "paint" that hardened and coated the barn like plastic. From that time on it became customary to paint barns red. Likewise schools took on this color as well because of the paint's availability and cheapness.

"Why Are Most Barns Red"? *Country Magazine* Premier Issue 1987.

What is "berm"?

Berm (also spelled "berme") refers to the shoulder of the road. It is common to see traffic signs in the southern United States that state "Soft Berm-Keep Off." The etymology can be traced back to Norman times, when berm meant the ridge between the edge of the moat around the castle and the fortress wall.

William Morris and Mary Morris, *Morris Dictionary of Word and Phrase Origins* (New York: Harper & Row, 1977), 55.

Where is the English Channel Tunnel located?

For centuries, the British have enjoyed geographic isolation from continental Europe. However, that isolation has come to an end with the opening of the Channel Tunnel, or "Chunnel." The train tunnel, a 31-mile corridor between Folkestone, England, and Calais, France, was officially dedicated on May 6, 1994, by Britain's Queen Elizabeth II (1926-) and French president Francois Mitterand (1916-1996). However, the first public run on high-speed trains through the tunnel occurred on November 14, 1994. The tunnel trip from Folkestone to Calais takes approximately 35 minutes, as opposed to 70 minutes by hovercraft or ferry. The tunnel lies 130 feet under the English Channel through an impermeable layer of chalk. It operates 24 hours a day, 365 days a year. Although most of the French are pleased with the opening of the Channel Tunnel, most British are concerned that the tunnel signals an end to British independence.

Richard W. Stevenson, "The Chunnel is Ready, But Are the English"? *New York Times* 30 January 1994. "Chunnel Passenger Train Makes Inaugural Run," *USA Today* 10 March 1994.

When was New York City's Empire State Building built?

The 102-story Empire State Building in New York City was started on March 17, 1930 and opened on May 1, 1931. Until 1972 it was the world's tallest building; then it was superseded by the Sears Tower in Chicago. Some interesting facts include:
Because of its height and air currents, snow drifts up to the top of the building.
The 102nd floor was originally designed to be a dirigible landing sight.
In 1986 two people parachuted off the top of the building.
In 1945 a military plane crashed into the building's 79th floor, killing 14.
Many movies have had scenes featuring the building but *King Kong* (1933) is the most famous.
In high winds the building can sway as much as 1.48 inches.
Fourteen people died during the building's construction.

"The Empire At 60," *USA Today* 22 April 1991.

What are the origins of plaster of Paris?

Plaster of Paris is in reality gypsum or especially calcined gypsum. Its name derives from the gypsum quarries of Montmartre, Paris.

Ivor H. Evans, *Brewer's Dictionary of Phrase and Fable, 14th ed.* (New York: Harper & Row, 1989), s.v. "plaster of Paris."

Who designed the Golden Gate Bridge?

Joseph B. Strauss (1870-1938), formally named chief engineer for the Golden Gate Bridge project in 1929, was assisted by Charles Ellis and Leon Moissieff in the design. An engineering masterpiece that opened to traffic in May of 1937, this suspension bridge spans San Francisco Bay, linking San Francisco with Marin County, California. It has a central span of 4,200 feet (1280.2 meters) with towers rising 746 feet (227.4 meters).

Donald C. Jackson, *Great American Bridges and Dams* (Washington, DC: Preservation Press, 1988), 278-80.

Who built the Brooklyn Bridge?

John A. Roebling (1806-1869), a German-born American engineer, constructed the first truly modern suspension bridge in 1855. Towers supporting massive cables, tension anchorage for stays, a roadway suspended from the main cables, and a stiffening deck below or beside the road deck to prevent oscillation are all characteristics of Roebling's suspension bridge. In 1867 Roebling was given the ambitious task of constructing the Brooklyn Bridge. In his design he proposed the revolutionary idea of using steel wire for cables rather than the less-resilient iron. Just as construction began, Roebling died of tetanus after his foot was crushed in an accident and his son, Washington A. Roebling (1837-1926), assumed responsibility for the bridge's construction. In 1883, 14 years later, with 20 lives lost during its construction, the bridge was completed. At that time, it was the longest suspension bridge in the world, spanning the East River and connecting New York's Manhattan with Brooklyn. The bridge has a central span of 1,595.5 feet (486.3 meters), with its masonry towers rising 276 feet (84.1 meters) above high water. Today the Brooklyn Bridge is among the best known of all American civil engineering accomplishments.

Daniel L. Schodek, *Landmarks in American Civil Engineering* (Cambridge: MIT Press, 1987), 132-42. Caroline Sutton and Duncan M. Anderson, *How Do They Do That?* (New York: Quill, 1982), 156-60. Irving Wallace et al., *The Book of Lists #2* (New York: William Morrow, 1980), 79.

Where is the longest bridge-tunnel in the world located?

Completed on April 15, 1964 after 42 months' work and $200 million and spanning a great distance of open sea, the Chesapeake Bay Bridge-Tunnel is a 17.5 mile (28.2 kilometer) combination of trestles, bridges, and tunnels that connect Norfolk with Cape Charles in Virginia. Its only rival for crossing so much open and deep water is the Zuider Zee Dam in Holland-a road-carrying structure of similar length, but without the same water depth and same length of open sea.

Nigel Hawkes, *Structures* (New York: Macmillan, 1990), 232. John H. Stephens, *The Guinness Book of Structures* (London: Guinness Superlatives, 1976), 260.

When was the first U.S. coast-to-coast highway built?

Completed in 1923, after ten years of planning and construction, the Lincoln Highway was the first transcontinental highway connecting the Atlantic coast (New York) to the Pacific (California). Its original length of 3,389 miles (5,453 kilometers) was later shortened by relocations and improvements to 3,143 miles (5,057 kilometers). Crossing 13 states-New York, New Jersey, Pennsylvania, Ohio, Indiana, Illinois, Nebraska, Colorado, Wyoming, Utah, Nevada, and California-in 1925, the Lincoln Highway became, for most of its length, U.S. Route 30.

Joseph N. Kane, *Famous First Facts, 4th ed.* (New York: Wilson, 1981), 549. Jean Labatut and J.L. Wheaton, *Highways in Our National Life* (Princeton, NJ: Princeton University Press, 1950), 94.

How much does the Leaning Tower of Pisa lean?

The Leaning Tower of Pisa, 184.5 feet (56.23 meters) tall, is about 17 feet (5.18 meters) out of perpendicular, increasing by about 1/20 inch (1.25 millimeters) a year. Begun by Bonanno Pisano in 1173 as a Romanesque-style campanile or bell tower for the nearby Baptistry, it was not completed until 1372. Built entirely of white marble, with eight tiers of arched arcades, it started to lean during construction. Although the foundation was dug down to 10 feet (3.04 meters) the builders did not reach bedrock for a firm footing. Ingenious attempts were made to compensate for the tilt by straightening up the subsequent stories and making the pillars higher on the south side than on the north to shift the tower's center of gravity. During the 1960s, cement was added to the foundation to strengthen it, but it is still threatened with collapse.

Charles J. Cazeau, *Science Trivia* (New York: Berkley Books, 1986), 65. Nigel Hawkes, *Structures* (New York: Macmilllan, 1992), 228. John H. Stephens, *The Guinness Book of Structures* (London: Guinness Superlatives, 1976), 104.

Who invented the geodesic dome?

A geodesic line is the shortest distance between two points across a surface. If that surface is curved, a geodesic line across it will usually be curved as well. A geodesic line on the surface of a sphere will be part of a great circle. Buckminster Fuller (1895-1983) realized that the surface of a sphere could be divided into triangles by a network of geodesic lines and that structures could be designed so that their main elements either followed those lines or were joined along them.

This is the basis of his very successful geodesic dome: a structure of generally spherical form, constructed of many light, straight structural elements in tension, arranged in a framework of triangles to reduce stress and weight. These contiguous tetrahedrons are made from lightweight alloys with high tensile strength.

An early example of a geodesic structure is Britain's Dome of Discovery, built in 1951. It was the first dome built with principal framing members intentionally aligned along great circle arcs. The ASM (American Society for Metals) dome built east of Cleveland, Ohio, in 1959-1960 is an open lattice-work geodesic dome. Built in 1965, the Houston Astrodome forms a giant geodesic dome.

Encyclopedia Americana (Danbury, CT: Grolier, 1990), 12:431. George W. Morgan, *Geodesic and Geodetic Domes and Space Structures* (Madison, WI: Sci-Tech Publications, 1985), 32-34. Anthony Pugh, *Polyhedra* (Berkeley: University of California, 1976), 56.

What is red dog?

Red dog is the residue from burned coal dumps. The dumps are composed of waste products incidental to coal mining. Under pressure in these waste dumps, the waste frequently ignites from spontaneous combustion, producing a red-colored ash, which is used for driveways, parking lots, and roads.

Victor J. Brown, *Engineering Terminology* (Chicago: Gillette, 1938), 172.

What is a theodolite?

A theodolite is an optical surveying instrument used to measure angles and directions, mounted on an adjustable tripod and has a spirit level to show when it is horizontal. Similar to the more commonly used transit, the theodolite gives more precise readings; angles can be read to fractions of a degree. It is comprised of a telescope that sights the main target, a horizontal plate to provide readings around the horizon, and a vertical plate and scale for vertical readings. The surveyor uses the geometry of triangles to calculate the distance from the angles measured by the theodolite. Such triangulation is used in road-and tunnel-building and other civil engineering work. One of the earliest forms of this surveying instrument was described by Englishman Leonard Digges (d.1571?) in his treatise, *A Geometrical Treatise Named Pantometria* (1571).

Oxford Illustrated Encyclopedia of Invention and Technology (Oxford: Oxford University Press, 1992), 353. *World Book Encyclopedia* (Chicago: World Book, 1990), 19:252. Harriet Wynter and Anthony Turner, *Scientific Instruments* (New York: Charles Scribner's Sons, 1975), 149.

Where is the steepest street in the world located?

Having a maximum gradient of 1 in 1.266, the world's steepest street is Baldwin Street in Dunedin, New Zealand.

In the United States, Lombard Street in San Francisco, California is the steepest as well as the most crooked street. It has eight consecutive 90-degree turns out of 20-feet radius.

Mark C. Young, ed., *The Guinness Book of Records 1995* (New York: Facts on File, 1994), 123.

Where was the first lighthouse built in the United States?

The first lighthouse built in the United States was Boston Lighthouse on Little Brewster Island in Boston Harbor. It was first lit in 1716 and, although destroyed in 1776 during the American Revolutionary War, was rebuilt on the same site in 1783 and still stands today.

The World Book Encyclopedia (Chicago: World Book, 1994), s.v. "lighthouse."

Why did St. Louis build a giant arch on its waterfront?

Gateway Arch was built on the western bank of the Mississippi and was meant to symbolize that St. Louis was the gateway to the West for pioneers during the nineteenth century. It is officially known as the Jefferson National Expansion Memorial because Thomas Jefferson negotiated the Louisiana Purchase, which made western expansion possible. Constructed of 17,246 tons of concrete and steel, the arch has a catenary shape-the curve assumed by a free hanging cord when it is held at both ends. Its simple geometric beauty is emphasized by its great size, for the arch rises 63 stories (630 feet) and spans an equal distance. Designed by Eero Saarinen, who won the commission in an international competition in 1948, it was not built until the sixties. The arch was first open to the public in July of 1967, and every year over 600,000 people ride the tram that runs through its interior to enjoy the view from the apex.

U.S. Department of the Interior National Park Service, *Questions and Answers about the Gateway Arch* (St. Louis, MO: Jefferson National Expansion Memorial, 1994), 1-2.

Which American Indians are known for their ironworking on high-rise construction projects?

The Mohawk Indians live in Canada on either the Caughnawaga Reserve or the Six Nations Reserve and on the St. Regis reservation in Franklin County, New York. The tribe, especially the Caughnawaga, has developed the world-wide reputation for working at great heights without fear ever since its men helped build a bridge span in Montreal in 1850. Many of the Indians are ironworkers in the construction industry and work on high-rise buildings and bridges. Ironworking is deeply ingrained in reservation heritage and folklore. As early as 1714 it was noted by an English traveller that the Mohawks had this uncanny unconcern and physical ease with heights.

"They will walk over deep Brooks, and Creeks, on the smallest Poles, and that without any fear of Concern. Nay, an Indian will walk on the Ridge of a Barn or House and look down the Gable-end, and spit upon the Ground, as unconcerned, as if walking on Terra firma."

The tradition is dangerous, as 33 died in the 1907 collapse of a bridge project in Quebec, and one or two die in job-related accidents each year.

Barbara Leitch, *A Concise Dictionary of Indian Tribes of North America* (Algonac, MI: Reference Publications, 1979), 284. Jane Polley, ed., *Stories Behind Everyday Things* (The Readers Digest Association, 1980), 314. *Wall Street Journal* 20 April 1992. *The World Book Encyclopedia* (Chicago: World Book, 1994), 13:688.

Which of Egypt's pyramids is the largest and what are its dimensions?

Egypt's largest pyramid was built as a burial tomb for King Khufu (known to the Greeks as Cheops) around 2500 B.C. during the "Old Kingdom." Called the Great Pyramid it was constructed over the 23 year reign of Khufu by 4,000 laborers working in gangs of 18 to 20 men. Built mostly of limestone the pyramid contains over two million stone blocks each weighing 2.5 tons. Originally the pyramid was 481 feet (147 meters) high but after losing some of its upper stones over the centuries it now stands at 450 feet (140 meters). The base of the Great Pyramid covers about 13 acres (5 hectares). So as to sail into the afterworld Khufu's body was carried into the pyramid accompanied by a cedar boat.

Lionel Casson, *Ancient Egypt* (New York: Time, 1965), 129-32. Barbara Mertz, *Temples, Tombs and Hieroglyphs* (New York: Peter Bedrick Books, 1978), 68-69.

When did an airplane crash into New York City's Empire State Building?

On the morning of July 28, 1945, a B-25 light bomber with pilot, copilot, and passenger took off from Bedford, Massachusetts, for Newark, New Jersey. In heavy fog over New York City, the plane crashed into the 78th floor of the Empire State Building. One of the plane's engines catapulted into an elevator shaft severing the cables and causing the elevator to plummet to the basement level. The other engine crashed through seven walls before coming out the opposite side of the building. Pieces of the plane and the building hailed down on sidewalk pedestrians. The plane's fuel tanks ignited and six floors and the sides of the building were engulfed in fire. Fourteen people were killed, including the plane's occupants.

Amy Wallace et al. , *The Book Of Lists #3* (New York: William Morrow, 1983), 91.

What was the cost of constructing the Erie Canal?

The Erie Canal, a man-made link from Lake Erie to the Hudson River, cost $7,770,000 in the early 1800s. The 363-mile long canal was easily financed, however, because of the general enthusiasm the project inspired. The Erie Canal Commission had no problem finding financial support for the project and it promptly paid back all of its debts due to the tremendous income the canal soon produced. Construction of the canal lasted from 1817 to 1825; the cost was completely paid off by 1836. The high volume of use enabled the Commission to decrease the tolls for using the canal.

Collier's Encyclopedia (New York: P. F. Collier, 1993), s.v. "Erie Canal." George E. Condon, *Stars in the Water: The Story of the Erie Canal* (Garden City, NY: Doubleday, 1974), 110.

How is common whitewash made?

Although it is not as durable as modern paints, whitewash is still a very practical paint to use on fences, curbs, trellises, and similar outdoor projects. The basic ingredient in it is lime paste which is made by soaking eight pounds of hydrated "spray lime" in three quarts of water. Dissolve two pounds of salt in 2-gallons of water and add this to one gallon of the lime paste. Stir and add enough water to make a thin paint.

An interior whitewash, or calcimine, can be made by dissolving -pound of animal glue in one quart of water and stirring this mixture into one gallon of lime paste. Add enough water to make a thin paint. The mixture may also be tinted with paint pigments.

Harris Mitchell, *1,200 Household Hints You Wanted to Know* (Toronto: Bestsellers, 1982), 168.

Which U.S. location has the most bridges?

With the possible exception of Venice, Italy, Pittsburgh, Pennsylvania is the bridge capital of the world. There are more than 1,700 bridges in Allegheny County's 731 square miles. The county has 2.3 bridges per square mile or one bridge for every mile of highway. Nationwide, there are approximately 564,000 bridges.

American Transportation Builder Winter 1981.

What is a yurt?

Originally a Mongolian hut, the yurt has been adapted in the United States as a low-cost structure which can be used as a dwelling. The foundation is built of wood on a hexagonal frame. The wooden lattice-work side walls have a tension cable of 3/16 inch airplane cable sandwiched between the wall pieces at the top to keep the walls from collapsing. The walls are insulated and covered with boards, log slabs, canvas, or aluminum siding. A shingle roof, electricity, plumbing, and a small heating stove may be installed. The interior can be finished as desired with shelves, room dividers, and interior siding. The yurt is practical and relatively inexpensive to erect.

Leonard Charney, *Build a Yurt* (New York: Macmillan, 1974), 134. James E. Churchill, *The Backyard Building Book* (Harrisburg, PA: Stackpole Books, 1976), 76-84.

When was the first shopping center built?

The first shopping center in the world was built in 1896 at Roland Park, Baltimore, Maryland. The world's largest shopping center is the West Edmonton Mall in Alberta, Canada, which covers 5.2 million square feet (480 thousand square meters) on a 121 acre (49 hectare) site. It has 828 stores and services with parking for 20 thousand vehicles.

One of the largest and most popular malls in the United States is the Mall of America. Located in Bloomington, Minnesota, the mall is spread out across 78 acres. Several large retailers are located at the mall, including Sears, Bloomingdale's, Macy's, and Nordstrom. In addition to these retailers, the Mall of America has over 400 specialty stores and dozens of restaurants, sports bars, and nightclubs.

AAA Tourbook: North Central (American Automobile Association, 1994), 66. *Guinness Book of Records 1992* (New York: Bantam Books, 1992), 305. Mark C. Young, ed., *Guinness Book of Records 1995* (New York: Facts on File, 1994), 101.

What is the BOCA code?

The Building Officials and Code Administrators (BOCA) International is a service organization which issues a series of model regulatory construction codes for the protection of public health, safety, and welfare. The codes are published in sections, such as the National Building Code, National Plumbing Code, and National Fire Prevention Code. They are designed for adoption by state or local governments and may be amended or modified to accomplish desired local requirements.

The BOCA National Building Code 1990, 11th ed. (Country Club Hills, IL: BOCA International, 1989), inside front cover, iii.

What is crown molding?

Crown molding is a wood, metal, or plaster finishing strip placed on the wall where it intersects the ceiling. If the molding has a concave face, it is called a cove molding. In inside corners it must be cope-jointed to insure a tight joint.

Robert E. Putnam, *Builder's Comprehensive Dictionary, 2d ed.* (Carlsbad, CA: Craftsman Book, 1989), 103.

What are the dimensions of the Eiffel Tower?

Now France's most instantly recognizable landmark, the Eiffel Tower was completed in 1889 in Paris by Gustave Eiffel (1832-1923), a French engineer, for the 100th anniversary of the French Revolution. For this momentous occasion, for which a huge exhibition-Exposition Universelle-was planned in Paris, Eiffel wished to erect something extraordinary made from modern materials. His design, a structure of wrought iron ribs, held together by rivets and resting on a solid masonry foundation, was initially denounced by some as a "tragic lamppost," but its elegance has come to be recognized by most.

It weighs 7,000 pounds and stands 985 feet 11 inches (300.5 meters) on a square base measuring 328 feet (100 meters) on each side. The first story platform is at 189 feet (57.6 meters), with sides 232 feet (70.7 meters) long. The second story platform is at 379 feet (115.5 meters), with sides 134 feet (40.8 meters) long. There is an intermediate platform at 643 feet (196 meters)-this is only a point to change elevators. The third story platform is at 905 feet (275.8 meters). Later a 66-foot (20-meter) television antenna was attached, which extended the tower's total height to 1052 feet (320.7 meters).

Ren Poirier, *The Fifteen Wonders of the World* (New York: Random House, 1961), 242, 248.

Where is the highest dam in the United States and what is its capacity?

Oroville, the highest dam in the United States, is an earth-fill dam that rises 754 feet (229.8 meters) and extends more than a mile across the Feather River, near Oroville, California. Built in 1968, it forms a reservoir containing about 3.5 million acre-feet (4.3 million cubic meters) of water. The next highest dam in the United States is the Hoover Dam on the Colorado River, on the Nevada-Arizona border. It is 726 feet (221.3 meters) high, and was, for 22 years, the world's highest. Presently, there are nine dams higher than the Oroville-the highest currently is the 1,098-foot (334.7-meter) Rogun(skaya) earth-fill dam, currently under construction, which also crosses the Vaksh River in Tadzhikistan.

Mark C. Young, ed., *Guinness Book of Records 1995* (New York: Facts On File, 1994), 103. John H. Stephens, *The Guinness Book of Structures* (London: Guiness Superlatives, 1976), 61-64. *World Book Encyclopedia* (Chicago: World Book, 1990), 14:864.

Communication

What is a computer hedgehog?

A computer hedgehog is a person whose knowledge and awareness of computers, computer systems, hardware, and software is limited to one type of machine, activity, or program.

Harold LeMay, *The Facts On File Dictionary of New Words* (New York: Facts on File, 1988), s.v. "computer hedgehog."

Which group of people were the first to develop an alphabet?

The first alphabet was developed by a group of Semites known as Canaanites during the second millennium B.C., who borrowed largely from Egyptian hieroglyphics (or picture writing) the symbols for their sounds. This alphabet of 30 symbols did not differentiate between vowels. The Phoenicians modified this alphabet to 22 letters. The Phoenicians were traders and this alphabet was disseminated throughout the Mediterranean area. Eventually other Semites and the ancient Greeks developed their own scripts based this model. The Greeks dropped three sounds and added their own symbols for the sounds and changed the direction of writing from left to right. In addition they added six new symbols: the vowels a, e, u, long e, and i to make the first alphabet to contain individual vowels and letters. This Greek alphabet was adapted by the Etruscans who migrated to Italy about 700 B.C. where they taught it to the Romans.

Joseph Naveh, *Origins of the Alphabet* (London: Cassell, 1975). Bridget Travers, ed., *World of Invention* (Detroit: Gale Research, 1994), s.v. "alphabet."

When was the first telephone directory issued?

The first telephone directory was issued in 1878 by the New Haven (Connecticut) District Telephone Company. It contained fifty listings.

David Louis, *fascinating facts:* (New York: Ridge Press, 1977), 51.

What technological development eliminated the need for the "Pony Express"?

In 1860 in an effort to promote a central mail route through the west as opposed to a more southerly one Senator William Gwin of California persuaded the freighting firm of Russell, Majors, and Waddell to set up a mail delivery service called the Central Overland California & Pike's Peak Express Company which came to be known as the "Pony Express." The central 1,966 mile route chosen by William Russell started at St. Joseph, Missouri and generally followed the Oregon-California trail through Nebraska, Wyoming, Utah, and Nevada before ending at Sacramento, California. Stations were established every fifteen miles along the relay route where the mail carriers would have two minutes to mount new horses. In the eighteen months of service from April 3, 1860 to November 20, 1861 the "Express" only missed one trip in its 10-day delivery service that carried in total 34,753 pieces of mail. Its best time between Fort Kearny and Fort Churchill was six days in November of 1860 when the news of U.S. president Abraham Lincoln's election was carried.

At first the service was weekly and cost five dollars for a half-ounce; this was later changed to semi-weekly at a cost of one dollar. The venture became a financial failure with losses amounting to thirteen dollars per letter. Although each trip might earn as much as a thousand dollars, the expense of maintaining 190 stations, 80 riders, and 500 horses exceeded that amount, costing the company sixteen dollars to deliver each letter for which it received only three dollars in fees per letter. The completion of cross-country telegraph lines on October 24, 1861 made Pony Express obsolete.

Dictionary of American History (New York: Charles Scribner's Sons, 1976), s.v. "pony express. " Mabel Loving, *The Pony Express Rides On!* (St. Joseph, MO: Robidoux Printing, 1961), 131-32. Jane Polley, ed., *Stories Behind Everyday Things* (Pleasantville, NY: Reader's Digest Association, 1980), 214. *The World Book Encyclopedia* (Chicago: World Book, 1994), s.v. "pony express."

When was the first transatlantic telephone call made?

The first official transatlantic telephone call marked the start of this service on January 7, 1927. W. S. Gifford, the president of the American Telephone and Telegraph Company, in New York City, telephoned Sir G. Evelyn Murray, the secretary of the British Post Office, in London, England. The technology used to create the new service involved both wires on land and transoceanic radio. Newswriters reflected on the potential impact of the transatlantic telephone: The *Schenectady Union Star* predicted that the new service would "go far toward making English more nearly the universal language."

Literary Digest 22 January 1927.

What does the term "widow" mean when referring to typography?

The word "widow" is used as a typographical term; it is used to describe the short line that is created when the last few words of a paragraph are placed at the top of a page. Copy editing or changing spacing is often used to eliminate a widow line. The term can also be applied to a single word or part of a word, when it stands alone on a line.

The Chicago Manual of Style (Chicago: University of Chicago Press, 1982), 681.

Who "runs" the INTERNET?

The INTERNET, a global computerized communications network has no headquarters, board of directors, or chief-executive-officer. In essence no single person, group of people or government agency "runs" the Internet, nor is its operation totally anarchistic. The INTERNET is a cooperative venture amongst various networks who provide money, hardware, software, maintenance and technical expertise. These various networks receive their funding from a wide variety of sources. The U.S. government however plays a role in the INTERNET via the National Science Foundation which provides federal dollars to burgeoning academic and research networks. An example of National Science Foundation involvement is NSFNET which connects mid-level networks that in turn connects universities and various organizations. International networks are also funded by other governments and organizations.

Tracy Laquey, *THE INTERNET COMPANION: A Beginner's Guide to Global Networking* (Reading, MA: Addison-Wesley Publishing, 1993), 27-28.

What were *Enigma* and *Purple* in World War II?

Enigma and *Purple* were the electric rotor cipher machines of the Germans and Japanese, respectively. The Enigma machine, used by the Nazis, was invented in the 1920s. The Japanese machine, called Purple by the Americans, was adapted from Enigma.

Cryptography-the art of sending messages in such a way that the real meaning is hidden from everyone but the sender and the recipient-is done in two ways: code and cipher. A code is like a dictionary in which all the words and phrases are replaced by codewords or codenumbers. A codebook is used to read the code. A cipher works with single letters, rather than complete words or phrases. There are two kinds of ciphers: transposition and substitution. In a transposition cipher, the letters of the ordinary message (or plain text) are jumbled to form the cipher text. In substitution, the plain text letters can be replaced by other letters, numbers, or symbols.

Bruce Norman, *Secret Warfare: The Battle of Codes and Ciphers* (Reston, VA: Acropolis Books, 1973), 13-14. Graham Yost, *Spy Tech* (New York: Facts On File, 1985), 216.

Who invented radio?

Guglielmo Marconi (1874-1937), of Bologna, Italy, was the first to prove that radio signals could be sent over long distances. Radio is the radiation and detection of signals propagated through space as electromagnetic waves to convey information. It was first called wireless telegraphy because it duplicated the effect of telegraphy without using wires. On December 12, 1901, Marconi successfully sent Morse code signals from Newfoundland to England.

In 1906, the American inventor Lee DeForest (1873-1961) built what he called "the Audion," which became the basis for the radio amplifying vacuum tube. This device made voice radio practical, because it magnified the weak signals without distorting them. The next year, DeForest began regular radio broadcasts from Manhattan, New York. As there were still no home radio receivers, DeForest's only audience was ship wireless operators in New York City Harbor.

Isaac Asimov, *Asimov's Biographical Encyclopedia of Science and Technology, 2nd ed.,* (Garden City, NY: Doubleday & Co., 1982), 650-51. Charles Panati, *Panati's Browser's Book of Beginnings* (Boston: Houghton Mifflin, 1984), 217-19.

Why do FM radio stations have a limited broadcast range?

Usually radio waves higher in frequency than approximately 50 to 60 megahertz are not reflected by the earth's ionosphere, but are lost in space. Television, FM radio, and high frequency communications systems are therefore limited to approximately line-of-sight ranges. The line-of-sight distance depends on the terrain and antenna height, but has usually a limitation of 50 to 100 miles (80 to 161 kilometers). FM (frequency-modulation) radio uses a wider band than AM (amplitude-modulation) radio to give broadcasts the quality of high fidelity. This is especially noticeable in music, which on FM radio has crystal clarity to high tones and rich resonance in base notes—all with a minimum of static and distortion. FM radio was invented by a professor of electrical engineering, Edwin Howard Armstrong (1891-1954) in 1933, and for his contribution Armstrong has been called the Father of FM. FM receivers became available in 1939.

Lee W. Churchman, *Survey of Electronics* (San Francisco: Rinehart Press, 1971), 66. Harry Harris, *Good Old-Fashioned Yankee Ingenuity* (Chelsea, MI: Scarborough House, 1990), 128-29. Charles Panati, *Panati's Browser's Book of Beginnings* (Boston: Houghton Mifflin, 1984), 220-22.

Who was the father of television?

The idea of television (or "seeing by electricity" as it was called in 1880) was offered by several people over the years, and several individuals contributed a multiplicity of partial inventions. For example, in 1897 Ferdinand Braun (1850-1918) constructed the first cathode ray oscilloscope, a fundamental component to all television receivers. In 1907, Boris Rosing proposed using Braun's tube to receive images, and in the following year Alan Campbell-Swinton likewise suggested using the tube, now called the cathode-ray tube, for both transmission and receiving. However, the key figure, frequently called the father of television was the Russian-born American, Vladimir K. Zworykin (1889-1982). A former pupil of Rosing, he produced a practical method of amplifying the electron beam so that the light/dark pattern would produce a good image. In 1923, he patented the iconoscope (which would become the television camera) and in 1924 he patented the kinoscope (television tube). Both inventions rely on streams of electrons for both scanning and creating the image on a fluorescent screen. By 1938, after adding new and more sensitive photo cells, Zworykin demonstrated his first practical model.

During the earlier twentieth century others worked on different approaches to television. The best-known is John L. Baird (1888-1946) who in 1936, used a mechanized scanning device, to transmit the first recognizable picture of a human face. Limitations in his designs made any further improvements in the picture quality impossible.

Isaac Asimov, *Understanding Physics* (New York: Dorset Press, 1988), 3:48-51. Carlo M. Cipolla, and Derek Birdsall, *The Technology of Man* (New York: Holt, Rinehart, and Winston, 1980), 236. Ian McNeil, *An Encyclopedia of the History of Technology* (London: Routledge, 1990), 744-46.

What name is used for a satellite dish that picks up TV broadcasts?

Earth station is the term used for the complete satellite receiving or transmitting station that picks up television broadcasts. It includes the antenna, the electronics, and all associated equipment necessary to receive or transmit satellite signals. It can range from a simple inexpensive receive-only earth station that can be purchased by the individual consumer, to elaborate, two-way communications stations that offer commercial access to the satellite's capacity. Signals are captured and focused by the antenna into a feedhorn and low noise amplifier. These are relayed by cable to a down converter and then into the satellite receiver/modulator.

Satellite television became widely available in the late 1970s, when cable television stations, equipped with satellite dishes, received signals and sent them to their subscribers by coaxial cable. Taylor Howard designed the first satellite dish for personal use in 1976. By 1984 there were 500,000 installations and in recent years that number has increased worldwide to 3.7 million.

Frank Baylin, and Brent Gale, *The Home Satellite TV Installation and Troubleshooting Manual* (Boulder, CO: Baylin¤Gale Productions, 1985), 3, 5, 307. James Harry Green, *The Dow Jones-Irwin Handbook of Telecommunications* (Homewood, IL: Dow Jones-Irwin, 1986), 448. Neil Schlager, ed., *How Products Are Made* (Detroit: Gale Research, 1994), 1:390.

How does a car phone work?

There are three parts to a cellular phone system: the installation in the car; the cell site; and the mobile telephone switching office. Each cell has at its center a cell site where the fixed radio receiver and transmitter are located. All the cell sites belonging to a particular system are connected together at a mobile telephone switching office, which ties them to the local phone system. As a call passes from one cell site and enters into another, the call is transferred to an adjoining cell without any noticeable interruption.

Josef Bernard, *The Cellular Connection* (Mendocino, CA: Quantum Publishing, 1987), 7.

What is digital audio tape (DAT)?

Digital audio tape or DAT, is a magnetic recording that produces a mathematical value for each sound based on the binary code. When the values are reconstructed during playback, the reconstructed sound is so much like the original that the human ear cannot distinguish the difference.

The Almanac of Science and Technology (San Diego, CA: Harcourt Brace Jovanovich, 1990), 247.

What is the lifespan of a CD-ROM disc?

Although manufacturers claim that a CD-ROM disc can last twenty years, the U.S. National Archives and Records Administration suggests that a lifespan of three to five years is maybe more accurate. The main problem is that the aluminum substratum on which the data is recorded is vulnerable to oxidation.

PRLC Technical Bulletin January/February 1992.

When was the first commercial communications satellite used?

In 1960 *ECHO 1*, the first communications satellite, was launched. Two years later, on July 10, 1962, the first commercially funded satellite, *Telstar 1*, (paid for by American Telephone and Telegraph) was launched into low earth orbit. It was also the first true communications satellite, being able to relay not only data and voice but television as well. The first broadcast, which was relayed from the United States to England, showed an American flag flapping in the breeze. The first commercial satellite (in which its operations are conducted like a business) was *Early Bird* which went into regular service on June 10, 1965, with 240 telephone circuits. *Early Bird* was the first satellite launched for Intelsat (International Telecommunications Satellite Organization). Still in existence, the system is owned by member nations-each nation's contribution to the operating funds are based on its share of the system's annual traffic.

Kenneth Gatland, *The Illustrated Encyclopedia of Space Technology* (New York: Orion Books, 1989), 90-92. Ian McNeil, *An Encyclopedia of the History of Technology* (London: Routledge, 1990), 747-48.

What is a fiber optic cable?

A fiber optic cable is composed of many very thin strands of coated glass fibers that transmit light through the process of cladding in which total internal reflection of light is achieved through the use of material that has a lower refractive index. Once light enters the fiber, the cladding layer inside it prevents light loss as the beam of light zigzags inside the glass core. Glass fibers can transmit messages or images by directing beams of light inside itself over very short or very long distances up to 13,000 miles (20,917 kilometers) without significant distortion. The pattern of light waves forms a code that carries a message. At the receiving end the light beams are converted back into electric current and decoded. Since light beams are immune to electrical noise and can be carried greater distances before fading, this technology is used heavily in telecommunications. Other applications include using medical fiber optic viewers, such as endoscopes and fiberscopes, to see internal organs; fiber optic message devices in aircraft and space vehicles; and fiber optic connections in automotive lighting systems.

Robert J. Cone, *How the New Technology Works* (Phoenix: Oryx Press, 1991), 30-33. Bridget Travers, ed., *World of Invention* (Detroit: Gale Research, 1994), s.v. "fiberoptics."

Why are most pencils yellow?

Painting pencils yellow became a sign of quality during the 1890s. The painting practice had originally been started as early as 1854 in Keswick, England, but most likely it was done to cover the imperfect wood used in some pencils. It was the American Koh-I-Noor Company whose successful, high-quality yellow pencil became so firmly established in the minds of users that any other color was assumed to be an inferior pencil. Yellow has thus become established as the preferred color for a writing pencil, as it has for school buses and highway signs. It makes them all highly visible-whether on a busy desk or highway.

Very early pencils were covered, square sticks of graphite (a soft black lustrous form of carbon) that left as much of a mark on the user's hand as on the paper. Later, in England and Germany, marking sticks were wrapped tightly with string to fashion pencils, with the string slowly unwound to expose more stick. In the sixteenth century the Germans inserted the sticks into grooves cut in narrow strips of wood.

As graphite supplies became scarce in the late eighteenth century, chemists sought ways to reduce the graphite content in pencils. In 1795 N.J. Conte (1755-1805) produced pencils made from ground graphite and clay that had been shaped into sticks and kiln-baked-a process still done to this very day. Today, although a pencil appears to be all one piece, it actually is formed from two pieces of wood glued together so well that the seams are not visible.

The development of the process of vulcanizing rubber in 1839 made feasible the attachment of the eraser. In 1858 Hyman L. Lipman of Philadelphia patented a pencil with an eraser glued to one end.

Harry Harris, *Good Old-Fashioned Yankee Ingenuity* (Chelsea, MI: Scarborough House, 1990), 121. Charles Panati, *Panati's Browser's Book of Beginnings* (Boston: Houghton Mifflin, 1990), 79. Henry Petroski, *The Pencil: A History of Design and Circumstance* (New York: Knopf, 1990), 138-40, 162-63.

Who was the father of cybernetics?

Norbert Weiner (1894-1964) is considered the creator of cybernetics. Derived from the Greek word "kubernetes," meaning steerman or helmsman, cybernetics is concerned with the common factors of control and communication in living organisms, automatic machines, or organizations. These factors are exemplified by the skill used in steering a boat, in which the helmsman uses continual judgement to maintain control. The principles of cybernetics are used today in control theory, automation theory, and computer programs to reduce many time-consuming computations and decision-making processes formerly done by people.

W. Ross Ashby, *An Introduction to Cybernetics* (New York: John Wiley & Sons, 1958), 1-5. Maurice Trask, *The Story of Cybernetics* (London: Studio Vista, 1971), 9.

Where did the term "bug" originate?

The slang term "bug" is used to describe problems and errors occurring in computer programs. The term may have originated during the early 1940s at Harvard University when a computer malfunctioned. A dead moth found in the system was thought to be the cause of the system's failure. This famous carcass, taped to a page of notes, is preserved with the trouble log notebook at the Virginia Naval Museum.

James W. Cortada, *Historical Dictionary of Data Processing: Technology* (Westport, CT: Greenwood Press, 1987), 49.

What is a computer "virus" and how is it spread?

Taken from the obvious analogy with biological viruses, a computer "virus" is a program that searches out other programs and "infects" them by replicating itself in them. When the programs are executed, the embedded virus is executed too, thus propagating the "infection." This normally happens invisibly to the user. A virus cannot infect other computers, however, without assistance. It is spread when users communicate by computer, often when they trade programs. The virus might do nothing but propagate itself and then allow the program to run normally. Usually, however, after propagating silently for a while, it starts doing other things—from inserting "cute" messages or destroying all of the user's files. Computer "worms" and "logic bombs" are similar to viruses, but they do not replicate themselves within programs as viruses do. A logic bomb does its damage immediately-destroying data, inserting garbage into data files, or reformatting the hard disk; a worm can alter the program and database either immediately or over a period of time.

In the 1990s, viruses, worms, and logic bombs have become such a serious problem, especially among IBM PC and Macintosh users, that the production of special detection and "innoculation" software has become an industry.

Alan Freedman, *The Computer Glossary, 5th ed.* (New York: AMACOM, 1991),346, 636-637, 657. Eric S. Raymond, *The New Hacker's Dictionary* (Cambridge: MIT Press, 1991), 371.

Who invented the COBOL computer language?

COBOL (common business oriented language) is a prominent computer language designed specifically for commercial uses, created in 1960 by a team drawn from several computer makers and the Pentagon. The best-known individual associated with COBOL was then-Lieutenant Grace M. Hopper (1906-1992) who made fundamental contributions to the U. S. Navy standardization of COBOL. COBOL works very well for the most common kinds of data processing for business-simple arithmetic operations performed on huge files of data. The language endures because its syntax is very much like English and because a program written in COBOL for one kind of computer can run on many others without alteration.

Understanding Computers: Illustrated Chronology and Index (New York: Time-Life Books, 1989), 47. Michael R. Williams, *A History of Computing Technology* (New York: Prentice-Hall,1985), 247.

Who invented the computer?

Computers developed from calculating machines. One of the earliest mechanical devices for calculating, still widely used today, is the abacus-a frame carrying parallel rods on which beads or counters are strung. Herodotus, the Greek historian who lived around 400 B.C., mentions the use of the abacus in Egypt. In 1617 John Napier (1550-1617) invented "Napier's Rods"-marked pieces of ivory for multiples of numbers. In the middle of the same century, Blaise Pascal (1623-1662) produced a simple mechanism for adding and subtracting. Multiplication by repeated addition was a feature of a stepped drum or wheel machine of 1694 invented by Gottfried Wilhelm Leibniz (1646-1716). In 1823 the English visionary Charles Babbage (1792-1871) persuaded the British government to finance an "analytical engine." This would have been a machine that could undertake any kind of calculation. It would have been driven by steam, but the most important innovation was that the entire program of operations was stored on a punched tape. Babbage's machine was not completed and would not have worked if it had been. The standards required were far beyond the capabilities of the engineers of the time, and in any case, rods, levers,and cogs move too slowly for really quick calculations. Modern computers use electrons, which travel at near the speed of light. Although he never built a working computer, Babbage thought out many of the basic principles that guide modern computers.

Based on the concepts of British mathematician Alan M. Turing (1912-54), the earliest programmable electronic computer was the 1,500-valve "Colossus," formulated by Max Newman (1897-1985), built by T.H. Flowers, and used by the British government in 1943 to crack the German codes generated by their coding machine "Enigma."

Edward De Bono, *Eureka!* (New York: Holt, Rinehart and Winston, 1974), 214. *Guinness Book of Records, 1992* (New York: Bantam Books, 1992), 287. *Purnell's Encyclopedia of Inventions* (London: Purnell & Sons, 1976), 96.

Who was the first programmer?

According to historical accounts, Lord Byron's daughter, Augusta Ada Byron, the Countess of Lovelace, was the first person to write a computer program for Charles Babbage's (1792-1871) "analytical engine." This machine, never built, was to work by means of punched cards that could store partial answers that could later be retrieved for additional operations, and that would print results. Her work with Babbage and the essays she wrote about the possibilities of the "engine" established her as a "patron saint," if not a founding parent, of the art and science of programming. The programming language called "Ada" was named in her honor by the U. S. Department of Defense. In modern times the honor goes to Commodore Grace Murray Hopper (1906-1992) of the U. S. Navy. She wrote the first program for the Mark I computer.

James Jespersen, *RAMS, ROMS, and Robots* (New York: Atheneum,1984), 59. Howard Rheingold, *Tools for Thought* (New York: Simon & Schuster, 1985), 31. Jack B. Rochester, *The Naked Computer* (New York: Morrow, 1983), 43, 45.

What does it mean to "boot" a computer?

Booting a computer is starting it, in the sense of turning control over to the operating system. The term comes from bootstrap, because bootstraps allow an individual to pull on boots without help from anyone else. Some people prefer to think of the process in terms of using bootstraps to lift oneself off the ground, impossible in the physical sense, but a reasonable image for representing the process of searching for the operating system, loading it, and passing control to it. The commands to do this are embedded in a *r*ead *o*nly *m*emory (ROM) chip that is automatically executed when a microcomputer is turned on or reset. In mainframe or minicomputers, the process usually involves a great deal of operator input. A cold boot powers on the computer and passes control to the operating system; a warm boot resets the operating system without powering off the computer.

Alan Freedman, *The Computer Glossary, 5th ed.* (New York: AMACOM, 1991), 68, 113, 647. Douglas R. Hofstadter, *Gdel, Escher, Bach: An Eternal Golden Braid* (New York: Vintage Books, 1979), 24, 293-94.

Who coined the term technobabble?

John A. Barry used the term technobabble to mean the pervasive and indiscriminate use of computer terminology, especially as it is applied to situations that have nothing at all to do with technology. He first used it in the early 1980s.

John A. Barry, *Technobabble* (Cambridge, MA: MIT Press, 1991), xiii, 3-5.

For what purpose was MADAM designed?

MADAM (Manchester automatic digital machine) is a chess-playing machine designed by Alan M. Turing (1912-1954) in 1950. Turing was one of the first individuals to program a computer to play chess. His machine was a very poor chess player and made foolish moves. After several moves the machine would be forced to give up. Today it is possible to play a fairly advanced game of chess with a computer. However, no machine has been designed that analyzes every possible strategy corresponding to any move. Even if a machine could play one million chess games per second, it would take 10108 years to play all the possible games.

The Biographical Dictionary of Scientists: Mathematicians (New York: Peter Bedrick Books, 1986), 126. Joseph Sinclair, *Mathematics As a Second Language, 4th ed.* (Redding, MA: Addison-Wesley, 1987), 344.

What is meant by *default*?

As used in computer, communication, and data processing systems, a default is the response that a system "assumes" in the absence of specific instructions. It can be a value (6), a condition (true), or an action (close file).

Dennis Longley and Michael Shain, *Van Nostrand Reinhold Dictionary of Information Technology, 3d ed.* (New York: Van Nostrand Reinhold, 1989), 148. Martin H. Weik, *Communications Standard Dictionary* (New York: Van Nostrand Reinhold, 1989), 253.

Why does a computer floppy disk have to be "formatted"?

A disk must first be organized to that data can be stored on it and retrieved from it. The data on a floppy disk or a hard disk is arranged in concentric tracks. Sectors, which can hold blocks of data, occupy arc-shaped segments of the tracks. Most floppy disks are soft-sectored, and formatting is necessary to record sector identification so that data blocks can be labeled for retrieval. Hard-sectored floppy disks use physical marks to identify sectors; these marks cannot be changed, so the disks cannot be reformatted. The way that sectors are organized and labeled dictates system compatibility: disks formatted for DOS computers can only be used in other DOS machines; those formatted for Macintoshes can only be used in other Macintoshes. Formatting erases any pre-existing data on the disk. Hard disk drives are also formatted before being initialized, and should be protected so that they are not reformatted unintentionally.

Chris De Voney, *MS-DOS User's Guide, 2nd ed.* (Indianapolis: Que Corp., 1987), 395-402. Alan Freedman, *The Computer Glossary, 5th ed.* (New York: AMACOM, 1991), 191, 246, 275, 359-60. Dennis Longley and Michael Shain, *Van Nostrand Reinhold Dictionary of Information Technology, 3rd ed.* (New York: Van Nostrand Reinhold, 1989), 223, 450, 512.

Which woods are used for telephone poles?

The principal woods used for telephone poles are southern pine, Douglas fir, western red cedar, and lodgepole pine. Ponderosa pine, red pine, jack pine, northern white cedar, other cedars, and western larch are also used.

U.S. Forest Products Laboratory, *Encyclopedia of Wood* (New York: Drake, 1977), 294.

Is anyone looking for extraterrestrial life?

A program called SETI (the Search for ExtraTerrestrial Intelligence) began in 1960, when American astronomer Frank Drake (b. 1930) spent three months at the National Radio Astronomy Observatory in Green Bank, West Virginia, searching for radio signals coming from the nearby stars Tau Ceti and Epsilon Eridani. Although no signals were detected and scientists interested in SETI have often been ridiculed, support for the idea of seeking out intelligent life in the universe has grown.

Project Sentinel which used a radio dish at Harvard University's Oak Ridge Observatory in Massachusetts was capable of monitoring 128,000 channels at a time. This project was upgraded in 1985 to META (Megachannel ExtraTerrestrial Array), thanks in part to a donation by filmmaker Steven Spielberg. Project META is capable of receiving 8.4 million channels. NASA began a ten-year search in October 1992 using radio telescopes in Arecibo, Puerto Rico and Barstow, California.

Scientists are searching for radio signals which stand out from the random noises caused by natural objects; such signals might repeat at regular intervals or contain mathematical sequences.

Life September 1992. *The Planetary Report* September/October 1985.

When was the 911 emergency telephone number established?

In 1967, the U.S. President's Commission on Law Enforcement proposed a common emergency number. The American Telephone and Telegraph Company then offered the digits "911" as an emergency telephone number for public safety agencies in 1968.

U.S. Department of Justice, Bureau of Justice Statistics, *911: A Primer for Planners* (Washington, DC: Government Printing Office, 1980).

What are "ack emma" and "pip emma"?

In the late 1800s and early 1900s during telephone communications and in the oral transliteration of code messages, letters were often given sounds in order to send messages clearly. Ack represented the letter "a"; emma, the letter "m"; and pip, the letter "p." For example, ack emma represented a.m., for morning, and pip emma represented p.m., for afternoon/evening.

J.A. Simpson and E.S.C. Weiner, eds., *The Oxford English Dictionary, 2d ed.* (Oxford: Clarendon Press, 1989), s.v. "ack," "emma," "pip."

When was the first public demonstration of color television?

The first public demonstration of color television took place in the Bell Telephone Laboratories in New York City on June 27, 1929. Objects such as the American flag, a watermelon, and roses were shown using three complete systems of photoelectric cells, amplifiers, and glow tubes. Each system had a different screen in red, blue, or green which were superposed using a system of mirrors to make one color picture from the three monochromatic images.

Albert Abramson, *The History of Television, 1880 to 1941* (North Carolina: McFarland & Co., 1987), 135, 137. Joseph Nathan Kane, *Famous First Facts, 4th ed.* (New York: H.W. Wilson, 1981), 645.

When was the telegraph first used in U.S. politics?

The first time the telegraph was used in politics was to report that James K. Polk (1795-1849) had been nominated as the Democratic candidate for the U.S. presidential nomination. After he was nominated on May 29, 1844, a telegram was sent from Baltimore, Maryland (site of the convention), to Washington, D.C.

Joseph Nathan Kane, *Facts About the Presidents: A Compilation of Biographical and Historical Information, 6th ed.* (New York: H. W. Wilson, 1993), s.v. "James Knox Polk." Charles Sellers, *James K. Polk: Continentalist 1843-1846* (Princeton, NJ: Princeton University Press, 1966), 2:98.

Which countries have the capability to build and launch satellites?

Several countries in the world have the technological capability to build and launch satellites. They are: Japan, Russia, China, India, Israel, South Korea, the United States, and France. The United States is the undisputed leader in mobile satellite navigation and tracking services, the development of new technology, and the creation of new markets for satellites.

The United States had over 60 percent of the world market for commercial communications satellites in 1994, followed by

France, Russia, the United Kingdom, Germany, Italy, and Canada.

U.S. Department of Commerce, *U.S. Industrial Outlook 1994* (Washington, DC: Government Printing Office, 1994), 28-1.

Who was the boy who made his bar mitzvah speech with the aid of a computer speech synthesizer?

During his bar mitzvah in 1985, 13-year-old Lee Kweller of Pittsburgh chanted ancient Hebrew melodies, led the congregation in prayer, and gave a speech all with the aid of a computerized speech synthesizer. Kweller has cerebral palsy and is unable to walk or talk.

William Marbach and Karen Springen, "The Gift of Voice Synthesis," *Newsweek* 4 November 1985

What role have scribes played in civilizations?

Before the invention of printing, a scribe was an official who wrote and copied books, letters, and documents by hand. In countries of today with high illiteracy rates, scribes can be found in markets, mosques, and public places where they read, write, and copy letters, documents and other communications for those who cannot do so themselves.

The World Book Encyclopedia (Chicago: World Book, 1987), s.v. "scribe."

Which materials were used for writing surfaces in ancient China?

The oldest records of ancient China were engraved on stone and bone, impressed on clay, and cast in bronze, but they of course were not in book form. The earliest books were made of bamboo or wood tablets that were connected by a string. Later, about the fifth century *B.C.*, silk became a new surface for writing and during the second century *A.D.* paper was introduced. The use of a new surface did not necessarily mean the old surfaces were abandoned; some were used concurrently as the list of time periods below indicates.

Bamboo and wood were used as writing surfaces from earlier times to third or fourth century A.D.

Silk was used as a writing surface from the fifth or fourth century B.C. to the fifth or sixth century A.D.

Paper was used from the second century A.D. to the present.

Ts'un-hsn Ch'ien, *Written on Silk and Bamboo* (Chicago: University of Chicago Press, 1962), 90-91.

What is the history of the TV satellite dish?

In the late 1970s cable television was becoming increasingly popular and like its name implies signals were delivered over wires. The DBS system however began providing wireless service to its subscribers via its "private earth stations" more commonly known as satellite dishes. Originally the dishes were regarded as an expensive novelty; Neiman-Marcus once offered one for $36,500. As the price of the dish dropped, its popularity rapidly increased as did lawsuits which contended owners were stealing TV signals to which they had not subscribed. The dishes were soon the focal point of the great "signal piracy" debate which was largely resolved in 1984 when U.S. Senator Barry Goldwater (1909-) sponsored a bill that allowed the reception of unscrambled signals but outlawed converters that could decode scrambled signals.

Philip Mattera, *Inside U.S. Business: A Concise Encyclopedia of Leading Industries,* (New York: IRWIN, 1994), 34-35.

What is the recipe for invisible ink?

Writing with invisible ink is simple. Pour some vinegar or lemon juice in a shallow bowl. Using a small paint brush or writing instrument, write the message with the vinegar or lemon juice on a clean sheet of white paper. What is being written will not be visible to the writer as well as to the reader. Let the sheet dry and then hold the paper close enough to a light bulb to warm it. Through the process of oxidation, the writing will soon appear as a faint brown scorching.

Ovid K. Wong, *Is Science Magic?* (Chicago: Childrens Press, 1989), 66-67.

What is "Hyperglot"?

"Hyperglot" is a computer product that teaches foreign languages. Different versions, such as the CD-ROM Learn to Speak Spanish, allow the user to select from 30 lessons. Each involve listening to the spoken language, reading notes on vocabulary and phrases, and recording and playing back your own pronunciation. Hyperglot has been on the market since 1989, and works on PCs with Microsoft Windows software as well as on Macintosh computers, each with the appropriate sound, memory, and processing requirements.

New York Times 20 September 1994.

How did the INTERNET originate?

The INTERNET, the global computerized communications network had its innocuous beginnings as ARPANET in 1969. ARPANET was originally an experiment in "packet-switched networking" by ARPA (the Advanced Research Projects Agency) which was part of the DOD (Department of Defense). ARPA, a network originally designed for work-sharing between remote computers later became DARPA (Defense Advanced Research Projects Agency). In 1980 MILNET (an unclassified military network) was created as an offshoot of ARPANET but communication was still possible between the two networks then called DARPA-INTERNET but later shortened to INTERNET.

Tracy Laquey, *THE INTERNET COMPANION: A Beginner's Guide to Global Networking* (Reading, MA: Addison-Wesley Publishing, 1993), 3-4.

In computer lingo what is a gopher?

In computer lingo a gopher is an interface system that allows uniform access to INTERNET resources. A gopher provides "smooth passage" into computer networks and their resources.

Tracy Laquey, *THE INTERNET COMPANION: A Beginner's Guide to Global Networking* (Reading, MA: Addison-Wesley Publishing, 1993), 106.

Which animals other than horses have been used to deliver the mail?

During the nineteenth century, cows hauled mail wagons in some German towns. In Texas, New Mexico, and Arizona, camels were used. In Russia and Scandinavia, reindeer pulled mail sleighs. The Belgian city of Lige even tried cats, but they proved to be unreliable.

Reader's Digest Practical Problem Solver (Pleasantville, NY: Reader's Digest Association, 1991), 161.

Who invented the Braille alphabet?

The Braille system, used by the blind to read and write, are combinations of raised dots that form characters corresponding to the letters of the alphabet, punctuation marks, and common words such as "and" and "the." Louis Braille (1809-1852), blind since the age of three, began working on developing a practical alphabet for the blind shortly after he started a school for the blind in Paris. He experimented with a communication method called night-writing, which the French army used for nighttime battlefield missives. With the assistance of an army officer, Captain Charles Barbier, Braille pared the method's 12-dot configurations to a 6-dot one and devised a code of 63 characters. The system was not widely accepted for several years; even Braille's own Paris school did not adopt the system until 1854 (two years after his death). In 1916, the United States sanctioned Louis Braille's original system of raised dots, and in 1932 a modification called "Standard English Braille, Grade 2" was adopted throughout the English-speaking world. The revised version changed the letter-by-letter codes into common letter combinations, such as "ow," "ing," and "ment," making reading and writing a faster activity.

Before Braille's system, one of the few effective alphabets for the blind was devised by another Frenchman, Valentin Hay (1745-1822), who was the first to emboss paper to help the blind read. Hay's letters in relief were actually a punched alphabet, and imitators immediately began to copy and improve on his system. Another letter-by-letter system of nine basic characters was devised by Dr. William Moon (1818-1894) in 1847, but it is less versatile in its applications.

How In the World (Pleasantville, NY: Reader's Digest Association, 1990), 280. Charles Panati, *Panati's Browser's Book of Beginnings* (Boston: Houghton Mifflin, 1984), 84-85.

Why do AM radio stations have a wider broadcast range at night?

This variation is caused by the nature of the ionosphere of the earth. The ionosphere consists of several different layers of rarefied gases in the upper atmosphere that have become conductive through the bombardment of the atoms of the atmosphere by solar radiation, by electrons and protons emitted by the sun, and by cosmic rays. These layers, sometimes called the Kennelly-Heaviside layer, reflect AM radio signals, enabling AM broadcasts to be received by radios that are great distances from the transmitting antenna. With the coming of night the ionosphere layers partially dissipate and become an excellent reflector of the short waveband AM radio waves. This causes distant AM stations to be heard more clearly at night.

Isaac Asimov, *Understanding Physics* (New York: Dorset Press, 1988), 45. Lee W. Churchman, *Survey of Electronics* (San Francisco: Rinehart Press, 1971), 64-66. *World Book Encyclopedia* (Chicago: World Book, 1990), 16:85.

Can radio transmissions between space shuttles and ground control be picked up by shortwave radio?

Amateur radio operators at Goddard Space Flight Center, Greenbelt, Maryland, retransmit shuttle space-to-ground radio conversations on shortwave frequencies. These retransmissions can be heard freely around the world. To hear astronauts talking with ground controllers during liftoff, flight, and landing, a shortwave radio capable of receiving single-sideband signals should be tuned to frequencies of 3.860, 7.185, 14.295, and 21.395 megahertz. British physics teacher Geoffrey Perry, at the Kettering Boys School, has taught his students how to obtain telemetry from orbiting Russian satellites. Since the early 1960s Perry's students have been monitoring Russian space signals using a simple taxicab radio and using the data to calculate position and orbits of the spacecraft.

Anthony R. Curtis, *Space Almanac* (Woodsboro, MD: ARCsoft, 1990), 278. *Science Digest January* 1984.

How does rain affect television reception from a satellite?

The incoming microwave signals are absorbed by rain and moisture, and severe rainstorms can reduce signals by as much as 10 decibels (reduction by a factor of 10). If the installation cannot cope with this level of signal reduction, the picture may be momentarily lost. Even quite moderate rainfall can reduce signals enough to give noisy reception on some receivers. Another problem associated with rain is an increase in noise due to its inherent noise temperature. Any body above the temperature of absolute zero (0 degrees Kelvin or -459 degrees Fahrenheitor -273 degrees Celsius) has an inherent noise temperature generated by the release of wave packets from the body's molecular agitation (heat). These wave packets have a wide range of frequencies, some of which will be within the required bandwidth for satellite reception. The warm earth has a high noise temperature, and consequently rain does as well.

D.J. Stephenson, *Newnes Guide to Satellite TV* (London: Newnes, 1991), 20.

What is high definition television?

The amount of detail shown in a television picture is limited by the number of lines that make it up and by the number of picture elements on each line. The latter is mostly determined by the width of the electron beam. To obtain pictures closer to the quality associated with 35 millimeter photography, a new television system HDTV (High Definition Television) has been developed which will have more than twice the number of scan lines with a much smaller picture element. Currently American and Japanese television has 525 scanning lines, while Europe uses 625 scanning lines. HDTV has received wide publicity in recent years, but it is currently in an engineering phase, and not yet commercially available.

The Japanese are generally given credit for being pioneers in HDTV, ever since NHK, the Japanese broadcasting company, began research in 1968. In fact, the original pioneer was RCA's Otto Schade who began his research after the end of World War II (1939-1945). Schade was ahead of his time, and decades passed before television pickup tubes and other components became available to take full advantage of his research.

HDTV cannot be used in the commercial broadcast bands until technical standards are approved by the U.S. Federal Communications Commission (FCC) or the various foreign regulating agencies. The more immediate problem however, is a technological one-HDTV needs to transmit five times more data than is currently assigned to each television channel. One approach is signal compression-squeezing the 30 megahertz bandwidth signal that HDTV requires into the 6 megahertz bandwidth currently used for television broadcasting. The Japanese and Europeans have chosen analog systems that use wave-like transmission to develop, while the Americans are basing their HDTV development on digital transmission systems.

Richard P. Brennan, *Dictionary of Scientific Literacy* (New York: John Wiley & Sons, 1992), 140-41. Andrew F. Inglis *Behind the Tube: A History of Broadcasting Technology and Business* (London: Focal Press, 1990), 473-87. *The New Book of Popular Science* (Danbury, CT: Grolier, 1988), 6:259.

What is the Dolby noise reduction system?

The magnetic action of the tape produces a background hiss-a drawback in sound reproduction on tape. A noise reduction system known as Dolby (named after its inventor R.M. Dolby [b. 1933]) is widely used to deal with the hiss. In quiet passages, electronic circuits automatically boost the signals before they reach the recording head, drowning out the hiss. On playback, the signals are reduced to their correct levels. The hiss is reduced at the same time becoming inaudible.

How in the World (Pleasantville, NY: Reader's Digest Association, 1990), 221.

How are compact discs (CDs) made?

The master disc for a CD is an optically flat glass disc coated with a photo resist. The resist is a chemical that is impervious to an etchant that dissolves glass. The master is placed on a turntable. The digital signal to be recorded is fed to the laser, turning the laser off and on in response to the binary on-off signal this product is called CD encoding. When the laser is on, it burns away a small amount of the resist on the disc. While the disc turns, the recording head moves across the disc, leaving a spiral track of elongated "burns" in the resist surface. After the recording is complete, the glass master is placed in the chemical etchant bath. This developing removes the glass only where the resist is burned away. The spiral track now contains a series of small pits of varying length and constant depth the master then undergoes an electroforming process in which a metal negative impression of the sound track is made. This metal negative becomes a die into which molten polycarbonate plastic is poured into. When cooled the plastic contains the positive impression of the original disc master track. It is cooled with a thin layer of aluminum and then a layer of acrylic plastic for protection. To play a recorded CD, a laser beam scans the three miles (five kilometers) of playing track and converts the "pits" and "lands" of the CD into binary codes. A photodiode converts these into a coded string of electrical impulses. In October 1982, the first CDS and CD players were marketed; they were invented by Phillips (Netherlands) Company and Sony in Japan in 1978.

Ira Flatow, *Rainbows, Curve Balls, and Other Wonders of the Natural World* (New York: Harper & Row, 1988), 217-21. *The New Book of Popular Science* (Danbury, CT: Grolier, 1988), 6:268. Neil Schlager, ed., *How Products Are Made* (Detroit: Gale Research, 1994), 1:148-52.

What is a Clarke belt?

Back in 1945, Arthur C. Clarke (b. 1917), the famous scientist and science fiction writer, predicted that an artificial satellite placed at a height of 22,248 miles (35,803 kilometers) directly above the equator would orbit the globe at the same speed with which the earth was rotating. As a result, the satellite would remain stationary with respect to any point on the earth's surface. This equatorial belt, rather like one of Saturn's rings, is affectionately known as the Clarke belt.

D.J. Stephenson, *Newnes Guide to Satellite TV* (London: Newnes, 1991), 10-11.

How does a telefax work?

Telefacsimile (also telefax or facsimile or fax) transmits graphic and textual information from one location to another through telephone lines. A transmitting machine uses either a digital or analog scanner to convert the black and white representations of the image into electrical signals that are transmitted through the telephone lines to a designated receiving machine. The receiving unit converts the transmission back to an image of the original and prints it. In its broadest definition, a facsimile terminal is simply a copier equipped to transmit and receive graphics images.

James Harry Green, *The Dow Jones-Irwin Handbook of Telecommunications* (Homewood, IL: Dow Jones-Irwin, 1986), 561-77.

Why are the letters all mixed up on the typewriter keyboard?

Although Christopher Latham Scholes did not invent the typewriter, he made it work more efficiently with his keyboard design. The standard keyboard (called QWERTY for the letter arrangement of the top letter line) as used today was established by Scholes in 1872. He rearranged the alphabetical keyboard, which was prone to having the letter bars jam, to one in which the letter arrangement made the bars hit the inked ribbon from opposite directions. The result was less jamming-whether it was from the letter arrangement or from the typist slowing down. Eventually the Remington Fire Arms Company bought the patent and mass-produced the machine in 1874. American writer Samuel Clemens (1835-1910), better known by his pen name Mark Twain, was one of the 400 customers who purchased Remington typewriters in 1874. The first 10 years of production had disappointing sales. One reason was the use of aniline-inked typewriter ribbons that would eventually fade. With the introduction in 1885 of permanent ink ribbons, the typewriter became an essential office item.

W.A. Beeching, *Century of the Typewriter* (New York: St. Martin's Press, 1974), 40. Patrick Robertson, *The Book of Firsts* (New York: Clarkson N. Potter, 1974), 193-94.

Who invented Liquid Paper?

Betty Nesmith Graham in 1951 started using a white paint to correct her typographical errors. After her coworkers began requesting bottles of the paint, Mrs. Graham started a small company to sell the paint. Over the years her small company grew to a large industry.

Ethlie Ann Vare, *Mothers of Invention* (New York: Morrow, 1988), 38-42.

What is a pixel?

A pixel (pix [for picture] element) is the smallest element on a video display screen. A screen contains thousands of pixels, each of which can be made up of one or more dots or a cluster of dots. On a simple monochrome screen, a pixel is one dot; the two colors of image and background are created when the pixel is switched either on or off. Some monochrome screen pixels can be energized to create different light intensities, to allow a range of shades from light to dark. On color screens, three dot colors are included in each pixel-red, green, and blue. The simplest screens have just one dot of each color, but more elaborate screens have pixels with clusters of each color. These more elaborate displays can show a large number of colors and intensities. On color screens, black is created by leaving all three colors off; white by all three colors on; and a range of grays by equal intensities of all the colors.

The most economical displays are monochrome, with one bit per pixel, with settings limited to on and off. High-resolution color screens, which can use a million pixels, with each color dot using four bytes of memory, would need to reserve many megabytes just to display the image.

Alan Freedman, *The Computer Glossary, 5th ed.* (New York: AMPCOM, 1991), 461.

A lot of people have heard of ENIAC, the first large electronic computer. What was MANIAC?

MANIAC (mathematical analyzer, numerator, integrator, and computer) was built at the Los Alamos Scientific Laboratory under the direction of Nicholas C. Metropolis between 1948 and 1952. It was one of several different copies of the high-speed computer built by John von Neumann (1903-1957) for the Institute for Advanced Studies (IAS). It was constructed primarily for use in the development of atomic energy applications, specifically the hydrogen bomb.

It was originated with the work on ENIAC (electronic numerical integrator and computer), the first fully operational large-scale electronic digital computer. ENIAC was built at the Moore School of Electrical Engineering at the University of Pennsylvania between 1943 and 1946. Its builders, John Prosper Eckert, Jr., and John William Mauchly (1907-1980), virtually launched the modern era of the computer with ENIAC.

James W. Cortada, *Historical Dictionary of Data Processing: Technology* (Westport, CT: Greenwood Press, 1987), 156, 258.

Is an assembly language the same thing as a machine language?

While the two terms are often used interchangeably, an assembly language is a more "user friendly" translation of a machine language. A machine language is the collection of patterns of bits recognized by a Central Processing Unit (CPU) as instructions. Each particular CPU design has its own machine language. The machine language of the CPU of a microcomputer generally includes about 75 instructions; the machine language of the CPU of a large mainframe computer may include hundreds of instructions. Each of these instructions is a pattern of one's and zero's that tells the CPU to perform a specific operation.

An assembly language is a collection of symbolic, mnemonic names for each instruction in the machine language of its CPU. Like the machine language, the assembly language is tied to a particular CPU design. Programming in assembly language requires intimate familiarity with the CPU's architecture, and assembly language programs are difficult to maintain and require extensive documentation.

The computer language C, developed in the late 1980s, is now frequently used instead of assembly language. It is a high-level programming language that can be compiled into machine languages for almost all computers, from microcomputers to mainframes, because of its functional structure.

Alan Freedman, *The Computer Glossary, 5th ed.* (New York: AMACOM, 1991), 33, 79, 354. Douglas R. Hofstadter, *Gdel, Escher, Bach: An Eternal Golden Braid* (New York: Vintage Books, 1979), 289-291. John Shore, *The Sachertorte Algorithm* (New York: Viking Penguin, 1985), 145-48.

What does *DOS* stand for?

DOS stands for disk operating system, a program that controls the computer's transfer of data to and from a hard or floppy disk. Frequently it is combined with the main operating system. The operating system was originally developed at Seattle Computer Products as SCP-DOS. When IBM decided to build a personal computer and needed an operating system, it chose the SCP-DOS after reaching an agreement with the Microsoft Corporation to produce the actual operating system. Under Microsoft, SCP-DOS became MS-DOS which IBM referred to as PC-DOS (personal computer), and which eventually was simply called DOS.

Paul Freiberger and Michale Swaine, *Fire in the Valley: The Making of the Personal Computer* (Berkeley: Osborne/McGraw-Hill, 1984), 269, 272, 276. Jerry M. Rosenberg, *Dictionary of Computers, Data Processing, and Telecommunications* (New York: John Wiley & Sons, 1984), 157.

What is the origin of the expression "Do not fold, spindle, or mutilate"?

This is the inscription on an IBM punched card. Frequently, office workers organize papers and forms by stapling or folding them together, or by impaling them on a spindle. Because Hollerith (punched) card readers scan uniform rectangular holes in a precise arrangement, any damage to the physical card makes it unusable. In the 1950s and 1960s, when punched cards became widespread, manufacturers printed a warning on each card; IBM's "Do not fold, spindle, or mutilate" was the best-known. In 1964, the student revolution at the University of California, Berkeley used the phrase as a symbol of authority and regimentation.

Scientific Quotations: The Harvest of a Quiet Eye (New York: Crane, Russak, 1977), 80.

What was the first major use for punched cards?

Punched cards were a way of programming, or giving instructions to, a machine. In 1801 Joseph Marie Jacquard (1752-1834) built a device that could do automated pattern weaving. Cards with holes were used to direct threads in the loom, creating predefined patterns in the cloth. The pattern was determined by the arrangement of holes in the cards, with wire hooks passing through the holes to grab and pull through specific threads to be woven into the cloth.

By the 1880s Herman Hollerith (1860-1929) was using the idea of punched cards to give machines instructions. Hollerith was issued a patent (no. 395,783) for his "apparatus for compiling statistics" on January 8, 1889. He built a punched card tabulator that processed the data gathered for the 1890 United States Census in six weeks at three times the speed of previous compilations. Metal pins in the machine's reader passed through holes punched in cards the size of dollar bills, momentarily closing electric circuits. The resulting pulses advanced counters assigned to details such as income and family size. A sorter could also be programmed to pigeonhole cards according to pattern of holes, an important aid in analyzing census statistics. Later, Hollerith founded Tabulating Machines Co., which in 1924 became IBM. When IBM adopted the 80-column punched card (measuring 7 and 3/8 by 3 and 1/4 inches, or 18.7 by 8.25 centimeters, and .007 inches, or .018 centimeters, thick), the de facto industry standard was set, which has endured for decades.

James W. Cortada, *Historical Dictionary of Data Processing: Technology* (Westport, CT: Greenwood Press, 1987), 308. John Graham, *Facts On File Dictionary of Telecommunications, rev. ed.* (New York: Facts On File, 1991), 127. *Understanding Computers: Illustrated Chronology and Index* (New York: Time-Life Books, 1989), 9, 11.

Who invented the computer mouse?

A computer "mouse" is a hand-held input device that, when rolled across a flat surface, causes a cursor to move in a corresponding way on a display screen. A prototype mouse was part of an input console demonstrated by Douglas C. Englehart in 1968 at the Fall Joint Computer Conference in San Francisco. Popularized in 1984 by the Macintosh from Apple Computer, the mouse was the result of 15 years devoted to exploring ways to make communicating with computers simpler and more flexible.

The physical appearance of the small four-sided box with the dangling tail-like wire suggested the informal name of "mouse," which quickly superseded its now forgotten formal name.

Compute August 1991. *Understanding Computers: Illustrated Chronology and Index* (New York: Time-Life Books, 1989), 62, 73.

What is a hacker?

A hacker is a skilled computer user. The term originally denoted a skilled programmer, particularly one skilled in machine code and with a good knowledge of the machine and its operating system. The name arose from the fact that a good programmer could always hack an unsatisfactory system around until it worked.

The term later came to denote a user whose main interest is in defeating password systems. The term has thus acquired a pejorative sense, with the meaning of one who deliberately and sometimes criminally interferes with data available through telephone lines. The activities of such hackers have led to considerable efforts to tighten security of transmitted data.

Ian R. Sinclair, *The HarperCollins Dictionary of Computer Terms* (New York: Harper Perennial), 105.

What is e-mail?

Electronic mail, also known as e-mail, uses communication facilities to transmit messages. Many systems use computers as transmitting and receiving interfaces, but fax communication is also a form of e-mail. A user can send a message to a single recipient, or to many. Different systems offer different options for sending, receiving, manipulating text, and addressing. For example a message can be "registered," so that the sender is notified when the recipient looks at the message (though there is no way to tell if the recipient has actually read the message). Many systems allow messages to be forwarded. Usually messages are stored in a simulated "mailbox" in the network server or host computer; some systems announce incoming mail if the recipient is logged onto the system. An organization (such as a corporation, university, or professional organization) can provide electronic mail facilities; there are also national and international networks. In order to use e-mail, both sender and receiver must have accounts on the same system or on systems connected by a network.

Don Cassel, *Understanding Computers* (Englewood Cliffs, NJ: Prentice-Hall, 1990), 147. Alan Freedman, *The Computer Glossary, 5th ed.* (New York: AMACOM, 1991), 217. Dennis Longley and Michael Shain, *Van Nostrand Reinhold Dictionary of Information Technology, 3d ed.* (New York: Van Nostrand Reinhold, 1989), 188.

How is a hard disk different from a floppy disk?

Both types of disk use a magnetic recording surface to record, access, and erase data, in much the same way as magnetic tape records, plays, and erases sound or images. A read/write head, suspended over a spinning disk, is directed by the Central Processing Unit (CPU) to the sector where the requested data is stored, or where the data is to be recorded. A hard disk uses rigid aluminum disks coated with iron oxide for data storage. It has much greater storage capacity than several floppy disks (from 10 to hundreds of megabytes). While most hard disks used in microcomputers are "fixed" (built into the computer), some are removable. Minicomputer and mainframe hard disks include both fixed and removable (in modules called disk packs or disk cartridges). A floppy disk, also called a diskette, is made of plastic film covered with a magnetic coating, which is enclosed in a nonremovable plastic protective envelope. Floppy disks vary in storage capacity from 100 thousand bytes to more than 2 megabytes. Floppy disks are generally used in minicomputers and microcomputers.

In addition to storing more data, a hard disk can provide much faster access to storage than a floppy disk. A hard disk rotates from 2,400 to 3,600 Revolutions Per Minute (rpm) and is constantly spinning (except in laptops, which conserve battery life by spinning the hard disk only when in use). An ultra-fast hard disk has a separate read/write head over each track on the disk, so that no time is lost in positioning the head over the desired track; accessing the desired sector takes only milliseconds, the time it takes for the disk to spin to the sector. A floppy disk does not spin until a data transfer is requested, and the rotation speed is only about 300 rpm.

Douglas Downing and Michael Covington, *Dictionary of Computer Terms, 2d ed.* (Hauppauge, NY: Barron, 1989), 131, 148. Alan Freedman, *The Computer Glossary, 5th ed.* (New York: AMACOM, 1991), 245-46, 275, 359-61. Nigel J. Hopkins, John W. Mayne, and John R. Hudson, *The Numbers You Need* (Detroit: Gale Research, 1992), 286-87.

When was the first United States satellite launched?

Explorer 1, launched January 31, 1958, by the U.S. Army was the first United States satellite launched into orbit. This 31-pound (14.06-kilogram) satellite carried instrumentation that led to the discovery of the earth's radiation belts, which would be named after University of Iowa scientist James A. Van Allen. It was launched four months after the world's first satellite, the Soviet Union's *Sputnik 1*. On October 3, 1957, the Soviet Union placed the large, 184-pound (83.5-kilogram) satellite into low earth orbit. It carried instrumentation to study the density and temperature of the upper atmosphere.

Wernher von Braun and Frederick I. Ordway III, *Space Travel: A History* (New York: Harper & Row, 1985), 170-73. Anthony R. Curtis, *Space Almanac* (Woodsboro, MD: ARCsoft, 1990), 13.

What is the Emergency Broadcast System?

The forerunner of the Emergency Broadcast System, Conelrad (Control of Electromagnetic Radiation) originated in the early 1950s. It was to limit broadcasting to only one station in an area and confine all broadcasting in the United States to two frequencies if the country was under attack. In 1964 it was replaced by the Emergency Broadcast System (EBS). The EBS is composed of AM, FM, and TV broadcast stations, low-power TV stations, and non-government industry entities operating on a voluntary, organized basis during emergencies at national, state, or local levels.

National Archives and Records Administration, Office of the Federal Register, *Code of Federal Regulations* (Washington, DC: Government Printing Office, 1993), 236-37. Sybil P. Parker, *McGraw-Hill Dictionary of Scientific and Technical Terms, 4th ed.* (New York: McGraw-Hill, 1989), s.v. "Conelrad." "Debris Adrift in Space ...Conelrad Warning System...Federal Aid to Rebuild Cities," *U.S. News & World Report* 24 November 1975.

What are chops?

Seals, such as those used on letters and documents, are call "chops" by the Chinese. One of the earliest known artifacts, the seal-a human being's way to inform the rest of the world "this is mine"-was invented over five thousand years ago and spans cultures.

Sarah Drummond, "Antiques: Seals," *Architectural Digest* October 1987.

Is there an information number to access toll-free numbers?

AT&T can provide information on toll-free numbers when called at 1-800-555-1212.

AT&T Toll-Free 800 Directory: Business Buyer's Guide (Bridgewater, NJ: AT&T, 1994), A4.

How does one get rid of the silverfish insect that feeds on books?

Since the silverfish insect likes moisture, make sure the area around the books is dry. Boric acid powder spread lightly behind and around the books will kill silverfish (and cockroaches). It may take several weeks for the boric acid to work. Insecticides are not recommended because they can damage books. A note of caution: It is not recommended placing boric acid where children or domestic animals can reach or walk.

Jane Greenfield, *The Care of Fine Books* (New York: Nick Lyons Books, 1988), 66-67.

When were adhesive postage stamps first used?

While Scotland claims to be the birthplace of adhesive postage stamps, they were probably first issued in Paris on April 8, 1653, by the Petite Poste, a short-lived postal service organized by Renouard de Villayer. Scotland claims the idea belonged to James Chalmers (1782-1853), a Dundee bookseller actively involved in postal reform, or to Rowland Hill (1795-1879), another postal reformer, who in 1837 proposed ". . . using a bit of paper . . . covered at the back with a glutinous wash . . . ." It was Rowland Hill who suggested the design of the first widely used adhesive stamp, the Penny Black of Great Britain, which bore a profile of Queen Victoria (1819-1901). This stamp went on sale on May 1, 1840.

James Mackay, *The Guinness Book of Stamps: Facts & Feats* (New York: Canopy Books, 1992), 72-74.

Energy and Related Industries

Which nations have the largest oil reserves?

According to the Energy Information Administration, U.S. Department of Energy, as of December 31, 1992, the ten countries with the largest crude oil reserves in barrels are as follows: Saudi Arabia, with 261.0 billion; the former Soviet Union, 186.9 billion; Iraq, 99.8 billion; Kuwait, 94.8 billion; United Arab Emirates, 65.1 billion; Venezuela, 63.3 billion; Iran, 61.3 billion; Mexico, 51.2 billion; Libya, 38.2 billion; and China, 29.6 billion. The United States had the eleventh largest reserves, with 23.7 billion barrels.

Robert Famighetti, ed., *The World Almanac and the Book of Facts 1995* (Mahwah, NJ: World Almanac, 1995), 167.

What are gasoline prices like in Europe?

Typically, gasoline prices are far higher in Europe than in North America. A report published in *The New York Times* in 1993 showed that prices ranged from a high in the Netherlands for premium leaded of $4.11/gallon to a low in Luxembourg of $2.88/gallon. Prices for regular unleaded ranged from a high in the Netherlands of $3.77/gallon to a low in Luxembourg of $2.45/gallon.

New York Times 9 May 1993.

What is the difference between passive solar energy systems and active solar energy systems?

Passive solar energy systems use the architectural design, the natural materials or absorptive structures of the building as an energy saving system. The building itself serves as a solar collector and storage device. An example would be thick-walled stone and adobe dwellings that slowly collect heat during the day and gradually release it at night. Passive systems require little or no investment of external equipment.

Active solar energy systems require a separate collector, a storage device, and controls linked to pumps or fans that draw heat from storage when it is available. Active solar systems generally pump a heat-absorbing fluid medium (air, water, or an antifreeze solution) through a collector. Collectors, such as insulated water tanks, vary in size, depending on the number of sunless days in a locale. Another heat storage system uses eutectic (phase-changing) chemicals to store a large amount of energy in a small volume.

William P. Cunningham and Barbara Woodhouse Saigo, *Environmental Science: A Global Concern* (Dubuque, IA: Wm. C. Brown, 1990), 377.

What is a meltdown?

A meltdown is a type of accident in a nuclear reactor in which the fuel core melts, resulting in the release of dangerous amounts of radiation. In most cases the large containment structure that houses a reactor would prevent the radioactivity from escaping. However, there is a small possibility that the molten core could become hot enough to burn through the floor of the containment structure and go deep into the earth. Nuclear engineers call this type of situation the "China Syndrome." The phrase derives from a discussion on the theoretical problems of a nuclear reactor if it were to undergo a meltdown, a scientist commented that the molten core could bore a hole through the earth, coming out-if one happened to be standing in America-in China. Ever since then, this scenario has been nicknamed the "China Syndrome." Although the scientist was grossly exaggerating, some took him seriously. In fact the core would only bore a hole about 30 feet into the earth, but this small distance would have grave repercussions. All reactors are equipped with emergency systems to prevent such an accident from occurring.

Ian Blair, *Taming the Atom* (Bristol, England: Adam Hilger, 1983), 170-71. *World Book Encyclopedia* (Chicago: World Book, 1990), 14:593.

Where is the oldest operational nuclear power plant in the United States?

The Yankee Plant at Rowe, Massachusetts, which was constructed in 1960, is the oldest United States power plant. The working life of a nuclear power plant is approximately 40 years, which is about the same as that of other types of power stations.

Nuclear News February 1992. Ian Blair, *Taming the Atom* (Bristol, England: Adam Hilger, 1983), 78.

What has been the effect of the Chernobyl accident on the Republic of Belarus?

Radioactive fallout from the nuclear plant accident at Chernobyl in April 1986 contained the isotopes cesium 137 and strontium 90 which contaminated an enormous geographical area including Belarus (then Byelorussia), Latvia, Lithuania, the central portion of the then Soviet Union, the Scandinavian countries, the Ukraine (where Chernobyl is located), Poland, Austria, Czechoslovakia, Germany, Switzerland, northern Italy, eastern France, Romania, Bulgaria, Greece, Yugoslavia, the Netherlands, and the United Kingdom. Roughly five percent of the reactor fuel or seven tons of fuel containing 50 to 100 million curies were released. The fallout, extremely uneven because of the shifting wind patterns, extended 1,200 to 1,300 miles (1,930 to 2,090 kilometers) from the point of the accident. However, Belarus received extensive contamination from the winds blowing in a northwesterly direction and still suffers the aftereffects of the fallout. Most animals had to be killed and crops destroyed to prevent their consumption by humans. More than two million people lived in the contaminated area in which detoxification, including the removal of contaminated top soil, has progressed slowly. The radioactive cesium 137 has a halflife of 30 years and strontium 90 has a halflife of 28 years. In southern Belarus, 150,000 people in 1990 still had not been evacuated from land considered uninhabitable because of the high residual radiation levels. Another 1.2 million people live on land considered unsafe. Almost a decade later in some areas, food still cannot be grown and must be imported. Estimates of the human effects of this fallout range from 28,000 to 100,000 deaths from cancer and genetic defects within the next 50 years.

Stephen K. Batalden and Sandra L. Batalden, *The Newly Independent States of Eurasia: Handbook of Former Soviet Republics* (Phoenix, AZ: Oryx, 1993), 49-50. William P. Cunningham and Barbara Woodhouse Saigo, *Environmental Science: A Global Concern* (Dubuque, IA: Wm. C. Brown Publishers, 1990), 354-55. E. Willard Miller, *Environmental Hazards: Air Pollution* (Santa Barbara, CA: ABC_CLIO, 1989), 67-68. *Oxford Illustrated Encyclopedia of Invention and Technology* (Oxford, England: Oxford University Press, 1992), 72.

What is a Franklin stove?

The Franklin stove, invented by Benjamin Franklin (1706-1790) in 1740, is a free-standing, enclosed unit usually made from cast iron. Being enclosed with limited air flow gives the stove controllable combustion and greater efficiency. Today, stoves of this type are often called "Franklin stoves."

Franklin's stove was built to heat rooms, and its most important feature was the flue, which doubled back and formed a sort of radiator, around which room air circulated. Since it was free-standing, there was more surface to radiate the heat, and none of its heat was wasted by being held in the fireplace's brickwork.

William Busha and Stephen Morris, *The Book of Heat* (Brattleboro, VT: Stephen Greene Press, 1982), 160-61. Mitchell Wilson, *American Science and Invention* (New York: Simon and Schuster, 1954), 22. Bridget Travers, ed., *World of Invention* (Detroit, MI: Gale Research, 1994), 596.

How do three-way light bulbs work?

Three-way light bulbs have two filaments, which are used separately for two of the light levels and are combined for the third. The highest wattage will always be the sum of the first two wattages (e.g., a 50/100/150 watt three-way bulb). These bulbs only work in specially designed sockets.

The principle of the light bulb (more correctly known as the incandescent filament lamp) is that if sufficient electric current can be passed through a conducting filament, the molecules of the filament become excited, the filament gets hot and eventually glows. Discovering the right substance to use for the filament enabled American inventor Thomas Alva Edison (1847-1931) to produce the first practical electric light. For 14 months he tested over 1200 filaments until on October 31, 1879, he discovered that charred cotton sewing thread was the answer. Edison obtained patent no. 223,898 for the light bulb. In England, prior to Edison's work, Joseph Wilson Swan (1824-1914) had designed a thin carbon filament in a vacuum tube in 1878, but Swan did not get his invention into production until 1881. Filaments today are made from tungsten, which resists melting below 6,170 degrees Fahrenheit (3,410 degrees Celsius).

Donald Clarke, *The Encyclopedia of How It Works* (New York: A & W Publishers, 1977), 136. Edward De Bono, *Eureka!* (New York: Holt, Rinehart and Winston, 1974), 147. Harry Harris, *Good Old Fashioned Yankee Ingenuity* (Chelsea, MI: Scarborough House, 1990), 172-72. Neil Schlager, ed., *How Products Are Made* (Detroit: Gale Research, 1994), 256-60.

What is a Leyden jar?

A Leyden jar, the earliest form of capacitor, is a device for storing an electrical charge. First described in 1745 by E. Georg van Kleist (c.1700-1748), it was also used by Pieter van Musschenbroek (1692-1761), a professor of physics at the University of Leyden. The device came to be known as a Leyden jar and was the first container that could store large amounts of electric charge. The jar contained an inner wire electrode that was in contact with water, mercury, or wire. The outer electrode was a human hand holding the jar. An improved version coated the jar inside and outside with separate metal foils with the inner foil connected to a conducting rod, terminating in a conducting sphere. This eliminated the need for the liquid electrolyte. In use, the jar was normally charged from an electrostatic generator. The Leyden jar is still used for classroom demonstrations of static electricity.

Encyclopedia Americana (Danbury, CT: Grolier, 1990), 17:280. *New Encyclopaedia Brittanica, 15th ed.* (Chicago: Encyclopaedia Brittanica, 1990), 18:189.

How much energy is saved by recycling one aluminum can?

Some sources indicate that one recycled aluminum can saves as much energy as it takes to run a television set for four hours or the energy equivalent of 1/2 gallon (1.9 liters) of gasoline.

Heloise: Hints for a Healthy Planet (New York: Perigee, 1990), 56.

How much money can be saved by lowering the setting on a home furnace thermostat?

Tests have shown that a 5 degree Farenheit reduction in the home thermostat setting for approximately eight hours will save up to 10 percent in fuel costs.

Robert L. Dalley, *Are You Burning Money?* (New York: Reston, 1982), 121.

What is the advantage of switching from incandescent to fluorescent light bulbs?

One 18-watt fluorescent bulb provides the light of a 75-watt incandescent bulb and lasts ten times as long. Even though the purchase price is higher, over its useful life, an 18-watt fluorescent light bulb saves 80 pounds of coal used to produce electricity. This translates into 250 fewer pounds of carbon dioxide released into the earth's atmosphere.

Diane MacEachern, *Save Our Planet* (New York: Dell, 1990), 34.

Is it more economical to run an automobile with its windows open rather than using its air conditioner?

At speeds greater than 40 miles (64.4 kilometers) per hour, less fuel is used in driving an automobile with the air conditioner on and the windows up than with the windows rolled down. This is due to the air drag effect-the resistance that a vehicle encounters as it moves through a fluid medium, such as air. In automobiles, the amount of engine power required to overcome this drag force increases with the cube of the vehicle's speed-twice the speed requires eight times the power. For example, it takes 5 horsepower for the engine to overcome the air resistance at 40 miles (64.4 kilometers) per hour; but at 60 miles (96.5 kilometers) per hour, it takes 18 horsepower; at 80 miles (128 kilometers) per hour, it takes 42 horsepower. Improved aerodynamics, in which the drag coefficient (measure of air drag effect) is reduced, significantly increases fuel efficiency. The average automobile in 1990 has a drag coefficient of about 0.4. In the early 1960s it was 0.5, on the average, to 0.47 in the 1970s. The lowest maximum level possible for wheeled vehicles is 0.15.

Richard P. Brennan, *Levitating Trains and Kamikaze Genes* (New York: Harper Perennial, 1990), 206-8. Jack Doo, *The Ultimate Owner's Manual* (Alhambra, CA: Edmund, 1991), 61.

What does the term *cooling degree day* mean?

It is a unit for estimating the energy needed for cooling a building. One unit is given for each degree Fahrenheit above the daily mean temperature when the mean temperature exceeds 75 degrees Fahrenheit.

The McGraw-Hill Dictionary of Scientific and Technical Terms 4th ed. (New York: McGraw-Hill, 1989), 431.

How much does a barrel of oil weigh?

A barrel of oil weighs about 306 pounds (139 kilograms).

Norman J. Hyne, *Dictionary of Petroleum Exploration, Drilling & Production* (Tulsa, OK: Penn Well, 1991), 33.

How much wood is in a cord?

A cord of wood is a pile of logs four feet (1.2 meters) wide and four feet (1.2 meters) high and eight feet (2.4 meters) long. It may contain from 77 to 96 cubic feet of wood. The larger the unsplit logs the larger the gaps, with fewer cubic feet of wood actually in the cord.

Pennsylvania Forests November-December, 1986. Charles Self, *Wood Heating Handbook* (Blue Ridge Summit, PA: TAB, 1977), 118.

When was the first oil well in the United States drilled?

The Drake well at Titusville, Pennsylvania, was completed on August 28, 1859 (some sources list the date as August 27). The driller, William "Uncle Billy" Smith, went down 69.5 feet (21.18 meters) to find oil for Edwin L. Drake (1819-1880), the well's operator. Within 15 years, Pennsylvania oil field production reached over 10 million 360-pound (163.3-kilograms) barrels a year.

Norman J. Hyne, *Dictionary of Petroleum Exploration, Drilling & Production* (Tulsa, OK: Penn Well, 1991), 585. Joseph N. Kane, *Famous First Facts, 4th ed.,* (New York: Wilson, 1981), 439. Ian McNeil, *An Encyclopedia of the History of Technology* (London: Routledge, 1990), 211.

When was offshore drilling for oil first done?

The first successful offshore oil well was built off the coast at Summerland, Santa Barbara County, California, in 1896.

Joseph N. Kane, *Famous First Facts, 4th ed.* (New York: Wilson, 1981), 438.

How much space does a recycled ton of paper save in a landfill?

Each ton of recycled paper saves more than three cubic yards of landfill space.

50 Simple Things You Can Do to Save the Earth (Berkeley, CA: Earth Works Press, 1989), 70.

How much wood is used to make a ton of paper?

In the United States, the small diameter wood bolts and pulpwood are mainly used for the manufacture of paper. It is usually measured by the cord or by weight. Although the fiber used in making paper is overwhelmingly wood fiber, a large percentage of other ingredients is needed. One ton of a typical paper requires two cords of wood, but also requires 55,000 gallons of water, 102 pounds of sulfur, 350 pounds of lime, 289 pounds of clay, 1.2 tons of coal, 112 kilowatt hours of power, 20 pounds of dye and pigments, and 108 pounds of starch, as well as other ingredients.

John G. Haygreen, *Forest Products and Wood Science, 2d ed.* (Ames: Iowa State University Press, 1989), 410-12.

What caused the explosion at the Union Carbide Pesticide Plant in Bhopal, India?

The explosion at the Union Carbide Pesticide Plant in Bhopal, India on December 3, 1984, is considered the worst industrial accident in history. Poorly maintained equipment, indifferent management, and faulty judgement all contributed to the disaster. The plant manufactured the pesticide Sevin, consisting of a mix of carbon tetrachloride, methylisocyanate (MIC), and alpha-naphthol. One of the 15,00-gallon MIC tanks was faulty; not only did it have a leak, but the refrigeration unit designed to keep the MIC cool and thus nonreactive was not turned on. The night of Sunday, December 2, a supervisor told a worker to clean a section of pipe that filtered crude MIC before it flowed into the storage tanks. The worker connected a hose to the pipe, allowing water to flow into the pipe, out the pipe drains, and onto the floor to the floor drain. Although the workers and supervisor knew that water reacts violently with MIC and that valves were leaking in both the storage tank and the pipe being washed, no one stopped the operation, and water flowed for three hours. By 11:30 that night, workers knew MIC was leaking because their eyes were watering and their noses detected the smell. Because minor leakages were a common occurrence at the plant, workers and supervisors did not become greatly alarmed. Around 12:45 the morning of December 3, the pressure gauge on the MIC tank indicated 55 pounds per square inch, only 15 points from the top of the scale. At last, a supervisor ordered all the water in the plant turned off, but by then it was too late. The water reacted with the MIC, and the leak burst open. The lethal gas spewed into the atmosphere, and chaos ensued. The explosion and its aftermath claimed 2,000 lives and caused 200,00 injuries.

Lee Davis, *Man-Made Catastrophes: From the Burning of Rome to the Lockerbie Crash* (New York: Facts on File, 1993), 253-57.

How long is the Trans-Alaska Pipeline and what does it connect?

The 800 mile (1,300 kilometers) Trans-Alaska Pipeline connects Prudhoe Bay on the Arctic Ocean with the ice-free port of Valdez on the Gulf of Alaska. The Alaskan pipeline project received approval in 1973 and was completed in 1977 at a cost of $8 billion.

Academic American Encyclopedia (Danbury, CT: Grolier, 1988), s.v. "Trans-Alaska Pipline."

How much did oil prices rise during the 1970s?

Oil prices skyrocketed by an average of 94.7 percent in 1979, from $12.84 a barrel at the beginning of the year to $25 a barrel at the end of 1979. Ten years earlier, oil had been priced at just two dollars a barrel.

Time 7 January 1980.

Why do newer electric power receptacles have a third hole?

In 1962 the third hole was added for grounding purposes. Previously, electrical plugs with two prongs could give the user a shock if a short circuit in the wiring or in the electrical device developed. Since 1962, "double-insulated" pronged plugs were developed (with fatter ends) that do not require a third prong for shock protection. But these new double-insulated prongs do require new wide-slotted receptacles.

Nell DuVall, *Domestic Technology* (Boston: G. K. Hall, 1988). 255. David Feldman, *Do Penguins Have Knees?* (New York: Harper Perennial, 1991), 191. *Technology and Culture* July 1986.

What was the Rasmussen report?

Professor Rasmussen of the Massachusetts Institute of Technology (MIT) conducted a study of nuclear reactor safety for the United States Atomic Energy Commission. The study cost four million dollars and took three years to complete. It concluded that the odds against a worst-case accident occurring were astronomically large-ten million to one. The worse case accident projected about three thousand early deaths and 14 billion dollars in property damage due to contamination. Cancers occurring later due to the event might number 1,500 per year. The study concluded that the safety features engineered into a plant are very likely to prevent serious consequences from a meltdown. Other groups criticized the Rasmussen report and in particular declared that the estimates of risk were too low. After the Chernobyl disaster in 1986, some scientists estimated that a major nuclear accident might in fact happen every decade.

Geoffrey Lean et al., *WWF Atlas of the Environment* (New York: Prentice-Hall, 1990), 119. Penelope ReVelle, *The Environment* (Boston: Willard Grant Press, 1991), 317-18.

What caused the Chernobyl accident?

The nuclear accident at the Chernobyl nuclear power plant in the Ukraine near the border with Byelorussia (now known as Belarus) on April 26, 1986, was the result of gross human error. On Friday, April 25, at 1:00 a.m., one of the four 1,000-megawatt reactors was reduced in power in preparation for an unauthorized experiment. The operators conducting the test shut off all of the emergency safety systems, in violation of regulations, in order to learn more about the plant's operation. During the process, an operator received a computer printout indicating the reactor was in great danger of overheating unless it was immediately shut down, but he dismissed it. Other warning signs appeared during the testing period, but the operators ignored them. Hydrogen gas formed from steam created by the water coolant of the overheated reactor caused one reactor to explode early on Saturday morning, a little more than 24 hours after the test began. A second explosion occurred from the hydrogen gas igniting from the heat generated during the meltdown of the reactor. The initial accident claimed 31 lives and more than 100,000 people were evacuated from the plant's vicinity. The long-term effects have yet to be determined.

Lee Davis, *Man-Made Catastrophes: From the Burning of Rome to the Lockerbie Crash* (New York: Facts On File, 1993), 263-67. Neil Schlager, ed., *When Technology Fails: Significant Disasters, Accidents, and Failures of the Twentieth Century* (Detroit: Gale Research, 1994), 529-36.

What actually happened at Three Mile Island?

The Three Mile Island nuclear power plant in Pennsylvania experienced a partial meltdown of its reactor core and radiation leakage. On March 28, 1979, just after 4:00 a.m., a water pump in the secondary cooling system of the Unit 2 pressurized water reactor failed. A relief valve jammed open, flooding the containment vessel with radioactive water. A backup system for pumping water was down for maintenance. Temperatures inside the reactor core rose, fuel rods ruptured, and a partial (52%) meltdown occurred, because the radioactive uranium core was almost entirely uncovered by coolant for 40 minutes. The thick steel-reinforced containment building prevented nearly all the radiation from escaping-the amount of radiation released into the atmosphere was one-millionth of that at Chernobyl. However, if the coolant had not been replaced, the molten fuel would have penetrated the reactor containment vessel, where it would have come into contact with the water, causing a steam explosion, breaching the reactor dome, and leading to radioactive contamination of the area similar to the Chernobyl accident.

Richard P. Brennan, *Dictionary of Scientific Literacy* (New York: John Wiley & Sons, 1992), 297-98. John May, *The Greenpeace Book of the Nuclear Age* (New York: Pantheon, 1989), 215-28.

How is the proper size of a room air conditioner determined?

In order to determine the proper size of window air conditioner needed for a room, multiply the square footage of the room or rooms to be cooled by 27. This figure will be the size air conditioner needed in British thermal units (BTU). BTU is a common energy measurement that represents the energy required to raise the temperature of one pound of water by one degree Fahrenheit.

P. H. Collin, *Dictionary of Ecology and the Environment* (Teddington, England: Peter Collin Publishing, 1988), 22. *Rodale's Complete Home Products Manual* (Emmaus, PA: Rodale Press, 1989), 8.

What inventions are credited to Benjamin Thompson, Count Rumford?

Benjamin Thompson (1753-1814), a physicist interested in caloric (heat) theory, invented a kitchen stove in which the fire was enclosed within the range to conserve heat. In the process, he invented the fireplace damper and smoke shelf, and redesigned the fireplace so that smoke went up the chimney rather than into the room. Known for his studies on heat and friction, he argued that heat is a form of motion. He developed a calorimeter and a photometer, a double boiler and a drip coffeepot, as well as a device to measure the power of gunpowder, and devised improvements in lighting. Thompson, a Loyalist born in Massachusetts, became a permanent exile after the American Revolutionary War. The Elector of Bavaria made Thompson a count in 1790 in gratitude for introducing Watt's steam engine, the potato, etc., to Bavaria.

Isaac Asimov, *Asimov's Biographical Encyclopedia of Science and Technology, 2d ed.* (Garden City, NY: Doubleday, 1982), 242-44. *The Biographical Dictionary of Scientists: Physicists* (New York: Peter Bedrick Books, 1984), 139-40. Martin Elkort, *The Secret Life of Food* (Los Angeles: Jeremy P. Tarcher, 1991), 164-66.

How did the electrical term volt originate?

The unit of voltage is the volt, named after Alessandro Volta (1745-1827), the Italian scientist who built the first battery. Voltage measures the force with which electrical charges are pushed through a material. Some common voltages are 1.5 volts for a flashlight battery; 12 volts for a car battery; 115 volts for ordinary household receptacles; and 230 volts for a heavy-duty household receptacle.

James Trefil, *1001 Things Everyone Should Know About Science* (New York: Doubleday, 1992), 134.

How much energy is saved by raising the setting for a house air conditioner?

For every one degree Farenheit the inside temperature is increased the energy needed for air conditioning is reduced by 3 percent. If all consumers raised the settings on their air conditioners by six degrees Farenheit, for example, 190 thousand barrels of oil could be saved each day.

50 Simple Things You Can Do to Save the Earth (Berkeley: Earth Works Press, 1989), 30. John Luetzelschwab, *Household Energy Use & Conservation* (Chicago: Nelson Hall, 1980), 168.

How much gasoline do underinflated tires waste?

Underinflated tires waste as much as one gallon out of every 20 gallons of gasoline consumed by an automobile.

Reader's Digest Consumer Advisor (Pleasantville, NY: Reader's Digest Association, 1989), 144.

When should a fluorescent light be turned off to save energy?

Fluorescent lights use much electric current getting started, and frequent switching the light on and off will shorten the lamp's life and efficiency. It is energy-efficient to turn off a fluorescent light only if it will not be used again within an hour or more.

A.J. Hand, *Home Energy How-To* (New York: Harper & Row, 1977), 2.

How is a heating degree day defined?

Early this century engineers developed the concept of heating degree days as a useful index of heating fuel requirements. They found that when the daily mean temperature is lower than 65 degrees Fahrenheit, most buildings require heat to maintain a 70 degrees Fahrenheit temperature. Each degree of mean temperature below 65 degrees Fahrenheit is counted as "one heating degree day." For every additional heating degree day, more fuel is needed to maintain a 70 degrees Fahrenheit indoor temperature. For example, a day with a mean temperature of 35 degrees Fahrenheit would be rated as 30 heating degree days and would require twice as much fuel as a day with a mean temperature of 50 degrees Fahrenheit (15 heating degree days). The heating degree concept has become a valuable tool for fuel companies for evaluation of fuel use rates and efficient scheduling of deliveries. Detailed daily, monthly, and seasonal totals are routinely computed for the stations of the National Weather Service.

Frank E. Bair, *The Weather Almanac, 6th ed.* (Detroit: Gale Research, 1992), 148.

What is a reformulated gasoline?

Oil companies are being required to offer new gasolines that burn more cleanly and have less impact on the environment. Typically, reformulated gasolines contain lower concentrations of benzene, aromatics, and olefins; less sulfur; a lower Reid Vapor Pressure (RVP); and some percentage of an oxygenate (non-aromatic component) such as Methyl Tertiary Butyl Ether (MTBE). MTBE is a high-octane gasoline blending components produced by the reaction of isobutylene and methanol.

Department of Energy, Energy Information Administration *The Motor Gasoline Industry: Past, Present, and Future* (Washington, DC: Government Printing Office, 1991), 37-38. *Road & Track* August 1991.

How is gasohol made?

Gasohol, a mixture of 90 percent unleaded gasoline and 10 percent ethyl alcohol (ethanol), has gained some acceptance as a fuel for motor vehicles. It is comparable in performance to 100 percent unleaded gasoline with the added benefit of superior antiknock properties (no premature fuel ignition). No engine modifications are needed for the use of gasohol.

Since corn is the most abundant United States grain crop, it is predominately used in producing ethanol. However, the fuel can be made from other organic raw materials, such as oats, barley, wheat, milo, sugar beets, or sugar cane. Potatoes, and cassava (a starchy plant) and cellulose (if broken up into fermentable sugars) are possible other sources. The corn starch is processed through grinding and cooking. The process requires the conversion of a starch into a sugar, which in turn is converted into alcohol by reaction with yeast. The alcohol is distilled and any water is removed until it is 200 proof (100 percent alcohol).

One acre of corn yields 250 gallons (946 liters) of ethanol; an acre of sugar beets yields 350 gallons (1,325 liters), while an acre of sugar can produce 630 gallons (2,385 liters). In the future motor fuel could conceivably be produced almost exclusively from garbage, but currently its conversion remains an expensive process.

V. Daniel Hunt, *The Gasohol Handbook* (New York: Industrial Press, 1981), 1, 4. John W. Lincoln, *Driving Without Gas* (Pownal, VT: Garden Way, 1980), 7. Caroline Sutton, and Duncan M. Anderson, *How Do They Do That?* (New York: Quill, 1982), 210-11.

What is cogeneration?

Cogeneration is an energy production process involving the simultaneous generation of thermal (steam or hot water) and electric energy by using a single primary heat source. By producing two kinds of useful fuels in the same facility the net energy yield from the primary fuel increases from 30-35 percent to 80-90 percent.

Oxford Illustrated Encyclopedia of Invention and Technology (Oxford: Oxford University Press, 1992), 81.

How many trees are saved by recycling paper?

One ton (907 kilograms) of recycled waste paper spares 17 trees.

Philip Nobile, *Complete Ecology Fact Book* (New York: Doubleday, 1972), 379.

Manufacturing and Mining

Did Christopher Columbus discover the cigar?

The explorer Christopher Columbus (1451-1506) and his crew were the first Europeans to discover the cigar when in 1492 they observed New World Indians smoking tobacco rolled in leaves. The Mayan Indian word for smoking was "sik'ar."

Jane Polley, ed., *Stories Behind Everyday Things* (Pleasantville, NY: Reader's Digest Association, 1980), 69.

Is it possible to build a concrete canoe that floats?

In 1985, engineering students from several colleges held a canoe race between concrete canoes. Teams from the United States Military Academy, Hudson Valley Community College, City College of New York, the New Jersey Institute of Technology, Union College, Nassau Community College, and Wentworth College constructed canoes designed to prove that concrete can float. To create the canoes, students designed a plywood mold resembling a standard canoe. A lining of wire fabric was placed in the mold and a thin layer of concrete was applied. Successive layers of concrete were then added for thickness. In order to increase buoyancy, lightweight substances known as aggregates were added to the concrete. Floatation materials such as styrofoam were also placed on the canoes.

New York Times 22 October 1985.

What is Kirlian photography?

Kirlian photography, sometimes called electrography or electrographic photography, is a technique using high-frequency, high-voltage, low-amp electricity to produce an image. In the photographs, objects appear surrounded by multicolored, glowing auras or biofields.

The technique, known since the late 1800s, is named after Semyon Kirlian, a Russian inventor-electrician who experimented with this photography in the early 1940s. Kirlian photographed his own hand for his first experiment and observed a strange glow surrounding the fingertips. Kirlian and his wife Valentina experimented with photographing live and inanimate objects. Their work was noted by the West in the 1960s.

Despite the lack of proof of any paranormal phenomena, some researchers claim the photographs are evidence of the existence of psychic energy. Others contend it reveals the etheric body. Critics argue it is only a discharge of electricity.

Rosemary Ellen Guiley, *Harper's Encyclopedia of Mystical and Paranormal Experience* (New York: HarperCollins, 1991), s.v. "Kirlian photography."

What is cordovan leather?

Cordovan is a very durable, nonporous leather made from horse hide. Used for the production of fine boots and shoes, the leather is usually finished in black or reddish-brown glossy finishes. The word is derived from the name of the city of Cordova in Spain, a center of world-renowned tanners.

Charlotte M. Calasibetta, *Fairchild's Dictionary of Fashion* (New York: Fairchild Publications, 1988), 333. Mary Brooks Picken, *The Fashion Dictionary, rev. ed.* (New York: Funk & Wagnalls, 1973), 229.

Who invented velcro?

Velcro is the invention of George de Mestral, a Swiss engineer. He got the idea around 1948 when he noticed how burdock burrs often cling to clothing. Granted U.S. patent number 2,717,437 in 1955, de Mestral opened the first factory to produce velcro in 1957. The name is derived from velvet (vel) and crochet (cro) from the French word for small hook. A velcro fastener consists of two nylon strips, one containing thousands of tiny hooks, the other, tiny eyes. Pressing the two together locks the hooks in the eyes. To perfect that simple idea required 10 years of continuous effort.

Inventive Genius (New York: Time-Life Books, 1991), 72. Charles Panati, *Panati's Extraordinary Origin of Everyday Things* (New York: Perennial Library, 1987), 317-18. Bridget Travers, ed., *World of Invention,* (Detroit, MI: Gale Research, 1994), 663.

What is nylon?

This is another name for polyhexamethyleneadipamide, a family of polyamide fibers, first developed by Wallace H. Caruthers (1896-1937) of the DuPont Corporation, and patented on February 16, 1937. This made-made material, called "Fiber 66" by DuPont, had both high strength and flexibility, as well as impact and wear resistance. Nylon's first practical consumer application product came in 1938, when the new polymer was introduced to the public in the form of toothbrush bristles. But nylon's use in stockings, made it an overwhelming commercial success, because although it was similar to silk in its properties nylon was far less expensive.

Introduced to the buying public on May 15, 1940, nylon stockings caused the consumers to line up for hours in advance at department stores, and near riots occurred in some areas. Three million dozens of women's nylon stockings were produced in 1940, but in 1941 restrictions on silk and nylon for wartime uses reduced its production. Hosiery was only available in rayon, cotton, and wool. After the end of World War II (1939-45), nylon remained the favorite over silk.

The two most common types of nylon in production are "Nylon 6.6" and "Nylon 6;" the difference is based on the number of carbons in the repeating units of its molecular structure. Nylon 6 accepts dyes better, has great elasticity and softness, but has a lower melting point (420 degrees Fahrenheit or 215.5 degrees Celsius) than Nylon 6.6 (482 degrees Fahrenheit or 250 degrees Celsius).

Encyclopedia of Textiles (New York: Prentice-Hall, 1980), 21-24, 568. Carl H. Snyder, *The Extraordinary Chemistry of Ordinary Things* (New York: John Wiley & Sons, 1992), 536-39. Milton N. Grass, *History of Hosiery* (New York: Fairchild Publications, 1955), 263-66. *Van Nostrand Reinhold Encyclopedia of Chemistry* (New York: Van Nostrand Reinhold, 1984), 635. Bridget Travers, ed., *World of Invention* (Detroit: Gale Research, 1994), 449.

What is the origin of blue jeans?

In 1860 Levi Strauss (1829-1902) arrived in San Francisco with bales of canvas cloth he intended to use to make tents and wagon coverings. He used this material to make overalls for the gold rush prospectors who complained that ordinary trousers wore out too quickly in their work environment. In the 1860s, Strauss replaced the canvas with denim, a type of softer twilled cloth called "serge de Nimes"—that was Manufactured in the city Nimes in southern France. The indigo dye minimized soil stains. In 1873 Strauss patented his pant style. In 1893 copper rivets were added to stress points, such as pockets, which tended to be pulled out by the weight of the tools the pockets held. In 1935 they became a fashion item. The term "jeans" denotes a twilled cotton cloth, similar to denim, that was used in the manufacturing of sturdy work clothing. The textile first was milled in Genoa, Italy, which French weavers called "Genes."

Charles Panati, *Panati's Extraordinary Origins of Everyday Things* (New York: Perennial Library, 1987), 302-3. Patrick Robertson, *The Book of Firsts* (New York: Clarkson N. Potter, 1974), 89.

When was the lawn mower invented?

The first mechanized mower was patented in 1830 by the English inventor Edwin Budding. This device was a 19-inch (48-centimeter) roller mower that used a set of rotating cutters operating against fixed ones-an adaptation of the rotary shearing machine used to cut nap off of cotton cloth. Previously, grass needed to be dampened first to give it enough "body" before it could be cut with a scythe. Budding's device could be used on dry grass. By the 1880s, the popularity of hand-powered mowers increased as their cost decreased. And in 1919, an American army colonel, Edwin George, produced the first gasoline-powered lawn mower.

Neil Schlager, ed., *How Products are Made; An illustrated Guide to Product Manufacturing* (Detroit, MI: Gale Research, 1994) 252-55. Charles Panati, *Panati's Extraordinary Origins of Everyday Things* (New York: Perennial Library, 1987), 162-63. Doreen Yarwood, *Five Hundred Years of Technology in the Home* (London: B.T. Batsford, 1983), 109.

Who invented the modern flush toilet?

In 1449, Thomas Brightfield of St. Martin's Parish in England, built a water closet flushed by water piped from a cistern. In 1586, English poet Sir John Harington (1561-1612) designed and installed a practical water-flushing system for cleaning toilets. In 1778, Englishman Joseph Bramah (1748-1814) invented the ball-valve and u-bend method. But it was not until 1861 that British sanitary engineer Thomas Crapper (1837-1910) offered his major innovation-a mechanism that shut off the flow of clean water when the tank filled. Previously, the supply of clean water had be turned on and off by the user, and many simply left it running continuously.

Tom Burnam, *The Dictionary of Misinformation* (New York: Perennial Library, 1986), 56. Nell DuVall, *Domestic Technology* (Boston: G.K. Hall, 1988), 363, 366. Richard B. Manchester, *Mammoth Book of Fascinating Information* (New York: A & W Visual Library, 1980), 452-56. Bridget Travers, ed., *World of Invention* (Detroit, MI: Gale Research, 1994), 634.

When was the window air conditioner invented?

The term "air conditioning" was first used by American physicist Stuart W. Cramer in 1907-years before a practical air-conditioning system was invented. The American inventor Willis Carrier (1876-1950) invented an air conditioning system in 1911, and commercial air conditioners were produced in 1914. A patent request was filed in 1931 by H.H. Schultz and J.Q. Sherman for an air conditioner to be placed on window ledges. Room air conditioners were available for home use in 1932, but because of economic constraints arising from the Depression and World War II (1939-19445) and the uneven spread of electrical power distribution systems widespread use was not feasible until after the war.

Nell DuVall, *Domestic Technology* (Boston: G.K. Hall, 1988), 247. Valerie-Anne Giscard d'Estaing, *World Almanac Book of Inventions* (New York: World Almanac Publications, 1985) 21. Charles Panati, , *Panati's Extraordinary Origins of Everyday Things* (New York: Perennial Library, 1987), 159-60. Bridget Travers, ed., *World of Invention* (Detroit: Gale Research Inc., 1994), 7.

Who invented the first electric iron?

The electric clothes iron was first invented in France in 1880. On June 6, 1882, Henry W. Seely of New York City received a patent on one which proved impractical, requiring too much reheating. In 1896, heavy electric irons with replaceable heating units were unsuccessfully sold by the Ward Leonard Electric Company. In 1903, Earl H. Richardson devised a small lightweight iron heated by a glowing wire wrapped around a brass core. He later reworked the design so that more heat was directed to the point, facilitating the smoothing of buttonholes and pleats. This iron became so popular that Richardson renamed his company "Hotpoint."

Daniel Cohen, *The Last Hundred Years: Household Technology* (New York: M. Evans & Co., 1982), 100-2. Kevin Desmond, *A Timetable of Inventions and Discoveries* (New York: M. Evans & Co., 1982), 1880, 1882. Harry Harris, *Good Old-Fashioned Yankee Ingenuity* (Chelsea, MI: Scarborough House, 1990), 118.

What is the Toxic Release Inventory (TRI)?

Toxic Release Inventory (TRI) is a government mandated, publicly available compilation of information on the release of over 300 individual toxic chemicals and 20 categories of chemical compounds by manufacturing facilities in the United States. The law requires manufacturers to state the amounts of chemicals they release directly to air, land, or water, or that they transfer to off-site facilities that treat or dispose of wastes. The U.S. Environmental Protection Agency compiles these reports into an annual inventory and makes the information available in a computerized database. In 1989, 22,560 facilities released 5.7 billion pounds of toxic chemicals into the environment. Over 189 million pounds of this total were released into the water; 2.4 billion pounds emitted into the air; 445 million pounds into landfills; 1.2 billion pounds into underground wells; 551 million pounds to municipal wastewater treatment plants; and 916 million pounds to treatment and disposal facilities (offsite).

Council on Environmental Quality, *Environmental Quality* (Washington,DC: Council on Environmental Quality, 1992), 152-53. *Toxics in the*

Community, 1988 (Washington, DC: U.S. Environmental Protection Agency, 1990), xxi, 14-15.

What are flue gas scrubbers?

The scrubbing of flue gases refers to the removal of sulfur dioxide and nitric oxide which are major components of air pollution. Wet scrubbers use a chemical solvent or lime, limestone, sodium alkali, or diluted sulfuric acid to remove the sulphur dioxide formed during combustion. Dry scrubbing uses either a lime/limestone slurry or ammonia sprayed into the flue gases.

E. Willard Miller, *Environmental Hazards: Air Pollution* 44-45.

What is a WOBO?

A WOBO-world bottle-is the first mass-produced container designed for secondary use as a building product. It was conceived by Albert Heineken of the Heineken beer family. The beer bottles were designed in a special shape to be used, when empty, as glass bricks for building houses. The actual building carried out with WOBOs was only a small shed and a double garage built on the Heineken estate at Noordwijk, near Amsterdam. Although not implemented, WOBO was a sophisticated and intelligent design solution to what has emerged as a major environmental issue in recent years.

Martin Pawley, *Building For Tomorrow: Putting Waste to Work* (San Francisco: Sierra Club Books, 1982), 152-54. Martin Pawley, *Garbage Housing* (New York: Halsted, 1975), 23, 25-30.

Who invented Tupperware?

In the 1940s, Earl S. Tupper (d.1983), an American molding engineer, saw the potential of using polyethylene for making bowls, food storage items, etc. In 1945, he produced his first item-a seven-ounce (207-milliliter) bathroom tumbler-in the Tupperware line, followed by polyethylene bowls that had a revolutionary new vacuum-creating seal. Tupper devised a marketing plan to sell the products through in-home sales parties in 1946. In 1958 Tupper sold his business to Rexall Drugs.

Charles Panati, *Panati's Extraordinary Origins of Everyday Things* (New York: Perennial Library, 1987), 129-30. Adrian Room, *Dictionary of Trade Name Origins* (London: Routledge & Kegan Paul, 1982), 176.

What is the National Inventors Hall of Fame?

The National Inventors Hall of Fame was founded in 1973 on the initiative of H. Hume Matthews, then chairman of the National Council of Patent Law Associations (now called the National Council of Intellectual Property Law Associations). The U.S. Patent and Trademark Office became a co-sponsor the following year. A foundation, created in 1977, administers this prize; which honors inventors who conceived great technological advances that contributed to the nation's welfare. Usually the recognition is for a specific patent. Thomas A. Edison (1847-1931), the first inductee, was honored for his electric lamp, U.S. patent number 223,898, granted January 27, 1880. Since then nearly a hundred other inventors have been inducted into the hall.

Encyclopedia of Associations, 27th ed., (Detroit: Gale Research, 1993), 1:579. *The National Inventors Hall of Fame 1990* (Washington, DC: U.S. Patent and Trademark Office, 1990), 2, 62. Timothy Lee Wherry, *Patent Searching for Librarians and Inventors* (Chicago: American Library Association, 1995), 9,11.

What is a Rube Goldberg contraption?

A Rube Goldberg contraption is an overengineered solution to a simple problem. Ruben Lucius Goldberg (1883-1970) was a skilled engineering draftsman, a stand-up comic, a reporter, and a cartoonist. His bizarre inventions mixed grand silliness with high seriousness. His devices used balloons, leaking hot water bottles, candle flames, pulleys, strings, levers, and various animals in elaborate schemes devised to accomplish simple tasks.

Inventive Genius (New York: Time-Life Books, 1991), 42.

Which scientific discoveries were made accidently?

Some accidental discoveries include velcro, penicillin, x-rays, dynamite, vulcanization of rubber, synthetic dyes, rayon, saccharin, and the discoveries of iodine and helium.

Royston M. Roberts, *Serendipity: Accidental Discoveries in Science* (New York: John Wiley & Sons, 1989), 31-33, 53-58, 66-74, 86-87, 94, 139, 150-59, 220-22.

Which patents were issued to Mark Twain?

The American writer Mark Twain whose real name was Samuel Clemens (1835-1910), was granted three patents. The first, patent number 121,992, issued in 1871 was for suspenders. His second, issued in 1873, was for his famous "Mark Twain's Self-Pasting Scrapbook." The third patent in 1885 was for an educational game that was to help players remember important historical dates.

Richard C. Levy, *The Inventor's Desktop Companion* (Detroit: Visible Ink Press, 1991), 9.

How did the bazooka get its name?

It was coined by American comedian Bob Burns (1893-1956). As a prop in his act he used a unique musical instrument that was long and cylindrical and resembled an oboe. When United States Army soldiers in World War II (1939-45) were first issued hollow-tube rocket launchers, they named them bazookas because of their similarity to Burns' instrument.

Science and Technology Illustrated (Chicago: Encyclopaedia Britannica, 1984), 354.

Who invented the Bowie knife?

A popular weapon of the American West, the Bowie knife was named after Jim Bowie (1796-1836), who was killed at the Alamo. According to most reliable sources, his brother Rezin Bowie might have been the actual inventor. The knife's blade measured up to two inches (5 centimeters) wide and its length varied from nine inches to 15 inches (23 to 38 centimeters).

Edward DeBono, *Eureka!* (New York: Holt, Rinehart and Winston, 1974), 218. David Wallechinsky, *The Book of Lists* (New York: Morrow, 1977), 89.

Who was known as the Cannon King?

Alfred Krupp (1812-87), whose father Friedrich (1787-1826) established the family's cast-steel factory in 1811, began manufacturing guns in 1856. Krupp supplied large weapons to so many nations that he became known as the "Cannon King." Prussia's victory in the Franco-German War of 1870-71 was largely the result of Krupp's field guns. In 1933 when Adolf Hitler came to power, this family business began manufacturing a wide range of artillery. Alfred Krupp (1907-67), the great-grandson of Alfred, supported the Nazis in power and accrued staggering wealth for the company. The firm seized property in occupied countries and used slave labor in its factories. After the war, Alfred was imprisoned for twelve years and had to forfeit all his property. Granted amnesty in 1951, he restored the business to its former position by the early 1960s. On his death in 1967, however, the firm became a corporation and the Krupp family dynasty ended.

Ian V. Hogg, *The Illustrated Encyclopedia of Artillery* (London: Stanley Paul, 1987), 184. William R. Manchester, *The Arms of Krupp 1587-1968* (Boston: Little, Brown, 1968), 93.

How did Big Bertha get its name?

This was the popular name first applied to the then powerful 42-centimeter (about 16.5 inches) howitzers used by the Germans and Austrians in 1914, the year World War I started. Subsequently the term included other types of huge artillery pieces used during World War I (1914-18) and II (1939-45). The large gun, which could fire shells a distance of six to eight miles, was built by the German arms manufacturer Friedrich A. Krupp (1854-1902), and was named after his only child, Bertha Krupp (1886-1957) by the gun's designer, Professor Rausenberger.

These large guns were used to destroy the concrete and steel forts defending Belgium in 1914, and their shells weighed 205 pounds (930 kilograms) and were nearly as tall as a man. Since it was slow and difficult to move such guns, the use of them was practical only in static warfare. In World War II, bomber aircraft took away this role of long-range bombardment from these cumbersome guns.

Ian V. Hogg, *The Illustrated Encyclopedia of Artillery* (London: Stanley Paul, 1987), 90. Norbert Muhlen, *The Incredible Krupps* (New York: Henry Holt, 1959), 113. *Weapons: An International Encyclopedia from 5000 B.C. to 2000 A.D.* (New York: St. Martin's Press, 1990), 188.

Who invented mine barrage?

In 1777, David Bushnell (1742?-1824) conceived the idea of floating kegs containing explosives which would ignite upon contact with ships.

Joseph Gies and Frances Gies, *The Ingenious Yankee* (New York: Thomas Y. Crowell, 1976), 22-23.

When and where was gunpowder probably invented?

The explosive mixture of saltpeter (potassium nitrate), sulfur, and charcoal called *gunpowder* was known in China at least by 850 A.D., and probably was discovered by Chinese alchemists searching for components to make artificial gold. Early mixtures had too little saltpeter (50 percent) to be truly explosive; 75 percent minimum is needed to get a detonation. The first use of the mixture was in making fireworks. Later, the Chinese used it in incendiary like weapons. Eventually it is thought that the Chinese found the correct proportions to utilize its explosive effects in rockets and "bamboo bullets." However, some authorities still maintain that the "Chinese gunpowder" really had only pyrotechnic qualities, and "true" gunpowder was an European invention. Roger Bacon (1214-1292) had a formula for it and so might have the German monk Berthold Schwartz (1353). Its first European use depended on the development of firearms in the fourteenth century. Not until the seventeenth century was gunpowder used in peacetime for mining and civil engineering applications.

Charles Panati, *Panati's Browser's Book of Beginnings* (Boston: Houghton Mifflin, 1984), 346-47. Dennis Sanders, *The First of Everything* (New York: Delacorte, 1981), 64. Robert Temple, *The Genius of China* (New York: Simon and Schuster, 1986), 224-29.

Is glass a solid or a liquid?

Even at room temperature, glass appears to be a solid in the ordinary sense of the word. However, it actually is a fluid with an extremely high viscosity. It has been documented that century-old windows show signs of flow. The internal friction of fluids is called viscosity. It is a property of fluids by which the flow motion is gradually damped (slowed) and dissipated by heat. Viscosity is a familiar phenomenon in daily life. An opened bottle of wine can be poured: the wine flows easily under the influence of gravity. Maple syrup, on the other hand, cannot be poured so easily; under the action of gravity, it flows sluggishly. The syrup has a higher viscosity than the wine.

Glass is usually composed of mixed oxides based around the silicon dioxide unit. A very good electrical insulator, and generally inert to chemicals, commercial glass is manufactured by the fusing of sand, limestone, and soda at temperatures around 2552 degrees Fahrenheit to 2732 degrees Fahrenheit (1400 to 1500 degrees Celsius). On cooling, the melt becomes very viscous and at about 932 degrees Fahrenheit (500 degrees Celsius, known as glass transition temperature), the melt "solidifies" to form soda glass. Small amounts of metal oxides are used to color glass, and its physical properties can be changed by the addition of substances like lead oxide (to increase softness, density, and refractive ability for cutglass and lead crystal), and borax (to lower significantly thermal expansion for cookware and laboratory equipment). Other materials can be used to form glasses if cooled sufficiently rapid from the liquid or gaseous phase to prevent an ordered crystalline structure from forming. Glasses such as obsidian occur naturally. Glass objects might have been made as early as 2500 B.C. in Egypt and Mesopotamia, and glass blowing developed about 100 B.C. in Phoenicia.

Encyclopedia of Physical Science and Technology (San Diego: Academic Press, 1987), 6:266. Frank N. Magill, *Magill's Survey of Science. Physical Science Series* (Englewood Cliffs, NJ: Salem Press, 1992), 6:2685. *Oxford Illustrated Encyclopedia of Invention and Technology* (Oxford, England: Oxford University Press, 1992), 156.

How is bulletproof glass made?

Bulletproof glass is composed of two sheets of plate glass with a sheet of transparent resin in between, molded together under heat and pressure. When subjected to a severe blow, it will crack without shattering. Today's bulletproof glass is a development of laminated or safety glass, invented by the French chemist Edouard Benedictus. It is basically a multiple lamination of glass and plastic layers.

George S. Brady, *Materials Handbook, 12th ed.* (New York: McGraw-Hill, 1986), 550. Freda Diamond, *The Story of Glass* (San Diego: Harcourt, Brace, 1953), 128-30.

Which metal is the main component of pewter?

Tin. Roman pewter has about 70 percent tin. The best pewter used for expensive articles today contains 100 parts tin, eight parts antimony, two parts bismuth, and two parts copper. This alloy is easy to work with, does not become brittle when repeatedly beaten, and can be worked cold. However, it is too soft to use for heavy tools or weapons, so its use is confined to domestic utensils.

Edward De Bono, *Eureka!* (New York: Holt, Rinehart and Winston, 1974), 87.

Is white gold really gold?

White gold is the name of a class of jeweler's white alloys used as substitutes for platinum. Different grades vary widely in composition, but usual alloys consist of from 20 percent to 50 percent nickel, with the balance gold. A superior class of white gold is made of 90 percent gold and 10 percent palladium. Other elements used may be copper and zinc. The main use of these alloys is to give the gold a white color.

George S. Brady, *Materials Handbook, 12th ed.* (New York: McGraw-Hill, 1986), 882. Paul W. Thrush, *A Dictionary of Mining, Mineral, and Related Terms* (Washington, DC: U.S. Bureau of Mines, 1968), 1235.

Where were the first successful ironworks in America?

Although iron ore in this country was first discovered in North Carolina in 1585, and the manufacture of iron was first undertaken (but never accomplished) in Virginia in 1619, the first successful ironworks in America was established by Thomas Dexter and Robert Bridges near the Saugus River in Lynn, Massachusetts. As the original promoters of the enterprise, they hired John Winthrop, Jr. from England to begin production. By 1645, a blast furnace had begun operations, and by 1648, a forge was working there.

James M. Swank, *History of the Manufacture of Iron in All Ages* (New York: Burt Franklin, 1965), 108-19.

From where do frankincense and myrrh originate?

Frankincense is an aromatic resin obtained by tapping the trunks of trees belonging to the genus *Boswellia.* The milky resin hardens when exposed to the air and forms irregular lumps—the form in which it is usually marketed.

Myrrh is a resin that comes from a tree trunk of the genus *Commiphora,* a native of Arabia and Northeast Africa.

Popular Encyclopedia of Plants (New York: Cambridge University Press, 1982), 97, 144, 231.

Who invented the fountain pen?

Invented by Lewis E. Waterman of the United States in 1883, the first practical fountain pen carried its own ink reservoir which could be replenished with an eyedropper. In 1913 the automatic or lever-filling reservoir became available.

The Encyclopedia Americana, intern. ed. (Danbury, CT: Grolier, 1994), 21:619. Andreas Lambrou, *Fountain Pens: Vintage and Modern* (London: Sotheby's Publications, 1989), 16.

Which country produces the most salt?

As of 1991, the largest producer of salt was the United States, with 36.3 million metric tons or 19.5 percent of the world production. China comes in second with 25.4 million metric tons or 13.7 percent of the world's total.

The New Encyclopaedia Britannica, 15th ed., "Micropaedia" (Chicago: Encyclopaedia Britannica, 1993), s.v. "mining."

Who invented the hot iron, used to remove the curl from African-American hair?

C.J. "Madame" Walker was credited with inventing a hot iron that successfully removed the curl from African-American hair. A laundry woman by trade, she had experimented with an oil treatment to straighten hair, but was not successful until her 1905 invention of the hot iron.

She marketed her invention very successfully, opening a cosmetology school to train workers, and purchasing a factory to make the iron. She also employing workers to demonstrate the "Walker System." Her invention made her quite wealthy and she later became famous for her philanthropy to organizations.

Afro-American Encyclopedia (North Miami, FL: Educational Book Publishers, 1974), s.v. "Walker, C. J. 'Madame.'"

How was glass discovered?

According to a story told by Pliny the Elder, glass was discovered accidentally by Phoenician saltpeter merchants. While camped on a beach by the Belus River in Phoenicia (present-day Israel), they used saltpeter blocks to hold a kettle above their campfire. The fire's heat caused the sand and saltpeter to fuse into a nitreous mass-surprising the merchants with an early form of glass.

Scientists and archaeologists dispute this story by citing a lack of proper heat and chemical ingredients for real glass. In addition, there is evidence that glass was made earlier in Egypt and Mesopotamia. Glass beads appeared there around 4,000 to 5,000 B.C.

Joan Mowat Erikson, *The Universal Bead* (New York: W. W. Norton, 1993), 118. Bridget Travers, ed., *The World of Invention* (Detroit, MI: Gale Research, 1994), 284.

Who invented the paper clip?

The paper clip that attaches sheets of paper together was patented by Johan Vaaler, a teacher from Aurskog, Norway in 1890.

Valerie-Anne Giscard d'Estaing, *The World Almanac Book of Inventions* (New York: World Almanac, 1985), 89. *Parade Magazine* 27 July 1986.

What was Fulton's Folly?

Robert Fulton (1765-1815) was an American inventor and engineer who played a major role in the development of steamboat transportation. In 1786 while studying art in London, Fulton became fascinated with England's bridges, canals, and factories. He soon began devoting more time to solving engineering problems and less time to the study of art. He became involved with mechanical dredges, boat-hauling equipment and underwater warfare and explosives. By 1802 the idea of steam-powered ships fascinated Fulton and he became involved in a steamboat venture with Robert R. Livingston, U.S. minister to France. He and Livingston in 1807 built the *Clermont,* a steam-powered paddle wheel boat which was derisively known as Fulton's Folly. The *Clermont,* however, was a mechanical and commercial success and carried passengers 150 miles up the Hudson River from New York to Albany in 32 hours. The *Clermont,* along with Fulton's substantial financial backing, a federal patent, and the subsequent Livingston-Fulton steamship monopoly, made Fulton a successful if not controversial entrepreneur. Court challenges to Fulton's monopoly grew as he expanded his operations westward, but the monopoly was finally broken in 1824 by U.S.

Supreme Court Chief Justice John Marshall's decision in *Gibbons* v. *Ogden.*

Dictionary of American History, rev. ed. (New York: Charles Scribner's Sons, 1976), s.v. "Fulton's Folly." *McGraw-Hill Encyclopedia of World Biography* (New York: McGraw-Hill, 1973), s.v. "Fulton, Robert."

What was the "Iron Maiden" in medieval England?

The "Iron Maiden" was a torture device used in medieval England. It is a metal casket, formed in the shape of a woman, that is filled with spikes.

Clarence L. Barnhart and Robert K. Barnhart, eds., *The World Book Dictionary* (Chicago: World Book, 1990), s.v. "iron maiden."

The World War II inflatable life jacket was named after which famous movie actress?

Bawdy and buxom comedienne Mae West (1892-1980) lent her name to the World War II (1939-1945) inflatable life jacket.

John Robert Elting, Dan Cragg, and Ernest L. Deal, *A Dictionary of Soldier Talk* (New York: Charles Scribner's Sons, 1984), s.v. "Mae West."

Are enzymes still used in detergents?

Enzymes are widely used in detergents because they are an ideal way to remove food, blood, and grass stains without damaging delicate fabrics. Enzymes are used in 80% of detergents in Western Europe, and, 60 percent in Japan. They are found in an encapsulated form in 40 percent of U.S. laundry detergents, but unencapsulated enzymes had been added to as many as 60 percent of all detergents in the United States until the end of the 1960s. After many consumers complained of skin irritation and rashes, in the early 1970s manufacturers ceased to add enzymes to consumer detergents. But detergent makers did not give up on them completely and developed an encapsulation technique for enzymes that eliminated skin contact.

The Almanac of Science and Technology (New York: Harcourt Brace Jovanovich, 1990), 176.

Where did the military tank get its name?

During World War I, when the British were developing the tank, they called these first armored fighting vehicles "water tanks" to keep their real purpose a secret. This code word has remained in spite of early efforts to call them "combat cars" or "assault carriages."

Jay M. Shafritz, *The Facts On File Dictionary of Military Science* (New York: Facts on File, 1989) 454.

Who developed the Universal Product Code?

Also called a bar code, the Universal Product Code (UPC) is a product description code designed to be read by a computerized scanner or cash register enabling the computer scanner at the retail checkout to find the price of that item. The UPC was developed by the Uniform Code Council in 1974. Located in Dayton, Ohio, the Council also administers the Uniform Communications Standard (UCS), Warehouse Information Network Standard (WINS), Voluntary Inter-Industry Communications Standard (VICSEDI), and Uniform Industrial Code. The UPC consists of 11 numbers in groups of "0"s (dark strips) and "1"s (white strips). A bar will be thin if it has only one strip or thicker if there are two or more strips side by side.

The first number describes the type of product. Most products begin with a "0"; exceptions to this are variable weight products such as meat and vegetables (2), health-care products (3), bulk-discounted goods (4), and coupons (5). Since it might be misread as a bar, the number 1 is not used.

The next five numbers describe the product's manufacturer. The following five numbers after that describe the product itself including its color, weight, size, and other distinguishing characteristics. The price of the item is not included; it is coded into the cash register separately.

The last number is a check digit which is used to tell the scanner if there is an error in the other numbers. The preceding numbers, when added, multiplied, and subtracted in a certain way will equal this number. If they do not, there is a mistake somewhere.

Robert E. Cone, *How the New Technology Works* (Phoenix, AZ: Oryx Press, 1991), 107. Nigel J. Hopkins, John W. Mayne, and John R. Hudson, *The Numbers You Need* (Detroit: Gale Research, 1992), pp. 173-74. Jeff Rovin, *Laws of Order* (New York: Ballantine, 1992), 48. Peggy Kneffel Daniels and Carol A. Schwartz, eds., *Encyclopedia of Associations, 2 ed.,* (Detroit: Gale Research, 1993), 40.

What is a "miner's canary"?

Both mice and birds have been used by miners to test the purity of the air in the mines. A canary two carried in a small cage, will show signs of distress in the presence of carbon monoxide more quickly than humans will, thus alerting the miner to toxic air. This method of safety was used prior to the more sophisticated equipment available today.

Bureau of Mines, *Bulletin No. 42, 1913* (Washington, DC: Bureau of Mines, 1913), 66.

When did the symbol of Smokey the Bear begin to be used for forest fire prevention?

A nationwide effort in wildfire prevention was begun in 1942. A poster featuring Smokey the Bear was circulated in 1945. The symbol soon became very popular. The slogan "Only you can prevent forest fires" was coined in 1947.

Fire Management Notes Fall 1982.

How does a four-stroke differ from a two-stroke engine?

A four-stroke engine functions by going through four cycles: 1) the intake stroke draws a fuel-air mixture in on a down stroke; 2) the mixture is compressed on an upward stroke; 3) the mixture is ignited causing a down stroke; and 4) the mixture is exhausted on an up stroke. A two-stroke engine combines the intake and compression strokes (1 and 2) and the power and exhaust strokes (3 and 4) by covering and uncovering ports and valves in the cylinder wall. Two-stroke engines are typically used in small displacement applications, such as chain saws and some motorcycles.

Reader's Digest Fix-It-Yourself Manual (Pleasantville, NY: Reader's Digest Association, 1978), 370-71.

Who invented the electron microscope?

The theoretical and practical limits to the use of the optical microscope were set by the wavelength of light. When the oscilloscope was developed, it was realized that cathode-ray beams could be used to resolve much finer detail because their wavelength was so much shorter than that of light. In 1928, Ernst Ruska (1906-88) and Max Knoll, using magnetic fields to "focus" electrons in a cathode-ray beam, produced a crude instrument which gave a magnification of 17 and by 1932 they developed an electron microscope having a magnification of 400. By 1937 James Hillier (b. 1915) advanced this magnification to 7,000. The 1939 instrument Vladimir Zworykin (1889-1982) developed gave 50 times more detail than any optical microscope ever could with its magnification up to two million. With this highly-resolved powerful magnification, the electron microscope revolutionized biological research, especially in the areas of cell structures, proteins, and viruses.

Carlo M. Cipolla and Derek Birdsall, *The Technology of Man* (New York: Holt, Rinehart and Winston, 1980), 236.

What are the six simple machines?

All machines and mechanical devices, no matter how complicated, can be reduced to some combinations of six basic, or simple, machines. The lever, the wheel and axle, the pulley, the inclined plane, the wedge, and the screw were all known to the ancient Greeks who learned that a machine works because an "effort," which is exerted over an "effort distance," is magnified through "mechanical advantage" to overcome a "resistance" over a "resistance distance." Some consider there to be only five simple machines, and regard the wedge as a moving inclined plane.

David Macauley, *The Way Things Work* (Boston: Houghton Mifflin, 1988), 14-73. Robert O'Brien, *Machines* (New York: Time, 1964), 16.

Who invented the compound microscope?

The principle of the compound microscope, in which two or more lenses are arranged to form an enlarged image of an object, occurred independently, at about the same time, to more than one person. Certainly many opticians were active at the end of the sixteenth century, especially in Holland, in the construction of telescopes, so that it is likely that the idea of the microscope could have occurred to several of them independently. In all probability, the date may be placed within the period 1590-1609, and the credit should go to three spectacle makers in Holland. Hans Janssen, his son Zacharias (1580-1638), and Hans Lippershey (1570-1619) have all been cited at various times as deserving chief credit. An Englishman, Robert Hooke (1635-1703) was the first to make the best use of a compound microscope, and his book, *Micrographia*, published in 1665, contains some of the most beautiful drawings of microscopic observations ever made.

Savile Bradbury, *The Evolution of the Microscope* (Elmsford, NY: Pergamon Press, 1967), 21, 39-67.

Who developed fiberglass?

Coarse glass fibers were used for decoration by the Egyptians in ancient times. Other developments were made during Roman times. Parisian craftsman Dubus-Bonnel was granted a patent for the spinning and weaving of drawn glass strands in 1836. In 1893, the Libbey Glass Company exhibited lampshades, at the World's Columbian Exposition in Chicago, that were made of coarse glass thread woven together with silk. However, this was not a true woven glass. Between 1931 and 1939, the Owens Illinois Glass Company and the Corning Glass Works developed practical methods of making fiberglass commercially. Once the technical problem of drawing out the glass threads to a fraction of their original thinness was solved—basically an endless strand of continuous glass filament as thin as 1/5000 of an inch—the industry began to produce glass fiber for thermal insulation and air filters, among other uses. When glass fibers were combined with plastics during World War II (1939-1945), a new material was formed. Glass fibers did for plastics what steel did for concrete-gave strength and flexibility. Glass-fiber-reinforced plastics (GFRP) became very important in modern engineering. Fiberglass combined with epoxy resins and thermosetting polyesters are now used extensively in boat and ship construction, sporting goods, automobile bodies, and circuit boards in electronics.

Freda Diamond, *The Story of Glass* (San Diego: Harcourt, Brace, 1953), 197-224. Valerie-Anne Giscard d'Estaing, *The World Almanac Book of Inventions* (New York: World Almanac, 1985), 274. *Oxford Illustrated Encyclopedia of Invention and Technology* (Oxford, England: Oxford University Press, 1992), 129.

Why is sulfuric acid so important?

Sometimes called "oil of vitriol," sulfuric acid has become one of the most important of all chemicals. It was little used until it became essential for the manufacture of soda in the 18th century. It is prepared industrially by the reaction of water with sulfur trioxide, which in turn is made by chemical combination of sulfur dioxide and oxygen by one of two processes (the contact process or the chamber process). Many manufactured articles in common use depend in some way on sulfuric acid for their production. Its greatest use is in the production of fertilizers, but it is also used in the refining of petroleum, and production of automobile batteries, explosives, pigments, iron and other metals, and paper pulp.

Ian McNeil, *An Encyclopedia of the History of Technology* (London: Routledge, 1990), 221-23. *Van Nostrand Reinhold Encyclopedia of Chemistry, 4th ed.* (New York: Van Nostrand Reinhold, 1984), 909-10. *World Book Encyclopedia* (Chicago: World Book, 1990), 18:967.

When was cement first used?

Cements are finely ground powders that, when mixed with water, set to a hard mass. The cement used by the Egyptians was calcined gypsum, and both the Greeks and Romans used a cement of calcined limestone. Roman concrete (a mixture of cement, sand, and some other fine aggregate) was made of broken brick embedded in a pozzolanic lime mortar. This mortar consisted of lime putty mixed with brick dust or volcanic ash. Hardening was produced by a prolonged chemical reaction between these components in the presence of moisture. With the decline of the Roman empire, concrete fell into disuse. The first step toward its reintroduction was in about 1790, when the English engineer, John Smeaton (1724-1792), discovered that when lime containing some clay was burnt, it would set under water. This cement resembled what previously had been made by the Romans. Further investigations by James Parker during the same decade led to the commercial production of natural hydraulic cement. In 1824, Englishman Joseph Aspdin (1799-1855) applied for a patent for what he called "portland cement," a material produced from a synthetic mixture of limestone and clay. He called it "portland" because it resembled a building stone that was quarried on the Isle of Portland off the coast of Dorset in England. The manufacture of this cement spread rapidly to Europe and the United States by 1870. Today, concrete is often reinforced or prestressed, increasing its load-bearing capabilities.

Walter H. Taylor, *Concrete Technology and Practice* (New York: McGraw-Hill, 1977), 3-4.

What is creosote?

Creosote is a yellowish poisonous oily liquid obtained from the distillation of coal tar. Coal tar constitutes the major part of the liquid condensate obtained from the "dry" distillation or carbonization of coal to coke. Crude creosote oil, also called dead oil or pitch oil, is used as a wood preservative. Railroad ties, poles, fence posts, marine pilings, and lumber for outdoor use are impregnated with creosote in large cylindrical vessels. This treatment can greatly extend the useful life of wood that is exposed to the weather.

George S. Brady, *Materials Handbook, 12th ed.* (New York: McGraw-Hill, 1986), 244. *Van Nostrand Reinhold Encyclopedia of Chemistry, 4th ed.* (New York: Van Nostrand Reinhold, 1984), 264-65.

Why is titanium dioxide the most widely used white pigment?

Titanium dioxide has become the predominant white pigment in the world because of its high refractive index, lack of absorption of visible light, ability to be produced in the right size range, and its stability and nontoxicity. It is the whitest known pigment, unrivalled in respect of color, opacity, stain resistance, and durability; it is also non-toxic. The main consuming industries are paint, printing inks, plastics, and ceramics, which together account for 60 percent to 70 percent of the total demand.

Encyclopedia of Chemical Technology, 3d ed. (New York: Wiley, 1978), 23:143. W. M. Morgans, *Outlines of Paint Technology* (New York: Halsted Press, 1990), 52. *The Timetable of Technology* (San Diego: Harvest Books, 1982), 28.

What is carbon black?

Carbon black is finely divided carbon produced by incomplete combustion of methane or other hydrocarbon gases (by letting the flame impinge on a cool surface). This forms a very fine pigment containing up to 95 percent carbon, which gives a very intense black color that is widely used in paints, inks, and protective coatings and as a colorant for paper and plastics.

Chambers Science and Technology Dictionary (Cambridge, England: Cambridge University Press, 1988), 133. *Van Nostrand Reinhold Encyclopedia of Chemistry, 4th ed.* (New York: Van Nostrand Reinhold, 1984), 170.

When was plastic first invented?

About 1850 Alexander Parkes (1813-1890) experimented with nitrocellulose (or guncotton). Mixed with camphor, it gave a hard but flexible transparent material, which he called "Parkesine." He teamed up with a manufacturer to produce it, but there was no call for it, and the firm went bankrupt. An American, John Wesley Hyatt (1837-1920), acquired the patent in 1868 with the idea of producing artificial ivory for billiard-balls. Improving the formula and with an efficient manufacturing process, he marketed the material, to make a few household articles, under the name "celluloid." Celluloid became the medium for cinematography: celluloid strips coated with a light-sensitive "film" were ideal for shooting and showing movie pictures. Celluloid was the only plastic material until 1904 when a Belgian scientist, Leo Hendrik Baekeland (1863-1944), succeeded in producing a synthetic shellac from formaldehyde and phenol. Called *bakelite*, it was the first of the "thermosetting" plastics (i.e., synthetic materials which, having once been subjected to heat and pressure, became extremely hard and resistant to high temperatures).

Edward De Bono, *Eureka!* (New York: Holt, Rinehart and Winston, 1974), 89.

Who made the first successful synthetic gemstone?

In 1902, Auguste Victor Louis Verneuil (1856-1913), synthesized the first man-made gemstone, a ruby. Verneuil perfected a "flame-fusion" method of producing crystals of ruby and other corundums within a short time period.

Edward De Bono, *Eureka!* (New York: Holt, Rinehart and Winston, 1974), 93. Kurt Nassau, *Gems Made by Man* (Radnor, PA: Chilton, 1980), 27.

What is the only unclad United States coin?

Like the first five-cent nickels authorized by the U.S. Congress on May 16, 1866, the nickels of today are the only unclad (without an exterior metal coating) United States coins. Except for a brief period during World War II (1939-45), the nickels have always been composed of three parts copper and one part nickel. During the war (1942-1945), a shortage of nickel caused that metal to be removed and the coins were made of 56 percent copper, 35 percent silver, and 9 percent manganese.

Marc Hudgeons, *The Official 1994 Blackbook Price Guide of United States Coins, 32nd ed.* (New York: Random House, 1993), 158, 168-73.

Who invented the wrist watch?

It is not known who invented the wrist watch. Queen Elizabeth I of England wore a watch heavily decorated with gold and jewels, and small miniature watches were made as early as 1790. In 1684 Christian Huygens produced a watch having a balance spring. However Robert Hooke claimed Huygens stole his idea. In 1761 English inventor John Harrison produced the first precise and completely portable watch. Harrison's design is the basis of most of the current spring-driven time pieces.

The Swiss industry began mass production of wrist watches around 1880 and introduced them to the United States in 1895. In 1907, Louis Cartier created a wrist watch for his friend, aviator Santos-Dumont, who used it while setting the first airborne speed record by traveling 220 meters in 21 seconds.

The wrist watch began gaining in popularity during World War I (1914-18) when French soldiers began attaching watches to their arms with watch chains. In 1923 the self-winding wrist watch was introduced by John Harwood who was able to mass produce them by 1929. By 1928, wrist watches were outselling pocket watches.

Valerie-Anne Giscard d'Estaing, *The Second World Almanac Book of Inventions* (New York: World Almanac, 1986), 285. Cooksey Shugart and Tom Engle, *The Complete Price Guide to Watches* (Cleveland, TN: Cooksey Shugart Publications, 1991), 363. Bridget Travers, ed., *World of Invention* (Detroit: Gale Research, 1994), 145.

In what year were American pennies made of zinc?

In 1943, during World War II, pennies were made of steel-coated zinc. They were followed in 1944 through 1946 by what are known as "Shell Case Cents," which were made from spent shell casings and were 95% copper and 5% zinc.

Marc Hudgeons, *The Official 1995 Blackbook Price Guide of United States Coins, 33d ed.* (New York: House of Collectibles, 1994), 158-59.

Who invented the sewing machine?

While Americans can take credit for the actual development of a practical sewing machine, the first developmental concepts occurred in Europe. For instance, the most indispensable ingredient-a needle with both the point and eye at the same end-was invented in 1755 by German mechanic Charles F. Weisenthal while he was working in London. In 1790 Thomas Saint, a London cabinetmaker, received a patent for a machine for stitching leather. By 1800 a German hosiery worker, Balthasar Krems, used a stitching machine to produce knitwear. In the years that followed, other inventions were developed that could be termed sewing machines, including a few in America. In 1829 a French tailor Barthelemy Thimmonier built a sewing machine that created a chain stitch linking the two pieces of fabric together and patented it in 1830. Twice he was on the verge of commercial success, but angry tailors, learning that the machine would put them out of work smashed his 80 machines in 1841. The revolution of 1848 squashed his second attempt to commercially build the machines with the financial assistance of Jean Marie Magnin. In the United States between 1843 and 1846 an American named Elias Howe, Jr., developed a practical two-thread machine using a shuttle, and he later successfully brought infringement of patent suits against subsequent manufacturers of sewing machines, including Isaac Singer, who had patented his more reliable sewing machine in 1851, which required fewer repairs. Singer's machine is considered to be the first labor-saving machine that could be found in an average U.S. household.

Brian Jewell, *Veteran Sewing Machines* (Cranbury, NJ: A. S. Barnes, 1975), 23-32. Lisa Mirabile, ed., *International Directory of Company histories* (Chicago, IL: St. James Press, 1990), 2:9.

How can books that have been water-damaged be restored?

The restoration of water-damaged books can be a painstaking process. Place irreplaceable materials in a freezer until a professional restorer can attend to them. Put less valuable books in an environment with relative humidity of less than 70 percent, wash the mud off, and stand the books up with their pages fanned. Riffling the pages occasionally hastens the drying process.

After 24 hours, insert white toweling or white paper every ten pages, and change the sheets as they become soaked. Try to separate sticking pages while they are still damp. Use a palette knife or thin butter knife for this procedure. To care for the binding, place wax paper between end papers and cover boards, then stack the books-front covers facing up-with white blotting paper or newspapers between them. Place four or five books in each stack and weigh the stacks down with bricks.

Mold can be treated by spraying or painting the pages with a solution of ten percent Thymol and 90 percent methyl or ethyl alcohol. Alternatively, a white paper treated with the solution can be placed between pages. The solution should be applied lightly to avoid dye running. Also, wear rubber gloves and perform this task in a well-ventilated area. Blotters can help to prevent ink from running. Place the books between two pieces of plastic screening or aluminum, then hold them under a tap to wash off mud, but be careful to watch for running ink.

"More Flood Damage Counsel from Cornell Librarian," *Library Journal* 1 December 1972.

How long of a line can the average pencil make?

A typical pencil contains enough graphite to trace a 35-mile-long line or write approximately 45,000 words.

Jane Polley, ed., *Stories Behind Everyday Things* (Pleasantville, NY: Reader's Digest Association, 1980), 245.

How much does the Big Ben bell in England weigh?

The bell that hangs in the tower of the Palace of Westminster in England weighs approximately 14 tons. When the work was commissioned in 1856 by Sir Benjamin Hall (whose name was affectionately given to the bell), no foundry in England had ever cast such a massive bell. For ten months, it hung in the palace yard for purposes of testing. A four-foot crack appeared soon afterwards, and Big Ben was recast. The second bell was placed in the tower's belfry in July of 1859 and also developed a few cracks. Upon the recommendation of the Astronomer Royal, the bell was turned on its mount slightly and a smaller hammer was installed. The original hammer is on display in the palace.

Even at 14 tons, Big Ben is still not the largest bell in England. In 1882, a 16.75-ton bell known as Great Paul was installed in St. Paul's Cathedral in London, England.

Hobbies January 1956.

How are coins produced?

The first step in producing a coin is the cutting of the die which is done by machine. Metal alloys are then prepared in varying mixtures. Alloys are melted in crucibles and poured into molds to form ingots. The ingots are in the form of thin bars and vary in size according to the denomination of coin. The width is sufficient to allow three or more coins to be cut from the strips. The ingots are next put through rolling mills to reduce the thickness to required limits. The strips are then fed into cutting presses which cut circular blanks (planchets) of the approximate size of the finished coin. The blanks are run through annealing furnaces to soften them; next through tumbling barrels, rotating cylinders containing cleaning solutions, and finally into centrifugal drying machines. The blanks are next fed into a milling machine which produces the raised or upset rim. The blank is now ready for the coining press. The blank is held firmly by a collar, as it is struck under heavy pressure varying from 40 tons for the one-cent pieces and dimes to 170 tons for silver dollars. Upper and lower dies impress the design on both sides of the coin. The pressure is sufficient to produce a raised surface level with that of the milled rim. The collar holding the blank for silver or clad coins is grooved. The pressure forces the metal into the grooves of the collar, producing the "reeding" on the finished coin.

Kenneth Bressett, ed., *1994 Handbook of United States Coins, 51st ed.* (Racine, WI: Western Publishing, 1993), 5-6.

What rigors must a watch pass to be called "shock-resistant," "water-resistant," or "antimagnetic"?

In 1968 the Federal Trade Commission established standards for the watch industry that must be met in order for watches to bear the labels "shock-resistant," "water-resistant," and "antimagnetic." In order to be called shock-resistant, a watch must be capable of surviving shocks that simulate a three-foot fall with the watch landing on its side or its face. To be water-resistant, a watch must be able to withstand water pressure at a depth of 33 feet for five minutes and 115 feet for five more minutes. An antimagnetic the watch must not react to magnetic fields generated by common household appliances. Under the same ruling, the word "proof" as in "waterproof" or "shockproof" is not allowed.

"When a Watch is Shock-resistant, Water-resistant, or Antimagnetic," *McCall's* April 1969.

When was permanent press invented?

"Permanent press" is a term used to describe a fabric or garment which retains its original shape through wear and laundering and needs no ironing. This means it will resist wrinkling and will retain creases and pleats indefinitely. Crease-resistance was first developed for cotton in 1932 by R.S. Willows and his research team for the Manchester textile manufacturer, Tootal Broadhurst Lee. Rather than laminating the fibers with synthetic resin solutions, Willows made the individual cotton fibers absorb the solution-giving the cotton yarn an elasticity that it otherwise lacked. The first products manufactured using this process were Tootal ties (marketed in autumn 1932) and dress fabrics (marketed in April 1933). In permanent press, the yarn is treated with a cross-linking chemical or reactant which is then cured (or fixed) by the application of heat. For garments needing creases or pleats, a post-cured process is used, giving the fabric "memory." Koret of California developed the process and received a patent in 1961 for its deferred cure process. The first application, in 1964, was for men's and boys' pants introduced to the consumer by Levi Strauss and McCampbell Graniteville Co.

Encyclopedia of Textiles (New York: Prentice-Hall, 1980), 187, 408, 411. Patrick Robertson, *The Book of Firsts* (New York: Clarkson N. Potter, 1974), 46.

How is silk made?

Silk fiber is a continuous protein filament produced by a silkworm to form its cocoon. The principal species used in commercial silkmaking is the mulberry silkworm (the larva of the silk moth *Bombyx mori*) belonging to the order Lepidoptera. The raw silk fiber has three elements-two filaments excreted from both of the silkworm's glands and a soluble silk gum called "sericin," which cements the filaments together. It is from these filaments that the caterpiller constructs a cocoon around itself.

The process of silkmaking starts with raising silkworms on diets of mulberry leaves for five weeks until they spin their cocoons. Then the cocoons are treated with heat to kill the silkworms inside (otherwise when the moths emerged, they would break the long silk filaments). After the cocoons are soaked in hot water, the filaments of five to ten cocoons are unwound in the reeling process, and twisted into a single thicker filament; still too fine for weaving, these twisted filaments are twisted again into a thread that can be woven. Other insects, of course, produce a kind of silk, e.g. spider's silk, but these generally are too sticky for commercial use.

Charles J. Cazeau, *Science Trivia* (New York: Berkley Books, 1986), 105-6. *Encyclopedia of Textiles* (Englewood Cliffs, NJ: Prentice-Hall, 1980), 125-37.

Who invented the zipper?

On August 29, 1893, a Chicago, Illinois, mechanical engineer, Whitcomb Judson, was awarded a patent for a "clasp-locker." The purpose of this fastener was to close high boots, replacing the long buttonhooked shoelaces of the 1890s. It consisted of a linear sequence of hook-and-eye locks. Judson displayed the invention at the 1893 Chicago World's Fair to drum up business, but it was ignored. Judson and his partner Lewis Walker did receive an order from the United States Postal Service for twenty zippered mail bags, but in use, the zippers jammed up so badly that the bags were discarded. In 1913 Gideon Sundback, a Swedish-American engineer, abandoned Judson's hook-and-eye arrangement to devise a smaller, lighter, more reliable "hookless fastener" with interlocking teeth (similar to today's zippers). The United States Army was Sundback's first customer in 1918. In 1923, when B.F. Goodrich introduced these hookless fasteners on its boots, it called the boots "zippers"-stemming from the "zip" sound the fastener made when closing. The name eventually applied to the hookless fastener itself.

Charles Panati, *Panati's Extraordinary Origins of Everyday Things* (New York: Perennial Library, 1987), 316-17.

Where should a smoke detector be located in the home?

The best location for a home smoke detector is on or near a ceiling close to the sleeping area and away from corners, windows, and doors. Another good location is at the top of a stairwell.

Reader's Digest Practical Problem Solver (Reader's Digest Association, 1991).

What is a fluting iron?

A household iron with grooves for pressing fabric into pleats or ruffles is called a fluting iron.

Nell DuVall, *Domestic Technology* (Boston: G. K. Hall, 1988), 201-2.

When was the first microwave oven sold?

Microwave cooking-the first absolutely new method of cooking food since fire was discovered—it has no application of fire or a fiery element, direct or indirect, to the food. Pure electromagnetic energy agitates the water molecules in food at almost 2,500 million times a second, producing friction and as a by-product, sufficient heat for cooking. Metal containers reflect microwaves and should not be used in cooking. The electronic tube that produces microwave energy-a magnetron-was invented by Sir John Randall and H.A. Boot during World War II to be used in radar. In 1946, a Raytheon engineer, Percy Spencer (1894-1970), discovered food was affected by the magnetron. Raytheon developed a very large, commercial microwave oven, the Radar Range, in 1947. Although it was the size of a refrigerator, its cooking space was modest. Before microminiaturization, electronic devices like the microwave oven required much space for vacuum tubes, wiring, etc.-making these devices very bulky. By 1952, the Tappan Company produced an oven with two speeds for the home, but it was still very expensive and large. During the 1960s the ovens became more available, less expensive, and smaller. But it took nearly 20 years for this new way of cooking to become popular.

Robert J. Cone, *How the New Technology Works* (Phoenix, AZ: Oryx Press, 1991). Howard Hillman, *Kitchen Science* (Boston: Houghton Mifflin Company, 1989), 19-20. Charles Panati, *Panati's Extraordinary Origins of Everyday Things* (New York: Perennial Library, 1989), 125-26. Bridget Travers, ed., *World of Invention* (Detroit: Gale Research, 1994), 421-22.

When was the electric washing machine and clothes dryer invented?

Electric washing machines appeared early in the 1900s. Electric wringer washers appeared in 1910. The Maytag Company, which introduced its electric Hired Girl wringer washer in 1911, added the vaned agitator to its machines in 1922. Although a wringerless model was marketed as early as 1926, wringer washers continued to be the industry standard until the early 1950s, when spin dry models became popular. The first manual clothes dryer, called a "ventilator" was made by the French inventor Pochan in 1799. It was a crank-operated container pierced with holes, which was suspended above an open fire-clothes would either dry or burn. Spin dryers, first developed around 1909, used centrifugal force to remove moisture, and about 1930 electric clothes dryers first appeared.

Ellis Mount and Barbara A. List, *Milestones in Science and Technology* (Phoenix, AZ: Oryx Press, 1987). Charles Panati, *Panati's Extraordinary Origins of Everyday Things* (New York: Perennial Library, 1987). Bridget Travers, ed., *World of Invention* (Detroit, MI: Gale Research, 1994), 145, 673.

Who invented scissors?

Although the inventor of scissors is unknown, they were developed in the ancient Near East around 1500 B.C. They made of bronze and specially designed for cutting fabric and other materials. Early spring-type scissors appeared in 500 B.C. Pivoted scissors, similar to those of today, were used in ancient Rome in 100 A.D.; but they were not used domestically in Europe until the sixteenth century. The modern cast-steel scissors were developed in England by Robert Hinchcliffe in 1761.

Nell DuVall, *Domestic Technology* (Boston: G.K. Hall, 1988), 164-65. Bridget Travers, ed., *World of Invention* (Detroit: Gale Research Inc., 1994), 537-38.

How do spray cans of deodorant, paint, air fresheners, whipped cream, and others, affect the atmosphere?

Every time a button is pushed on a spray can using fluorocarbon propellant, a tiny bit of the propellant is released into the air. The fluorocarbon drifts hundreds of miles into the earth's upper atmosphere where it changes some ozone into oxygen creating a "hole" that lets through more ultraviolet light to the earth's surface. This creates health problems for humans such as cataracts and skin cancer, and disturbs delicate ecosystems (for example, plants produce less seed). Currently propellants have been changed to hydrocarbons, such as butane. Chlorofluorocarbons-organic compounds containing chlorine and fluorine-have been banned in aerosols and are being phased out elsewhere.

Geraldine Woods, *Pollution* (New York: Franklin Watts, 1985), 26.

How much newspaper must be recycled to save one tree?

One 35-to 40-foot (10.6-to 12-meter) tree produces a stack of newspapers 4 feet (1.2 meters) thick; this much newspaper must be recycled to save a tree.

Heloise Hints for a Healthy Planet (New York: Perigree, 1990), 67.

Who invented the tin can?

The English inventor, Peter Durand, created the tin canister in 1810. The cans were handmade and expensive. Machine-stamped cans were introduced in 1847. In 1959 Ermal Cleon Fraze (1913-1989) invented the pull-top can.

Harry Harris, *Good Old-Fashioned Yankee Ingenuity* (Chelsea, MI: Scarborough House, 1990), 127. Dennis Sanders, *The First of Everything* (New York: Delacorte, 1981), 17. E. Joseph Stilwell, et al., *Packaging for the Environment* (New York: AMACOM, 1991), 77.

When was the first world's fair?

The Great Exhibition of the Works of Industry of All Nations, commonly referred to as the Great Exhibition of 1851 or the Crystal Palace Exhibition, was the first true world's fair. It opened May 1, 1851, and closed October 15, 1851.

John E. Findling, *Historical Dictionary of World's Fairs and Expositions, 1851-1988* (Westport, CT: Greenwood, 1990), xv, 3.

What are the ten outstanding engineering achievements of the last 25 years?

The National Academy of Engineering lists them as follows:
The Moon Landing
Application Satellites
Microprocessors
Computer-Aided Design and Manufacturing
CAT Scan
Advanced Composite Materials
Jumbo Jets
Lasers
Fiber-Optic Communication
Genetically Engineered Products

Engineering and the Advancement of Human Welfare (Washington, DC: National Academy Press, 1989), 1.

What are the areas of critical technology?

There are 22 areas of technological development that the United States considers to be critical to the prosperity and security of the country. They are aeronautics; applied molecular biology; ceramics; composites; computer simulation; data storage; electronic and photonic materials; energy; environment; flexible computer integrated manufacturing; high-definition imaging and displays; high-performance computing/networking; high-performance metals and alloys; intelligent processing equipment; materials processing; medicine; micro-and nano-fabrication; microelectronics and optoelectronics; sensors and signal processing; software; surface transportation; and systems-management.

The World Almanac and Book of Facts 1992 (New York: World Almanac, 1991), 200.

Who invented the Xerox machine?

After 20 years of experimentation, American physicist Chester F. Carlson (1906-1968) developed in 1938 a method of copying that used dry powder, electric charge, and light. Because nothing moist was used in the process, the procedure was called xerography (meaning "dry writing" in Greek). But Carlson could not interest the industry of this new method until the Haloid Company of Rochester, New York, acquired his patent. The company, which later became the Xerox Corporation, gave the first public demonstration of this copier at the annual meeting of the Optical Society of America, in Detroit, Michigan, on October 22, 1948.

Carlson's new method used static electricity as the basis of the xerographic process. An electrostatic charge is induced on an insulating photoconductive surface in darkness. Then this surface is exposed to light reflecting from the original (similar to a photographic plate). The resultant charge pattern is dusted with a charged powder (called toner) that is attracted to the pattern but rejected by the background. The powder pattern (the image of the original) is transferred to ordinary paper with an electrostatic charge and "fixed" on the paper by either heat or by chemicals. Finally the xerographic surface is cleaned and ready for reuse. Today, copy paper is used, which forms the photo conductive surface and consequently becomes the final copy.

Isaac Asimov, *Asimov's Chronology of Science and Discovery* (New York: Harper and Row, 1989), 598. Edward De Bono, *Eureka!* (New York: Holt, Rinehart and Winston, 1974), 61-62.

What is a donkey engine?

A donkey engine is a small auxiliary engine which is usually portable or semi-portable. It is powered by steam, compressed air, or other means. It is often used to power a windlass or lift cargo on shipboard.

The McGraw-Hill Dictionary of Scientific and Technical Terms, 4th ed. (New York: McGraw-Hill, 1989), 569.

Which warfare innovations were introduced during the American Civil War?

Barbed wire, trench warfare, hand grenades, land mines, armored trains, ironclad ships, aerial reconnaissance, submarine vessels, machine guns, and even a primitive flamethrower were products of the American Civil War (1861-65).

Michael Newton, *Armed and Dangerous* (Cincinnati: Writer's Digest Books, 1990), 17.

When was the Colt revolver patented?

The celebrated six-shooter of the American West was named after its inventor, Samuel Colt (1814-62). Although he did not invent the revolver, he perfected the design which he first patented in 1835 in England and then the United States in the following year. Colt had hoped to mass-produce this weapon, but failed to get enough backing to acquire the necessary machinery. Consequently, the guns, made by hand, were expensive and attracted only limited orders. In 1847, the Texas Rangers ordered one thousand Colt pistols enabling Colt to finally set up assembly line manufacture in a plant in Hartford, Connecticut.

New Illustrated Science and Invention Encyclopedia (Westport, CT: Stuttman, 1988), 24:3241.

What was the Manhattan Project?

The Manhattan Engineer District was the formal code name for the U.S. government project to develop an atomic bomb during World War II (1939-1945). It soon became known as the Manhattan Project-a name taken from the location of the office of Colonel James C. Marshall, who had been selected by the U.S. Army Corp of Engineers to build and run the bomb's production facilities. When the project was activated by the U.S. War Department in June 1942, it came under the direction of Colonel Leslie R. Groves (1896-1970).

The first major accomplishment of the project's scientists was the successful initiation of the first self-sustaining nuclear chain reaction, done at a University of Chicago laboratory on December 2, 1942. The project tested the first experimental detonation of an atomic bomb in a desert area near Alamogordo, New Mexico on July 16, 1945. The test site was called Trinity, and the bomb generated an explosive power equivalent to between 15,000 and 20,000 tons (15,240 and 20,320 tonnes) of TNT. Two of the project's bombs were dropped on Japan the following month (Hiroshima on August 6 and Nagasaki on August 9, 1945) resulting in the Japanese surrender to end World War II (1939-1945).

Don E. Beyer, *The Manhattan Project* (New York: Watts, 1991), 36. Richard Rhodes, *The Making of the Atomic Bomb* (New York: Simon and Schuster, 1986), 436-42.

Who invented the machine gun?

The first successful machine gun, invented by Richard J. Gatling (1818-1903), was patented in 1862 during the American Civil War (1861-65). Its six barrels were revolved by gears operated by a hand crank, and it fired 1,200 rounds per minute. Although there had been several partially successful attempts at building a multi-firing weapon, none were able to overcome the many engineering difficulties until Gatling. In his gear-driven machine, cocking and firing were performed by cam action. The U.S. Army officially adopted the gun on August 24, 1866.

The first automatic machine gun was a highly original design by Hiram S. Maxim (1840-1915). In 1884, the clever Maxim designed a portable, single-barreled automatic weapon that made use of the recoil energy of a fired bullet to eject the spent cartridge and load the next.

The original "tommy gun" was the Thompson Model 1928 SMG. This 45 caliber machine gun, designed in 1918 by General John Taliaferro Thompson (1860-1940), was to be used in close-quarter combat. The war ended before it went into production however, and Thompson's Auto Ordnance Corporation did not do well, until the gun was adopted by American gangsters during Prohibition. The image of a reckless criminal spraying his enemies with bullets from his hand-held "tommy gun" became a symbol of the depression years. The gun was modified several times and was much used during World War II (1939-45).

George M. Chinn, *The Machine Gun* (Washington, DC: Department of the Navy, 1951), 1:24, 48-63, 123-49. John Ellis, *The Social History of the Machine Gun* (London: Croom Helm, 1975), 149-65. *Weapons: An International Encyclopedia from 5000 B.C. to 2000 A.D.* (New York: St. Martin's Press, 1990), 149.

Does catgut really come from cats?

Catgut does not come from cats, but rather from the smooth side of sheep intestines or casings. It is used for the strings of tennis rackets and musical instruments, surgical thread, etc. Today nylon has become a substitute for the tough cords of catgut in many instances. There is no simple explanation for the derivation of the misnomer "catgut," but possibly it is a corruption of the word "kitgut," as the product was originally called. A "kit" is an old name for a small violin as well as the name for an immature cat; and "gut" is a synonym for intestines.

Henry Hendrickson, *The Henry Holt Encyclopedia of Word and Phrase Origins* (New York: Henry Holt, 1987), 105. Malcolm D. Whitman, *Tennis: Origins and Mysteries* (New York: Derrydale Press, 1932), 126-32.

How are colored fireworks made?

Fireworks existed in ancient China in the ninth century A.D. where saltpeter (potassium nitrate), sulfur, and charcoal were mixed to produce the dazzling effects. Magnesium burns with a brilliant white light and is widely used in making flares and fireworks. Various other colors can be produced by adding certain substances to the flame. Strontium compounds color the flame scarlet and barium compounds produce a yellowish-green color; borax produces a green color, and lithium a purple color.

Gardner D. Hiscox, *Henley's Twentieth Century Book of Formulas, Processes, and Trade Secrets* (New York: NY Books, 1963), 609. William C. Vergara, *Science in Everyday Life* (New York: Harper & Row, 1980), 267.

What is crown glass?

In the early 1800s, window glass was called crown glass. It was made by blowing a bubble, then spinning it until flat. This left a sheet of glass with a bump, or crown, in the center. This blowing method of window-pane making required great skill and was very costly. Still, the finished crown glass produced a distortion through which everything looked curiously wavy, and the glass itself was also faulty and uneven. By the end of the nineteenth century, flat glass was mass-produced and was a common material. The cylinder method replaced the older method, using compressed air to produce glass which could be slit lengthwise, reheated, flattened on an iron table under its own weight. New furnaces and better polishing machines made the production of plate-glass a real industry. Today, glass is produced by a float-glass process especially needed for the manufacture of high-quality flat glass for large areas and industrial uses. The float glass process, invented by Alistair Pilkington, in 1952, departs from all other glass processes where the molten glass flows from the melting chamber into the float chamber which is a molten tin pool approximately 160 feet (49 meters) long and 12 feet (3.5 meters) wide. During its passage over this molten tin, the hot glass assumes the perfect flatness of the tin surface and develops excellent thickness uniformity. The finished product is as flat and smooth as plate glass without having been ground and polished.

Edward De Bono, *Eureka!* (New York: Holt, Rinehart and Winston, 1974), 94. Freda Diamond, *The Story of Glass* (San Diego: Harcourt Brace, 1953), 111-12. R.W. Douglas and Susan Frank, *A History of Glassmaking* (London: G.T. Foulis, 1972), 133-61. *Handbook of Glass Manufacture, 3d ed.,* (New York: Ashlee, 1984), 2:711. *World Book Encyclopedia* (Chicago: World Book, 1990), 8:219.

When were glass blocks invented?

Glass building bricks were introduced in 1931. They were invented in Europe in the early 1900s as thin blocks of glass supported by a grid. They have been in and out of favor since they were introduced. They are small, the largest being 12 inches by 12 inches (30 centimeters by 30 centimeters). They offer the following advantages: they allow natural light to filter through, but their patterns can afford privacy; they have the insulating value of a 12 inch-thick (30 centimeters) concrete wall; they absorb outside noise; and they are much more secure than ordinary flat glass.

Nell DuVall, *Domestic Technology* (Boston: G.K. Hall, 1988), 254. Bob Pennycook, *Building With Glass Blocks* (New York: Doubleday, 1987), 1, 3-4.

How thick is gold leaf?

Gold leaf is pure gold which is hammered so thin that it can take typically 300,000 units to make a stack one inch high. The thickness of a single gold leaf is .0000035 inches (3-millionths of an inch), although this may vary widely according to which manufacturer makes it. Also called gold foil, it is used for architectural coverings and for hot-embossed printing on leather.

Charlotte M. Calasibetta, *Fairchild's Dictionary of Fashion* (New York: Fairchild Publications, 1988), 254. Raymond Le Blanc, *Gold-Leaf Techniques* (Cincinnati: ST Publications, 1986), 2.

What is German silver?

Nickel silver, sometimes known as German silver, is a silver-white alloy composed of 52 percent to 80 percent copper, 10 percent to 35 percent zinc, and 5 percent to 35 percent nickel. It may also contain a small percent of lead and tin. There are other forms of nickel silver, but the term "German silver" is the name used in the silverware trade.

George S. Brady, *Materials Handbook, 12th ed.* (New York: McGraw-Hill, 1986), 539-40. *The McGraw-Hill Dictionary of Scientific and Technical Terms, 4th ed.* (New York: McGraw-Hill, 1989), 1273. Paul W. Thrush, *A Dictionary of Mining, Mineral, and Related Terms* (Washington, DC: U.S. Bureau of Mines, 1968), 490.

What products are made from horsehair?

Products made from horsehair, include baskets, belts, bird nests, hair and industrial brushes, buttons, carpet, curlers, fishing lines, furniture padding, hats, lariats, fishing nets, plumes for military hats or horse bridles, surgical sutures (during the Civil War), upholstery cloth, bows (for violin, cello, and viola) whips, and wigs.

Marjorie Congram, *Horsehair: A Textile Resource* (Martinsville, NJ: Dockwra Press, 1987), 81-82.

In coal mining what is meant by damp?

In coal mining, damp is a poisonous or explosive gas in a mine. Carbon monoxide is known as white damp, and methane is known as firedamp. Blackdamp is formed by mine fires and explosion of firedamp in mines. It extinguishes light and suffocates its victims. The average blackdamp contains 10 percent to 15 percent carbon dioxide and 85 percent to 90 percent nitrogen.

L. Harold Stevenson, *The Facts On File Dictionary of Environmental Science* (New York: Facts On File, 1991), 68. Paul W. Thrush, *A Dictionary of Mining, Mineral, and Related Terms* (Washington, DC: U.S. Bureau of Mines, 1968), 108.

Who was the greatest U.S. inventor?

Thomas Alva Edison (1847-1931) is considered the most prolific inventor of the United States. He owned 1,093 patents, including the incandescent electric lamp, the phonograph, the carbon telephone transmitter, and the motion-picture projector. His first patent was obtained in 1868 for an electrical vote recorder. He established his laboratory at Menlo Park, New Jersey, in 1876, then moved the research laboratory to West Orange, New Jersey, in 1887. Edison's last patent was granted posthumously in 1933, for a holder for an article to be electroplated.

Matthew Josephson, *Edison: A Biography* (New York: McGraw-Hill, 1959), 296. *The National Inventors Hall of Fame* (OH: National Inventors Hall of Fame, 1993), 2-3. Trevor I. Williams, *The History of Invention* (New York:

Facts On File, 1987), s.v. "Edison." *The New Encyclopaedia Britannica, 15th ed., "Micropaedia"* (Chicago: Encyclopaedia Britannica, 1993), s.v. "Edison, Thomas Alva."

How does a lie detector or polygraph work?

A lie detector or polygraph is a machine that measures bodily changes in blood pressure, pulse, galvanic skin response, and rate and depth of breathing and records these changes on a moving graph. It is believed that lying causes anxiety which in turn causes small but immediate and measurable physiological changes. Usually the respondent is asked non threatening questions at first to calm the respondent and to establish the normal pattern of bodily reactions. Then key questions are periodically inserted. Abrupt physiological changes could indicate that the subject is lying. However, the machine cannot unfailingly detect a lie and the results must not be used conclusively. John Larsen in the 1920s created the first continuous-recording polygraph, which tracked a respondent's changes in heart rate, blood pressure, and respiration. In the 1930s Leonard Keeler improved Larsen's invention by adding a galvanometer hooked to electrodes which when placed under the respondent's fingertips would record changes in perspiration rate.

Bridget Travers, ed., *World of Invention* (Detroit, MI: Gale Research, 1994), 376-77. *McCall's* April, 1969.

Who invented glue, from what material was it made, and what was its first use?

Glue was invented by the Romans, who made it by boiling down mistletoe juice. The substance was spread on trees to catch birds.

John May et al. , *Curious Trivia* (New York: Dorset Press, 1984), 103.

Who invented the paper bag?

In 1872 Luther C. Cromwell was the first to make a square-bottomed paper bag. This was a boon to shoppers of all kinds.

Dennis Sanders, *The First of Everything: A Compendium of Important, Eventful, and Just-Plain-Fun Facts About All Kinds of Firsts* (New York: Delacorte Press, 1981), 10.

What is the history of the umbrella?

Umbra is the Latin word for shade, and umbrellas were originally used as sunshades. Evidence of their use dates back to the twelfth century B.C. in Mesopotamia, Egypt, and China. Because early umbrellas were made of leather and were both costly and heavy, they were used only by royalty or the rich. The owner of an umbrella needed to be able to afford servants or slaves to carry it.

By the seventeenth century, the leather of umbrellas was replaced by lighter-weight cloths such as silk, and the ribs were made of whalebone, so umbrella owners could carry them unaided. Now umbrellas became useful as a shield from the rain as well as sun but were still not accepted by all. Men considered them effeminate, and the well-to-do considered them a poor substitute for a carriage. During the eighteenth century, Jonas Hanway is credited with introducing the umbrella into wide use in rainy Britain. During the 1850s, Samuel Fox invented an even lighter-weight metal umbrella, which became generally popular. After World War I, sunshine was considered healthy, tanned skin became desirable, and umbrellas were used primarily as protection from rain.

Rudolph Brasch, *How Did It Begin?* (New York: David McKay, 1966), 119-22.

What is a Molotov Cocktail?

A Molotov Cocktail is an incendiary device made by filling a glass bottle or jar with gasoline and inserting a rag wick in its mouth. The bottle is quickly turned upside down, just long enough to saturate the wick with the fluid. The wick is lit and when the bottle is smashed against a hard surface it shatters setting the target aflame. The use of the Molotov Cocktail originated during the Spanish Civil War and was used extensively during the Soviet-Finnish War of 1939-40 and World War II (1939-45) by guerilla and partisan forces.

Named after Vyacheslav M. Molotov (1890-1987), a veteran of the Soviet Politburo and close political ally of Soviet leader Joseph Stalin (1879-1953). Molotov at one time held the high position of Commissar for Foreign Affairs and was deeply involved with negotiating the Soviet-German Nonaggression Pact of 1939.

Thomas Parrish, ed., *The Simon and Schuster Encyclopedia of World War II* (New York: Simon and Schuster, 1978), s.v. "Molotov cocktail."

Who was Candido Jacuzzi?

The popular Jacuzzi whirlpool bath was named for its inventor, Candido Jacuzzi. Born in northeastern Italy, Jacuzzi emigrated to the United States with his seven brothers and six sisters. They created a family business, Jacuzzi Brothers Inc., beginning in a small machine shop. The company flourished and opened factories in six different countries, making a wide range of products and developing more than 50 patents that are widely used in industry. Jacuzzi created his design for a whirlpool bath in 1949, when his son Kenneth was diagnosed with rheumatoid arthritis. In answer to his son's need for hydrotherapy, Jacuzzi developed the first pump for use in a bathtub. Formerly, such therapy was only available at medical facilities and spas.

Glenn Fowler, "Candido Jacuzzi, 83, Is Dead. Inventor of Whirlpool Bath," *New York Times* 10 October 1986.

What was the job of a "powder monkey"?

The name "powder monkey" was once used to describe boys who were used in forts and on warships to supply guns with powder. It also identifies a worker who is expert in the use of explosives, particularly in the construction industry.

Clarence L. Barnhart and Robert K. Barnhart, eds., *The World Book Dictionary* (Chicago: World Book, 1990), s.v. "powder monkey."

What was a fustibal?

The fustibal, also known as the fustibalus, was a sling that is part of a staff. The meter-long weapon was used to throw pebbles and stone or metal pellets a distance of more than 550 feet. It was used during the ancient period and in the late Middle Ages. Examples of the fustibal were included in Leonardo da Vinci's *Codex Atlanticus.*

Leonid Tarassuk and Claude Blair, eds., *The Complete Encyclopedia of Arms & Weapons: The Most Comprehensive Reference Work Ever Published On Arms And Armor From Prehistoric Times To The Present—With Over 1,250 Illustrations* (New York: Simon and Schuster, 1982), s.v. "fustibalus."

Who is known as the father of the British civil engineering profession?

Thomas Telford (1757-1834), the first president of the Institute of Civil Engineers, is the father figure of the British civil engineering profession. Telford established the professional ethos and tradition of the civil engineer-a tradition followed by all engineers today. He built bridges, roads, harbors, and canals. His greatest works include the Menai Strait Suspension Bridge and Pont y Cysyllte Aqueduct, the Gotha Canal in Sweden, the Caledonian Canal, and many Scottish roads. He was the first and greatest master of the iron bridge.

Keith Ellis, *Thomas Telford* (Duluth, MN: Priory Press, 1974), 15. John H. Stephens, *The Guinness Book of Structures* (London: Guinness Superlatives, 1976), 224-25.

How does police RADAR work?

The Austrian physicist, Christian Doppler (1803-1853), discovered that the reflected radio waves bouncing off a moving object are returned at a different frequency (shorter or longer waves, cycles, or vibrations). This phenomenon, called the Doppler effect, is the basis of police RADAR. Directional radio waves are transmitted from the RADAR device. The waves bounce off the targeted vehicle and are received by a recorder. The recorder compares the difference between the sent and received waves, and translates the information into miles per hour and displays the speed on a dial.

Bruce F. Bogner, *Vehicular Traffic Radar: Handbook for Attorneys* (Mount Holly, NJ: Brehn, 1979), 4. Herman Schneider, *The Harper Dictionary of Science in Everyday Language* (New York: Harper & Row, 1988), 90.

How is underground coal mined?

There are two basic types of underground mining methods: room and pillar and longwall. In room and pillar mines, coal is removed by cutting rooms, or large tunnels, in the solid coal, leaving pillars of coal for roof support. Longwall mining takes successive slices over the entire length of a long working face. In the United States, almost all of the coal recovered by underground mining is by room and pillar method. Coal seams in the United States to range in thickness from a thin film to 50 feet (15 meters) or more. The thickest coalbeds are in the western states, ranging from 10 feet (3 meters) in Utah and New Mexico to 50 feet (15 meters) in Wyoming. Other places such as Great Britain, use the longwall method.

David J. Cuff, *The United States Energy Atlas, 2d ed.,* (New York: Macmillan, 1986), 19, 21.

What is a green product?

Green products are environmentally safe products that contain no chlorofluorocarbons, are degradable (can decompose), and are made from recycled materials. Deep-green products are those from small suppliers who build their identities around their claimed environmental virtues. Greened-up products come from the industry giants and are environmentally improved versions of established brands.

Buzzworm: The Environmental Journal November/December 1991. *Environment* November 1991.

How does a breathalyser determine the alcohol level of the breath?

Breathalysers used by police are usually electronic, using the alcohol blown in through the tube as fuel to produce electric current. The more alcohol the breath contains, the stronger the current. If it lights up a green light, the driver is below the legal limit and has passed the test. An amber light means the alcohol level is near the limit; a red light above the limit. The device has a platinum anode which causes the alcohol to oxidize into acetic acid with its molecules losing some electrons. This sets up the electric current. Earlier breathalysers detected alcohol by color change. Orange-yellow crystals of a mixture of sulfuric acid and potassium dichromate in a blowing tube turn to blue-green chromium sulfate and colorless potassium sulphate when the mixture reacts with alcohol, which changes into acetic acid (vinegar). The more crystals that change color, the higher the alcohol level in the body.

How in the World? (Pleasantville, NY: Reader's Digest Association, 1990), 251.

What does "cc" mean in engine sizes?

Cubic centimeters (cc), as applied to an internal combustion engine, is a measure of the combustion space in the cylinders. The size of an engine is measured by theoretically removing the top of a cylinder, pushing the piston all the way down and then filling the cylinder with liquid. The cubic centimeters of liquid displaced (spilled out) when the piston is returned to its high position is the measure of the combustion volume of the cylinder. If a motorcycle has four cylinders, each displacing 200 ccs, it has an 800 cc engine. Automobile engines are sized essentially the same way.

Mary Blocksma, *Reading the Numbers* (New York: Penguin, 1989), 124-26.

What is a power take-off?

The standard power take-off is a connection that will turn a shaft inserted through the rear wall of a gear case. It is used to power accessories such as a cable control unit, a winch, or a hydraulic pump. Farmers use the mechanism to pump water, grind feed, or saw wood. A power take-off drives the moving parts of mowing machines, hay balers, combines, and potato diggers.

Herbert L. Nichols, *Moving the Earth, 3d ed.,* (Greenwich, CT: North Castle Books, 1976), 15-4. *World Book Encyclopedia* (Chicago: World Book, 1990), 19:360, 457.

How did Frank B. Gilbreth use his cyclograph?

The American engineer and efficiency expert, Frank Bunker Gilbreth (1868-1924) used his cyclograph, or "motion recorder," to refine his study of time and motion. An ordinary camera and a small electric bulb was all he needed to show the path of movement. The light patterns reveal all hesitation or poor habits interfering with a worker's dexterity.

Siegfried Giedion, *Mechanization Takes Command* (New York: Oxford University Press, 1948), 103.

Who invented thermopane glass?

Thermopane insulated window glass was invented by C.D. Haven in the United States in 1930. It is two sheets of glass that are bonded together in such a manner that they enclose a captive air space. Often this space is filled with an inert gas which increases the insulating quality of the window. Glass is also one of the best transparent insulating materials because it allows the short wavelengths of solar radiation to pass through it, but prohibits nearly all of the long waves of reflected radiation from passing back through it.

George R. Drake, *Weatherizing Your Home* (New York: Reston, 1978), 153-54. Nell DuVall, *Domestic Technology* (Boston: G.K. Hall, 1988), 254.

How is dry ice made?

Dry ice is composed of carbon dioxide, which at normal temperatures is a gas. The carbon dioxide is stored and shipped as a liquid in tanks that are pressurized at 1073 pounds per square inch. To make dry ice, the carbon dioxide liquid is withdrawn from the tank and allowed to evaporate at a normal pressure in a porous bag. This rapid evaporation consumes so much heat that part of the liquid carbon dioxide freezes to a temperature of minus 109 degrees Fahrenheit (minus 78 degrees Celsius). The frozen liquid is then compressed by machines into blocks of "dry ice" which will melt into a gas again when set out at room temperature.

It was first made commercially in 1925 by the Prest-Air Devices Company of Long Island City, New York through the efforts of Thomas Benton Slate. It was used by Schrafft's of New York in July 1925 to keep ice cream from melting. The first large sale of dry ice was made later in that year to Breyer Ice Cream Company of New York.

Joseph N. Kane, *Famous First Facts, 4th ed.* (New York: Wilson, 1981), 316. Caroline Sutton and Duncan M. Anderson, *How Do They Do That?* (New York: Quill, 1982), 154.

What is solder?

Solder is an alloy of two or more metals used for joining other metals together. The most common solder is called half-and-half, or "plumber's" solder, and is composed of equal parts of lead and tin. Other metals used in solder are aluminum, cadmium, zinc, nickel, gold, silver, palladium, bismuth, copper, and antimony. Various melting points to suit the work are obtained by varying the proportions of the metals.

Solder is an ancient joining method, mentioned in the Bible (*Isaiah* 41:7). There is evidence of its use in Mesopotamia some five thousand years ago, and later in Egypt, Greece, and Rome. For the near future, it appears that as long as a combination of conductors, semiconductors, and insulators is used to build electrical and magnetic impulse circuitry, solder will remain indispensable.

George S. Brady, *Materials Handbook, 12th ed.* (New York: McGraw-Hill, 1986), 750-52. Howard H. Manko, *Solders & Soldering, 2d ed.* (New York: McGraw-Hill, 1979), xv.

Who developed the process for making ammonia?

Known since ancient times, ammonia has been commercially important for more than 100 years and has become the second largest chemical in terms of tonnage production and the first chemical in value of production. The first breakthrough in the large-scale synthesis of ammonia resulted from the work of Fritz Haber (1863-1934). In 1913 Haber found that ammonia could be produced by combining nitrogen and hydrogen with a catalyst (iron oxide with small quantities of cerium and chromium) at 131 degrees Farenheit (55 degrees Centigrade) under a pressure of about 200 atmospheres. The process was adapted for industrial-quality production by Karl Bosch (1874-1940). Thereafter, many improved ammonia-synthesis systems, based on the Haber-Bosch process, were commercialized using various operating conditions and synthesis loop-designs. One of the five top inorganic chemicals produced in the United States, it is used in refrigerants, detergents, and other cleaning preparations, explosives, fabrics, and fertilizers. A little over 75 percent of ammonia production in the United States is used for fertilizers. It has been shown to produce cancer of the skin in humans, in doses of 1,000 milligrams (or one gram) per kilogram (2.2 pounds) of body weight.

Van Nostrand Reinhold Encyclopedia of Chemistry, 4th ed. (New York: Van Nostrand Reinhold, 1984), 58-59. Ruth Winter, *A Consumer's Dictionary of Household, Yard and Office Chemicals* (New York: Crown Publishers, 1992), 50.

How is sandpaper made?

Sandpaper is a coated abrasive which consists of a flexible-type backing (paper) upon which a film of adhesive holds and supports a coating of abrasive grains. Various types of resins and hide glues are used as adhesives. The first record of a coated abrasive is in thirteenth century China, when crushed seashells were bound to parchment using natural gums. The first known article on coated abrasives was published in 1808 and described how calcined, ground pumice was mixed with varnish and spread on paper with a brush. Most abrasive papers are now made with aluminum oxide or silicon carbide, although the term sandpapering is still used. Quartz grains are also used for wood polishing. The paper used is heavy, tough, and flexible, and the grains are bonded with a strong glue.

George S. Brady, *Materials Handbook, 12th ed.* (New York: McGraw-Hill, 1986), 698. *Coated Abrasives: Modern Tool of Industry* (New York: McGraw-Hill, 1958), 7-8. *World Book Encyclopedia* (Chicago: World Book, 1990), 21:401.

Who invented dynamite?

Dynamite was not an accidental discovery but the result of a methodical search by the Swedish technologist Alfred Nobel (1833-1896). Nitroglycerine had been discovered in 1849, by the Italian organic chemist Ascanio Sobriero (1812-1888), but it was so sensitive and difficult to control that it was useless. Nobel sought to turn nitroglycerine into a manageable solid by absorbing it into a porous substance. During 1866-1867, he tried an unusual mineral, kieselguhr, and created a dough-like controllable explosive. Nobel also invented a detonating cap incorporating mercury fulminate with which nitroglycerine could be detonated at will. Nobel made a great fortune and bequeathed it to a foundation for awarding prizes for contributions to science, literature, and the promotion of peace.

Edward De Bono, *Eureka!* (New York: Holt, Rinehart and Winston, 1974), 76-77. *Dictionary of Scientific Biography* (New York: Charles Scribner's Sons, 1973), 10:132.

Who invented teflon?

In 1938, the American engineer Roy J. Plunkett (b. 1910) at DuPont de Nemours, discovered the Polymer of TetraFluorEthylene (PTFE) by accident. This fluorocarbon is marketed under the name of Fluon in Great Britain and Teflon in the United States. Patented in 1939 and first exploited commercially in 1954, PTFE is resistant to all acids and has exceptional stability and excellent electrical insulating properties. It is used in making piping for corrosive materials, in insulating devices for radio transmitters, in pump gaskets, and in computer microchips. In addition, its non-stick properties make PTFE an ideal material for surface coatings. In 1956, French engineer Marc Gregoire discovered a process whereby he could fix a thin layer of teflon on an aluminum surface. He then patented the process of applying it to cookware, and the no-stick frying pan was created.

Valerie-Anne Giscard d'Estaing, *The Second World Almanac Book of Inventions* (New York: World Almanac, 1986), 12, 272. Charles Panati, *Panati's Extraordinary Origins of Everyday Things* (New York: Perennial Library, 1987), 105-7.

How can plastics be made biodegradable?

Plastic does not rust or rot. This advantage in its usage becomes a liability when it must be disposed. Degradable plastic has starch in it so that it can be attacked by starch-eating bacteria to eventually disintegrate the plastic into bits. Chemically degradable plastic can be broken up with a chemical solution that dissolves it. Used in surgery biodegradable plastic stitches slowly dissolve in the body fluids. Photodegradable plastic contains chemicals that slowly disintegrate in light over a period of one to three years. Twenty-five percent of the plastic yokes used to package beverages are made from a photodegradable plastic called Ecolyte.

How in the World? (Pleasantville, NY: Reader's Digest Association, 1990), 130.

Which metals are used to make today's United States coins?

Current United states coins are composed of the following metals:

Penny—Since 1982, zinc core with copper coating
Nickel—Since 1946, 75% copper, 25% nickel; the only non-clad U.S. coin
Dime—Since 1965, 75% copper, 25% nickel outer covering with an interior of pure copper
Quarter—Since 1965, 75 % copper, 25% nickel outer covering with an interior of pure copper
Half dollar—Since 1971, three parts copper/one part nickel outer covering with an interior of pure copper

Mark Hudgeons, *The Official 1994 Blackbook: Price Guide of United States Coins* (New York: Random House, 1993), 39, 156-59, 173.

Who invented the safety pin?

The modern safety pin was invented by American Walter Hunt (1796-1859) in 1849. He patented the design and sold the rights for $400. Straight pins of iron and bone can be traced back to 3000 B.C. By the sixth century B.C., Greek and Romans were using the fibula, a pin with the middle coiled which produced tension and provided the fastener with a spring-like opening action. A forerunner of the modern safety pin, the fibula was used to attach draped garments.

Valerie-Anne Giscard d'Estaing, *The Second World Almanac Book of Inventions* (New York: World Almanac, 1986), 16. Charles Panati, *Extraordinary Origins of Everyday Things* (New York: Harper & Row, 1987), 313. Bridget Travers, ed., *World of Invention* (Detroit: Gale Research, 1994), s.v. "pin."

Who invented the self-winding watch?

The earliest mention of self-winding watches was published in 1651 and described a belt which rose and fell with the breaths of the person wearing it, thereby acting as a perpetual spring for the watch hanging from it. The earliest device to become common was patented in 1780 by an Englishman named Louis Recordon, who invented a pedometer type of self-winding device. A weight at the end of a lever moved up and down as a person walked. The up-and-down motion enabled the watch to be wound. The same type of device was also used by A. L. Breguet, who is generally credited with inventing the self-winding watch.

G. H. Baillie, *Watches: Their History, Decoration and Mechanism* (London: Methuen, 1929), 335-41.

Who was the first woman inventor in the United States?

Mary Kies was the first woman to be granted a patent in the United States, on May 5, 1809. She invented a method of weaving straw with silk or thread. Before the United States become a nation, the first American invention recognized by the British government was patented by a man, but the records state that the process was "found out by Sibylla his wife." This patent was granted to Thomas Masters in 1715 for an invention for cleaning and curing Indian corn.

Joseph Nathan Kane, *Famous First Facts* (New York: H. W. Wilson, 1981), s.v. "Patent."

Transportation

What is the busiest domestic airline route in the United States?

According to the *Travel Industry World Yearbook*, the most heavily traveled domestic airline route in the United States is between New York and Los Angeles. Approximately 2,998,000 passengers annually fly this route.

Les Krantz, *America By the Numbers: Facts and Figures From the Weighty to the Way-out* (Boston: Houghton Mifflin, 1993), 11.

Did a collision occur between an airplane and a fish?

The first known in-flight collision between a commercial jetliner and a fish occurred near Juneau, Alaska, on March 30, 1987. An Alaska Airlines Boeing 737 flew close to an eagle which dropped what was believed to be a salmon or cod on top of the plane. The collision was confirmed by the Federal Aviation Administration.

Pittsburgh Press 2 April 1987.

What are "Black Star Airports"?

The Federation of Airline Pilots (FAP), describe "Black Star Airports" as the most dangerous airports to fly in and out of. Chicago's Midway, Los Angeles' International and Boston's Logan airport consistently make this FAP list of Black Star Airports.

Les Krantz, *What The Odds Are* (New York: HarperPerennial, 1992), 268.

In the year 1992 was there an increase in automobile seat belt use in contrast to that for the year 1982?

According to the National Highway Traffic Safety Administration, automobile seat belt use increased from 11 percent in 1982 to 62 percent in 1992.

USA Today 30 December 1992.

What was the only ocean liner to serve in both World War I and II?

The *Aquitania* was the only ocean liner to serve in both World War I and II. The four-funneled ship was commissioned by the United States as an armed merchant cruiser in August of 1914, in its first year of service. It was also used as a hospital ship and troopship from 1915-19. From 1939-48 it was again used as a troopship; and from 1948-49, the ship carried war brides and emigrants to Canada. The *Aquitania* was broken up in 1950.

Frederick Emmons, *The Atlantic Liners, 1925-70* (New York: Drake Publishers, 1972), 13.

What percent of road travel in the United States is on interstate highways?

According to the U.S. Federal Highway Administration, 1.2 percent of roadways in the United States are interstate highways, but they handle 23 percent of the travel. In total, there are 3.9 million miles of roads in America.

"Interstates get a workout," *USA Today* 1 May 1992.

What was the *Elizabeth II*?

The *Elizabeth II* was a ship that sailed in Sir Walter Raleigh's expeditions to the New World. It was used for his second voyage, in 1585, from Plymouth, England, to Roanoke Island in what is now North Carolina. The ship is thought to have carried colonists and supplies to a site that Raleigh had previously designated for a military colony. The garrison was established to bolster England's claim to the New World.

A North Carolina historic site is now home to a recreation of the *Elizabeth II*. The ship is based on common 16th-century designs used by the English. A 69-foot, square-rigged sailing ship, it is used for tours and exhibits depicting life on the sea in the 1500s. This version of the *Elizabeth II* was built to celebrate America's 400th anniversary.

Come Aboard Elizabeth II (Manteo, NC: North Carolina Historic Sites, n.d.).

What safety feature became mandatory on U.S. cars in 1967?

Motor Vehicle Safety Standard No. 209 was established in 1967, requiring seat belt assemblies in U.S. motor vehicles. That included "passenger cars, multipurpose passenger vehicles, trucks and buses."

Federal Register 1 March 1967.

What are the "doomsday planes"?

The Cold War produced a fleet of U.S. jets known as the "doomsday planes." Four Air Force 747s were prepared for use in nuclear attacks on the Soviet Union. With the end of the Cold War, these planes were given a new assignment, as a flying control center to be used in coordinating the response to natural disasters. The "doomsday planes" are still equipped to perform in the event of a nuclear attack, but can also be used for this new purpose. Housed at an Air Force base in eastern Nebraska, the planes carry advanced communications equipment that was previously a military secret. The planes are also outfitted to accommodate the president and his advisors in a "senior-level room." These facilities offer a combination of sophisticated technology, an expert crew, and the ability to respond quickly in the event of an emergency.

Kevin Robbins, "'Doomsday' Jets Have New Task," *Pittsburgh Post Gazette* 30 July 1994.

How are U.S. highways numbered?

The main north-south interstate U.S. highways always have odd numbers of one or two digits. The system, beginning with Interstate 5 on the West Coast, increases in number as it moves eastward, and ends with Interstate 95 on the East Coast.

The east-west interstate highways have even numbers. The lowest numbered highway begins in Florida with Interstate 4, increasing in number as it moves northward, and ends with Interstate 96. Coast-to-coast east-west interstates, such as Routes 10, 40, and 80, end in zero. An interstate with three digits is either a beltway or a spur route.

U.S. routes follow the same numbering system as the interstate system, but increase in number from east to west and from north to south. U.S. Route 1, for example, runs along the East Coast; U.S. Route 2 runs along the Canadian border. U.S. route numbers may have anywhere from one to three digits.

Mary Blocksma, *Reading the Numbers* (New York: Penguin, 1989), 97-98.

Which city had the first traffic light?

On December 10, 1868, the first traffic light was erected on a 22-foot-high (6.7-meter) cast-iron pillar at the corner of Bridge Street and New Palace Yard off Parliament Square in London, England. Invented by J.P. Knight, a railway signaling engineer, the light was a revolving lantern illuminated by gas, with red and green signals. It was turned by hand using a lever at the base of the pole.

Cleveland, Ohio, installed an electric traffic signal at Euclid Avenue and 105th Street on August 5, 1914. It had red and green lights with a warning buzzer as the color changed.

Around 1913, Detroit, Michigan, used a system of manually operated semaphores. Eventually the semaphores were fitted with colored lanterns for night traffic. New York City installed the first three-color light signals in 1918; these signals were still operated manually.

Edward De Bono, *Eureka!* (New York: Holt, Rinehart and Winston, 1974), 39. Patrick Robertson, *The Book of Firsts* (New York: Clarkson N. Potter, 1974), 191-92. *Traffic Engineering Handbook, 2d ed.* (Washington, DC: Institute of Traffic Engineers, 1959), xi-xii.

Who created the Liberty ship?

The Liberty ship of World War II (1939-45) was the brainchild of Henry J. Kaiser (1882-1967), an American industrialist who had never run a shipyard before 1941. The huge loss of merchant tonnage during the war created an urgent need for protection of merchant vessels transporting weapons and supplies, and the Liberty ship was born. It was a standard merchant ship with a deadweight tonnage of 10,500 long tons and a service speed of eleven knots. They were built to spartan standards and production was on a massive scale. Simplicity of construction and operations, rapidity of building, and large cargo carrying capacity were assets. To these, Kaiser added prefabrication, and welding instead of riveting. The ships were a deciding factor on the side of the Allies. In four years 2,770 ships with a deadweight tonnage of 29,292 thousand long tons were produced.

Peter Kemp, *The History of Ships* (New York: Galahad, 1979), 255. L. A. Sawyer and W. H. Mitchell, *The Liberty Ships* (Cambridge, MD: Cornell Maritime Press, 1979).

Why did the *Titanic* sink?

On its maiden voyage from Southampton, England, to New York, the British luxury liner, *Titanic*, sideswiped an iceberg at 11:40 p.m. on Sunday, April 14, 1912, and was badly damaged. The 882-foot-long (268.8-meter) liner, whose eight decks rose to the height of an 11-story building, sank two hours and forty minutes later. Of the 2,227 passengers and crew, 705 escaped in 20 lifeboats and rafts; 1,522 drowned.

Famous as the greatest disaster in transatlantic shipping history, circumstances made the loss of life in the sinking of the *Titanic* exceptionally high. Although Captain E.J. Smith was warned of icebergs in shipping lanes, he maintained his speed of 22 knots, and did not post additional lookouts. Later inquiries revealed that the liner *Californian* was only 20 miles (32.18 kilometers) away and could have helped, had its radio operator been on duty. There was an insufficient number of lifeboats, and those available for use were badly managed, with some leaving only half-full. The only ship responding to distress signals was the ancient *Carpathia*, which saved 705 people.

Contrary to a long-held belief, the Titanic had not been sliced open by the iceberg. When Dr. Robert Ballard (b. 1942) from Woods Hole Oceanographic Institution descended to the site of the sunken vessel in the research vessel *Alvin* in July of 1986, he found that the ship's starboard bow plates had buckled under the impact of the collision. This caused the ship to be opened up to the sea.

Ballard found the bow and the stern more than 600 yards apart on the ocean's floor, and speculated on what happened after the collision with the iceberg. "Water entered six forward compartments after the ship struck the iceberg. As the liner nosed down, water flooded compartments one after another, and the ship's stern rose even higher out of the water, until the stress amidships was more then she could bear. She broke apart ..." and the stern soon sank by itself.

James Cornell, *The Great International Disaster Book, 3rd ed.* (New York: Charles Scribner, 1982), 403-5. Michael Davie, *Titanic: The Death and Life of a Legend* (New York: Alfred Knopf, 1987), xiii. *National Geographic* October 1987.

What is a Sopwith Camel and why is it so called?

The most successful British fighter of World War I, the Sopwith Camel was a development of the earlier Sopwith Pup, with a much larger rotary engine. Its name "camel" was derived from the humped shape of the covering of its twin synchronized machine guns. The highly maneuverable Camel, credited with 1,294 enemy aircraft destroyed, proved far superior to all German types as dogfighters, until the introduction of the Fokker D. VII in 1918. Altogether, 5,490 Camels were built by Sopwith Aircraft. Its top speed was 118 miles (189 kilometers) per hour and it had a ceiling of 24,000 feet (7,300 meters).

Michael J. H. Taylor and John W. R. Taylor, *Encyclopedia of Aircraft* (London: Weidenfeld & Nicolson, 1978), 205-206.

What do the numbers mean on automobile tires?

The numbers and letters associated with tire sizes and types are complicated and confusing. The "Metric P" system of numbering is probably the most useful method of indicating tire sizes. For example, if the tire had P185/75R-14, then "P" means the tire is for a passenger car. The number 185 is the width of the tire in millimeters. Seventy-five is the aspect ratio, i.e., the height of the tire from the rim to the road is 75 percent of the width. "R" indicates that it is a radial tire. Fourteen is the wheel diameter. Thirteen and fifteen inches are also common sizes.

Nigel J. Hopkins, John W. Mayne, and John R. Hudson, *The Numbers You Need* (Detroit: Gale Research, 1992), 206.

How does an air bag work to prevent injury in an automobile crash?

An air bag, stored in the steering wheel or dashboard, is activated during a frontal collision involving a force roughly equivalent to hitting a solid barrier head-on at about 12 miles (19.31 kilometers) per hour. Sensors trigger the release of chemicals (sodium azide and nitrogen) that inflate the bag fully in about 1/30 of a second after impact to create a protective cushion. Immediately the airbag begins to deflate and the harmless nitrogen gas escapes through holes in the back, so that it is out of the way almost at once.

Richard P. Brennan, *Dictionary of Scientific Literacy* (New York: John Wiley & Sons, 1992), 4-5. *Consumers' Research Magazine* January 1991.

What is the origin of the term taxicab?

The term taxicab is derived from two words-taximeter and cabriolet. The taximeter, an instrument invented by Wilhelm Bruhn in 1891, automatically recorded the distance traveled and/or the time consumed. This enabled the fare to be accurately measured. The cabriolet is a two-wheeled, one-horse carriage which was often rented.

The first taxicabs for hire were two Benz-Kraftdroschkes operated by "Droschkenbesitzer" Dtz in the spring of 1896 in Stuttgart, Germany. In May of 1897 a rival service was started by Friedrich Greiner. In a literal sense, Greiner's cabs were the first "true" taxis because they were the first motor cabs fitted with taximeters.

New Encyclopaedia Britannica, 15th ed. (Chicago: Encyclopaedia Britannica, 1990), 11:585. Patrick Robertson, *The Book of Firsts* (New York: Clarkson N. Potter, 1974), 173.

When is it more economical to restart an automobile rather than let it idle?

Tests by the Environmental Protection Agency have shown that is it more economical to turn the engine off rather than let it idle if the idle time would exceed 60 seconds.

Robert Sikorsky, *How to Get More Miles Per Gallon in the 1990's* (Blue Ridge Summit, PA: TAB, 1991), 15.

What do the octane numbers of gasoline mean?

The octane number is a measure of the gasoline's ability to resist engine knock (pinging caused by premature ignition). Two test fuels, normal heptane and isooctane, are blended for test results to determine octane number. Normal heptane has an octane number of zero and isooctane a value of 100. Gasolines are then compared with these test blends to find one that makes the same knock as the test fuel. The octane rating of the gasoline under testing is the percentage by volume of isooctane required to produce the same knock. For example, if the test blend has 85 percent isooctane, the gasoline has an octane rating of 85. The octane rating that appears on gasoline pumps is an average of research octane determined in laboratory tests with engines running at low speeds, and motor octane, determined at higher speeds.

Chambers Science and Technology Dictionary (Cambridge, England: Cambridge University Press, 1988), 622. *Reader's Digest Consumer Adviser* (Pleasantville, NY: Readers Digest Association, 1989), 143.

What are the odds on being killed on a motorcycle?

1,250 to 1 are the odds on being killed on a motorcycle.

The Odds on Virtually Everything (New York: G. P. Putnam's Sons, 1980), 162.

Which United States manned space flight was the longest?

It was Skylab SL-4, which lasted 84 days, 1 hour, 15 minutes and 31 seconds, from November 16, 1973 to February 8, 1974. During this time, the three-man crew, Gerald Carr, Edward Gibson, and William Pogue, observed Comet Kohoutek and set records for time spent on experiments in every discipline from medical investigations to materials science. The longest single Soviet stay in space was accomplished by cosmonauts Vladimir Titov (b. 1947) and Musa Manarov (b. 1951) during *Soyuz TM4.* Their space flight aboard the space station Mir lasted 366 days (December 21, 1987-December 21, 1988).

Anthony R. Curtis, *Space Almanac* (Woodsboro, MD: ARCsoft, 1990), 37-38. *Space Flight: The First 30 Years* (Washington, DC: NASA, 1991), 20.

What were the first monkeys and chimpanzees in space?

On a United States *Jupiter* flight on December 12, 1958, a squirrel monkey named Old Reliable was sent into space, but not into orbit. The monkey drowned during recovery.

On another *Jupiter* flight, on May 28, 1959, two female monkeys were sent 300 miles (482.7 kilometers) high. Able was a 6-pound (2.7-kilograms) rhesus monkey and Baker was an 11-ounce (0.3-kilograms) squirrel monkey. Both were recovered alive.

A 37-pound chimpanzee named Ham was used on a *Mercury* flight on January 31, 1961. Ham was launched to a height of 157 miles (253 kilometers) into space, but did not go into orbit. His capsule reached a maximum speed of 5,857 miles (9,426 kilometers) per hour and landed 422 miles (679 kilometers) downrange in the Atlantic Ocean where he was recovered unharmed.

On November 29, 1961, the United States placed a 37.5 pound chimpanzee named Enos into orbit and recovered him alive after two complete orbits around the earth. Like the Soviets, who usually used dogs, the United States had to obtain information on the effects of space flight on living animals before they could actually launch a human into space.

David Baker, *The History of Manned Space Flight* (New York: Crown Publishers, 1982), 62-64. *Life* 8 June, 1959. Neil McAleer, *The OMNI Space Almanac* (New York: World Almanac, 1987), 15. Nicholas Roes and William E. Kennedy, *The Space-Flight Encyclopedia* (Chicago: Follet, 1968), s.v. "Enos," "Ham."

Who was the first African American in space?

Guion S. Bluford, Jr. (b. 1942) became the first African American to fly in space during the Space Shuttle *Challenger* mission STS-8 (August 30-September 5, 1983). Astronaut Bluford, who holds a Ph.D. in aerospace engineering, made a second shuttle flight aboard *Challenger* mission STS-61-A/Spacelab D1 (October 30-November 6, 1985). The first African-American man to fly in space was the Cuban cosmonaut, Arnaldo Tamayo-Mendez, who flew aboard *Soyuz 38* and spent eight days aboard the Soviet space station *Salyut 6* during September 1980. Dr. Mae C. Jemison became the first African-American woman in space on September 12, 1992 aboard the Space Shuttle *Endeavour,* mission Spacelab-J.

Ray Spangenburg and Diane Moser, *Space People From A-Z* (New York: Facts on File, 1990), 7-8, 72.

Who were the first married couple to go into space together?

Astronauts Jan Davis and Mark Lee were the first married couple in space. They flew aboard the space shuttle *Endeavor* on an eight-day mission which began on September 12, 1992. Ordinarily NASA bars married couples from flying together. An exception was made for Davis and Lee because they had no children and had begun training for the mission long before they got married.

The New York Times 21 September 1992.

Why did Amelia Earhart dub the last plane she flew as the "Flying Laboratory"?

American famous pilot, Amelia Earhart (1897-1937), referred to the Lockheed Electra that she flew on her last, and presumably fatal flight in 1937 as the "Flying Laboratory" because it was so well outfitted. On this particular flight, Earhart was to study human reactions and mechanical performance at high altitudes and extreme temperatures over long intervals and to gather microscopic samples from the upper air.

Edward T. James, ed., *Notable American Women 1607-1950: A Biographical Dictionary* (Cambridge, MA: Belknap Press of Harvard University Press, 1971), s.v. "Earhart, Amelia Mary."

Who were the first American astronauts?

The first American astronauts were those selected for the Mercury program in 1959. They were Walter M. "Wally" Schirra, Jr.; Donald K. "Deke" Slayton; John H. Glenn, Jr.,; M. Scott Carpenter; Alan B. Shepard, Jr.; Virgil I. "Gus" Grissom; and Leroy Gordon "Gordo" Cooper, Jr. Alan Shepard became the first American in space on May 5, 1961, when he flew for fifteen minutes. John Glenn became the first astronaut to orbit the earth. He went around the earth three times on February 20, 1962. Deke Slayton never flew a Mercury capsule but did take part in the subsequent Apollo program in 1975. Of the 23 launches for the Mercury program, thirteen carried no crew, four carried animals, and six carried astronauts. the 1983 film "The Right Stuff" detailed the lives of these astronauts during the Mercury program.

The Carnegie Library of Pittsburgh, ed., *Science and Technology Desk Reference: 1,500 Answers to Frequently-Asked or Difficult-to-Answer Questions* (Detroit: Gale Research, 1993), 551-52. Anthony R. Curtis, *Space Almanac, 2d ed.* (Houston: Gulf Publishing, 1992), 82-86. Carol Greene, *Astronauts* (Chicago: Childrens Press, 1984), 12-13. Jay Robert Nash and Stanley Ralph Ross, *The Motion Picture Guide, 1927-1983* (Chicago: Cinebooks, 1986), s.v. "Right Stuff, The."

How beneficial are automobile seat belts?

Safety belts are 45 percent effective in preventing fatalities and 50 percent effective in preventing moderate to critical injuries. In 1991, 52 percent of unrestrained automobile occupants were killed while only 29 percent of those using seat belts were.

Accident Facts 1993 Edition (Itasca, IL: National Safety Council, 1993), 60. *Current Health* 2 April 1994.

What names have been given to presidential planes?

The first presidential planes were the *Dixie Clipper* (unofficial; borrowed to fly to Casablanca in 1943) and the *Sacred Cow* (official), when Franklin D. Roosevelt (1882-1945) was President. The *Sacred Cow's* call sign was the last four digits of its registered tail number, 42-107451. The call sign was preceded by the prefix "Army" (changed to "Air Force" in 1947); if a ranking VIP was aboard, the prefix became "Special Flight" or its phonetic initials, "Sam Fox." Thus it was called "Air Force 7451" or "Sam Fox 7451." Harry Truman's (1884-1972) plane was the *Independence*, with a call sign of "Sam Fox 6505." President Dwight Eisenhower's (1890-1969) planes were "Sam 8610" and "Sam 7885." Mamie Eisenhower named the planes *Columbine II* and *Columbine III* after the flower of her home state, Colorado. However, during Eisenhower's presidency it was decided that the president's personal radio call sign should be "Air Force One" for quick and positive identification. President John F. Kennedy (1917-1963) had an unnamed plane, "3240," during his first year of presidency, but when the Boeing 707 was added in 1962, the public began referring to the presidential plane as *Air Force One*, the same as the call sign. Therefore any Air Force plane with the President aboard is now referred to as "Air Force One." Other aircraft such as helicopters are referred to as "Marine One" or "Army One." Craft with the Vice President aboard carry the designation "Two." President Richard Nixon (1913-1994) began using the name *Spirit of '76* in 1971 for his primary plane in honor of the Bicentennial and President Ford (1913-) continued the practice, but he usually called it *Air Force One.* Today, two Boeing 707s are actually used, with one designated as the primary plane.

Bill Lambrecht, "'Air Force One' To Be Two 747s," *St. Louis Post Dispatch* 24 August 1990. Lu Ann Paletta and Fred L. Worth, *The World Almanac of Presidential Facts* (New York: World Almanac, 1988), 143, 150, 156. J.F. ter Horstand Ralph Albertazzie, *The Flying White House: The Story of Air Force One* (New York: Coward, McCann & Geoghegan, 1979) 10-13, 63-67.

What was the M-551 Sheridan Airborne Light Tank used in Desert Shield?

The M-551 Sheridan Airborne Light Tank was used by the U.S. 82nd Airborne Division in Operation Desert Shield. It was the first of U.S. tanks to arrive in Saudi Arabia at the onset of the Persian Gulf Crisis in January of 1991. The tank weighs 16 tons and can move at a rate of 65 kilometers per hour. The gun includes a 152 millimeter gun/launcher and uses 20 cannon rounds, 10 Shillelagh missiles ammunition. Due to problems with its main armament's recoil its use is limited.

Desert Shield Fact Book, 2d ed. (Bloomington, IL: Game Designers' Workshop, 1991), 4.

What famous locomotive engineer rode the *Cannonball Express* into the history books?

John Luther Jones of Cayce, Kentucky, is better known to the world as "Casey Jones," the railroad engineer celebrated in song and legend along with the *Cannonball Express.* Jones died a heroic death in April of 1900 after the *Cannonball Express* crashed into a stalled train, but not before Jones' desperate actions to stop the *Express* saved the lives of his fireman and many other people.

Irving Wallace et al. , *The Book of Lists #2,* (New York: William Morrow, 1980), 461.

Who was "Wrong Way" Corrigan?

"Wrong Way" Corrigan (1907-1995) was an American aviator who earned the nickname in July of 1938 by arriving in Ireland and announcing to authorities he thought he had been flying toward California. Douglas Corrigan took off from New York in a small plane that had been specifically modified to carry an extra supply of fuel. He also brought along a twelve foot pole so he could reach out the window and de-ice the wings. The grave navigational error seemed to be a publicity stunt that he hoped would net him steady work as a pilot. A movie of the incident was made, starring the aviator himself, but Corrigan faded into obscurity after serving in World War II (1939-45) as a civilian pilot.

Bill Bullock, "Do You Remember ... ? "Wrong Way" Corrigan," *Flying* January 1952.

What two major cities were connected by the once famous American highway Route 66?

The once famous American highway, Route 66, connected Chicago with Los Angeles. Actually starting at Chicago's Grant Park, the 2,400-mile highway crossed three time zones and eight states on its way to becoming an American cultural icon. The man most responsible for the highway was Cyrus Stevens Avery, an Oklahoma entrepreneur who did much in the World War I era to develop roads and highways in that region of the country. In 1921 he was elected president of the Associated Highways Associations of America and in 1924 became an important figure in the American Association of State Highway Officials. Acting as a representative of that organization, he persuaded various federal officials to study the feasibility of a national trans-Mississippi highway. Avery was hired as a highway consultant to the Federal government and he laid the groundwork for what was to become the United States Highway System, of which the future Route 66 was an integral part. Route 66 became a vital element in the American landscape during World War II (1939-45) with soldiers traveling to western bases, and in the post-War era with new residents traveling to the burgeoning west and California. In 1960 the hit television series *Route66* made the highway a cultural icon. The show featured Martin Milner as Tod Stiles and George Maharis as Buz Murdock, two slightly disenchanted wanderers who searched for love, adventure, and the meaning of life from behind the steering wheel of a Corvette convertible. Route 66 still has a romantic impact on America, something Michael Wallis described as "An inspiration to.... a nation of dreamers....A broken chain of concrete and asphalt...has forever meant going somewhere."

Tim Brooks and Earle Marsh, *The Complete Directory to Prime Time Network TV Shows, 1946-Present* (New York: Ballantine Books, 1992), s.v. "Route

66." Michael Wallis, *Route 66: The Mother Road* (New York: St. Martin's Press, 1990), 1-7.

What is a possible location of Amelia Earhart's missing airplane?

On July 1, 1937, world-renowned aviatrix Amelia Earhart and her navigator, Fred Noonan, were continuing the first circum-equator around-the-world flight in a Lockheed 10-E Electra and had left New Guinea. However, midway through the flight over the Pacific Ocean, all radio contact with Earhart and Noonan was lost. A Coast Guard search of Earhart's intended flight path failed to turn up any sign of Earhart, Noonan, or their plane. The fate of Amelia Earhart and Fred Noonan remains one of the most enduring mysteries in aviation history.

In 1989, a group of searchers from the International Group for Historic Aircraft Recovery made an expedition to the remote Pacific island of Nikumaroro. Nikumaroro is located about 300 miles south of Earhart's intended destination, Howland Island. A search of Nikumaroro revealed an aluminum box of the type and vintage used by aviators in the 1930s. The searchers also found a shoe heel and sole that resembled the style of shoes worn by Earhart. Also, a battered aluminum fragment with rivet holes was found on the island. Tests of the fragment revealed that it could possibly be a part of Earhart's Lockheed Electra. However, the lack of a serial number on the fragment has made positive identification impossible. Although these discoveries are encouraging, the bodies of Earhart and Noonan have not been found. The discovery of their bodies or the Lockheed Electra would finally solve the mystery.

The Encyclopedia Americana, International ed. (Danbury, CT: Grolier, 1990), s.v. "Earhart, Amelia." *Pittsburgh Press* 4 January 1991. *Pittsburgh Press* 5 September 1991.

What was the worst marine disaster in U.S. history?

The worst marine disaster in U.S. history was the boiler explosion and subsequent burning of the sidewheeler *Sultana* on the Mississippi River, eight miles north of Memphis, Tennessee on April 17, 1865. Overburdened with more than 2,500 passengers—including former prisoners of war returning north—the old steam boilers could not cope with the enormous load—the ship's legal limit was 376—and burst, tearing apart the *Sultana* setting her on fire. An estimated 1,400 to 1,700 people died in the explosion, or from the fire, or drowning.

Russell Ash, *The Top Ten of Everything* (London: Dorling Kindersley, 1994), 246-47. Woody Gelman and Barbara Jackson, *Disaster Illustrated* (New York: Harmony Books, 1976), 74.

What is a rogallo wing?

A rogallo wing is a sail-like device, invented by Professor Francis Rogallo of the National Space Academy in the 1950s during his research on space capsule reentry. This flexible wing led to the sport of hang-gliding.

Coles Phinizy, "I'm Icarus -Fly Me," *Sports Illustrated* 10 December 1973.

Who was the first woman to fly solo across the Pacific Ocean from east to west?

Betty Miller made aviation history on May 12, 1963 when she became the first woman to fly solo across the Pacific Ocean from east to west. She made the 7,000 mile crossing, from Oakland, California to Brisbane, Australia, flying a twin engine Piper light aircraft.

New York Times 13 May 1963.

Who made the first nonstop transatlantic flight?

The first nonstop flight across the Atlantic Ocean, from Newfoundland, Canada, to Ireland, was made by two British aviators, Capt. John W. Alcock (1892-1919) and Lt. Arthur W. Brown (1886-1948), on June 14-15, 1919. The aircraft, a converted twin-engine Vickers Vimy bomber, took 16 hours 27 minutes to fly 1,890 miles (3,032 kilometers). Later Charles A. Lindbergh (1902-1974) made the first solo crossing flight on May 20-21, 1927, in the single-engine Ryan monoplane *Spirit of St. Louis* with a wing spread of forty-six feet and a chord of seven feet. The plane weighed 5,135 pounds and was propelled by a 225-horsepower Wright Whirlwind motor. His flight from New York to Paris covered a distance of 3,609 miles (5,089 kilometers) and lasted 33-hours. The first woman to fly solo across the Atlantic was Amelia Earhart (1897-1937) who flew from Newfoundland to Ireland May 20-21, 1932.

Kenneth Colegrove, *Dictionary of American History, rev. ed.* (New York: Charles Scribner's Sons, 1976), s.v. "Lindbergh's Atlantic Flight." *Encyclopedia of Aviation* (New York: Scribners, 1977), 12-13, 64, 119.

Where is the black box carried on an airplane?

Actually painted bright orange to make it more visible in an aircraft's wreckage, the black box carried on an airplane is a tough metal and plastic case containing two recorders. Installed in the rear of the aircraft-the area most likely to survive a crash-the case has two shells of stainless steel with a heat-protective material between the shells. The case must be able to withstand high velocity impact, contract with seawater and a temperature of 2,000 degree Fahrenheit (1,100 degree Celsius) for 30 minutes. Inside it, mounted in a shockproof base, is the aircraft's flight data and cockpit voice recorders. The flight data recorder provides information about airspeed, direction, altitude, vertical acceleration, engine thrust, and rudder and spoiler positions from sensors that are located around the aircraft. The data is recorded as electronic pulses on stainless steel tape which is about as thick as aluminum foil. When the tape is played back, it generates a computer printout. The cockpit voice recorder records the previous 30 minutes of the flight crew's conversation and radio transmission on a continuous tape loop. If a crash does not stop the recorder, vital information can be lost.

Ira Flatow, *Rainbows, Curve Balls, and Other Wonders of the Natural World Explained* (New York: Harper & Row, 1988), 231. *How In the World* (Pleasantville, NY: Reader's Digest Association, 1990), 99-100. James E. Tunnell, *Latest Intelligence* (Blue Ridge Summit, PA: TAB, 1990), 27.

Why did the dirigible *Hindenburg* explode?

Despite the official U.S. and German investigations into the explosion, it still remains a mystery today why the dirigible *Hindenburg* burned. The most plausible explanations are structural failure, St. Elmo's Fire, static electricity, or sabotage. Built following the great initial success of the *Graf Zeppelin*, the *Hindenburg*, was intended to exceed all other airships in size, speed, safety, comfort, and economy. At 803 feet (244.75 meters) long, it was 80 percent as long as the liner *Queen Mary*, and it was 135 feet (41.1 meters) in diameter, and could carry 72 passengers in its spacious quarters.

In 1935 the German Air Ministry virtually took over the Zeppelin Company to use it to spread Nazi propaganda. Following its first flight in 1936, the airship became very popular with the flying public. No other form of transport could carry passengers so swiftly, reliably, and comfortably between continents. During 1936 1,006 passengers flew over the North Atlantic Ocean in the *Hindenburg.* But on May 6, 1937, while landing at Lakehurst, New Jersey, its hydrogen fuel burst into flames, and the airship was completely destroyed. Of the 97 people aboard, 62 survived. With this disaster commercial dirigible air travel ended. The current day blimps are similar in shape but are not the same as the Zeppelins, which were rigid airships.

Ken Dallison, *When Zeppelins Flew* (New York: Time-Life Books, 1969), 30-31, 47, 50-51. Louis C. Gerken, *Airships: History and Technology* (Chula Vista, CA: American Scientific Corp., 1990), 331-53. Tom Stacey, *The Hindenburg* (San Diego: Lucent, 1990), 52-53.

What is the difference between an amphibian plane and a seaplane?

An amphibian plane has retractable wheels that enable it to operate from land as well as water, while a seaplane is limited to water take-offs and landings, having only pontoons without wheels. Because its landing gear cannot retract, a seaplane is less aerodynamically efficient than an amphibian.

Encyclopedia of Aviation (New York: Scribners, 1977), 172-73. *World and United States Aviation and Space Records* (Washington, DC: National Aeronautic Association of the USA, 1991), 138.

When was the B-17 Flying Fortress introduced?

A Flying Fortress prototype first flew on July 28, 1935, and the first Y1B-17 was delivered to the Air Corps in March 1937 followed by an experimental Y1B-17A fitted with turbo-supercharged engines in January 1939. An order for 39 planes was placed for this model under the designation B-17B. In addition to its bombing function, the B-17 was used for many experimental duties, including serving as a launching platform in the U.S.A.A.F. guided missile program and in radar and radio-control experiments. It was called a "Flying Fortress" because it was the best defended bomber of World War II (1939-45). Altogether, it carried thirteen 50 caliber Browning M-2 machine guns, each having about 700 pounds (317.5 kilograms) of armor-piercing ammunition. Ironically, the weight of all its defensive armament and manpower severely restricted the space available for bombs.

Jane's All the World's Aircraft 1947 (London: Sampson Low Marston, 1977), 192-93. Mike Jerram, *The World's Classic Aircraft* (London: Frederick Muller, 1981), 110, 113. David A. Wragg, *A Dictionary of Aviation* (Reading, ENG: Osprey, 1973), 49.

Has there ever been a nuclear-powered automobile?

In the 1950s Ford automotive designers envisioned the Ford Nucleon, which was to be propelled by a small atomic reactor core, located under a circular cover at the rear of the car. It was to be recharged with nuclear fuel. The car was never built.

Yearbook of Science and the Future 1991 (Chicago: Encyclopaedia Britannica, 1990), 22.

What was the first car manufactured with an automatic transmission?

The first of the modern generation of automatic transmissions was General Motors' Hydramatic, first offered as an option on the Oldsmobile during the 1940 season. Between 1934 and 1936, a handful of 18 horsepower Austins were fitted with the American-designed Hayes infinitely variable gear. The direct ancestor of the modern automatic gearbox was patented in 1898.

Anthony Harding, *The Guinness Book of Car Facts and Feats* (London: Guinness Superlatives, 1980), 32, 252.

When was the Michelin tire introduced?

The first pneumatic (air-filled) tire for automobiles was produced in France by Andr (1853-1931) and Edouard Michelin (1859-1940) in 1885. The first radial-ply tire, the Michelin X, was made and sold in 1948. In radial construction, layers of cord materials called plies are laid across the circumference of the tire from bead to bead (perpendicular to the direction of the tread centerline). The plies can be made of steel wires or belts which circle the tire. Radial tires are said to give longer tread life, better handling, and a softer ride at medium and high speeds than bias or belted bias tires (both of which have plies laid diagonally). Radials give a firm, almost hard, ride at low speeds.

Automotive Encyclopedia, rev. ed. (South Holland, IL: Goodheart-Willcox, 1989), 589-90. Anthony Harding, *The Guinness Book of the Car* (London: Guinness Superlatives, 1987), 11.

What is a Johnson bar on a locomotive?

A Johnson bar is the reverse lever of a locomotive. The expression "To put the Johnson bar against the running board" means to get speed.

Ramon F. Adams, *The Language of the Railroader* (Norman: University of Oklahoma Press, 1977), 87, 120.

When was the first railroad in the United States chartered?

The first American railroad charter was obtained on February 6, 1815, by Colonel John Stevens (1749-1838) of Hoboken, New Jersey, to build and operate a railroad between the Delaware and Raritan rivers near Trenton and New Brunswick. However, lack of financial backing prevented its construction. The Granite Railway built by Gridley Bryant was chartered on October 7, 1826. It ran from Quincy, Massachusetts, to the Neponset River-a distance of three miles (4.8 kilometers). The main cargo was granite blocks used in building the Bunker Hill Monument.

Barbara Berliner, *The Book of Answers* (Englewood Cliffs, NJ: Prentice-Hall, 1990), 8. John Marshall, *Rail: The Records* (London: Guinness Books, 1985), 16. O. S. Nock, *Encyclopedia of Railways* (London: Octopus Books, 1977), 52.

What is the world's longest railway?

The Trans-Siberian Railway, from Moscow to Vladivostok, is 5,777 miles (9,297 kilometers) long. If the spur to Nakhodka is included, the distance becomes 5,865 miles (9,436 kilometers). It was opened in sections and the first goods train reached Irkutsk on August 27, 1898. The Baikal-Amur Northern Main Line, begun in 1938, shortens the distance by about 310 miles (500 kilometers). The journey takes approximately seven days, two hours and crosses seven time zones. There are nine tunnels, 139 large bridges or viaducts, and 3,762 smaller bridges or culverts on the whole route. Nearly the entire line is electrified.

In comparison, the first American transcontinental railroad, completed on May 10, 1869, is 1,780 miles (2,864 kilometers) long. The Central Pacific Railroad built eastward from Sacramento, California, and the Union Pacific Railroad built westward to Promontory Point, Utah, where the two lines met to connect the line.

Mark C. Young, ed., *Guinness Book of Records 1995* (New York: Facts On File, 1994), 124. John Marshall, *The Guinness Railway Book* (London: Guiness Books, 1989), 62-64. Ian McNeil, *An Encyclopedia of the History of Technology* (London: Routledge, 1990), 574.

What was the railroad velocipede?

In the nineteenth century, railroad track maintenance workers used a three-wheeled handcar, called a railroad velocipede, to speed their way along the track. The handcar was used for inter-station express and package deliveries and for delivery of urgent messages between stations that could not wait until the next train. Also called an "Irish Mail," this 150-pound (68-kilogram) three-wheeler resembled a bicycle with a sidecar. The operator sat in the middle of the two-wheel section and pushed a crank back and forth, which propelled the triangle-shaped vehicle down the tracks. This manually powered handcar was replaced after World War I by a gasoline-powered track vehicle. This, in turn, was replaced by a conventional pickup truck fitted with an auxiliary set of flanged wheels.

Technology and Culture July 1976.

How was early macadam different from modern paved roads?

Macadam roads developed originally in England and France and are named after the Scottish road builder and engineer, John Louden MacAdam (1756-1836). The term "macadam" originally designated road surface or base in which clean, broken, or crushed ledge stone was mechanically locked together by rolling with a heavy weight and bonded together by stone dust screenings which were worked into the spaces and then "set" with water. With the beginning of the use of bituminous material (tar or asphalt), the term "plain macadam," "ordinary macadam," or "waterbound macadam" was used to distinguish the original type from the newer "bituminous macadam. Waterbound macadam surfaces are almost never built now in the United States, mainly because they are expensive and the vacuum effect of vehicles loosens them. Many miles of bituminous macadam roads are still in service, but their principal disadvantages are their high crowns and narrowness. Today's roads that carry very heavy traffic are usually surfaced with very durable portland cement.

Clarkson H. Oglesby and R. Gary Hicks, *Highway Engineering* (New York: John Wiley, 1982), 652. John S. Scott, *Dictionary of Civil Engineering* (New York: Halsted Press, 1981), 169, 298. *Standard Handbook for Civil Engineers, 3d ed.* (New York: McGraw-Hill, 1983), 16-40 -16-41.

Which woods are used for railroad ties?

Many species of wood are used for ties. The more common are oaks, gums, Douglas fir, mixed hardwoods, hemlock, southern pine, and mixed softwoods.

U.S. Forest Products Laboratory, *Encyclopedia of Wood* (New York: Drake, 1977), 298.

Did physical changes occur in the astronauts' bodies when they were in space?

The astronauts grew 1-to 2 inches taller. This height increase was due to spinal lengthening and straightening. Their waist measurements decreased by several inches, due to an upward shift of the internal organs in the body. The calves of their legs became smaller because the muscles of the legs forced blood and other fluids toward the upper part of the body, thus decreasing the girth measurement around the thighs and calves.

William R. Pogue, *How Do You Go to the Bathroom in Space?* (New York: Tom Doherty Associates, 1985), 11.

Who was the "father" of the Soviet space program?

Sergei P. Korolev (1907-1966) made enormous contributions to the development of Soviet manned space flight, and his name is linked with their most significant space achievements. Trained as an aeronautical engineer, he directed the Moscow group studying the principles of rocket propulsion, and in 1946 took over the Soviet program to develop long-range ballistic rockets. Under Korolev, the Soviets used these rockets for space projects and launched the world's first satellite in October 4, 1957. Besides a vigorous unmanned interplanetary research program, Korolev's goal was to place men in space, and following tests with animals his manned space flight program was initiated when Yuri Gagarin (1934-1968) was successfully launched into earth orbit.

The Cambridge Encyclopedia of Space (New York: Cambridge University Press, 1990), 34.

When did the Volkswagen Beetle first appear?

The Volkswagen Beetle, affectionately called "the Bug" was designed by Ferdinand Porsche in the mid-1930s but not built until 1945. The German automobile manufacturer stopped making Beetles in 1978, although approximately 100 per day are still built and sold in Mexico. Over 21 million have been built since 1945. In 1994 a new Beetle prototype was unveiled, and in 1998 they were available to the public for purchase.

David Feldman, *Why Do Clocks Run Clockwise? and other Imponderables: Mysteries of Everyday Life* (New York: Harper & Row, 1987), 192-94. Jerry Flint, "The return of the Bettle?," *Forbes,* 9 May 1994. Helen Kahn, "Foreign firm can be sued via U.S. unit," *Automotive News* 20 June 1988. *World Book Encyclopedia* (Chicago: World Book, 1994), s.v. "Volkswagen."

Who was the first person in the U.S. to die as the result of an automobile accident?

The first person to die from an automobile accident was Henry H. Bliss, a 68-year-old real estate broker. He was knocked down and run over by a car as he was getting off a streetcar in New York City on September 13, 1899.

Joseph Nathan Kane, *Famous First Facts: A Record of First Happenings, Discoveries, and Inventions in American History, 4th ed.* (New York: H. W. Wilson, 1981), s.v. "automobile fatality."

What type of steamboat was designed especially for use on the Mississippi River?

The first type of steamboats in the early nineteenth century had a paddle wheel on each side and a deep, V-shaped hull. Called "sidewheelers," they were ideal for deep eastern rivers like the Hudson. Sidewheelers did not work well on the Mississippi River because it was deep in some parts, shallow in others, and uprooted trees on the bottom of the river damaged the boats' hulls. A new type of steamboat, the "sternwheeler," was designed with a flat hull which prevented the boat from getting stuck on sandbars. The wheel was located at the back or stern, and it was protected from the river bottom by the hull.

Pam Zeck and Gerry Zeck, *Mississippi Sternwheelers* (Minnesota: Carolrhoda Books, 1982), 2-3, 5.

Who was the first person to fly solo around the world?

Wiley Post (1899-1935) was the first person to make a solo flight around the world. In 1933 he flew a single-engine Lockheed Vega called the *Winnie Mae* for 15,596 miles in 7 days, 18 hours, and 49 minutes with the help of a new automatic pilot system that allowed him to rest. Two years earlier, he and navigator Harold Gatty had flown the same plane around the world in a record 8 days, 15 hours, and 15 minutes. Congress authorized the Smithsonian to pay Post's widow $25,000 for the *Winnie Mae.* The bill for the purchase had been introduced in Congress before Post died, but the funds came after he was killed in a plane crash in Barrow, Alaska, with his friend and famed American humorist and social critic Will Rogers on August 15, 1935. The plane he was attempting to fly across Siberia had been built from parts of other planes and carried no name.

Bryan B. Sterling and Frances N. Sterling, *Will Rogers and Wiley Post: Death at Barrow* (New M. Evans, 1993), 101-5, 110-11, 310-11. *The World Book Encyclopedia* (Chicago: World Book, 1994), s.v. "Post, Wiley, "Rogers, Will."

When and why was the two-bag carry-on limit implemented on U.S. airplanes?

The Federal Aviation Administration (FAA) enacted a two-bag carry-on limit in 1987 as a safety measure. Passengers had been injured by items falling from crammed overhead bins. Most airlines were lax about the rule until they found that people trying to find places for luggage were slowing down flights. The size of the carry-on luggage is usually limited to 45 linear inches. Travelers should check each airline to find out whether it counts or does not count laptop computers, briefcases, and infant strollers as the second piece of luggage.

Lisa I. Fried, "You Can't Take it With You," *Frequent Flyer* October, 1994.

What were the names of the United States presidential yachts?

The first vessel that can be considered a presidential yacht was the *River Queen*, a 181-wooden side-wheeled steamboat. It was rented for $241 per day for Abraham Lincoln's (1809-1865) use during the latter part of the American Civil War (1861-1865) in 1865.

Fifteen years later, while Rutherford B. Hayes (1822-1893) was U.S. president the *Despatch*, a 174-foot brigantine, was overhauled and refitted for use as a presidential yacht. It continued to serve during the administrations of U.S. presidents Garfield (1831-1881), Arthur (1829-1886), Cleveland (1837-1908) and Harrison (1773-1841). In 1891 the *Despatch* was wrecked off the Virginia coast.

The *Despatch* was replaced by the *Dolphin*, a 256--foot steel cruiser. The *Dolphin* served seven U.S. presidents, from Harrison to Harding (1865-1923), finally being decommissioned in 1921.

Serving simultaneously with the *Dolphin* were the *Sylph* and the *Mayflower*. The *Sylph* was a 123-foot, 8-inch power yacht first used by President McKinley (1843-1901) and last used by Woodrow Wilson (1856-1924) during his 1913-1921 term. The *Mayflower*, a 318-foot steam yacht, was first used by Theodore Roosevelt (1858-1919). In 1929 Herbert Hoover (1874-1964) dispensed with the vessel as an economy measure.

The next presidential yacht, the *Sequoia* was also dispensed with as an economy measure. In 1933, while Franklin D. Roosevelt (1882-1945) was president, this 104-foot motor yacht was officially commissioned as a presidential yacht. It served until 1977 when Jimmy Carter (1924-) concluded the $800 thousand annual cost was not justified.

In 1936, also during Franklin D. Roosevelt's administration, the *Potomac* was a presidential yacht. It was a 165-foot long cutter which Harry S. Truman (1884-1972) agreed to replace in 1945 with the *Williamsburg*. The *Williamsburg* was a 243-foot, 9-inch long yacht last used by Dwight Eisenhower (1890-1969) in 1953.

When Eisenhower retired the *Williamsburg* he authorized the refitting of two tenders as presidential yachts. The *Barbara Anne* was a 92-foot, 3-inch ship renamed the *Honey Fitz* by John F. Kennedy (1917-1963) and then the *Patricia* by Richard Nixon (1913-1994). The *Susie E.* was 64 feet long and later renamed the *Patrick J.* by Kennedy and the *Julie* by Nixon. Nixon ordered both vessels decommissioned in 1969 as economy measures.

Fred E. Crockett, *Special Fleet: The History of the Presidential Yachts,* (Camden, ME: Down East Books, 1985), 16-90.

When did dining car service begin on U.S. railroads?

The first known instance of meals being served on a U.S. train was January 10, 1853, aboard a Baltimore and Ohio Railroad train from Baltimore to Wheeling, Virginia, when the passengers were fed a catered meal at tables and benches before the trip. The first dining cars on regularly scheduled passenger trains were used in 1863 on the Philadelphia, Wilmington, and Baltimore Railroad. The food, however, was prepared before the trip. George M. Pullman (1831-1897) is credited with developing the first railway dining car in which the food was prepared on the train en route. His first restaurant car was introduced in 1868.

Will C. Hollister, *Dinner in the Diner, 2d ed.* (Los Angeles: Trans-Anglo Books, 1965), 9-12.

Where is the safest place to sit on an airplane?

According to a *New York* magazine investigation, the back of an airplane is the safest place to sit. In an examination of airline crashes from 1978 to 1987, statistics revealed that persons sitting in the rear third of an airplane survived 55 percent of all crashes. Persons sitting in the front third of an airplane survived 40 percent of crashes, while passengers sitting in the middle third of an airplane only survived 38 percent of airline crashes.

USA Today 22 August 1989.

Which United States city had the first subway?

The first subway system in the United States was constructed in Boston, Massachusetts. Built between 1895 and 1897, it was 1.5 miles long and used trolley streetcars, acquiring conventional subway trains later.

The New Encyclopaedia Britannica, Micropaedia, 15th ed. (Chicago: Encyclopaedia Brittannica, 1989), s.v. "subway."

Who are the "99s"?

The "99s" began with a group of women flyers who joined together in 1929 to form an organization of licensed women pilots. Of the 126 eligible licensed women pilots, 99 decided to join the organization, hence its name, "The Ninety-Nines." The organization came into being as the result of the August 1929 "Women's Air Derby." Some called it a powder-puff derby, but the event was actually a grueling 2,800 mile race beginning in Los Angeles and ending in Cleveland. Associated with Cleveland's National Air Races, the contest offered a first prize of $2,500, a large amount in the 1920s. Preliminary meetings of the 99s were held in November and December of 1929 and the fledgling organization's first president was famed flyer Amelia Earhart (1897-1937). Headquartered in Oklahoma City, the 99s boasted 6,400 worldwide members by the mid 1990s.

Mary Cadogan, *Women with Wings* (Chicago: Academy Chicago Publishers, 1993), 87-9. David Roberts, "The 99s: The Right Stuff Then and Now," *Smithsonian* August 1994.

What was the name of the Wright brothers' plane?

The first airplane to be flown successfully by Orville Wright (1871-1948) and his brother Wilbur (1867-1912) was named the *Flyer*. This plane was also called the *Whopper*, a name given to it by the Wrights' nephew. Previous crafts built by the pair had been gliders; when they perfected their glider design, they fitted it with an engine to create a self-powered machine. The plane was built during the summer of 1903 and Orville Wright became the first man to sustain a controlled airplane flight on December 17, 1903 at Kitty Hawk, North Carolina. The first flight lasted 12 seconds and covered some 120 feet.

John W. R. Taylor and Kenneth Munson, *History of Aviation* (New York: Crown Publishers, 1972), 47. John Evangelist Walsh, *One Day at Kitty Hawk: The Untold Story of the Wright Brothers and the Airplane* (New York: Thomas Y. Crowell, 1975), 199.

What was the speed of railroad trains in 1860?

In 1860 trains in the United States' eastern Cotton Belt were able to run at speeds approaching 25 miles per hour. This improvement over earlier speeds was the result of improved tracks and rail cars. Further improvement would not occur until steel rails replaced the less reliable wrought-iron ones.

Ulrich Bonnell Phillips, *A History of Transportation in the Eastern Cotton Belt to 1860* (New York: Columbia University Press, 1908), 383.

What western American railroad is celebrated in song and named after three cities?

The Atchison, Topeka and Santa Fe Railroad was originally chartered in 1859 to connect Atchison and Topeka, Kansas, and was named after three cities of the "Old West." By 1889 the railroad connected Chicago with the Pacific Coast and had over 7,000 miles of rail. By the middle decades of the twentieth century, it was the first railroad in mileage with 13,000 miles of rail.

Dictionary of American History, rev. ed. (New York: Charles Scribner's Sons, 1976), 6:32.

Who was the last survivor of the *Titanic* sinking, and when did she die?

Marjorie Newell Robb, the last living survivor of the *Titanic*, died in 1992 at the age of 103.

USA Today 15 June 1992.

What was the purpose of Thor Heyerdahl's voyage in July of 1970?

In 1970, modern-day Norwegian explorer and anthropologist Thor Heyerdahl (1914-) demonstrated that the ancient Egyptians could have traveled to the Caribbean area as early as 5,000 years ago. Traveling in the *Ra II*, a sail boat made of papyrus reeds, he and an eight-man crew completed the 3,200-mile Atlantic Ocean crossing in 57 days. They departed from Safi, Morocco, on May 17 and arrived in Bridgetown, Barbados, on July 12. Accompanied by a tug boat, the *Ra II* survived the rough seas and difficulties in charting its course. Heyerdahl had made an unsuccessful attempt to cross the Atlantic in *Ra II's* predecessor, the *Ra*, in 1969.

Heyerdahl had devoted most of his career attempting to prove his controversial theory that transmigration by primitive cultures over the oceans had occurred long before the Europeans sailed in these areas. His voyage on the raft *Kon-Tiki* in 1947 was made to show that the Pacific Islands inhabitants could have migrated from South America. The *Ra* expedition was made to prove that an early westward voyage could have been made across the Atlantic Ocean. Some scholars disagree with Heyerdahl's theories, using linguistic differences, etc. as counter-evidence to his claims.

Richard Bolander, *World Explorers and Discoverers* (New York: Macmillan, 1992), 224-25. *New York Times* 13 July 1970.

What is the zero milestone?

The zero milestone is a point in Washington, DC, from which all public highways are supposed to be measured. It is marked by a block of stone and is on the Ellipse, 900 feet south of the White House. Legislation for the zero milestone was enacted in 1920, but the stone was put in place in 1923.

"Zero Milestone Stands Near White House," *Pittsburgh Press* 26 June 1968.

Which state has the most miles of roads?

Texas lays claim to the most road mileage with 305,692 miles (491,858 kilometers) lacing through the Lone Star State. California is a distant second with 164,298 miles (264,355 kilometers) of roads. On the other end of the scale, only three states have less than 10,000 miles (16,090 kilometers) of roads: Delaware, Hawaii, and Rhode Island. The total road mileage count for the United States is 3,876,501 miles (6,237,290 kilometers).

MVMA Motor Vehicle Facts and Figures '91 (Detroit: Motor Vehicle Manufacturers Association of the United States, 1991), 84.

Who made the first supersonic flight?

Supersonic flight is defined as flight at or above the speed of sound. The speed of sound is 760 miles (1,223 kilometers) per hour in warm air at sea level. At a height of about 37,000 feet (11,278 kilometers), the speed of sound is only 660 miles (1,062 kilometers) per hour. The first person credited with traveling faster then the speed of sound (Mach 1) was Major Charles E. (Chuck) Yeager (b. 1923), of the U.S. Air Force. On October 14, 1947, he attained Mach 1.45 at 60,000 feet (18,288 meters) while flying the Bell *X-1* rocket research plane designed by John Stack and Lawrence Bell. This plane had been carried aloft by a B-29 and released at 30,000 feet (9,144 meters). In 1949 the Douglas *Skyrocket* became the first supersonic jet-powered aircraft to reach Mach 1 when Gene May flew at Mach 1.03 at 26,000 feet (7,925 meters).

Encyclopedia of Aviation (New York: Scribners, 1977), 184-85.

What is avionics?

Avionics, a term derived by combining aviation and electronics, describes all of the electronic navigational, communications, and flight management aids with which airplanes are equipped today. In military aircraft it also covers electronically-controlled weapons, reconnaissance, and detection systems. Until the 1940s, the systems involved in operating aircraft were purely mechanical, electric, or magnetic, with radio apparatus being the most sophisticated instrumentation. The advent of RADAR and the great advance made in airborne detection during World War II (1939-45) led to the general adoption of electronic distance-measuring and navigational aids. In military aircraft such devices improve weapon delivery accuracy and in commercial aircraft they provide greater safety in operation.

Encyclopedia of Aviation (New York: Scribners, 1977), 20-21. *The Illustrated Science and Invention Encyclopedia* (Westport, CT: H. S. Stuttman, 1983), 2:206-10. *Science and Technology Illustrated* (Chicago: Encyclopaedia Britannica, 1984), 3:328

Which type of wood was used to build Noah's ark?

According to the Bible, Noah's ark was made of gopher wood. This is identified as Cupressus sempervirens, one of the most durable woods in the world. Also called the Mediterranean cypress, the tree is native throughout southern Europe and western Asia. It grows up to 80 feet (24.38 meters) tall. Similar to this tree is the Monterey cypress (Cupressus macrocarpa), which is restricted to a very small area along the coast of central California. It can become as tall as 90 feet (27.43 meters) with horizontal branches that support a broad, spreading crown. When old, this tree looks very much like the aged cedars of Lebanon.

Thomas H. Everett, *Living Trees of the World* (New York: Doubleday, 1968), 35. Rutherford Platt, *1001 Questions Answered About Trees* (New York: Dodd, Mead, 1959), 31.

When were the first nuclear-powered vessels launched?

A controlled nuclear reaction generates tremendous heat, which turns water into steam for running turbine engines. The USS *Nautilus* was the first submarine to be propelled by nuclear power, making her first sea run on January 17, 1955. It has been called the first true submarine since it can remain underwater for an indefinite period of time; as a nuclear reactor requires no oxygen to operate, only the crew's need for oxygen limits the submersion time. The *Nautilus*, 324 feet (98.75 meters) long, has a range of 2,500 miles (4,022.5 kilometers) submerged, a diving depth of 700 feet (213.36 meters), and can travel submerged at 20 knots.

The first nuclear warship was the 14,000-ton cruiser USS *Long Beach*, launched on July 14, 1959. The USS *Enterprise* was the first nuclear-powered aircraft carrier. Launched on September 24, 1960, the *Enterprise* was 1,101.5 feet (335.74 meters) long, and designed to carry 100 aircraft.

The first nuclear-powered merchant ship was the *Savannah*, a 20,000-ton vessel, launched in 1962. The United States built it largely as an experiment and it was never operated commercially. In 1969 Germany built the *Otto Hahn*, a nuclear-powered ore carrier. The most successful use of nuclear propulsion in nonnaval ships has been as icebreakers. The first nuclear-powered icebreaker was the Soviet Union's *Lenin*, commissioned in 1959.

Edward Horton, *The Illustrated History of the Submarine* (London: Sidgwick & Jackson, 1974), 150-60. Peter Kemp, *Encyclopedia of Ships and Sailing* (Dobbs Ferry, NY: Stanford Maritime, 1989), 99. Patrick Robertson, *The Book of Firsts* (New York: Clarkson N. Potter, 1974), 13, 171, 243, 244.

Why was the designation *MiG* chosen for the Soviet fighter plane used in World War II?

The *MiG* designation, formed from the initials of the plane's designers, Artem I. Mikoyan and Mikhail I. Gurevich, sometimes is listed as the Mikoyan-Gurevich MiG. Appearing in 1940 with a maximum speed of 400 miles (643.6 kilometers) per hour, the MiG-3, a piston-engine fighter, was one of the few Soviet planes whose performance was comparable with Western types during World War II. One of the best-known fighters, the MiG-15, first flown in December 1947, was powered by a Soviet version of a Rolls-Royce turbo jet engine. This high performer saw action during the Korean Conflict (1950-1953). In 1955 the MiG-19 became the first Soviet fighter capable of supersonic speed in level flight.

Jane's Encyclopedia of Aviation (New York: Portland House, 1989), 655. Michael J. H. Taylor and John W. R. Taylor, *Encyclopedia of Aircraft* (London: Weidenfeld & Nicolson, 1978), 164-65. David W. Wragg, *A Dictionary of Aviation* (Reading, ENG: Osprey, 1973), 192-93.

Who invented the culin device on a tank?

In World War II (1939-45), U.S. tank man Sergeant Curtis G. Culin devised a crossbar welded across the front of the tank with four protruding metal tusks. This device made it possible to break through the German hedgerow defenses and save thousands of lives. In the hedgerow country of Normandy, France, countless rows or stands of bushes or trees surrounded the fields, limiting tank movement. The culin device, also known as the "Rhinoceros," because its steel angled teeth formed a tusk-like structure, cut into the base of the hedgerow and pushed a complete section ahead of it into the next field, burying any enemy troops dug in on the opposite side.

James Cary, *Tanks and Armor in Modern Warfare* (New York: Franklin Watts, 1966), 206. R. P. Hunnicutt, *Sherman: A History of the American Medium Tank* (San Rafael, CA: Taurus Enterprises, 1978), 310-11.

How does VASCAR work?

Invented in 1965, VASCAR (Visual Average Speed Computer and Recorder) is a calculator that determines a car's speed from two simple measurements of time and distance. No RADAR is involved. VASCAR can be used at rest or while moving to clock traffic in both directions. The patrol car can be behind, ahead of, or even perpendicular to the target vehicle. The device measures the length of a speed trap and then determines how long it takes the target car to cover that distance. An internal calculator does the math and displays the average speed on an LED readout. Most police departments now use several forms of moving RADAR which are less detectable and more accurate.

Popular Science September 1990.

When was the air bag invented?

Patented ideas on air bag safety devices began appearing in the early 1950s. U.S. patent 2,649,311 was granted on August 18, 1953, to John W. Hetrick for an inflated safety cushion to be used in automotive vehicles. The Ford Motor Company studied the use of air bags around 1957, and other undocumented work was carried out by Assen Jordanoff before 1956. There are other earlier uses of an air bag concept, including a rumored method of some World War II pilots inflating their life vests before a crash.

In the 1970s, General Motors geared up to sell 100,000 air bag-equipped cars a year in a pilot program to offer them as a discounted option on luxury models. GM dropped the option after only 8,000 buyers ordered air bags in three years. As of September 1, 1989, all new passenger cars produced for sale in the United States were required to be equipped with passive restraints (either automatic seatbelts or air bags).

Motor Trend August 1970. *MVMA Motor Vehicle Facts and Figures '91* (Detroit: Motor Vehicle Manufacturers Association of the United States, 1991), 3. *Status Report* 6 October 1990.

What information is available from the vehicle identification number (VIN), body number plate, and engine on a car?

The Vehicle Identification Number (VIN) are coded numbers that reveal the model and make, model year, type of transmission, plant of manufacture and sometimes even the date and day of the week a car was made. The form and content of these codes is not standardized and often changes from one year to the next for the same manufacturer. Various components of a car may be made in different plants so a location listed on a VIN may differ from one on the engine number. The official shop manual lists the codes for a particular make of car.

Catalog of American Car ID Numbers 1970-79 (Sidney, OH: Amos Press, 1991), 1-1, 2-1.

Which colors of cars are the safest?

Tests at the University of California concluded that either blue or yellow is the best color for car safety. Blue shows up best during daylight and fog; yellow is best at night. The worst color from the visibility standpoint is gray. In another study by Mercedes-Benz in Germany, white ranked the highest in all-around visibility, except in situations of completely snow-covered roads or white sand. In such extremes, bright yellow and bright orange ranked second and third respectively in visibility. The least visible car color in the Mercedes-Benz test was dark green.

Jean Carper, *Stay Alive* (New York: Doubleday, 1965), 282. National Safety Council, *Accident Facts, 1989* (Washington, DC: National Safety Council, 1989), 73.

What is a pedicar?

As a response to the concern of energy conservation, the pedicar was introduced in 1973. It was a pedal-powered, all-weather one passenger vehicle with straight-line pedal action, disc brakes, five forward speeds plus neutral and reverse. Costing about $550 in 1973, the vehicle was conceived as an alternative to the automobile. It had a speed of 8 to 15 miles (12.9-24.1 kilometers) per hour and was developed mainly for fun use around parks, resorts, college campuses, country clubs, and similar protected areas.

Popular Mechanics May 1974.

What is the process known as hydrocarbon cracking?

Cracking is a process that uses heat to decompose complex substances. Hydrocarbon cracking is the decomposition by heat, with or without catalysts, of petroleum or heavy petroleum fractions (groupings) to give materials of lower boiling points. Thermal cracking, developed by William Burton in 1913, uses heat and pressure to break some of the large heavy hydrocarbon molecules into smaller gasoline-grade ones. The cracked hydrocarbons are then sent to a flash chamber where the various fractions (groupings) are separated. Thermal cracking not only doubles the gasoline yield, but has improved gasoline quality, producing gasoline components with good anti-knock characteristics.

Michael Allaby, *Dictionary of the Environment, 3rd ed.* (New York: New York University Press, 1989), 103, 204. *The Motor Gasoline Industry: Past, Present, and Future* (Washington, DC: U.S. Department of Energy, Energy Information Administration, 1991), 49.

Did raising the speed limit on rural interstate highways from 55 to 65 miles per hour have an effect on the accident and death rate?

There was an estimated 20 percent to 30 percent increase in deaths on those roads and a 40 percent increase in serious injuries when the speed limit was raised from 55 miles (88.5 kilometers) per hour to 65 miles (104.5 kilometers) per hour on rural interstate highways.

Susan P. Baker et al. , *The Injury Fact Book, 2d ed.* (New York: Oxford University Press, 1992), 251.

When and what was the first animal sent into orbit?

A dog erroneously listed by the Western press as having the name Laika, was aboard the Soviet *Sputnik 2*, launched November 3, 1957, and became the first animal sent into orbit. The dog's breed was a "Laika" (a female Samoyed husky); her name was Kudryavka (or Kudyarka or Limorchik). This event followed the successful Soviet launch on October 4, 1957 of *Sputnik 1*, the first man-made satellite ever placed in orbit. Laika was a very small female dog and became the first living creature to go into orbit. She was placed in a pressurized compartment within a capsule that weighed 1103 pounds (500 kilograms). After a few days in orbit, she died, and *Sputnik 2* reentered the earth's atmosphere on April 14, 1958.

The Cambridge Encyclopedia of Space (New York: Cambridge University Press, 1990), 48. Anthony R. Curtis, *Space Almanac* (Woodsboro, MD: ARCsoft, 1990), 425. Gerald L. Wood, *Guinness Book of Pet Records* (London: Guinness Books, 1984), 39.

What were the first words spoken by an astronaut after touchdown of the lunar module on the Apollo 11 flight and while standing on the moon?

On July 20, 1969, at 4:17:43 p.m. Eastern Daylight Time (20:17:43 Greenwich Mean Time), Neil A. Armstrong (b. 1930) and Edwin E. Aldrin, Jr. (b. 1930), landed the lunar module *Eagle* in the moon's Sea of Tranquility, and Armstrong radioed: "Houston, Tranquility Base here. The *Eagle* has landed." Several hours later, when Armstrong descended the lunar module ladder and made the small jump between the *Eagle* and the lunar surface, he announced: "That's one small step for man, one giant leap for mankind." The article "a" was missing in the live voice transmission, and was later inserted in the record to amend the message to "one small step for *a* man."

Kenneth Gatland, *The Illustrated Encyclopedia of Space Technology* (New York: Orion Books, 1989), 171.

Who was the first woman in space?

Valentina V. Tereshkova-Nikolaeva (b. 1937), a Soviet cosmonaut, was the first woman in space. She was aboard the *Vostok 6*, launched June 16, 1963. She spent three days circling the earth, completing 48 orbits. Although she had little cosmonaut training, she had been an accomplished parachutist and was especially fit for the rigors of space travel.

The United States space program did not put a woman in space until 20 years later when, on June 18, 1983, Sally K. Ride (b. 1951) flew aboard the space shuttle *Challenger* mission STS-7. In 1987, she moved to the administrative side of NASA and was instrumental in issuing the "Ride Report" which recommended future missions and direction for NASA. She retired from NASA in August 1987 to become a research fellow at Stanford University after serving on the Presidential Commission that investigated the *Challenger* disaster. Currently, she is the director of the California Space Institute at the University of California San Diego (UCSD) and professor of physics at UCSD.

Ray Spangenburg and Diane Moser *Space People From A-Z* (New York: Facts on File, 1990), 61, 72. *Who's Who in Science and Engineering 1994-1995* (New Providence, NJ: Marquis Who's Who, 1994), s.v. "Ride, Sally Kristin."

Where are the world's longest roads?

The longest driveable road in the world is the Pan-American Highway, which is over 15,000 miles in length and extends from Northwest Alaska to Brasilia, Brazil.

In the United States US-20 is the longest. It runs 3,370 miles from Boston, Massachusetts, to Newport, Oregon.

Peter Matthews, ed., *The Guinness Book of Records 1994* (New York: Facts On File, 1993), 122-23.

In what year did the Model T Ford touring car first appear and how much did it cost?

While actually a 1909 model, the Model T Ford touring car was introduced on October 8, 1908. It cost $850, weighed approximately 1,200 pounds, and could cruise up to 45 miles per hour. The vehicle had an engine of 20 horsepower and a two-speed transmission.

George H. Dammann, *90 Years of Ford* (Osceola, WI: Motorbooks International, 1993), 34, 37.

Are any U.S. battleships still in service?

There are no more U.S. battleships in action. According to *Webster's Dictionary*, a battleship is defined as a warship of the largest and most heavily armed and armored class usually having at least 10-inch armor and carrying in the main battery guns of 12-inch or larger caliber. The last battleship, *USS Missouri* or *Mighty Mo*, was decommissioned in 1992. It cost $38 million a year to operate by 1992. The *USS Missouri* can be brought back into action if needed in the future, as it will be at the "mothball" yard at Bremerton, Washington, the Navy's inactive ship facility. Three other battleships-*Iowa, New Jersey* (used in Vietnam), and *Wisconsin*-are also there.

USS Missouri was the last battleship to be built and the last to join the Pacific fleet in World War II (1939-45). It served as the flagship for Admiral W. F. Bull Halsey and saw action at Iwo Jima and Okinawa. It was the site of the formal surrender by the Japanese in Tokyo Bay on September 2, 1945. Redeployed to Korea in 1950 and in 1952, and mothballed in 1955, it was recommissioned in 1986 with electronic gear added.

USS Missouri statistics during World War II:
Cost-$100,000,000
Speed-33 knots
45,000 tons
887 feet long with a 108-foot beam
2,700 men at wartime strength
16-inch, 66-feet-long guns which could throw a 2,700-pound armor-piercing missile 23 miles.

The Encyclopedia Americana, intern. ed. (Danbury, CT: Grolier, 1994), s.v. "warships," "World War II." *Journal of Commerce* 27 March 1992. *Webster's Third New International Dictionary of the English Language, Unabridged* (Springfield, MA: Merriam-Webster, 1986), s.v. "battleship."

Who was the first person to jump from great heights using a parachute?

The first parachute jump was made from a tower by Sebastien Lenormand in 1783. Andr Garnerin jumped at an altitude of 3,000 feet from a balloon using a 30-foot wide parachute in Monceau Park in Paris, France, in 1797. On July 24, 1808, a parachute was first used in an emergency when Polish aviator Jodaki Kuparento had to escape his burning balloon. Since then parachutes have become standard safety equipment for aviators.

Academic American Encyclopedia (Danbury, CT: Grolier, 1988), s.v. "parachute." Laurence J. Peter, *Peter's Almanac* (New York: William Morrow, 1982).

What is significant about Promontory Point, Utah?

On May 10, 1869, the American transcontinental railroad link was completed at Promontory Point, Utah. The Union Pacific Railroad coming west from Nebraska and the Central Pacific line coming east from California were joined together by a railroad spike made of gold. Wielding a silver sledge hammer Leland Stanford, president of the Central Pacific Railroad, drove the spike into the final railroad tie made of polished California laurel. Along with the railroad a transcontinental Western Union telegraph line was also completed. Two locomotives, *Jupiter* and *119* advanced along the lines and gently touched noses when scheduled train runs from Boston to Oakland, California, began in 1870, this accelerated the development of the American West.

Dictionary of American History, rev. ed. (New York: Charles Scribner's Sons, 1976), s.v. "Promontory Point." *Webster's Guide To American History: A Chronological, Geographical, and Biographical Survey and Compendium* (Springfield, MA: G. & C. Merriam, 1971), 258-59.

How were United States battleships named during World War II?

During World War II (1939-45), U.S. battleships were named for American states; U.S. aircraft carriers, for battles; U.S. cruisers, for American cities; U.S. destroyers, for dead war heroes; U.S. submarines, for fish; U.S. ammunition ships, for mythological gods; and U.S. tugboats, for Native American tribes.

Fred L. Worth, *The Trivia Encyclopedia* (New York: Bell Publishing, 1974), 245.

What happened to the *Edmund Fitzgerald*?

Launched in 1958, the *Edmund Fitzgerald* was a 729-foot Great Lakes ore carrier-the largest Great Lakes freighter of its time. On November 10, 1975, the *Edmund Fitzgerald* had departed from

Superior, Wisconsin, with a cargo of 26,000 tons of taconite iron pellets, bound for Detroit. At around 7:00 p.m., the *Edmund Fitzgerald* encountered a fierce winter storm on Lake Superior. Waves were reported as high as 25 feet, and strong northwest winds averaged 60 to 65 miles per hour. The captain of the *Edmund Fitzgerald* radioed a distress signal to a freighter that was sailing approximately ten miles behind it, indicating that the *Fitzgerald* was taking on water. When the *Edmund Fitzgerald* was approximately 15 miles northwest of Whitefish Point, Michigan, in eastern Lake Superior, she disappeared from radar. A search conducted on the morning of November 11 discovered lifeboats and other debris from the *Fitzgerald*, but there was no sign of the crew. The *Fitzgerald* had sunk in approximately 500 feet of water and the bodies of Captain Ernest McSorley and 28 crewmembers were never recovered.

Agis Salpukas, "Ship Lost with 29 in Lake Superior," *New York Times* 11 November 1975.

What is a travois?

A travois was used by Native Americans for transporting goods and, sometimes, people. It consisted of two long poles with a "bed" of skin, wicker, or canvas draping between them. The ends of the poles were attached to a horse by leather strips and the goods were placed on the bed. The travois was then dragged behind the horse. A scaled-down travois could be attached to a dog, and the sick or elderly often rode on a travois behind a horse.

Lotsee Patterson and Mary Ellen Snodgrass, *Indian Terms of the Americas* (Englewood, CO: Libraries Unlimited, 1994), s.v. "travois."

Who was the first woman to fly at the speed of sound?

The first woman to fly at the speed of sound was Jacqueline Cochran (1910-80). Born in Pensacola, Florida, around 1910, she flew a Canadian Sabre jet faster than Mach 1, the speed of sound in May 1953.

Phyllis Read and Bernard L. Witlieb, *The Book of Women's Firsts* (New York: Random House, 1992), 95-97.

What was the first federally funded highway in the United States?

The first federally funded highway in the United States was the National Road, the official origins of which date back to 1806. Also called the Cumberland Road, or the Great National Pike, the road originated in Cumberland, Maryland; the first stretch reached Wheeling, West Virginia and opened for use in 1818. Built of crushed and compacted stone, the National Road eventually extended to Illinois by 1840. It cost the federal government over $6.8 million and was the only such large-scale, publicly funded transportation effort for more than a century.

Dennis Sanders, *The First of Everything* (New York: Delacorte, 1981), 72.

When was the wreck of the *Huron?*

The *Huron*, a 541-ton ship in the service of the U.S. Navy was wrecked in 1877. The ship had been built in 1874.

Edward W. Callahan, ed., *List of Officers of the Navy of the United States and of the Marine Corps from 1775-1900* (New York: L. R. Hamersly, 1901), 738.

What two cities did the famed Santa Fe Trail connect?

The famed Santa Fe Trail linked Franklin and, later, Independence, Missouri, with Santa Fe, New Mexico. The trail was a heavily used nineteenth-century overland trade route especially following the Mexican War.

Academic American Encyclopedia (Danbury, CT: Grolier, 1988), s.v. "Santa Fe Trail."

When was the first non-stop, unrefueled airplane flight around the world?

Dick Rutan (b. 1943) and Jeana Yeager (b. 1952) flew the *Voyager*, a trimaran monoplane, in a closed circuit loop westbound and back to Edwards Air Force Base, California, December 14-23, 1986. The flight lasted 9 days, 3 minutes, 44 seconds and covered 24,986.7 miles (40,203.6 kilometers). The first successful round-the-world flight was made by two Douglas World Cruisers between April 6 and September 28, 1924. Four aircraft originally left Seattle, Washington, and two went down. The two successful planes completed 27,553 miles (44,332.8 kilometers) in 175 days-with 371 hours 11 minutes being their actual flying time. Between June 23 and July 1, 1931, Wiley Post (1900-35) and Harold Gatty (1903-57) flew around the world, starting from New York, in their Lockheed Vega, *Winnie Mae.*

David Mondey, *The Guinness Book of Aircraft* (London: Guinness, 1988), 103, 108-9, 126.

When was the first full-scale wind tunnel for testing airplanes used?

The first full-scale wind tunnel for testing airplanes began operations on May 27, 1931, at the Langley Research Center of the National Advisory Committee for Aeronautics, Langley Field, Virginia. This tunnel, still in use, is 30 feet (9.14 meters) high and 60 feet (18.29 meters) wide. A wind tunnel is used to simulate air flow for aerodynamic measurement; it consists essentially of a closed tube, large enough to hold the airplane or other craft being tested, through which air is circulated by powerful fans.

Joseph N. Kane, *Famous First Facts, 4th ed.* (New York: Wilson, 1981), 703.
Joseph L. Nayler, *Aviation: Its Technical Development* (Chester Springs, PA: Dufour Editions, 1965), 268.

Who designed the *Spruce Goose*?

Howard Hughes (1905-76) designed and built the all-wood H-4 Hercules flying boat, nicknamed the *Spruce Goose.* The aircraft had the greatest wingspan ever built and was powered by eight engines. It was only flown once-covering a distance of less than one mile at Los Angeles harbor on November 2, 1947, lifting only 33 feet (10.6 meters) off the surface of the water.

After the attack on Pearl Harbor on December 7, 1941, and the subsequent entry of the United States into World War II (1939-45), the U.S. government needed a large, cargo-carrying airplane that could be made from non-critical wartime materials, such as wood. Henry J. Kaiser (1882-1967), whose shipyards were producing Liberty ships at the rate of one per day, hired Howard Hughes to build such a plane. Hughes eventually produced a plane that weighed 400,000 pounds (181,440 kilograms) and had a wingspan of 320 feet (97.5 meters). Unfortunately, the plane was so complicated that it was not finished by the end of the war. In 1947, Hughes flew the boat himself during its only time off the ground-supposedly just to prove that something that big could fly. Today the plane is on public exhibition in Long Beach, California.

Encyclopedia of Aviation (New York: Scribners, 1977), 97. *Milestones of Aviation* (Washington, DC: Smithsonian Institution, 1989), 188.

Why is the right side of a ship called starboard?

In the time of the Vikings, ships were steered by long paddles or boards placed over the right side. They were known in Old English as steorbords, evolving into the word starboard. The left side of a ship, looking forward, is called port. Formerly the left side was called larboard, originating perhaps from the fact that early merchant ships were always loaded from the left side. Its etymology is Scandinavian, being *lade* (load) and *bord* (side). The British Admiralty ordered *port* to be used in place of *larboard* to prevent confusion with *starboard.*

Charles E. Funk, *Horse Feathers and Other Curious Words* (New York: Harper, 1958), 13. W.A. McEwan and A.H. Lewis, *Encyclopedia of Nautical Knowledge* (Centreville, MD: Cornell Maritime Press, 1953), 278.

Who invented the automobile?

Although the idea of self-propelled road transportation originated long before, Karl Benz (1844-1929) and Gottlieb Daimler (1834-1900), are both credited with the invention of the gasoline-powered automobile, because they were the first to make their automotive machines commercially practicable. Benz and Daimler worked independently, unaware of each other's endeavors. Both built compact, internal-combustion engines to power their vehicles. Benz built his three-wheeler in 1885; it was steered by a tiller. Daimler's four-wheeled vehicle was produced in 1887.

Earlier self-propelled road vehicles include a steam-driven contraption invented by Nicolas-Joseph Cugnot (1725-1804), who rode the Paris streets at 2.5 miles (four kilometers) per hour in 1769. Richard Trevithick (1771-1833) also produced a steam-driven vehicle that could carry eight passengers. It first ran on December 24, 1801, in Camborne, England. Londoner Samuel Brown built the first practical four-horsepower gasoline-powered vehicle in 1826. The Belgian engineer J.J. Etienne Lenoire (1822-1900) built a vehicle with an internal combustion engine that ran on liquid hydrocarbon fuel in 1862, but he did not test it on the road until September 1863, when it travelled a distance of 12 miles (19.3 kilometers) in three hours. The Austrian inventor Siegfried Marcus (1831-1898) invented a four-wheeled gasoline-powered handcart in 1864 and a full-size car in 1875; the Viennese police objected to the noise that the car made, and Marcus did not continue its development. Edouard Delamare-Deboutteville invented an eight-horsepower vehicle in 1883, which was not durable enough for road conditions.

John Day and C. Eng, *The Bosch Book of the Motor Car* (New York: St. Martin's Press, 1976), 14-15. *Guinness Book of Records 1992* (New York: Bantam Book, 1992), 357. Patrick Robertson, *The Book of Firsts* (New York: Clarkson N. Potter, 1974), 99-100.

Which vehicle had the first modern automobile air conditioner?

The first air-conditioned automobile was manufactured by the Packard Motor Car Company in Detroit, Michigan, and was exhibited November 4-12, 1939, at the 40th Automobile Show in Chicago, Illinois. Air in the car was cooled to the temperature desired, dehumidified, filtered, and circulated. The first fully automatic air conditioning system was Cadillac's "Climate Control," introduced in 1964.

Anthony Harding, *The Guinness Book of the Car* (London: Guinness Superlatives, 1987), 28. Joseph N. Kane, *Famous First Facts, 4th ed.* (New York: Wilson, 1981), 51.

What is the difference between a medium truck and a heavy truck?

Medium trucks weigh 14,001 to 33,000 pounds (6,351 to 14,969 kilograms). They span a wide range of sizes and uses from step-van route trucks to truck tractors. Common examples include beverage trucks, city cargo vans, and garbage trucks. Heavy trucks weigh 33,001 pounds (14,969 kilograms) or greater. Heavy trucks include over-the-road 18-wheelers, dump trucks, concrete mixers, and fire trucks. These trucks have come a long way from the first carrying truck, built in 1870 by John Yule, which moved at a rate of 0.75 miles (12 kilometers) per hour.

Patrick Robertson, *The Book of Firsts* (New York: Clarkson N. Potter, 1974), 108. *Versatility of Trucks* (Detroit: Motor Vehicle Manufacturers Association, 1991), 8.

When were tubeless automobile tires first manufactured?

In Akron, Ohio, the B. F. Goodrich Company announced the manufacture of tubeless automobile tires on May 11, 1947. Dunlop was the first British firm to make tubeless tires in 1953.

Anthony Harding, *Car Facts and Feats* (London: Guinness Superlatives, 1975), 206. Patrick Robertson, *The Book of Firsts* (New York: Clarkson N. Potter, 1974), 133.

What was the route of the *Orient Express?*

The luxury train service, called the *Orient Express*, was inaugurated in June of 1883 to provide through connection between France and Turkey. It was not until 1889 that the complete journey could be made by train. The route left Paris and went via Chalons, Nancy, and Strasbourg into Germany (via Karlsruhe, Stuttgart, and Munich), then into Austria (via Salzburg, Linz, and Vienna), into Hungary (through Gyor and Budapest), south to Belgrade, Yugoslavia, through Sofia, Bulgaria and finally to Istanbul (Constantinople), Turkey. It ceased operation in May of 1977. In 1982 part of the line, the *Venice-Simplon-Orient Express*, went into operation.

O. S. Nock, *Encyclopedia of Railways* (London: Octopus Books, 1977), 239.

What is the world's fastest train?

The world's fastest train is France's TGV (Train Grande Vitesse or train of great speed) with a top speed of 320.2 miles per hour and an average speed of 132 miles per hour. However, soon it could be outdistanced by the MAGLEV (magnetic levitation) trains of Japan and Germany, which can travel between 250 to 300 miles per hour. These trains run on a bed of air produced from the repulsion or attraction of powerful magnetic fields (based on the principle that like poles of magnets repel and unlike poles (north and south) attract). The German Transrapid uses conventional magnets to levitate the train. The principle of attraction in magnetism, the employment of wing-like flaps extending under the train to fold under a T-shaped guideway, and the use of electromagnets on board (that are attracted to the nonenergized magnetic surface) are the guiding components. Interaction between the train's electromagnets and those built on top of the T-shaped track lift the vehicle 3/8 inch (1 centimeter) off the guideway. Another set of magnets along the rail sides provides lateral guidance. The train rides on electromagnetic waves. Alternating current in the magnet sets in the guideway changes their polarity to alternately push and pull the train along. Braking is done by reversing the direction of the magnetic field (caused by reversing the magnetic poles). To increase train speed, the frequency of current is raised.

The Japanese MLV002 uses the same propulsion system; the difference is in the levitation design in which the train rests on wheels until it reaches a speed of 100 miles (161 kilometers) per hour. Then it levitates four inches (10 centimeters) above the guideway. The levitation depends on superconducting magnets and a repulsion system (rather than the attraction system that the German system uses).

Richard P Brennan, *Levitating Trains and Kamikaze Genes* (New York: Harper Perennial, 1990), 218-20. Mark C. Young, ed., *Guiness Book of Records 1995* (New York: Facts On File, 1994), 123.

What is a standard gauge railroad?

The first successful railroads in England used steam locomotives built by George Stephenson (1781-1848) to operate on tracks with a gauge of 4 feet 8.5 inches (1.41 meters) probably because that was the wheel spacing common on the wagons and tramways of the time. Stephenson, a self-taught inventor and engineer, had developed in 1814 the steam-blast engine that made steam locomotives practical. His railroad rival, Isambard K. Brunel (1806-59), laid out the line for the Great Western Railway at 7 feet 0.25 inches (2.14 meters), and the famous "Battle of the gauges" began. A commission appointed by the British Parliament decided in favor of Stephenson's narrower gauge, and the Gauge Act of 1846 prohibited using other gauges. This width eventually became accepted by the rest of the world. The distance is measured between the inner sides of the heads of the two rails of the track at a distance of 5/8 inch (1.58 centimeters) below the top of the rails.

O. S. Nock, *Encyclopedia of Railways* (London: Octopus Books, 1977), 11-12. Charles Panati, *Panati's Browser's Book of Beginnings* (Boston: Houghton Mifflin, 1984), 311. *Standard Handbook for Civil Engineers, 3rd ed.* (New York: McGraw-Hill, 1983), 15-19.

How does a cable car move?

A cable runs continuously in a channel between the tracks located just below the street. The cable is controlled from a central station and usually moves about 9 miles (14.5 kilometers) per hour. Each cable car has an attachment on the underside of the car, called a grip. When the car operator pulls the lever, the grip latches onto the moving cable and is pulled along by the moving cable. When the operator releases the lever, the grip disconnects from the cable and comes to a halt when the operator applies the brakes. Also called an endless ropeway, it was invented by Andrew S. Hallide (1836-1900) who first operated his system in San Francisco in 1873.

Charles A. Smallwood et al. , *The Cable Car Book* (Berkeley, CA: Celestial Arts, 1980), 6-7. *World Book Encyclopedia* (Chicago: World Book, 1990), 3:7.

What is Belgian block?

Belgian block is a road-building material, first used in Brussels, Belgium, and introduced into New York about 1850. Its shape is a truncated pyramid with a base of about five or six inches square (13-15 centimeters) and a depth of seven to eight inches (18-20.5 centimeters). The bottom of the block is not more than one inch (2.5 centimeters) different from the top. The original blocks were cut from trap-rock from the Palisades of New Jersey.

Belgian blocks replaced cobblestones mainly because their regular, shape allowed them to remain in place better than cobblestones. They were not universally adopted, however, because they would wear round and create joints or openings which would then form ruts and hollows. Although they provided a smooth surface compared to the uneven cobblestones, they still made for a rough and noisy ride.

Austin T. Byrne, *A Treatise on Highway Construction* (New York: John Wiley and Sons, 1896), 81-82. Harwood Frost, *The Art of Roadmaking* (New York: Engineering News Publishing, 1910), 314-15.

Who was the first man in space?

Yuri Gagarin (1934-1968), a Soviet cosmonaut, became the first man in space when he made a full orbit of the earth in *Vostok I*, on April 12, 1961. Gagarin's flight lasted only 1 hour and 48 minutes, but as the first man in space, he became an international hero. Partly because of this Soviet success, U.S. president John F. Kennedy (1917-1963) announced on May 25, 1961, that the United States would land a man on the moon before the end of the decade. The United States took its first step toward that goal when it launched the first American into orbit on February 20, 1962. U.S. Astronaut John H. Glenn, Jr. (b. 1921) completed three orbits in *Friendship 7* and travelled about 81,000 miles (130,329 kilometers). Prior to this, on May 5, 1961, Alan B. Shepard, Jr. (b. 1923) became the first American to man a spaceflight, aboard *Freedom 7*. This suborbital flight reached an altitude of 116.5 miles (187.45 kilometers).

The Cambridge Encyclopedia of Space (New York: Cambridge University Press, 1990), 50-55.

What is the message attached to the *Voyager* spacecraft?

Voyager 1 (launched September 5, 1977) and *Voyager 2* (launched August 20, 1977) were unmanned space probes designed to explore the outer planets and then travel out of the solar system. A gold-coated copper phonograph record containing a message to any possible extraterrestrial civilization that they may encounter was attached to each spacecraft. The record contained both video and audio images of earth and the civilization which sent this message to the stars.

The record began with 118 pictures. These showed the earth's position in the galaxy; a key to the mathematical notation used in other pictures; the sun; other planets in the solar system; human anatomy and reproduction; various types of terrain (seashore, desert, mountains); examples of vegetation and animal life; people of both sexes and of all ages and ethnic types engaged in a number of activities; structures (from grass huts to the Taj Mahal to the Sydney Opera House) showing diverse architectural styles; and means of transportation—roads, bridges, cars, planes, and space vehicles.

The pictures are followed by greetings from Jimmy Carter (1924-), then president of the United States, and Kurt Waldheim, then Secretary General of the United Nations. Brief messages in 54 languages, ranging from ancient Sumerian to English, was included as was a "song" of the humpback whales.

The next section is a series of sounds common to the earth. These include thunder, rain, wind, fire, barking dogs, footsteps, laughter, human speech, the cry of an infant, and the sounds of a human heartbeat and human brainwaves.

The record concludes with approximately 90 minutes of music— "Earth's Greatest Hits." The musical selections were drawn from a broad spectrum of cultures and include such diverse pieces as a Pygmy girl's initiation song; bagpipe music from Azerbaijan; the First Movement of the Fifth Symphony, by Ludwig von Beethoven; and "Johnny B. Goode" by Chuck Berry.

It will be tens or even hundreds of thousands of years before either *Voyager* comes close to another star, and perhaps the message will never be heard; but it is a sign of humanity's hope to encounter life elsewhere in the universe.

Murmurs of Earth: The Voyager Interstellar Record (New York: Random House, 1978).

Who made the first golf shot on the moon?

Alan B. Shepard, Jr. (b. 1923), commander of "Apollo 14," launched on January 31, 1971, made the first golf shot. He attached a six iron to the handle of the contingency sample return container, dropped a golf ball on the moon, and took a couple of one-handed swings. He missed with the first, but connected with the second. The ball, he reported, sailed for miles and miles.

William David Compton, *Where No Man Has Gone Before* (Washington, DC: Superintendent of Documents, 1980), 209.

What was the worst disaster in the U.S. space program and what caused it?

Challenger mission STS 51L was launched on January 28, 1986, but exploded only 73 seconds after lift-off. The entire crew of seven was killed and the *Challenger* was completely destroyed. The crew members included:
Francis R. "Dick" Scobee—commander
Michael J. Smith—pilot
Sharon Christa Corrigan McAuliffe—educator
Judith A. Resnik—mission specialist
Ronald E. McNair—mission specialist
Ellison S. Onizuka—mission specialist
Gregory B. Jarvis—engineer

The investigation of the *Challenger* tragedy was performed by the Rogers Commission, established and named for its chairman, former Secretary of State William Rogers. The consensus of the Rogers Commission (which studied the accident for several months) and participating investigative agencies is that the accident was caused by a failure in the joint between the two lower segments of the right solid rocket motor. The specific failure was the destruction of the seals that are intended to prevent hot gases from leaking through the joint during the propellant burn of the rocket motor. The evidence assembled by the commission indicated that no other element of the space shuttle system contributed to this failure.

Although the commission did not affix blame to any individuals, the public record made clear that the launch should not have been made that day. The weather was unusually cold at Cape Canaveral and temperatures had dipped below freezing during the night. Test data had suggested that the seals (called O-rings) around the solid rocket booster joints lost much of their effectiveness in very cold weather.

Gene Gurney, *Space Shuttle Log* (Blue Ridge Summit, PA: TAB, 1988), 269. Frank N. Magill, *Magill's Survey of Science: Space Exploration Series* (Englewood Cliffs, NJ: Salem Press, 1992), 4:1813. Marcia Smith, *Space Activities of the United States and Other Launching Countries/Organizations: 1957-1991* (Washington, DC: Library of Congress, Science Policy Research Division, 1992), CRS-35.

What was the U.S. national speed limit during the energy crisis of the 1970s?

In order to conserve fuel during the energy crisis, a temporary national highway speed limit of 55 miles per hour was enacted on January 2, 1974, by U.S. President Richard M. Nixon (1913-1994). Receipt of federal highway aid funds was made conditional on compliance by the states. The speed limit was made permanent when President Gerald Ford (1913-) signed a new bill on January 4, 1975, but was later raised to 65 miles per hour in 1991 for interstate highways outside an urbanized area of 50,000 or more in population.

"The Energy Crisis," *Facts on File* 23-31 December 1973. "The Energy Crisis," *Facts on File* 1-12 January 1974. *Facts on File* 11 January 1975. *United States Code, 1988 ed.* (Washington, DC: Government Printing Office, 1993), 4:443.

Which cities still have streetcars?

Streetcar lines still operate in the U.S. cities of Boston, Cleveland, Dallas, New Orleans, Newark, Philadelphia, Pittsburgh, Portland, San Diego, San Francisco, and Seattle. Canadian cities include Calgary, Edmonton, and Toronto. Hong Kong has double-deckers and an overhead trolley system. Some areas of central and eastern Europe, Russia, and South America still operate streetcars. Many streetcars were replaced by cars, buses, and most recently, light-rail systems.

The Encyclopedia Americana, international ed. (Danbury, CT: Grolier, 1994), s.v. "streetcar." *The New Encyclopaedia Britannica, 15th ed., "Micropaedia"* (Chicago: Encyclopaedia Britannica, 1994), s.v. "streetcar." *World Book Encyclopedia* (Chicago: World Book, 1994), s.v. "streetcar."

Why were German submarines called U-boats?

The term "U-boat" is translated from the German *U-boot*, short for *unterseeboot*, which means literally undersea boat. The U-boat was a German submarine used in World War I and II to destroy enemy shipping.

Merriam-Webster's Collegiate Dictionary, 10th ed. (Springfield, MA: Merriam Webster, 1993), s.v. "U-boat." *The New Encyclopaedia Britannica, 15th ed., "Macropaedia"* (Chicago: Encyclopaedia Britannica, 1993), s.v. "U-boat."

Which is bigger, an oil tanker or an aircraft carrier?

The largest oil tanker is the *Jahre Viking*, formerly the *Happy Giant*, which is 1,471 feet long.

The largest aircraft carriers are of the Nimitz class. The United States Navy aircraft carriers USS *Nimitz, Dwight D. Eisenhower, Carl Vinson, Theodore Roosevelt, George Washington*, and *Abraham Lincoln* are 1,092 feet long. Each can carry 5,986 personnel.

Passenger ships are a close third. The *Norway* is 1,035 feet, 7.5 inches in length. It can carry 2,022 passengers and a crew of 900.

Mark C. Young, ed., *The Guinness Book of Records 1995* (New York: Facts on File, 1994), 110-12.

Why did it take so long for the Wright Brothers' plane to be exhibited at the Smithsonian Institution?

The historic flight by Wilbur (1867-1912) and Orville Wright (1871-1948) was made on December 17, 1903, near Kitty Hawk, North Carolina, but the plane was not exhibited at the Smithsonian Institution until 1948. Because of a dispute with the Institution about the invention of the first airplane, Orville decided instead to lend the plane to the Science Museum at South Kensington, near London, in 1928. The dispute was settled to Orville's satisfaction in 1942, but World War II (1939-1945) delayed transport of the plane until after the war. It was unveiled at an exhibit which opened on December 17, 1948.

Aircraft of the National Air and Space Museum, 3d ed. (Washington, DC: Smithsonian Press, 1985). C.D.B. Bryan, *The National Air and Space Museum, 2nd ed.* (New York: Harry N. Abrams, 1988), 22-23. Omega G. East, *Wright Brothers: National Memorial, North Carolina* (Washington, DC: Government Printing Office, 1961), 60.

Index

A

B

C

D

E

F

H

I

J

K

L

M

N

O

P

Q

R

S

T

U

V

W

Index

X

Y

Z